Discovering
CHILD DEVELOPMENT

Carol Lynn Martin
Arizona State University

Richard Fabes
Arizona State University

PEARSON

A and B

Boston   New York   San Francisco
Mexico City   Montreal   Toronto   London   Madrid   Munich   Paris
Hong Kong   Singapore   Tokyo   Cape Town   Sydney

W9-BZP-713

Executive Editor: *Karon Bowers*

Series Editorial Assistant: *Deborah Hanlon*

Senior Developmental Editor: *Lisa McLellan*

Senior Marketing Manager: *Pamela Laskey*

Manufacturing Buyer: *Megan Cochran*

Composition and Prepress Buyer: *Linda Cox*

Cover Coordinator: *Linda Knowles*

Editorial Production Administrator: *Anna Socrates*

Editorial Production Service: *Susan McNally*

Text Designer: *The Davis Group, Inc.*

Illustrations: *William Melvin; Network Graphics*

Photo Research: *Helane M. Prottas, Posh Pictures*

Electronic Composition: *Omegatype Typography, Inc.*

For related titles and support materials, visit our online catalog at www.ablongman.com

Between the time Website information is gathered and then published, it is not unusual for some sites to have closed. Also, the transcription of URLs can result in unintended typographical errors. The publisher would appreciate notification where these errors occur so that they may be corrected in subsequent editions.

CIP Data not available at time of publication

ISBN: 0-205-45462-3

Photo credits appear on page 642, which constitutes a continuation of the copyright page.

Printed in the United States of America

10 9 8 7 6 5 4 3 2 1   VHP   10   09   08   07   06   05

Brief Contents

To the Student   xxi

Preface   xxiii

PART 1   INTRODUCTION TO CHILD DEVELOPMENT   1

    1   Introduction to Child Development   2

    2   Understanding and Studying Child Development   28

PART 2   PRENATAL AND NEONATAL DEVELOPMENT   60

    3   Biological Foundations of Development   62

    4   Prenatal Development and Birth   88

PART 3   INFANT AND TODDLER DEVELOPMENT   128

    5   Physical Development and Health in Infancy and Toddlerhood   130

    6   Cognitive and Language Development in Infancy and Toddlerhood   166

    7   Social and Emotional Development in Infancy and Toddlerhood   204

PART 4   EARLY CHILDHOOD DEVELOPMENT   242

    8   Physical Development and Health in Early Childhood   244

    9   Cognitive and Language Development in Early Childhood   268

    10   Social and Emotional Development in Early Childhood   298

PART 5   LATE CHILDHOOD DEVELOPMENT   338

    11   Physical Development and Health in Late Childhood   340

    12   Cognitive and Language Development in Late Childhood   366

    13   Social and Emotional Development in Late Childhood   402

PART 6   ADOLESCENCE   442

    14   Physical Development and Health in Adolescence   444

    15   Cognitive Development in Adolescence   484

    16   Social and Emotional Development in Adolescence   512

Glossary   554

References   560

Name Index   624

Subject Index   633

Contents

To the Student   xxi

Preface   xxiii

About the Authors   xxix

part one   *Introduction to Child Development*   1

1   Introduction to Child Development   2

NURTURING CHILDREN   FOSTERING CHILDREN'S CONCERN
AND CARING FOR OTHERS   4

What Is Child Development?   4

What Are Some Critical Issues in the Study of Child Development?   5

Influences on Child Development   5

FROM RESEARCH TO PRACTICE   DO EARLY EXPERIENCES INFLUENCE
LATER DEVELOPMENT? THE CASE OF THE DUTCH FAMINE OF 1944–1945   6

Teasing Out the Roles of Nature and Nurture   8
Continuity versus Discontinuity   10
Critical and Sensitive Periods   10
Individual Differences in Development—Stability and Change   11

What Are the Historical Roots of the Study of Child Development?   11

Children of Antiquity   11
Children as Miniature Adults: Medieval Children   12
Early Philosophical Roots of Childhood   12
Charles Darwin: Evolution and Child Development   13
G. Stanley Hall: Pioneer in the Study of Development   14

**What Changes in Contemporary American Life Influence the Study
of Child Development?**   14

Changes in Family Structure   14
Children of Same-Sex Parents   17
Ethnic and Racial Diversity   18

DEBATING THE ISSUE   HOW DO IMMIGRANT CHILDREN
AFFECT AMERICAN LIFE?   19

Poverty and Child Development   20

How Can We Capture the Diversity of Children's Development?   21

Try It Out 24 ▪ Key Terms and Concepts 25 ▪ Sum It Up 25

Visual Summary   26

2 Understanding and Studying Child Development 28

How Do Theories Explain Child Development? 29
Scientific Theories 30
Evaluating Theories of Development 30

What Are the Major Biology-Based Theories of Child Development? 31
Evolutionary Theories 31
Ethological Theory 32
Neurodevelopmental Approaches 33

What Are the Major Psychoanalytic Theories of Child Development? 33
Freud's Psychosexual Theory 33
Erikson's Psychosocial Theory 35

What Are the Major Environment-Based Theories of Child Development? 36
Classical Conditioning 36
Operant Conditioning 38
Social Learning Theory 38

What Are the Major Cognition-Based Theories of Child Development? 39
Piaget's Cognitive Developmental Theory 39
Vygotsky's Theory of Cognitive Development 41
Information Processing Theory 42

What Are the Major Contextual Theories of Child Development? 43
Bronfenbrenner's Ecological Theory 43
Dynamic Systems Theory 44

How Is Child Development Studied? 46
Scientific Reasoning and the Scientific Method 46
Topics in Developmental Science 46
Research Strategies 47

FROM RESEARCH TO PRACTICE HOW CAN RESULTS FROM DIFFERENT STUDIES BE COMBINED? 48

NURTURING CHILDREN PROTECTING CHILDREN INVOLVED IN RESEARCH 52
Measuring Change over Time 52
Measuring Children's Behavior 54

DEBATING THE ISSUE DO GIFTED CHILDREN BECOME WELL-ADJUSTED ADULTS? 55

Try It Out 56 ■ **Key Terms and Concepts 56** ■ **Sum It Up 57**

Visual Summary 58

part two

Prenatal and Neonatal Development   60

3 Biological Foundations of Development   62

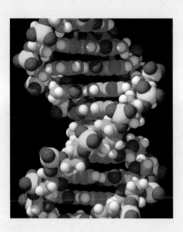

How Do Genes Influence Development?   63

Hunting for Genes: The Human Genome Project   63
DNA: The Secret to Life   64
Genes and Chromosomes   65
Sex Determination: Girl or Boy?   66
Genetic Transmission Patterns   66

DEBATING THE ISSUE   SELECTING OUR BABIES: SHOULD THE SEX OF A CHILD BE PRESELECTED?   68

Genomes to Life Project   72

How Do Genes and Environments Work Together?   72

Gene Expression   72
Genes and Exposure to Different Environments   74
Gene–Environment Interactions   74

What Are Common Chromosomal Abnormalities?   75

Down Syndrome   75
Sex Chromosome Abnormalities   76

How Are Genetic Diseases Detected?   77

Genetic Technology   78
Genetic Counseling   79

NURTURING CHILDREN   TREATING A DISEASED FETUS   80

How Does Conception Occur, and What Can Be Done to Overcome Infertility?   80

Ovulation   80

FROM RESEARCH TO PRACTICE   INFINITE EGGS?   82

Spermatogenesis   82
Fertilization   82
Overcoming Infertility   83

Try It Out 85   ■   Key Terms and Concepts 85   ■   Sum It Up 85

Visual Summary   86

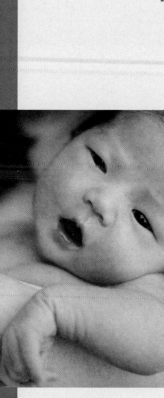

4 Prenatal Development and Birth   88

How Does Prenatal Development Proceed?   89

Overview of Prenatal Development   89
The Germinal Stage   90
The Embryonic Stage   91
The Fetal Stage   94

What Conditions Influence Pregnancy and Prenatal Development?   96

Diseases   97
Drugs   98

DEBATING THE ISSUE   SHOULD THERE BE LIMITS
TO NEONATAL TREATMENT?   100

Environmental Hazards   103
Maternal Conditions   103
Protective Factors   105
Cultural Influences on Pregnancy   106

How Is a Baby Born?   107

The Birth Process   107
Birthing Methods   110
Birth Complications and Related Procedures   112

How Is Childbirth Experienced?   113

The Mother's Perspective   114
The Father's Perspective   115
The Newborn's Perspective   116
Cultural Differences in the Experience of Childbirth   116

NURTURING CHILDREN   BONDING AT BIRTH   117

What Are the Characteristics of a Newborn?   118

Physical Appearance   118
Behavioral Assessment of Neonates   119

Why Are Some Newborns at Risk?   120

Consequences of Low Birthweight and Prematurity   121
Neonatal Intensive Care   122
Caregiving and High-Risk Infants   123

FROM RESEARCH TO PRACTICE   RISK AND PROTECTIVE
FACTORS IN THE LONG-TERM EFFECTS OF PRENATAL
ALCOHOL EXPOSURE   123

Try It Out 124 ▪ Key Terms and Concepts 124 ▪ Sum It Up 125

Visual Summary   126

part three

Infant and Toddler Development   128

5   Physical Development and Health in Infancy and Toddlerhood   130

How Do Infants and Toddlers Develop Physically?   131
Growth Patterns of Infants and Toddlers   131
Infant States and Sleep Patterns   133

How Do Infant Brains Develop?   136
Early Brain Development   136
Key Brain Structures   139
Brain Plasticity   139
Environmental Effects on Brain Development   140

How Do Infants' Perceptual Abilities Develop?   142
The Visual World of Newborns and Infants   142
Perception of Faces   143
Perception of Moving Objects   144
Depth Perception   144
The Infant's World of Sound   145
The Infant's World of Taste, Smell, and Touch   145

FROM RESEARCH TO PRACTICE   DO NEWBORNS PREFER TO HEAR THEIR OWN LANGUAGE?   146
The "Dance of Perception"   147

How Do Motor Skills Develop in Infants and Toddlers?   148
Neonatal Reflexes   149
Gross Motor Skills   149
Fine Motor Skills   155
Bowel and Bladder Control   156

What Factors Influence Infant Health and Safety?   157
Promoting Healthy Development and Growth   157
Avoiding Accidents   157

DEBATING THE ISSUE   SHOULD BABIES BE TAUGHT TO SWIM?   158
Infant Mortality   158
Infant Nutrition   158

NURTURING CHILDREN   PREVENTING SIDS   159
Failure-to-Thrive Infants   162

Try It Out 162 ■ **Key Terms and Concepts 162** ■ **Sum It Up 163**

Visual Summary   164

6 Cognitive and Language Development in Infancy and Toddlerhood   166

How Do Cognitive Abilities Develop During Infancy and Toddlerhood?   167

Piaget's Sensorimotor Stage   167

Beyond Piaget: Newer Research on Early Cognitive Abilities   172

DEBATING THE ISSUE   WHAT DO INFANTS KNOW, AND HOW DO THEY KNOW IT?   177

The Social Contexts of Early Learning and Cognitive Development   179

The Cultural Contexts of Early Learning and Cognitive Development   180

How Do Infants and Toddlers Learn, Remember, and Process Information?   180

Learning Through Contingency and Association   180

Learning What's Familiar: Habituation and Novelty Responses   181

Developing Long-Term Memory   182

How Do Infants and Toddlers Develop Language Skills?   184

Before the First Words   185

First Words   186

Development of Vocabulary   187

Solving the Mystery of Word Meaning   187

FROM RESEARCH TO PRACTICE   CAN BABIES COMMUNICATE THROUGH HAND SIGNALS?   188

First Sentences   191

Early Talkers and Late Talkers   191

How Is Children's Language Acquisition Explained?   192

Learning-Based Theories   192

Innate Theories: Biological Influences   193

NURTURING CHILDREN   PROMOTING LANGUAGE DEVELOPMENT   195

Social Interaction Theories   196

Genie's Outcomes   197

The Resilient and Fragile Aspects of Language Development   198

Try It Out 200   ▪   Key Terms and Concepts 201   ▪   Sum It Up 201

Visual Summary   202

7 Social and Emotional Development in Infancy and Toddlerhood   204

How Do Emotions Develop During Infancy and Toddlerhood?   205

Developing a Sense of Trust   206
Smiling and Laughter   206
Anger and Temper Tantrums   210

NURTURING CHILDREN   SOOTHING A CRYING INFANT   211

Shame, Pride, and Other Self-Conscious Emotions   211
Play and Emotional Development   213

How Does Temperament Influence Development During Infancy and Toddlerhood?   213

The Structure of Temperament   214
Contributions of Temperament to Infant Development   215
Cultural Perceptions of Temperament   217

How Do Parent–Infant Attachments Influence Development?   217

FROM RESEARCH TO PRACTICE   WHAT ARE THE EARLY ROOTS OF SHYNESS?   218

Attachment Theory   219
The Development of Attachment   219
Assessing Patterns of Attachment   221
Caregiver and Child Factors Affecting Attachment   225
The Role of Culture in Attachment   226
Consequences of Attachment   227
Attachment to Fathers   228

How Does Day Care Influence Infants' and Toddlers' Development?   229

Patterns of Day-Care Use   229
Effects of Day Care   230

DEBATING THE ISSUE   HOW DOES MOM'S WORKING AFFECT CHILDREN'S DEVELOPMENT?   231

Guidelines for Quality Day Care   232
Culture and Day Care   233

Why Are Children Abused and Neglected?   233

Definitions of Child Abuse and Neglect   234
Incidence of Child Abuse and Neglect   234
Characteristics of Victims and Abusers   235
Effects of Child Abuse and Neglect   237
Preventing Child Abuse and Neglect   238

Try It Out 239 ■ **Key Terms and Concepts 239** ■ **Sum It Up 239**

Visual Summary   240

part four   *Early Childhood Development*   *242*

8   Physical Development and Health in Early Childhood   244

How Do Children's Bodies and Brains Develop During Early Childhood?   245

Changing Body Size and Appearance   245
Brain Development   246

How Do Children's Motor Skills Improve During Early Childhood?   249

Gross Motor Skills   249

DEBATING THE ISSUE   AUTISM AND THE BRAIN—ARE GIRLS' AND BOYS' BRAINS DIFFERENT?   249

Fine Motor Skills   251
Handedness   253
Cultural and Racial Influences on Motor Development   254

What Are the Nutritional Needs and Sleep Patterns for Young Children?   254

Nutritional Needs and Eating Habits   254

NURTURING CHILDREN   HELPING YOUNG CHILDREN BECOME HEALTHY EATERS   256

Undernourishment and Malnourishment   256
Sleep Patterns and Problems   258

FROM RESEARCH TO PRACTICE   SLEEPINESS AND CHILDHOOD INJURIES   261

What Are the Health and Safety Needs of Young Children?   262

Diseases: Close-up on Asthma   262
Accidents   263
Environmental Hazards   264

Try It Out 265   ■   Key Terms and Concepts 265   ■   Sum It Up 265

Visual Summary   266

9 Cognitive and Language Development in Early Childhood   268

How Do Young Children Think and Solve Problems?   269

Piaget's View of Preoperational Thinking   269

Evaluating Piaget's View of Preoperational Development   273

Vygotsky's View of the Social Context of Cognitive Development   274

Evaluating Vygotsky's Theory of Social Cognitive Development   276

The Information Processing Approach   276

Young Children's Theory of Mind   278

DEBATING THE ISSUE   CAN YOUNG CHILDREN'S EYEWITNESS TESTIMONY BE BELIEVED?   279

Young Children's Understanding of Pretend and Real   280

Cultural Influences on Young Children's Thinking   281

What Changes Occur in Young Children's Language Development During Early Childhood?   282

Vocabulary   282

Young Children's Language Styles   283

Grammar: Beyond Two-Word Sentences   283

Understanding Conversational Rules   285

The Social Context of Language Development   285

Language Development in Bilingual Children   286

NURTURING CHILDREN   HELPING CHILDREN TO LEARN LANGUAGE   287

How Does Early Childhood Education Influence Development?   287

Parents as Teachers   287

Young Children's Educational Experiences   288

Early Intervention and Young Children's Cognitive Development   290

FROM RESEARCH TO PRACTICE   WHEN ARE YOUNG CHILDREN PREPARED TO START SCHOOL?   291

Try It Out 295 ▪ Key Terms and Concepts 295 ▪ Sum It Up 295

Visual Summary   296

10 Social and Emotional Development in Early Childhood   298

How Does Self-Awareness Change During Early Childhood?   299

The Psychosocial Crisis of Initiative Versus Guilt   299
Developing Self-Concept   300
Developing Self-Esteem   301

How Do Young Children Develop a Concept of Gender?   302

FROM RESEARCH TO PRACTICE   WHAT FACTORS AFFECT POSITIVE SELF-ESTEEM IN AFRICAN AMERICAN AND LATINO CHILDREN?   303

Young Children's Gender Stereotypes   304
Young Children's Gender-Typed Play Preferences   304
Contemporary Theories of Gender Development   306

How Do Emotions Develop During Early Childhood?   308

Controlling and Regulating Emotions   308
Dealing with Conflict, Anger, and Aggression   311
Developing Caring Feelings and Actions   313

How Do Parenting Behaviors and Family Context Influence Young Children's Development?   315

Disciplining Young Children   315
Influences on Parents' Use of Discipline   317
Parenting Styles   318
The Effects of Divorce on Young Children's Development   320

DEBATING THE ISSUE   DOES CUSTODY MAKE A DIFFERENCE?   325

How Do Peer and Sibling Relationships Develop During Early Childhood?   325

Young Children's Friendships   326
Young Children at Play   328
Young Children's Sibling Relationships   330

How Does Television Influence Young Children's Emotional and Social Development?   332

Effects of Television on Family Life   332
Effects of Television Violence on Children's Aggression   332

NURTURING CHILDREN   SUPERVISING CHILDREN'S TELEVISION VIEWING   333

Effects of Television on Children's Prosocial Behavior   334

Try It Out 334   ■   Key Terms and Concepts 335   ■   Sum It Up 335

Visual Summary   336

part five *Late Childhood Development*   *338*

11 Physical Development and Health in Late Childhood   340

How Do Children's Bodies and Brains Develop During Late Childhood?   341

Brain Development   341
Body Size and Appearance   342
Bone Health   342
Tooth Development and Oral Health   344
Physical Health Concerns   344

How Do Motor Skills and Physical Fitness Develop During Late Childhood?   347

Motor Skills   347
Physical Fitness and Sports   348

FROM RESEARCH TO PRACTICE   DO BOYS AND GIRLS HAVE DIFFERENT PHYSICAL SELF-CONCEPTS?   349

What Are the Nutritional Needs and Concerns of School-Age Children?   350

Nutritional Needs   350
Undernutrition   351
Childhood Obesity: Generation XL   352

DEBATING THE ISSUE   SHOULD SCHOOLS ALLOW VENDING MACHINES THAT DISPENSE JUNK FOOD?   353

NURTURING CHILDREN   HOW CAN CAREGIVERS PROMOTE CHILDREN'S PHYSICAL ACTIVITY?   355

What Are the Health and Safety Concerns of Late Childhood?   356

Diseases   356
Accidents and Injuries   360
Personal Safety   361

Try It Out 362   ■   **Key Terms and Concepts 362**   ■   **Sum It Up 363**

Visual Summary   364

12 Cognitive and Language Development in Late Childhood   366

How Do School-Age Children Think and Solve Problems?   367

Children's Logical Problem Solving   367
Children's Understanding of Categories and Concepts   368
Children's Understanding of Seriation   369
Culture as a Context for Children's Cognitive Development   370
Information Processing in School-Aged Children   370

What Characteristics Define Children's Intelligence and Creativity?   371

FROM RESEARCH TO PRACTICE   ARE THERE CULTURAL DIFFERENCES IN CHILDREN'S REASONING?   372

Measuring Intelligence   373
Understanding the Limits of IQ Scores   373
Identifying the Components of Intelligence   374
Creativity in Children   376
Family and Cultural Influences on Intellectual Development   377

How Do Language and Literacy Develop During the School Years?   379

Development of Syntax   380
Development of Semantics   380
Development of Pragmatics   381
Children's Literacy   381

How Do School-Age Children Understand the Social World?   383

Social Perspective Taking: Communicating with Others   383
Children's Understanding of Others' Beliefs and Feelings   384
Children's Understanding of Race and Prejudice   385

NURTURING CHILDREN   REDUCING PREJUDICE IN CHILDREN   386

How Does Schooling Influence Children's Cognitive Development?   387

Opportunities for Active Learning   387
Multicultural and Multilingual Education   387
Teachers' Bias in Achievement Expectations   388

DEBATING THE ISSUE   HOW SUCCESSFUL IS BILINGUAL EDUCATION?   389

Students with Special Needs   390

Try It Out 398 ■ Key Terms and Concepts 398 ■ Sum It Up 399

Visual Summary   400

13 Social and Emotional Development in Late Childhood   402

How Do Children's Selves Develop During Late Childhood?   403
Erikson: Industry Versus Inferiority   404
Influences on Children's Perception of Self   404

How Do Emotions Develop During Late Childhood?   406
Fear and Anxiety in Late Childhood   406
Stress and Coping   407

NURTURING CHILDREN   HELPING CHILDREN COPE WITH DISASTER   410
Children's Responses to Community Violence   411

What Emotional and Psychological Disturbances Affect Children in Late Childhood?   413
Antisocial Behavior   413

FROM RESEARCH TO PRACTICE   HOW DO FAMILIES CONTRIBUTE TO CHILDREN'S ANTISOCIAL BEHAVIOR?   416
Childhood Depression   416

What Changes Take Place in Moral Development During Late Childhood?   418
Piaget's Theory of Moral Development   419
Kohlberg's Theory of Moral Development   421
Culture and Morality   425
Gender and Morality   426

How Do Children's Family Relationships Change During Late Childhood?   427
Reduced Parent–Child Interaction   427
Reduced Parental Supervision   427
Increased Importance of Sibling Relationships   429
Only Children   430

What Factors Influence School-Age Children's Peer Relationships?   430
Peer Rejection   431
Bullying and Being Bullied   431

DEBATING THE ISSUE   ARE SCHOOLS SAFE?   433
Development of Social Competence   434

How Does School Affect Social and Emotional Development in Late Childhood?   436
Influence of the School Environment   436
Influence of Teacher–Child Relationships   437

Try It Out 438 ▪ Key Terms and Concepts 438 ▪ Sum It Up 439

Visual Summary   440

part six

Adolescence   *442*

14 Physical Development and Health in Adolescence   444

What Is Adolescence?   445
  Historical Perspectives on Adolescence   446
  Cultural Perspectives on Adolescence   447

How Do Adolescents Develop Physically and Sexually?   448
  Brain Development   448

FROM RESEARCH TO PRACTICE   ADOLESCENT SLEEP
AND DEVELOPMENT   450
  The Adolescent Growth Spurt   451
  The Process of Puberty   452

DEBATING THE ISSUE   DOES PUBERTY INTENSIFY
ADOLESCENTS' GENDER ROLES?   454
  Adolescents' Responses to Physical and Sexual Maturation   456
  Psychological Reactions to Pubertal Events   460

What Are the Health and Safety Concerns for Young Adolescents?   462
  Nutrition   462
  Fitness and Sports Participation   462
  Eating Disturbances and Disorders   465
  Adolescents and Chronic Illnesses   469
  Death in Adolescence   470
  Sexual Health Concerns   474

NURTURING CHILDREN   CHARACTERISTICS OF EFFECTIVE
SEX EDUCATION PROGRAMS   480

Try It Out 480 ▪ Key Terms and Concepts 481 ▪ Sum It Up 481

Visual Summary   482

15 Cognitive Development in Adolescence   484

How Do Young Adolescents Think and Reason?   485

Reaching Cognitive Maturity: Formal Operational Thinking   485

Adolescent Egocentrism   488

Social Cognition: Thinking About People and Relationships   489

Political and Religious Thinking   492

How Does School Influence Early Adolescent Development?   493

Adaptation to a Change in Schools   493

Transition to High School   494

NURTURING CHILDREN   DEVELOPMENTALLY APPROPRIATE MIDDLE SCHOOLS   495

What Factors Influence Adolescents' Perceptions of Academic Competence?   498

Gender Differences in Adolescents' Cognitive Abilities and Achievement   498

DEBATING THE ISSUE   SHOULD TEENS WORK?   499

Explaining Gender Differences in Academic Abilities and Achievement   502

Cultural Influences on Academic Achievement   506

FROM RESEARCH TO PRACTICE   WHAT FACTORS PROMOTE THE ACADEMIC ACHIEVEMENT OF ADOLESCENTS FROM IMMIGRANT FAMILIES?   508

Try It Out 509   ■   Key Terms and Concepts 509   ■   Sum It Up 509

Visual Summary   510

16 Social and Emotional Development in Adolescence   512

How Do Older Adolescents Develop a Sense of Self and Identity?   513

Changes in Self-Concept During Adolescence   513
Self-Esteem During Adolescence   515
Gender Influences on Self-Development   515
Adolescent Identity Formation   516
Development of Adolescent Autonomy   521

How Do Family Relationships Change During Early Adolescence?   523

Parenting and Adolescent Development   524
The Bidirectionality of Parent–Adolescent Relationships   525
Parent–Adolescent Conflict   526

FROM RESEARCH TO PRACTICE   WHAT ROLES DO MOTHERS
AND FATHERS PLAY IN TEENS' PEER RELATIONSHIPS?   527

What Are the Characteristics of Adolescent Peer Relationships?   528

DEBATING THE ISSUE   DO FRIENDS LEAD TEENS INTO TROUBLE?   528

The Adolescent Peer Culture   529
Friendships During Adolescence   531
Peer Popularity and Rejection   531
Dating and Romantic Relationships   532
Sexual Relationships in Adolescence   533

How Do Mass Media Influence Adolescents' Development?   537

Popular Music   537
Computers   538

What Types of Behavior Problems Occur During Adolescence?   541

Antisocial Behavior   541
Depression   541
Substance Use and Abuse   542

NURTURING CHILDREN   PREVENTING TEENAGE DRUG USE   547

What Factors Influence Adolescents' Vulnerability and Resilience?   547

Try It Out 549 ■ Key Terms and Concepts 551 ■ Sum It Up 551

Visual Summary   552

Glossary   554

References   560

Name Index   624

Subject Index   633

To the Student

Our goal in writing this book was to explain how children develop, from conception through adolescence, and to explore the impact that individual characteristics, biological factors, personal relationships, social policies, and cultural values and beliefs have on a child's development. We do this by focusing on scientific research that examines the relationships children have with people and with their environments and how these relationships influence a child's cognitive, physical, social, and emotional development.

One of the best ways to understand what this book teaches is to first analyze the facts and issues that are presented and then apply them to your own life. Understanding the central role of relationships in development may lead you to new insights about your own childhood, as well as those of infants, children, and adolescents around you. Not only will you find the study of child development more meaningful; you will also be in a position to make better-informed decisions about issues related to children and their development.

Carol Lynn Martin
Richard Fabes

Preface

Children say and do amazing things—on a really hot day in Georgia, our niece recently described herself as being "soaking hot." When he was 4 years old, our nephew Brandon thought macaroni cooked in the oven at 25 degrees. Children's ordinary everyday activities are driven by fascinating developmental processes, such as when infants throw and drop objects off their high chairs—they do this acting as little scientists who are interested in exploring the properties of the things they drop. Our goal in writing this textbook was to convey a sense of wonder and discovery at the mysteries of child development. To accomplish this, we present reader-friendly and research-based discussions of child and adolescent development for students who are likely being exposed to this material for the first time. Our intention was to light the fire of students' interest in children, promote a passion for nurturing and caring for children, and illustrate the excitement of scientific explorations into the important issues involving the well-being of children, teens, and families.

Our Goals: From Research to Practice

Good science and its application are the centerpieces of this book. We have written our text to emphasize a scientific approach to child development. We also stress the application of science in helping to solve the real-world problems of children. Throughout the text, we focus on the various ways in which research discoveries can be practically applied in everyday living. In addition, we constantly reinforce the idea that development is shaped by the continuous interplay between individuals and their ever-changing environments.

The primary goals of *Discovering Child Development* are as follows:

- To encourage students to think critically about research and issues in child development
- To relate scientific research on children to real-life experiences
- To acknowledge the uniqueness of each child and to describe the impact that people, contexts, and experiences have on how they develop
- To consider child development within different biological, familial, social, and cultural backgrounds

Text Organization

This textbook is divided into six parts based on the sequence of developmental changes, from conception through adolescence. The text follows a chronological approach and emphasizes the critical changes that take place in physical, cognitive, and social development.

Part 1 introduces key themes and terminology in the study of child development, including the conceptual, historical, and scientific foundations of the field. Students receive a basic orientation to the major issues concerning development, research methods, and general theories of development.

Part 2 discusses the origins of development, including heredity and genetics; how life begins and the course of prenatal development; and childbirth. Part 3 focuses on the astonishing changes and accomplishments of infants and toddlers. Special attention is given to understanding these accomplishments as they occur within the context of early relationships, especially caregiving relationships.

Part 4 focuses on early childhood and includes perspectives on physical, cognitive, and socio-emotional development during the preschool years. Part 5 covers the period of childhood from the time children enter school until they begin puberty. The chapters in Parts 4 and 5 highlight the expanding abilities that develop during childhood and their links to the broadening scope of relationships found in peer and school environments. Part 6 provides in-depth coverage of adolescent development, again emphasizing physical, cognitive, and socio-emotional development and how these domains relate to and affect one another. Particular emphasis is placed on the changing nature of interpersonal relationships during adolescence.

Learning Aids

The variety of learning aids provided in this text is designed to promote critical thinking, enhanced understanding, and an appreciation for the complexities of children's lives and development. Many of the learning-related features incorporated into this text have been class-tested with students for effectiveness and appeal. In addition to the tried-and-true pedagogy that is typical of child development texts, we also include one particularly innovative feature—end-of-chapter visual summaries. We believe that this new feature will become standard practice for texts like this one in the years ahead because it will help focus students' attention on important summary information, while offering particular help to students who tend to consolidate and learn information visually. Below is an outline of the learning features in each chapter:

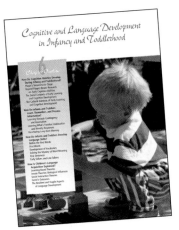

- ■ **Chapter outline.** Each chapter begins with a detailed outline to help students navigate their way through the chapter. The main chapter headings are framed as key questions, which are answered in the paragraphs that follow.

- ■ **Key terms and marginal glossary.** Key terms are boldfaced in the narrative where they first appear and then are defined in the margin. The key terms are also listed in the end-of-book glossary.

- ■ **Try It Out exercises.** These chapter-closing activities provide meaningful opportunities for relating chapter content to firsthand experience. These applications and activities are designed to make the material more personally and professionally relevant.

- ■ **Illustrations.** We worked hard to appeal to visual learners in our text, and have filled it with beautifully rendered illustrations that visually highlight important—and sometimes challenging—concepts.

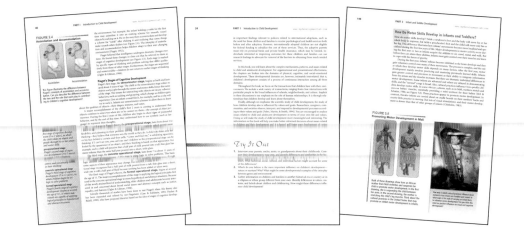

- **Visual summaries: A new twist on an old standby!** In lieu of traditional text-based end-of-chapter summaries, we close each chapter with an eye-catching, pedagogically useful chapter review. These two-page spreads summarize the key topics covered in the chapter by using text, photos, figures, and tables to present material in the most engaging way. More traditional end-of-chapter summaries are provided in the *Instructor's Manual*.

- **Sum It Up:** We've also added summary review questions at the end of each chapter to reinforce learning and review the material.

Special Features

Along with the learning aids embedded in each chapter are special features designed to engage students' interest and highlight important influences on children's development.

- **A Developmental Mystery.** Every chapter begins with a thought-provoking "developmental mystery" to hook the student's interest and to highlight the complexities of child development.

- **From Research to Practice.** These features present findings from cutting-edge scientific research in child development and walk students through the practical applications of that research. **Thinking It Through** questions close each feature, urging students to think critically about the research.

- **Debating the Issue.** These sections focus on contemporary policy issues that represent critical points of controversy in the field. **Thinking It Through** questions close each feature, encouraging students to analyze and express opinions on these issues and develop the skills needed to evaluate policy, research, and media issues in the field.

- **Nurturing Children.** These sections show the impact of various research findings on decision making and problem solving related to children in real-world contexts. These direct applications to the areas of education, parenting, health, and safety are particularly relevant to students pursuing careers in working with and caring for children.

Supplements

For the Instructor

Child Development Classroom Kit (Volumes I and II):   We have streamlined our supplements package for instructors by placing all of our print supplements in two easy-to-use volumes. Organized by chapter, each volume contains the relevant chapters from the instructor's manual, with detailed chapter outlines, lecture topics, and classroom demonstrations; the Grade-Aid Study Guide, with activities, practice tests, and other learning aids for students; the Test Bank, containing over 2,000 multiple-choice, true/false, fill-in, and essay questions; and sample slides from the Martin/Fabes PowerPoint presentation. The Classroom Kit is an invaluable tool, providing support and classroom management solutions for new and experienced instructors alike.

Child Development Classroom Kit CD-ROM: This exciting new supplement for instructors will bring together electronic copies of the Instructor's Manual, the Test Bank, the Grade-Aid Study Guide, the PowerPoint presentation, images from the text, and video clips for easy instructor access. Highly practical, the CD will be organized by chapter and searchable by key terms.

Test Bank and TestGenEQ: Prepared by Carol Lynn Martin and Richard Fabes of Arizona State University, this thoroughly reviewed test bank provides questions that target the key concepts from the text. The test bank has over 2,000 multiple-choice, true/false, fill-in, and essay questions, each with answer justification, page reference, difficulty ranking, and type designation to help professors prepare appropriate exams for their students. The test questions for the Martin/Fabes text can be found in print form in the Classroom Kit and digitized on our Classroom Kit CD-ROM. This supplement is also available in TestGen computerized version, on a multiplatform CD-ROM for Windows and Macintosh, for use in creating tests in the classroom.

Instructor's Manual: Written by Shelley Moore of Douglas College, this helpful teaching companion features at-a-glance grids, handouts, lecture enhancements, detailed chapter outlines, activities for the classroom, and other valuable course organization material for new and experienced instructors.

PowerPoint: Developed by Cynthia K. S. Read, Tarrant County Community College, the PowerPoint presentation is an interactive tool for use in the classroom, containing a comprehensive lecture outline and images from the textbook. This outline can be displayed to the class using a computer and an overhead projector with an LCD panel, printed and made into overhead transparencies, or printed and distributed individually to students. The PowerPoint is available through our IRC (www.ablongman.com/irc) website and can also be found on the Child Development Classroom Kit CD-ROM.

Video: A completely new Allyn & Bacon "Insights into Human Development" video is available to accompany the *Discovering Child Development* text. The video highlights important high-interest topics in child development and across the life span. Ask your local sales representative how to obtain a copy.

The Transparency Package for Human Development: Designed to enhance your classroom presentations, the transparency package contains color acetate transparencies drawn from the Martin/Fabes text and other relevant sources.

Digital Media Archive for Human Development: This comprehensive source of images includes charts, graphs, maps, tables, and figures, with audio clips and related Web links.

MyDevelopmentLab: MyDevelopmentLab is a state-of-the-art interactive and instructive solution for human development. This multimedia resource can be used to supplement a traditional lecture course or to administer a course entirely online. It is an all-inclusive tool, a text-specific e-book plus multimedia tutorials, audio, video, simulations, animations, and controlled assessments to completely engage students and reinforce learning. Fully customizable and easy to use, MyDevelopmentLab meets the individual teaching and learning needs of every instructor and every student. Visit the site at www.mydevelopmentlab.com.

For the Student

Grade-Aid with Practice Tests: The Grade-Aid Study Guide, a comprehensive interactive workbook, has been written by Denise Bodman of Arizona State University. It offers students a variety of guided activities and resources to reinforce their reading. Learning tools for each chapter include the following:

- "Before You Read," containing a brief chapter summary and chapter learning objectives
- "As You Read," offering a collection of demonstrations, activities, and exercises
- "After You Read," consisting of two short practice quizzes and one comprehensive practice test

- "When You Have Finished," presenting Web links for further information and a crossword puzzle using key terms from the text

Companion Website with Online Practice Tests: This website contains Online Practice Tests created by Carol Lynn Martin and Richard Fabes that connect the textbook to the Internet, and contain flash cards, learning objectives, and web links for each chapter, which help students review and retain key concepts from the text. Visit this site (www.ablongman.com/martinfabes1e).

Development Journey through Childhood and Adolescence CD-ROM (0-205-39568-6): This multimedia learning tool, developed by Dr. Kelly Welsh, Kansas State University, can be packaged with the text or sold separately. It includes eight interactive units that cover prenatal development through adolescence and uses video, audio, and animation to introduce biological, cognitive, and psychosocial changes. Video clips include footage such as live birth, kids demonstrating new physical and social skills, and a teen mom discussing the realities of pregnancy. Flash and 3-D video animations teach students about the inner workings of the human body, including the reproductive organs, conception, and pregnancy. Several exercises for students are included, such as drag-and-drop activities, multiple-choice quizzes, flash-card glossary terms, journal writing, and quick-response exercises called "Mad Minutes."

Tutor Center: The Tutor Center at www.aw.com/tutorcenter (access code required) provides students free, one-on-one, interactive tutoring from qualified psychology instructors on all material in the text. The Tutor Center offers students help with understanding major principles as well as methods for study. During Tutor Center hours, students can obtain assistance by phone, fax, Internet, and e-mail. For more details and ordering information, please contact your Allyn & Bacon publisher's representative.

MyDevelopmentLab: MyDevelopmentLab is a state-of-the-art interactive and instructive solution for human development. This multimedia resource can be used to supplement a traditional lecture course or to administer a course entirely online. It is an all-inclusive tool, a text-specific e-book plus multimedia tutorials, audio, video, simulations, animations, and controlled assessments to completely engage students and reinforce learning. Fully customizable and easy to use, MyDevelopmentLab meets the individual teaching and learning needs of every instructor and every student. Visit the site at www.mydevelopmentlab.com.

Study Card for Child Development, Chronological, © 2005—Colorful, affordable, and packed with useful information, Allyn & Bacon/Longman's Study Cards make studying easier, more efficient, and more enjoyable. Course information is distilled down to the basics, helping students quickly master the fundamentals, review a subject for understanding, or prepare for an exam.

Research Navigator: Allyn & Bacon's Research Navigator™ is the easiest way for students to start a research assignment or research paper. Complete with extensive help on the research process and three exclusive databases of credible and reliable source material including EBSCO's ContentSelect Academic Journal Database, New York Times Search by Subject Archive, and "Best of the Web" Link Library, Research Navigator™ helps students quickly and efficiently make the most of their research time.

Acknowledgments

A project of this type and magnitude requires the contributions and efforts of many individuals. First, we thank our families, particularly our parents, for providing us with examples of nurturance, love, strength, and support. This book is dedicated to them with our love and thanks. We especially acknowledge Carol's mother, Carolyn Ivey Martin, who did not survive her battle with cancer to see the final product. We miss her greatly and recognize that her love of being a mother colored much of our thinking about why it is important to nurture and cherish children.

We owe special thanks to Lisa McLellan, senior development editor, whose attention and faith in this book were exceptional and encouraging. We also thank Anna Socrates and Susan McNally, who helped mold and guide the form and structure of the book. Without their help, the book would not be what it is. Thanks also to Jennifer Trebby for her help with the supplemental materials and to all the members of the production team (listed at the beginning of the book) who did such a fine job editing and designing the book. We also are grateful to other Allyn & Bacon team members—Karon Bowers, Wendy Gordon, and Nancy Forsyth—for their confidence, support, and advice on various aspects of the book.

Many people helped us develop the content and materials for the book. In particular, Denise Bodman not only served as co-author on some of the supplemental materials but also provided us with feedback and enthusiasm, as did Barb and Bob Weigand. We also wish to thank our colleagues in the Department of Family and Human Development at Arizona State University, particularly our colleague Dr. Laura Hanish, for providing a supportive and stimulating environment in which to work and in helping us maintain our research in light of the demands of this project.

We also have benefited greatly from the ideas, insights, and issues brought up by the many reviewers of this textbook. We would like to thank the following individuals for their feedback on drafts of our chapters of *Discovering Child Development* in various stages of development:

Jackie Adamson, South Dakota School of Mines & Technology
Anita Anderson, University of the Incarnate World
Sharon Antonelli, San Jose City College
Harry Avis, Sierra Community College
Phoebe Baker, Tulsa Community College
Elise Barrett, Durham Technical Community College
Daniel Bellack, Trident Community College
Jannette Benson, University of Denver
Michael Bergmire, Jefferson College
Mary Bernadette, Concordia University
Tanisha Billingslea, Cameron University
Linda Bird, University of Michigan
Sandra Burkhardt, Saint Xavier University
Barry Bussewitz, Solano Community College
Tena Carr, San Joaquin Delta College
Dianna Chiabotti, Napa Valley College
Andrea Clements, East Tennessee State University
Margaret Coberly, University of Hawaii
Timothy Croy, Eastern Illinois University
Denise Davidson, Loyola University–Chicago
Derek de la Pena, University of Houston
Linda Dersheid, Northern Illinois University
Christyn Dundorf, Portland Community College
Martha M. Ellis, Collin Community College
Laurel Engholm, Southwestern College
Linda Estes, St. Charles Community College
Diane K. Feibel, University of Cincinnati–Raymond Walters College
Marie Fero, Eastern Illinois University
Sally Fiala, Visalia Unified School District
Diane Finley, Prince George's Community College
Linda E. Flickinger, St. Clair County Community College
Pamela Flores, Nassau Community College
Tom Frangicetto, Northampton Community College
Janet Fuller, Mansfield University

Albert H. Gardner, University of Maryland
Eugene Geist, Ohio University
Thomas Gerry, Columbia Green Community College
Pamela Guerra-Schmidt, Modesto Junior College
Kristine Hagen, Virginia Commonwealth University
Sharon B. Hamill, California State University–San Marcos
Lisa Hensley, Texas Wesleyan University
Martha Herndon, The University of Tennessee at Martin
William Higgins, University of Tennessee–Knoxville
Debra L. Hollister, Valencia Community College
David Hurford, Pittsburg State University
Kevin Keating, Broward Community College
John S. Klein, Castelton State College
Allison Larsen, Arizona State University
Sara Lawrence, California State University
Jennifer Lento, University of San Diego
Cathy Litty, Western Carolina University
Ron Lumson, Hudson Valley Community College
Kevin MacDonald, California State University–Long Beach
Barbara Matthews, Palm Beach Community College
Mary Ann McLaughlin, Clarion University of Pennsylvania
Leslie B. Minor-Evans, Central Oregon Community College
Kathryn Markell, Cardinal Stritch University
Rebecca Martin, University of Connecticut
Kerri Modry-Mandell, University of Arizona
J. Ann Moylan, California State University–Sacramento
Lynn Marie Nagle, Mount Aloysius College
Glenda K. Hill Nanna, Charleston Southern University
Karen Olson, St. Louis Community College

Shana Pack, Kentucky Wesleyan College
Rob Palkovitz, University of Delaware
Maribeth Palmer-King, Broome Community College
Sherri Addis Palmer, Truman State University
Richard Passman, University of Wisconsin–Milwaukee
Peggy Perkins, University of Nevada–Las Vegas
John A. Prange, Irvine Valley College
Joe M. Price, San Diego State University
Thomas G. Reio, Jr., University of Maryland
Barbara Reynolds, College of the Sequoias
Diane Roni, Southern Connecticut State University
Randall J. Russac, University of North Florida
Marcia Rysztak, Lansing Community College
Paul Schwartz, Mount St. Mary College
Michael F. Shaughnessy, Eastern New Mexico University
Michael Sontag, Lander University
Patricia D. Stanley, Louisiana State University–Shreveport
Ann Szalda-Petree, University of Montana
Tod Thorgersen, New Jersey City University
Kathleen Torsney, William Patterson University
Susan Troy, Northeast Iowa Community College
James Turcott, Kalamazoo Valley Community College
Linda Venekamp, Dakota State University
Elisa Vele, Albert Einstein College of Medicine
Judy Wendt, Blue Mountain Community College
Amy Williamson, Moraine Valley Community College
Lois Willoughby, Miami Dade College
Patty Wilhite, Northeast Louisiana University
Kevin M. P. Woller, Rogers State University
Peggy Wroten, Northeast Mississippi Community College

A final note of thanks is expressed from each of us to the other—without the love, patience, and companionship we have, it would have been almost unthinkable to take on this kind of project. Without each other, the job would have been much lonelier—and much less fun!

About the Authors

Carol Lynn Martin, Ph.D., is professor of child development at Arizona State University, where she has been for more than 15 years. She is a member of the Society for Research in Child Development and the National Council on Family Relations and a fellow of the American Psychological Association. Martin has been associate editor for *Developmental Psychology* and was a member of the editorial board of *Child Development*. She has written over 50 articles and book chapters, including a co-authored chapter in the new edition of the *Handbook of Child Psychology*. Most of these publications are in the areas of gender-role development and the cognitive processes underlying it. She is married to Richard Fabes, and away from work she enjoys yoga, tennis, traveling, and reading.

Richard A. Fabes, Ph.D., is professor of child development at Arizona State University, where he has been for more than 20 years. He is the chair of the Department of Family and Human Development and is a member of the Society for Research in Child Development, National Council on Family Relations, and American Psychological Association. Fabes has been an associate editor of *Merrill-Palmer Quarterly* and has been a member of the editorial boards of several widely known scientific journals, including *Developmental Psychology* and *Psychological Bulletin*. He has written over 100 articles, book chapters, or edited books, including a co-authored chapter in the new edition of the *Handbook of Child Psychology*. Most of these publications are in the areas of socio-emotional development of young children. He is married to Carol Martin, and away from work he enjoys tennis, traveling, and music.

part

1

Introduction to Child Development

For most people, caring for a child is one of life's most rewarding experiences—there is nothing more important than nurturing and understanding children. One of the purposes of this textbook is to give you a better understanding of the need for caring adults in children's lives. In this text, you will find a wide range of scientifically based information that will be both personally and professionally valuable. Even if you already have children of your own or have experience in caring for children, there is still much to learn about them. By devoting some time and effort, you can become better informed about the changing needs of children and the role that caring adults can play in helping them develop and reach their potential.

Introduction to Child Development

Chapter Outline

What Is Child Development?

What Are Some Critical Issues in the Study of Child Development?
Influences on Child Development
Teasing Out the Roles of
      Nature and Nurture
Continuity Versus Discontinuity
Critical and Sensitive Periods
Individual Differences in Development—
      Stability and Change

What Are the Historical Roots of the Study of Child Development?
Children of Antiquity
Children as Miniature Adults:
      Medieval Children
Early Philosophical Roots of Childhood
Charles Darwin: Evolution and
      Child Development
G. Stanley Hall: Pioneer in the
      Study of Development

What Changes in Contemporary American Life Influence the Study of Child Development?
Changes in Family Structure
Children of Same-Sex Parents
Ethnic and Racial Diversity
Poverty and Child Development

How Can We Capture the Diversity of Children's Development?

A DEVELOPMENTAL MYSTERY

In 1999, Angela Arenivar was a finalist in the Scripps National Spelling Bee. Hundreds of regional middle-school spelling champs converged on Washington, DC, for this competition. Angela was just one of these outstanding young spellers, but her story is especially fascinating because her parents had illegally crossed into the United States from Mexico many years earlier, and her mother and father never learned to speak English. How does a child who grows up in a poor family with parents who do not speak the language become an English spelling bee champion? Despite these odds, Angela (now a college student) was determined to succeed. As other contestants turned to computerized study tools and expensive coaches, Angela invented games to teach herself the spelling bee words. For her, mastery of the English language and a victory at the regional bee proved that she belonged in her culture, and her background and accomplishments inspired filmmakers to give her a starring role in the documentary film *Spellbound*.

Angela Arenivar was a finalist in the National Spelling Bee despite the fact that her parents could not speak English. What do children like Angela tell us about development and children's abilities to overcome potential barriers to growth and development?

Angela's story reflects one of the grand mysteries of child development: children whose backgrounds and experiences seemingly work against them can somehow overcome obstacles to achieve outstanding accomplishments. Does Angela's success reflect her own characteristics and qualities, such as being bright, hardworking, and able to concentrate? Or does her ability to overcome the odds reflect her family life and personal relationships? Or is her success based on some combination of these two factors? Answering questions like these is an important part of discovering child development.

What motivates people to do the things they do? Many movies, books, and documentaries have tried to answer this question. Often people look to a person's childhood to get clues about his or her attitude or behavior, whether good or bad. In Angela's case, nothing unusual or special would lead us to predict that she would be a finalist for a national spelling bee. In fact, her circumstances would lead most of us to predict just the opposite—research tells us that children from impoverished backgrounds and from environments in which English is not the dominant language often have difficulty doing well in school (see the section Poverty and Child Development). But clearly, some children, such as Angela, break the mold and succeed. Predicting which children will overcome such obstacles is virtually impossible. Similarly, predicting which children will grow up to be criminals or delinquents is also extremely difficult because such individuals are rare.

Nevertheless, trying to figure out how children and adults become who they are is intriguing. Like many people, scientists and practitioners who study and work with children are interested in these questions: What effects does environment have on people? How important are early experiences in shaping later behavior? Can children's development and behavior be changed? Development is complex, and many factors influence who we are and what we become; knowledge and ongoing research about this process form the essence of this book. Studying and understanding the broad and diverse influences on children's development can be very rewarding. Such studies focus on not only what can go wrong, but also, increasingly, on what can go right in development, such as attainment of competence and wisdom (Masten & Curtis, 2000; Pasupathi, Staudinger, & Baltes, 2001; see also boxed feature). This endeavor has relevance and meaning! Adults can make a difference in children's lives. Understanding children, their development, and the factors that can lead to positive and negative outcomes can empower us to help them reach their potential as successful, productive, and happy individuals.

NURTURING CHILDREN
FOSTERING CHILDREN'S CONCERN AND CARING FOR OTHERS

Although our culture tends to focus on the problems of children and families (such as aggression, drug abuse, or depression), researchers who study child development also focus on the development of positive qualities and characteristics. Considerable research now exists concerning how children develop caring feelings for others (Eisenberg, Fabes, & Spinrad, 2005). These studies suggest that the following activities can help children develop concern and caring feelings for others:

- Draw the child's attention to other people's feelings. Encourage the child to imagine how he or she would feel in someone else's situation.
- Talk to children about the impact of their actions on other people's feelings, including your own.
- Explain why other people feel the way they do and why they often do the things they do.
- Let the child know that you expect her or him to be considerate and

responsible and that these qualities are important to you.
- Give approval when the child is considerate and helpful; show disapproval when he or she is not.
- Share your own feelings of concern and sympathy with the child. Stress the good feelings that come from caring about other people.

What Is Child Development?

child development *changes in physical, social, emotional, and intellectual functioning over time, from conception through adolescence*

developmental domains *the three main areas of development: physical, cognitive, and social–emotional development*

physical development *growth and change in a person's body and bodily functions*

cognitive development *development of mental processes used to process information, grow in awareness, solve problems, and gain knowledge*

social–emotional development *development of processes related to interactions with other people*

Child development involves changes in physical, social, emotional, and intellectual functioning over time, from conception through adolescence. Changes include physical alterations in size, shape, and function, and these alterations can be either progressive or regressive (Magnusson, 1995). Time and change work in concert to shape who we are.

In this book, child development is presented in terms of functionally defined age-related stages: prenatal development, infancy and toddlerhood, early and middle childhood, and adolescence. These stages reflect a contemporary view of development and will help you conceptualize the complex, interdependent changes that take place across childhood. In each stage, changes occur in three main areas of development called **developmental domains. Physical development** involves growth and change in a person's body and bodily functions. Included in this developmental domain is the study of physiological and motor development as well as the impacts of illness, nutrition, and health. **Cognitive development** involves mental processes used to process information, grow in awareness, solve problems, and gain knowledge. This developmental domain encompasses the study of brain functioning, perception, memory, learning, thinking, and language. **Social–emotional development** involves processes related to interactions with other people. Included in this domain is the study of relationships, emotions, personality, and moral development.

Is any single domain more important than others? Some people might think so. For example, many parents and educators believe that being smart and doing well in school (the cognitive domain) are the most important aspects of successful development (Zill, 1999). Parents are much less certain about the role of social and emotional growth in healthy development (Zero to Three, 1997). But does emphasizing the intellect build the best bridge from childhood to adulthood? Consider the story of William James Sidis, a child prodigy whose intellectual gifts were "off the charts." Born in 1898, William learned to read when he was 18 months old. By the age of 6, he could read several languages. At that point, he was required by law to go to school, where he moved through all seven grades of elementary school in just 6 months. Over the next couple of years, he was taught at home until he went to high school, from which he graduated in 3 months. At the age of 11, William entered Harvard University, and a few months later he delivered a brilliant speech to the Harvard Math Club.

You may think that things looked pretty good for William. Unfortunately, this was the high point of his life. Although he received his bachelor's degree from Harvard at the age of 16, he never put it to use. He went to graduate school for a year and then went to law school, but he never received a degree from either. He taught at a university for a short period of time and then turned against his schooling and intellectual accomplishments. He spent the rest of his life working at mindless, low-paying jobs, moving from one position to another. He never married, and he was filled with bitterness and loneliness. When he died at the age of 46, William was alone, obscure, penniless, and miserably maladjusted (Montour, 1977).

The story of William James Sidis reveals that no single developmental domain is more important than another. Although he was clearly smart, his lagging social development created serious adjustment problems. Each domain is important at each stage of development, and this book examines each stage in terms of the three developmental domains and the interrelationships among them.

What Are Some Critical Issues in the Study of Child Development?

The study of child development deals with how children change and become who they are, though scientists who address these critical issues often disagree about the wellsprings of behavior and personality. This topic also attracts the interest of the general public and the news media. For example, in a series of tragic events that occurred from December 1997 to April 1999, young students in Kentucky, Arkansas, Oregon, and Colorado opened fire on classmates. In the worst of these cases—the tragedy in Littleton, Colorado, in the spring of 1999—13 people were killed, booby traps and bombs were planted, and the teens who masterminded this violent assault took their own lives. Immediately, local

FIGURE 1.1
Developmental Domains

Physical Development

Cognitive Development   Social Development

Children's development can be broken into three separate domains: physical, cognitive, and social. Although we separate them for the sake of discussion, they are all interconnected. Can you identify the kinds of changes that occur in each and how these may relate to changes in other domains?

and national media gathered the experts to discuss the events. Laypeople also tried to make sense of the tragedy. The questions they asked were familiar ones: How could this happen? What caused the kids to do these terrible deeds? Was it something in their upbringing or something within them? The answers are elusive, but to begin to answer them we must understand children and adolescents and the influences that affect their development.

Influences on Child Development

Developmental changes are brought about by a variety of mechanisms. Some occur largely through the unfolding of a person's genetic code. These changes are referred to as **maturation,** and they involve a series of preprogrammed transformations in the form, structure, or function of an individual. One vivid example of maturation is the physical change associated with puberty; in this stage, genetically inherited instructions guide development of the adolescent's nervous system. Changes in other domains of development (such as social and intellectual changes) and in other aspects of life, such as diet, exercise, or stress, are associated with maturation.

Environmental factors also influence human development (Harris, 1995). Because environmental stimuli bombard children every moment of every day, their potential for affecting development is great. This influence begins very early; for example, if a pregnant woman is exposed to environmental toxins or radiation, it can affect her unborn child and influence its development. The effects of these early environmental exposures can be devastating and permanent.

maturation   *changes brought about largely through the unfolding of a person's genetic code*

FROM RESEARCH TO PRACTICE
DO EARLY EXPERIENCES INFLUENCE LATER DEVELOPMENT?
THE CASE OF THE DUTCH FAMINE OF 1944–1945

FROM RESEARCH . . .

Do early experiences influence later development? This critical question in child development research is difficult to answer. For example, according to one hypothesis, many diseases of later life are thought to originate when a person is developing in the mother's womb. This notion reflects the belief that an adverse prenatal environment permanently changes the physiology, metabolism, and organ structure of the developing child, making it susceptible to disease later in life (Rosenboom et al., 2003). But how can we study this hypothesis? One way is to find and examine applicable historical examples. One such case occurred during World War II, when the Nazis carried out an inhuman operation of revenge for a Dutch railroad workers' strike that slowed German troop reinforcements in 1944. To retaliate, the Nazis imposed an embargo on transports to the Netherlands. This embargo included the transport of food, producing a famine that continued until the spring of 1945. During that time, 40,000 pregnant Dutch women and their unborn children were exposed to severe malnutrition and starvation. By studying these children, scientists gained important insights into the effects of malnutrition during pregnancy on the development of children.

As babies, the effects of malnourishment were dramatic—those exposed to malnourishment during the second or third trimesters had higher-than-normal death rates in their first weeks of life, and the rate continued to climb until they were 3 months old. Once these babies reached the age of 1 year, their risk of death returned to normal levels (Diamond, 1990).

Adults who had experienced the famine as babies were physically smaller and more likely to have defects of the central nervous system. In particular, those who were exposed to famine during the first trimester of pregnancy showed greater evidence of brain abnormalities, heart disease, obesity, and mental illness (Hulshoff-Pol et al., 2000; Roseboom et al., 2003). These findings suggest that early prenatal malnutrition may adversely influence susceptibility to later disease. Nutritional deficiencies during early pregnancy program a child's physiological functioning to prepare for survival in the hostile prenatal environment, but this programming significantly increases the risk of poor physical and mental health later in life (Hobel & Culhane, 2003).

But even more sobering was the effect starvation had on the generation of children born to these famine babies. Examination of the birth records revealed that women who were born to mothers starved during the Dutch famine of World War II gave birth to underweight babies. Thus, the babies were affected by the starvation of their grandmothers two generations earlier. Somehow the grandmothers' starvation had very long-term effects. The lesson of the Dutch famine is that harm from prenatal malnourishment is not limited to the generation that experiences it directly, but may be felt generations later (Diamond, 1990).

. . . TO PRACTICE

Such findings highlight the importance of proper nutrition and other health practices during pregnancy—not only for the developing child but also for future generations. Eating properly, getting sleep and exercise, and avoiding stress and harmful substances and situations all contribute to healthy pregnancies (as you will learn in Chapter 4). But is it enough to begin these practices when a woman finds out that she is pregnant? Increasingly, evidence is pointing to preparing for pregnancy—perhaps even as much as two years in advance (March of Dimes, 2004).

THINKING IT THROUGH

1. What cause-and-effect relationships are implied in this case?

2. What problems might researchers encounter in using historical events for drawing conclusions about cause-and-effect relationships?

3. What are the implications of these findings for mothers today?

The environment also influences behavior through **learning,** changes that occur as the result of observation, experience, instruction, or practice. Learning affects a wide range of activities, behaviors, and attitudes—sports, attitudes toward people of different races, achievement in school, and aggressiveness, to name only a few. Learning also influences the process by which children become members of a social group, a family, a community, a tribe, or a team. The process by which children learn social roles and become members of

learning   *changes that occur as the result of observation, experience, instruction, or practice*

groups is referred to as **socialization.** By teaching them the values, beliefs, customs, and expectations of their society, socialization helps most children get along cooperatively in the social and cultural contexts in which they find themselves.

Some developmental changes are relatively permanent, such as the development of the skeletal system, whereas other changes may be more fleeting, such as the use of a particular cognitive strategy to add numbers. Many people make the mistake of assuming that changes caused by biological agents (such as drugs or hormones) are irreversible, whereas those caused by social agents (such as family interactions or schooling) can be modified. However, some changes brought about by biological agents can be reversed. For example, the very serious brain damage caused by the genetic disease phenylketonuria (PKU) can be prevented by altering the child's diet. On the other hand, a child may never overcome the intellectual deficits caused by parents who are too depressed to interact with her or him.

The extent to which biological/genetic and environmental factors influence development has been, and continues to be, hotly debated in the field of child development. This controversy is often referred to as the **nature versus nurture debate.** Those who support the nature side of the debate emphasize the role of biological/genetic factors, whereas those on the nurture side emphasize the role of the environment.

How children come to understand the values and customs of their culture reflects the process of socialization. As this picture indicates, parents are important agents of socialization. Can you identify other socialization agents?

The Wild Boy of Aveyron: A Case for Nurture?

One way to examine the effects of biology and the environment is to study children who are deprived of human contact. Do these children develop like children who have contact with others? If so, then genetic inheritance must be the major factor in their development, and the role of the social environment in producing normal behavior is small. Or does their behavior become what we consider human only after contact with other humans? Of course, conducting an experiment that isolates children in this way is out of the question ethically. But in some rare instances, it has been possible to study children abandoned early in development and left to survive on their own.

The Wild Boy of Aveyron stands out as one of the most famous and well-documented cases of such a child. The Wild Boy was captured by hunters in 1798 and placed in a hospital in Aveyron (in the countryside outside Paris), where he was diagnosed as a "congenital idiot." At the time of his capture, the boy was about 12 years old and probably had been living alone in the wild since the age of 3 or 4.

Initial descriptions of the boy's behavior aroused much curiosity; he was described as a savage, subject to fits of anger, nervous spasms, and convulsions. He slept according to the sun; was restless, shy, and wild; sought escape at every opportunity; did not talk but growled and grunted; bit and scratched; and showed little affection. He disliked sleeping in a bed; was not bothered by cold temperatures or foul smells; ate berries, roots, and raw chestnuts; and disliked sweets. In short, the Wild Boy, who came to be known as Victor, lacked all elements of "civilized" human behavior (Malson, 1972).

Eventually Victor was brought under the care of Jean Itard, a French physician. Itard argued that Victor's retardation was the result of lack of experience and contact with humans. He believed that if Victor was given proper remedial experience, he would become normal and civilized. Itard set out to provide educational experiences for Victor and show that the environment is the major influence on development.

Under Itard's care, Victor's behavior did change. He lost some of his wildness and made important intellectual strides. He learned to dress himself, use table utensils to eat, and express basic emotions. Although he never learned to speak, he learned to identify various letters. Interestingly, he learned to express simple wants and needs through writing. By the end of five years with Itard, however, Victor's behavior was by no means "normal." Compared to other children of his own age, Victor was still severely intellectually and socially retarded. Itard stopped the experiment because he felt that not enough progress had been

In this photo from the 1970 movie *L'Enfant Sauvage,* the Wild Boy of Aveyron is being trained to speak. Why did Itard attempt to socialize the boy? What questions does this case raise about the study of child development?

socialization *the process by which children learn social roles and become members of groups*

nature versus nurture debate *controversy over the extent to which biological/genetic and environmental factors influence development*

made (Itard, 1972a/1801, 1972b/1806). Victor lived out his life with the woman who had been caring for him at the hospital, and he died in 1828.

Scientifically, we can conclude little about Itard's natural experiment. Certainly, Victor's condition improved, but the best we can say is that the results are inconclusive. We do not know enough about Victor prior to the time he was captured to answer the nature versus nurture question. Perhaps Victor had some biological condition that impaired his ability to learn and become socialized. His tendency toward "fits of convulsions and spasms" may have been the reason he was abandoned in the first place (Frith, 1989).

Medical Wonders: A Case for Nature?

Itard tried to use the unusual case of Victor to study the extent to which environmental influences contribute to development. Other unusual cases have been used to explore the degree to which biological processes contribute to development. Such is the case of Brandi Binder. When she was 6 years old, the entire right side of her cortex (the outer layer of the brain) was removed because of severe epileptic seizures. Because the right side of the cortex controls the muscles on the left side of the body, she lost motor control over half of her body. Yet after seven years of intensive therapy in motor skills, math, and music, Brandi became proficient in skills ordinarily associated with the right cortex of the brain. Thus, Brandi's brain was plastic enough to compensate for the loss of half of her cortex. Brandi's brain rearranged many of its connections to allow her to regain function in areas normally controlled by the right brain. Unfortunately, function was not restored to all areas—she still cannot use her left arm (Nash, 1997).

Cases like Brandi's tell us that if there is a way to compensate for severe damage, the brain will find it and attempt to restore things to normal. But like the case of Victor, Brandi's case provides only limited help in resolving the nature versus nurture debate. Brandi's recovery proves that biology and physiology are not the sole or dominant influences on early development. Without environmental factors such as intense therapy (ranging from leg lifts to musical drills), Brandi would never have recovered to the extent that she did. Her environmental experiences may have determined how her brain rewired itself (Jacobs, 1997).

Teasing Out the Roles of Nature and Nurture

Modern child development researchers use sophisticated techniques and strategies, such as adoption and twin studies, to address questions of nature versus nurture. Additionally, the essence of the debate has changed somewhat: now it does not concern whether nature or nurture has an influence—we know that both do—but rather how nature and nurture work together to influence development (Gottlieb, 1997; Rutter et al., 1997).

Determining the genetic and environmental bases for characteristics and behaviors is challenging, particularly for complex human attributes such as intelligence, mental illness, or personality. Much of our knowledge about the genetic transmission of physical characteristics has been acquired by studying insects and animals, but they provide poor models for studying complex human behaviors and characteristics. Another problem is that the environment is difficult to assess or control. Despite these difficulties, behavioral genetics researchers use a variety of techniques to assess the roles that genetics and the environment play in human behavior.

Adoption Studies

An adopted child carries the genetic inheritance of his or her biological parents but is raised by parents who are genetically unrelated to him or her. This situation provides a natural opportunity to study genetic influences. If an adopted child's behavior more closely resembles that of the parents who raised him or her, this suggests that the family environment plays a strong role in that particular behavior. In contrast, if an adopted child behaves in ways more similar to the actions of biological parents, this suggests that genetic factors play a strong role in that behavior (Plomin, Fulker, Corley, & DeFries, 1997).

Twin Studies

Another way to tease out the roles that nature and nurture play in development is to study twins. **Monozygotic (MZ) twins,** often called *identical twins,* share the same genetic

monozygotic (MZ) twins *twins who share the same genetic code because they developed from one fertilized egg, which divided into two separate individuals; identical twins*

code because they developed from one fertilized egg, which divided into two separate individuals. **Dizygotic (DZ) twins,** often called *fraternal twins,* developed from two separate eggs fertilized by two separate sperm cells. DZ twins may be very similar or very different genetically, just like any two siblings. On average, about 50 percent of their genetic code is shared. Both kinds of twins experience the same prenatal environment, are born at the same time, and usually live in the same family, so they share many similar environmental factors. Because MZ and DZ twins differ in the degree to which they share genetic codes but tend to have similar environments, they provide a way to estimate how genes and environment interact to influence development (Wachs, 1992).

Identical twins share the same genetic structure. Even so, they often are very different from each other. What does this tell us about the influence of nature versus nurture?

If a particular characteristic has a strong environmental component and a weak genetic component, MZ twins should be no more alike than DZ twins regarding that characteristic. If a characteristic has a strong genetic component, then MZ twins should be more alike based on that characteristic than are DZ twins. Geneticists determine **heritability**—an estimate of the degree to which variation of a characteristic in a population is influenced by genetic factors—by comparing the degrees of similarity of MZ and DZ twins (Plomin, 1994). Studies of twins have shown that height, for example, is largely genetically determined. MZ twins are quite similar in height, usually differing by only about $1/3$ inch. DZ twins are less similar in height, usually differing by about $1^1/_2$ inches (Mange & Mange, 1994). The heritability estimate suggests that 90 percent of the variation in height is due to genetic factors. Twins' weights vary much more than their heights do, suggesting that environmental factors play a larger role in determining weight.

Such findings suggest that the correspondence of certain physical traits increases as the degree of genetic relatedness increases. But does this relationship apply to complex human characteristics? The answer seems to be yes. For example, the risk of a person's developing schizophrenia (a serious mental illness) increases when close family members have the disorder (Gottesman, 1991). The closer the relative, the greater the risk. The risk of developing schizophrenia is greatest when an MZ twin has developed the disorder, but this risk does not reach 100 percent. This finding suggests that although genetic factors may predispose someone to schizophrenia, nongenetic factors (such as family experiences or stress-related factors) may need to be present for the illness to manifest itself (Gottesman, 1991). Findings such as these reinforce the importance of exploring how genes and the environment work together to influence development.

Twin and Adoption Methods Combined

Sometimes researchers combine the twin and adoption study methods, looking at the similarity or dissimilarity of twins who are reared apart. From these studies, researchers have concluded that many aspects of personality have a sizable genetic component, with roughly 50 percent of the variability in personality accounted for by heredity (Tellegen, 1988). The remaining 50 percent of the variability in personality is attributable to environmental factors, including shared experiences (such as experience in the same family) and nonshared experiences (such as influences of different teachers or friends). MZ twins raised together tend to be no more alike than MZ twins reared apart, suggesting that nonshared environments influence personality development to a greater extent than do shared experiences.

Shared environments, however, play a greater role in the development of intelligence (Plomin et al., 1997). Studies conducted on twins raised together and apart have shown that intelligence test scores are most closely related for MZ twins who are raised together. About 50 percent of the variability in intelligence can be attributed to genetic inheritance and 50 percent to environmental influences. Even the shared prenatal environment of twins contributes to their similarities and may partly explain why DZ twins have higher resemblance in intelligence than do ordinary siblings (Devlin, Daniels, & Roeder, 1997).

Twin and adoption studies help us understand that genes and the environment are complexly interwoven. For instance, genes may influence exposure and susceptibility to

dizygotic (DZ) twins *twins who develop from two separate eggs fertilized by two separate sperm cells; fraternal twins*

heritability *an estimate of the degree to which variation of a characteristic in a population is influenced by genetic factors*

different kinds of environments. Children who are genetically predisposed to be active will search out peers who are active, thereby affecting their development by changing their environment (Rutter et al., 1997).

Continuity Versus Discontinuity

Another major issue in child development concerns the course of development: does it occur gradually and smoothly or in a series of abrupt and separate changes? Some developmental scientists focus on gradual changes and view development as **continuous**—as seen in the development of vocabulary, whereby children slowly add more and more words over time (see Figure 1.2a). Other scientists view development as **discontinuous** and focus on the acquisition of qualitatively new patterns of behavior—as seen in the transition from crawling to walking (see Figure 1.2b). These qualitatively different patterns in development are called *stages*, and, as you will see, many theories of development (such as Piaget's) are stage theories.

The advantage of using stages to represent development is that they help organize information in a meaningful way. The disadvantage of stage theories is that they gloss over the inconsistencies, complexities, and irregularities of development (Aylward, 1997; Flavell, 1982). Changes that seem abrupt, such as a child's first step, may actually be the culmination of a long, gradual process (Thelen, 1989). For instance, infants increasingly kick their legs in rhythm until they begin to crawl and walk. These early leg kicks reveal a continuity in development, setting the stage for what appears to be a rather sudden shift in the infant's development—namely, the beginning of upright self-movement (Thelen & Smith, 1998). When viewed in this manner, development is best conceived of as a dynamic and complex pattern of both gradual and abrupt changes.

Critical and Sensitive Periods

Another important issue is whether there exist **critical periods** of development—specific periods during which a particular event or stimulus has the greatest impact on develop-

continuous development
view of development as smooth and gradual

discontinuous development
view of development as abrupt and unstable, made up of qualitative stages and changes

critical periods   *periods of time during which a particular event or stimulus has to occur to have an impact on development*

FIGURE 1.2
Views on the Nature of Developmental Change

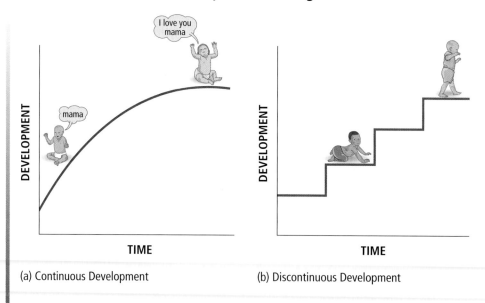

(a) Continuous Development   (b) Discontinuous Development

Some developmental scientists view change as a smooth trajectory (a), whereas others view it as a series of discrete stages (b). Still others believe that change consists of both discrete stages and smooth trajectories. Which of these models best fits your view of developmental change?

ment. According to the critical period view, individuals are unusually influenced by specific types of stimulation at certain times. If the stimulation is received during the critical time period, development is affected. If the needed stimulation is received at the wrong time, its impact may be lessened or even nonexistent (Wachs, 1992).

Evidence for critical periods has been well documented in many animals. For example, a critical period immediately after birth has been established for imprinting in ducklings—they follow the first moving object they see right after birth, which usually is the mother duck. The strongest evidence for critical periods in child development comes from studies of language development. Children who do not have sufficient exposure to language before the age of 6 or 7 years, like Victor, may never acquire a language (Newport, 1991).

For most aspects of development, however, the concept of critical periods appears to be too narrow (Bornstein, 1989). The case of Brandi Binder shows that children are remarkably resilient and can compensate for inadequate or inappropriate stimulation during important times in development. Many developmental scientists use the term **sensitive periods** to refer to times that are optimal for the development of certain behaviors or functions but, unlike critical periods, are not defined as necessary (Shavinina, 1997). The concept of sensitive periods acknowledges that it is possible for development to occur later, although it may be more difficult or incomplete then (Wachs, 1992).

Ducklings follow the first moving object they see. Here, they follow Konrad Lorenz, who used principles such as critical and sensitive periods to explain development. What role do critical and sensitive periods play in human development?

Individual Differences in Development—Stability and Change

Another vital issue in the field of child development is sorting out universal versus individual developmental characteristics and events. Because children are all members of the same species, they are alike in many ways—they have similar basic physical form, functions, and abilities. However, as soon as children are born (and even before), differences among them are noticeable. Also, although children share biological and cultural characteristics, every child is unique. Even identical twins, who share identical genetic information, are different in many respects. Are individual differences stable and permanent, or do they change over time? Do fussy children grow up to be fussy adolescents and adults? Do shy children grow up to be shy adolescents and adults? As you will learn, individual differences tend to be consistent, but human behavior is amazingly flexible and subject to change over time and across different situations.

What Are the Historical Roots of the Study of Child Development?

The desire to understand children is not new. As you will soon learn, the Greek philosopher Plato addressed issues related to the nature versus nurture debate. Although critical issues related to child development are not necessarily new, the use of scientific methods to address them is relatively recent—only about 100 years old. Before then, cultural and social factors in Western civilization limited scientific inquiry into child development. In addition, the study of child development has been influenced by changing views concerning the nature, role, and status of children in society.

Children of Antiquity

In ancient Greece and Rome, children were viewed as helpless and incapable of caring for themselves, as well as lacking in self-control and prone to disobedience. Therefore a heavy emphasis was placed on discipline (Borstelmann, 1983). Children were meant to serve the interests of the gods through their families and society; they had no status independent of such considerations.

sensitive periods *periods of time that are optimal, but not necessary, for the development of certain behaviors or functions*

Children also were viewed as naive and easily susceptible to corruption. In ancient Greece, Plato (808 BC) addressed these concerns by proposing drastic measures. Convinced that the citizens of Athens had succumbed to a decadent society and were unfit to rear children, Plato proposed that children be separated from their parents early in life and reared under state control. Selective screening would ensure that only those individuals of the highest moral character would rear and train children. Plato believed that socialization and the environment are critical factors in development and that development is a continuous process. Although his contention that children should be reared by professional caregivers rather than parents seems undesirable by today's standards, it reflects the belief that children are important to the future of a society—a view held by most people today.

Children as Miniature Adults: Medieval Children

During the European Middle Ages, children were not recognized as distinct from adults. As soon as a child could live without the constant attention and help of a caregiver (at about the age of 6 or 7), she or he belonged to adult society (Aries, 1962). Evidence of this lack of distinction between children and adults is seen often in the art of the times, wherein children are depicted as miniature adults. Medieval artists did not represent physical differences other than size in the bodies and dress of adults and children.

This lack of a distinction between children and adults did not mean that children were neglected or forsaken. It simply reflected the historical context of the Middle Ages: compared to our way of life, the lives of children and families during this period were harsh and difficult, and the attitudes toward children reflected these conditions. Children's labor was considered a necessity, and because infant mortality was so high—one half to two thirds of all children died during infancy—adults were reluctant to recognize children as special individuals (Jaffe, 1997). Children worked like adults, dressed like adults, and could legally be married, crowned, or hanged like adults. Distinctions were not made between activities appropriate for children and for adults because it was believed that children generally did not have needs beyond those of adults. Although this view has been challenged (Elkind, 1986; Pollock, 1983), it exemplifies how the conceptualization and treatment of children are intricately bound to the historical context in which they are raised.

Early Philosophical Roots of Childhood

A more enlightened view of childhood arose during the Renaissance (late fourteenth and early fifteenth centuries) and the Reformation (fifteenth and sixteenth centuries). More children were living to adulthood, and helping them acquire knowledge and skills at an early age became more important. During the sixteenth through eighteenth centuries, a new way of looking at childhood emerged. In particular, two philosophers, writing about 100 years apart, took an interest in the welfare of children and recognized that their needs differ from those of adults. The two philosophers, John Locke and Jean-Jacques Rousseau, argued that childhood is an important period that sets the stage for what one becomes later in life. But at the same time, Locke's and Rousseau's views on the primary influence and process of development differed, reflecting the nature versus nurture debate.

John Locke: The Tabula Rasa

John Locke (1632–1704) proposed that a child is like a blank slate, or *tabula rasa* in Latin, upon which experiences in life write their story. Through interactions with

Notice how the children in this painting are depicted as miniature adults. What differences would you expect to see if they were accurately portrayed? What does this artwork tell us about the conceptualization of children during this period?

people and objects in the environment, each child develops his or her unique character and abilities. Locke emphasized the long-term impact of early experiences and the responsibility parents bear for their children's character formation.

> *The great mistake I have observed in people's breeding their children is that the mind has not been made obedient to discipline and pliant to reason when it was most tender, most easy to be bowed.*
>
> —John Locke (1690/1964)

This quotation reflects Locke's belief that the environment is the driving force in development. By promoting children's obedience and curiosity, parents encourage their children to develop into rational, attentive, and affectionate people. Through the experiences provided by parents, children are socialized into their culture.

Jean-Jacques Rousseau: Innate Morality

Jean-Jacques Rousseau (1712–1778) also challenged the notion that children are merely miniature and inferior adults. In contrast to Locke, however, Rousseau emphasized the importance of internal, or innate, forces. He believed that from the time they are born, children possess an intrinsic character that is perfect and good. The role of adults, in Rousseau's view, is to let the natural positive forces in children emerge without restraint:

> *God makes all things good; man meddles with them and they become evil.*
>
> —Jean-Jacques Rousseau (1762/1911)

Because of his emphasis on letting the natural qualities of the child dictate his or her development, Rousseau is humorously referred to as the "grandfather of permissive parenting." Children should be allowed to naturally unfold, with little pressure from adults (although he did sometimes advocate that parents carefully regulate their children's experiences). In emphasizing the inborn, natural qualities of development, Rousseau placed greater importance on internal (nature) rather than external (nurture) processes (Synnott, 1988).

Locke and Rousseau set the stage for the modern scientific study of child development. They assigned children a special status and argued that early experiences shape later development.

Charles Darwin: Evolution and Child Development

With his theory of evolution, Charles Darwin (1809–1882) radically changed the way scientists thought about child development. In *Origin of Species* (published in 1859), Darwin proposed the revolutionary ideas that various species had a common ancestor and that species either die out or change to meet the demands of their changing environments. Darwin's views challenged the ingrained theological view that child behavior is created in a fixed and perfect form. Instead, Darwin believed that human behavior evolved slowly over time.

Darwin's theory is based on the concept of **natural selection**—the idea that in nature, individuals who are best adapted to their surroundings survive and reproduce, and the adaptive characteristics of those individuals are passed on to the next generation. After many generations, the traits of these individuals become increasingly prevalent in the population (Darwin, 1859).

The impact of Darwin's work continues to be dramatic and pervasive. The possibility that human behavior reflects evolutionary adaptation and selection is a part of many theories of development. Furthermore, Darwin's emphasis on common ancestors has led to comparisons between the development of human behavior and the development of similar behaviors in other species (Berman, Rasmussen, & Suomi, 1994).

natural selection   *the process, in nature, whereby individuals who are best adapted to their surroundings survive and reproduce, and the adaptive characteristics of those individuals are passed on to the next generation*

Locke, Rousseau, Darwin, and Hall all had important influences on the early study and conceptualization of child development. Can you identify their contributions? Can you discuss their views on the influence of nature versus nurture?

G. Stanley Hall: Pioneer in the Study of Development

Up to 100 years ago, most studies of child development consisted of philosophical treatises (such as those written by Locke and Rousseau) and biographical diaries written by parents about their infant children (Darwin, 1877). Then, at the beginning of the twentieth century, G. Stanley Hall (1844–1924) pioneered the application of scientific procedures to the study of child development. For example, he was the first to use questionnaires with children. Although his early attempts were somewhat haphazard, his research illustrated how scientific methods can be used to understand children.

Hall was the first scientist to focus attention on adolescent development and to define adolescence as a separate period of life. He also wrote one of the first developmental textbooks. Thus, Hall's work directly stimulated significant areas of contemporary developmental study: scientific aspects of the study of development, adolescence, and early childhood education (Cairns, 1998).

What Changes in Contemporary American Life Influence the Study of Child Development?

Just as historical changes affected the study of children, contemporary changes in American population and culture have an impact on the study of child development. This impact reminds us that the study of child development is influenced by the contexts in which researchers work. Changes in family composition and increasing cultural diversity, for example, have stimulated new research.

Changes in Family Structure

Family life in the United States has been changing dramatically. Even the concept of what a family is has undergone change. The prevalence of the traditional **nuclear family,** in which the biological mother and father and their children live together, has been declining for some years. In 1970, 40 percent of all US households consisted of children living with their biological parents. By 2000, this figure had dropped to 24 percent (US Census, 2001b).

The fastest-growing type of family in the United States in recent years is the **single-parent family,** in which children live with only their mother or their father. The primary cause of single-parent families is divorce, and 90 percent of single-parent families are headed by women. In 1960, only 9 percent of children under the age of 18 lived with a single parent. By 2002, the proportion of single-parent children had jumped to nearly one

nuclear family *family structure in which the biological mother and father and their children live together*

single-parent family *family structure in which children live with only their mother or their father*

FIGURE 1.3
Children Living in Different Types of Families, by Race: 2002

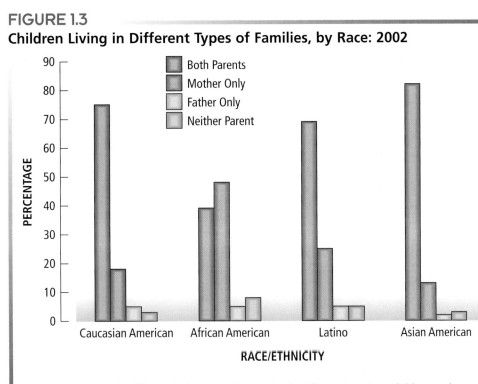

Notice the dramatic differences between the graphs for African American children and those for Caucasian American, Asian American, and Hispanic children. What are the major differences, and what factors might account for them?

Source: US Census Bureau, 2003.

quarter of all US children (US Census Bureau, 2003), and, with the exception of Asian American children, the proportion was even larger for minority children (see Figure 1.3). As you can see, the percentage of minority children living in single-parent families is especially high for African American children. This is due primarily to the higher rate of African American children living with mothers who were never married.

Another family type that has become increasingly common is the **blended family**—formed when a widowed or divorced person remarries. If the remarried husband or wife or both have children from a former marriage, a **stepfamily** is formed. About 29 percent of African American children, 15 percent of Hispanic children, and 17 percent of Caucasian American children live in stepfamilies; almost all of these children live with their biological mother (US Census Bureau, 2001b). Census estimates suggest that by 2007 stepfamilies will outnumber traditional nuclear families. It is estimated that about one third of all children can expect to live with a biological parent and a stepparent for at least one year before the age of 18 (Dainton, 1993; DeLongis & Preece, 2002).

An **extended family** consists of one or more parents, one or more of the parents' children, and one or more other relatives (grandparents, aunts, uncles, etc.) living together in one household. This type of family is more common among certain ethnic groups. For example, sharing a residence with extended family members has long been a characteristic of African American families (Garcia Coll, 1990). Similarly, many Mexican American families include aunts and uncles, grandparents, cousins, in-laws, and sometimes even close friends. Extended family members exchange a wide range of goods and services, including child care, nursing, and emotional support (Muller & Espenshade, 1985).

Table 1.1 identifies some important changes in US households since 1970 and some that are projected to occur by 2010. Fewer households are headed by a married couple, the

blended family *family structure formed when a widowed or divorced person remarries*

stepfamily *family structure formed when a person who has children from a former marriage remarries*

extended family *family structure consisting of one or more parents, one or more of the parents' children, and one or more other relatives living together in one household*

TABLE 1.1

Household Comparisons: 1970 Versus 2000 Versus 2010 (Projected)

	1970	2000	2010
Percent of households made up of married couples	71%	53%	52%
People per household	3.14	2.59	2.53
Families headed by women with no husband present	5.6 million	12.3 million	13.9 million
Families headed by men with no wife present	1.2 million	3.9 million	4.7 million
Families with no children under 18 at home	44%	54%	59%

Source: US Census Bureau, 2001b.

average household consists of fewer people, and there are more families without children under the age of 18. These trends are expected to continue throughout this decade (US Census Bureau, 2001b).

The following story of Cassie and her mother reveals another important change in the structure of US families:

> At 7:40 A.M., four-year-old Cassie sidles in, her hair half-combed, a blanket in one hand, a fudge bar in the other. "Pleeese, can't you take me with you?" Cassie pleads. "You know I can't take you to work," her mother replies. Cassie's shoulders drop in defeat and she is resigned to her mother's imminent departure. As her mother later explained, she continually feels that she owes Cassie more time than she actually gives her. She has a time-debt to her daughter and she sometimes finds herself indulging Cassie with treats or softened rules in exchange for missed time together. (Hochschild, 1997, adapted from pp. 3–4)

Parents, particularly mothers, are working more than ever before. In 1950, only about 13 percent of married mothers with children under age 17 worked for pay. Currently, almost 70 percent do so, and about 60 percent of mothers who have children age 3 or younger are in the workforce (US Department of Labor, 2004). In addition, the number of hours that both men and women put in at work has increased since 1980; more women particularly are working over 40 hours per week. For example, in 1979, 14 percent of women worked more than 40 hours per week. In 2002, that figure increased by more than 50 percent—to about 25 percent of women (US Department of Labor). Moreover, women moving into the workforce are less likely than ever to move out of it. And parents feel the pressure of this time drain—in one study 57 percent of fathers and 55 percent of mothers reported feeling guilty that they spent too little time with their children (Hochschild, 1997).

With the increased number of families with parents who work outside the home, young children are spending more time with nonparental caregivers. Figure 1.4 outlines the changes in enrollments in preschool programs since 1965 for 3- and 4-year-old children; as you can see, there has been a steady increase. More than 4 million children under the age of 6 now attend some type of preschool program. These findings strongly suggest that preschool enrollments are large, growing, and here to stay (National Research Council, 2001).

These changes in US households reflect trends in values, technology, and demographics that have occurred since 1970. Together, they significantly affect children's environments. Scientists interested in the study of child development must be attentive to these changes.

Children of Same-Sex Parents

Historically, people in Western cultures have believed that the most favorable home environments were those provided by traditional two-parent families. Although rarely stated explicitly, it is most often assumed that the parents in such families are heterosexual (Patterson, 1992). In the contemporary United States, however, this is not always the case—many children grow up in homes in which the parent or parents are gay or lesbian.

Estimates of the number of gay and lesbian parents in the United States range from 2 million to 8 million, and estimates of the number of children of gay and lesbian parents range from 4 million to 14 million (Patterson, Fulcher, & Weinright, 2002; Savin-Williams & Esterberg, 2000). The exact figures are difficult to determine because many gay and lesbian parents conceal their sexual orientation out of fear of discrimination and prejudice (Saffron, 1996). In most cases, children are born as a result of a heterosexual relationship between biological parents. After one parent acknowledges her or his sexual orientation, separation or divorce may occur, and the children are then raised in a gay or lesbian home (Falk, 1989). However, an increasing number of children, conceived through donor insemination, are now being born into lesbian homes (Chan, Raboy, & Patterson, 1998). And more recently, certain cities and states (such as San Francisco, Massachusetts, and Oregon) have permitted same-sex marriages—which mobilized those against such marriages and led to a debate about a constitutional ban against them (as well as several states passing laws in the 2004 election outlawing such marriages). Nonetheless, it is clear that the number of children of gay and lesbian parents is substantial and will continue to increase.

Much of the research on children reared in same-sex households has been generated in the past 20 years, often in the context of custody disputes. Concerns about children's sexual development, the quality of parenting provided by gay and lesbian parents, and the stress and ridicule these children might face have been raised by those who believe that children in these families are at risk and that homosexuals should be denied the rights and privileges of having a family (Focus on the Family, 1992). The scientific evidence presents a different picture, however.

Research on children from same-sex households suggests that they are no different from children reared by heterosexual parents (Fitzgerald, 1999; Medeiros, 2003; Patterson, 2003). Children's performance on standard developmental and psychological tests gives no indication as to whether they have a homosexual or a heterosexual parent. Thus, children raised by gay and lesbian parents appear to be just as healthy and well adjusted as those raised by heterosexual couples (Tasker, 2002); no evidence suggests that their development is compromised in any respect (Patterson, 2002). The evidence to date indicates that the home environments provided by gay and lesbian parents are as likely as those provided by heterosexual parents to support and enable children's growth and development.

Of course, lesbian and gay parents are as diverse in backgrounds, personalities, and values as are heterosexual parents. Having addressed the negative assumptions and popular prejudices that underlie concerns about gay and lesbian parenting, researchers now are exploring issues raised by the emergence of different kinds of lesbian and gay families with children (Patterson & Chan, 1999).

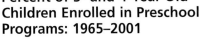

FIGURE 1.4

Percent of 3- and 4-Year-Old Children Enrolled in Preschool Programs: 1965–2001

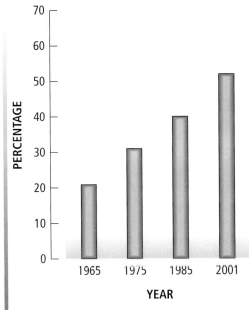

Notice the consistent increase in preschool enrollments from 1965 to 2001. What factors contributed to this change?

Source: National Center for Educational Statistics, 1998.

These two mothers are interacting with their child. What does the research on children from same-sex homes show about their psychological health and adjustment? In what ways is developmental research able to dispel misconceptions about parenting?

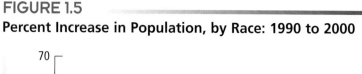

FIGURE 1.5
Percent Increase in Population, by Race: 1990 to 2000

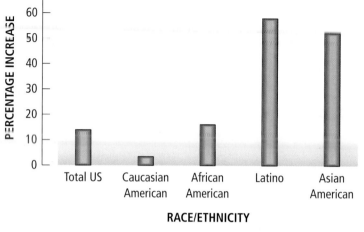

Notice the large percentage increases over the decade of the 1990s in Hispanic and Asian American individuals in the US population. What factors contributed to these changes, and what impact are they likely to have on children and families in the United States?

Source: US Census Bureau, 2001c.

Ethnic and Racial Diversity

In addition to paying more attention to changes in family structure, researchers have become more sensitive to cultural and ethnic influences on child development. This adjustment in part reflects the fact that the US population is more diverse than ever before. According to current and projected data collected by the US Census Bureau (2001c), Caucasian Americans are the slowest-growing segment of the US population, and their contribution to the total population growth in this country is becoming smaller (see Figure 1.5). From 1990 to 2030, the percentage of total population growth accounted for by Caucasian Americans is expected to decrease. By the year 2050, Caucasian Americans will represent only a slight majority. As seen in Figure 1.5, the Hispanic population is the fastest-growing group, and by the year 2025 it will be the largest minority group in the United States. Similarly, the Asian population in the United States is expected to increase at a considerable pace through the year 2050.

Although birthrates generally are higher for minority groups than for Caucasian Americans, almost one third of the current growth in minority groups is caused by immigration. By 2050, the net increase in population due to immigration is projected to be 82 million (US Census Bureau, 2001d). Increased diversity in the US population demands greater sensitivity to human variety and the culturally diverse environments in which children are raised. However, relatively few studies of minority children, adults, and families have been conducted (Arms, Davidson, & Moore, 1992).

The task of researching the impact of diversity is complicated by the considerable variation that exists within, as well as between, minority groups (McAdoo, 1993). For example, Hispanic people from Puerto Rico reside primarily in cities of the Northeast, are a relatively young group (median age is 23.3 years), and have not done well economically in the United States. In contrast, Hispanic people from Cuba reside primarily in urban areas of the Southeast (particularly Florida), are relatively older (median age is 39.1 years), and generally have done well economically, particularly those who immigrated prior to 1980 (Ortiz, 1995). As a result, the development of individuals in these two Hispanic groups is influenced in different ways by the backgrounds, experiences, values, and beliefs of their different subcultures.

A further complication in researching the role of diversity in development is the lack of agreement on the terminology used to identify groups. For example, in one poll 30 percent of respondents indicated that they wished their race to be identified as African American, whereas the majority listed Black as their choice (Roper Organization, 1993). These findings reflect a difference not only in label preference but also in the concepts of race and ethnicity. Although no clear, unambiguous definitions of these terms exist, **race** primarily refers to a group whose members share a genetic heritage (Curran & Renzetti, 1996). **Ethnicity** primarily refers to a group whose members share a common cultural heritage and a sense of belonging (Yetman, 1991). Ethnicity is considered to be a social construct, whereas race is considered relatively less so. For example, most (but not all) Americans of African descent are grouped racially as Black; however, the term *African American* refers to an ethnic group, most often to people whose ancestors experienced slavery in the United

race   *a group whose members share a genetic heritage*

ethnicity   *a group whose members share a common cultural heritage and a sense of belonging*

DEBATING THE ISSUE

HOW DO IMMIGRANT CHILDREN AFFECT AMERICAN LIFE?

 No group of children in America is expanding more rapidly than children of immigrant families (Urban Institute, 2004). In the past two decades, the number of immigrant children in public schools has grown by nearly 8 million. Since 1990, the number of children from immigrant families grew by 47 percent, compared with only 7 percent for US-born children of US-born parents (Office of Immigration Statistics, 2002). Today, approximately 12 million children in the United States are immigrants or were born to immigrant parents. Most immigrant children come from Central and South America, the Caribbean, and Asia (Camarota, 2001). These children come to the United States with or to join other family members.

It is not surprising that immigrants and their impact on US society have caught the attention of the public, as well as that of government officials (National Research Council, 1998). In a poll taken in 2001, 65 percent of respondents favored a moratorium on legal immigration (Zogby International, 2002). Their concerns may be based on public anxiety about the high cost of providing services to new immigrants. But is this concern justified?

Although legal immigrants and refugees may receive benefits such as food stamps and health care, the average household incomes of legal immigrants and refugees who enter the United States generally are *higher* than those of US-born Americans (Fix & Passell, 1994). Considering the taxes that an immigrant and his or her dependents are likely to pay over a lifetime, the United States actually gains revenue from immigrants (Glastris, 1997). However, the economic status of *undocumented* immigrants is so poor that when the immigrant population in the United States is examined as a whole, the immigrants are less well off than US-born Americans. Thus, many beliefs about immigrant children and their families are based on those immigrants who are in the United States *illegally*.

Another misconception about immigrants is that they are at risk for poor educational outcomes because of limited proficiency in English. Yet research shows that immigrant children do well in school and often stay in school longer than do their US-born peers with similar backgrounds (McDonnell & Hill, 1993). The academic performance of many immigrant children exceeds that of the average US-born child, despite the fact that immigrant children often come from disadvantaged or war-torn backgrounds. In the future, the United States will be even more racially, ethnically, and culturally diverse (Sahlman, 2002). With increased research, other negative beliefs and stereotypes about immigrants may be dispelled. Far from being a fringe element of the American population, immigrant children and their families form an increasingly large core of US society.

THINKING IT THROUGH

1. What factors contribute to negative views about the impact of immigrants on US society?

2. What do you think US immigration policy should be? Should the United States accept many immigrants into the country? Why or why not?

3. How does immigration influence theory and research about child and adolescent development?

States (Soberon, 1996). Thus, not all Blacks in the United States are African American (for example, some are from Haiti and others from the Caribbean).

Similar confusion exists over the terminology used to refer to people of Mexican or Spanish descent. Consider the following terms (Campos, 1996; Office of Management and Budget, 1995; Soberon, 1996):

- *Spanish:* Used to refer indiscriminately to any person who speaks Spanish. This term is imprecise because it includes people from many different countries and continents (America, the Caribbean, Europe).

- *Latino/Latina:* Used to refer to people in the United States originating from or having a heritage related to Latin America (Central or South America). Because *Latin* refers to the fact that a romance language (Spanish, Portuguese, French) is the native tongue of the majority of Latin Americans, this term may not be appropriate for people from that region who do not speak a romance language (such as native Indians).

Tiger Woods created a controversy when he declined to identify himself as being of one race or another. Many individuals are, like Woods, multiracial, and their increasing numbers reflect the fact that the population of the United States is becoming more diverse.

■ *Mexican:* Used to refer to the inhabitants of Mexico. The term may be appropriate for Mexican citizens working in or visiting the United States, but it is not appropriate for people of Mexican descent who are citizens of the United States.

■ *Mexican American:* Commonly used to recognize US citizens who are descendants of Mexicans. The term may be inappropriate for those who identify themselves as having a Spanish rather than a Mexican heritage or for those who do not view themselves as Americans by choice.

■ *Chicano/Chicana:* Used to refer to descendants of inhabitants of Mexico. Preferred by certain political activists and those who seek to create a new identity, it is reflective of a unique culture.

■ *Hispanic:* Used to refer to people of Mexican, Puerto Rican, Cuban, Central and South American, and other Spanish culture or origin, regardless of race. This term is used by the US Census Bureau as an encompassing ethnic classification with many subgroups.

Another controversy concerns how to classify persons who identify with more than one race. Consider, for example, the case of Tiger Woods, who in 1997 became the youngest golfer ever (at age 21) to win the Masters golf tournament. Woods' father is African American (but also part Native American and Caucasian), and his mother is Asian American (from Thailand). Woods caused a stir when he refused to identify himself as a Black. Instead, he coined a term, saying he was "Cablinasian"—a mixture of Caucasian, African American, Native American, and Asian (Padilla, 1997).

Woods' situation points out a dilemma faced by an increasing number of people: what do people of mixed races call themselves? For the most part, the term **multiracial** has been used to refer to people like Woods who are of two or more races. And there are more multiracial individuals today than in the past. In 1960, there were about 150,000 interracial marriages in the United States, compared with 1.5 million in 1990 (OMB, 1995). Today, about 2.4 percent of the US population (about 7 million people) can be considered multiracial (US Census Bureau, 2001c). For these individuals, a single category often does not reflect how they think of themselves.

The amazing diversity of people has only just begun to be recognized in theories and research on child development (Spencer, 1990). Although many developmental processes (such as motor or language development) probably emerge in similar fashion across racially and ethnically diverse populations, our understanding of child development needs to be expanded to consider factors and situations that may be unique to a particular group (such as lifestyle or food choices). For instance, for children of color, explicit attention needs to be paid to the unique circumstances they face, such as racism and stereotyping. Clearly, the "one size fits all" model of development is inadequate, and identifying and integrating the experiences and circumstances that are not shared by the majority population will provide a fuller and more inclusive understanding of child development (Garcia Coll et al., 1996).

Poverty and Child Development

In 2003, more than 12 million children in the United States lived in families on or below the poverty line (the federal definition of poverty in 2002 was a family of four with an income of no more than $18,400; Gershoff, 2003). These parents are typically unable to provide their children with basic necessities such as stable housing, health care, and adequate meals. Like Angela in the opening story of this chapter, these children face increased difficulties in being successful and developing optimally. Although Angela was able to overcome these obstacles, many children are not as fortunate and suffer significantly.

multiracial *a term used to describe people who are of two or more races*

Living in low-income households exacts a toll on children's overall healthy development (Evans & English, 2002). The intellectual, social, and physical development of these children lags behind that of their more affluent peers. For example, in a study examining children in both low- and higher-income settings, performance on standardized tests increased as the income in a child's family increased (see Figure 1.6). Researchers have gathered evidence that poverty is associated with a variety of risk factors (such as poor nutrition, exposure to environmental toxins, and trauma and abuse) that hinder optimal brain development (National Center for Children in Poverty, 1999). Additionally, the incidence of mental retardation is about six times higher among children who are raised in chronic poverty than among those raised in middle- and upper-income families (Baumeister & Baumeister, 1989). Thus, poverty has the potential to adversely affect intellectual development and performance in school. In fact, racial and ethnic differences in IQ and school achievement all but disappear once adjustments are made for economic and social-class differences (Brooks-Gunn, Klebanov, & Duncan, 1996).

The impact of poverty also depends on unique characteristics of the child. Some children may be more vulnerable and less able to withstand the risks associated with growing up in an impoverished environment. Bradley and colleagues (1994), for instance, found that the percentage of low-birthweight children (children who weigh less than 5½ pounds at birth) living in poverty who adapt to the changing demands of their environments was exceptionally low (about 10%). This was significantly lower than the 40 percent incidence of adaptiveness in low-birthweight children born into more affluent homes. These findings are particularly noteworthy, given that Bradley and his colleagues did not include children with serious medical problems. Findings such as these provide evidence that certain environmental conditions such as poverty can increase the vulnerability of an already vulnerable child.

The problems of poverty are intergenerational, complex, and enduring. For example, women living in poverty receive less prenatal care and have more difficulties with their pregnancies. Not surprisingly, they are more likely to give birth to premature and unhealthy babies, who then face high rates of illness and all the other debilitating conditions associated with poverty (Owens & Shaw, 2003). The cumulative effects of poverty on many aspects of development make it all the more important to find ways to keep families out of the poverty cycle.

FIGURE 1.6

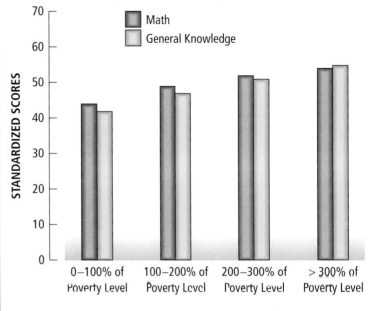

General Knowledge Test Scores by Income Group

Performance on standardized tests improves as the income level of children's families increases. Can you identify some reasons why this might be so?

Source: Gershoff, 2003.

How Can We Capture the Diversity of Children's Development?

Given the diversity and variability that exist in children, families, and their environments, the best way to study and understand children and their development is to focus specifically on this diversity. Thus, development can be best viewed from a **transactional perspective,**

transactional perspective
the view that development occurs as the result of the interplay between the diverse qualities that individuals bring to their environments and the diverse environments that individuals experience

which holds that development results from the interplay between the diverse qualities that individuals bring to their environments and the diverse environments that individuals experience. Development is a product of the continuous interactions between the child and his or her social context (Sameroff, 1989). Although it has long been recognized that children's environments significantly affect their development, equal emphasis must be given to the effects that children have on their environments.

Figure 1.7 provides an example of dynamic transactions between children and their environments (Sameroff, 1987). According to this model, a complicated childbirth may make a mother anxious and nervous about her fragile newborn child. The mother's anxiety during the first months of the infant's life may cause her to be uncertain and inappropriate in her interactions with the infant. In response to such inconsistency, the infant may develop some irregularities in feeding and sleeping patterns. These irregularities might decrease the pleasure the mother obtains from the relationship and, as a result, cause her to spend less time with her infant. One outcome of her withdrawal may be

FIGURE 1.7
Example of Transactional Model

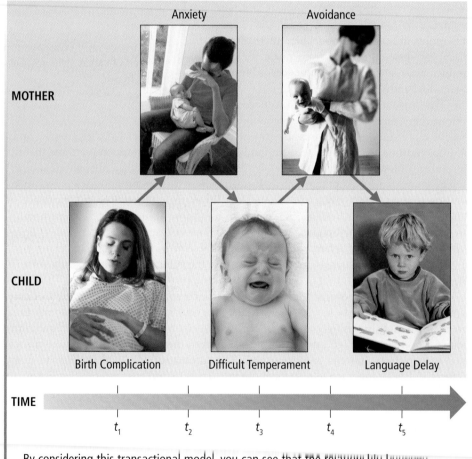

By considering this transactional model, you can see that the relationship between birth complications and language delay is complex. The model depicts different transactions that may occur between birth and the subsequent delay of language.

Source: Sameroff, 1987 (p. 278). Copyright © 1987. This material is used by permission of John Wiley & Sons, Inc.

that the infant is exposed to less talk, which hinders the acquisition of language. In this example, the developmental outcome (delayed language of the child) is not caused by the complicated birth or by the mother's subsequent anxiety; the most direct cause is the mother's avoidance. But you can see from this example that such a conclusion would be a serious oversimplification of a complex sequence of transactions that occurred over time.

Our understanding of the complex interaction between individuals and their environments is still rudimentary (Bronfenbrenner & Ceci, 1994), but the diversity of individual and environmental factors makes it likely that development is multiply determined. No single influence determines the outcomes of development, and similar developmental outcomes can be produced in a variety of ways. Additionally, individual and environmental factors, and their interaction, change as children mature. For example, the interactions of infants and their environments are qualitatively different depending on whether or not the infant has developed the ability to crawl or walk (Campos, Kermoian, & Zumbahlen, 1992). The ability to crawl or walk creates a sense of control as well as increasing the risk of falling and getting hurt. Thus, infants who can move about their environments have different experiences than those who cannot.

Because the transactional model emphasizes the divergent nature of development, it leads us to expect that parents belonging to a particular ethnic or cultural group share beliefs and practices that overlap with, but differ in some respects from, those of parents from other cultures. Thus, children in minority families might be exposed to caregiving environments characterized by cultural beliefs and caregiving practices that differ from those of the Caucasian American culture. For example, Hispanic mothers engage in predominantly nonverbal interactions with their infants, whereas Caucasian American mothers engage in more verbally oriented interactions (Hurtado, 1995). Whereas Caucasian American mothers are likely to emphasize parenting goals that relate to the development of children's confidence and independence, Hispanic mothers are more likely to value parenting goals that emphasize respectful, obedient behavior (Harwood et al., 1996). These differences reflect the fact that parental belief systems are influenced by cultural values regarding what constitutes desirable behavior.

Differences in parental beliefs also are found in other cultures. For example, the Digo and Kikuyu are two East African cultures that have different beliefs about infant capacities (DeVries & Sameroff, 1984). The Digo believe that infants can learn within a few months after birth, and they begin to teach their infants at that time. The Kikuyu, in contrast, believe that serious education is not possible before the second year of life, and they delay education until that time. Thus, caregivers from different cultures and subcultures have different beliefs, goals, reactions, and expectations about their children, and these beliefs uniquely influence children's development.

The complexity of issues related to child development also has important implications for social policy. Individuals concerned about children's welfare and well-being can make a difference by formulating and influencing policies that affect child development. For example, in the United States, nearly 60,000 children have been adopted from foreign countries since 1992, and the number of adoptions increases annually by about 18 percent. Many of these children come from countries where they were institutionalized for at least 8 months and where they likely experienced some combination of adverse conditions and malnutrition (Johnson, 2001; US State Department, 2000). Many of these children reach their adoptive families in poor medical health and with varying degrees of developmental problems. Despite these experiences and problems, many internationally adopted children make excellent progress. Unfortunately, many do not. To address this issue, developmental scientists have begun to study the factors that make a difference in these children's lives (Gunnar, Bruce, & Grotevant, 2000). Their research is resulting in important findings relevant to policies related to international adoptions, such as the need for these children and families to receive psychological and health services both before and after adoption. However, internationally adopted children are not eligible for federal funding to subsidize the cost of these services. Thus, the adoptive parents must rely on personal funds and private health insurance, which may be limited. Individuals interested in improving outcomes for these children and families can use research findings to advocate for removal of the barriers to obtaining these much needed services.

In this book, you will learn about the complex mechanisms, patterns, and issues related to child and adolescent development. For organizational and presentational effectiveness, the chapters are broken into the domains of physical, cognitive, and social–emotional development. These developmental domains are, however, intimately interrelated; that is, children's development consists of a process of continuous interaction among all three domains.

Throughout the book, we focus on the transactions that children have with their environments. We include a wide variety of transactions, ranging from close interactions with particular people to the broad influences of schools, neighborhoods, and culture. Implicit in these discussions is our emphasis on the role of human relationships. It is through relationships that children develop and learn about themselves.

Finally, although we emphasize the scientific study of child development, the study of how children develop also is influenced by values and goals. Researchers, caregivers, communities, and societies observe, interpret, and respond to developmental processes according to their values and goals (Fabes, Martin, & Smith, 1994). You are encouraged to analyze issues related to child and adolescent development in terms of your own life and values. Doing so will make the study of child development more meaningful and interesting. The information in this book will help you make better-informed decisions about issues related to children and their development and, it is hoped, will foster your development of caring attitudes and behaviors.

Try It Out

1. Interview your parents, uncles, aunts, or grandparents about their childhoods. Compare their development to your own, and identify differences and similarities in the factors, environments, and relationships that likely influenced their development and yours. What historical, social, cultural, and individual factors might account for some of the differences?
2. Which do you believe is the more important influence on children's development—nature or nurture? Why? What might be some developmental examples of the interplay between genes and environment?
3. Gather information on children and families in another historical era or country or in a religious or ethnic group different from your own. Identify differences in values, customs, and beliefs about children and childrearing. How might these differences influence child development?

Key Terms and Concepts

blended family (15)
child development (4)
cognitive development (4)
continuous development (10)
critical periods (10)
developmental domains (4)
discontinuous development (10)
dizygotic (DZ) twins (9)
ethnicity (18)
extended family (15)
heritability (9)
learning (6)
maturation (5)

monozygotic (MZ) twins (8)
multiracial (20)
natural selection (12)
nature versus nurture debate (7)
nuclear family (14)
physical development (4)
race (18)
sensitive periods (11)
single-parent family (14)
social–emotional development (4)
socialization (7)
stepfamily (15)
transactional perspective (21)

Sum It Up

What is child development?

- What kinds of changes occur during the time from birth through adolescence? (pp. 4–5)

What are some critical issues in the study of child development?

- What are some of the influences on the child development process? (pp. 5–8)

- What kinds of studies have been used to examine influences on child development? (pp. 8–9)

What are the historical roots of the study of child development?

- What were the concepts of childhood held by Plato, Locke, and Rousseau? (pp. 12–13)

- How did Charles Darwin change the way scientists think about development? (pp. 13–14)

What changes in contemporary American life influence the study of child development?

- How has the idea of family changed in the last 20 years? (pp. 14–17)

- How has US culture changed during the last 20 years? (pp. 18–21)

Can we capture the diversity of children's development?

- What is the transactional perspective on development? (pp. 21–23)

Parents are important agents of socialization.

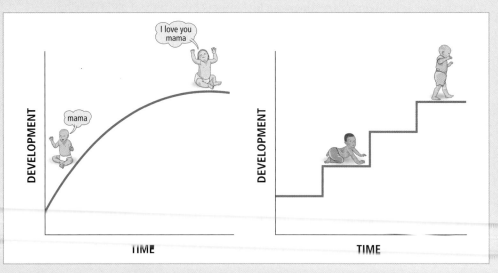

Physical Development

Cognitive Development   Social Development

FIGURE 1.1   **Developmental Domains**

CRITICAL ISSUES IN CHILD DEVELOPMENT

The study of child development includes critical questions and issues such as the role of biology versus experience as influences on development, how early experiences influence later development, continuity and change in development, and the wide range of individual differences in development. These issues guide research and theory. (Refer back to pages 5–11).

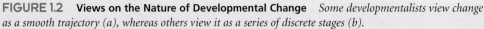

FIGURE 1.2   **Views on the Nature of Developmental Change**   *Some developmentalists view change as a smooth trajectory (a), whereas others view it as a series of discrete stages (b).*

TABLE 1.1

Household Comparisons: 1970 Versus 2000 Versus 2010 (Projected)

	1970	2000	2010
Percent of households made up of married couples	71%	53%	52%
People per household	3.14	2.59	2.53
Families headed by women with no husband present	5.6 million	12.3 million	13.9 million
Families headed by men with no wife present	1.2 million	3.9 million	4.7 million
Families with no children under 18 at home	44%	54%	59%

The percentage of households made up of married couples has decreased significantly since 1970, and families headed by a single mother will have nearly tripled by 2010.

CONTEMPORARY CHANGES

No single model of development fits all children and their families. Contemporary research and theory in child development must account for the large changes in family makeup that have taken place in recent years. Today, children live in families that are much more diverse than those of the past. (Refer back to pages 14–24).

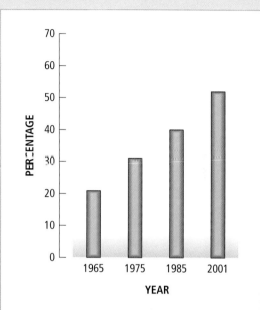

FIGURE 1.4 **Percent of 3- and 4-Year-Old Children Enrolled in Preschool Programs: 1965–2001** *Notice the consistent increase in preschool enrollments from 1965 to 2001.*

More children are being raised by same-sex parents.

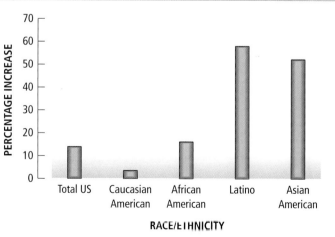

FIGURE 1.5 **Percent Increase in Population, by Race: 1990 to 2000** *Notice the large percentage increases over the decade of the 1990s in Latino and Asian American individuals in the US population.*

Understanding and Studying Child Development

Chapter Outline

How Do Theories Explain Child Development?
Scientific Theories
Evaluating Theories of Development

What Are the Major Biology-Based Theories of Child Development?
Evolutionary Theories
Ethological Theory
Neurodevelopmental Approaches

What Are the Major Psychoanalytic Theories of Child Development?
Freud's Psychosexual Theory
Erikson's Psychosocial Theory

What Are the Major Learning-Based Theories of Child Development?
Classical Conditioning
Operant Conditioning
Social Learning Theory

What Are the Major Cognition-Based Theories of Child Development?
Piaget's Cognitive Developmental Theory
Vygotsky's Theory of Cognitive Development
Information Processing Theory

What Are the Major Contextual Theories of Child Development?
Bronfenbrenner's Ecological Theory
Dynamic Systems Theory

How Is Child Development Studied?
Scientific Reasoning and the Scientific Method
Topics in Developmental Science
Research Strategies
Measuring Change over Time
Measuring Children's Behavior

A DEVELOPMENTAL MYSTERY

Three teachers are discussing a puzzle that has come up at their school: Tamika, a 9-year-old girl in the third grade who used to be calm and controlled, now becomes easily frustrated when interacting with others and hits other children when she gets upset. Tamika's third-grade teacher, Rob, her second-grade teacher, Cathy, and the music education teacher, Mary, all have different theories about the reasons behind the change in Tamika's behavior.

"She wasn't like that last year," Cathy points out. "She was fairly impulsive and never sat still for very long, but she wasn't especially aggressive toward the other children. Something must have changed."

"I know there's stress at home," Rob replies. "Her parents are divorcing."

"That's it, then," notes Cathy. "Tamika's acting out her repressed feelings about the impending divorce. That would explain why she lashes out and why she cries so easily. We should refer her for counseling."

"I don't know," says Rob. "That's a troubled family. Tamika gets exposed to a lot of anger at home on a daily basis. Maybe she has learned that's the way people are supposed to act toward each other. I think we should refer the family to the social worker."

"But plenty of kids experience far worse than Tamika and don't turn aggressive," Mary states. "I think we need to look at the causes of her impulsivity and aggressiveness. She might have some problem with her health. We really ought to refer her to a neurologist for testing."

"This is confusing," Cathy says. "Which way should we go?"

"Maybe it's 'all the above,'" Rob suggests. "But where should we start?"

Like the three teachers, you may wonder about the causes of your own and others' behavior. As you learned in Chapter 1, questions about the origins of behavior fascinate developmental scientists as well. To what extent is our behavior due to biological factors or to the ways we are raised in our families? Can a poor family environment be overcome by positive experiences with friends and in school? Just as Tamika's teachers developed ideas about the causes of her behavior, developmental scientists formulate theories or hypotheses about the causes of behavior and then use them to design studies about development and make sense of their findings.

How Do Theories Explain Child Development?

Babies delivered by cocaine-addicted mothers are exposed to drugs before they are born. They are likely to be raised in disorganized homes with drug-abusing parents who probably will not be able to provide them with warmth, shelter, food, and nurture. What is the best way to improve the lives of these children? Are these infants' brains permanently damaged by drug exposure during critical periods of development? Should children born in this situation be taken away from their mothers? Should the children receive social support within their families to help them overcome the problems of being raised in a disadvantaged environment? Think about your response to the problem of how to improve the lives of "crack babies". What would you do first? What priorities would you set for providing support for these children?

Theories of child development help developmental scientists decide what to focus on when they study or work with children. Each theory provides a framework for investigation and suggests its most central factors. Recall from Chapter 1 the story of Victor, the Wild Boy of Aveyron. Faced with the challenge of explaining and treating the Wild Boy's behavior, Itard relied on a theory for guidance. Itard believed that development is shaped by the environment and that Victor's savage behavior was due to the savage environment he grew up in. Without a theory, Itard would have had no way to explain what caused Victor's behavior, nor would he have been able to plan ways to help Victor become civilized. Theories are important because they provide the tools researchers need to organize and understand the complexities of development.

Theories are not just for researchers. In everyday life, people develop implicit theories to help them understand and explain other people's behavior. For instance, in the introduction to Chapter 1, you learned about Angela Arenivar, who was a finalist in the Scripps National Spelling Bee despite the fact that her parents did not speak English. People are curious about cases like Angela's and want to understand how she was able to overcome obstacles. Similarly, people are curious about individuals like Tamika in the introduction to this chapter and want to understand the origins of problem behaviors. Personal theories about why people behave as they do also influence interactions with others and guide many major decisions.

Scientific Theories

The informal theories that we use every day are simpler versions of the formal theories that scientists use. Some people believe that scientific theories are elaborate ideas with little relevance to the real world. But this belief is wrong—theories are the backbone of developmental research and very much connected to the real world. A scientific **theory** is a set of ideas structured to organize and explain facts. In contrast, a **fact** is an objective statement of truth. Facts may be single observations or summaries of many observations. For instance, your height is a fact with which any physician would agree. Facts are based on supporting evidence and have been proved true.

Facts need to be distinguished from **opinions**—an individual's thoughts and feelings about a given topic; they may or may not be based on fact. All of us, from time to time, blend our opinions with the facts and consider the resulting viewpoint to be actual fact. A person's thoughts and feelings are important; nevertheless, they do not change a fundamental principle: thoughts and feelings, no matter how sincere or strong, do not change the facts.

Theories organize and give meaning to facts by describing how they fit together. Theories also guide future research by suggesting which investigative leads scientists should pursue. As noted earlier, it is a fact that many unborn children are exposed to crack cocaine. Should scientists focus their research on the effects of the drug on the child or on the child's later experiences in a drug-abusing family? Research based on biological theories might assess how biochemical changes associated with drugs influence development (Holzman & Paneth, 1994). Research based on environmental theories might focus on the stressful conditions associated with living in drug-addicted families (Black et al., 1994). Both kinds of theories—biological and environmental—have proved important in understanding that early drug exposure does not necessarily cause permanent, irreversible damage. We now know that supportive family environments can buffer children from the devastating effects of early drug exposure (Leventhal et al., 1997).

Different theories provide different frames of reference for interpreting facts, and people tend to interpret facts in ways that fit the theory they hold. As you will soon learn, there are many theories of human development, each of which presents a unique perspective. Because human behavior is so complex, it is unlikely that any single theory will be able to explain all of it (Miller, 1993).

theory *a set of ideas structured to organize and explain facts*

fact *an objective, provable statement*

opinions *thoughts and feelings about a given topic*

empirically based *based on observation and experimentation*

Evaluating Theories of Development

Developmental scientists consider whether a theory explains the available facts about the real world of child development. The more facts it explains, the better the theory is. A good theory also is understandable, predicts future events, provides practical guidance, and stimulates the growth of new knowledge. A good theory is **empirically based,** meaning that it is based on observation and experimentation. Thus, a good theory is testable—

TABLE 2.1
Categorization of Theories of Human Development

CATEGORY	DESCRIPTION	THEORIES INCLUDED
Biology-based theories	Emphasis on inherited biological factors and processes	Evolutionary theories Ethological theories Attachment theory Neurodevelopmental theories
Psychoanalytic theories	Emphasis on unconscious internal drives and interactions with others	Freud's psychosexual theory Erikson's psychosocial theory
Learning-based theories	Emphasis on the role of the external world	Classical conditioning Operant conditioning Social learning theory
Cognition-based theories	Emphasis on the role of cognition and processing of information	Piaget's theory Vygotsky's theory Information processing theory
Contextual theories	Emphasis on the interaction between individuals and their environments	Ecological theory Dynamic systems theory

researchers can determine whether its propositions are correct. If a theory is untestable, its usefulness and accuracy cannot be determined (Thomas, 1996).

Different theories of development present distinct perspectives on the developmental issues discussed in Chapter 1 (such as nature versus nurture and continuity versus discontinuity). The major theories and approaches used to study child development are categorized in terms of these issues in Table 2.1 and in the following sections.

What Are the Major Biology-Based Theories of Child Development?

Many theories focus on the biological factors that underlie development—including both evolutionary processes and physiological development, such as the functioning of the brain. Biology-based theories assume that powerful organic or inherited forces influence behavior.

Evolutionary Theories

As you learned in Chapter 1, Darwin's theory of evolution is based on the idea that individuals who have characteristics that promote survival and reproduction are more likely to pass these characteristics on to future generations. For instance, early primates who had physical characteristics such as opposable thumbs and an upright stance had increased chances of surviving because they were better able to adapt to the environment and gather food than were individuals without those characteristics. Likewise, the ability to communicate, reason, and cooperate increased chances for survival. Thus, the capacities for social behavior and reasoning, along with physical characteristics, underwent natural selection (Darwin, 1877).

Today, **evolutionary theories** influence many areas of research on development, including studies of social behavior and mate selection (Buss, 1998). In these studies, researchers focus on the behaviors they believe promote the survival of the species. Likewise, evolutionary developmental theorists consider the aspects of child development that promote survival (Bjorklund & Pellegrini, 2000; Geary & Bjorklund, 2000). For instance, evolutionary developmental theorists speculate that the limited capacity of children's memory is advantageous for language acquisition because it helps children focus on the most essential features of language. Computer simulations of language learning confirm this

evolutionary theories *explanations of development that focus on how behaviors promote the survival of the individual and the species*

FIGURE 2.1
Infant and Adult Faces

Notice how infants of many different species have similar facial features, such as a small nose, a large forehead, and big eyes. Ethologists believe that these features are cues that evolved to elicit caregiving behavior from parents. These facial features make infants appear lovable and attractive to caregivers.

speculation (Cangelosi & Parisi, 2001). In such a simulation, a computer is used to play out a theory. Researchers have used simulations to reconstruct the origins and evolutionary stages of human language. In addition, evolutionary theorists explain children's play activities, aggression, and lack of inhibition by focusing on each one's survival value (Bjorklund & Pellegrini, 2000).

Ethological Theory

Ethological theory, derived from Darwin's ideas about evolution, focuses on the causes and adaptive value of behavior, considering both the evolutionary history of the species and the social context. Ethologists have been influential in proposing that during critical periods in development a specific type of learning occurs rapidly. For example, as you learned in Chapter 1, newborn ducklings have a critical period during which they learn to follow the first moving object they see. Because this object usually is their mother, this inherited tendency (called imprinting) increases their chances of survival.

Ethological research has focused on questions such as how adults become attached to infants, why infants prefer to look at human faces, and how facial expressions communicate emotions and intentions. For instance, developmental ethologists are concerned with why infants of many different species have similar facial features, such as a small nose, a large forehead, and big eyes (see Figure 2.1). Ethologists proposed that these features are visual cues that have evolved to elicit caregiving behavior from parents. Research has confirmed this idea with respect to human infants (Zebrowitz, Kendall-Tackett, & Fafel, 1991); even adults who have a "baby face" are perceived by others as being more childlike in their behavior (Zebrowitz & Montepare, 1992).

One of the most famous applications of ethological theory was proposed by John Bowlby (1907–1990). Based on ethological principles, Bowlby developed an influential theory about the importance of early relationships for the developing child. According to Bowlby's **attachment theory,** all children become emotionally attached to their caregivers, regardless of the treatment they receive from them. Attachments form as infants give cues to which caregivers respond, increasing the likelihood of infant survival.

Research today focuses on the quality of the attachment. Over the first few years of life, children develop inner working models about themselves and others, based on the kind of care they receive. For example, a child who receives sensitive and consistent caregiving comes to view himself or herself as worthy. Children's inner working models become internalized views or expectations about relationships with others and provide a basic roadmap for subsequent interactions with people (Crittenden & Claussen, 2000). Although many researchers focus on the social aspects of attachment, the conceptual foundation for attachment remains based on the survival value of attachments—they bring infants into contact with caregivers who can provide for their needs during a period in which infants are entirely dependent on others for survival.

Recent research on attachment theory supports the idea that inner working models are influential in later development. Infants who have strong emotional ties with their caregivers are more likely than other children to explore their environments readily, to maintain contact with their caregivers, to become independent, and to have good self-esteem (Thompson, 1998). Researchers also are exploring how these early attachments influence dating, marriage, friendships, and parenting later in life (Crowell & Treboux, 2001).

ethological theory *explanation of development that focuses on the causes and adaptive value of behavior, considering both the evolutionary history of the species and the social context*

attachment theory *explanation of development that focuses on the quality of the early emotional relationships developed between children and their caregivers*

Neurodevelopmental Approaches

Neurodevelopmental approaches to the study of development focus on the relationship of brain development to behavior and thinking. How the brain develops and how the different parts of the brain function provide a broad basis for understanding how biology and environment both contribute to development. Studies of brain development point to the importance of the early years of children's lives (MacLean, 1985). For instance, early in development, the brain depends on environmental input to fine-tune itself so that it is maximally sensitive to its environment (Jacobs, 1997). That is, a child's experiences help determine the patterns of connections in the brain (Elbert, Heim, & Rockstroh, 2001). Early experiences, then, have a crucial role in determining how the brain wires itself, which in turn influences how the individual later responds to stimuli.

Neurodevelopmental theories focus on how the brain influences behavior and development. These theories also emphasize the importance of early experience and how early experience influences the organization and functioning of the brain.

What Are the Major Psychoanalytic Theories of Child Development?

Psychoanalytic theories of development originate in the belief that the most important causes of behavior are rooted in the unconscious drives and forces that develop within the mind of an individual. Although today psychoanalytic theories are not often used to guide research, they continue to influence the ways people think about human behavior. Freudian notions underlie much of the thinking about developmental issues.

Freud's Psychosexual Theory

Sigmund Freud (1856–1939) was a Viennese physician whose training stressed biological determinism—the view that all human activity has biological or neurological causes. Freud also was influenced by Darwin's theory of evolution and Newton's law of physics (that energy cannot be created or destroyed). These influences led Freud to postulate that human behavior arises from the dynamic internal energy that is the result of our evolutionary heritage (Green, 1989). Freud called this fixed pool of energy the **libido**—the source of action and sexual desire.

According to Freud, the human personality, or psyche, consists of three structures: the id, the ego, and the superego. The **id** represents the primitive and instinctual components of the psyche that are unconscious, irrational, and uncontrolled. The id is driven by the pleasure principle—it seeks immediate gratification and avoids pain and distress (Freud, 1923/1960). Because the demands of the id are irrational, they often do not match what the environment provides. For example, because infants cannot feed themselves when they become hungry, immediate gratification may not be available. Infants may seek gratification by crying, sucking, and maybe even hallucinating. However, the reality of the world eventually forces changes in the id. It transforms a portion of itself into a new personality structure—the ego.

The **ego** is the source of reason and operates according to the reality principle, which is based on the conditions and demands of the real world. The ego seeks to fulfill the demands of the id in ways that are acceptable to society. The ego does not, however, represent an internalized set of social rules. This aspect of the psyche develops out of the ego and becomes the superego.

The **superego**, which represents one's conscience, moral standards, and code of social conventions, demands strict adherence to cultural expectations. When its demands are disobeyed, the superego punishes the individual by producing guilt, shame, and fear.

An individual's behavior depends on the dynamic interactions of these three structures. For instance, the ego may need to negotiate a settlement among conflicting demands: those of the id—which insists on immediate fulfillment of selfish desires, and the superego—which demands that individuals perfectly follow an unrealistic set of moral social

neurodevelopmental approaches *explanations of development that focus on the relationship of brain development to behavior and thinking*

psychoanalytic theories *explanations of development that focus on the unconscious drives and forces that develop within the mind*

libido *the source of action and sexual desire*

id *the part of the psyche that is primitive and instinctual*

ego *the part of the psyche that is the source of reason and operates within the conditions and demands of the real world*

superego *the part of the psyche that represents one's conscience, moral standards, and code of social conventions*

FIGURE 2.2
Freud's Theory of Psychosexual Development

Oral (Birth–1 year)	Anal (1–3 years)	Phallic (3–6 years)	Latency (6 years–puberty)	Genital (puberty–adulthood)
Id is the only psychic structure operating. Pleasure principle operates unconsciously. Erogenous zone is the mouth.	Ego develops as the result of conflicts with the social world. Reality principle operates. Erogenous zone is the anus.	Superego develops as the result of the conflict over the sexual desire for the opposite-sex parent and the rivalry of the same-sex parent. Erogenous zone is the genital region.	Libido becomes dormant. Focus is on the development of skills necessary for adult functioning. There is no particular erogenous zone.	Focus is on mature sexual functioning and reproduction. Erogenous zone is the genital area.

Sigmund Freud developed a psychosexual theory of development based on the idea that internal forces and energy change across five stages. Can you identify these changes and the contributions that Freud's theory made to today's thinking about child development?

values. Consider a person who becomes hungry while shopping in a store. The desires of the id unconsciously push the individual to seek food, regardless of the situation. In this case, the person spots a candy bar at the checkout stand. The id pushes harder for its hunger to be immediately satisfied ("eat the candy bar NOW!"). The superego, however, responds by creating a sense of guilt about eating the candy without paying for it and fear of being caught shoplifting. The ego resolves this conflict by finding a compromise: the person will buy the candy bar and then eat it. Thus, the demands of the id are met in ways that do not violate the demands of the superego.

Freud's theory of **psychosexual development** is a stage theory of development, based on how the libido is transformed into different structures and modes of expression (see Figure 2.2). During each stage, the increased sensitivity of a particular area of the body makes it an erogenous zone where libidinal energy is invested and pleasure is experienced (Freud, 1920/1965). Different erogenous zones are activated over the course of development as the child's genetic blueprint unfolds.

The ideas put forth by Freud on the importance of early development and the role that parents play in influencing children's personalities have become ingrained in our culture. One of his most enduring contributions is his concept of the unconscious—the idea that forces of which we generally are not aware do influence our behavior. His notion that *defense mechanisms*—such as repression and projection—protect individuals from anxiety and fear also has become widely accepted. His belief that early experiences and patterns of social interaction can produce mental illness led him to develop *psychoanalysis*—a form of therapy designed to help individuals recover memories of the early interactions that influence their behavior.

Notwithstanding these contributions, there are serious problems with Freud's theory. Most important, the theory is not based on solid scientific evidence. In fact, although Freud proposed a developmental theory, he never really studied children; he obtained his evidence

psychosexual development
Freud's stage theory of development, based on how the libido is transformed into different structures and modes of expression

from his patients' recollections, during psychoanalysis, of their childhoods. Furthermore, many aspects of Freud's theory are unmeasurable and therefore untestable—how does one measure libidinal energy or identify the source of the superego? Inherent in Freud's discussion of the libido and its source of gratification is the notion that infants and young children are sexual beings and derive erotic pleasure from their interactions. This notion was (and still is) very controversial. Freud developed his theory during a period in history when society held very restrictive views about sexuality. Other Freudian concepts reflect cultural biases, such as the implication that male sexuality has a superiority that makes it a source of envy and jealousy for females (Horney, 1967).

Erikson's Psychosocial Theory

Erik Erikson (1902–1994) was a German-born psychoanalyst who extended and refined Freud's theory of development. Erikson accepted Freud's theory of psychosexual development but believed that, for several reasons, it was incomplete:

- It gave too little recognition to social and cultural influences.
- It failed to recognize developmental changes beyond adolescence.
- It did not give enough emphasis to ego development.
- It focused primarily on the development of neurotic and maladaptive behavior and did not give enough consideration to *healthy* development.

Erikson argued that during development, individuals go through a series of eight **psychosocial crises** that reflect a struggle between two conflicting personality characteristics. These crises represent critical periods in personality development (Erikson, 1968) and in social/emotional development. They are governed by the *epigenetic principle*—the belief that everything that develops is controlled by a preset genetic plan (Erikson, 1968). The sequence and type of crisis at each stage are fixed; individuals can do nothing to prevent a crisis from occurring or to change or speed up the sequence of crises. Erikson believed, however, that these crises manifest themselves differently from person to person. For example, although all infants experience the natural conflict between trust and mistrust during the first year of life, individual circumstances affect the outcome of the crisis. Imagine how differently trust is experienced by an infant who has warm clothing and adequate food and by an infant who is left alone for hours with only a bottle or who is constantly hungry and ignored by caregivers. Thus, the level of attention given to infants may affect their development of basic trust (Wallerstein & Goldberger, 1998). What kind of trust did Victor, the Wild Boy, develop when he was abandoned at a young age? What kind of autonomy did he develop? The resolution of each crisis results in the development of a sense of competence or incompetence, which then affects the course of the individual's development.

Erikson's major contribution was his detailed definitions of psychosocial stages and the crisis associated with each one, shown in Table 2.2. Each stage builds on the preceding ones and paves the way for subsequent stages, and the outcome of one stage is not permanent but can be altered by later experiences. In addition, Erikson recognized cultural differences (Erikson, 1963) and contributed significantly to the study of adolescence, especially the process by which adolescents form personal identities (Erikson, 1968). Another critical aspect of Erikson's theory that differs from Freud's is his emphasis on the role of the ego rather than that of the id. As a result, Erikson's theory is more positively oriented than Freud's and focuses on healthy outcomes to a greater extent. For example, Erikson places a great deal of emphasis on the development of *identity*—the external reflection of one's ego. Unfortunately, though, apart from research on adolescent identity, there is little research on childhood and adult psychosocial crises. Moreover, many of Erikson's theoretical propositions, like other psychoanalytic ideas, are difficult, if not impossible, to test (Green, 1989).

psychosocial crises   *in Erikson's lifespan theory, the struggles that occur at the various stages of development between two conflicting personality characteristics*

TABLE 2.2
Erikson's Psychosocial Theory of Development

STAGE (CRISIS)	RESULTS OF POSITIVE RESOLUTION OF CRISIS	AGES
Trust vs. Mistrust	Ability to predict and depend on one's own behavior and the behavior of others	0–1 year
Autonomy vs. Shame/Doubt	Ability to do things for oneself	2–3 years
Initiative vs. Guilt	High and realistic sense of ambition and independence	3–6 years
Industry vs. Inferiority	Active and satisfying involvement in activities	7–12 years
Identity vs. Identity Diffusion	Determination of one's identity	12–18 years
Intimacy vs. Isolation	Ability to commit to another and establish a close, loving relationship	20s
Generativity vs. Stagnation	Incorporation of the needs of others into one's personal life	20s–50s
Integrity vs. Despair	Healthy adjustment to aging and mortality	50s and beyond

Source: Adapted from Erikson, 1959.

What Are the Major Learning-Based Theories of Child Development?

Learning-based theories maintain that the environment in which people live and the experiences they have are major determinants of behavior. According to this view, people are relatively passive in responding to the environments they are exposed to during their lives. Behavioral changes occur only when the environment is changed. Learning-based studies focus on factors that determine how behavior changes in response to everyday events.

Classical Conditioning

Ivan Pavlov (1849–1936), a Russian physiologist, was the founder of modern learning theory. While studying dogs' digestive systems, he made an important accidental discovery. When food was placed on a dog's tongue, the dog salivated as a reflex response to the food. Pavlov noticed that after a while, dogs also salivated when they saw the food coming. For this to happen, the dogs must have learned to associate the sight of food with the taste of the food. Thus, they learned a conditioned response to a previously neutral stimulus. Many people have noticed a similar pattern of conditioning in their pets—cats often come running at the sound of a can opener because they have associated the sound of the can opener with food (Crain, 1992).

In Pavlov's studies, the typical **classical conditioning** procedure was to present, over several trials, a *conditioned stimulus*—for example, a bright light—paired with an unconditioned stimulus, such as food. The food is an *unconditioned stimulus* because it automatically elicits a response, the *unconditioned response* of salivation. The light begins as a neutral stimulus, but with repeated pairings the dog learns to associate it with the food, thereby producing a *conditioned response*—salivating when the light goes on (Kehoe & Macrae, 1998).

The principles of classical conditioning were first applied to humans by John Watson (1878–1958). Watson argued that infants naturally respond with fear to only two events: suddenly losing support (fear of falling) and sudden loud noises. How, then, do children develop fear of snakes or dogs or the dark? Freud would have argued that a child's fear of snakes reflects his or her repressed, unconscious drives and instincts. For Watson, the answer was that children learn to be fearful through classical conditioning.

To test this idea, Watson and colleagues conditioned an 11-month-old boy named Albert to fear a white rat (Watson & Raynor, 1920). At first, Albert was not afraid of the

classical conditioning
Pavlov's theory of how responses to neutral stimuli become conditioned

rat. But then Albert was shown the rat while a loud noise was made. After four pairings of these two stimuli, Albert was shown the rat by itself, and he whimpered and withdrew from it. A few days later, Albert was tested to see whether he had generalized his fear to other objects or animals. He had indeed become fearful of all kinds of furry animals and objects, such as rabbits and fur coats (Crain, 1992). Classical conditioning can thus help explain children's development of common fears such as that of going to visit the doctor (see Figure 2.3).

Watson also found a method to decondition fears. He used *systematic desensitization* to decondition the fears of a young child named Peter. Peter was afraid of many animals, furry things, and mechanical objects. When Peter was relaxed and eating in his high chair, Watson would bring in a caged animal and leave it visible in the distance. The animal was gradually brought closer, allowing Peter to associate the pleasant feelings of eating with the presence of the animal. Over repeated and gradual exposures, Peter eventually lost his fear of the animal,

FIGURE 2.3
An Example of Classical Conditioning

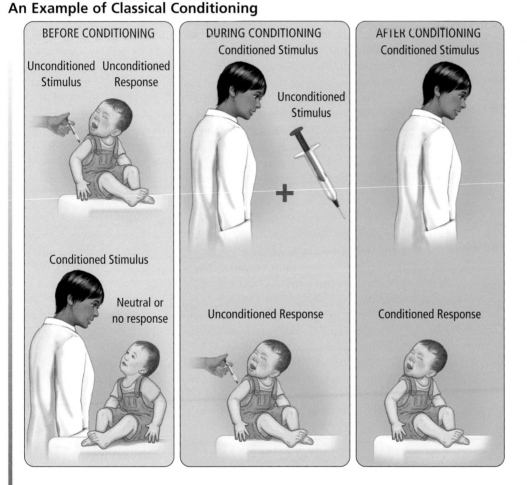

At first, the pain of the vaccination the child receives naturally elicits crying, but the sight of the doctor does not. After the child associates the doctor with the vaccination, the sight of the doctor elicits fear and crying. Thus, the child is classically conditioned to fear the doctor. Using classical conditioning principles, how might you recondition and eliminate the child's fear of the doctor?

This picture illustrates the concept of negative reinforcement. By using an umbrella, the aversive condition of getting wet in the rain is removed. Thus, the use of the umbrella is reinforcing and should increase its use in future rain storms (if you remember to carry your umbrella with you).

Operant Conditioning

B. F. Skinner (1905–1990) was concerned with how the environment shapes people's behaviors. **Operant conditioning** focuses on how the consequences of a behavior affect the likelihood that the behavior will be repeated. For instance, if an infant is praised when he or she takes a first step, the infant will be more motivated to take another step.

The principles of operant conditioning have been studied extensively and applied effectively to many kinds of human behavior. Behavior is more likely to occur after the presentation of **positive reinforcement** (such as food or praise). Behavior also is more likely to occur with **negative reinforcement,** which consists of removing a negative, or aversive, condition. Seat belt alarms are an example of an effective negative reinforcer: once the seat belt is hooked, the annoying buzzing stops, thereby increasing the chances that one will use seat belts in the future.

In contrast, **punishment** is the application of unpleasant consequences to decrease the likelihood that a behavior will be repeated. Some parents use scolding or spanking as punishment, in the hope that these consequences will reduce undesirable behaviors. Punishment also may take the form of extra work, revoking privileges, or disapproval. Studies show, however, that punishment often is effective for only a short time and may have unintended negative side effects (such as increasing anxiety and timidity). A more effective strategy for reducing unwanted behavior may be **extinction,** in which all positive consequences are withheld (Crain, 1992).

Have you ever wondered how animals in the movies or on television learn to do difficult routines on cue? Animal trainers use the principles of operant conditioning to train them. A complex sequence of behaviors is learned through **shaping**—a process of rewarding behaviors that approximate the desired result. A small step toward a larger goal is rewarded a few times, and then the next step is rewarded. For example, getting children to put their toys away can be shaped by rewarding them first when they approach the toys, then when they pick them up, and then when they attempt to put them away (Green, 1989). Similarly, animals are rewarded for performing small tasks, which are eventually developed into a complex string of actions.

Social Learning Theory

Consider this scenario: four-year-old Todd watches as his friend Ian puts on high heels and a fancy dress. Several children begin to comment on Ian's appearance, telling him he shouldn't dress up in girls' clothes. They tease him and won't play with him for the rest of the day.

In this story, Ian may have learned a hard lesson; the consequences of dressing in girls' clothing can be severely negative, and he may therefore be unlikely to do it again in the future. But what does Todd learn from observing Ian? Does Todd need to experience the teasing to recognize that putting on "girls' clothes" might lead to negative outcomes? According to Albert Bandura (b. 1925), much of children's learning occurs by watching the consequences that others experience for their behaviors, through a process called **vicarious reinforcement.** From his observation of Ian, Todd learns that boys shouldn't dress up in girls' clothes. Knowledge of such consequences guides children's and adults' future behavioral choices (Bandura, 1977).

Bandura's **social learning theory** is based on his idea that individuals are greatly influenced by other people. In addition to being affected by vicarious reinforcement, Bandura believes that children and adults imitate, or model, the behavior of other people. Through *modeling,* individuals learn new behaviors, the contexts appropriate for those behaviors, and their consequences. Consider how children often mimic the actions of superheroes from movies and television. How are they able to do this?

Four processes are involved in modeling the behavior of others:

- *Attention:* A child must pay attention to models to be able to imitate their behavior. The models most likely to capture attention are those with power, prestige, or charisma.

operant conditioning *learning based on the principle that the consequences of a behavior affect the likelihood that the behavior will be repeated*

positive reinforcement *presentation of stimuli that increase the likelihood that a behavior will recur*

negative reinforcement *removal of a negative or aversive stimulus, which increases the likelihood that a behavior will recur*

punishment *application of unpleasant consequences to decrease the likelihood that a behavior will be repeated*

extinction *reducing unwanted behavior by withholding all positive consequences*

shaping *the process of rewarding behaviors that approximate the desired behavior*

vicarious reinforcement *learning by watching the consequences of other people's behaviors*

■ *Retention:* To imitate another person's behavior later on, a child must have a way to represent the behavior in her or his memory so that it can be retrieved when necessary.

■ *Motor reproduction:* To successfully reproduce another's behavior, a child must have the motor control or abilities to carry out the action. Imitation provides the pattern for a behavior but not the actual skill to accomplish it.

■ *Reinforcement and motivation:* Successful imitation requires that the behavior have the desired consequences, causing the child to want to repeat it.

Social learning theory often has been used to explain the impact of television on children's behavior. Popular television characters attract children's attention, and children may learn to act inappropriately by observing the behaviors of these powerful models (American Medical Association, 1996). Based on the four processes described above, what might be effective strategies for reducing children's modeling of inappropriate behavior? for increasing their modeling of positive behaviors?

Imitation and modeling are powerful ways to learn or alter behavior. In this picture, the younger sibling is trying to imitate the behavior of her older brother. What factors contribute to whether or not a child imitates or models someone else's behavior?

What Are the Major Cognition-Based Theories of Child Development?

Cognition-based theories emphasize the role of mental processes such as memory, decision making, and information processing in influencing development. Studies of cognitive development focus on how thinking and reasoning change over time and the effects of these changes on development. Cognition-based theories assume that an essential feature of development is that individuals strive for greater understanding of the world around them.

Piaget's Cognitive Developmental Theory

Jean Piaget (1896–1980) was a Swiss scientist who became interested in the question of how we come to know and understand the world around us. While administering intelligence tests to French schoolchildren, Piaget noticed a pattern in the reasons children gave for correct and incorrect answers on the tests. He speculated that children of different ages use different kinds of thought processes. Piaget also observed the development of his own children and became convinced that children's thinking is very different from that of adolescents and adults (Crain, 1992; Miller, 1993). This idea became the central tenet of his theory.

Piaget's View of Intelligence

Piaget defined intelligence as an active process in which people acquire information by interacting with objects, ideas, and other people. From these interactions, individuals develop better ways of adapting to life's challenges. According to Piaget, cognitive development is a process of developing the intellectual means to adapt to the environment (Langer & Killen, 1998).

When children interact with people and objects in the world, changes occur in their conceptions of the world. Children's abilities to interact with the environment are based on their **schemes**—cognitive guides, or blueprints, for processing information. A child gathers information about an object or person by applying a scheme and using it to sort and organize the information. The schemes that children use change over time. Infants use schemes, such as sucking and grasping, that are based on their senses. Young children use schemes that are based on the appearances of objects. As children grow older, they develop more complex and abstract schemes. For instance, a high school student may have a scheme for solving algebraic equations.

Changes occur rapidly when information is being processed about the world. An infant who first holds a rattle has to apply schemes to the rattle to try to solve the problem of what this object is. Children develop problem-solving abilities through two continually occurring processes of adaptation: **assimilation,** or directly processing information that fits a scheme, and **accommodation,** or changing the scheme to fit the new information from

social learning theory *Bandura's theory that individuals are greatly influenced by observing and imitating other people*

schemes *cognitive guides, or blueprints, for processing information about the world*

assimilation *directly processing information that fits a scheme*

accommodation *changing a scheme to fit new information from the environment*

FIGURE 2.4
Assimilation and Accommodation

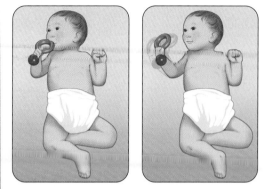

Assimilation   Accommodation

This figure illustrates the difference between Piaget's concepts of assimilation and accommodation. Can you describe the difference between the two and the role that each play in contributing to children's cognitive development?

sensorimotor stage *Piaget's first stage of cognitive development (0 to 2 years), in which the child relates to objects and people through his or her senses and motor skills*

preoperational stage
Piaget's second stage of cognitive development (2 to 7 years), in which children begin to think in symbols but are egocentric and perceptually bound in their thinking

concrete operational stage
Piaget's third stage of cognitive development (7 to 11 years), in which children begin to use logic to solve problems

formal operational stage
Piaget's fourth stage of cognitive development (begins at around the age of 11), in which individuals are capable of applying logical principles to hypothetical and abstract situations

the environment. For example, the infant holding a rattle for the first time may assimilate it into an existing scheme for smooth, round objects by sucking on it. He or she may then accommodate and develop a scheme for "rattle" after shaking it and realizing that some things make sounds when shaken (see Figure 2.4). The interplay of assimilation and accommodation helps children adapt to their ever-changing environment (Piaget, 1952)

Piaget believed that intelligence undergoes dramatic changes over time. He found these changes so clear-cut that he referred to them as stages of cognitive development (see Figure 2.5). Each stage is marked by specific types of thinking and problem solving that differ qualitatively from those of other stages. Furthermore, the stages are sequential and nonreversible—children do not return to earlier stages of thinking (Zigler & Gilman, 1998).

Piaget's Stages of Cognitive Development
Piaget's first stage, the **sensorimotor stage,** begins at birth and lasts until about 2 years of age. The child in the sensorimotor stage relates to objects and people through the senses and motor skills, hence the name of the stage. The means for interacting with objects are innate reflexive behaviors, such as sucking and grasping, which change as children gain experience. Give an infant a small block, for example, and he or she will try to suck it. Infants use sensorimotor schemes to allow them to learn about the qualities of objects—their shapes, textures, and tastes.

A major accomplishment of the child's first 2 years is coming to understand that objects continue to exist even when she or he cannot see them—the concept of *object permanence.* During the first 2 years of life, children also begin to show signs of purposeful behavior, and by the end of this time, they understand how to use symbols (such as language) to represent their thoughts.

The second stage in Piaget's theory, the **preoperational stage,** lasts from about 2 to 7 years of age. Children in the preoperational stage think in symbols, which permit more flexibility and planning in their problem solving. These children are egocentric in their thinking—they believe that everyone sees the world as they do. A child who hides only her or his face behind a curtain and then yells, "Come and find me," is exhibiting egocentric thinking: if I can't see you, you can't see me! Children in the preoperational stage can be fooled by the appearance of an object, and their thinking is based on that appearance. For example, such a child will perceive that a half pint of milk poured into a tall, thin glass has more volume than the same half pint poured into a short, wide glass.

The third stage, the **concrete operational stage,** lasts from 7 to about 11 years of age. The major accomplishment of this stage is using logic to solve problems. This basic logic involves understanding that things maintain their essential attributes even though some aspects of their appearance may change. For instance, a child in the concrete operational stage recognizes that a half pint of milk poured from a tall, thin glass into a short, wide one is still a half pint of fluid because nothing has been added or taken away.

The final stage of Piaget's theory, the **formal operational stage,** begins at around the age of 11. The major accomplishment of this stage is applying the logical principles first used in the concrete operational stage to more hypothetical and abstract situations. Because of this newly attained level of understanding, older children and adolescents become interested in and concerned about broad social issues and abstract concepts such as justice, equality, and fairness (Zigler & Gilman, 1998).

Literally thousands of studies have been done to test Piaget's ideas. His theory also has been expanded and refined by *neo-Piagetians* (Case & Edelstein, 1993; Fischer & Bidell, 1998), who have proposed theories based on the idea of stages of cognitive develop-

FIGURE 2.5
Piaget's Stages of Cognitive Development

Sensorimotor Stage (0–2 years)	**Preoperational Stage** (2–7 years)	**Concrete Operational Stage** (7–11 years)	**Formal Operational Stage** (11 years and beyond)

Motoric knowledge Lack of understanding that objects continue to exist when not in view Present orientation	Symbolic representation Planning Thinking and problem solving guided by perception and appearances Egocentric thinking	Logic used in problem solving Logic applied only to concrete objects and events	Logic applied to hypothetical and abstract problems Concern with concepts like justice, equality, and fairness

Piaget described four stages of cognitive development. The stages represent qualitative differences in how children and adolescents reason and think. Can you identify these stages and the major features of children's thinking at each stage?

ment while giving more emphasis than Piaget did to the way information is processed in the brain. For instance, Case argues that children's thinking is organized into central conceptual structures—networks of concepts that allow for thinking about a variety of situations (Case & Okamoto, 1996). These structures change during development, as connections between different parts of the brain increase, thereby enlarging memory capacity.

Vygotsky's Theory of Cognitive Development

Lev Vygotsky (1896–1934) was a Russian psychologist whose work with children with disabilities gave him an interest in issues of development (Rieber & Hall, 1998). He proposed a theory of development based on the idea that children use psychological tools such as language, numbering systems, and maps to develop higher levels of thinking; he found language particularly important because it allows children to develop new ideas and to regulate their behavior. Vygotsky argued that people use language to engage in internal dialogues that help them solve difficult tasks. For instance, you may say to yourself that when you finish reading this section, you will take a break. Through the self-direction of your internal dialogue, you continue reading, thereby regulating your behavior and promoting the learning of the material. Vygotsky regarded this internal, or private, speech as a critical element in cognitive development and learning.

More than Piaget, Vygotsky emphasized the influence of social interaction on development. A 3-year-old boy, for example, may be unable to discuss a trip he took to the zoo, but given a series of prompts by his mother, he can describe the animals he saw and the foods he ate during his trip. The mother acts as a skilled helper in using language to describe experiences. Similarly, a teacher may provide the information and support a student needs to carry out long division. The distance between what a child can do unaided and what a child

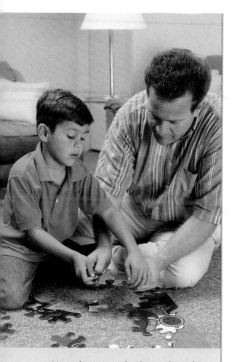

Vygotsky proposed a theory about the important role that social interactions and caregivers have in facilitating learning in children. What is the father in this photograph doing to help the son to put this puzzle together?

can do through interaction with skilled helpers is called the **zone of proximal development.** Within this zone a person's potential for new learning is strongest.

The idea that children learn through social interactions with skilled helpers suggests that everyday experiences play a crucial role in children's development. Through routine interactions, caregivers and teachers provide meaningful assistance to children in developing cognitive, social, and emotional skills (Stringer, 1998). For instance, caregivers often describe problem-solving strategies to children to help them guide their own behavior. As they grow older, children repeat these guidance messages to themselves, aloud at first. These messages later become the silent inner speech that is used to guide behavior (Vygotsky, 1934/1986).

Information Processing Theory

Studies of cognitive development have stimulated efforts to understand how people take in, remember, and use information from their experiences (Keil, 1998). **Information processing theory** is based on the idea that people have limited capacities for learning but can flexibly apply strategies to find ways around those limitations (Munakata, 1998; Siegler, 1996, 1998).

The human information processing model, shown in Figure 2.6, has three parts. The **sensory register** allows people to very briefly retain visual, auditory, and other information taken in through the senses. **Short-term memory** holds information long enough for the person to evaluate and selectively act on inputs. The capacity of short-term memory is limited: only a few bits of information can be remembered (Bjorklund, 1995). **Long-term memory,** however, has an unlimited capacity for storing information over lengthy periods of time. In long-term memory, information becomes linked to earlier memories, associations, and visual representations, creating networks that aid in recall. Individuals consciously link or classify ideas and use memory aids (such as rehearsal) to retrieve information.

Information processing theory has been particularly useful for understanding why children and adults remember information differently. For instance, 4-year-old children are less likely than adults to use memory aids and thus are less likely to process information so that it is retained in long-term memory. The theory also is helpful in understanding other

zone of proximal development *Vygotsky's term for the distance between what a child can do unaided and what a child can do through interaction with skilled helpers*

information processing theory *explanations for development that are based on the idea that people have limited capacities for learning but can flexibly apply strategies to find ways around those limitations*

sensory register *the part of the information processing system that allows people to very briefly retain information taken in through the senses*

short-term memory *the part of the information processing system that holds information long enough for the person to evaluate and selectively act on the input*

FIGURE 2.6
Information Processing System

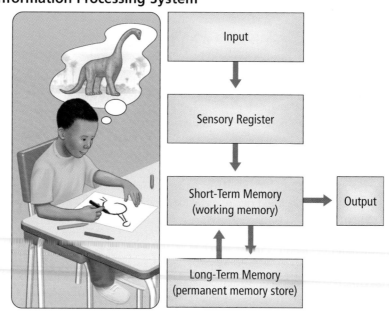

This diagram depicts the three parts of the information processing system. Can you explain what these parts are and how they work together?

changes, such as increased attention to relevant features, that occur in information processing as we grow older.

What Are the Major Contextual Theories of Child Development?

Contextual theories emphasize the interaction between the biological and environmental forces that influence behavior and development in particular contexts. Although these theories are diverse, each is based on the idea that to truly understand child development, one must study children in their historical, social, and cultural contexts. Development occurs when a child acts within the environment to produce change.

Bronfenbrenner's Ecological Theory

What happens to children raised in neighborhoods with drive-by shootings, drug dealing, and poor access to health care? How do societal values influence children's development? Urie Bronfenbrenner (b. 1917) used a concept from earth science—ecology—to outline the interplay between the child and his or her immediate social and physical environment. As shown in Figure 2.7, the child's experiences are viewed as subsystems within larger systems, or a set of nested structures (Bronfenbrenner, 1979).

FIGURE 2.7
Bronfenbrenner's Ecological Model

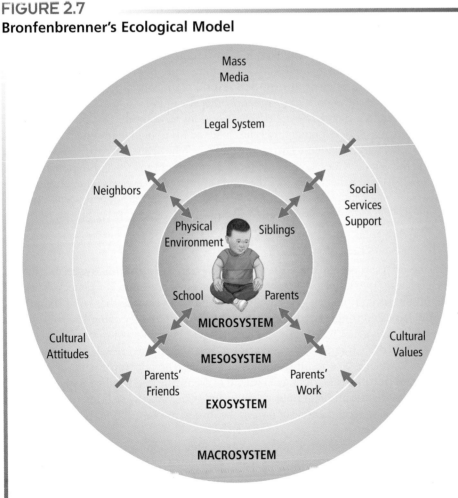

Notice that the different spheres contain different types of influences. Bronfenbrenner believed that these different levels of influence interact to affect a person's development and behavior. This model depicts the complexity of contextual theories of development.

long-term memory   *the part of the information processing system that has an unlimited capacity for storing information over long periods of time*

The innermost circle in the **ecological model** in Figure 2.7 represents the child's **microsystem** (immediate environment) and includes influences such as physical objects (toys and technology), the structure of the environment, and the roles of and relationships among family members (Bronfenbrenner & Morris, 1998). This immediate environment has important effects on development. In a classic series of studies of the microsystem, Caldwell and colleagues (Bradley & Caldwell, 1976; Elardo, Bradley, & Caldwell, 1975) found that the quality of 6-month-old infants' physical and intellectual environments (such as the presence of appropriate play materials and opportunities for daily stimulation) related to their intellectual performance 4 years later. Similar results have been obtained in more recent studies (Brooks-Gunn, 1995).

The middle sphere of the ecological model is the **mesosystem,** which encompasses the connections among settings including the child and how these connections influence the child—for example, how a child's relationships at school affect her or his relationships with extended family members. One of the first studies of mesosystem influences found that children whose parents were actively involved in their hospital care were less emotionally distressed (both while in the hospital and at home up to a year later) than were children whose parents were allowed only brief visits (Prugh et al., 1953). Introducing people from one of the children's settings (the family) into another (the hospital) helped ease the transition between them.

The next circle, the **exosystem,** represents the linkages among settings, one of which does not include the child, and how these influence development. External settings include parents' social worlds, such as their employment, church attendance, and friends, and the physical environment beyond the immediate setting, such as neighborhood conditions. Researchers studying the exosystem have found, for instance, that children who live in violent neighborhoods have difficulty sleeping, have impaired cognitive performance, and often are aggressive, depressed, and fearful (Gorman-Smith & Tolan, 1998; Horn & Trickett, 1998). The outermost circle, the **macrosystem,** represents larger societal values, historical changes, and social policies (Bronfenbrenner, 1986).

Bronfenbrenner's ecological model is based on his assumption that the environment plays a decisive role in development. But the child and his or her environment are not separate. The child interacts with the environment of which he or she is a part, and these interactions are the engine of development (Bronfenbrenner & Evans, 2000; Bronfenbrenner & Morris, 1998). Children meet their environment most directly in everyday situations (micro- or mesosystem interactions), but these are embedded in the larger physical, social, and cultural contexts (the exosystem), which also affect their development (Magnusson, 1995).

Dynamic Systems Theory

One of the newest theories in the study of development is **dynamic systems theory** (Thelen & Smith, 1998). Its basic ideas come from research done outside the social sciences, largely in physics and biology. Dynamic systems theorists assume that complex systems form from basic and simple conditions without requiring a master plan (Thelen & Smith, 1994, 1998). This is a new way of thinking about development. Rather than unfolding from a master plan coded by genes, development is believed to involve self-organization, in which systems change as a result of their interactions. The individual parts of a system, called **control parameters,** interact in ways that eventually lead to advancement to a new level or a new form. Control parameters can include external as well as internal factors. In this way, dynamic systems theory emphasizes the strong interconnections between children and their environments.

Consider the development of walking as a dynamic system (see Figure 2.8). Walking is a motion of coordinated leg movements that is performed easily by most people. Walking also is highly variable and complex because it requires constant readjustments to allow for different surfaces and different speeds. How does a child develop these coordinated motions and learn to adjust them as needed? A child has acquired many components of

ecological model   *Bronfenbrenner's model of the different spheres of influence*

microsystem   *the inner sphere of the ecological model, which represents the immediate environment and includes influences such as physical objects, the structure of the environment, and the roles of and relationships among family members*

mesosystem   *the middle sphere of the ecological model, which encompasses the connections among settings that include the child and how these connections influence the child*

exosystem   *the part of the ecological model that represents the linkages among settings, one of which does not include the child, and how these influence development*

macrosystem   *the outermost sphere of the ecological model, which represents societal values and attitudes*

dynamic systems theory   *a theory based on the idea that complex systems form from basic and simple conditions without adhering to a master plan for development*

control parameters   *the individual parts of a dynamic system*

walking—balance, coordination of the legs, stepping abilities, and leg strength—before she or he actually walks. At some point, these separate pieces come together, and the child is able to propel herself or himself across the floor for a few steps, usually with great concentration and little grace.

The slowest, or last-developing, part of a system is called the **rate-limiting component;** when it develops, the system evolves into a new form (Thelen, 1989). For many children, the last part of the "walking puzzle," the rate-limiting component, is leg strength. When their legs develop adequate strength, balance improves, enabling them to shift their weight back and forth on one leg as they take a step. If assistance is provided to reduce the input of the rate-limiting (leg strength) component, such as by putting children into a walker, they can easily walk earlier than development normally would allow. Once children are walking unaided, practice at using all the parts of the system together leads to smoother and better performance. As you can see from this example, a new behavior—walking—emerges out of several different systems that eventually work together to produce this new ability. Later, with further adjustments and development of individual pieces of the motor system, brain, and body, the child will move to another new form—running.

Although the dynamic systems approach is based on ideas formed outside the developmental sciences, the theory fits very well with the idea that development involves transactional experiences, from which universal developmental domains are constructed (Horowitz, 2000).

Dynamic systems approaches are based on the idea that complex behaviors arise from simple components. What components are involved in a toddler's first steps? How might these components vary from one child to another?

FIGURE 2.8
A Dynamic Systems Model of Walking

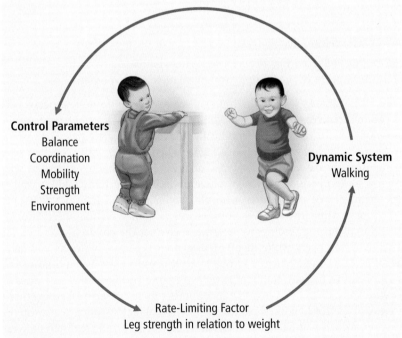

Control Parameters
Balance
Coordination
Mobility
Strength
Environment

Dynamic System
Walking

Rate-Limiting Factor
Leg strength in relation to weight

In this model, the different elements involved in walking are considered to be control parameters. The slowest-developing aspect is the rate-limiting component, which limits the speed at which the behavior is acquired. Once this aspect develops, the system evolves into a new form—walking.

rate-limiting component
the slowest, or last-developing, part of a dynamic system

How Is Child Development Studied?

Theories guide researchers by helping them to raise interesting and important questions. Once a question has been formulated, scientists set out to answer it using a well-defined approach called the *scientific method.*

Consider 4-year-old Bridget. She is a typical preschooler. Her best friend is Ivanna, and she seldom plays with boys. Bridget, like many other children, prefers to play with children of the same sex. Scientists have been trying to discover why children prefer same-sex play-mates (Maccoby, 1998; Martin, 1994; Martin & Fabes, 2001), but how do they investigate a question like this? Finding an answer requires application of scientific reasoning and use of the scientific method.

Scientific Reasoning and the Scientific Method

Scientific reasoning is similar to good everyday problem solving. When you need to solve a problem, you apply logical reasoning to minimize the number of possible explanations, with the ultimate goal of finding one probable explanation (Overton, 1998). Scientific reasoning is designed to produce results that are objective (they are measurable and observable by others), reliable (they can be replicated repeatedly), and valid (they accurately describe the phenomenon in question).

To solve the many mysteries of child development, researchers use the scientific method. This method involves four steps:

1. *Formulating a hypothesis:* Through observation and study, a scientist develops an educated expectation, or hypothesis, about the phenomenon or behavior he or she is interested in.

2. *Designing a study:* The scientist strategically designs a study that tests the hypothesis. The study may involve many different methods, such as structured interviews, observations, or experiments in the laboratory.

3. *Collecting evidence:* The scientist uses the strategy that he or she has designed to collect information that will test the accuracy of the hypothesis.

4. *Interpreting and reporting the evidence:* The scientist analyzes the data and interprets the patterns of the findings as they relate to the hypothesis.

Consider this hypothesis: children prefer to play with same-sex peers because they have common interests. If this hypothesis is accurate, we would expect children to play more often with same-sex peers during gender-typed activities. For instance, a girl would be more likely to play with other girls when playing with a kitchen set than when playing on swings, a non-gender-typed activity. To test this hypothesis, a scientist might design a study in which a team of observers watches certain children while they play and notes the sex of the children who play with them and their activities. After a specified amount of time, the scientist summarizes and analyzes the observations. The scientist then interprets the findings to determine whether the children were more likely to play with same-sex peers while involved in gender-typed activities as compared to non-gender-typed activities. When Maccoby (1998) investigated this hypothesis, she did not find support for it. Instead, children played with same-sex playmates regardless of the type of activity. Thus, this same-sex preference appears to be caused by factors other than shared interests. When a hypothesis is not confirmed, scientists often learn interesting new information, which may change theories and help them formulate different hypotheses to test.

Topics in Developmental Science

Think about some of the headlines that you have seen related to child development or some of the issues that you have discussed with your friends. Should children go to preschool?

How do teen gangs form? Can babies learn before they are born? Developmental scientists are interested in these questions and many more. What determines the areas or topics they choose to study?

The topics that developmental scientists study have changed over time, and the "hot" topics of developmental science also evolve over time (Horowitz, 2000). The scientific study of child development grew out of concerns about the welfare of children, and very practical questions formed the initial focus of research. Trends then changed for many years, becoming more focused on topics related to children's learning (Schwebel, Plumert, & Pick, 2000).

Just as research topics have changed over time, so too have the ways in which they are evaluated as significant or less important topics by both the lay public and other scientists. Recently, topics that have practical, everyday importance in the lives of children have received increasing attention (Lerner, Fisher, & Weinberg, 2000; McCall & Groark, 2000). The newsworthiness of the topic, the severity of a problem (e.g., HIV infection in babies), and the number of people affected by it also influence which topics are evaluated as having high priority (Fabes, Martin, Hanish, & Updegraff, 2000).

Traditionally, research topics have been described as falling into one of two camps—basic developmental research and applied developmental research. Basic developmental research is designed to answer broad, fundamental questions, such as the following:

This picture depicts a common scene: boys playing with other boys. Although the tendency of boys to play with other boys and girls to play with other girls is widely recognized, the reasons for it remain unclear. Can you identify the steps in the scientific method that would allow researchers to test their ideas about the reasons for these play preferences?

- What are the causes of developmental disabilities?
- How is language acquired?
- What emotions are infants born with?

Applied developmental research is designed to solve practical problems, such as the following:

- How to treat children with developmental delays
- How to improve the language skills of children who suffer head injuries
- How to help parents cope with chronically ill infants

Both types of research are necessary for understanding child development. Basic research lays the foundation for the applied research that follows. Additionally, applied research often produces questions that can be answered only through basic research (Herrmann, 1998).

Today, there is a movement toward integrating the basic and applied approaches. Basic researchers can consider the implications of their research for applied issues. Applied scientists can ground their research on applied problems in basic research findings. And basic research can be conducted within the context of an applied problem. For instance, research on children's high accident rates when driving ATVs led to the idea that children's understanding of their own abilities varies depending on their familiarity with the demands of a situation. Children are most at risk for making errors (and possibly injuring themselves) when they are learning a new skill or acting within a new environment (Schwebel et al., 2000). When research is done in this way, the complementary roles of applied and basic research become even more apparent.

Research Strategies

For both basic and applied developmental research, scientists have developed methods, or research designs, to help them determine whether their hypotheses are correct. No single research design is perfect; each has advantages and disadvantages. The following qualities vary according to the design of the study:

- Degree of control and structure
- Degree to which cause and effect can be determined
- Degree to which the findings of the study can be generalized to other people or settings
- Degree to which the findings directly apply to real-life events and processes

Table 2.3 outlines how these qualities apply to the six different types of research designs discussed in this chapter.

How do scientists select the methods they believe will be most useful in investigating a problem? First, the theory that guides their research may lead them to choose a particular method. Ethologists, for instance, choose methods that allow them to collect data in natural settings because they are interested in observing the adaptive functions of behaviors as they occur in everyday situations. Learning theorists are more likely to choose controlled

FROM RESEARCH TO PRACTICE
HOW CAN RESULTS FROM DIFFERENT STUDIES BE COMBINED?

FROM RESEARCH . . .

Few single studies can assess the diversity of factors that influence development, no matter how well designed or analyzed. As a result, scientists review and synthesize studies that accumulate in a particular area of child development (Sutton, Abrams, & Jones, 2001). In the traditional method of reviewing and consolidating the information in many studies, a researcher's subjective interpretation played a defining role. But another researcher, reviewing the same literature, might not reach a similar conclusion—clearly, a new method was needed. Researchers now rely on the relatively new practice of meta-analysis to more objectively interpret the meaning of information gleaned from large numbers of studies (Cooper & Hedges, 1994; Sutton et al., 2001).

In meta-analysis a clear set of guidelines for using statistical principles to summarize the results of previous studies is employed, making the process of reviewing child development literature (or any research literature) more scientific and objective. The goal of meta-analysis is to make the research review process as systematic and replicable as any other piece of scientific work; any disagreement about such a review now tends to focus on method rather than the reviewer's opinion (Wanner, 1992).

The use of meta-analysis has increased dramatically. This method has been employed to address many important topics in child development, such as developmental changes (Fabes & Eisenberg, 1996), the impact of parents and peers (Gershoff, 2002; Leaper, Anderson, & Sanders, 1998), sex differences (Lautenbacher, 2004), and health behaviors (such as the treatment of influenza; Cooper et al., 2003).

. . . TO PRACTICE

One important application of meta-analysis is the assessment of treatment programs. Meta-analysis can help practitioners make important decisions about treatment options for various mental and physical health problems. For example, Lipsey (1995) examined the effectiveness of different approaches to the treatment of juvenile delinquency. The issue concerned whether punishment or rehabilitation produced better outcomes. Lipsey used meta-analysis to examine the effectiveness of different treatment strategies, summarizing over 400 different studies. In general, Lipsey found that the most effective treatments emphasized rehabilitation (employment, job skills, counseling). Programs emphasizing punishment not only were less effective but actually produced greater subsequent rates of delinquency. Thus, the use of meta-analysis can help translate research into practice and help make important, real-life decisions.

THINKING IT THROUGH:

1. What problems does a scientist face when he or she wants to review several studies in an area of human development?

2. How can two reviewers, looking at the same literature, come to two different conclusions?

3. How can results from meta-analyses be useful for practitioners?

TABLE 2.3
Comparing Different Research Strategies

METHOD	CONTROL AND STRUCTURE	DETERMINATION OF CAUSALITY	GENERALIZES WELL	DIRECT APPLICATION TO REAL LIFE
Case studies	No	No	No	Yes
Clinical interviews	No	No	Possibly	Possibly
Survey studies	No	No	Possibly	No
Naturalistic studies	No	No	Possibly	Yes
Correlational studies	No	No	Possibly	Possibly
Experimental studies	Yes	Yes	Possibly	Possibly

settings, such as laboratory experiments, in which they can manipulate conditions to study the effects of reinforcement on specific behaviors.

Second, the research question may dictate the best methods, leading scientists to adopt different methods at different times. For example, when first investigating a question, a scientist might examine behaviors in a natural setting. After formulating a testable hypothesis, he or she may then move to a more controlled environment where cause and effect can be tested.

Case Studies

In a **case study,** the researcher collects information about aspects of a person's life, such as medical history, family background, school grades, friendships and relationships, intelligence and achievement, personality characteristics, or dreams and desires. The advantage of this design is that it allows an in-depth view of the person. The disadvantage is that the information may not be generalized to other people because of unique features of the person (Yin, 1994).

One of the earliest case studies was Charles Darwin's detailed diary study of his infant son's behavior (Darwin, 1877). Other important case studies have been based on the lives of famous people such as Mahatma Gandhi (Erikson, 1969). Case studies may feature people who are unusual or who have a noteworthy condition, such as Victor the wild boy (see Chapter 1). More recently, a case study of a severely neglected and abused child named Genie provided insights into child development under extremely harsh conditions (Curtiss, 1977; see Chapter 6).

Clinical Interviews

In a **clinical interview,** the researcher asks detailed questions in interaction with the participant. The goal of the clinical interview is to identify how the individual thinks about a given topic. In the following example (Piaget, 1946/1969, p. 207), the researcher is exploring the child's understanding of age. This interview reveals a common misunderstanding held by young children: that age is directly related to size.

Experimenter: Are you the same age? [as his older sister]

Filk (boy, age 5): No, because we weren't born at the same time.

Experimenter: Who was born first?

Filk: She was.

Experimenter: Will you be the same age as her one day, or will the two of you never be the same age?

Filk: Soon I will be bigger than her, because men are bigger than women. Then I shall be older.

case study *method in which the researcher collects information about aspects of a person's life*

clinical interview *method in which the researcher asks detailed questions while interacting with the participant*

Jean Piaget developed a comprehensive theory about how children move through different stages in cognitive development. Many of his studies involved using the clinical interview method. What are the main components of this method and how can it produce useful information about children's development?

survey study *method in which a number of people respond to a set of structured questions*

naturalistic study *method in which researchers observe the behavior of people in their natural environments*

correlational study *method in which researchers compare participants on two variables to determine whether the variables relate to each other*

correlation coefficients *calculated measures of the relations between variables*

experimental study *method in which scientists bring people into a manipulated laboratory situation and then note the effects of the manipulation*

random sampling *selecting participants for a study at random*

random assignment *randomly assigning people to groups in a study so that the effects of uncontrolled variables will be the same for all groups*

independent variable *condition that is assumed to be the cause of the behavior and is manipulated by the scientist*

The data obtained in a clinical interview may be biased by participants' telling the experimenter what they believe the experimenter wants to hear (Garbarino & Stott, 1992). Also, the method can be used only with language-proficient participants and thus is not useful with very young children or with children who have language problems. The advantage of this method is its flexibility. The clinical interview can be used to probe for new information or to gain insights into people's thoughts and feelings.

Survey Studies

A **survey study** is used to determine how a number of people respond to a set of structured questions. A survey may be conducted by phone, in person, on the Internet, or by mail. An advantage is that data for many people can be obtained easily, but a disadvantage is that people often respond inaccurately as they try to present themselves in the most positive way (Cozby, 2004).

If you have answered questions for a telephone poll, you have been involved in a survey study. Survey studies are popular for gathering data about demographics (age, income, marital status), beliefs and attitudes, leisure activities, political beliefs, and consumer choices. Several large-scale surveys have been done involving adults. One is the General Social Survey, which covers topics such as attitudes, life satisfaction, health, religion, sex, and race. Another is the National Health Interview Survey, designed to obtain information about eating and health habits. The National Survey of Children is one of the few large-scale studies of a broad range of topics focused on children. Every decade, the US Census Bureau conducts one of the largest surveys, encompassing almost the entire US population, and the results have important consequences for funding and political representation for cities and states.

Naturalistic Studies

In a **naturalistic study,** researchers observe the behavior of people in their natural environments—homes, schools, malls, or parks. Because researchers are watching people in their familiar everyday settings, the people tend to behave normally. A disadvantage of naturalistic studies is the difficulty of generalizing from one setting to another setting. In addition, the researcher has no control over the naturalistic setting, making it virtually impossible to determine cause and effect.

Fabes and colleagues (2003) conducted a year-long naturalistic study in preschool and kindergarten classrooms. They observed children's social behavior on the playground, in classrooms, at lunch, and while alone. From these observations, they described how boys and girls interacted. For instance, they concluded that both sexes tend to play in same-sex groups but that certain children tended to cross gender lines more than others. Fabes's data did not enable him to draw cause-and-effect conclusions, though, because he could not systematically control for variables that might explain why children behaved as they did.

Correlational Studies

Are children who watch more television more aggressive? This important research hypothesis has been difficult to test. Because so many children watch television, it is difficult to find children who do not watch it to serve as a comparison group. In such cases, researchers use correlational studies. A **correlational study** compares participants (children, in this case) on two variables to determine whether the variables relate to each other: are children who watch more television more likely to be aggressive than children who watch less television?

To uncover patterns in variables, researchers use **correlation coefficients**—calculations of the relations between variables. Correlation coefficients range from +1.0 to −1.0. A positive score represents a positive relationship between variables (a high score on one variable is related to a high score on the other). Zero represents no relationship between variables, and a negative score represents an inverse relationship between variables (a high score on one variable is related to a *low* score on the other). Figure 2.9 illustrates positive and negative correlations.

Although correlational studies demonstrate how variables are related, they cannot reveal whether one causes the other. In the example of television viewing and aggression, for instance, it is impossible to conclude whether television viewing causes children to be more aggressive. It may be that children who are aggressive are more inclined to watch television than are less aggressive children. Or television viewing and aggression may each be related to a third variable that has not been considered, such as parental supervision. Perhaps when parents do not supervise their children closely, the children watch more television and are also more aggressive, even though the two behaviors are not causally linked (Cozby, 2004).

Sometimes correlational studies provide the only ethical way to study a topic. For example, the most scientifically sound way to study the effects of spanking on children would be to have one group of parents spank their children and another group to refrain from spanking. But this would not be ethical. A correlational study allows researchers to ask parents about spanking practices and examine the data in relation to their children's behavior.

Experimental Studies

How, then, do scientists investigate whether television viewing causes aggression? To determine causality, scientists must use an **experimental study,** creating a manipulated situation in a laboratory and noting the effects of the manipulation. The causes of behavior are easier to determine with experimental rather than with correlational methods because the scientist controls the sequence of events and any extraneous variables that may influence the findings in unexpected ways.

Scientists gain control over extraneous variables in several ways. One way is by trying to hold constant all factors that may influence behavior. For instance, in a study of television violence, a scientist might hold constant the characteristics of the experimenter, the ages of the participants, the lighting, and the time of day during which participants are tested.

Not all variables can be easily controlled, however, especially characteristics of people. Scientists want to ensure that the effects of uncontrollable variables are randomly distributed across the groups involved in the study. For instance, a child's upbringing may influence his or her likelihood of being aggressive with other people, but it is impossible to identify and control all the variables related to a child's upbringing in a given study. To minimize the effects of these variables, scientists use randomization. They select participants at random, a procedure called **random sampling,** and they randomly assign people to groups, a procedure called **random assignment.** In this way, the effects of upbringing and other uncontrolled variables will be approximately the same for all groups in the study.

When designing an experimental study, scientists determine the variable whose effects they want to test. This is the **independent variable,** the one thought to be the cause of the behavior and the one that the scientist will manipulate. Thus, if the independent variable is exposure to violent programming, one group of children will watch a violent program, and the other will watch a nonviolent one. The children who watch the violent program are in the **experimental group,** whereas the children watching the nonviolent program are in the **control group.** All other variables are kept the same for both groups. The researcher then assesses whether children who received the independent variable (exposure to violent programming) differ from those who did not. The behavior thought to be affected by the independent variable is the **dependent variable**—in this case, aggressive behavior following the television viewing. Thus, in experimental studies, the "cause" is the independent variable, and the "effect" is the dependent variable (Cozby, 2004).

Although the experimental method allows scientists to determine cause and effect, it has disadvantages. The major disadvantage is that laboratory situations tend to be artificial. People may respond quite differently in a laboratory setting than they do in real life. Findings from experimental studies may be very relevant for real life, but care must be taken in interpreting them if the experimental manipulation is not realistic.

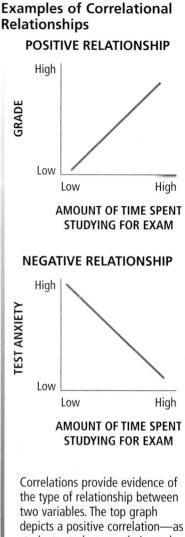

FIGURE 2.9
Examples of Correlational Relationships

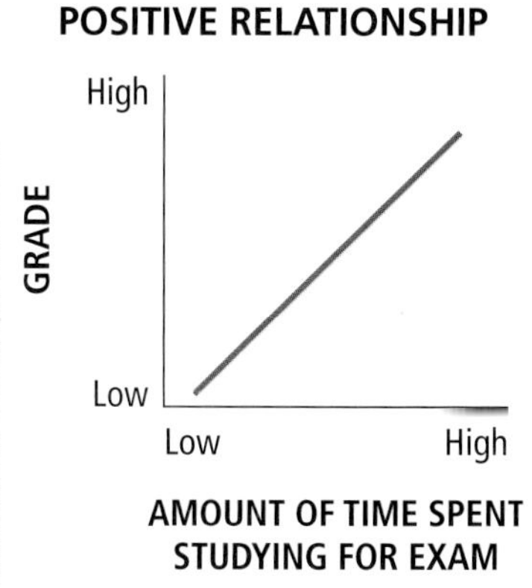
POSITIVE RELATIONSHIP
GRADE
High
Low
Low
High
AMOUNT OF TIME SPENT STUDYING FOR EXAM

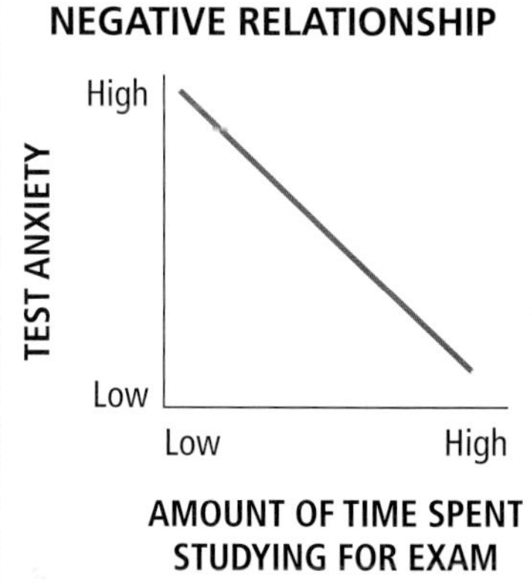
NEGATIVE RELATIONSHIP
TEST ANXIETY
High
Low
Low
High
AMOUNT OF TIME SPENT STUDYING FOR EXAM

Correlations provide evidence of the type of relationship between two variables. The top graph depicts a positive correlation—as students study more, their grades improve. The bottom graph depicts a negative correlation—as students study more, their anxiety about test performance decreases. Correlational research, however, cannot tell us the reasons for these relationships.

experimental group *group that receives the independent variable*

control group *comparison group that is treated in the same way as the experimental group but does not receive the independent variable*

dependent variable *the behavior thought to be affected by the independent variable*

NURTURING CHILDREN
PROTECTING CHILDREN INVOLVED IN RESEARCH

To understand children's development, we must study them. But special care must be taken because children are more vulnerable to stress and less able to evaluate what participation in a research program may mean. As a result, scientists who study child development follow strict guidelines for the ethical treatment of the participants in their studies. Before running a study, scientists submit a plan for the study to the institutional review board at their college or university. This board is responsible for granting approval for and overseeing studies that involve human participants. To obtain approval, scientists must comply with the American Psychological Association's guidelines for research with human participants and the guidelines for children developed by the Society for Research in Child Development. The guidelines for research with children include the following:

■ *Protection from harm:* Each child must be protected from potential physical and psychological harm. No treatment or experimental condition can cause harm.

■ *Protection of well-being:* If, in the course of research, information that may seriously affect a child's well-being comes to the researcher's attention, the investigator has a responsibility to discuss the information with experts in the field so that the parents may arrange necessary assistance for their child.

■ *Informed consent:* Each child and his or her parents have the right to know the procedures that will be used in the study and decide whether or not to be involved in it. Informed consent also requires a description of the risks and benefits of the study.

■ *Privacy:* Children involved in studies have the right to maintain their privacy. This is accomplished by allowing children to remain anonymous when they participate in studies, typically by assigning identification numbers rather than using names and by analyzing data at a group rather than an individual level.

■ *Right to beneficial treatments:* Children have the right to receive any treatment that is found to be effective when used in a study. If a child is a member of a nontreated control group, she or he has the option of receiving the treatment as soon as the treatment is found to be successful.

THINKING IT THROUGH

1. What special protections, in addition to those extended to adults, must be provided for children who participate in research?

2. What scientific risk is entailed in informing research participants about the specific nature of the study, the hypotheses, and the methods before the study begins?

Measuring Change over Time

Many of the most interesting questions in child development involve change over time. Is an outgoing and affectionate toddler likely to grow up to be a teenager who has many friends? Do active children become active adults? To answer these questions, scientists use methods that assess change over time.

One method for assessing change is the **cross-sectional study.** As Figure 2.10 illustrates, in cross-sectional studies, individuals of different ages are tested at the same point in time, and the results from each age group are compared. For instance, a researcher interested in developmental changes in memory capacity might test children who are 4, 8, 12, and 16 years old. Children at each age would be shown a group of objects and later asked what they remembered about the objects. By averaging the memory scores for children at each age, researchers could get an idea of how memory capacity changes.

Cross-sectional studies are limited in their ability to identify age-related changes, however. In these studies, the people in each age group make up a **cohort,** or unique birth group. The scientist may be unaware of important differences between cohorts that may affect the results of a study. For instance, suppose a comparison of computer skills among 10-year-olds and 60-year-olds reveals that more of the 10-year-olds are highly skilled. The scientist might be tempted to conclude that as people grow older, they lose computer skills. However, these

cross-sectional study *method in which individuals of different ages are tested at the same point in time and the results from each age group are compared*

cohort *a group of individuals who are the same age or who experience similar events at the same time*

FIGURE 2.10
Cross-Sectional Design

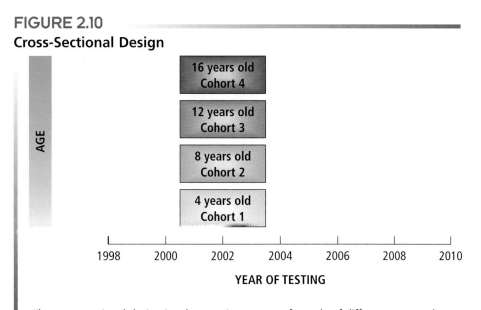

The cross-sectional design involves testing groups of people of different ages at the same point in time. What are the strengths and weaknesses of this design?

two cohorts have experienced different periods of history, which affected their exposure to computers in the first place.

Another method for assessing change over time is the **longitudinal study** (see Figure 2.11), in which the same group of individuals is tested at different points in time. When the results at the different points in time are compared, developmental changes become apparent. Problems of longitudinal studies include a tendency for some individuals to drop out and for test scores to improve because of repeated testing. Longitudinal studies also have limited ability to identify age-related changes. Any findings may reflect the particular cohort rather than age-related changes. These studies also are expensive and time consuming (Willett, Singer, & Martin, 1998).

FIGURE 2.11
Longitudinal Design

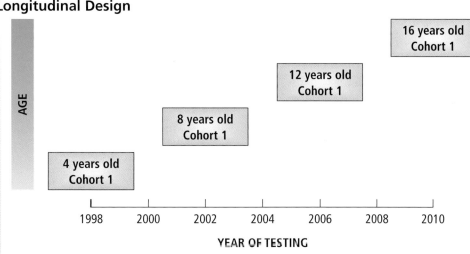

The longitudinal design involves testing the same people repeatedly at several different points in time. What are some limitations of longitudinal designs?

longitudinal study *method in which the same group of individuals is tested at different points in time*

FIGURE 2.12
Cohort-Sequential Design

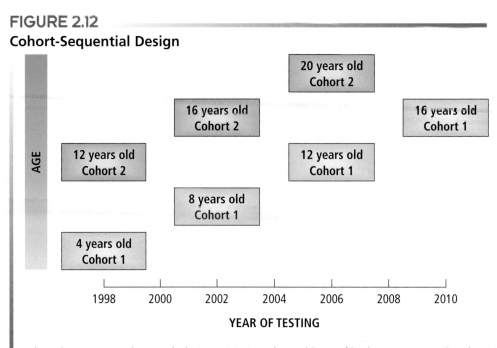

The cohort-sequential research design minimizes the problems of both cross-sectional and longitudinal designs. The same children are tested at several points in time, but new participants are added at each time point to prevent the problems of repeated testing and attrition.

To minimize problems with cross-sectional and longitudinal designs, scientists may combine the two strategies, in a **cohort-sequential research design.** In this design, illustrated in Figure 2.12, a cross-sectional study is expanded so that data are collected from the same cohorts at different points in time. Children of different ages are involved and studied over time, including at least two different cohorts. Such a design assists in disentangling age and cohort effort and determining whether age changes reoccur in other cohorts. Another advantage to this design is that new participants can be added at each point in time to prevent the problems caused by repeated testing and attrition.

Measuring Children's Behavior

Developmental scientists have devised many ways to measure variables such as aggression, memory, intelligence, and stress. Four broad categories of measures are used. *Physiological measures* record responses of the body, such as heart rate, hormone production, and galvanic skin response (sweating), which are used to assess arousal and anxiety. Activity in different parts of the brain can be assessed by recording electrical activity. Brain cell activity is recorded through sensitive electrodes placed at various locations on the person's head and scalp. Many of these methods are used with infants and young children.

Behavioral measures involve the direct assessment of behavior through observation. For example, to investigate whether children have preferences for certain toys, observers watch them play to see if they choose one type of toy over another. To assess whether mothers and fathers respond to their children differently, observers watch and record how parents play with their children.

Self-reports are a third type of measure. Rather than observe children as they play with dolls or cars, a scientist might ask them which toy they prefer. Self-reports include ques-

cohort-sequential research design   *a cross-sectional study expanded so that data are collected from the same cohorts at different points in time*

DEBATING THE ISSUE
DO GIFTED CHILDREN BECOME WELL-ADJUSTED ADULTS?

 Remember the case of William James Sidis, the child prodigy discussed in Chapter 1? Many people believe that gifted children are like William—odd and socially awkward. But is this perception true? One attempt to examine this issue was launched in 1920, when Lewis Terman (1877–1956) began a longitudinal study of gifted children. He was interested in discovering the origins and outcomes of being a genius. He was particularly interested in testing the popular belief that geniuses grow up to be maladjusted. This study is one of the classic longitudinal studies (Terman, 1925). Over 1,000 highly intelligent (IQ scores of 140 and above, or 40 points over the average) children from California were followed from school age through the rest of their lives. Terman was involved in the study until the children were in their 40s and 50s (Terman & Oden, 1959), and then new researchers took over the study to

continue following Terman's "Termites," as the participants called themselves.

Terman's participants were successful at all stages of their lives. As children, they did well in school, had satisfactory peer relationships, and showed early and intense interests in science and literature. Many more of the gifted participants finished college and obtained graduate degrees than did members of comparison groups with normal-range IQ scores. With respect to social adjustment and maturity, the gifted participants were similar to comparison groups of nongifted people. Almost all of them married, and many had children. In their 40s, the gifted participants were at the peak of their careers.

The Termites included many distinguished scientists, doctors, lawyers, and inventors. One participant learned 15 languages, and two others were awarded over a hundred patents. Generally, the participants seemed contented with their lives. The gifted participants did not grow up to

be criminals or alcoholics; in fact, their rates of criminal behavior and alcoholism were much lower than those for the general population. Even in their 70s, many of the participants had active and intellectually stimulating lives (Shurkin, 1992).

THINKING IT THROUGH

1. Why is it important to test common-sense beliefs? In what ways does Terman's study dispel the myth that geniuses are eccentric?

2. If you were designing a study of the psychological adjustment of gifted children, what kinds of measures might you include in your study? Why is it difficult to measure adjustment?

3. Why are longitudinal studies difficult to conduct? What factors make them expensive? How do you keep participants interested in being in the study?

tionnaires in which people respond to questions about their behavior, attitudes, beliefs, values, and habits. Self-report measures are the easiest type of information to gather, but people may not make accurate reports or may not remember the information they are asked to report on.

Projective measures indirectly assess individuals' psychological states. The typical strategy is to show a participant an ambiguous scene, such as a picture of a boy standing by a fireplace, looking sad. The participant is then asked to make up a story about the boy. Or a child may be asked to draw a person or a family. From these stories and drawings, researchers infer the person's thinking and feelings. This method yields only subjective data, however, which might vary in interpretation from researcher to researcher.

Consider, too, the special challenges involved in testing hypotheses relevant to infants and young children. Many of the techniques used with older children and adults, such as questionnaires and projective measures, are impossible to use with infants and young children because they do not have the necessary verbal skills. Whereas older children can provide some insight into their own thinking and experience, this kind of response is very difficult for younger children to make, even when they have some skill with words. Testing infants, in particular, is difficult because they are often crying, asleep, or drowsy, making them unresponsive to any kind of testing. Adhering to ethical guidelines also is problematic when testing young children and infants, because it is difficult to assess a nonverbal child's refusal to participate.

As you can see, developmental scientists face many challenges as they choose a research question, a theoretical basis, a set of methods, and the types of measures. But studying how behavior develops and changes over time can be rewarding and meaningful work.

Try It Out

1. Think about your own behavior. Can you think of examples of behaviors that you learned through operant conditioning? through social learning? Describe how you might have acquired these behaviors.
2. Consider the development of a child born to a drug-addicted mother. Think about the kinds of microsystem, exosystem, and macrosystem influences that could potentially play a role in the child's development. Now discuss how interventions could be used at each of these levels to improve the developmental outcome for the child.
3. Design an individual or collaborative research project using one of the research strategies described in this chapter. Begin by posing a question about child development that you wish to answer. Try to formulate a hypothesis, and then consider these questions. What methods will you use to test it? Who will your participants be, and how many will you need? What information will you need, where and how will you get it, and in what form will you record it? What ethical issues will you need to consider? What might be some applications of your findings?

Key Terms and Concepts

accommodation (39)
assimilation (39)
attachment theory (32)
case study (49)
classical conditioning (36)
clinical interview (49)
cohort (52)
cohort-sequential research design (54)
concrete operational stage (40)
control group (51)
control parameters (44)
correlational study (50)
correlation coefficients (50)
cross-sectional study (52)
dependent variable (51)
dynamic systems theory (44)
ecological model (44)
ego (33)
empirically based (30)
ethological theory (32)
evolutionary theories (31)
exosystem (44)
experimental group (51)
experimental study (50)

extinction (38)
fact (30)
formal operational stage (40)
id (33)
independent variable (50)
information processing theory (42)
libido (33)
longitudinal study (53)
long-term memory (43)
macrosystem (44)
mesosystem (44)
microsystem (44)
naturalistic study (50)
negative reinforcement (38)
neurodevelopmental approaches (33)
operant conditioning (38)
opinions (30)
positive reinforcement (38)
preoperational stage (40)
psychoanalytic theories (33)
psychosexual development (34)
psychosocial crises (35)
punishment (38)
random assignment (50)

random sampling (50)
rate-limiting component (45)
schemes (39)
sensorimotor stage (40)
sensory register (42)
shaping (38)
short-term memory (42)

social learning theory (39)
superego (33)
survey study (50)
theory (30)
vicarious reinforcement (38)
zone of proximal development (42)

Sum It Up

How do theories explain child development?

- What is the function of a scientific developmental theory? (pp. 29–30)

What are the major biology-based theories of child development?

- What is the difference between evolutionary and ethological theories of development? (pp. 31–33)
- Describe the neurodevelopmental approach to the study of development. (p. 33)

What are the major psychoanalytic theories of child development?

- How do Freud's and Erikson's theories differ? (pp. 33–35)

What are the major learning-based theories of child development?

- Who were the three most influential learning-based theorists, and how do their theories differ? (pp. 36–38)
- What is the major emphasis of social learning theory? (p. 38)

What are the major cognition-based theories of child development?

- Describe one major theory of cognitive development (pp. 39–42)

What are the major contextual theories of child development?

- Describe the differences between Bronfenbrenner's ecological theory and dynamic systems theory. (pp. 43–45)

How is child development studied?

- What research strategies are available for testing hypotheses? (pp. 47–52)
- What are the different measures used to study children's development? (pp. 54–55)

Chapter
Summary
2

TABLE 2.1
Categorization of Theories of Human Development

CATEGORY	DESCRIPTION	THEORIES INCLUDED
Biology-based theories	Emphasis on inherited biological factors and processes	Evolutionary theories Ethological theories Attachment theory Neurodevelopmental theories
Psychoanalytic theories	Emphasis on unconscious internal drives and interactions with others	Freud's psychosexual theory Erikson's psychosocial theory
Learning-based theories	Emphasis on the role of the external world	Classical conditioning Operant conditioning Social learning theory
Cognition-based theories	Emphasis on the role of cognition and processing of information	Piaget's theory Vygotsky's theory Information processing theory
Contextual theories	Emphasis on the interaction between individuals and their environments	Ecological theory Dynamic systems theory

Neurodevelopmental theories focus on how the brain influences behavior and development.

THEORIES OF CHILD DEVELOPMENT

No single theory accounts for all of development, and different theories have different strengths, weaknesses, and foci. (Refer back to pages 29–45)

Mass Media
Legal System
Neighbors
Social Services Support
Physical Environment — Siblings
School — Parents
MICROSYSTEM
Cultural Attitudes
Cultural Values
MESOSYSTEM
Parents' Friends
Parents' Work
EXOSYSTEM
MACROSYSTEM

FIGURE 2.7 **Bronfenbrenner's Ecological Model** *This model depicts the complexity of contextual theories of development.*

FIGURE 2.5 **Piaget's Stages of Cognitive Development** *Jean Piaget developed a comprehensive theory about how children move through different stages in their cognitive development.*

Sensorimotor Stage (0–2 years)

Motoric knowledge

Lack of understanding that objects continue to exist when not in view

Present orientation

Preoperational Stage (2–7 years)

Symbolic representation

Planning

Thinking and problem solving guided by perception and appearances

Egocentric thinking

Concrete Operational Stage (7–11 years)

Logic used in problem solving

Logic applied only to concrete objects and events

Formal Operational Stage (11 years and beyond)

Logic applied to hypothetical and abstract problems

Concern with concepts like justice, equality, and fairness

TABLE 2.3
Comparing Different Research Strategies

METHOD	CONTROL AND STRUCTURE	DETERMINATION OF CAUSALITY	GENERALIZES WELL	DIRECT APPLICATION TO REAL LIFE
Case studies	No	No	No	Yes
Clinical interviews	No	No	Possibly	Possibly
Survey studies	No	No	Possibly	No
Naturalistic studies	No	No	Possibly	Yes
Correlational studies	No	No	Possibly	Possibly
Experimental studies	Yes	Yes	Possibly	Possibly

RESEARCH METHODS

Child development researchers use a variety of methods to study children's behavior. Each method has advantages and disadvantages, and these vary according to the specific type of study and the age of the children involved. In addition, researchers are careful to protect the rights of children in research as children lack adult awareness of the issues involved in research participation and therefore cannot also provide informed consent. (Refer back to pages 46–56).

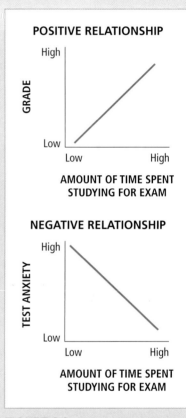

POSITIVE RELATIONSHIP

GRADE (Low to High) vs. AMOUNT OF TIME SPENT STUDYING FOR EXAM (Low to High)

NEGATIVE RELATIONSHIP

TEST ANXIETY (Low to High) vs. AMOUNT OF TIME SPENT STUDYING FOR EXAM (Low to High)

FIGURE 2.9 Examples of Correlational Relationships *Correlations provide evidence of the type of relationship between two variables.*

Many of Jean Piaget's studies involved using the clinical interview method.

part

2

Prenatal and Neonatal Development

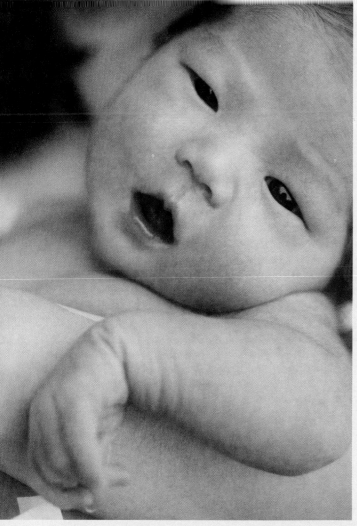

The miracle of life and its development captures the attention, fancy, and amazement of parents as well as poets, writers, and scientists. From a single fertilized cell, a complex individual made up of trillions of cells develops. Parents-to-be all over the world wonder whether their unborn child is a boy or a girl and whether the child is healthy. Most children are born healthy, but some are born with serious disorders due to genetic or environmental factors. The costs associated with complicated births and pregnancies are considerable—for parents, children, and society as a whole.

Once children are born, the demands of parenting and caregiving begin. Growth and development are rapid in the early years of life, and many changes result from the birth of a child. Newborns are not as helpless and passive as we once thought them to be. Thanks to new research, our ideas about newborns have changed. Babies actively strive to meet their needs for food, comfort, and social interactions.

Biological Foundations of Development

3

Chapter Outline

How Do Genes Influence Development?
Hunting for Genes: The Human Genome Project
DNA: The Secret to Life
Genes and Chromosomes
Sex Determination: Girl or Boy?
Genetic Transmission Patterns
Genomes to Life Project

How Do Genes and Environment Work Together?
Gene Expression
Genes and Exposure to Different Environments
Gene–Environment Interactions

What Are Common Chromosomal Abnormalities?
Down Syndrome
Sex Chromosome Abnormalities

How Are Genetic Diseases Detected?
Genetic Technology
Genetic Counseling

How Does Conception Occur, and What Can Be Done to Overcome Infertility?
Ovulation
Spermatogenesis
Fertilization
Overcoming Infertility

A DEVELOPMENTAL MYSTERY

When Carmen was born in a small village on a lake in Venezuela, her parents did not know whether she would grow up to be afflicted with "El Mal." According to local legends, German and Spanish sailors, whose trading ships regularly sailed to a nearby port city in the early 1800s, also visited the small villages on the lake. Some of the sailors slept with the local women; some stayed and lived there. One of these sailors, as the story goes, left behind El Mal. El Mal is Huntington's disease, a serious neurological dis- order causing severe wasting of the nervous system over many years, usually striking in middle age. The descendants of these families, living in many villages in the area, numbered about 3,000 in the late 1970s; about 100 of them had the disease already, and half of them were at risk for developing it. As Carmen grew older, she wondered if she or her children would get the disease or if they would be spared. Why do so many people in these villages contract El Mal?

How Do Genes Influence Development?

Carmen's mystery reflects the impact that genetic inheritance can have. Legends are built to explain such phenomena. El Mal, or Huntington's disease, is only one of many diseases strongly influenced by a person's genetic inheritance, and in this case, by a single gene. But the impact such diseases can have are sometimes devastating and people need to know beforehand so that they can prepare for the disease. Geneticists are interested in identifying which genes may influence the development of a disease or characteristic as well as how the gene or combinations of genes influence development. Once these questions can be answered, researchers hope to have at their fingertips the means to prevent and treat many serious human conditions. But genes control more aspects of development than diseases: many human characteristics are influenced by genetic inheritance. For many parents, it is only after the second child is born that they begin to marvel at how their two children could be so different from each other, though raised with similar expectations and goals. One possibility is that children inherit different genetic patterns, which then predispose them to behave in certain ways. Like many parents, scientists are interested in these differences, and they study genetic inheritance to learn how people develop in their appearance, thinking, and behavior.

Hunting for Genes: The Human Genome Project

We are fortunate to live in the twenty-first century, which is being dubbed the "biology century." Never have so many exciting findings about genetics been made in such a short time. Over the past decade, the *Human Genome Project (HGP),* involving the coordinated efforts of many scientists all over the world, took on the massive job of mapping the human genome. One day in February 2001, in a room packed with reporters, scientists from the HGP gave a press conference. During this important media event, they announced that they had succeeded in developing the first initial sequencing of the human genome. They also announced a major surprise—that the human genome had been found to contain around 30,000 genes, considerably below the initial estimate of 100,000 (Baltimore, 2001).

By mapping genes, scientists can begin to examine how genes code development. This knowledge can be used in many ways—for instance, in developing more effective treatments for diseases.

What is the human genome? A person's complete set of DNA is his or her **genome.** The human genome is essentially a book of instructions that tells how to put together series

genome *a person's complete set of DNA*

FIGURE 3.1
The Building Blocks of Life

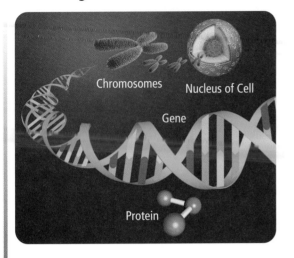

Chromosomes are found within each cell and are made up of DNA, and on the DNA strands are genes. Genes provide the message about how and which proteins should form. Proteins are the building blocks of life.

Source: U.S. Department of Energy Human Genome Program, 2004.

of amino acids, which make up specific proteins. These proteins are the building blocks of life—they trigger chemical reactions in every part of the body and are essential to life itself. The human genome "book" contains an enormous amount of information, equivalent to the information found in 5,000 books the size of this textbook! This gigantic recipe for human life is contained within the microscopic nucleus of a tiny cell that would fit easily into the period at the end of this sentence (Ridley, 1999).

Virtually every human cell carries this genetically programmed blueprint for development. If we look deep within each cell, into its nucleus, we would find rod-shaped bundles called **chromosomes.** Chromosomes are made up of tightly coiled ribbons of **DNA,** or deoxyribonucleic acid and proteins. Genetic information is outlined by the genes, which are arranged in specific locations on the "arms" or "legs" of chromosomes. For instance, researchers have located a gene on chromosome 10 involved in hormone production whose presence increases the risk of breast cancer for women. The number of chromosomes varies dramatically across species. In normal humans, each cell contains 46 chromosomes that work together in pairs: one chromosome of the pair is inherited from the mother and the other from the father.

The challenge of discovering the sequence of genes in humans began in 1990, when the Department of Energy and the National Institutes of Health proposed a joint project to the US Congress—the HGP—in which a 16-nation group of scientists would completely map the human genome in 15 years. At the time, the task seemed formidable. Nonetheless, the initial working draft of the human genome was completed in 2003, earlier than expected.

Whose genes are being mapped in this project? DNA was extracted from 20 individuals, but the DNA of only 5 of them has been used as the prototypic genome. You may wonder whether it makes sense to unravel the code of just a few specific individuals. Actually, individuals share 99.99 percent of their genetic code with other individuals, and people of different sexes, races, and national descent may have more in common genetically than people of the same sex or race or national descent. The categories of sex and race that are so important culturally reflect only a very tiny portion of our genes. For these reasons, knowing the genetic map of one individual provides insights into the genetics of all humans.

DNA: The Secret to Life

To understand how genetic information is provided for each cell, it is important to understand how DNA is structured and how it works. DNA is a double helix structure consisting of two backbones, like a twisted ladder, and each rung of the ladder is made up of a combination of two chemical substances called bases. The bases are labeled A, T, C, and G (to represent their chemical names), and these bases always match up the same way: C with G and A with T. The combinations of these bases signal to the body which types of proteins to form. The proteins include hormones and enzymes, and they are used in building cells, cell functioning, muscle contractions, digestion, and growth.

The secret to the coding of information on the chromosome lies in the sequencing of the bases along the ladder of DNA. DNA can duplicate itself, and this explains why almost every cell in the body contains genetic information. **Genes** are the labels given to portions of the DNA that encode specific genetic information, and they vary in length from the smallest sequences of a few thousand bases to the largest with several million bases, with the average gene having about 3,000 bases. Each gene encodes a specific protein. Chromosomes consist of genes and some proteins, but it is the genes themselves that provide the actual genetic code. Surprisingly, very little of the human genome is made up of genes.

To pass on the coded information, DNA breaks apart in the middle of the rungs, pulling apart the pairs of bases that "fit" together. New matching bases then attach them-

chromosomes *the structures on which genes reside*

DNA *a double helix consisting of two backbones, like a twisted ladder, whose rungs are made up of chemical combinations; the basis of chromosomes*

genes *the portion of DNA that encodes specific genetic information*

FIGURE 3.2
Double Helix

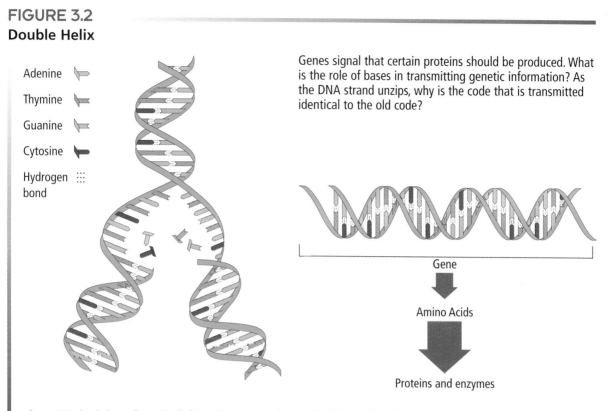

Adenine

Thymine

Guanine

Cytosine

Hydrogen
bond

Genes signal that certain proteins should be produced. What is the role of bases in transmitting genetic information? As the DNA strand unzips, why is the code that is transmitted identical to the old code?

Gene

Amino Acids

Proteins and enzymes

Source: Kosslyn & Rossenberg, *Psychology: The Brain, The Person, The World,* 2/e. Published by Allyn and Bacon, Boston, MA. Copyright © 2004 by Pearson Education. Reprinted by permission of the publisher.

selves to the half of the old ladder and its rungs, forming a new strand of DNA that is identical to the old one. In this way, the new cell has the same genetic information as the original cell and can produce the same proteins.

Genes and Chromosomes

To understand the actions of genes, consider how a child comes to have his or her specific complement of genes. The process begins as sex cells—ova and sperm—develop within the child's mother and father. Most cells multiply by creating exact duplicates of themselves through **mitosis.** Mitosis is a type of cell division that gives rise to two daughter cells, each with identical chromosomes and genotypes. The process of mitosis involves one duplication of chromosomes (one set for each daughter cell) and one cell division to split the material into the two daughter cells (see Figure 3.3a). When cell division occurs, the DNA "unzips" and duplicates itself. Each resulting cell contains the full complement of 23 pairs of chromosomes. **Gametes,** which are sex cells (ova and sperm), however, undergo a process called **meiosis,** which involves creating sex cells with half the genetic complement (so that they are able to join with other gametes). Meiosis involves an extra step: there is one duplication of chromosomes, then two daughter cells split off, each with a full set of genetic material. Then these cells undergo another division, such that the resulting four cells contain half the complement of chromosomes: one member of each pair of chromosomes (see Figure 3.3b). Once conception occurs, the chromosomes of the ovum and sperm align so that the newly developing child obtains half of his or her genes from each parent. Thus, genes provide a unique plan for development, incorporating genetic information from each parent.

In a **karyotype** analysis, a geneticist photographs chromosomes and then aligns each chromosome with the other member of its pair, and the pairs are ordered by size and structure. The first 22 pairs of chromosomes, called **autosomes,** account for most aspects of development. Within these, the largest chromosomes are in the first pair, where each chromosome

mitosis   *a type of cell division that gives rise to two daughter cells, each with identical chromosomes and genotypes; involves one duplication of chromosomes and one cell division*

gametes   *the sex cells (ova and sperm)*

meiosis   *the process of cell replication undergone by ova and sperm; involves one duplication and one division of chromosomes, resulting in cells with a full set of genetic material, which undergo another division so that the final four cells each contain half the complement of chromosomes*

karyotype   *a photograph of chromosomes, used by geneticists to align each chromosome with the other member of its pair*

autosomes   *the first 22 pairs of chromosomes, which account for most of the body's cells*

FIGURE 3.3

Mitosis and Meiosis

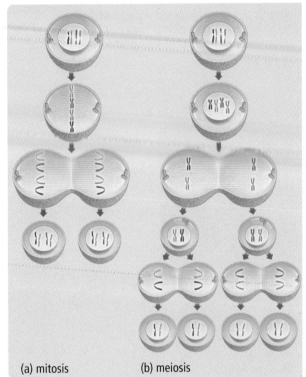

(a) mitosis   (b) meiosis

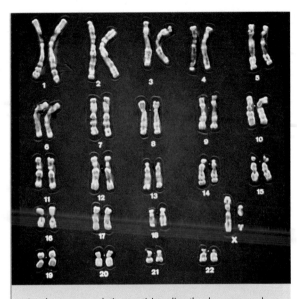

In a karyotype analysis, geneticists align the chromosomes by pairs and identify them by number. Notice that the first pairs of autosomes tend to be larger than the higher-numbered pairs. You can see that in the sex chromosomes for this male (the 23rd pair), the X chromosome is much larger than the Y chromosome. What factors determine whether a boy or a girl is conceived?

Mitosis and meiosis are processes involved in the creation of new cells. Notice that meiosis, which produces sex cells, involves an extra cell division. Why is an extra cell division needed?

contains about 3,000 genes, and the smallest are in the 22nd pair, which contains far fewer genes. The 23rd pair, called the **sex chromosomes,** is unique in that the members may not match. For human females, the sex chromosomes normally consist of two X chromosomes. For males, the sex chromosomes normally consist of an X and a Y chromosome, which are given different labels because they look and function differently (Mange & Mange, 1994). The X chromosome is quite large; it contains about 2,000 genes. The Y chromosome is the smallest of all the chromosomes, with only about 200 genes, and most of these encode male-specific characteristics (Tilford et al., 2001).

Sex Determination: Girl or Boy?

In some royal families, the monarchy can be passed on only to a son, so the pressure to give birth to a male child is high. How is the sex of a child determined before birth? The key is the father. Remember that females have the XX pattern in the 23rd pair of chromosomes—that means they carry only ova with X's and can contribute only X's to the genetic pairing. In contrast, males have the XY pattern, meaning that some of a father's sperm are X sperm and some are Y sperm. If an X ovum and X sperm unite, then a girl is born; if an X ovum and a Y sperm unite, then a boy is born.

Genetic Transmission Patterns

How likely is it that a child will be tall like his father or have the same color of eyes as his mother? Certain physical characteristics such as a cleft chin and hundreds of diseases are determined by the action of a single gene, making it possible to predict whether they will occur in offspring. Many other characteristics, diseases, and behaviors have genetic components, but the transmission patterns are more complex and difficult to determine because they are caused by multiple genes. Although many human characteristics follow complex patterns of transmission, it is still important to understand the more straight-

sex chromosomes *the 23rd pair of chromosomes, which accounts for a person's sex*

forward genetic transmission patterns since a number of diseases and physical characteristics are passed on from one family member to another in this way.

Genotypes and Phenotypes

A person's **genotype,** or genetic code, influences his or her **phenotype,** which is the outward expression of the genotype. For instance, a person who carries a gene for a disease may not end up having the disease—how genes work is more complex than simply providing a genetic code that is carried out in the person's body. For this reason, genotypes and phenotypes do not have a one-to-one correspondence. For example, a person can carry a gene for a certain characteristic but have it masked by the presence of another gene. In this case, the masked gene is part of the genotype but is not exhibited in the phenotype of the person.

To understand how genetic information is passed on, remember that genes work in pairs and that certain types of genes are more likely to be exhibited in the phenotype than others. Each autosomal gene comes in two copies, called **alleles,** one from each parent. Each parent may contribute identical copies of a gene, or identical alleles, to their child, in which case the child is **homozygous** for the trait. Or each parent may contribute a different copy of the gene to their child, in which case the child is **heterozygous** for the trait.

As an illustration of the action of genes, consider a girl who is heterozygous for a cleft chin, having received the gene for a cleft chin from her dad and a "normal," non-cleft chin gene from her mother. This girl will have a cleft chin because the gene for that trait is dominant. An allele whose code is exhibited in the phenotype is called a **dominant gene.** For dominant genes to be exhibited in the phenotype, only one copy needs to be present. An allele that is not exhibited in the presence of a dominant allele is a **recessive gene,** such as the gene for a non-cleft chin. How genes are manifested is very complex, but a simple way to think about it is that the dominant gene overrides the recessive allele. For a recessive characteristic to be exhibited, both alleles in the pair must be recessive. For instance, if a child inherits the homozygous pattern of a non-cleft chin gene from her mother and a non-cleft chin gene from her father, she will not have a cleft chin.

Until recently, it was assumed that characteristics such as eye color, hair color, the ability to curl the tongue, and height were the result of the action of a single gene. Today, however, geneticists believe that each of these characteristics is determined by multiple genes. Although dark eye colors tend to be dominant over light eye colors, it is possible for two blue-eyed parents to give birth to a brown-eyed child (Eiberg & Mohr, 1987).

Dominant Transmission

Some physical features and characteristics are transmitted through dominant genes, such as cleft chin, hair on the middle digit of the fingers or toes, tune deafness, and white hair streaks (see Table 3.1). Most physical characteristics, such as hair color, height, nose shape,

FIGURE 3.4
Sex Determination

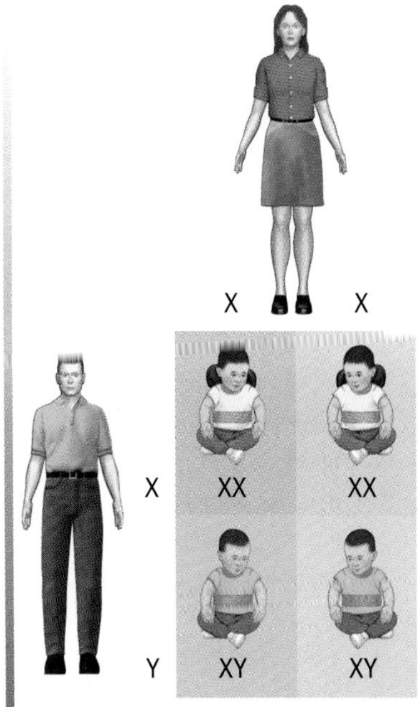

Which parent determines the sex of the child?

TABLE 3.1
Dominant and Recessive Traits

DOMINANT TRAITS	RECESSIVE TRAITS
Achoo syndrome (sneezing in response to a bright light)	Normal
Cleft chin	Non-cleft chin
Curved fifth finger	Straight fifth finger
Double rows of eyelashes	Single row of eyelashes
Piebald trait (a shock of white hair)	Normal hair coloring
Tune deafness	Normal tune perception

Source: Adapted from McKusick, 1998.

genotype   *a person's genetic code*

phenotype   *the outward expression of the genotype*

alleles   *different forms of each gene*

homozygous   *describing inheritance of a trait to which both parents contributed identical copies of the gene*

heterozygous   *describing inheritance of a trait to which each parent has contributed a different copy of the gene*

dominant gene   *a gene whose code is expressed when only one copy of the gene is present*

recessive gene   *a gene whose code is not expressed in the presence of a dominant gene*

DEBATING THE ISSUE

SELECTING OUR BABIES: SHOULD THE SEX OF A CHILD BE PRESELECTED?

 If you could, would you want to select or know the sex of your baby before the baby was born or even conceived? If so, you are not alone: according to one survey, 80 percent of Americans say they would do whatever was needed to ensure that the sex of their child was the one they wanted (Pooler, 1991).

In the past, a variety of approaches were tried to increase the likelihood of having a girl or a boy. Certain foods or douches were used in hopes of promoting the survival of one type of sperm over the other. In the 1980s and 1990s, a popular method was developed in which intercourse was varied based on the differences between the qualities of X and Y sperm (Shettles & Rorvik, 1984). These methods have not been proven successful scientifically.

Recent scientific and technological advances have made it easier to predetermine the sex of a child and to do so with a high degree of certainty. One method involves increasing the number of either X or Y sperm that are available before intercourse. Dr. Lawrence Johnson of the US Department of Agriculture developed a method of separating X and Y sperm, based on the fact that X sperm are significantly larger than Y sperm (Johnson et al., 1993). Once sorted, the sperm can be used in intrauterine or in vitro fertilization. In the first human attempts using this method, X sperm were preselected, and they found a 93

percent success rate in having girls (Fugger, Black, Keyvanfar, & Schulman, 1998). Today the company that holds the patent on the technique reports a 92 percent success rate for having a daughter and a 76 percent success rate for having a son. An even more successful but very controversial method is preimplantation genetic diagnosis (PGD), which involves undergoing in vitro fertilization, developing embryos, and then genetically testing them to determine their sex. Only embryos of the right sex would then be implanted in the mother.

Sexual selection provides important options for families who have X-linked disorders. Many human diseases are X-linked, and remember that these diseases are passed on only to sons. To avoid having a diseased child, parents can undergo sex selection and increase the odds of giving birth to a daughter, who is likely to be normal (or could be a carrier but not diseased). However, sex selection can also be used for "family balancing"—to control the gender mix or order in the family; for example, parents might decide to have an older son and younger daughter.

In the United States, there are no laws against sex selection. Ethical concerns have been raised about its widespread use, however (Parens & Knowles, 2003). What if all families decide that boys are more desirable than girls, or if they decide that a sister having an older brother is better than the reverse? Certain groups may place a higher value

on controlling the sex of offspring in order to pass on a name or choose the sex more likely to help care for elderly parents. With widespread use of sex selection, an imbalance of the sexes may result. Is this a new form of sex discrimination? And what are the consequences of an imbalance in the ratios of females and males? Maybe it will influence marriage or divorce rates. Medical researchers are concerned about the "slippery slope" of parents determining more and more of the characteristics of their children. Might parents ask for a blue-eyed, blond girl and a brown-eyed, tall, and muscular son? A rigorous debate is needed on whether sex selection should be used for the purpose of family balancing.

THINKING IT THROUGH

1. What reasons might parents have for choosing the sex of their children? Do you think the risk of passing on an X-linked disease a valid reason for sperm sorting? Why or why not?

2. What might be some negative consequences of allowing people to choose the sex of their children?

3. If people routinely chose the sex of their children, do you think they would choose boys or girls more often? Why?

and earlobe types are determined by more than one gene (see below) and do not reflect simple transmission patterns. It is interesting that few serious genetic diseases are transmitted by dominant genes. This is because diseased offspring would not survive long enough to transmit the characteristics to their own children. But some genetic diseases, such as Huntington's disease (called El Mal in the chapter introduction), are transmitted by a single dominant gene (on the fourth chromosome) and are maintained in the population because they often do not strike until middle age.

As described at the beginning of the chapter, dominant transmission poses serious problems for those like Carmen, who may carry the dominant gene for a disease.

For example, suppose Carmen learns that her mother had Huntington's disease. Based on the possible combinations of genetic pairs contributed by her parents, she has a 50 percent chance of having the dominant gene for Huntington's (see Figure 3.5). And if Carmen carries the disease, her children have a 50 percent chance of carrying it as well. In the past, Carmen would have had to decide about having children before she knew whether or not she had the gene. Now she can be tested for Huntington's, but the decision to take the test can be agonizing because there is no known cure for the disease. For this reason, few members of families that carry the disease choose to take the test.

Recessive Transmission

The birth into the Deford family of the first girl in over 50 years was greeted with much celebration and joy. Alex Deford was a healthy girl at birth but soon was sick all the time. At 4 months, Alex was tested and found to have *cystic fibrosis (CF)*, a serious recessive genetic disease. Because no one in the family had CF, they were shocked at the news. As Alex grew older, her health deteriorated. She had difficulty breathing, lost weight, and developed heart and liver problems. She was continually in and out of the hospital. Alex died when she was only 10 years old (Deford, 1986).

CF is the most common autosomal recessive disease among Caucasians, affecting about 1 in 2,000 newborns. It is the leading genetic cause of childhood death. About 1 in 20 people is heterozygous for CF; such a person has one copy of the disease gene but also has the normal, dominant gene that masks the effect of the recessive gene. A child with the disease has identical recessive genes—in this case, two CF genes. About 50 percent of people with CF die by the age of 24. There currently is no cure for CF, although gene therapies are being developed.

Approximately 500 characteristics and diseases are transmitted through recessive genes. Unlike dominant characteristics and diseases, which 50 percent of the offspring are likely to have, recessive characteristics and diseases like CF can remain hidden for generations because they are not expressed unless both parents contribute the gene to their child (see Figure 3.6).

People who are heterozygous for a recessive disease or characteristic do not have the recessive disease or characteristic but are **carriers.** A child whose parents are both carriers has a 25 percent chance of having the recessive disease or characteristic and a 50 percent chance of being a carrier.

FIGURE 3.5
Dominant Transmission: Huntington's Chorea

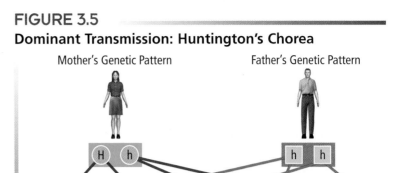

Dominant Transmission: Huntington's Chorea

The father is homozygous, with two healthy copies (h) of the gene, but the mother is diseased because she has one diseased copy (H) of the dominant Huntington's gene. As you can see, the offspring of these two parents have a 50 percent chance of being healthy and a 50 percent chance of being diseased.

FIGURE 3.6
Recessive Transmission: Cystic Fibrosis

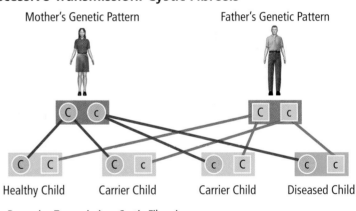

Recessive Transmission: Cystic Fibrosis

The father and mother are carriers because they each have one copy of the cystic fibrosis gene (c). Their offspring have a 25 percent chance of being healthy, a 50 percent chance of being carriers, and a 25 percent chance of having the disease because it takes two copies of the cystic fibrosis gene (cc) to have the disease.

carriers   *people who are heterozygous for a recessive disorder*

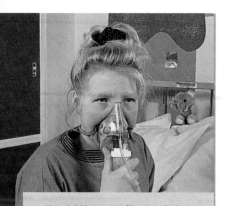

This child has cystic fibrosis, which is a very serious recessive genetic disease with no known cure. How can parents minimize their chance of giving birth to a child with a genetic birth defect?

Because recessive transmission requires that both parents pass on the recessive gene, recessive diseases and characteristics tend to be more prevalent in groups that are isolated or that intermarry. For instance, people of Mediterranean origin are more at risk for *beta thalassemia*, an untreatable but prenatally detectable disease that accounts for hundreds of thousands of childhood deaths a year worldwide. Jewish people from central and eastern Europe and certain groups of French Canadians are more at risk for *Tay Sachs disease*, a serious and untreatable illness that often leads to death within the first two years of life. The risk for Jewish and French Canadian groups is about 1 in 6,000 births, as compared to 1 in 550,000 births among non–Jewish American and non–French Canadian populations. Individuals with African heritage, especially those from West Africa, are more at risk for *sickle cell anemia*, a disease of the blood that causes painful joint swelling, anemia, and infections and may lead to an early death. For African Americans, the risk of having both genes for the disease is about 1 in 500 (Mange & Mange, 1994).

The genes that cause diseases such as sickle cell anemia do not die out of the population because they confer genetic advantages as well as disadvantages, thus favoring a kind of genetic diversity called **balanced polymorphism.** For example, although few individuals with sickle cell anemia survive to reproduce, those who are heterozygous for the disease are resistant to malaria. Because they increase the likelihood of survival for those who are heterozygous, genes like those for sickle cell anemia are preserved in a population (Plomin, DeFries, McClearn, & Rutter, 1997).

FIGURE 3.7

Sex-Linked Transmission: Color-blindness

Mother's Genetic Pattern   Father's Genetic Pattern

X X   X y

X X   X y   X X   X y

Normal Girl   Healthy Boy   Carrier Girl   Diseased Boy

Sex-Linked Transmission

The mother carries the gene for a sex-linked disease like color blindness on one of her X chromosomes (X). The daughters have a 50 percent chance of being normal non-carriers of the disease gene and a 50 percent chance of being carriers, with one disease copy and one normal copy of the gene. None of the daughters will have the disease, because those with a disease copy (XX) will have one normal copy of the gene to mask the disease copy. The sons have a 50 percent chance of being normal and a 50 percent chance of being diseased, because those with a disease copy (XY) will not have a normal gene on their Y chromosome to suppress the disease gene.

balanced polymorphism *a kind of genetic diversity in which the genes that cause diseases provide certain genetic advantages as well as disadvantages*

Sex-Linked Transmission

Remember that the size of chromosomes varies from relatively small chromosomes in pair 1 to very large chromosomes in pair 22. The X chromosome is a relatively large chromosome that contains genetic information for many different characteristics and systems, including vision, hearing, the muscular system, the nervous system, teeth, and skin. Most X-linked genes have nothing to do with sex differentiation. In contrast, the Y chromosome is one of the smallest chromosomes, and it carries very limited genetic information, mainly about sexual development. The size differential between the X and Y chromosomes causes another type of transmission pattern, called sex-linked or X-linked transmission.

One of the clearest examples of X-linked genetic transmission concerns *hemophilia*, which causes excessive bleeding due to failures in blood clotting. This genetic disease was frequently observed among members of European royalty. The pattern of transmission is recessive, but with a twist. In this case, as is true for virtually all cases of sex-linked transmission, the gene for the disease is found on the X chromosome. Recessive transmission is different on the sex chromosomes than it is on the autosomes. On the autosomes, two recessive copies of the gene must be present for the characteristic to be expressed. This is not true on the sex chromosomes. Because the Y chromosome is smaller than the X, it does carry enough genetic material to match, gene for gene, the information on the X chromosome. A single recessive gene on the unmatched segment of the X chromosome may be expressed because there is no corresponding gene on the Y to suppress it. Figure 3.7 shows how sex-linked transmissions of conditions such as hemophilia, baldness, and color blindness occur. With sex-linked transmission, females are more likely to be carriers and males are about three times more likely to have the disease or condition. For example, **fragile X syndrome**—a common cause of mild to moderate mental retardation—a sex-linked disease which occurs in 1 in 1,250 males and 1 in 2,500 females (Plomin, DeFries, et al., 1997). Fragile X syndrome stems from a mutated region near the tip of the long arm of the X chromosome. At this point on the chromosome, the more copies there are of a particular amino acid (trinucleotide, CGG), the more severe the retardation. Individuals with fragile X syndrome may have protruding ears, a prominent jaw, unusual speech, and poor eye contact.

Genetic Imprinting

Remember that genes work in pairs, with one allele contributed by the mother and one by the father. Until the 1980s, geneticists assumed that the outcomes of recessive and dominant transmission did not depend on whether the alleles were from the father or the mother. However, after conducting experiments using mice and by carefully analyzing human genetic disorders, geneticists have found a surprising pattern: the expression of some diseases depends on whether the allele was transmitted by the mother or the father (Reik et al., 1987; Sapienza & Hall, 1995; Swain, Stewart, & Leder, 1987). **Genetic imprinting** occurs when gene expression depends on the origins of the genes. Rather than the two parental alleles working together in the typical manner, in some specific regions of the genome, chemical agents inactivate genetic information if it is received from one parent but not if it is received from the other. In these cases, only one parent's genetic information is used in determining the genetic pattern for the child (see Figure 3.8).

Parent-of-origin effects on genetic transmission are involved in a number of serious diseases such as certain cancers (Christofori et al., 1995; Li et al., 1995) and some birth defects, such as spina bifida (Chatkupt et al., 1992). Remember Huntington's disease, presented earlier as an example of one of the few severe autosomal dominant diseases? Research has shown that the severity of the disease depends on whether the dominant gene was inherited from the father or mother. Cases with early onset tend to involve inheriting the gene from the father; later onset tends to involve inheriting the gene from the mother.

Two of the most well-studied diseases that exhibit genetic imprinting are Prader-Willi syndrome (which involves severe growth problems, obesity, slow-moving actions, and mental retardation) and Angelman syndrome (originally called the "happy puppet" (in French) because, although they exhibit severe mental retardation, people with the disease laugh excessively and move in jerky, puppetlike ways; Hall, 1990; Sapienza & Hall, 1995). What is particularly interesting is that these very different diseases result from genetic action on the identical place on chromosome 15. When the disease-producing genetic pattern is inherited from the father, it results in Prader-Willi syndrome; when it is inherited from the mother, it results in Angelman syndrome.

Each parent contributes to the genetic development of the child, and genetic imprinting illustrates why the genetic contributions of each parent are unique and vital to development. The extent to which genetic imprinting is involved in human development is being studied, and it is not yet known how many genetic disorders are influenced by genetic imprinting. Researchers suggest that at least 10 to 20 percent of mouse genes are subject to imprinting, but it is not clear how many human genes are (Hitchens & Moore, 2002; Mange & Mange, 1994).

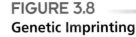

FIGURE 3.8
Genetic Imprinting

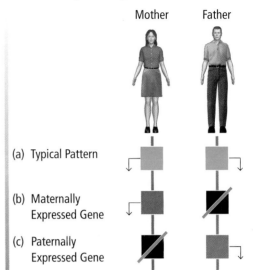

Hypothetical examples illustrating (a): the typical pattern of genetic expression in which both mother's and father's alleles contribute to outcome, (b) maternally expressed gene in which father's allele is inactivated and only mother's allele contributes to the outcome, and (c) paternally expressed gene in which mother's allele is inactivated and only father's allele contributes to the outcome. Mother's contributions for 3 gene pairs are on the left on the dark pink line and father's contributions are on the right. Genes are represented by boxes, and arrows indicate that the gene is active.

fragile X syndrome *a condition passed on by sex-linked transmission and characterized by protruding ears, prominent jaw, unusual speech, poor eye contact, and mild to moderate retardation*

genetic imprinting *situation in which gene expression depends on the origins of the genes*

Polygenic Transmission

When a new baby is born, parents often wonder how much the baby will look like each of them. Will he have blond hair like me or brown hair like his dad? Will he be as tall as his father or shorter like me? For many physical features, as well as a number of genetic diseases, the simple genetic transmission types are not enough to explain inheritance patterns. A child's height is determined by **polygenic transmission,** which involves the combined effect of multiple genes to produce the outcome. Height is not coded on a single gene: instead, the combined size of all of the body parts from head to foot determines the height of an individual. So a person's height is a result of the combination of the genetic information guiding the development of many individual body parts. Other characteristics, such as skin color, nose shape, and eye color, are influenced by multiple genes. Similarly, a predisposition for colon cancer or diabetes appears to be coded by multiple genes, and an environmental stimulus may be required for the disease to be manifested.

Genomes to Life Project

Identifying the sequence of the human genome is a crucial step in understanding human development. Once sequencing is complete, the next step is even more far-reaching—namely, to develop a fundamental, comprehensive, and systemic understanding of life. This is the goal of the most ambitious biological program yet proposed, called the Genomes to Life Project. Rather than concentrate on individual life components, such as genes and other DNA sequences, this new program intends to consider an integrated view of biology at a whole-systems level. The plan for this ten-year program is to use DNA sequences as the starting point for tackling questions about the most fundamental and essential processes of life. How do organisms develop, survive, carry out their normal lives, and reproduce? Scientists will consider how biology and environmental factors interact over time in dynamic and transactional ways to produce development.

How Do Genes and Environment Work Together?

The nature versus nurture issue is well illustrated by considering how genes and environments work together to produce human development. A child's phenotype unfolds during development, when genes and gene products interact with each other and with environmental factors. Genes and environmental factors interact to produce the many variations we can observe among different people.

Gene Expression

After seeing how single genes can cause so many different disorders, it is easy to conclude that genes alone determine development. However, from what is known about genes in animals and plants, it is clear that possession of a gene is not a guarantee that it will be expressed the same way in every individual. Remember that virtually all the cells in our bodies contain the same genetic material, but we know that, despite having similar genetic material, a cell in the brain does not function the same way as a cell in the liver. This is because different genes are being "turned on" in different cells, producing different proteins, which then lead to different functions. When a gene is expressed—when it is turned on and its chemical products are produced—these products interact with the elements of the internal environment (e.g., other gene products) and external environment (e.g., nutrition, climate, exercise),

When and How Do Genes Express Themselves?

Some genes control the expression of other genes. These genes are called **regulator genes** because they influence how and when other genes are turned on so that their proteins are produced. Some gene regulation is short term and responds to the environment, whereas

polygenic transmission *combined effect of multiple genes*

regulator genes *genes that control the expression of other genes*

other types of regulation are long term. Regulator genes play an important role in genetic expression although little is known yet about how they work.

Some genes, such as those determining blood types, are directly expressed in essentially the same way, regardless of the context or outside conditions. Other genes may be expressed fully, partially, or not at all, depending on circumstances. Furthermore, some genes do not express themselves except under particular circumstances. For example, Siamese cats have a gene that expresses itself differently, depending on the environmental conditions, especially temperature—the lower the temperature, the darker the fur and the more extensive the dark areas. Apparently, the enzyme that produces the pigment to darken the fur (which is coded by the gene) works more effectively at lower temperatures, farther from the center of the body. Thus, Siamese cats vary in how much dark fur appears on their paws, ears, and faces. Similarly, many human dominant traits for diseases are variable in their expression, allowing some individuals to have a very mild form of a disease while others have more serious forms.

Scientists are focusing attention on finding out when and how different genes express themselves so that they can better control and intervene in faulty genes. The environment plays an important role in how and when genes are expressed. Also, the particular genes that are expressed vary depending on the developmental stage of the organism. Researchers have discovered, for instance, that out of 1,800 genes in strawberries, about 200 change their expression depending on whether the strawberry is green or fully ripe (Aharoni et al., 2000).

Range of Reaction

The degree to which genes are influenced by the environment varies, depending on the type of gene. Some genes place a narrower range of possibilities on phenotypes than other genes, and the range of possibilities is called the **range of reaction.** Genes can place restrictions on the range of possible phenotypes that a person can display in response to different environments. For instance, a person who has genes that grow long bones—someone with a genetic predisposition to be tall—may or may not become tall, depending on the environment. A person with the predisposition to tallness who does not get adequate nutrition will not grow up to be as tall as she would have with adequate nutrition. A person with a genetic predisposition to be short can have a healthy diet and still not grow tall because tallness was outside the range of reaction of this person's genetic code. When the range of reaction of genes is very narrow, the phenotype may be **canalized,** meaning that genetic constraints have limited phenotypic variation so that development follows specific outlines, or "canals," along the developmental pathway. For example, most people develop arms despite challenges from environments; the phenotype of having arms is strongly canalized. However, a genetic predisposition for some types of cancers are not strongly canalized; cancer will occur only under certain environmental conditions.

It can be difficult to grasp these concepts in relation to humans. They are, however, clearly illustrated in animal studies, wherein scientists have experimentally manipulated genetic and environmental conditions. The classic study of range of reaction was done with two groups of genetically modified rats (Cooper & Zubek, 1958). Over many generations of breeding, scientists had changed the genetic inheritance of two groups of rats. One group had been bred to be maze bright (they could solve mazes quickly); the other group had been bred to be maze dull. When both groups were given a very enriched and stimulating environment, the environment made little difference for the maze-bright rats but improved the performance of the maze-dull rats. In contrast, a very restricted environment was found to be detrimental to the performance of the maze-bright rats but not for the maze-dull rats. In this case, it is clear that the influence of the environment depended upon the genetic predisposition of the rats.

What accounts for two people with similar genetic endowments showing different phenotypes? In this case, why do you think the child is taller than the parent?

range of reaction *the range of possibilities of phenotypic variation displayed in response to different environments*

canalized *genetically limited phenotypic variation*

FIGURE 3.9

Gene–Environment Correlations

Passive G–E Correlation   Evocative G–E Correlation   G–E Correlation

1. What accounts for children being exposed to environments that relate to their genetic endowment when there is a passive G–E correlation?

2. What characteristics elicit positive versus negative responses from others in evocative G–E correlations?

3. How do children search out environments that match their genetic endowment in active G–E correlations?

Genes and Exposure to Different Environments

A person's genetic predisposition also influences the kinds of environments they are exposed to. Three gene–environment (G–E) correlations describe how a particular genotype can determine a child's exposure to different sorts of environments (Scarr & McCartney, 1983).

Parents, because they share genetic material with their child, often provide a rearing environment that matches the child's genotype, creating a **passive G–E correlation.** Because the parents' own behavior is influenced by their genetic inheritance, this inheritance then influences the kind of environment in which the child is raised. Parents who enjoy reading are likely to provide their child with a rearing environment that encourages reading. Parents who are athletic are likely to encourage their children to participate in sports, and these children probably have some genes that help them be better athletes.

Another type of gene–environment correlation involves how the child's own genes influence others directly. Children's genotypes draw responses from others, giving rise to an **evocative G–E correlation.** A child who actively engages with other people by smiling, laughing, looking at them, and being pleasant is more likely to be responded to and treated positively by teachers and others. This child's genetic predisposition to be positive and sociable gives rise to many more social experiences, thereby reinforcing the genetic predisposition through environmental action.

The third type is an **active G–E correlation,** created when people seek out environments compatible with their genotype. Children who are relatively inactive may seek out others who are quiet and studious, while avoiding sports. This behavior is called *niche building* because it involves selecting for oneself the aspects of the environment that are most comfortable and then learning from exposure to those environments.

As people grow older, the influence of these different types of correlations changes. Because infants and children spend so much time with their parents, it is not surprising that passive G–E correlations are very influential to development in youth. As children grow into adolescents and adults, however, passive G–E correlations are less important, while active G–E correlations gain importance. Evocative G–E correlations continue to exert an influence on development all through life.

Gene–Environment Interactions

Not only do people differ in the kinds of exposure they have to different environments, but there are also gene–environment interactions, which involve genetic sensitivity to particu-

passive G–E correlation *situation in which parents provide a rearing environment that matches the child's own genotype*

evocative G–E correlation *situation in which the child's genotype draws responses from others*

active G–E correlation *situation in which the child seeks out environments compatible with his or her genotype*

lar environmental factors. Investigating the causes for a child's behavior is complicated by the fact that various types of G–E interactions influence development (Scarr & McCartney, 1983). Although single genes can be the cause of certain diseases or characteristics, most physical features, disorders, and behaviors are likely influenced by multiple genes and by genes in interaction with environmental agents, as discussed earlier. Many characteristics, such as skin color, are due to polygenic inheritance. Also, **gene–environment interactions,** in which the influence of a gene varies depending on its environment, account for many aspects of development.

A classic example of gene–environment interaction is PKU (phenylketonuria). This is the most well-known inherited form of moderate mental retardation, which occurs in about 1 in 10,000 births. When it is untreated, people with PKU tend to have IQ scores below 50. PKU is a single-gene recessive disorder (carried on chromosome 12), and the gene for the disease interferes with the metabolism of a specific amino acid, phenylalanine. When a person is homozygous for the PKU allele, they are unable to metabolize phenylalanine in food. This then builds up and causes severe damage to the developing brain. Phenylalanine does not harm children who do not carry the PKU allele. What is particularly interesting is that children who have the PKU gene can avoid retardation by avoiding foods with phenylalanine (e.g., red meat). You can see that the environment—exposure to phenylalanine—is a critical component for even recognizing that one is carrying the PKU gene. When phenylalanine is avoided, the PKU gene has no deleterious effect (see Figure 3.10).

Consider a more complicated example involving a gene–gene–environment interaction and bladder cancer. Leslie inherits the two genes (NAT1 and NAT2), and she smokes. Compared to her smoker friend Jerry, who did not inherit NAT1 and NAT2, Leslie has a much greater chance of developing bladder cancer. This is because the NAT2 gene reduces Leslie's ability to metabolize carcinogens and the NAT1 gene transforms compounds into carcinogens more rapidly than normal—and tobacco smoke provides the chemicals that become transformed into carcinogens (Taylor & Bell, 1998). If Leslie never smoked, her NAT1 and NAT2 genes might not cause her any serious problems. In this case, the environmental input—smoking—is as central to getting cancer as are the genes, and neither, by itself, can be accurately labeled as the cause of bladder cancer.

FIGURE 3.10
Gene–Environment Interaction: PKU

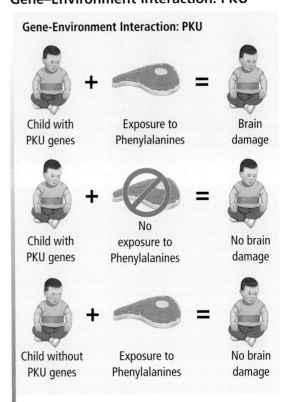

Gene-Environment Interaction: PKU

Child with PKU genes	+	Exposure to Phenylalanines	=	Brain damage
Child with PKU genes	+	No exposure to Phenylalanines	=	No brain damage
Child without PKU genes	+	Exposure to Phenylalanines	=	No brain damage

How does the PKU gene influence a child's predisposition to be influenced by the environment? What are the likely outcomes for a child with PKU genes if there is no environmental exposure to phenylalanines?

What Are Common Chromosomal Abnormalities?

The chances that a healthy mother will give birth to a healthy infant are high. Nonetheless, 3 to 5 percent of newborns have some type of genetic or chromosomal abnormality. Genetic disorders are due to flaws in one or two genes. In contrast, chromosomal abnormalities occur when a child is born with missing or extra chromosomes. Most embryos with genetic or chromosomal abnormalities do not survive until birth—they are spontaneously aborted, or miscarried, before the mother even knows she is pregnant.

Down Syndrome

A common chromosomal abnormality is *Down syndrome,* which occurs in about 1 in 900 live births (March of Dimes, 2000). About 90 percent of children with Down syndrome have 47 chromosomes rather than the normal 46, with an extra number 21 chromosome (referred to as *trisomy 21*). This excess genetic material results from the failure of chromosomes to

gene–environment interactions *genetic sensitivity to particular environmental factors*

Down syndrome children tend to be identifiable by their facial features, such as a large tongue, wide-spaced eyes, and a round face. What risk factors increase a couple's chance of giving birth to a child with Down syndrome?

separate during meiosis. About 5,000 children are born each year with Down syndrome, and more than 350,000 people in the United States currently have Down syndrome (National Down Syndrome Society, 2000).

Most children with Down syndrome have certain physical characteristics, including wide-spaced eyes, a large protruding tongue, short stature, a round face, folds in the corners of their eyes, and unusual creases on the palms of their hands (Hassold & Patterson, 1998). Children with Down syndrome also often have heart and eye defects and may have immunological problems that make them susceptible to diseases. These physical problems account for the lower life expectancy for individuals with Down syndrome, but life expectancy has increased from an average of 15 years in the 1940s to 55 or more years today (March of Dimes, 2000).

Children with Down syndrome have mental retardation, with intelligence scores ranging from 20 to 80 (100 is an average score), but most are in the mild to moderate retardation range (Plomin, DeFries, et al., 1997; Robinson, Goodman, & O'Brien, 1984). Language skills are severely impaired (Fowler, Gelman, & Gleitman, 1994). By adolescence, language skills remain at the level of a 3-year-old (Plomin, DeFries, et al., 1997). About 50 percent of children with Down syndrome have visual or hearing impairments, some of which are correctable with glasses or surgery. About 50 percent of these children develop behavioral problems as they grow older, especially boys with limited or no language skills (Tager-Flusberg, 1994).

Young mothers have little risk of giving birth to infants with this abnormality—only 1 in 2,400 live births of infants with Down syndrome occurs for mothers under 20 years of age. By age 35, the risk increases to 1 in every 365 births; and by age 40, the risk is 1 in 110 live births (National Down Syndrome Society, 2000). The most common cause of Down syndrome is a failure of sex cell division during the formation of ova (Mange & Mange, 1994; Plomin, DeFries, et al., 1997).

Sex Chromosome Abnormalities

Sex chromosome abnormalities include having an extra X or Y chromosome and lacking an X chromosome. Through karyotype analyses, many more cases of sex chromosome abnormalities can now be identified.

Turner's Syndrome

Girls born with *Turner's syndrome* are missing either the second X chromosome (45, X) or part of the second X chromosome, usually as a result of cell division abnormalities in the father's sperm (Mange & Mange, 1994). Estimates vary, but there may be 1 case of Turner's syndrome in every 2,500 births (Plomin, DeFries, et al., 1997). Girls with Turner's syndrome lack ovaries and have immature external genitalia. They tend to be short, with broad chests and wide (webbed) necks. This condition often can be identified at birth, but many cases are not identified until the girls reach puberty and fail to menstruate. Early identification is useful because hormone therapy can help. Girls with Turner's syndrome have normal verbal skills but often have poor skills in spacial relations, difficulty sustaining attention and remembering information, and delayed social skills (McCauley, Kay, Ito, & Treder, 1987). They are also prone to heart, kidney, and thyroid problems (Turner Syndrome Society of the US, 2001).

Trisomy-X Syndrome

The chromosome disorder 47,XXX affects girls who are born with an extra X chromosome; it occurs in approximately 1 out of 1,000 female births. These females are phenotypically normal but may have a slightly lower intelligence level than 46,XX females (Hartl, 1994). They often are quiet and passive, and they may have delayed development of speech and motor skills. Females with 47,XXX are usually fertile, although they may reach menopause at an earlier age than 46,XX females do.

Klinefelter's Syndrome

Boys born with an extra X chromosome have *Klinefelter's syndrome* (XXY). This is probably the most common chromosomal variation found in humans (Klinefelter Syn-

TABLE 3.2
Some Chromosome Abnormalities

ABNORMALITY	CHROMOSOMAL PATTERN	OUTCOME
Down Syndrome Children born with an extra chromosome 21 or an extra piece of a chromosome	47 (XX or XY)	Wide-spaced eyes, large protruding tongue, short stature, a round face, folds in the corners of the eyes, unusual creases on the palms of the hands, heart and eye defects, immunological problems, mental retardation
Turner's Syndrome Girls missing the second X chromosome in the sex chromosomes	45, X	Lack of ovaries, immature external genitalia, short and broad chest, webbed neck, poor spatial skills, delayed social skills
Trisomy-X Syndrome Girls born with an extra X chromosome in the sex chromosomes	47, XXX	Normal phenotype, slightly lower IQ, quiet and passive demeanor, delayed development of speech and motor skills
Klinefelter's Syndrome Boys born with an extra X chromosome in the sex chromosomes	47, XXY	Sterility, long limbs, immature testes, lack of development of masculine physical characteristics at puberty (e.g., body hair), possible female-like breast development, possible mental retardation, language and attention deficits
XYY Syndrome Boys with one or more extra Y chromosomes in the sex chromosomes	47, XYY or 48, XYYY	Normal phenotype, tall height, severe acne, poor coordination, impulsive behavior, lower intelligence

drome & Associates, 2001). This disorder occurs at a rate of 1 or 2 cases per 1,000 births (Plomin, DeFries, & McClearn, 1990). Boys with Klinefelter's syndrome are sterile and tend to have long limbs and immature testes (Sotos, 1997). Because they lack adequate male hormones, they do not develop masculine characteristics at puberty, such as facial and body hair, and may have female-like breast development. Early hormone replacement therapy can produce a more typical male pattern of development. Mental retardation may also occur (Jones & Cahill, 1994). Boys with Klinefelter's syndrome often have language deficits, attention problems, and reading difficulties (Rovet et al., 1996).

XYY Syndrome
Boys born with *XYY syndrome,* characterized by one or more extra Y chromosomes, appear normal (Jones & Cahill, 1994). These boys are tall, have severe acne during adolescence, are poorly coordinated, and may exhibit impulsive behaviors and lower intelligence (Kumra et al., 1998). The more Y chromosomes a boy has, the lower his intelligence is likely to be.

XYY patterns are caused by cell division problems during sperm production. About 1 in 1,000 births results in a boy with extra Y chromosomes (Plomin, DeFries, & McClearn, 1990). In the 1960s, researchers identified a higher-than-expected frequency of the XYY pattern in inmates of a maximum security prison. The hypothesis was proposed that having an extra Y chromosome produces aggressive and antisocial behavior. Later studies revealed, however, that this hypothesis is wrong: male prisoners in general, regardless of the nature of their crime, are likely to have XYY patterns. These findings suggest that lower intelligence and impulsive behavior, rather than aggressiveness, may land XYY men in prison (Sutton, 1988).

How Are Genetic Diseases Detected?
In the past, family planning was limited to the ability to choose whether or not to have a child. Today, with tremendous advances in the ability to detect genetic and chromosomal abnormalities, more options are available to help families plan for the future. Fortunately,

in most cases the outcome of genetic testing is favorable, and families can be assured that they will have a child who is no more at risk for health problems than other children (Mange & Mange, 1994).

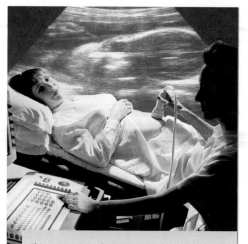

This woman is undergoing an ultrasound procedure. What advantages are associated with this procedure compared to other prenatal tests?

Genetic Technology

Genetic and chromosomal disorders account for many problems that affect the health and well-being of infants. Because of the significance of these disorders for infant health, many technologies have been developed to assess the status of infants even before they are born. Some of these technologies, such as ultrasound imaging, involve visual examination of the unborn child to determine physical defects. Other technologies, such as amniocentesis, require obtaining genetic material that is used to test for genetic and chromosomal problems.

Ultrasound Imaging

A painless and virtually risk-free procedure for identifying some developmental problems is **ultrasound,** in which video images of the fetus and its internal organs are produced from the echoes of sound waves. Ultrasound can detect heart conditions and physical deformities. Ultrasound is used with other techniques when an accurate image of the fetus's location is needed. Studies show that ultrasound helps identify possible birth defects when performed by physicians with extensive training in fetal diagnosis (Crane et al., 1994), and many women want an ultrasound as part of their routine pregnancy exams (Stephens, Montefalcon, & Lane, 2000).

Chorionic Villus Sampling

Since the 1980s, **chorionic villus sampling (CVS)** has been successfully used to assess genetic material in fetal cells. Either by inserting a needle through the mother's abdominal wall or by inserting a catheter through the mother's cervix, cells are removed from the projections on the chorionic membrane (a layer of protective cells surrounding the fetus); these are then analyzed for genetic defects (Wapner, 1997).

CVS can be done during the first trimester of pregnancy, usually 9 to 12 weeks after conception. The risk of problems associated with CVS is very low (Salihu, Boos, & Schmidt, 1997), particularly when it is performed after the eighth week of pregnancy by experienced medical personnel (Wilson, 2000). The early detection that CVS affords gives couples more time to consider their options—such as whether to continue or terminate the pregnancy.

FIGURE 3.11
Amniocentesis

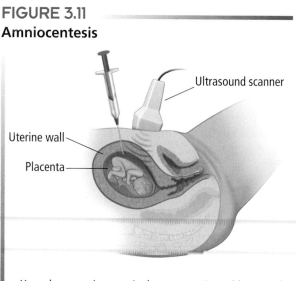

Ultrasound scanner

Uterine wall

Placenta

How does amniocentesis detect genetic problems in the fetus? What are the disadvantages to using this method of genetic testing?

Source: McAnulty and Burnette, 2004.

Detection of Alpha Fetoprotein

The mother's blood contains *alpha fetoproteins (AFP),* which can be used to screen for several developmental problems during pregnancy. Testing for AFP usually occurs between the 16th and 18th weeks of pregnancy. If the mother has a high level of alpha fetoproteins, the fetus may have a neural tube defect (such as spina bifida), which then can be confirmed through ultrasound. If the mother's alpha fetoprotein level is low, the fetus may have a chromosomal abnormality (such as Down syndrome), which must be confirmed through genetic testing (Akbas et al., 2001).

Amniocentesis

A common method of detecting genetic problems during prenatal development is **amniocentesis,** in which a long, thin needle is inserted through the mother's abdominal wall into the fluid-filled amniotic sac surrounding the fetus. The amniotic fluid contains some skin cells of the fetus; some fluid is removed, and then these cells are examined to determine whether genetic defects are present. In addition, the analysis determines whether biochemical or metabolic imbalances are present. The sex of the child also may be identified. Studies show that the risk of amniocentesis for the unborn child is small (Simpson & Elias, 1994). The major drawback is that the test is done relatively late in pregnancy (15 to 19 weeks), and obtaining the results takes several weeks. The advantage is that it is a very accurate method of identifying a variety of prenatal developmental problems (Wilson, 2000).

Genetic Counseling

Despite the many advances that science has made in detecting genetic and chromosomal abnormalities, tens of thousands of children are born each year with birth defects. Birth defects occur in 1 of every 33 births and are the leading cause of infant death, accounting for about 22 percent of all infant deaths (March of Dimes, 2000). Table 3.3 lists the incidence of the most common types of birth defects.

Genetic counselors help couples determine the likelihood of having children with birth defects, assist them in making decisions about conception, and provide counseling for families who have given birth to infants with genetic problems. Genetic counseling is recommended for individuals in the following situations (Mange & Mange, 1994):

- Individuals who have children with a genetic disorder
- Individuals with a known genetic disorder who would like to start families
- Women who have had repeated miscarriages
- Older pregnant women

TABLE 3.3
Incidence of Common Birth Defects

BIRTH DEFECT	ESTIMATED INCIDENCE
Structural/Metabolic	
Heart and circulation	1 in 115 births
Muscles and skeleton	1 in 130 births
Genital and urinary tracts	1 in 135 births
Nervous system and eyes	1 in 235 births
Chromosomal disorders	1 in 600 births
Down syndrome	1 in 900 births
Respiratory tract	1 in 900 births
Cleft lip/palate	1 in 930 births
Spina bifida	1 in 2,000 births
Metabolic disorders	1 in 3,500 births
Congenital Infections	
Syphilis	1 in 2,000 births
HIV infection	1 in 2,700 births
Rubella	1 in 100,000 births
Other	
Fetal alcohol syndrome	1 in 1,000 births
Rh blood incompatibility	1 in 1,400 births

Note: All numbers are based on the best available estimates, which underestimate the incidence of many birth defects.

Source: March of Dimes, 2000.

ultrasound *a procedure used to identify some developmental problems, in which video images of the fetus and the fetus's internal organs are produced from the echoes of sound waves*

chorionic villus sampling (CVS) *a procedure used to assess genetic material in fetal cells, in which cells are removed from the projections on the chorionic membrane*

amniocentesis *a procedure used to determine whether genetic defects are present, in which amniotic fluid is collected and fetal cells are genetically tested*

NURTURING CHILDREN
TREATING A DISEASED FETUS

Their first son died when he was only 7 months old. He died of an X-linked recessive disease called *severe combined immunodeficiency,* which strikes approximately 1 out of every 100,000 babies. Because it is X-linked, it strikes boys more often than girls. The disease produces a very weak immune system, increasing the child's susceptibility to infections. Most infants born with this disease die within the first year of life. When the woman became pregnant again, she was concerned that her second child would also have the disease. Using chorionic villus sampling, doctors tested the unborn child's DNA. The child, another son, was affected. In a medical first, the child was treated for the disease in utero by Dr. Alan Flake, a pediatric surgeon at Children's Hospital of Philadelphia. Using the unaffected father's bone marrow, Flake gave the fetus three transplants of cells by ultrasound guided injections at 16, 17, and 18 weeks. At birth, the child seemed normal except for an easily treated rash. At 11 months, he showed no signs of the immune disease and was healthy.

Medical treatment for unborn children, or *fetology,* is a relatively new medical specialty. To date, medical treatments such as blood and bone marrow transfusions, insertion of drainage tubes, and surgical repairs have been performed in utero. Although risks are involved in these prenatal treatments, early treatment can prevent symptoms of a disease and may even eliminate the disease entirely (Flake et al., 1996). Similar techniques may soon be used to treat other genetic disorders such as sickle cell anemia. With improvements in technology and medical science, it is likely that fetologists will be able to treat more and more cases in the future.

■ Couples at risk for genetic diseases because of their ethnicity or ancestry

■ Couples at risk for genetic diseases because the two individuals are related to each other

Genetic counseling begins with an accurate medical history and diagnosis. Karyotype analyses may be done to determine the genetic patterns of the parents, and a pedigree analysis may be carried out to determine genetic diseases of other family members. Genetic counselors use this information to help families make difficult decisions about conception, pregnancy, and birth.

How Does Conception Occur, and What Can Be Done to Overcome Infertility?

For the many people who have difficulties in conceiving a child, research on reproduction is a fundamental source of hope. Answers to questions about how to maintain viable eggs and sperm and how to improve the chances of fertilization literally hold the secret to life for these couples. In this section, you will learn how ova and sperm develop and how information about the development of these sex cells is being used to broaden the frontiers of reproductive science.

Ovulation

For pregnancy to occur, a human egg, or **ovum,** and a sperm cell must meet and share their genetic material. This process begins with ovulation. Each month, a woman releases at least one ovum from her ovaries during ovulation, as a normal part of the menstrual cycle. In addition to ensuring that ovulation takes place, the menstrual cycle initiates changes in the uterus that prepare it to receive a fertilized ovum.

The average menstrual cycle is approximately equal to a lunar month in length but can vary greatly, from 25 to 35 days. At birth, females have approximately 400,000 to 500,000 immature ova in each ovary, and typically no new ova develop after birth. With an average cycle of 28 days, a women ovulates about 13 ova per year, or 481 ova in the

ovum   *a human egg*

FROM RESEARCH TO PRACTICE
INFINITE EGGS?

FROM RESEARCH . . .

In 1998, a 25-year-old young woman named Ouarda Touirat from Belgium was diagnosed with cancer. She knew that she would be undergoing chemotherapy and radiation treatments to eliminate the cancer cells. She also knew that if she could be cured of cancer, she wanted to have children. Unfortunately, the treatment to destroy cancer cells also would make her infertile. How could she maintain her fertility while also treating her cancer?

For this young woman, and many others who want to maintain fertility despite treatments for cancer, hope is on the horizon. Scientists have made tremendous breakthroughs in finding ways to produce new mature ova in women. New research shows that it is possible to induce immature ova to develop into viable mature ova by grafting frozen ovarian tissue into the body. To do this, the ovarian tissue is removed and frozen; then, when the treatment is completed, the ovarian tissue is inserted into the body again (Oktay et al., 2004). The challenges scientists face in doing this are tremendous. One challenge is how to successfully freeze ova. These large, watery cells can get freezer burn, explode, or die from the process of being frozen. Another challenge is how to induce immature ova into

maturity. Although obstacles in inducing this tissue to produce mature ova still need to be resolved, success seems close at hand. A rhesus macaque monkey has given birth to a baby through this method.

. . . TO PRACTICE

When Ouarda underwent cancer treatment, she decided to have an ovary removed and frozen before treatment. As expected, she was made infertile by the cancer treatment. Five years later, in 2003, after being declared cancer free, she was ready to try to get pregnant despite her infertility. With the help of Dr. Jacques Donnez, Ouarda was made fertile again by undergoing a transplant of her own frozen ovarian tissue into her body. After about 3 to 4 months, mature ova were being produced from the previously frozen immature ova. Happily, she is the first woman who has given birth following an ovarian tissue transplant. She is now 32 years old, and she gave birth in September 2004 to a healthy girl, Tamara (Boseley, 2004; Donnez et al., 2004; Horsey, 2004). Other researchers have also reported success with ovarian transplants and are awaiting similar pregnancies (Oktay et al., 2004). Another use of this method may be to prolong fertility: women could decide to freeze their ovarian tissue when they are young and then have it reim-

planted when their fertility decreases later in life. This method, if it becomes readily available, may provide families with much more control over their fertility than ever before. Rather than suffer from much reduced or even nonexistent fertility in their 40s and 50s, older women may be able to conceive easily with ova frozen when they were 25— at the peak of their fertility.

THINKING IT THROUGH

1. What are the ethical challenges involved in changing women's fertility in this way? Who decides which women may use this method? Could women choose to use someone else's ovarian tissue, just as some women use donor eggs for in vitro fertilization?

2. What additional medical risks might be associated with this procedure? Consider, for instance, that for women with cancer who undergo this procedure, the ovarian tissue that is removed prior to the cancer treatment may contain cancerous cells that are then reintroduced into her body years later.

3. How might this procedure help women who have difficulty conceiving? Do you think advances in this procedure can help women without cancer conceive more easily?

approximately 37 years of her reproductive life (Jones, 1997). How these ova are selected to reach full maturation from the thousands contained in a woman's ovary remains a mystery. Solving this mystery is important for many women who have difficulty getting pregnant and for women who have to undergo treatments that can cause their ovaries to stop functioning. New research suggests that ova can be induced to mature (see feature box).

Each menstrual cycle is divided into three main phases. The first is the *menstrual phase* (lasting 4 to 5 days), when menstruation (the "period") takes place. Menstruation occurs because the lining of the uterus degenerates and is expelled in a bloody discharge.

The second phase is the *follicular phase,* in which the lining of the uterus grows back and thickens, influenced by the female hormone estrogen. This phase continues until ovulation, which occurs on about day 14 of a 28-day cycle or day 16 of a 30-day cycle (Rathus, Nevid, & Fichner-Rathus, 1993). This is the time of the month when a woman is most likely to get pregnant.

The last phase is the *luteal phase,* lasting from ovulation until the beginning of the next menstruation (usually about 14 days). During this phase, different hormones are secreted (such as progesterone) that prepare the uterus for the arrival of a fertilized ovum. If fertilization does not occur, the ovum disintegrates and is washed out of the body in the menstrual flow. If fertilization does occur, the fertilized ovum embeds itself in the uterine lining, menstrual cycles usually stop during pregnancy (Jones, 1997).

Spermatogenesis

After puberty, men produce sperm in their testes on a daily basis throughout their lives (about 100 sperm are produced per second). Sperm develop in a process called **spermatogenesis,** which requires about 72 days to produce a mature sperm cell (Rathus et al., 1993). In early stages, each immature sperm cell contains 46 chromosomes, including one X and one Y sex chromosome. These then divide into two; each resulting cell has 23 chromosomes, including either an X or a Y sex chromosome. These mature sperm, called **spermatozoa,** are fully functional and capable of fertilizing a human ovum.

Approximately 200 to 500 million sperm are released at each ejaculation (Wong & Perry, 1998). A man is considered fertile if there are approximately 60 million sperm in a normal ejaculation, 60 percent of them are normal in shape and size, and 40 percent are mobile (Institute of Medicine, 1990).

Fertilization

The mature ovum is one of the largest cells in the human body, with a diameter of approximately 190 micrometers (about the size of a period printed on this page). As shown in Figure 3.12a, the two primary layers are an outer protective layer of cells and an inner nucleus that contains 23 chromosomes—the genetic material of the woman. Each month during her reproductive lifetime, an ovum matures and is released during ovulation. Once released, the ovum enters the fallopian tube and is moved toward the uterus by cilia, small hairlike structures lining the tube. The ovum cannot propel itself and depends on the cilia to move it to the uterus (Glass, 1994). For fertilization to occur, an ovum must be penetrated by a sperm cell within 24 to 48 hours after ovulation.

A healthy sperm cell is about 0.0002 inch long and is composed of a head, body, and tail (see Figure 3.12, b and c). The head contains the genetic material, and the tail moves the sperm through the woman's reproductive system. The body contains the energy production system for moving the tail (Wong & Perry, 1998).

As noted earlier, males produce X and Y sperm. Remember that if an X sperm fertilizes the ovum, a girl is conceived; if a Y sperm fertilizes the ovum, the child will be a boy. Thus, the father's sperm determines the child's sex (the mother contributes only X chromosomes).

Once ejaculated, the sperm begin a long journey through the female reproductive tract. Of the millions of sperm that are ejaculated, only 100 to 1,000 actually reach the ovum. Many sperm get sidetracked and do not successfully complete the journey. Others are weak or damaged and are unable to navigate the very long distance to the ovum. In a sense, a "survival of the fittest" test eliminates many genetically weak sperm. For fertilization to occur, sperm must reach and penetrate the ovum within about three days of ejaculation. The ovum appears to play a role in attracting sperm to it, but how this is done is unclear.

spermatogenesis *the process by which sperm develop*

spermatozoa *mature spermatids that are fully functional and capable of fertilizing a human ovum*

FIGURE 3.12
Ovum and Sperm

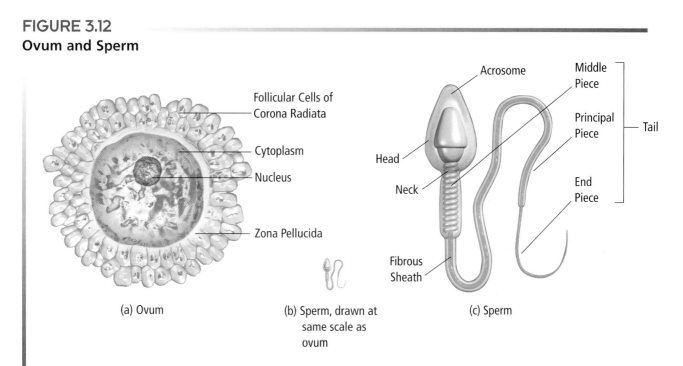

(a) Ovum

(b) Sperm, drawn at same scale as ovum

(c) Sperm

The ovum is much larger than the sperm. The chromosomal material is in the nucleus of the ovum and in the head of the sperm. Can you explain the processes by which ova and sperm are produced?

After three days or so, the fertilizing abilities of sperm decline, although in rare cases sperm can survive longer than six days (Jones, 1997).

Fertilization begins when a sperm penetrates the outer layer of an ovum. Once this happens, the ovum releases a secretion that thickens its outer layer, preventing other sperm from penetrating it. After penetration, the head of the sperm sinks into the nucleus of the ovum and the corresponding chromosomes align in pairs. Fertilization is complete once the chromosomes from the sperm and ovum combine to form 23 pairs that carry unique genetic instructions (Moore, 1998).

Overcoming Infertility

About 8.5 percent of couples who want children are unsuccessful in their efforts. Infertility is defined as being unable to conceive after 12 months of unprotected intercourse or being unable to carry a fetus to term (Institute of Medicine, 1990; Keel, May, & DeJonge, 2000). For about 50 percent of infertile couples, the conditions that complicate conception are related to the mother; abnormal ovulation, damaged ovaries, and endometriosis are a few. Another 20 percent of infertile couples have conception problems that are attributed to the father—low sperm count, hormone deficiency, and sperm antibodies. For the remaining 30 percent, there are complications involving both parents or unknown factors (Centers for Disease Control, 2003). Parents who are having difficulty conceiving, however, have many options, including surgery, hormone therapy, and artificial insemination, to remedy their situation.

Couples spend almost $3 billion each year trying to overcome fertility problems. In addition to surgery, traditional medical procedures, and adoption, several new procedures for "assisted reproduction" are now available.

■ *Intrauterine insemination:* Sperm are provided by a partner or donor, and near the time when the woman is ovulating, a doctor uses a syringe to deposit the sperm into the woman's uterus. This procedure is repeated as many times as necessary to achieve fertilization and is often successful. About 8,000 children in the United States are conceived though the use of intrauterine insemination each year.

■ *In vitro fertilization (IVF):* In 1978, baby Louise, a normal baby girl, was born in England after fertilization in a test tube. The basic procedure is to obtain an ovum directly from the woman's ovary, fertilize it with sperm in a culture dish, and then transfer the zygote(s) to the woman's uterus. Women are usually treated with hormones to induce ovulation of more than one egg, which increases the chances of success but also has resulted in many multiple pregnancies. The success rate for in vitro fertilization has improved significantly over the past few years (Centers for Disease Control, 2001a). This is by far the most common form of assisted reproduction and is necessary when the women's fallopian tubes are damaged.

■ *Gamete intrafallopian transfer (GIFT):* Sperm and an ovum are deposited into the woman's fallopian tube, and then fertilization occurs as it would normally. The rate of success is higher for this procedure than for in vitro fertilization, probably because more of the eggs are fertilized and developed in the natural environment of the fallopian tube.

■ *Intracytoplasmic sperm injection (ICSI):* When poor-quality sperm are the problem for conception, a tiny injection of sperm into the egg is done microscopically by the physician, using a very fine pipette. Even sperm that are immobile have been inserted into eggs in this way, and the procedure has resulted in pregnancies and healthy babies.

■ *Embryo transfer:* If both partners are infertile, embryo transfer may be a suitable option. In this procedure, donors provide both sperm and an ovum. Once the ovum is fertilized, the zygote is transferred to the woman. This procedure is rare, and its success rate is low.

■ *Surrogate mothers:* A surrogate mother is artificially inseminated with sperm from the man, carries the fertilized egg through pregnancy and birth, and then gives up the child.

Although the overall success rates vary depending on the reason for infertility, the age of the woman, the quality of the clinic, and the type of eggs used, a sizable portion of births in the United States results from one of these forms of assisted reproduction. About 14 percent of births in the United States are now attributable to assisted reproduction methods, and the rates of twins has increased due to these procedures (Reynolds et al., 2003). In one year, about 100,000 assisted reproductive procedures were reported in the United States, and out of these, 29 percent produced a live birth of one or more children (Wright et al., 2004). The most successful methods involve freshly fertilized embryos, with eggs from younger mothers.

Assisted reproductive techniques are not a solution for all couples. Procedures can be time consuming, expensive, and physically and emotionally demanding. Most physicians recommend that couples begin with the less-expensive and less-invasive procedures, progressing to the more aggressive methods later (Keel et al., 2000). These methods often result in the birth of twins or triplets, and this factor needs to be taken into consideration. A growing body of evidence suggests that fewer embryos need to be transferred, and this may cut down on multiple births in the future (Gerris et al., 2002; Jain, Missmer, & Hornstein, 2004). Although 90 percent of children born through the help of assisted reproductive technologies are healthy, about twice as many are at risk for major birth defects or low birthweight as compared to other babies. Furthermore, these techniques have generated important ethical and moral questions. For example, what happens to their frozen embryos when a couple divorces? What happens when a surrogate mother decides that she cannot give up the baby after having carried it for 9 months? Until these questions are resolved, interested couples need to be aware that uncertainties exist and take steps to minimize undesired consequences (Robertson, 1996).

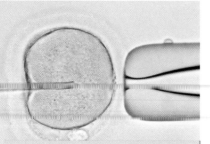

In this procedure, sperm are inserted directly into the ovum. In what types of situations would this procedure be more beneficial than typical IVF?

Try It Out

1. Review how you are similar to and different from your grandparents, parents, and siblings. To what extent do you think genes versus family environment contributed to those differences? Discuss with your family members the genetic factors in your family history that might be relevant to your medical history. What might you do to offset genetically related health risks?
2. What factors contribute to a couple's ability to conceive? How do these factors differ for women and men? Collect information on techniques that help couples who have trouble conceiving. Which of these procedures would you personally consider?
3. Collaborate with classmates on a research project to identify (a) factors that can prevent conception, (b) ethical dilemmas in genetic counseling, or (c) ethical dilemmas in assisted reproduction.

Key Terms and Concepts

active G–E correlation (74)
alleles (67)
amniocentesis (79)
autosomes (65)
balanced polymorphism (70)
canalized (73)
carriers (69)
chorionic villus sampling (CVS) (79)
chromosomes (64)
DNA (64)
dominant gene (67)
evocative G–E correlation (74)
fragile X syndrome (71)
gametes (65)
gene–environment interactions (75)
genes (64)
genetic imprinting (71)
genome (63)

genotype (67)
heterozygous (67)
homozygous (67)
karyotype (65)
meiosis (65)
mitosis (65)
ovum (80)
passive G–E correlation (74)
phenotype (67)
polygenic transmission (72)
range of reaction (73)
recessive genes (67)
regulator genes (72)
sex chromosomes (66)
spermatogenesis (82)
spermatozoa (82)
ultrasound (79)

Sum It Up

How do genes influence development?
■ What is the function of a gene? (pp. 64–65)

How do genes and environments work together?
■ Compare and contrast passive, evocative, and active G-E correlations. (p. 74)

What are common chromosomal abnormalities?
■ How does trisomy 21 occur? (p. 76)

How are genetic diseases detected?
■ For which individuals is genetic counseling recommended? (p. 79)

How does conception occur, and what can be done to overcome infertility?
■ What new procedures are available to help overcome infertility problems? (p. 84)

Chapter Summary 3

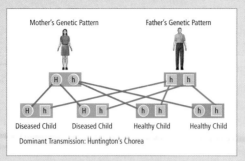

FIGURE 3.5   Dominant Transmission: Huntington's Chorea

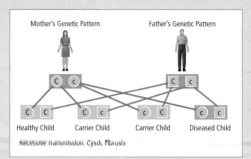

FIGURE 3.6   Recessive Transmission: Cystic Fibrosis

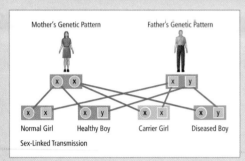

FIGURE 3.7   Sex-Linked Transmission: Color-blindness

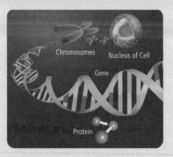

FIGURE 3.1   **The Building Blocks of Life**   *Proteins are the building blocks of life, and genes provide the message about how and which proteins should form.*

GENETIC INFLUENCES

The human genome is the book of instructions for human life, written by genes on chromosomes. Genes provide information about how proteins, the building blocks of the body, are to be constructed. Many physical characteristics and diseases result from information coded by a single gene, which can be expressed through a dominant, recessive, or sex-linked pattern. Multiple genes complexly determine most personality, behavioral, and intellectual traits. (Refer back to pages 64–72.)

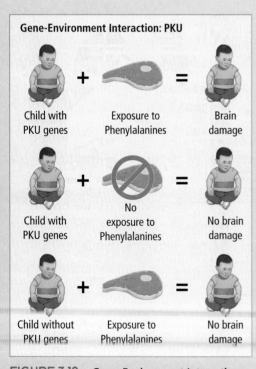

FIGURE 3.10   **Gene–Environment Interaction: PKU**   *What are the likely outcomes for a child with PKU genes if there is no environmental exposure to phenylalanines?*

GENE–ENVIRONMENT CORRELATIONS AND INTERACTIONS

Much recent genetics research has focused on the expression of genes: What causes certain genes to turn on? Why do some genes express themselves while others do not? Under what conditions do genes become expressed? Gene–environment correlations illustrate how genetic predispositions influence exposure to the environment. (Refer back to pages 72–75.)

Passive G–E Correlation   Evocative G–E Correlation   G–E Correlation

FIGURE 3.9   **Gene–Environment Correlations**   *How do the different types of gene–environment correlations influence the kinds of environments children are exposed to?*

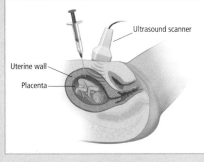

FIGURE 3.11 **Amniocentesis** *One way genetic disorders can be detected is through amniocentesis.*

TABLE 3.2

Some Chromosome Abnormalities

ABNORMALITY	CHROMOSOMAL PATTERN	OUTCOME
Down Syndrome Children born with an extra chromosome 21 or an extra piece of a chromosome	47 (XX or XY)	Wide-spaced eyes, large protruding tongue, short stature, a round face, folds in the corners of the eyes, unusual creases on the palms of the hands, heart and eye defects, immunological problems, mental retardation
Turner's Syndrome Girls missing the second X chromosome in the sex chromosomes	45, X	Lack of ovaries, immature external genitalia, short and broad chest, webbed neck, poor spatial skills, delayed social skills
Trisomy-X Syndrome Girls born with an extra X chromosome in the sex chromosomes	47, XXX	Normal phenotype, slightly lower IQ, quiet and passive demeanor, delayed development of speech and motor skills
Klinefelter's Syndrome Boys born with an extra X chromosome in the sex chromosomes	47, XXY	Sterility, long limbs, immature testes, lack of development of masculine physical characteristics at puberty (e.g., body hair), possible female-like breast development, possible mental retardation, language and attention deficits
XYY Syndrome Boys with one or more extra Y chromosomes in the sex chromosomes	47, XYY or 48, XYYY	Normal phenotype, tall height, severe acne, poor coordination, impulsive behavior, lower intelligence

CHROMOSOMAL AND GENETIC ABNORMALITIES

One of the most common chromosomal abnormalities is Down syndrome, which results from an extra chromosome on the twenty-first pair. Sex-linked chromosomal abnormalities are characterized by extra or missing sex chromosomes. Children with these disorders usually have abnormal development of sex organs and often have behavioral problems. Genetic disorders can be detected by using ultrasound imaging, chorionic villus sampling, and amniocentesis. (Refer back to pages 75–80.)

CONCEPTION AND INFERTILITY

Fertilization occurs when an egg and sperm cell meet and share their genetic material. The window of time for fertilization is only a few days around ovulation. For those couples who have difficulty conceiving, new procedures for "assisted reproduction" include artificial insemination, in vitro fertilization, gamete intrafallopian transfer, embryo transfer, and involvement of surrogate mothers. Rates of success vary. (Refer back to pages 80–84.)

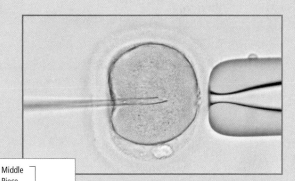

In this procedure, sperm are inserted directly into the ovum.

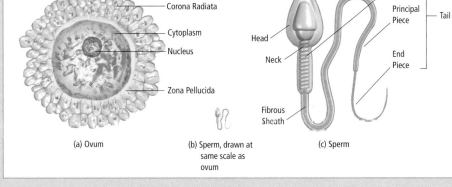

FIGURE 3.12 **Ovum and Sperm**

Prenatal Development and Birth

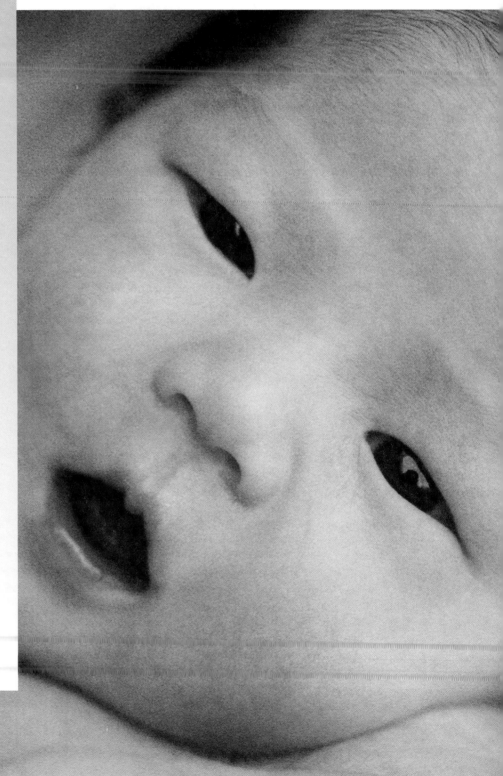

4

Chapter Outline

How Does Prenatal Development Proceed?
Overview of Prenatal Development
The Germinal Stage
The Embryonic Stage
The Fetal Stage

What Conditions Influence Pregnancy and Prenatal Development?
Diseases
Drugs
Environmental Hazards
Maternal Conditions
Protective Factors
Cultural Influences on Pregnancy

How Is a Baby Born?
The Birth Process
Birthing Methods
Birth Complications and Related
    Procedures

How Is Childbirth Experienced?
The Mother's Perspective
The Father's Perspective
The Newborn's Perspective
Cultural Differences in the Experience
    of Childbirth

What Are the Characteristics of a Newborn?
Physical Appearance
Behavioral Assessment of Neonates

Why Are Some Newborns at Risk?
Consequences of Low Birthweight and
    Prematurity
Neonatal Intensive Care
Caregiving and High-Risk Infants

A DEVELOPMENTAL MYSTERY

And suddenly, there she was—my new baby daughter. How did this miracle happen? Just a few months ago, it was just the 2 of us—and suddenly that changed. As I watched my new mother-to-be change in shape and size over the 9 months, I marveled and wondered at what was growing inside of her. How does this happen? From two separate cells, a single life is sprung. That fertilized cell multiplies and multiplies. Not only does that cell increase in number, but from that single cell many different types of cells form—hair cells, liver cells, brain cells, skin cells. . . . What a marvel. But more mysteriously, this produces an integrated, whole, and complex individual. And here she was in my arms—my daughter had arrived and although my prayers were answered, the questions behind the mystery are bigger than ever.

—Anonymous father's diary of the birth of his daughter

The words of this new parent reflects the fact that the miracle and mystery of life and its development are captivating. It captures the attention, fancy, and amazement of parents, as well as poets, writers, and scientists. From a single fertilized cell, a complex individual made up of trillions of cells develops. Parents-to-be all over the world wonder whether their unborn child is a boy or girl and whether the child is healthy. Most parents have very vivid memories of when they discovered that a baby was on the way. When couples receive the news about pregnancy, thoughts generally focus on the excitement and joy of having a child and on the external signs of the pregnancy. And all the while, their developing child's genetic endowment, transmitted at conception, is guiding prenatal development as the child grows from a single cell into a complex, functioning human being. But as the father's diary entry above reflects, prenatal development and birth remain a mystery that rivals any story ever told.

How Does Prenatal Development Proceed?

From the time the sperm and egg unite, miraculous changes occur that culminate in the birth of an infant. How these changes are brought about, what influences them, and how to maximize optimal outcomes are questions that confront parents and scientists. In this section, you will learn that prenatal development is made up of many complex and interrelated processes working together to produce a human infant.

Overview of Prenatal Development

In most Western cultures, birth is considered the beginning of a person's lifetime (Rosenblith, 1992). At birth, however, infants already have been influenced by their genetic makeup and the qualities of their prenatal environment. An understanding of the changes that take place during prenatal development is needed to fully understand later development.

Prenatal development, which begins at conception and ends at birth, proceeds through three stages.

- The **germinal stage** begins at conception and lasts until the fertilized egg implants itself in the uterine wall (usually about two weeks). Cell division and differentiation are the main qualities of this stage.

- The **embryonic stage** begins at implantation and lasts until about eight weeks. The developing child is referred to as an *embryo*. During this stage, the major organs and body parts develop almost daily. This stage is the most critical time in prenatal development; it is when environmental damage is most likely to occur.

germinal stage *the first stage of prenatal development, which begins at conception and lasts until the fertilized egg implants itself in the uterine wall*

embryonic stage *the second stage of prenatal development, which begins at implantation and lasts until about eight weeks*

■ The **fetal stage** begins at about eight weeks and lasts until birth. The developing child is referred to as a *fetus*. During this stage, elaboration of the existing organs and structures occurs and the brain develops rapidly.

The Germinal Stage

The fertilized ovum, called the **zygote,** takes two to three days to reach the uterus. During this time, the zygote divides several times through mitosis, producing cells that are identical to the zygote. The first cell division occurs within about 24 hours after fertilization. By the time the zygote reaches the uterus, it consists of 12 to 16 cells that are beginning to separate into two layers. The inner layer of cells develops into the infant, and the outer mass

FIGURE 4.1

Early Timetable of Prenatal Development

Sun	Mon	Tue	Wed	Thur	Fri	Sat
			1 Last menstrual period.	2	3	4
5	6	7	8	9	10	11
12	13	14 Ovulation occurs (ovum lasts up to 24 hours; sperm lasts up. to 6 days)	15 Fertilization occurs.	16	17	18
19	20 Zygote adheres to uterine wall.	21 Implantation begins.	22	23	24 Implantation ends.	25
26	27	28 Amnion, chorion, placenta, and umbilical cord begin to develop.	29 First menstrual period is missed.	30		

fetal stage   *the third and final stage of prenatal development, which begins at about eight weeks and lasts until birth*

zygote   *the fertilized ovum*

Early in prenatal development, the major changes involve cell growth and differentiation. At this point, the mother may not even know she is pregnant. What signs would mothers look for to tell if they are pregnant during these early phases?

Source: Adapted from Jones, 1997.

of cells eventually forms the structures that support the developing infant, such as the umbilical cord and placenta (Wong & Perry, 1998). Figure 4.1 outlines the major changes of early prenatal development.

After two or three days of floating freely in the uterus, the zygote implants itself in the wall of the uterus. The cells of the outer layers of the zygote develop hairlike projections that burrow into the lining of the uterus. Eventually, these hairlike structures will transfer nutrients to the zygote. The connections established by implantation provide a source of nutrients for the zygote until the support structures are fully functional. This process is complete during the second week, and the zygote, measuring no more than 1 millimeter in diameter, now consists of a few thousand cells. Implantation also triggers hormonal changes that prevent menstruation and provide the woman with some of the first noticeable signs that she is pregnant.

Ectopic Pregnancies

Usually implantation takes place in the uterus, but sometimes it occurs outside the uterus—most commonly in a fallopian tube, but occasionally in the abdomen or ovary. This condition, known as an **ectopic pregnancy** (outside the uterus), occurs in about 1 of every 100 pregnancies (Wong & Perry, 1998). The main cause of ectopic pregnancies is damaged fallopian tubes. Ectopic pregnancies cause abdominal pain and irregular vaginal bleeding and are dangerous to the health of the mother if not terminated.

Multiple Pregnancies

Another complication of fertilization occurs when multiple pregnancies (such as twins) develop. In the United States, twins occur in about 1 in every 80 pregnancies, but in other parts of the world, the incidence varies, with a much higher rate in West Africa, for example, and a much lower rate in Japan. The incidence of twin pregnancies is up to four times greater than the rate of twin births, though, because often one of the embryos spontaneously aborts early in development (Jones, 1997).

Rates of twin births generally are greater than they were ten years ago. As you can see in Figure 4.2, as the age of the mother increases, the rates of twin births increase, becoming particularly high for mothers who are 45 to 49 years of age (National Center for Health Statistics, 2003). Notice the dramatic increase in twin births to older mothers since 1990—almost 600 percent. More than one third (34 percent) of all births to mothers of ages 45 to 49 were twin births. This high rate of twins among older women likely results from the use of fertility drugs by women who decided to delay pregnancy and then needed to overcome the greater difficulty in getting pregnant.

Multiple pregnancies involving more than two children are even rarer than twins. Triplets occur once in every 8,000 to 9,000 pregnancies, and quadruplets occur once in every 700,000 pregnancies (Grant, 1993). Because of the increased use of fertility drugs, the incidence of giving birth to 3 or more babies has quadrupled since 1980. The higher rates of multiple pregnancies among Caucasian American women likely result from the use of fertility drugs. With increasing numbers of fetuses in a pregnancy, the chance of survival and good outcomes decreases. But today's medical technology makes it more probable that multiple infants will survive—as in the case of Bobbi McCaughey, who in 1997, gave birth to seven babies after she took fertility drugs to get pregnant (visit http://mccaugheyseptuplets.com).

The Embryonic Stage

Once implantation occurs, the embryo and its support structures take shape and begin to function. Figure 4.3 identifies the major accomplishments of prenatal development. From the inner mass of cells, two membranes form that surround and protect the embryo. The first is the **amnion,** which grows over the embryo and becomes filled with *amniotic fluid.* The amount of amniotic fluid is about 5 to 10 milliliters after eight weeks of development and increases through pregnancy to a maximum of 1,000 to 1,200 milliliters (Wong & Perry, 1998). This sac and its fluid provide the developing embryo with shock-absorbing protection.

ectopic pregnancy *a pregnancy that occurs outside the uterus*

amnion *a membrane that grows over the embryo and becomes filled with amniotic fluid, which protects the embryo*

FIGURE 4.2
Rates of Twin Births by Age of Mother: 1980 to 2001

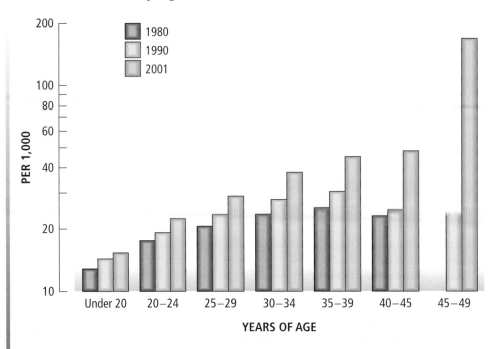

Notice that the rate of twins increases with the age of the mother primarily only for those giving birth in 2001. Also notice the dramatic increase for the oldest mothers in 2001. What factors likely contributed to these increases?

Note: The birth rate for women 45–49 years of age for 1980 is not shown because of the small number of twin births. Rates are plotted on a log scale.

Source: National Center for Health Statistics, 2003a.

FIGURE 4.3
Milestones & Characteristics of Prenatal Development

.17 in.	1.25 in.	3–4 in.	6.5–7 in.	10–11 in.
0 g	1 g	28 g	113 g (4 oz)	227–454 g (.5–1 lb)
Backbone and vertebrae form. Primitive heart forms and starts to beat. Arm and leg buds form. Embryo is not yet distinguishable as human.	Bone cells appear. Arms and legs become distinct. Fingers and toes form. Major blood vessels form. Internal organs continue to develop.	Eyes form, but eyelids are fused shut. Ears form. Arms and legs are fully formed. Heartbeat can be detected. External genitalia develop. Fingernails and toenails form.	Head is large relative to rest of body. Face takes on human features. Movements may be detected by mother.	Head and body hair are visible. Head is less disproportionate to rest of body. Brain develops rapidly. Periods of sleep alternate with periods of alertness.
1 month	2 months	3 months	4 months	5 months

As you can see, changes early in prenatal development are more rapid than those later in development.

Source: Bennett and Brown, 1993; Jones, 1997; Moore, 1998.

The second membrane is the **chorion,** which grows to surround the embryo after about one month of development. The chorion helps form the **placenta,** a mass of tissue through which nutrients and waste products are exchanged between the mother and the developing embryo. The placenta is made up of fine blood vessels (called *capillaries*) from the mother's and embryo's circulatory systems. The mother's blood does not directly mix with that of her developing child. The developing embryo is connected to the placenta by the **umbilical cord,** the lifeline of the embryo, which consists of two arteries and one vein.

The third week of prenatal development begins with the formation of three layers of cells. The outer layer is the *ectoderm,* which later becomes the skin and nervous system. The middle layer is the *mesoderm,* which becomes the muscles, bones, and circulatory system. The inner layer is the *endoderm,* which becomes the digestive system and lungs. The formation of these layers reveals the remarkable nature of early development. Early development involves not only the change from a single cell into a creature that ultimately consists of several trillion cells but also increasing cell differentiation. Our many different types of cells—hair cells, liver cells, brain cells, and so on—all form from a single cell. About 21 days after fertilization, the ectoderm begins to form a groove that develops into the *neural tube.* This tube eventually becomes the central nervous system. The front portion of the tube becomes the brain, and the back forms the spinal cord.

Within a few weeks, the embryo is about a half inch long and looks more like a salamander than a human being. In fact, early in development it is almost impossible to distinguish embryos of different species. By the end of the embryonic period (at about eight weeks), however, human embryos look distinctively different than embryos of other species.

During the embryonic period, the brain, nervous system, circulatory system, and sensory organs develop. At four weeks, the heart, although still just a tube, begins to flutter and then beat. Arms and legs appear, first as buds and later as limbs. The liver, pancreas, and major divisions of intestines develop at around this time, and the embryo's face begins to form, although at this age the face is still unrecognizable. By eight weeks, the fingers and toes are visible and are noticeably webbed. At the end of eight weeks, the embryo weighs about 0.03 ounce and is slightly over one inch in length.

chorion   *a membrane that grows to surround the embryo after about one month of development and helps form the placenta*

placenta   *the structure through which nutrients and waste products are exchanged between the mother and the developing embryo*

umbilical cord   *the lifeline of the embryo, consisting of two arteries and one vein*

11–14 in.	13–17 in.	16.5–18 in.	18–20 in.
567–681 g (1.25–1.5 lb)	1135–1362 g (2.5–3 lb)	2100 g (6 lb)	3178–3405 g (7–7.5 lb)
Layers of the cortex of the brain develop. Skin is wrinkled. Skin is pink because blood vessels are visible.	Fetus becomes viable. Eyelids open and eyelashes form. Teeth form.	Fat deposits form. Body is more rounded. Skin unwrinkles. Testes in boys descend into scrotum.	Body hair is shed. Nails reach tips of fingers and toes. Growth rate slows down. Fetus moves into position for birth.
6 months	7 months	8 months	9 months

FIGURE 4.4

Changes in Body Proportion During Prenatal Development

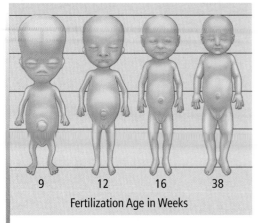

9   12   16   38
Fertilization Age in Weeks

Notice that as the embryo and fetus grow, the size of the head relative to the rest of the body changes. What other aspects of developmental change can you identify in this figure?

Reprinted from *The Developing Human*, 6/E, by K. L. Moore, © 1998, with permission from Elsevier.

cephalocaudal development
the principle that growth occurs from the head downward

proximodistal development
the principle that body parts closer to the central axis of the body develop first, while those farther away from the center of the body develop later

quickening *fetal movements during pregnancy*

age of viability *the point at which postnatal survival is likely*

Development during the embryonic period proceeds according to two important principles. The first is that growth occurs from the head downwards—a principle referred to as **cephalocaudal development** (see Figure 4.4). The second is that body parts closer to the central axis of the body develop first, while those that are farther away from the center of the body (such as the hands) develop later. This principle is referred to as **proximodistal development.**

By the end of the embryonic period, 95 percent of the major body structures are developed and some are even functioning, although they are incapable of sustaining the embryo independent of the mother. Because the organs and body systems are forming during the embryonic period, it is a time of great vulnerability to environmental influences.

The Fetal Stage

The transition from an embryo to a fetus is gradual and signifies that the developing child is unquestionably recognizable as human. The fetal stage is marked by growth and elaboration of the structures that developed earlier. This is the final and longest phase of prenatal development—extending from about the ninth week after fertilization until birth.

Around the 16th week of prenatal development, many mothers first feel the movements of the unborn child. These fetal movements, known as **quickening,** are dramatic signs of pregnancy. More than a positive pregnancy test, a bulging abdomen, or even the sound of the fetal heartbeat, the movements of the fetus signal and confirm the presence of the life inside the woman. Quickening is one of the greatest sources of joy during pregnancy, and lack of fetal movements can be a source of great anxiety (Eisenberg, Murkoff, & Hathaway, 1999).

Growth during the fetal stage is very rapid, especially during the third and fourth months. The rate of growth is greater than at any other time before or after birth. By 16 weeks, the fetus is three to four times larger and over a hundred times heavier than it was at the end of the embryonic period. It is 6 to 7 inches long and weighs about 4 ounces (Jones, 1997). As the fetus enlarges, the mother's uterus, or womb, grows; as a result, it is around the 16th week that her condition becomes obvious to others (see Figure 4.5).

Important body changes occur during the third and fourth months. The fetus develops a penis or vagina at the beginning of the third month. In males, the process begins when the testes secrete the male hormone testosterone, which causes a group of cells to develop into the penis, scrotum, and seminal vesicles. In females, because testosterone is not secreted, these cells develop into the fallopian tubes, uterus, and vagina. Thus, boys' and girls' sex organs have the same origins but develop differently, depending on the presence or absence of testosterone (Wong & Perry, 1998).

The nervous system also develops rapidly during the early part of the fetal period. By the fifth month, the cells of the brain have migrated to their proper locations and formed connections with other brain cells. These connections allow brain cells to communicate with one another and to control some bodily functions. The fetus displays simple reflexes such as sucking and swallowing and can react to disturbances of its environment, such as loud noises made outside but near the mother's uterus (Jones, 1997). Such reactions indicate that the fetus is not simply an unreactive mass of tissue but a responsive being, capable of learning (Joseph, 2000).

An important milestone is reached as the fetus enters the last trimester of prenatal development. Prior to this point, a fetus born prematurely has a poor chance of surviving. At about seven months, survival is possible with intensive care because the fetus's lungs and nervous system are developed enough to support breathing. Thus, the seventh month marks the **age of viability**—the point at which postnatal survival is likely (Moore, 1998).

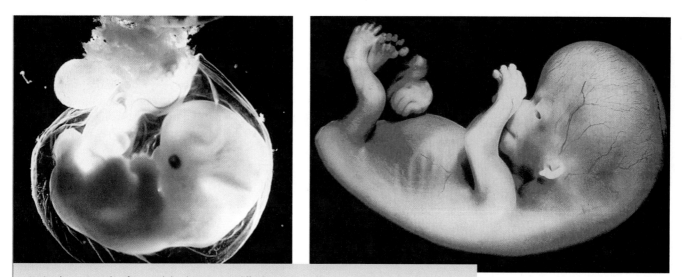

Notice that at 5 weeks of prenatal development it is difficult to distinguish human embryos from those of others species. But by 8 weeks, the embryo is beginning to look more human in its physical features. Why are embryos most susceptible to damaging environmental influences during these periods of time?

FIGURE 4.5
Growth and Change of Fetus and Mother

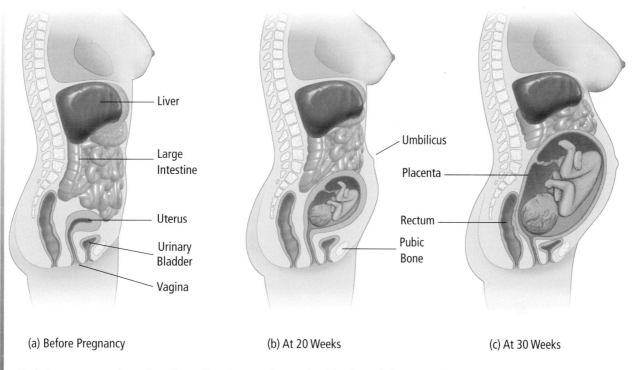

(a) Before Pregnancy

(b) At 20 Weeks

(c) At 30 Weeks

Early in pregnancy, the embryo is small and causes few noticeable physical changes in the mother. Later in pregnancy, the physical changes in the mother increase as the baby grows larger. Can you describe how the mother's and the embryo's systems are connected?

Source: The Developing Human, 6/E, by K. L. Moore, © 1998, with permission from Elsevier.

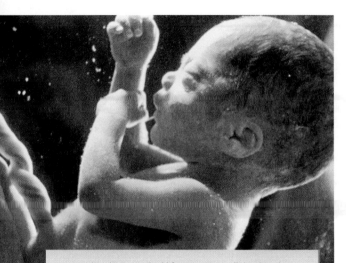

Notice that the 8-month-old fetus is quite well developed at this point. What major changes occur during the last trimester?

During the last three months, the finishing touches of prenatal development are completed. At 30 weeks, the eyelids open to reveal fully formed eyes with pupils that respond to light. By 35 weeks, the hands have a firm grasp and the hair is growing. Increased production of fat makes the body more rounded and less wrinkled (Sadler, 2000). This increase in fat improves control of body temperature. By the end of the last trimester, the average newborn is about 20 inches long and weighs 7 to 7½ pounds.

What Conditions Influence Pregnancy and Prenatal Development?

Although genetic and chromosomal disorders cause some birth defects, about 80 percent of birth defects are caused by environmental problems during prenatal development. The unborn child has at least two lines of protection from environmental influences. The first is the amniotic fluid, which protects the fetus from physical injuries. The second line of protection is the **placental barrier,** created by blood vessel walls that separate the maternal and fetal circulatory systems. This barrier acts as a filter, blocking many harmful agents from entering the blood supply of the child. The placental barrier effectively blocks large agents, such as bacteria, but not smaller agents, such as viruses. The mother's hormones, any alcohol she drinks, and the nicotine from any cigarettes she smokes are among the substances that can cross the placental barrier. Thus, the protection provided by the placental barrier is incomplete.

Alcohol and cigarettes are examples of **teratogens**—agents that cross the placental barrier and cause or increase the incidence of physical malformations and behavioral and cognitive deficits in children. Many teratogens have been identified, including diseases such as smallpox and HIV, environmental agents such as X-rays and pesticides, and drugs such as cocaine and alcohol. Although the effects of teratogens vary, the severity of these effects depends on at least three factors:

■ *When the teratogenic exposure occurs:* A particular teratogen will affect a zygote, an embryo, and a fetus differently. If the zygote is exposed to a teratogen, a spontaneous abortion may occur. As you can see in Figure 4.6, teratogenic exposure during the embryonic period is particularly harmful. During the embryonic stage, organs and body structures, which are undergoing rapid development, are likely to be damaged. Teratogenic exposure at the fetal stage, when the brain is developing quickly, may damage the nervous system and brain, affecting later behavior or intelligence.

■ *Amount of teratogenic exposure:* Some teratogens, especially alcohol and drugs, are dosage dependent; that is, the more the mother takes, the greater the likelihood that the developing child will be affected. Similarly, the longer the exposure to teratogens, the greater the likelihood that development will be disrupted.

■ *Fetal characteristics:* Important individual differences occur in fetal reactions to a teratogen. Depending on constitution, some fetuses will perish under the influence of a particular teratogen, while others may suffer severe or mild complications.

placental barrier   *a line of protection for the unborn child, created by blood vessel walls that separate the maternal and fetal circulatory systems*

teratogens   *agents that cross the placental barrier and cause or increase the incidence of physical malformations and behavioral and cognitive deficits*

These three factors operate together to determine the degree to which teratogens influence the developing child. Some effects are direct (for example, the fetus is exposed to alcohol when the mother drinks), and some are indirect (for example, the fetus receives less oxygen while the mother is smoking). Because many teratogenic effects occur before women even know they have conceived, a good strategy to ensure healthy offspring is for women to avoid teratogens if there is any possibility that they may be pregnant—that is, if they have had unprotected intercourse.

FIGURE 4.6
Critical Periods for Teratogenic Effects

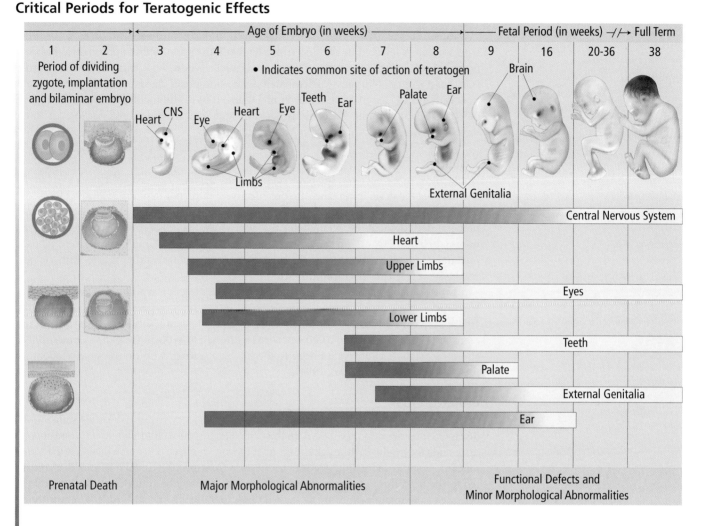

The timing of teratogen exposure is crucial. Notice that teratogens have the most impact during the embryonic stage, except on certain body parts such as the brain and ears, which continue to be at risk for teratogenic effects because they continue to grow and develop during the fetal period.

Note: Dark portions denote highly sensitive periods; light portions denote less sensitive periods.

Source: The Developing Human, 6/E, by K. L. Moore, © 1998, with permission from Elsevier.

Diseases

About 3 to 5 percent of birth defects are caused by infectious diseases transmitted to the developing child (Thorogood, 1997). Several diseases have a dramatic impact on the developing child, even when they produce only mild symptoms in the mother. The diseases most likely to influence prenatal development are caused by viruses. Approximately 5 percent of women who are pregnant are affected by viral diseases (Gibbs & Sweet, 1994).

Rubella

The placental barrier does not provide complete protection for the developing child. During a mini-epidemic of rubella—a form of measles—in the 1960s, 30,000 fetuses and newborns died and over 16,000 children were born deaf or blind (Rosenblith, 1992). Rubella causes flu-like symptoms so mild that pregnant women may not even realize they are ill. Nonetheless, rubella crosses the placental barrier and interferes with normal development during early pregnancy. If the mother has rubella during the first 12 weeks of pregnancy, the child has about an 80 percent chance of showing some effects. At 13 to 14 weeks, the risk drops to about 50 percent; by the end of the second trimester, the risk is 25 percent (Cunningham et al., 2001).

Rubella is the best-known congenital infection that can cause birth defects. If a pregnant woman is infected in the first trimester, her baby has a one-in-four chance of being born with one or more features of congenital rubella syndrome (deafness, mental retardation, heart defects, blindness). Fortunately, with widespread vaccination, this syndrome is now rare in the United States (March of Dimes, 2004). The incidence of rubella-related defects is higher among Hispanic Americans and African Americans because of lower immunization rates (Office of Minority Health, 1998).

Syphilis

Unlike most other bacteria, the bacteria that cause syphilis can cross the placental barrier and damage the developing child. Before effective treatments, syphilis accounted for about one third of stillborn children. Unlike most teratogens, syphilis is more dangerous in later prenatal development, especially after the 18th week. Syphilis causes lesions on the eyes, leading to blindness, and on the skin and mucous membranes. Children who were exposed prenatally to syphilis also suffer retarded growth, liver damage, and problems with the nervous system (Fletcher & Gordon, 1990).

In most states, prenatal health care includes testing for syphilis and other sexually transmitted diseases. Although antibiotics reduced the rates of new cases of syphilis in the 1960s, prenatal syphilis infection continues to be a problem (National Center for Health Statistics, 2001a). About 1 in 2,000 newborns is affected by syphilis (March of Dimes, 2004), and most of these children are born to low-income women who do not receive adequate prenatal care (Gibbs & Sweet, 1994).

Pediatric AIDS

Pregnant women infected with the human immunodeficiency virus (HIV) often transmit the disease to their developing children. In the United States, most children with HIV are born to drug-addicted mothers, although the number of women infected through heterosexual transmission is rapidly increasing (Centers for Disease Control, 2001b). HIV is usually transmitted to the fetus through the placental barrier but also may be transmitted during delivery because of the infant's exposure to vaginal fluids and during breast-feeding (Committee on Pediatric AIDS, 1998). HIV-infected infants are likely to have impaired brain growth (Epstein et al., 1986), bacterial and viral infections, cognitive deficits, and weak muscles (Byers, 1989).

The first case of AIDS in the United States was reported in 1981; now, there are almost 800,000 AIDS sufferers (Centers for Disease Control, 2001b). Thus, more and more children are being exposed to this disease prenatally. An estimated 120,000 to 160,000 women in the United States are living with the virus, and many do not know they are infected. Each year, about 6,000 to 7,000 of these women give birth. Approximately 15,000 children in the United States have contracted HIV, and about 3,000 have died. About 90 percent contracted the virus from their mothers during pregnancy or birth (March of Dimes, 2004). Studies suggest that mothers with AIDS who take the medication AZT during pregnancy are much less likely to transmit the virus to their newborns (Morris, 1998).

Drugs

In the United States, 90 percent of pregnant women take some type of drug during pregnancy (Cunningham et al., 2001), including over-the-counter medications, prescriptions, and illicit drugs. Drugs influence the mother's entire body and are transmitted to the developing child during pregnancy.

Thalidomide

During her pregnancy, my mother was prescribed thalidomide to alleviate severe morning sickness symptoms. My mother took thalidomide twice, two teaspoons total.

Thalidomide caused my birth disabilities, necessitating thirty-two operations over my life and nine years accumulated time spent in the hospital before I was 16, in a different city from where my parents lived.

—Randy Warren (founder and CEO of the Thalidomide
Victims Association of Canada, Thalidomide Workshop, 1997)

The negative consequences of drugs are best illustrated by the thalidomide tragedy. In Europe in the 1950s, over 10,000 children were born with arms or legs missing, hands growing from their shoulders, or feet growing from their hips. Medical researchers pinpointed the cause of these defects: the mothers had taken a mild sedative called thalidomide, prescribed to them by their doctors during early pregnancy to control nausea and insomnia (Kalter, 2003). The US Food and Drug Administration had not approved the use of thalidomide because of lack of testing, so most families in the United States were spared its tragic consequences (Bower, 1995).

The timing of thalidomide ingestion was significant (Beckman & Brent, 1986). Because thalidomide interferes with development of the skeletal system, its effects are most obvious during the late embryonic period, when arms and legs are forming. As Randy Warren's story illustrates, even a very small amount of a teratogen can have very serious consequences during this time. Once developed, the embryo's arms and legs are not affected by thalidomide.

Although it was banned worldwide, thalidomide has been discovered to be effective in treating a variety of diseases (Neiger, 2000). In a controversial move, the Food and Drug Administration in 1998 approved the use of thalidomide to treat leprosy. To avoid the tragic consequences of thalidomide on developing embryos, a number of safeguards have been instituted. Men who take thalidomide must practice birth control and cannot donate blood or semen. Women can begin taking thalidomide only after a negative pregnancy test. Then they are tested every week for the first month and every two to four weeks after that. In addition, they must use two forms of effective birth control at the same time for at least one month before receiving thalidomide and must continue until one month after their last dose (Center for the Evaluation of Risks to Human Reproduction, 1999b).

Alcohol

Over 5 million women in the United States drink alcohol during pregnancy, and each year more than 40,000 babies are born with some degree of alcohol-related damage (March of Dimes, 2004). When a pregnant woman drinks, her unborn child is exposed to the teratogen ethanol—the active ingredient in alcoholic beverages. Because the fetus is less able to metabolize ethanol than the mother is, the fetus's exposure may be longer and more intense. Even low and sporadic levels of alcohol consumption during pregnancy may increase the risk of congenital anomalies in the offspring, and this risk increases with increasing levels of alcohol consumption (Martinez-Frias, Bermejo, Rodriguez-Pinilla, & Frias, 2004). Heavy drinkers and binge drinkers also have a much higher risk of giving birth to a child with **fetal alcohol syndrome (FAS),** a constellation of problems marked by physical deformities and intellectual deficits. Characteristics of FAS include the following (Streissguth, 1997):

- Abnormally flat face and nose
- Narrow head
- Delayed and retarded physical growth
- Heart defects
- Cognitive deficits
- Hyperactivity

The most serious and consistent feature of FAS is mental retardation. In a longitudinal study of 500 children with FAS, followed until age 7, the children were found to have an average IQ score of 65, compared with a normal score of about 100 (Streissguth et al., 1989). Women who drink alcohol moderately (one or two drinks per day) may be at risk for giving birth to children with **fetal alcohol effects (FAE)**. These children have

This 8-year-old child has fetal alcohol syndrome. He has the typical facial abnormalities associated with the syndrome, including a flat nose and small, narrow head. In some states, mothers who drink or take drugs during pregnancy are charged with child abuse. Do you agree or disagree with this policy? Why?

fetal alcohol syndrome (FAS)
a constellation of problems, including physical deformities and intellectual deficits, that may occur if a mother drinks heavily during pregnancy

fetal alcohol effects (FAE)
the effects, including mildly retarded physical development and learning disabilities, that may occur if a mother drinks moderately during pregnancy

DEBATING THE ISSUE

SHOULD THERE BE LIMITS TO NEONATAL TREATMENT?

Rapid improvements in medical care for newborns have led to an increase in survival rates for very small and very low birthweight infants. The advent of neonatal intensive care procedures has also increased the number of high-risk newborns who survive but have disabilities (Hack et al., 1995). In addition to ethical issues, there also is a medical question concerning the provision of extensive medical treatment to extremely immature newborns. Is there a limit to the effectiveness of treatment? Several studies have investigated infant survival rates to determine whether a cutoff point exists in treatment effectiveness. In a study of infants born from 1988 to 1991 at 22 to 25 weeks' gestation, it was found that outcome depended on gestational age. As the table shows, the likelihood of survival varied dramatically with age, as did the chance of having severe brain damage (Allen, Donohue, & Dusman, 1993). The researchers concluded that aggressive medical care (such as resuscitation) is indicated for infants born in the 25th gestational week but not for those born in the 22nd gestational week. To determine the indicated treatment level for those in between, the researchers recommended opening discussions with parents, health care providers, and society at large. Concerns about which infants receive intensive medical care are likely to become more pressing as scarce health care resources are evaluated and reallocated.

THINKING IT THROUGH

1. How does society determine which—and whether—very small and very early newborns will receive expensive and demanding medical interventions?

2. Should parents be asked to consider the costs to society of caring for a high-risk infant whose chances of surviving are very low? Why or why not?

3. Because medical interventions for very small or early infants are expensive, should society make certain these interventions are available to all who need them? Why or why not?

Nutrition is an important part of good prenatal care. Can you identify lifestyle factors that influence prenatal development?

slightly retarded physical development and may have learning disabilities (O'Mally & Nanson, 2002), and these effects may be long term (Baer et al., 2003).

Binge drinking may be more injurious than consistent low levels of drinking (Abel, 1996). The timing of fetal exposure to ethanol also is important. For example, facial anomalies and mental retardation are more likely to occur if the mother drinks early in pregnancy (Maier & West, 2001). Some evidence suggests that women who quit drinking during pregnancy may prevent FAS or FAE in their newborns (Coles, 1994). No one knows how much alcohol consumed during pregnancy is *too* much, so physicians recommend total abstinence.

Caffeine

Until recently, it was difficult to determine whether caffeine consumed by a pregnant woman acted as a teratogen. Some studies suggested that just two cups of coffee could increase the risk of miscarriage; others found no effect, even when large amounts were consumed. Part of the difficulty in assessing the effects of caffeine arose from researchers' need to rely on participants' own reports of caffeine use, which often are faulty. A new method is now available, in which assessments are made of the blood levels of a substance produced when caffeine is broken down by the liver. This method is assumed by researchers to be a more accurate barometer of caffeine consumption. When this method was used in a large study involving over 40,000 women and the risks associated with other factors likely to increase the risk of miscarriage (e.g., smoking) were taken into account, the results showed that only large amounts of caffeine increased miscarriage risk for women. Two cups of coffee a day did not increase miscarriage risk. But women who consumed five or more cups of coffee a day were more than twice as likely to miscarry as women who consumed less caffeine or none at all (Klebanoff et al., 1999). Thus, women should monitor the amount of caffeine they ingest during pregnancy, especially during the third trimester, when it might be related to slow and retarded growth (Vik et al., 2003). It is important to remember that caffeine is found not only in coffee but also in a variety of foods, including tea, chocolate, and many carbonated beverages.

Cigarettes

Despite warnings about the dangers of cigarette smoking, approximately 12 percent of pregnant women smoke (March of Dimes, 2004). The highest rates generally are found among mothers of 15 to 25 years of age. Caucasian mothers are more likely to smoke during pregnancy than are minority mothers, especially at younger ages (National Center for Health Statistics, 2001a). With each puff, they expose themselves and their unborn children to toxic substances. Even secondhand smoke puts a fetus at risk and should be avoided (Goel et al., 2004).

Smokers ingest over 2,500 chemicals in each cigarette, including known carcinogens. Some of these chemicals pass through the placenta and influence the unborn child. For example, carbon monoxide and nicotine deprive the child of oxygen, adversely influencing brain development. The danger to fetuses is especially severe when mothers smoke a pack or more per day.

Males who smoke may decrease their sperm production, making conception less likely. Women who smoke during pregnancy increase their risk of having a spontaneous abortion, premature birth, and complications in delivery (Cnattingius, 2004). Infants born to smokers are smaller and less likely to survive.

Some studies report that children of smokers have deficits in motor coordination, brain development, physical growth, and spatial and reading abilities, as well as increased irritability (Brook, Brook, & Whiteman, 2000; Kallen, 2000). However, these outcomes also are influenced by related lifestyle factors such as alcohol use, socioeconomic status, and nutrition (Barr, Streissguth, Darby, & Sampson, 1990). Smoking also has long-term effects (Fergusson, Horwood, & Lynskey, 1993; Lassen & Oei, 1998). In an important classic study, children whose mothers smoked during pregnancy were more likely to fail in school and have learning deficiencies than were children whose mothers did not smoke. As indicated in Figure 4.7, the more a mother smoked, the more likely the child was to fail at school (Newman & Buka, 1991).

Because the effects of smoking are dosage related, they can be minimized if mothers reduce the number of cigarettes they smoke and reduce their exposure to secondhand smoke. In fact, if all pregnant women in the United States stopped smoking, there would be an estimated 10 percent reduction in infant deaths (March of Dimes, 2004). Smokers who enroll in smoking cessation programs and reduce their smoking tend to give birth to normal-birthweight babies, but this does not prevent all smoking-related deficits (Lindley, Becker, Gray, & Herman, 2000). Ideally, women should stop smoking before they become pregnant.

FIGURE 4.7

Smoking Among Mothers During Pregnancy and School Failure and Learning Problems for Children at Age 7

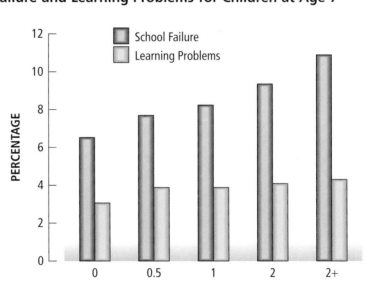

Notice that the rates of school failure and learning problems in children depend on whether and how much the mother smoked during pregnancy. School failure seems to be more influenced by maternal smoking than learning problems are. What can be done to decrease the rates of smoking among pregnant women?

Source: Adapted from Newman and Buka, 1991.

Cocaine

The impact of illicit drug abuse and addiction on children in the United States is particularly devastating. Among pregnant women, about 4 percent reported using illicit drugs in the month prior to their interview (Department of Health and Human Services, 2003). This rate was significantly lower than the rate among women who were not pregnant (10.4 percent). The full extent of the effects of prenatal drug exposure on a child is still not known completely, but science has shown that babies born to mothers who use drugs during pregnancy are often delivered prematurely, have low birthweights and smaller head circumferences, and are often shorter in length than infants not exposed to drugs in utero. Estimating the actual consequences of maternal drug use is difficult, and determining the specific hazard of a particular drug to the unborn child is even more problematic, given that more than one substance is typically used.

Cocaine is one of the most commonly used illicit drugs. In a study of 400,000 admissions of women to drug treatment facilities in 1993, the second most common reason for admission (following alcohol use, at 44 percent) was use of cocaine, especially crack cocaine, at 26 percent (National Center for Health Statistics, 1996). About 1.7 million Americans currently use cocaine at least once per month, and over 45,000 pregnant women smoke crack cocaine each year. Although overall use of cocaine has decreased somewhat in the past few years, rates among inner-city and minority groups have increased (Department of Health and Human Services, 2003). Federal law mandates drug testing of all newborns.

Women who use cocaine during pregnancy have more miscarriages, stillbirths, and lower-birthweight babies than do other women (Kuhn et al., 2000), and this is especially true for mothers who use crack cocaine (Richardson, Hamel, Goldschmidt, & Day, 1999). Infants born to cocaine-using mothers are more at risk for physical deformities, especially of the heart and circulatory system (Chavkin, 2001), and their brain development may be adversely affected (Scher, Richardson, & Day, 2000).

After birth, infants exposed to cocaine prenatally seldom experience symptoms of withdrawal from the drug, but they may be irritable and have attention-span, language, and motor-development problems (Bandstra et al., 2004; Singer et al., 2002). They also may show less interest in learning than other infants do (Alessandri, Sullivan, Imaizumi, & Lewis, 1993). Although research suggests that some children who were exposed to cocaine prenatally may have cognitive deficits, these deficits greatly depend on the family environment (Singer et al., 2004). For example, children born to mothers who use cocaine also are at greater risk of abuse and neglect than children of nonusers, and abuse and neglect, in turn, are linked to cognitive deficits (Leventhal et al., 1997). Some studies suggest that the home environment (Hurt et al., 2001) and poverty are the major risks for young children (Van Beveren, Little, & Spence, 2000). The long-term effects that can be attributed directly to a mother's cocaine use are difficult to pinpoint because, as noted previously, cocaine use is associated with many other risk factors (Brown et al., 2004). In addition, because cocaine users tend to use other illicit drugs, alcohol, and/or tobacco, it is difficult to differentiate the effects that are due specifically to cocaine (Frank et al., 2001).

Heroin

Heroin (and other narcotics such as morphine and codeine) crosses the placental barrier, and infants of mothers who use heroin are born addicted to the drug and undergo withdrawal (Yanai et al., 2000). Addicted newborns experience sleep disturbances, hyperactivity, convulsions, fever, sweating, vomiting, diarrhea, and even death. Heroin-exposed infants are small and have behavioral problems such as irritability and excessive crying. These effects are evident at four months after birth, but research has not consistently found narcotic effects on behavior after about one year of age (Fabris, Prandi, Perathoner, & Soldi, 1998).

Because drug-addicted parents expose their children to many risk factors, it is difficult to disentangle the effects due solely to prenatal exposure to the drug. In an interesting study, Wilson (1989) compared heroin-exposed infants with unexposed infants raised by addicted parents. Children's intelligence related to the home environment; those with the lowest IQs were those raised by addicted parents. Thus, the effects of prenatal drug exposure may be exacerbated by caregivers who continue to use drugs and tend to have disorganized and chaotic lifestyles (Eyler & Behnke, 1999).

Environmental Hazards

Lead, pesticides, radiation, and chemicals are environmental agents that may cross the placental barrier and affect the developing fetus. These environmental agents may be hazardous to people of any age and increase the risk of cancer later in life. However, they are particularly hazardous to prenatal development.

Radiation

Radiation is a powerful teratogen. Over 30 types of birth defects, many involving the central nervous system, have been related to prenatal exposure to high levels of radiation. The most common effects are microencephaly (abnormally small brain and skull) and mental retardation. The severity and type of effect depend on the amount of radiation received and on the timing of the exposure. Following World War II, Japanese women survivors who had been closest to the sites of the atomic bomb explosions and had received high levels of radiation gave birth to physically deformed and mentally retarded children (Otake & Schull, 1984). Although diagnostic X-ray procedures involve much less radiation, a risk for birth defects remains, especially for fetuses between 8 and 15 weeks of age (Cunningham et al., 2001).

Chemical Hazards

Every day we are surrounded by potentially dangerous chemicals in air, water, food, and the products we use. Unfortunately, pregnant women may not even be aware that they have been exposed to harmful chemicals. For example, in the 1950s, an industrial plant in Japan dumped mercury waste into the ocean, polluting the water and fish. Children born to mothers living nearby suffered severe retardation and irreversible physical and neurological impairments. Pregnant women often unknowingly expose their unborn children to high levels of lead, contained in paint, auto emissions, and coatings on blinds and shades; this is especially true for poor women (Rothenberg et al., 1999). Research now suggests that many common products, ranging from food preservatives to insecticides and even some cosmetics, pose risks to unborn children.

Maternal Conditions

In addition to biological and teratogenic factors that affect the developing child, characteristics of the mother can pose risks to the unborn child. A mother's physical, psychological, and social characteristics can affect the fetus by influencing her health or by altering the chemistry of her blood.

Maternal Age

More than ever before, women delay having their first child. As shown in Figure 4.8, birth rates have been dropping among women in their early 20s but increasing among women in their early 30s and early 40s—particularly Caucasian American and Asian American women (National Center for Health Statistics, 2003a). Today it is not uncommon for a woman to have her first child or start a second family after 40.

Pregnancy risks increase as the mother gets older (Reichman & Pagnini, 1997). Mothers over 35 are at increased risk for having a child

This 37-year-old woman is having her first child. What factors contribute to the increase in the number of older women starting families?

FIGURE 4.8

Changes in Birth Rates By Age and Race/Ethnicity of Mother

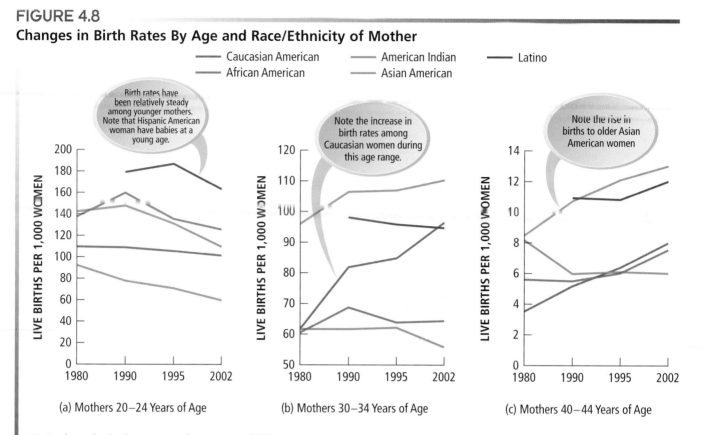

(a) Mothers 20–24 Years of Age

(b) Mothers 30–34 Years of Age

(c) Mothers 40–44 Years of Age

Notice how the birth rates vary for women of different races/ethnicities. For young mothers, birth rates have been dropping somewhat, although more Hispanic American women have babies at a young age than do women of other ethnicities. In both groups of older mothers, there are more Asian American women than women of other ethnicities. Changes over time are seen mainly for older Caucasian American and Asian American mothers. What factors have contributed to these changes in birth rates?

Note: Data for Hispanic mothers were not available until 1990.

Source: National Center for Health Statistics, 2001a, 2003a.

with Down syndrome. They also risk developing high blood pressure, gestational diabetes, and cardiovascular disease, all of which are usually controllable. Additionally, older mothers are somewhat more likely to miscarry (Astolfi & Zonta, 1999). When an older mother eliminates as many risk factors as possible and undergoes extensive prenatal testing, however, her chances of delivering a healthy newborn are virtually as good as those for a younger mother (Yagel et al., 1998).

Maternal Stress

A pregnant woman's psychological condition influences the health of her unborn child. Like any other major life transition, pregnancy and delivery produce a moderate amount of stress, as parents-to-be adjust to new demands and responsibilities. Stress can cause changes in the mother's blood chemistry. Research has shown that mothers who are stressed or emotionally upset produce hormones that cross the placental barrier and affect the fetus (Monk et al., 2000). Extreme and prolonged conditions of stress increase the risk for miscarriage, difficult labor and delivery, and prematurity (Glover, 1997).

Parity

Parity, or the number and spacing of children a woman bears, also affects prenatal development. Generally, a woman's endocrine system takes four years to return to prepregnancy condition (Cunningham et al., 2001). Infants born before the endocrine system recovers may be

parity   *the number and spacing of children a woman bears* at a disadvantage; a pregnancy within three months of delivery is classified as a high-risk pregnancy (Eisenberg et al., 1999). Infants conceived after the period of recuperation have a better prenatal environment than do firstborn children. Blood circulation is richer after a first pregnancy, and later-born children suffer fewer birth defects and complications. Furthermore, labor and delivery are quicker and less demanding for later-born children. However, the advantages of this enhanced prenatal environment are lost if later births follow too closely.

Protective Factors

Couples can increase their chances of delivering a healthy baby. Several important protective factors have been identified. Let's look at a few of these factors.

Nutrition

Good nutrition during pregnancy is essential. Proper nutrition and weight gain increase the likelihood of giving birth to a healthy baby (Cnattingius, Bergstrom, Lipworth, & Kramer, 1998). Women need not "eat for two"; usually a woman needs only about 300 additional calories (American College of Obstetricians and Gynecologists, 2000). Pregnant women have some special nutritional needs, though. To produce more blood, they need increased levels of iron, protein, and folic acid; to help fetal bones grow, they need more calcium and phosphorus. Ideally, women of average weight should gain approximately 30 pounds during pregnancy.

Even before they become pregnant, women should keep in mind the importance of good nutrition. For instance, in the early 1990s, researchers recognized that many birth defects could be prevented if women took folate, a B vitamin found in a variety of foods, both before and during the first weeks of pregnancy. During the early weeks of pregnancy, before women know they are pregnant, the neural tube is forming. If supplies of folate are insufficient, the child is at risk of developing two types of serious and common birth defects called neural tube defects. One defect is anencephaly, in which most or all of the brain tissue does not form. If the child is not stillborn, she or he will die shortly after birth. The other defect is spina bifida, in which the spinal column does not become fully enclosed. Spina bifida causes neurological problems and may cause mental retardation. Its effects range in severity; most children with this defect live into adulthood. Approximately 2,500 infants are born each year in the United States with neural tube defects, and about half of these cases are caused by inadequate folate intake by the mother (March of Dimes, 2004). The US Public Health Service recommends that all women of childbearing age consume 400 micrograms of folate daily to reduce their risk of having a child with neural defects. For pregnant women, the recommended amount is 800 micrograms daily. Folate is found in liver, dark leafy vegetables, broccoli, citrus fruits and juices, wheat germ, and dried beans and peas. Since 1998, folic acid has been added to breads and other grain products. Many multivitamins contain folate.

Exercise

Exercise also provides important benefits, especially to the mother and her well-being (Paisley, Joy, & Price, 2003). Regular exercise gives pregnant women more energy, builds bones and muscles, and generally improves health. It may also improve women's ability to cope with childbirth pain (American College of Obstetricians and Gynecologists, 2000).

Prenatal Care

One of the most important ways women can protect their unborn children is to have regular prenatal checkups, which can prevent complications or deal with them promptly and effectively. The number of women who receive prenatal care has steadily increased, and such care has been associated with lower rates of birth complications (March of Dimes, 2004). Unfortunately, not every woman receives adequate prenatal care.

Exercise is one way a woman can increase the chances of a health pregnancy and delivery. Can you identify other protective factors?

Social Support

Pregnancy is a family affair. A supportive and nurturing environment protects a pregnant woman and her unborn child by creating favorable conditions for them. Having a sympathetic partner, relatives, or friends helps minimize the negative effects of stress. Additionally, having a source of social support helps a woman deal with the physical demands or complications that arise during pregnancy.

Cultural Influences on Pregnancy

In every culture, reproduction and pregnancy are fundamental issues of human existence. Although reproduction and pregnancy are biological events that are similar all over the world, the experience and treatment of these events differ dramatically across cultures. In most Western cultures, pregnancy represents a major transition into adult life. Unlike marriage, pregnancy and birth are irreversible processes and mark a break from childhood (Fogel, 1997). But other cultures view pregnancy and birth differently. For example, West Africans view pregnancy as a divine gift, primarily signifying a couple's purity and strength (Nsamenang, 1992). Infertility among West African couples is interpreted as proof that the couple is being punished by their ancestors (Nsamenang, 1987). Most West Africans indicate that they would prefer to die in poverty and be survived by children than to die rich and childless (Nsamenang & Laosebikan, 1981).

Women's Responses

Culture also affects the impact of pregnancy and the changes it brings for the parents-to-be. The fact that responses to pregnancy differ across cultures and subcultures tells us that this biological condition is interpreted through the lens of cultural values and beliefs and institutions. In North America, many women become preoccupied with weight gain and physical appearance during the later stages of pregnancy because the culture values slenderness. North American women report feeling that they had lost control of their bodies and become embarrassingly conspicuous. Some pregnant women believe they look less attractive sexually and worry about being attractive to their partners (Fogel, 1997). In contrast, on the island of Yap in Micronesia, females are desired for their fertility, and the largeness of a pregnant woman is a symbol of her ability to produce children. In the Yap culture, the increased size associated with pregnancy is highly valued, so women do not worry about looking big during pregnancy (Lingenfelter, 1993).

Men's Responses

In the United States, men and women differ somewhat in their reactions to pregnancy. In one study, most mothers and fathers reported that they anticipated and were curious about the upcoming birth, but fathers expressed less anxiety and less pleasure about the pregnancy than did mothers. Mothers were more likely to say they talked to or loved the unborn child (Mercer et al., 1988). Some expectant fathers experience a sympathetic pregnancy, known by the French term *couvade*. During his partner's pregnancy, the father may suffer symptoms for which there is no recognized physiological basis, including increased or decreased appetite, weight gain, diarrhea or constipation, and headaches or toothaches. Onset is usually during the third gestational month, and the symptoms usually go away after childbirth (Holditch-Davis, Harris, Sandelowski, & Edwards, 1994). In most Western cultures, *couvade* is seen as an expression of anxiety about the pregnancy, ambivalence about being a father, or envy over the attention the expectant mother receives during her pregnancy (Klein, 1991).

Pregnancy and birth are biological events that occur similarly worldwide. However, the changes that occur during pregnancy and birth are viewed differently, depending on cultural expectations. In this photo, Australian Aboriginal women are performing a "baby smoking" ceremony. What might be the purpose of this ceremony?

In some non-Western cultures, *couvade* refers to a custom whereby expectant fathers identify with their mates and make sacrifices of their own during the pregnancy. In India, for example, when the wife of a Brahman becomes pregnant, the husband traditionally stops chewing betel palm leaves until his wife gives birth. In the Philippines, an expectant father stops eating sour fruit a week before the delivery to prevent the newborn from being born with stomach problems. An expectant father in the Ifugao tribe of the Philippines is not supposed to disturb his unborn child by cutting wood during his wife's pregnancy (Meltzer, 1981).

Unfortunately, not all men share the feelings of their pregnant partners. The likelihood of extramarital sex increases during pregnancy (Thorpe, Dragonas, & Golding, 1992), and about 1 in 6 pregnant adult women is physically abused by her partner (Parker, McFarlane, & Socken, 1994). Thus, in addition to cultural differences, there are individual differences in how men (and women and children) react to pregnancy (Clinton, 1986).

How Is a Baby Born?

For most individuals, the birth of a child into the family is an unforgettable and mysterious event, and family members continue to tell stories about the birth of their babies long after the children have grown up. Even children marvel at the birth of a baby and the early changes that occur. Most people's family and personal lifestyles are altered dramatically by the arrival of a newborn.

The birth of a child is a complex and exciting event. For approximately nine months, the expecting parents, family members, and friends anticipate the event. During that time, the unborn child has been developing in preparation for life outside the mother's womb. But even with nine months' notice, many expecting parents are caught off guard by the events associated with birth.

The Birth Process

When a woman finds out she is pregnant, her doctor will count 280 days from the first day of her last period and pronounce this to be her due date. Only about 3 percent of all women give birth on their due date, but over 45 percent give birth within one week before or after that date. Although most children are delivered from 37 and 41 weeks' gestation, a sizable number are delayed or arrive preterm, and the proportion is greater for minorities (especially African American children) than for Caucasians. Girls tend to be born a few days earlier than boys, and women who have shorter menstrual cycles tend to have shorter pregnancies, although the reasons for these differences are not clear (Jones, 1997).

One of the many unanswered questions surrounding childbirth is what causes it to begin. Much of our present understanding of how labor begins comes from observations of sheep. For some time, sheepherders in Idaho had noticed that pregnant ewes grazing in certain pastures failed to give birth on time. Looking for the causes of this delay, researchers discovered that the newborn lambs had underdeveloped adrenal and pituitary glands. These abnormalities occurred because the pregnant ewes were eating plants containing high levels of a chemical that crossed the placenta and harmed the glandular development of the fetus. As a result, the fetus secreted lower-than-normal levels of adrenal steroid hormones. Subsequent research confirmed that fetal steroids initiate labor. Injections of fetal hormones into pregnant ewes any time during the second half of their pregnancy resulted in early delivery (Nathanieisz, 1995).

Like the sheep, human newborns who are delivered early tend to have larger adrenal glands and those delivered late tend to have underdeveloped glands. However, the mother's body also may trigger labor by releasing prostaglandins, a group of fatty acids widely distributed throughout body tissues (Cunningham et al., 2001). Other evidence suggests that oxytocin, a hormone secreted by the mother's pituitary glands, stimulates uterine contractions and hastens labor. In fact, many women are given synthetic oxytocin (pitocin) to hasten labor contractions. Other evidence indicates that along with hormones, maturation of the placenta controls the onset of labor (Jones, 1997). The variety of possible causes of birth suggests that we still have much to learn about the factors that determine when birth occurs.

Women all over the world experience the same general biological changes associated with birth. About two to three weeks before birth, many women report that they suddenly can breathe more easily and feel more comfortable. This relief is referred to as **lightening** and occurs when the fetus drops into the pelvic cavity, decreasing pressure on the mother's diaphragm. In a few hours to a week before the onset of labor, the baby's head moves further down into the mother's pelvis in preparation for birth. The birth process is divided into three stages (see Figure 4.9): (1) dilation of the cervix, (2) birth of the baby, and (3) expulsion of the placenta, or "afterbirth." The first stage lasts the longest, but the length of each stage varies considerably from birth to birth. For mothers who are having their first child, the entire birth process usually lasts from 10 to 16 hours. The average length of time is shorter (6 to 11 hours) for women who have previously given birth. Any duration up to 24 hours is considered normal (Wong & Perry, 1998).

FIGURE 4.9
Childbirth

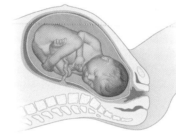
(1) The second stage of labor begins.

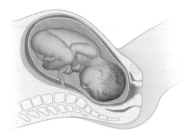
(2) Further descent and rotation.

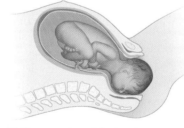
(3) The crowning of the head.

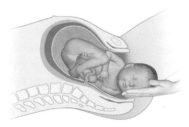
(4) Anterior shoulder delivered.

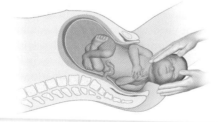
(5) Posterior shoulder delivered.

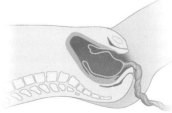
(6) The third stage of labor begins with separation of the placenta from the uterine wall.

lightening *sensation that occurs when the fetus drops into the pelvic cavity, decreasing pressure on the mother's diaphragm*

Although we do not know what causes birth to begin, the stages of birth have been clearly identified. Can you describe the different stages and what happens during each?

Source: McAnulty and Burnette, 2004.

- Women carrying twins, triplets, or other multiple fetuses

Women who are at risk have limited options because they must have the full range of support systems available in case of an emergency.

To provide couples with more choices in birthing methods, birthing centers have been developed. These centers provide an out-of-hospital, family-centered setting where labor and delivery are treated as normal life events to be shared with whomever the mother likes. Many centers encourage mothers to walk, eat, drink, and get into positions that are comfortable for them during labor and delivery. Certified nurse–midwives provide most of the care, but many centers have close connections with hospitals in case of an emergency. Only women with low-risk pregnancies are accepted at birthing centers.

Lamaze Childbirth

During World War II, Russian doctors were faced with a problem; they did not have any pain medication they could administer to women who were giving birth. To help these women through labor and delivery, they applied the principles of classical conditioning (see Chapter 2). Through breathing and muscular relaxation, they conditioned the women to respond positively to their contractions (Wong & Perry, 1998). These techniques were adopted by Dr. Fernand Lamaze and introduced around the world.

Lamaze classes usually involve six weekly sessions in which the participants prepare for birth by learning the following information:

- How the childbirth process works
- How to breathe during labor and delivery to control pain and discomfort
- How to focus on relaxing thoughts and feelings
- How fathers or other partners can help in labor and delivery

FIGURE 4.10

Historical Trends in the U.S. in Infant and Maternal Mortality

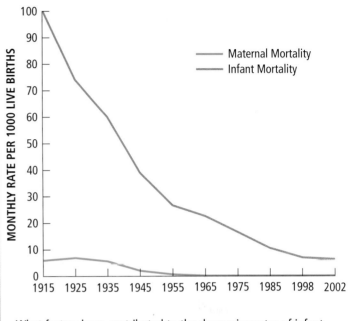

What factors have contributed to the decreasing rates of infant and maternal mortality in the United States?

Source: National Center for Health Statistics, 2001a, 2003b.

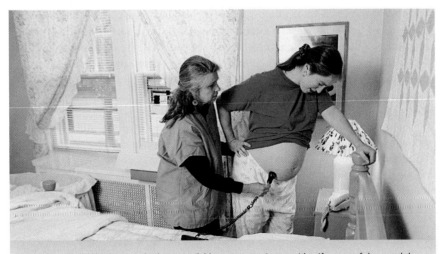

A wide variety of birthing methods are available to parents. Can you identify some of these and the alternatives they provide?

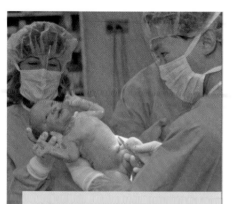

If there were potential complications with the birth of your child, would you lean toward choosing a cesarean section or waiting and trying alternative approaches?

TABLE 4.1

Conditions Most Commonly Associated with the Use of Cesarean Sections

1. Unfavorable shape of pelvis
2. Breech presentation
3. Placenta previa (placenta is attached near the opening of the cervix)
4. Cord prolapse (compressed or ruptured umbilical cord)
5. Fetal distress (significant increase or decrease in fetal heart rate)
6. Eclampsia (pregnancy-induced hypertension)
7. Prolonged labor
8. Diabetes

Source: Adapted from National Center for Health Statistics, 2001a.

cesarean section   *procedure by which the fetus is delivered through an incision in the mother's abdomen*

The goal of the classes is to help women manage the pain of labor and delivery and to maximize parents' enjoyment of the birth of their children.

Leboyer Method

A complementary birth approach was developed by Dr. Frederick Leboyer, a French physician. The focus of this technique is on the infant's, rather than the parents', birth experience. Leboyer developed techniques that minimize the infant's trauma of being born by mimicking the conditions of the mother's womb. The bright lights of the operating room are replaced with dim, indirect lighting; the temperature of the usually cool delivery room is raised so that it is closer to the mother's body temperature. After delivery and before the umbilical cord is cut, the naked infant is placed on the mother's bare belly, providing direct physical contact. The infant is then given a warm bath, in an effort to re-create the experience of the prenatal environment.

How well do the Lamaze and Leboyer methods meet their goals? The existing evidence is conflicting. Some research reports that when parents are Lamaze trained, mothers experience less pain and parents have more positive feelings about the birth experience (Leventhal, Leventhal, Shacham, & Easterling, 1989; Mackey, 1990). Other research fails to find such differences (Copstick, Taylor, Hayes, & Morris, 1986; Hodnett & Osborn, 1989). Part of the reason for these different findings is that parents are individuals with different needs and no program will consistently meet the needs of all parents. Some couples who try the Lamaze or the Leboyer childbirth technique do not succeed in having unmedicated births (Shute, 1997). When this happens, they often feel guilty for not being tough enough or angry because they were not told how much it would hurt.

Despite the conflicting evidence, it appears that alternative birthing techniques, if properly supervised, can be safe, enjoyable, and satisfying (Galotti, Pierce, Reimer, & Luckner, 2000). The best advice for parents-to-be is to choose a birth method carefully—obtain all available information on the method, just as you would when choosing a physician or hospital.

Birth Complications and Related Procedures

The experience of childbirth is usually positive for family members, as they celebrate the entry of a healthy newborn into the world. But childbirth can be stressful and frightening for some families. Many complications can occur during delivery.

Cesarean Sections

Most births involve the fetus descending through the mother's vagina, however, many do not. In a nonvaginal birth, known as a **cesarean section,** the fetus is delivered through an incision in the mother's abdomen. In general, a cesarean section is used whenever it is believed that further delay in delivery would seriously compromise the health of the fetus. Table 4.1 lists some of the conditions most commonly associated with cesarean sections.

Although the conditions for performing cesarean sections have not changed much in recent years, the number of cesarean sections performed in the United States has increased dramatically since the 1970s. Figure 4.11 shows that cesarean deliveries accounted for about 5 percent of all deliveries in 1970 but about 22 percent in 1999 (National Center for Health Statistics, 2001a). About 900,000 cesarean deliveries are performed each year in the United States, making it the most common type of major surgery performed. European rates are about one fourth to one half the US rates (Korte & Scaer, 1992).

Many factors account for the rise in cesarean births. By the 1960s, increasing emphasis was being placed on the health of the fetus. At the same time, advances in medical care had made cesarean deliveries safer to perform. As a safe alternative to normal deliveries, cesarean sections became a practical way to improve the outcome of difficult pregnancies. Another contributing factor was the rising number of repeat cesareans. More than 98 percent of women in the United States who have had a cesarean delivery undergo cesareans for subsequent pregnancies (National Center for Health Statistics, 2001a). Furthermore, doctors' concerns about being sued for malpractice, should something go wrong with the delivery, increased the likelihood that a cesarean section would be used at the slightest indication of fetal distress (Korte & Scaer, 1992).

In 95 percent of all births, the fetus is delivered in the head-down position. In about 4 percent of births, however, the fetus is positioned with buttocks or feet leading the way (National Center for Health Statistics, 2001a). This position is referred to as the **breech presentation.** Breech deliveries usually involve longer periods of labor but often occur with no difficulties. Sometimes, however, breech presentation requires cesarean delivery. In 1 out of 200 births, the fetus is positioned with shoulders and arms leading the way— known as the **transverse presentation.** In these cases, a cesarean delivery almost always is necessary (Cunningham et al., 2001).

Today most parents and doctors are urged to exercise caution in the use of cesarean sections, which represent major surgery. Compared to a normal delivery, it is costly, involves a longer recovery period, has a higher risk of infection, and may be more likely to make infants or their mothers ill (Haynes de Reght, Minkoff, Feldman, & Schwartz, 1986). Even women who have had previous cesarean sections can usually have subsequent vaginal deliveries. Alternative methods are available for dealing with fetal distress and prolonged labor, and these can be tried before moving forward with surgery. However, when the mother or her unborn child is at risk, complications can be avoided with early and aggressive surgical intervention.

Induced Labor

During some pregnancies, situations arise in which the prolongation of the pregnancy is not in the best interests of either the mother or the fetus. In these situations, labor may be induced. Almost 20 percent of women who delivered in 1999 had induced labor, twice the 1990 level. The rate of induction has increased every year since 1989 (National Center for Health Statistics, 2001a). Pitocin or other medications may be given to start labor and delivery. These drugs have been found to be effective (Prysak & Castronova, 1998), and studies show no higher chances that infants delivered after labor is induced will develop physical problems (Alexander, Bloom, McIntire, & Leveno, 1999). However, because labor may signal the maturity of the fetus, its absence may indicate that the fetus is not quite ready for life outside the mother's womb. Although there clearly are times when allowing a pregnancy to continue is dangerous for mother or child, decisions to induce labor must be made carefully.

How Is Childbirth Experienced?

Mothers, fathers, and newborns experience childbirth differently. As with all the major life events, the birth of a child has a lasting impact on the family, and mothers, fathers, and newborns each face a different set of challenges as they adjust to the changes brought about by birth.

FIGURE 4.11
Percentage of Cesarean Deliveries By Year

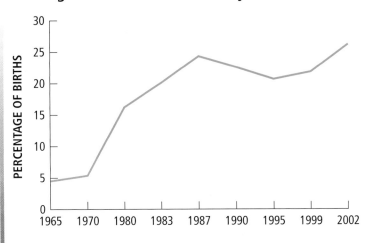

What factors have contributed to the increased rates of cesarean deliveries since 1970? What factors should a mother and her doctor consider before deciding on a cesarean delivery?

Source: Adapted from National Center for Health Statistics, 2001a, 2003a; Taffel, Placek, and Moien, 1989.

breech presentation *fetal position in which the buttocks or feet lead the way*

transverse presentation *fetal position in which the shoulders and arms lead the way*

Actress Brooke Shields suffered from postpartum depression. What factors contribute to these feelings of intense sadness and anxiety following childbirth?

The Mother's Perspective

The experience of birth is intense and mixed. Although having a baby is a joyous time for most women, many new mothers feel anxious, fragile, and overwhelmed after giving birth. The "baby blues" are not an inevitable part of having a baby, but they are very common, affecting about 70 to 80 percent of women giving birth. New mothers often cry unexpectedly and feel sad or angry without knowing why. A number of factors contribute to these blues, including the following (Eisenberg et al., 1999):

- *Biological changes:* The postpartum period is a time of great changes in a woman's body. Levels of female hormones drop sharply after childbirth.

- *Fatigue:* The strains of labor, delivery, and care of the newborn, combined with a loss of sleep, contribute to mothers' feelings of being overwhelmed and exhausted.

- *Loss of attention:* The baby takes center stage, and mothers no longer receive the attention they had while pregnant.

- *Increased demands at home:* New mothers may feel overwhelmed by the responsibilities at home, particularly if there are other children in the family.

- *Sense of anticlimax:* After the long pregnancy and all the excitement it generated, the "big event" may not live up to the mother's expectations.

- *Feelings of inadequacy:* Concern about her ability to care for the newborn may raise the mother's levels of confusion, guilt, and anxiety. In addition, changes in her physical appearance and body may raise the mother's doubts about her attractiveness.

For most mothers, these feelings usually begin a day or so after birth and peak three or four days later, but they rarely last more than a week or two and go away without the need for treatment. For actress Brooke Shields, known for her signature smile and upbeat attitude, the "blue" feelings associated with birth did not subside quickly or easily. For someone beautiful, talented, and living what seemed to be the picture-perfect life, what could go so wrong that would send her into a deep, troubling psychological state? In Shields's case, she was suffering from postpartum depression.

In contrast to the baby blues, **postpartum depression** is marked by intense feelings of sadness, anxiety, or despair that disrupt the new mother's ability to function and interact with her child (Epperson, 1999). Postpartum depression can affect the newborn child. In one study, newborns of mothers who experienced postpartum depression showed poor motor activity and were more irritable (Abrams, Field, Scafidi, & Prodromidis, 1995).

It is not known why some women become depressed after childbirth and others do not. One important factor is biology. Because some women are more sensitive to the biological changes that accompany birth, they may be more prone to postpartum depression. Stressful life events (unwanted pregnancy, single parenthood, lack of social support) and delivery complications also increase the chances of experiencing postpartum depression (Hagen, 1999; Logsdon, McBride, & Birkimer, 1994). Not surprisingly, lack of sleep and problems with the newborn's sleeping patterns are associated with this condition (Hiscock & Wake, 2001). If depression and anxiety do not go away and they begin to interfere with the mother's functioning, treatment may be needed (Charbol et al., 2002).

Research findings tell us that, all in all, it is common for mothers to experience a brief period of fear and anxiety after childbirth. Such feelings are quite common and do not mean that the new mother is a failure or mentally ill. For the most part, these feelings are the result of the changes, both physical and psychological, brought about by the birth of a child.

postpartum depression
intense feelings of sadness, anxiety, or despair experienced by a mother after the birth of a child

The Father's Perspective

Probably one of the most memorable moments with Jeremy was being able to be there for his birth and to hold him for the first time right after he was born. To cradle a newborn life in your arms that you know is yours and that you created—you really can't describe it. You don't want to put him down. You don't want to let him go. A lot of other experiences have come since then, but that has got to be one of the most enjoyable.

—Anonymous father's online story of the birth of his son

As this birth story reveals, for most contemporary fathers, experiencing the birth of a child does not mean pacing the hospital hallway with a pocketful of cigars to hand out as soon as word comes down. Today, many fathers take an active role in the birth process. In childbirth classes, fathers frequently serve as coaches for their partners, providing both physical and emotional support.

How a father experiences the birth of his child is strongly influenced by his emotional reactions and the degree to which he believes he is able to support his partner. Many men report that assisting in the birth of their child was a wonderful experience but at the same time made them feel helpless, particularly in dealing with their partner's labor. The more involved fathers become in the birth process, the more often they report feelings of closeness to their spouse and to their newborn child (Doherty, 1997).

Notice how comfortable the father in this photo appears to be in holding his newborn and how alert the baby is. How do fathers experience birth? How has fathers' experience of birth changed in the past 50 years?

Compared with fathers of the past, today's fathers show a high level of expectation of participating in the care of newborns and a high degree of confidence in their ability to do so (Fox, Bruce, & Combs-Orne, 2000). Even before they become fathers, men have considerable expectations about fatherhood. In one study (Marsiglio, Hutchinson, & Cohan, 2000), men who were not yet fathers were asked about their perceptions of becoming a father. Most of the men were receptive to the idea (fatherhood readiness) and had relatively clear visions of what to expect once they became fathers (fatherhood visions).

Having a baby has a significant effect on fathers' concepts of themselves. In a classic study in which new fathers were compared to men who were not yet fathers, Cowan and colleagues (1985) found that several aspects of the new fathers' self-concepts changed in the direction of becoming more mature. These new fathers described themselves as being more aware of their personal relationships and using more tact and skill in managing family problems. Additionally, new fathers place more importance on their role as father and less on their role as spouse (Strauss & Goldberg, 1999). Of course, not all fathers "mature"—some regress, becoming jealous over the loss of attention and freedom, and some suffer from a type of postpartum depression (Antonucci & Mikus, 1988). Men's interactions with their partners and other family members significantly contribute to their perceptions of themselves as fathers and influence how they respond to the birth of a child (Marsiglio et al., 2000). Thus, men's attitudes and beliefs about fatherhood are influenced by those individuals who are most meaningful in their lives.

The father's involvement in the birth also influences how mothers feel about the experience. Fathers who are supportive during labor and birth have partners who are less anxious and distressed and are not as likely to need medication (Biller, 1993). Although the determinants of a father's level of involvement in the birth process and with his very young child are complex, fathers with greater psychological, social, and economic resources tend to be more involved and more satisfied with their involvement (Daly, 1993; Woodworth, Belsky, & Crnic, 1996).

FIGURE 4.12

Comparison of Stress Hormone Levels

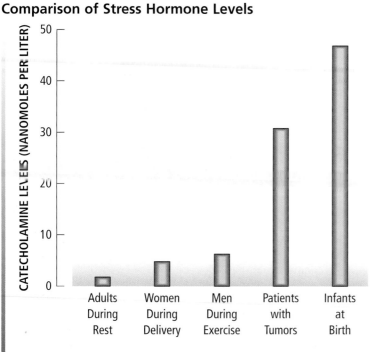

Why are stress hormone levels so high at birth? Notice that women giving birth have relatively low stress hormone levels.

Source: Adapted from Lagercrantz and Slotkin, 1986.

The Newborn's Perspective

How does the newborn experience birth? Most of us would imagine that birth is a gruelling and frightening experience. The baby is squeezed through the birth canal for several hours, during which time his or her head is compressed and put under considerable pressure. Then the baby is delivered from the warm, moist, and protected environment of the womb into a bright, loud, and chaotic world. As Figure 4.12 shows, newborns produce "stress" hormones, called *catecholamines,* at levels 20 times higher than those found in adults—levels higher even than those found in adults who have serious medical conditions (Lagercrantz & Slotkin, 1986).

Despite these conditions, the stress of a normal delivery usually is not harmful (Gunnar, 1989). Evidence suggests that the fetus is well equipped to withstand this stress and that the chemicals produced by the stress may prepare the newborn to survive outside the mother's womb. For example, the surge in stress hormones helps clear the newborn's lungs and promotes normal breathing. Additionally, the surge in hormones increases the newborn's metabolism and energy supply (Slotkin, Kudlacz, Hou, & Seidler, 1990). One result is that the newborn is born alert and aroused. By causing this alertness, the hormonal surge may promote the development of emotional

ties between parents and their newborn during the first hours of life (Slotkin & Seidler, 1989). Birth by cesarean section does not lead to the surge in stress hormones, raising another concern about the overuse of this procedure.

Cultural Differences in the Experience of Childbirth

Societies have unique responses to the event of birth, based on their beliefs, values, and customs. Even labor and labor pain vary from culture to culture, as do women's physiological reactions to childbirth (Mander, 2000; Scopesi, Zanobini, & Carossino, 1997). In the United States, birth generally is considered a very private affair, with only a few people involved. Until recently, this meant that mothers went through almost the entire birth process in the presence of only medical personnel. Only in the past 20 years or so have fathers and other close family members or friends attended births. At the other extreme, the Jahara of South America believe that the birth of a child is an event of interest to the entire community. They celebrate birth as a public event—mothers give birth under a shelter and in full view of the entire village, even small children (Fogel, 1997).

In Holland, midwives play a much greater role in childbirth than they do in the United States. In fact, midwives in Holland are part of the medical establishment and have belonged to the medical profession since 1972, along with general practitioners, dentists, pharmacists, and obstetricians. Midwifery training in Holland has always been of very high quality, with strict criteria for entry into the profession. These criteria have given midwives a more professional status than they have in the United States. This status is reflected in the Dutch word for *midwife,* which means "wise woman" (Smulders, 1999).

In developing countries, about two thirds of all births take place outside of health care facilities. In almost half of the births, mothers deliver alone or are attended by untrained traditional birth attendants or family members. A wide variety of traditional beliefs is associated with birth. For example, in many countries, people believe that all life from the pla-

NURTURING CHILDREN
BONDING AT BIRTH

When mothers and newborns spend time together right after birth, do they create a special bond that then helps the baby develop? Conversely, are children who are deprived of early bonding, because they were adopted or sick, at risk for later developmental problems or even child abuse? These questions arose in the 1960s, after two decades during which mothers generally gave birth in cold and sterile hospital rooms, usually after taking pain medications that decreased their awareness of the birth process. Once the baby was born, she or he was whisked away to a nursery. Every four hours or so during the four or five days that mother and child stayed in the hospital, a nurse would bring in the baby for Mom to feed. Thus, early contact between mother and child was limited.

Because of their concerns about these childbirth procedures, researchers in the 1970s (Klaus, Kennell, Plumb, & Zeuhlke, 1970) compared mothers and newborns who went through this typical procedure to a group of mothers and newborns who had extended contact immediately after birth. After one month, the mothers with extended contact were more likely to be responsive to their newborns. Based on these results, it was proposed that a sensitive period immediately follows birth, during which mothers and infants can bond through close physical contact. When bonding is interrupted, parenting failures are more likely, and the child is at greater risk for abuse, neglect, and poor parenting.

As a result of these findings, many positive changes have occurred in birthing practices, such as allowing babies to room in with their mothers. Although the scientific basis for bonding has not held up over time (Goldberg, 1983; Myers, 1984), for mothers who may be at risk for developing poor relationships with their newborns, having extra time with their infants may promote healthy interactions (Perusse, Neale, Heath, & Eaves, 1994).

No one denies the importance of parents' and infants' spending time together. Establishing a healthy parent–child relationship has many phases; spending the first minutes or hours together may be one of them. If parents miss this first step, they still have many other opportunities to develop healthy parent–child relationships. There is no evidence of a critical period for human bonding—success or failure in the parent–child relationship does not hinge on a few brief moments in time (Goldberg, 1983). The emotional tie between infants and their significant caregivers develops over a long period of time and does not depend only on early interactions.

centa must be transferred to the newborn; otherwise, the baby may die. Therefore, the cord is cut only after pulsations stop or after the delivery of the placenta. In some areas, the cord is milked, especially if the baby is not breathing, in order to bring the baby's soul back from the mother (World Health Organization, 1999).

In Turkey, after a mother gives birth, she receives presents of gold and the child receives various gifts. The mother is not supposed to go out from her house for 40 days. If she works, she has a holiday of 40 days automatically. Relatives, friends, and neighbors are all helpful. During the first three days, only close relatives come to visit; but in the following days, others come also, bearing presents. In Anatolia (the peninsula of land that constitutes the Asiatic portion of Turkey), there is a custom of planting trees in the names of newly born children. Chestnut, mulberry, or apple trees are planted for girls, poplar or pine trees for boys. Planting trees is a kind of investment for them, as the trees can be used in negotiating their marriages when they grow up (Yenen, 1997).

In many cultures, specific ceremonies surrounding birth reflect the traditions and values of the culture. Morris Opler (1995) describes one interesting example of such a ceremony for children born into the Jicarilla Apache Indian tribe. This event usually is conducted within four days of birth, to bond the child both to the family and to protective supernatural powers. Called "water has been put on the top of his head," the ceremony marks the first time water touches the baby. Only water mixed from sacred "male" and "female" rivers is used. The newborn is bathed in the sacred water, and songs are sung. The parents' and siblings' faces are painted with red ochre. This face painting is like a prayer and is considered a blessing in Jicarilla culture. When all have been painted, the singer presents the newborn to the father, saying, "This is your baby." This announcement publicly establishes the sacred obligation of the father to his newborn child and his mate. The father then gives the baby to the mother.

Birth rituals and traditions illustrate how one's culture attributes meaning to birth. Because birth is such a powerful and profound event in most people's lives, many customs

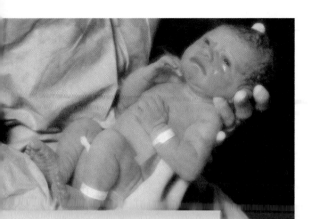

Newborns look different than those you see on television. Can you describe the general physical appearance of a newborn?

have developed that link it to the fabric of culture. These customs signify that birth is a social as well as a physical event and highlight the significance a culture places on bringing forth new life. Perhaps the remarkable thing is the ability of parents and newborns to adapt to the diversity of rituals different cultures prescribe.

What Are the Characteristics of a Newborn?

The adjustments a newborn must make to a new world are complex and demanding. After nine months as a protected and dependent being inside the mother's womb, the newborn must adapt to life outside. The term **neonate** refers to infants who are making this adjustment—usually within their first one to two months. To survive, newborns must accomplish four major tasks:

■ *Breathing on their own:* The newborn's first challenge is to obtain the oxygen necessary for survival. To do this, the infant must switch from relying on oxygen provided by the blood in the umbilical cord to breathing on his or her own. A newborn's mouth and nose are filled with fluid before birth, and this fluid must be drained and the airways opened for breathing. Childbirth itself forces some of the fluid out during the tight squeeze through the birth canal. The doctor or nurse clears out the remaining fluid to help the baby breathe.

■ *Changing blood circulation:* The infant's circulation pattern must also change to allow for breathing. Before birth, the placenta supports the infant. When the link to the mother is severed, circulation changes so that blood flows, for the first time, to the lungs. This change shifts the pressure of blood in the heart, which then changes the direction of blood flow. This is why newborns have irregular heartbeats and unstable blood pressure.

■ *Controlling body temperature:* Unlike the uterine environment, which has a steady, warm temperature, the environment outside the womb is susceptible to extreme changes in temperature. To survive, infants must control their body temperature and adjust to shifting temperatures.

■ *Ingesting food:* During prenatal development, the fetus obtains nutrients through the placenta. After birth, the newborn must obtain nourishment in a different way—through the mouth. Normally, infants quickly adapt to oral feeding because they are capable of sucking when they are born and their digestive systems are developed enough to process the nutrients they need.

Physical Appearance

Many parents are surprised by the appearance of their newborn child—he or she does not look like the babies they've seen on television! Newborns on average range in length from 19 to 21 inches, and their length at birth depends more on the size of the mother's uterus than on genetic inheritance. This is why a small mother can carry the child of a very large father. The average weight for newborns is 7 to 7½ pounds. After a vaginal delivery, the baby's head often is misshapen, the face swollen, and the nose flattened from the pressures of moving through the birth canal. The newborn also may be covered in a white, waxy covering, called the **vernix caseosa,** which provides protection from bacteria. Many infants have uneven coloring, often having bluish or grayish fingers, nose, and feet as a result of poor blood circulation. Because of the presence of maternal hormones, the newborn may have enlarged genitalia.

She had microscopic fingernails, a scrawny, funny ducktail hairdo, and tiny replicas of a wizened old man's hands She had weighed six pounds, fifteen ounces at birth, and had been twenty-one-and-one-half inches long. I leaned over and started whispering

neonate   *an infant who is in the first one to two months of life*

vernix caseosa   *a white, waxy covering that provides the newborn child with protection from bacteria*

TABLE 4.2
Apgar Scoring System

SIGN	0 RATING	1 RATING	2 RATING
Heart rate	Absent	Slow (below 100)	Over 100
Respiration	Absent	Slow and irregular	Good, crying
Skin color	Blue or pale	Extremities blue, trunk pink	Completely pink
Muscle tone	Limp	Some flexion of extremities	Active movements
Reflex response	No response	Grimace	Vigorous crying

Source: Adapted from Apgar, 1953.

to her and stroking her head. She looked up at me and I kept whispering, Amazing. Forty-eight hours ago she hadn't even been born. (Greene, 1984, pp. 11–12)

Like most new parents, Bob Greene began his assessment of his newborn with a quick examination of her size, fingers, and head. Medical personnel also do a quick examination of the general well-being of the infant, to determine whether any type of emergency intervention is needed. The most commonly used procedure was developed by an anesthesiologist, Dr. Virginia Apgar. The **Apgar Scale** is a simple and effective method of diagnosing potential problems in full-term and preterm newborns (Hegyi et al., 1998). At 1 minute and 5 minutes after birth, the baby is examined for five vital signs: respiration, reflex responsiveness, muscle tone, color, and heart rate (see Table 4.2).

To test her new system, Dr. Apgar attended hundreds of births and meticulously recorded her findings. Newborns who scored from 8 to 10 usually emerged from the birth canal with a lusty cry and adjusted on their own. Babies who scored from 4 to 7 needed help or close observation until their scores improved. Those who scored from 0 to 3 were limp and unresponsive. To survive, they needed CPR. For example, a child who has been oxygen deprived during labor and delivery is likely to have blue- or gray-colored skin, may have arms and legs that droop because of lack of muscle tone, and may not be breathing immediately after birth. Fortunately, only 1.4 percent of newborns have Apgar scores of less than 7, although the rate is twice as high for African American babies as it is for Caucasian babies (2.4 versus 1.2 percent; National Center for Health Statistics, 2001a).

Behavioral Assessment of Neonates

A neonate's behavior provides insight into his or her development and health. For this reason, many instruments have been developed to assess their behavior. The most widely used instrument is the **Neonatal Behavioral Assessment Scale,** developed by a pediatrician, Dr. T. Berry Brazelton, to measure a newborn's responses to the environment, especially reactions to others. The assessment is conducted with simple equipment by a trained examiner, who reviews the newborn's reflexes, motor capabilities, abilities to control attention and behavior, and responses to interaction with others. For instance, to assess cuddliness, the examiner holds the baby close and assesses to what extent the baby relaxes or curls up to cuddle. To assess self-quieting abilities, the examiner observes the actions a baby takes after he or she has become fussy: does the baby suck his or her thumb to settle down?

The scale is used to identify newborns who have difficulties adjusting to their new environment outside the womb. After difficulties are identified, appropriate interventions can be developed. For instance, a neonate with impaired brain development may be hypersensitive to stimulation and react in a disorganized manner. Better control over the kinds of stimulation the infant receives may help the baby develop the ability to organize responses to the environment. The scale provides useful information even for infants who are not at

Apgar Scale *a method of diagnosing potential problems in newborns, in which five vital signs are examined: respiration, reflex responsiveness, muscle tone, color, and heart rate*

Neonatal Behavioral Assessment Scale *a measure commonly used to assess a newborn's responses to the environment*

FIGURE 4.13

Low-Birthweight and Preterm Births, by Race/Ethnicity

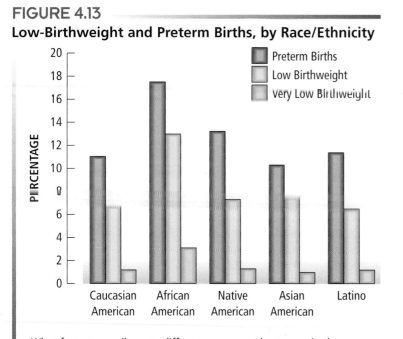

What factors contribute to differences among the groups in the percentages of low-birthweight and preterm births?

Source: Adapted from National Center for Health Statistics, 2003a.

risk because it helps identify each baby's capacity for receiving and using stimulation from the environment (Brazelton, Nugent, & Lester, 1987).

Why Are Some Newborns at Risk?

Although most babies are born healthy, some newborns face risky health situations right from the start. For example, children who are born too early or too small may have difficulty making the adjustment from the prenatal environment to the postnatal world. An important distinction is made between infants who are **preterm** (or **premature**)—those born prior to 37 weeks' gestation—and infants who have **low birthweight**—those born after 37 weeks' gestation but weighing less than 5 pounds. Low birthweight usually is a more significant risk factor than prematurity, accounting for 75 percent of poor postnatal outcomes (Fanaroff, Martin, & Miller, 1994). Prematurity is a risk factor largely because of the many disabilities often associated with it (Allen, 1993). A baby born at 30 weeks takes 8 weeks to reach the same developmental level as a baby born at 38 weeks. The combination of being both preterm and of low birthweight places a newborn at the greatest risk for negative outcomes (Bardin, Zelkowitz, & Papageorgious, 1997).

Rates of low-birthweight and premature babies vary by racial/ethnic group (National Center for Health Statistics, 2003). As depicted in Figure 4.13, African American mothers have a higher incidence of low-birthweight, very low birthweight (less than 3.3 pounds), and premature deliveries than any other ethnic group. The reason for this difference is unclear, but some factors that increase its likelihood among African Americans seem not to affect other ethnic groups, even other minority groups. A list of the factors that place a newborn at risk for poor developmental outcomes appears in Table 4.3.

Over the past decade, annual rates of preterm births in the United States have increased almost 14 percent, from 10.2 to 11.6 percent of all births. The current preterm birth rate is over 50 percent higher than the Healthy People 2010 objective set by the US Department of Health and Human Services. Had the target been attained, more than 150,000 of the over 540,000 cases of prematurity that year would have been prevented. About 23,000 of the preterm infants born in 1999 were born two to three months premature and weighed less than 1,000 grams (2.3 pounds). These infants are referred to as "kilogram kids," and they spend their first few months fighting for their lives. In the past, virtually all of these newborns died. More recently, almost 9 out of every 10 infants who weigh less than 500 grams at birth do not live, whereas about 75 percent of those who weigh 1,000 grams survive (National Center for Health Statistics, 2001a). However, poor postnatal development remains a concern, particularly for those weighing less than 600 grams (Lemons et al., 2001).

Prematurity and low birthweight interact with cultural and social variations in caregiving environments to influence children's developmental outcomes. For instance, Bradley and colleagues (1994) found that the percentage of low-birthweight children living in poverty who were adaptive and resilient was very low (about 10 percent). This percentage is considerably lower than the 40 percent of preterm children from more affluent, non-poverty households who were adaptive and resilient. These findings are particularly noteworthy given that the researchers did not include children with serious chronic medical problems (such as cerebral palsy). The odds that a premature, low-birthweight child living

preterm or **premature**   *term describing infants born prior to 37 weeks' gestation*

low birthweight   *term describing infants born after 37 weeks' gestation but weighing less than 5½ pounds*

TABLE 4.3
Factors That Place Newborns at Risk for Poor Developmental Outcomes

BIOLOGICAL RISK FACTORS	ENVIRONMENTAL RISK FACTORS
Prematurity	Poverty/unemployment
Intracranial hemorrhage	No medical insurance
Growth retardation	Teenage mother
Brain abnormalities	Mental retardation or emotional disturbance in parent or caregiver
Biochemical abnormalities	Substance abuse by caregiver
Infections	History of child abuse or neglect in family
Lung disease	Family dysfunction
Neonatal seizures	Lack of parenting skills
Maternal substance abuse during pregnancy	Parent–child separation (divorce, maternal incarceration)

Source: Adapted from Allen, 1993.

in poverty will show early evidence of the ability to tolerate adverse conditions are "for all practical purposes, nil" (Bradley et al., 1994, p. 357). These findings provide evidence that certain environmental conditions, such as poverty, can increase the vulnerability of an already vulnerable child (Fang, Madhavan, & Alderman, 1999).

Consequences of Low Birthweight and Prematurity

Most infants who are born too early or weigh too little at birth develop normally and become healthy, thriving children. The positive outcomes for many of these children relate to the plasticity of an infant's nervous system, which recovers from trauma more quickly and easily than an adult's nervous system does. Nonetheless, as a group, these infants are more likely to show a variety of physical problems, including the following (Hack, Klein, & Taylor, 1995):

- Subnormal growth
- Mental retardation
- Blindness
- Deafness
- Cerebral palsy (a brain disorder involving loss of control over motor functions)
- Health problems (asthma, kidney dysfunction, diabetes)

The smallest infants are at a higher risk for having low intelligence scores and deficits in cognitive abilities when they grow up, even when neurological and social risk factors are taken into account (Doussard-Roosevelt et al., 1997). Very low birthweight babies (weighing less than 3.3 pounds) are particularly at risk for problems in specific areas, such as memory and fine motor skills, with verbal abilities being less impaired (Hack, Taylor, Klein, & Eiben, 1994; Schothorst & van Engeland, 1996). Low-birthweight babies also have more difficulties in school, and the number of difficulties seems to increase as the weight of the child at birth decreases. Very low birthweight children are particularly vulnerable to problems in mathematics and specific learning disabilities (Koller et al., 1997; Taylor, Klein, & Hack, 1994); in addition, they have an increased risk of needing special education classes (Hack et al., 1995). Very low birthweight children who are premature show the greatest impairments in intelligence, motor performance, and attention (Korkman, Liikanen, & Fellman, 1996).

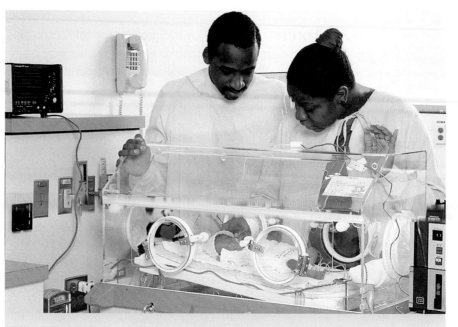

Notice that this infant is in an incubator, which helps keep him warm. How has technology improved the survival chances of newborns needing intensive care? What ethical issues does this technology raise?

Very low birthweight children also may have more behavior problems than other children do, and the lower the birthweight, the more problems reported (McCormick, Gortmaker, & Sobol, 1990). The problems include hyperactivity, poor social skills, and conduct disorders (Young, 1996).

Neonatal Intensive Care

Most preterm newborns with developmental problems are put in a neonatal intensive care unit. The first step is to stabilize the newborn's body temperature and place her or him in an isolette to prevent loss of warmth. If respiratory problems are evident, the newborn is given oxygen. Heart, respiration, and other vital signs are closely monitored. Treatment for apnea or infection is given. After the infant is stabilized, she or he can be moved to an intermediate-level care facility. Upon reaching 5½ pounds, babies graduate from their special care facilities and can go home.

Approximately 2 to 9 percent of newborns require intensive care, and most of these are very low birthweight infants (Hack et al., 1995; Widerstrom, Mowder, & Sandall, 1991). Most of these newborns spend 15–50 days receiving special care in the neonatal intensive care unit, with the longest stays for the lightest babies (Gottfried, 1985). Changes in medical care, especially neonatal intensive care, have dramatically improved the survival rates for very low birthweight infants (Hobar & Lucey, 1995).

Not long ago, newborns in intensive care units experienced the frantic pace of hospital life and continuous monitoring, without their special developmental needs or their families' needs taken into account (Young, 1996). Today medical personnel are more sensitive to these newborns' special requirements and attempt to provide a setting that mimics the conditions of the prenatal environment. Lights are turned down, infants are swaddled in hammocks, and medical personnel know when to encourage or limit interactions with the infants. Most important, parents are encouraged to be involved in their infant's care (Gottwald & Thurman, 1990). Breast-feeding and supplemental touching and caressing appear to be particularly valuable for premature and low-birthweight babies (Bier et al., 1997; Browne, 2000). These interventions effectively shorten the length of the premature infant's stay in intensive care.

FROM RESEARCH TO PRACTICE
RISK AND PROTECTIVE FACTORS IN THE LONG-TERM EFFECTS OF PRENATAL ALCOHOL EXPOSURE

FROM RESEARCH . . .

Researchers have shown that high rates of prenatal alcohol exposure are related to long-term problem behaviors and outcomes. For example, prenatal alcohol exposure has been found to be significantly associated with alcohol problems at 21 years of age (Baer et al., 2003). However, not all children develop such problems, and we know little about the risk and protective factors that exaggerate or limit such adverse life outcomes.

To address this issue, researchers have examined how social factors influence the effects of prenatal alcohol exposure. In one such study (Streissguth et al., 2004), over 400 patients enrolled in a fetal alcohol follow-up study. All of the participants had been diagnosed with FAS and were between 6 and 51 years of age when the study took place. Based on interviews with the patients and/or parents, the adverse life outcomes (such as expulsion from school, trouble with the law, alcohol/drug problems, etc.) and risk/protective factors (such as experience of abuse and neglect, percentage of life spent in a stable, nurturing home, IQ, etc.) were identified.

The results revealed that patients in the study generally had a lifetime of adverse life outcomes that supports the poor long-term prognosis for individuals exposed to high prenatal levels of alcohol. For example, from childhood to adulthood, inappropriate sexual behavior (exposing oneself, promiscuity, etc.) was the most frequent adverse problem behavior identified. Problems with alcohol or drug use, disrupted school experiences, legal or psychiatric confinement, and trouble with the law increased dramatically from childhood into adolescence and adulthood.

Significantly, this study also identified some risk and protective factors that increased or reduced the likelihood that patients experienced adverse outcomes. For example, growing up in a stable, nurturing household decreased the odds of problem outcomes whereas being a victim of abuse increased the odds of problems later in life. One of the strongest predictors of adverse outcomes was a late diagnosis: the longer the delay in receiving the diagnosis, the greater the odds of adverse outcomes.

. . . TO PRACTICE

These findings reveal the importance of the social environment in determining the degree of adverse outcomes for those exposed to high prenatal levels of alcohol. Stable and nurturing family environments promote positive adaptive behaviors, and such family situations also increase the chances that medical help will be sought—increasing the chances of an early diagnosis. These factors help reduce the long-term problems associated with prenatal alcohol exposure and provide a strategy for working with this at-risk group: interventions for these children need to target the entire family.

THINKING IT THROUGH

1. By definition, mothers who expose their unborn children to high levels of alcohol have a problem with alcohol abuse. How does alcohol abuse affect a mother's ability to parent and help her vulnerable child?

2. How might stable and nuturing families improve the quality of life for children who were exposed to high levels of prenatal alcohol?

3. Can you identify other risk or protective factors that might influence the effects of prenatal alcohol exposure?

Caregiving and High-Risk Infants

Even in the best of circumstances, adjusting to the birth of a child is difficult and stressful for parents and other family members. Adjusting to the birth of a high-risk infant means additional emotional, psychological, and physical challenges. Seeing an infant in an intensive care unit can be frightening and overwhelming, and parents often are not prepared for this experience. Preterm and very low birthweight babies look different from healthy, full-term babies; the tubes, machines, and isolettes appear foreign and unsettling to most parents (Fleming et al., 1994; Singer et al., 1999). Even in well-functioning families, parents who give birth to fragile children experience chronic or recurrent stress (Clubb, 1991; DeMier et al., 2000).

Once a high-risk infant is taken home, the family faces many new challenges. The baby may have short-term health care needs, such as a need for someone to monitor apnea episodes, or long-term needs, such as a need for a ventilator. High-risk newborns require a great deal of parents' time and energy, and many parents report that family life deteriorates: spouses have less time for each other, and parents have less time to attend to the needs of their other children (Diehl, Moffitt, & Wade, 1991). Family functioning also can be affected by financial concerns, which mount as the care for the fragile child continues. For families with high-risk infants, problems with finances are a common source of stress (Wegener & Aday, 1989).

In interactions with their parents, preterm infants are less responsive, alert, and active than their full-term peers are. Yet parents of preterm infants take a more active role in interactions than parents of full-term infants do (Goldberg & DiVitto, 1995). For example, parents of preterm infants stay closer, hold and touch the infant more, and provide more stimulation. These findings suggest that parents of a preterm infant sometimes compensate for the low responsiveness of their infant by taking more direct action to engage the infant. This provides a basis for secure parent–infant relationships as the preterm infant gets older and healthier. Nonetheless, parents of very low birthweight infants or preterm infants who have a lasting illness (such as a heart defect) are more likely to have difficulties establishing secure relationships with their newborn (Feldman et al., 1999; Plunkett et al., 1986).

Try It Out

1. Interview a woman who is pregnant with her first baby. Ask her how she feels about the pregnancy. How does she feel about her own physical and emotional condition? Are any of her concerns based on cultural beliefs and attitudes? To what extent does she engage in behaviors that promote healthy development of the unborn child? What concerns does she express about the health of the baby? After your interview, consider what conditions in the baby's total environment might influence prenatal development.

2. How have birthing practices changed over time? Talk to your parents and their friends about their childbirth experiences, and compare them to those of parents who have given birth within the last ten years. What changes have occurred in attitudes, practices, and technology? How have these changes altered the experience of childbirth? What type of birth method would you choose? Why?

3. Re-read the section on low-birthweight and at-risk newborns. Consider the impact that having an at-risk baby would have on a family. Try thinking about how parents' expectations of having a healthy, cuddly baby would contribute to the difficulties of dealing with an at-risk newborn. What factors might influence how parents respond to this situation and how they cope with the demands of caring for a fragile baby?

Key Terms and Concepts

age of viability (94)	cesarean section (112)
amnion (91)	chorion (93)
Apgar Scale (119)	crowning (110)
Braxton-Hicks contractions (109)	ectopic pregnancy (91)
breech presentation (113)	embryonic stage (89)
cephalocaudal development (94)	epidural block (109)

episiotomy (110)

false labor (109)

fetal alcohol effects (FAE) (99)

fetal alcohol syndrome (FAS) (99)

fetal stage (90)

germinal stage (89)

lightening (108)

low birthweight (120)

molding (110)

Neonatal Behavioral Assessment
   Scale (119)

neonate (118)

parity (104)

placenta (93)

placental barrier (96)

postpartum depression (114)

premature (120)

preterm (120)

proximodistal development (94)

quickening (94)

teratogens (96)

transverse presentation (113)

umbilical cord (93)

vernix caseosa (118)

zygote (90)

Sum It Up

How does prenatal development proceed?

■   What goes on during the germinal stage of prenatal development? (p. 89)

■   What is the age of viability of a fetus? (p. 94)

What conditions influence pregnancy and prenatal development?

■   What is a teratogen? What can influence its effects? (p. 96)

■   Which infectious diseases can seriously affect the health and well-being of the developing child? (p. 97)

■   What are some other major potential hazards to mother and fetus? (pp. 98–104)

How is a baby born?

■   What are some common birthing methods? (pp. 110–112)

■   What can be done when birth complications occur? (pp. 112–113)

How is childbirth experienced?

■   What are some of the mother's positive and negative experiences of childbirth? (p. 114)

■   What can influence the father's experience of the event? (p. 115)

What are the characteristics of a newborn?

■   What four tasks must newborns accomplish in order to survive? (p. 118)

Why are some newborns at risk?

■   What are some of the consequences of low birthweight and prematurity? (p. 121)

.17 in.	1.25 in.	3–4 in.	6.5–7 in.	10–11 in.
0 g	1 g	28 g	113 g (4 oz)	227–454 g (.5–1 lb)
Backbone and vertebrae form. Primitive heart forms and starts to beat. Arm and leg buds form. Embryo is not yet distinguishable as human.	Bone cells appear. Arms and legs become distinct. Fingers and toes form. Major blood vessels form. Internal organs continue to develop.	Eyes form, but eyelids are fused shut. Ears form. Arms and legs are fully formed. Heartbeat can be detected. External genitalia develop. Fingernails and toenails form.	Head is large relative to rest of body. Face takes on human features. Movements may be detected by mother.	Head and body hair are visible. Head is less disproportionate to rest of body. Brain develops rapidly. Periods of sleep alternate with periods of alertness.
1 month	2 months	3 months	4 months	5 months

FIGURE 4.3 **Milestones and Characteristics of Prenatal Development**

PRENATAL DEVELOPMENT

From the moment of fertilization, dramatic and complex changes occur. Early in prenatal development, the basic structures and organs form. Later in prenatal development, elaboration and refinement of these basic structures and organs take place. At all stages of prenatal development, the developing child is susceptible to teratogenic influences. Regular and early checkups, healthy eating and lifestyle, and avoidance of toxic environments can increase the odds of sustaining a healthy pregnancy. (Refer back to pages 89–107.)

CHILDBIRTH

The birth of a child usually is a joyous and memorable event. The factors that trigger birth remain unclear, but the birth process involves three stages: labor, delivery, and expulsion of the afterbirth. How individuals react and view birth varies from individual to individual, from family to family, and from culture to culture. Thus, although birth is a biological process, how it is perceived is influenced by social and environmental factors. (Refer back to pages 107–118.)

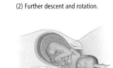

(1) The second stage of labor begins.

(2) Further descent and rotation.

(3) The crowning of the head.

(4) Anterior shoulder delivered.

(5) Posterior shoulder delivered.

(6) The third stage of labor begins with separation of the placenta from the uterine wall.

FIGURE 4.9 **Childbirth**

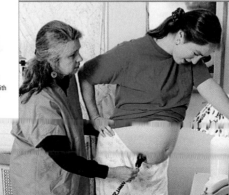

A wide variety of birthing methods are available to parents.

Fathers participate much more actively in the birth and early rearing of newborns than they did 50 years ago.

11–14 in.	13–17 in.	16.5–18 in.	18–20 in.
567–681 g (1.25–1.5 lb)	1135–1362 g (2.5–3 lb)	2100 g (6 lb)	3178–3405 g (7–7.5 lb)
Layers of the cortex of the brain develop. Skin is wrinkled. Skin is pink because blood vessels are visible.	Fetus becomes viable. Eyelids open and eyelashes form. Teeth form.	Fat deposits form. Body is more rounded. Skin unwrinkles. Testes in boys descend into scrotum.	Body hair is shed. Nails reach tips of fingers and toes. Growth rate slows down. Fetus moves into position for birth.
6 months	7 months	8 months	9 months

What factors increase the chances of having a healthy baby?

- Good nutrition
- Regular exercise
- Regular prenatal checkups
- Social support from family and friends

NEWBORNS

Newborn babies must make adjustments to life outside the womb. There is considerable variation in how newborns make this adjustment. For some newborns, this adjustment is extremely difficult due to factors that put them at risk— such as being born too early or being born with a low birthweight. New technologies and procedures have increased the chances of these at-risk newborns to survive and thrive. (Refer back to pages 118–129.).

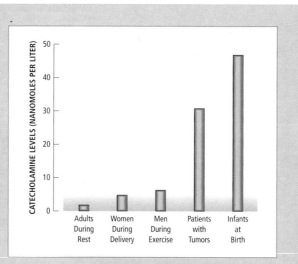

FIGURE 4.12   **Comparison of Stress Hormone Levels**

TABLE 4.3

Factors That Place Newborns at Risk for Poor Developmental Outcomes

BIOLOGICAL RISK FACTORS	ENVIRONMENTAL RISK FACTORS
Prematurity	Poverty/unemployment
Intracranial hemorrhage	No medical insurance
Growth retardation	Teenage mother
Brain abnormalities	Mental retardation or emotional disturbance in parent or caregiver
Biochemical abnormalities	Substance abuse by caregiver
Infections	History of child abuse or neglect in family
Lung disease	Family dysfunction
Neonatal seizures	Lack of parenting skills
Maternal substance abuse during pregnancy	Parent–child separation (divorce, maternal incarceration)

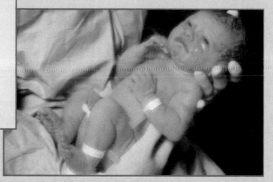

Newborns look different than those you see on television.

127

Part

3

Infant and Toddler Development

*F*rom the moment they are born, infants are bombarded by sights, sounds, smells, and tactile sensations. A major task of the first two years of life is to develop ways of making sense of and organizing these sensations. As the brain develops and infants gain experience, they increasingly acquire abilities to integrate and understand words and to coordinate their eyes and hands so that they can reach out to grab something they want.

Infants also face the task of developing ways of interacting with their social world. Parents, caregivers, siblings, other family members, and friends interact with infants, and the quality of these interactions has important implications for infants' development. In turn, infants' actions and responses affect how others interact with them. This reciprocal interaction forms the basis for much of the development that occurs during this stage of life. Unfortunately, very young children also are at risk for accidental injury, illness, and maltreatment.

Physical Development and Health in Infancy and Toddlerhood

Chapter Outline

How Do Infants and Toddlers Develop Physically?
Growth Patterns of Infants and Toddlers
Infant States and Sleep Patterns

How Do Infant Brains Develop?
Early Brain Development
Key Brain Structures
Brain Plasticity
Environmental Effects on Brain Development

How Do Infants' Perceptual Abilities Develop?
The Visual World of Newborns and Infants
Perception of Faces
Perception of Moving Objects
Depth Perception
The Infant's World of Sound
The Infant's World of Taste, Smell, and Touch
The "Dance of Perception"

How Do Motor Skills Develop in Infants and Toddlers?
Neonatal Reflexes
Gross Motor Skills
Fine Motor Skills
Bowel and Bladder Control

What Factors Influence Infant Health and Safety?
Promoting Healthy Development and Growth
Avoiding Accidents
Infant Mortality
Infant Nutrition
Failure-to-Thrive Infants

A DEVELOPMENTAL MYSTERY

After a difficult labor, instead of coming into the world fussing and kicking, Shawna was quiet, and her arms and legs were limp and floppy. As a 3-month-old, Shawna did not hold her head up when lying on her stomach. She had difficulty sitting upright. As Shawna's first birthday approached, like many other parents, Shawna's parents anxiously awaited her first steps. When Shawna was still not walking by age 1 1/2, her parents were very concerned. The pediatrician diagnosed Shawna with a motor development disorder, and she received intervention to help her overcome this challenge. Today, as a 5-year-old, Shawna is active, chases her dog around the yard, and swims with her friends in the neighborhood. What might have happened to Shawna's motor development and brain development if she had not received early intervention to improve her motor skills?

Growth and physical development are important indicators of young children's health. Fortunately, for Shawna, her parents noticed this and got her the help she needed. Early physical development is highly noticeable to most parents and adults, but growth patterns vary greatly from child to child, and from culture to culture.

How Do Infants and Toddlers Develop Physically?

Growth in height and weight and dramatic changes in motor skills occur rapidly during the first two years of life, more rapidly than for older children. Infants' proportions are different from those of older children and adults. Their heads are much larger relative to the size of their bodies. A newborn's head is about one quarter of his or her body size, whereas an adult's head makes up about 12 percent of his or her body size. Relative to head size, infants have a large forehead, small flat nose, and large eyes. They have a distinctive body shape as well, with a protruding stomach; short, bowed legs; and relatively high amounts of fat (Cratty, 1999).

Growth is an indication of children's health. Pediatricians use growth charts to follow changes in children's height and weight over time and to compare one child's growth to that of other children. After a visit to the pediatrician, you can hear a parent ask another, "At what percentile is your child's height?" The parent is asking where the child falls in comparison with other children of the same age. Pediatricians determine this by using growth charts like those shown in Figure 5.1. Each curved line on the charts represents a different growth pattern. If a mother hears that her child is at the fifth percentile in height, it means that her child is growing more slowly than other children—only 5 percent of children of the same age are shorter. The blue line in the middle represents an average growth pattern. If a child is in the 50th percentile, half of the other children are taller and half shorter. The top line represents the growth of a child in the 95th percentile, who is taller (or heavier) than almost all other children. For most children, growth patterns remain similar over time, so a child who is average in height at age 3 is likely to be average at age 5.

Growth Patterns of Infants and Toddlers

By their first birthday, most children gain 15 pounds and grow 9 inches. After prenatal growth, there is no other period of life in which children grow as quickly as they do during the first year. As you can see in Figure 5.1, infant boys and girls continue to grow rapidly during the first three years, and their growth patterns are similar. By age 2, boys reach about 50 percent and girls 53 percent of their adult height. Birth weight usually doubles by 5

FIGURE 5.1

Growth Charts for Height and Weight (birth to 36 months)

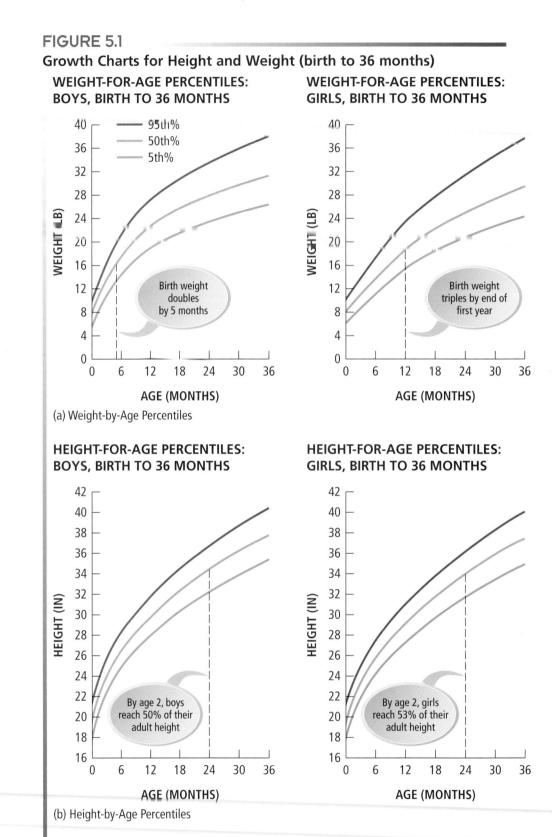

WEIGHT-FOR-AGE PERCENTILES: BOYS, BIRTH TO 36 MONTHS

WEIGHT-FOR-AGE PERCENTILES: GIRLS, BIRTH TO 36 MONTHS

95th%
50th%
5th%

Birth weight doubles by 5 months

Birth weight triples by end of first year

(a) Weight-by-Age Percentiles

HEIGHT-FOR-AGE PERCENTILES: BOYS, BIRTH TO 36 MONTHS

HEIGHT-FOR-AGE PERCENTILES: GIRLS, BIRTH TO 36 MONTHS

By age 2, boys reach 50% of their adult height

By age 2, girls reach 53% of their adult height

(b) Height-by-Age Percentiles

Notice that infants tend to grow very rapidly in both weight and height. Girls and boys show similar growth patterns in the first two years of life.

Source: Developed by the National Center for Health Statistics in collaboration with the National Center for Chronic Disease Prevention and Health Promotion, 2000.

months, triples by the end of the first year, and quadruples by about 30 months of age. It takes ten years for children to reach half their adult weight.

Genetic factors play a major role in determining a child's growth pattern, especially for height and body type and to a lesser extent for weight. Generally, tall parents have children who are tall, and short parents have children who are short.

The conditions in which a child is raised also influence growth patterns. Children who do not receive adequate nutrition during their early years do not achieve optimal height. Changes in diet can alter trends, however. For example, because of improved diets, Japanese children born after World War II grew too large to fit into the school desks that their parents had used as children. Americans, too, are taller than their ancestors because of improved diets; children born after World War II tend to be about 1 inch taller than their parents (Roche, 1979).

Infant States and Sleep Patterns

Infants experience changes of state—they move from crying and fussing into watchful wakefulness, and from being drowsy to sleeping. Researchers have identified how infants move from one state to another and have described how being in certain states influences the ways that infants interact with others and learn about their world. One of the most common states for young infants is sleep, and it is a topic of much concern to caregivers who worry about whether their children are sleeping enough and at the right times.

Arousal States

If you have ever spent time with a young infant, you have probably observed rapid changes in her or his **state of arousal**—the degree to which the infant is alert, attentive, and awake. Infants rapidly drift in and out of wakefulness, excitement, drowsiness, and sleep. As shown in Table 5.1, these different states can be described in terms of six major categories, from high to low arousal: fussing/crying, nonalert waking, alert waking, drowsiness/sleep–wake transition, active sleep, and quiet sleep (Thoman & Whitney, 1990).

Understanding states of arousal is important for several reasons:

- States of arousal influence infants' interactions with others and with their environment. In a quiet alert state, infants learn better and seem particularly tuned in to the environment.

- Infant states of arousal provide information about individual differences. Some infants sleep more than others whereas some are more alert, and these differences

TABLE 5.1
Infant States of Arousal

STATE	DESCRIPTION	TIME IN STATE (WHILE ALONE)
Fussing/crying	Low-intensity fussing or higher-intensity crying	3%
Nonalert awake	Eyes open but unfocused, body movements, isolated fussing	3%
Alert awake	Attentive, looking around, eyes open	7%
Drowsiness/sleep–wake transition	Little motor activity, eyes closing and opening	7%
Active sleep	Eyes closed, uneven breathing, rapid eye movements, smiling, grimacing	50%
Quiet sleep	Eyes closed, regular and slow respiration, limited activity	30%

Source: Adapted from Thoman and Whitney, 1990.

state of arousal *degree to which an infant is alert, attentive, or awake*

are seen even during prenatal development (Groome et al., 1997). These differences in states of arousal also provide insight into the behavioral traits of young infants. As you will learn, some infants are passive and react little to their environment, whereas others are more responsive and easily irritated.

■ The regularity of states of arousal provides a window on the maturity of the nervous system. Neonates who are very irregular in their states of arousal are at risk for later developmental problems. (Thoman, 1990)

Infant states vary depending on the qualities of the caregiving they receive. In a classic study, Sander and colleagues (1972) found that newborns cried more and showed altered arousal patterns when they were introduced to new caregivers who responded differently than their previous caregivers had. These findings suggest that infant states of arousal develop through an interaction between their biological tendencies, such as the maturation level of the nervous system, and their environment, such as the quality of caregiving they receive.

Sleep Patterns

You get so tired. In the middle of the night something interrupts your sleep; it is that cry again, and you don't know how you're going to make it out of bed to hold the baby. (Greene, 1984, p. 21)

A newborn child averages about 16 hours of sleep a day. Nonetheless, as Bob Greene's diary entry reveals, parents of newborns often are bleary-eyed and tired because they do not get enough sleep. This is because newborns do not sleep 16 hours all at one time. In Figure 5.2 you can see that the typical adult sleeps for one long period of about 7 to 8 hours and is awake for the rest of the day. In contrast, the typical newborn sleeps six or seven times a day for about 2 to 3 hours at a time (Thoman & Whitney, 1989). Even this figure is somewhat misleading because newborns may fall asleep for a few minutes or a few hours at almost any time of the day. By the end of two weeks, neonates begin to sleep somewhat longer during the night than during the day, and parents use a wide variety of techniques to help infants fall asleep (Toselli, Farneti, & Salzarulo, 1998). As infants grow older, the time they spend sleeping decreases, and the timing of sleep also changes. Older infants sleep more hours at night and fewer hours during the day, matching adult patterns more closely.

The length of time an infant sleeps at night may be an indicator of brain development (Zaiwalla & Stein, 1993). Indices of brain activity show that changes in sleeping and waking occur in the first months of life (Hoppenbrouwers et al., 1988). For instance, the brain activity patterns associated with drowsiness are not found in very young infants but are found in infants of 5 to 8 months of age (Berg & Berg, 1987). The changes in sleep–wake cycles may signal important changes in the brain's ability to process information, which increase the infant's responsiveness to his or her environment (Sigman, Beckwith, Cohen, & Parmelee, 1989).

Night waking is common in infants. During the first few months, infants awaken on average every 3 to 4 hours at night, often because they are hungry and uncomfortable. Infants typically require parents to soothe and feed them, and they often fall asleep soon after being fed or changed. By 8 or 9 months, about 70 percent of children "sleep through the night" (Anders, Halpern, & Hua, 1992), although this is an inaccurate label. In observational studies of

FIGURE 5.2

Sleep Patterns Across the Life Span

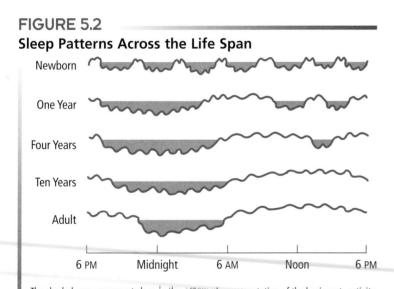

The shaded areas represent sleep in this schematic representation of the basic rest–activity cycle superimposed on the sleep–wake cycle.

Notice how the sleep patterns of newborns are different from those of older children and adults. What factors contribute to these differences?

Source: Bornstein and Lamb, 1992. Reproduced with permission of the authors.

sleep, almost all children whom parents describe as sleeping through the night actually awaken during the night, usually after 6 or 7 hours, and yet they are able to fall asleep on their own—that is, they are able to self-soothe, and because of this, they do not need to awaken their parents (Anders, 1979; Anders & Keener, 1985). Optimally, at some point during the first year, infants should be able to self-soothe, both to fall asleep and when they awaken at night.

Why do some children learn to fall asleep and to self-soothe when they awaken whereas many others do not? The answers are not clear yet for this problem that affects many families: during a child's first two years of life, sleep problems are the most frequent complaint of parents during visits to health professionals (Ferber, 1986a, b). The regulation of sleep is complex, influenced by both the qualities of the individual child and his or her relationships (infant–parent). Repeated patterns of interaction between infants and their caregivers influence how children fall asleep and their likelihood of learning to self-soothe after waking at night. The child's temperament, nursing patterns, and health influence his or her ability to settle into longer sleep durations; infant illnesses, family stress, and changes in sleeping environments have an effect on night waking (Bernal, 1973). The use of sleep aids, such as pacifiers or thumbs, can reduce night waking (Paret, 1983), and children quite commonly use them to help soothe themselves (Burnham, Goodlin-Jones, Gaylor, & Anders, 2002). In one study, problem sleepers at 8 months showed different sleep behaviors than "good" sleepers. Problem sleepers were more likely to be put into their cribs already asleep, they were unlikely to use sleep aids, and they were more likely to signal to their parents when they were awake. Problem sleepers were also more likely to be boys than girls. Good sleepers were more likely to be put into their cribs awake and then fell asleep, they were more likely to use sleep aids, and they were less likely to signal to their parents when they were awake. Interestingly, these problem sleepers were not identified as such early in life, suggesting that sleep problems may not be consistent over the early years (Anders et al., 1992).

Sleep problems also affect toddlers and young children (Anders, Goodlin-Jones, & Sadeh, 2000; Davis, Parker, & Montgomery, 2004). Young children who do not sleep enough hours during the night are often found to have behavioral problems (e.g., Lavigne et al., 1999), but at this point it is unclear whether the behavior problems cause the lack of sleep or the lack of sleep contributes to the behavior problems (or both).

Where do infants sleep in most countries in the world? How might early sleeping arrrangements and cultural values influence children's ability to sleep through the night?

Families, Culture, and Sleep: Cosleeping with Babies

In the United States, most newborns sleep alone. In many countries, infants and mothers sleep together during the first few years of life. For instance, in a study of 12 communities, only in the United States did young infants regularly sleep away from parents (Whiting & Edwards, 1988). Cosleeping occurs in both technologically advanced and less advanced societies. For instance, Japanese babies sleep next to their mothers in early childhood and often continue to sleep with a member of the family until they are 15 years old. Cosleeping is not due to limited space but rather to cultural beliefs about the importance of having a sleeping partner.

One study compared the sleeping patterns and beliefs of US parents and Highland Mayan parents (Morelli, Rogoff, Oppenheim, & Goldsmith, 1992). The typical pattern in US Caucasian families was sleeping separately. After 3 months of sleeping near parents in a crib or bassinet, about 60 percent of infants in the United States moved to their own room, and by 6 months, 80 percent of infants had their own room for sleeping. In contrast, 100 percent of the Mayan mothers slept in bed with their infants, and more than half of the fathers did as well. Infants tended to sleep with their mothers until the next child was born.

Mayan parents differed from US parents in their beliefs about sleeping arrangements. Mayan families believe that cosleeping is the only reasonable way for babies and parents to sleep. When hearing about the US style of separate sleeping, some Mayan parents were shocked and strongly disapproved, suggesting that this pattern may be tantamount to child neglect. US parents reported that they believed separate sleeping arrangements are necessary because parents needed to go back to work and because it fostered independence in their children. Furthermore, many US parents worried that sleeping together would be a difficult habit to break and that it might be unsafe (the baby might be crushed).

The cultural differences between Mayan and US families may relate to problems in sleeping. In the United States, parents commonly report that infants have difficulty sleeping, and a number of programs have been designed to train infants to soothe themselves and regulate their own sleep (Ferber, 1986a, b). In Mayan families, infants go to sleep easily, and parents do not complain of sleep difficulties. Perhaps the bedtime difficulties reported by US parents relate to infants being separated from the social interactions of family life to sleep alone in their own rooms. Additionally, mothers nurse their infants three times more frequently when they sleep together (McKenna et al., 1994). The cosleeping that occurs in so many other cultures allows infants to be involved in social interactions since they sleep when others do, and it may alleviate the child's fears and ease their transition to sleep (Morelli et al., 1992).

How Do Infant Brains Develop?

By the time a baby is born, the parts of the brain that control many important survival-related functions, such as breathing, swallowing, sucking, and maintaining a heartbeat, are functioning. The sensory areas of the brain also develop early, allowing newborns to smell, taste, feel, see, and hear things going on around them. Only later do areas of the brain develop that are thought to be involved in regulating emotions, acquiring language, and reasoning. During early infancy, the size of the brain increases dramatically, and it becomes capable of controlling more and more complex behaviors.

About half of all human genes are involved in building the brain by providing the codes for its basic structures and functions (Robinson, 1996). Once brain development has been set in motion, the genetic code goes only so far before the child's environment makes a tremendous impact. An infant who has an enriched environment, in which she or he is exposed to many people, to music, to language, and to play opportunities, develops under optimum conditions.

Early Brain Development

To understand early development requires an understanding of how the brain develops before and after birth. Some of the most interesting new ideas about development concern how early brain development occurs and how the environment and biology play roles in shaping the brain. You may be surprised to learn that the environment actually shapes the way the brain forms, and in turn, the structure of the brain influences how children interpret information and learn about the world around them.

Formation and Migration of Neurons

One of the most intriguing developmental mysteries that scientists are beginning to unravel is how the brain is built. Remember from Chapter 4 that a newborn's nervous system and brain begin to form from the neural tube. Very early in prenatal development, the neural tube generates a large number of **neurons,** the nerve cells that make up the communication system of the brain (Begley, 1996). These brain cells migrate outward to specific areas of the brain to form its structure. By the end of the seventh month of prenatal development, most of the neurons that will be used to construct the brain have been formed and have moved into place. The formation of neurons and their movement or migration to form the parts of the brain are considered "progressive" because they provide increasing organization and structure. If, however, fewer neurons form or if they do not move into place, the size of the brain will be stunted and brain functioning will be impaired. For most infants, these processes occur normally. By the time a newborn is born, the brain has over 100 billion neurons (Nash, 1997).

neurons *the nerve cells that make up the communication system of the brain*

FIGURE 5.3
Brain Cell and Synaptic Connection

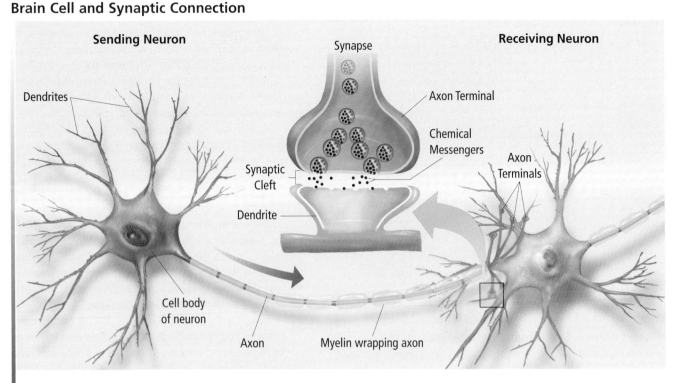

The dendrites of the neuron receive messages, and the axons send messages. How are these messages sent?

Neurons have to be linked to provide efficient information flow between the senses and the brain. Let's review how the basic building blocks of the brain—the neurons—work. As you can see in Figure 5.3, a neuron is composed of a cell body, many **dendrites** for receiving messages, and a long **axon** for sending messages. After migrating to their appropriate locations in the nervous system, neurons spin out axons and dendrites that allow for the transmission of information among them. For example, neurons transmit the information to your central nervous system and brain that you have burned your finger on a hot stove. Information is transmitted through electrical impulses that travel down the length of a neuron, causing it to produce a chemical response to the impulse. This chemical messenger then transmits the information from one neuron to the next through small gaps, or spaces, between the cells, called **synapses.** These impulses travel quickly—fast enough to ensure that the finger is withdrawn before it is seriously burned on the hot stove.

Forming Connections Among Neurons
The newborn brain is bombarded with a wealth of new sensory information, and for this information to be processed, neurons must become wired to one another. The amount of new information causes infants' neurons to form synaptic connections at a very fast rate (see Figure 5.4), producing a very interesting developmental pattern. At this point, the "blooming" of neuronal connections occurs: each neuron produces many different connections with other neurons. Just as the formation and migration of neurons add structure to the brain, so does this blooming of connections. **Synaptogenesis** is the creation of new neural connections, or synapses. Each of these progressive events increases the organization and development of the brain.

Given that the major structures and connections of the brain are beginning to be formed during infancy, it is easy to understand why unfavorable environments (such as prenatal exposure to drugs or alcohol) can disrupt these events and have such serious consequences for development (see Figure 5.5).

dendrites   *parts of a neuron that are located on the cell body and receive messages from other neurons*

axon   *long part of a neuron that is located at the cell base and sends messages to other neurons*

synapses   *small gaps, or spaces, between the cells through which information is transmitted from one neuron to the next*

synaptogenesis   *the creation of new neural connections, or synapses*

FIGURE 5.4

Development of Neural Connections, from Birth Through 15 Months of Age

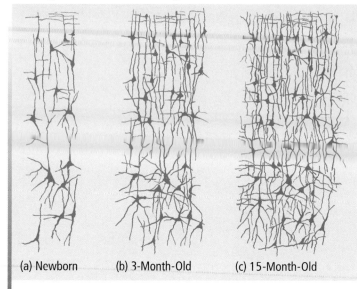

(a) Newborn   (b) 3-Month-Old   (c) 15-Month-Old

What differences are apparent in the depictions of neural connections of young children at different ages? What factors contribute to these differences?

When neuronal connections are first made, information is moved along these pathways relatively slowly, compared to later in development. Another critical process in brain construction, which occurs in the early years of brain development, helps speed information flow. Called **myelination,** it provides neurons with a sheath of smooth layers of fatty proteins (myelin). These fatty proteins wrap themselves around the axons; to imagine this, think of a thin pancake or a tortilla being wrapped around a long, thin cord. Electrical impulses travel about three times faster along myelinated pathways. Myelination begins during prenatal development for parts of the spinal cord. In the brain, myelination occurs first in the parts that control reflexes and later in the parts that control voluntary movements (Cratty, 1999). After birth, those parts of the brain that process sensory information (such as the visual system) myelinate first, and the parts that control attention, memory, self-control, and learning myelinate later. The most dramatic changes in myelination occur before 2 years of age, although some continue into adulthood (Sampaio & Truwit, 2001). Research has linked myelination to behavioral and cognitive development. For instance, particular brain locations in the cortex (the outer

FIGURE 5.5

Development of the Brain

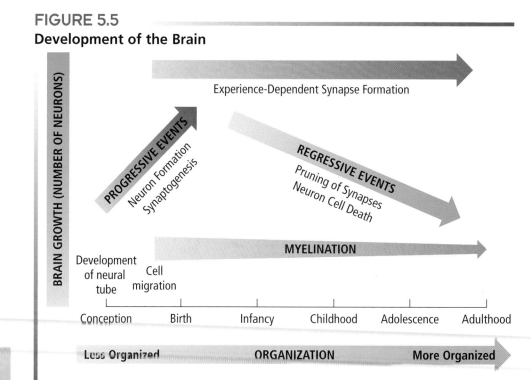

myelination *the process in which a neuron is sheathed in a smooth layer of fatty proteins (myelin)*

This model illustrates different events in brain development. How does this model help you understand the impact that children's environment can have on their development?

layer of the brain) are myelinated at 15 to 24 months of age, which corresponds to the time when children make tremendous advances in cognitive and language skills (Konner, 1991).

Neuron Death and Synapse Loss

You may be surprised to learn that the wiring of the brain involves losing many neurons and losing connections between neuronal pathways. These "regressive" events are some of the many intriguing features of brain development. During early development, the brain generates about two to three times more neurons and connections between neurons than are needed to survive and function. *Pruning,* the process whereby some little-used neural connections are eliminated, then takes place to decrease the number of cells and connections (see Figure 5.5). Although cells and connections are lost, those that are maintained are reorganized and strengthened, and the brain becomes increasingly organized.

Pruning is influenced by both genetic and environmental factors; the connections lost during pruning are those that are not reinforced by the child's environment. "Neurons that fire together, wire together" (Courchesne, Chisum, & Townsend, 1994). That is, this developmental event appears to be guided by the "use it or lose it" principle: only the connections that are most frequently used and most adaptive to the environment survive, and connections that are not used disappear (Singer, 1995). Early experiences play a crucial role, therefore, in the formation of neural pathways (Greenough & Alcantara, 1993; Greenough, Black, & Wallace, 1987).

The timing of the "blooming" and later "pruning" of neuronal connections varies according to the region of the brain (Huttenlocher, 1979; Huttenlocher & Dabholkar, 1997). Connections for the visual areas bloom during the first months of life; pruning starts in the infant and toddler years and lasts until the preschool period. In the auditory and language parts of the brain, blooming and pruning occur somewhat later, with peak overproduction occurring late in the first year of life and pruning occurring through young childhood. For the areas of higher cognitive functioning, blooming of connections occurs at approximately 1 year of age, but it is not until later in adolescence that the number of connections has been pruned to match adult levels. Over most of early childhood and into the adolescent years, the parts of the brain responsible for higher cognitive functioning undergo rapid changes in both progressive and regressive events.

Key Brain Structures

The size of the brain changes very quickly during the first few years of life. When a baby is 6 months of age, her or his brain weighs approximately half of what an adult brain weighs; by the time she or he reaches 2 years of age, the weight of the baby's brain is almost 80 percent of that of an adult brain.

The largest part of the brain is the cerebral cortex, which has many folds, or convolutions, throughout its surface. The cerebral cortex controls higher thought processes such as problem solving, consciousness, and language. The cortex is the last part of the brain to finish growing. Because of its slower rate of growth, the cortex is more susceptible to environmental influences than other parts of the brain. The cerebral cortex is divided into two halves, called hemispheres, each of which has areas specialized for certain functions. For most people, the left hemisphere is specialized for language processing, whereas the right hemisphere is specialized for recognizing spatial relationships (reading maps, for instance). Hemispheric development occurs unevenly. The left hemisphere develops rapidly around the age of 2; the right hemisphere develops later. Also, the two hemispheres are not fully connected until later (see Chapter 7).

Brain Plasticity

Infant brains are more flexible than adult brains. The flexibility, or plasticity, of the brain allows it to become fine-tuned through interaction with its environment. Because of this plasticity, infant brains adjust to many different situations and can recover from serious assaults. We know about the benefits of brain plasticity from clinical cases. Recall from Chapter 1 the case of Brandi Binder, who, because of severe epileptic seizures, had to have the entire right side of her cortex removed when she was 6 years old. Still, she managed to become talented in art, math, and music. It is likely that many functions associated with the parts of her brain that were removed were redeveloped in other parts of the brain; that is, new neuronal connections were made. This is why we think of young people as having "plastic" brains. With age, some of this plasticity is lost. Adults who undergo Brandi's operation lose much more functioning because other parts of their brains are unable to take over the functioning of the damaged or removed parts (Goodman & Whitaker, 1985).

Environmental Effects on Brain Development

Because of the rapid growth of the brain at this time, children's experiences during infancy and toddlerhood play an important role in helping to "wire" the brain. Our genetic inheritance sets up sensitive periods that act as windows of opportunity for particularly influential learning. The nature of early experiences helps determine how many and which types of neuronal connections are maintained during synaptic pruning. As a consequence of the child's experiences, the brain fine-tunes its neuronal connections to respond to the child's environment. Early experiences actually change the structure and functioning of the brain. In fact, experience may be the chief architect of the brain (Nash, 1997).

Two types of environmental influences are critical to the brain. One is called *experience-expectant,* meaning that development will not happen unless a particular experience occurs during this critical period (Greenough & Black, 1992). Early on, the normal unfolding of developmental processes in the brain relies on environmental experiences presumed to occur for most individuals at a particular time. For instance, overproduction of synapses commonly happens when infants are handled, talked to, and looked at—common experiences for most infants. Not being handled or talked to would be unusual and would contribute to atypical brain development. The other type of environmental influence is called *experience-dependent;* unlike experience-expectant processes, it is based on experiences that are not highly typical. For example, infants whose parents make a concerted effort to expose them to as many varied experiences as possible—zoos, museums, libraries, and plays, for instance—have an "enriched" environment compared to that of many infants and toddlers. From these experiences, infants receive additional environmental stimulation, and this then influences their brain development.

Just because children's brains are more plastic than adults' brains does not mean they are immune to the influence of negative environmental events. Because of the rapid growth of the brain during the early years of life, children are vulnerable to the effects of the environment (Nelson & Bloom, 1997). Unfavorable conditions such as poor nutrition or exposure to drugs or diseases increase the risk of problems in brain development, especially when experience-expectant processes are disrupted. Disruptions of growth and development during the brain's growth spurt can have a variety of serious outcomes:

- Permanent reduction in brain size
- Reduction in the number of neurons
- Reduced myelination of cells
- Decreased numbers of synaptic connections

Damage or disruption in the development of the brain during the early years may increase the likelihood that a child will have difficulties in school, lack the ability to handle

How is brain development influenced by the qualities of stimulation that animals receive? Are these same environmental effects found in humans? What are the implications of this research for how infants are raised, especially in child-care facilities?

stress well, and have poor motor and sensory functioning (Cratty, 1986). One source of such disruption is inadequate stimulation during sensitive periods. For example, infants who have depressed mothers and who receive less social interaction have brains that are less active (Nash, 1997). Animal studies support the idea that environmental stimulation has a strong effect on brain development. Experience-expectant learning is disrupted when cats are not exposed to the visual stimulation they normally would receive, and they become unable to process certain kinds of visual information (Hubel & Wiesel, 1979). Experience-dependent processes have also been demonstrated. Animals that live in enriched environments—with playmates and toys to interact with—have 25 percent more connections between neurons than do animals in impoverished environments (Greenough, Black, & Wallace, 1987). In humans, intensive early intervention has been shown to improve brain structure and functioning (Als et al., 2004). Research on early intervention, using foster care placement of institutionalized abandoned children in Bucharest, Romania, is being done to provide clues about which aspects of brain development are most influenced by early experiences (Zeanah et al., 2003).

Research on brain development in rats, cats, and humans has popularized the idea that the first three years of life are the most critical for brain development. Although focusing the lay public's attention on the critical events of early life may be beneficial in that parents, teachers, and others become more aware of potentially damaging events in young children's lives, this increased attention also has a downside. First, there are other times of life when the brain is susceptible to influence—in particular, during prenatal development. For example, during cell migration (6 to 24 weeks prenatal), the brain is highly vulnerable to teratogens, drug and alcohol exposure, and malnutrition (Thompson & Nelson, 2001). Second, there are few truly critical periods in human development. Instead, most are best characterized as being sensitive periods, in that the time periods are broader and more flexible (Bornstein, 1989). Third, recent research suggests that brain development and brain plasticity continue in important ways into adolescence and adulthood, and these time periods should not be ignored (Greenough & Black, 1992; Gould, 1999; Kempermann, Kuhn, & Gage, 1997; Thompson & Nelson, 2001).

The implications of the newest research on brain development are profound. The idea that the environment is central in fine-tuning the brain suggests that experience may be even more important than previously thought in influencing both healthy and unhealthy developmental outcomes.

How Do Infants' Perceptual Abilities Develop?

When they are first born, infants perceive sights, sounds, textures, smells, and tastes, but their abilities to experience these sensations are not as fully developed as older infants' or children's. Newborns' senses of taste and smell are more developed after birth than their senses of vision and hearing are. Decorating a newborn child's room with pale yellow and pink may appeal to adults but is unlikely to be within the child's sensory range. Because their sensory systems are not yet fully developed, low-intensity stimuli, such as pale colors and soft sounds, may not be noticed at all. For newborns, stimuli that are moderately intense are the "gentle magnets" that draw their attention (Stern, 1992). As infants grow older, they perceive a wider range of stimuli and begin to make sense of the sights, sounds, smells, tastes, and tactile sensations that bombard them. From this array of stimuli, they perceive and begin to make sense of their world by selecting some types of information and ignoring others. Infants actively sort and organize information into meaningful units, and their ability to make meaning from the stimulation they receive is due to the maturation of the nervous system and brain (Kellman & Banks, 1998).

The Visual World of Newborns and Infants

Because the womb is a dark place, fetuses have little exposure to visual information before birth. Until the 1960s, people did not really know what or how newborns could see. Many parents have noticed that their newborns stare at them right after birth and sometimes follow movements with their eyes. But just what does the world look like to a newborn?

Newborns have poor visual acuity; what they see at 20 feet is what an adult with good vision sees at 300 to 800 feet (Aslin, 1987). The optic nerve and parts of the brain that process visual information are not fully developed at birth. Furthermore, the newborn's eye is shorter in length than an adult's eye, leading to less detailed encoding of information (Dannemiller, 2001). Visual acuity improves rapidly within six months, but it does not reach adult levels until 4 to 6 years of age (Maurer & Lewis, 2001). You may wonder how scientists determine what a young infant can see. Developing methods to assess nonverbal infants has been a challenge. A variety of methods have been designed, all of which tap into the kinds of behaviors that infants can perform: look at objects, suck on pacifiers, and turn their heads. In studying visual acuity, Fantz and his colleagues developed a clever method that capitalizes on infants' preferences for looking at patterns rather than solid colors (Fantz, Ordy, & Udelf, 1962; see Figure 5.6). Infants are presented with two stimuli—one is a solid gray block of color, and the other is a pattern of black-and-white stripes varying systematically in width. Fantz assumed that when infants stopped showing a preference for the striped pattern (as the presented stripes got narrower), the limits of their visual acuity had been reached. Imagine what this test might look like to a very young infant: In the first presentation, the stripes are quite wide, and so the infant focuses on the striped pattern. As the stripes become very narrow, however, they no longer appear to be stripes to the infant's eye; instead, they are seen as gray, like the other stimulus. So both stimuli look the same to the infant, and neither attracts more interest than the other.

Soon after birth, although their vision is blurry, neonates can see and track slow-moving objects within their visual range—about 7 inches in front of the face. While tracking an object, newborns move their eyes with jerky motions, which are gradually replaced with smoother movements as they gain control of their eye muscles.

When adults visually scan objects, their eyes make very small, rapid movements to shift from one point of fixation to another. These movements allow them to take in visual information about the whole object, collecting enough small images to recognize an object for what it is.

Just as adults do, newborns systematically scan objects, especially faces. A few simple rules sum up how neonates visually scan the world around them (Haith, 1980):

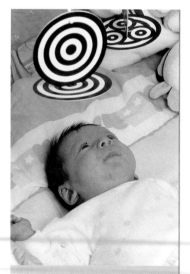

Notice how intensely this neonate is looking at the mobile. What features of the mobile make it effective in catching the visual attention of the newborn?

- They look for edges, using broad, jerky sweeps across their visual field.

- If they find an edge, they keep looking at it.

- They sweep their eyes across the edge again and again.

- If they cannot continue scanning one edge, they look for another.

As infants grow older, their scanning moves from the external edges to the more internal parts. Generally, younger infants attend to the most striking aspect of an object—the part that is moving, the brightest part, or the largest part. This is why mobiles that are bright and feature high-contrast colors are the ones young infants find most attractive. Parents holding a newborn often notice that she or he seems to look above their eyes. This is due to the newborn's fascination with areas of highest contrast—the hairline or eyebrows. However, newborns often look right into a caregiver's eyes because the eyes are very striking and appealing.

Important changes occur in the development of the eye and the visual pathways to the brain over the first months of life, all of which improve the visual capabilities of young infants (Dannemiller, 2001). With increased visual acuity, development of their visual system, and better control of eye movements, infants between 2 and 4 months expand the range of their attention to include stimuli that are colorful, meaningful, and patterned. By 2 months of age, infants discriminate red, blue, and green (Adams, 1989). They perceive patterns in place of the simple lines and shapes seen by newborns; that is, they observe the relationships among the lines and shapes. Several studies indicate that by 3 months of age, infants take notice of patterns that are "different" or misaligned, but 1-month-old infants do not (Van Griffin & Haith, 1984). These findings suggest that between 1 and 3 months, infants begin to see the organization of visual displays rather than only their details.

FIGURE 5.6
Testing Infants' Visual Acuity

How do newborns see the striped patterns as compared to how older infants see them? What changes allow the older infants to see differently?

Source: Fantz, Ordy, and Udelf, 1962.

Perception of Faces

As infants gradually develop greater control over the movements of their eyes, they are able to seek out and fix their attention on objects that appeal to them. This increased control results from the maturation of the nervous system, and, significantly, caregivers respond to these changes with increased attention and affection toward the infant. Caregivers often report that their infant is looking at them "for the first time" and that this represents an expression of affection on the part of the infant. Caregivers find this immensely appealing. They cannot tell you what has changed but are aware that something is different. This interplay shows how changes in the maturation of the infant's nervous system bring about changes in the infant's social and emotional relationships (Bertenthal, 1996).

FIGURE 5.7

Face and Nonface Stimuli Used to Study Infants' Face Preferences

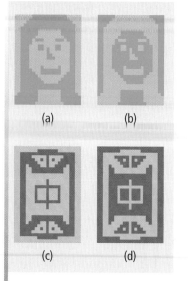

(a)   (b)

(c)   (d)

Early studies of face preferences compared infants' responses to faces and to other patterns, but it was unclear whether the complexity of the stimuli influenced their responses. To ensure that the amount and complexity of visual information did not bias their results, Dannemiller and Stephens (1988) controlled for the amount of dark and light areas in each figure that infants were shown. Infants show face preferences even when the information is controlled.

Source: Dannemiller and Stephens, 1988.

visual cliff apparatus   *a two-level "cliff" with a checker-board pattern, covered with Plexiglas, used to create an illusion of depth*

Infants' preference for faces increases as they grow older and learn to recognize how a whole face should look. By 12 weeks of age, infants prefer faces over nonface stimuli, even when the complexity of the two pictures is equal (Dannemiller & Stephens, 1988; see Figure 5.7). By 5 months, infants treat their own faces as familiar, social stimuli (Legerstee, Anderson, & Schaffer, 1998), suggesting that they recognize themselves through facial cues.

When shown schematic drawings of faces, infants exhibit a preference for looking at typical faces rather than faces with distorted features (Maurer & Barrerra, 1981). Surprisingly, even infants as young as 3 months prefer attractive adult faces over less attractive ones (Langlois et al., 1987; Samuels & Ewy, 1985), and by 6 months they prefer attractive faces of infants and adults of diverse races (Langlois, Ritter, Roggman, & Vaughn, 1991).

Although young infants recognize and prefer to look at faces, they are not very good at reading emotions displayed on faces. Until they are about 6 months old, they recognize only simple and clearly displayed emotional expressions. For instance, they recognize a smile only if it is broad and open-mouthed (Kuchuk, Vibbert, & Bornstein, 1986). Not until they are 18 to 24 months old do infants understand that facial expressions reflect others' emotional states (Repacholi & Gropnik, 1997; Saarni, Mumme, & Campos, 1998).

Infants are born with capacities that direct them to learn about and orient themselves to people and events that are crucial for their survival. Infants are especially attentive to faces, particularly when held close. They prefer curved lines and moderate complexity, as found in faces, and areas of high contrast, as found in eyes and mouths. Caregivers elicit the infant's attention by holding their face close to the infant's face in the same orientation and by interacting with the infant. The infant's visual capabilities combine with the caregivers' tendencies to interact with the baby in ways that provide mutually rewarding visual interactions.

Perception of Moving Objects

Infants prefer to watch moving objects rather than stationary ones. When shown moving and stationary objects or patterns, infants prefer to look at patterns or objects that move at a moderate rate. Infants' abilities to detect motion improve in the first 3 months; by about 6 months of age, infants are good at coordinating their movements with the movements of objects (Aslin, 1987). For instance, they will grasp at a moving object within a 20th of a second of the moment it touches their hand (von Hofsten, 1983).

Infants also recognize and prefer complex patterns of motion made by people (such as walking or running). To test infants' abilities in this area, researchers devised an unusual experiment in which a person was outfitted with small lights to mark the locations of the major joints (such as shoulders and hips). The outfitted person was then filmed running and walking in a very dark room so that only the points of lights were visible on the film. When shown these moving light displays along with computer-generated lights moving in nonhumanlike patterns, infants from 3 to 5 months of age preferred to watch the human patterns of motion (Bertenthal, Proffitt, Kramer, & Spetner, 1987).

Depth Perception

Does an infant recognize that stairs drop off? Will he or she try to crawl down the stairs or be afraid of falling? The classic study of depth perception involved placing infants on a **visual cliff apparatus,** a two-level "cliff" with a checkerboard pattern covered with Plexiglas to create an illusion of depth. On the "cliff" end, the checkerboard pattern drops off several feet, but the Plexiglas continues on the same level. If an infant can detect height, will she or he crawl over the "edge" of the cliff?

By 7 months, most infants avoid the cliff area of the apparatus, even when their mother calls them from across the "abyss." This suggests that infants of this age respond to changes in depth (Walk & Gibson, 1961). Prior to this age, infants often show interest in the cliff but may or may not avoid it. Seven-month-old crawling babies begin to show fear of heights, and infants who push themselves around in walkers also develop a fear of the cliff (Bertenthal & Campos, 1984).

Infants detect depth and distance before they can crawl, probably because of changes that occur in the visual system between 3 and 7 months of age. Depth and distance are better perceived when the viewer is able to compare images from both eyes. At birth, the visual system receives input from both eyes in the same part of the brain, but by 6 or 7 months, separate locations develop for input from each eye (Kellman & Banks, 1998).

Researchers use looming and zooming objects to assess infants' responses to distance. Around 3 months of age, infants respond to looming objects—those that seem to be coming toward them—by blinking. When an object is zooming away from them, they do not blink (Banks, 1988). Seven-month-old infants begin to use visual cues to determine depth (Kellman & Banks, 1998). The relative size of an object, for example, provides information about whether the object is close or far away.

Why will this infant avoid crawling over the "cliff"? What changes must take place in the visual system for an infant to be able to detect depth?

The Infant's World of Sound

The structures needed for hearing are more developed at birth than are the structures needed for vision. By 1 year of age, an infant's auditory system generally is similar to an adult's (Kellman & Banks, 1998). But what do newborns hear? From birth, babies can hear sounds that are whispered, but not sounds softer than that; adults can hear much softer sounds (Nozza, 1995). Newborns cannot hear sounds of short duration as well as adults can, and they prefer relatively high-pitched sounds, such as the sound of a woman's voice (Fernald, 1985). Even newborns can localize sounds; for instance, they can identify the location of a rattle by hearing that the sound is coming from the left side rather than the right side (Aslin, Jusczyk, & Pisoni, 1998). Newborns' localization ability is relatively crude at birth but improves dramatically between birth and 6 months of age (Aslin & Hunt, 2001). Infants seem particularly attuned to human voices, especially the sound of their own mother's voice (DeCasper & Spence, 1986). Newborns prefer the sounds they were exposed to during prenatal development. Within two days of birth, infants show a preference for hearing their own language rather than another language (see Research to Practice box). They tend to prefer to listen to speech sounds, even in languages other than their own, rather than to nonspeech sounds (Werker & Vouloumanos, 2001). They also prefer the sounds of intrauterine heartbeats to many other sounds, and they prefer melodies their mother sang during pregnancy to other melodies. Prenatal exposure to sounds appears to "set" infants' preferences for sounds after they are born (Aslin, 1987).

The Infant's World of Taste, Smell, and Touch

Infants have well-developed senses of taste, touch, and smell. Even at birth, these abilities are evident.

Taste

Newborns can distinguish among tastes that are sweet, salty, bitter, and sour. They prefer sweet solutions over all other tastes, and they show disgust or distress when tasting something bitter or sour (Rosenstein & Oster, 1988). Although their numbers increase after birth, taste buds form early in prenatal development, suggesting that this sensory system functions even before birth. Early in life, babies have a wider distribution of taste buds than adults do—taste buds are found even on the tonsils and in the back of the throat. Further confirmation of the early functioning of the sense of taste comes from the findings that premature newborns pucker their lips when they taste something sour (Tatzer, Schubert, Timischl, & Simbruner, 1985), and premature and full-term neonates are calmed by sweet-tasting substances (Smith & Blass, 1996; Zeifman, Delany, & Blass, 1996). Recently, scientists have

FROM RESEARCH TO PRACTICE
DO NEWBORNS PREFER TO HEAR THEIR OWN LANGUAGE?

FROM RESEARCH . . .

As you have learned, newborns have preferences for certain sounds; they like to listen to their mother's voice, heartbeats, and stories that they heard to while they were still in the womb. Do unborn children also pay attention to the language that they hear spoken? Can they distinguish it from another language? If a mother and father speak only English during pregnancy, will their newborn prefer to listen to English?

Eight 2-day-old infants who were born into monolingual English homes and eight 2-day-old infants who were born into monolingual Spanish homes were tested to determine whether they could discriminate between their own and another language. A contingent reinforcement procedure was used, in which infants learned to control the presentation of audio recordings of women speaking in either Spanish or English by sucking on a pacifier that was connected to a computer. The harder and longer the infants sucked, the longer they could control the length of time they heard the voices. After spending about 12 minutes learning

how to control the voices through sucking, 12 of the 16 infants showed the expected pattern: they activated the recordings in their native language for longer periods than they did the recordings in the foreign language (Moon, Cooper, & Fifer, 1993). The two days over which the infants were exposed to their native language after birth may have influenced their preferences, but the researchers believe that it is more likely that their prenatal experiences determined their preferences for their native language.

. . . TO PRACTICE

Although it is not yet demonstrated that prenatal exposure can have long-term impact on infants' speech, a possible implication of these findings is that infants will show more interest in speakers of their native language than in speakers of other languages. If they show more interest in them, they may learn more quickly from native speakers. This research suggests that parents should talk to their infants, even before they believe that they can understand what they are saying. Infants may be

particularly tuned into their own parents' speech patterns and language. Long before the baby is able to speak, the child is learning the sounds and rhythms of their native language. Parents and other native speakers of the language may become compelling promoters of language learning in babies.

THINKING IT THROUGH

1. Why would newborns have a preference for their own language?

2. What differences would you expect in the findings if *2-month-old* infants were studied instead of *2-day-old* infants? Would it be more difficult to determine when the infants' preferences developed? Explain your answer.

3. Why did the researchers use infant sucking behavior to answer their research questions? What other behaviors could they have measured as indicators of preferences?

4. What other practical implications can you think of for this type of research?

confirmed that flavors from the mother's diet during pregnancy are transmitted to the amniotic fluid and swallowed by the fetus. Exposure to flavors prenatally and through breast milk enhances infants' enjoyment of solid foods with those flavors during weaning (Mennella, Jagnow, & Beauchamp, 2001).

Smell
Newborns can distinguish between smells such as those of vinegar and alcohol. They turn away and make faces when presented with strong or unpleasant smells (vinegar) and turn toward more pleasant smells (Lipsitt, Engen, & Kaye, 1963).

Smells may be one of the first and most basic connections between neonates and their caregivers (Fabes & Filsinger, 1988). Within six days after birth, infants will turn their heads toward the smell of their mother's breast milk rather than that of other mothers (MacFarlane, 1975). Breast-fed infants show particular sensitivity to their mother's smells, such as her perfume and underarm odor (Cernoch & Porter, 1985; Porter, Makin, Davis, & Christensen, 1992). Mothers have a similar sensitivity to their infant's smells and can identify the smell of their infant soon after birth. When presented with clothing worn by their own baby and identical clothing worn by other babies, mothers are most likely to pick the clothing of their own baby by the smell (Porter, Cernoch, & McLaughlin, 1983).

Touch

Early in prenatal development, the fetus responds to a light touch—moving, for instance, when touched by an instrument. The parts of the nervous system that process information about touch develop very early. At birth, the presence of reflex responses to touch suggests that the newborn is particularly sensitive on the face, hands, soles of the feet, and abdomen (Reisman, 1987). Newborns are sensitive to changes in temperature and respond to cooling temperatures by waking up and moving around, which increases their heat production. A full-term newborn may sweat when the temperature is hot, but a preterm infant does not, suggesting that the cooling mechanism of sweating matures more slowly than do other responses to temperature (Harpin, Chellappah, & Rutter, 1983). When infants are hungry, they will root toward warmth. For example, when warm glass tubes are held close to their cheeks, they move their heads and open their mouths toward the tubes (Reisman, 1987). This finding suggests that temperature cues are used by infants to locate nourishment.

How do infant facial expressions indicate their sensory capabilities? How fully developed are infants' abilities to distinguish different tastes?

The extent to which infants experience pain has important consequences for their treatment. For many years, medical personnel assumed that infants were buffered from pain, at least for a short time after birth. Because of this assumption, they avoided giving newborns anesthesia or pain medication for surgical procedures, to reduce the risk of complications. Today, however, we know that newborns do experience pain. When they are circumcised or receive injections, infants become distressed. They hold their breath and cry, their arms and legs and torsos become rigid, their faces show "pain" expressions, and they have difficulty sleeping (Anand & Hickey, 1987). Infants' bodies respond to surgical procedures by producing more stress hormones (Gunnar, Fisch, Korsvik, & Donhowe, 1981). When infants need to undergo surgical procedures, the American Academy of Pediatrics (1989) recommends that physicians use anesthesia and analgesics, following the same guidelines as for other high-risk groups. These procedures effectively and safely reduce the pain and distress experienced during surgery (Stang et al., 1997).

The "Dance of Perception"

Infants respond to meaningful stimuli, and their responses facilitate the development of close relationships. Babies curl up in a caregiver's arms, look at the caregiver and appear interested in what they see, and respond to the caregiver's touch. When an infant cries, the mother's breasts respond with increased blood flow, facilitating milk production. In turn, a caregiver's responses reinforce and shape the infant's subsequent responses. Thus, as in a dance, each partner mutually leads and follows the other's responses.

Additionally, caregivers respond to babies in ways that facilitate interactions. By holding a baby in the crook of the arm, they place the baby at just the right distance for the baby's eyes to focus. By speaking in a high-pitched, melodious voice, they draw the baby's attention and soothe any distress. As this "dance of perception" between the young infant and a caregiver continues, each partner in the dance fine-tunes his or her responses to adapt to the other's nuances.

What is this mother doing to facilitate interaction with her baby? What do babies do to contribute to interactions?

How Do Motor Skills Develop in Infants and Toddlers?

How do motor skills develop? Tickle a newborn's foot and the baby will move his or her whole body in response, but tickle a preschooler's foot and the child will move only his or her leg. This difference illustrates how infants' movements become more localized and specialized during the first few years of life. Major developments in motor activity occur during the first year or two as infants acquire the abilities to sit, crawl, stand, and walk. But before they can attain these abilities, infants must gain control over their muscles and learn to cope with the forces of gravity.

During the first year, infants' reflexes become inhibited as the brain develops and they gain voluntary control over many of their movements. The process is complex, and the rate at which they develop motor skills depends on many factors. After the first year, motor development mainly involves practicing and mastering previously learned skills. Infants gain greater control and precision in movement as their ability to integrate information from the senses and the muscles increases. But there are dramatic individual differences in motor development. Some infants are advanced and others are delayed in demonstrating skills, and the "normal" range is broad. Also, cultural practices influence how quickly children develop motor skills. In some African cultures, such as in Mali, mothers stretch and exercise babies' muscles, essentially providing a mini-workout for their babies (Bril & Sabatier, 1986; see Figure 5.8). These practices appear to promote motor development. In contrast, Navaho infants are carried about on cradle boards on their mothers' backs and receive little practice in moving (but lots of visual stimulation), and their motor development is slower than that of other groups of infants (Chisholm, 1983).

FIGURE 5.8
Promoting Motor Development in Mali

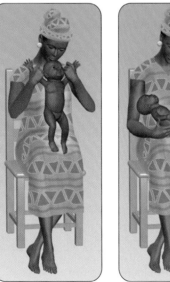

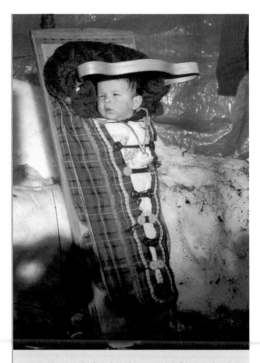

Both of these drawings show how an African mother from Mali stretches and suspends her child to promote motor development. In the first drawing, she is suspending the child between her arms. In the second drawing, the mother is stretching the child's leg muscles. Think about the cultural practices in the United States that may promote or inhibit motor development in infants.

One way in which cultural practices influence development is how infants are handled and moved. In what ways is this style of carrying an infant likely to influence motor development? Do you think this style has positive influences on visual and cognitive development?

Neonatal Reflexes

Infants are born with simple, coordinated, unlearned responses called **reflexes,** which provide limited ways for them to interact with their environment. Some reflexes aid survival because they orient the infant toward food or protection. Protective reflexes include coughing, sneezing, blinking, and muscle withdrawal (see Table 5.2).

Feeding reflexes include the rooting and sucking reflexes. The *rooting reflex* is seen when you rub your finger against a newborn's cheek: the baby turns toward the stimulation in search of a nipple to suck. The *sucking reflex* is seen whenever something touches an infant's lips: the baby tries to suck on it. Sucking is a surprisingly complex behavior that involves coordinating breathing and swallowing as well as coordinating the movements of the tongue, lips, and jaw to create a vacuum.

Other reflexes include the *Moro reflex,* a startle reaction to loud noises in which infants fling their arms out and then draw them in, arch their backs, and extend their legs. The *palmar grasping reflex* is elicited by touching the inside of the baby's hand, which causes the fingers to curl around the object. Parents of newborns are often surprised at how powerful this grasp reflex is—newborns can be lifted by using their grasping reflex.

Because reflexes help a newborn survive, an assessment of reflexes provides important insights into problems that some babies may face. An infant's reflexes can be used as indicators of the development of the nervous system. Reflexes that are too strong or too weak or that do not show expected developmental changes may indicate that the child has a problem. Babies who have been exposed to medications during delivery may fail to show some of the reflexes, such as sucking, but catch up soon after birth. As the infant's brain develops, the infant begins to take control of actions, and some reflexes disappear, usually between 4 and 8 months. The normal development of reflexes has been charted, and deviations from this pattern may signal that an infant has neurological problems. For instance, infants who have brain damage caused by cerebral palsy may continue to show a reflex after it should have disappeared (Allen, 1996).

Gross Motor Skills

Infants use gross motor skills to move about and explore their worlds. These skills involve movements of large muscles groups in the body, such as moving the legs to walk around and controlling the head and body enough to sit up. Many basic, important gross motor skills develop during infancy and toddlerhood. Although the sequence of events tends to be uniform across children, large individual variations exist in how quickly children move through these developmental phases. In general, motor control precedes in a cephalocaudal direction, moving from development of motor control of the head to the feet. Also, head, trunk, and arm control appears before children are able to coordinate their hands and fingers, showing the proximodistal trend of development.

Lifting the Head and Sitting

Infants can raise the head before they learn to stand up. The cephalocaudal trend is apparent in the development of motor control and stability in that infants first gain control over the head, later the trunk, and even later, balance, enabling them to stand and walk.

Caregivers often are cautioned to support the head when they hold a newborn. There are good reasons for this. At birth, infants have little control over head and neck muscles and cannot hold up their head. Within a month, most infants can hold up their head if someone supports the base of the neck. Three-month-old Kirra can raise her chest off the floor when placed on her stomach. In another two to three months, she gains enough control over her

FIGURE 5.9

Development Is Proximodistal and Cephalocaudal

Development is Proximodistal and Cephalocaudal

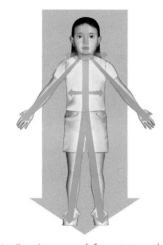

The Development of Gross Motor Skills

Proximodistal development proceeds from the spinal column outward. Cephalocaudal development proceeds from the head to the feet. Which term describes the pattern of development that occurs when children are able to control their arms before their fingers? What about when they learn to hold the head up before they learn to walk?

reflexes   *simple, coordinated, unlearned responses*

TABLE 5.2
Some Neonatal Reflexes

NAME	STIMULUS	RESPONSE	DEVELOPMENTAL COURSE
Blink	Puff air at baby	Closes eyes	Permanent
Sucking	Place object in infant's mouth	Sucks rhythmically	Changes to voluntary sucking by 2 months
Stepping	Hold baby under the arms in upright position, with feet on the ground; move baby forward	Steps by alternating legs	Disappears at 2 to 3 months
Babkin	Gently squeeze baby's palms with baby lying on back	Closes eyes, opens mouth, and turns head to middle of body	Disappears around 3 to 4 months
Rooting	Tickle baby's cheek with finger or nipple	Turns head toward finger or nipple and tries to suck	Disappears around 3 to 4 months
Tonic neck	Lay baby down flat	Turns head to one side, with arm and leg extended on that side and other arm and leg bent inward	Disappears around 3 to 4 months
Palmar grasp	Press finger against baby's palm	Grasps the finger	Declines after 3 to 4 months

NAME	STIMULUS	RESPONSE	DEVELOPMENTAL COURSE
Moro	Make sudden loud noise or let infant's head drop slightly	Arches back, throws arms out, and then draws them in, legs extended	Disappears around 5 to 6 months
Swimming	Place infant belly down in water	Moves arms and legs rhythmically, exhales through mouth	Disappears around 6 months
Babinski	Gently stroke sole of baby's foot from heel to toe	Spreads out and curls toes, turns foot inward	Changes at 12 months

Source: Adapted from Prectl and Beintema, 1965.

upper trunk to be able to sit with support. By the time she is 7 or 8 months old, Kirra's control extends to her lower trunk, and she can sit erect (Gallahue & Ozmun, 1995).

Crawling, Creeping, and Standing

Five-month-old Manuel is lying on his stomach. When he reaches for a toy in front of him, this motion causes his head and chest to rise, and then his outstretched arm pulls him forward. For many infants, within months, these motions will turn into crawling, in which he will move with his stomach on the floor. Several months later, when he is stronger and more coordinated, Manuel's crawling will change into creeping, in which he will move on his hands and knees without his stomach's touching the floor. Like most infants, Manuel will be able to stand at about 6 months, but only while someone holds him up under the arms. He will then begin to stand by holding onto furniture and pulling himself up. By 11 to 13 months, Manuel will stand well on his own.

Why Babies Aren't Crawling

Developmental milestones such as crawling and turning over are used by parents and caregivers to determine whether their child is on track for a healthy developmental outcome. Surprisingly, some of these developmental markers are changing. If you were raising a child even ten years ago, you would have expected to see your child begin crawling around 6 to 8 months of age. Today many infants are not crawling at all, or, if they are, they begin much later than babies did in the past. Many babies are not turning over when they usually did either. Should parents be concerned? Not according to developmental specialists who have conducted several studies of this change in infant motor development. The change is apparently an unexpected consequence of the public health campaign started in 1994 to reduce sudden infant death syndrome (SIDS) by teaching parents to place infants on their backs when they sleep. This campaign has been effective: SIDS deaths have dropped by about 40 percent since the program began.

Are the babies who are sleeping on their backs experiencing slower than normal development? Will their development be delayed? When researchers studied the slower-to-crawl babies, they found that these babies were normal in every other way; they sat up and walked when they were expected to do so. Pediatricians, caregivers, and parents need to be aware that today, crawling and turning over are not good markers of developmental status. Instead, language skills are considered superior indicators of whether a baby's development is on track or delayed (Davis, Moon, Sachs, & Ottolini, 1998).

When do you think this infant will begin walking? What factors contribute to an infant's developing this motor skill? Why do some infants walk before others?

Walking

Eleven-month-old Sheri was playing in a wading pool with her older sister. Much to the surprise of her parents, Sheri stood up, holding on to the side of the pool, and then let go of the edge and took her first steps. The excitement and story surrounding her first steps are now a part of Sheri's family history.

Like Sheri's family, most families respond to an infant's first steps with excitement, recognizing that walking is the most spectacular feat of early motor development. The increased mobility infants gain when they learn to walk leads to many new opportunities for learning, as well as danger. The relationship between infants and their caregivers changes once this important developmental milestone is reached.

Learning to walk progresses in stages. Not long after infants start to creep and pull themselves to a standing position, they begin to **cruise**—moving around while holding onto things for support. At 10 to 15 months, children make tentative and unsteady efforts to walk unassisted, usually with their arms held shoulder high and their feet spread apart and pointed outward. This first walking motion involves wobbly movements as children shift their weight from one foot to the other to move forward, giving them an unsteady toddling motion. Gradually, they lower their arms, turn their feet forward, and narrow their stance (Cratty, 1999). During their second year, children try many variations in their movements, including walking sideways, backwards, and on their toes.

Children's motor development, especially with respect to walking, is well described by a dynamic systems perspective (see Chapter 2). Recall that this perspective focuses on how each action is made up of bits and pieces of experience and how an action is dynamic because it changes every time it is performed (Adolph, 1997; Fogel, 1997). For instance, infants can walk on smooth floors as well as carpets because the complex actions required for each step are subtly adjusted to accommodate the different types of floor (Thelen & Smith, 1994). Rather than assume that advances in motor development are accounted for solely by maturation of the brain, dynamic systems theory assumes that the components leading to motor actions act in concert to produce changes, with each component important and necessary for producing change.

Research shows that infants have many of the motor capabilities involved in walking long before they put them all together and begin to walk. But why don't infants walk earlier? One reason is that they are unable to support their weight on one leg. Watch as adults walk and you will see that they shift all their weight from one leg to the other. Thus, each leg must be able to support the weight of the body, which requires muscle strength and balance. As infants' fat-to-muscle ratio changes over the first year, they achieve a critical combination of strength and balance that enables them to put the necessary components together to walk (Fogel & Thelen, 1987). Because infants' fat-to-muscle ratios vary, the timing of walking varies from one child to the next. When Sheri was in water, her body was lighter and she could walk, even though these actions were not yet possible on dry land. Dynamic systems theory is useful for explaining how a minor change in balance and strength results in the reorganization of capabilities to develop a much more complex behavior—walking.

Implications of Walking for Infants and Their Families

When infants begin to walk, new worlds open up to them. At the same time, a new emotional climate develops in the home. For example, once they can move about by themselves, infants react with increased frustration and anger when they cannot quite reach an attractive goal or an object they set out to get (Campos, Kermoian, & Zumbahlen, 1992). Their increased ability to locomote also heightens infants' sensitivity to the presence of caregivers. Infants who can walk show greater levels of distress when separated from caregivers and greater affection when in their presence.

Parents, too, change their emotional reactions once infants begin to walk. The expression of anger increases; some parents report that the onset of walking coincides with the first time they express anger toward their infants. As they see their infants develop in-

cruise *in infant development, to move around while holding on to things for support*

dependence, parents increasingly hold them responsible for their actions, expecting the infants to comply when told "No, stop that!" Parents also express more affection toward their walking infants, as a result of the pride they feel in their infants' new accomplishments (Campos et al., 1992).

Walking provides a good example of the transactional and interrelated nature of the domains of development. To be able to walk, children must accomplish a series of complex motor and physical tasks involving coordination, balance, and strength. Moving about freely changes children's expectations about what they can do, thereby changing their emotional responses. The new level of independence children achieve as walkers changes their parents' expectations about them. Thus, changes in childrens' physical development can bring about changes in their social and emotional relationships with others.

Early Motor Skills as Markers for Developmental Risks

At 15 months, Katie was unable to walk. She had lagged behind other children in sitting, crawling, and walking. Even when she began walking at 18 months, her movements were unusually awkward. Her mother, Kathy, expressed her concerns to her pediatrician, and Katie was diagnosed with *hypotonia,* or low muscle tone. "I had my suspicions that something was wrong, but I thought, well, maybe she's just

Why does being in the pool make walking easier for her? Why is walking considered a dynamic process in which many factors come together to permit the skill to emerge?

FIGURE 5.10
The Interrelated Domains of Development

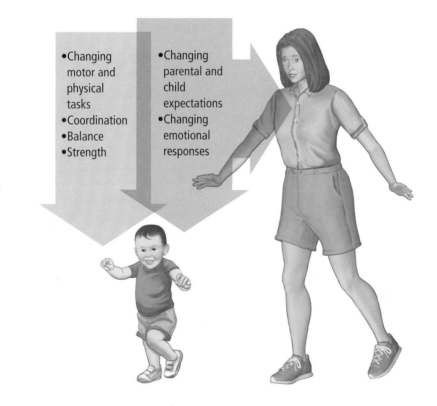

- Changing motor and physical tasks
- Coordination
- Balance
- Strength

- Changing parental and child expectations
- Changing emotional responses

When a child begins to walk, it is a marker that she has mastered certain motor skills. How does this change relate to changes in other domains, such as her relationships with her caregivers and her control over her actions? How do caregivers' expectations about her change once she begins to walk?

a slow walker. . . . When I found out that Katie wasn't perfect, I couldn't help but think of the limitations she would face. I worried that she wouldn't be in a ballet or run cross country, and it broke my heart." When her second child, Kylie, was born and by six months also appeared to have motor development problems, Kathy decided not to "wait and see" with Kylie. Both girls underwent early intervention to alter their movements and to facilitate better ways to move about in their environments. Now both children are doing quite well. Their mom says, "They can do whatever they want without limitation" (Warfield, 2002).

In the past, children with motor development delays and disorders often were not identified until age 3 or 4, which meant that they missed out on early intervention to help them practice and develop motor skills. Not surprisingly, it is easier to address delays in

TABLE 5.3
Typical and Atypical Motor Development

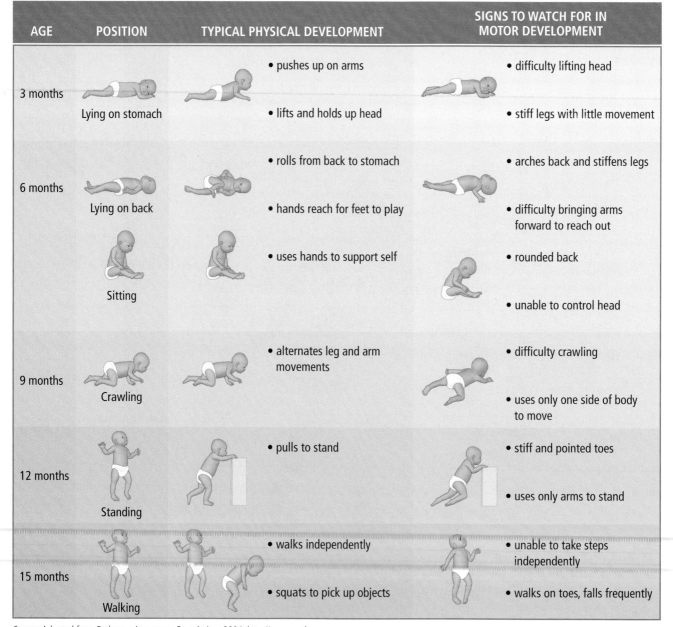

AGE	POSITION	TYPICAL PHYSICAL DEVELOPMENT	SIGNS TO WATCH FOR IN MOTOR DEVELOPMENT
3 months	Lying on stomach	• pushes up on arms • lifts and holds up head	• difficulty lifting head • stiff legs with little movement
6 months	Lying on back Sitting	• rolls from back to stomach • hands reach for feet to play • uses hands to support self	• arches back and stiffens legs • difficulty bringing arms forward to reach out • rounded back • unable to control head
9 months	Crawling	• alternates leg and arm movements	• difficulty crawling • uses only one side of body to move
12 months	Standing	• pulls to stand	• stiff and pointed toes • uses only arms to stand
15 months	Walking	• walks independently • squats to pick up objects	• unable to take steps independently • walks on toes, falls frequently

Source: Adapted from Pathways Awareness Foundation, 2004; http://www.pathwaysawareness.org

children's development if problems are identified early. Based on developmental research, there is now a diagnostic tool for early detection, which involves a trained evaluator who assesses the infant several times to evaluate motor behaviors in various positions (Kong, 1992; Prechtl et al., 1997). Normal babies tend to show variability and can adapt to different positions; children at risk for motor development tend to show a lack of variability, do not adapt to different postures, and may show the same behavior repeatedly (see Table 5.3). For example, when a typical 5-month-old is placed on her stomach on the floor, she will hold her head up and support herself on her elbows. In contrast, an at-risk child is likely to be unable to lift her head, cannot support herself on her arms, and cannot move out of the position (Stein, Bennett, & Abbott, 2004).

Fine Motor Skills

Gross motor skills allow children to explore their worlds by moving about; fine motor skills allow children to manipulate and interact with objects. Being able to reach for a toy or use fingers and thumb together to pick up a Cheerio are examples of the fine motor skills that develop during infancy. The development of fine motor skills has a very important impact on another domain of development, namely, cognitive development. Being able to grasp and reach for objects enables children to explore more thoroughly the properties of objects.

Reaching

Young infants are unable to reach for or grasp objects they are interested in, although they show different hand and arm motions when objects and people are nearby than when they are not (Ronnqvist & Hofsten, 1994). In the first few months of life, infants typically show **prereaching** behaviors in which they reach their arms toward the object but do not contact it—instead, they usually hold their hands in fists that seem to aim in the direction of the object. When presented with objects in different locations, newborns direct more of their arm movements toward the objects, indicating that they are beginning to master basic movements (Bloch, 1990). This research reveals a surprising degree of coordination in fine motor movements among newborns.

After several months, infants' skills at reaching become more highly coordinated (Smitsman, 2001). By about 3 months, infants watch an object intently as they reach toward it, and their hands adjust to fit the size of the object even before contact is made (von Hofsten, 1984; von Hofsten & Spelke, 1985). The dynamic system involved in reaching is very evident: to reach for an object requires controlling arm and hand movements. Vision plays a role, in that children use information about where objects are located to direct their reaches (Jonsson & von Hosten, 2003; Rosander & von Hofsten, 2004; Spelke & von Hosten, 2001). But more central to development is children learning to recognize and control the feeling of the arms as they move through space. Children differ in their muscle control and their speed of reacting (Thelen et al., 1993; Thelen, Corbetta, & Spencer, 1996). Not surprisingly, first reaches often miss their mark; smooth reaching takes practice. Some children move quickly and with intensity; to have a controlled reach, they must bring their intense motions under control. Other children move too tentatively, and they must learn to move with more forcefulness to reach their target. The nature of the object children reach for also matters. For instance, when children reach for objects that they are going to throw, they approach them quickly; in contrast, if they are reaching for an object to insert into a small opening in a container, they move much more slowly. When reaching for moving or spinning objects, infants adjust their reach (Morrongiello & Rocca, 1989; von Hofsten & Lindhagen, 1979; von Hofsten et al., 1998; Wentworth, Benson, & Haith, 2000). This suggests that children's reaching motions are guided in part by their expectation of what they will do with the object and the orientation of the object in space (Claxton, Keen, & McCarty, 2003).

Grasping

Newborns have the grasping reflex that allows them to hold on to objects (such as a parent's finger), but this reflex drops out quickly. If they are handed an object, 3-month-olds can hold

FIGURE 5.11

Prereaching

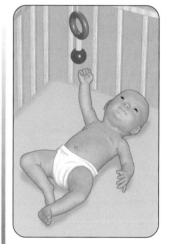

What behavior is this child demonstrating? In what ways do these early, uncoordinated behaviors promote later coordinated motor development?

prereaching *a child's effort to reach the arms toward an object without being able to contact it*

FIGURE 5.12
Grasping Reflexes

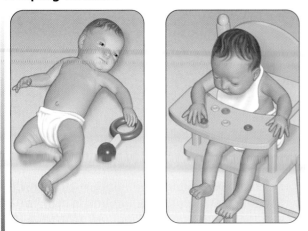

Which type of grasp is each of these babies showing? How do these grasps differ in the way the thumb is used? Which grasp requires more coordinated motions?

it in an *ulnar grasp,* which is a clumsy grasp with the fingers folded over the object. By the end of the first year, infants have a much more coordinated grasping movement, called the **pincer grasp,** which involves using the forefinger and the thumb in opposition to pick up small objects. This action also becomes more skilled until children are able to pick up tiny pieces of cheese or a single Cheerio off their plate. Just as reaching involves both children's own motor skills and the qualities of the object they are reaching for, so does grasping. A child who is trying to grasp an object will orient the hand in the best manner to grab hold of the object, depending on its properties. A child moving toward a toy with a handle at the top will move the hand so that it can best grasp the handle (Robinson, McKenzie, & Day, 1996).

How do infants explore objects that they grasp and reach for? Their styles of exploration change dramatically from 2 to 5 months of age. When handed an object to explore, most 2-month-olds will immediately move the object to the mouth to explore it. By 5 months of age, few bring it to the mouth first; most bring it to the eyes for a good look. However, once they have had a good look at the object, they often will continue to explore it with the mouth, and with a combination of both. These findings suggest that infants use multiple modes of learning about objects as they grow older (Rochat, 1989).

Caregivers encourage and respond to the changes in children's motor skills (Danis, Bourdais, & Ruel, 2000). Before infants are able to grasp and reach for objects, adults will show them objects and demonstrate their qualities, such as shaking a rattle or making a squeaky toy make a squeak. They also give babies toys to play with so that they can explore them even before they can reach for them. When infants can reach, parents tend to hold toys steady and within reach so that babies are encouraged to try to reach for them. Although it may not seem important, how parents hold infants plays a role in how infants explore objects. Think about an infant lying on her back—she probably has little access to toys or to visual stimulation. Now think about an infant who is being held sitting up; his hands are free to explore, and he can easily see people and objects in the room (Fogel et al., 1993).

Bowel and Bladder Control

During the first year of life, infants have no control over the muscles involved in elimination and have little, if any, awareness of the physical signs that signal elimination. In the middle of the second year, many children make the connection between the feelings of impending elimination and their outcome (Leach, 1997). The potential to be toilet trained increases at the end of the second year or the beginning of the third year, once toddlers can anticipate elimination. Control over bowel movements usually is accomplished earlier than bladder control.

When to start toilet training is a serious concern for many parents. Junko was very anxious because her son, who had just turned 3, was not yet toilet trained. She wondered what she should do about this. Research shows that there are large individual differences in when children become toilet trained (Taubman, 1997). Most children learn to control their bladders and bowels when they are ready, just as they learn to sit and walk. For example, shortly after Junko voiced her concerns, her son seemed to spontaneously become toilet trained.

When Junko's son was ready for toilet training, he responded positively and quickly to it. Starting to train him earlier would have lengthened the process and probably not produced earlier bowel or bladder control. Four percent of children are toilet trained by age 2, 60 percent are trained by age 3, and only 2 percent are not trained by age 4. Boys generally

pincer grasp *using the forefinger and the thumb in opposition to pick up small objects*

take longer to be trained than girls do. If a child is not trained by 42 months, caregivers may want to seek the advice of a pediatrician (Blum, Taubman, & Osborne, 1997).

What Factors Influence Infant Health and Safety?

Infants' health issues vary depending on their age, genetic inheritance, condition at birth, and living conditions. The leading causes of death for children under 1 year of age are congenital anomalies, sudden infant death syndrome (SIDS), and disorders related to low birthweight or premature birth (see Chapter 4). After children learn to walk, the leading cause of death is physical injuries, which account for about one third of all deaths of children 1 to 4 years of age (Brenner et al., 2001; National Center for Health Statistics, 2001c). Many health problems that children experience can be prevented through vaccines to ward off diseases and safety devices to prevent injuries. Another health issue for young children is exposure to environmental hazards, such as lead and radon gas. Children who live in impoverished environments are most at risk for health and safety problems because of a lack of health care and the unsafe conditions in which they live (Bellinger & Adams, 2001).

Promoting Healthy Development and Growth

In order to promote children's healthy development and growth, the American Academy of Pediatrics (1991) recommends six "well-child" visits during the first year of life, six visits over the next four years, and then a visit every other year until the age of 20.

In the United States, all states require that children receive basic immunizations before entering school. During the first years of life, the recommended immunizations include vaccines to protect against hepatitis B; diphtheria, tetanus, and pertussis; measles, mumps, and rubella; polio; influenza; varicella (chicken pox); and pneumonia (Centers for Disease Control, 2004). Some of these vaccines are given together in one vaccine injection (such as diphtheria, tetanus, and pertussis), and most require multiple injections over a span of time for full protection. The vaccines are safe and very rarely cause side effects. Approximately 20 percent of children under age 3 do not receive immunizations, and inner-city children of low-income families are least likely to be immunized (National Center for Health Statistics, 2001b). Not receiving vaccinations can have serious consequences such as placing children at risk for many serious and life-threatening diseases. For instance, 1 out of 30 children with measles get pneumonia, and some children die from measles (Centers for Disease Control, 2004). Unfortunately, many US children lack access to health care, and the number of children without any form of health insurance has increased over the past 25 years (US Census Bureau, 2002). Hispanic children are less likely to have health insurance than Caucasian American or African American children (US Census Bureau, 2001c). The lack of health insurance among Hispanic children may be due to cultural factors—because of social and cultural barriers (such as limited English proficiency or fear of deportation), immigrant families may not seek health coverage.

Avoiding Accidents

Infants and toddlers are at risk for many kinds of accidents. Before they crawl, infants may fall off changing tables or beds or get caught in crib rails; they can suffocate on soft bedding materials or on pillows. Baby appliances such as walkers, rockers, and jumpers can cause injuries if used improperly (Smith, Bowman, Luria, & Shields, 1997). Unsupervised crawling and walking infants may hurt themselves by falling down stairs, falling into swimming pools, or walking into the street. Infants and toddlers also may be hurt or killed in car accidents. Caregivers need to be particularly cautious about car safety; babies should be restrained in car seats attached to the back seat. Infants and toddlers also may be poisoned by dangerous chemicals in the house. Because very young children are eager to explore, caregivers should make sure their homes are childproof.

What types of accidents are most commonly experienced by toddlers? What steps can caregivers take to prevent accidents?

DEBATING THE ISSUE

SHOULD BABIES BE TAUGHT TO SWIM?

Drowning is one of the most common accidents of childhood. In addition to falling into swimming pools, rivers, and lakes, children have drowned by toppling into toilets or buckets with just a few inches of water in them. In an effort to "drownproof" them, some parents enroll their children in infant swimming programs. Other parents place their infants in these classes because they believe that there is a critical period for learning to swim.

These programs should be viewed with caution for several reasons. First, parents must realize that their children will never be "drownproofed" because no one, regardless of age or skill, is completely safe around water (American Academy of Pediatrics, 2000; Langendorfer, 1987). Second, scientific evidence does not support the idea of a critical period for acquiring swimming skills. Third, although few experience this rare condition, some babies will suffer hyponatremia (water intoxication) if they ingest large quantities of water during swimming. Symptoms of hyponatremia are lethargy, weakness, vomiting, and seizures, and victims may die (Burd, 1986). A more common problem is that children may catch giardia, an intestinal parasite that causes severe diarrhea. Because of these concerns, the American Academy of Pediatrics (2000) recommends that parents wait until children are 3 or 4 years old before enrolling them in organized aquatic programs (Gallahue & Ozmun, 1995).

THINKING IT THROUGH

1. Why might people think that infancy is an ideal time to teach swimming skills?

2. What were your experiences in and around water as a baby or young child? If you can swim, when and under what circumstances did you learn to swim?

3. What guidelines might you follow to prevent the accidental drowning of an infant or toddler in your care?

Infant Mortality

Many infants worldwide do not live long enough to celebrate their first birthday. In 2001, Angola and Afghanistan had two of the highest rates of infant mortality in all the world. In the United States, the infant mortality rate was relatively low, with only 7 children out of 1,000 not surviving until their first birthday. However, despite the excellent medical facilities in the United States, the US infant mortality rate is still higher than that of many other developed countries—20 countries have lower rates (UNICEF, 2001).

Within the United States, some groups have much higher rates of infant mortality than others do. Compared with the mortality rate for Caucasian American infants—6.0 deaths per 1,000 live births—mortality rates are 136 percent higher for African American infants and 45 percent higher for Native American Indian infants. The mortality rate for Hispanic infants is comparable to that for Caucasian American infants, whereas Asian American infants have a mortality rate that is 16 percent lower (National Center for Health Statistics, 2001a). Why the infant mortality rates for these groups differ is as yet unknown, but one likely reason is differences in access to and use of prenatal and postnatal care. Cultural values and family support are important, too, as evidenced by the lower rates of infant mortality among Hispanic infants, despite lower socioeconomic status and less prenatal care (Balcazar, Peterson, & Krull, 1997).

Infant Nutrition

In the 1940s and early 1950s, pediatricians recommended that parents feed their infants on a rigid 4-hour schedule, with the idea that this routine would increase infants' self-regulation of hunger. Today most pediatricians recommend feeding "on demand"—that is, feeding infants whenever they are hungry. Feeding on demand allows infants to control their own nutritional intake and satisfaction (Drewett, 1993).

NURTURING CHILDREN
PREVENTING SIDS

After the first few days of life, the most common cause of unexpected death in infants is sudden infant death syndrome (SIDS). When an infant dies in his or her sleep and there is no other ready explanation, SIDS is often the diagnosis. SIDS strikes nearly 5,000 babies in the United States each year (American Academy of Pediatrics, 2001). Other possible causes of death, such as child abuse and overheating, must be ruled out. SIDS is not well understood; apparently, many different factors can cause an infant to die during the first months after birth. Some of the suspected causes of SIDS include drug use by the mother during pregnancy, an undetected fast-acting viral or bacterial infection, oxygen deprivation during pregnancy, hormonal imbalance, and cigarette smoking in the home. More infants die of SIDS within the first few months of birth than later, suggesting that infants may be less susceptible to SIDS once certain developmental changes have occurred. Certain infants seem to be at risk for SIDS: boys, infants with brothers or sisters who died of SIDS, preterm infants, low-birthweight infants, infants with low Apgar scores, and infants with respiratory problems (Barness & Gilbert-Barness, 1992).

To reduce the likelihood of an infant's dying of SIDS, recommendations to parents include placing the infant in a face-up position rather than a face-down position to sleep, using a firm mattress, avoiding overdressing or overheating the infant, breast-feeding when possible, and maintaining regular health care visits (Association of SIDS and Infant Mortality Programs, 1998).

Infants grow most rapidly in the first year, so adequate nutrition during that period is essential. Most infants obtain adequate nutrition from breast milk or formula. Human milk has evolved to provide the best nutrition for an infant, and it changes in composition to match the infant's needs. Even a mother who is malnourished produces milk that is sufficient to meet her infant's nutritional needs for the first few months of life (Brown, Robertson, & Akhtar, 1986).

Benefits of Breast-Feeding to Infants

Human milk provides all the protein needed by a baby for the first six months of life. It also contains a balance of amino acids and minerals that differs from that in other nutritional sources. Human milk contains more cholesterol than cow's milk or formulas, and cholesterol is essential for promoting myelination within the brain (Uauy & Peirano, 1999). Also important for brain development is human milk's higher concentration of lactose, which provides the fuel needed by the infant's rapidly growing brain. Although human and cow's milk are both low in iron, the iron in human milk is absorbed better, reducing the likelihood of iron deficiencies. Human milk also is more digestible than cow's milk.

Breast milk also provides an array of protective benefits to infants. Breast-fed infants are more resistant to infections than are bottle-fed infants. One reason is cleanliness. Contaminants are more likely to be a problem with bottle-feeding, especially in countries that have very hot climates (which promote bacteria growth) or have contaminated water (Lifshitz, Finch, & Lifshitz, 1991). Another reason is that breast milk contains substances that fight off infections. Breast-feeding is especially useful in transferring the mother's immunities to the infant in the first weeks of life and stimulating the infant's own immune system. During the first few days of the baby's life, the mother's breasts produce **colostrum,** a pre-milk substance containing antibodies that protect the baby from infections. The advantages of breast-feeding may last a long time; breast-fed infants have less risk of some diseases later in life, including coronary artery disease, allergies, and diabetes (Lifshitz et al., 1991).

Findings from several studies suggest that breast feeding helps minimize the risk of obesity in children. In a study of 15,000 children of ages 9 to 14, children who were breast-fed as babies were found to be less likely to grow up to be overweight than were

colostrum *a pre-milk substance containing antibodies from the mother that protect the baby from infections*

formula-fed babies, even when potential confounding influences (such as the amount of time spent watching television, physical activity, and maternal weight) were controlled (Gillman et al., 2001). Also, the influence of breast-feeding on weight may become evident in early childhood, although the research evidence to support this trend is less clear-cut (Hediger, Overpeck, Kuczmarski, & Ruan, 2001; von Kries et al., 1999).

Breast-fed newborns tend to be more irritable, reactive, and physiologically adaptive than bottle-fed babies. Research shows that this is an optimal pattern of responsiveness (DiPietro, Larson, & Porges, 1987). Longer-term effects of breast-feeding include scoring slightly higher on intelligence tests, even when family economic backgrounds are taken into account (Fergusson, Beautrais, & Silva, 1982). Babies breast-fed longer than eight months show increases in IQ and reading comprehension scores at 8 and 18 years of age as well (Horwood & Fergusson, 1998). It is unclear, however, whether it is the composition of breast milk or the interpersonal interactions involved in breast-feeding that affect later cognitive development (Doyle et al., 1992; Lucas et al., 1992). One study suggests that the association between breast-feeding and parental characteristics (such as IQ) explains why children's intelligence scores improve with breast-feeding. As well as being more likely to provide breast-feeding opportunities, mothers who have higher IQs provide more educational opportunities and enrichment for their children. Thus, their children are more likely to perform well on IQ tests (Jacobson, Chiodo, & Jacobson, 1999). These findings do not detract from the many health advantages associated with breast-feeding. And the possible intellectual benefits of breast-feeding do not mean that caregivers should be overly concerned if they cannot or do not breast-feed. As you will learn, many other factors, such as providing an enriching intellectual environment, play important roles in influencing children's intellectual growth.

Benefits of Breast-Feeding to Mothers

In addition to conveying nutritional and protective benefits to infants, breast-feeding also has benefits for mothers. Many women enjoy breast-feeding their infants because of the pleasure and closeness they experience during feeding sessions. Women who breast-feed lose more weight and experience nonpainful uterine contractions, which help them recover from childbirth more quickly than women who do not breast-feed. Breast-feeding also delays ovulation, which is beneficial for mothers who do not use or have limited access to birth control. Convenience also is a factor. Breast milk does not need to be heated up or cooled down; it is portable and usually plentiful. And breast-feeding is less expensive: in the United States, breast-feeding saves $400 in food purchases in the first year (Smolin & Grosvenor, 2000). In developing countries, families attempting to bottle-feed may spend

TABLE 5.4
Benefits of Breast-Feeding for Infants and Mothers

FOR INFANTS	FOR MOTHERS
Source of protein and iron	Contact and intimacy with infant
Source of cholesterol and lactose (good for brain development)	Increased weight loss
Resistance to infections	Faster recovery from childbirth
Protection against diseases even later in life	Delayed ovulation
Minimized risk of obesity	Convenience
Slightly higher IQ and improved reading comprehension	Less expense

50 percent of their income on infant formula (Lifshitz et al., 1991). Also, parents do not have to worry about the potentially fatal consequences if formula is limited or water is contaminated.

For women who find breast-feeding difficult and painful, trained lactation consultants can improve the likelihood of success. However, breast-feeding is not an option for all women. For example, it is difficult to maintain while working outside the home, although breast pumps allow women to express their milk for later use. Some women are advised not to breast-feed because of the medication they are taking or diseases they might transfer to their infants through breast milk. Mothers with AIDS, for instance, may pass the disease on to their infants through their milk (Sizer & Whitney, 1997). Additionally, breast-feeding can be demanding on mothers—using a bottle allows other family members to help and participate in the care of the infant. Bottle-feeding requires less energy from infants and so may be preferable for weak babies.

When caregivers decide to use bottle-feeding, it is very important that they select a specially formulated infant formula. Using cow's milk or other types of milk can lead to serious nutritional deficiencies (Smolin & Grosvenor, 2000).

Prevalence of Breast-Feeding

In the 1970s, only about 25 percent of new mothers in the United States breast-fed their babies; today, about 64 percent of mothers breast-feed in the early weeks of life (Li et al., 2002; Ryan, 1997). Breast-feeding has become especially popular among college-educated, higher-income women (Life Sciences Research Office, 1995). Mothers also are breast-feeding for longer periods of time than they did in the 1970s. Today, 29 percent more mothers breast-feed for 6 months and 16 percent for one year (NHANES, 2002). African American women are less likely to breast-feed than are Mexican American and Caucasian women (NHANES, 2002). Experts on nutrition would like to increase to 75 percent the number of mothers who breast-feed for the first few weeks and increase to 50 percent the number who continue until the babies are 4 to 6 months old (Sizer & Whitney, 1997).

Notice that the mother is holding the infant and gazing at him. Beyond providing infants with optimal nutrition, what aspects of breast-feeding may be pleasant for mothers and encourage attachment for infants?

Weaning and Feeding Infants and Toddlers

The recommended timing for introducing solid foods into an infant's diet has changed since the 1970s, when mothers were encouraged to offer cereal to infants as young as 6 weeks of age. Pediatricians now recommend delaying solid foods until the child has reached at least 13 to 14 pounds (double the average birthweight) or is between 4 and 6 months old. Before that time, infants' digestive systems are not sufficiently developed to digest starchy foods. Undigested solid foods may sensitize the child to proteins that cause food allergies and may result in kidney malfunction. Infants signal their readiness for solid foods by demanding to be fed more frequently than every 2 hours and by drinking large quantities of milk (Lifshitz et al., 1991). Although "baby teeth" begin to erupt between 5 and 9 months of age and most infants have six teeth by their first birthday, their first foods need to be soft because infants are unable to chew well until their second year.

Children need high-calorie foods because they have high energy needs to support their rapid growth. Most parents start by introducing cereals, which are digested easily and rarely cause food allergies. Later, fruits and vegetables are added to an infant's diet. Protein foods such as cheese, yogurt, egg yolks, and pureed meats can be introduced at 6 to 8 months. Whole eggs, milk, and more table foods can be introduced when babies are 1 year old (Sizer & Whitney, 1997).

Throughout the toddler years, children make a gradual transition to their family's regular diet and develop more mature eating habits and skills. Toddlers need to eat frequently,

Notice that this baby has smeared his face with food. Can you identify when children should be weaned and the reasons associated with this?

failure to thrive (FTT)   *a term used to describe infants and children who do not grow at the expected rates*

and their diet must include nutrient-dense foods to ensure that their nutritional needs are met while they are growing rapidly. For example, low-fat milk is not appropriate for an infant. Reducing fat and cholesterol in the diet, restricting high-calorie foods, and limiting between-meal snacks may be recommended for many older children and adults, but for infants such restrictions can contribute to inadequate nutrition and failure to thrive (Smolin & Grosvenor, 2000).

Failure-to-Thrive Infants

Failure to thrive (FTT) is a term used to describe infants and children who do not appear to be ill or abnormal but who do not grow at the expected rates (Casey, 1992). Children whose growth is below normal or whose growth rate slows down drastically may be FTT infants (Lifshitz et al., 1991).

The most common causes of FTT are *undernutrition,* the condition of not having enough food to eat, and *malnutrition,* the condition of not receiving the appropriate nutrients. The quality of the interactions children have with their caregivers also may be a factor (Powell, Low, & Speers, 1987). Once treated with adequate nutrition and calories, FTT children return to normal growth patterns (Bithoney & Newberger, 1987), although children with FTT generally are shorter and lighter than those without FTT, even 14 years after the initiation of treatment (Oates, Peacock, & Forrest, 1985).

Failure to thrive is more than a growth problem. Children with FTT also are likely to display abnormal behaviors; be passive, inactive, and withdrawn; show little expression of emotion; avoid close physical contact and cuddling; and show unusual eating behaviors (Powell et al., 1987).

Mothers of FTT children may be depressed or may have serious psychological problems that interfere with caregiving activities, including feeding. Families of children with FTT often have disorganized homes and experience social isolation or multiple stressors (Casey, 1992).

Several studies show that FTT children lag behind their peers in language development, reading, verbal intelligence, and social maturity, even years after treatment. The outcome for the individual child depends on how long the child had FTT, the ongoing quality of caregiving, and the child's home environment (Casey, 1992).

Try It Out

1. At what age did you first walk unassisted? In what physical environment and social context did you accomplish this feat?
2. Observe an infant or toddler to identify his or her perceptual abilities. You might interact with or test the baby informally to try to determine perception of colors, patterns, faces, movement, or depth.
3. Investigate and report on a nutrition, health, or safety issue concerning infants or toddlers. For example, you might research a topic such as immunizations, baby foods, SIDS, lead exposure, baby toys, furniture and appliances for babies, infant car seats, or FTT babies.

Key Terms and Concepts

axon (137)

colostrum (159)

cruise (152)

dendrites (137)

failure to thrive (FTT) (162)

myelination (138)

neurons (136)

pincer grasp (156)

prereaching (155)
reflexes (149)
state of arousal (133)

synapses (137)
synaptogenesis (138)
visual cliff apparatus (144)

Sum It Up

How do infants and toddlers develop physically?

■   Describe some states of infant arousal. (pp. 133–135)

How do infant brains develop?

■   What are the progressive and regressive events of brain development? (p. 136)

■   Describe the formation and migration of neurons. (pp. 136–138)

How do infants' perceptual abilities develop?

■   What changes occur in visual acuity between 1 and 6 months? (pp. 142–144)

■   By what age do infants begin to discriminate colors; recognize patterns; prefer faces, especially attractive ones; and recognize human-generated motion? (pp. 142–144)

■   How do infants begin to recognize depth and distance? (pp. 144–145)

■   Why does an infant's auditory sense mature so much more rapidly than visual acuity? (p. 145)

■   What tastes can newborns distinguish? (p. 145)

How do motor skills develop in infants and toddlers?

■   Describe the sequence the development of motor skills in infants and toddlers. (p. 148)

■   What are the differences between a reflex, a gross motor skill, and a fine motor skill? (pp. 149–155)

What factors influence infant health and safety?

■   What is the leading cause of death for children after they learn to walk? (p. 157)

■   What are some of the benefits of breastfeeding to infants? (pp. 159–161)

■   Describe some of the difficulties experienced by a failure-to-thrive child. (p. 162)

FIGURE 5.1 **Growth Charts for Height and Weight (birth to 36 months)** *Notice that infants tend to grow very rapidly in both weight and height.*

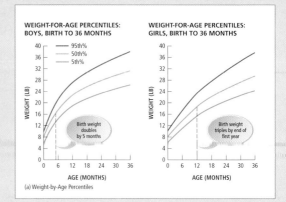

WEIGHT-FOR-AGE PERCENTILES: BOYS, BIRTH TO 36 MONTHS

WEIGHT-FOR-AGE PERCENTILES: GIRLS, BIRTH TO 36 MONTHS

Birth weight doubles by 5 months

Birth weight triples by end of first year

(a) Weight-by-Age Percentiles

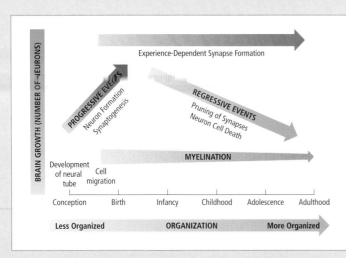

FIGURE 5.5 **Development of the Brain** *This model illustrates different events in brain development.*

PHYSICAL AND BRAIN DEVELOPMENT

Physical growth is very rapid during this time. The brain is also growing quickly, and its growth depends on the environment in which the child is raised. As the brain grows, it is vulnerable to the environment, which influences how it is wired and which neuronal connections are lost. Enriched environments (books, parks, talking to child) help develop more neural connections; impoverished environments (lack of stimulation) hinder brain development. (Refer back to pages 131–141.)

PERCEPTUAL DEVELOPMENT

Newborns can see, hear, taste, touch, and smell, and they can feel pain. However, not all sensory systems are fully developed at birth. Taste and smell more fully developed than vision and hearing. (Refer back to pages 142–149.)

Newborns prefer sweet solutions over all other tastes, and they show disgust or distress when tasting something bitter or sour.

FIGURE 5.6 **Testing Infants' Visual Acuity** *This test uses infant preferences for patterns to test their visual acuity.*

FIGURE 5.8
Promoting Motor Development in Mali

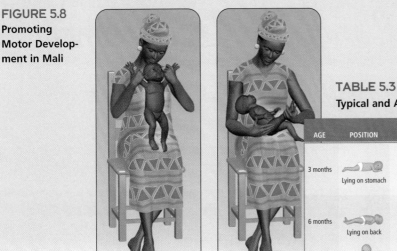

TABLE 5.3
Typical and Atypical Motor Development

AGE	POSITION		TYPICAL PHYSICAL DEVELOPMENT		SIGNS TO WATCH FOR IN MOTOR DEVELOPMENT
3 months	Lying on stomach		• pushes up on arms • lifts and holds up head		• difficulty lifting head • stiff legs with little movement
6 months	Lying on back		• rolls from back to stomach • hands reach for feet to play		• arches back and stiffens legs • difficulty bringing arms forward to reach out
	Sitting		• uses hands to support self		• rounded back • unable to control head
9 months	Crawling		• alternates leg and arm movements		• difficulty crawling • uses only one side of body to move
12 months	Standing		• pulls to stand		• stiff and pointed toes • uses only arms to stand
15 months	Walking		• walks independently • squats to pick up objects		• unable to take steps independently • walks on toes, falls frequently

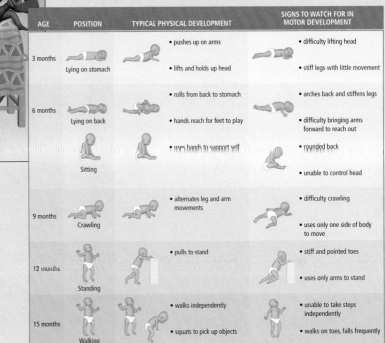

MOTOR SKILLS

The basic developmental trends are represented in motor development. Development proceeds from head to toe (cephalocaudal development) and from the spine outward (proximodistal development). (Refer back to pages 148–157.)

HEALTH AND SAFETY

Good nutrition, health care, and immunizations are important to promote health. Risks to health include car accidents, drowning, poisoning, and falling. (Refer back to pages 157–162.)

Infants and toddlers are at risk for many kinds of accidents

TABLE 5.4

Benefits of Breast-Feeding for Infants and Mothers

FOR INFANTS	FOR MOTHERS
Source of protein and iron	Contact and intimacy with infant
Source of cholesterol and lactose (good for brain development)	Increased weight loss
Resistance to infections	Faster recovery from childbirth
Protection against diseases even later in life	Delayed ovulation
Minimized risk of obesity	Convenience
Slightly higher IQ and improved reading comprehension	Less expense

165

Cognitive and Language Development in Infancy and Toddlerhood

Chapter 6 Outline

How Do Cognitive Abilities Develop During Infancy and Toddlerhood?
Piaget's Sensorimotor Stage
Beyond Piaget: Newer Research on Early Cognitive Abilities
The Social Contexts of Early Learning and Cognitive Development
The Cultural Contexts of Early Learning and Cognitive Development

How Do Infants and Toddlers Learn, Remember, and Process Information?
Learning Through Contingency and Association
Learning What's Familiar: Habituation and Novelty Responses
Developing Long-Term Memory

How Do Infants and Toddlers Develop Language Skills?
Before the First Words
First Words
Development of Vocabulary
Solving the Mystery of Word Meaning
First Sentences
Early Talkers and Late Talkers

How Is Children's Language Acquisition Explained?
Learning-Based Theories
Innate Theories: Biological Influences
Social Interaction Theories
Genie's Outcomes
The Resilient and Fragile Aspects of Language Development

A DEVELOPMENTAL MYSTERY

Imagine a girl raised for 10 years under the most extreme isolation: little contact with anyone except for offers of food and water and basic care; hearing no sounds except for the occasional dog barking in the distance; nothing much to look at except one barely furnished room; and no caring parents to hug and nurture her. How might development occur under such horrible conditions? Hearing no human language, how would this affect her own language development? Having no adults to guide her, how would this affect her intellectual development?

To what extent does the early development of intellectual and language skills require human interaction and exposure to stimulation in one's environment (such as changing sights, sounds, and touch)? This mystery has intrigued both scientists and the general public. Recall the story of the *Wild Boy of Aveyron* you read about in the opening chapter. His case revealed the potential for the lack of human contact to have dramatic effects on the development of intellectual and language skills. Sadly, these kinds of cases still occur; several children have been raised under similar circumstances. These cases tell us that infant cognitive and language abilities are closely tied to their social environments.

How Do Cognitive Abilities Develop During Infancy and Toddlerhood?

Jean Piaget developed a theory that described how children become problem solvers beginning in infancy, and this theory about cognitive development provided parents, teachers, and other professionals with freshly original insights about children. Particularly remarkable is how infants and children differ from older children, according to his theory. For most people, understanding infancy is challenging, but Piaget provided keys to help unlock the secrets of how infants and toddlers think. Remember from Chapter 2 that Piaget believed that a stage perspective best captured the changes that occur in thinking and that children move through these stages progressively, with each stage providing a different lens through which the world can be viewed.

Piaget's Sensorimotor Stage

What is problem solving or thinking for an infant? When do children begin to show that their actions have purpose? One of Piaget's most significant contributions to understanding development was his description of how, over the course of less than 2 years, infants' behavior undergoes amazing changes from nonpurposeful movements to purposeful experimenting to find out about the qualities of objects. At 2 months, infants do not reach out to grab a rattle, but by 18 months, as an experiment in learning, they will try every possible action to make a rubber ducky squeak. During the first 2 years of life, infants move from narrow and repetitive reflex actions to the flexible use of symbols to represent objects and people. During this time, infants and toddlers also come to recognize that other people and objects are separate from themselves. At 8 to 12 months, infants begin to show the first signs of truly intelligent behavior; for example, they plan and try out different actions to obtain a goal. According to Piaget, these changes characterize the first period of cognitive development: the *sensorimotor stage* (see Chapter 2). Piaget described the rapid changes that infants and toddlers undergo in terms of six substages

TABLE 6.1
Substages in the Sensorimotor Stage

SUBSTAGE	AGE	CHARACTERISTICS
Substage I	Birth to 1 month	Practices reflex actions
Substage II	1 to 4 months	Engages in primary circular reactions—repetitive actions centered on the infant's body
Substage III	4 to 8 months	Uses visually guided reaching for greater exploration
		Engages in secondary circular reactions—repetitive actions centered on objects
Substage IV	8 to 12 months	Shows first signs of intelligence by using intentional behavior to solve problems
Substage V	12 to 18 months	Engages in tertiary circular reactions—modified repetitive actions designed to explore qualities of objects
Substage VI	18 to 24 months	Achieves greater flexibility in problem solving by using symbols to represent objects

(Piaget, 1936/1963). Each substage builds on the skills acquired in the previous ones (see Table 6.1).

The sensorimotor stage lasts from birth until approximately the age of 2. Its name derives from Piaget's belief that infants learn about the world through their senses and their actions. For example, infants try to mouth most anything they touch in an effort to learn the qualities of the objects. April, when she was 5 months old, persistently sucked on the face of a watch worn by the adult who was holding her, in an attempt to "understand" its qualities. By using senses and actions, and being constrained to these forms of learning, infants gain a distinct type of understanding of the world. Piaget believed that infants' type of understanding—sensorimotor understanding—was the basis for a whole stage of development and that it differed from the types of learning that older children and adults use. Since ways of learning and problem solving change during infancy, Piaget also devised substages to describe the precise subtle changes that occur over the course of the first 2 years of life.

FIGURE 6.1
Sensorimotor Schemes

What automatic reflexive scheme is this infant using?

primary circular reactions
repetitive actions that are centered on an infant's own body and motions

Substage I: Using Reflexive Schemes (Birth to 1 Month)
In substage I, neonates spend their time using the reflexive behaviors that they were able to perform at birth. As you learned in Chapter 5, many neonatal reflexes, such as grasping, looking, and sucking, help them survive. Piaget viewed these reflexes as the basic schemes, called *sensorimotor schemes*, that provide children with ways to interact with and know about the world around them. Infants' first knowledge of the world is derived from these schemas. For example, through their experiences in applying the "sucking" scheme, infants come to know the shape of an object (see Figure 6.1). By grasping a toy, infants come to know its shape. In Piagetian terms, infants assimilate information by using schemes.

Although sensorimotor schemes are repetitive and automatic behaviors, they are not applied rigidly: infants can adapt them to fit a particular situation, such as changing the shape of their lips to fit a differently shaped nipple. According to Piaget, infants accommodate their schemes to meet the demands of different situations. At this point, however, infants' behavior is not purposeful—they do not have goals in mind while exercising reflex actions.

Substage II: Exploring Movements of the Body (1 to 4 Months)
In substage II, infants act somewhat more purposefully. By 2 to 3 months, many infants recognize that their actions have specific effects. They discover these effects through repetitive actions, which Piaget described as **primary circular reactions**—repetitive actions that are centered on an infant's own body and motions. These actions, such as thumb sucking, first occur accidentally, but infants find them pleasurable and so continue the actions (see

FIGURE 6.2
Primary Circular Reactions

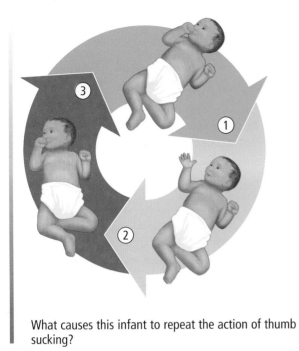

What causes this infant to repeat the action of thumb sucking?

FIGURE 6.3
Secondary Circular Reactions

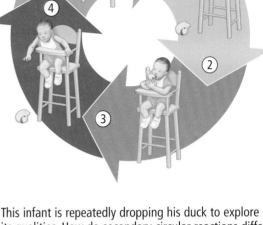

This infant is repeatedly dropping his duck to explore its qualities. How do secondary circular reactions differ from primary circular reactions?

Figure 6.2). For example, Piaget described how his son Laurent began sucking his thumb. Laurent's hand accidentally landed near his mouth while he was being held. Seeing this interesting object, Laurent tried to suck on it, but his arm slipped away. After many tries, Laurent moved his arm so that his thumb was near his mouth, and he began sucking his thumb (Piaget, 1936/1963).

Substage III: Exploring Objects (4 to 8 Months)

At around 4 months, infants begin to combine primary circular reactions into more coordinated patterns. For instance, they coordinate schemes so that they can grasp objects they see. To do this, infants must connect what they see, the movements of their arms, and the movements of their hands. This coordination of vision and movement schemes allows infants much more flexibility to explore.

An example illustrates the new means of learning available to infants in substage III. During a meal, 7-month-old Noah drops a spoon off the edge of his tray onto the floor. He finds the sound interesting, so he repeats this action each time his mother puts the spoon back on his tray. Noah's behavior indicates that he is using a new way to explore the qualities of objects—in this case, the spoon. Noah, like other infants in substage III, demonstrates that he can use a new type of circular reaction, called a secondary circular reaction. **Secondary circular reactions** are repetitive actions focused on the qualities of objects, such as the noises they make or their shapes and colors. Like primary circular reactions, these reactions begin accidentally, but through them infants explore the characteristics of objects rather than those of their own body. The sound a spoon makes when it hits the floor or the sound a plastic duck makes when squeezed becomes the focus of attention, and infants will repeat the action time and time again to reproduce this interesting property (see Figure 6.3).

Infants in this substage want to make appealing sights and sounds continue. Piaget (1936/1963) describes how, at 7 months, his son Laurent used all his skills to make an interesting event happen again. After watching his father drum on a tin box, Laurent turned

secondary circular reactions
repetitive actions focused on the qualities of objects, such as the noises they make or their shapes and colors

toward the box, shook his arm in front of the box, and shook his head, trying out all of his movements to make the phenomenon reoccur.

Infants become goal oriented and more tuned in to their environments as they mature cognitively. Because of these changes, everyday activities become increasingly challenging and interesting. The highly repetitive, structured, and predictable games that caregivers and infants often engage in during feeding, bathing, and diapering provide infants with opportunities to learn contingencies and elicit smiles of obvious pleasure. In turn, caregivers respond positively to the increased pleasure displayed by infants, creating a mutually rewarding context for interactions.

Substage IV: Active Problem Solving (8 to 12 Months)

There was that first long stage when she didn't pick anything up at all, and everything had to be handed to her. Now it's different. If she is playing with a toy, and it slips out of her hand, she will follow it with her eyes; we can see her wondering what has become of it. A month ago it would have stayed on the floor, no longer a part of her consciousness; now, most of the time, she will return to it and pick it up again. She understands that even though it's out of her hand for the moment, it's still a part of her world.

—Bob Greene, journal entry about Amanda at 8 months
(1984, p. 229)

Amanda's behavior illustrates one of the two major events that mark this substage of development—she recognizes the permanence of an object, namely, her toy. The second major event of substage IV is showing intelligent behavior. According to Piaget, infants in substage IV show the first signs of intelligence, marked by the intentional application of schemes to reach a goal. Like substage III infants, substage IV infants use familiar schemes, but they are now purposeful in applying them. Also, infants are able to combine actions to solve problems, which Piaget called the **coordination of secondary circular reactions**. Older infants set out to accomplish a task and often have a goal in mind before starting an action. One indication of purposeful behavior in infants is the desire to complete activities they begin. Unlike a younger infant, who might be easily distracted by other interesting objects, an infant in substage IV who fails to accomplish his or her task is likely to be upset. For instance, 10-month-old Stacie becomes upset after her father picks her up and moves her away from the cat she is trying to catch. A few months earlier, Stacie would have been easily distracted by this bold movement and would have happily lost interest in the cat. Unfortunately for the cat, Stacie now has a preset goal, and her actions are focused on achieving it. Similarly, Amanda is no longer fooled by the disappearance of the toy that slips from her hand; now she wonders where it has gone and will recognize and play with it if it is handed back to her.

Amanda's understanding that her toy continues to exist even out of her sight signals an important change in her cognitive development. Knowing that people and objects have an independent existence beyond one's own perception of them is called an understanding of **object permanence.** Infants are not born with this understanding; they have no idea that objects or people continue to exist outside of their own perception of them. When Bob Greene's daughter was younger, she did not bother to look for objects she dropped because they were no longer part of her consciousness. This lack of understanding of object permanence extends to infants' bodies: they are unaware that the objects flying in front of their face are their own arms and hands.

Over the first 2 years of life, infants gradually develop an understanding of object permanence by coming to realize that objects have form, depth, and solidity. Toward the end of the sensorimotor period, infants become capable of acting on that knowledge by actively searching for objects that have disappeared from their field of vision. Piaget assumed that an important indicator of infants' understanding of object permanence was whether they tried to find a hidden object. Based on the studies he conducted on infants' searching strategies, Piaget outlined how infants develop an understanding of object permanence and how this understanding relates to the substages of sensorimotor cognitive development.

coordination of secondary circular reactions *infants' ability to combine actions to solve simple problems*

object permanence *the concept that people and objects have an independent existence beyond one's own perception of them*

▓ In substages I and II (0 to 4 months), infants show no evidence of realizing the independent existence of objects. An infant who drops a rattle outside her or his field of vision will not cry in frustration or even look for the toy. If someone covers a toy with a cloth while an infant in substage I or II watches, the infant does not try to uncover it; as far as the infant is concerned, the toy has disappeared.

▓ In substage III (4 to 8 months), infants search for an object that is partially in view but not one that is completely hidden. Because infants at this age do not search for hidden objects, Piaget suggested that they still do not realize the permanence of objects.

▓ Infants' behavior during substage IV (8 to 12 months) is puzzling and intriguing. They show some understanding of object permanence, but their understanding is far from complete. For example, Vonnie's mother hides a doll under a washcloth several times, and Vonnie finds it. Then Vonnie watches her mother hide the doll under a washcloth and, from there, under a blanket. Where will Vonnie look for the doll? You might guess that she would look under the blanket, assuming that the last hiding place is the best bet for finding the toy. Substage IV infants, however, show a surprising pattern: they look in the first place the object was hidden. Thus, Vonnie looks under the washcloth. The tendency to search in the first hiding place (A) while ignoring the second place (B) is called the **A-not-B error** (see Figure 6.4).

FIGURE 6.4
A-not-B Error

Where do children who show the A-not-B error look for the duck? What factors might explain why infants continue to look in the same but inaccurate place for the hidden object?

Why would an infant like Vonnie search in the first hiding spot? This question has intrigued researchers for years. According to Piaget, infants remember the object as an "object + action"—that is, the object takes on the characteristics of the action performed on it. In this case, the doll becomes doll-under-a-washcloth, and an infant with this concept is unlikely to search for doll-under-a-washcloth by looking under a blanket. Research shows that this error may be due to infants' inability to inhibit actions they have performed before (such as searching in the A hiding place) until a certain level of brain development has occurred (Diamond, 1991).

Substage V: Creative Problem Solving (12 to 18 Months)

Infants in substage V are creative problem solvers. For the first time, they are capable of applying entirely new strategies to solve problems rather than simply using combinations of previously learned schemes. Infants' creativity during this substage stems from the use of **tertiary circular reactions,** in which infants systematically modify their behaviors with objects in subtle ways to explore the effects of those modifications (see Figure 6.5 on page 172). Noah, who had earlier dropped a spoon off his high chair to explore the qualities of the spoon, begins to explore these qualities in a new way as he grows older. He now experiments with different trajectories of the spoon: dropping it, throwing it gently, and flinging it across the room. Noah acts as a budding scientist, interested in finding out how variations in his behavior influence the qualities of the spoon. Now he might squeeze a toy duck to make it quack, then sit on it, and finally bite it to find out what happens.

The ability to conduct tertiary circular actions provides children with the means to learn from their actions. Because infants in substage V are capable of trying many ways to solve a problem, they are more likely to hit upon a successful solution than are younger infants who use more rigidly applied schemes.

A-not-B error *infants' tendency to search in the first hiding spot (A) while ignoring the second (B)*

tertiary circular reactions *subtle modifications infants make in their behavior with objects so as to explore the effects of those modifications*

FIGURE 6.5
Tertiary Circular Reactions

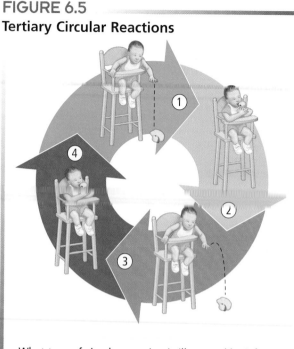

What type of circular reaction is illustrated by infants who drop things off their high chairs in different ways? How does this ability differ from earlier circular reactions? How might parents change their view of this behavior by knowing that it is a signal of their child's cognitive ability?

FIGURE 6.6
Using Symbolic Representation

When children can think about objects and people in symbolic ways, how does their thinking change?

symbolic representation
the use of mental symbols to represent objects

Changes occur in children's understanding of object permanence during this substage. By the time they reach substage V, infants are capable of searching for hidden objects that have been moved several times. The only limit to their understanding is that they must see each movement of the object to be able to find it.

Substage VI: Using Symbols to Represent Reality (18 to 24 Months)

After 18 months of age, toddlers develop a new and important ability that changes the way they approach and solve problems. Substage VI toddlers begin to use mental symbols to represent objects, a strategy called **symbolic representation.** They no longer need to act out a sequence of events to discover the outcome—they can imagine the actions beforehand. Thus, problem solving now can take place inside the child's mind before he or she takes any action (see Figure 6.6).

Piaget described how his daughter Lucienne solved a problem by using mental symbols. Piaget inserted a metal chain into a matchbox and then handed the matchbox to Lucienne. The matchbox was left partially open, and Lucienne began exploring the box by turning it over. She then tried to grasp the chain through the opening. When those actions were unsuccessful, she tried a new way to solve the problem: she inserted her index finger into the opening, grabbed a small part of the chain, and then pulled the whole chain out. Piaget then repeated this experiment, this time leaving a smaller opening in the matchbox. Lucienne tried to solve the problem the same way she did before, but this time her solution did not work because the opening was too small. She then paused and seemed to think about how to solve the problem. During this pause, Piaget noticed that Lucienne was opening her mouth, at first a little and then wider and wider. This indicated to him that Lucienne recognized that she needed to increase the size of the opening in the matchbox so that her finger would fit in it. Lucienne then used her finger to widen the opening and successfully applied her previous scheme of grasping the chain. She did not have to try many different actions before finding a solution; Lucienne "thought" through the problem, using symbols for the object and actions, and decided which actions were most likely to be successful.

Toddlers in substage VI thus rely less on motor actions and more on symbols for solving many everyday problems. With their increased use of symbols, toddlers are more capable than infants of carrying out tasks such as thinking about the past and future, thinking about problems quickly and flexibly, and remembering actions to use in new situations.

By 18 months, toddlers in substage VI have a fully developed concept of object permanence. They now can follow multiple movements of objects, even when the movements cannot be seen. For instance, when Sean watches his mother place a toy cow in a plastic cup and then place the plastic cup under a blanket, he still knows where the cow is. Although Sean does not see that the cow is hidden under the blanket, he infers that the cow continues to exist even though it is hidden in the cup and then infers that the cow must still be wherever the cup is, which in this case is under the blanket.

Beyond Piaget: Newer Research on Early Cognitive Abilities

Piaget's view that children have a different problem-solving perspective than adults do has provided researchers with a world of ideas about how to investigate cognitive development.

Many investigators have tried to replicate Piaget's findings by using simpler tests to ensure that the developmental changes he described accurately reflect children's cognitive abilities. These researchers have wondered whether Piaget underestimated children's abilities because some of the tasks he presented to them were difficult. The newer studies suggest that Piaget developed an accurate description of the sequence of children's stages of development, but that he may have underestimated the ages at which children come to exhibit more advanced abilities.

Furthermore, not all researchers agree with Piaget's conclusions about development. Rather than believe that complex cognitive abilities develop gradually over infancy and childhood, "neo-nativist" scientists think that some of these abilities are innate; that is, infants are born with cognitive abilities to understand space, language, and objects, and the environment only has to present the proper stimulation to make these abilities appear (Baillargeon, 1987, 1994; Gopnik & Wellman, 1994; Karmiloff-Smith, 1992; Newport, 1991; see also Debating the Issue on page 177). According to this view, the brain processes information in ways attuned to learning about particular features of the environment (such as language) more quickly (Bjorkland, 1995). Because of this heightened sensitivity to certain aspects of the environment, certain domains or modules of expertise develop more quickly than others, and in different ways. To investigate these views, scientists have devised clever techniques of exploring what children know about the world. Consider what method you would use to investigate infants' or toddlers' understanding of math or gravity. These are just some of the challenges that researchers face in exploring children's cognitive abilities.

Reassessing Object Permanence

When Amanda recognized that her dropped toy continued to exist, she exhibited early understanding of object permanence. However, when Piaget formally tested children's abilities to find toys after several moves, he used very challenging tasks: children had to watch him move the toy and hide it several times. The search task requires that infants coordinate several schemes, including their vision and reaching schemes, to find a hidden object. Maybe infants younger than 18 months understand object permanence but could not master the coordination of schemes well enough to demonstrate their understanding in such a task. The issue of children's *performance versus competence* is a recurring one in developmental research. Researchers often have to infer what infants or children know from what they do; if their actions are limited, inferences about their knowledge may be inaccurate. A solution to this problem is to simplify the tasks that infants and children are asked to perform. Rather than having infants search for hidden objects, an alternative approach is to examine their visual attention to different objects. Remember that infants pay more attention to surprising and novel experiences than to familiar ones. Based on this preference, researchers have devised clever visual attention studies that allow them to assess infants' understanding of objects without the performance demands involved in Piaget's search studies.

In one of these studies (Baillargeon & Graber, 1988), 7- to 8-month-old infants were shown objects that appeared and disappeared. During one of these presentations, however, the sequence of events was "impossible." As depicted in Figure 6.7 on page 174, infants first saw an object located on one of two placemats. Next, a screen was pushed in front of each placemat, hiding the object from the infant's view. Fifteen seconds later, a hand reached behind one of the two screens and pulled out the object. For one event, the object was pulled from behind the screen that covered the placemat on which the infant had seen the object—the "possible sequence." For the other event, the object was pulled out from behind the screen that had *not* hidden the object—the "impossible sequence." Infants stared longer at, and were more surprised by, the impossible sequence than the possible one. This result indicates that the infants remembered the location of the hidden object and were surprised when it was not where it was supposed to be.

By using simplified methods, researchers have found evidence of object permanence in even younger infants (Haith & Benson, 1998; Munakata, McClelland, Johnson, & Siegler, 1997). Additionally, 5-month-old infants were more surprised and paid more attention when a wall appeared to move *through* a solid object than when the wall stopped upon

FIGURE 6.7

Baillargeon and Graber's Possible and Impossible Events

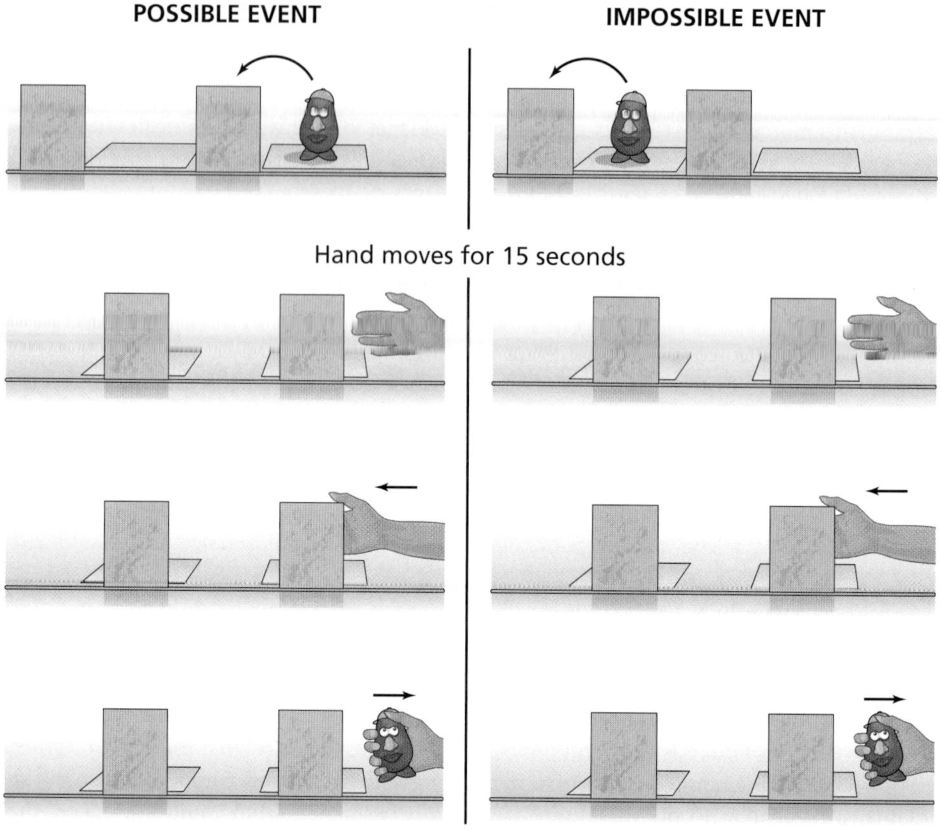

Infants in this study were shown possible and impossible events to determine whether they had an understanding of object permanence. In the possible event, the screen on the right covers the object, and a hand reaches behind the screen and removes the object. In the impossible event, the screen on the left covers the object, but the hand reaches behind the screen on the right and removes the object. Infants were surprised by and paid more attention to the impossible event. How can we use this reaction to determine what infants know?

Source: Baillargeon and Graber, 1988. Copyright © 1988 by the American Psychological Association. Adapted with permission.

coming into contact with the object (Baillargeon, Spelke, & Wasserman, 1985). Other studies have shown that 3- and 4-month-old infants understand basic principles of objects and motion, such as gravity and inertia (Spelke, Breinlinger, Macomber, & Jacobson, 1992). These studies suggest that very early in life, children develop basic concepts about the world that are then expanded and elaborated on later in development (see Table 6.2). Piaget, however, was accurate in describing how infants act on objects around them. By 6 to 12 months, infants begin to demonstrate in their actions what they know about objects (Goubet & Clifton, 1998). This change is likely due to development of the frontal cortex of the brain (Diamond, 1991). It is not until the end of their second year, however, that infants can completely integrate their knowledge of objects with their actions (Small, 1990).

Thousands of studies have tested Piaget's ideas about cognitive development. Although much of his work has been substantiated, some findings have led to conclusions different from those Piaget originally suggested. For example, infants' abilities are more variable and context-dependent than Piaget initially proposed. Also, as you have seen, infants' understanding of object permanence is more complex and cumulative than Piaget thought.

TABLE 6.2
Stages in Understanding of Object Permanence

STAGE	AGE	KNOWLEDGE	ACTION OR LIMITATION
Stages I & II	0 to 4 months	Loses awareness of objects when they disappear By 3 to 4 months, understands inertia and gravity	Loses interest and does not search
Stage III	4 to 8 months	Recognizes continued existence of hidden objects Understands solidity of objects	Cannot find completely hidden objects
Stage IV	8 to 12 months	Remembers last location of a hidden object	Shows A-not-B error—will search for object in the first hiding place but not the second Cannot inhibit reach to first hiding place
Stages V & VI	12 to 24 months	Recognizes complex hiding patterns	Can search for and find hidden objects, even if they are hidden in two places

Furthermore, the idea that the brain may be specialized for learning about certain features of the world has gained support in studies of object permanence.

Infants' Understanding of Number Concepts

Infants' cognitive accomplishments include more than problem solving and the understanding of objects. Research has demonstrated something few people thought possible: infants have a basic understanding of the concept of numbers. Wynn (1992) used a version of the possible–impossible event procedure to explore infants' understanding of numbers. After being habituated to displays of one or two items, one group of 5-month-old infants watched an "addition situation," in which one object was added to another, and another group watched a "subtraction situation," in which one of two objects was removed (see Figure 6.8 on page 176). In both situations, one outcome was a possible event and one was impossible. In the addition situation, for instance, a screen was lifted to hide one Mickey Mouse doll. Infants then saw a hand place another identical mouse doll behind the screen. In the possible event, the screen dropped to reveal two dolls (1 + 1 = 2). In the impossible version, the screen dropped to reveal only one doll (1 + 1 = 1). Infants spent more time looking at the impossible event; that is, they stared longer at 1 + 1 = 1 than at 1 + 1 = 2. These findings suggest that even 5-month-old infants have a basic understanding of addition and subtraction. However, more recent studies have not consistently supported Wynn's original findings. In some cases, infants were unable to show numerical competencies by adding and subtracting small numbers of objects when a computer display of the events was used (Wakeley, Rivera, & Langer, 2000a). The discrepant findings may suggest that the numerical abilities of young infants are more fragile and inconsistent than Wynn's initial study demonstrated (Wakeley et al., 2000a, b), or they may be due to the use of different methods to assess infants' abilities (Wynn, 2000). Furthermore, very young infants may simply have basic visual concepts of what a number of objects looks like and exhibit surprise when objects do not match these expectations (Haith & Benson, 1998). Recent studies suggest that the number of objects may also influence whether infants can discriminate number: in one study, infants were able to discriminate larger numbers (e.g., 4 versus 8) but not smaller numbers of objects (2 versus 4) (Xu, 2003).

Perception in Early Cognitive Development

People must be able to categorize information into coherent units, or concepts, to handle the wealth of stimulation around them. Perception plays an important role in how information is categorized, and its role is particularly important in infancy. What is not yet clear is the role of perception in forming more abstract concepts (e.g., about groups of people), which infants begin to do after about a year when they start to name objects and people and recognize how objects are used (Madole, Oakes, & Cohen, 1993). The controversy

FIGURE 6.8
Wynn's Possible and Impossible Events

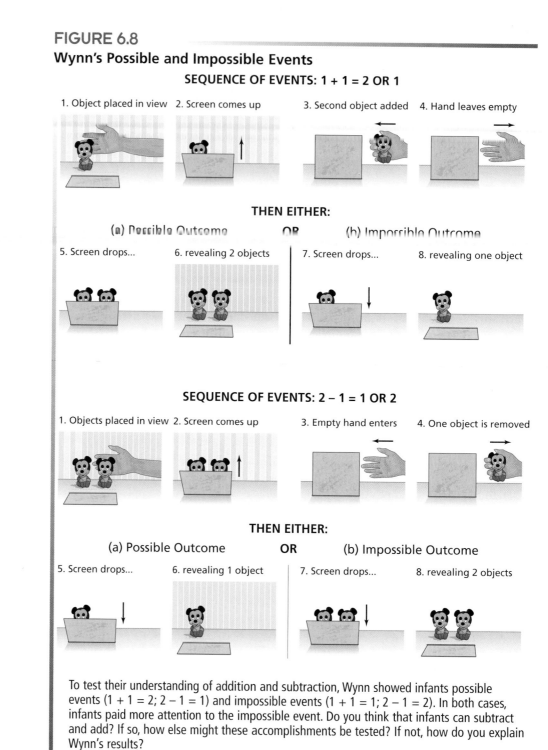

SEQUENCE OF EVENTS: 1 + 1 = 2 OR 1

1. Object placed in view   2. Screen comes up   3. Second object added   4. Hand leaves empty

THEN EITHER:

(a) Possible Outcome   OR   (b) Impossible Outcome

5. Screen drops...   6. revealing 2 objects | 7. Screen drops...   8. revealing one object

SEQUENCE OF EVENTS: 2 − 1 = 1 OR 2

1. Objects placed in view   2. Screen comes up   3. Empty hand enters   4. One object is removed

THEN EITHER:

(a) Possible Outcome   **OR**   (b) Impossible Outcome

5. Screen drops...   6. revealing 1 object | 7. Screen drops...   8. revealing 2 objects

To test their understanding of addition and subtraction, Wynn showed infants possible events (1 + 1 = 2; 2 − 1 = 1) and impossible events (1 + 1 = 1; 2 − 1 = 2). In both cases, infants paid more attention to the impossible event. Do you think that infants can subtract and add? If so, how else might these accomplishments be tested? If not, how do you explain Wynn's results?

Source: Wynn, 1992.

about the formation of concepts involves two viewpoints. (1) concepts arise from perception versus (2) conceptual categorization involves higher-order thinking and language.

Some researchers believe that infants develop basic concepts about the world around them from perceptual knowledge alone (Quinn, 2002; Quinn & Eimas, 1996; Rakison, 2003). According to this view, infants' early concepts come from their perceptions of objects. For instance, a child may come to form the concept of a dog by seeing that dogs

DEBATING THE ISSUE
WHAT DO INFANTS KNOW, AND HOW DO THEY KNOW IT?

 One of the hottest debates in infancy research is what infants know and how they know it. Although there are many angles of the debate, two prominent positions are the Piagetian and neo-nativist views. Piagetian and neo-Piagetian views are based on Piaget's ideas about development: there are stages in development, there is relative consistency within a stage, and children's movement from stage to stage is abrupt. The structure of the stage constrains learning for children. A child cannot view the world from a further advanced stage.

In contrast, according to the neo-nativist view, abilities develop in a modular, domain-specific fashion, with some domains showing more advanced development than others (Gelman & Williams, 1998). Each domain is governed by a coherent set of operating principles, and within each, the same rules are applied. Core domains, acquired earlier in life, are those that infants are particularly attuned to, such as learning about

people, how objects move in space, and language (Gopnik, Meltzoff, & Kuhl, 1999). Learning in some areas is more constrained than in others.

Underlying this debate is the nature versus nurture issue: are infants born with adult abilities, or do they learn them over time? Piagetian scientists tend to assume that development proceeds by the maturation of the brain in interaction with stimulation from the environment. Neo-nativists assume that the wiring of the brain and the human capacity to process information are the key constraints and facilitators of learning, although they too believe that environmental input is needed for normal development to occur.

Different problems of development are taken up by these two groups of researchers. Piagetian researchers focus on how children change as they move through different stages of development; neo-nativists tend to focus on identifying the early abilities that infants can demonstrate. For people who work with children, these two perspectives offer dif-

ferent insights. The Piagetian perspective provides guidelines about the levels of cognitive development that would be expected from children at different stages and would suggest enriching their environments to promote development. The neo-nativist perspective suggests that children will develop more unevenly; the types of abilities likely to be shown will vary, depending on the particular skill being assessed.

THINKING IT THROUGH

1. Why do you think some researchers moved away from the Piagetian view of cognitive development?

2. Describe how the methods used in research and the age groups that are studied by these two groups are likely to be different.

3. Describe the ways that a practitioner might apply each of these perspectives to working with a child.

---

move around and bark. Even information that cannot be easily perceived through object properties, such as concepts of above and below, may be categorized by using perceptual cues (Quinn, 2003). The early parsing of the world into perceptually distinct categories may lay the foundation from which more adult conceptions of objects develop (Markman, 1989; Millikan, 1998). This view challenges the idea that children need language or different mental processes to form abstract categories (Quinn, 2003).

Other researchers believe that the "perception only" view is limited because it cannot account for concepts involving class membership on the basis of the roles or functions that people or objects serve (Mandler, 2003). Instead, these researchers view perceptual categories and conceptual concepts as being distinct (Hespos & Baillargeon, 2001; Mandler, 1992; Spelke, 1992; Spelke & Hespos, 2002). According to their view, perceptual categorization involves noticing physical similarities among objects, and conceptual categorization involves developing abstract schemas about objects, which may be based in part on perceptual features.

Mandler proposed that conceptual categorization can develop based on an initial input from perceptual categorization. Mandler observed that infants as young as 6 months old spend a great deal of time looking back and forth between two new objects as if contemplating similarities and differences between them (Ruff, 1986), and this scrutiny increases with age (Mandler, 1990). What are infants doing during these intense visual inspections?

FIGURE 6.9
Relational Play

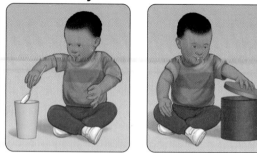

What concept does a child understand when able to place a lid on a container or a spoon in cup? What type of play is this?

Mandler believes that infants may be comparing similarities and differences between objects and forming **image schemas**—primitive notions, based on the visual appearance of objects, that lay a foundation for thinking about those objects (see Figure 6.9). For instance, infants may have an up–down schema, a container schema, and a part–whole schema. A container schema has an interior, an exterior, and a boundary; infants with a container schema understand that containers hold things and are surprised if they do not. Infants may use image schemas to develop perception-based concepts that help them quickly learn about the world without requiring actions on their part. These image schemas become the groundwork for more complex and abstract ideas about objects.

Regardless of whether concepts form directly from perception or whether the process is more complex (Oakes & Madole, 2003), by 10 months of age, infants begin to understand the relationships between objects such as a lid and a pot. Evidence of this understanding comes from **relational play,** in which children perform actions that demonstrate their understanding of the relationship between two objects (Fenson, Kagan, Kearsley, & Zelazo, 1976)—for example, a child might place a spoon in a cup or a lid on a box. Perception of objects plays a part in this aspect of cognitive development in that babies are more likely to recognize the roles of objects when the objects are more perceptually distinct, such as when a lid and a box are different colors (Bates, Carlson-Luden, & Bretherton, 1980).

Babies also are capable of understanding categories when the members of different categories are perceptually distinct. By 10 months, infants show abilities to form categories similar to those used by adults (e.g., gender categories for male and female faces) (Younger & Fearing, 1999). By 15 months of age, infants will pick up objects that belong to the same category before they pick up objects belonging to another category—for example, first picking up pictures of cats and then pictures of dogs (Levy, 1999; Mandler & Bauer, 1988; Oakes, Plumert, Lansink, & Merryman, 1996). By 18 to 24 months, toddlers can sort objects from two categories into spatially distinct groups (Gopnik & Meltzoff, 1992).

As young infants form an understanding of categories, it may be impossible to distinguish which categories are based on what they have seen versus those based on more abstract concepts or rules (Cohen, 2003). A useful strategy may be to focus on the basic processes that underlie categorization, recognizing that, with age, infants have a broader pool of features on which to base categorization, they can take advantage of more information in different contexts, and they gain background knowledge that helps them make sense of potential categories (Oakes & Madole, 2003).

Understanding the Differences Among People
Like recognizing categories based on physical differences, the understanding that people differ from one another emerges during the first few years of life. One method of assessing infants' understanding of differences among people is to determine whether they recognize that not all people have the same preferences or desires. Researchers who investigated this problem used a simple food-preference task. They placed in front of infants a bowl of goldfish crackers and a bowl of raw broccoli (Repacholi & Gopnick, 1997). All the babies preferred the crackers to the broccoli. Then an adult reached over and tasted each food. With some babies, the adult showed a preference for the broccoli over the crackers. Then the adult placed the bowls near the infant and asked for some food. How did the infant determine which food to give to the adult? If the infant understood that some people, including this particular adult, like broccoli, the infant would hand her or him more broccoli. If, instead, the baby assumed that all people like what the baby likes, then the baby would offer crackers to the adult. Repacholi and Gopnik (1997) found that 14-month-old babies handed the adult crackers, thereby showing no evidence of understanding differences among people's desires, whereas 18-month-olds did make such distinctions.

image schemas *primitive notions, based on the visual appearance of objects, that lay a foundation for thinking about them*

relational play *actions demonstrating an understanding of the relationship between two objects*

The Social Contexts of Early Learning and Cognitive Development

Much of infants' knowledge of the world is gained through their many daily interactions with others, particularly caregivers. The Russian scientist Lev Vygotsky believed that social interactions are essential for learning and that infants develop cognitive skills through interactions with others more skilled than themselves (Vygotsky, 1978). Older children and adults serve as role models for thinking, provide stimulating environments for children, and encourage children's learning by guiding them to find solutions to problems.

In Vygotsky's view, children develop cognitive abilities through socially mediated learning. As you learned in Chapter 2, Vygotsky used the concept of the *zone of proximal development* to represent the range of learning that a child is capable of with help from more skilled and experienced partners (Rogoff, 1990). Through interactions with skilled

Parents in rural areas differ from parents in urban areas in their methods of scaffolding. How might this Guatemalan parent provide scaffolding for her children?

partners, children expand their cognitive competencies. Children's cognitive development is influenced by daily interactions within a cultural community (Rogoff, 1990). Parents and other adults in the community involve children in guided participation in everyday activities, which become the context for an "apprenticeship in thinking." Through these apprenticeships, children learn about their own culture and develop enhanced cognitive skills. Adults from all over the world use many of the same methods to guide their children's participation in daily events.

Scaffolding

Caregivers provide structure and support for children's thinking through informal teaching methods called **scaffolding.** Just as steel and wooden scaffolding provides the support needed to construct a building, caregivers' cognitive scaffolding provides the support children need to extend their current skills to a higher level of competence. The type of scaffolding used by caregivers changes as infants' understanding increases, and it varies according to the caregiver's preferences (Bruner, 1983). For instance, caregivers often help infants interpret situations through their actions, emotions, and tone of voice. With older children, some mothers prefer a social style of scaffolding in which they draw attention to themselves ("watch me do it"), whereas other mothers use an activity-oriented method in which they draw attention to objects or events ("find the piece of the puzzle that matches the color of the one next to it") (Bornstein & Tamis-LeMonda, 1990).

Mothers and fathers are equally effective in supplying scaffolding for their children's emerging skills (Connor, Knight, & Cross, 1997), and they begin these interactions soon after the child's birth. By 2 months of age, infants already have developed a basic understanding of what patterns to expect in these interactions. In one study (Murray & Trevarthen, 1986), mothers and their 2-month-old infants were videotaped, and the babies were given the chance to watch their mothers live on a video monitor as their mothers interacted with them. The babies responded positively by making eye contact and moving their mouths. When the live video was replaced with a taped replay of their mothers' reactions in a former exchange, the babies were distressed and looked away. Although the mothers were responding as they had before, their responses were not contingent on their infants' actions—they were not in synchrony—and this was distressing to the babies.

Joint Attention

Like synchrony, joint attention between "teacher" and "learner" facilitates cognitive development. Because they share a focus of attention, caregivers and infants have a common ground for interpreting and understanding interactions (Rogoff, 1998). By about 6 months, infants

scaffolding *informal teaching methods that provide structure and support for children's thinking*

and their caregivers begin to share and negotiate learning tasks during play. Ten- to 12-month-old infants and their caregivers work out the details of interactions quite well and are well practiced in their routine interactions (Corkum & Moore, 1998; Rogoff, 1990). The ability of parents to successfully engage their children in joint attention on a task influences their children's later cognitive development. Toddlers whose mothers engage them in effective joint attention at 6 and 12 months have comparatively higher IQs (Hunter, McCarthy, MacTurk, & Vietze, 1987). In general, caregivers who are responsive and sensitive to their children's interactions encourage cognitive development (Bornstein & Tamis-LeMonda, 1997).

The Cultural Contexts of Early Learning and Cognitive Development

Do caregivers all over the world use scaffolding to encourage their children's cognitive development? To answer this question, Rogoff and colleagues (Rogoff, Mistry, Goncu, & Mosier, 1993) examined the use of scaffolding by middle-class parents in cities in Utah and Turkey and by parents in small communities in India and Guatemala. In all four communities, the two parents and their children jointly took part in structured learning situations.

Striking cultural variations in the use of scaffolding were found. In Utah and Turkey, parents were more likely to provide verbal instructions and activity lessons that were removed from the ordinary context of adult life. For instance, parents in these communities interacted with their children around toys and games but did not take their toddlers into their workplaces. In India and Guatemala, however, children were less likely to receive direct instruction during play but were more likely to be observant of, and take primary responsibility for, learning and participating in adult activities. These differences relate to the expectations and demands of the children's communities. In communities in which children spend most of their time with their parents, the children are expected to learn the specific economic skills of their parents, such as weaving, and their training involves watching and participating in these activities. In communities in which children spend less time with their parents, the children are expected to learn varied skills and to spend years in school. The focus is on motivating children to learn through praise and verbal instruction. Both methods of scaffolding produce the desired result of socializing children to become effective members of the community in which they are raised (Rogoff et al., 1993).

How Do Infants Learn, Remember, and Process Information?

Think back as far as you can—what do you remember? Can you remember your parents taking you home from the hospital right after you were born? Can you remember being injured as a toddler? Most people can remember events that happened to them when they were 3 or 4 but not what happened to them earlier in life. What is interesting is that infants can remember information, sometimes for long periods of time. How do infants with limited experiences remember information, and what conditions are likely to produce memories? And, if we can remember events early in life while they are happening, how do we explain the paradox that adults do not remember their experiences as infants? Many answers to these questions come from research on learning and memory that has been conducted from an information processing perspective. This approach is concerned with what people learn, how they remember information, and the situations that increase the likelihood of remembering.

Learning Through Contingency and Association

In Chapter 2, you learned about Albert, the young boy who was conditioned to be afraid of a white rat. Albert initially was unafraid of the rat, but when researchers paired a loud, unpleasant noise with the rat, Albert learned to associate the two. After making that association, he responded to the sight of the rat with fear, even when no noise occurred.

Human newborns as young as 2 hours old can be trained through classical conditioning methods to expect a contingency. In one study, newborns were gently stroked on the head for 10 seconds before they were fed sweetened water. Initially, the stroking had no effect on sucking behavior, but once infants learned the association, stroking caused them to orient the head, pucker the lips, and suck more than infants who had not been provided with the same contingency (Blass, Ganchrow, & Steiner, 1984). When the infants in the contingency group were given a different contingency—they were stroked, but the feeding was stopped—they often cried, became angry, or whimpered, indicating that their expectancies had been violated.

Infants also learn through operant conditioning, in which they associate their actions with particular consequences (see Chapter 2). When a baby experiences a pleasant or rewarding consequence for a behavior, he or she is likely to act in the same way again. In studies of infants, the actions most commonly measured are sucking, kicking, gazing, and head turning. Infants are particularly quick to learn about consequences that have to do with feeding or that allow them to hear their mother. For instance, infants have been taught that if they suck longer or harder, they can listen to a sound they like, such as their mother's voice (DeCasper & Fifer, 1987). They have learned to associate their behavior (sucking) with a positive consequence (hearing the mother's voice).

Learning What's Familiar: Habituation and Novelty Responses

When infants find something fascinating, they turn their attention to this stimulus and gaze intently at it. Beyond sensing objects and perceiving their forms, what do infants gain from such focused attention? Scientists who use information processing theories to explore cognitive changes in children are interested in whether differences exist in the ways that infants and children pay attention to stimuli and what kinds of information they acquire.

To gain her infant's attention, Marta repeatedly dangles a stuffed bear in front of her daughter, Celina, and then removes it. At first, her daughter stares at the bear for a long time, but with continued presentations, Celina looks at the bear for shorter periods of time, as if she is getting bored. This behavior provides evidence of **habituation**—a decrease in attention to a stimulus that has been presented repeatedly (Bornstein & Ludemann, 1989). Now Marta replaces the bear with a clown, and Celina shows renewed interest. Celina's increase in attention to this new stimulus after habituation to a previous stimulus, a response called **dishabituation,** shows that she distinguishes between the two stimuli, the bear and the clown (see Figure 6.10).

When babies habituate and then dishabituate, they demonstrate that they can make a perceptual distinction between objects. For instance, they can distinguish between a dog and a horse. However, habituation and dishabituation do not tell us exactly what it is that infants notice or respond to. These processes also show that infants remember, at least for a short time, an object they have been shown and can compare that memory with a new stimulus (Schneider & Bjorklund, 1998). To assess infants' short-term memories, researchers use habituation–dishabituation tasks and measure visual behavior, sucking rates, and heart and respiration rates. Because infants cannot use words to tell us about their perceptions, thoughts, and memories, the habituation task is important in assessing these abilities.

Evidence of habituation is found very early in life: newborns habituate to repeated visual presentations (Slater, Mattock, Brown, & Bremner, 1991). The fact that habituation occurs so early allows researchers to test what kinds of things infants discriminate, including social

FIGURE 6.10
Habituation and Dishabituation

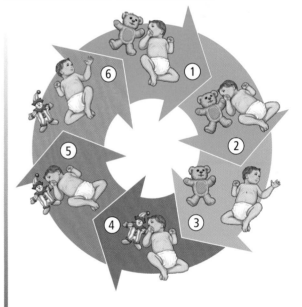

When children are repeatedly shown an object like the teddy bear in this example, they gradually lose interest in it and stop looking at it for very long, a reaction called habituation. If a new object is introduced, such as the clown, children will show interest in it (a reaction called dishabituation), but this interest also will decline after repeated presentations (another case of habituation).

habituation *decrease in attention to a repeatedly presented stimulus*

dishabituation *renewed attention after habituation, caused by presentation of a new stimulus*

categories. For example, in one study, infants habituated to faces of men and dishabituated when presented with faces of women. This finding suggests that by 9 months of age, infants distinguish between the appearances of men and women (Leinbach & Fagot, 1993).

As infants grow older, they habituate to new stimuli more quickly. A newborn might take 5 to 10 minutes to habituate, but a 6-month-old habituates in 30 seconds (Bornstein, 1985). Among infants of the same age, the rate of habituation varies, and these differences are stable over the first 3 years. Faster habituation may reflect an ability to process information more effectively, which may be critical to memory later in life (Schneider & Bjorklund, 1998).

Developing Long-Term Memory

Fetuses can learn associations in the last months of prenatal development and remember them after birth. Newborns are capable of learning basic survival-related information, such as the sources of nourishment and the smells and sounds of their mother. However, young infants have fragile memories—they are unlikely to remember information for very long, and their memories are constrained by the context of learning. Marked improvements occur at 2 to 3 months and at 6 to 10 months of age. These improvements are linked to increased myelination of the neurons, the increased number of synapses formed in the brain, development of the frontal cortex, and increased attention span. Another improvement occurs at around 18 to 20 months of age, when babies use language to aid memory.

Repeated Exposure Helps Memory

Try to remember experiences that occurred during the first 3 years of your life. Few people, if any, can do this. The inability to recall events that occurred very early in life is called **infantile amnesia.** Why do we remember so little from our earliest years? Initial research on this question suggested that young infants need repeated exposure to ensure memory that lasts for even a few days. In one study, mothers repeated phrases to their 2-week-old infants 60 times a day for 2 weeks. After over 800 exposures, infants remembered the information for almost 2 days (Ungerer, Brody, & Zelazo, 1978). If it takes this many exposures to learn and recall something for 2 days, it is no wonder that we remember so few early childhood experiences! Encouraging them to reenact events or parts of events, though, can remind very young children of past experiences and inoculate them against forgetting these experiences over long periods of time (Hudson & Sheffield, 1998).

Familiar Contexts Aid Memory

Research has shown that memory is improved when the procedures used to create associations are familiar to children. Consider 6-month-old Yi Ling, who participates in an experiment in which one end of a ribbon is tied to her leg and the other end to an interesting mobile above the crib. After 5 minutes, Yi Ling recognizes the contingency: when she kicks, the mobile turns (Rovee-Collier & Fagen, 1981). Two weeks later, Yi Ling returns to the laboratory, and the mobile-and-string setup is tried again. Will Yi Ling remember that kicking her foot makes the mobile move? Unlike many of the testing situations used in early research to assess infants' long-term memory, this situation closely resembles her everyday experiences, and she remembers the contingency (see Figure 6.11).

When infants are placed in familiar situations and are motivated to remember, they learn with less repetition (or fewer exposures) and remember for longer periods of time. For instance, in a series of studies, 2- and 3-month-old infants were trained in two 9-minute sessions to learn the contingency that leg kicking will make a mobile turn. When their memories were tested within 1 or 2 weeks of learning the contingency, most babies remembered it, but the longer the time between learning and testing, the less likely they were to remember. Generally, 2-month-old infants remembered the contingency when tested 1 week after learning it. The 3-month-old infants remembered it 2 weeks later, but after that time they acted as though they had never seen the mobile (Rovee-Collier et al., 1981). Other studies show that older infants, like Yi Ling (6 months), can remember the contingency up to 7 weeks later when reminders are given (Rovee-Collier & Shyi, 1992).

infantile amnesia   *inability to recall events that occurred very early in life*

Situational Cues Aid Memory

Infants, like all learners, remember best when the testing conditions are similar to the original learning situation. Thus, infants' memories are context-bound—that is, strongly tied to situational cues. The importance of these cues to infant memory has been confirmed by another series of leg-kicking studies. In these studies, some infants were shown a reminder (a moving mobile) on day 13 after they first learned the kicking contingency—1 day before they were likely to completely forget it. The "reminded" infants remembered the contingency better the next day than did infants who had not been reminded about their earlier learning or those who had been shown only a still mobile or a ribbon (Hayne & Rovee-Collier, 1995). Similarly, when infants were tested in an environment that differed from the one in which learning took place, such as a crib with a different colored bumper, they were less likely to remember the contingency than when they were tested in the same environment (Butler & Rovee-Collier, 1989; Hayne, Rovee-Collier, & Perris, 1987).

Reminders Help in Memory Retrieval

Deferred imitation, in which a delay occurs between seeing an action and imitating it (see Chapter 4), provides evidence of infants' long-term memory because it requires that the infant have a way of representing an observed action in memory and recalling it. By 6 weeks of age, infants not only imitate the facial expressions of those in their immediate presence but also show evidence of deferred imitation of behaviors, imitating behaviors that occurred in the past (Meltzoff & Moore, 1994). Infants' ability to imitate someone after a delay indicates that they remember something about that individual. Similarly, a child who watches his father make cookies and the next day pretends to make cookies is showing that he

FIGURE 6.11
Familiar Contexts Aid Memory

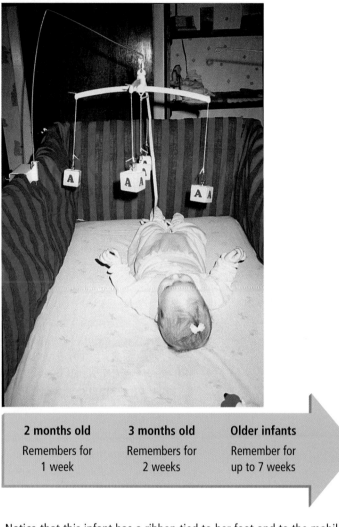

2 months old	3 months old	Older infants
Remembers for 1 week	Remembers for 2 weeks	Remember for up to 7 weeks

Notice that this infant has a ribbon tied to her foot and to the mobile. She has learned that when she kicks, she turns the mobile. Why is this method useful for assessing infants' memories? What factors influence whether infants will remember the contingency?

remembered the previous day's cookie-making actions. Research indicates that infants' abilities to engage in deferred imitation improve during their first 2 years. Infants from 11 to 20 months old show deferred imitation of novel actions for up to 12 months (Meltzoff, 1995).

Longitudinal studies support the finding that infants are capable of long-term memory. In one study, 6-month-old infants were trained to reach for a toy whenever it made a noise. The training took place in a laboratory room under two situations—with the lights on and with the lights off. Two years later, the same children and other children serving as a control group were asked if they remembered being in the earlier study. None of them did. Some of the children were reminded of the earlier study by being shown the toys that had been used. Then, while sitting with their mothers, the children were tested in the dark and in the light to see whether they would reach for the toy that made the sound, as they had done 2 years before. The children who had participated in the earlier study were much more likely than the children in the control group to reach for the toy (Perris, Myers, & Clifton, 1990). This study shows that unusual situations may be memorable to young children for a long period of time, especially when the events are novel and involve smells, sounds, and movements.

From these studies we can conclude that changes in infant memory can be described using three principles (Hayne, 2004):

- Older infants remember longer than younger infants.

- Older infants use a wider range of cues to help them remember than do younger infants.

- Forgotten memories can be retrieved through the presentation of reminders.

Age-related changes in memory capabilities likely play an important role in infantile amnesia, since early memories are fleeting and fragile as compared to those shaped by memory capabilities later in infancy and early childhood (Hayne, 2004). Infantile amnesia also may occur because adults are seldom in situations that resemble those of infancy to trigger memory, adults and infants represent information differently, and brain development and cognitive abilities differ for adults and infants (Hayne & Rovee-Collier, 1995; Schneider & Bjorklund, 1998). Age-related changes in children's self-concept also may account for infantile amnesia. Specifically, only when a child develops a cognitive sense of self as a person at around the age of 2 can memories be organized around the experiences that happened to "me" (Howe & Courage, 1997); some scientists, however, believe that this development may happen more gradually and later in childhood (Nelson & Fivush, 2004).

How Do Infants and Toddlers Develop Language Skills?

Language is a social tool consisting of a complex set of rules for using symbols (Owens, 1996). With a limited number of words, we can generate an infinite number of different messages. Thus, language is creative and flexible, and children show evidence of this when they generate words to say things they probably have never heard. For example, when 24-month-old Brandon experienced his first snowfall, he referred to it as "milk rain"—generating his own unique description of the event. Language also can be used to refer to events that happened in the past or to describe future events.

Infants are exposed to language during social interactions, even before they understand what individual words mean. When adults carry on a conversation in front of a young infant, the infant is likely to hear them speaking over 100 words a minute, making 12 to 30 sounds per second (Lieberman, 1984). How do infants make sense of all these sounds and words? With exposure to speech, infants learn to recognize speech sounds, words, and what words mean. Before they even utter a word, children practice many skills that relate to mastering language. During the first year, infants' language production consists of cooing, babbling, and gesturing—using sounds and motions to communicate their desires. In the second year, the range and flexibility of infants' language abilities expand rapidly as they begin to use their first words and phrases to express themselves. By the time they are 5 years old, most children are competent speakers of their native language.

To become speakers of a language, children must be able to master four language-related domains (Gleason, 1993):

- **Distinguish sounds and sound patterns.** A child who is a competent speaker of a language recognizes and distinguishes the basic sounds of that language, or **phonemes.** In English, examples of phonemes include the /sh/ sound, which is distinct from the /s/ sound. Competence in language also involves being able to produce these sounds so that others can understand them.

- **Learn the meanings of words. Semantics** refers to the meanings associated with words. Children accomplish an amazing feat when they learn how to use cues from others and from the environment to make sense of a sound and associate it with a particular word.

- **Learn to put words together. Syntax** is the grammar, or rules, of a language. Competent speakers of English realize that "I store am going" is not a grammatical sen-

phonemes   *the sounds of a language that are the basis for word construction*

semantics   *the meanings associated with words*

syntax   *the grammar, or rules, of a language*

FIGURE 6.12
Milestones of Early Language Development

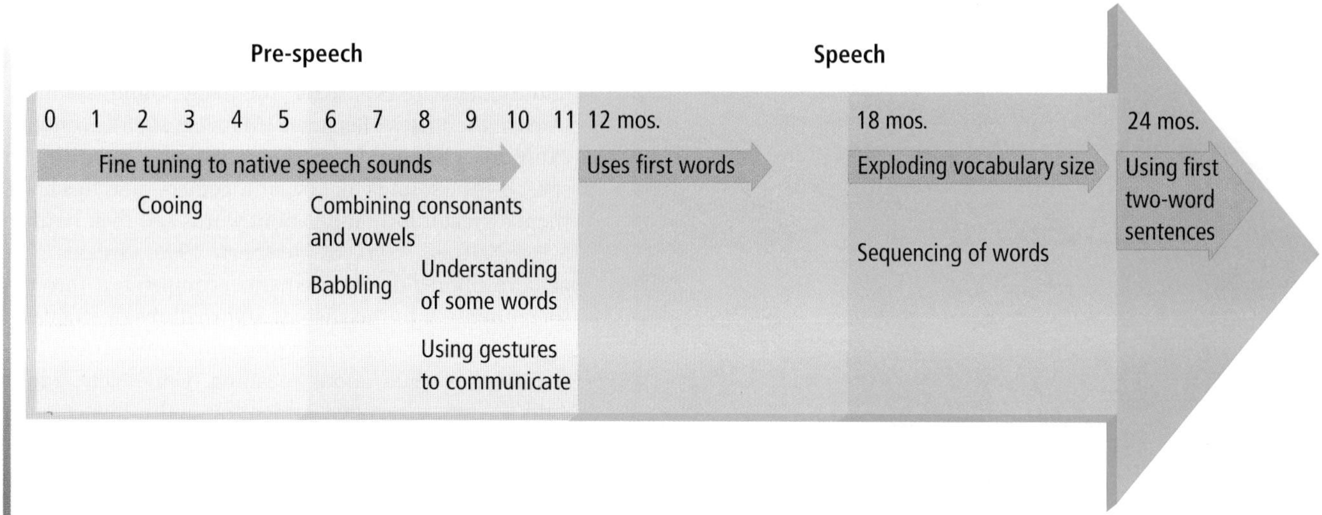

Pre-speech		Speech	

0 1 2 3 4 5 6 7 8 9 10 11	12 mos.	18 mos.	24 mos.
Fine tuning to native speech sounds	Uses first words	Exploding vocabulary size	Using first two-word sentences
Cooing			
Combining consonants and vowels		Sequencing of words	
Babbling Understanding of some words			
Using gestures to communicate			

Notice that language is considered to be developing even before children speak. What is happening during the prespeech period that facilitates children's language development?

tence. As part of mastering language, children must learn to arrange words in meaningful order and use the parts of speech as prescribed by the rules of the language.

- ■ *Learn to use language in a social context.* **Pragmatics** refers to the practical rules guiding the use of verbal and nonverbal communication in differing situations. A child who commands his grandmother to take him to the playground has not yet learned that in this situation the polite use of language, rather than a command, is more likely to bring success. To become competent speakers, children must learn the rules of using language with others, such as waiting for pauses in conversations to speak and taking turns in a discussion.

Before the First Words

Infants are actively engaged in learning language. Before they utter words, infants must become proficient in distinguishing and producing the sounds of their native language, and they need to identify individual words and their meanings from the streams of sounds they hear spoken around them (see Figure 6.12).

Distinguishing the Sounds of Speech

Children must be able to discriminate the sounds of language before they can put sounds together in a meaningful way. Each language uses a subset of the 100 to 150 possible phonemes; for instance, English uses about 45 phonemes (Owens, 1996). Languages differ in terms of the number and types of phonemes they contain (Menyuk, 1988).

Because each language involves only some of the sounds that are possible, scientists have asked whether infants learn to hear only the sounds from their native language or have the ability to hear all sounds. Research has demonstrated a surprising pattern—newborns are able to discriminate and attend to the sounds from all languages, but by 10 months of age, infants no longer attend to phonemes unless the phonemes occur in the speech they hear every day (Werker & Tees, 1984). Infants therefore appear to have a sensitive period in which their capabilities are fine-tuned to the particular language (or languages) they are exposed to early in life (Best, 1995). The processes underlying this fine tuning and the extent to which it occurs have yet to be determined (Aslin, Jusczyk, & Pisoni, 1998; Jusczyk, 1997).

pragmatics *the practical rules guiding the use of verbal and nonverbal communication in differing situations*

When infants cannot say what they want, they use gestures. How does this infant's pointing at an object indicate that he understands cause-and-effect relationships?

Children also acquire **phonemic awareness**—knowledge of permissible and nonpermissible strings of sounds in their native language. For instance, English combines *s* + *p* in words such as *speak* and *spring* but not *s* + *r*. As they listen to the language around them, infants and toddlers are exposed to the many sound combinations of their native language (Menyuk, 1988). From this exposure, children learn the statistical regularities in speech—the sounds that occur together—and this helps them extract information about words and their boundaries (Saffran, Aslin, & Newport, 1996). Infants also achieve phonemic and semantic competence through their attention to the rhymes and rhythms of language. For example, *intonation*—rising and falling speech patterns—gives clues about meaning. Universally, adults tend to use exaggerated intonation and a higher pitch when speaking to infants. Caregivers use rising intonations when they want infants to pay attention to something (Fernald, 1989).

Producing the Sounds of Speech

By 2 months of age, many infants make their first noncrying sounds. They begin **cooing,** making soft, repetitive vowel sounds such as "aah" and "ooh." Around 6 months of age, infants begin to produce sounds combining consonants and vowels, such as "ba" and "da." Between 6 and 10 months of age, they begin **babbling,** repeating consonant–vowel combinations such as "mama" and "dada." Many caregivers interpret these babbles as words, but at this age infants do not associate these sounds with particular meanings.

Intentional Communication

Ten-month-old Ray looks at his father, points to a teddy bear, and grunts. The message is clear: he wants his father to hand him the teddy bear. Even before they utter a word, infants communicate their needs through gestures and vocalizations. As they grow older, children add verbal interactions as another way to communicate (Owens, 1996).

Infants' abilities to communicate develop in concert with their cognitive abilities and based on the responses they receive to their communication attempts. For instance, the cognitive ability to understand cause-and-effect relationships goes hand in hand with realizing that behavior can be used to achieve an effect or a goal. A 10-month-old infant understands cause and effect and uses gestures to communicate needs and desires. In response, caregivers demand more precise communication from their older infants; they expect them to communicate more directly, such as by pointing to objects.

First Words

Children's ability to understand language, called **receptive language,** precedes their ability to produce language, or **expressive language** (see Figure 6.13). For example, long before they can utter the word *cat,* infants respond to "Where's the cat?" by looking at the cat. Many children understand single words at around 8 to 9 months of age (Owens, 1996). This is most reliably demonstrated by their response to being called by their name or to being told "No!"

Although infants communicate through gestures and produce and respond to word-like sounds during the first year, they usually do not begin to say real words until they are about 12 months old (Bloom, 1998). Children's first attempts to speak real words are important because they signal that the child understands the symbolic significance of words. Speaking words is not an easy task. To produce a word, children must be able to recognize the sounds that make up the word and the order in which these sounds need to be

phonemic awareness *knowledge of permissible and nonpermissible strings of sounds in one's native language*

cooing *making soft, repetitive vowel sounds such as "aah" and "ooh"*

babbling *repeating consonant–vowel combinations, such as "mama" or "dada," two or more times*

receptive language *children's understanding of language*

expressive language *children's ability to produce language*

produced. They must remember the sounds and integrate them into a smooth-flowing word.

First words usually are the names of common objects or people. The importance of children's social environment as a setting for language development is apparent: their first words often describe the important people and objects with which they are most familiar, such as *mama, dada,* names of pets, or names of categories (*hat, doggie*). For some children, first words include action words (*bye-bye, all gone*) and, of course, the word *no* (Bloom, 1994; Nelson, 1981).

The ability to say words indicates a remarkable increase in children's level of abstract thinking—they now understand the correspondence between a mental concept and the set of sounds (the word) that has been assigned to that mental concept (Woodward & Markman, 1998). In addition, their first words are packed with meaning. A child's first words are **holophrases,** individual words that convey as much meaning as sentences. For instance, a child is likely to say "doggie" to announce that the dog is entering the room or to convey her desire that the dog come play with her. *Doggie* means much more than simply "the dog."

FIGURE 6.13
Receptive Language Precedes Expressive Language

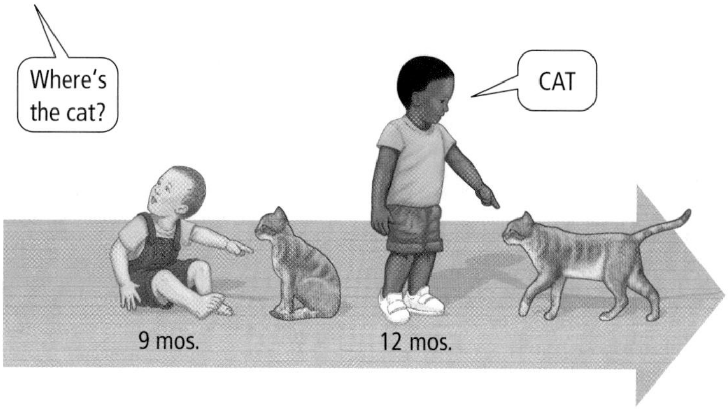

Children understand more words than they can speak, and these words make up their receptive language. The words they can speak when they are trying to communicate an idea make up their expressive language.

Development of Vocabulary

Once children understand the sound–word connection (between 12 and 18 months), they add around 3 words per month to their vocabulary. After 18 to 24 months, a vocabulary "explosion" often occurs, in which children quickly acquire a large number of words at a rapid rate (Bates, O'Connell, & Shore, 1987; see Figure 6.14 on page 189). They also begin to use words for social rituals, such as saying "bye-bye" (Gopnick, 1988). Around age 2, children include words that indicate an understanding of success ("hooray") and failure ("uh-oh") (Gopnick & Meltzoff, 1986). Because children's vocabularies are limited, they invent new words by, for instance, changing a noun to a verb. A child who sits in a rocker chair might say, "Rocker me, Mommy" (Clark, 1997).

Solving the Mystery of Word Meaning

Every time children hear a new word, they must act like detectives, trying to solve the mystery of the meaning that is intended. Young children are smart word learners and understand the meanings of novel nouns quickly (Akhtar, Carpenter, & Tomasello, 1996), and they use many kinds of input to make sense of word meaning (Hollich et al., 2000). One way children learn word meanings is through **fast mapping,** in which they learn to associate the sound of the word with the concept the word stands for, sometimes in a single exposure (Markson & Bloom, 1997). Mappings are more likely to occur, and are more accurate, for concrete objects than for abstract information (Rice, 1990). Children's abilities to attend and remember enhance their ability to learn new words (Samuelson & Smith, 1998). Children also use cues from social interactions to attach meaning to new words (Tomasello, Strosberg, & Akhtar, 1996).

When they are first learning to speak, children learn words slowly, while at the age of 2, they acquire about 10 words a day on average (Golinkoff et al., 2000). Similarly, the speed of the mapping process increases with age, such that preschoolers are more likely

holophrases *individual words that convey as much meaning as whole sentences*

fast mapping *associating the sound of a word with the concept the word stands for, sometimes in a single exposure*

FROM RESEARCH TO PRACTICE
CAN BABIES COMMUNICATE THROUGH HAND SIGNALS?

Most 1-year-olds are limited in their ability to express their desires because they know only a few words. Does this mean that infants are unable to let their caregivers know when they are cold or what they want to eat? For most infants, these would be difficult messages to convey. Some babies, however, have learned how to communicate complex messages through the use of simple gestures, called *baby signs.*

FROM RESEARCH . . .

Baby signing as an area of study arose from Linda Acredolo's experience with her 1-year-old daughter, Kate, who began to sign for flowers by wrinkling her nose and sniffing. With encouragement, Kate learned 29 signs in the next 6 months and became able to communicate many complex ideas. As she grew older and her verbal skills developed, she stopped using signs.

Because of her experience with Kate, Acredolo and her colleague, Susan Goodwyn, began a study of baby signs in 140 families. They found that children who used signs were helped in their language development rather than hindered and that their parents responded more positively toward them because of their increased ability to communicate their needs to sleep or eat or have a book read to them. They also found that girls were more likely to develop signs than boys and that parent–child interactions were important in helping children to learn signs. By 16 to 18 months of age, children averaged about 4 signs that they used frequently (Acredolo & Goodwyn, 1988). Infants who use signs may be less frustrated because their needs can be addressed more quickly. For example, one child in the study who was afraid of dogs could easily signal this fear to parents and be comforted promptly.

Baby Signs

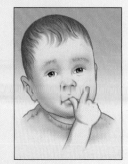 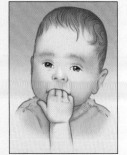 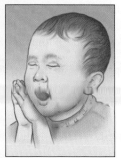

Drink/Bottle
Description:
Thumb to mouth, tilting up
Mimics a drinking motion

Possible Situations:
To request a bottle; to request juice or water.

Food/Eat
Description:
Fingertips to lips
Depicts putting food in mouth

Possible Situations:
To request something to eat; to label food or someone eating.

Sleep
Description:
Head tilted, hands against cheek
Mimics head on pillow

Possible Situations:
Request to take a nap; request to go to bed

Baby signs are often related to the activities and immediate needs of the infant. Many of the signs are made by miming the action to be communicated or by indicating a part of the body (for example, *noisy* might be indicated by pointing to the ear). Which signs do you think infants are most likely to use?

Source: Acredolo and Goodwyn, 1996.

. . . TO PRACTICE

Infants can be encouraged to use signs they invent themselves, or caregivers can teach signs to children. For instance, *noisy* can be represented by pointing a finger to the child's ear, *go out* by pretending to turn a doorknob, and *cold* by hugging the arms to the body. Acredolo and Goodwyn recommend that caregivers start with a few simple physical signs, say the words as they make the signs, and repeat the signs often to increase the likelihood of the child's using them (Acredolo & Goodwyn, 1996).

THINKING IT THROUGH

1. Why might effective nonverbal communication benefit infants and toddlers and their relationships with parents?

2. How might effective nonverbal communication promote the development of language and thinking?

3. What signs and signals did you learn and use as a young child? What five signs would you regard as the most important to teach a baby?

FIGURE 6.14
Growth of Young Children's Vocabulary

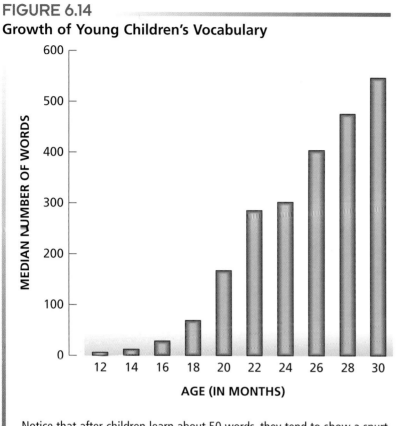

Notice that after children learn about 50 words, they tend to show a spurt in vocabulary learning. How do you think children learn so many words so quickly? What role do caregivers play in this learning?

Note: Data for 8 to 16 months and for 18 to 30 months came from different samples of children.
Source: Fenson et al., 1994.

than toddlers to learn words in a single exposure. In one study, children were asked to play a hiding game with a puppet. They were shown three objects—two familiar objects and one new object called a *koob*—and three hiding places. The children were asked to hide each object in a designated spot. After hiding the two familiar toys, the children were directed to "hide the koob under the bowl." They were then asked questions about the objects and the objects' names. The results revealed that almost all of the children fast-mapped the name *koob* to the new object (Dollaghan, 1985).

Over- and Underextending Meaning

Although fast mapping helps children learn new words, it does not provide solutions to more subtle aspects of word meaning (Woodward & Markman, 1998). Listen to young children's speech and you will note that their use of words is often quite different from adults'—especially the way they relate a word to a class of objects. Sometimes children use words to refer to objects or things that are outside the bounds of the category named by the word, in a process called **overextension** (Anglin, 1985). A child who uses the word *doggie* to refer to all furry animals with four legs—a cat, a dog, a lamb—is overextending the bounds of the meaning of the word. The child is nonetheless demonstrating the ability to map a set of sounds (doggie) to a meaningful grouping (small furry animals). The tendency to overextend words is very common among young children (Woodward & Markman, 1998). When children use words to refer to a smaller group than the word actually names, they are exhibiting

overextension *the use of words to refer to objects or things that are outside the bounds of the category named by the word*

FIGURE 6.15

Examples of Children's Mapping of Words to Categories

(a) An Overextended Category: *doggie*

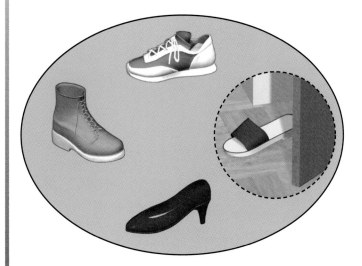

(b) An Underextended Category: *shoe*

When children overextend, their use of a word extends beyond the category named by the word. In (a), the child has extended "doggie" to mean any animal with hair. When children underextend, their use of a word is narrower than the category named by the word. In (b), the child has narrowed the meaning of "shoe" to only shoes in closets—not shoes on people's feet.

underextension   *the use of words to refer to fewer items than the word actually names*

underextension (MacWhinney, 1989). For instance, a child who uses *shoe* to refer only to the shoes in the closet but not to the shoes he or she wears is underextending the range of the meaning of *shoe* (Clark, 1981; see Figure 6.15). Children pay particular attention to the forms of objects and their functions when trying to solve the mystery of word meaning.

Learning Levels of Meaning

Children also must determine the level of meaning intended by a word (Woodward & Markman, 1998). When Kurt was 2 and first met his friend's cat, Simon, he heard the labels "Simon," "cat," and "animal." Each label is correct, but each has a different level of meaning. How does Kurt know which word stands for the individual animal and which stands for the whole category of small, furry creatures?

One way that children learn the meanings associated with alternative words for the same object is through cues that others provide in their speech. When children hear the cue word *the*, they know that the following word refers to a category of objects rather than a single unique object (Callanan, 1989). When Kurt heard "See the cat," he had a way to recognize that *cat* must refer to the category rather than a name. In contrast, when he heard "This is Simon," the preceding words acted as a cue that *Simon* was the proper name of the object (Gelman & Taylor, 1984).

Another way that children resolve the category-level problem is through certain assumptions they make about words and objects. Around age 2, children make the assumption that only one name applies to each object. When they hear a new word associated with an object, they assume that word is the name of the object (Merriman & Bowman, 1989). Given another word, they are unlikely to think it is also the name of the object. Instead, they assume that it refers to another aspect of the object. Children show an order of preference for mapping new words to objects and attributes. They first assume the new word is an object name. If it is not an object name, they then assume the new word refers to a part of the object. If that is not correct either, they assume the word refers to an unusual aspect of the object, such as its texture or shape (Marcus et al., 1992). Using these assumptions and the cues others give, children eventually learn that multiple labels can be used to represent people and objects (Deak & Maratsos, 1998; Hall & Graham, 1998).

As you might suspect, it is difficult for children to understand the meanings of words that refer to abstract concepts—such as *tall* and *short, high* and *low*—because these words are not associated with any particular object (Woodward & Markman, 1998). Think about a child who hears the word *tall* associated with a building and with a person. What will this child likely infer about its meaning? A person may be tall relative to a chair but short in comparison to a building. *Tall* is not associated with a person in the same way that *adult* might be. So it is not surprising that children have difficulty mastering these descriptive terms.

First Sentences

At about 18 months, many children begin to produce sequences of words, usually separated by long pauses. By the end of the second year, these sequences give way to true sentences (Bloom, 1998). The shift from using holophrases to actually producing sentences marks another tremendous accomplishment of the toddler years. In true sentences, children do not randomly string words together. Instead, the order of the words represents their first application of grammar—the use of rules to convey meaning in language. Constructing sentences is taxing and requires much effort for young children; this probably explains why early sentences are produced haltingly and why children often repeat the same sentence over and over with only minor changes (Cartwright & Brent, 1997).

Two-word sentences contain the information that is available in each word as well as the information implied in the order of the words (Braine, 1963). Children's early sentences emphasize meaning and usually refer to actions or objects (Bloom, 1998). When discussing actions, children talk about who performs the action, where it is done, and the object used to perform it. When discussing objects, children talk about the names and characteristics of the objects, their locations, and their ownership. A construction that children commonly use is an agent and its action, such as "daddy go" or "doggie bark." Examples of 2-year-olds' two-word sentences are shown in Table 6.3.

Children's earliest sentences are called **telegraphic speech** because they contain only the most essential and informative words and seldom include less informative words, such as *a, an,* or *the.* Telegraphic speech gradually becomes elaborated as children develop more sophisticated language skills.

Early Talkers and Late Talkers

Early talkers are children between 11 and 20 months of age who are in the top 10 percent for vocabulary production (Bates, Dale, & Thal, 1995). The variations in when children begin to talk relate to language competence 5 years later, although long-term studies beyond this time frame have yet to be conducted. Interestingly, early-talking children can be described as "saying everything they know." Whereas most children have significantly better comprehension of information than production of speech, early talkers are normal in comprehension but exceedingly high in their production of speech (Bates et al., 1995).

TABLE 6.3
Examples of Children's Two-Word Sentences

SEMANTIC RELATION	ENGLISH	GERMAN	SAMOAN
agent–action	teddy fall	puppe kommt (doll comes)	pa'u pepe (fall doll)
action–object	hit ball	tur aufmachen (door open)	tapale 'oe (hit you)
possessor–possession	mama dress	mein ball (my ball)	lol a'u (candy my)
rejection–action	no wash	nicht blasen (not blow)	le 'ai (not eat)

Source: Adapted from de Villiers and de Villiers, 1992.

telegraphic speech *early language in which only highly informative words are used and less informative words are neglected*

In contrast, children who are at the bottom of the vocabulary production scale relative to their peers have mixed developmental outcomes. Many of these children will appear normal in language development within about a year or so; for that reason, language specialists have not wanted to label them as having any type of language disorder. Instead, they are labeled "late talkers" (Paul, 1991; Rescorla & Schwartz, 1990). About half of late talkers continue to show delayed language development, especially those in families with lower socioeconomic status, those with the greatest delays, and those with the smallest expressive vocabularies (Paul, Spangle-Looney, & Dahm, 1991). Nonetheless, the long-term outcome for these children is unclear: many show normal-range language development later in childhood, but some continue to show evidence of delayed language development (Bates et al., 1995).

How Is Children's Language Acquisition Explained?

How do most children quickly and easily develop the skills needed to speak sentences and understand the rules of a language? Many different explanations have been proposed. Some emphasize the special role of the human brain in interpreting language, whereas others emphasize the role of rewards for grammatical speech. To better understand the issues of language development, consider the true story of Genie, a girl who was denied exposure to language, along with provision of other basic needs, for 11 years (Rymer, 1993).

One day in 1970, a slumped and disheveled child weighing approximately 60 pounds entered a welfare office in Los Angeles with her almost-blind mother. What social workers thought might be an autistic child of 5 or 6 years turned out to be a 13-year-old who had been hidden away in a back room since the age of 2. Genie's father believed she was brain damaged and forced her to live virtually alone for her whole life. Genie's only contacts with humans were brief and unpleasant; her father would sometimes bark at her, but little was ever said to her directly. She was strapped into a crib at night and onto a potty chair for most of her days.

Genie was immediately removed from this horrible environment and admitted to a children's hospital. She was weak, unable to walk very well, and not toilet trained. Psychologists, social workers, linguists, and therapists all worked with Genie, trying to assess her capabilities and help her develop the social, emotional, and intellectual skills that should have been a natural part of her upbringing. In addition to her physical problems, Genie could not utter more than a few sounds. Would she be able to learn language and adapt to her new environment? The following sections explore the theoretical stances on language acquisition and how these theories might predict outcomes for Genie.

Learning-Based Theories

Learning-based theories emphasize a child's environment as the key to developing language skills. The leading proponent of this theory was Skinner (1957), who suggested that children learn language through reinforcement of correct and grammatical forms of speech. Other behaviorists suggest that language is learned through observation—by watching and listening to others (see Chapter 2).

Reinforcement-Based Theories

Rewards and punishment are involved in important ways in language development: caregivers encourage infants to talk and reinforce their talking with praise, affection, and attention. Thus, reinforcement motivates children's communication efforts (Owens, 1996). Imitation also is important to language acquisition in that children grow up speaking the language they hear around them; they imitate idioms and dialects. For instance, children in parts of the South might say, "I'm fixin' to go to school," meaning that they are getting ready to go to school.

Environment-Based Theories

More recent learning-based views assume that rewards are less central than exposure to the environment. The types of regularities that children hear in speech provides the input for them to begin to recognize the qualities of language. For instance, as discussed earlier in this chapter, studies have found that after only a few minutes of exposure to particular pairings of speech sounds, 8-month-old infants recognize the sounds that go together more often in speech than those sounds that do not (Saffran et al., 1996). For instance, in the United States, babies are more likely to hear the sound "da" used, such as in the words "Dada" or "day" or "Saturday" and seldom hear the sound "sb." Studies of "statistical learning" of which sounds go together appear to provide an important mechanism for learning language (Marcus, Vijayan, Rao, & Vishton, 1999), because it provides a mechanism to help infants begin to recognize the patterns underlying speech. However, it is not yet clear how well these processes work for more complex aspects of language (Altmann, 2002; Werker et al., 2004).

Learning-based theories of language acquisition are based on the idea that parents encourage and reward their children's use of language. What forms of language are parents likely to reward, and what types do they not reward?

Objections to Learning-Based Theories

Although they are useful in explaining some aspects of language acquisition, learning-based theories do not adequately explain the development of grammar. Parents seldom reward or punish grammatical aspects of children's speech; they are more likely to reinforce children for *what* they say rather than *how* they say it (deVilliers & deVilliers, 1992). Also, children produce so many new and unusual sentences that it is unlikely that they have heard and borrowed them from others or been reinforced for these sentences (Clark, 1997). For instance, after taking a bath, 30-month-old Jake told his mother that he was "barefoot all over," referring to the fact that he was naked. It is unlikely that Jake had ever heard anyone refer to being naked in this way.

To the extent that observational learning, rewards, and punishments account for language development, the prognosis for Genie would be somewhat hopeful. If she was presented with many instances of speech from the concerned people trying to help her and was rewarded for producing grammatically correct sentences, she might slowly acquire language, although it could take years of training for her to become a competent speaker of English.

Innate Theories: Biological Influences

In contrast to Skinner's ideas about learning and language development, biological theories suggest that a special capacity for understanding language resides within the human brain. The dominant biological theory was proposed by Noam Chomsky (1965, 1986), who argued that children are born with a **language acquisition device (LAD)** in their brain that allows them to understand the properties—the universal grammar—of all human languages. The LAD acts as a guide, or blueprint, for recognizing language input and detects the regularities in language. Children develop a sense of universal grammar merely by being exposed to language.

Evidence for Chomsky's Theory

Some indirect evidence in support of Chomsky's ideas comes from similarities in the ways that children all over the world acquire language. Scientific evidence supports Chomsky's assumptions about the importance of the brain in language acquisition. Although the LAD part of the brain has not been identified, people with various kinds of brain damage show

language acquisition device (LAD) *Chomsky's idea that there is a part of the brain that allows children to understand the properties of all human languages*

very specific language disorders, which suggests that different aspects of language are processed in specific locations in the left hemisphere of the brain. For instance, people with damage to Broca's area of the brain (see Figure 6.16) can express meaning but are unable to produce sentences that reflect grammatical rules. Damage to Wernicke's area does not prevent people from forming grammatically correct sentences, but they convey nothing meaningful in their sentences. Recent studies suggest that the brain is involved in very complex ways in processing language (Maratsos, 1998; Seidenberg, 1997). For instance, studies using brain-imaging techniques show that different sites within the brain are activated for processing nouns and for processing verbs (Damasio & Damasio, 1992). More recently, consistent with Chomsky's ideas, Pinker (1994) argued that language is a human instinct, wired into our brains by evolution. In this view, the brain has a special module for language learning, with sensitivities to the sounds and patterns of language (Fodor, 1983). According to this view, learning and the environment, although playing important roles in language, cannot account for all the types of language rules that children learn. Direct evidence in support of these ideas is difficult to obtain. No studies of language development have been designed to definitively address the question of whether humans are born with a special capacity for understanding language.

Critical Periods for Language Development

Biological factors, specifically brain development, seem to play a powerful role in language acquisition. According to Lenneberg (1967), there is a critical period for language development, from about the age of 2 to puberty, during which the brain is primed for processing language. Without exposure to language during this critical period, a person will never learn to use it, because thereafter the brain loses its ability to acquire language through simple exposure.

FIGURE 6.16
Language-Related Areas of the Brain

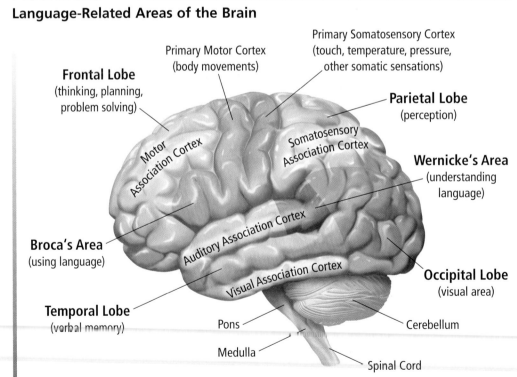

The brain areas in bold show the parts of the brain that are thought to be heavily involved in processing language-related information. What does recent research tell us about the complexity of language processing?

NURTURING CHILDREN
PROMOTING LANGUAGE DEVELOPMENT

Parents powerfully influence their children in many ways—one way is through helping them to learn language. The stimulation that parents and other caregivers provide for infants and toddlers sets the stage for them to develop effective communication skills. Even though genetics plays a role in language development, and the brain is prewired to be sensitive to the sounds and rhythms of language, language learning requires stimulation and input from the child's social environment. Watching television is not a particularly good way for children to learn language; human interaction seems to be the key for promoting language growth. Human interaction is essential because parents are able to fine-tune their speech—to speak child-directed language—in ways that most appeal to infants and children.

What can parents do to help their children learn to communicate through language?

■ Ensure that your child is healthy. Make sure your child can hear well, and treat ear infections quickly so that children do not lose language input.

■ Keep it interesting. By varying the pitch of your voice, you can maintain your child's attention.

■ Speak simply. By using shorter words and sentences, parents provide a simple model of good grammar that children can model.

■ Speak clearly. Use clear pronunciation of words so that the child hears an accurate representation of the word.

■ Label objects and people. Children want to know what everything is. Provide your child with labels so that he or she has a word to associate with each object or person.

■ Be prepared to answer (simply) hundreds of questions. As your child begins to speak, he or she will initiate conversations with anyone at any time. They will ask "why" over and over. Your child wants to practice language and needs a partner. Be a good partner, and provide short and simple answers to questions.

■ Provide a rich language environment. Read to your child, introduce new words, play word games, listen to music, and go to the library (even before your child can read).

Source: Adapted from Golinkoff & Hirsh-Pasek, 1999.

Brain development, especially of areas believed important in language learning, occurs rapidly in the first years of life, and these developmental changes may be necessary to children's acquisition of language (Bates, Thal, & Janowsky, 1992; Huttenlocher, 1990; Pinker, 1994). Other evidence in support of Lenneberg's critical period hypothesis has been obtained in studies of immigrants' language abilities. When people move to the United States from other countries, they are placed in a new environment and need to learn a new language to function effectively. How easily do non-English-speaking immigrants learn to speak English? Research on second-language learning suggests that age at arrival in a foreign country relates to mastery of the language, even after decades of practice. In one study, Korean children who arrived in the United States before age 7 mastered English as well as native English-speaking children did; those who arrived here between 8 and 15 years of age were less capable; and adolescents and adults who arrived between 17 and 39 years of age did not master English very well at all (Johnson & Newport, 1989). These findings suggest that learning a new language is easier for children than it is for adults.

Biologically based theories have dominated much of the scientific thinking about language development. Although these theories explain many interesting features of language development, they may not provide the whole explanation. Language development occurs more gradually than is implied by innate theories, and the universal features that Chomsky believes underlie all languages have been difficult to identify (Moerk, 1989).

The case of Genie was a natural test of innate biological theory because Genie was not exposed to language during the critical period. According to biologically based theories, the prognosis for Genie would be pessimistic. Genie might be unable to acquire language, even with rigorous training.

Social Interaction Theories

Caregivers support language acquisition in many important ways beyond rewarding children and providing models for language use. Social interaction theories suggest that the social context of language is a fundamental part of language development (Bohannon & Warren-Leubecker, 1989). Thus, children acquire language in interaction with parents and other skilled speakers of the language. Many studies confirm the importance of social interaction in language acquisition. For instance, a child may watch foreign-language television for hours a day but will not learn the language unless he or she interacts with others using that language (Bloom, 1998).

Children's active participation in social interactions is also vital to developing complex forms of language. Language acquisition seems to require children's participation in the activities that the language is helping to create (Cole, 1992). For children to acquire anything more than the basics of language, they must actively take part in everyday social interactions using language.

Language Acquisition Through Exposure

Another way in which caregivers foster children's language acquisition is through exposure. By talking to them, caregivers expose infants to the rules, contexts, and patterns of language. Early in language development, mere exposure makes a critical difference (Owens, 1996). In a 2-year longitudinal study of US families with toddlers, Hart and Risley (1995) found that the average family spent 28 minutes an hour interacting with their child when he or she was very young and even more time when the child began to speak words. Parents addressed their children an average of 325 times per hour, although the rate varied from 56 to 793 times per hour (Hart & Risley, 1995). Thus, in a 14-hour day, one child may hear about 700 utterances, while another hears over 11,000 utterances! Over several years, the language environments of these two children will grow even more discrepant. It is no wonder that the researchers found that by age 3, children exposed to more utterances per day knew more words than children exposed to fewer (Hart & Risley, 1995). The powerful message of this research is that the sheer quantity of language interactions to which a child is exposed in her or his social environment makes a difference in early language development.

Child-Directed Speech

Another role of caregivers is to provide many examples of language near the child's own level of understanding. They talk to and interact with their children in specific ways that seem to facilitate language development (Vygotsky, 1986/1934). The version of language that caregivers use with their children has been termed **child-directed speech** or *motherese;* it consists of simple, repetitive sentences spoken in attention-getting ways. Child-directed speech is spoken in a loud, high-pitched voice and uses exaggerated intonations to direct and maintain the child's attention. This speech has a simple vocabulary, uses repetition, and focuses on present events. Many studies indicate that not only caregivers but also older children use child-directed speech (Hoff-Ginsberg, 1986). Even mothers of deaf infants use child-directed sign language (Masataka, 1996, 1998).

In child-directed speech, words that may be difficult for the child to understand are modified; for instance, a parent might say "tummy" for *stomach* and "grandpa" for *grandfather.* Caregivers also simplify the grammar in sentences and use active constructions, such as "baby eats carrots" rather than "the carrots are going to be eaten by the baby." In these ways, child-directed speech exposes children to simplified language that is still more complex than what they may already understand and use (Bruner, 1983).

Studies suggest that use of child-directed speech is related to enhanced language skills in children (Gleitman, Newport, & Gleitman, 1984). Further studies show that infants

child-directed speech *a special version of language that caregivers use with their children; also called motherese*

whose mothers try to elicit language from them ("Tell me what this is called" and "Is that a horse or a cow?") develop larger vocabularies than many of their peers do (Jones & Adamson, 1987). A longitudinal study of language development in the first 3 years of life indicated that children whose mothers allow them to take turns in conversations learn language more rapidly (Menyuk, Liebergott, & Schultz, 1995).

Caregivers differ in their use of child-directed speech. Compared to older mothers, adolescent mothers speak fewer words to their infants, and their infants vocalize less than those of older mothers (Culp, Osofsky, & O'Brien, 1996). Additionally, children of depressed mothers, who do not use exaggerated intonation patterns when talking to their infants and who are less responsive, verbalize less than children of nondepressed mothers (Bettes, 1988). Although caregivers all over the world use child-directed speech, cultural differences are apparent in its specific forms (Ingram, 1989). For instance, Korean mothers emphasize action-oriented speech rather than object-oriented speech with their infants. Korean infants understand more verbs than do English-speaking infants (Choi & Gopnick, 1995).

Teaching by Expansion

Caregivers use subtle methods to illustrate complex forms of grammar—for instance, **expansion** of the child's own utterances. When an infant says, "cup," a caregiver is likely to respond by saying, "Yes, that is your cup." By expanding the child's one or two words to a complete sentence, the caregiver is presenting the child with an opportunity to understand and acquire the complexities of the language.

Caregivers' use of expansions and child-directed speech act as scaffolding for learning language. The scaffolding changes as parents offer ever more advanced versions of the language, thereby providing an optimal language-learning environment for children. The social context, especially active interactions with caregivers, provides children with a learning environment that supports their language development. However, it is unlikely that the social context fully explains all aspects of language development. Not all children have optimal social interactions, and yet most children learn language.

According to social interaction theories, Genie's prognosis would be somewhat hopeful. Genie had little exposure to people during her early years and so had few opportunities to engage in language within a social context. Over time, Genie might gradually gain language skills through intensive social interactions with concerned caregivers if they provide motivation and appropriate levels of child-directed language and expansions of her speech.

Genie's Outcomes

Soon after Genie appeared in the welfare office, she began working with Susan Curtiss, a graduate student in linguistics. Curtiss kept records of Genie's vocalizations and conducted testing of her language skills (Curtiss, 1977). At first, Genie's vocalizations were high-pitched, monotone whimpers or squeaks. After many outings with Curtiss, Genie acquired new words that represented some of her favorite things, such as *pail* for the plastic containers she liked to play with and *store* for the places she liked to visit.

Genie quickly developed a variety of social skills, and she learned a number of new vocabulary words in a relatively short time. One year after Genie was admitted to the hospital, her grammar resembled that of an 18-month-old child; 6 months later, she was using

Why are social interactions important in language development? What do caregivers do to simplify their speech, and how might this help children learn language more quickly?

expansion   *taking young children's simplified language and adding complexity and completeness to it*

plurals and could produce some 2- and 3-word sentences. The linguists working with Genie were excited about the possibility that she would learn grammar despite being beyond the critical period, but in 3 more years Genie's speech did not improve very much. Unlike most 3-year-olds, Genie could not correctly form complex sentences using *why, where,* or *what.* For example, she produced word strings such as "Where is may I have a penny?" or "I where is graham cracker on top shelf" (Rymer, 1993). Genie also had difficulty recognizing how to use grammatical markers such as *-ed* and *s.*

In tests conducted to assess Genie's brain functioning, researchers discovered an abnormality: her left hemisphere, which for most people is involved in processing language, did not function at all. Her right hemisphere processed language. Genie's brain could not handle language input normally. After living with a string of researchers and foster parents, Genie today lives in a home for adults with mental impairments. Now in her forties and without the special attention researchers provided, Genie seems to have lost her hard-won social skills along with her battle to acquire language (Rymer, 1993).

How can we explain Genie's developmental successes and failures? It is difficult to draw firm conclusions because of the severe physical and emotional abuse and neglect she suffered at the hands of her parents. The abuse, including malnourishment, may have interfered with her ability to learn language. Or she may have been brain damaged in some way before the abuse started, the brain damage hampering her ability to learn language and causing her father to think she was mentally retarded. Despite developing cognitive and social skills, Genie may have found it hard to learn grammar and syntax because of her brain dysfunction. In addition, Genie missed the early years of language learning, possibly limiting her ability to ever acquire language skills. Genie's story suggests that exposure to language may be important for normal brain development, as well as for language acquisition. For many years Genie lacked the stimulus of social interaction and appropriate language models to observe and follow. She was never reinforced for using language, and she never heard child-directed speech. Thus, in the triumph and ultimate tragedy of Genie's story, you can see how each theory of language acquisition provides insights about how children acquire and learn to use language.

The Resilient and Fragile Aspects of Language Development

Genie's case is useful for illustrating that despite horrifying early conditions, some aspects of language development can be resilient, whereas others are not. Rather than assume that there is a strictly controlled critical period in learning language, most researchers today understand that aspects of language development vary in their vulnerability to environmental conditions.

In general, language learning is remarkably resilient, even under extreme conditions. Although Genie had difficulty with syntax—especially understanding and using grammatical markers correctly—she developed a large vocabulary, even including words that were unusual

Most deaf children are born to hearing parents. What kind of language input do they receive? How do these children learn language?

for a child first developing language (such as words for emotions or for many variations in color hues; Curtiss, 1977). Language need not be spoken to be acquired. Children who are exposed from birth to conventional sign languages (such as American Sign Language) learn language at the same rate and in the same pattern as children acquiring spoken language (Lillo-Martin, 1999; Newport & Meier, 1985).

Unfortunately, not all children have exposure to a rich and varied linguistic environment. About 90 percent of deaf children are born to hearing parents and thus are not exposed to sign language early in life. With no exposure to sign language until much later in life, these children have no usable linguistic input. But even with such limited language exposure, these children find a way to communicate, using gestures to express their desires. The gestures these children use, called "home signs," are more complex than those used by hearing children to supplement their spoken language, and they are not imitations of the gestures used by the hearing parents; home signs follow the patterns expected for early language use (Goldin-Meadow, 1997).

Deaf children who have not been exposed to sign language and who cannot use speech have been studied in Taiwan and the United States (Goldin-Meadow & Mylander, 1998). Both the Taiwanese and the US children used gestures to communicate in various ways with their hearing parents—to make requests and comments, to talk about past and present, and to ask questions. Children in both countries tended to develop series of gestures akin to sentences, and the order of the gestures followed neither Mandarin nor English word order. The findings concerning deaf children's development of home signing suggests that some linguistic properties are not transmitted from one generation to another but instead result from attempts to communicate (National Research Council and Institute of Medicine, 2000).

Language learning is resilient to even relatively extreme variations in the amount of input to the language learner. Hearing children raised by deaf parents lack the usual spoken language input but typically acquire spoken language with only about 5 to 10 hours a week of exposure to hearing speakers. Furthermore, these children do not mimic idiosyncrasies of their deaf parents' speech but instead regularize their language based on the norms of the spoken language they are learning. Although blind children lack the means to visually associate objects with the spoken words they hear, they do not experience difficulties in language development (Schiff-Myers, 1988). Apparently, language development does not depend on a mapping of words onto the physical world.

Even variations in biological conditions may not deter language development. As important as the brain is for language development, children who experience major brain damage may still acquire language. Surprisingly, children who have damage to the left cortex of the brain may recover language use as long as the damage occurs early in life (Feldman, MacWhinney, & Sacco, 2002). When both hemispheres are damaged, speech and language difficulties are more likely to result (National Research Council and Institute of Medicine, 2000).

Genie's case also demonstrates, however, that not all aspects of language development are resilient. Evidence concerning the timing of linguistic exposure suggests that some aspects of language development are more fragile and vulnerable to environmental conditions. Generally, exposure to a language early in life results in better proficiency in the language than does later exposure. For instance, deaf children of hearing parents who receive no linguistic input until later in life are typically greatly impaired in their use of syntax, just as Genie was, even when these children do not experience the same sorts of physical and social deprivation that Genie did (Curtiss, 1989; Newport, 1991). Similarly, even after 30 years of exposure to American Sign Language, native signers (exposed at birth) outperform early learners, and early learners (before age 6) outperform late learners (after age 12).

Second-language learning also is affected by the timing of input. Research has illustrated that the influence of early input is not tightly time-bound, however. This sensitive period is not a window that closes at 6 or 7, but rather one that seems to close more gradually over many years. Furthermore, unlike the resilient aspects of language, which are learned in consistent patterns across individuals, the fragile aspects of language are much more variable. Some individuals master the complexities of a second language even relatively late in life; many others do not. The conclusion that can be drawn from the evidence on deaf isolates, second-language learning, and cases like Genie's is that the ability to acquire language diminishes with age (Stromswold, 2000).

Studies of brain activity support the notion that some aspects of language development are fragile. When studies have assessed event-related brain potentials (called ERPs), which provide indications about the processing of information in the brain, different patterns have been found for early versus late language learners. Among Chinese–English bilingual speakers, the parts of the brain that deal with semantic aspects of language (e.g., nouns and verbs) were relatively unaffected by delays in exposure, but the parts of the brain that process grammatical markers of language (e.g., prepositions and conjunctions) were markedly different, depending on the delay in exposure to the second language (Weber-Fox & Neville, 1996). This finding suggests that the parts of the brain that deal with grammar are more modifiable, and thus more vulnerable to variations in language exposure, than the parts that deal with meaning (National Research Council and Institute of Medicine, 2000).

Try It Out

1. Visit with a toddler and a preschool child. Ask the toddler to tell you about something he or she did that day. Compare this story to the story you hear from the preschool child. What factors influence the differences in the qualities of their stories? What roles do memory and experience likely play in the differences you notice?

2. Talk to the parents of these children. At what age did the children first use words to communicate? What were their first words and sentences, and in what social and cultural contexts did they say them? Did the parents use child-directed language with their babies?

3. Go online and explore the types of programs available for stimulating cognitive development in infants and toddlers. What do these programs stress? From what you have learned about development, evaluate whether the recommended types of training are based on good scientific evidence. What recommendations would you make to parents who want to enrich their child's environment?

4. Watch children's television on Saturday morning. Are any programs geared toward very young children? What are the features of these programs? What qualities of television programming may be enriching for language or cognitive development in infants and toddlers, and what qualities might be detrimental?

Key Terms and Concepts

A-not-B error (171)
babbling (186)
child-directed speech (196)
cooing (186)
dishabituation (181)
expansion (197)
expressive language (186)
fast mapping (187)
habituation (181)
holophrases (187)
image schemas (178)
infantile amnesia (182)
language acquisition device (LAD) (193)
object permanence (170)
overextension (189)

phonemes (184)
phonemic awareness (186)
pragmatics (185)
primary circular reactions (168)
receptive language (186)
relational play (178)
scaffolding (179)
semantics (184)
secondary circular reactions (169)
symbolic representation (172)
syntax (184)
telegraphic speech (191)
tertiary circular reactions (171)
underextension (190)

Sum It Up

How do cognitive abilities develop during infancy and toddlerhood?

■   What changes occur during the sensorimotor period of development as described by Piaget? (pp. 167–172)

■   Describe a child's understanding of object permanence. (pp. 170, 173)

■   According to Vygotsky's zone of proximal development, what kinds of experiences are likely to expand the range of children's cognitive abilities? (p. 179)

How do infants and toddlers learn and remember?

■   What are the roles of classical and operant conditioning in infant learning? (pp. 180–181)

■   What is habituation, and how can we tell it is occurring? (p. 181)

How do infants and toddlers develop language skills?

■   What are the four domains of language mastery? (pp. 184–185)

■   How do children communicate before they can talk? (p. 185)

■   What kinds of words are the first ones infants produce? (pp. 186–187)

■   How do children use fast mapping? (p. 187)

How is children's language acquisition explained?

■   How does an innate theory of language acquisition differ from a learning theory of acquisition? (pp. 192–195)

■   What role do social interactions play in children's language development? (pp. 196–197)

■   Which aspects of language development are most vulnerable to environmental influence? (pp. 198–200)

TABLE 6.1
Substages in the Sensorimotor Stage

SUBSTAGE	AGE	CHARACTERISTICS
Substage I	Birth to 1 month	Practices reflex actions
Substage II	1 to 4 months	Engages in primary circular reactions—repetitive actions centered on the infant's body
Substage III	4 to 8 months	Uses visually guided reaching for greater exploration
		Engages in secondary circular reactions—repetitive actions centered on objects
Substage IV	8 to 12 months	Shows first signs of intelligence by using intentional behavior to solve problems
Substage V	12 to 18 months	Engages in tertiary circular reactions—modified repetitive actions designed to explore qualities of objects
Substage VI	18 to 24 months	Achieves greater flexibility in problem solving by using symbols to represent objects

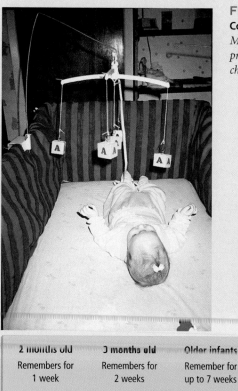

FIGURE 6.4 **Object Permanence** *Children's understanding of objects undergoes dramatic changes during infancy and toddlerhood. Infants move from having no concept of the permanence of objects to having a partial understanding. Only later in infancy do they acquire a full understanding of object permanence.*

COGNITIVE ABILITIES

During the sensorimotor stage, infants rely on their senses and their actions to learn about the world. Early in this stage, infants use reflexes such as sucking and grasping to learn about the qualities of objects. Later in this stage, infants explore objects in more varied ways. (Refer back to pages 167–180.)

FIGURE 6.11 **Familiar Contexts Aid Memory** *Memory improves when the procedures are familiar to children.*

INFANT LEARNING AND MEMORY

Learning and memory improve with age in infants, and a number of factors influence their memory. (Refer back to pages 180–184.)

FIGURE 6.6 **Using Symbolic Representation**

2 months old	3 months old	Older infants
Remembers for 1 week	Remembers for 2 weeks	Remember for up to 7 weeks

What factors influence infants' long-term memory?

- Repeated exposure
- Familiar contexts
- Situational cues
- Reminders

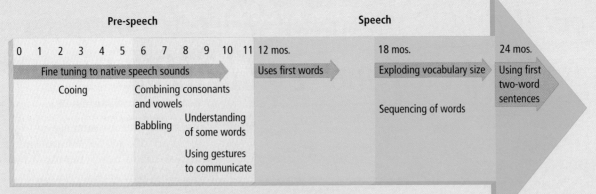

FIGURE 6.12 **Milestones of Early Language Development** *Notice that language is considered to be developing even before children speak.*

LANGUAGE DEVELOPMENT

Language development moves from the prespeech stage, during which infants learn the sounds of language and how to segment streams of sounds into words, to the speech stage, during which infants use words to communicate. (Refer back to pages 184–192.)

FIGURE 6.13 **Receptive Language Precedes Expressive Language** *Children understand more words than they can speak, and these words make up their receptive language.*

LANGUAGE ACQUISITION

Many different explanations have been proposed to help us understand how most children quickly and easily develop the skills needed to speak sentences and understand the rules of language. (Refer back to pages 192–200.)

Social interactions in everyday life play an important role in children's language development by providing a rich language-learning environment.

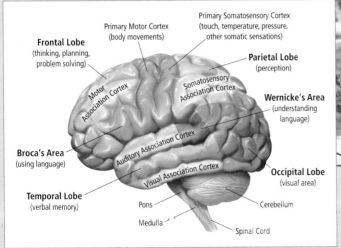

FIGURE 6.16 **Language-Related Areas of the Brain**

Learning theories emphasize the roles of modeling and reinforcement in language development.

Social and Emotional Development in Infancy and Toddlerhood

7

Chapter Outline

How Do Emotions Develop During Infancy and Toddlerhood?
Developing a Sense of Trust
Smiling and Laughter
Crying
Anger and Temper Tantrums
Shame, Pride, and Other Self-Conscious Emotions
Play and Emotional Development

How Does Temperament Influence Development During Infancy and Toddlerhood?
The Structure of Temperament
Contributions of Temperament to Infant Development
Cultural Perceptions of Temperament

How Do Parent–Infant Attachments Influence Development?
Attachment Theory
The Development of Attachment
Assessing Patterns of Attachment
Caregiver and Child Factors Affecting Attachment
The Role of Culture in Attachment
Consequences of Attachment
Attachment to Fathers

How Does Day Care Influence Infants' and Toddlers' Development?
Patterns of Day-Care Use
Effects of Day Care
Guidelines for Quality Day Care
Culture and Day Care

Why Are Children Abused and Neglected?
Definitions of Child Abuse and Neglect
Incidence of Child Abuse and Neglect
Characteristics of Victims and Abusers
Effects of Child Abuse and Neglect
Preventing Child Abuse and Neglect

A DEVELOPMENTAL MYSTERY

Two 11-month-old boys, Jamal and Kyle, are at a birthday party for another child who is turning 1. Although both boys find themselves in a similar situation, their reactions are dramatically different. Jamal is curious and interested in the goings-on at the party. He easily separates from his mother and explores the interesting new environment. When a balloon bursts suddenly and makes a loud noise, he becomes upset and goes to her for comfort. Once in her arms, he is quickly soothed and soon smiles and returns to exploration and play. In contrast, Kyle is timid and fearful in this new situation and does not explore his new environment. Kyle clings to his mother and becomes upset when separated from her, even for a short time. But when his mother picks him up to comfort him, Kyle pushes and fusses in her arms and becomes angry. When the loud balloon pops, he becomes intensely distressed but is not easily comforted by his mother.

Why do Jamal and Kyle react so differently to the same situation? The answer to this mystery reflects, in part, the fact that during infancy and toddlerhood, children encounter a wider social world that brings them in contact with new situations and people, but how they react to these situations varies dramatically from one child to the next.

During the period of infancy and toddlerhood children make major strides in the development of social and emotional competencies (Saarni, Mumme, & Campos, 1998). Infants and toddlers must develop the social and emotional skills that allow them to get and hold the attention of adults and other important figures in their lives, express affection and annoyance when appropriate, establish relationships, and adapt to the demands of increasingly complex environments. Establishing trust and some measure of independence are important outcomes (Erikson, 1968). The characteristics infants and toddlers bring to these environments—and the ways significant people treat them—have important consequences for their development, and Jamal and Kyle reflect how the consequences may differ. For many children like Jamal, infancy and toddlerhood are times of exciting growth, change, and challenge. For children like Kyle, however, this period is often fraught with insecurity, uncertainty, and sometimes even victimization.

How Do Emotions Develop During Infancy and Toddlerhood?

For many years, people believed that newborns and young infants expressed only one emotional state—general excitement (Bridges, 1932)—and that other emotions appeared gradually with age and experience. Newer research suggests, however, that many of the basic emotions are present at birth. As you can see from Figure 7.1, the basic emotions of interest, sadness, and disgust are present at birth, and joy, anger, surprise, and fear develop during the first eight months. Although researchers sometimes disagree as to the precise timetable for the development of emotions (Malatesta, 1990), it is clear that by the end of the first year of life, infants have a wide range of emotional capacities and express emotions in increasingly complex ways (Kochanska, Coy, Tjebkes, & Husarek, 1998).

Children also become more social and independent over the first two years of life—the clingy behavior of infants eventually is replaced by more mature forms of social behavior, such as making a verbal request or moving about to get something. Children's behavior also changes in response to the demands of their environments. Very young infants often get the attention of their parents by crying, but older infants use other means, such as showing a toy to a parent or expressing affection, as they face increased expectations for age-appropriate behavior.

FIGURE 7.1

The Appearance of Emotions in the First Year of Life

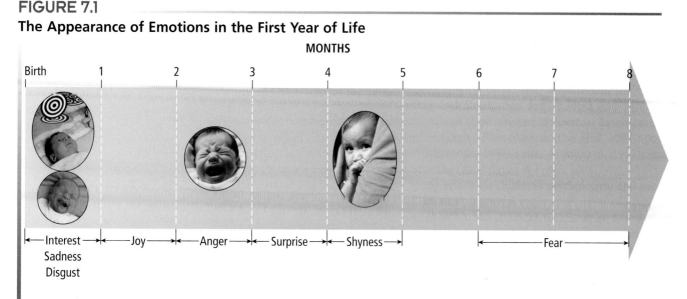

Notice that within the first 6 to 8 months of life, many of the basic emotions develop. Can you identify the main changes that take place in emotional development during the first year of life?

Source: Adapted from Izard and Malatesta, 1987.

Developing a Sense of Trust

According to Erikson's theory of psychosocial development, the first stage of development involves one of the important components of positive emotionality and personality—the development of a basic sense of trust. This sense of trust about oneself and one's world develops in the first year of life. During this time, the infant is faced with a conflict between mistrust in the world and a tendency to trust that his or her basic needs will be met. The primary task of this stage is to develop trust without completely eliminating the capacity for mistrust. If the proper balance is achieved, the child will develop positive emotions, the strong belief that, even when things are not going well, they will work out well in the end. This ability helps us get through disappointments throughout our lives and sets the stage for a positive emotional life. A sense of trust requires a feeling of physical comfort and a minimal amount of fear and apprehension about the future. Trust in infancy sets the stage for a lifelong expectation that the world will be a good and pleasant place to live. If the child's world is unpredictable and if caregiving is inconsistent or rejecting, Erikson believed the child is likely to be mistrustful and anxious, fraught with negative emotions and misgivings about his or her world (Erikson, 1969).

The reactions of Jamal and Kyle at the beginning of this chapter could be explained by a general difference in trust and mistrust. Jamal seems to have developed a strong sense that his world will be okay despite the new and unexpected situations and events of the birthday party. In contrast, Kyle is anxious and wary and responds negatively to change and uncertainty, perhaps because he does not trust that he will be protected and taken care of.

Smiling and Laughter

When you're drawing up your list of life's miracles, you might place near the top the first moment your baby smiles at you. Today, she looked right at me. And she smiled. Her toothless mouth opened, and she scrunched her face up and it really was a grin. The sleepless nights, the worries, the crying—all of a sudden it was all worth it. She

TABLE 7.1
The Development of Smiling and Laughing

AGE	RESPONSE	STIMULATION	TIME TO ONSET	CONDITIONS
Smiling				
Neonate	Corners of mouth	No external stimulation		Due to nervous system fluctuations
Week 1	Corners of mouth	Low-level, modulated sound	6–8 sec	During sleep, boosting of tension
Week 2	Mouth pulled back	Low-level, modulated voices		When drowsy, satiated
Week 3	Grin, includes eyes	Moderate-level voices	4–5 sec	When alert, attentive (nodding head with voices)
Week 4	Grin, active smile	Moderate or moderately intense sounds	Reduced	Vigorous tactile stimulation effective
Weeks 5–8	Grin, active smile, cooing	Active stimulation, first visual stimulation	Less than 3 sec	Nodding head, flicking lights, stimulation that must be followed
Weeks 9–12	Grin, active smile, cooing	Inactive visual stimulation, moderately intense	Short	Trial-by-trial effects, recognition
Laughter				
Month 4	Laughter	Multisensory, vigorous stimulation	1–2 sec	Touch, tickling, auditory
Months 5–6	Laughter	Intense auditory stimulation and touch	Immediate	Items that may previously have caused crying
Months 7–9	Laughter	Social, visual stimulation	Immediate	Tactile, auditory decline
Months 10–12	Laughter	Visual, social	Immediate or anticipatory	Visual incongruities, active participation

Source: Sroufe and Waters, 1976. Copyright © 1976 by the American Psychological Association. Adapted with permission.

is no longer just something we are nursing and carrying along—somewhere inside, part of her knows what's going on, and that part of her is telling us that she's with us. (Greene, 1984, pp. 33–34)

As Bob Greene's journal entry suggests, an infant's smile and laughter not only conveys a sense of well-being and pleasure but also reminds us that young infants have meaningful internal states (Greenspan & Greenspan, 1985). In fact, smiling and laughing may be one of the most significant aspects of social and emotional development during the first year of life.

Smiling

Similar to many other aspects of early development, smiling develops through a series of maturational changes (Super & Harkness, 1991; see Table 7.1). As you can see, newborn children sometimes smile, but their smiles are not enduring or strong and occur most often while they are asleep. Such a smile is called an **endogenous smile** because it is triggered by changes in nervous system activity. Endogenous smiles are reflexive and involve only the lower facial muscles.

By 2 to 3 weeks, infants smile when gently stimulated by high-pitched sounds or by soft stroking of their abdomens. This gentle stimulation increases the level of nervous system excitement and elicits a tiny reflex smile (Sroufe, 1977). This reflex smile is labeled an **exogenous smile** because it is triggered by external stimuli (Wolff, 1963).

endogenous smile *smile that is triggered by changes in nervous system activity and involves only the lower facial muscles*

exogenous smile *smile that is triggered by external stimuli*

This 1-month-old infant's reflex smile involves just the muscles of her lower face. Notice that only her mouth is smiling—her eyes are not. To get the full effect, cover half of the picture with your finger. What does the mouth convey to you? What do the eyes convey?

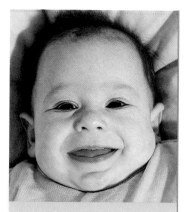

The social smile of this 3-month-old child involves the entire face—the grin extends from cheek to cheek, and the eyes are bright and wide open. What changes occur in parents' responses when their infant begins to smile like this?

social smile *smile that is triggered by social stimuli (such as the mother's face)*

social referencing *using caregivers as a source of information about how to respond in an uncertain emotional situation or condition*

Over the next few weeks, infants smile when they are fully awake and attentive. These alert smiles are fuller and more expressive than the earlier ones and may be a response to a combination of visual, tactile, and auditory stimulation (Stack & LePage, 1996). Playing pat-a-cake, for example, might elicit 20 to 30 smiles, whereas auditory or visual stimuli alone might elicit only 8 to 10 smiles (Rosenblith, 1992).

By 6 to 8 weeks, an important change takes place—the **social smile** first appears. Now the infant smiles upon seeing Mother's or Father's face or hearing her or his voice. Social smiles are longer lasting and involve the entire face; the grin goes from cheek to cheek, and the eyes widen and brighten (Izard & Malatesta, 1987).

At about 10 weeks of age, infants' smiling becomes *instrumental*—they use their smiles to achieve a goal, such as getting Mom, Dad, or other caregivers to smile back (Bower, 1982). Smiles are powerful social reinforcers for both infants and caregivers. When an infant smiles, the caregiver tends to smile back and repeat the behavior that elicited the smile. Infants learn about the power of their smiles, and they begin to use them to gain control over their environment (Brazelton, 1991). For example, 10-month-old infants are more likely to smile at their mother when the mother is attentive to them than when she is not, suggesting that infant smiling is responsive to the social context (Jones, Collins, & Hong, 1991; Schneider, 1997). Additionally, the mutually reinforcing smiles between an infant and his or her caregiver foster the development of attachment. Thus, consistent with ethological theory, smiling appears to be a genetic adaptation that promotes close contact and emotional ties between infants and their caregivers.

Laughter

Infants' laughter appears at about 4 months of age. At first, laughing occurs in response to physical stimulation, such as tickling or being swooped up high in Mom's or Dad's arms (Sroufe & Waters, 1976). After 6 months of age, infants increasingly laugh at visual and social stimuli, such as playing peek-a-boo or seeing a sister make a funny face. As toddlers, children laugh at events that earlier made them cry, such as seeing Dad wear a mask. These milestones reflect the child's developmental progression from laughter based on physical stimulation to laughter based on cognitive interpretations (Snow, 1989). Laughing also is mutually reinforcing and fosters positive feelings and interactions between the infant and others in the social environment.

Cross-Cultural Similarities and Differences

Although the development of smiling and laughter is similar across cultures, the behaviors that parents use to elicit smiling do vary. For example, American mothers rely largely on toys and objects to elicit smiling from their infants, whereas Japanese mothers are likely to engage infants in social stimulation. Mothers in both cultures are equally effective in eliciting these smiles, but they do it in different ways (using toys versus using touch or physical contact) because of different culture-based parenting goals. In the United States, mothers place high value on promoting autonomy and independent exploration of the object world. Japanese mothers, in contrast, place high value on strengthening mutual dependency and making the infant an extension of themselves. Thus, they engage their infants differently (Bornstein, Tal, & Tamis-LeMonda, 1991).

Social Referencing

Toward the end of the first year, infants have been observed to "check back" to caregivers when confronted with novel situations or uncertain conditions, a process called **social referencing.** Infants specifically assess the caregiver's emotional appraisal of the situation as a guide to their own behavior (Klinnert et al., 1983). The way in which the caregiver responds has been found to directly influence the child's behavior (Ainsworth, 1992). Thus, if parents respond to an uncertain situation (such as approaching a dog) without showing distress or fear, an infant is likely to smile or laugh. If parents respond with protest and facial expressions of anxiety, the infant is likely to become scared and cry. In this way, infants may "catch" emotional responses from their parents or others.

Crying

Crying is an infant's most effective way of communicating. This is true from the moment the child is born—the cries of the newborn tell the mother, doctor, and nurse that the newborn's lungs have filled with air. The cries also tell something about the status of the newborn's nervous system. Differences in pitch, duration, or pattern of crying may reveal abnormalities in a newborn's functioning. For example, newborns with high-pitched, shrill cries may have *cri du chat* (cry of a cat) syndrome, indicating brain damage or other nervous system disorders (Baird, Campbell, Ingram, & Gomez, 2001). Crying is the mechanism by which infants communicate their needs—such as expressing that they are hungry, wet, or cold. Infants who are placid and rarely cry may be at risk of poor growth because their parents are not always made aware of the need to feed them (Skuse, Wolke, & Reilly, 1992).

Crying begins as a reflex response that has survival value and progressively becomes more controllable. Moreover, the significance of crying changes over the course of infancy and toddlerhood (Barr, Hopkins, & Green, 2000).

From birth, crying is an infant's most effective way of communicating. How should caregivers respond to infants' crying? What consequences might be associated with such responses?

Characteristics of Cries

Mothers frequently report that they can distinguish different types of cries that their infants make. Researchers also have identified different characteristics of infants' crying (Wasz-Hockert, Michelsson, & Lind, 1985; Wolff, 1969).

■ The *basic cry* is a rhythmic pattern of crying followed by a brief silence, a short inhalation whistle, and then another brief silence.

■ *Anger cries* differ from the basic cry in that excess air forced through the vocal cords gives the cry a more breathy sound.

■ The *pain cry* is distinguishable through its sudden and loud onset and duration, followed by a period of breath holding.

■ A fourth cry—the *hunger cry*—is similar to the basic cry, but it tends to be rhythmic and have a braying sound, accompanied by kicking in the same rhythm as the crying (Wolff, 1969).

Despite the fact that many caregivers and some researchers believe that it is possible to tell, from the sound alone, the specific cause of an infant's cry, the research evidence is mixed (Gustafson, Wood, & Green, 2000).

The amount of crying varies dramatically from infant to infant and from day to day (St. James-Roberts & Plewis, 1996). Crying increases over the first six weeks of life and then decreases. Figure 7.2 shows that crying peaks in the first three months and then decreases by about half by the end of the first year. On the average, infants cry more in the first three months of life than at any other time, averaging about 2 hours of crying each day. Although some babies cry more than others, what most infants have in common is a period of fussiness late in the day, beginning at 3 to 12 weeks (McGlaughlin & Grayson, 2001; Zeskind, 1985). Figure 7.2 also reveals that infant crying initially is greatest in the evening, when the infant's nervous system overloads (Amato, 1997), and then shifts toward feeding times as the infant gets older (St. James-Roberts & Halil, 1991). These patterns are similar across different Western cultures (St. James-Roberts, 1993).

Like smiling, crying progresses from being a response to internal sources of stimulation to a response to external ones (Snow, 1989). During the neonatal period, infants cry primarily because of physical needs—because they are hungry, in pain, or physically uncomfortable. Additionally, during some periods infants cry for no apparent reason. As infants get older, their crying gradually becomes more related to cognitive and emotional conditions than to physical ones (Lester, 1985). For example, older infants might cry because they are scared or angry or because they do not want to be left alone. Caregivers' perceptions of infant crying change based on age—as infants get older, caregivers perceive more complex and individualized needs and motives in the cries they hear (Leger, Thompson, Merritt, & Benz, 1996).

FIGURE 7.2
Patterns of Crying in the First Year of Life

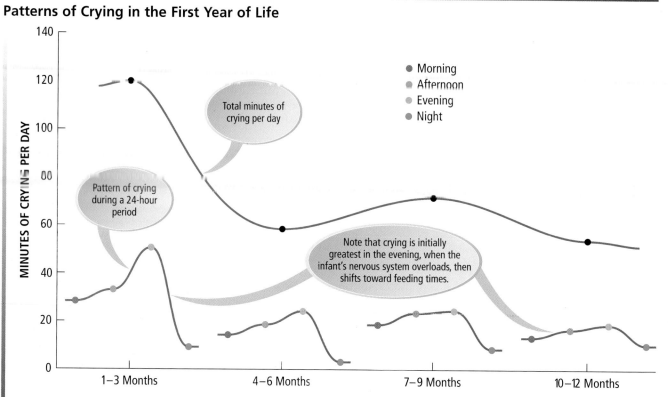

Both the total amount of crying and the times of day during which crying occurs change over the first year of life. What developmental changes might account for these differences?

Source: St. James-Roberts and Halil, 1991. Reprinted with the permission of Cambridge University Press.

Culture and Infant Crying

People in different cultures, and in the same culture at different times, have contrary ideas about appropriate responses to a crying infant. In some cultures, crying is thought to be good for the infant. Some Mexican mothers believe that crying cleanses the child of illness or disease and that letting the child cry strengthens the lungs and nervous system (Atkin, Olvera, Givaudan, & Landeros, 1989). In other cultures, caregivers believe that infants should not cry and that their needs should be constantly and consistently attended to. For example, traditional Navaho caregivers believe that infants should be kept calm and quiet. To prevent crying, they often wrap infants onto a cradle board for the first ten months of life. These swaddled infants, who are in a lower state of arousal, sleep longer and cry less (Chisholm, 1989).

Anger and Temper Tantrums

Although there is some debate as to when infants first express anger, it is clear that by the end of the first year children can and do become angry (Buss & Goldsmith, 1998). At about 9 months of age, infants begin to develop a sense of control, and angry crying and temper tantrums are signals of their frustration when things are not to their liking (Wolf, 1996). As infants move beyond the first year of life, they become aware of, and are frustrated by, the limits they experience. For example, 14-month-old Ethan used to play happily in his high chair and car seat, but he now cries and flails his arms and legs when put in either one. Ethan is a physically active infant who is mobile and agile. The restrictiveness of the car seat and high chair is frustrating, and he reacts angrily to it. Similarly, 16-month-old Josephina enjoys playing with her mother's car keys. But her smiles turn to screams of protest when

NURTURING CHILDREN
SOOTHING A CRYING INFANT

Caregivers are very motivated to soothe crying infants and often try a variety of techniques (Wikander & Helleday, 1996). Here are some effective ones to consider:

■ *Holding a crying infant:* Picking up and holding a crying infant is one of the most effective methods to get the infant to stop crying. Holding the infant up high, in a front-to-front position so that the infant looks over the caregiver's shoulder, is one of the most effective positions.

■ *Providing auditory stimulation:* Talking, singing, or providing background noise are effective methods of soothing a crying infant. The kind of auditory stimulation depends in part on the age of the infant. For newborns, nonsocial auditory stimulation is most effective (the humming noise of a clothes dryer or vacuum cleaner). For older infants (more than 3 months of age), social auditory stimuli, such as the caregiver's voice, is more effective than nonsocial stimuli.

■ *Providing visual stimulation:* After 3 to 4 months of age, visual stimulation is effective. At this age, seeing the face of a caregiver or a toy will soothe a crying child. After 4 months of age, the combination of both visual and auditory stimulation is more effective than either one alone. At this age, presenting an attractive toy that makes noise often soothes a crying infant.

■ *Rhythmic physical stimulation:* Providing the infant with rhythmic physical stimulation, such as rocking or patting, is often effective. Generally, rocking an infant from side to side is more effective than rocking the infant up and down. Additionally, increasing the pace of rocking is more effective than decreasing the pace. Many parents have found that taking their crying infant for a ride in the car is soothing, partially because of the rhythmic stimulation provided by the movement of the car.

■ *Use of a pacifier:* A pacifier is effective in soothing a crying infant because it stimulates the sucking response, which is incompatible with crying. The rhythmic nature of sucking helps the infant reorganize his or her behavior and calm down.

■ *Removing distressing stimuli:* Changing a wet diaper, feeding a hungry infant, or removing a scratchy blanket or other irritant will reduce crying.

None of these techniques work all of the time with every infant, and techniques that were effective for newborns become less effective with older infants. Thus, it is no wonder that caregivers complain that as soon as they figure out how to soothe infants, they change, and caregivers have to figure them out all over again.

Source: Adapted from Amato, 1997; Hogg, 2001.

---

her mother needs the keys and takes them from her. Josephina becomes rigid, throws herself to the ground, and kicks and yells. These behaviors give an infamous reputation to the toddler years, commonly referred to as the "terrible twos and threes."

Three important changes that take place during the toddler years contribute to the defiant reputation toddlers have (Hoyt, 1996; Schaefer & DiGeronimo, 1995):

■ *Increased ability to express anger:* As toddlers' communication skills increase, so does their ability to express anger and frustration. Their vocabulary grows dramatically although they have not yet learned to censor themselves. They now are more capable of telling caregivers when things are not to their liking. The amount of angry crying decreases, but defiant language increases (Kopp, 1992).

■ *Limitations in social understanding:* Although toddlers have many increased capacities, they do not yet understand concepts such as waiting, sharing, or patience. Thus, hunger, boredom, or fatigue can cause angry outbursts.

■ *Strivings toward autonomy:* Toddlers increasingly strive to express their newfound abilities and their desire to be individuals (Erikson, 1968). This independence often conflicts with what is required of them or what is best for them. For example, 30-month-old Dori constantly struggles with her mother over getting dressed. Dori wants to wear only her red skirt and cries angrily when she has to wear anything else.

Shame, Pride, and Other Self-Conscious Emotions

Erikson's second stage of psychosocial development also has important implications for early emotional development. Erikson (1969) believed that during late infancy and through

Notice the look of shame and guilt on this 2-year-old's face. Once children understand that behavioral standards exist, self-conscious emotions appear. What other changes bring about the development of self-conscious emotions?

the toddler years, children must deal with the psychosocial conflict of autonomy versus shame and doubt. After gaining trust in their caregivers, infants begin to discover that their behavior is their own. They start to assert their sense of independence and autonomy. As they do, they develop a sense of pride and independence in their actions and abilities. If infants are restrained too much or punished too harshly, they are likely to develop a sense of shame, doubt, and uncertainty in dealing with the world.

It is during the second year of life that children become more aware of their emotions. By 18 to 24 months of age, children understand that emotions are connected with what one wants or does not want (Wellman & Woolley, 1990). Toddlers' temper tantrums illustrate that young children can and do use an emotional reaction to try to get what they want. Thus, children's first understanding of emotions is based on associations with their desired goals and outcomes (Stein & Trabasso, 1989).

Over the course of the second year, toddlers begin to express **self-conscious emotions,** such as pride, shame, embarrassment, and guilt. Self-conscious emotions are those that involve injury to or enhancement of one's sense of self (Tangney, 1999). For example, at about 24 months, children show signs of embarrassment when they are caught violating a rule—they may lower their eyes, hang their head, and hide their face with their hands.

Self-conscious emotions require several important advances in self-awareness and cognitive development. For these emotions to develop, children must have the following characteristics (Lewis, 1993):

- A conscious awareness of themselves as distinct from others
- A recognition that certain rules are to be followed and standards or expectations are to be met
- The ability to evaluate their behavior in relation to these standards
- A sense of responsibility for meeting or not meeting these standards

To determine whether children have accomplished these important steps in self-recognition and awareness, Michael Lewis and colleagues developed an ingenious test (Lewis & Brooks-Gunn, 1979), using a mirror and a dab of rouge. In general, most babies love mirrors. If you hold a baby in front of a mirror, she or he may smile, pat the glass, or even try to lick the reflection. In their study, the researchers asked each mother of a young baby to pretend to wipe dirt off her baby's face while she was really putting a dab of rouge on the tip of the baby's nose. Then each baby was placed in front of the mirror. Would these babies notice the red spot? Would they recognize that something was different about their faces and try to wipe the red spot off?

Before 15 months of age, babies don't seem to recognize themselves as themselves in the mirror. Typically, these young babies stared at their reflections, but they didn't react differently when they saw the rouge spots. By 24 months, every baby tried to touch or wipe his or her nose. These babies had reached a new level of self-awareness and seemed to understand that certain rules or expectations had been violated—they showed clear signs of being embarrassed by the spot of rouge. Also, only those babies who touched their red nose in the mirror showed embarrassment (Lewis, Sullivan, Stanger, & Weiss, 1989).

These experiments show that a certain level of self-awareness and self-recognition is needed before children experience emotions like embarrassment. When children see themselves as responsible for success in meeting a standard, they experience pride. When they view themselves as responsible for failing to meet a standard or follow a rule, they may feel guilt, embarrassment, or shame. Thus, at about age 2, children have gained a rudimentary understanding that their behaviors lead to others' approval or disapproval, and they feel emotions that reflect this anticipation (Frolund, 1997). Three-year-olds still depend on others' reactions for these feelings; for example, they beam with pride because Mom is proud of them. After age 3, children begin to react independently to these standards; they feel pride or shame as they develop the ability to reflect on and compare their behaviors to standards they set for themselves. It is not until about 8 years of age that children say they feel

self-conscious emotions
those emotions that involve injury to or enhancement of one's sense of self (such as pride and shame)

proud or ashamed of themselves independently of others' approval or disapproval (Stipek, Recchia, & McClintic, 1992).

From toddlerhood on, girls are more likely than boys to show shame when they fail at a task (Lewis, Alessandri, & Sullivan, 1992). What is particularly interesting about this finding is that girls often show more shame than boys do even though they perform as well as the boys; that is, girls show more shame than boys do despite a lack of difference in their abilities. Research indicates that the same is true in adulthood: women express more shame than men do (Tangney, 1990).

These findings suggest that gender differences in the expression of shame appear early and persist throughout life. One reason is that girls and women are more likely than boys and men to be taught to assume personal responsibility for failure (Dweck & Leggett, 1988). Additionally, girls are more likely than boys to receive negative feedback from caregivers and teachers (Lewis, 1987). Thus, there is good reason to believe that early socialization experiences account for the gender differences in the expression of shame and other self-conscious emotions (Fredrickson, 1998).

Play and Emotional Development

Fifteen-month-old Ben tries to get his 4-year-old sister's attention by taking one of her dolls and offering it to her. When his sister fails to respond, he drops the doll and laughs. When his sister again fails to respond, he does this a second and third time. Soon his sister tells him to stop bothering her, and Ben becomes upset and takes the doll to the kitchen, where his mother is. He shows the doll to his mother, and she asks, "Is the doll hungry?" Ben first looks sad, then smiles and says, "Yes." His mother gives him a piece of carrot, which Ben tries to feed to the doll. When he cannot get the carrot in the doll's mouth, he gets upset until his mother suggests that he put the baby to sleep. Ben then puts the baby on the chair and puts a napkin over it.

Ben's story provides vivid evidence that many of children's early emotional responses occur in the context of play. Even before the toddler years, infants smile and laugh when Mother plays with them while they are being bathed or diapered. Play provides young children with the opportunity to experiment with emotions in a relatively stress-free environment (Sutton-Smith, 1998).

Play also provides young children with an opportunity to learn about their world. Ben, for example, learned that he can use play to attract others' interest and attention. It may not always work and sometimes produces feelings of frustration and sadness, but Ben's understanding of the world is enhanced by these playful interactions (Sutton-Smith, 1994).

Infants' and toddlers' play often is repetitive and ritualistic. Initially, it revolves around the child's body and physical actions, such as when 6-month-old Teri repeatedly splashes water in the bath and laughs each time. By 12 months, children begin to use objects and involve others in their play (Goncu, 1993). These playful interactions can be emotionally intense, and they can quickly lead to anger and aggression because of the egocentric and impulsive nature of toddlers. But even these negative interactions help children learn about their emotional worlds—they provide children with opportunities to gain self-control and cope with negative social interactions and feelings (Eisenberg, Fabes, & Guthrie, 1997).

How Does Temperament Influence Development During Infancy and Toddlerhood?

As you have just learned, the type, degree, and intensity of emotions babies express differ dramatically from one baby to the next. Thus, from the moment of birth, infants differ in their responses to their environment. Some babies cry frequently and intensely; others rarely cry, and when they do their cries are relatively quiet. Other babies are relatively calm and happy and seem to get on a schedule very quickly and adapt easily to changes in their environment. In contrast, other babies are unpredictable and do not easily adjust to change. Many researchers consider these differences to be linked to biological and genetic processes that predispose a person to respond in certain enduring and characteristic ways to the environment, a predisposition known as **temperament** (Wachs & King, 1994).

An important aspect of temperament is consistency. Temperament sometimes shows stability from infancy to adolescence and even adulthood (Caspi & Silva, 1995; Caspi et al., 1995). Research suggests that temperamental differences are present prenatally: for example, very active fetuses are more unpredictable and unadaptable as infants (DiPietro, Hodgson, Costigan, & Johnson, 1996). The heritability of temperament distinguishes it from the closely related concept of personality, which refers to a person's unique behavioral, motivational, and temperamental ways of responding. Personality therefore is a broader term, and a person's personality is more likely to be a product of diverse influences (Rothbart & Bates, 1998; Strelau, 1994).

The Structure of Temperament

What qualities make up a person's temperament? This question has received the attention of many researchers, but they have yet to come up with a single agreed-upon set of qualities that represent the structure of temperament. Instead, a variety of components of temperament have been identified (Buss & Plomin, 1984; Rothbart, 1989); the most well known are the nine enumerated in Thomas and Chess's longitudinal studies of infants and children (1970, 1977):

1. *Rhythmicity:* The regularity of basic functions, such as sleep, wakefulness, excretion, and hunger
2. *Activity level:* The intensity and frequency of motor movements
3. *Approach–withdrawal:* The degree to which a child accepts or rejects new people, objects, or situations
4. *Persistence:* The amount of time a child devotes to an activity
5. *Adaptability:* How quickly and easily a child adjusts to change
6. *Quality of mood:* The extent to which a child expresses positive or negative emotions
7. *Distractibility:* The degree to which stimuli in the environment can alter a child's behavior
8. *Threshold of responsiveness:* The intensity of stimulation needed to elicit a response
9. *Intensity of reaction:* The energy level of a child's response

More recent research on temperament suggests that a smaller number of components make up temperament. Researchers found that many elements that constituted Thomas and Chess's components overlapped considerably, suggesting that some components measured similar aspects of temperament (Rothbart & Bates, 1998). Today's researchers have sought to define a clearer, more precise structure of temperament. Mary Rothbart and her colleagues identified a shorter list of six reliable, nonoverlapping temperamental constructs (Rothbart & Mauro, 1990):

1. *Fearful distress,* reflecting a child's tendency to withdraw and become distressed in new situations or circumstances
2. *Anger/frustration,* reflecting the degree to which a child becomes angry or frustrated when his or her needs or desires are not met
3. *Positive affect,* reflecting the amount of positive emotion, pleasure, and excitement shown by a child
4. *Activity level,* reflecting a child's level of gross motor activity and energy

temperament *the predisposition to respond in certain enduring and characteristic ways to one's environment*

5. *Attention span/persistence,* reflecting a child's ability to maintain focus and interest

6. *Regularity,* reflecting the predictability of a child's behavior

As you can see, some of Thomas and Chess's original nine dimensions are not included here. For example, according to this list, positive and negative emotions stand as distinct components of temperament. Intensity of responding is now subsumed within other constructs and does not stand on its own. These newer components help in defining the aspects of temperament that come into play in a given situation. For example, suppose an infant who experienced a bath for the first time became intensely upset but lay in the bath water placidly while crying. How would the earlier category of "intensity of responding" be coded? In this case, the infant responded with intense emotions but did not show intensity in gross motor activity. The old system would not differentiate between these two reactions; Rothbart's new dimensions do a better job of capturing the distinct responses.

Consistency of Temperament

Temperamental traits are thought to be stable and enduring throughout the life span. To the extent that this is true, children who are active and angry as infants can be expected to be active and angry as older children, adolescents, and adults. For example, an infant who is high in positive affect and low in fearful distress will enjoy his or her first bath. As a pre-schooler, this child likely will play happily with new peers, and as a school-aged child she or he likely will look forward to beginning a new school year.

Although there is considerable evidence that temperament is consistent across development (Braungart-Rieker & Stifter, 1996; Caspi & Silva, 1995), it does not always follow a predictable course. Thomas and Chess (1985) found that some children in their study showed consistency in temperamental traits, whereas other children were consistent in certain aspects of temperament but inconsistent in others. Some children changed completely in regard to a number of temperamental qualities. These findings suggest that the expression of one's temperament may be modifiable and that socialization and other environmental influences affect what we observe in others (Wachs & King, 1994).

Goodness of Fit

One newer addition to temperament theory is called **goodness of fit**—a measure of the match between a child's temperament and the demands of his or her environment (family, school, child-care setting). This has proved to be one of the most important elements of temperament theory. High goodness of fit exists when the demands and expectations of the family members and others in an individual's life are compatible with one's temperament, abilities, and characteristics (Chess & Thomas, 1999). The match between parents' and children's temperamental qualities influences goodness of fit. For example, in the chapter opening story, Kyle reacts loudly and intensely when frustrated or scared by new events and people. Kyle's mother is easily frustrated and anxious herself. She is quickly distressed by Kyle's behavior because she expects and wants him to be more like Jamal. Thus, this poor fit results in conflict and strain between Kyle and his mother.

Because parents cannot change or determine a child's temperamental style, parenting needs to be molded around the child's temperament. Parents who try to make a child fit their concept of the "perfect child" usually end up frustrated. A better approach is to observe and learn about the child and then shape reactions to a given situation that take into account the child's own characteristics. Thus, understanding a child's temperament, as well as understanding one's own, can help a parent or caregiver achieve goodness of fit and reduce frustration and annoyance for everyone (Carey & Jablow, 1999).

Contributions of Temperament to Infant Development

Temperament theorists believe that temperament has a profound influence on the course of an individual's development (Molfese & Molfese, 2000). For example, a child's temperament has an impact on how he or she learns about his or her environment. A child who responds with fear and distress to new situations and people is more likely to avoid them

goodness of fit *the match between a child's temperament and the demands of his or her environment*

FIGURE 7.3

Effects of Temperamental Qualities on Positive or Negative Adjustment

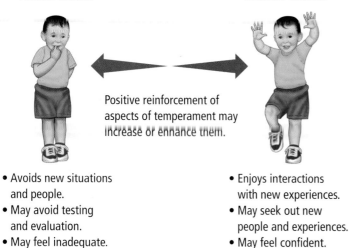

Fearful Toddler   **Fearless Toddler**

Positive reinforcement of aspects of temperament may increase or enhance them.

- Avoids new situations and people.
- May avoid testing and evaluation.
- May feel inadequate.

- Enjoys interactions with new experiences.
- May seek out new people and experiences.
- May feel confident.

Temperament refers to a person's genetic predisposition to respond to the environment in characteristic ways. Notice the differences in the ways that these two toddlers tend to respond to their environments. How might these differences influence later development and adjustment?

than is a child who is less fearful. A child low in fearfulness not only does not experience fear when exposed to new situations and people but also may experience pleasure in interactions with strangers. If this is so, the child may develop a conditioned approach to future interactions with strangers. You can see how positive reinforcement in these situations can magnify initial temperamental differences and how this might influence future adjustment (Rothbart & Bates, 1998). Similarly, children who are high in fearful distress might actively avoid situations in which they are tested and evaluated (such as school). This may lead to feelings of inadequacy and to future avoidance of these situations (Posner & Rothbart, 2000). Thus, temperamental qualities can be related to both positive and negative adjustment and outcomes (see Figure 7.3).

Children's development of conscience and morality also may be related to temperament. Kochanska (1995; Kochanska, Murray, & Harlan, 1999) has found that these qualities are related to children's ability to control their behavior and attention. Temperament also influences how children respond to their parents' efforts to socialize them (Kochanska, 1997). For fearful toddlers, gentle discipline (using encouragement rather than threats) appears to promote conscience development. For fearless toddlers, who are often unaroused by gentle discipline, alternative socialization practices—perhaps those that capitalize on positive mother–child relationships (secure attachment)—are more likely to promote conscience and morality development. Thus, temperament and socialization practices interact in a transactional way to influence the development of children's conscience and morality.

Some temperament theorists have tried to identify different patterns of temperamental responding to classify types of children and their development. For example, by identifying different combinations of temperamental traits, Thomas and Chess (1985) tried to classify infants based on three temperament groups:

1. *Easy*—infants who behave predictably and respond positively to new situations
2. *Difficult*—infants who are irregular in their schedules and bodily functions, are slow to adapt to change, cry longer and louder than other infants, and generally are wary of new people or situations
3. *Slow-to-warm-up*—infants who tend to be active but initially do not respond well to new situations or people

Although these categories have some appeal, research has not supported their usefulness. For example, about one third of all children cannot be classified based on the three temperament groups. In addition, most children display a wide range of responses to the environment and do not fit neatly into a particular category. "Easy" children are not always easy, and "difficult" children are not difficult in all situations (Thomas & Chess, 1985). Because of these issues, the whole concept of a "difficult" temperament has been questioned (Bates, 1987). Does a difficult temperament refer to a pattern of traits in the child or a social perception of the caregiver? What is considered difficult by one caregiver may not be considered difficult by another, although a broadly difficult temperament at 18 months is predictive of behavior problems ten years later (Guerin, Gottfried, & Thomas, 1997).

Another problem in classifying temperament is the difficulty of measuring it objectively. Typically, parents or caregivers rate children on various characteristics. Because such ratings may be influenced by a person's relationship with the child or a person's own temperamental qualities, different raters of the same child sometimes perceive the child to have different temperamental qualities. To avoid such problems, researchers have begun to use observational methods (Goldsmith & Rieser-Danner, 1990), as well as physiological measures, to assess temperament. For example, infants at day care who were rated as higher in social fearfulness showed higher levels of cortisol (a hormone associated with stress) than those children low in social fearfulness (Watamura, Donzella, Alwin, & Gunnar, 2003). This finding suggests that infants and toddlers who are more socially fearful may find day care particularly challenging and experience more stress. Having a more reactive stress physiology is believed to underlie a more fearful, anxious temperament (Kagan, Reznick, & Snidman, 1987). Researchers hope these new methods will provide greater insight into the role that the nervous system plays in the expression of temperamental qualities.

Why are some children shy and others not? How can caregivers help children overcome tendencies toward shyness?

Cultural Perceptions of Temperament

In addition, the perception of an infant's temperamental qualities is influenced by cultural factors. For example, caregivers in areas of Brazil where infant mortality is very high because of impoverished conditions show a preference for difficult infants (Schepher-Hughes, 1987). This preference is based on the perception that difficult infants are "stronger" than placid, easy infants and are more likely to survive harsh conditions. Similarly, difficult infants born into the Masai tribe in Kenya are preferred over easy infants because they are viewed as potential "warriors" for the tribe, a role that is highly valued (DeVries, 1984). Thus, the links between infant temperament and caregivers' perceptions and beliefs are influenced by the context in which they live (Wachs & Kohnstamm, 2001).

How Do Parent–Infant Attachments Influence Development?

Researchers who focus on children's temperaments believe that children's own biological dispositions are the touchstone to understanding their development. Other researchers believe that the quality of parent–infant relationships is the key. Let's now look at this aspect of early development.

During infancy and toddlerhood, more than at any other time, children depend on their parents to meet their basic needs. Although the influence of parents is just one of many, most people believe that different childrearing experiences early in development relate to differences in the way children turn out. Primary among these early parental influences is **attachment**—an enduring emotional tie characterized by a tendency to seek and maintain closeness to a specific figure (the attachment figure), particularly under conditions of stress. Children's patterns of attachment to their caregivers help explain individual differences.

As you have learned, young children perceive and respond to their environments differently. Some infants' strong sense of security enables them to explore their world, even in situations that are new and potentially stressful. Other infants' anxiety and uncertainty inhibit their ability to cope successfully with new and demanding situations. Based on the work of John Bowlby (1969) and Mary Ainsworth (1973), attachment theory accounts for such individual differences by emphasizing the caregiver–child relationship.

attachment *an enduring emotional tie characterized by a tendency to seek and maintain closeness to a specific figure (the attachment figure), particularly under conditions of stress*

FROM RESEARCH TO PRACTICE
WHAT ARE THE EARLY ROOTS OF SHYNESS?

My daughter and I have never been close. I gave up my career to do special things with her and we oftentimes clash. She prefers doing things alone instead of playing with me. She now is very passive at school, does not want group attention, prefers to play alone, but likes to watch others play. I feel that Julie was born this way. (Rubin & Asendorpf, 1993, pp. 3–4)

FROM RESEARCH . . .

In this excerpt from a letter, a mother comes to the conclusion that her daughter's shyness and social withdrawal have a genetic basis, were present from birth, and are part of her temperament. This mother's conclusion is consistent with research findings on the early roots of shyness. For example, Kagan and colleagues (Kagan, 1989; Kagan, Snidman, & Arcus, 1993) found that about 15 to 20 percent of healthy 1- to 2-year-old Caucasian children are extremely and consistently shy, timid, and fearful when they encounter unfamiliar situations. These children hesitate in their approach to objects, remain quiet with new people, and stay close to their mother. Longitudinal studies indicate that over 75 percent of these children retain this shyness through the eighth year of life (Kagan et al., 1993). By contrast, approximately 30 percent of Caucasian children are fearless, uninhibited, and outgoing. They approach objects without hesitation, talk spontaneously to unfamiliar persons, and spend little time close to their mothers. In comparing shy children with those who are not, Kagan found that a combination of temperamental traits, including high

motor activity and frequent crying upon novel stimulation, predicts early shyness. These qualities are thought to reflect differences in inherited physiological processes. Using these predictors, Kagan and colleagues identified two groups of infants, who were seen at 4 and 14 months of age. At 4 months, one group of infants showed frequent and vigorous motor activity, such as flexing and extending their limbs, arching the back, and crying frequently. The second group of infants showed low levels of motor activity and rarely cried (Kagan et al., 1993). At 14 months, the two groups of infants were observed in situations likely to produce fearful reactions, such as being presented with a noisy metal robot. Over 60 percent of the infants who were active and cried a lot at 4 months were fearful at 14 months. In contrast, only 12 percent of the infants who were low in temperamental reactivity at 4 months were fearful at 14 months.

These findings suggest that some children have a biological predisposition to respond with fear and withdrawal to new or strange environments. The relationship between the 4-month profile of motor activity and crying and later signs of shyness was not due to differences in gestational age at birth, health, or stressful conditions. Instead, it appears that the children's nervous systems made them vulnerable to anxiety and distress.

. . . TO PRACTICE

The findings of this study do not mean that children cannot learn to control these feelings and the urge to withdraw. The environ-

ment appears to play a more substantial role in helping children overcome their tendencies toward shyness than in making them shy in the first place (Kagan et al., 1993). For example, parents can model outgoing social behavior for their child. Caregivers who want their children to act more outgoing are wise to monitor their own behavior and act outgoing whenever possible in front of the children. Invite friends and family members over, visit neighbors, and speak to pleasant-looking strangers in grocery store lines. The more practice shy children get at interacting with unfamiliar people, the faster the shyness will decrease. However, this exposure will work best if it is gradual. Whenever possible, let the child get used to the setting and people before encouraging the child to interact. Rewarding the child after doing so will increase the child's tendency to do so again.

THINKING IT THROUGH

1. Were you or one of your siblings shy as a young child? (Offer evidence for your answer.) If so, what were some consequences of shyness for your (or your sibling's) development?

2. What learning principles might explain how shyness develops in children?

3. Why was it important for Kagan to control for gestational age, health, and stress in studying shyness? What roles might these factors play in the development of shyness?

In contemporary Western societies, attachment theory is widely regarded as one of the most promising theories of personality and social development (Colin, 1996).

Attachment Theory

Attachment refers to a long-lasting relationship; it is not a product of transient enjoyment or comfort. For most people, the best example of attachment is the tie that usually develops between an infant and his or her primary caregiver (most often the mother). Evidence of this attachment is seen in a child's attempts to seek out and maintain contact with his or her primary caregiver and in the child's distress when separated from that person.

Attachment is distinct from bonding (see Chapter 4), which generally refers to the caregiver's tie to the infant. Some scientists believe that there is a sensitive period in the first hours or days after birth during which bonding must occur (Klaus & Kennell, 1982). Evidence for this sensitive bonding period in humans is scarce. Human parents have the ability to bond with their child even if they do not have contact with the child early in life. Adopting parents, for example, form deep and meaningful emotional ties to their adopted children (Edens & Cavell, 1999; Juffer & Rosenboom, 1997), even when the adoption occurs years after the child is born (Brodzinsky, Lang, & Smith, 1995).

When not stressed, infants are curious and naturally seek interaction with their environments. They explore their world contentedly if an attachment figure is present but become distressed and stop exploring when separated from this person (Posada et al., 1995). Infants do not have to be in physical contact with the attachment figure for exploration and curiosity to occur—just knowing that the attachment figure is near seems sufficient. Thus, infants use the attachment figure as a base from which they attend to, learn about, and explore their world. When a threat arises, the attachment figure serves as a base of security and safety.

As Bowlby (1969) noted, attachments also give rise to the views that individuals develop about themselves and others. Through their attachments, children develop an "internal working model" that consists of general expectations of their own worthiness and the availability of others. This model serves as a basis for future relationships (Griffin & Bartholomew, 1994). Infants whose needs are neglected or ignored come to expect that their needs will be neglected or ignored in the future. In turn, this expectation may lead these children to avoid intimate personal relationships because they believe they cannot rely on others to be available. Attachments therefore not only represent the past experiences of children but also relate to how children construct their own representations of relationships. This internal working model subsequently affects their interactions with others (Thompson, 1998).

Not all infants form the same kind of attachment or internal working model of relationships. For example, infants differ in their ability to use an attachment figure as a secure base and in the intensity and quality of emotions they feel toward this figure. Caregivers likewise differ considerably in how they respond to infants and in the feelings they hold toward them.

The Development of Attachment

Based on Bowlby's theory (1969) and on Mary Ainsworth's (1973) observations of infants in Uganda (Africa) and Baltimore, the development of early attachment relationships has been broken down into four phases (see Table 7.2). The first three phases take place during infancy and toddlerhood. Despite the large cultural differences between African and US infants, the sequence of the development of attachment was found to be very similar, and subsequent research on infants raised in other cultures confirmed these basic findings (Colin, 1996).

The Preattachment Phase

During the first eight weeks of life, infants are sometimes referred to as "asocial" because both social and nonsocial stimuli produce positive responses. Infants at this age rarely

TABLE 7.2
Phases of Attachment

	AGE 0–2 MONTHS	AGE 2–6 MONTHS	AGE 7–12 MONTHS	AGE 48 MONTHS
Phase	Preattachment	Attachment-in-the-making	Clear-cut attachment	Goal-corrected partnership
Characteristics	Nondiscriminate responses to caregivers Reflexive rather than voluntary behavior Positive response to both social and nonsocial stimuli	Clear preference for social stimuli Positive response to familiar caregivers but not to unfamiliar ones No single attachment preference observable	Clear preference for a single attachment figure Evidence of stranger and separation anxiety	Recognition that caregivers have feelings or goals that may be different from the child's Attempts to change caregivers' plans and goals and become a partner in planning how the relationship proceeds

protest when caregivers leave and do not distinguish among the various caregivers who attend to them (Thompson, 1998).

This first phase is called the *preattachment phase,* in reference to the fact that young infants do not discriminate in their responses to caregivers. Little evidence suggests that infants consistently prefer the primary caregiver to any other person. Recall from Chapters 4 and 5 that infants are drawn to human faces and to the human voice but at first do not associate these with any particular person. Although infants' responses generally are reflexive rather than voluntary, their reflexive behaviors strengthen the emotional tie with caregivers and draw caregivers to them.

The Attachment-in-the-Making Phase

After a period of indiscriminate responding, infants around 2 to 6 months of age gradually begin to direct their responses to familiar rather than unfamiliar people. This shift characterizes the second phase. In this *attachment-in-the-making phase,* infants more often smile at, look at, reach for, and are soothed by familiar rather than unfamiliar people.

Despite increased preference for familiar caregivers, infants at this phase do not have full-fledged attachments. By definition, attachments cannot occur until the child understands that people and objects have an independent existence—that is, when the infant develops object permanence. For a young infant, when a parent is "out of sight" the parent is "out of mind." Thus, in the second phase of attachment, infants may recognize caregivers and respond with a delight and pleasure that they do not show to strangers, but attachment has not yet fully developed.

The Clear-Cut Attachment Phase

Important changes that take place at around 7 months of age enable infants to develop clear-cut attachments with their primary caregivers. Evidence of these changes comes from studies of infants who are placed in foster care. If infants are placed prior to 7 months of age, they usually adapt to a new caregiver quite easily. In contrast, infants placed in foster care after 7 months of age do not adjust quickly or easily (Colin, 1996). These findings provide evidence of developing attachment; disruption of this attachment elicits specific adverse responses.

In addition to developing object permanence at around this age, infants become able to develop goals—they make planned efforts to achieve contact with the attachment figure, such as protesting when separated or lifting their arms to be picked up. These early efforts at making contact and influencing caregivers are primitive, however. An infant may pull a book out of Mother's hand if she is reading or may pull the telephone cord while Father is talking. As children mature, they develop more sophisticated and acceptable forms of achieving contact. Nevertheless, in both cases, children are developing ways of satisfying their own needs for help and comfort (Maccoby, 1980).

Two vivid characteristics of clear-cut attachment appear during this phase. The appearance of stranger anxiety and separation anxiety are important markers of the increasing emotional tie the infant has with her or his caregiver. Although these anxieties can cause stress and discomfort for caregivers, they reflect the infant's greater awareness of the importance of the primary caregiver. Let's look in detail at these phenomena.

Stranger Anxiety. A wary and fearful reaction to strangers, **stranger anxiety** appears at about 7 months. Until that time, infants often respond positively to strangers, but after forming attachments they soon become fearful of them. The intensity of this response peaks at about 8 to 10 months and gradually declines during the second year of life (Thompson, 1998). Stranger anxiety may not completely subside; even some 4-year-old children show signs of wariness when encountering a stranger, particularly in an unfamiliar setting.

Although most children show some stranger anxiety, this wariness of strangers is not universal or consistent. For example, an infant is less likely to respond negatively to a stranger if the caregiver is holding the child, if the caregiver greets the stranger in a warm and pleasant tone of voice, or if the caregiver talks to the child about the stranger in a soothing voice (Gunnar, 1980). Additionally, infants who are exposed regularly to large numbers of adults show less stranger anxiety (Colin, 1996). Infants with little experience with strangers, on the other hand, may associate them with negative experiences, such as going to the doctor for a vaccination.

Separation Anxiety. The protests that accompany an infant's separation from the attachment figure reflect **separation anxiety.** Protests over the departure of the attachment figure usually peak in frequency and strength between 12 and 18 months of age but commonly remain strong through the second year of life (Colin, 1996). Studies of infants in diverse cultures reveal similar patterns: before 7 or 8 months of age, infants rarely protest when separated from their caregivers. Separation anxiety then increases during the second year of life and declines thereafter (Kagan, 1976). Infants protest and show distress when attachment figures depart and express joy and relief when reunited with them. These responses are not shown when strangers depart or reappear. Thus, separation from attachment figures represents a significant source of stress for infants—and their caregivers (Deater-Deckard, Scarr, McCartney, & Eisenberg, 1994).

The final phase of attachment shown in Table 7.2, the goal-corrected partnership, is not reached until 4 years of age, when children begin to negotiate relationships more directly. This phase is discussed in Chapter 10.

Assessing Patterns of Attachment

How does a researcher study the attachment between infant and caregiver? One problem is that it is difficult to conduct the types of experiments that are required. For example, infants cannot be deliberately separated from their mothers to determine the effects of separation, nor can they be reared in total isolation. Such limitations led one curious researcher to develop a seminal series of studies in which infant monkeys were taken away from their mothers at birth and raised either in isolation or with wire-mesh models that resembled monkey mothers (Harlow, 1958, 1959). The results showed that monkeys who were deprived of contact with their mothers later experienced serious adjustment problems. But when the mothers of infant monkeys were replaced by the wire-mesh substitute, the infant monkeys formed a strong attachment to the substitute. In addition, Harlow compared infant monkeys' attachment to cloth-covered versus wire mother-substitutes and found

stranger anxiety *a wary and fearful reaction to strangers*

separation anxiety *a response in which negative protests accompany separation from attachment figures*

FIGURE 7.4

Infant Monkeys' Responses to Cloth and Wire "Mothers"

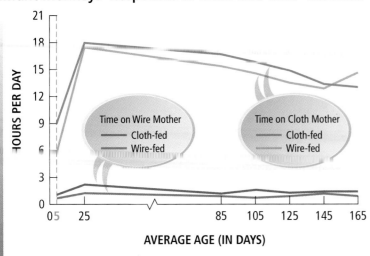

The results show a clear attachment to and preference for the cloth mother, regardless of which mother fed the infant. What do these findings imply about attachment in both infants and humans? What ethical questions do such experiments raise?

Source: Adapted from Harlow, 1959.

that the monkeys clearly showed a stronger attachment to the cloth-covered substitute (see Figure 7.4), regardless of whether the infant was fed on the wire or cloth mother substitute. Such findings suggest that something in the physical contact between mothers and infants might contribute to attachment and that feeding itself is not the critical factor.

To be blunt, these studies involved considerable cruelty. Moreover, Harlow's work does not tell us much about human attachment, and some researchers (Ainsworth, 1984) questioned how much these studies actually teach us about attachment. As a result, researchers became convinced that they had to find a way to study human attachment within the guidelines of conducting ethical research. Subsequently, Mary Ainsworth and colleagues developed the most common method of assessing attachment; it is based on the characteristic responses of infants to the presence or absence of caregivers and strangers. Ainsworth intended to create a situation that would activate infant attachment behavior that is not routinely observed in the home. The **Strange Situation** is a procedure used with infants between 11 and 18 months of age (Ainsworth, Blehar, Waters, & Wall, 1978). Carried out in an environment that is unfamiliar to the infant, it consists of eight 3-minute episodes involving exploration, separation, and reunion sequences with a caregiver (usually the mother) and an adult stranger. Table 7.3 describes the eight episodes of the Strange Situation.

Episode 1 involves establishing rapport. During Episode 2, observers assess the extent to which the infant uses his or her mother as a secure base for exploring the new room and toys. Reactions to a stranger are assessed in Episode 3. Separation anxiety is assessed in Episode 4, when the mother leaves the infant with the stranger. In Episode 6, separation responses are observed in a more stressful context, when the infant is left alone. If the infant becomes highly upset, these episodes are terminated early. The infant's responses to being reunited with the mother are observed in Episodes 5 and 8, and the infant's ability to be soothed by the stranger is assessed in Episode 7. Thus, Ainsworth devised a series of episodes that allow researchers to compare and contrast infants' responses to the presence and absence of their mother (or other caregiver) and to the presence and absence of a stranger. Based on the responses observed over the eight episodes of the Strange Situation, four patterns of attachment were identified (see Figure 7.5).

Secure Attachment

The first type of attachment, a relatively common one, is referred to as **secure attachment.** When securely attached infants and their mothers go through the Strange Situation, the children tend to explore the new room and the new toys right away (Episode 2). They often vocalize and show the toys to their mother. When the stranger comes in during Episode 3, they look intensely at her, move closer to their mother, and resume their play. When their mother leaves, secure infants stop playing and become upset. When the stranger tries to comfort them, they accept the contact and stop crying but show little interest in playing. Upon their mother's return, they smile, rush to meet her, and eagerly accept her comfort. Afterward, they return to playing with the toys.

Strange Situation   *a procedure used to assess infants' attachment behavior under conditions of increasing stress due to separations from caregivers and strangers*

secure attachment   *pattern in which infants use their attachment figures as a secure base, obtaining comfort from their presence and becoming distressed by their absence*

TABLE 7.3
Ainsworth's Strange Situation Procedure

EPISODE	PROCEDURE
Setup	Appropriate for infants 11–18 months old, the procedure requires an unfamiliar room with two chairs, an attractive collection of toys, and space for the infant to move about.
	Two chairs and the toys are on the three points of a triangle, far enough apart so that the observer can determine whether the infant is nearer the caregiver, the toys, or the other adult.
Episode 1	Experimenter shows caregiver where to put infant and where to sit, then leaves.
	If necessary, caregiver gets infant to start playing with the toys.
Episode 2	Caregiver does not initiate interaction with infant but may respond if necessary.
Episode 3	Stranger enters, sits quietly for 1 minute, talks with caregiver for 1 minute, and engages infant in interaction or play for 1 minute.
Episode 4	Caregiver exits. Stranger lets infant play.
	If infant needs comfort, stranger tries to provide it.
	If infant cries hard, the episode is terminated early.
Episode 5	Caregiver calls to infant from outside the door; caregiver enters, greets infant, and pauses. If infant needs comfort, caregiver may provide it.
	When infant is ready to play with the toys, caregiver sits in a chair.
	If infant is very upset and needs extra time, the episode can be extended.
Episode 6	Caregiver exits. Infant is left alone.
	If infant cries hard, the episode is terminated early.
Episode 7	Stranger enters, greets infant, and pauses. If infant is OK, stranger sits.
	If infant needs comfort, stranger tries to provide it.
	If infant cries hard, the episode is terminated early.
Episode 8	Caregiver calls to infant from outside the door; caregiver enters, greets infant, and pauses.
	If infant needs comfort, caregiver may provide it.
	Caregiver lets infant return to play when ready.

Source: Adapted from Colin, 1996.

FIGURE 7.5
Patterns of Attachment

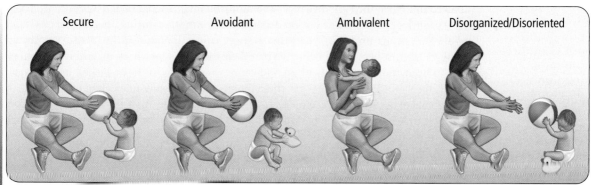

Researchers have identified four basic patterns of attachment. What factors influence the type of attachment that develops between a child and his or her caregivers?

When left alone during Episode 6, secure infants stop playing and begin to cry. When the stranger enters during Episode 7, they resist attempts to be comforted. Their mother's final return is met with clear signals to be picked up, and their distress is soothed right away. Secure infants then resume playing with the toys until the end of the final episode.

Based on these qualities of response, secure infants appear to use their mother as a secure base from which they can separate to some degree and explore their environment. Securely attached infants seek out their attachment figures, obtain much pleasure and comfort from their presence, and are distressed and bothered by their absence. Approximately 68 percent of middle-class American infants are classified as securely attached infants.

Avoidant Attachment

The second pattern of attachment is referred to as **avoidant attachment.** Infants who fall into this pattern show conspicuous avoidance of contact or interaction with their caregiver. These infants readily separate from their mother and explore the toys during Episode 2. The entrance of the stranger during Episode 3 often is met with a smile. When their mother leaves, avoidant infants continue to play contentedly during her absence. During Episode 5, they react neutrally to their mother's return and quickly turn back to the toys. In contrast to secure infants, avoidant infants do not seek physical contact with their mother when she returns. When left alone during Episode 6, they become unhappy and fussy. This negative response disappears when the stranger enters. When their mother returns in the final episode, avoidant infants barely take notice of her.

On first glance, avoidant infants appear to be very independent. They do not respond to the presence or absence of their mother. They clearly dislike being left alone but are as easily calmed by the stranger as they are by their mother. Does this mean that avoidant infants are indifferent to their attachment figures? After much consideration, Ainsworth and colleagues concluded that avoidant infants might be masking the insecure distress they feel and suppressing their impulses to seek comfort from their mother. Studies that examine the physiological responses of these infants show that they are aroused—their heart rates rise during the stressful segments of the Strange Situation (Sroufe & Waters, 1977). Their behaviors may suggest that these infants are unresponsive, but their internal responses reveal the discomfort they feel (Colin, 1996). Approximately 20 percent of infants are classified as exhibiting avoidant attachment.

Ambivalent Attachment

The third attachment pattern is called **ambivalent attachment.** During Episode 2, ambivalent infants are reluctant to leave their mother's side and explore the new room and toys very little. They are noticeably anxious when the stranger enters. When their mother first leaves, these infants cry angrily and reject the stranger's attempts to comfort them. When their mother returns, she is greeted with a cry and clear signals that they want to be picked up. When their mother picks them up, the infants wrap their arms around her but also push, kick, and cry. The second departure of the mother during Episode 6 elicits immediate and strong protests. When the stranger comes in, ambivalent infants scream and struggle against being held by her. When their mother is sent back in, ambivalent infants cry to her with their arms held up, indicating that they want to be picked up. But again, when their mother picks them up, these infants scream even louder, cling to her skirt, and thrash out at her. When picked up again, they continue to be upset and are stiff and uncomfortable in her arms. After a period of time, they begin to relax in her arms and eventually resume playing with the toys.

Ambivalent infants' behavior toward their mother is inconsistent. They appear to want to be comforted by their mother but also seem to receive little comfort once in her arms. These infants' responses are ambivalent—simultaneously desiring and resisting their mother's contact and comfort. About 12 percent of infants are classified as ambivalently attached.

avoidant attachment   *pattern characterized by conspicuous avoidance of contact or interaction with the caregiver*

ambivalent attachment   *pattern characterized by inconsistent behavior toward a caregiver*

Disorganized/Disoriented Attachment

A fourth pattern of attachment was later added to Ainsworth's original classification system (Main & Solomon, 1990). The **disorganized/disoriented attachment** classification was developed in response to the concern that a high percentage of infants who had been abused and/or neglected were classified as securely attached (Crittenden, 1988). Many researchers doubted that maltreated infants could have secure attachments, and closer examination of their behaviors in the Strange Situation revealed some abnormalities (van IJzendoorn, Schuengel, & Bakermans, 1999).

Infants classified as disorganized/disoriented in their attachments have no coherent strategy for handling separations from and reunions with their mother. Consequently, their behavior is inconsistent, disorganized, and disoriented. For example, when Brooks was assessed in the Strange Situation, she first approached her mother after reunion and then froze and became dazed, avoiding her completely. When her mother returned, she began to cry. During the exploration phase (Episode 2), Brooks approached her mother with a toy but then became apprehensive toward her.

Why infants like Brooks, who have been abused and neglected, might react to the Strange Situation with this type of behavior is clear: they have the same need for contact and warmth from the caregiver that other children have, but their prior experiences of maltreatment have taught them that the caregiver may ignore or punish their bids for contact (Crittenden & Ainsworth, 1989). Thus, Brooks's inconsistent and disorganized responses reflect both her need for closeness and her expectations of her mother's aversive responses. About 15 percent of infants from normal middle-class families develop disorganized attachment behavior (van IJzendoorn et al., 1999), and these children are at risk for future adjustment problems (Moss, St. Laurent, & Parent, 1999).

Caregiver and Child Factors Affecting Attachment

What determines the type of attachment formed? Researchers have found that two influences are particularly important: (1) the sensitivity of the caregiver and (2) characteristics of the child.

Caregiver Sensitivity

Based on her research, Ainsworth concluded that what matters the most to the development of attachment is the caregiver's sensitive responsiveness to the infant (De Wolff & van IJzendoorn, 1997). Sensitive responsiveness includes the ability to notice signals from the infant, interpret these signals accurately, and then respond appropriately. So it is not surprising that sensitive parenting is an important predictor of a child's development of a secure attachment (Atkinson et al., 2000; Braungart-Rieker, Garwood, Powers, & Wang, 2001). Securely attached infants come to believe that their signals will elicit the help they need and that their needs will be met (Isabella, 1993). Insensitive caregiving does not necessarily mean coldness or hostility; it refers to caregivers who fail to respond accurately and supportively to their infants' needs. For example, infants whose mothers are depressed are unlikely to have their needs met and will therefore be more likely to develop insecure attachments (Cicchetti, Rogosch, & Toth, 1998; Martins & Gaffan, 2000). Insensitive caregivers teach infants that their signals are ineffective (Susman-Stilman, Kalkose, Egeland, & Waldman, 1996).

Thus, caregiver sensitivity also is reflected in the degree to which caregiver's and infant's behaviors are in **synchrony**—that is, the degree to which gaze, attention, vocalization, and emotional expressiveness of caregiver and baby occur in "packages" of coordinated activity. Synchrony reflects the degree to which the caregiver's and baby's behaviors occur responsively to produce a state of mutual enjoyment and engagement (Moore & Dunham, 1995). The caregiver's synchronized responses tend to be specific to the situation; for example, infant vocalization is met with increased vocalizations if the infant's emotion is positive, but the caregiver provides postural adjustments and soothing vocalizations if the

disorganized/disoriented attachment *pattern characterized by lack of a coherent strategy for handling separations from and reunions with the caregiver*

synchrony *degree to which caregiver's and baby's behaviors occur together and are coordinated to produce a state of mutual enjoyment and engagement*

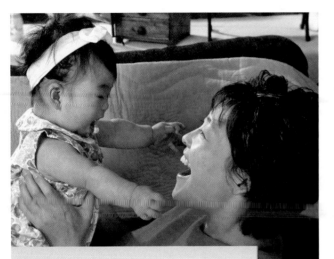

Notice how the caregiver and child in this picture are engaged with each other. Can you describe how this type of "synchrony" promotes attachment and bonding?

infant is scared (Lohaus et al., 2001). This caregiver–child synchrony contributes to the development of attachment by helping the child become an effective partner in interactions with predictable, appealing elements of behavior.

Infant Characteristics

Ainsworth and her colleagues believe that the quality of attachment depends solely on the caregiver's behavior. Other researchers, however, believe that characteristics of the infant influence the caregiver's behavior (Belsky, 1999). Remember that theories of temperament suggest that infants react very differently to the same stimulus; for example, some infants are more responsive to their environments, and some are more resistant to being held and cuddled (Seifer et al., 1996). Such characteristics may shape the behaviors of caregivers. Infants who like to be held, cuddled, and looked at foster the caregiver's sensitivity, whereas those who are difficult to soothe or easily overstimulated may discourage it (Bridges, Connell, & Belsky, 1988; Seifer & Schiller, 1995; see Figure 7.6).

Additional evidence of the role that infant characteristics may play in the formation of attachment comes from studies of children with disabilities or who are at risk. For example, deaf or blind infants often are slow to develop secure attachments to their mothers (Meadow-Orlans & Spencer, 1999). Compared with nondisabled children, these infants may respond in ways that are less likely to promote sensitive caregiving. Blind infants, for instance, cannot use their gaze to attract their caregivers the way sighted infants can. Similarly, very low birthweight preterm infants are more likely to be insecurely attached because they are less socially responsive and more difficult to soothe than are full-term infants (Mangelsdorf et al., 1996). Although disabled and at-risk infants can form healthy attachments, their behaviors do not encourage caregiver responsiveness to the extent that other infants' behaviors do.

FIGURE 7.6

Effects of Infant Characteristics on Parents' Behavior

Although it is clear that parental behaviors influence children, an infant's behavior also influences her or his parents. Can you identify some examples of how this might be true?

The Role of Culture in Attachment

Attachment theory was proposed as a universal theory of human development. However, because childrearing goals, values, and behaviors vary from culture to culture, attachments may not have the same meaning in different cultures (Crittenden & Claussen, 2000). For example, infants who rarely experience separation from their mothers may react differently to the Strange Situation than do infants who experience separation more frequently. Japanese infants, who are encouraged to be dependent on their mothers, are more likely than US infants to cry and become passive when left alone. Correspondingly, Japanese mothers are more likely than US mothers to hold and maintain contact with their infants (Rothbaum et al., 2000; Takahashi, 1990). Because of the increased stress experienced by Japanese infants in the Strange Situation, a higher percentage of Japanese infants than US infants are classified as ambivalently attached (32 percent and 16 percent, respectively).

Research has confirmed different patterns of attachment in infants from different cultures (Miyake, Chen, & Campos, 1985). Figure 7.7 shows how the percentages of infants classified as secure, avoidant, and ambivalent vary from one culture to the next. In Ger-

FIGURE 7.7
Cultural Differences in Patterns of Attachment in Children

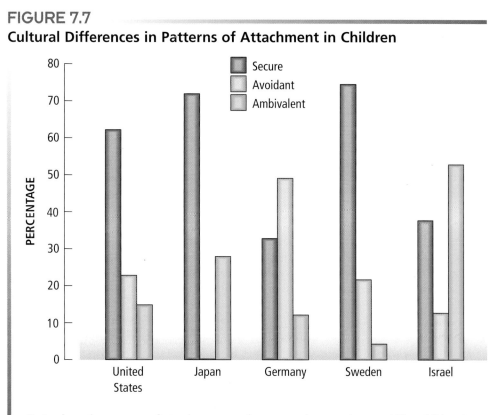

Notice how the patterns of attachment vary from one culture to the next. What childrearing and cultural factors contribute to these differences?

Source: Miyake, Chen, and Campos, 1985.

many, for example, where parents press infants to behave independently and rebuff their bids for contact, a sizable percentage of children are classified as avoidant. In contrast, in Japan, where mothers value contact and dependency, almost no children are classified as avoidant. In Israel, where children have only infrequent contact with unfamiliar people, almost half of the infants are classified as ambivalent. Compare this to the patterns of attachment found in Sweden, where children are exposed to large numbers of unfamiliar people.

American cultural diversity also leads to differences in attachment behaviors and patterns. European American mothers place a great deal of emphasis on self-confidence and self-reliance. These values reflect the individualism of traditional European American culture. In contrast, Puerto Rican mothers place more emphasis on respect, obedience, and remaining connected with others (Harwood, Miller, & Irizarry, 1995). As a result, Puerto Rican infants are more likely to be classified as ambivalently attached than are European American infants.

Consequences of Attachment

How much does the nature of early attachment matter to children's later development? The answer to this question is the subject of debate. Kohlberg and Kramer (1969) questioned the impact of early relationships on later development unless these relationships are extreme and traumatic. They maintained that the quality of early relationships is greatly transformed by the cognitive changes that take place later in life and it is therefore difficult to imagine how an infant's attachment early in life can have a strong effect on his or her development later in life.

What roles do fathers take in caregiving, and how do these roles differ from the ones mothers often take? Do differences in roles influence infants' tendencies to become attached to their fathers?

Other researchers, however, believe that the nature of early attachment plays an important role in influencing later development (Sroufe, Carlson, Levy, & Egeland, 2003). Children who have secure attachments see themselves as lovable and feel their needs will be met. They act in ways that are consistent with this benevolent view of the world (Belsky, Spritz, & Crnic, 1996). In contrast, children with insecure attachments tend to develop a dramatically different internal working model of themselves and their environments. They believe that the world is unsupportive, inconsistent, and rejecting. These beliefs, feelings, and behaviors link their past experiences and attachments with the present (Carlson, Sampson, & Sroufe, 2003).

Some support has been found for a link between early attachment and later development. For example, some studies have found that securely attached children have better social skills, tolerate frustration more successfully, and express a wider range of emotions than children who are not securely attached (Arend, Gove, & Sroufe, 1979; Bohlin, Hagekull, & Rydell, 2000; Mikulincer, Shaver, & Pereg, 2002). Children with secure attachments as infants have been found to approach their environments with interest and pleasure, are comfortable in seeking help from others, follow directions easily, and seldom cry, fuss, or become angry when encountering frustrating circumstances (Elicker, Englund, & Sroufe, 1992). Securely attached children also tend to remember positive events better than negative ones, whereas the reverse is true for insecurely attached children (Belsky et al., 1996), and tend to perform better in school (Aviezer, Sagi, Resnick, & Gini, 2002).

Although these studies appear to provide support for the effects of attachment on later development, the findings are inconsistent and relatively weak when the scientific evidence is examined as a whole (Belsky & Cassidy, 1994). In some cases, researchers have failed to replicate the findings; and when the findings have been replicated, the effects have tended to be small (Booth, Rose-Krasnor, & Rubin, 1991; Easterbrooks & Goldberg, 1990; Frankel & Bates, 1992). The inconsistency of these findings suggests that although the nature of early attachment may be an important factor in children's lives, other factors (such as family income, disability, temperament, etc.) also influence later adjustment and functioning (Thompson, 1999).

Attachment to Fathers

In the United States, fathers spend considerably less time interacting with their infants than do mothers (Kazura, 2000), and this difference has been found across a wide range of culturally diverse populations (Fracasso, Lamb, Schoelmerich, & Leyendecker, 1997). There are, however, large individual differences among fathers, with some being very involved in caregiving and others almost completely disengaged (Jain, Belsky, & Crnic, 1996; Lewis & Lamb, 2003). As children get older, the father's involvement increases (Coltrane, 1995; Cooksey & Fondell, 1996).

Not only do fathers and mothers spend different amounts of time with their infants, but they also interact differently. Fathers typically interact as playmates, rather than as protectors, comforters, or care providers (Bornstein & Tamis-LeMonda, 1997). When infants need caring for, many fathers let mothers take over (Parke, 1995). But despite these differences in the nature of the interactions of US mothers and fathers with their young children, infants do develop secure attachments with fathers, and fathers play an important role in children's early social and emotional development (Belsky, 1996; Skogstad, 2003).

Research comparing infants' responses to mothers and fathers in the Strange Situation suggests that infants cry when both mothers and fathers leave the room, but they do not cry when strangers leave the room. When reunited with either parent, most infants show relief and comfort. Exploration of the room generally is greater when either mothers or fathers are present than when they are gone (Colin, 1996). Although infants' reactions tend to be less intense with their fathers, they nonetheless treat fathers as attachment figures who serve as secure bases (Doherty, 1997). When given the opportunity, fathers have as much capacity as mothers do to form intimate ties with their infants, to be sensitive to their needs, and to be competent in nurturing them (Beitel & Parke, 1998). Longitudinal research, however, has found that fathers' sensitivity during playful interactions with their infants may be a better predictor of children's long-term attachment representation than the early infant–father attachment security (Grossman et al., 2002). Thus, it appears that how fathers play with their infants is a key factor in making an early difference in children's adjustment and outcomes.

Do infants who are securely attached to their mother also develop a secure attachment to their father? According to an analysis of studies that examined the relationship between infant–mother and infant–father attachment, there is some consistency (Fox, Kimmerly, & Schafer, 1991). Infants who are securely attached to one parent generally are securely attached to the other parent, and infants who are insecurely attached to one parent are insecurely attached to the other. Thus, mothers and fathers generally provide caregiving behaviors that mutually support the development of attachment. This consistency also suggests that one sensitive parent may buffer the infant from deficiencies in the other parent's behavior, thereby promoting secure attachments to both parents (Colin, 1996).

How Does Day Care Influence Infants' and Toddlers' Development?

As you have just learned, the quality of an infant's attachment depends in part on the quality of parenting received. Quality of parenting is a function of both the amount and the nature of the time infants and caregivers spend together. But in the United States, more and more children are placed in day care, where they interact with nonparental caregivers. Concerns have been raised about the impact of this on children's development.

In the United States, there are almost 20 million children under the age of 5, and both parents of about 12 million of these children work outside the home (US Census Bureau, 2002). This situation is radically different from that of the 1950s, when only 12 percent of married women with preschool children worked outside the home. Until 1975, the Census Bureau did not even collect labor force data on mothers with infants or toddlers because it was assumed that few mothers worked (National Issues Forum, 1989). Now, about 60 percent do so, largely for economic reasons. The increase in the number of working mothers with children less than 3 years of age is especially dramatic. More than half of all mothers with children under age 1 are in the workforce, either full or part time (US Department of Labor, 2001a). The rapid entry of women into the labor force over the past few decades has altered the way very young children are raised, and the demands for—and concerns about—day care have soared.

Patterns of Day-Care Use

Although it is popularly believed that most infants and toddlers with working mothers are cared for in group day-care centers, most are cared for in homes by relatives, such as fathers, mothers, siblings, grandparents, uncles, aunts, or cousins (Ehrle, Adams, & Tout, 2001). As Figure 7.8 indicates, children under age 3 are more likely to be cared for by relatives than are older children. Young children are more likely to be cared for by relatives, particularly the father, if the mother works part time rather than full time (National Center for Education Statistics, 2003). Mothers who work full time are more likely to rely on organized day-care centers or nonrelatives to care for their children (US Census Bureau, 2002). As shown in Figure 7.9, day-care

FIGURE 7.8

Day-Care Arrangements for Children of Employed Mothers, by Children's Age

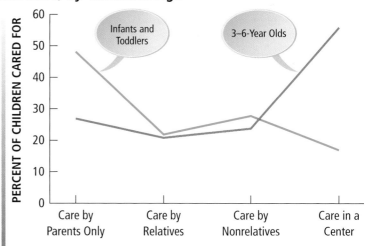

Compare the figures for infants and toddlers to those for preschool children. Notice especially the increase in the percentage of older children who receive care from someone other than a relative. What factors contribute to these differences?

*Some children participate in more than one type of arrangement, so the sum of all arrangement types exceeds 100 percent.

Source: National Center for Education Statistics, 2003.

FIGURE 7.9

Day-Care Arrangements, by Work Status of Mother

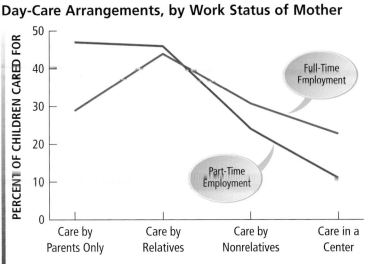

Notice the differences between child-care arrangements for children whose mothers work versus those whose mothers do not. Can you identify some reasons for these differences?

Note: Some children participate in more than one type of arrangement, so the sum of all arrangement types exceeds 100 percent.

Source: US Census Bureau, 2002.

FIGURE 7.10

Day-Care Arrangements, by Ethnicity

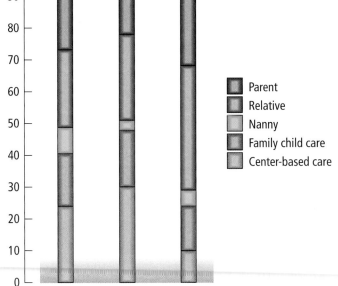

What are the most noticeable differences in the graphs? How might ethnic differences contribute to differences in day-care use?

Source: Ehrle, Adams, and Tout, 2001.

arrangements for infants and toddlers vary by whether or not there are two parents in the household. Children in single-parent families are more likely to be taken care of by relatives, whereas children in two-parent families are more likely to receive care from a parent or a nanny or in family- or center-based care facilities (US Census Bureau, 2002).

Child-care arrangements for infants and toddlers also differ based on ethnic group. As depicted in Figure 7.10, African American children are most likely to be cared for in center-based programs, whereas Hispanic children are likely to be cared for by family members (either parents or relatives). Caucasian children are more likely than either minority group to be cared for by nannies. These differences reflect differences in income, access to child-care arrangements, and the values and standards held by each ethnic group.

With the exception of government-sponsored programs for children from poor families, child care (particularly infant care) in the United States is privately owned and operated (Lamb, Sternberg, & Ketterlinus, 1992). Nationwide regulations have never been mandated by the federal government, and existing state and local regulations generally establish only minimal requirements to ensure that children are protected from harm (Phillips, Lande, & Goldberg, 1990; Scarr, 1998). According to the National Institute of Child Health and Development (NICHD) Early Child Care Research Network's comprehensive study of child care (2000), which conducted observations of over 600 child-care settings of all kinds (grandparents, in-home care, child-care homes, and centers) in nine states, most centers were judged to be only fair in quality. Overall, only 11 percent of the settings were considered excellent. Poor-quality care was more likely in centers serving infants and toddlers (10 percent) than in centers serving older children (4 percent). Infants from high-income families, as well as those from low-income families that receive subsidies, are more likely to receive high-quality day care than are infants from middle-income families (Vandell & Wolfe, 2000). Clearly, findings such as these suggest that plenty of room for improvement remains.

Effects of Day Care

With so many infants and toddlers spending so much time away from their parents, particularly their mothers, how might children's development in general, and their attachments in particular, be affected? As you might expect, this question is not easily answered.

Attempts to examine the effects of early child care have led to contradictory conclusions. The

DEBATING THE ISSUE

HOW DOES MOM'S WORKING AFFECT CHILDREN'S DEVELOPMENT?

 One of the most striking pieces of evidence of the changing roles of women in the latter part of the twentieth century is the tremendous increase in the number of women participating in the paid labor force. Women's participation in the labor force tripled from 1950 to 1985; by the century's end, women accounted for about 50 percent of the total workforce (US Department of Labor, 2001a). Increasingly, women with children are pursuing employment outside of the home. As you learned in Chapter 1, about 56 percent of mothers with children age 1 or younger are in the workforce (US Department of Labor, 2001a).

But what impact does mothers' employment have on their young children? A large body of research has focused on comparing children whose mothers are employed with those whose mothers are at home full time. This research generally has found no consistent differences in cognitive, social, or emotional development between these two groups of children (Hoffman &

Youngblade, 1999). Although some researchers have raised concerns about the impact of maternal employment on infants' and toddlers' attachment (Belsky, 1990), this concern has been debated and challenged (Clarke-Stewart, 1989). In fact, there is some evidence that maternal employment may be beneficial for certain groups of children. For example, daughters of employed women have been found to have higher academic achievement, to have greater independence, and to be more assertive than those of unemployed women (Aube, Fleury, & Smetana, 2000). Studies of children from low-income households have consistently found that maternal employment is associated with better socioemotional and cognitive functioning, for both boys and girls (Hoffman & Youngblade, 1999).

In general, these findings suggest that, in itself, maternal employment is not a cause for alarm and does not harm young children's physical or psychological well-being. One set of factors that seems to be particularly important concerns the quality of women's experiences on the

job. Although women have made important strides in the workforce, in many ways the work of women tends to be characterized by less status, less pay, and less power than the work of men, even for women with higher levels of education. Moreover, women are more likely to be victims of sexual harassment and discrimination than are men (Aube et al., 2000). Social and economic policies that promote women's greater job equity and satisfaction likely will facilitate positive outcomes associated with maternal employment. For example, in 1993, the Family and Medical Leave Act was passed. This act provides unpaid leave for a limited period of time at key moments in a family's life—such as when a baby is born or a family member becomes ill. Such policies enhance women's (and men's) abilities to meet the needs of their family without prejudice to their job. Greater satisfaction with their ability to meet the demands of home and work is likely to result, improving the chances of positive outcomes for children and families (Aube et al., 2000).

---

results from several studies show that day care may benefit low-income children and have benign, sometimes even beneficial, effects on middle-class children (Clarke-Stewart, Allhusen, & Clements, 1995; Hausfather, Toharia, LaRoche, & Engelsmann, 1997; NICHD, 2002). Day care generally enhances the intellectual performance of low-income children, increases their curiosity and concentration, and fosters independence, social competence, and cooperativeness (Caputo, 2003; NICHD, 1996, 2003a). But the results from other studies have not been as positive. For example, some studies report that day care increases children's aggression and decreases their compliance (NICHD, 2003b).

Beginning in the late 1980s, the accumulation of evidence regarding the impact of infant day care on mother–infant attachment led some researchers to conclude that day care has adverse effects on attachment. Specifically, Belsky (1988, 1990) concluded that infants may be at risk for insecure attachments if they spend more than 20 hours per week in nonmaternal care during their first year of life. When observed in the Strange Situation, infants with early extended day-care experiences were more likely to avoid and ignore their mothers.

Belsky's conclusions have drawn intense criticism (Clarke-Stewart, 1992). One criticism is that Belsky's conclusions are too strong: the majority of infants with early extended day-care experiences are securely attached to their mothers (Thompson, 1991). Other researchers note that it is not day care itself that leads to insecure attachments but rather the comparatively greater stress that parents who rely on early extended infant care may be experiencing. Families under stress report that they spend less time researching day-care options, need

More young children than ever before are being cared for by someone other than their parents. What social changes contribute to this increase in nonparental care? How do you feel about this? What factors should parents consider when looking for high-quality care for their young children?

longer hours of day care for their infants, and accept poorer quality day care (Lamb, 1998).

Howes (1990) found that the quality of care was a better predictor of later functioning than was the age at which children entered day care. Secure relationships with day-care teachers have been found to enhance children's play, competence, and social relationships (Howes, Hamilton, & Matheson, 1994). And the more recent large-scale study by NICHD found that early child care itself did not harm mother–infant attachment (NICHD, 2002). Additionally, family factors were more strongly predictive of positive outcomes for young children in day care than are child-care factors (NICHD, 2003b). Thus, what transpires in a young child's family appears to be more important than the day care itself in determining how children are affected by day care.

This debate highlights the need for affordable, high-quality day care (Vandell & Wolfe, 2000). Even Belsky (1990) notes that affordable, high-quality day care is not as available as it needs to be and that it is inappropriate to conclude that only mothers can care for their infants or that day care is bad for infants. High-quality day care clearly has positive effects on children's intellectual and verbal development, especially when children come from impoverished and unstimulating environments. Poor-quality day care may have negative effects (Burchinal & Caskie, 2001; Lamb, 1998; NICHD, 2000b). Evidence from countries such as Sweden, where high-quality infant day care is readily available, also shows that infants with high-quality day care experience have more positive developmental outcomes (such as greater social skills and intellectual competence) than do infants without such experience (Andersson, 2003). In the United States, where most child care is a for-profit enterprise, parental decisions regarding day care are more often determined by cost and availability than by quality (Blau, 2001).

Guidelines for Quality Day Care

Given the importance of high-quality care, it is critical that parents be able to judge the quality of day-care programs. The following guidelines, based on research (American Red Cross, 2001; Zero to Three, 2004), can be used to judge a program's quality:

▪ *Safety:* Child-care settings should be safe. Look for fences around the outdoor playground and well-constructed play equipment. Dangerous and toxic substances should be locked out of the children's reach. Electrical outlets and radiators should be covered. The child-care workers should wash their hands before feeding, handling food, diapering, and washing surfaces. A system for identifying the parent or guardian responsible for picking up the child should be well established and adhered to.

▪ *Adult/child ratios and group size:* The more adults present, the more individual attention children receive. Younger children need more adults present than do older children. The total size of the group also is important. There should be no more than 8 in a group for infants and no more than 20 in a group for 5-year-olds. For each adult, there should be no more than the following number of children:

3–4 infants or toddlers	8–9 4-year-olds
4–6 2-year-olds	8–10 5-year-olds
7–8 3-year-olds	

▪ *Staff training and program:* Licensing and training requirements vary from state to state. Although compliance does not guarantee quality, the program should be in compliance with state requirements. Some professional organizations (such as the National Association for the Education of Young Children) accredit programs that meet high standards of quality. Ask for evidence of such accreditation. Qualified staff should have some direct education in early childhood education or child development.

■ *Curriculum:* The materials provided to children should be appropriate for their age and level of development. For infants and toddlers, there should be soft, washable, colorful toys that can be looked at or sucked. There should be no small parts that could come off and be swallowed. Preschoolers should have access to books as well as toys, blocks, and equipment that emphasizes gross motor development.

These are just a few of the factors that parents need to consider when determining the quality of a day-care program. Finding high-quality day care takes time and effort. Parents should look at many programs and talk to relatives, friends, neighbors, and parents familiar with the programs. They should visit programs at various times; if a program discourages such visits, they probably should look elsewhere. It is essential for parents to remember that this critical decision requires considerable attention and thought.

Culture influences how children are cared for and raised. Can you identify some of the ways in which cultural differences contribute to differences in child care?

Culture and Day Care

Variations in caregiving and day care for infants and children in different countries and communities reflect different political, cultural, and social values (Johnson et al., 2003; Rosenthal, 1999). In the People's Republic of China, many day-care policies reflect the collectivist values mandated by the central government as well as traditional values emphasizing obedience and respect. Because of China's overpopulation problems and one-child policy, most contemporary families are made up of six adults (four grandparents and two parents) and one child. The child therefore becomes the center of adult attention and care. To cultivate the correct socialistic spirit, day care is designed to train children in developing self-control, good habits, and obedience (Lee, 1992). By 2 or 3 years of age, children are learning how to satisfy others and behave according to formal and rigid standards, which mandate behaviors rarely expected of toddlers from Western cultures (such as sharing).

Very different child care conditions exist for children and families in Brazil, where three quarters of the people live in impoverished urban areas. Intense urbanization has not been matched by corresponding increases in job, educational, health, or housing opportunities. Often, small children are confined in cramped spaces with little food, while adults and older siblings work long hours. Thus, there is great need for *creches* (day care), but only about 23 percent of preschool-age children attend such programs. For the very young, such care is even less available; only about 10 percent of infants and toddlers attend *creches* (Campos, 1992). As you might imagine, in most of the *creches*, particularly those serving low-income families, children are placed in large groups supervised by relatively untrained staff. Although some improvements have been made, the unfavorable economic conditions and overcrowding lead to rigid routines in the *creches*, with little tolerance for child initiative and autonomy (Goncalves, 1990).

In the Kenyan community of Morongo, where infant mortality is very high, infants and toddlers are never left alone. An infant is carried by his or her mother until about 6 months of age, at which time the child is taken care of by others in the family or community. This "dense caretaking environment" in early childhood reflects the Morongon child-care strategy, which seeks to maximize survival in a high-mortality context during the most vulnerable period of the child's life (LeVine et al., 1994). The differences among child care in China, Brazil, and Kenya demonstrate how child care and its impact on children are influenced by the broader cultural, social, political, economic, and physical environments in which children and families find themselves (Morelli & Verhoef, 1999).

Why Are Children Abused and Neglected?

The study of children's attachments and relationships to parents and other caregivers highlights the important role that sensitive, nurturing, and responsive caregiving plays in influencing early social and emotional development (Volling, McElwain, Notaro, & Herrera,

2002). For most children, experiences with the adults in their lives are generally positive, but some children experience the horror and tragedy of being the victim of abuse and neglect. Consider Katy's story:

> *Katy was shaken so hard as a baby that her brain was smashed inside her skull. The damaged areas eventually had to be cut out, leaving her with half a brain. A stroke at age 4 left her partially paralyzed. Tests revealed problems with Katy's pituitary gland and thyroid. She goes to the hospital twice a week for 2 hours of occupational and speech therapy. Her sister, Micki, escaped the wrath of their angry father; while Micki was getting taller and slimmer, Katy was squat. Micki stands as testimony to what Katy's life might have been.* (Adapted from Bland, 1997)

Katy's story is one of the thousands of cases of abuse and neglect that take place each year. The media have flooded us with stories of infants and children who have been abandoned, beaten, or killed by their caregivers; deprived of essential emotional and physical comfort; or sexually molested and abused. Such reports have increased the public's awareness of the incidence and severity of child abuse. In 1976, only 10 percent of Americans surveyed considered child abuse to be a problem; less than 20 years later, that figure had risen to over 90 percent (Finkelman, 1995). Although the stories attract tremendous attention and outrage, they fail to reveal the complex interplay of factors that make up the causes and consequences of child abuse and neglect.

Definitions of Child Abuse and Neglect

Four categories of child maltreatment generally are distinguished:

1. **Physical abuse,** in which caregivers cause death, serious physical harm, or imminent risk of serious harm to children
2. **Sexual abuse,** in which caregivers engage in sexual activity with children
3. **Neglect,** in which children's physical or emotional well-being is jeopardized by the failure to provide shelter, clothing, or protection
4. **Psychological maltreatment,** in which caregivers emotionally abuse children by threatening them or conveying that they are worthless, unloved, or unwanted (Berliner & Elliot, 1996; Kolko, 1996; Lutzker, 2000)

According to the scientific evidence, psychological maltreatment often is the strongest predictor of harmful developmental outcomes for a child (Hart, Brassard, & Karlson, 1996).

Caregivers who maltreat children often abuse or neglect them in more than one way (Belsky, 1993). In one study (Kaufman & Cicchetti, 1995), not one of the 70 physically abused children had experienced physical abuse alone. Each type of maltreatment has its own rates of occurrence, factors that influence it, and potential consequences. Because researchers and therapists tend to focus on one type of abuse or another, we know little about the extent to which different types of child abuse and neglect share common factors or respond to different types of treatment (Widom, 2001).

Incidence of Child Abuse and Neglect

The findings of the Third National Incidence Study of Child Abuse and Neglect (Sedlak & Broadhurst, 1996) indicated a sharp increase in the scope of the child maltreatment problem. Using a broad definition of maltreatment, this study estimated that the total number of US children who were reported as abused or neglected in 1994 was 2,815,600. By 1999, over 3 million children were reported abused or neglected (National Clearinghouse on Child Abuse and Neglect, 1999). This total reflected a 98 percent increase since 1986. The incidences for the various categories of abuse had increased as follows:

- The number of sexually abused children had risen from 133,600 to 300,200 (a 125 percent increase).

physical abuse   *abuse that causes death, serious physical harm, or imminent risk of serious harm*

sexual abuse   *abuse that involves engaging in sexual activity*

neglect   *failure to provide shelter, clothing, or protection for a child*

psychological maltreatment *emotional abuse caused by threatening harm or conveying to an individual that she or he is worthless, unloved, or unwanted*

- The number of neglected children had increased from 917,200 to 1,961,300 (a 114 percent increase).

- The number of physically abused children had increased from 311,500 to 614,100 (a 92 percent increase).

Although rates of child victimization have decreased somewhat since the mid-1990s, the rates are still considerably higher than they were a quarter of a century ago (National Child Abuse and Neglect Data System, 2001). Sadly, not all cases of alleged child abuse and neglect are investigated: in only 28 percent of the cases of child abuse and neglect did an investigation take place.

Characteristics of Victims and Abusers

What are the characteristics of both victims of child abuse and neglect and child abusers?

Victims of Child Abuse and Neglect

Certain children face greater risk of experiencing abuse than others do. Of course, these children are not responsible for their abusive conditions; however, they possess characteristics known to increase the chance that abuse will occur. The following are some findings about how child and family characteristics are related to child abuse and neglect (Goodman, Emery, & Haugaard, 1998; Kapitanoff, Lutzker, & Bigelow, 2000; Widom, 2001; Wiese & Daro, 1996):

- *Gender:* Girls are sexually abused more often than boys are. This gender difference in the incidence of sexual abuse leads to higher rates of abuse in general for girls.

- *Age:* Young children are more at risk for maltreatment than are older children. The lower rates as children get older reflect the reality that older children have more opportunities to escape, defend themselves, or retaliate.

- *Temperament:* Children with difficult temperamental qualities (such as negative moods or intense crying) may tax parental tolerance, increasing the risk of abuse.

- *Income:* Children living in families that earn less than $15,000 annually are 25 times more likely to experience some form of maltreatment than are children in families earning $30,000 or more. (This statistic may be due to reporting bias.) Once income is controlled, any differences in race and ethnicity generally disappear.

- *Family size:* Children from large families are more likely to be abused and neglected than children from small families.

- *Disabilities:* Children with disabilities are four to ten times more likely to experience abuse or neglect than their nondisabled peers are. Similarly, children with medical or health problems (such as birth complications, prematurity, or asthma) are more likely to experience abuse or neglect.

These findings tell us that some children are more at risk than others for maltreatment, often because they place more stress or demands on parents. Yet although they may not do so evenly, child abuse and neglect cross all social class, racial, religious, and educational boundaries (Sidebotham, 2000; Wolfner & Gelles, 1993).

Characteristics of Child Abusers

The image most people have of a child abuser is a person with a serious psychological disturbance, but the research evidence does not support this conclusion. In fact, less than 10 percent of child abusers evidence extremely disturbed symptoms (Murphy & Smith, 1996). What, then, are the characteristics of those who commit child abuse and neglect? From the existing research (Kolko, 1996; Lutzker, 1998, Reder & Duncan, 2000; Sedlak & Broadhurst, 1996), the following conclusions can be drawn:

- Parents are more likely than any other group to abuse children (see Figure 7.11). Although the popular press highlights cases in which nonparental caregivers and foster parents perpetrate abuse, they are the adults least likely to do so.

FIGURE 7.11

Perpetrators of Child Abuse

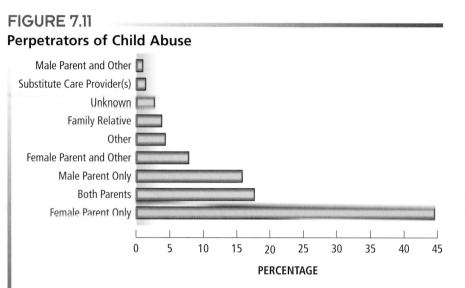

There is a dramatic difference between the rates at which child abuse is perpetrated by parents—especially mothers—and all others. What impact might such findings have for intervention and prevention programs?

Source: US Department of Health and Human Services, 1999.

■ Because mothers carry the major responsibility for child care, they tend to abuse children more often than fathers do (although fathers are more often involved in sexual abuse). However, the severity of the injury or impairment that a child experiences as a result of maltreatment is not related to the sex of the perpetrator.

■ Probably because children most often live with their biological parents, biological parents are responsible for the majority of the cases of child abuse and neglect. Sixty-two percent of abuse cases and 91 percent of neglect cases are perpetrated by biological parents.

■ Single parents have a particularly high rate of committing abuse and neglect.

■ Children are more likely to be abused by younger than by older caretakers.

■ Adults who commit child abuse tend to be isolated, lack family and peer support networks, and not be involved in community activities.

■ Abusive adults have limited knowledge of caregiving, have unrealistic expectations for children's behavior, find childrearing difficult, have a low tolerance for infant behaviors (such as crying), and tend to use harsh disciplinary practices.

■ Although committing child abuse is not consistently associated with alcohol use, it is associated with drug use. The rate of child maltreatment is about 46 percent higher for drug users than for those who do not use drugs.

One of the most consistently reported findings regarding characteristics of child abusers is that they are likely to have experienced abuse themselves when they were children (Heyman & Slep, 2002). Approximately 30 percent of abused children grow up to be abusive, compared with 4 percent of the general population (Maxfield & Widom, 1996). Additionally, child abuse often occurs in a general context of family violence. When a child is abused, it is likely that a spouse is also abused (Appel & Holden, 1998; Margolin, Gordis, Medina, & Oliver, 2003). Domestic violence appears to promote negative views of children and of being a parent, increasing the risk of child abuse (McGuigan, Vuchinich, & Pratt, 2000). Child abuse thus frequently reflects an atmosphere of violent and abusive family relationships (Slep & O'Leary, 2001).

Together, these findings present a complex picture of the person who commits child abuse and neglect. Although they suggest that some individuals are more at risk than others for committing child abuse, the potential for acting abusively is present in varying degrees in many individuals (Reder & Duncan, 2000). No single profile fits all child abusers.

To address the complex causes of child abuse, Belsky (1980, 1993) developed an ecological model showing different pathways leading to child maltreatment (see Figure 7.12). According to Belsky, child maltreatment is most likely to occur when the stressors outweigh the supportive conditions in a person's environment. These stressors and supports take many forms and include a variety of parent factors (personality, attitudes), child factors (temperament, age, health condition), family and community factors (stress, family structure, social support), cultural norms (attitudes toward parenting and toward violence), historical developments (children's rights), and evolutionary factors (fitness).

As an illustration of the broad array of factors that influence child abuse and neglect, consider the case of Amos. Amos was born to parents who were fundamentalist in their religious beliefs and who approached parenting with a traditional and physical style of parenting (Melzak, 1992). At the time of Amos's birth, his mother was preoccupied with

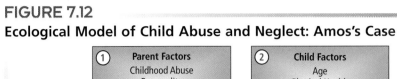

FIGURE 7.12
Ecological Model of Child Abuse and Neglect: Amos's Case

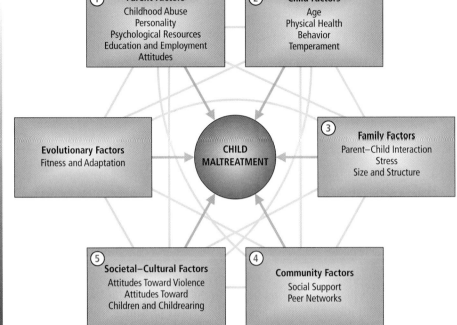

This model illustrates how different contextual factors might interact to increase children's risk for abuse and neglect. How does this model help us understand the dynamics of child maltreatment? How might it be used to design effective interventions and prevention programs?

Source: Belsky, 1993.

her new relationship with Amos's father and with a custody battle she was having over her eldest son from a prior marriage. Amos's mother was an insecure, intelligent, anxious woman, and his father was a gentle, quiet man who often was humiliated by his wife (1, Figure 7.12). Amos was described as an active, difficult-to-manage child who did not sleep regularly and did not live up to his elder brother's model of maturity, obedience, and self-control (2). Beginning sometime after his first birthday, Amos was beaten at home by both parents and sometimes by his grandparents (3). When Amos began preschool, he often got in trouble and was severely beaten with a belt by his parents for doing so (4). The parents reported that this was how they were punished when they were children (5).

The case of Amos reveals the complex factors that contribute to abuse. Amos's parents came from a background where physical punishment and physical control of children were acceptable. The fact that Amos also was beaten by his grandparents and that intense physical punishment was used by the grandparents to discipline Amos's parents when they were children reflects an intergenerational history of abuse. Additionally, because of the stress associated with the new marriage and the custody battle, Amos's parents had limited abilities to cope with the stress of childrearing. Faced with a sensitive, impulsive, and out-of-control little boy, Amos's parents were overwhelmed.

Amos's case supports Belsky's (1993) proposal that child abuse and neglect are multiply determined by the interaction of processes associated with various individual, familial, cultural, and historical factors. There is no one cause of child maltreatment, and no single determining factor or profile of a child abuser or a victim has emerged from the literature. The most consistent conclusion seems to be that child abuse, its causes, and its consequences result from the transaction of risk and protective factors that exist at multiple levels (Korbin et al., 1998; Stockhammer, Salzinger, Feldman, & Mojica, 2001). The exact conditions that contribute to child abuse, however, vary from family to family, from situation to situation, and from culture to culture.

Effects of Child Abuse and Neglect

In the United States, over 1,400 children annually die from maltreatment, over 3 children every day, and the rate is up almost 30 percent since 1985 (US Department of Health and

Human Services, 2004). Younger children are more at risk of loss of life from maltreatment than are older children—86 percent of the fatalities from maltreatment occurred in children under 5 years of age, and 43 percent occurred in children under 1 year of age. As Katy's story at the beginning of this section reveals, even if young children survive maltreatment, it can have irreparable effects on their development.

Even when there is no evidence of neurological or physical impairment, the consequences of child abuse can be devastating (Administration for Children and Families, 2002). Abused and neglected children sometimes show delayed intellectual development, particularly in the area of verbal intelligence (Zigler, Finn-Stevenson, & Hall, 2002); poor school performance (Kendall-Tackett & Eckenrode, 1997; Leiter & Johnsen, 1997); and deficits in attention and information processing (Zurbriggen & Freyd, 2004).

Child abuse and neglect also have strong effects on children's psychological and social development, and these consequences are extremely powerful in the early stages of development (Lutzker, 2000; Oddone-Paolucci, Genuis, & Violato, 2001). Early child abuse and neglect may harm the development of children's attachments, sense of security, self-esteem, and emotional stability (Trickett & McBride-Chang, 1995). Children who have been abused or neglected also may have negative mental health outcomes, such as depression, anxiety disorders, and aggressiveness (Cuffe & Shugart, 2001; McCloskey et al., 1995). A consistent finding is that sexually abused young children exhibit inappropriate sexual behavior (Zurbriggen & Freyd, 2004).

Preventing Child Abuse and Neglect

As the number of victims increases, awareness of the need to prevent child abuse and neglect is growing. Unfortunately, most efforts are devoted to helping children only after a major incident of maltreatment has been identified. Yet because of the high financial and human costs associated with child maltreatment, preventing it is critical (Daro, 2000).

Prevention is commonly categorized as primary, secondary, or tertiary. **Primary prevention** is directed at the population as a whole. Educational programs that sensitize society to basic issues of maltreatment or that provide essential parenting skills to all individuals before they become parents are examples of primary prevention programs (Daro, 1996, 2000). **Secondary prevention** targets a specific segment of the population thought to be at high risk for child maltreatment. Generally, these programs are designed to provide support for poor single mothers and fathers, helping them cope with the demands of child rearing. **Tertiary prevention** is directed at situations in which child maltreatment already has occurred. The goal is to prevent or decrease its reoccurrence. Providing training programs in parenting skills to individuals who have committed child abuse is an example of tertiary prevention.

Most prevention efforts focus on parent training (Edgeworth & Carr, 2000; Sanders, Cann, & Markie-Dadds, 2002). Training parents in child management (such as discipline techniques), child care, and self-control skills (such as managing frustration and anger) has been effective in promoting positive parent–child interactions (Britner & Reppucci, 1997). There also is some evidence that parent training reduces parental distress, thereby reducing the chances of abuse and neglect (Shifflett & Cummings, 1999). When parenting programs are combined with efforts to provide families with services that address critical family needs—such as child care, mental health counseling, social support, and home improvements—the effectiveness of the intervention is improved (Reuter, Conger, & Ramisetty-Mikler, 1999; Striefel, Robinson, & Truhn, 1998).

Unfortunately, given that reports of child abuse and neglect are increasing, it seems that prevention efforts have been relatively ineffective (Emery & Laumann-Billings, 1998). In fact, there is some evidence that one third or more of the abusive parents served by prevention programs maltreated their children while in these programs (McFarlane, Doueck, & Levine, 2002). To date, most interventions have been designed to address child abuse and neglect using secondary or tertiary prevention rather than primary prevention. In Scandinavian countries such as Norway, nationwide primary prevention programs provide support and services to all families. In these countries, rates of child abuse and neglect can be over 10 times lower than those in the United States (UNICEF, 2003). Thus, it appears we can do something about the rates of child abuse and neglect in the United States, but it will take broader interventions and policies to make a difference.

primary prevention *efforts targeted at the population as a whole, to sensitize people to basic issues or to provide particular skills*

secondary prevention *efforts targeted at a specific segment of the population thought to be at high risk*

tertiary prevention *efforts directed at preventing or decreasing the reoccurrence of an event that has already occurred*

Try It Out

1. How would you describe your temperament? What were some social, emotional, and behavioral expressions of your temperament when you were young? How would you characterize your pattern of attachment with your primary caregiver? How do you think this pattern might have influenced your social and emotional development?

2. At a playground, observe infants and toddlers interacting with their parents. Using factors associated with different types of attachments, try to determine what kind of attachment each child has. What behaviors do you focus on? What factors affect your judgments?

3. Arrange to observe infants and toddlers in a day-care program at the beginning and the end of the day, when they are being dropped off and picked up. Observe and record the behavior and social and emotional responses of parents, children, and day care workers. Before you observe, however, develop a research design. What will be your research question? What, exactly, will you observe, when, and for how long? How will you systematize and interpret your observations to answer your research question?

Key Terms and Concepts

ambivalent attachment (224)
attachment (217)
avoidant attachment (224)
disorganized/disoriented attachment (225)
endogenous smile (207)
exogenous smile (207)
goodness of fit (215)
neglect (234)
physical abuse (234)
primary prevention (238)
psychological maltreatment (234)
secondary prevention (238)

secure attachment (222)
self-conscious emotions (212)
separation anxiety (221)
sexual abuse (234)
social referencing (208)
social smile (208)
Strange Situation (222)
stranger anxiety (221)
synchrony (225)
temperament (214)
tertiary prevention (238)

Sum It Up

How do emotions develop during infancy and toddlerhood?

■ What is the difference between an endogenous and exogenous smile? (p. 207)

How does temperament influence development during infancy and toddlerhood?

■ List and describe the six temperamental constructs as defined by Rothbart and colleagues. (p. 214)

■ Give an example of both high and low goodness of fit. (p. 215)

How do parent–infant attachments influence development

■ List and describe the characteristics of the four phases of attachment. (pp. 219–220)

■ What factors influence the types of attachments that form between caregiver and child? (pp. 222–225)

How does day care influence infants' and toddlers' development?

■ How does culture play a role in variations in caregiving and day care environments? (p. 233)

Why are children abused and neglected?

■ List and describe the four categories of child maltreatment. (p. 234)

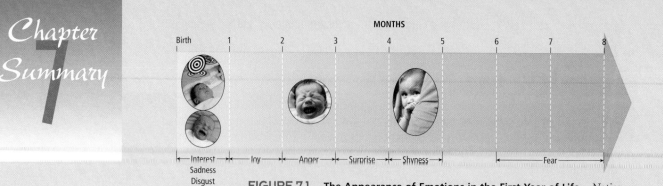

FIGURE 7.1 **The Appearance of Emotions in the First Year of Life** *Notice that within the first 6 to 8 months of life, many of the basic emotions develop.*

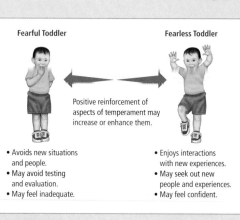

FIGURE 7.3 **Effects of Temperamental Qualities on Positive or Negative Adjustment** *Temperament refers to a person's genetic predisposition to respond to the environment in characteristic ways.*

EMOTIONAL DEVELOPMENT AND TEMPERAMENT

Many of the most common emotions are present at birth or develop quickly after that. From the moment of birth, infants differ in their responses to the environment. These differences are thought to be due to genetic differences in how children react to the world around them. (Refer back to pages 205–217.)

ATTACHMENT

Differences in how children react to their worlds can be thought of as a function of the quality of the relationships children form with significant caregivers. These attachments are thought to provide children with an internal representation of the world and an expectation about how their needs and emotions will be dealt with. Depending on the sensitivity of caregivers, different types of attachments are formed (secure, ambivalent, avoidant, and disorganized/disoriented). (Refer back to pages 217–229.)

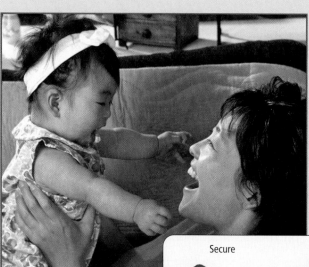

Notice how the caregiver and child in this picture are engaged with each other.

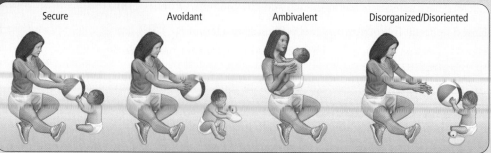

FIGURE 7.5 **Patterns of Attachment** *Researchers have identified four basic patterns of attachment.*

More young children than ever before are being cared for by someone other than their parents.

Factors used to judge a day care program's quality

- Safety
- Adult/child ratios and group size
- Staff training
- Curriculum

CHILD CARE

Because both parents are more typically joining the workforce, child care plays an increasingly important role in children's development. Although a wide variety of types of child care exist, the quality of such care determines its impact on a child. (Refer back to pages 229–233.)

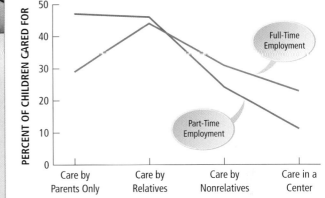

FIGURE 7.9 **Day-Care Arrangements, by Work Status of Mother** *Notice the differences between child-care arrangements for children whose mothers work versus those whose mothers do not.*

CHILD ABUSE

Unfortunately, many children are abused and neglected, especially younger children. Abuse and neglect come in many forms, but they all have the potential to seriously damage children's growth and health. (Refer back to pages 233–239.)

Definitions of child abuse and neglect

- Physical abuse
- Sexual abuse
- Neglect
- Psychological maltreatment

FIGURE 7.12 **Ecological Model of Child Abuse and Neglect** *This model illustrates how different contextual factors might interact to increase children's risk for abuse and neglect.*

① **Parent Factors**
Childhood Abuse
Personality
Psychological Resources
Education and Employment
Attitudes

② **Child Factors**
Age
Physical Health
Behavior
Temperament

Evolutionary Factors
Fitness and Adaptation

CHILD MALTREATMENT

③ **Family Factors**
Parent–Child Interaction
Stress
Size and Structure

⑤ **Societal–Cultural Factors**
Attitudes Toward Violence
Attitudes Toward
Children and Childrearing

④ **Community Factors**
Social Support
Peer Networks

Part
4

Early Childhood Development

During early childhood, children experience an increase in the complexity with which they think about and participate in their worlds. Although family members, particularly parents, remain important, children begin to experience life outside the family. They are increasingly exposed to non–family members and influences such as school and television. Most of these experiences involve peers, and most peer interactions take place in the context of play.

Children make significant advances in their cognitive development in early childhood. Their reasoning becomes more abstract and less bound by motor actions. Their language and communication skills increase, and they can ask and answer many rich and complex questions. Their reasoning, however, remains limited compared to that of older children and adults. Young children's thinking is dominated by their own perceptions, feelings, and perspectives. They have difficulty understanding that others have views different from their own. These new ways of thinking set the stage for even more advanced forms of reasoning and understanding.

The world of the 3- to 7-year-old child is different from that of older children and adults: a young child may think that a moving plastic duck is alive, that a broken cookie doesn't taste as good as an unbroken one, or that the stars shine so that he or she can see at night. Children view the world through their own perspective, and they tend to be easily fooled by what things look like—they fail to recognize the more stable features of objects. Children's physical development is not as dramatic as it is during infancy, but the changes are still very apparent—they no longer have their "babyish" appearance. Unlike infants, preschoolers can dress themselves, draw pictures, throw a ball, and run forward and backward. Language development occurs rapidly during this time, as children master many complexities of grammar and the use of language. As you will see in Part IV, cognitive, language, and motor skills develop best in the context of social interactions with caregivers and other adults in the community.

Physical Development and Health in Early Childhood

8

Chapter Outline

How Do Children's Bodies and Brains Develop During Early Childhood?
Changing Body Size and Appearance
Brain Development

How Do Children's Motor Skills Develop During Early Childhood?
Gross Motor Skills
Fine Motor Skills
Handedness
Cultural and Racial Influences on Motor
   Development

What Are the Nutritional Needs and Sleep Patterns of Young Children?
Nutritional Needs and Eating Habits
Undernourishment and Malnourishment
Sleep Patterns and Problems

What Are the Health and Safety Needs of Young Children?
Diseases: Close-Up on Asthma
Accidents
Environmental Hazards

A DEVELOPMENTAL MYSTERY

Rob, a 7-year-old boy, feels his face splashed by water as Alex bumps him at the water fountain. In a situation like this one, most people's brains would help them accurately read social cues showing that no harm was intended; instead, Alex slipped and bumped into Rob. But Rob's brain works differently. He assumes the worst—that Alex is trying to hurt him, and Rob feels threatened. Instead of brushing this encounter off, Rob gets angry. He vows never to be friends with Alex.

Rob suffered child abuse when he was younger. Could Rob's abuse cause physical changes in the brain that make him react so negatively to Alex? Many abused children respond the way Rob does—does his brain interpret other people's emotions in a distinct way? Did his early abuse change the way his brain is structured and how it functions?

How children's physical development relates to their social experiences, and how family and social experiences influence physical development are fascinating developmental issues. Research on these issues shows how closely interconnected are children's physical and social lives.

How Do Children's Bodies and Brains Develop During Early Childhood?

Physical growth slows down in young children compared to their growth earlier in life, but nonetheless many important physical changes occurr during these years. Bodies continue to grow taller, stronger, and more coordinated. Most important are the changes that go on in the brain. Inside children's brains, the sheaths of fat that cover the neuronal connections grow quickly, allowing for faster and more efficient transfer of information. All of these physical changes provide children with increased competencies to function in the world.

Changing Body Size and Appearance

Remember the general physical characteristics of infants, which we discussed in Chapter 5—protruding stomach, short bowed legs, and a large head relative to body size. Compared to infants, the most notable physical feature of preschool children is that they lose their babyish appearance. Body fat decreases to approximately 12 percent of body weight, the stomach flattens as muscles strengthen, arms and legs grow longer and slimmer, and the body grows in size relative to the head.

During the preschool years, growth is not as rapid as it is during the infant years, but most children grow approximately 3 inches per year and gain 4 pounds per year. Girls and boys are very similar in their patterns of physical growth and development during the preschool years. The average 3-year-old boy is 38 inches tall and weighs 33 pounds, and the average 3-year-old girl is slightly smaller and lighter (Tanner, 1975).

Some children grow taller and develop more quickly than other children. What factors account for these differences? As you have learned, children's genetic endowment influences growth and development, with taller children being born to taller parents. In the United States, African American children tend to be taller than Caucasian American children, and both groups tend to be taller than Asian American children. However, children born in the United States, regardless of ethnic and racial background, tend to be taller than almost

Here you see an older child playing with her younger brother. What physical differences do you notice between them? Compare head size to body size—whose head is relatively larger? Who looks more babyish?

all other children around the world (Cratty, 1986). In addition to genetic endowment, good nutritional habits and better health care tend to foster taller children.

Brain Development

During the preschool years, a child's brain develops quickly, reaching 75 to 90 percent of adult size by age 5.

The Brain's Growth Spurt

In the first few years after birth, brain size increases markedly (Johnson, 2001). Remember from your reading in Chapter 5 that the two hemispheres of the brain develop at different times. The left hemisphere develops rapidly at around the age of 2; the right hemisphere, with its visual recognition systems, does not develop at the same rate. The growth spurt for the right hemisphere occurs at around the age of 4 or 5 (Dorsting, 1994; Fischer & Rose, 1994). Also at around age 5, the connections between the two hemispheres increase in number and become more efficient, allowing children to better coordinate functions involving both sides of the brain and body (Huttenlocher, 1990; 1994). The brain grows larger during this time because the neurons grow more interconnections, increasing the number and size of nerve endings (Nosphitz & King, 1991).

Increase in Myelination

Another change is an increase in myelination, which allows information to move more quickly between the cells in the brain. Remember that different parts of the brain myelinate at different times (see Chapter 5) and that myelination relates to the functioning of the area. Myelination occurs as **glial cells,** which provide physical and functional support for neurons, send out extensions that are wrapped around the axons of some neurons of the central nervous system. Remember from Chapter 5 that glial cells become wrapped around the axons of the neurons during myelination (see Figure 8.1). Although for many years the glial cells were considered to only have a supportive function for neurons, it is now acknowledged that these cells play a more active role in brain functioning (Lo Turco, 2000) by participating in transmitting chemical signals through the brain and controlling the establishment and maintenance of synapses between neurons (Ullian, Sapperstein, & Christopherson, 2001; Yuan & Ganetsky, 1999). Additional evidence about the role of myelin comes

glial cells _cells that provide physical and functional support for neurons_

prefrontal cortex _the front part of the brain, which is involved in planning, social behavior, and working memory_

FIGURE 8.1

Axon Wrapped by Glial Cells

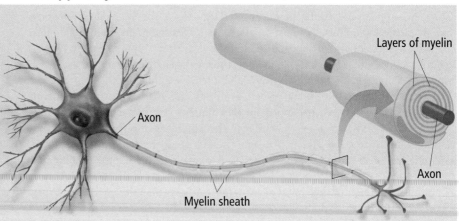

In what ways do glial cells function in the brain? Why does myelination improve the functioning of a neuron?

from brain imaging studies of people with psychological disorders. In one such study, the density of glial cells in certain parts of the brains of people with schizophrenia, bipolar disorder, and major depression was lower than that of unaffected people. It may be that the lower density of glial cells contributes to atrophy of neurons in the cortex for some people with psychological disorders (Uranova, Vostrikov, Orlovskaya, & Rachmanova, 2004).

The Developing Prefrontal Cortex

By early childhood, some areas, such as the sensory areas, of the brain have already been myelinated; and soon after, the motor areas begin to myelinate. In childhood, myelination of the prefrontal cortex is occurring, and this pattern of brain development continues until adolescence. The **prefrontal cortex** is the area in the front of the brain (see Figure 8.2), which is thought to be involved in complex cognitive behaviors. The rate of development of many children's skills and abilities may depend on myelination. For instance, the areas of the brain involved in hand–eye coordination are not completely myelinated until around the age of 4 or 5 (Konner, 1991; Tanner, 1978).

The continuing development of the prefrontal cortex throughout childhood and into adolescence means that this part of the brain has the most prolonged period of development of all the regions of the brain. Given the complexity and size of the prefrontal region, it is not surprising that there is no single accepted view about the functions that it controls. Nonetheless, evidence suggests that the prefrontal region of the brain plays a role in three different types of functions:

■ Goal setting and planning of sequences of actions

■ Inhibiting responses that are inappropriate

■ Working memory (keeping information available and accessible for short periods of time while it is being used) (Fujii & Graybiel, 2003; Hauser, 1999; Miller & Cohen, 2001)

Given that the functions associated with the prefrontal cortex are continuing to develop over childhood, and that this part of the brain is the last to develop, it should not be surprising that children have yet to reach adult-like levels of planning, behaving appropriately, and remembering. Nonetheless, during early childhood, children's abilities to plan improve, their behavior becomes more appropriate, and the function of their working memories is enhanced. The improvements that children show in these areas may enable them to successfully navigate the transition into formal schooling that would have been impossible just a year before.

Evidence of the importance of the prefrontal cortex has come from many different sources. For example, scientists have recognized that violent offenders often have impaired prefrontal areas (Bergvall, Wessely, Forsman, & Hansen, 2001). Additional evidence of the role of this part of the brain comes from case studies of people who sustained damage to the brain early in life. In one study, two individuals with damage to the prefrontal cortex that occurred before 16 months of age (in one case, due to a car accident) were tested as young adults. They showed normal basic cognitive abilities but were very severely impaired in social behavior, moral reasoning, and sensitivity to future consequences of decisions. They generally were unable to plan for the future. For instance, when playing a gambling game, they did not follow the typical pattern of opting for smaller immediate rewards and larger long-term gains; rather, they persisted in choosing response options that provided high immediate rewards but higher long-term loss (Anderson et al., 1999). It appears that early damage to this part of the brain causes long-term consequences for social behavior and the ability to set goals and execute plans to achieve them.

FIGURE 8.2

The Prefrontal Cortex

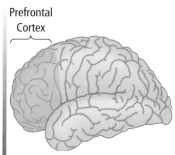

What is the role of the prefrontal cortex? How quickly does this area of the brain develop?

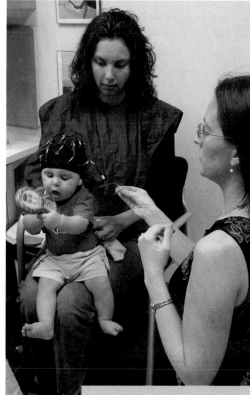

What aspect of brain functioning is measured with this device?

FIGURE 8.3
Experience Dependent Plasticity

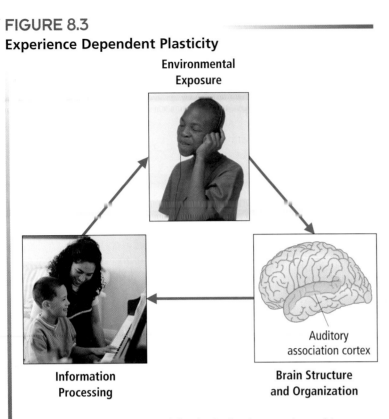

Environmental Exposure

Information Processing

Auditory association cortex

Brain Structure and Organization

Many studies have illustrated that brain development is sensitive to environmental exposure. What does this sensitivity imply about raising children in high- or low-quality environments? Why might environmental effects on the brain be long lasting?

Event Related Potentials (ERP) *a sharp increase in electrical activity in the brain that is created by exposure to a particular stimulus*

experience-dependent plasticity *a shift in the wiring of the brain based on the type of environment the person is exposed to*

auditory cortex *the part of the brain that responds to complex musical tones*

Experience-Based Changes in Brain Organization

Just as early damage can influence the way the brain is wired for assessing planning, early negative experiences can impact how the brain becomes organized, which in turn influences how information is interpreted (see Figure 8.3). In the mystery that opened the chapter, we speculated that Rob's brain is different from those of many other children in the way it processes information about emotion. How might this happen? In a study of the influence of early negative experience on development, the brain electrical activity of children who had been physically abused was compared with that of children who had not been abused; during the study, the children watched people displaying different types of emotions such as anger, happiness, fear, and sadness. The children wore a cap with electrodes that measure **Event Related Potential** (ERP), which is a sharp increase in electrical activity in the brain that is created by exposure to a particular stimulus. When children recognize a particular expression, they respond with a sudden burst of electrical activity. Compared to children who had not been abused, children who had been physically abused were very quick to detect that a face showed anger, yet they were slower to detect sadness. The abused children probably had more exposure to anger in their homes and had come to associate expressions of anger with their parents' high-intensity aggressive outbursts and even physical injury (Pollak & Sinha, 2002).

Thus, the abused children seemed equipped with an "early detection system," an adaptive and protective brain mechanism that forewarns them about impending parental anger. Unfortunately, the same system may hinder these children in their peer relationships, as described in the chapter opening, because they might be quick to jump to the conclusion that someone intends to harm them. In terms of brain development, these results are an example of **experience-dependent plasticity,** by which the wiring of the brain changes pattern based on the type of environment a person experiences.

Early music training also changes the organization and functioning of the human brain. Using functional magnetic resonance imaging of the brain, in which blood flow to functioning areas of the brain is registered, researchers have discovered that children who have had early musical training tend to have an expanded **auditory cortex,** the part of the brain that responds to complex musical tones (Rauschecker, 1999). Neurodevelopmental research indicates that features of the environment—either positive (such as musical training) or negative (such as physical abuse)—influence brain development in complex ways during the early years.

Experience-dependent plasticity allows each person's brain to become finely attuned to their own experiences and environments. Just as infants' exposure to chronic stress and unpleasant parenting experiences can interfere with their brain development (see Chapter 5), the paths of development in young children's brains can also be shifted by experiencing non-optimal environments.

How Do Children's Motor Skills Improve During Early Childhood?

Consider the following scenario. Tracy, age 4, throws a large red ball to her 15-month-old sister, Kim. Kim reaches for it but is unable to catch it. Kim leans forward to retrieve the ball and toddles unsteadily. Tracy runs toward her, picks up the ball, hands it to Kim, and says, "Now you throw it to me." Kim tries to throw the ball, but it falls out of her hand and rolls away. Leaner and taller preschoolers like Tracy move more quickly and steadily than do toddlers like Kim, and they can run, jump, and throw a ball with good accuracy.

Gross Motor Skills

The development of children's brains lays the groundwork for other forms of development, including how they move about, control their bodies, and use their hands. As their brains develop, vision and balance improve, allowing children to gain more control over motor skills. For instance, after a year of coordinating all the systems required for standing and walking, toddlers take another year to perfect walking. Soon after, children begin trying many variations in their movements, including walking sideways, walking backward, and walking on their toes. New skills are emerging rapidly in the third year. With little training, children learn to run, throw balls, ride tricycles, use a slide, and jump. By age 4, they can turn somersaults and walk up and down stairs, alternating their feet. By age 5, children can jump rope, skate, and skip, alternating their feet. By age 6, they throw and catch balls and can climb and swing with ease (see Figure 8.4). Both girls and boys show similar patterns of motor development.

DEBATING THE ISSUE

AUTISM AND THE BRAIN—ARE GIRLS' AND BOYS' BRAINS DIFFERENT?

Prenatal hormones are known to influence the structure and development of the human brain differently for males and females, although debate continues as to the extent of these differences and how they translate into behavior. Adding to the debate is a new book on sex differences in the brain by autism researcher Simon Baron-Cohen (2003) of Cambridge University. He theorizes that the female brain is predominantly wired for empathy and the male brain for understanding and building systems, a distinction he calls "empathizing—systematizing." According to Baron-Cohen, autism, the neurological disorder that affects social interaction and communication, may be an extreme male version of the brain. Interestingly, boys are

diagnosed with autism more often than girls are. People with autism show deficits in social interaction, while at the same time they show a strong drive to systematize. For instance, a particular 5-year-old autistic boy may be capable of memorizing dozens of car registrations and explaining which car belongs to which house, but he would be unable to initiate a conversation.

Of course, this theory does not tell us how autistic children might come to be this way; it may be that male hormones play a role, but further research is needed to explain the origins of autism, including where in the brain structure the sexes differ and how those differences might be demonstrated in everyday life. Furthermore, no one, even Baron-Cohen, believes that all males think in one way and all females think in the other way.

Careful attention to individual differences in children is important in trying to assess their competencies.

THINKING IT THROUGH

1. What additional evidence would be needed to support Baron-Cohen's conclusion?

2. Can you imagine a disorder that could be described as an extreme version of the tendency Baron-Cohen sees in the female brain? What would this disorder be like?

3. Is the empathizing—systematizing distinction a useful way to think about the balance of competencies of individuals? Why or why not?

FIGURE 8.4
Milestones in Motor Development

	2–3 YEARS OF AGE	3–4 YEARS OF AGE	4–5 YEARS OF AGE	5–6 YEARS OF AGE
GROSS MOTOR SKILLS	• Runs forward well • Jumps in place with two feet together • Stands on one foot with aid • Walks on tiptoe • Kicks a ball forward	• Runs around obstacles • Walks on a line • Balances on one foot for 5–10 seconds • Hops on one foot • Rides tricycle • Throws ball overhead • Catches a bounced ball	• Walks backward toe to heel • Jumps forward 10 times without falling • Walks up and down stairs independently • Turns somersault	• Runs lightly on toes • Walks on balance beam • Hops 6 feet • Skips on alternate feet • Jumps rope • Skates
FINE MOTOR SKILLS	• Strings four large beads • Turns single pages • Snips with scissors • Holds crayon with thumb and finger (not fist)	• Builds tower of nine small blocks • Drives nails and pegs • Copies circle • Manipulates clay (rolls it into balls and snakes) • Eats with a spoon • Uses one hand consistently in most activities	• Cuts on line continuously • Copies cross and square • Prints some capital letters • Dreses self • Draws tadpole figures	• Cuts out simple shapes • Copies triangle • Copies first name • Draws letters • Colors within lines • Uses adult grasp of pencil • Unzips a zipper • Has well-established handedness

Children's motor skills change dramatically during young childhood. What factors account for these changes?

Adapted from Learning Disabilities, ___. Available at http://www.ldonline.org/ld_indepth/early_identification/motorskills_milestones.html

One key factor in the development of motor skills is the development of children's visual systems. Areas of the brain associated with the ability to focus the eyes and with eye movements continue to develop through early childhood. The development of visual pathways, combined with improving communication between the hemispheres, results in advances in eye–hand coordination and allows preschoolers to become better at understanding left–right directions.

Another important factor for motor development is balance, which contributes greatly to the proliferation of skills that children exhibit during the preschool years. Children with visual or inner-ear problems may have difficulty integrating the sensory information necessary for good balance (Hatton, Bailey, Burchinal, & Ferrell, 1997). A lack of balance interferes with the stability they need to perform more complex skills such as kicking and throwing. Practice, imitating others, and others' expectations and encouragement also play important roles in motor development. For example, children with older siblings develop motor skills more rapidly than other children do (Samuels, 1980).

Although some children take longer to develop motor skills than others, a small group of children are clumsy—they are unable to coordinate parts of their bodies for activities such as throwing a ball, hopping, or drawing. Because clumsy children may be improperly labeled as learning disabled or may suffer from teasing, early identification of motor development problems and referral to treatment programs can benefit children. Other children may show significant delays in motor development, such as not being able to hop on one foot by age 6 or being unable to jump across a small object at 4 years, and these children benefit from early identification so that their motor development delays can be addressed (Bertenthal & Clifton, 1998).

Running and Jumping

Very young children sometimes appear to be running; however, it is not until they are 2 to 3 years of age that they show true running, during which both feet leave the ground. Even then, they are not well-controlled runners; they are unable to stop or start quickly. By the time children are 4 to 5 years old, their running ability has greatly improved, and most can run twice as fast as they did when they were 2 (Cratty, 1986).

What changes occur in running (or jumping) during young childhood? How do changes in the visual system and in ability to balance influence the development of this motor skill?

Children's first attempts at jumping are one-footed steps off an object, usually occurring at around 18 months of age. By age 2, most children can use a two-footed takeoff to propel themselves off an object, but they are not very efficient in using their arms to enhance their motion. By age 4, most children can jump on level ground, using their arms appropriately to help propel them. And by age 5, most children can jump a distance of 3 feet (Cratty, 1986).

Throwing and Catching

Throwing and catching a ball are complex motor skills that develop in stages over the early childhood period (Marques-Bruna & Grinshaw, 1997). Throwing gradually comes to involve more of the body and greater body rotation. Mature throwers rotate around the central axis of their body and shift their weight forward. In contrast, 2- to 3-year-olds often use a rigid underhand toss with no body movement. By 3 years, children can throw overhand with some body rotation, but they keep their feet firmly on the ground. By age 5 or 6, most children step with the opposite foot and shift their weight when throwing, and their speed and accuracy improve with age.

Throwing proceeds from a toddler's accidental letting go of an object to a 2 to 4-year old's variable throws (pictured here). How will this child's throwing technique improve by the age of 6?

Children's ability to catch a ball also develops during childhood, with better visual tracking of the ball, more flexible positioning of their arms during the "catch," and faster reaction times. Very young children tend to hold their arms stiffly in front of them to catch a ball and sometimes close their eyes or turn their head away to avoid the ball. By 4, most children watch the ball coming and hold their hands open to receive it. By 5 to 6 years of age, most children hold their arms and elbows flexibly to absorb the force of the ball.

Fine Motor Skills

To be able to cut with a pair of scissors or fold pieces of paper, children must organize the coordination of their hands and eyes, using the small muscles in their hands precisely. These fine motor skills develop markedly during the early childhood period.

Differentiation, Coordination, and Control

Although infants can grasp small objects between the forefinger and thumb, precise movements of individual fingers take several more years to achieve (Geraldson & Hopkins, 1997). Biological factors play a role in finger differentiation: children with brain damage often cannot use each finger individually and instead use their hands as though they were encased in a fingerless mitt (Cratty, 1986).

The developmental progression in fine motor skills from less to more differentiation, coordination, and control is apparent during the preschool years. This is the same type of developmental pattern we saw with infants. Remember that young infants move their whole body when stimulated; as they grow older, they can respond only by using the arm or leg that is stimulated. Increasing differentiation is apparent in motor development during early childhood as well. For instance, 2-year-olds can scribble while holding a crayon in their fist, but by age 2½, they can scribble while holding the crayon between thumb and fingers. Also, by age 2, children can put on some articles of clothing, turn pages in a book, and construct towers consisting of six to eight blocks. Three-year-olds have better-developed fine motor skills: they can eat with a spoon, copy a circle, and pour from a pitcher. By age 4, children can dress themselves, draw tadpole-like human figures (see Figure 8.5), and cut on a line with scissors. Most 5-year-olds can fasten buttons, draw letters, unzip a zipper, and string beads. With increasing age, each skill is performed more competently as children gain experience through practice and as their brains, visual systems, and coordination improve with age.

FIGURE 8.5
Tadpole People

About how old were the children who drew these "tadpole" people? What physical characteristics do these children represent in their drawings? What aspects of the physical development of young children do the drawings represent?

Source: From *Artful Scribbles* by Howard Gardner. Copyright © 1980 by Howard Gardner. Reprinted by permission of Basic Books, a member of Perseus Books Group, L.L.C.

Developmental Changes in Drawing

Why do young children all over the world draw tadpole-like human figures? Researchers interested in children's art have examined thousands of drawings by children to analyze the developmental changes in drawings as children grow older. The progression begins with scribbles, usually starting at around 18 months, often done with a crayon held in the fist. Scribbling provides sensory enjoyment, but also the child is interested in the marks that he or she makes. Early scribbles may represent movements, such as hopping a crayon across a page to represent a rabbit's movements (Winner, 1986). First scribbles are challenging because children have difficulty with placing the marks exactly where they intend them to go. Drawing movements are large and imprecise, involving the whole arm, with little finger or wrist control. Rhythmic, repetitive motions are common in first scribbles. With practice, children gain more and more control, and they can use finer discrimination of the muscles, moving only the fingers and wrist rather than the whole arm. Full control, however, is very difficult and does not occur until much later (Cratty, 1986).

There are over 20 different basic scribbles that children tend to draw, and their placement of scribbles on a page is not random (Kellogg, 1970). At around the age of 3, children begin to recognize certain familiar features—seeing their dog, a cow, or a house in their scribbles. These features were not intentionally drawn; rather, they are identified by shape similarities that occur by accident. For example, after noticing that his scribbles looked like noodles, one 2-year-old boy labeled his drawing as "chicken pie and noodles" (Winner, 1986).

At age 2 to 3, children undergo a major milestone in drawing; they begin to use lines to represent the boundaries of things, and this development leads to the drawing of shapes, such as primitive squares, circles, rectangles, and crosses (Kellogg, 1970). Soon after, they begin to combine these shapes into aggregates to form realistic drawings of common objects or people (Barrett & Eames, 1996). These drawings do not reflect reality to any great degree. Young children are not good at representing depth, and they often include things in their pictures that are not really visible based on realistic perspective (e.g., all the wheels of a car; Cox & Littleton, 1995).

Often children's first attempts at combining shapes is to draw a person—a tadpole person, one with arms and legs growing out of the circular body–head lump. Eyes, mouths, and noses are included in early tadpole drawings of people. Even belly buttons are often included in the head/body area. Why do children draw like this? Do they think people look like this, with no bodies or necks? One possibility is that children draw what they see on their own bodies. If you look down, you see arms coming out of your head. Maybe that is what children draw. Or is it just easy and convenient to draw tadpoles? Some research suggests that this is the case: when given blocks or tiles to "build" a person, children include heads and trunks (Cox, 1992). As children grow older, their tadpoles give way to more realistic-looking people with arms and legs that have shape, necks, body shape, and shoulders (Cox, 1992).

In the preschool years, children's drawings are fanciful: the sky and ground may not meet, grass may be purple, and dogs may be orange. All perspectives may be represented in a drawing—the right profile, the left profile, and the front view, all at the same time. Whereas younger children are not concerned about proportion or perspective, by age 6 or 7, children strive to make their drawings look more realistic. Some children learn to solve the problem of representing perspective to their satisfaction, but some children get discouraged because they are unable to do this well (Gardner, 1980).

Cultural Influences on Drawing

How does culture influence children's drawing? Some cultures value drawing as art whereas others show no evidence of drawing. In studies of children's art in different cultures (e.g., Alland, 1983), children who are given drawing materials and whose cultures value drawing tend to spend time enjoying drawing, and they gain experience in it. Also, children's drawings reflect aspects of the culture in which they are raised (Hondt, Cambier, & Vandewiele, 1989). For instance, girls in Africa draw earrings on women, but few European girls do this (Hondt et al., 1989). Japanese children tend to draw complex and harmonious pictures as

FIGURE 8.6
Cultural Differences in Drawing

Is it surprising that children from different countries draw different types of pictures? How does culture influence drawing content and style?

compared to North American children (Alland, 1983). Swazi children in Africa draw their mothers taller than their fathers when their fathers do not live with them, probably suggesting that their mothers have taken on increased importance in their lives (Booth & Matuga, 2003).

Children who have had little experience in drawing, when given the opportunity, tend to scribble and experiment in many different ways. Their attempts to draw people may look like stick figures or tadpole people, even among older children; children in remote villages in Papua New Guinea, where there is no pictorial art, tend to do this (Martlew & Connolly, 1996). When they draw, children imitate the designs and compositions they see around them in fabrics, written letters or numbers, or the art they are exposed to. American preschoolers tend to incorporate letters and numbers into their drawings; Taiwanese children include Chinese characters in theirs (Crosser, 2004). Similarly, just like their parents, Australian Aboriginal children draw "dream-time" stories about the land of their ancestors, but to us, these images appear to be abstract dot paintings (see Figure 8.6). For the children, the dots represent hills, streams, animals, and campsites.

Handedness

Parents often wonder whether their children will be right- or left-handed. Handedness is influenced more by genetics than environment (McManus & Bryden, 1992), and most children and adults (92 percent) are right handed (Coren & Porac, 1977). Infants do not show strong hand preferences; instead, they vary the use of their hands. Stable preferences emerge for most children at around 3 to 4 years of age. The links between hand preferences and brain development have become more obvious as researchers examine competencies and handedness (Annett, 1993; Coren & Halpern, 1991; Geschwind & Galaburda, 1985, 1987). Some evidence suggests that an early (4 to 6 months of age) and strong hand preference may indicate that the infant has a neurological problem (Harris, 1992). Hand preferences are related to how the brain is organized. Children with right-hand preferences tend to have stronger lateralization of their brains, meaning that their left hemisphere is more strongly dominant for language processing and their right for spatial tasks. In contrast, children with left-hand preferences tend to have less lateralized brains, meaning that the two hemispheres show less specialization of function. These differences, in turn, have been found to relate to some of children's competencies, particularly in language. Using a battery of nine language tests on 135 school-age children, researchers in Greece found that right-handed children showed superior language skills as compared to left-handed children (Natsopoulos, Kiosseoglou, Xeromeritou, & Alevriadou, 1998).

What factors might explain why some African American children show advanced motor skills?

To test a preschooler's hand preference, it is best to use a task that is somewhat challenging because either hand may be used for a simple task, such as reaching for an object. For children, the tasks commonly used to assess handedness include writing, drawing, eating, pointing, and throwing. However, an indeterminate number of children and adults are ambidextrous—they switch preferred hands, depending on the task they need to do. Even for the same task, they will sometimes prefer the right hand and other times the left hand (Porac, Coren, & Searleman, 1986). For many generations, left-handedness was actively discouraged in schools. Even today, our environment is structured to favor right-handers, but parents are encouraged to let children's natural handedness prevail (Coren, 1993).

Cultural and Racial Influences on Motor Development

You may be thinking that one aspect of development that is not influenced by culture is motor development. However, even motor development varies, depending on one's culture. Children with African origins typically are more advanced in motor development than children with European origins: they throw farther, balance better, and run better (Cratty, 1986). The reasons for these differences are varied and complex. Genetic factors may play a role, specifically in influencing the length and proportions of arms, legs, and the overall body size. Cultural factors—including parenting practices, nutrition, and the perceived importance of motor skill development—also play a role, however. Mothers in Nigeria, Uganda, Sierra Leone, India, and Pakistan encourage their children to walk and stand up more quickly and train them in motor development. For instance, Nigerian and West Indian mothers use passive stretching movements, massage, and active encouragement in the first year of a child's life to promote motor development (Hopkins, 1991) (see Chapter 5). Interestingly, in two African groups that do not encourage early motor development (the Baganda and the Somia), the infants and children show slower development of motor skills than do Caucasian children in the United States (Kilbride, 1980).

Cultural and biological factors likely interact to influence children's motor development. For instance, African American infants show early motor precocity and are especially reactive, which may, in turn, contribute in a transactional way to caregivers' encouragement of their motor skills (Rosser & Randolph, 1989). In other words, as these children exhibit high levels of motor skills, their parents may further encourage these skills, which in turn further promotes skill development.

What Are the Nutritional Needs and Sleep Patterns of Young Children?

Children's physical, motor, and cognitive development depend on being in good health, having adequate nutrition, and getting rest each night (Georgieff & Rao, 2001). Children who do not eat well or sleep well are likely to have a variety of problems, including being at risk for accidents, being less likely to learn new information, and being less likely to have the energy to play and practice their motor skills.

Nutritional Needs and Eating Habits

As children grow older, their nutritional requirements change to meet different growth and activity needs. Remember that infants and toddlers need more fat in their diets than do young children because their brains and bodies are growing so quickly. The healthful diet for young children is somewhere between that of toddlers and adults. Young children

Do you think that each of these children is eating a healthy lunch? What strategies can caregivers use to encourage preschoolers to eat more healthful meals?

require a relatively high number of calories because they are very active—they are running, jumping, and climbing. However, because the rate of growth slows in childhood, their appetite may not be as strong as it was when they were infants and toddlers. Young children are often finicky eaters, and caregivers worry that children are not eating enough to obtain adequate nutrition. However, the nutritional requirements of young children can be met with small, healthful meals. An average preschooler requires about 1,700 calories per day, with less than 35 percent of the calories coming from fat.

Children over the age of 2 need a varied diet that includes whole grains, vegetables, fruits, milk and high-protein foods, and moderate fat. Compared with infants and toddlers, young children need more energy and protein because of their greater body size. The fat content of young children's diets should be gradually reduced from the levels of toddlerhood; much of this reduction in fat can be achieved by using reduced-fat dairy products (Smolin & Grosnevor, 2000). The ideal level of fat is about 35 percent of calories in a preschooler's diet (for adults, the recommended level is 30 percent). A healthful diet for a young child includes the following:

- Two servings each of milk, meat, fruit
- Three servings of vegetables
- Six servings of bread and grains (USDA, 2004)

Children of ages 2 to 4 need fewer calories than older children do, and their servings' sizes should be about two thirds of the size of portions for older children. Young children tend to get these servings in different ways than adults and older children do. They often eat luncheon meats and ground beef rather than fish; they are less likely to eat salads and more likely to drink fruit juice and eat whole fruit. Overall, many preschoolers' diets do not meet the recommended servings from the meat, fruit, and grain groups. For instance, preschoolers tend to eat only 1½ servings of vegetables instead of the 3 that are recommended (USDA, 2004).

Caregivers face a variety of challenges in providing healthful, safe diets for young children. Until age 4, many children have difficulty swallowing and chewing, and so they are at risk for choking on foods such as grapes, cherries, raisins, popcorn, and hard candies. To prevent choking, these foods should be avoided or cut into smaller pieces. Also, some children, such as 4-year-old Erin, are finicky eaters and want to eat only "slurpy noodles." Caregivers find it challenging to deal with young children's strong food preferences—for instance, a desire to eat only peanut butter and jelly sandwiches every day. How do parents

NURTURING CHILDREN
HELPING YOUNG CHILDREN BECOME HEALTHY EATERS

To help caregivers make better food selections for their children, several consumer groups have assessed popular children's foods. In one assessment of children's convenience foods, ten non-diet foods were identified by nutritionists as having relatively low fat, low sodium, and low cholesterol. These healthful foods were tested and found to be foods that young children enjoyed. The nutritionists discovered, however, that many foods that are tasty to children, especially convenience soups, are high in sodium (salt). Parents can increase the nutritional value of these foods by adding a vegetable side dish (Sizer & Whitney, 1997). The following table presents information on some of these relatively healthy convenience foods.

Calories, Fat, and Sodium in Convenience Foods That Children Enjoy

Convenience Food	Calories	Fat (%)	Sodium (mg)
Light vegetable pizza	240	26	500
Fat-free deli sliced turkey breast (1 oz)	360	33	225
Fish fillets (3 oz)	130	21	220
BBQ chicken meal	370	7	670
Chicken nuggets, corn, pudding	360	33	500
Prepared rice or noodle dishes	420	10	760

ensure that children get adequate nutrition? One strategy is to provide small amounts of varied foods at every meal. As children gain familiarity with different foods, they are more likely to eat them. Give the child four choices of new foods to try, and let the child help select them. Children also need several small snacks during the day, and at these times healthful choices can be encouraged. Exposure to others in the family who are eating healthful foods is useful, too. Creativity in food preparation also helps: making foods into interesting shapes, giving foods special names to encourage eating, and letting children help prepare foods may be useful strategies for encouraging healthy nutrition (see the Nurturing Children box).

Undernourishment and Malnourishment

Inadequate nutrition is implicated in more than half of child deaths worldwide (UNICEF, 2001). Almost 200 million of the world's children below 5 years of age are underweight and likely to be suffering from undernourishment. Undernourishment is more common in parts of Africa and Asia than elsewhere in the world (Pollitt et al., 1996; UNICEF, 2001). Undernourishment is closely associated with economic impoverishment, limited health care and educational opportunities, and poor living conditions. When food is scarce, children's diets consist largely of cereals and legumes, and they eat few fruits, vegetables, and animal products. Thus, undernourished children often are malnourished as well—they do not receive adequate proteins, vitamins, and minerals.

kwashiorkor *a form of protein energy malnutrition in which only protein is deficient*

marasmus *a form of protein-energy malnutrition involving severe body wasting*

Deficiencies from Inadequate Diets

Children in developing nations are more likely than children in the United States to have inadequate diets. Children in Africa, South and Central America, the Near East, and the Far East are at risk for protein-energy malnutrition (PEM), which ranges from pure protein deficiency, called **kwashiorkor,** to energy deficiency, called **marasmus.** In the language of the Ga tribe of the African Gold Coast, *kwashiorkor* means "the disease that the first child gets when a second child is born." With the birth of a new sibling, children who have been fed protein-rich breast milk are switched to a watered-down version of the diet that the adults eat. This diet is low in protein and high in fiber, so it is difficult to digest. Because children grow more quickly than adults, their protein requirements are higher and the effects of protein deficiency are more evident. Children with kwashiorkor have stunted growth, susceptibility to infection, and bloated stomachs. Bloating is due to fluids that accumulate in the stomach because there is not enough protein to maintain the fluids in the blood.

Marasmus, which means "to waste away," is due to a deficiency of energy. Children with marasmus are emaciated because their body fat has been used to provide energy. Marasmus has devastating effects on development: early energy deficiencies cause decreases in intelligence and learning ability that persist throughout life. Children may develop marasmus because of limited access to food; for instance, marasmus can result from being fed diluted infant formula by caregivers trying to stretch limited supplies. Protein-energy malnutrition is a major public health problem. Approximately one third of children under the age of 5 in developing countries are underweight, and about 10 percent have body wasting (World Health Organization, 1997). Nutritional supplements can be given to counteract the cognitive and other developmental problems associated with nutritional deficiencies (Grantham-McGregor, Ani, & Fernald, 2001).

Approximately 13 million children in the United States are malnourished—about 1 in 4—and most of these children are from low-income families (UNICEF, 2001). A common problem for young children who do not eat enough meats and green vegetables is lack of iron, which results in chronic fatigue. Serious iron deficiencies lead to **iron-deficiency anemia,** a common nutrient deficiency. Some children may be malnourished even though they consume enough calories. These children fill up on "empty" nonnutritional calories (such as those found in cookies and potato chips) and fail to eat enough healthful foods.

Undernutrition among preschoolers and school-age children is a serious health concern because of the many adverse consequences associated with it. Undernourished children tend to have stunted growth and delayed motor development (Simeon & Grantham-McGregor, 1990). They also are at risk for cognitive disabilities such as low levels of attention, learning impairments, and poor academic and school-related performance (Hurtado, Claussen, & Scott, 1999; Wachs, 1995).

Functional Isolation

Why do undernourishment and malnourishment have such pervasive and negative effects on children? One idea that may explain these effects is **functional isolation**—malnourished children become increasingly disengaged from their social and physical environments (Brown & Pollitt, 1996). Functional isolation results from direct and indirect effects of poor environment and inadequate nutrition. If children's diets lack iron, for example, their brain development will be impaired and delayed (Georgieff & Rao, 2001). Diminished brain development—accompanied by attempts to reduce energy expenditures by withdrawing from stimulation—influences children's behavior. The children may become more wary, easily tired, less attentive, and less playful, and they rarely show delight and pleasure (Lozoff et al., 1998; Lozoff et al., 2000). Because these children are not very responsive, caregivers do not interact with them much. Caregivers expect less from these children, so the children receive even less stimulation. Over time, they withdraw from their physical and social environments, increasing the likelihood that outcomes will be poor (see Figure 8.7).

Some children with inadequate nutrition live in families that cannot afford the food they need. However, many children lack nutritious diets even when food is abundant. Because of increased demands on family time, families often stop for fast food meals or prepare high-fat convenience foods at home, thereby including high levels of fat and sodium in the diet. Caregivers can limit children's fat and sodium intake by screening convenience foods based on their labels, curtailing fast food consumption, and carefully selecting the fast foods that are offered.

iron-deficiency anemia *a nutrient deficiency common among infants and toddlers*

functional isolation *increased disengagement from social and physical environments that may result from a poor environment and inadequate nutrition*

FIGURE 8.7

Bidirectional Model of Outcomes for Children with Nutritional Developmental Problems

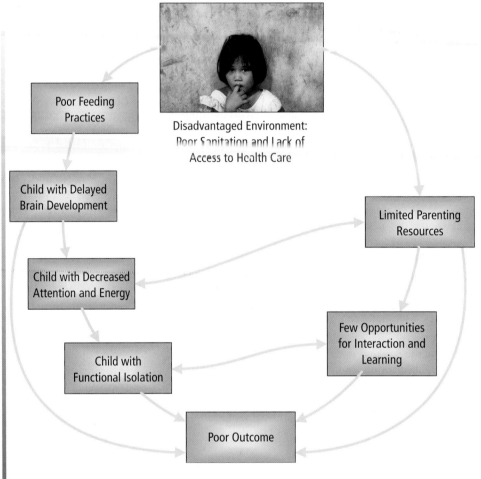

Notice that a disadvantaged environment has multiple effects, both direct and indirect, on children's development. The bidirectional effects can be seen in the interplay between children's having less energy and paying less attention and caregivers' having limited resources and lowered expectations. Each factor is an action as well as a reaction to the other factors.

Source: Lozoff et al., 1988.

Sleep Patterns and Problems

Sleep is a natural part of everyone's life—so much so that survival may depend on it. Rats that are deprived of sleep die within two to three weeks, a time frame similar to death due to starvation (Rechtschaffen et al., 2002). Thus, sleep is no less important to young children's healthy development than are food, drink, safety, and exercise.

Typical Sleep Requirements

As you have already learned, sleep during early infancy is quite different than the sleep of adults, but this changes at around 6 months of age, when the proportion of REM (rapid eye movement) and NREM sleep becomes more adultlike. In newborns, the amount of sleep is equally divided between night and day. Nighttime sleep gradually consolidates over the first three years into a single uninterrupted block of time, and daytime sleep decreases

FIGURE 8.8
Typical Sleep Requirements in Childhood

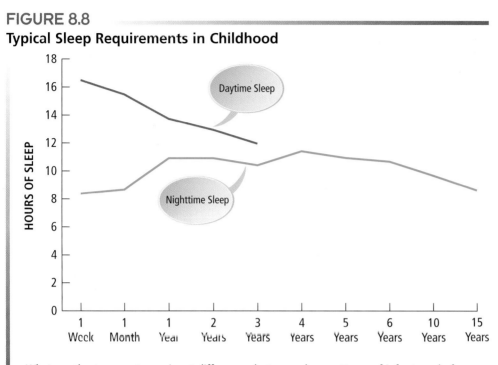

What are the two most prominent differences between sleep patterns of infants and of young children?

Source: Adapted from Ferber, 1985.

during this time (see Figure 8.8). By the age of 4, most children no longer take a daytime nap. In addition, across the period of childhood, the overall amount of required sleep diminishes so that by the time a child is age 15, his or her sleep patterns are similar to that of an adult (Thiedke, 2001).

Although sleep is controlled by physiological processes, cultural, familial, and other factors dramatically influence children's sleep habits. As you can see in Figure 8.8, total sleep duration declines rapidly across childhood; however, wake-up times are more consistent across ages (Ishihara & Miyake, 1998). Such findings suggest that the time at which children go to sleep is more age-dependent, but the time at which they wake up is determined more by environmental factors. School and parents' work schedules have a great impact on sleep during childhood.

Sleeping Through the Night

Sleeping through the night is a critical milestone that most parents eagerly look forward to. Although most children are able to sleep through the night by 6 months of age, it is a milestone that is not always maintained once it is achieved. Children who previously slept through the night can suddenly have difficulties doing so—but this is usually due to social rather than maturational factors (Thiedke, 2001). Studies indicate that night awakenings are common during early childhood, with about one child in three up to 4 years of age having difficulty sleeping through the night and requiring intervention by a parent to return to sleep (Adair & Bauchner, 1993).

When young children have trouble sleeping, it is difficult to know whether the problem is the cause or consequence of other problems. For example, as you will soon learn, sleep problems are related to a variety of behavior and health problems in children (Dahl, 1996; Sadeh, Raviv, & Gruber, 2000). But just as sleep problems might be a symptom of other problems or significant stress in a child's life, adjustment problems also might result from or be exaggerated by insufficient sleep, fatigue, and sleepiness.

Sleep Problems

Sleep problems are extremely common in children and often are the cause of tremendous worry, frustration, anger, and distress at home. In Western countries, estimates of sleep problems range from 10 to 45 percent for children (Stores, 1999), and few differences have been found between boys and girls (Kahn et al., 1989). The large discrepancy in the rates of sleep problems is due to the different methods, samples, and definitions used to define sleep disorders (Liu et al., 2000).

Studies of sleep problems among children in non-Western countries also reveal considerable, but lower, rates. For example, Liu and colleagues (2000) found that rates of sleep problems among Chinese children averaged around 12 percent. Such findings may reflect cultural and/or biological differences. Chinese parents and children, for instance, are much more likely to share a bed than is the case for families in Western cultures. By some estimates (Liu, Liu, & Wang, 2003), over half of young Chinese children share a bed with their parents. In Western countries, most parents and professionals focus on the hazards of bed sharing—such as impeding the development of autonomy, fostering dependency on parents, or interfering with parents' sexual intimacy. In contrast, Asian cultural beliefs about childrearing stress the development of interdependence, conformity, and family closeness. Consider the fact that almost 75 percent of Korean mothers approved of bed sharing for their children between 3 and 6 years of age (Yang & Hahn, 2002). The main reasons for bed sharing were "to look after the child while sleeping" and "child too young to sleep alone." These reasons are very unlikely to be given by Western parents and reflect cultural differences in beliefs and childrearing. Thus, the lower rates of sleep problems in Asian cultures are likely due to differences in cultural background and parental responsiveness, as well as differences in genetic characteristics (Liu et al., 2000).

During early childhood, many types of sleep problems begin to appear, and these differ from the more general problems of scheduling sleep for infants and young toddlers (such as problems associated with nighttime feeding). For example, during early childhood, nightmares and night terrors often appear. Although they share some commonalities, important differences characterize the two phenomena. Nightmares—bad dreams—are relatively common during childhood—almost all children experience them occasionally. They usually begin at around the age of 2 but are most common for children of 3 to 6 years of age. Nightmares usually take place during light sleep. Many children wake themselves up with their own movements or by talking, yelling, or crying, reactions that only add to the fright. Children who have awakened themselves may be very frightened, and they may be difficult to calm. They may not want to go back to sleep.

Some children have nightmares more often than others. One child may have bad dreams only a few times per year, and another may have them more frequently. Nightmares often come in phases, such as a succession occurring every night for a week or more, and then none at all for weeks or months. Although it is unclear why children have nightmares, they usually involve some kind of anxiety regarding a threat to the child's well-being (such as being lost or threatened). Nightmares generally affect girls more than boys, but most often do not present enduring or serious problems.

Night terrors (or pavor nocturnes) are different from nightmares and are characterized by repeated episodes of abrupt awakening, usually with a panicky scream, and accompanied by intense anxiety, disorientation, unresponsiveness, and an inability to remember details about the event. Children with night terrors often scream uncontrollably and wake themselves up. Often they are confused and inconsolable for up to 30 minutes before finally relaxing and going back to sleep (Thiedke, 2001). Night terrors are more likely to occur during times of stress or fatigue but typically are limited to short periods of time and then disappear.

Why is daytime tiredness a serious issue for children? In what ways does getting adequate sleep improve children's lives?

night terrors *sleep disturbance characterized by repeated episodes of abrupt awakening, accompanied by intense anxiety, disorientation, unresponsiveness, and an inability to remember details about the event*

FROM RESEARCH TO PRACTICE
SLEEPINESS AND CHILDHOOD INJURIES

In studies of adults, sleepiness has been found to be a factor related to vehicle injuries and accidents (Sagberg, 1999). But is there a similar pattern for children—is sleepiness related to the incidence of children's unintentional injuries and accidents? According to some recent research (Valent, Drusaferro, & Barbone, 2000), inadequate sleep and lack of daytime naps may increase the risk of injury for young children.

FROM RESEARCH . . .

To examine this issue, Italian researchers examined 292 injured children who came to a children's emergency center of a hospital in northern Italy. Information on the injury was collected at the hospital. In addition, for each child, sleep information was collected for the 48 hours before the injury occurred. The researchers then compared the sleep status of each child for the first 24 hours before the injury to the last 24 hours before the injury. That is, they compared sleep patterns during hours 1–24 to the patterns reported during hours 25–48 (the day before the injury occurred). By doing this, the researchers could use each child as their own comparison. Thus, the researchers could control for factors such as personality, age, sex, or other child-specific characteristic that may influence sleep patterns.

During the study, more boys (62 percent) than girls (38 percent) came to the emergency room to have an injury treated. Falls were the leading cause (43 percent), followed by injuries due to striking or being struck by objects or people (16 percent) and bicycle accidents (13 percent). Falls were particularly likely to be the cause of injury for those children under the age of 6 years. There were few differences between boys and girls for the types of accidents that caused an injury. Additionally, injuries were more likely to occur late in the day (4:00 to 7:00 P.M.) and during weekends.

When the researchers examined the sleep data, a significant pattern emerged. Comparisons of daily sleep highlighted that more children had less sleep the day before the injury than they did during the 24 hours before that. In general, sleeping fewer than 10 hours per day was associated with an 86 percent increase in children's risk of injury. For injuries that occurred between 4:00 P.M. and midnight, children who had been awake for at least 8 hours were four times more likely to be injured than those who were not. These differences were greatest for children 3 to 5 years of age and primarily for boys rather than girls.

. . . TO PRACTICE

The findings clearly point out the danger of not getting enough sleep, particularly for young children and for boys. When children get adequate nighttime rest, as well as sleep during daytime naps, unintentional accidents and injuries are less likely to occur. Because such injuries account for a large percentage of deaths among children and because injuries to children carry high human and financial costs associated with treatment, hospitalization, and recuperation (Kraus, Peek-Asa, & Blander, 1997), preventing such injuries is an important goal. Helping children get more sleep may be a relatively effective way to reduce the possible physical, psychological, and financial costs associated with young children's accidents and injuries.

THINKING IT THROUGH

1. Why might lack of sleep put children at risk for injuries?

2. Why do you think boys are at the most risk for injuries?

3. Do you think sleepiness would increase the chance of some types of injuries more than others?

Excessive sleepiness is also a problem for many young children (and for many older children, teens, and adults as well). Images of young children asleep during group activities or at their desk at school have led to increased concern and speculation about the implications of not getting enough sleep. Most studies suggest that sleepiness has a detrimental effect on children's behavior. Tired, sleepy children often have trouble focusing attention and staying alert, and they may be moody or hyperactive (Archbold, Giordani, Ruzicka, & Chervin, 2004; Sadeh, Gruber, & Raviv, 2002). Sleepiness has been linked to increases in behavioral difficulties (such as fighting, irritability, aggression; Fallone, Owens, & Deane, 2002). Children who are sleepy also are at risk for injury (see From Research to Practice box; Valent, Brusaferro,

& Barbone, 2001). Improving sleep helps improve behavior—treatment of sleep problems does lead to systematic betterment in young children's mood, performance, and learning (Fallone et al., 2002). Thus, sleepiness in children is likely to result in a variety of problems and significant consequences across many developmental domains.

What Are the Health and Safety Needs of Young Children?

Most children breeze through their early years with a few illnesses and maybe some scrapes and cuts, but healthy on the whole. Fortunately, in most industrialized countries young children experience good health, largely due to advances in controlling many life-threatening diseases through immunization. The health risks for young children tend to be preventable, involving car accidents, drownings, and injuries and diseases due to exposure to unhealthy or unsafe environments.

In the United States, children today are generally healthier than children of 20 years ago. Death rates from diseases such as influenza and pneumonia have decreased. Many dangerous and contagious childhood diseases (measles and polio, for instance) were virtually eliminated in the United States by the 1980s through routine vaccinations given during childhood. However, some caregivers, especially those from low-income families, have not ensured that their children receive these vaccinations, with the result being that 1 in 5 children is not protected against rubella, polio, mumps, and measles (Centers for Disease Control, 1999). Diseases reemerge in the population if children do not receive their sequence of vaccinations (Kassianos, 1998). Worldwide, many of these diseases remain serious public health concerns. Because children who are somewhat older are more likely to contract many of these diseases, we will discuss them in more depth in Chapter 11.

Diseases: Close-Up on Asthma

> *Except for my asthma, I was a pretty normal child. I enjoyed sports, playing with my friends, tormenting my little brother, and all the other things little boys do. When I was about 10 years old, I was diagnosed with asthma. I was playing outside during winter, and when I went inside, I started wheezing. It took me an hour to catch my breath again, and by that time, I didn't want to go back outside. My parents got worried and took me to the doctor, who told us it was asthma. . . . All that seems like a very long time ago. I do not need to use my medicines much anymore because I have learned over the years how to live with my asthma and control it. Though I have asthma, I exercise frequently. I run and lift weights. I also played saxophone for over 8 years (high school and college). I played the baritone sax, which requires a lot of lung power. That was probably my greatest asthma success.* (Joe, a 23-year-old man recalling his childhood problems and current life dealing with asthma)

The most common long-term childhood disease is **asthma,** which is a disease that causes difficulty with breathing. The number of children who have asthma has increased dramatically, and the number of children who have died of it has tripled over the past 20 years, so it is not surprising that asthma is considered to be a major public health problem of increasing concern in the United States (CDC, 2004c). Many missed days of school are due to asthma, it is the third leading cause of hospitalization of children, and treating asthma in children costs roughly $3 billion a year. Children with asthma have an inflammation of the bronchial tubes (leading from the trachea into the lungs), which causes difficulty with breathing. Most of the time, children with asthma breathe normally, but an asthma attack may occur when they encounter a "trigger" for their asthma. When this happens, the bronchial tubes narrow, making it difficult to draw air into the lungs (see Figure 8.9). People having an asthma attack might feel as if they are breathing through a straw, and they may wheeze, cough, and feel tightness in the chest. It may take several days for the bronchial tubes to return to normal. Without treatment, asthma tends to get worse over

asthma   *a disease that causes difficulty with breathing*

FIGURE 8.9
The Anatomy of Asthma

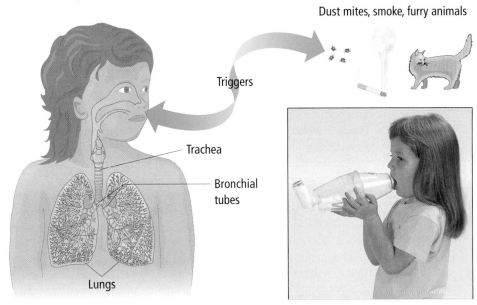

For children who have asthma, what triggers an attack, and why is breathing so difficult? Which parts of the airway are particularly affected by asthma?

time. The triggers that can set off an asthma attack are many: dust mites, pollen, mold, allergic reactions to animal dander, having a cold or the flu, exercise, cockroaches, smoking, and cold weather, to name a few.

About 5 million children in the United States have asthma. In one large-scale survey, about 15 percent of children were found to have asthma; many of those were of school age or adolescents. The likelihood of having asthma appears to be related to genetic and environmental factors, such as whether a parent smokes, a family history of asthma, and even income levels, with asthma rates being higher in low-income families. Consider the risk of exposing children to smoking: in households with smokers, 20 percent of children were reported to have asthma; in households with no smokers, the rate dropped to 15 percent (Macdonald, Pertowski, & Jackson, 1996). There is no cure for asthma, but the symptoms can be controlled through the use of inhalers to help open airways and through medications to reduce allergic reactions to triggers. A number of intervention programs have been designed to decrease the rates of asthma attacks in children, and they target smoking, frequent washing of bedding to reduce asthma triggers, education, and management (e.g., Carter, Perzanowski, Raymond, & Platts-Mill, 2001; CDC, 2003). Many children with asthma have grown up to become successful athletes, illustrating that the symptoms of asthma can be successfully managed.

Accidents

The leading cause of death in the preschool years is accidents, often automobile accidents. Four deaths and over 600 injuries a day in the United States are due to accidents (National Center for Injury Prevention and Control, 2004). In the United States, children are required to wear seat belts. Placing children in age-appropriate restraints for riding in the car reduces serious and fatal injuries by more than half (National Center for Injury Prevention and Control, 2004). Until they are age 5, children should travel in special car safety seats that protect them from injuries (American Academy of Pediatrics, 1999b). For young children of ages 4 to 8 (over about 40 pounds), booster seats are recommended so that seat

What can caregivers do to protect children around pools? What other sources of drowning danger are found in homes?

belts can be raised to the correct level on their bodies. Automobile manufacturers offer airbags and side-impact protection. Because the force of an opening airbag can harm children, young children should always be in the back seat of the car. Disarming airbags is not recommended. Restraint laws have been quite effective in protecting children: children who are not restrained are much more likely to die in automobile accidents than are children who are properly restrained (American Academy of Pediatrics, 1999b; Decker, Dewey, Hutcheson, & Schaffner, 1984; National Center for Injury Prevention and Control, 2004).

The second leading cause of death and injury of children is drowning. In the United States, about 350 children under the age of 5 and about 1,000 under the age of 14 died from drowning (Centers for Disease Control, 2002). Many more are treated in hospital emergency rooms each year, and some of these children suffer brain damage from being submerged under water. Among children of ages 1 to 4, most drownings occur in home swimming pools. Unlike what you may think, these children did not drown while swimming. Instead, they were last seen in their homes, had been out of sight for less than 5 minutes, and were in the care of one or both parents at the time (Present, 1987). This shows that "it only takes a minute" for a child to get in trouble when it comes to water. Children can drown in the time it takes to answer the phone. A layered protection approach is considered the best safety for pools: use barriers (fences and alarms) around the pool, door alarms to indicate that someone has gone outside, and power safety covers over the pool, and then provide adult supervision of the child at all times when around or in the pool. Flotation devices and swimming lessons do not make children drownproof. And remember that pools are not the only water danger for children: they can drown in large buckets, in bathtubs, and in toilets. Safety tips to prevent in-home drownings include the following:

- Never leave a young child alone in a bathtub.
- Keep the toilet lid down, and keep children out of the bathroom when unsupervised.
- Empty all containers that contain liquids immediately after use.
- Install and use safety covers on spas or hot tubs. (Consumer Product Safety Alert, 2004)

Environmental Hazards

Accidental poisonings have decreased markedly over the past 20 years; nevertheless, 500,000 children ingest some type of poison every year, and 2,000 die from the poison. Lead poisoning is a common health problem for young children in the United States. Although the incidence of lead poisoning has decreased, it continues to be a significant health issue. About 2 percent of young children (approximately 400,000) have a toxic level of lead in their blood (Centers for Disease Control, 2004b). Lead can be found everywhere—in paints, gasoline, foods, water, dust, and soil. The most common route of exposure for children is through lead-based paint in older homes. Children with high levels of lead are at risk for many behavioral problems. They may be hyperactive, impulsive, easily frustrated, or withdrawn. Even low levels of exposure increase the risk for social withdrawal and disinterest (Mendelsohn et al., 1998). Children who live in older neighborhoods and homes or who play on old playground equipment may be exposed to lead. Not surprisingly, children who live in the inner city are more likely to suffer elevated lead levels and anemia than are other children (Adams et al., 1998). In some of these neighborhoods, 20 percent of children have unhealthy levels of lead in their blood (Centers for Disease Control, 2004b).

A child who lives with parents who smoke cigarettes suffers an overwhelming health risk from **secondhand smoke,** that is, the smoke that is released into the air by someone smoking. Cigarette smoke is a toxic soup of more than 4,000 chemical compounds (including cynanide and carbon monoxides), about 70 of which are known cancer-causing agents (National Cancer Institute, 2001). The evidence is clear: children who are exposed to high levels of secondhand smoke are more likely to have ear infections, bronchitis, and pneumonia, and children with asthma experience more severe attacks. Exposure to secondhand smoke can make healthy children sick. Children who do not have asthma are likely to begin

secondhand smoke *smoke that is released through the burning of a cigarette*

to show symptoms of the disease if they are exposed to secondhand smoke (US Environmental Protection Agency, 1992). From 200,000 to 1 million children with asthma experience increased symptoms because of exposure to secondhand smoke (Environmental Protection Agency, 2004). Children and infants are particularly vulnerable to the negative effects of secondhand smoke because their lungs are still developing, they have higher breathing rates than adults, and they have little control over their indoor environments. Children can be protected from secondhand smoking by not allowing anyone to smoke in the home, and if parents are unable to quit, they should smoke outside (not just with a window open or in another room) so that the child has little exposure to the smoke.

Try It Out

1. Go to a playground, and observe children of different ages as they play. Are the preschool children able to throw, jump, and catch with greater maturity than the younger children? How can you tell that their behavior is more highly developed? Do you notice some children who seem less skilled for their age than others?
2. Watch Saturday morning television for children, and notice the kinds of food advertisements that are shown. Then go to the grocery store, and read the nutritional information on these foods. Are children being encouraged to eat and drink nutritious foods? If not, how might you remedy this situation if you were a parent?
3. Select a safety issue that is of concern to you, and write a brochure for parents, educating them about the issue. Make sure that you include reasons why parents should take the issue seriously. Provide practical suggestions that parents can implement in their homes to make their children more safe.

Key Terms and Concepts

asthma (262)
auditory cortex (248)
Event Related Potentials (248)
experience-dependent plasticity (248)

functional isolation (257)
glial cells (246)
iron-deficiency anemia (257)
kwashiorkor (256)

marasmus (256)
night terrors (260)
prefrontal cortex (246)
secondhand smoke (264)

Sum It Up

How do children's bodies and brains develop during early childhood?

▪ List and describe the three different functions attributed to the prefrontal cortex. (p. 247)
▪ What does the continuing development of the prefrontal cortex mean for children's ability to plan, behave appropriately, and remember? (p. 247)

How do children's motor skills develop during early childhood?

▪ How does culture influence children's drawing? (pp. 252–253)
▪ How is handedness related to language skills? (p. 253)

What are the nutritional and sleep patterns for young children?

▪ What are the nutritional needs of young children? (pp. 254–256)
▪ Describe the concepts of kwashiorkor, marasmus, and iron-deficiency anemia. (p. 257)
▪ How does culture play a role in sleep problems? (p. 260)

What are the health and safety needs of young children?

▪ What are some measures to take to prevent children from drowning? (p. 264)

Here you see an older child playing with her younger brother. What physical differences do you notice between them?

FIGURE 8.3 **Experience Dependent Plasticity**

Environmental Exposure

Information Processing

Brain Structure and Organization

Auditory association cortex

DEVELOPING BODIES AND BRAINS

Physical growth is fairly rapid during early childhood and is affected by many factors, including genetic inheritance, nutrition, family income, and ethnic group. A child's brain also develops in structure and function during this time. New neural connections form, and the increase in myelination of the axons allows for more efficient communication. In addition, the prefrontal cortex continues to undergo changes. (Refer back to pages 245–248.)

DEVELOPING MOTOR SKILLS

Preschool children make tremendous advances in gross and fine motor skills. These improvements are due to brain development, a better sense of balance, and increased eye–hand coordination. Motor development is influenced by practice, parental expectations, imitation, genetic inheritance, and culture and ethnicity. (Refer back to pages 249–254.)

	2–3 YEARS OF AGE	3–4 YEARS OF AGE	4–5 YEARS OF AGE	5–6 YEARS OF AGE
GROSS MOTOR SKILLS	• Runs forward well • Jumps in place with two feet together • Stands on one foot with aid • Walks on tiptoe • Kicks a ball forward	• Runs around obstacles • Walks on a line • Balances on one foot for 5–10 seconds • Hops on one foot • Rides tricycle • Throws ball overhead • Catches a bounced ball	• Walks backward toe to heel • Jumps forward 10 times without falling • Walks up and down stairs independently • Turns somersault	• Runs lightly on toes • Walks on balance beam • Hops 6 feet • Skips on alternate feet • Jumps rope • Skates
FINE MOTOR SKILLS	• Strings four large beads • Turns single pages • Snips with scissors • Holds crayon with thumb and finger (not fist)	• Builds tower of nine small blocks • Drives nails and pegs • Copies circle • Manipulates clay (rolls it into balls and snakes) • Eats with a spoon • Uses one hand consistently in most activities	• Cuts on line continuously • Copies cross and square • Prints some capital letters • Dresses self • Draws tadpole figures	• Cuts out simple shapes • Copies triangle • Copies first name • Draws letters • Colors within lines • Uses adult grasp of pencil • Unzips a zipper • Has well-established handedness

FIGURE 8.4 **Milestones in Motor Development** *Children's motor skills change dramatically during young childhood.*

By the time children are 4 to 5 years old, their running ability has greatly improved, and most can run twice as fast as they did when they were 2. And by 4, most children can jump on level ground, using their arms appropriately to help propel them.

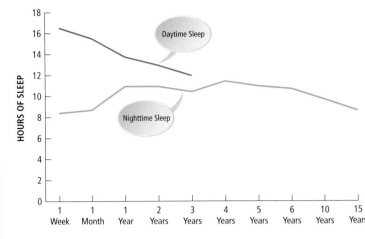

FIGURE 8.8 **Typical Sleep Requirements in Childhood** *Nighttime sleep gradually consolidates over the first three years into a single uninterrupted block of time, and daytime sleep decreases during this time. During early childhood, many types of sleep problems—such as nightmares and night terrors—begin to appear.*

Children over the age of 2 need a varied diet that includes whole grains, vegetables, fruits, milk and high protein foods, and moderate fat. Sometimes, children are undernourished and/or malnourished because they do not receive adequate nutrition.

NUTRITIONAL AND SLEEP NEEDS

Children's physical, motor, and cognitive development depends on being in good health, having adequate nutrition, and getting rest each night. (Refer back to pages 254–262.)

HEALTH AND SAFETY ISSUES

Most children breeze through their early years with a few illnesses and maybe some scrapes and cuts, but healthy on the whole. The health risks for young children tend to be caused by incidences that can be prevented—car accidents, drownings, and injuries and diseases due to exposure to unhealthy or unsafe environments. (Refer back to pages 262–265.)

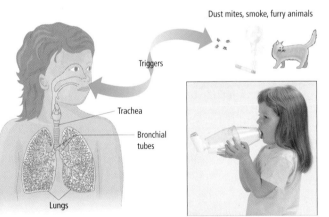

FIGURE 8.9 **The Anatomy of Asthma** *The most common long-term childhood disease is asthma, which is a lung disease that can be life threatening. It causes problems where the airways in the lungs get blocked, causing the lungs to get less air than usual.*

The leading cause of death in the preschool years is accidents. Caregivers can minimize the risks of accidents to children in a variety of ways.

Cognitive and Language Development in Early Childhood

9 Chapter Outline

How Do Young Children Think and Solve Problems?
Piaget's View of Preoperational Thinking
Evaluating Piaget's View of Preoperational Development
Vygotsky's View of the Social Context of Cognitive Development
Evaluating Vygotsky's Theory of Social Cognitive Development
The Information Processing Approach
Young Children's Theory of Mind
Young Children's Understanding of Pretend and Real
Cultural Influences on Young Children's Thinking

What Changes Occur in Young Children's Language Development During Early Childhood?
Vocabulary
Young Children's Language Styles
Grammar: Beyond Two-Word Sentences
Understanding Conversational Rules
The Social Context of Language Development
Language Development in Bilingual Children

How Does Early Childhood Education Influence Development?
Parents as Teachers
Young Children's Educational Experiences
Early Intervention and Young Children's Cognitive Development

A DEVELOPMENTAL MYSTERY

Felicity is 2 ½ years old and she is participating in a developmental study. She is shown a scale model of a living room. Under a chair in this scale model, the experimenter hides a miniature doll. Felicity is then ushered into a living room that looks exactly like the scale model except that it is full size. Felicity is asked to find where the doll is hidden in the room. As her parents watch, Felicity wanders around the room but never looks under the chair. Her parents are sur-

prised—she is unable to find the hidden doll. When she returns to the model, she is asked to find the doll and she is successful.

Why can't Felicity find the doll in the large room? Does she fail to grasp that the scale model represents the actual living room? If so, why? What are the implications of young children not being able to understand that things can be used to represent other things?

Young children have mastered many skills that infants have not: They understand the permanence of objects and can use language flexibly. Their newly developed skills do not make them perfect problem solvers or speakers of their language—they still have many skills yet to master. Children's social experiences and family life provide many opportunities for learning new skills and enhancing cognitive and language development.

How Do Young Children Think and Solve Problems?

Four-year-old Ginny, like other children of her age, can identify many kinds of dinosaurs. She knows that some dinosaurs ate only plants and others only meat. She is more knowledgeable about dinosaurs than many adults are. She also can easily be fooled by appearances: she thinks that a tall, thin glass holds more grape juice than a small, wide glass of the same volume. Ginny thinks differently than infants, older children, and adults. When it comes to dinosaurs, she is an expert; but when it comes to understanding the physical laws of nature, she is a novice with little understanding of the world. To fully understand young children's thinking, we must consider the physical, social, and cultural contexts they experience, as well as how they interpret problem-solving situations.

The following section addresses the major theoretical approaches used to understand children's thinking:

- Piaget's theory of cognitive development, which concentrates on children's different view of the world
- Vygotsky's sociocultural perspective, which views children's thinking as guided by their social interactions with others
- The information processing approach, which considers the constraints and limitations on children's thinking and on their memories

Piaget's View of Preoperational Thinking

According to Jean Piaget, young children have made tremendous strides in their understanding of the world, and their thinking is qualitatively different from that of infants. As you learned in Chapter 6, infants do not fully understand that objects continue to exist when they are not directly experiencing them, but young children have no difficulty comprehending object permanence. Infants experience the world in the here and now, with

Children are able to mimic the behavior of others, even days after it occurs. What is required for a child to show deferred imitation of a ballet move? How are symbols involved in deferred imitation?

little comprehension of the past or future, but preschoolers can think about the future and discuss the past.

Young children have moved into the *preoperational stage* of cognitive development (2 to 7 years of age). At this stage, they use **symbolic representations**—they can mentally represent objects and people and manipulate these representations. Children first show this ability at the end of the sensorimotor period (see Chapter 6). Because of their ability to use symbolic representations, young children are not confined, as infants are, to thinking in the present. Young children's symbolic capacities are illustrated in how they play, what they remember, and their increasingly sophisticated use of language. For instance, children in the preoperational stage often imitate behaviors they have seen in the past. Four-year-old Lynna provides an example of deferred imitation. Days after she saw her friend Maria trying a ballet pose, Lynna tried the same pose for the first time. Lynna remembered Maria's actions from days earlier and reproduced them.

Children at this stage show remarkable ability to communicate with language, which requires the use of symbols. Young children's thinking is no longer dominated by motor actions; they can use symbols to manipulate information mentally, allowing for faster and more flexible thinking. Before an action occurs, children can anticipate the outcome. Unlike infants, preschoolers have better memories of past events such as a family trip, and they can plan for the future, thinking about whom they will invite to a birthday party that is still weeks away.

According to Piaget, young children, unlike older children, adolescents, and adults, are preoperational thinkers because they are unable to apply **operations**—actions internalized as symbols that can be reversed and coordinated. For instance, young children do not recognize that a broken cookie has the same amount of cookie in it as an unbroken cookie. The cookie does not lose matter when it is transformed from being whole to broken. Young children fail to apply the operation of identity—that this shape can be reversed (in their minds at least) back into its original shape and therefore it must retain the same volume it had before it was transformed. As you can tell from this example, the ability to use operations is based on the ability to apply basic logic to problem solving. Children in the preoperational stage are able to internalize actions in symbols but cannot yet reverse and coordinate these symbols.

Understanding Symbols

In the developmental mystery that opened the chapter, Felicity was unable to recognize that hiding a miniature doll under the chair in the model provided a hint about the hiding place for the doll in the normal-size room. Why is she unable to understand that the model of the living room represented the full-size room and that it held the answer to where the toy was hidden? This fundamental issue relates to how children recognize and use symbols. A number of fascinating studies have been conducted on children's use of symbols in this way. What is particularly intriguing is the clear developmental differences in how well children perform on this type of task. About 75 to 90 percent of 3-year-old children show errorless retrieval of the object hidden in the living room, but children just 6 months younger consistently perform poorly on this task (about 15 to 20 percent errorless retrieval) (DeLoache, 1987, 1991; DeLoache, Kolstad, & Anderson, 1991; Dow & Pick, 1992; Marzolf & DeLoache, 1994). To be able to use symbols, such as models or photographs or maps, children must detect and mentally represent the relation between the symbol and what it stands for. Children who have this ability are more likely to use the information from a scale model to find the hidden toy than children who do not have this ability. Why do younger children have more difficulty with this task?

It is not that they cannot use symbols. Children at this age understand that words or actions can be used to represent objects in language, and they are not fooled by some types of symbolic representation. For instance, even when very realistic photographs of objects (such as a bottle) are presented to young children, they are not fooled into thinking that the photo is the real object, as are toddlers and infants (DeLoache, Pierroutsakos, & Troseth, 1997). By age 2, children can use pictures as a source of information in a retrieval task, even though they cannot use scale models (DeLoache, 1991), and they can use symbols in play

symbolic representations *mental representations of objects and people that can be manipulated in the mind*

operations *actions internalized as symbols that can be reversed and coordinated*

dual representation *the ability to mentally represent something both as itself and standing for something else*

conservation tasks *tasks used to assess children's use of operations, in which children must decide whether a transformed object is the same as or different from what it was before*

identity concept *the essential "sameness" of an object despite physical changes to it*

irreversibility *the inability to understand that an operation can be undone, returning something to its original form*

(Lillard, 1993; Tomasello, 1999). Another more likely possibility is that the ability needed for successfully navigating the scale model task is **dual representation,** that is, the ability to mentally represent both facets of a thing—the thing as a real object and the thing as it stands for something else (see Figure 9.1; DeLoache, 2000; DeLoache, Pierroutsakos, & Uttal, 2003). To understand scale models, a child must "see" the model itself and then "see through" the model to understand that it stands for the room (DeLoache, 2000). Children's general level of cognitive development and their experiences with symbols contribute to increased abilities to understand and use scale models.

Inability to Conserve

To illustrate the difference between operational and preoperational thinking, Piaget used **conservation tasks.** These are tasks like the one described above, in which children are shown an object, watch a transformation of that object, and then decide whether the transformed object is the same as or different from what it was before it was transformed. For instance, 4-year-old Jason is shown two balls of clay, both of which are exactly the same size and shape. One ball is then rolled out into a long, thin snake shape, and Jason is asked to decide if one piece has more clay in it than the other or if they have the same amount. His answer may come as a surprise to many adults: he is likely to say that the long, skinny shape has more clay in it than the ball.

In recognizing that the snake and the ball have the same amount of clay, adults apply basic logical principles regarding the conservation of matter. In contrast to Jason, older children and adults understand that an object transformed into a new form contains the same amount of matter so long as nothing is added or taken away. Older children and adults understand the **identity concept,** which involves recognizing the essential "sameness" of an object, despite physical changes to it.

Jason, like other preschool children, does not consistently apply the idea of identity to problem-solving experiences. Because young children do not use logical operations, their reasoning often seems flawed to us. One limitation in young children's thinking is **irreversibility**—the inability to understand that an operation can be undone so that something is returned to its original form. Also, young children's thinking exhibits **centration**—the tendency to focus attention on the most obvious and striking characteristic of an object while ignoring others (see Figure 9.2). They see the snake as having more clay than the ball, for example, because it is longer. Young children centrate on the length of the snake while ignoring its comparative thinness. Their thinking is guided by appearances—what things look like—rather than by logic. Eight-year-old Carol used to take advantage of her 4-year-old sister's tendency to centrate on size (and lack of knowledge of money) by trading big nickels for her sister's small dimes. To her younger sister, bigger meant more.

Static Thinking

The focus on one dimension also is obvious in children's **static thinking**—their tendency to attend to the outcome rather than to the changes that produced the outcome. For example, a preschool child may watch her friend dress in a monster costume at Halloween and then focus only on the final state; that is, she may become scared of the monster who has magically replaced her friend. Children may even make up unbelievable stories about what happened during such a transition. When asked what had happened to her friend, the child might say that her friend had gone home. Young children often exhibit static thinking when they tell stories; they focus on only the beginning of the story and its end. Three-year-old Erin's favorite story is "Once upon a time there was a princess. The end."

FIGURE 9.1
Dual Representation

What developmental changes occur in children's abilities to understand and use symbols such as scale models and maps?

What limitations in children's thinking during the preoperational stage cause them to have difficulty understanding transformations like this?

centration   *the tendency to focus attention on the most obvious and striking characteristic of an object while ignoring others*

static thinking   *the tendency to attend more to the outcome than to the changes that produced the outcome*

FIGURE 9.2
Centration Examples

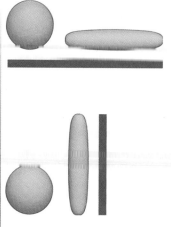

In each example, children centrate on different dimensions. Why is this so?

FIGURE 9.3
Class Inclusion

Preschoolers have difficulty comparing an entire class with a subclass. When asked whether there are more dogs or more brown dogs, preschoolers answer that there are more brown dogs. Why is understanding the comparison of two subclasses easier than comparing a class with a subclass?

transductive reasoning *the inference that if two particular examples or events occur together, they must be causally related*

class inclusion *part–whole relations of categories*

Precausal Reasoning

Young children's reasoning about the causes of events does not match adults'. Adults reason *inductively,* from particular examples to the general principle, or *deductively,* from the general principle to the specific example. For instance, inductive reasoning would suggest that if every swan you've ever seen is white, then all swans are white. Deductive reasoning would be used to determine that if all swans are white, and this bird is a swan, then this bird must be white. Piaget argued that young children are more likely than adults to use a different form of reasoning, called **transductive reasoning.** Transductive reasoning suggests that if two particular examples or events occur together, they must be causally related. For example, when Joshua sees his mother pick up her bagged lunch and leave for work, he may believe that the bagged lunch caused her to leave the house. Because the events occurred at the same time, he believes that one caused the other. Also, young children seem to infer that all things happen for a reason, so they search to find a cause, even when events are unrelated or arise by chance.

Understanding Concepts and Categories

Preschoolers' simple classifications of objects and people are based on partial concepts (sometimes called preconcepts) that allow them to make distinctions among global categories, such as animals, food, and people (Mandler, Bauer, & McDonough, 1991). In simple situations, young children can categorize on the basis of a single attribute, but their ability to vary strategies when necessary is limited (Freund, Baker, & Sonnenschein, 1990). Young children's ability to understand differences within a category also is limited. They may distinguish between dogs and elephants, for example, but have difficulty distinguishing different kinds of dogs.

Young children also have difficulty understanding some of the more complex aspects of categorization. They have trouble with multiple classification; that is, they fail to understand that one person or object may belong to multiple categories simultaneously (Winer, 1980). For instance, they may not understand how their mother can also be a daughter. Young children also have difficulty with categorization problems involving **class inclusion,** or part–whole relations of categories. When 4-year-old Elsie is shown ten brown dogs and five white dogs and is asked whether there are more brown dogs or more white dogs, she is likely to answer the question correctly. However, when asked whether there are more brown dogs (a subclass) or more dogs (the whole class), she is likely to say there are more brown dogs. Elsie's answers show that she can make comparisons within a classification level (brown versus white dogs), but she cannot make comparisons across different levels of classification (brown dogs versus all dogs combined; see Figure 9.3). A number of factors influence how well young children perform on class inclusion problems, such as whether the child has been trained in how to perform the task, whether information used in the categories is made salient, whether it is familiar, and whether the information from the categories is prototypical of the category (Brainerd & Kaszor, 1974; Greene, 1991; Wilkinson, 1976). For instance, children are more likely to answer questions about categories correctly when presented with robins and blue jays (both typical examples of birds) rather than with chickens and ducks (both atypical examples of birds) (Lane & Hodkin, 1985). These variations suggest that children have an understanding of part–whole relationships but may have difficulty activating that knowledge to solve a wide range of problems until they are older (Bjorklund, 1995).

Although Piaget described some of the changes that occur in children's classification abilities, other researchers have provided additional insights about them. Whereas very young children often group objects based on perceptual characteristics (e.g., size), slightly older children also form groups based on themes (e.g., saying that a horse and apple go together because horses eat apples). Children continue to use perceptual and thematic groupings as they grow older, but they also gain the ability to use conceptual or taxonomic groupings, which are based on category membership. For instance, a 7-year-old may classify a horse and a dog together as animals and an apple and a banana together as foods. Even with these changes, young children continue to use a variety of methods of classifying information (Bjorklund, 1995).

Egocentrism

One of the most interesting aspects of preschoolers' thought is their tendency toward **egocentrism;** they assume that their own perspective is shared by other people. Preschoolers rely on their own perception of events rather than recognizing that other people may have a different perception. The result is that they fail to take another person's point of view into account (Piaget & Inhelder, 1958). Egocentrism is evident in many aspects of preschoolers' thinking. For example, when 3-year-old Kirra pulled a blanket over her head and announced that we should try to find her, she exhibited egocentric thinking. She reasoned that if she could not see us, we could not see her.

Piaget and Inhelder (1958) designed a special task, called the *three-mountain task,* to assess whether children can adopt another's point of view (see Figure 9.4). In this task, a child and a doll sit at opposite sides of a table, with a view of a scene of three mountains varying in size and appearance. From the child's perspective, the tallest mountain has a different location in the scene than it does from the doll's perspective. The child examines the scene from each position around the table, including the doll's, and then is shown pictures representing all views. When asked which view the doll sees, preschoolers are likely to select the scene that best matches the view from their seat, not the doll's seat. Their egocentric thinking leads them to believe that others see things the way they do.

Children's lack of ability to recognize another's point of view influences their social interactions. Young children often have difficulty communicating effectively, especially on the telephone, because they do not understand that the other person does not see what they see or know what they know. Also, they may have difficulties dealing with others' emotions because they do not understand that others feel differently than they do.

Another feature of egocentric thought is **animism**—attributing lifelike qualities to objects that are not alive. By the preoperational stage, children recognize that most inanimate objects are not alive, but they have difficulty with inanimate objects that move freely. A 4-year-old girl, asked whether a river is alive, may assert that it is alive because the water moves. When children talk about the moon being happy or the sun going to sleep, their comments suggest that they believe that the moon or sun is alive. According to Piaget, the egocentric thinking of children in the preoperational stage inhibits their ability to distinguish between things that are alive and those that are not. Children focus on their own view of the object and their perception of it, and this distracts them from attending to the features that determine whether or not something is alive. A child may consider a wind-up plastic duck to be alive because the child pays attention to the movement—how it looks from his or her view—rather than assessing whether the duck is breathing or whether it moves because it propels itself.

Evaluating Piaget's View of Preoperational Development

Piaget's ideas about development were unlike those of his predecessors; they were so unusual and surprising that many studies were designed to replicate his findings. Even with children from other countries, Piaget's ideas have been confirmed when the same procedures have

FIGURE 9.4
Three-Mountain Egocentrism Task

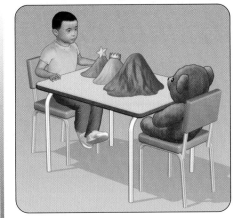

Why will this 3-year-old assume that the stuffed animal sees exactly what he sees? What term did Piaget give to this kind of thinking? Does this experimental result mean that a young child is not capable of taking the perspective of another person? Why or why not?

egocentrism   *the assumption, characteristic of most preschoolers, that their own perspective is shared by other people*

animism   *attributing lifelike qualities to objects that are not alive*

Can this child imagine what the world would look like to her doll? Why does using familiar objects improve children's abilities to demonstrate their understanding of conservation and perspective taking?

been used. Children go through the stages described by Piaget, in the order he outlined. Nonetheless, Piaget may have underestimated children's abilities in some ways. Many of Piaget's tasks may have been too demanding or confusing for preschool children. Developmental researchers have simplified Piaget's tasks to explore whether children will perform the simpler tasks the same way they do the more difficult versions (Gelman & Baillargeon, 1983). The implication is that if children show higher levels of problem-solving ability on simplified tasks, we must reconsider the meaning of Piaget's earlier research.

Children's egocentric thinking has been examined using tasks simpler than the three-mountain task. In one set of studies conducted by Hughes (cited in Donaldson, 1978), children were shown a four-room house without a roof. Two police officer dolls were placed in different locations in the house, and the children were asked to hide a boy doll from the officers' sight. Piaget's theory would predict that preschool children could not succeed at this task, just as they do not succeed at the three-mountain task. Surprisingly, most of the 3-year-olds and almost all of the 4-year-olds were successful in placing the boy doll in a position that neither adult doll could see. Making the task more understandable and providing some practice may improve children's ability to adopt another's perspective. Even 3-year-old children are able to imagine others' perspectives on tasks that involve familiar scenes (such as a pond or farmhouse with animals) and familiar characters (such as Grover from *Sesame Street*) (Borke, 1975).

Young children also are more likely to demonstrate an understanding of conservation when tasks are simplified. When children do not witness the transformation (making the snake from clay), they sometimes respond as though they have conserved (Rose & Blank, 1974). Some children can be trained to conserve, especially when simpler tasks are used, but younger children respond less to training than do older children (Case, 1998).

Animistic thinking is less evident when children are asked about familiar concrete objects (such as dolls and rocks) rather than the less familiar objects Piaget used (such as the sun or moon). In tasks with familiar objects, young children recognize the qualities associated with being alive earlier than Piaget expected. For instance, young children realize that movement, growth, and emotions are associated with people but not with rocks or dolls (Massey & Gelman, 1988; Rakison & Poulin-Dubois, 2001).

When familiar and comfortable situations are used for testing, children's understanding of causality also is more sophisticated than Piaget believed (Bullock, 1984). For instance, most preschool children know that causes precede outcomes, or effects. When shown an apparatus in which a Snoopy doll pops up if a marble is dropped into the left side but not the right side, 3-year-old children understand that the cause (dropping the marble) must occur prior to the effect (Snoopy's appearance) and select the correct side in which to drop the marble (Bullock & Gelman, 1979; Bullock, Gelman, & Baillargeon, 1982).

Children exhibit higher levels of categorization skills under simplified conditions. They can solve some kinds of class-inclusion problems when the wording is changed or when simpler versions of the task are used. For instance, young children recognize that a person would have more to color in a picture if he or she colored the whole bird rather than just its wings (Siegler, 1998).

These studies show that Piaget underestimated young children's capabilities to solve problems by using logical principles. Nevertheless, his theory still provides us with a good description of many of the ways in which young children's thinking differs from that of older children and adults. Piaget's ideas about preoperational development are a good starting point for understanding children's problem solving, and they guide us in the right direction for conducting new studies on how young children think about the problems they face every day.

Vygotsky's View of the Social Context of Cognitive Development

As you learned in Chapter 6, infants gain knowledge through interactions with other people. The social context continues to play an important role in young children's cognitive development. In Piaget's view, children are explorers who discover many interesting and valuable ideas through their interactions with people and objects. According to the Russian psychologist Lev Vygotsky, children and caregivers discover ideas together (Martin, 2000).

Just as parents can scaffold infants' and toddlers' learning of language, parents of preschoolers can promote cognitive development through the use of a scaffolding system. Remember that scaffolding involves providing children with some support for their learning. In this way, cognitive scaffolding provides a continually evolving, moderately challenging learning environment, which changes in response to the child's developing cognitive competencies.

Scaffolding involves many different strategies, including engaging the child's attention, reducing the number of steps in a task, motivating the child, and demonstrating the skill to be performed (Berk & Winsler, 1999; Karpov & Haywood, 1998). To see how caregivers' scaffolding strategies work, consider the way Anita helps her 4-year-old daughter Rachel with a challenging animal puzzle. To make the task easier, Anita breaks it into more manageable units. After turning all the pieces right side up, Anita suggests that Rachel select the pieces that have straight edges because these pieces make up the border of the puzzle. Then Anita gives Rachel strategies for putting the pieces together. As Rachel selects each piece, Anita describes the color and the animal on the piece, giving Rachel clues to help her decide where the piece might fit. At each step, Anita provides subgoals for finishing the puzzle, which help Rachel avoid frustration. She also suggests ways to think about the puzzle pieces, providing Rachel with keys to the thinking process.

Anita is extending Rachel's problem-solving abilities and understanding about puzzles by working within Rachel's zone of proximal development, or the range in learning that Rachel is capable of with help from Anita (Chapter 6). The next time they work on a puzzle, Anita waits to see whether Rachel turns the pieces right side up before suggesting this strategy. Anita also is less likely to discuss the colors of each piece, and Rachel is more likely to mention these qualities herself as she tries to fit pieces together. Anita and Rachel continually renegotiate strategies, with Anita tuning in to Rachel's skills each time they play.

If Anita tried the same strategies with a much more challenging game, Rachel probably would not complete the game. Both probably would feel frustrated in their efforts because they would be working outside of Rachel's zone of proximal development. If Anita tried the same strategies with a simple game that Rachel had already mastered, Rachel's cognitive skills would not be facilitated. By working within the frame of Rachel's abilities and providing a nurturing context, Anita gives Rachel a challenging experience, and Rachel's problem-solving abilities improve (Tappan, 1998).

When Rachel works on the puzzles, an interesting thing takes place: Rachel talks out loud to herself. Her tendency to talk about the puzzle aloud when she is alone demonstrates Vygotsky's idea of **private speech**, which individuals speak to themselves when solving problems. Piaget assumed that children's tendency to talk to themselves simply indicated egocentrism, and so he labeled this **egocentric speech.** Vygotsky, however, believed that private speech is an internalized voice that helps guide thinking. In solving the puzzle, Anita suggested strategies ("Let's put the straight-edged pieces together first"), which Rachel used to put the puzzle together. Later, when Rachel worked on the puzzle alone, she repeated out loud the strategies that her mom had proposed. Over time, these conversations become internalized and children can, on their own, use them to help direct their behavior (Winsler, Diaz, & Montero, 1997).

Recent research has confirmed and expanded upon the idea of private speech (Duncan & Pratt, 1997). Children use private speech more often to direct their actions than to make egocentric remarks. As children grow older, their private speech becomes quieter (Berk, 1994).

FIGURE 9.5
Vygotsky's Private Speech

This round piece goes here.

Children use their own internal dialogue when trying to solve problems. How do children learn to do this, according to Vygotsky?

private speech *Vygotsky's term for speech directed toward the self, used when solving problems*

egocentric speech *Piaget's term for speech directed toward the self*

Evaluating Vygotsky's Theory of Social Cognitive Development

Vygotsky's theory has become increasingly popular in the United States over the past 20 years (Thomas, R. M., 2000). Although he did not live long enough to develop a very elaborate theory, Vygotsky's ideas about the role of the social context in cognition have garnered much empirical support and have encouraged researchers to study how children think in various cultures (Rogoff, Mistry, Concu, & Mosier, 1993), and in many different types of social contexts (Rogoff, 1990). The theory is considered to be helpful for both directing researchers and for providing practical guidance about how to encourage cognitive development in young children.

The Information Processing Approach

After 4-year-old Drea made a trip to Disneyland with her parents, she was unable to explain what she saw there as they rode home in the car. Should her parents be concerned, or should they recognize that this is simply a limitation of the thinking of 4-year-olds? Information processing research in young children has been conducted to assess how and what children remember, whether they are more likely to remember a trip to Disneyland or to a familiar place, and how it is that some children become amazing experts at remembering things that even their parents do not understand. Another concern is when children begin to understand that others have thoughts and feelings, just as they do. At what point in development are children able to recognize what others think and feel? Finally, when do children come to understand the difference between what's real and what's pretend? Many people assume that children recognize the unrealistic nature of television and movies, but when and how do children learn to distinguish between fantasy and reality?

Young Children's Memory

Four-year-old Abe and 8-year-old Sophie just visited the zoo with their parents. On the car ride home, Abe says he saw a bear and some snakes. Sophie recites a much longer list; she reports that they also saw elephants, birds, monkeys, zebras, kangaroos, and lions. The children's parents remember even more of the animals than either of the children. This example illustrates a typical pattern that was also illustrated by Drea in the previous example: young children remember less than older children do. Information processing approaches to understanding children's thinking have focused attention on what children forget and what they remember. For instance, they consider whether young children simply fail to pay attention or whether older children have special capabilities for remembering.

Have you ever noticed that as soon as you read a phone number out of the telephone book and dial it, you forget it? Conversely, are you surprised at how vividly you remember some things? Many people say they can remember exactly what they were doing when they heard that Princess Diana of Great Britain was killed in an automobile crash in Paris. Most people have vivid memories of what they were doing when they heard about the horrific events of September 11, 2001. However, these same people may not remember what they ate for lunch the day before. Why are some memories so vivid, whereas others are so fleeting?

People have different ways to store memories, which determine the likelihood that the memories will be remembered later. In Chapter 2, you learned that the memory system has three components: sensory storage, short-term memory, and long-term memory. A phone number you want to dial immediately after looking it up would be held briefly in short-term memory; it would never be transferred to long-term memory because you have no need to remember it for a longer time period. In contrast, an event such as your wedding or an automobile accident you

Describe the differences in what these children are likely to remember about a trip to Disneyland. Why do these differences occur?

witnessed is likely to be moved into long-term memory because it is reviewed, involves visual imagery, evokes emotions, and may be important to remember. Like older children and adults, young children have a three-component memory system that allows them to store information in their memories. Why, then, do they remember less than older children and adults do?

All humans have limits on their capacities to process information. When people are distracted, tired, or presented with too much information, they will not remember it as well. However, young children's capacities are more limited than older children's and adults' for three basic reasons:

Over time, as children experience the same events repeatedly, they begin to learn the scripts involved in them. What kind of script does this child likely have?

■ *Tendency to be easily distracted:* Young children are more easily distracted than older children are. Children who are distracted by loud noises or colorful scenes will not pay as much attention as children who can focus their attention more systematically. Attention to relevant information increases between 3 and 8 years of age (DeMarie-Dreblow & Miller, 1988).

■ *Failure to use memory strategies:* Memory strategies are techniques used to improve memory, such as rehearsal (reviewing information), organization (clustering information into groups of similar objects or into meaningful categories), and elaboration (thinking of associations among objects). These strategies help move information into long-term memory. Consider how you study for an exam. To increase the likelihood of doing well, you might rehearse new terms and try to think of ways to relate them to meaningful concepts. For instance, you might study terms concerning prenatal development in the order in which developments occur month to month. The use of such strategies develops during childhood. Toddlers show evidence of using very simple precursors to memory strategies (DeLoache, Cassidy, & Brown, 1985). Preschoolers begin to develop memory strategies, but use rehearsal, organization, or elaboration only rarely to help them remember information.

■ *Lack of awareness of memory:* Young children are unlikely to use metacognition; that is, they are less likely than older children to be aware of memory and to monitor their memory performance. At around age 5, children begin to be aware of their learning processes, probably because of their school experiences, and this awareness grows throughout childhood. The better children monitor their memory and learning processes, the more likely they are to store and retrieve information effectively (Siegler, 1998).

Young Children's Understanding of Everyday Events

By the time a child is 5 years old, she or he may have taken hundreds of baths, eaten at fast food restaurants many times, and helped bake cookies a dozen times. What do children remember from these kinds of events? Do they understand that the actions involved in everyday interactions take place in some order? Do they understand which pieces of information are essential and which are not? For instance, in a fast food restaurant, a child can order a hamburger one day and chicken pieces the next, but in both cases, she or he must place the order and pay before picking up the food. The causal sequence of events is crucial, although the type of food is not (Schlottmann, 1999).

The concepts that people form about routines involved in everyday interactions and events may be thought of as **scripts.** As children experience these activities, they have opportunities to learn the sequencing of events (Nelson, 1986). By the age of 3, children begin to develop rudimentary scripts. For example, 3-year-old Jenny may describe the script for grocery shopping as "First, we go to the store, and then we pick out food we like." This basic script has little detail, but it reveals Jenny's understanding that going to the store

scripts *concepts that people form about routines involved in everyday interactions and events*

happens before picking out food. As children mature, they develop more elaborate scripts with more details and more sequencing of events (Farrar & Goodman, 1992; Mandler, 1993). For instance, a 5-year-old may remember the script for going to the store as driving to the store, parking the car, getting a cart for the food, picking out food, paying, going to the car, going home, and putting the groceries away (Hudson, Shapiro, & Sosa, 1995). Children's first successes at planning future events are based on their script-based knowledge of events (Hudson & Fivush, 1991).

Children's memory for everyday routines and activities influences how they remember specific information. Young children may inaccurately remember an uncommon event by distorting their memories in the direction of a familiar script. For instance, children who have eaten at a nice restaurant may inaccurately report that the food was paid for before they ate because this is what they have experienced in fast food restaurants. Familiarity with the fast food restaurant script colors their memory (Siegler, 1990). As children grow older they become better able to distinguish between actual and script memories.

Parents help children develop and remember scripts by asking them to recall past events and by asking questions about the activities that occurred (Hudson, 1990). In this way, parents provide children with hints about what kinds of information are important to remember and give them cues about the ordering of events (Nelson, 1993; Price & Goodman, 1990).

Young Children as Experts

Despite their limitations in remembering information, young children are able to learn a large amount of information on topics that interest them. Some children learn enough information in an area to become experts, such as developing a vast store of knowledge about dinosaurs or becoming a chess whiz. One study focused on a 4 ½-year-old dinosaur expert who had been exposed to information about dinosaurs for a little over a year. This child could name and recognize over 40 types of dinosaurs and describe where they lived, their diets, and their forms of locomotion (Chi & Koeske, 1983).

Why do some children become experts on dinosaurs? How does their knowledge of dinosaurs differ from that of someone who is not an expert?

Children and adults who are experts on a specific topic retain more details about that topic and think about that topic both more extensively and differently than other people (Chase & Simon, 1973). Most important, an expert organizes information differently. For instance, chess experts are better than nonexperts at remembering the positions of chess pieces in real games, but they do not have an advantage when the pieces are randomly arranged on the board (Chi, 1978). This suggests that a chess expert's better memory for chess is due not to better memory abilities overall but to a better understanding of chess.

Just as experts remember information relevant to their area of expertise better than novices do, children remember familiar information better than unfamiliar information (Harris, Durso, Mergler, & Jones, 1990). When information is familiar, children can apply new strategies more efficiently. With practice, these strategies become more automatic and require fewer processing demands. Because processing demands are minimal, children develop the capacity to apply memory strategies to unfamiliar content (Siegler, 1998).

Young Children's Theory of Mind

Tammy, age 3, played a trick one day with the help of her father. She called for her uncle to come into the room, knowing that as soon as he opened the door wide enough to enter, he would be hit by the pillow that she and her father had balanced on the top of the door. For Tammy to enjoy this trick, she had to recognize that her uncle did not know what was about to happen and would be surprised when the pillow dropped on him—which he was.

DEBATING THE ISSUE

CAN YOUNG CHILDREN'S EYEWITNESS TESTIMONY BE BELIEVED?

 In 1988, Margaret Michaels was convicted of sexually abusing preschool children at the school where she worked in New Jersey (*State v. Michaels,* 1988). She was accused of molesting children during regular school hours over a period of seven months. None of the alleged acts had been noticed by staff or parents, and none of the children had reported any instances to their parents. The first suspicion occurred when a 4-year-old former student told a nurse who was taking his temperature rectally, "That's what my teacher does to me." This started a series of investigations, and many other children began to disclose similar stories, but only after they had been repeatedly interviewed by caseworkers. On the basis of testimony provided by 19 child witnesses, Michaels was convicted of 115 counts of sexual abuse and sentenced to serve 47 years in prison. An appeals court reversed her conviction, and the New Jersey State Supreme Court upheld this reversal (*State v. Michaels,* 1994), ruling that in order to retry the case, the prosecution would first have to convince the court that the child witnesses could provide reliable testimony. The prosecution then dropped all charges against Michaels (Ceci & Bruck, 1995).

The Michaels case is not an isolated one. There have been many similar cases, some of which you may remember because of the extensive media coverage they received. Often the sole witnesses are preschool-age children who disclose the abuse only after a long delay and after intensive interviewing. Usually, no corroborative evidence is found, and the defendants maintain their innocence (Ceci & Bruck, 1995). Can the testimony of young children be believed?

Children can be reliable witnesses, but many conditions influence the accuracy of their testimony:

- *Suggestibility and vulnerability to leading questions:* Existing research indicates that preschoolers are more vulnerable than older children to leading questions and are more suggestible. This is not to say that young children cannot provide accurate and reliable testimony, but they are more susceptible to a variety of factors that contribute to unreliable testimony (Ceci & Bruck, 1998). A child who is repeatedly asked about how her teacher touched her in a "bad" place may be led into believing that this happened, even if it did not.

- *Desire for approval from adults:* Young children are very reliant on adults for approval and are eager to please them. It is common for a preschooler to provide a desired answer to an adult's question just to win the adult's approval (Garbarino & Stott, 1992). For example, when an adult asks young children to select a suspect from a series of photographs that does not contain a picture of the actual suspect, children rarely acknowledge that they do not recognize any of the photographs. They are likely to make a false identification because they want to please the adult. This is true even when children are warned that the lineup may not contain a picture of the suspect (King & Yuille, 1987).

- *Repeated questioning:* Young children's testimony is less likely to be distorted after one interview than after several interviews (Ceci & Bruck, 1995). Constant questioning,

and sometimes leading questions, may cause children to think that they are supposed to answer in certain ways. Repeating questions to young children may make them feel that their previous answers were wrong. A child who initially answered that the teacher didn't do anything "bad" may eventually say that the teacher *did* do something bad, simply because an adult asked repeatedly. The child may think that if his or her initial answer had been okay, then the adult would not have asked the question again and again. Children's desire to please adults may lead them to change their answers to what they believe the adult wants rather than what is accurate.

Of course, older children and adults also are suggestible and vulnerable to leading questions. However, because of their limited memory skills, dependency on adults, and limited experiences, young children are more easily influenced. The impact of persistent and suggestive questioning is likely to have an especially powerful effect on children (Ceci & Bruck, 1998).

THINKING IT THROUGH

1. Why did prosecutors drop their appeal in the Margaret Michaels case?

2. What are the three main factors that can lead to inaccuracy in children's testimony, and why do they decrease accuracy?

3. How can young children's reports of sexual abuse be obtained with the fewest inaccuracies?

These children have dressed up to play store. At this age, what do they understand about what is real and what is pretend?

Tammy's behavior indicates that she has some understanding of mental states—what people know, think, and feel. Preschoolers often use the words *think, pretend,* and *imagine,* providing clues that they have ideas about the inner mental events that people experience (Bartsch & Wellman, 1995). An understanding of inner mental events means that children have developed a **theory of mind;** that is, they understand that people think, imagine, pretend, and wonder about the world around them.

Developing a theory of mind represents a tremendous accomplishment whereby children learn to separate the external world from the inner workings of the mind (Wellman & Gelman, 1998). This achievement influences many aspects of children's lives, including how they distinguish pretend and real events, understand deception and lies, interpret other people's behavior, and distinguish between beliefs and desires. For instance, children who have a theory of mind are likely to understand how to anger or entertain a younger sibling (Dunn, 1988) and how to ensure that their communications have been understood (Shwe & Markman, 1997). The extent to which children all over the world develop a theory of mind is unclear. Cultural factors such as schooling, emphasis on science, and group cohesiveness may influence how and whether members of a culture develop and use beliefs about others' minds and behaviors (Gauvain, 1998; Lillard, 1998).

For North American children, whose understanding of theory of mind has been studied the most extensively, understanding of inner mental states increases in sophistication during early childhood. Three- and 4-year-old children realize that people, but not objects, can think and that thinking is an internal process. By 5 years of age, children tend to believe that people think by using their brains and realize that one can think about things that are not present (Flavell, Green, & Flavell, 1987). In addition, young children's theory of mind gives rise to fantasy play, as they now can pretend and imagine what others feel or think (Taylor & Carlson, 1997).

The method most commonly used to assess children's understanding of others' minds is the false-belief task (Wimmer & Perner, 1983). In the "Maxi" task, candy is hidden in a box while the child and another person, Maxi, watch. Maxi then leaves the room. While Maxi is gone, the treat is moved to another container. The question for the child is "When Maxi returns, will he know where the treat is hidden?" Usually, 4-year-olds recognize that Maxi will look where the candy was originally hidden, since that is the situation as Maxi experienced it. However, 3-year-olds usually cannot solve the problem, instead stating that Maxi will look in the new hiding place. This shortcoming in thinking suggests that younger children do not understand others' beliefs. Many studies have confirmed this developmental trend, including studies of children of Baka pygmies living in the rain forests of Cameroon (Avis & Harris, 1991). Young children appear to be unable to "read the minds" of others (Wellman, 1990).

Children are capable of misleading someone intentionally, using their theory of mind. To mislead someone, children must understand that the other person does not know what they know. When simple and concrete situations are used, even 3-year-olds can intentionally mislead someone (Chandler, Fritz, & Hala, 1989). However, young children's understanding of mental states is not sophisticated, nor is it applied consistently. They may be poor at inferring from a situation what others are thinking (Flavell et al., 1995). For example, Tammy continued to try to fool her uncle, not recognizing that he now knew the pillow trick. Preschool children also fail to realize that people tend to focus their thinking on one topic at a time rather than on many

theory of mind *the understanding of inner mental events—that people think, imagine, pretend, and wonder about the world around them*

Young Children's Understanding of Pretend and Real

Given that children spend much of their time playing "make believe" and watch many hours of fantasy situations on television, it is important to determine how well they can distinguish between pretend and real situations. The answer depends on the type of fantasy–reality comparison that is made. Children often are quite capable of making these distinctions. When 2½-year-old children are involved in fantasy play using make-believe substances such as "tea" in a cup, they recognize the fantasy nature of the play and respond appropriately—maybe even wiping up imaginary spilled tea after they watch another "spill" it (Harris & Kavanaugh, 1993; Leslie, 1987). Similarly, by age 3, young children understand the difference between a real object and a "play" toy (Woolley & Wellman, 1990).

Children do, however, have difficulty identifying an object when its appearance conflicts with its true identity. When children are shown a deceptive object, such as a sponge that looks like a rock, they are confused by the object's appearance and do not pay attention to its true nature (Flavell, 1988). At age 3, most children do not distinguish the appearance of deceptive objects from their reality, even after training (Taylor & Hort, 1990). However, in simplified situations, even 3-year-olds may recognize these distinctions (Rice et al., 1997). Children's ability to make more difficult discriminations increases with age (Flavell, Green, & Flavell, 1987). By age 5, children generally make these distinctions, even in cognitively demanding situations (Martin & Halverson, 1983). The boundaries children draw between fantasy play and reality also become more differentiated between 2 and 6 years of age: whereas younger children might scare themselves by playing monster, older children will not (DiLalla & Watson, 1988).

In what way is this child taking primary responsibility for learning to weave? By what means do children learn the scripts associated with their culture? How would cultural differences change this scene if you were learning to weave?

Cultural Influences on Young Children's Thinking

Just as caregivers provide learning environments for children's cognitive development, so too do the communities or cultures in which children are raised (DiMaggio, 1997). Children's learning takes place through active participation with others. One can think of children as apprentices who are actively involved in organizing and supporting their own learning experiences by working with other people in everyday cultural activities (Rogoff et al., 1993). Through apprenticeships with adults, children essentially become experts on their own culture; they learn the skills, the background knowledge, and the values and norms of their community.

Given the great diversity of cultures and communities, it is not surprising that children's exposure to their own culture results in specific experiences and scripts that differ from those of children raised in different cultures. How do children learn the specific cognitive skills and values associated with their own culture?

■ *Through exposure:* To learn cultural scripts, children need exposure to the situations associated with the scripts. In their day-to-day experiences and interactions with others, children are exposed to their culture's values regarding particular skills (Jacobs & Eccles, 2000). For instance, the Inuit, who live near the Arctic Circle, often demonstrate the value of knowing one's whereabouts as a survival skill, and so their children learn to use spatial skills to navigate their environment.

■ *Through practice:* Children also learn cultural scripts through practice (DiMaggio, 1997). A young child raised in a rural environment, for example, is more likely than a city child to learn about the care of farm animals. Similarly, children who are raised with the cultural expectation that they will learn certain skills, such as weaving, receive many opportunities to practice such skills.

■ *Through regulation:* Cultural differences in childrearing practices include variations in the extent to which adults control and regulate children's roles in everyday activities. Children may be allowed or required to observe a valued activity before practicing it. As children become more accomplished and skilled, adults may increase children's involvement. Providing graded levels of exposure to valued activities helps children learn the details needed to perform them (Rogoff et al., 1993).

■ *Through encouragement:* Adults provide different learning experiences for children by encouraging them to become involved in certain activities (Cole, 1997). Encouragement may be indirect and social or direct and material. In Zimbabwe, many parents encourage their children to learn about marketing because trading is an important part of daily life. In contrast, young children in the United States receive little parental encouragement to become involved in trading. Thus, children from Zimbabwe develop sophisticated cognitive scripts for and knowledge of trading more readily than do children from the United States.

■ *Through assignment of responsibility:* Cultures vary in the extent to which parents and adults structure the learning environment. In some cultures, adults provide structure by guiding children's attention, motivation, and involvement and by providing lessons in important activities. This greater level of parental involvement is typical in societies in which children's participation in adult life is delayed until they are much older. Children learn skills that are assumed to help them later, when they take on adult roles (Rogoff et al., 1993). In other cultures, children direct their own attention and motivation and determine for themselves their level of involvement in adult activities. The role of adults is to provide feedback in response to children's requests but not to try to direct the children. For instance, in a Mayan Indian town in Guatemala, children routinely observe their mothers' involvement in adult economic activities—for example, weaving and sewing. Children are responsible for watching the activities and deciding whether and when to enter into them. While the mothers respond to children's questions and requests, typically they do not give direct instruction (Rogoff et al., 1993). Children raised in traditional Native American cultures learn through quiet observation. A Navaho girl may decide she is ready to weave after spending time watching her mother but without receiving direct instruction in weaving (Collier, 1988).

What Changes Occur in Young Children's Language Development During Early Childhood?

Children's language use involves symbols, just as does cognition. By age 2, children begin to use the symbols of words to stand for the things they represent. This use of symbols grows in sophistication such that most children are competent speakers of their native language by the age of 5. They have learned many of the subtleties of language; for example, they can distinguish between two similarly worded sentences that have quite different meanings, such as "The bird is in the tree" and "The bird is in the dark." They learn the meanings of thousands of words during the early preschool years. Language development is a primary focus of socialization in a culture. **Social communicative competence** is the ability to effectively convey an intended message to others (Wilcox & Terrell, 1985). Children whose social communicative competence is low are at risk for problem behaviors and poor social relationships (Rice, Hadley, & Alexander, 1993).

Vocabulary

Children's vocabularies expand rapidly during the preschool years and even faster during the school years. Researchers estimate that before first grade, children learn about 5 words a day, but in first grade to third grade, they learn twice that a day. Using a large sample of words from an English dictionary and asking children about the meaning of these words, researchers have estimated the numbers of words children recognize and how their vocabularies change with age. Children average about 10,000 words in their vocabulary by first grade (Anglin, 1993).

Although young children have a much larger vocabulary than toddlers do, they still experience the frustration of not being able to get adults to understand their meaning. There are some words that children want to say but cannot. Some sounds are difficult for them to produce, and children around the world will avoid words that they find difficult to say (Ingram, 1989). Often children create words to better express themselves. For instance, a 4-year-old said, "Try to be more rememberful, Mom" when disappointed by his mother's

social communicative competence   *the ability to effectively convey an intended message to others*

forgetfulness (Clark, 1993). Children also use words creatively (and differently than adults) to convey meaning. Our 3-year-old niece, Erica, used the word *soaking* as a stand in for *very*—she described herself as "soaking tired" or "soaking cold."

Even with their larger vocabularies, young children continue to be faced with the problem of not knowing as many words as the adults around them know. Just as they did when they were younger, these children find ways to express themselves, using general-purpose nouns such as *thing* or general-purpose verbs such as *do* to describe objects and actions. They also create new words, as noted above. One method of word creation is to add -*er* to the end of a term to indicate an agent taking a particular action. For instance, one child added -*er* to the end of *hang* to refer to a person who hangs pictures as "a hanger." Another method is to coin terms by making nouns into verbs when trying to pick food up from his plate, one child said, "I'm gonna fork this" (Clark, 1993).

Much of the research on children's word learning focuses on how children learn about words for concrete objects that they can see and touch. But how do children solve the mystery of word meaning for verbs? Think about how much more difficult it is to figure out the meaning of a word such as *push* than that of a word such as *cat*. Verbs are more difficult to learn than nouns are; hence, children's early vocabularies have many more nouns than verbs. To learn verbs, children appear to employ a process called **syntactic bootstrapping,** in which they use the structure of a sentence to provide cues about the meaning of the novel verb (Gleitman & Gillette, 1995). (The word *bootstrapping* refers to "pulling yourself up by the bootstraps.") Suppose a parent says, "Look! The dog is gorping the cat." The child is likely to assume that *gorping* is something that one agent does to another. If the parent says instead, "Look! The dog and cat are gorping," the child is more likely to assume that gorping involved a mutual action (Naigles, 1990).

After hearing her parents describe her as soaking wet, how might this girl use the word *soaking*?

Young Children's Language Styles

The types of vocabulary words that children use are influenced by their language styles. Two types of language styles have been identified in middle-class US families. Children with a **referential language style** develop a vocabulary that includes many object names and use these labels to name the things in their environments. Children with an **expressive language style,** however, use words to regulate social interactions with adults and have fewer object names in their vocabulary (Nelson, 1973). The vocabulary explosion is likely to occur at the end of the second year for children with a referential style, who quickly add many names of things to their vocabulary at this time (Goldfield & Reznick, 1990).

All children use both referential and expressive styles of language on occasion, but some children emphasize one style over the other. Mothers of expressive children direct and control their children's actions through the use of language. For instance, a mother might say, "Say goodbye to your grandmother." In contrast, mothers of referential children comment on aspects of the environment and name activities and objects their children interact with—for example, naming the different toys a child picks up during play (Goldfield, 1987). A child's interests may contribute to the mother's use of language. The mother of a child who shows special interest in a certain toy may encourage that interest by providing names more freely than does the mother of a child who shows less interest (Bridges, 1986).

Grammar: Beyond Two-Word Sentences

As children grow older, their understanding and use of language become increasingly sophisticated. Sentences grow longer than two words, allowing children much more flexibility in communicating their ideas and desires. Between 2 and 3 years of age, many children form sentences of three words or more, using an agent–action–recipient word order to convey meaning. For instance, they might say, "I hugged the cat." Three-year-olds can use

syntactic bootstrapping
children's use of the structure of sentences to provide cues about word meaning

referential language style
language style focused on developing a vocabulary that includes many object names

expressive language style
language style focused on using words to regulate social interactions with adults

FIGURE 9.6

Referential Language Style Versus Expressive Language Style

What is the major difference between these two types of language styles? How do parents influence the development of these styles?

negatives such as *no, not, can't,* and *don't*. They may ask questions using *what* and *where*, but they are unlikely to form questions using *why* or *how*.

During the preschool years, children show evidence of trying to discover and apply grammatical regularities to their speech (Owens, 1996). It appears that children use many language cues to develop increasingly sophisticated knowledge about syntax. For instance, children pay close attention to the ends of words; this helps them understand past tense and plurals. They also pay close attention to word order, and they attempt to preserve the word order they hear in the adult speech directed to them. Children's vocabularies provide a way for them to use what they already know to learn the rules of language. In **semantic bootstrapping,** children use what they know about the meaning of words to help them decipher the syntactic structure of language (Pinker, 1984). For instance, actions indicate verbs, and persons and objects form categories indicated by nouns. Consider what a child might think about these unfamiliar words: *grom* and *floom*. If the child heard, "Reba grommed the house," the child might consider that *grom* is an action that can be done on houses; therefore, it could mean "to clean the house." If the child heard, "The floom is pink," the child might consider that *floom* must refer to objects that have color, so *flooms* could be "flowers." These bootstrapping techniques are imperfect; nonetheless, they provide children with a way of using previous knowledge to inform their language development.

During young childhood, children gain mastery over many rules of grammar, indicating past tense by adding *-ed* to the end of a verb and forming the plural by adding *-s* to the end of a noun. Their application of these rules becomes obvious when they use them in situations in which the rules do *not* apply, in a process called **overregularization.** At around 3 to 4 years of age, English-speaking children may begin to apply the rules for regular forms to irregular cases. Children overregularize infrequently, and when they do, it tends to be with words that parents do not use often (Fenson et al., 1994; Marcus et al., 1992). A child might say, "My teeths hurt" or "I breaked my toy." Caregivers' attempts to correct overregularizations are often ineffective. For example, when 3-year-old Brenda said, "I goed to school today," her mother tried to correct her by saying, "You mean you went to school today." Without missing a beat, Brenda replied, "Yeah, I goed to school today."

Even in completely unfamiliar situations, children assume that rules for regular plural forms apply. In one study, children were first shown a picture of a birdlike creature called a *wug* and then shown a picture depicting two of the creatures. The children were asked to finish the sentence "There are two _____." Most children said, "There are two *wugs*" (Berko, 1958). They assumed that the plural of *wug* would follow the regular form and be *wugs*.

An interesting twist on children's application of grammatical rules is that younger children correctly use the appropriate plurals and past tenses for even the irregular forms. It appears that very young children memorize the irregular forms and reproduce them accurately. Later, when they learn the rules for the regular forms, they assume that these apply to the irregular forms. Even later, they learn to distinguish between the regular forms and the irregular forms and produce both correctly.

At around 4 years of age, children begin to use connectives to conjoin two events in a compound sentence, such as "You watch television, and I'll play with my doll." Use of the connective word *and* is one of the first ways in which children combine simple sentences. As they mature, children learn to form more complicated sentences in which two events occur sequentially in time, such as "Let's go to the store and buy some cookies." Even later, children form sentences expressing causality. Children use *and* as an all-purpose connective word, but they begin to add others, such as *then* and *when* to represent temporal orderings of events and *because* and *so* to represent causal events (Bloom, 1998).

Five-year-old children have an amazing mastery of language and can use language to entertain and tell stories. Nonetheless, subtle aspects of syntax elude them, and they struggle with some forms of grammar such as the past tense of *be* (*was* and *were*), possessive pronouns (*his, her, your*), and infinitives ("I want *to go* now") (Owens, 1996). Children gain mastery over the more complex and subtle aspects of grammar and vocabulary during the school years.

Understanding Conversational Rules

Six-year-old Robbie sat at the dinner table with a group of adults, patiently trying to find a time to break into the conversation to make a point. By the time he found an opening in the conversation, he had forgotten what he wanted to say. For adults, most of the rules of conversation are so ingrained that they do not think about them. They know when they can take a turn in the conversation. But young children face the challenge of learning to follow conversational rules while at the same time applying the rules for forming sentences. This is one aspect of language development.

Young children are surprisingly good at following basic conversational rules. Even at the age of 2, most children realize that they should begin speaking once someone has spoken to them, and they recognize that certain statements require specific answers (yes or no) (Bloom, Rocissano, & Hood, 1976). By the age of 4, many children are aware that they must adjust their speech to fit the speaker; in other words, they must be mindful of whether the person they are speaking to can understand them. For instance, young children shorten their sentences, simplify their vocabulary, and speak more slowly when talking to even younger children (Tomasello & Mannie, 1985). The ability to adjust to the level of the listener continues to develop during childhood. It is important to remember, though, that these skills are not used all the time by all speakers: even adults are not always mindful of the capabilities of their listeners.

How might this child describe the broken toy? Why do children overregularize?

The Social Context of Language Development

Social experiences continue to play an important role in children's language acquisition after infancy (Huttenlocher, 1998; Wilcox, Hadley, & Ashland, 1996). Parents direct children's language exposure when they read to children or engage in a scripted activity such as a tea party. They provide opportunities for children to be involved in conversations by asking them to comment on activities and experiences. For instance, to prompt Sarah to begin a conversation with her father, Sarah's mother asks her at the dinner table, "Can you tell Daddy about the toy we bought for Erin?" Both parents are likely to continue to focus her attention on this topic by asking questions about the shopping trip. Caregivers use more sophisticated and complex forms of expansion as a way of encouraging children to pay attention to the grammatically challenging aspects of their speech (Bloom, 1998). Caregivers also socialize politeness in children's language. A father might say to his child, "Say, 'Please may I have a cookie,'" to encourage appropriate manners (Gleason, Ely, Perlmann, & Narasimhan, 1996).

Beyond parent-directed language activities is the larger social context of language use, which involves both the child and the caregiver as active agents who negotiate the activities of daily living (Ninio & Snow, 1996; Tomasello, 1992; Tomasello & Akhtar, 1995). Children play a more active role in directing speech than early research suggested. In fact, children may be the primary force in directing language interactions and often take the lead in their everyday conversations with adults and caregivers (Bloom, Margulis, Tinker, & Fujita, 1996). Caregivers are more likely to respond to children than to initiate conversations with them.

As children grow older, they spend more time with their siblings, and this new, expanded social context influences language development. Siblings' speech among themselves

This child speaks Spanish at home and English at school. How is this child's language development similar to or different from that of children who only know one language?

is different from caregivers' speech to children—it is more playful and includes more reciprocal verbal interchanges (Brown & Dunn, 1992). Having a variety of language partners, each with a particular language style and vocabulary, encourages and supports children's language development.

Thus, language learning occurs in a social context, driven by children's need to communicate and share meaning with others. Caregivers, siblings, peers, and teachers all contribute to learning by responding to the meanings children communicate, providing scripted language experiences, and being responsive partners in communication. Children's desire to communicate, opportunities to connect with others through language, and changes in cognitive development converge to facilitate language development (Bloom, 1998).

Language Development in Bilingual Children

A boy named Christian was born in Germany to an American Estonian father and an American mother. The mother generally spoke to Christian in English, the father mainly spoke to him in Estonian, and the nanny and other children in the neighborhood spoke to him in German. Christian's parents spoke to each other in English. Whereas most children hear one name or label associated with each noun early in their development, Christian often heard two or three different labels. Do you think this situation would be confusing for Christian?

For many years researchers have been intrigued by bilingual (two-language) and trilingual (three-language) language learning. As you can imagine, researchers have been interested in how children keep the languages straight and whether the children fall behind in learning. Although many researchers concluded that bilingual children (who have been studied more than trilingual ones) tend to develop language skills comparable to those of other children, at first they believed that the best strategy in the home was relatively unmixed language exposure, in which one language was associated with one person and the other with another person. The assumption was that the association between the language and its source (a particular person) would provide cues to the child about which language was appropriate to use. However, more recent work on this topic suggests a different conclusion: that most bilingual children receive both mixed and unmixed language input and that children are able to use these rich input sources in combination with their cognitive and language skills to make sense of the two languages (Bhatia & Ritchie, 1999). Overall, bilingual children develop language skills in the same order and the same time frame as do children exposed to only one language. Bilingual children have some advantages over other children, although the advantages are not uniform across areas (Bialystock, 1999, 2001, 2002). Christian's language learning for English was similar to other children's. However, within a few years, he was speaking German, English, and Estonian. For bilingual speakers, the pragmatics of using language are complex. They have to learn the circumstances under which they should use each language. In Christian's case, he could use the predominant language spoken by each of his parents as a cue in deciding which language to speak to them. With people he did not know, he used appearance to help him decide which language to speak. For instance, while living in the United States, he spoke German to an unfamiliar blond woman because, he said, she looked German. Both children and adult bilingual people frequently engage in **code switching**—alternating use of two or more languages to communicate their ideas. Just as most children are sensitive to the perceived language capabilities of the people they talk to, bilingual children use social cues and information about the target's language preferences—for instance, whether the other person uses one or two languages—to help them select a method of communication. The language they employ depends on the

code switching   *the alternate use of two or more languages*

NURTURING CHILDREN
HELPING CHILDREN TO LEARN LANGUAGE

Caregivers find many ways to provide an optimal learning environment for pre-school children's language acquisition (Owens, 1996). The following are some important strategies for helping children learn language.

■ *Recast and expand children's own sentences into longer and more correct forms:* If a child says, "The dinosaur walked in the woods," a caregiver might expand and recast the sentence by saying "That dinosaur walked a long time in the woods, didn't it?" Or a parent might expand a child's statement "I breaked my new doll" into "I'm sorry that you broke your new doll." These variant forms of sentences maintain the basic meaning but display it in a new sentence structure, as well as in correct grammatical form. Children learn more rapidly

about language when parents use these methods (Farrar, 1990). Caregivers can use more complex expansions with preschoolers than with toddlers (Hoff-Ginsberg, 1985).

■ *Maintain the child's attention to verbal tasks:* Children learn about conversations when caregivers provide topic continuity and reintroduce topics.

■ *Build language activities into everyday routines:* For example, while baking cookies, a caregiver might describe every step in the process. By using language skills for everyday activities, children develop scripts for these events that include the use of language.

■ *Provide a moderately challenging language environment for the child:* Caregivers should not adjust their language level down to the child's

at all times, but instead should regularly expose the child to a combination of moderately challenging and highly challenging language environments.

■ *Encourage the child to experience many language partners:* Children who are encouraged to speak to a wide range of social partners are more likely to hear varied types of input at different levels than are children who speak with fewer partners.

■ *Support the child's own style of language learning:* Some children are likely to imitate others, and some children tend to avoid imitation. Some children like to make a game out of naming objects. Try to determine the methods the child uses and then incorporate them into everyday language experiences.

setting, the person they are talking to, and the nature of the idea to be expressed (Edwards, 2004; Hamers, 2004). Bilingual children learn to code switch at an early age, and these skills come in part from observing the use of language by others around them (Bhatia & Richie, 1999; de Houwer, 1995; Hamers, 2004).

How Does Early Childhood Education Influence Development?

Young children's cognitive development is influenced by the stimulation and interactions that caregivers provide for them. Some of these interactions are very direct, such as those discussed earlier in which caregivers provide scaffolding for their children. Caregivers also act as teachers and facilitators of learning by providing stimulating environments for their children. Outside the home, children experience opportunities to learn in preschool and kindergarten settings.

Parents as Teachers

How do children grow up to become gifted or talented in a particular cognitive area? Do their parents treat them in any special ways to help encourage their talents? Not surprisingly, parents play a very important role in encouraging the cognitive abilities of their children. In a fascinating study of 25 famous mathematicians, it was discovered that 21 of these talented individuals had experienced early intellectual stimulation (Fowler, 1986). For example, the father of René Descartes (1596–1650; credited with unifying algebra and

How can trips to the library promote cognitive development? What else can parents do to help their children become talented and gifted?

geometry) began René's intensive intellectual stimulation when he was only 14 months of age. Blaise Pascal (1632–1662; credited with developing the first calculating machine and famous for his work on probability theory) and Karl Gauss (1777–1855; considered to be the father of modern mathematics) had parents who intensively schooled them to calculate, read, and write early and engaged them in many intellectual discussions. Almost all of these great mathematicians were, as children, exposed to highly intellectual adults who stimulated their cognitive development.

Parents promote cognitive development by constructing an optimal learning environment in the home—they provide materials, experiences, and encouragement that help children to become curious explorers of their worlds. An instrument designed to measure these aspects of a stimulating environment is called the Home Observation for Measurement of the Environment (HOME) Scale (see Table 9.1). Studies using the HOME Scale have investigated the roles in children's cognitive development of parental encouragement of learning and the physical environment to which the child is exposed (Bradley, 1999). Higher scores on the HOME Scale relate to better outcomes for children. When children are exposed to a large variety of learning materials in a safe environment and when they receive encouragement for learning, they score higher on tests of language development and cognitive development than do children with less stimulating environments (Bradley, Burchinal, & Casey, 2001). African American, Caucasian American, and Hispanic American children show similar relationships between HOME features and cognitive development (Bradley et al., 1989).

During the early years, parents can encourage children's cognitive development in many ways. Probably the most important one is spending time with children (see Table 9.2). Although most parents are aware of the importance of reading to their children, not all parents routinely provide this type of experience. Many children are read to very little or not at all during the early years, and how often children are read to varies by income level and the race/ethnicity of the family (see Figure 9.7).

Young Children's Educational Experiences

Since the first public nursery schools for children were opened in the United States in the early 1900s, the idea of an education-oriented setting for young children has become increasingly popular. Even with fewer children being born today in the United States than in

TABLE 9.1
Assessing the Home Environment

CRITERIA	SAMPLE EVIDENCE OF POSITIVE ENVIRONMENT
Stimulation of academic behavior	Child is encouraged to learn colors.
Variety in daily stimulation	Child is frequently taken on outings with other family members.
Access to toys and games or stimulation	Home has toys and games.
Encouragement of maturity	Child is encouraged to be responsible and sociable.
Language stimulation	Parent teaches child about language through the use of games, books, puzzles.
Punishment methods	Parent does not spank or slap child during visit.
Physical environment	Rooms are clean and uncluttered.
Pride and acceptance	Parent is proud of child.

TABLE 9.2
Stimulating Young Children's Intellectual Development

Read to children, and let them see you read.

Visit the library, and allow children to select their own books.

Set limits on television viewing to encourage conversational skills and reading.

Provide pencils, crayons, and markers for children to practice drawing and writing.

Ask children questions, and listen to their answers.

Take children to museums, art galleries, and historical sites.

Encourage children to think critically and solve problems.

Explore and play with children.

past decades, enrollment in preschools has risen dramatically, from about 20 percent of preschool-age children in the 1970s to about 50 percent today.

A good preschool uses developmentally appropriate practices. This means that the activities are based on knowledge about the developmental level of children within a particular age range. At the same time, a good preschool encourages and recognizes the unique qualities that each child brings to the educational experience. Activities in the preschool curriculum foster children's physical, social, cognitive, and emotional development.

A good preschool does not mimic older children's elementary education classes. Instead, it is geared specifically for the active young child. Rather than sitting at desks and being guided by a teacher, children should be encouraged to actively explore their environments. Some children might play with water containers, others listen to a story, and still others build a block fortress. Teachers can facilitate children's involvement by asking questions or offering suggestions. A good preschool focuses on the individual needs of each child and on enhancing children's self-esteem and self-control.

The effectiveness of preschool programs has been studied extensively. High-quality preschool programs have low student–teacher ratios, a well-educated staff, and developmentally appropriate activities. Children in such programs show advances in cognitive and social skills compared with children from the same kind of backgrounds who do not attend preschools (Clarke-Stewart, 1984). This is especially true for disadvantaged children (Burchinal, Lee, & Ramey, 1989). In one study, the cognitive and social advantages of preschool were still apparent after three years of elementary school (Howes, 1988b). Children who attended high-quality preschools had fewer behavior problems and better academic skills in first grade than did children who did not attend high-quality preschools.

Clearly, a major issue for parents must be the quality of care that their children receive. Given the importance of a good preschool, it is essential that parents learn how to assess the quality of preschools so that children have the optimal early childhood education experience. Table 9.3 outlines some of the features that parents should look for.

Children's first experience with formal schooling usually occurs in kindergarten. The first kindergartens, opened in the

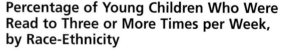

FIGURE 9.7
Percentage of Young Children Who Were Read to Three or More Times per Week, by Race-Ethnicity

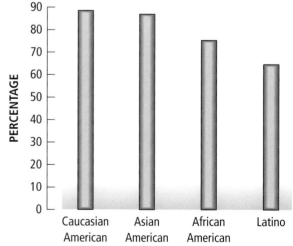

What generalizations can you draw from this figure? What factors may contribute to the differences found among the racial-ethnic groups?

Source: National Center for Education Statistics, 1999.

TABLE 9.3
Indicators of a High-Quality Preschool

Licensing/ Accreditation	The program is licensed by the state. If the program is accredited by the National Association for the Education of Young Children, it is a top-notch program.
Setting	There is a safe, fenced, outdoor play area, well equipped for many activities. The indoor area has space for many different activities and a wide variety of toys, books, puzzles, and games.
Teacher– Child Ratio	The number of children supervised by a team of two teachers is not greater than 18 to 20. Each teacher is responsible for no more than 8 to 10 children.
Teacher Qualifications	Teachers have college-level training in child development or early childhood education.
Parent Involvement	Parents are encouraged to drop in to observe the children and participate in activities with them. Teachers frequently review and discuss children's development with parents.

mid–nineteenth century, were designed to nurture young children. Today in the United States, kindergarten has become another tier of the public education system. Many people believe that children's cognitive development needs to be accelerated, and one means of doing so is to increase the academic emphasis in kindergarten. These people see preschools and kindergartens as obvious places to begin academic training and promote readiness for school. Many experts in child development, however, oppose an emphasis on early academic training in reading, writing, and arithmetic (Charlesworth, 1989; Elkind, 1987, 1988), primarily for two reasons. One reason relates to the belief that children learn best when they are actively involved in learning. Good kindergarten and preschool programs lay the foundation for later cognitive skills by encouraging developmentally appropriate play and supplying hands-on experiences. Another reason is that children who are pushed academically at a young age may lose interest in learning, which has serious long-term consequences for their education.

Early Intervention and Young Children's Cognitive Development

Young children's cognitive development is stimulated and nurtured when they are exposed to intellectually challenging environments and have positive role models to emulate. For instance, children are more likely to be interested in reading if they observe their parents routinely reading for pleasure in the home. Unfortunately, not all children have such ideal conditions for cognitive development. Many young children live in stressful, distracting environments that lack intellectual stimulation. These children do not have the kinds of early experiences that foster the development of competent intellectual performance and achievement. For instance, they may not be taken to libraries or read to often because the parents are overworked or in poor health. Can these unstimulating environments be overcome or supplemented?

Notice that the children in this class are not sitting at desks, studying. How do children learn in preschool? What are some developmentally appropriate methods for encouraging cognitive development in preschool children?

Head Start

Project Head Start originated in 1965, during America's "War on Poverty," and was designed to serve preschool-age children from economically disadvantaged backgrounds. In 2002,

FROM RESEARCH TO PRACTICE
WHEN ARE YOUNG CHILDREN PREPARED TO START SCHOOL?

"By the year 2000, all children in America will start school ready to learn." These words were uttered in 1989 by then President George H. Bush and the state governors, who established this as the top goal for American education. Few argued with this goal, but how *readiness* was to be defined and how this goal was to be reached were hotly debated (Gredler, 1997; Shepard, 1997).

FROM RESEARCH . . .

Readiness to learn has been conceptualized as the level of development at which a child is prepared to undertake the learning of specific material and content. For most preschoolers, learning is an active and enjoyable process. Most enter kindergarten ready to learn, but this readiness does not always guarantee success in school (Lewit & Baker, 1995).

Historically, chronological age has served as the major criterion for school entry. In the United States, although some children enter kindergarten at age 4, the majority enter at between 5 and 6 years of age, with about 6 percent held back each year to begin school after they are 6 (National Center for Education Statistics, 2001a). The tendency to hold children back has been increasing; in recent years, almost 16 percent of first-grade children were held back for one year (Brent, May, & Kundert, 1996). Because some aspects of development, such as language skills, are strongly correlated with age, older children, particularly boys, do better in school during the early grades than do younger classmates (US Department of Education, 1998). However, these differences tend to disappear by third grade (Stipek & Byler, 2001). Age generally is not a good predictor of academic success (Morrison, Alberts, & Griffith, 1997).

Although there is no agreement as to what constitutes readiness for school,

being physically healthy, having adequate communication skills, having an interest in learning, being able to sit still, and controlling one's impulses have been identified as key components (Child Trends, 2001; Huffman, Mehlinger, & Kerivan, 2000; Lewit & Baker, 1995). According to a large-scale study of kindergartners and their parents (US Department of Education, 1993), only 63 percent of kindergartners had all of these school-readiness qualities. These findings are in line with a more recent study in which kindergarten teachers said that about half of their students were not ready to participate successfully in school (Rimm-Kaufman, Pianta, & Cox, 2000). Boys are less likely to be ready for school than girls are. They are less likely than girls to be able to pay attention for a sustained period of time, they have more language difficulties, and they are more active and have more behavior problems than do girls (US Department of Education, 2001). In addition, when teachers were asked to compare the readiness of their current students with that of their students five years ago, only 25 percent said that today's kindergartners were more ready; 42 percent said fewer students were ready now than before (US Department of Education, 1993).

. . . TO PRACTICE

School readiness does not reside solely with children. Families, schools, and communities have the responsibility to ensure children's school readiness (Carlton & Winsler, 1999). Supportive environments that promote healthy, concerned, developmentally appropriate interactions with young children are likely to produce the most active and eager learners in kindergarten and beyond (May & Kundert, 1997). Parents can do many things to promote school success in their children:

- Parents are children's first teachers. They should devote time each day to help their child learn.
- Children should receive the nutrition, physical activity, and health care they need to enter school with healthy minds and bodies.
- Parents should monitor children's media viewing.
- Parents should encourage literacy by providing access to books and by reading to their child.
- Parents should ensure that their children have access to high-quality preschools to prepare them for school.

Schools play an important role in ensuring that children make smooth transitions into kindergarten. They can encourage more contact between preschools and kindergartens, as well as more contact between parents and schools before and after the child enters school. School also can provide parents with contact information about community services. Communities also must make investments in children's school success by providing support and education for parents, promoting children's health care and immunizations, supporting supplemental food programs for children, encouraging campaigns to educate the public about child safety, and addressing parents' and children's psychological challenges (Child Trends, 2001).

THINKING IT THROUGH

1. How can parents and teachers work together to promote young children's school readiness?

2. What individual characteristics of young children enhance their readiness to enter school?

3. In your opinion, what are the most important qualities that determine a young child's readiness to enter kindergarten? What factors put children at risk for not being ready to enter school?

almost 50,000 Head Start classrooms were serving over 900,000 children. The program has serviced almost 17 million children since 1965. The majority of families with children in Head Start had an annual income of less than $9,000. Of the children enrolled in Head Start, 33 percent were African American, 28 percent were Caucasian American, 30 percent were Hispanic American, 3 percent were Native American, and 2 percent were Asian American. Head Start serves about 30 percent of all eligible children (Administration for Children and Families, 2002).

Children living in low-income families are at risk for failure in school because these families may not give priority to academic values or encourage children to think critically. The families simply may not have the resources to promote cognitive development. Head Start programs were developed to overcome these problems. Children begin Head Start classes at age 3 and can continue for two years. Although Head Start is more than an educational program, one of its stated goals is to provide environmental interventions that stimulate children's cognitive growth. For this reason, much of the research on the effectiveness of Head Start has focused on the intellectual performance of the young children enrolled in the program (Raver & Zigler, 1997).

Studies of the immediate effects of Head Start showed that young children's IQ scores rose by at least 10 points and that their achievement levels sometimes rose after just a few weeks of attending Head Start (Datta, 1985). Unfortunately, findings on long-term effects were not as optimistic. Research found that young children attending Head Start did not continue to do better on cognitive tests or in school (Nieman & Gaithright, 1981). These reports dashed the hopes of those who believed that early intervention in the form of intellectually stimulating preschools could improve children's success in school permanently. In fact, plans were drawn up to discontinue Head Start (Lubeck, DeVries, Nicholson, & Post, 1997).

Fortunately, parents of the preschoolers enrolled in Head Start protested, and their actions saved the program. Soon afterward, new research was undertaken using more sophisticated designs and techniques. These studies show that in the first two years, the effects of Head Start are impressive: children begin Head Start at a great disadvantage compared to their peers, but they leave showing strong improvements in vocabulary knowledge and early writing skills. Spanish-speaking children make significant gains in English vocabulary without losing Spanish vocabulary. Children showed improvements in their social skills and reductions in hyperactive behavior (Tarullo et al., 2003). Although these studies found that young children who attend Head Start show an initial boost in intellectual performance that sometimes lasts for years, this initial boost often fades over time (Barnett, 1998).

Why might children's intellectual performance fade over time? One answer may be the formal education these children receive after the preschool years. Low-income families often live in communities where schools do not receive adequate funding. These children thus may find themselves in inferior educational settings and less than stimulating environments. The drop in performance may therefore be a by-product of the relatively poor school environments disadvantaged children encounter (Zigler & Styfco, 1998). Most children involved in Head Start classes are being raised in families facing many severe life challenges (see Figure 9.8). About one quarter of Head Start parents have major psychological depression, and their children have more behavior problems and some areas of lower academic performance than other Head Start children. About 10 percent of Head Start children witness violent crimes in their neighborhoods, and the more crime they witness, the more behavior problems, such as aggression, they exhibit. On the other side, however, about two thirds of Head Start parents attend parent–teacher conferences, and parental involvement is positively related to children's positive school behavior and academic performance (Tarullo et al., 2003). Being involved in Head Start may buffer parents and children from the challenging aspects of their lives, but once the program is over, this buffering ends.

FIGURE 9.8
Percentage of Head Start Families with Various Risk Factors

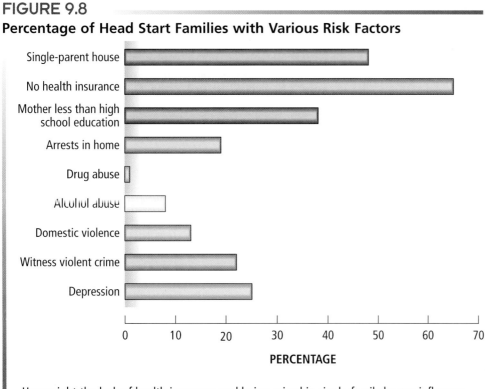

How might the lack of health insurance and being raised in single-family homes influence children in Head Start? How might support be given to these families to make their lives easier?

Source: Head Start FACES, 2000.

The research also showed, however, that important lasting effects of Head Start exist in other areas. Specifically, participants of Head Start were found to compare favorably in the following ways with low-income children who did not attend Head Start (Consortium for Longitudinal Studies, 1983; Gamble & Zigler, 1989):

- They were less likely to be assigned to special education classes.
- They were less likely to be held back a grade in school.
- They had fewer school absences.

The focus on the intellectual benefits of Head Start for disadvantaged young children obscures the benefits in other areas. Preschoolers who attend Head Start show improved physical health, nutritional status, family interactions, and social–emotional behaviors (Raver & Zigler, 1997; Tarullo et al, 2003). Thus, there are considerable benefits to the early interventions provided by Head Start (Fantuzzo & Mohr, 2000).

Head Start is expanding its services to include children younger than 3 years of age (Early Head Start). The rationale for this extension is clear: waiting until a child is 3 or 4 years old is too late (Kagan & Neuman, 1998). With children beginning Head Start earlier, it may be possible to provide preventive services that are more effective than the remedial services provided after problems arise. Children who are healthy, who have positive relationships with caregivers, and who receive adequate stimulation have the foundations for learning in preschool and beyond (Zigler, 1999).

Why has *Sesame Street* been successful in promoting the intellectual growth of preschool children all around the world?

Sesame Street

Television reaches many eligible children that Head Start does not reach. Because of its wide acceptance and use, television is viewed by educators as a "teacher" in every home. Between 1960 and 1970, Congress passed legislation funding the construction of public educational television stations and the development of educational programming. Today public television provides a wide range of educational programming, and almost every US family has access to these programs.

Most children know and recognize the characters Grover and Big Bird, attesting to the popularity of the highly successful educational program *Sesame Street*. In the United States, 77 percent of preschool children watch the show at least once a week (Public Broadcasting Service, 1999). *Sesame Street* was the first educational program that combined the attention-holding qualities of commercial television with developmentally appropriate educational material designed to help prepare children for school. The goal of *Sesame Street* is to promote the intellectual growth of preschoolers, particularly disadvantaged preschoolers.

Sesame Street is successful in teaching children many skills; regular viewing increases young children's understanding of numbers, letters, and vocabulary and boosts their reasoning skills. Children from varied racial, social, geographic, and educational backgrounds all seem to learn from watching *Sesame Street* (Children's Television Workshop, 1991; Rice, Huston, Truglio, & Wright, 1990). Measurable effects have been found 10 to 12 years later, and many effects have been found to be consistent across different cultures and countries (Fisch, Truglio, & Cole, 1999). In addition, mothers of preschoolers are pleased with the educational benefits provided by it (Yankelovich & White, 1989).

The influence of *Sesame Street* is stronger on 3-year-old children than on 5-year-olds, suggesting that the effects of *Sesame Street* may be greatest when children first begin to watch it. The effects of *Sesame Street* also are stronger the more often children watch it (Sell, Ray, & Lovelace, 1995). Early on, some critics of *Sesame Street* argued that its apparent effectiveness was due to children's watching the show with parents who used the television show as a means to teach their children (Cook et al., 1975). However, in later research (Rice et al., 1990), parents reported that they watched *Sesame Street* with their preschoolers only 25 percent of the time that the preschoolers watched it. Thus, 75 percent of the time preschoolers spent watching *Sesame Street* was without their parents. *Sesame Street* provides young children with valuable educational experiences that they can profit from on their own, as well as when they watch with their caregivers (Comstock & Paik, 1991).

Sesame Street is not just an American phenomenon. The show has been adapted for use all over the world and is recognized as beneficial in many countries. In its various adaptations, *Sesame Street* plays in over 80 countries around the world. In each country, *Sesame Street* has been tailored to meet educational goals specific to children in that cultural setting:

- The Arabic version of *Sesame Street*, *Iftah Ya Simsim*, focuses on bridging the gap between the informal language that Arabic-speaking children are exposed to in their homes and the classic Arabic language used in the schools. *Iftah Ya Simsim* makes learning formal Arabic fun as well as interesting (Ezzaki, 1990).

- In Portugal, *Sesame Street* is called *Rua Sesamo*. Because only 30 percent of children in Portugal go to preschool, *Rua Sesamo* plays an even greater role in early education than *Sesame Street* does in the United States (Brederode, 1990).

- The Turkish version of *Sesame Street* is called *Susam Sokagi*. In Turkey, concern about illiteracy—particularly among women and people who live in rural areas—is great. One goal of *Susam Sokagi* is to get mothers to watch with their children, so that both the mothers and the children will learn to read and write (Sahin, 1990).

The variations in *Sesame Street* reflect cultural differences in values, education, and economic conditions. Regardless of the culture, research evidence shows that *Sesame Street*, in its different versions, successfully meets the wide variety of educational needs of children in various countries (Children's Television Workshop, 1991).

Try It Out

1. Try some Piagetian tasks with a 4- or 5-year-old child. Ask the child about why the stars shine at night. Does the child give an egocentric response? Try a conservation task with the child. Does the child think a piece of clay that is long like a snake has more clay in it than one shaped like a ball? Give the child a choice between a broken and an unbroken cookie, and see if he or she thinks the unbroken one would taste better.
2. Listen to a parent and young child in a problem-solving situation. Who is directing the conversation? Does the parent encourage politeness, expand the child's sentences to make them more complex, or repeat the child's ideas back to her or him? In what ways does the parent help in the child's problem solving and use of language?
3. Watch *Sesame Street* with a young child. What features of the show are appealing to him or her? Notice what the child does during the show—such as imitating the characters' actions, singing the songs, or practicing the lessons.
4. Talk to a young child about common, everyday events. Does the child recognize the order of events and their timing? Then ask about less familiar events, and see if the child has an understanding of their temporal sequence. Why might his or her understanding of these two types of events be different? What factors do you think influence children's understanding of events?

Key Terms and Concepts

animism (273)
centration (271)
class inclusion (272)
code switching (286)
conservation tasks (270)
dual representation (271)
egocentric speech (273)
egocentrism (273)
expressive language style (283)
identity concept (270)
irreversibility (270)
operations (270)

overregularization (284)
private speech (275)
referential language style (283)
scripts (277)
semantic bootstrapping (284)
social communicative competence (282)
static thinking (271)
symbolic representations (270)
syntactic bootstrapping (283)
theory of mind (280)
transductive reasoning (272)

Sum It Up

How do young children think and solve problems?

- According to Piaget, why are young children preoperational thinkers? Give an example. (p. 270)
- Describe and give an example of Vygotsky's idea of egocentric speech. (p. 275)
- Why is young children's capacity to process information more limited than older children and adults' capacity to process information? (p. 277)

What changes occur in young children's language development during early childhood?

- List and describe the two types of language styles identified in middle-class U.S. children. (p. 283)

How does early childhood education influence development?

- What are some ways to stimulate young children's intellectual development? (p. 289)

FIGURE 9.5 **Vygotsky's Private Speech** *Children use their own internal dialogue when trying to solve problems.*

This round piece goes here.

Preoperational thinking is best illustrated using conservation tasks. These tasks show that young children tend to be fooled by the appearance of an object, rather than recognizing that transformations do not change the identity of the object.

THINKING AND PROBLEM SOLVING

The major theoretical approaches used to understand children's thinking are Piaget's theory of cognitive development, which concentrates on children's different view of the world; Vygotsky's sociocultural perspective, in which children's thinking is thought to be guided by their social interactions with others; and the information processing approach, which considers the constraints and limitations on children's thinking and on their memories. (Refer back to pages 269–282.)

LANGUAGE DEVELOPMENT

By the age of 5, most children are competent speakers of a language and have mastered the basics of semantics, syntax, and pragmatics. (Refer back to pages 282–187.)

Cat!

Hello, kitty cat!

FIGURE 9.6 **Referential Language Style Versus Expressive Language Style**

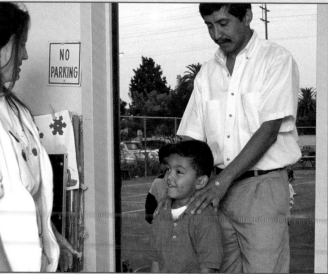

This child might talk about her "broked toy". These types of overregularizations illustrate that children are trying to understand and form rules about language.

Bilingual children develop language skills in the same order and the same time frame as children exposed to only one language.

Young children have some understanding of pretend versus real situations. They are more likely to confuse pretense and reality when an object's appearance conflicts with its true identity.

Children tend to have good memories for scripted events, especially those they experience frequently. Children's ability to remember scripts increases with age, especially as reflected in better memory for details and sequencing.

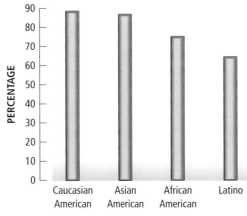

ΕARLY CHILDHOOD ΕDUCATION

Children can be encouraged to develop their cognitive skills through exposure to daily activities with caregivers, through preschool and kindergarten programs, and through educational television. (Refer back to pages 287–295.)

Children's cognitive development is influenced by their caregivers, who transmit cultural information and direct their learning experiences

FIGURE 9.7 **Percentage of Young Children Who Were Read to Three or More Times per Week, by Race-Ethnicity**

Activities in the preschool curriculum foster children's physical, social, cognitive, and emotional development.

Sesame Street has been successful in promoting intellectual growth of preschool children all around the world.

Social and Emotional Development in Early Childhood

Chapter Outline 10

How Does Self-Awareness Change During Early Childhood?
The Psychosocial Crisis of Initiative Versus Guilt
Developing Self-Concept
Developing Self-Esteem

How Do Young Children Develop a Concept of Gender?
Young Children's Gender Stereotypes
Young Children's Gender-Typed Play Preferences
Contemporary Theories of Gender Development

How Do Emotions Develop During Early Childhood?
Controlling and Regulating Emotions
Dealing with Conflict, Anger, and Aggression
Developing Caring Feelings and Actions

How Do Parenting Behaviors and Family Context Influence Young Children's Development?
Disciplining Young Children
Influences on Parents' Use of Discipline
Parenting Styles
The Effects of Divorce on Young Children's Development

How Do Peer and Sibling Relationships Develop During Early Childhood?
Young Children's Friendships
Young Children at Play
Young Children's Sibling Relationships

How Does Television Influence Young Children's Emotional and Social Development?
Effects of Television on Family Life
Effects of Television Violence on Young Children's Aggression
Effects of Television on Young Children's Prosocial Behavior

A DEVELOPMENTAL MYSTERY

Two boys, Barry and Hector, both age 5, watch as their teacher introduces a new computer game that allows them to create their own insects and learn about them in the process. Hector eagerly waits while the teacher sets up the game, but Barry is noticeably reluctant and nervous. Both boys are able to put the first two or three parts of the insect together, but after that the game becomes more difficult. Barry tries to add the next piece. After some unsuccessful attempts he pounds on the table, begins to sob, and cries out, "I hate this, I can't do it!" In contrast, Hector persists at the game until he discovers the correct movements to make the pieces fit. He smiles proudly, shouts, "I did it!", and starts another game. Barry, however, clearly feels bad and is quiet and withdrawn for some time afterward.

Barry and Hector do not differ in intelligence or in physical skills—they are both bright, healthy children. What factors produce these different reactions? Why does Barry give up at the first sign of failure or frustration? And why does Hector persevere through difficult periods with a desire to find the answer, regardless of how much frustration may be involved? This mystery reflects some of the more important processes reflected in social and emotional development during early childhood.

During early childhood, children's social and emotional lives become increasingly complex as they encounter a broader array of people, situations, and environments than they did when they were younger. This rich variety of interactive partners and contexts provides young children with many opportunities to learn about social interactions, their own and others' emotions, and their capabilities and characteristics. The mystery surrounding Hector's and Barry's reactions reflects the fact that although preschoolers' social and emotional lives are often playful and positive, they also can be tumultuous and uncertain.

How Does Self-Awareness Change During Early Childhood?

During early childhood, dramatic changes occur in children's awareness and image of themselves and in their feelings of self-worth. For some children, these changes lead to a positive view of self: they see themselves as active, independent, and persistent. For other children, these changes lead to a negative view of self, filled with uncertainty, helplessness, and failure.

The actions and feelings of Barry and Hector in the opening mystery are not rare or unique. Barry has difficulty coping with challenging and possibly frustrating events. His negative view of himself contributes to feelings of inadequacy and defeat. In contrast, Hector's positive self-image helps him face the challenge of the game without becoming upset and frustrated. He views himself as being able to solve problems without fear of failure. (Verschueren, Buyck, & Marcoen, 2001).

The Psychosocial Crisis of Initiative Versus Guilt

Erikson (1968) believed that during early childhood, a new psychosocial crisis arises—one in which preschool children eagerly begin and direct new projects and activities but sometimes feel bad when their efforts result in failure or criticism. As young children's physical, cognitive, and social skills improve, they formulate their own goals and desires and are increasingly capable of developing plans to reaches them. Sometimes, of course, the goals and actions of a child run counter to parental or social rules. As a result, children must learn

Erikson believed that during early childhood a new psychosocial crisis arises—one in which preschool children eagerly begin and direct new projects and activities but sometimes feel bad when their efforts result in failure or criticism. Can you explain the psychosocial crisis of initiative versus guilt?

to balance their eagerness for more adventure and more responsibility with learning to control impulses. This conflict of balance reflects Erikson's third stage of psychosocial development—**initiative** (a willingness to take on responsibilities and learn new skills) versus **guilt** (feelings of failure and becoming anxious when trying new things). During this period, children begin to interact with environment in a more adultlike manner as their motor and language skills develop. They learn to maintain an eagerness for adventure and play while controling impulsive behavior. If the child's social world is encouraging, but consistent in discipline, children will learn to accept this control without guilt. If not, children may develop a sense of guilt and may come to believe that it is wrong to be independent and act on their own. Thus, when 4-year-old Triana wants to use her father's delicate but attractive laptop computer, her father can encourage her desire to gain computer skills by positively yet firmly monitoring and guiding her so that she can develop confidence without fear that her actions will produce a severe reaction from her father.

Developing Self-Concept

By age 2, most toddlers recognize themselves as individuals—they can state their own name, identify themselves in a mirror, and distinguish and label themselves in pictures that include other children of the same age and same sex (Snow, 1990; Wolf, 1990). At this age, children begin to develop a **self-concept**—referring to an individual's beliefs about the attributes and capacities she or he possesses (Coopersmith, 1967; Lynch, 1981).

Important advances in self-concept are made during early childhood as children develop an awareness of their own characteristics. Three-year-old children first describe themselves in global terms, based on external qualities ("I'm fast") rather than psychological qualities ("I'm kind"). This global tendency leads young children to think that if they are good at drawing, they also are good at puzzles, running, or singing; that is, self-definitions are generalized to other contexts. By 4 years of age, children's judgments are more specific and differentiated (Measelle, Ablow, Cowan, & Cowan, 1998). They acknowledge that they are good at one skill, but not so good at others. Or they may acknowledge that they are good at doing something in one situation but not in other situations (Harter, 1998). For instance, older preschoolers may believe that they are good at puzzles but not at drawing or that they are good at playing basketball with other preschoolers but not with older children.

Young children have a more difficult time developing an understanding of their internal psychological qualities. They often describe themselves in an all-or-none fashion, failing to recognize that traits can co-occur. Thus, children ages 3 to 5 view themselves as either good or bad, but not *both* good and bad. Likewise, young children believe that they cannot feel both happy and sad at the same time (Ruble & Dweck, 1995).

Older children and adults recognize that their characteristics and traits are fairly stable over time and situations. Preschoolers, however, rarely describe themselves in terms of stable traits, and when they do, they use very global terms (Harter, 1999). Instead, their descriptions are likely to be based on characteristics and behaviors that change from time to time ("I'm clean" or "I'm happy").

Based on our discussion of cognitive development in Chapter 9, we could say that preschoolers lack "conservation of self." Just as young children do not recognize that a ball of clay retains its identity (contains the same amount of clay) when it is transformed from a ball to a snake, they do not recognize that their identity can be consistent in different situations and at different times (Bales & Sera, 1995). One consequence of this lack of recognition is that young children often overestimate their abilities, remaining confident even in the face of negative feedback (Pomerantz & Ruble, 1997; Stipek, Recchia, & McClintic, 1992). Given young children's tendencies to inaccurately estimate their abilities, caregivers should be skeptical when young children claim that they can do something that seems too advanced for them.

initiative *psychosocial crisis involving a willingness to take on responsibilities and learn new skills*

guilt *psychosocial crisis involving feelings of failure and becoming anxious when trying new things*

self-concept *an individual's beliefs about the attributes and capacities she or he possesses*

Developing Self-Esteem

Self-concept and self-esteem are closely related. Although self-concept refers to the mental picture we develop about ourselves, **self-esteem** refers to the value we attach to the mental pictures of ourselves (Coopersmith, 1967). Children with high self-esteem have positive feelings about themselves—they see themselves as confident, worthy, and effective. Children with low self-esteem have negative feelings about themselves—they feel uncertain, timid, and sad.

As children enter early childhood, they are increasingly capable of making judgments about themselves, but these judgments are global and vary depending on the situation. Young children's self-esteem revolves around feelings of good and bad—feeling "good" when they succeed in a task and feeling "bad" when they fail (Ruble & Dweck, 1995). For example, 5-year-olds Hector and Barry show clear signs of making evaluative judgments. Hector persists at a challenging computer game, is elated when he succeeds, and is motivated to play the game again. Barry feels bad when he begins to fail, becoming frustrated and helpless. Their evaluations of themselves are based on meeting a single standard, such as completing or failing at a task. As children get older (around age 7 or 8), they move away from this global good–bad evaluation of themselves and begin to make more complex assessments, evaluating themselves in comparison to others or in relation to the difficulty of the task (Pomerantz, Ruble, Frey, & Greulich, 1995). With age, children become more focused on distinguishing unique aspects of themselves (Daniels, 1998; Mintz, 1995).

Research suggests that self-esteem can be understood as a combination of two qualities: worthiness (feelings of being valued) and competence (feelings of being effective). Mruk (1999) put these two qualities on a matrix and used the various combinations of high and low worthiness and competence to identify four types of self-esteem. The matrix is presented in Figure 10.1.

For the first two types of self-esteem, high self-esteem and low self esteem, there is a match between feelings of competence and worthiness. A combination of high competence and high worthiness results in high self-esteem. Children with high self-esteem are better prepared to face challenges because they have acquired feelings about themselves that are associated with success and positive worth. In contrast, children with low self-esteem feel unworthy and have ineffective interactions, producing feelings of unhappiness and anxiety.

In Mruk's two other types of self-esteem, there is a discrepancy between feelings of worthiness and competence. These types of self-esteem demand that children "defend" their sense of self against others' view of them. Defensive self-esteem I combines high worthiness and low competence. Children with this pattern feel valued despite the fact that they lack the accomplishments or abilities to be successful. Thus, worthiness is not deserved. Children who possess this pattern of self-esteem often behave in ways that might be labeled spoiled, stuck-up, or self-centered.

The other discrepant type of self-esteem, defensive self-esteem II, combines high competence and low worthiness. In this case, children may be quite skilled, but their feelings of unworthiness distort their view of themselves. They tend to worry about performance and failure (performance anxiety), and they have difficulty experiencing satisfaction in their achievements. These children feel they must constantly prove their worth (Mruk, 1999).

FIGURE 10.1
Matrix of Self-Esteem

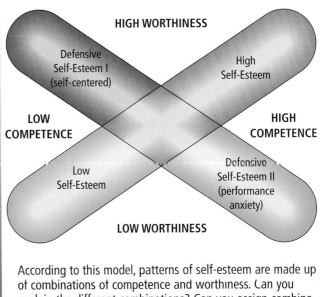

According to this model, patterns of self-esteem are made up of combinations of competence and worthiness. Can you explain the different combinations? Can you assign combinations to yourself and people you know?

Source: Mruk, 1999. Springer Publishing Company, Inc., New York 10012. Used with permission.

Notice how this young child's smile reveals the pride she feels in her accomplishment. How does this pride contribute to her self-concept and self-esteem?

self-esteem *the value an individual attaches to the mental picture of himself or herself*

Young children derive their feelings of competence and worthiness primarily from significant others, especially parents and other caregivers. Statements and expressions that affirm (or disaffirm) a child's accomplishments and value are rooted in how significant others regard the child and his or her particular behaviors and achievements. In a sense, competence is a measure of how effectively the child responds to the world, and worthiness is a measure of how the world responds to the child. In both cases, the values and judgments of children's social environments influence their self-esteem.

How Do Young Children Develop a Concept of Gender?

During the preschool years, children come to understand which gender group they belong to and that this is a stable part of one's self-concept (Frable, 1997). Learning this fundamental aspect of the self is only the beginning. Children also learn about the roles and expectations associated with their own and the other sex. These beliefs, roles, and expectations are shared cultural constructs, but each child develops her or his own set of individual beliefs about the sexes.

An important part of young children's self-concept is **gender identity**—the understanding and acceptance that one is a boy or a girl. Gender identity is based on the understanding that there are different sexes and that a person's gender group is stable over time and situations (Kohlberg, 1966). For most children, understanding of gender progresses through three stages:

1. By about 30 months of age, children engage in **gender labeling**—they label themselves and others according to their gender group. At this time, children call themselves *boys* and *girls* and use pronouns that correctly match the gender group.

2. By 3 to 4 years of age, children understand **gender stability**—they know that gender is stable over time. A boy who has achieved gender stability knows that he will always be a boy and will grow up to be a man, not a woman.

3. By 4 to 5 years of age, children understand **gender consistency**—they know that gender does not change despite changes in appearance or activities. For instance, a child who has achieved gender consistency understands that a boy who dresses as a girl remains a boy despite his appearance.

Not all children develop gender identity easily. Because of certain genetic disorders, a small number of children are born with ambiguous-looking genitals. Early research found that children with such genitals have problems developing gender identity if their gender group is assigned late in childhood (Money & Ehrhardt, 1972). However, some of these children have fewer problems if they are assigned to a gender group early in life (by 18–36 months), are raised consistently with their gender group assignment by their parents, and are given surgical or hormonal support for the assigned gender group. Surprisingly, even children who are raised to be one sex but are genetically the other sex can develop a stable gender identity. This is not always the case, however, and research has been undertaken to decide how best to determine gender group assignments (Bradley, Gillian, Avinoam, & Zucker, 1998; Diamond & Sigmundson, 1997).

Questions regarding the relative contributions of biological and social influences to gender identity development are being raised because of a rare genetic disorder first found in children in the Dominican Republic. In this disorder, boys are born with female-looking genitals and are usually raised as girls. At puberty, the male hormone testosterone is released, and these children develop masculine features and attributes. Thus, after being raised as girls, these children suddenly look like boys. Surprisingly, many of these children adjust to a male gender identity with little difficulty, probably because in their culture being a male is more highly valued than being a female. These cases suggest that a stable gender identity may not be fully developed until adolescence and that raising a child to be one sex does not always offset the biological influence of genes (Imperato-McGinley, Peterson, Gautier, & Sturla, 1979).

gender identity *understanding and acceptance that one is a boy or a girl*

gender labeling *labeling oneself and others on the basis of gender group*

gender stability *understanding that gender is stable over time*

gender consistency *understanding that gender does not change despite changes in appearance or activities*

FROM RESEARCH TO PRACTICE
WHAT FACTORS AFFECT POSITIVE SELF-ESTEEM AMONG AFRICAN AMERICAN AND LATINO CHILDREN?

FROM RESEARCH . . .

Because self-esteem is influenced by what other people think, it is sometimes assumed that minority children have lower levels of self-esteem than Caucasian American children. What is not considered, however, is that many minorities do not compare themselves to the larger society. Their self-esteem may be based less on what the general society thinks of them than on the perceptions of their family and friends and other important people in the minority community (vanLaar, 2001). Some current research has identified the factors that account for the healthy development of self-esteem in African American and Latino children.

African American Children.

African American children are likely to live in close proximity to their relatives, who often are an important source of affection, care, and support. The additional caregiving also serves as a source of comfort and help in times of stress (Brodsky & DeVet, 2000). The increased support and nurturance provided by this extended family network promote positive self-esteem.

The presence of a father plays an especially important role in the development of self-esteem among African American children—particularly African American boys. An African American child who lives in a home where the father is absent is likely to exhibit low self-esteem (Espinoza & Ehrlich, 1989).

African American children with a poor sense of ethnic identity—recognition and acceptance of membership in an ethnic group—suffer from low self-esteem (Ogbu, 1991). Some people believe that young children are "color blind," but as early as 4 years of age, children are capable of distinguishing different ethnic groups (Aries &

Moorehead, 1989). Children whose parents teach them about being African American and instill in them a sense of pride show healthy and positive self-esteem (Bowman & Howard, 1985). These parents help their children cope with the negative stereotypes and harassment they encounter (Walker, Taylor, McElroy, & Phillip, 1995).

Latino Children.

Like African American families, Latino families provide supportive and nurturing environments that often buffer children against the assaults that occur in the broader society (Scolis, 1995; Valdez, 1996). Latinos place a high value on family support (McDermott, 2001; Sabogal, Marin, & Otero-Sabogal, 1987), and this support is provided not only by parents but also by grandparents, uncles, aunts, and cousins. Often, no sharp distinction is made between relatives and friends, with friends being considered family if a close relationship has been formed (Chilman, 1993). The term *compadrazo* is often used to describe this relationship. Children living in these relatively large families have extensive networks of support and nurturance that protect and enhance their self-esteem.

Another important characteristic of Latino families that helps their children develop positive relationships and self-esteem is their traditional preference for smooth and pleasant social relationships. The term *simpatía* refers to the high regard the Latino culture has for feelings and actions geared to safeguarding the dignity of individuals by showing respect and striving for harmony. This does not mean that Latino families and children do not express anger, aggression, or frustration. However, when situations have the potential for conflict, particularly among family members or friends, solutions are sought that avoid confrontation, hurt feelings, and loss of self-respect. *Simpatía* and supportive extended families foster the development

of positive self-esteem among Latino children (Marin, 1994).

. . . TO PRACTICE

Fostering a positive sense of self among young minority children will help them understand where they come from and feel proud of it—it contributes to a sense of belonging. As minority children develop positive feelings toward self as well as racial and cultural identity, they gain confidence in who they are and how they can participate in different groups. A strong, positive sense of self also helps these children deal with the inevitable harshness of the real world—including discrimination, prejudice, and racism. Thus, understanding the need to promote positive self-esteem among minority children should translate into practices and policies that enhance their adaptiveness, competence, and strength so that they can achieve and thrive.

Although minority children generally have positive and healthy self-esteem, they face greater threats to their self-esteem than do Caucasian American children. These threats appear to be due to economic and social conditions rather than minority status *per se*. Thus, addressing the roots of the social and economic conditions that many minority children face may promote the development of strong and positive concepts of themselves.

THINKING IT THROUGH

1. How does being a member of a minority group influence self-esteem differently than being a member of a majority group?

2. How do parents and other family members influence minority children's self-esteem?

Children often prefer toys and activities that reinforce their own gender identity. What factors contribute to this preference? How might children be encouraged to play with more cross-sex toys?

Young Children's Gender Stereotypes

Gender stereotypes are the beliefs people share about the typical characteristics of males and females. As early as age 2½, children have learned basic stereotypes about the sexes, including information about appearance and activities. For instance, young children think that girls have long and curly hair and that they cry a lot (Intons-Peterson, 1988). They think that boys are taller and stronger than girls and hit people more (Kuhn, Nash, & Brucken, 1978). Young children even believe that softness is associated with being female and hardness with being male (Leinbach, Hort, & Fagot, 1997). Young children do not, however, think that males and females differ in personality, except in very concrete terms such as being strong or being nice.

Gender stereotypes influence children in many ways. First, children (and adults) use them to make judgments about other people, especially when their information about the other people is limited (Martin, 1989; Martin, Woods, & Little, 1990). These judgments often have to do with familiar activities and roles. For instance, 4-year-old Claudia decides that her new neighbor, Polly, might be fun to play with because she is a girl and therefore will probably like the kinds of things that Claudia likes.

Second, young children's stereotypes influence what they remember. Generally, children remember information that fits their stereotypic beliefs (Stangor & McMillan, 1992). After being shown pictures of girls and boys engaged in many activities, children better remember the pictures of children engaged in stereotypic activities (such as a boy playing with a car) than those of children engaged in counter-stereotypic activities (such as a boy playing with a doll). Young children also remember more about people of the same sex than about people of the other sex (Signorella, Bigler, & Liben, 1998).

Several studies have shown that children experience memory distortions; that is, they misremember information with a bias toward their stereotypes (Martin & Halverson, 1983; Signorella & Liben, 1984). For example, when 5- to 9-year-old children of both sexes saw television commercials of a boy playing with a doll and a girl playing with a truck, over half the children distorted the sex of the actor in one of the commercials and 25 percent distorted the sex of the actor in both commercials (Stangor & Ruble, 1989).

Many caregivers hope that their children will not learn gender stereotypes if they see many examples of people who break from stereotypic expectations. The fact that children distort information to fit their gender stereotypes, however, makes this effort difficult. Rather than breaking stereotypes, children's memories respond in ways that confirm them. It seems unlikely that caregivers can effect change merely by exposing children to examples of people engaging in counter-stereotypic behaviors and activities. Instead, parents and caregivers may need to take more active measures, such as teaching children that not all people believe gender stereotypes or act on the basis of them (Bem, 1983).

Young Children's Gender-Typed Play Preferences

By 2 years of age, girls and boys show preferences for different toys (Ruble, Martin, & Beerbaum, in press). By the age of 3 or 4, girls play more often than boys with dolls, tea sets, art materials, and domestic toys (ironing boards, kitchen sets). One reason children prefer stereotypic toys and activities is because they have a history of playing with them and are familiar with them. Also, parents give children toys that are gender-stereotyped and encour-

gender stereotypes *beliefs people share about the typical characteristics of males and females*

age them to play with them (Ruble et al., in press). Children also prefer toys and activities that reinforce their own gender identity. For example, when a toy that children have never seen before is described as a toy that is liked by others of their own sex, both girls and boys prefer that toy. If the new toy is described as being liked by members of the other sex, the toy often is avoided (Bradbard, Martin, Endsley, & Halverson, 1986).

Children are particularly likely to avoid toys gender-stereotyped for the other sex if they are discouraged from or punished for playing with them (Langlois & Downs, 1980). This avoidance reaction is so strong that children will stay away from even very attractive toys if they think the toys are intended for the other sex (Martin, Eisenbud, & Rose, 1995). For instance, Joe chose to play with a deflated football rather than a new kitchen set. Ian happily played with a race car until the helmet of the driver fell off, revealing a woman with long blonde hair. Ian immediately dropped the car like a "hot potato." Such findings suggest that children use stereotypic expectations to decide whether or not they like specific toys. These expectations prevent children from learning about the toys and activities used by the other sex (Boston & Levy, 1991).

Similarities and Differences Between Young Girls and Boys

Gender stereotypes are based on beliefs about differences between the sexes in behavior, appearance, and personality. But to what extent do boys and girls really differ? Observable differences between the behaviors of boys and girls generally have not been found before age 2 (Huston, 1983). Thus, if you were brought into a room full of young infants and could not tell by their appearance which were boys and girls, you would not consistently be able to distinguish girls from boys based on their behavior. Interestingly, although there are no noticeable differences between very young boys and girls, parents often say that their young sons and daughters *are* different. Based on these perceptions, parents may interact with their sons and daughters differently, thereby setting the stage for sex differences to emerge.

In a classic review, Maccoby and Jacklin (1974) concluded that there are four sex differences found consistently in children and adolescents. On average, males have better visual–spatial skills (such as map-reading skills), have better mathematical reasoning abilities, and are more physically aggressive, whereas females have better verbal skills. Maccoby and Jacklin (1974) also noted that these differences tend to be small and highly variable within each sex—girls, for example, are as different from one another as they are from boys.

The results of recent research suggest that sex differences occur in more areas than Maccoby and Jacklin originally identified (Ruble et al., in press). For instance, boys tend to be more active than girls (Eaton & Enns, 1986), although the level of activity varies considerably depending on the situation and age. Boys also are more likely to take risks (Ginsburg & Miller, 1982) and engage in rough play, such as wrestling (Braza, Braza, Carreras, & Munoz, 1997; Pellegrini & Smith, 1998). Gender differences in forms of play increase with age, are observed in cultures all around the world (Whiting & Edwards, 1988), and are even found in monkeys, apes, and rats (Meaney, 1988).

Boys throw a ball with considerably more accuracy and velocity than girls do, whereas girls have better fine eye-motor skills and flexibility (Thomas & French, 1985). Girls and boys also exhibit different types of nonverbal communication (Hall, 1984). Girls are more likely than boys to smile, and boys are more likely than girls to stare at others.

Gender differences also are found in social behavior and personality. Girls generally are more socially oriented, are more easily influenced, and are seen by teachers as more dependent than boys (Ruble et al., in press). Boys tend to show more aggression and anger, and girls show more fear (Eisenberg, Martin, & Fabes, 1996).

The reasons for these differences are complex. As you will soon learn, many different theories have been proposed to explain why males and females differ. Some of these theories focus on the effects of biological and physiological differences (Kimura, 1993; Levy &

Heller, 1992), whereas others focus on environmental and social factors (Bussey & Bandura, 1992) or cognitive processes (Martin, 1991).

Contemporary Theories of Gender Development

Several contemporary theoretical approaches attempt to explain the critical changes that affect children's gender development. Each theory provides insight into why boys and girls behave differently and the ways they use their knowledge of gender. Although the theories differ in the aspects of gender they emphasize, all the theories consider gender to be an important part of development.

Biological Theories

Biological theories focus on specific physiological or biochemical processes that affect gender development. The biological influences that have been studied most extensively concern the actions of hormones, and the most commonly studied hormones are androgens, especially testosterone. These hormones often are referred to as "male hormones" because they occur at higher levels in males than in females. When animals are exposed to androgens during prenatal development, they show more male-typical behaviors, such as aggression, and fewer female-typical behaviors, such as nurturance (Collaer & Hines, 1995). Prenatal androgens are thought to masculinize the brain as it develops, making it more sensitive to some types of environmental stimulation and less sensitive to others. As a result, males and females may be predisposed to develop different skills, abilities, and personalities.

Levels of hormones vary in humans, and some children are exposed to higher than normal prenatal levels of androgens, usually because of genetic disorders. An example is girls who have congenital adrenal hyperplasia (CAH). These girls may be born with somewhat masculinized genitals, but they usually are raised as girls and receive treatment and sometimes surgery to offset the masculine hormones. Parents report that their daughters with CAH behave as tomboys and prefer to play with boys' toys (Berenbaum & Snyder, 1995). Many researchers believe that the behavior of girls with CAH is the result of their exposure to high prenatal levels of androgens.

Biological theories suggest that children's abilities, behaviors, and personality may all be influenced by levels of hormones, especially those that are present during prenatal development. Some people worry that if biological factors influence gender development, then there is no way to change girls' or boys' behavior. However, this is not the case—some biological influences can easily be changed. Furthermore, most researchers believe that even if gender development is influenced by biological factors, environmental factors such as socialization and reinforcement can influence the course of a child's development (Hoyenga & Hoyenga, 1993).

Social Learning Theories

The basis of social learning theories is that children learn gender roles through two processes: direct learning and observation. In direct learning, children learn gender roles from the rewards and punishments they receive (Mischel, 1966). Children may be rewarded for exhibiting stereotypic traits and engaging in stereotypic activities and be punished for behaving in ways deemed gender inappropriate. Thus, their gender-related behavior is conditioned. For instance, when Jason is teased for playing with a baby doll, he discovers that this behavior is regarded as inappropriate for him and quickly learns to avoid baby dolls in favor of trucks or blocks.

Many research studies have shown that boys and girls receive different rewards and punishments for gender-related behaviors. Parents and peers reward girls and boys for different activities, but in both cases, stereotypic activities are encouraged more than counter-stereotypic ones (Trice & Rush, 1995). Interestingly, boys are more likely than girls to be punished for engaging in cross-sex behaviors and activities, suggesting that boys are held to more rigid standards than are girls (Burnett, Anderson, & Heppner, 1995). Parents treat their sons and daughters differently by presenting gender-stereotypic toys and assigning gender-stereotypic chores (Lytton & Romney, 1991; Ruble & Martin, 1998). Girls are more likely to be assigned kitchen and cleaning chores, and boys are more likely to be assigned yard work. Surprisingly, there is little evidence that parents treat boys and girls differently in other ways, such as encouraging daughters to be dependent or encouraging sons to be aggressive and dominant.

Children also learn gender roles by observing others (Bandura, 1977). When Lucas observes children tease Jason for playing with a doll, he too learns that boys should avoid dolls. By observing the consequences that befell Jason, Lucas learns without directly experiencing the same consequences. As children experience consequences, they develop expectations that can then guide their future behavior (Bussey & Bandura, 1999).

Children do not pay equal attention to, and learn equally from, everyone. A reasonable supposition would be that children observe and imitate the behavior of others of the same sex, which would explain why girls act differently than boys. It is not so simple, though. Children imitate a same-sex model if the model is familiar but not if the model is unfamiliar. However, they will imitate behaviors if they view many same-sex models, even if they do not know the people (Bussey & Bandura, 1984; Bussey & Perry, 1982). Because children pay attention to people who are prestigious or nurturant—such as sports and movie stars, teachers, and family members—they are likely to imitate these individuals (Lockwood & Kunda, 1997). Sometimes children imitate the behaviors of other-sex people; girls are more likely to do this than boys. Boys will imitate girls only if they are shown to be powerful (Bussey & Bandura, 1984).

Cognitive Theories

Cognitive theories contribute to our understanding of gender development by considering children to be actively involved in learning gender roles and motivated to adhere to them (Ruble & Martin, 1998). The earliest cognitive theory was proposed by Kohlberg (1966) and is based on the idea that children's understanding of gender emerges as part of their general cognitive development. Kohlberg argued that children's understanding of gender provides the key to the development of gender-stereotypic behavior. As children learn about their gender, they are motivated to behave in ways that are consistent with their gender group. Kohlberg believed that once children develop the idea that gender is a stable attribute, they will show stronger stereotypic behavior, pay more attention to same-sex models, and have better memory for stereotypic information than do children who lack basic gender knowledge (Stangor & Ruble, 1987).

A recent extension of cognitive–developmental theory is gender schema theory. People use **gender schemas,** which are mental representations about the sexes, to guide their behavior and thinking (Bem, 1981; Martin, 1991; Martin & Halverson, 1981). As children interact with their world, their experiences are filtered through gender schemas. Over time, many events come to be interpreted through these male–female schemas. Children then behave according to their interpretation of what it means to be male or female.

Most children have extensive gender schemas, which become more elaborate as they grow older. For instance, as part of her gender schema, 4-year-old Shawntel has information that girls like to make cookies and paint their toenails and boys like to play with trucks and spaceships. With this information, she can form ideas about what is appropriate for her to do.

Gender schemas influence what children pay attention to, what they remember, and how they behave (Martin, 1991). The influence of gender schemas is best summarized by the principle of **schematic consistency,** referring to the tendency of children's behavior and thinking to match their schemas (see Figure 10.2). For instance, children pay more attention to and better remember information if it is relevant to their own gender group (Signorella, Bigler, & Liben, 1998).

gender schemas *mental representations about the sexes*

schematic consistency *the tendency of children's behavior and thinking to match their schemas*

FIGURE 10.2
Model of Gender Schematic Processing

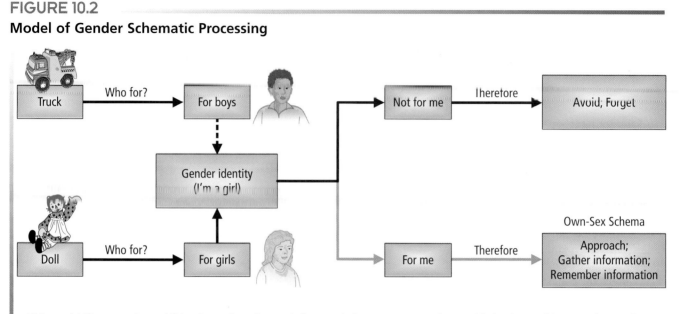

This model illustrates how children's gender schemas influence their memory, attention, and behavior. In this example, a girl decides to play with a doll because she believes it is a toy appropriate for girls. How does this model help in understanding the influence of gender schemas and stereotypes?

Source: Martin and Halverson, 1981. Reprinted by permission.

How Do Emotions Develop During Early Childhood?

As you saw in Chapter 7, even newborns express a variety of emotions. During early childhood, children's emotional lives become increasingly differentiated and rich. Young children become better at communicating their emotions, more emotionally responsive to others, and more aware of emotions in themselves and others.

Controlling and Regulating Emotions

> *While watching a cartoon DVD by himself, 4-year-old Matt becomes emotionally aroused and scared during a scene in which scary-looking sharks with big teeth are chasing the main characters. Very softly Matt begins to sing a song he knows from his preschool: "If you're happy and you know it clap your hands . . ." Matt quietly claps his claps and continues to sing this verse until the scary scene is over. Matt then settles down and relaxes, quits singing, and quietly watches the rest of the movie.*

Matt's story reveals that young children can be troubled by the emotional situations they experience. Emotions can be stressful—negative as well as positive emotions can exceed a child's ability to cope and respond appropriately. As a result, children's actions or thoughts can become disorganized and disruptive (Eisenberg & Fabes, 1992). When this happens, the emotional arousal and feelings need to be managed and controlled. Matt's singing and clapping during the scary scene reflect his attempts to modulate his fear and anxiety. By doing something that made him feel better, he quieted his negative emotional reactions so that he could continue to watch the movie, despite the scary material. Matt's ability to alter his emotional response to a situation is referred to as **emotion regulation** (see Figure 10.3).

Emotional reactions and responses are unavoidable and sometimes potentially overwhelming. Negative emotions (such as fear, anger, sadness) need to be managed (Denham,

emotion regulation   *ability to alter emotional responses to a situation*

1998). And there are many ways to regulate and control emotions—children can distract themselves from the source of the emotion, they can turn to others for care and comfort, or they can avoid a situation they know will be too emotionally arousing. In addition, at times a situation calls for children to heighten rather than dampen the expression of emotion, and this too is a type of emotion regulation—children often show more anger than they are feeling in order to win an argument or will cry more piteously than they actually feel to obtain something they want. Consider this story:

> *Sharon and Margie are both trying to get other children to come and play with them. Sharon looks at the other children and says quietly; "Hey . . . let's play this now." In contrast, Margie opens her eyes wide, waves her arms, and shouts to the other children with glee and excitement in her voice, "WOW . . . this is great! COME ON! Let's play this now!"*

Which child is more likely to succeed in attracting others to play with her? Margie, of course—she can elevate her positive emotions to convey the fun associated with her play and in a way that accurately (but not overwhelmingly) reflects the emotionality of the situation. This too is an example of emotion regulation.

Across the preschool years, children become more and more successful at controlling and regulating their own emotions. During play with other children, during quiet times with family or at school, at a house of worship, or at a wedding or birthday party for another, children must learn to modulate their emotional impulses and excitement in order to get along with others and act appropriately. Although children develop the ability to control their emotions before preschool (for example, infants learn to divert their gaze from something that is too emotionally distressing; Tronick, 1989), it is during early childhood that adults increasingly expect children to do so (Denham, 1998). In a classic study of younger and older children's ability to regulate emotion, Harris, Olthof, and Terwogt (1981) showed that even young children understood that it is possible to change their feelings. When asked how emotions could be changed, young children suggested leaving a situation or changing it, whereas older children also indicated that they could change how they feel by thinking different thoughts. Thus, as children get older, their strategies for regulating emotions become more abstract and sophisticated.

As you have seen, one can regulate emotions by hiding them, intensifying them, or otherwise altering the way they are expressed. To do this, children must understand the rules associated with how emotions should or should not be displayed. These rules are referred to as **display rules**—reflecting a child's recognition that there are times when it is not appropriate to express the emotions he or she is feeling. Thus, rules govern what type of emotion should be displayed in particular social circumstances. Even during early childhood, children have been found to understand that emotions should sometimes be masked. For example, in an ingenious research design, Saarni (1984) presented children with a situation in which they expected to receive an attractive prize. When they received it, however, the prize was either broken or appropriate for a much younger child. In this situation, children generally are taught to be thankful for the intention behind the gift rather than the gift itself. All of us can remember receiving a birthday or holiday gift from an aunt or grandparent that was disappointing and being told not to display the disappointment but to show gratitude for the thought behind the gift. Thus, the display rule for children would be to mask disappointment and show positive regard toward the act of giving the gift. Using this

FIGURE 10.3
Emotion Regulation

In this figure, the young girl is distracting herself from the scary television scene by singing to herself. Can you identify how young children regulate their emotions?

display rules *rules regarding how emotions should or should not be displayed*

method, young children (boys especially) showed more negative emotions when receiving an unappealing prize than did older children. Such findings suggest that although young children can control and modulate their emotions, they are more likely to use display rules as they get older.

As you have seen in the stories of Barry and Hector and of Margie and Sharon, preschoolers differ in their patterns of emotion regulation. When exposed to angry and scary events, some young children may freeze, try to run away, become aggressive, cry, or even smile. How can we explain such variation in how individual children regulate emotional reactions?

Certainly, a child's temperament plays a role. Eisenberg and Fabes (1992) identified two important temperamental dimensions that underlie emotion regulation:

1. *Emotional intensity:* Reflecting differences in the degree to which children respond to emotional events

2. *Regulatory processes:* Reflecting differences in processes that allow children to voluntarily inhibit, focus, and/or shift their attention or behavior

As you can see in Table 10.1, a child's tendencies in these two areas are thought to influence his or her emotional regulation abilities and subsequent emotional and social reactions. For example, a child who responds intensely to emotional situations and has low regulatory processes is unlikely to regulate his or her emotions very well and is likely to become aggressive or act out when emotionally aroused (Fabes et al., 1999). A child who responds intensely and is overly regulated is likely to be anxious, shy, and withdrawn. Optimal emotion regulation occurs when children are responsive to emotional situations but are able to modulate that stimulation such that the emotion does not become unbridled or excessively inhibited (Eisenberg & Fabes, 1992).

Although children's characteristics such as temperament are important factors in determining differences in emotion regulation, parents and other social agents also influence how children respond to emotional situations. Children who have positive and warm relationships with their parents feel more emotionally secure and, as a result, are more emotionally regulated (Cummings, Goeke-Morey, & Papp, 2003). In addition, parents actively teach and coach their children about emotions. For example, when children laugh at someone in a wheelchair, they may be taken aside and told that "We don't laugh at people who are hurt; it is mean and cruel!" Thus, parents teach children the display rules they need to know so that they can behave appropriately and effectively. In addition, parents often give their children strategies for coping with emotions. When 5-year-old Aletha had to wait a long time before her father came home and the family could go out to see a movie, her

TABLE 10.1
A Temperament Model of Emotion Regulation

LEVEL OF EMOTIONAL INTENSITY	LEVEL OF REGULATION		
	LOW	MODERATE	HIGH
Low	Flat emotion; unresponsive and passive in emotional situations	Placid; low to average expressiveness; resilient; low in aggression	Inhibited and passive; nonexpressive; unsociable and prone to withdrawal; somewhat flat affect
High	Uncontrolled, active behavior; prone to aggression, frustration, and anger	Appropriately expressive; socially competent; resilient; low in aggression	Inhibited; shy; prone to anxiety, fear, and sadness

Source: Adapted from Eisenberg and Fabes, 1992.

mother suggested that she read a book as a way to distract herself and thereby modulate her rising frustration. As you have seen before, parents and other social agents have both direct and indirect influences on their children's emotion regulation. This is particularly true during early childhood when children are more dependent on others to address situations that are likely to be emotionally intense.

Dealing with Conflict, Anger, and Aggression

As young children become actively involved in social relationships, it is not surprising that they encounter more situations that elicit conflict, anger, frustration, and aggression. During the second year of life, young children begin to confront their parents and siblings with increasing frequency. For example, conflicts between children and their mothers double in frequency between 18 and 24 months of age (Dunn & Munn, 1987). Children's aggressive acts also increase during the first three years of life, although the patterns vary, depending on the type of aggression studied.

Children's conflicts at this age revolve primarily around possession of objects and space. The frequency of conflicts increases during the preschool years. What factors account for this increase?

Young Children's Angry Conflicts

Most expressions of anger and aggression occur in the context of interactions with others. For young children, conflicts involve struggles over objects and possessions (Fabes & Eisenberg, 1992; O'Brien et al., 1999). As children mature, their conflicts increasingly have social causes, such as being rejected, ignored, or challenged (Ross & Conant, 1992). Angry tantrums and outbursts peak at about 2 years of age and are relatively uncommon after age 4. For 2-year-olds, the most common cause of anger is parents' attempts to establish household routines (such as for eating or sleeping). Among older preschoolers, anger is likely to be caused by difficulties with playmates (Laursen, Hartup, & Koplas, 1996), and how children respond influences how much they are liked by their peers (Murphy & Eisenberg, 1996).

Changes in the frequency of conflicts reflect changes in children's cognitive and social competencies. As children grasp social rules and order, they respond to violations of these with anger and frustration. Children's developing sense of autonomy during the second and third years also intensifies their negative reactions to others' attempts to control them. During this time, children begin to understand that rules can be questioned (Dunn & Slomkowski, 1992). In addition, their enhanced understanding of intentions makes it more likely that children will hold others responsible for their actions when there is no indication that the behavior was accidental. Holding others responsible increases the chance that a child will become angry when someone acts in a way that she or he does not like. These factors combine to increase the significance of others' behaviors in relation to young children's goals and desires.

Children respond to conflict in a variety of ways that change over the course of early childhood (Sandy & Cochran, 2000). When a conflict occurs, young children might become physically aggressive, try to reason out a solution, stand around, cry or throw a tantrum, go for help, or try to assert themselves (such as by taking back a toy that was taken from them). Interestingly, physical aggression in response to conflict is rare among young children; less than 20 percent of conflicts include acts of aggression such as hitting or kicking. As language develops, children increasingly rely on verbal strategies, such as negotiating, to resolve conflicts (Ross & Conant, 1992). In addition, as children gain a better understanding of social relationships, they begin to look for ways to resolve conflicts that do not damage their ongoing interactions—that is, they try to find a cooperative solution (Ashley & Tomasello, 1998; Verbeek, Hartup, & Collins, 2000).

Young Children's Aggression

Aggression is commonly defined as a behavior intended to harm or injure another (Grusec & Lytton, 1988). Although infants get angry and sometimes strike people and objects, it is difficult to say they are aggressive. Consider the following excerpt from Piaget (1952), describing what happened when he offered a matchbox to his 7-month-old son Laurent, but held his other hand in front of the matchbox so that Laurent could not reach it:

> I present a box of matches above my hand, but behind it, so that he cannot reach it without setting the obstacle aside. But Laurent, after trying to remove or lower it, . . . suddenly tries to hit my hand as though to remove or lower it. . . . Laurent tries to reach the box, and bothered by the obstacle, he at once strikes it, definitely lowering it until the way is clear. (Piaget, 1952, p. 217)

Laurent's behavior looks very much like aggression, but is it? It is unlikely that Laurent intended to harm his father; rather, it is more likely that he treated his father's hand as an obstruction that needed to be removed. Laurent's goal seems to have been focused more on possessing the interesting object than on inflicting harm or pain.

Near the end of the second year, things begin to change. Maccoby (1980) identified at least five kinds of information a child must master before the child's behavior can be judged as aggressive:

- That other people experience distress and feel pain
- That the child's own actions can cause distress
- Which actions cause distress in other people
- How to carry out distress-producing actions
- That distress can cause other people to act the way the child wants them to

These types of information are learned during early childhood, some earlier than others (Loeber & Hay, 1997). As children master these types of information, their ability to act aggressively increases. By the end of early childhood, most children have learned alternatives to aggressive behaviors, and those who have not are at increased risk of becoming aggressive teens or adults (Tremblay, 2001).

Different kinds of aggression have been identified. Physical aggression, such as hitting, kicking, and pushing, decreases between 2 and 4 years of age, while verbal aggression, such as threatening and name calling, increases (Coie & Dodge, 1998). The aggressive behavior of children 4 to 6 years of age often is aimed at the retrieval of objects or territory (Fabes & Eisenberg, 1992). This type of aggression is referred to as **instrumental aggression**— aggression used for a specific purpose. Kindergarten children (6 to 7 years of age) show less overall aggression, but they are more likely to be aggressive in ways that are designed to harm another person. This type of aggression is sometimes called **hostile aggression,** referring to the fact that it is directed against another person and is often used in retaliation for another's actions. Because hostile aggression requires that a child understand others' intentions, it occurs less often in younger children (Atkins et al., 2001).

Gender Differences in Aggression

The issue of gender differences in aggression has been of interest for decades (for an early example, see Green, 1933). In several reviews (Hyde, 1984; Knight, Fabes, & Higgins, 1996; Maccoby & Jacklin, 1980), boys were found to be both more physically and more verbally aggressive than girls. These findings are not restricted to studies conducted in the United States. Boys have been found to be more aggressive than girls in Switzerland, Ethiopia, Kenya, India, the Philippines, Mexico, and Japan (Smith & Green, 1974; Whiting & Whiting, 1975). Thus, there is considerable evidence that boys are more aggressive than girls. The cross-cultural consistency of these findings suggests that there may be biological contributions to aggressive behavior.

instrumental aggression *aggression used for a specific purpose*

hostile aggression *aggression directed against another person, generally in retaliation for his or her actions*

Is it possible that girls express aggression differently than boys do? Crick and Rose (2000) suggest that girls may exhibit unique forms of aggression that have been overlooked in past research. Crick agrees that boys may be more physically and verbally aggressive than girls. She argues, however, that because girls are more likely than boys to focus on establishing close relationships with others, they are more likely than boys to harm others through relational aggression. **Relational aggression** is designed to damage someone's relationships with others by withdrawing friendship, excluding someone from a group, and so on. Several studies have found that girls use relational aggression more than boys do (Crick & Grotpeter, 1995; Fabes, Eisenberg, Smith, & Murphy, 1996). Findings have been consistent across a wide range of ages and across a variety of cultures (Rys & Bear, 1997; Tomada & Schneider, 1997), suggesting that *both* young boys and young girls are aggressive, but they display distinct forms of aggression.

Developing Caring Feelings and Actions

A recently divorced father drops off his 3- and 4-year-old daughters, Aimee and Erin, at his former wife's house. Aimee and Erin burst out of the car and run into the waiting arms of their mother. The father clearly is sad, and Erin, the older daughter, notices her father's sad expression, becomes sad herself, and goes to tell her dad that she will miss him. She hugs him and says, "Things will be okay."

Erin feels sorry for her father and attempts to comfort him, an example of prosocial emotions and actions. **Prosocial behavior** refers to voluntary actions intended to benefit another person. Prosocial emotions motivate prosocial behavior (Eisenberg & Fabes, 1998). As you will see, during early childhood prosocial emotions and actions increasingly become part of the ways in which children relate to others.

Prosocial Emotions: Empathy and Sympathy

Empathy refers to an emotional state that matches another person's emotional state—for instance, feeling bad because someone else feels bad (Eisenberg & Strayer, 1987). In contrast, **sympathy** involves feeling sorry or concerned for other people because of their emotional states or conditions (Eisenberg & Fabes, 1999). When Erin felt sad at the sight of her father's sadness, she was displaying empathy. When she felt sorry for him, she was displaying sympathy. Sympathy frequently, but not always, results from empathy.

Empathy and sympathy are important to study because they often motivate prosocial behaviors and actions (Roberts & Strayer, 1996). Because of Erin's feelings of empathy and sympathy for her father, she felt compelled to help him feel better. The link between sympathy or empathy and prosocial behavior has been confirmed by research in the United States (Eisenberg & Fabes, 1998; Miller, Kozu, & Davis, 2001) and in countries as diverse as Germany (Trommsdorff, 1995), Brazil (Eisenberg, Zhou, & Koller, 2001), and Japan (Ando, 1987).

Empathy appears fairly early and increases across childhood (Hoffman, 2000). Although infants cannot distinguish their own feelings and needs from those of others, they occasionally respond to others' emotions. For example, they often cry when they hear the cry of another infant (Sagi & Hoffman, 1976), although this tendency is not consistent or universal (Zahn-Waxler, Radke-Yarrow, Wagner, & Chapman, 1992).

Early in childhood, children tend to act and think in an egocentric manner. Thus, they are likely to respond to another's distress in ways that they themselves might find comforting. When 3-year-old Thomas saw his mother crying, he became sad and brought her his favorite stuffed animal to cheer her up. In this situation, Thomas projected his own needs onto his mother. Thomas's response is not purely egocentric, however, because his attempt to cheer up his mother is based on empathy for his mother's emotional state.

As children develop the capacity to take the perspective of others, they become increasingly aware that other people's feelings are independent of, and sometimes different from, their

relational aggression *aggression designed to damage someone's relationships with others, by withdrawing friendship, excluding someone from a group, and so on*

prosocial behavior *voluntary actions intended to benefit another person*

empathy *an emotional state that matches another person's emotional state—for instance, feeling bad because someone else is feeling bad*

sympathy *feeling sorry or concerned for other people because of their emotional states or conditions*

During the preschool years, children's prosocial emotions and behaviors become more advanced and appropriate. Children become genuinely concerned about the well-being of others. What can be done to foster and promote such feelings and behavior?

own. Four-year-old Erin's response to her father's sadness reflected her understanding of her father's needs, and she responded appropriately. Until later childhood, however, children's empathic and sympathetic responses are limited to the feelings of familiar persons in familiar or directly observed situations. Preschoolers, for example, are most likely to be emotionally responsive to everyday events (such as getting scratched or being made fun of) that cause distress to familiar people or animals (Szagun, 1992). During later childhood, the scope of children's concerns widens to include the conditions of unknown others who are less fortunate than they are (Damon, 1988; Hoffman, 2000).

Helping, Sharing, and Acting Responsibly

Prosocial actions appear early in development (Dunn, 2001; Hay et al., 1999). Two-year-olds share toys and food with others, often without prompting. They also begin to help take care of their younger siblings and spontaneously help with some household chores (Garner, Jones, & Palmer, 1994; Rheingold, 1982). For example, 2-year-old Maggie responds to the cries of her younger sister by saying, "Sister is crying; let's go to her. Let me hold her. You'd better nurse her, Mommy. Does she have to burp?" Maggie is trying to comfort and care for her younger sister. Maggie's ability to meet the needs of her baby sister is limited, but her responses show genuine concern for her sister's well-being and a desire to help. Across the preschool years, these acts of caring become more common. Preschoolers also act in more responsible ways; they are more likely to comply with parents' requests and are less likely to ignore or defy parental demands (Power, McGrath, Hughes, & Manire, 1994). Evidence suggests that individual differences in prosocial behavior have their origins in early childhood (Eisenberg, Guthrie et al., 1999).

Reasons and motives for helpful and responsible behaviors also change during early childhood. When asked why they share or help, young preschoolers often explain their behavior by referring to the other person's needs ("I gave him some crackers because he's hungry") or practical reasons ("I helped clean up because the table was dirty"). Thus, they appear to be motivated by an understanding of another's situation or needs. At other times, children focus on the task at hand or other practical aspects of the situation (Eisenberg, 1992). Older preschoolers occasionally justify prosocial behaviors by referring to their relationship with the person who needs help ("I helped her carry the toys because she's my friend") or their desire for others' approval ("I gave him some of my blocks so he'll like me"). Four- and 5-year-olds also justify prosocial behavior on the basis of selfish reasons ("If I share with him, the teacher will let me play outside"). With maturity, children recognize the social nature of helping relationships. It is not until later childhood that children's reasons for helping become altruistic, reflecting the desire to help others without any apparent personal gain or benefit (Damon, 1988).

Socialization of Prosocial Emotions and Behavior

Caregivers have considerable influence on young children's prosocial responses (Carlo, Fabes, Laible, & Kupanoff, 1999). Children who have warm and secure relationships with their caregivers are more likely to show prosocial feelings and behaviors (Kestenbaum, Farber, & Sroufe, 1989). In contrast, if the parents express anger and hostility and use physical punishment, the children are less empathic and less prosocial (Denham, Renwick-DeBardi, & Hughes, 1994; Denham, Zoller, & Couchoud, 1994).

When caregivers frequently talk to and reason with children about prosocial activities and the importance of feeling concern for and helping others, the children are more empathic and prosocial (Buchanan & Hudson, 2000). Children also learn about acting prosocially by watching the actions of their caregivers. But parents' talk must be backed by action; parents or caregivers who preach prosocial behavior but do not model it have little effect on children's prosocial development (Bryan & Walbek, 1970). Children also can learn to be uncaring by imitating the selfish or uncaring behaviors modeled by adults (Eisenberg, 1992).

How Do Parenting Behaviors and Family Context Influence Young Children's Development?

During early childhood, children's attachments change significantly. Preschoolers come to understand that caregivers have feelings and plans that often differ from their own. This understanding enables preschoolers to attempt to change caregivers' plans and goals. Ainsworth (1973) referred to this new type of attachment relationship as a **goal-corrected partnership.** In this new, emerging relationship, the child becomes a partner in planning how the relationship develops. This change in attachment places greater emphasis on how caregivers respond to children's more active behaviors. Caregivers' behaviors influence children's development in many other ways (Parke & Buriel, 1998). For example, through parents or their substitutes, young children learn the ways and values of their society (Bugental & Goodnow, 1998).

Disciplining Young Children

When you think of the term *discipline,* punishment may be the first thing that comes to mind. However, punishment is only one type of discipline. In the context of childrearing, **discipline** refers to any attempt by parents to alter children's behaviors or attitudes. The goal of discipline is to help children develop self-control and act in ways that society deems acceptable and appropriate. Before the age of 2, children are rarely disciplined. After children reach the age of 2, however, disciplinary encounters dominate parent–child interactions, and parents increasingly expect children to be able to obey their rules. According to one estimate (Minton, Kagan, & Levine, 1971), almost half of all parent–child interactions after the age of 2 center on discipline, and disciplinary encounters between parent and child occur an average of 9 times per hour.

Children may behave appropriately for different reasons. **Compliance** occurs when children obey and act appropriately because they know that they are being watched or will be rewarded or punished for their actions. **Internalization** occurs when children's obedience is based on internal controls and standards that they have incorporated into their own expectations of themselves. That is, they act appropriately because they want to (internalization), not because they have to (compliance).

How discipline is used influences whether or not children internalize standards. Discipline is more effective if it is *consistent* (Deal, Halverson, & Wampler, 1989), is not threatening to the child's well-being (Weiss & Dodge, 1992), and occurs as soon as possible after the child's misbehavior (Grusec, 1988). Supportive discipline does not create anxiety, helps children see the consequences of their actions, and aids internalization and adaptation (Pettit, Bates, & Dodge, 1997).

Although there are many ways to discipline children, the most common methods fall into three general categories:

■ **Power assertion** encompasses attempts by parents to use physical force or threats of physical force to control children's behavior. It includes physical punishment, taking away of privileges or possessions, and threatening such acts. About 90 percent of parents report using some type of power assertion technique at some time over the course of their children's lives (Simons, Johnson, & Conger, 1994). Spanking is a form of power assertion. Boys are spanked more often than girls, mothers do more spanking than fathers, children under the age of 7 are spanked more often than older children, and African American mothers (but not fathers) spank more often than Caucasian American mothers (Day, Peterson, & McCracken, 1998).

goal-corrected partnership *an attachment relationship in which the child becomes a partner in planning how the relationship develops*

discipline *attempts by parents to alter children's behaviors or attitudes*

compliance *obedience brought about by external pressures (such as the knowledge that one will be rewarded or punished for actions)*

internalization *obedience based on internal controls and standards that children have incorporated into their own expectations of themselves*

power assertion *disciplinary techniques in which parents use physical force or threats of physical force to control children's behavior*

Caregivers vary considerably in their attitudes toward and choices about discipline. Even within a family, mothers and fathers may have very different approaches to discipline. Can you identify some of the factors that contribute to such differences?

Although spanking remains a widely used discipline technique in most American families, it is the subject of considerable debate. In a large-scale analysis of existing studies, Gershoff (2002) examined both positive and negative behaviors in children who were spanked and found strong associations between spanking and negative behaviors, such as increased child aggression and antisocial behavior. Additionally, the more often or more harshly children were spanked, the more likely they were to be aggressive or to have mental health problems. The single desirable association was that spanking was associated with increased immediate compliance on the part of the child. These findings reflect the underlying controversy in the use of spanking—it can be effective in getting children to do what parents want, but it also raises concerns that spanking might escalate into physical maltreatment or lead to problem behaviors in the child.

Gershoff also found that a variety of situational factors, such as the parent–child relationship, can moderate the effects of corporal punishment. Spanking varies across parents—they differ in how frequently they use it, how forcefully they administer it, how emotionally aroused they are when they do it, and whether they combine it with other techniques. Each factor influences the effects of spanking on children

Although these findings do not justify a blanket injunction against mild to moderate disciplinary spanking (Baumrind, Larzelere, & Cowan, 2002), they do underscore the fact that it should be used with caution (if at all). Spanking does not teach children right from wrong. Although it makes children afraid to disobey when parents are present, they may feel free to misbehave if they believe they can get away with it.

The effects of power assertive discipline vary for children of different ethnic and racial backgrounds. For example, African American parents report using harsh and punitive parenting more often than do Caucasian American parents, but the use of such parenting practices does not appear to have the same detrimental consequences for African American children that it does for Caucasian American children (Kelley, Power, & Wimbush, 1992; McLoyd, Cauce, Takeuchi, & Wilson, 2000). These differences likely result from differences in attitudes about the use of punishment—African American parents are more accepting of its use than are Caucasian American parents (Heffer & Kelly, 1987). Attitude differences are due in part to differences in socioeconomic status and hence in stress levels; they may also relate to the belief of many African American parents that such parenting practices will help prepare their children for the harsh treatment they are likely to receive from society as they grow older (Snyder, 1996). These findings reflect the fact that parenting and its effects on children vary according to cultural values and the conditions in which parents and children find themselves.

Reinforcing good behavior also is a type of power assertive discipline because it is based on a difference in power between parents and their children. Just like the overuse of punishment, the overuse of rewards can have detrimental effects on children. In one study, children whose parents relied on rewards to get them to act appropriately were less helpful and generous when rewards were no longer offered (Fabes et al., 1989). Children may see rewards as "bribes" and comply only to get the rewards rather than because of their internal motivation (Kohn, 1993).

love withdrawal *disciplinary techniques by which parents ignore, withhold affection from, or express lack of love for the child*

inductive reasoning *disciplinary techniques by which parents use reasoning and verbal communication for the purpose of changing children's behavior*

■ **Love withdrawal** refers to a parent's attempts to gain obedience by ignoring or isolating the child, withholding affection, or expressing lack of love for the child. Love withdrawal can be effective in the short term because of the threat of losing the caregiver's love. In the long term, however, the constant anxiety about being rejected or abandoned has negative consequences for children's internalization (Grusec & Goodnow, 1994; Magai, Hunziker, Mesias, & Culver, 2000).

■ **Inductive reasoning** is a disciplinary technique in which parents use reasoning and verbal communication for the purpose of changing children's behavior (McGrath, Wilson, & Franssetto, 1995). Parents' use of inductive reasoning may include the following: explanations of rules and standards expected of children ("You need to stay close to me because you might get lost"), moral persuasion ("It's nice to help others"), personal appeals ("It will make Mommy happy if you help your brother"), explanations of the hurtful consequences of children's actions for others ("It hurt your sister's feelings when you wouldn't let her play with you"), and character attributions ("A kind boy like you helps his friend"). During early childhood, as children develop the cognitive ability to understand their parents' reasoning, parents begin to favor the use of inductive reasoning (Kuczynski, Kochanska, Radke-Yarrow, & Girnius-Brown, 1987). Children whose parents use inductive reasoning tend to be more prosocial and popular and have more internalized values and acceptable behavior (Eisenberg & Murphy, 1995; Hart, DeWolf, Wozniak, & Burts, 1992).

Influences on Parents' Use of Discipline

The reasons a parent chooses one disciplinary technique over another are not entirely clear. Parents have different beliefs and values about how to discipline children and what is or is not effective. Additionally, parents' use of discipline depends on a variety of factors—such as the characteristics of the child and the situation (Grusec, Goodnow, & Kuczynski, 2000).

Characteristics of the Child

Parents use different disciplinary techniques with different children. They are more likely to use power assertion with their sons than with their daughters because they often expect their sons to be harder to control (Leve & Fagot, 1997). Similarly, parents are more likely to use power assertion with children who are difficult to manage than with children who are easy to manage (Greenwald, Bank, Reid, & Knutson, 1997). Parents are more likely to reason with older children, who can recognize and respond to parents' intentions. Moreover, as children mature, they are less tolerant of parental demands in areas they regard as outside the legitimate control of parents, such as the types of clothes they wear and the appearance of their rooms. Thus, parental discipline changes in response to children's increasing autonomy and cognitive development (Smetana, 1988).

A similar trend is found in other cultures. For example, in mainland China, early childhood is divided into two periods: *budongshi,* the age of innocence (the first 6 years), when children lack cognitive understanding, and *dongshi,* the age of understanding (after age 6). Chinese parents rely on power assertive techniques during *budongshi* but use them less often once children reach *dongshi* (Stevenson, Chen, & Lee, 1992).

Nature of the Misbehavior

The discipline parents use varies depending on the nature of the child's misbehavior. For example, parents might use a combination of power assertion and inductive reasoning in response to lying and stealing, whereas they might use inductive reasoning alone when children fail to show concern for others (Grusec, Dix, & Mills, 1982; Trickett & Kuczynski, 1986). Parents also are more likely to use spanking and removal for dangerous misbehaviors than for behaviors that are merely annoying (Socolar & Stein, 1996).

Cultural, Ethnic, and Social Values

Disciplinary methods vary across cultures and among ethnic groups, in part because of different parenting goals and values. For example, many Hispanic Americans and Asian Americans believe that children should be obedient, so they use power assertive discipline more than other groups of parents do (Carter & Middlemiss, 1992). In contrast, Japanese mothers tend to indulge their children, with the intention of promoting a strong sense of dependency on the family—an outcome that is valued more in Japanese than in American culture (Azuma, 1986).

Among Aka pygmies, a hunter–gatherer tribe in the tropical rain forests of central Africa, parents seldom use power assertion. They are accepting of and responsive to their children but do not firmly or consistently enforce standards for behavior. Because of the demands of their environment, Aka children must be able to care for themselves at an early

How are parents' abilities to rear competent children challenged when the family lives in poverty?

age. Aka parents value the development of autonomy more than obedience and respect for elders, and their disciplinary practices reflect these values (Hewlett, 1992).

Contextual and social factors also influence parents' choice of discipline. One factor that is associated with power assertive parenting, as noted earlier, is socioeconomic status. In general, parents with low incomes, regardless of their ethnic background, are likely to stress obedience and use power assertion (Fox & Solis-Camera, 1997; Kelley, Sanchez-Hucles, & Walker, 1993). Parents' ability to rear competent children may be undermined by the stress and strain of the undesirable conditions associated with poverty (McLoyd, 1998b). Poverty diminishes parents' psychological well-being and their capacity for supportive parenting (McLoyd, 1998b). Such adults are more likely to experience physical and mental health problems than are their economically advantaged counterparts. In addition, parents with low incomes face a variety of negative life conditions—the threat of eviction, criminal assault, poor nutrition, inadequate housing, and so on—that increase their frustration and stress (Hashima & Amato, 1994). Poverty also is associated with single-parenting, and those who have to care for children alone face additional stress (Chase-Linsdale et al., 1999; Huston, 1991).

As a family's economic situation worsens, the parent or parents exhibit less nurturance and more negative discipline toward the children (Elder, Conger, Foster, & Ardelt, 1992; Lamb, 1999). Low-income parents are more likely to issue commands without explanation, less likely to consult children about their wishes, and less likely to reward children for behaving in desirable ways (Conger et al., 1994; McLoyd, 1998a). This is especially true if low-income parents do not have a network of social support—friends or relatives they can rely on (Hashima & Amato, 1994). Not surprisingly, these parenting practices can have negative consequences for the well-being of their children.

However, not all parents who live in poverty are depressed or disengaged parents. Many effectively buffer their children from the potentially detrimental effects of poverty (McLoyd, 1998b). When low-income parents have the psychological strength to manage the demands of being a parent, they can and do provide their children with supportive and responsive parenting behaviors (Jack, 2000). It is important to remember that stress in any family, regardless of how much money the family might have, can undermine the quality of parenting. Unfortunately, poverty places increased stress on parents and thus potentially influences their parenting negatively.

Parenting Styles

Although parents' disciplinary methods vary, certain consistencies are apparent. One of the most prominent studies of parents' styles of discipline was carried out by Diana Baumrind. In a long-term study of how parents influence children's development, Baumrind identified two important parenting characteristics (Baumrind, 1967, 1971, 1989). One is **demandingness**—the tendency to exert firm control over children, requiring them to act in mature and appropriate ways. The other is **responsiveness**—the tendency to be warm, accepting, and willing to take into account the wishes and feelings of the child. On the basis of these two characteristics, Baumrind identified three main parenting styles, and Maccoby and Martin (1983) added a fourth (see Figure 10.4).

Authoritarian Parenting

Authoritarian parenting is characterized by parents' efforts to shape, control, and judge the behaviors and attitudes of their children according to rigid standards of conduct. These parents usually value obedience and favor harsh, forceful measures, including physical punishment, to ensure that children comply with their rules. These parents discourage verbal give-and-take, believing that children should accept their word for what is right. Thus, authoritarian parents are high in demandingness and low in responsiveness. They set the rules, and children are to obey them because the parents say so. Preschoolers from authoritarian homes have low levels of self-control and independence, and they tend to be aggressive, anxious, and resistant to correction (Baumrind, 1971; Kochanska & Askan, 1995).

demandingness   *the tendency of parents to exert firm control over children, requiring them to act in mature and appropriate ways*

responsiveness   *the tendency of parents to be warm, accepting, and willing to take into account the wishes and feelings of the child*

authoritarian parenting   *a style of parenting in which parents try to shape, control, and judge the behaviors and attitudes of their children according to rigid standards of conduct*

Permissive Parenting

Parents who practice **permissive parenting** make few demands on their children—they are accepting and tolerant of their children's impulses and desires. These parents view themselves as resources to be used as their children wish rather than as agents responsible for shaping or altering their children's behavior. Permissive parents avoid the use of force to accomplish their goals and thus are low in demandingness and high in responsiveness. Because permissive parents fail to set limits on their children's behavior, preschoolers raised by permissive parents resemble those from authoritarian homes. They tend to be relatively immature, demanding, rebellious, impulsive, aggressive, and less socially competent (Baumrind, 1971).

Authoritative Parenting

Authoritative parenting is exhibited by parents who encourage verbal give-and-take and share with their children the reasons behind discipline and household rules. These parents value conformity to their rules and exert consistent and firm—but not excessive—control to bring it about. Authoritative parents are loving and supportive, and they recognize the importance of children's individual interests and needs. Authoritative parents can be classified as high in demandingness and high in responsiveness (Baumrind, 1996). Preschool children raised in authoritative homes tend to be friendly, cooperative, socially competent, confident, and self-reliant (Dekovic & Janssens, 1992; Hinshaw et al., 1997).

Thus, authoritative parenting produces the best outcomes for children. But why is that the case? Baumrind (1989) argues that the optimal parent–child relationship at any stage of development is characterized by reciprocity—the tendency to engage in mutual give-and-take. Authoritative parenting is associated with a pattern of family functioning in which children are required to be responsive to parental demands and parents accept a reciprocal responsibility to be as responsive as possible to the reasonable demands of their children. Authoritative parents maintain a balance between structure and control on the one hand and warmth and respect on the other, and they encourage the same balance in their children. In Western cultures, this balance represents competent parenting, and parents who cannot provide the necessary control and guidance have children who are difficult to manage (Belsky, Woodworth, & Crnic, 1996a; Gray & Steinberg, 1999).

Because different cultures hold different values, it is not surprising that the degree to which parents are authoritative or authoritarian differs across cultures and subcultures. Authoritative parenting is more prevalent in two-parent nondivorced families than in single-parent families or stepfamilies (Hetherington & Clingempeel, 1992). Authoritarian parenting is more common among families experiencing financial difficulties and among ethnic minorities (Steinberg, Mounts, Lamborn, & Dornbusch, 1991). Moreover, parents who adhere to conservative religious beliefs tend to adhere to an authoritarian parenting style more often than do parents who are less conservative in their religious beliefs (Day, Peterson, & McCracken, 1998). Authoritarian parenting also is more common in cultures emphasizing collectivist, rather than individualist, values (Rudy & Grusec, 2001). These findings indicate that parenting styles and their impact on children are influenced by family circumstances and cultural beliefs and attitudes.

Uninvolved Parenting

Maccoby and Martin (1983) expanded Baumrind's classification of parenting by adding uninvolved parenting. **Uninvolved parenting** describes the style of parents who make few demands on their children but are unresponsive or rejecting as well. Uninvolved parents do whatever they can to minimize the costs of being a parent and put little time

FIGURE 10.4

Classification of Baumrind's Parenting Styles

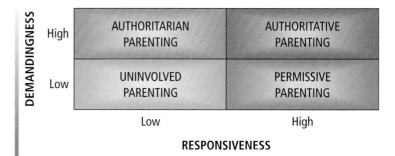

Parenting styles are based on differences in demandingness and responsiveness. Can you describe the qualities of parents within each classification and the impact the different styles have on children?

permissive parenting *a style of parenting in which parents make few demands on their children—they are accepting and tolerant of their children's impulses and desires*

authoritative parenting *a style of parenting in which parents encourage verbal give-and-take and share with their children the reasons behind discipline and household rules*

uninvolved parenting *a style of parenting in which parents make few demands of their children and are unresponsive or rejecting*

TABLE 10.2
Divorce Rates in Selected Countries
(divorces per 1,000 married women)

COUNTRY	1960	1970	1988	1998
United States	9.2	14.9	20.7	20.1
France	2.9	3.3	8.4	8.9
Canada	1.8	6.3	12.9	10.0
Denmark	5.9	7.6	13.1	11.4
Japan	3.6	2.9	5.4	7.9
Netherlands	2.2	3.3	8.1	7.5
Sweden	5.0	6.8	11.7	11.4
United Kingdom	2.0	4.7	12.3	12.5

Source: National Center for Health Statistics, 1990; *Miami Herald,* 1998.

and effort into interactions with their children. Parents' efforts relate more to their own immediate comfort and convenience than to the long-term development of the child. For example, these parents are unlikely to establish and enforce rules about bedtime or children's diets. At the extreme, uninvolved parents may be neglectful. Parental depression is sometimes related to uninvolved parenting; depressed parents tend to be withdrawn, disengaged, and unresponsive to their children (Lee & Gotlib, 1995). As you might expect, children from homes where the parents are uninvolved, neglectful, or depressed do not fare very well. They tend to be noncompliant, aggressive, withdrawn, and insecure in their attachments to others (Egeland & Sroufe, 1983; Miller et al., 1993).

The Effects of Divorce on Young Children's Development

Divorce is more commonplace today than at any time in the past. Although marriage is still viewed as a lifelong commitment, many people believe that couples who are unhappy should not be forced to stay together, not even for the sake of the children. When a sample of young parents was interviewed in 1962, half of them said that couples with children should stay together, even if they did not get along. Now, only 15 percent give that same answer (Whitehead & Popenoe, 2003).

Divorce rates in the United States generally increased from 1960 to 1988 and have stabilized since 1998. Over 1 million divorces are granted each year (Centers for Disease Control, 2001a). This trend is not unique to the United States. Table 10.2 presents divorce rates in selected countries for 1960, 1970, 1988, and 1998. As you can see, before stabilizing or even declining some, the divorce rates increased over time in all countries listed, in some cases more than tripling. Although similar trends are seen in all countries, divorce rates in the United States continue to be among the highest in the world.

Young Children's Understanding of Divorce

Divorce and separation are difficult concepts for children to grasp. Divorce is an abstract concept, and children's understanding of divorce is influenced by their ability to understand abstract ideas (Hetherington & Clingempeel, 1992).

Preschoolers have difficulty distinguishing between inner motives and outward appearances. They see divorce as one parent's moving away—they do not understand the complex motivations underlying the behaviors of both parents (Johnston, Breunig, Garrity, & Baris, 1997). Preschoolers view parents as possessions that belong to them and have only vague notions as to how parents relate to each other. They do not understand why their parents have to live apart or that divorce is usually permanent. School-age children, however, are more likely to understand the motives of their parents and that divorce is a permanent state in which parents grow apart from each other (Kurdek, 1988).

Young children's conception of *family* is concrete and is limited to those people who live together (Wedemeyer, Bickhard, & Cooper, 1989). The idea of blood relations is often too abstract for them to understand. When Dad leaves home because of a divorce or separation, it is not uncommon for young children to consider him no longer a family member. This reasoning reflects their tendency to focus on the observable qualities of a situation rather than the underlying and unseen qualities. Older children come to define families and family transitions such as divorce in psychological rather than physical terms (Mazur, 1993).

Divorce can be emotionally upsetting and frightening to young children. Because they are more dependent on the people they live with than are older children, the possibility of abandonment poses a more serious threat to them. The egocentric nature of young children's thinking leads them to see themselves as at least partly to blame for their parents' separation. Children who feel this way may try to undo the situation by making amends. Similarly, when a parent stops visiting, the young child may think that it is because of something he or she did and feel unloved or rejected. Older children are more likely to recognize that the reasons for the divorce have little to do with them and that the divorce reflects the incompatibility of their parents (Kurdek, 1988).

In families that have experienced divorce, parents often have to adopt roles and responsibilities that they did not have before. What roles do divorced fathers adopt?

Effects of Divorce on Young Children's Behavior and Adjustment

Over the past decade or so, researchers have come to understand that divorce is not a single event—rather, it is a complex process that does not begin with the dissolution of the marriage. Often, divorce is a lengthy sequence of events, involving "predivorce" experiences that may be as important for determining children's welfare as is the separation itself. Additionally, children do not react uniformly to divorce; their reactions depend on their age and developmental stage, their temperament, the way the process is managed by their parents, and the conditions associated with the breakup (such as the economic impact and the amount of lingering conflict) (Furstenberg & Kiernan, 2001).

Divorce can generate painful emotions, uncertainty, and confusion (Guidubaldi, 1988; Maccoby & Mnookin, 1992). Divorce forces mothers, fathers, and children to adapt to changes that can affect nearly every aspect of their lives. Two households must be established where there was only one before. Family finances and schedules are radically altered. Family loyalties are divided. Parental roles and responsibilities change dramatically.

Nearly all children react with shock and are extremely upset when they learn of their parents' breakup. Even when parents are openly fighting, young children often do not grasp the significance of these behaviors and cannot envision a separation. Most parents do not inform their young children of an impending separation until shortly before it occurs (Furstenberg & Cherlin, 1991).

In a series of longitudinal studies, Wallerstein and colleagues (Wallerstein & Kelly, 1975, 1976, 1980; Wallerstein & Lewis, 1998) found that children respond to divorce differently, according to age. Young preschoolers (2½ to 3½ years) are likely to show increased aggression; middle preschoolers (3½ to 4½ years) are likely to show increased irritability, aggression, self-blame, and confusion; and older preschoolers (5 to 6 years) are likely to show increased anxiety and aggressive behavior. Many of these negative behaviors ended within a year or two for children who experienced stable caregiving environments. However, 44 percent of the preschoolers continued to show emotional distress and poor psychological adjustment a year or two following the divorce.

Because of findings such as these, some researchers have labeled the first two years following a divorce as a "crisis period" for children and adults (Chase-Linsdale & Hetherington, 1990; Hetherington & Stanley-Hagan, 1999a). Young children have special needs during this crisis period. First, they need additional emotional support as they try to adapt to the new and frightening challenges brought about by their parents' divorce. Second, they need the predictable daily structure of their pre-divorce home life. Many single parents, however hard they may try, cannot meet these needs. Parents often lack the emotional energy to comfort children as they try to sort out their own anger, depression, and anxiety. The increased demands of single-parenthood often cause schedules to change from day to day. As a result, young children lose some of the support and structure they need, which may increase their aggression, fear, and uncertainty. In young children, the increased stress and confusion can result in regressed behavior, such as bed-wetting or sleep problems, that did not exist before the divorce (Benedek & Brown, 1995).

The adverse consequences of divorce appear to be greater for young boys than for young girls (Chase-Linsdale & Hetherington, 1990). It is possible that boys fare worse because they typically live with their mother, and there is some evidence that children adjust better after a divorce if they reside with the same-sex parent (Emery, 1988). Girls may be no less affected by divorce, though. Their responses (depression and withdrawal) may simply be less noticeable than boys' responses (aggression and hostility), and problems stemming from divorce may not appear until years after the breakup (Furstenberg & Cherlin, 1991)

For the sake of the children, should parents stay together in an unhappy marriage? This question has been asked repeatedly by parents, researchers, clinicians, and policy makers. The answer is complex. It is clear that high levels of parental conflict put children at greater risk for developing psychological and behavioral problems (Hetherington, 1999a). It is also clear, however, that divorce puts children at risk for a variety of poor developmental outcomes. If the stresses on family processes associated with an unhappy marriage can be reduced by a divorce, then the divorce may be advantageous. But the diminished resources that result from a divorce, coupled with inept parenting, may cause children to be better off if their parents stay in an unhappy marriage (Hetherington, 1999b). Most of the scientific research shows that, although growing up in a divorced family elevates the risk for certain kinds of problems, divorce by no means dooms children to having a terrible life. Additionally, research suggests that many of the problems in children that have been attributed to divorce were actually present prior to the divorce (Amato, 2000).

Factors That Affect Young Children's Adjustment to Divorce

Several factors influence how well children adapt to a divorce. Some of the important research findings can be summarized in terms of the following main factors (Hetherington, Bridges, & Insabella, 1998):

▨ *Amount of conflict between the parents:*   Children who are exposed to overt parental conflict (both before and after a divorce) have more adjustment problems (Cummings & Davies, 1996; Davis, Hops, Alpert, & Sheeber, 1998). When parents have hostile battles in front of young children, children's stress and anxiety increase. In fact, there is some indication that moving from a household with two parents who always are fighting in front of the children to a stable one-parent household can lead to better adjustment for children (Peterson & Zill, 1986). When divorced parents maintain civil and cordial relationships, children's adaptation to divorce is enhanced (Walsh & Stolberg, 1989).

▨ *Effectiveness of the parents:*   A critical factor in children's short- and long-term adjustment to divorce is how effectively the ex-spouses (particularly the custodial parent) function as parents. Divorced parents experience more stress because of the increased demands and more limited resources they face, and as a result, the relationships between parents and their children can deteriorate. In divorced families, parent–child relationships generally are more negative (especially between mothers and their sons) and parenting is less authoritative than in nondivorced families (Parke & Buriel, 1998). Mothers tend to become more authoritarian after a divorce, whereas fathers become more permissive. The better able parents are to cope with the disruptions brought about by a divorce, the less likely they are to dramatically alter their parenting styles and the more capable they are of providing their children with the structure, consistent discipline, and love they need (Katz & Gottman, 1997).

▨ *Characteristics of the child:*   Some children react more negatively to divorce than others do. As discussed earlier, age and sex are important determinants of children's responses. Recall from earlier discussions that children's reactivity to and resiliency in stressful environments vary. Children who are sensitive to changes in their environment and do not readily adapt may be more affected by divorce than are children whose temperaments are more adaptive to change. Similarly, children who are moody and irritable may react to divorce more negatively than children who are less emotionally sensitive and less easily upset (Monahan, Buchanan, Maccoby, & Dornbusch, 1993). Children's perception of the quality of the relationship between their parents also influences their response to marital conflict and divorce (Fincham, 1998).

■ *Relationship of the child with the noncustodial parent:* Young children's adjustment to divorce is enhanced when both parents are able to maintain relationships with them. In many cases, the father, who often is the noncustodial parent, may break off the relationship with his children, or the mother may actively try to undermine this relationship. Loss of the father's relationship generally has a greater impact on boys than on girls. Also, the younger the child is when separated from a parent, the more affected the child is by the loss (Stanley, Weikel, & Wilson, 1986). When a noncustodial parent is able to maintain an active and supportive parenting relationship, children are better off. Part of the reason for this is that noncustodial parents who maintain regular contact with their children also are likely to keep paying child support (Peters, Argys, Maccoby, & Mnookin, 1993). Additionally, the more often a father sees his children, the better he feels about the visits and the less likely problems are to occur (Arditti & Keith, 1993). Despite visitation and custody arrangements, contact with noncustodial parents drops off sharply over time. According to some estimates, by the end of the second year after a divorce, only 1 child in 6 sees his or her father as often as once a week, and close to half have not seen their father at all over the course of the preceding year (Furstenberg & Cherlin, 1991).

Child Custody Arrangements

Until recently, the dominant legal standard for awarding custody of children, particularly young children, favored mothers. This practice was based on the "tender years" doctrine, which assumed that child care during the early years should be undertaken by women (Maccoby & Mnookin, 1992). Today, however, the "best interests of the child" standard has replaced the tender years doctrine in most states (Krauss & Sales, 2001). This doctrine is based on the notion that the custody arrangement should be the one that best suits the child. The increased recognition that fathers' involvement with their children is beneficial to them is a reason many states have adopted joint-custody statutes (Wallerstein & Corbin, 1999).

Several types of custody arrangements are available (see Table 10.3). They vary in the degree to which both parents are involved in physical care of and decision making for the

TABLE 10.3
Types of Custody Arrangements

TYPE OF CUSTODY	DESCRIPTION
Sole legal custody	Custodial parent is assigned all legal rights, duties, and powers and is responsible for all decisions regarding child's welfare. Noncustodial parent has limited rights and powers.
Sole physical custody	Custodial parent has primary physical custody of child. Noncustodial parent is usually awarded visitation rights.
Joint legal custody	Both parents retain rights to make decisions regarding child's health and welfare.
Joint physical custody	Both parents retain rights to share in day-to-day physical care of child. Child spends substantial amount of time with each parent.
Divided custody	Each parent has child for a portion of the year or in alternating years. Each parent has legal rights and makes decisions when child is with that parent.
Split custody	Each parent has sole legal and physical custody of one or more children. Noncustodial parent has visitation rights.

Source: Kelly, 1994.

FIGURE 10.5

Custody Arrangements for African American and Caucasian American Children

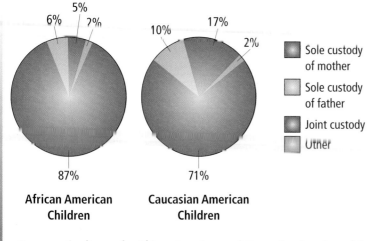

African American
Children

Caucasian American
Children

Sole custody
of mother

Sole custody
of father

Joint custody

Other

Compare the figures for African American and Caucasian American children. Notice that joint custody and father custody are more common among Caucasian American children than among African American children. What factors contribute to these differences?

Source: National Center for Health Statistics, 1995.

children. As you can see in Figure 10.5, most children are placed in the sole custody of the mother (National Center for Health Statistics, 1995). Joint custody is awarded in a small number of cases; the percentage of arrangements in which sole custody is given to the father is even smaller. The figure also shows that African American children are more likely than Caucasian American children to be placed in sole custody of their mother.

Young Children's Adjustment to Remarriage

When parents remarry, children must share them with a widening circle of other people—stepparents and stepsiblings. After a divorce, between 70 and 80 percent of parents remarry (Coleman, Ganong, & Fine, 2000).

More than half of all Americans alive today have been, are now, or eventually will be in one or more stepfamily situations during their lives. One third of all children are expected to become stepchildren before they reach the age of 18, and about 1 of every 3 Americans is a stepparent, stepchild, stepsibling, or some other member of a stepfamily. African American children are most likely to live in stepfamilies—32 percent of African American children live in stepfamilies, versus 16 percent of Hispanic children and 15 percent of Caucasian children (Arnold, 1998).

Currently, the vast majority of stepfamilies (86 percent) are composed of a biological mother and a stepfather (Hetherington & Stanley-Hagan, 1999b). The dramatic increase in the number of people living in stepfamilies is largely due to America's increasing divorce rate. Two thirds of the people who are divorced and widowed choose to remarry, and the number of stepfamilies has grown proportionately. The other major reason for the increase in stepfamilies is the fact that more children are being born out of wedlock. One third of children entering stepfamilies do so after birth to an unmarried mother, a situation that is four times more common in African American stepfamilies than in Caucasian stepfamilies. The mode of entry into stepfamilies varies with the age of the child. Most preschoolers who enter stepfamilies do so after nonmarital birth; 16 percent become members of a stepfamily through parental remarriage following divorce. About half of the stepfamilies into which children over the age of 10 enter are formed when a parent remarries following a divorce (Arnold, 1998).

The changes brought about by remarriage are dramatic (Mason, 1998). Newly remarried parents report experiencing twice the stress of nondivorced parents. The changing dynamics of family life after remarriage lead to changes in parenting behaviors. For example, mothers report that they are less emotionally responsive to their children and more punitive in their discipline than they were before remarrying (Hetherington, Hagan, & Anderson, 1989). The changes associated with stepfamily life may put some children at risk for poor outcomes (Nicholson, Fergusson, & Horwood, 1999).

In contrast to the findings on divorce, girls have more problems than boys in making the transition to the new family. Young girls, who are likely to have enjoyed a good relationship with their single mother, may become angry and resentful of the new husband. Competition for the mother's time and attention increases the daughter's rivalry with the stepfather, regardless of how supportive the new father is (Hetherington & Stanley-Hagan, 2000).

Young children seem to adapt more readily to their parents' remarriages than do older children and adolescents (Hetherington & Stanley-Hagan, 2000). Because young children

■ In **parallel play,** the child engages in an activity that another is engaged in at the same time and place, but each child is still playing separately. The children play side by side but not *with* each other. Parallel play is commonly observed in preschoolers.

■ In **associative play,** the child engages in play that involves other children, but each child has a different goal. Associative play involves a considerable amount of social interaction, turn-taking, and expressive communication. Associative play is occurring when two children draw pictures at the same table, sharing crayons and commenting on each other's picture. Each child has his or her own design and goal in mind, but they share and socialize with each other as they draw. Associative play is common among 3- and 4-year-olds.

In this example of parallel play, notice how these children are playing the same thing but are not taking notice of each other. What factors contribute to the development of more advanced forms of social play?

■ In **cooperative play,** two or more children engage in a play activity with a common goal that requires social interaction. For instance, two children might dig through sand with their bare hands, opposite each other, with the goal of meeting in the middle to form a tunnel. Cooperative play represents the highest level of social play.

It is best not to think of these categories as discrete developmental stages of play. Although their play becomes increasingly social and interactive as children develop, even toddlers engage in cooperative play, and most children display a blend of all varieties of play (Howes & Matheson, 1992). Also, the kind of play children engage in is not always a measure of social maturity. For example, the meaning of solitary play depends on what the child is doing (Coplan & Rubin, 1998; Coplan et al., 1994) and on the physical environment (Frost, Shin, & Jacobs, 1998). Solitary play may be appropriate for a 4-year-old child when cutting and pasting paper but not when engaging in pretend play. Thus, if a child is engaged alone in an activity that is best done as a group, then solitary play may be detrimental to the child's development.

Variations in Play Across Cultures

Although play is universal among children, there are differences in the amounts and kinds of play observed across and within cultures (Roopnarine, Lasker, Sacks, & Stores, 1998). Families in various cultures encourage different types of play and attach different meanings to play activities. For instance, differences were apparent in a study that compared how Japanese and American mothers interacted with their young children in a free-play situation (Tamis-LeMonda et al., 1992). Japanese mothers encouraged their young children to engage in pretend play—suggesting, for example, that the child kiss a doll or offer the doll some food. American mothers emphasized the functional uses of the toys—"Push the bus"—and spoke more about the toys as objects than did Japanese mothers. Japanese mothers viewed the play situation as an opportunity to teach their children how to interact with others, whereas American mothers used play to teach their children about the world and how to explore it on their own (Tamis-LeMonda et al., 1992).

The amount of time children spend in various play activities also is influenced by their cultural environments. For example, American children and young children growing up in the Marquesas Islands in the South Pacific allocate different amounts of time to various play activities. Figure 10.6 presents a breakdown of these differences. As you can see in this

parallel play *play in which two or more children engage in the same activity at the same time and place, but each child still plays separately*

associative play *play in which various children engage, but with different goals*

cooperative play *play in which two or more children engage, with a common goal that requires social interaction*

FIGURE 10.6

Percentages of Time Marquesan and American Children Spend in Different Types of Play

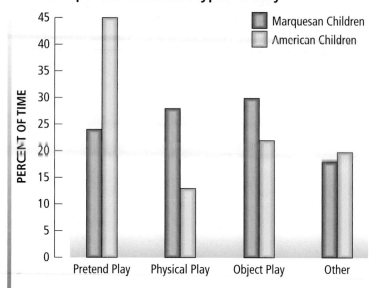

What differences do you see when you compare the figures for Marquesan and American children? What accounts for the high rate of pretend play among American children?

figure, Marquesan children spend considerably less time in pretend play and more time in physical and object play than do American children. This difference is due in part to cultural differences in their views of social status. Because Marquesan children are taught to be cautious about forming status hierarchies, they avoid play that requires distinct leaders, preferring activities that do not require much individual competition (Martini, 1994). Pretend play requires cooperation and structure; Marquesan children are more likely to engage in types of play that do not include these elements. They prefer play that is object oriented (pounding rocks to make noise) or physical (searching for insects or eels, chasing waves). Their preferences reflect the cultural values of the society in which they are reared.

The culture children grow up in also influences the amount of time they spend immersed in the different forms of play. Marquesan children almost never play alone, whereas American children spend about 35 percent of their time engaged in solitary play (Martini, 1994). Because the play of American preschoolers is almost always supervised by adults who set limits, they are not exposed to the dangers Marquesan children face. Large play groups are necessary for the protection and safety of Marquesan children.

Young Children's Sibling Relationships

Almost 80 percent of children in the United States have siblings (Dunn, 1992). But the arrival of a new brother or sister is not an easy adjustment for children, and it sometimes leads to increased withdrawal, aggression, or dependency (Teti, 1992). There is evidence that mother–child attachment security decreases following the birth of a sibling (Teti et al., 1996). These negative reactions are especially likely among preschool-age children who have a limited understanding of their relationship to the new baby. Young children may react strongly to the stress brought about by the new demands. Furthermore, because parents often pay a lot of attention to the newborn, at the expense of the preschooler, the preschooler may feel neglected.

When siblings are similar in age, marked changes in the nature of their relationship begin to appear during early childhood. Between 3 and 4 years of age, children become more interested in their siblings (Brown & Dunn, 1992)—they collaborate, cooperate, and play together with increasing frequency. They also fight and struggle more than they did before, and they get along better with friends than with each other (Volling, Youngblade, & Belsky, 1997).

Dynamics of Sibling Relationships

Siblings spend considerable time interacting with one another and therefore influence one another in a variety of ways. Siblings are a source of comfort and support, as well as conflict and antagonism, and they serve as role models, helping children learn new behaviors. Positive sibling relationships foster healthy adaptation in a variety of settings (Richman, Stevenson, & Graham, 1982). Negative sibling relationships also have pervasive effects. For example, children who are aggressive with their siblings are likely to have poor peer relationships (Dishion, 1990).

Sibling relationships change as children move through different developmental periods. When siblings are more than a few years apart in age, the older sibling assumes roles that are more parentlike than peerlike, often acting as teacher and caregiver for the younger brothers and sisters (Brody, Stoneman, MacKinnon, & MacKinnon, 1985; Dunn, 1988). During early childhood, children begin to share intimate feelings and thoughts with their siblings and are quite dependent on each other for companionship and support. Older siblings often become particularly important to young children in families that have recently immigrated to the United States, especially when the parents have less understanding of the new culture than the older siblings do (Perez-Granados & Callanan, 1997). During later childhood and adolescence, friends and peers take on more of these roles, and siblings are less important sources of intimacy and support. This is not to say that siblings are not important after early childhood, but their relative importance compared to peers decreases somewhat (Buhrmester, 1992).

This child is looking at her baby brother. In what ways do siblings influence child development?

Differences in the Quality of Sibling Relationships

As early as young childhood, striking differences in sibling relationships appear. Some siblings are very close, others extremely antagonistic. There are at least three factors influencing the quality of sibling relationships (Dunn, 1992):

1. *Temperaments of the siblings:* The temperamental qualities of the siblings influence the level of conflict between them. Children who are active, intense, or unadaptable in temperament are likely to have antagonistic sibling relationships (Miller, Volling, & McElwain, 2000). The temperament match between siblings also is important: siblings who are temperamentally similar are more likely to have positive relationships (Boer, 1990; Munn & Dunn, 1988).

2. *Parental treatment:* Negative relationships between siblings often are attributed to the parents' favoritism toward one of the siblings (Brody, Stoneman, & McCoy, 1992; McHale, Crouter, McGuire, & Updegraff, 1995). Often it is difficult to avoid treating children differently, especially if siblings are of different ages. If 4-year-old Erin is sent to bed earlier than her 9-year-old sister Sarah, for example, she may accuse her parents of favoring her sister. But if they are both sent to bed at the same time, Sarah may find this unfair because she was not allowed to stay up so late when she was 4. Although the ages and sexes of the siblings significantly affect the degree to which differential treatment disrupts sibling relationships (McHale et al., 2000), the effects become more profound if one sibling is treated with less warmth and affection or with more punishment. That child is more likely to behave in an aggressive, rivalrous, and unaffectionate manner toward his or her sibling (Boer, Goedhart, & Treffers, 1992; Volling & Elins, 1998). Children are less likely to respond negatively if they perceive that the differential treatment was justified (Kowal & Kramer, 1997).

3. *Family life events:* Sibling relationships can be influenced by stressful events affecting the family, such as divorce, job loss, or death (Erel, Margolin, & John, 1998). For example, sibling relationships often deteriorate in families that experience a divorce. Because of changes in caregiving following a divorce, older siblings are likely to engage in more caretaking behavior with their younger siblings; younger siblings may reject this caregiving, thereby setting the stage for conflict (MacKinnon, 1989). Sibling relationships also may become more hostile as siblings compete for the limited time and attention of their parents (Beaudry, Simard, Drapeau, & Charbonneau, 2000). The stress and new demands of making the transition to school also are likely to negatively affect siblings' relationships (Dunn, 1992). Stress also exacerbates parents' tendencies to treat siblings differently, thereby increasing the possibility of conflicted sibling relationships (Crouter, McHale, & Tucker, 1999).

How Does Television Influence Young Children's Emotional and Social Development?

You learned in Chapter 9 that television viewing affects young children's cognitive development. As you might expect, children's social development also is influenced by television. Television plays a central role in the life of most contemporary families and often provides people with common points of reference for relating to others. Many of the themes in young children's play revolve around what they see on television.

During early childhood, many children begin to spend a large amount of time watching television, and long-term relations have been found between early television viewing and later adjustment (Anderson et al., 2001). The amount of time children spend watching television and the content of many television programs have generated concerns and questions about the impact of television on family life and children's emotional and social development.

Effects of Television on Family Life

The acceptance and popularity of television began slowly and then exploded. In 1950, only 5 percent of US households owned a television set, but within ten years, almost 90 percent of households owned one (Van-Evra, 1998). Today, only 2 percent of households do not own a television set, and about two thirds of households own two or more sets.

Time spent watching television has steadily increased. The television set is now on for an average of almost 7 hours per day (A. C. Nielsen Media Research, 2003). Although almost everyone watches some television, low-income families watch more television than middle- or upper-income families; television is relatively cheap entertainment, and low-income families may not have the money to spend on other sources of entertainment (Huston et al., 1992).

Most children are exposed to television from the time they are born. As you can see in Figure 10.7, children's television viewing time increases during the preschool years to an average of 2.5 hours each day and continues to increase through the elementary school years. Viewing time peaks at about 4 hours per day just before the start of adolescence, when competing activities reduce the number of hours spent in front of the television set (Condry, 1989). When computers, DVDs, and video games are taken into account, children today spend an average of 5 hours a day in front of "video screens" (Woodward & Gridina, 2001). Similar patterns have been found in other countries (Liebert & Sprafkin, 1988).

Effects of Television Violence on Young Children's Aggression

Despite efforts at regulation, children's television still contains a good deal of violent content (Federman, 1998). Violent acts typically are defined as any deliberate acts of physical or verbal force to achieve a goal. In 1997, 61 percent of all television programs had some form of violence, and over half of all violent acts were lethal (Federman, 1998). For children's programs, the rates of violence also are high. By some estimates, children's shows contain 20 to 25 violent acts per hour (Murray, 1995). By the time they reach adolescence, children have witnessed over 100,000 acts of televised violence, including over 20,000 murders (American Psychological Association, 1993). In addition, children's programs tend to depict violence

FIGURE 10.7

Hours of Television Viewing, by Age

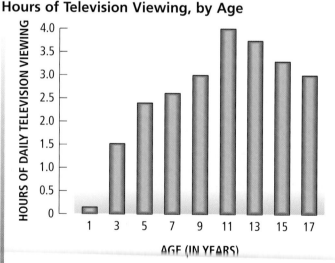

Notice the increase in rates of viewing early in development. What factors contribute to this increase? Why does television play such a large role in everyday family life?

Source: Figure from *Televison and the American Child* by G. Comstock and H. Paik, copyright © 1991 by Academic Press, reproduced by permission of the publisher.

in ways that glamorize and reward it. These depictions frequently involve (1) a perpetrator who is an attractive role model (such as a super hero), (2) violence that seems justified, (3) violence that goes unpunished, (4) minimal consequences to victims, and (5) violence that seems realistic to the viewer (Federman, 1998).

Young children hold mixed views about the violence in television programs. Some find the violence attractive. Some do not view a program as being violent unless there is bloodshed. Others disapprove of the violent behaviors portrayed and realize that the violent themes and messages conflict with what is good. Thus, young children interpret and define television violence in different ways, and these differences affect their responses to it (Wilson & Smith, 1998).

Scientific evidence supports a relationship between children's exposure to violent television content and their own aggressive and risky behaviors and attitudes (Jason, Kennedy-Hanaway, & Brackshaw, 1999; Potts, Doppler, & Hernandez, 1994). This relationship has been demonstrated in studies of thousands of children of different ages and backgrounds, using a variety of procedures and methods (Hearold, 1986; Paik & Comstock, 1994). The link between television violence and children's aggression has been found worldwide (Huesmann & Eron, 1986).

With literally thousands of studies showing a relation between television violence and children's aggressive behaviors and attitudes, what conclusions can be drawn? Several important themes are highlighted in the research (Huston & Wright, 1998; Jason et al., 1999):

Television viewing, which increases during the preschool years, has important effects on children's development and family life. Can you identify these effects? How are they produced?

- Children's aggressive tendencies are likely to be increased by violence on television when it is portrayed realistically (Atkin, 1983), when it is portrayed by human rather than cartoon characters (Hayes & Casey, 1992), when it is not subject to critical commentary (Peracchio, 1993), and when the aggressive behavior is seen as justified or rewarded (Perry, Perry, & Rasmussen, 1986).

- Increased arousal after viewing violent television disposes children to behave more impulsively (Zillmann, 1982), and implied violence elicits as much arousal as does actual violence (Kalamas & Gruber, 1998).

NURTURING CHILDREN
SUPERVISING CHILDREN'S TELEVISION VIEWING

Given the attractiveness of television and its dominant role in American family life, what guidelines can caregivers follow to establish positive viewing habits in children? Here are some practical ideas (Center for Media Literacy, 1995; Murray, 1995; Public Broadcasting Service, 2003):

- *Start early:* The younger children are, the easier it is to establish positive television viewing habits.
- *Set daily limits:* Most professionals suggest that children be limited to a maximum of 2 hours of television per day.

- *Encourage planned viewing:* Have children select programs you approve of from television schedules.
- *Don't locate a television set in a child's room:* It encourages isolated television viewing.
- *Remember that children learn from their caregivers and other role models:* If caregivers watch a lot of television, children are likely to watch a lot of television.
- *Watch television with children:* Encourage children to discuss what they see on television and how they feel about it. Let them know what you think about it.

- *Talk to children about television advertising:* Tell children that the purpose of advertising is to sell as many products as possible to as many viewers as possible.
- *Read to children rather than watching television:* Reading to children fosters more intimate interactions and enhances children's appreciation of books and reading.
- *Use V-chip technology:* This technology allows caregivers to block out shows that are offensive or inappropriate for children.

- Children who are abused, emotionally disturbed, or predisposed to act aggressively are more influenced by television violence than others are (Sprafkin, Gadow, & Abelman, 1992).

- Television violence can have long-term consequences. Children with high levels of exposure to television violence were likely to be aggressive 10 years later and were more likely to be arrested or convicted for violent crime or abuse 22 years later than children with less exposure to television violence (Eron, 1982; Eron, Huesmann, Lefkowitz, & Walder, 1996).

Although exposure to television violence relates to children's aggressive behaviors and attitudes, many factors influence this relationship. Debate continues about the extent to which we can conclusively say that television violence *causes* increased aggression in children (Josephson, 1995).

Effects of Television on Young Children's Prosocial Behavior

Not all behavior on television is violent or aggressive; acts of kindness and cooperation are common. Rates of prosocial behaviors generally are comparable to rates of aggressive and violent behaviors (Greenberg et al., 1980).

Some of the programs designed for young children (such as *Sesame Street, Clifford, Between the Lions,* and *Mr. Rogers' Neighborhood*) specifically focus on teaching prosocial behavior. Soon after these shows were introduced, scientists became interested in determining their effectiveness in increasing children's prosocial behavior. They found that preschoolers who watched characters on *Sesame Street* or *Mr. Rogers' Neighborhood* cooperated with and helped each other more than those who did not (Friedrich-Cofer et al., 1979; Singer & Singer, 2001). However, simply exposing young children to prosocial television characters is not enough to strongly influence their prosocial behavior (Singer & Singer, 2001). The extent to which young children learn prosocial lessons and behaviors from television depends on two factors related to presentation:

- *Environmental cues and supports:* A parent or teacher may need to supplement prosocial television programming with related materials (puppets, costumes) that promote role playing. Verbal discussions and labeling of prosocial behavior also are effective, but role playing is most effective in helping young children apply television content to their own behavior (Friedrich & Stein, 1975).

- *Competing messages in the program:* In many television programs, characters display both prosocial and aggressive behaviors. Story lines often continue over several programs, with characters displaying conflicts and maladaptive behaviors as well as helpful and sympathetic responses. Young children learn best when the prosocial message clearly replaces aggressive behavior. Combined prosocial and aggressive messages sometimes lead to increased aggressive behavior in children, perhaps because children find the aggressive action more interesting and memorable than the prosocial lessons contained in the program (Lovelace & Huston, 1983).

Without environmental cues and clearly contrasting depictions of prosocial behavior, young children may not be able to apply the prosocial lessons they watch on television to their own lives.

Try it Out

1. Using Baumrind's definitions, describe the parenting styles of your parents. Identify the specific parenting behaviors that you used to classify your parents in one of the four categories. Discuss the difficulties you had in classifying them. What effects do you think your parents had on your development? What style of parenting will you use with your own children?

2. Arrange to observe preschool children playing on a playground. What kinds of play can you identify? Who do the children play with? What kinds of activities do they engage in with their peers? Why are some children more likely than others to play with peers?

3. Watch some children's television shows, and record the numbers of aggressive and pro-social acts. How did you define them? What kinds of characters displayed them? What impact might these televised acts have on young children's development?

Key Terms and Concepts

associative play (329)
authoritarian parenting (318)
authoritative parenting (319)
compliance (315)
cooperative play (329)
demandingness (318)
discipline (315)
display rules (309)
emotion regulation (308)
empathy (313)
gender consistency (302)
gender identity (302)
gender labeling (302)
gender schemas (307)
gender stability (302)
gender stereotypes (304)
goal-corrected partnership (315)
guilt (300)
hostile aggression (312)

inductive reasoning (316)
initiative (300)
instrumental aggression (312)
internalization (315)
love withdrawal (316)
onlooker play (328)
parallel play (329)
permissive parenting (319)
power assertion (315)
pretend play (328)
prosocial behavior (313)
relational aggression (313)
responsiveness (318)
schematic consistency (307)
self-concept (300)
self-esteem (301)
solitary play (328)
sympathy (313)
uninvolved parenting (319)

Sum It Up

How does self-awareness change during early childhood?

- What do the authors mean when they say preschoolers lack "conservation of self?" Give an example. (p. 300)

How do young children develop a concept of gender?

- Name the three stages of gender understanding in children. (p. 302)
- Compare and contrast the three categories of gender development theory: bio-logical, social learning, and cognitive. (pp. 306–307)

How do emotions develop during early childhood?

- What role does temperament play in regulating emotion? Describe the two impor-tant underlying temperamental dimensions in emotion regulation. (p. 310)

How do parenting behaviors influence young children's development?

- What are the most common categories of parental discipline? (p. 315)

How do peer and sibling relationships develop during early childhood?

- In what ways do peer relationships differ from family relationships? (p. 325)

How does television influence young children's emotional and social development?

- How does television violence affect children's aggressive tendencies? (p. 333)

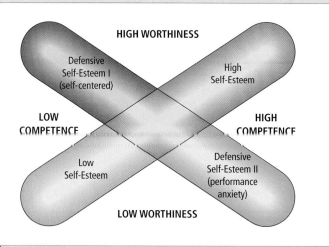

FIGURE 10.1 **Matrix of Self-Esteem** *Patterns of self-esteem are made up of combinations of competence and worthiness.*

Children often prefer toys and activities that reinforce their own gender identity.

SELF-AWARENESS AND GENDER CONCEPT

During early childhood, dramatic changes occur in children's awareness and image of themselves and in their feelings of self-worth. During the preschool years, children also come to understand that gender is a stable part of their self-concept. (Refer back to pages 299–308.)

EMOTIONAL DEVELOPMENT

During early childhood, children's emotional lives become increasingly differentiated and rich. Young children become better at regulating and communicating their emotions, more emotionally responsive to others, and more aware of emotions in themselves and others. (Refer back to pages 308–315.)

FIGURE 10.3 **Emotion Regulation** *In this figure, the young girl is distracting herself from the scary television scene by singing to herself.*

During the preschool years, children's prosocial emotions and behaviors become more advanced and appropriate.

Children's conflicts at this age revolve primarily around possession of objects and space.

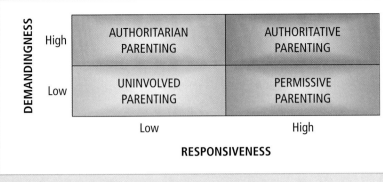

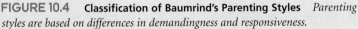

FIGURE 10.4 **Classification of Baumrind's Parenting Styles** *Parenting styles are based on differences in demandingness and responsiveness.*

In this example of parallel play, notice how these children are playing the same thing but are not taking notice of each other.

INFLUENCE OF FAMILIES AND PEERS

As preschoolers become more independent and active, parental disciplinary efforts increase. The nature of the misbehavior, characteristics of the child, and cultural and ethnic values influence caregivers' choice of disciplinary practices. As young children widen their social relationships, peers become increasingly more important influences in their lives. (Refer back to pages 315–331.)

IMPACT OF TELEVISION

During early childhood, many children begin to spend a large amount of time watching television, and long-term relations have been found between early television viewing and later adjustment. (Refer back to pages 332–334.)

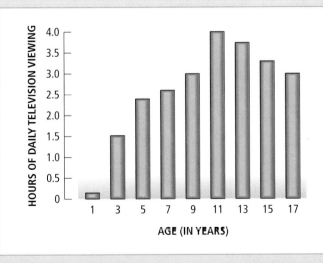

Television viewing, which increases during the preschool years, has important effects on children's development and family life.

FIGURE 10.7 **Hours of Television Viewing, by Age** *Notice the increase in rates of viewing early in development. Children who watch more television have lower reading comprehension and interest in reading and decreased readiness for school.*

Part

5

Late Childhood Development

During late childhood, the years from 5 to 11, which are also known as the school-age years, children undergo pervasive changes affecting their physical and psychological well-being. New contexts provide additional challenges. When children enter school, they are exposed to a wide variety of new intellectual and social demands. Teachers, other students, principals, classes, homework, and extracurricular activities play significant roles in children's lives. Family members remain important, but the amount of time children spend with family members drops, and time spent in school and with peers increases. Thus, children experience important changes in environment and social transactions.

School-age children often find their performance compared to that of others. They are evaluated by teachers, and their parents receive reports about their performance and behavior in school. Tests, homework, and assignments take up a good deal of children's time and are sources of comparison with others. New acquaintances, friends, and enemies develop. Many of these challenges and stressors were not present before children entered school. Thus, during late childhood, children have to develop new coping strategies to deal with the demands placed by their changing environment. Though many children cope easily and adjust well, some are overwhelmed and lack the skills and support to cope effectively. Children's cultural backgrounds affect how they handle these demands and influence the types of challenges they face.

Physical Development and Health in Late Childhood

Chapter Outline

How Do Children's Bodies and Brains Develop During Late Childhood?
Brain Development
Body Size and Appearance
Bone Health
Tooth Development and Oral Health
Physical Health Concerns

How Do Motor Skills and Physical Fitness Develop During Late Childhood?
Motor Skills
Physical Fitness and Sports

What Are the Nutritional Needs and Concerns of School-Age Children?
Nutritional Needs
Undernutrition
Childhood Obesity: Generation XL

What Are the Health and Safety Concerns of Late Childhood?
Diseases
Accidents and Injuries
Personal Safety

A DEVELOPMENTAL MYSTERY

Stories would circulate like wildfire in the neighborhood—"Did you hear about Davey Williams? He got it. He was fine last week but woke up a couple days ago, weak and achy. Today he can't breathe on his own, so he's in an iron lung at the hospital." Because of stories like this, which unfortunately were very common in 1952, children were kept prisoners in their own homes. Parents would not allow their children to play with large groups of children, so few children went to camp or played sports. The cause of the fear was polio—a disease causing muscle paralysis and sometimes death. Why were some children more likely to contract the disease? How could polio be stopped? These mysteries drove the medical community to find a cure or a way to prevent the disease.

Polio is one of the many diseases that strike during childhood, and thanks to effective vaccines, for children in many parts of the world this disease is preventable. However, children in less well developed countries continue to be at risk for this and many other diseases. In part, where children live influences their health, although there are similarities in physical and motor development for children all over the world.

How Do Children's Bodies and Brains Develop During Late Childhood?

During late childhood, children's bodies and brains continue to grow and develop, but the physical changes are not as pronounced as those of early childhood. Although growth is slower during this period, motor and physical abilities improve significantly. The brain continues to develop, particularly the frontal lobes. During the school years, children's bones and teeth undergo important changes that have long-term impact on their health. Some children experience serious problems involving their sensory capabilities; others encounter less serious issues that also may raise concerns about physical well-being.

Brain Development

In school-age children, the brain continues to undergo growth and change. During the school years, the functioning of a child's brain improves (Black, 1998). Information is processed more efficiently because of increased myelination of the nerve fibers of the brain and increased lateralization of the two hemispheres of the brain. Remember that not all parts of the brain undergo myelination at the same time. During childhood and adolescence, the prefrontal cortex is still undergoing dramatic developmental changes in myelination, and these changes are thought to relate to higher cognitive functions such as planning, setting goals, and inhibiting inappropriate behavior. Because the brain is still developing, it is not surprising that children's goal setting and planning have yet to reach their maximum levels. By the age of 6, most children's brains have reached a level of development that allows children to learn in a school classroom environment. During the school years, the brain also continues to undergo changes in neural connections. Redundant synaptic connections between neurons continue to be pruned, especially in the areas involved in higher cognitive functioning, increasing the organization of the brain (Case, 1992). These changes may relate to the continuing development of problem solving, memory, and understanding of language that occurs during childhood (Byrnes & Fox, 1998; Diamond, 2000).

To what extent do individual differences in growth remain stable over time?

Body Size and Appearance

Children grow more slowly during the school years than they did as younger children—usually about 2 to 3 inches and 3 to 6 pounds a year—and this slower rate of growth continues until preadolescence (see Figure 11.1, a and b). During the elementary school years, boys and girls develop very similarly: the arms and legs grow longer relative to the trunk of the body, and the body lengthens and fills out. One effect of this slower growth rate is that children have time to become accustomed to their bodies. This brings about gains in motor control and coordination (Gallahue & Ozmun, 1995).

At this age, individual differences among children's bodies are striking, and these differences tend to remain relatively constant over time. Research shows that, generally, children's body builds remain about the same through childhood and into adolescence. Height is usually more constant than weight and musculature, which are more influenced by exercise and diet. (We will discuss children's weight later in the chapter.)

What is the relation between body build and athletic ability? Observations of Olympic athletes suggest that certain sports require particular body builds. For instance, most gymnasts are short and small-boned, whereas most volleyball players are tall. Although in many countries trainers try to select the "perfect" body build for each type of athletic performance (especially for early identification of possible Olympic athletes), predicting the performance of an average-looking child based only on his or her body shape and size is very difficult (DiGirolamo, Geis, & Walker, 1998). How muscular a child is, however, does relate to physical performance: children who are more muscular usually perform physical tasks somewhat better than children who are less muscular.

Bone Health

Although parents seldom consider bones when they think of their children's health, building healthy bones is essential for lifelong health, especially in preventing a common disease of older people known as osteoporosis. **Osteoporosis** involves a serious loss of bone density, leaving bones at risk for fractures later in life. For bones made fragile with osteoporosis, much of the bone tissue has disappeared, so that even bending over to tie a shoe can break a bone in the spine.

To understand why bone health is important, it is essential to recognize that bones are living tissue that undergoes constant change as parts of old bone are removed and replaced by new bone. One way to think about bone development is like a bank account in which deposits and withdrawals of bone mass are made. During childhood and adolescence, many more deposits of bone mass are made than withdrawals, even as the skeleton grows in size and density. These deposits depend on diet and exercise. In the mid-20s, bones reach their maximum density, or **peak bone mass.** Ideally, you want to make many deposits into your "bone account" during the early years, so that more bone is available in the account when you grow older. Over time, your body withdraws from the account by absorbing some of the calcium in the bones when blood levels of calcium are low, so maintaining optimal calcium in the diet is needed for bone health.

Many factors influence bone mass. Boys tend to have greater bone mass than girls do, African American girls have higher bone mass than Caucasian girls do, calcium deficiencies reduce bone mass, and physical activity improves bone mass. Just as muscles get stronger as we use them, the more work bones do, the stronger they become. To promote bone health, weight-bearing exercises such as walking, running, dancing, soccer, skateboarding, basketball, and jumping rope are best. Even when bones stop growing, physical activity helps to strengthen and thicken them.

osteoporosis *a disease that involves a serious loss of bone density*

peak bone mass *the highest density of bone a person has in life*

FIGURE 11.1
Growth Charts for Height and Weight (ages 5–11)

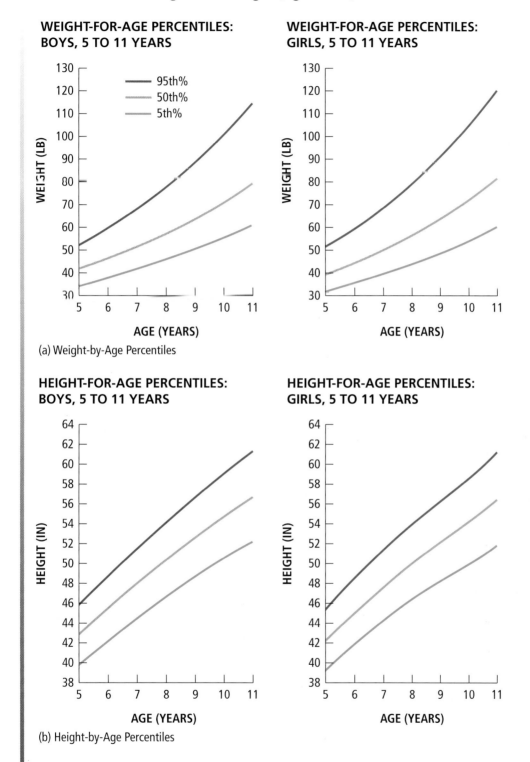

(a) Weight-by-Age Percentiles

(b) Height-by-Age Percentiles

Compared to younger children, what changes in physical development do school-age children undergo? How do developmental patterns differ for girls and boys?

Source: National Center for Health Statistics, 2000.

FIGURE 11.2
Bone Health

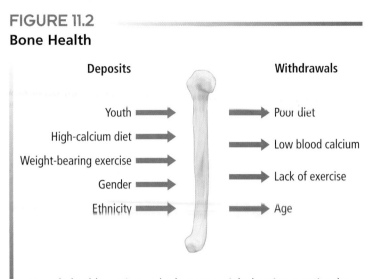

How do healthy eating and adequate weight-bearing exercise during the school years contribute to later bone health?

Most children have good dental health, but some do not. Which children are at risk for poor dental health, and why?

For children, the most critical and influential factors that can be controlled are diet and exercise. Young children tend to get adequate calcium, but only one fifth of girls and about one half of boys of ages 9 to 19 get enough calcium to ensure optimal bone mass. Encouraging children to eat a calcium-rich diet and to engage in plenty of physical activity will go a long way to improving bone health (National Institute of Arthritis and Musculoskeletal and Skin Diseases, 2002). Public health programs have been developed to help improve bone health in children, especially girls, since they are much more at risk for developing osteoporosis than are boys (Centers for Disease Control, 2004a).

Tooth Development and Oral Health

During early childhood, baby teeth are replaced by permanent adult teeth, leaving children with temporary gaps in their smiles. It is vitally important that children have healthy teeth and gums (American Dental Association, 2003). Strong, healthy teeth enable children to chew properly and speak clearly, and they give children's face its shape. Tooth decay, if left untreated, can lead to problems in eating, speaking, school absences, and even the ability to learn (US Department of Health and Human Services, 2001).

Even though children today have much better oral health than those in the past, you may be surprised to learn how many children have dental caries (cavities). Children are 5 to 8 times more likely to have cavities than to have asthma, which is the most common chronic disease in children. More than half of children have cavities by the second grade.

The children most likely to suffer from high levels of oral disease are those who live in poverty, those who do not have medical insurance, children with disabilities, some racial/ethnic minority populations, and children with HIV infection (Office of the Surgeon General, 2000).

Having regular dental checkups will help ensure that children maintain good oral health. For most children, twice-a-year visits are recommended. During the visit, children have their teeth cleaned, receive a fluoride treatment to strengthen the teeth and prevent cavities, and learn to care for their teeth. Dental sealants may be applied to teeth to protect them from decay. Encouraging children to floss, brush their teeth regularly, and avoid foods with high sugar content are steps that caregivers can take to improve children's oral health. Some foods have surprising amounts of sugar. For instance, fruit juice is a common high-sugar source. For children from 7 to 18 years of age, fruit juice intake should be limited to 8 to 12 ounces per day (American Academy of Pediatrics, 2003).

Physical Health Concerns

During the school years, some children experience chronic health problems, such as speech and hearing problems or visual impairments, that require attention from caregivers and support professionals. Other children experience less serious physical conditions, such as growing pains and bed-wetting, but these also raise concerns about the child's health.

Hearing Problems

Hearing involves the ears and brain as they interpret patterns in the movement of air molecules. Sounds can be described by their frequency (pitch) and their intensity (loudness). Frequency is measured in hertz (Hz). People who hear within the normal range can discern sounds that have frequencies from 20 to 20,000 Hz, and most everyday sounds register 250 to 6,000 Hz. Vowel sounds such as /ŭ/, which tend to be low in frequency, are usually easier to hear than some consonants, such as the /sh/, /h/, and /f/ sounds, which have higher frequencies. Someone who has a hard time hearing high-frequency sounds will have difficulty interpreting speech. Loudness is measured in decibels (dB), and a person with normal hearing typically hears sounds of 0 to 140 dB. Just to give some comparisons, a whisper is about 30 dB, conversations are about 50 to 60 dB, and a loud rock concert may reach 110 dB.

What types of accommodations will be helpful for educating a child who is deaf?

Hearing impairments can involve either frequency or loudness or both. The severity of the problem is based on how well a person can hear the frequencies and intensities associated with speech, and it ranges from mild to moderate, severe, or profound. Hearing loss can affect one or both ears.

During the 2002–2003 school year, almost 72,000 US children from 6 to 21 years of age got special education services under the hearing impairment category. Another 1,600 received services under the deaf blind category. The total number of children affected by hearing loss is likely to be higher than these numbers indicate because they may receive services under other special education categories (US Office of Special Education Programs, 2003). In a study of children in Atlanta, 11 of every 10,000 children were deaf or hard of hearing, and the impairment was found more commonly in older children and in boys, especially African American boys. About one quarter also had other disabilities (Van Naarden, Decoufle, & Caldwell, 2000).

Speech Problems

Most school-age children have easily mastered language and are able to communicate quite well, although poor articulation can be a common speech problem. A small group of children, however, struggle with speech, especially in communicating their ideas in a smooth, flowing pattern. In the early stages of learning to speak, many children speak haltingly, with many revisions in their sentences, false starts, and frequent use of *uh* and *um.* This is normal. However, some children begin **stuttering,** meaning that they have excessive disruptions in the rate, rhythm, and forward flow of speech. Some danger signs that indicate that a child is developing a stutter include the following:

- Repeated syllables or sounds ("t-t-t-t-time")
- Prolonged sounds ("mmmmmmmmmama")
- Tremors in the small muscles around the mouth, eyes, or jaw as the child tries to say the word he or she is stuck on
- Visible signs of struggle when trying to produce a word (e.g., squeezing the eyes shut, rapidly blinking)
- Fear or avoidance of speaking (Hearing, Speech, and Deafness Center, 2004)

Boys are three times more likely to begin stuttering than girls are, the condition usually begins in early in life, and most children begin stuttering for no obvious reason or cause. Only about 5 percent of children begin stuttering, and for fewer than 1 percent will the condition persist for a long time. Children who show signs of stuttering should be evaluated by a speech/language pathologist, and parents are likely to be given advice about how to deal with the condition effectively. For instance, parents are advised not to complete the sentence or word for the child and not to let others tease him or her. Parents also are encouraged to show interest in what the child is saying and to try to keep the child interested in talking by making speech fun and rewarding the child through games, songs, and rhymes. Children may or may not be given treatment for stuttering; treatments tend to be very effective in reducing or stopping stuttering. Better outcomes are seen for children who have stuttered for a shorter amount of time, and that is one reason why early intervention is important.

stuttering *excessive disruptions in the rate, rhythm, and forward flow of speech*

What changes in educational materials are particularly effective for educating blind children?

Vision Problems

Imagine what it is like to be a child whose vision is poor: you are unable to watch your sister play soccer, and you can see only a blur in front of you in class. Such a child's eyesight cannot be corrected within a normal range, so daily tasks can be impossible to do. Vision impairment changes how a child understands what is going on in the world and how she or he functions in it. Fortunately, such impairments are uncommon in young children, but it is somewhat more common in older children. Two thirds of children with vision impairment have some other form of disability, such as mental retardation, cerebral palsy, hearing loss, or epilepsy (CDC, 2004f). Vision impairment is often caused by damage to the eye itself, which limits its ability to process visual information, but it may also be due to improper shape of the eye or to brain damage that interferes with how visual information is processed. In a recent study of older children in Atlanta, most of the causes of blindness were due to problems that occurred before the child was a month old. In particular, a common cause of visual impairment in children is retinopathy of prematurity, which involves abnormal blood vessel growth or scarring of the retina; this often affects children born prematurely or at a very low birthweight (Mervis, Yeargin-Allsopp, Winter, & Boyle, 2000). Many children with vision impairment will need supportive services for their entire lives (Holbrook, 1996).

Growing Pains?

About 10 to 15 percent of children from ages 8 to 12 experience what some physicians call growing pains (Oberklaid et al., 1997; Walco, 1997). The evidence is unclear about whether these are truly growing pains; they may instead simply be a result of active children's running, jumping, and climbing. Surprisingly, the condition is most likely to occur in children of ages 6 to 13, when growth is relatively slow. These pains tend to occur in the late afternoon or evening and are mainly located in the muscles in front of the thighs, in the calves, or behind the knee. No redness or swelling is associated with these pains, leading some physicians to wonder if they may result from bone growth. Children with these types of pains tend to feel better when massaged or cuddled, but children with other serious medical conditions that affect muscles do not usually like to be handled. Applying heat, doing stretches, and taking doses of ibuprofen can alleviate the pains (Baxter & Dulberg, 1988; Manners, 1999). Research has shown that these children may be prone to pain in general, since they have more headaches and abdominal pain than other children do (Walco, 1997). Even though the condition is painful, experiencing growth pains is unlikely to represent a serious problem, but caregivers should notify a physician if the child has difficulty walking or has pains only on one side; these may be symptoms of more serious conditions.

Bed-Wetting

Bed-wetting, or *nocturnal enuresis,* is a common problem that is troubling for children and their caregivers. About 5 to 7 million children in the United States experience bed-wetting, and the problem occurs three times more frequently in boys than in girls (Thiedke, 2003). Children who lose bladder control in the middle of the night are diagnosed with nocturnal enuresis only after age 5 because before that time, loss of control is extremely common. At age 5, 15 to 25 percent of children wet the bed at night, but with each additional year of maturity, the percentage of bed wetters declines. By age 12, only 8 percent of boys and 4 percent of girls have this problem.

There are many causes for bed-wetting. Often, a genetic link underlies the condition: when both parents were bed wetters as children, their children have a 77 percent risk of being bed wetters. When only one parent was a bed wetter, the risk drops almost by half. Most children who have nocturnal enuresis have parents who also had the condition (Norgaard et al., 1997). Some children who wet their beds may have a bladder disorder; others may have a maturational delay in the nighttime secretion of a hormone that suppresses the production of urine, which thereby increases the amount of urine in the bladder at night (Deitt et al., 1999). But why do children with this delay fail to get up to go to the bathroom? One possibility, for which little evidence yet exists, is that children who wet their beds at night have a sleep disorder or disturbance. Although sleep studies show very little difference between bed wetters and non–bed wetters, parents of bed wetters report that these children are very deep sleepers compared to their siblings (Neveus et al., 1999).

Children who wet their beds at night after age 5 should be evaluated by a physician. Depending on the type of bed-wetting and the underlying cause, different treatments may be recommended. One effective method involves a small alarm bell that awakens the child during bed-wetting, reminding the child to visit the bathroom. Another method is a nose spray that suppresses urine production at night. Some parents use responsibility training or positive reinforcements to reduce bed-wetting. Although it is a fairly common strategy, parents should avoid shaming or punishing the child for this problem (Thiedke, 2003).

FIGURE 11.3
Causes of Bedwetting

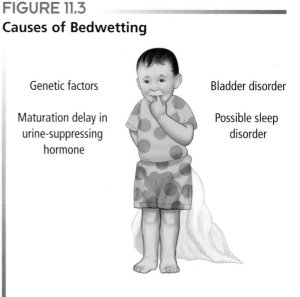

Genetic factors

Maturation delay in urine-suppressing hormone

Bladder disorder

Possible sleep disorder

What factors contribute to bed-wetting in children?

How Do Motor Skills and Physical Fitness Develop During Late Childhood?

During late childhood, children become more coordinated, stronger, and more agile, and they fine-tune the motor skills they developed earlier in life. Yet during this time, many children may become less physically fit. Maintaining physical fitness becomes a challenge during the school years because many children spend much of their time in sedentary activities such as watching television and using computers.

Motor Skills

During the early school years, children show remarkable improvements in motor skills (Cowden, Sayers, & Torrey, 1998). Whereas young children have difficulty jumping, older children can jump without losing their balance. A 6-year-old might throw a ball 10 feet, but an 11-year-old can throw one 30 feet (Cratty, 1986). Older children have more strength, agility, and balance than younger ones do. In each of these areas, gains can be seen every year until preadolescence, when they slow down. One reason for these dramatic improvements is that body growth has slowed, so children have time to become accustomed to their bodies and can use them more effectively. Yet increased coordination and agility do not make all physical activities easy to learn. Children need considerable practice to master tasks that require high levels of hand–eye coordination, such as striking a ball with a bat.

In what ways are school-age children's motor skills more sophisticated than those of young children?

During the school years, children also gain better control of fine motor movements. Their writing becomes neater, and their ability to master difficult and intricate tasks, such as knitting or playing a musical instrument, increases. Some of the changes in children's fine motor control may relate to the changes in myelination that the brain is undergoing during these years.

School-age girls and boys perform similarly in almost all motor activities, although there are some differences. Boys generally have somewhat more upper-body strength than girls do, and boys throw faster and more accurately than girls do (Thomas & French, 1985). Both boys and girls engage in vigorous physical activities, but boys are more likely than girls

Why is exercise so important for children's health? What can caregivers do to promote physical activity in children?

to engage in rough-and-tumble play, which involves pretend fighting and roughhousing (DiPietro, 1981). Girls are more flexible in their hip joints and so may be more agile than boys (Plimpton & Regimbal, 1992). Biological factors and the different experiences of boys and girls may account for some performance differences. Boys' leisure activities involve more sports than do girls', giving them more time to practice motor skills (Cratty, 1986). Children vary tremendously in their motor development, with some children showing more sophisticated skills at an earlier age.

Physical Fitness and Sports

Since the 1950s, when fitness comparisons showed that 55 percent of American children were unfit versus only 15 percent of European youth, much attention has been paid to assessing and improving children's fitness in the United States. Concerns about children's fitness are still warranted today—more than half of children and adolescents are not vigorously active on a regular basis (Surgeon General, 1996).

As a way to promote children's health, the Centers for Disease Control (2003b) and the Surgeon General of the United States recommend that children spend at least 30 to 60 minutes in physical activity per day on all or most days of the week. Even better is for children to spend more than 60 minutes per day engaged in physical activity. Some activity each day should consist of short bouts of about 10 to 15 minutes and should include moderate to vigorous physical activity. School-age children should not spend extended periods of time being inactive (CDC, 2003b).

Reasons for Lack of Fitness

Why are so many children physically unfit? One reason is that many children prefer sedentary activities, such as watching television or playing video games. In a national study of how children spend their time with media (Vandewater et al., 2004), children were found to spend much more time watching television than engaging in physical activities (see Fig-

FIGURE 11.4
Minutes in Each Activity Per Day

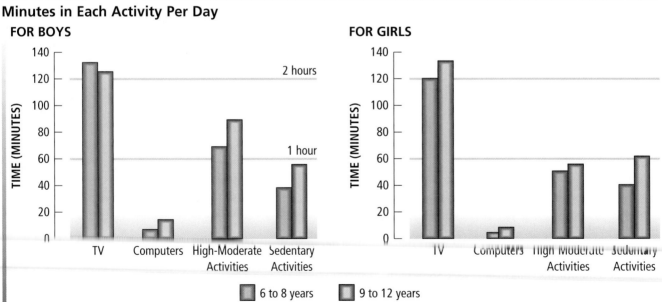

What differences are apparent between girls and boys? What differences are apparent between younger and older children?

Source: Reprinted from *Journal of Adolescence*, Vol. 27, No 1, Vandewater, Shim, and Caplovitz, "Linking Obesity and Activity Level," pp. 71–85, Copyright 2004, with permission from Elsevier.

FROM RESEARCH TO PRACTICE
DO BOYS AND GIRLS HAVE DIFFERENT PHYSICAL SELF-CONCEPTS?

FROM RESEARCH . . .

Even though many more girls are involved in sports now compared to 20 years ago, girls' levels of participation are still not comparable to those of boys, and girls tend to stop playing sports earlier than do boys. Is this because girls do not have the same feelings of competence about their physical selves? Early research on this topic grouped together many different facets of self-concept, such as fitness, appearance, health, grooming, sporting competence, body image, and physical activity, but more recently, researchers have recognized that these facets should be investigated separately. The Physical Self Description Questionnaire (PSDQ; Marsh & Redmayne, 1994) assesses ten areas:

1. Appearance (being attractive)
2. Strength (having well-developed muscles, being strong)
3. Endurance (being able to run a long way without stopping)
4. Health (not getting sick very often)
5. Coordination (being good at coordinated movements)
6. Physical activity (doing lots of physical activity regularly)
7. Body fat (not being overweight)
8. Sports (being good at sports)
9. Flexibility (being able to bend and turn one's body easily in different directions)
10. Global self-esteem (overall positive or negative feeling about oneself)

In a study of over 1,000 children 10–14 years old living in Norway, girls and boys were found to differ on most aspects of physical self-concept (Klomsten, Skaalvik, & Espnes, 2004). Boys rated themselves higher on global self-esteem, global physical, appearance, body fat, sport competence, physical activity, endurance, strength, coordination, and health. Girls and boys did not differ on flexibility, which is somewhat surprising, since girls tend to be more flexible than boys are. Children's feelings of self-worth were related to their self-rating of physical attractiveness. Girls, especially the older girls, were more concerned about their appearance than boys were.

. . . TO PRACTICE

How might these findings be used to develop interventions to change the way children feel about their physical selves? Given these findings, it might be particularly important to target young girls, to try to influence their physical self-concepts before they become negative. Programs could provide role models of very strong and physically powerful sports figures, such as tennis stars Venus and Serena Williams or Olympic swimmer Cynthia Beard. Another strategy would be to increase girls' involvement in sports so that they develop more realistic views of their physical capabilities.

THINKING IT THROUGH

1. What factors do you think contribute to girls' poor physical self-concept?

2. Should intervention programs be designed to reduce media exposure to thin, attractive female role models while increasing exposure to strong female role models? Do you think this would have an impact on girls' self-images? Why or why not?

3. How might girls' view of themselves as less physically strong and competent than boys influence the types of sports they choose to play? How might these beliefs influence girls to drop out of sports when they reach adolescence?

ure 11.4). Some girls may avoid physical activity because they are not confident about their physical abilities (see from Research to Practice). Another reason is that a significant number of children live in urban settings that limit opportunities for exercise. Schools also contribute to lack of fitness in children. US children get 20 to 40 percent of their total physical activity at school, and many children are active only during physical education classes. However, in many schools the time spent in PE classes has decreased, such that some classes average only 10 minutes per week of moderate exercise (Simons-Morton, Taylor, Snider, & Huant, 1993). Because of political, financial, and educational priorities, many children are not getting the opportunity to engage in physical activity during PE classes (Robinson & Killen, 2001).

Influence of Sports Participation

Although many children are sedentary, the rise in the popularity of sports participation over the past 20 years has been phenomenal. Approximately 46 million children and adolescents in the United States participate in some type of sport (Griffin, 1998). In a US national survey, about 40 percent of 9- to 13-year-old children were reported by their parents to be involved in an organized physical activity in the preceding week, but children from minority ethnic groups and those from lower-income families were half as likely to be involved in organized sports. The major barrier to participation for these families was the expense involved. Children's favorite activities were baseball or softball, soccer, and basketball (CDC, 2003b). When children are involved in organized sports, they gain both physical and social skills. Besides simply enjoying themselves, children benefit from regular activity and establish habits and skills that help them enjoy physical activities throughout their lives (Telama, Yang, Laakso, & Viikari, 1997). In team sports, children also learn how to cooperate with other children.

Children's involvement in sports can also have a downside: they can sustain injuries, from sprained ankles to spinal cord injuries. There is no clear evidence, however, that these injuries occur more often in organized sports than in free play (Bijur et al., 1995). In fact, children who play on trampolines or who do in-line skating are particularly at risk of injury (American Academy of Pediatrics, 1998; Smith & Shields, 1998). Some organized sports are riskier than others. Children who are involved in gymnastics, baseball, or basketball, for instance, are more likely to be injured than children who play other sports (O'Neill & Micheli, 1988).

Another downside is that sports injuries may damage the growth of children's long bones, which can result in permanent joint deformities or delay in growth. However, these injuries are relatively infrequent and rarely associated with involvement in organized sports. Children's sports injuries are more likely to be due to overuse, in which repetitive action causes stress and strain to the joints and muscles. Most of these injuries can be successfully treated, and few result in permanent damage (Watkins & Peabody, 1996).

Because of fear of injuries, pediatricians used to urge parents not to let their children participate in organized sports too early. Today the focus is on improving sports safety. For example, the Consumer Product Safety Commission (1996) recommends that softer balls and new kinds of batting helmets be used to reduce the number of baseball-related injuries.

What Are the Nutritional Needs and Concerns of School-Age Children?

Just like younger children, school-age children need to maintain a healthful diet to promote optimal health and growth. Unfortunately, many children of school age tend to be overweight, causing serious threats to their present and future health.

Nutritional Needs

Because of time and work pressures, many adults eat poorly; unfortunately, children often eat what their parents eat. The typical American diet, based on frequent trips to fast-food restaurants, is high in calories, fat, and sodium, and low in calcium and fiber-containing foods (such as fruits, vegetables, and whole grains). This kind of diet is associated with many chronic diseases, including heart disease, some types of cancer, diabetes, hypertension, and stroke. Just like adults, children suffer the negative effects of unhealthful eating (Sizer & Whitney, 1997).

Because children continue to grow in size and weight throughout the elementary school years, a healthful diet is essential for optimal growth. During these years, children need approximately double the calories and protein (per pound) that adults need. Children also need to obtain adequate zinc, calcium, and iron because these minerals are crucial for facilitating growth (Lifshitz, Finch, & Lifshitz, 1991).

The US Department of Agriculture has developed a food pyramid to depict a healthful balance of foods (see Figure 11.5). On the top of the pyramid—at the most narrow point—are the foods to be used most sparingly, including fats and sweets. The next level shows that it is ideal to eat each day approximately 2 to 3 servings of milk, yogurt, and cheese and 2 to

3 servings of meat, poultry, beans, eggs, and nuts. On the next level, the pyramid shows that it is ideal to have each day 3 to 5 servings of vegetables and 2 to 4 of fruit. The widest part of the pyramid is reserved for foods that can be consumed more frequently, such as breads, cereals, and pasta (US Department of Agriculture, 1998). Compared to the pyramid, the typical American diet differs in two areas: it includes fewer fruits and vegetables and many more sweets and fats. The typical American diet would topple the pyramid (Sizer & Whitney, 1997). Although the food pyramid is a good point of reference for healthful eating, it is being revised because the USDA is concerned that it promotes eating more carbohydrates than may be healthful.

Adult standards of healthful eating are not entirely appropriate for children. For instance, nutritional guidelines for adults recommend avoiding fats and cholesterol, but these are essential for the healthy development of children, especially for optimal brain development. Children on reduced-fat diets may develop nutritional deficiencies. Red meat and eggs, often avoided by health-conscious adults, are excellent sources of minerals such as iron and zinc, essential for children's growth. Avoidance of red meats may contribute to the prevalence of iron deficiencies in children, who need more iron for their weight than adults do.

FIGURE 11.5
The Food Pyramid

Fats, Oils & Sweets
USE SPARINGLY

▪ Fat (naturally occurring and added)
▽ Sugars (added)

These symbols show fats and added sugars in foods.

Milk, Yogurt & Cheese Group
2–3 SERVINGS

Meat, Poultry, Fish, Dry Beans, Eggs & Nuts Group
2–3 SERVINGS

Vegetable Group
3–5 SERVINGS

Fruit Group
2–4 SERVINGS

Bread, Cereal, Rice & Pasta Group
6–11 SERVINGS

The food pyramid provides guidance about healthful eating. How does a fast-food diet fare in comparison to the recommended diet? What parts of the pyramid are lacking in most children's diet?

Source: US Department of Agriculture, 1998.

To address deficiencies in consumption of vegetables and fruits, a current campaign reminds people to eat "Five a Day"—five helpings of fruits and vegetables per day. Also, *Dietary Guidelines for Americans* (2000) provides many ways to promote healthful diets, such as eating sensible portions; including a variety of grains, fruits, and vegetables; and limiting the consumption of foods high in sugars and fats.

Undernutrition

Children who fail to receive the nutrients they need are adversely affected in academic and social domains. In a national US study, children who reported that their families did not have enough food to eat were more likely to repeat a grade, had lower arithmetic scores, were more likely to have seen a psychologist, were more likely to have been suspended from school, and had more difficulty getting along with other children (Alaimo, Olson, & Frongillo, 2001). In the United States, approximately one third of children experience either short-term or chronic hunger (Kleinman et al., 1998).

Because of the importance of good nutrition for improving children's educational opportunities, free lunch and breakfast programs have been instituted in schools in many developing countries, and food supplementation in schools began in the United States as early as the 1890s (Levinger, 1986). Children in the United States who have been given school breakfasts are more likely to attend school and show improvements in language, mathematics, and reading (Myers et al., 1989). Overall, it appears that supplemental food programs help children have more positive attitudes toward school, perform better in school, increase time on tasks, and improve attendance (Grantham-McGregor et al., 2001).

Although serious consequences arise from undernutrition, that is, the failure to receive adequate nutrition, the most common nutritional concern for school-age children in the

Based on the food pyramid, what foods are US children lacking? Do you think the slogan of "Eat Five a Day" will prove effective in promoting different eating habits in children?

What health risks do overweight children face? What are the psychological consequences associated with being overweight?

United States is overeating. Children who eat a low-quality diet that is high in calories may suffer a variety of health and psychological problems.

Childhood Obesity: Generation XL

Overweight children trudge through their school years on the way to an adult life rife with health problems. They are victims of an epidemic of childhood obesity in the United States, and yet public policy makers are tiptoeing around one of the root causes of their disease: too much eating of the wrong kinds of foods. (Generation XL: An obesity epidemic, 2003).

The media has dubbed today's overweight children as Generation XL. Unfortunately, there are many more overweight children than there used to be, and this condition poses serious health risks for children. According to a national report on nutrition in the United States, children from 6 to 11 years of age are heavier and fatter today than they were 20 years ago (Ogden, Flegal, Carrol, & Johnston, 2002). Those children (and adults) who weigh more than 20 percent over their ideal weight (based on height, sex, and body composition) are defined as **obese** (Wisniewski & Marcus, 1998). Obesity in children is considered an epidemic of growing proportions. National surveys show that the number of children who are overweight has doubled over the past 20 to 30 years and that about 15 to 20 percent of children are overweight (CDC, 2002b). The increase in weight has occurred for children and adolescents, and for girls and boys in each ethnic group. However, Latino and African American children are particularly at risk for being overweight (Strauss & Pollack, 2001). In longitudinal studies, estimates vary but show that from 40 to 80 percent of very overweight school-age children go on to become overweight adults, so being overweight as a child may represent a lifelong health risk (Guo et al., 1994; Whitaker et al., 1997).

Physical and Psychological Health Consequences of Obesity

The physical and psychological health consequences associated with obesity are serious. The most immediate risk is for social discrimination. Children who are overweight may experience teasing or exclusion by their peers, and this type of social rejection may lead to feelings of low self-worth and depression (Graber, Petersen, & Brooks-Gunn, 1996; Thompson, Heinberg, Altabe, & Tantleff-Dunn, 1999). How children feel about their bodies, referred to as their body image, is influenced by how heavy they are. From 6 to 8 years of age, sex differences in body image typically appear; girls show more body dissatisfaction than boys do, are more likely to consider a thin body ideal, and express more of a desire to be thinner (Grogan, 1999; Hill & Pallin, 1998; Ricciardelli & McCabe, 2001; Sands et al., 1997; Schur, Sanders, & Steiner, 2000; Tiggemann & Wilson-Barrett, 1998). For both sexes, body image relates to weight; heavier children have more negative body images (Thomas, Ricciardelli, & Williams, 2000).

Obese children are at risk for serious health problems, including asthma, liver disease, cancer, orthopedic problems, high blood pressure, and respiratory diseases, that result in shorter life spans (Belamarich et al., 2000; Dietz, 1998; Gunnell et al., 1998; Must & Strauss, 1999; Rossner, 1998; Torgan, 2002). One particularly startling trend is that children who are obese have shown an alarming increase in the incidence of type 2 diabetes (Freedman et al., 1999; Sinha et al., 2002). **Type 2 diabetes** involves an insensitivity to insulin, which causes an imbalance in how the body handles the consumption of sugar. This form of diabetes had been called adult-onset diabetes because previously it had been much more common in middle age or older overweight adults. But today, because so many children are overweight, this disease is beginning to strike at much younger ages. Consider that in 1982, only 4 percent of children were diagnosed with type 2 diabetes; today the number is closer to 16 percent. Obese African American, Asian, American Indian, and Latino children are at higher risk for developing type 2 diabetes than are other children.

Another serious concern recently identified in children is **metabolic syndrome,** a combination of obesity, high blood pressure, problems with metabolizing blood sugar, and high

obesity   *having a weight 20 percent more than ideal weight*

type 2 diabetes   *an insensitivity to insulin causing an imbalance in how the body handles sugar consumption*

metabolic syndrome   *a combination of obesity, high blood pressure, diabetes, and high cholesterol*

cholesterol (Brage et al., 2004). This combination of factors greatly increases the risk of heart disease, but thus far, it has been studied mainly in adults.

Causes of Obesity

Why do children become obese? Genetics plays a significant role—children inherit a predisposition for obesity from their parents. This is unlikely to account for the dramatic shift in the numbers of children who are overweight, however. It is suspected that the environment, particularly what the child eats and how much exercise the child engages in, plays a significant role in the recent changes in children's weight.

In what ways has the supersizing of food contributed to weight problems for people in the United States?

Even though more low-fat foods have become available over the past 15 years, their potential benefits may be offset by cultural changes in food preparation and family meals, which likely play a role in the problem. In the 1930s, all food was prepared from scratch. Today, with the development of a wide variety of frozen foods and the convenience of microwave ovens, children can take a more active role in choosing what they want to eat and even preparing the food, and they can do this without any parental guidance. Another cultural shift is in how much food is eaten outside the home. About one third of family meals are prepared outside the home, and these meals tend to be higher in calories than those made at home. Even school lunches and the food available in schools may contribute to overeating and poor nutrition (see Debating the Issue).

Compared to 20 years ago, Americans today consume an additional 200 calories per day (Schlosser, 2002). It is no wonder that obesity and overweight have become more common. Cultural shifts also have occurred in portion sizes, influencing how much food is eaten both within and outside the home. A muffin of today is not a muffin of ten years ago. Food portions are much larger today than in the past (Young & Nestle, 1995, 2002). When Jewish bakers first introduced bagels to the United States from Poland, these baked goods weighed 1.5 ounces and contained 116 calories. Today's bagel is three times bigger in size and calories—it may have over 300 calories. Muffins today are over three times the standard serving size, servings of pasta are

DEBATING THE ISSUE

SHOULD SCHOOLS ALLOW VENDING MACHINES THAT DISPENSE JUNK FOOD?

Childhood obesity has increasingly become a US public health concern. To what extent do schools contribute to children's poor eating habits? One way in which schools exacerbate the obesity problem is through the selection of foods they make available to children. Hard candy, doughnuts, potato chips, and soda are commonly found in school vending machines, allowing children to select foods of poor nutritional choices that are high in fat, salt, and sugar.

Why do schools allow companies to place vending machines on the school grounds and stock them with such poor food choices? The answer is money. Schools make thousands of dollars from their contracts with these companies, and

the money pays for computers, sports programs, and many after-school activities. Some schools make over $100,000 per year, according to one report. As school budgets have been cut, the money from vending machines gives schools financial flexibility that they may not have otherwise.

About two dozen states are considering total bans or limits on vending machine products, and about 20 other states already restrict students' access to junk food until after lunch. California was the first state to ban the sale of soft drinks in elementary and junior high schools. Other alternatives are to restrict what is offered in vending machines, such as stocking machines with more healthful alternatives such as granola

bars, fruit, water, yogurt, and milk (Chang, 2004).

THINKING IT THROUGH

1. Do you think schools should continue to offer children of all ages a full range of food choices, including unhealthful junk foods? Why or why not?

2. Do you think placing restrictions on certain types of foods would increase children's healthful eating?

3. How should schools balance short-term financial needs with the long-term health risks of obesity?

FIGURE 11.6

Prevalence of Overweight Children and Television Viewing: 1971–2000

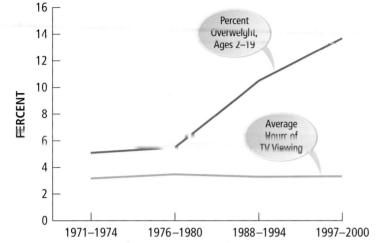

As you can see from this figure, television watching has remained at about the same level while the numbers of overweight children has increased. These data bring into doubt that television viewing directly causes overeating.

Source: Reprinted from *Journal of Adolescence,* Vol. 27, No 1, Vandewater, Shim, and Caplovitz, "Linking Obesity and Activity Level," pp. 71–85, Copyright 2004, with permission from Elsevier.

FIGURE 11.7

The Vicious Cycle of Poor Food Choices and Inactivity

This figure does not imply that television is necessarily the cause of becoming overweight. Why might it be the reverse, that is, that children who are overweight enjoy watching TV more? And, explain why the link between TV and weight may be a problem for only a subset of children.

often five times the standard serving size, and cookies are seven times the standard portion size! The standard order of French fries offered at a popular fast-food chain in the 1950s is now labeled small and is one third the weight of the largest size available in 2001.

Sedentary lifestyles also contribute to problems with weight in children. Fewer children play in their neighborhoods than in the past. Studies show that active children have less body fat than sedentary children do and that obese children are less active than those who are lean (CDC, 2001d; Rowland, 1991). Only about half of US children participate in physical education classes at school.

One controversial topic among scientists is the role of television in children's weight. A popular hypothesis among many scientists (e.g., Chen & Kennedy, 2001; Dietz, 2001) and the general public is that television watching, video games, and computers keep children glued to their seats rather than up and moving—the "couch potato hypothesis." In addition, the "exposure to junk food hypothesis" posits that children who watch lots of television are exposed to hundreds of food commercials, mainly for unhealthful foods, and these ads may make children want to consume those foods and encourage their parents to buy them.

Some evidence has been found in support of each of these ideas. In a national survey of school-age children, researchers found that the more time children watched television, the heavier they were, lending some support to the "couch potato hypothesis." For instance, among children who watched less than 1 hour per day, about 10 percent were obese; among children who watched more than 5 hours per day, 20 percent were obese (Dietz & Gortmaker, 1985). However, some of the more recent studies do not find the same link between television viewing and weight, especially when important demographic factors are taken into account (Robinson, 1998; Robinson & Killen, 1995; Vandewater et al., 2004). And the increase in obesity in children does not correspond to increased amounts of time spent watching television (see Figure 11.6). This evidence suggests that for a certain subset of children—perhaps those who are at risk because of their genetic inheritance—TV watching is risky behavior. For many other children, however, it is not. Alternatively, television viewing may be a consequence of weighing more. Further longitudinal research is being conducted to discover whether only certain children are at risk and how such patterns change over time.

Evidence has also been found in support of the "exposure to junk food hypothesis." The more children watch ads for unhealthful foods, the more they request them and the more their parents buy these foods for them (Taras et al., 1989). You can see how a cycle could form—children watch television, see ads for unhealthful foods, eat those foods, experience an energy slump, and lack the motivation to get up and turn off the television (see Figure 11.7).

Psychological factors and contextual factors also play a role in weight gain. Stress, and particularly family distress, contributes to obesity. Children in families experiencing chronic stress are more at risk for obesity because of the tendency to eat and the low activity levels that accompany stress (Dietz & Gortmaker, 1985; Lifshitz et al., 1991). Even schools may play a contextual role in obesity. School lunches provide children with a limited set of food choices, and these choices may contribute to either healthful or unhealthful eating.

Helping Children Lose Weight

Caregivers can help children lose weight in a number of ways (see Nurturing Children). First, they can exercise control over what their children eat; parents who show little control over children's consumption of foods tend to have children who weigh more and eat more unhealthful foods (Lederman, Akabas, & Moore, 2004). Second, they can limit television viewing. Unplugging the television may encourage children to play and exercise more. When television watching has been limited (reduced by a quarter to a half) in intervention programs to prevent obesity, children's levels of body fat also decreased (Robinson, 1999). Parents should get moving themselves, to provide good role models for exercise; exercising provides good family time together. Parents can promote activity rather than exercise. We often think of exercise as punishment instead of fun. It is not necessary to enroll a child in sports or dance classes; parents need only encourage their children to move and play.

Formal programs also have shown some success, especially those involving multiple components. These programs involve parents, teachers, and health workers, and they include education about nutrition, counseling, and opportunities for physical activity (Golan, Weizman, Apter, & Fainaru, 1998; Robinson & Killen, 2001). The Centers for Disease Control recently launched a program called VERB, a campaign to encourage children of ages 9 to 13 to get active in safe and exciting ways (CDC, 2003b). Schools, media, parents, and children can get support for increased physical activity. Children can access a website (VERBNow.com) where they create their own "virt" and give it a name (e.g., Astro Tennis Star; see Figure 11.8). This virtual character survives only by being "fed" energy. To

NURTURING CHILDREN
HOW CAN CAREGIVERS PROMOTE CHILDREN'S PHYSICAL ACTIVITY?

With the rise in childhood obesity and the serious health problems associated with it, many caregivers are concerned about how to promote healthier lifestyles in their children. Many parents ask how to encourage their children to exercise more often. The recommended level of exercise for children is 30 to 60 minutes daily of physical activity. However, even shorter stretches of physical activity provide health benefits. How can parents move children away from the television and off the couch to the outdoors (Mayo Clinic, 2003; Summerfield, 2000; Torgan, 2002)?

Here are a number of ways in which parents can promote physical activity:

- Limit television viewing, and remove television sets from children's bedrooms.

- Encourage schools to require physical education classes for children.
- Encourage your child to join sports teams.
- Plan family activities that involve exercise—go for a hike, toss a ball, ride bicycles together, walk around the mall together.
- Make exercise fun: don't just run, but run like a gorilla, walk like a spider, or stretch like a cat.
- Vary the activities you do together as a family, and let the child choose which activity to do each week, such as bowling, hiking, or hitting balls at batting cages.
- Check on community activities: do a 5K walk–run with your child, or swim together at the community pool.

- Play games with your child, such as tag or Simon Says—it will benefit both you and your child.
- Give your child the job of walking the dog.
- Give your child physically active chores to do.
- Practice motor skills with your child, and explore many different activities so that he or she will develop a lifelong love of physical activity and sports.
- Plan family vacations around activities such as hiking, skiing, snorkeling, or camping.

FIGURE 11.8
VERBnow.com

One of the major factors contributing to obesity in children is lack of adequate exercise. Do you think the VERB program will be effective in increasing children's level of exercise?

Source: www.verbnow.com. VERB is a trademark of DHHS, CDC. Copyright © 2004. All rights reserved.

give it energy, children have to engage in activities, and they report how much they do each day, enabling their virt to move to different levels. As the virt says, "You move, I move. If you sit on the couch, I get mad." This program allows children to monitor their own activity, and it provides interesting information about a variety of sports and activities. Parents also have a related website with hints about how to promote fun activities and find resources relating to activities, sports, and nutrition (VERBparents.com).

What Are the Health and Safety Concerns of Late Childhood?

School-age children are generally healthy. They suffer mainly from bumps, bruises, broken bones, colds, and stomachaches typical of childhood. Most health problems that school-age children encounter result from accidental injuries, most of which are preventable. In the United States, it is rare for children to die during the school years. As you can see in Figure 11.9, boys are more likely to die than girls, and African American children, in particular, have higher death rates than do other groups of children. Though school-age children are at risk for contracting a number of serious diseases, US children have exceptionally good health, as compared to children in many other countries, largely because of vaccinations against serious childhood diseases.

Diseases

Sore throats, runny noses, upset stomachs, and allergies makes childhood seem like a constant state of illness, yet these problems, although common and recurring, are not life threatening. But though most children experience common colds and flu, some also experience more serious life-threatening diseases such as measles, chicken pox, and asthma. As you have already learned, many of these diseases have been almost eradicated in the United States, but they remain very serious problems in many other countries in the world.

Chicken Pox

I remember my mom wrapping my hands in oven mitts so I wouldn't scratch myself. The blisters from the chicken pox were all over me, and they itched like crazy. My mom kept me away from my sister and told me over and over not to scratch because I would scar myself. (Author's childhood memory of chicken pox).

Chicken pox is one of the most prevalent childhood diseases, occurring most frequently among children of about 2 to 8 years of age. It takes about two weeks from the time of exposure for symptoms to appear. This highly contagious disease begins with a slight fever and tiredness; then the distinctive blisterlike rash appears and spreads over the body. My mother was right—breaking the blisters can result in scarring, so children must not scratch them. Until the blisters develop a crust, about 5 to 7 days after they first appear, the disease is very contagious, since the blisters release the virus that spreads the disease. Treatment consists of acetaminophen, lukewarm baths, and possibly an antihistamine to reduce itching. If the child's fever persists for more than four days or runs very high, more intensive treatments may be needed. Vaccines are now available for chicken pox, and this has greatly decreased the number of US children who contract the disease.

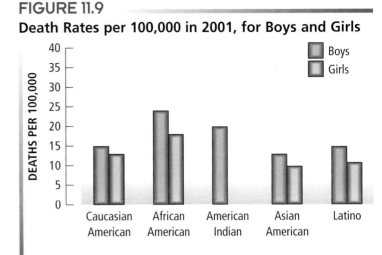

FIGURE 11.9

Death Rates per 100,000 in 2001, for Boys and Girls

What are the leading causes of death among children? Why are some children more at risk than others?

Source: National Vital Statistics Reports, 2003.

*No reliable data were available for American Indian girls.

Measles

Measles is one of the most contagious childhood diseases, and worldwide, it poses a serious public health problem. Before the widespread use of vaccines against measles beginning in 1963, 90 percent of children got it at some point during childhood. Today far fewer children contract the disease in the United States and many other countries, but still almost 1 million children die of measles per year, most of them in Africa (Quadros, 2004).

Loss of appetite, fever, runny nose, tiredness, and coughing mark the early stages of the disease. Then tiny spots appear in the mouth, and a day or so later, the child's temperature shoots up, the oral spots disappear, and an itchy rash appears behind the ears and on the neck and cheeks. The final stage is marked by a high fever, red eyes, extensive rash, and severe cough. About five days after the rash first appears, symptoms disappear, and the disease is no longer contagious. Unfortunately, measles is easily spread because it is most contagious during the 3 to 5 days before any symptoms appear, so it is difficult to know that a child has the disease. Treatment involves isolation, bed rest, and acetaminophen to reduce the fever.

Because of effective vaccinations, measles is rare in the United States today. Nonetheless, cases still occur, and the highly contagious nature of the disease is evident in how fast it spreads. In the 1980s, studies of measles showed that a single vaccine often did not confer complete protection: some children who received single vaccinations got the disease anyway. For that reason, states began to recommend two doses of the vaccine for children. Even with that knowledge about disease prevention, the largest recent epidemic of measles occurred in the late 1980s, and 55,000 children were stricken. Scientists discovered that most children who got the disease were unvaccinated, again confirming the need for widespread use of measles vaccine. When this took place, the number of cases of measles dropped by 98 percent. Most US cases are now caused by measles brought in from other countries. The last large reported outbreak occurred in 2003 in a boarding school in Pennsylvania, where 11 cases were confirmed. The boy who brought the disease to the school had recently traveled from Lebanon, where measles was circulating. Although he had gotten vaccinations, he showed symptoms and then spread the disease to others. The importance of receiving the recommended double-dosage vaccination was made clear in this case: the rate of contracting measles was 67 percent among unvaccinated students and 1 percent among vaccinated students (CDC, 2004c). All US states but one require the two doses of vaccine for children attending school; however, exemptions related to religion or philosophy are allowed in many states, placing the unvaccinated children at higher risk for contracting the disease. Because of the effectiveness of vaccination programs, only 42 confirmed cases of the measles were reported in 2003(CDC, 2004c).

Mumps

Mumps is a viral disease typically found in children from 5 to 9 years old. Mumps begins with a headache, muscle pains, low fever, loss of appetite, and tiredness. Then an earache and swelling and tenderness in the glands begin. Some children have additional serious complications, including abdominal pain, meningitis (about 10% of the cases), or inflammation of the testes. Treatment involves acetaminophen to ease the pain and fever and adequate fluid intake. There is a vaccine for mumps, and it is highly effective in decreasing the numbers of cases in a population as long as a significant portion of people receive the vaccine. In the United States, the last large outbreak of mumps was associated with a dropoff in the number of children who had received vaccinations. In countries where vaccinations are not given, such as many places in Africa, mumps continues to be a public health concern for children.

Polio

Richard Daggert contracted polio as a child in 1953. He remains in a wheelchair today. He remembers his excitement about hearing about a new polio vaccine: "I was in the hospital at the time when they made the public announcement, and everybody was overjoyed. All of us kids, we would have yelled if we could have, but most of us were on respirators, so we couldn't make a lot of noise. But it was very good news."

As described in the chapter opener, this viral infection was a cause of fear and tragedy well into the 1950s. Parents watched as neighborhood children were struck down, some so seriously that they had to use respirators ("iron lung" machines) to help their paralyzed lungs breathe. The crippling disease seemed to occur at random in the summer, when children played in groups together. One day a child was running around the neighborhood; the next day, the child was paralyzed. Some children suffered severe symptoms such as full paralysis; some experienced very mild symptoms such as muscle weakness.

Thanks to the medical breakthroughs achieved by Jonas Salk, an experimental polio vaccine was developed and field-tested in 1954. One million children—called the Polio Pioneers—took part in the test of the vaccine: half were given the real vaccine and half were given a placebo. The whole country held its breath to find out the results. Happily, by 1955, the vaccine was found to be both safe and effective. Because of this achievement in medicine, children in the United States have avoided one of the most debilitating diseases of childhood. The 45,000 cases of polio reported in the two years before the development of the vaccine declined to fewer than 1,000 within nine years (Arnold, 2004).

Today few US children have to worry about contracting polio, but children in other parts of the world are not so lucky. For the past 15 years, 20 million volunteers from 200 countries have been involved in the largest public health campaign ever launched, the Global Polio Eradication Initiative to stamp out polio from the world. Their efforts have yielded remarkable results: when they began, they faced 350,000 cases of polio in 125 countries; in 2003, 700 cases were reported, mainly in six countries—Nigeria, India, Niger, Afghanistan, Pakistan, and Egypt (see Figure 11.10). Nonetheless, polio remains a major public health concern because it is so contagious and because many children are no longer

FIGURE 11.10
Polio Around the World

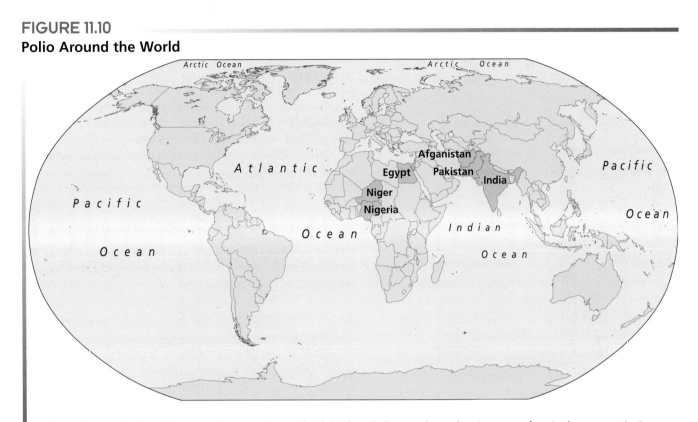

What efforts are being taken to eradicate polio worldwide? What challenges do eradication teams face in these countries?

being vaccinated, thereby increasing the numbers of children who are susceptible to contracting it. Even today, in parts of Africa, epidemics of polio threaten to paralyze thousands of children for life.

The goal of the eradication initiative is to vaccinate every child in the world. In the race to beat polio, medical personnel have to do what seems impossible: they must gain access to every child in the world within a brief period of time, including children who live in remote rural areas as well as in war-torn countries. A synchronized immunization campaign began in October 2004 for all the countries that had significant numbers of polio cases in the past few years. In Africa, more than 1 million polio vaccinators in 23 African countries immunized 80 million children in just over four days (World Health Organization, 2004). Other countries launched similar efforts at the same time. Only time will tell whether polio will be completely eradicated by these bold efforts.

HIV/AIDS

AIDS threatens children's lives in many ways. First, many children acquire the disease from their infected mothers during prenatal development, and about half of them develop full-blown AIDS. In the United States, estimates suggest that about 9,000 children have been diagnosed with AIDS since 1998 (CDC, 2003a), and about 8,000 were infected through exposure to their mothers' disease (see Figure 11.11). Treatments exist to prevent the spread of AIDS from mothers to children, but unfortunately, not all mothers have access to these treatments, and this is particularly true for mothers in developing countries. Second, many children are being orphaned by the deaths of their parents from AIDS. Third, when family members are struck with the disease, children are often pressed into the care of sick and dying parents, have to drop out of school, and often lose access to material goods and health services (UNAIDS, 2002). Each of these problems is a worldwide public health concern.

FIGURE 11.11

Estimated Numbers of Diagnoses of AIDS in Children Under 13 by Exposure Category from 1998–2002 (US)

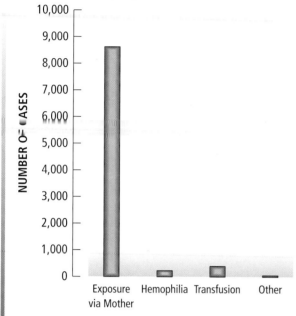

As you can see, the vast majority of AIDS cases in children are due to exposure to the virus through the mother. How can this type of AIDS transmission be stopped so that fewer children contract the disease?

Source: CDC, 2003.

Why is wearing a bicycle helmet so effective in preventing deaths and serious injuries? What methods are successful in increasing the use of helmets among school-age children?

An estimated 40 million people in the world are living with AIDS today, and 3 million of them are children (UNAIDS, 2002). It is estimated that another 13 million children have lost one or both parents to AIDS, and many of these children live in sub-Saharan Africa. By 2010, the number is expected to reach 25 million. Given that AIDS infections are on the increase, public health officials expect that this epidemic will continue to cause long term and large-scale suffering for children all over the world.

Local, national, and governmental agencies have mobilized to help the children orphaned by AIDS. Strategies of assistance include helping extended families provide support for orphans, enlisting the aid of community-based groups, keeping children in school so that they can provide for themselves as they grow up, encouraging governments to develop policies to provide essential services to vulnerable children, and increasing awareness of the magnitude of the problem to create an environment of support for these children (UNAIDS, 2002).

Accidents and Injuries

School-age children run fast, play hard, ride bicycles and scooters, and engage in a variety of sports. It should come as no surprise that they suffer from injuries from these activities. What may be more of a surprise is how often children are injured and die from other forms of accidents, especially motor vehicle accidents.

Motor Vehicle Accidents

The leading cause of death among US children of ages 5 to 14 is motor vehicle injuries, and this is considered the greatest pressing public health problem facing US children today. Every 90 seconds, a child in the United States is killed or injured in a motor vehicle. About 2,000 children per year die, and another 300,000 are hurt (CDC, 2004b). Many children over the age of 5 ride unrestrained in cars, greatly increasing their risk of injury and death from an accident. As discussed in Chapter 8, the dangerous force of exploding airbags means that children below the age of 12 should ride in the backseat. Children of ages 4 through 8 should ride in booster seats to increase their safety.

Bicycle and Scooter Accidents

Children of ages 5 to 15 are at risk for injuries and death due to bicycle accidents. About 200 children die each year, and over 100,000 children are treated in emergency departments, because of head injuries sustained while bicycling (CDC, 2002a). Almost every bicyclist who dies in an accident was not wearing a helmet. Programs involving bicycle education, helmet giveaways, and enforcement of helmet requirements have been effective in increasing the number of school-age children who wear helmets.

Scooters (both motorized and nonmotorized) have been increasing in popularity, and the number of children showing up in emergency rooms with broken arms and legs, as well as face and head injuries due to scooter accidents (over 80,000 estimated in 2001), has increased dramatically. Even some deaths have been attributed to use of scooters (US Consumer Product Safety Commission, 2001). Wearing helmets and knee and elbow pads and avoiding riding in traffic and at night can decrease injury risks. Also, the American Academy of Pediatrics recommends that only older children (age 8 and older) be allowed to ride scooters, given the risk of injury associated with them (American Academy of Pediatrics, 2002).

Playground Injuries

Playgrounds can be risky places for young children (Sacks et al., 1989). Over 200,000 children age 14 and younger are treated for playground accidents each year in the United States. About half of these are severe—fractures, internal injuries, concussions, dislocations, and even amputations (Tinsworth & McDonald, 2001). Children of ages 5 to 9 have higher rates of emergency department visits for playground injuries than any other age group, and most of these injuries occur at school (Phelan, Khoury, Kalkwarf, & Lanphear, 2001). Climbing equipment is the leading cause of injuries at school; swings are the culprit at home (Tinsworth & McDonald, 2001). Playgrounds in low-income neighborhoods are riskier for children because of unsafe conditions than are playgrounds in higher-income areas (Suecoff, Avner, Chou, & Crain, 1999). The National Program for Playground Safety recommends the following strategies to prevent playground injuries:

What are effective ways to prevent playground injuries?

- Improve adult supervision of children on playgrounds.
- Educate the public about age-appropriate playground equipment.
- Build playgrounds with protective surfaces to reduce injuries related to falls.
- Improve the maintenance of equipment and surfaces.

Personal Safety

A child walks down the street on her way to school, and a man stops her and asks her to help him find his lost puppy. She takes his hand, follows him to his car, and never shows up for dinner that night. This is a parent's worse nightmare—a stranger abducts a child. As horrific as this scenario is, it is a relatively rare occurrence (see Figure 11.12). Very few children are abducted by strangers; most children who are missing are runaways or thrown-away children (Shutt, Miller, Schreck, & Brown, 2004). Out of the children who are abducted, most are taken by a parent or trusted caregiver from their own homes, and the vast majority of these cases involve custody disputes. An alarming number of abducted children are taken by other people known to the family, suggesting that acquaintances can also be a danger to children.

Child abduction patterns change dramatically from early childhood to later childhood. In early childhood, children are victimized more often by family members and acquaintances in protected circumstances (e.g., in their homes). In later childhood, victimization rates triple, and girls are more at risk for abduction than boys are, largely because sex is a motive for abductions in this age group. In most cases involving school-age children, either acquaintances or strangers are the most likely offenders; in cases involving older school-age children, the risk of stranger abduction increases, and children are more likely to be abducted from playgrounds, parks, and malls. These differences are likely due to several factors. First, school-age children are more independent than younger children and are more

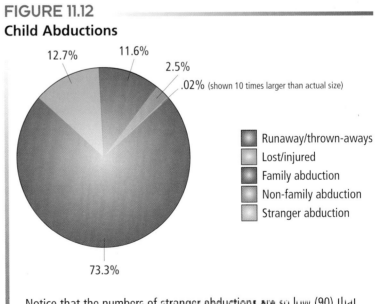

FIGURE 11.12
Child Abductions

12.7%   11.6%   2.5%
.02% (shown 10 times larger than actual size)

- Runaway/thrown-aways
- Lost/injured
- Family abduction
- Non-family abduction
- Stranger abduction

73.3%

Notice that the numbers of stranger abductions are so low (90) that they are barely represented in this figure. Most of the cases of missing children are runaways or thrownaway children. Why do stranger abductions gain our attention?

Source: Sedlak, Finkelhor, Hammer, and Schultz, 2002.

often unsupervised in their activities. Some children, especially older school-age girls, are considered especially vulnerable prey: mature enough to be sexually desirable but also young enough to be easily controlled and exploited. Offenders tend to have a history of sexual misconduct, impulsive and violent behavior, substance abuse, and poor social skills.

When children go missing for any reason, federal law requires that their names be entered into a national database of missing persons. If a threat to the child is suspected because either a stranger or an abusive parent abducted him or her or the runaway child is suicidal, the child's name is flagged for automatic transmittal to the FBI and to the National Center for Missing and Exploited Children. These groups assist local and state authorities in finding the child (Lord, Boudreaux, & Lanning, 2001). The first few hours after the abduction are critical, and children who have been abducted are more likely to be recovered if parents can provide a few key pieces of information about the child: weight, eye color, height, and a recent photo. Parents also can teach children about personal safety to help prevent abductions. Rather than using a "stranger danger" approach that emphasizes wariness of all strangers, most professionals today recommend teaching children about safety without causing unwarranted fear. Good safety practices for children include the following:

- Knowing their address, home phone number, and parents' work numbers, as well as how to use 911 for emergencies
- Letting parents know where they are and being supervised by an adult or accompanied by a friend when away from home
- Saying no any time they feel threatened or uncomfortable
- Knowing that appropriate strangers (store clerks, police officers) can provide assistance if children are lost or need help
- Knowing boundaries of places that are okay to go to (Nemours Foundation, 2002)

Try It Out

1. Watch children play an organized sport such as soccer or softball. What benefits do you think the children are deriving from participation in the sport? What kinds of cognitive and social skills are fostered? Is it likely that different sports encourage different sorts of cognitive and social skills in children? Why or why not?
2. Visit a park, and watch the children who are riding scooters and bicycles. How many are wearing helmets and following good safety practices? How might caregivers and teachers encourage children to follow good safety practices?
3. Watch children's television on Saturday morning. How many advertisements for food do you see? What kinds of foods are children being encouraged to buy? What is the nutritional value of the foods children are being encouraged to eat? Do you think advertisements for vegetables and fruits would effectively increase children's healthful eating? Why or why not?

Key Terms and Concepts

metabolic syndrome (352)
obesity (352)
osteoporosis (342)

peak bone mass (342)
stuttering (345)
type 2 diabetes (352)

Sum It Up

How do children's bodies and brains develop during late childhood?

- By what age have children's brains reached the level of development to learn in a school environment? (p. 341)
- What is the relation between body build and athletic ability? (p. 342)

How do motor skills and physical fitness develop during late childhood?

- Describe the differences between school-age boys' and girls' motor skills. (pp. 347–348)

What are the nutritional needs and concerns of school-age children?

- Why is obesity in children considered an epidemic of growing proportions? (p. 352)
- How can caregivers help children control and/or lose weight? (p. 355)

What are the health and safety concerns of late childhood?

- List and describe five practices children can follow for personal safety. (p. 362)

Chapter Summary

Children grow more slowly during the school years than they did as younger children— usually about 2 to 3 inches and 3 to 6 pounds a year.

During the school years, some children experience chronic health concerns that require attention from caregivers and support professionals, as speech and hearing problems, or visual impairments.

FIGURE 11.2 **Bone Health** *Building healthy bones is essential for lifelong health.*

DEVELOPING BODIES AND BRAINS

Children's brains and bodies are growing during this time, although growth is slower than it was in early childhood. Important physical changes occur in the development of bones and teeth. (Refer back to pages 341–347.)

MOTOR SKILLS AND PHYSICAL FITNESS

Older children become increasingly competent in motor skills during the school years, and their strength, agility, and balance are better than those of younger children. Motor developmental skills are improved because physical growth has slowed and children have time to become accustomed to their bodies and can use them more effectively. Fine motor skills also improve as children develop better hand–eye coordination. (Refer back to pages 347–350.)

School-age children's motor skills are more sophisticated than young children's.

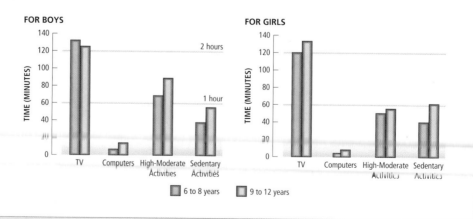

FIGURE 11.4 **Minutes in Each Activity Per Day** *Girls tend to be more sedentary than boys at this age.*

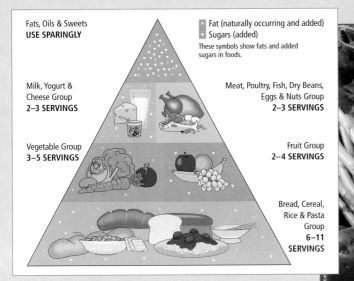

Fats, Oils & Sweets
USE SPARINGLY

▲ Fat (naturally occurring and added)
▼ Sugars (added)
These symbols show fats and added sugars in foods.

Milk, Yogurt & Cheese Group
2–3 SERVINGS

Meat, Poultry, Fish, Dry Beans, Eggs & Nuts Group
2–3 SERVINGS

Vegetable Group
3–5 SERVINGS

Fruit Group
2–4 SERVINGS

Bread, Cereal, Rice & Pasta Group
6–11 SERVINGS

FIGURE 11.7
The Vicious Cycle of Poor Food Choices and Inactivity *This figure does not imply that television is necessarily the cause of becoming overweight. Why might it be the reverse, that is, that children who are overweight enjoy watching TV more?*

NUTRITIONAL NEEDS AND CONCERNS

Many school-age children have problems with being overweight. Contributing factors include heredity, lack of exercise, and poor eating habits. (Refer back to pages 350–356).

HEALTH AND SAFETY CONCERNS

School-age children are generally healthy in the United States but not in other parts of the world, where many contagious and dangerous diseases still strike children. Motor vehicle accidents are the number one killer of children. Many of these deaths could be prevented by using simple child car restraints. (Refer back to pages 356–362.)

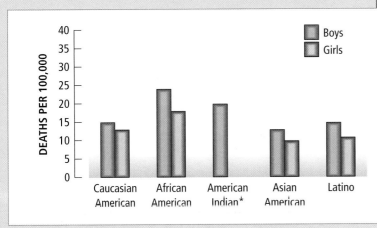

There are many effective ways to prevent playground injuries.

FIGURE 11.9 **Death Rates per 100,000 in 2001, for Boys and Girls** *What are the leading causes of death among US children?*

*Note: No reliable data were available for American Indian girls.

Cognitive and Language Development in Late Childhood

12

Chapter Outline

How Do School-Age Children Think and Solve Problems?
Children's Logical Problem Solving
Children's Understanding of Categories and Concepts
Children's Understanding of Seriation
Culture as a Context for Children's Cognitive Development
Information Processing in School-Age Children

What Characteristics Define Children's Intelligence and Creativity?
Measuring Intelligence
Understanding the Limits of IQ Scores
Identifying the Components of Intelligence
Creativity in Children
Family and Cultural Influences on Intellectual Development

How Do Language and Literacy Develop During the School Years?
Development of Syntax
Development of Semantics
Development of Pragmatics
Children's Literacy

How Do School-Age Children Understand the Social World?
Social Perspective Taking: Communicating with Others
Children's Understanding of Others' Beliefs and Feelings
Children's Understanding of Race and Prejudice

How Does Schooling Influence Children's Cognitive Development?
Opportunities for Active Learning
Multicultural and Multilingual Education
Teachers' Bias in Achievement Expectations
Students with Special Needs

A DEVELOPMENTAL MYSTERY

Lawrence entered the room wearing his backpack. Upon seeing the examiner, his mother whispered, "Say hello, Lawrence." "Say hello, Lawrence," he echoed, and then, "My name's Lawrence, Lawrence P. What's your name? My name's Lawrence P. I'm ten and a half years old.". . . The experimenter asked Lawrence what he liked to do after school. After repeating her name again, the examiner said she used to play basketball after school when she was his age and asked Lawrence if he liked sports. "Yeah, I like sports. I like sports. My name's Lawrence, Lawrence P. I'm ten and a half years old. What's your name?" (Sigman & Capps, 1997)

Lawrence's behavior and speech are unusual for a child his age. Why does Lawrence repeat his name so often and seem so unresponsive to his social environments?

Lawrence is autistic. Scientists are busy trying to understand why this disorder has such a severe impact on daily functioning—even simple things such as carrying on a conversation with another person. Developmental scientists have been in the forefront of unraveling the mystery of autism as well as in trying to discover how typically-developing children think, solve problems, and use language to communicate.

How Do School-Age Children Think and Solve Problems?

At roughly age 6 or 7, most children move to the next stage of thinking identified by Piaget—called *concrete operations*—and continue to function at this level until they are about 11 or 12 years of age. In the concrete operational stage of cognitive development, children show remarkable advances in their thinking and problem-solving strategies. For the first time, they can apply logic to solve problems in an adultlike manner. School-age children's thinking is more flexible and reversible and less egocentric than preschoolers'. The older child considers multiple dimensions of a problem rather than focusing on only one dimension, as children in the preoperational stage do. These advances allow for more sophisticated and systematic methods of solving problems. Older children's problem solving is somewhat more constrained than the problem solving of adolescents and adults, though, because older children can apply logic only to concrete or familiar situations.

Children's Logical Problem Solving

According to Piaget, the best indicator of concrete operational thinking is a child's use of logical principles. These principles are most vividly demonstrated when children solve conservation problems. As you learned in Chapter 9, the understanding of the conservation of mass is assessed by showing children two identical balls of clay and then rolling one ball into a snake. To demonstrate this understanding, children must infer that the two shapes still contain the same amount of clay even though they look different. Preschool children do not draw this conclusion. Centrating on one dimension (such as length), they assume that the snake must have more clay in it than the ball because it is longer. Between 6 and 7 years of age, children begin to solve conservation problems. To do so, they must be able to do the following (Siegler, 1998):

- *Mentally represent the action:* Through concrete operational thinking, children can mentally visualize the changes that occur in conservation tasks. In the clay example, they recall how the clay was transformed from a ball into a snake.

■ *Focus on more than one dimension:* Children in the concrete operational stage have the ability to think about both the length and the height of the clay, rather than focusing on only one dimension.

■ *Recognize that appearances can be deceiving:* Unlike preschoolers, who are easily deceived by the appearances of objects, children in the concrete operational stage recognize that what they see can sometimes be misleading. They can use logic to override misleading appearances.

According to Piaget, an older child draws the same conclusion as an adult about the clay by applying operations. Most children who correctly answer conservation questions use the concept of identity; that is, they reason that because no clay was added or removed, there has to be the same amount, regardless of any apparent changes in appearance (see Chapter 9).

Children also use other concepts, such as reversibility and compensation, to solve conservation problems. **Reversible thinking** reflects an understanding that actions can be undone or reversed. For instance, in a conservation task, the child can mentally return the changed object to its original form (the snake can be made back into the ball). Through **compensation,** the child decides whether one change offsets another—that is, is a change in the height of a piece of clay compensated for by a change in its width?

Children master many kinds of conservation during the school years (Goswami, 1998), including conservation of number. In one conservation of number task, a child is shown two rows of five dimes, placed 1 inch apart, and watches as an adult spreads the dimes in the second row 2 inches apart. Which row contains more dimes, or do they contain the same number? Children who conserve number respond that the two rows contain the same number of dimes. Children who do not conserve number respond that the longer row has more dimes.

Other types of conservation tasks are shown in Figure 12.1. Most children understand conservation of solid and liquid quantity, number, and length by the age of 6 or 7 years. Children can solve area and weight conservation problems by age 8 or 9 and volume conservation problems at about 10 or 11. The exposure children have to different types of conservation tasks may explain why they learn them at different rates.

Children's Understanding of Categories and Concepts

During the concrete operational stage, children's understanding of categories and concepts becomes more sophisticated. Unlike preschool children, who are inflexible in classifying objects, children in the concrete operational stage can vary their strategies when necessary (Freund et al., 1990). In addition, they no longer have difficulty with class inclusion problems—making comparisons between a whole class of objects and subsets within the class. Recall the class inclusion problem discussed in Chapter 9, in which children were asked to compare the whole class "dogs" with the subclass "brown dogs." Unlike his 4-year-old sister Tammy, 8-year-old Jonathan understands that the category "dogs" is more inclusive than the subset based on the dogs' color.

Older children's ability to consider several dimensions at once is illustrated by their solutions to multiple classification problems. Children are shown an array of objects that differ in two or more ways and are asked to select the missing object that best fits the array. To accurately answer the question, children must consider the two dimensions of the objects simultaneously. In Figure 12.2, for example, the objects in a matrix differ in shape and color. After examining the objects and their layout, children are asked to place an object in the blank space. A child who has mastered multiple classification will choose a blue triangle as the solution.

In a classic study comparing classification strategies of preschoolers and older children, Inhelder and Piaget (1964) found that most preschoolers used only one dimension in selecting the missing object; that is, they might select any blue shape or a triangle of any color. In contrast, older children tended to select the object that satisfied both criteria.

reversible thinking   *the understanding that actions can be undone or reversed*

compensation   *the understanding that one change can offset another*

FIGURE 12.1
Examples of Different Types of Conservation Tasks

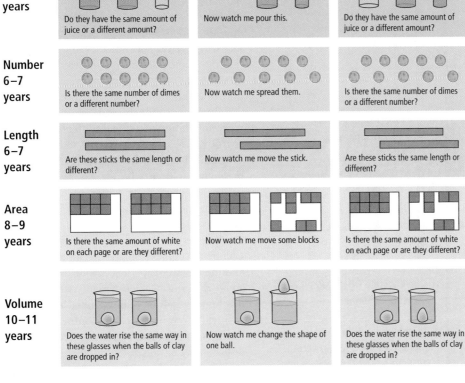

	Step 1	Step 2	Step 3
Solid quantity 6–7 years	Do they have the same amount of clay or a different amount?	Now watch me roll this into a snake.	Do they have the same amount of clay or a different amount?
Liquid quantity 6–7 years	Do they have the same amount of juice or a different amount?	Now watch me pour this.	Do they have the same amount of juice or a different amount?
Number 6–7 years	Is there the same number of dimes or a different number?	Now watch me spread them.	Is there the same number of dimes or a different number?
Length 6–7 years	Are these sticks the same length or different?	Now watch me move the stick.	Are these sticks the same length or different?
Area 8–9 years	Is there the same amount of white on each page or are they different?	Now watch me move some blocks	Is there the same amount of white on each page or are they different?
Volume 10–11 years	Does the water rise the same way in these glasses when the balls of clay are dropped in?	Now watch me change the shape of one ball.	Does the water rise the same way in these glasses when the balls of clay are dropped in?

What cognitive advances must children make to solve conservation problems? At what stage of cognitive development are most children when they start first grade?

Children's Understanding of Seriation

Seriation involves ordering stimuli along a quantitative dimension (such as length). Older children understand the logic of serial position, but younger children do not. When 4-year-old Tammy is shown a group of sticks that vary in length and asked to arrange them in order from the longest to the shortest, she is likely to arrange them slowly in a discontinuous way, usually by comparing pairs of sticks (see Figure 12.3).

Children like Tammy in the preoperational stage do not understand the comparative length of a number of objects and are likely to be distracted by other dimensions, such as visual alignment. As a result, they cannot accurately place all the sticks in sequence by height. But children like 8-year-old Jonathan in the concrete operational stage can

seriation   *the ordering of stimuli along a quantitative dimension (such as length)*

FIGURE 12.2
Example of a Multiple Classification Task

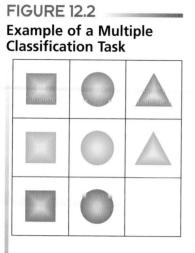

Pick the picture that fits in the blank.

In this task, children are asked to classify objects on two dimensions. Why might young children classify objects in this task differently than older children? What stage of cognitive development does mastery of the task indicate? Consider how mastery of the multiple classification task may relate to concept development and the understanding of categories.

Source: Inhelder and Piaget, 1964.

FIGURE 12.3
Example of a Seriation Task

(a) The Array of Sticks the Child Is Presented with and Asked to Arrange in Order from Longest to Shortest

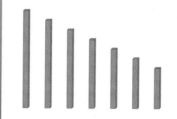

(b) The Preoperational Child's Attempt at Seriation

(c) The Concrete Operational Child's Attempt at Seriation

What skills enable concrete operational children to seriate correctly? How do those skills transfer to academic tasks in the school years?

control for apparent height by aligning the bases of the sticks and focusing on their actual length.

Culture as a Context for Children's Cognitive Development

Culture and community influence children's cognitive development in a number of ways (see Chapter 9). Children are exposed to scripts of daily activities and events valued in their culture, and they have opportunities to practice and learn how to carry out activities valued by their community. To what extent do cultural variations influence children's performance on cognitive tasks?

Children from nonindustrial cultures often fall behind children from industrialized cultures in the ability to conserve, to take others' perspectives, and to understand causal relationships (Segall, Dansen, Berry, & Poortinga, 1990). Based on these findings, some researchers wondered whether concrete operational thinking may be characteristic only of children in industrialized countries.

To understand why children from nonindustrialized cultures perform differently on these cognitive tasks, two issues need to be considered. The first has to do with communication. Not surprisingly, children who are interviewed in their native language show better performance than children interviewed in a language they use but do not know as well (Nyiti, 1982).

The second issue has to do with experience. Children's cognitive abilities relate to their culture and the types of experiences they have in it. If the ability does not match experience well, its development may be slower. If the cognitive ability matches well with experience, its development may be advanced. Children in nonindustrialized societies may display more advanced development than children in industrialized societies if the cognitive tasks selected tap into specialized experiences of their own culture. For instance, when 9- to 12-year-old children from Zimbabwe were evaluated on their understanding of profit, over three quarters of the children understood the need to sell a product for more than one paid for it. In comparison, only about half of the same-age Scottish children understood the concept. This difference is likely due to the Zimbabwe children's greater experience in helping their families buy and sell things in the public market (Jahoda, 1983).

When children are tested in appropriate situations and when their own cultural "specialties" are assessed, the results support the notion that people in every culture reach concrete operational levels of understanding. The differing patterns that have been found are related to communication difficulties and to the types of tasks that are used to assess cognitive development.

Information Processing in School-Age Children

Information processing theorists consider the human mind a complex, symbol-manipulating system that processes many kinds of information (Chen & Siegler, 2000). The changes that occur in children's thinking and problem solving are believed to be due to increased capacities, use of different strategies, and a stronger knowledge base. Furthermore, information processing theorists assume that developmental transitions from one level of thinking to another reflect improvements in the synchronization of processing in different regions of the brain (Chen & Siegler, 2000).

Strategies for Remembering

Recall from Chapter 9 that one reason very young children have poor memories is that they fail to use the memory strategies of rehearsal, organization, and elaboration to help them remember information. During the school-age years, children become more likely to use two of these strategies—rehearsal and organization (elaboration is not typically used until adolescence).

Given the task of remembering a group of objects they have been shown, older children are apt to repeat a whole list of words in their minds to help them remember the names of the objects; younger children tend to repeat the name of only one object at a time (Ornstein, Naus, & Liberty, 1975). When children are trained to use rehearsal strategies, they can improve their memory (Cox et al., 1989).

Similarly, whereas older children will organize information into conceptual categories to help their memory, younger children fail to do so. Though younger children can be encouraged to use organizational strategies on specific tasks, they seldom generalize their use to new situations. And when they do, often they do not gain much advantage from the strategies, suggesting that the effectiveness of an organizational strategy depends on becoming familiar with it (Bjorklund, Miller, Coyle, & Slawinski, 1997). Thus, although younger children are able to employ organizational strategies, they tend not to use them.

Peruvian child vendors are business whizzes compared to most European children of the same age. What accounts for their better understanding of commerce and business practices?

Learning How to Learn

Children's own thinking and problem solving produce information that then leads to changes in their thinking. That is, the outcomes of their thinking contribute information that helps them modify their strategies for future problem solving. For example, children use many different types of strategies to solve mathematics problems, and through their attempts, they learn which strategies are more effective for particular types of problems (Siegler & Shipley, 1995). Furthermore, the knowledge base that children have acquired through prior learning influences how new information is stored and integrated into their previous knowledge, as well as the speed with which information is processed (Bjorklund, 2000). Children who are "experts" in a certain domain, such as dinosaurs or chess or tennis, are better able to chunk information related to that domain into meaningful units, thereby increasing their memory for the information (McPherson & Thomas, 1989). They are then able to engage in faster and more efficient processing of domain-related information.

As children move through the school years, their metacognition improves—that is, their awareness and knowledge about how to learn. They become more knowledgeable about how to learn information and how to apply useful strategies that increase learning. For instance, after having been given information about solving a difficult problem, children given different but similar problems showed a learning-to-learn effect. They were much more likely to solve the new problems than were children who had not received any hints (Brown & Kane, 1988; Brown, Kane, & Long, 1989). Children develop the ability to use the knowledge they gain in one context in another situation.

What Characteristics Define Children's Intelligence and Creativity?

A pair of twins is given a date in the future—say, August 17, 3040. Almost instantly, they announce the day of the week on which the date falls. Or give them a 30-digit number to remember, and they can report it back as accurately as if it had only three digits (Sacks, 1970). In another case, a young boy sets up a laboratory in his basement in which he invents burglar alarms and fixes radios. As an adult, he deciphers a Mayan Indian code and solves physics

FROM RESEARCH TO PRACTICE
ARE THERE CULTURAL DIFFERENCES IN CHILDREN'S REASONING?

FROM RESEARCH . . .

Do children all around the world reason in the same way? Attempts to answer this question have sent researchers to many different countries to ask children about how they think and solve problems. One of Piaget's students, Pierre Dasen (1973), conducted a study of Australian Aboriginal children. The Aborigines were the first inhabitants of Australia. Today, many Aborigines still live in harsh environments, covering a very large territory as they move from place to place in search of water and food. Because they are continually on the move, they own few objects. They have an active and complex spiritual life, which includes elaborate rituals, myths, and symbolic art forms. For instance, they draw and paint maplike scenes that they call "dreamtime stories," containing symbols for important physical features in the environment and for movements between locations. These scenes bear no obvious resemblance to landscape scenes drawn by European artists.

Aware of the many differences between the lives of Aboriginal and most European children, Dasen set out to determine whether they differed in how they reasoned about the world. For the study, Dasen tested Aboriginal children from 8 to 14 years of age who had been in school. Several of Piaget's tasks were used. The tasks assessed conservation skills, spatial understanding, and the ability to view a scene from another person's perspective. In one spatial task, the child was shown a landscape scene with an animal in it. The child then had to find where the animal would be in a second scene, which was the original scene shifted by 180 degrees. The second spatial task involved a bottle half-filled with water, which was tilted (with the water level hidden behind a screen). The child had to match the water level to a series of pictures.

For European children, the ability to understand the liquid conservation task appeared at around the age of 6 or 7. Aboriginal children showed the same changes as the European children in moving from preoperational thinking to concrete operational thinking, but the shift to understanding liquid conservation did not occur until 10 to 13 years of age. Some Aboriginal adolescents and adults even failed the liquid conservation task. Similar results were found for the other conservation tasks.

Although the Aboriginal children were "behind" European children in their level of understanding of conservation, their understanding of the spatial task was quite advanced. Aboriginal children moved through the stages of understanding this task more quickly than European children did.

. . . TO PRACTICE

To interpret these results, Dasen considered the different cultures of the two groups of children. In European countries, quantification of amounts is important. Children may learn these skills more quickly because they are of value in their culture. Children in European countries count many things, and they begin doing so when they are young. In contrast, Aboriginal culture places less value on quantification. Counting things beyond five is unusual. Because of this cultural difference, it is not surprising that European children can solve conservation problems earlier than Aboriginal children can.

The differences in spatial tasks also may reflect cultural variations in lifestyles. European children tend to be more sedentary and certainly are not nomadic like the Aboriginal children. Aboriginal children travel through difficult landscapes, often separately, and meet up again at the end of the day. Finding water is crucial for survival. Without good spatial skills, they would be unable to roam as freely in search of food or to find water as easily. Their spatial abilities are also fostered and reinforced by their "dreamtime stories," in which they attach meaning to physical features of the landscape.

Applying these findings to working with children in different cultures requires understanding what types of cognitive skills a culture values, what skills are practiced and needed while living in the culture, and the types of lifestyles that children have in these cultures. By examining these aspects of culture, a much fuller context becomes available for understanding the types of cognitive skills that children exhibit.

THINKING IT THROUGH

1. How did Dasen's study reveal the impact of culture on children's development of cognitive skills?

2. Why do European children learn conservation of quantities at an earlier age than Australian Aboriginal children do? Why is the reverse true for spatial skills?

3. How do you think Aboriginal and European children would compare on other tests of reasoning?

problems (Feynman, 1985). These people seem to be extraordinarily gifted, and we might assume they have high levels of intelligence. But to what extent do these capabilities actually relate to intelligence? In the cases just discussed, not very well: although the young inventor, Richard Feynman, grew up to win the Nobel Prize in physics, the twins had low IQ scores (around 60) and were institutionalized.

If you ask people on the street what makes someone intelligent, they are likely to suggest that there are three facets to intelligence: practical problem-solving abilities (reasoning logically), verbal abilities (reading comprehension, being a good conversationalist), and social abilities (being sensitive to social cues). Many scientists, but not all, agree that there are several different types of intelligence.

Measuring Intelligence

Few children graduate from high school without having taken at least one intelligence test. Intelligence tests were first developed at the beginning of the twentieth century by Alfred Binet and Theodore Simon. These tests were designed for practical reasons, especially to differentiate between those children who would benefit from standard schooling and those who might need special types of instruction.

Today many types of intelligence tests exist, but the most popular individual test for school children is the Wechsler Intelligence Scale for Children–Third Edition, or WISC–III (Sattler, 2001). The WISC has two major components. The first component is verbal intelligence, which is measured by assessing general world knowledge ("How many pennies make a dime?"), vocabulary, comprehension of written passages, digit span memory (how many numbers the child can remember), and arithmetic. The second component is performance intelligence. To assess performance intelligence, many different tasks are used, including finding what is missing in a picture, arranging pictures in order so that they tell a sensible story, arranging blocks to reproduce a particular design, and unscrambling pieces of objects. The child receives scores on the two major components. The WISC also provides a profile of skills that the child possesses.

Intelligence quotient (IQ) was originally used to express the relationship between the number of items passed and the child's age. The method used today compares a child to other children of the same age. This method assumes that intelligence is normally distributed across the population (see Figure 12.4), with most people falling in average ranges and fewer people falling in the upper and lower ends of the scale. Children who score 100 have an IQ equal to or greater than that of 50 percent of children of the same age. Children with a score of 70 have an IQ equal to or greater than that of about 3 percent of children of the same age (Bjorklund, 1995).

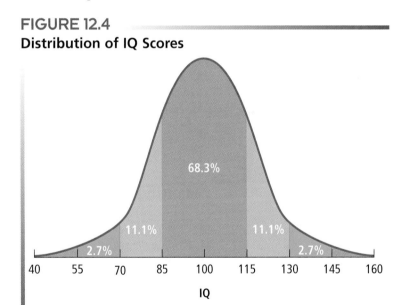

Would you consider a successful artist to be intelligent? Does intelligence involve knowing math and science only?

FIGURE 12.4
Distribution of IQ Scores

Intelligence is assumed to be normally distributed in the population. Explain what this means. What percentage of children have an IQ greater than 130?

Understanding the Limits of IQ Scores

For many children, especially highly verbal children, IQ scores predict school achievement and success (Sattler, 2001). IQ tests also accurately identify children who need special help in school and those who are especially bright. Yet despite these encouraging results, the usefulness of IQ tests has been questioned. For example, IQ scores do not predict life out-comes for many individuals. People who score high on IQ tests tend to complete more years of school and have more prestigious occupations (Morris & Levinson, 1995), but within nor-mal ranges, IQ does not relate to success in a career (McClelland, 1993). Career success is due to many factors such as motivation and social skills (Sternberg & Wagner, 1993).

Because IQ scores do not always predict life success, IQ testing has come under scrutiny in federal courts and several state legislatures. Furthermore, IQ tests may not be used simi-larly for all children. In California, for example, because disproportionate numbers of African American children were placed in special education classes on the basis of IQ scores, the court has banned the use of these scores for student placement. The irony here is that tests designed to help decide a child's placement are now banned from the use for which they were designed (Weinberg, 1989).

The reasons IQ tests are questioned are many, but one of the most common reasons is that they are culturally biased—that is, they test material that is more important or famil-iar to people from one culture than people from another (Ogbu, 1994). For many years, researchers have attempted to develop culture-free tests in which general abilities are assessed rather than the knowledge that has been acquired through one's specific culture. One example is the Raven Progressive Matrices Test, which presents material in pictorial form. Although this test eliminates many of the problems of culture-bound tests, such as heavy reliance on language skills, it still relies on some culturally relevant material. For instance, it requires children to recognize that three-dimensional objects can be represented in two dimensions, which is not a typical skill for children in nonliterate societies (Dere-gowski, 1980). Another alternative has been to try to devise tests that are culture-fair—that is, they assess aspects of functioning that are common to all cultures. These tests, however, still favor the skills of some cultures over the skills of other (Anastasi, 1988).

Today many educators and researchers believe that the assumptions underlying IQ tests are flawed and that the best approach is to use an IQ test as only one part of a com-prehensive assessment of an individual's functioning (Howe, 1997). Instead of using an IQ test as the sole indicator of a child's abilities, an educator should carry out a full assessment of each child, taking into consideration her or his everyday behavior outside of school, opportunities for schooling, and classroom performance (Weinberg, 1989). In fact, some scientists suggest that a better indicator of children's developmental status is social or emo-tional IQ (Salovey & Sluyter, 1997).

Identifying the Components of Intelligence

When Steven was growing up, I didn't know he was a genius. Frankly, I didn't know what the hell he was. I'm really ashamed, but I didn't recognize the symptoms of tal-ent. For one thing—and he'll probably take away my charge accounts for saying this—Steven was never a good student. Once, his teacher told me he was "special"—and I wondered how she meant it. (Leah Adler, mother of award-winning director Steven Spielberg)

Whether an individual succeeds in life may depend on aspects of functioning that are not captured in the typical IQ test. For that reason, several theorists have proposed that people differ in various components of intelligence. For instance, in his *triarchic theory of intelligence*, Robert Sternberg (1985) proposes that people differ in three components that relate to how they process information (see Figure 12.5):

■ *Analytical intelligence:* This type of intelligence is similar to the standard view of intel-ligence. It involves problem solving, encoding and interpreting information, choosing strate-gies for solving problems, and the capacity to gain and store new information in memory. The analytical component is involved in solving the following problem: Cake is to ice cream as eggs are to (a) bacon or (b) pie. Solving this analogy first requires encoding the words and their meanings. Next, the relation between cake and ice cream has to be inferred (often eaten together). Then the relation between cake and eggs has to be determined (both foods) and then related to the choices. For this analogy, the reasoning might be that eggs and bacon are often eaten together just as cake and ice cream are.

■ *Creative intelligence:* This type of intelligence involves insights, synthesis, and the ability to react to new situations and stimuli. Being able to apply existing knowledge to new problems is an example of using creative intelligence. Older children, children with higher IQs, and children with greater expertise are better able to apply information from one situation to another (Siegler, 1998).

■ *Practical intelligence:* This type of intelligence could be called "street smarts" because it involves the ability to understand and deal with everyday tasks. This intelligence operates in the real world, and people who have it are successful in adapting to and shaping their environments to suit their own needs.

Sternberg's approach to intelligence focuses on how people interact with and adapt to their environment and how they process information about it. Research has demonstrated that individuals differ in these three types of intelligence and that the triarchic theory provides a useful way to think about changes in intelligence as children grow older.

In contrast to Sternberg's focus on processing strategies, Gardner (1983; 1999) emphasizes *multiple intelligences*—that is, intellectual domains in which individuals may have different strengths. As you can see in Table 12.1, Gardner proposed eight "frames of mind," or distinct areas of skill that are relatively independent of one another. In any of these, a person can display talent or genius. Only three of these frames of mind are assessed in standard IQ tests (Simonton, 1994). The frames-of-mind approach is useful for thinking about intelligence across cultures and throughout time. In some cultures, it may be adaptive to

FIGURE 12.5
Sternberg's Triarchic Theory of Intelligence

What type of intelligence is this child likely to be using if he is solving an analogy problem? Can children who have "street smarts" be considered intelligent according to Sternberg?

TABLE 12.1
Gardner's Eight Frames of Mind: Examples of Abilities and People Who Exemplify Them

FRAME OF MIND	ABILITIES	PEOPLE
Linguistic	Good conversationalist; has learned several languages; writes well	Katie Couric, Christine Amanpour
Logical–mathematical	Able to solve logical and mathematical problems; analytical	Marie Curie, Albert Einstein
Musical	Plays several instruments; understands music theory; composes music	Wolfgang Mozart, Bono
Spatial	Good at visualizing, solving visual problems, and negotiating directions; artistic	Pierre Renoir
Bodily–kinesthetic	Good athlete or dancer; has good motor skills	Tiger Woods
Interpersonal	Socially competent; understands others' feelings	Sigmund Freud
Intrapersonal	Knows himself or herself	Mahatma Gandhi
Naturalistic	Can categorize and draw upon features of the environment	John Horner

Source: Adapted from H. Gardner, 1983.

FIGURE 12.6

Christene's Puzzle: Is It Creative?

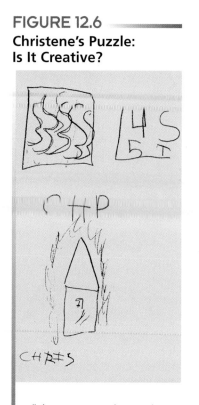

"The answer to the puzzle is me! These lines stand for my wavy hair, the numbers show that I'm four going on five, and the rest doesn't stand for anything at all!" Do you think this puzzle depicts creativity? How might this puzzle fit the definition of creativity?

Source: Amabile, 1993.

savants   *people who show exceptional abilities in one domain of intelligence but have retarded mental development in some other domains*

prodigies   *children who show exceptional abilities at a very young age in one domain of intelligence but not necessarily in others*

creativity   *novel and appropriate behavior that is different from what the person has done or seen before*

divergent thinking   *thinking that moves in many directions to produce many ideas or alternatives*

convergent thinking   *thinking that attempts to find a single correct answer to a problem*

have good spatial skills so that one can be a successful hunter. In most Western cultures, linguistic and logical–mathematical skills are especially valued. Each person is seen as having a unique blend of these intelligences. These skills are often used together, and they can complement one another to help people solve problems (Gardner, 1999).

The eight frames of mind were identified from research on brain-damaged individuals and from studies of exceptional children as well as on experimental psychological tasks. Individuals who have particular forms of brain damage due to strokes or injury will exhibit normal skills in some areas but have extremely limited skills in other areas. For instance, a person with damage to the frontal lobes of the neocortex may have very limited interpersonal skills but intact logical–mathematical functioning. Similarly, some children—such as the twins who could associate days with dates—are known as **savants** because they show exceptional abilities in one domain of intelligence but are incompetent in some other domains. One popular example of a savant is the autistic man played by Dustin Hoffman in the movie *Rain man*. He could memorize the cards perfectly during a game of blackjack but could not carry on a conversation with his brother. Children called **prodigies** show exceptional abilities at a very young age in one domain but not necessarily in others. Wolfgang Amadeus Mozart was a musical prodigy who composed keyboard pieces at age 5, published a composition by age 7, and wrote symphonies and operas by age 15. Otherwise, he was a typical, playful child and teenager (Simonton, 1994). Michael Jackson could sing and dance amazingly well at a very young age, but he may not be particularly advanced in other areas.

The concept of multiple intelligences has inspired many educational innovations in North America, including the ideas that it is important to match instruction to learning styles, provide instruction in more than one way, and encourage student specialization (Gardner & Hatch, 1989; Kornhaber, 2001; Krechevsky & Seidel, 1998). The theory has been criticized, however, for its static view of student competence (Klein, 1997).

Creativity in Children

Four-year-old Christene and her mother were waiting for their dinner at a restaurant. Using the pad and pen they brought along, Christene drew a puzzle for her mother to solve. After her mother tried but could not solve the puzzle, Christene explained, "The answer to the puzzle is me! These lines stand for my wavy hair, the numbers show that I'm four going on five, and the rest doesn't stand for anything at all!" (Amabile, 1993, p. 18)

Creativity is novel and appropriate behavior, different from what the person has done before or seen before (Amabile, 1993). According to this definition, Christene's actions would be considered creative because the puzzle includes a novel and appropriate representation of herself (see Figure 12.6)

Because the creativity of a work of art or a solution to a problem is defined by the culture in which it occurs (Csikszentmihalyi, 1996), it is difficult to assess creativity (Runco & Pritzker, 1999). The most commonly used tests, designed by E. P. Torrance (1966), involve assessments of **divergent thinking,** that is, thinking that moves in many directions to produce many ideas or alternatives. In divergent thinking, many creative possiblities are generated, and this type of thinking differs from **convergent thinking,** which involves trying to find a single correct answer to a problem. Divergent thinking is assessed using both verbal and graphic tests. In the verbal section, the student is asked to think of as many uses as possible for objects like a tin can or paper clip. In the graphic section, the student is presented with a page covered with 30 lines and asked to create different drawings from these lines. Responses are scored for three aspects: how many answers are given (which measures fluency), unusualness of answers (which assesses originality), and number of categories of responses (which assesses flexibility; Sattler, 2001). Research shows that children who score well on these tests are more likely to have creative achievements later in life, although the relationship is not strong (Torrance, 1988).

Some researchers who have studied creativity think that anyone can be creative in the right situation (Amabile, 2001; Hennessey & Amabile, 1988; Mellou, 1996). Four components appear to be needed for creativity:

▪ *Domain skills:* Creativity requires a solid background and ability in the particular domain of interest. For example, a scientist is unlikely to make a creative breakthrough in understanding cellular functioning without an extensive knowledge of biology.

▪ *Creative working style:* A creative working style is characterized by a dedication to working well, ability to concentrate, willingness to work hard, and persistence when roadblocks occur in thinking.

▪ *Creative thinking style:* Creative thinking includes "breaking set"—that is, being willing to drop old ways of thinking to try new ways. Creative thinking also involves perceiving things freshly, or taking a different perspective on the problem than most people would take (Feldman, 1999; Runco, 1999; Russ, 1996).

▪ *Intrinsic motivation:* Creativity is facilitated when people are internally interested in and challenged by the problem (Amabile, 2001; Hennessey & Amabile, 1988; Martindale, 2001).

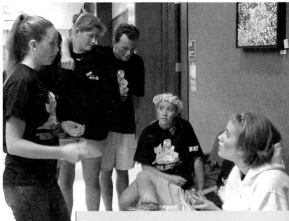

Destination Imagination, a non-profit organization, teaches creative thinking, problem-solving, and teamwork to kids of all ages.

Family and Cultural Influences on Intellectual Development

Children's intelligence and achievement are influenced by the kind of family and community in which they grow up (see Figure 12.7). Some children grow up in a home with many disadvantages. These children may have a difficult time developing their full intellectual potential. Other children have the advantages of good housing, health care, and nutrition and supportive caregivers, which increase their chances for optimal intellectual development.

The Impact of Poverty on Children's Intellectual Development

The incidence of mental retardation is about six times higher among children who are raised in chronic poverty than among children who are raised in middle- and upper-income families (Baumeister & Baumeister, 1989). Children raised in poverty also are likely to be undernourished, have substandard housing, be ill more often, receive less health care, and come from more disorganized families than children from wealthier backgrounds (Aber, Jones, & Cohen, 2000; Huston, 1999). Thus, poverty has the potential to adversely affect children's intellectual development and performance in school. Racial and ethnic differences in IQ and school achievement all but disappear once adjustments are made for economic and social differences (Brooks-Gunn, Klebanov, & Duncan, 1996).

The problems of poverty are intergenerational, complex, and enduring. For example, women living in poverty receive less prenatal care and have more difficulties with their pregnancies. Not surprisingly, they are more likely to give birth to premature and unhealthy babies, who then face high rates of illness and all the other debilitating conditions associated with poverty (McLoyd, 1998a). The cumulative effects of poverty on many aspects of development make it all the more important to find ways to keep families out of the poverty cycle.

The Role of the Family in Children's Giftedness

Families and communities play a role in the development of gifted children. Studies of the early lives of remarkably accomplished young adults showed that these young people shared many family characteristics, even though they had diverse talents, as they ranged from concert pianists and neurologists to

FIGURE 12.7

Influences on Children's Intellectual Development

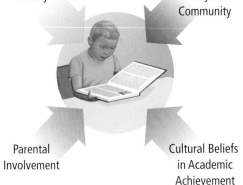

Impact of Poverty

Role of Family and Community

Parental Involvement

Cultural Beliefs in Academic Achievement

Children vary in how quickly they learn to read. Which of the factors shown in this diagram do you think play the largest role in influencing how quickly a child learns to read?

Latino parents have high expectations for their children's school performance. How do parents provide support and encouragement for their children in school?

Olympic swimmers. In most cases, the family was intact and parents went to enormous lengths to help their children succeed at whatever task they undertook. Below are some of the characteristics that are commonly found in families of successful and talented children (Feldman, 1999; Howe, 1999):

- Parents value success and encourage children to do their best.

- Parents supervise practice sessions and training.

- Parents encourage active pursuits; they do not encourage television viewing or other passive pursuits.

- Parents devote time and energy to their children by reading to them, playing games with them, teaching them, checking homework, and supervising practice sessions.

- Family life is firmly structured, and children are required to share in responsibilities at home.

It is the parents who first introduce many children to the area in which they eventually excel, and often the parent is talented in this area as well. With parental encouragement and informal teaching, children can develop a high level of skill at home. The parents of gifted children realize the importance of practice and are sensitive to the need to support and encourage their children's practice (Strom, Strom, Strom, & Collinsworth, 1994). Although the families involved in these studies differed from one another in many ways, the one constant factor was the encouragement and support the parents gave their children.

In a longitudinal study, information was obtained about the lives of children from 1 to 8 years of age. At age 8, some of the children were identified as being gifted. When the early lives of the gifted children were compared with those of the other children, surprisingly few differences were found. Gifted and nongifted children had similar personalities, similar rates of behavioral and emotional problems, and similar social relationships. However, gifted and nongifted children's families differed. Gifted children's parents were more highly educated, and their families showed healthier functioning. Gifted children had more learning opportunities, more educational stimulation, more exposure to books, and more trips to libraries than children who were not gifted (Gottfried, Gottfried, Bathurst, & Guerin, 1994).

The Roles of Parental Involvement and Cultural Beliefs in Academic Achievement

For many years, American children have not performed as well as Chinese and Japanese children in most academic areas. Several factors, including classroom strategies and cultural beliefs and ceremonies, contribute to these differences (DeCorte, Greer, & Verschaffel, 1996; Stevenson, 1998a). Families also contribute to the differences found in the performance levels of children in different cultures.

In an extensive research program, Harold Stevenson and his colleagues investigated mathematics achievement among first- and third-grade children in three large cities—Sendai, Japan; Minneapolis, Minnesota; and Taipei, Taiwan (Stevenson & Lee, 1990). Although the children's performance did not differ much in the first grade, by the third grade, the Asian children were far outperforming the American children. The researchers found dramatic differences between the Asian and the American families. Parents in Japan and Taiwan mobilized their resources to help their children as soon as the children entered school. For instance, the percentage of parents who bought their children mathematics workbooks varied from 58 percent in Japan and 56 percent in Taiwan to only 28 percent in the United States. Almost all of the Japanese (98 percent) and Taiwanese (95 percent) children had their own desk and work space at home, compared to only 28 percent of the American children. The Asian parents monitored their children's homework more than the American parents did. And, although the Asian children were performing quite well overall, their parents expressed more concerns with the school system than American parents did. Another clue to the success of the Asian students may be the interpretation parents placed on good mathematics performance. Asian parents were likely to attribute good mathematics skills to hard work, whereas American parents were more likely to attribute these skills to natural ability (Stevenson, 1998b; Stevenson, Lee, & Mu, 2000).

Parents' involvement, especially in holding high aspirations and expectations for their children, plays a significant role in children's academic achievement (Fan & Chen, 2001). Research suggests that families' attitudes toward and encouragement of education are important factors in the lives of children from diverse ethnic groups within the United States (Stevenson, Chen, & Lee, 1993). In a large-scale study of African American, Caucasian American, and Latino children in Chicago schools, mothers' and children's attitudes toward school were investigated, as well as children's school achievement in reading and mathematics (Stevenson, Chen, & Uttal, 1990). In early elementary grades, African American and Latino children had lower school achievement scores than Caucasian American children did; by fifth grade, these differences had disappeared for mathematics but not for reading. Differences in children's mathematics achievement in fifth grade related to the mother's educational level, rather than the child's ethnicity. Children whose mothers had lower levels of education did not perform as well in mathematics as children whose mothers had higher levels of education. Overall, minority children were more positive in some of their attitudes about school. For instance, African American children tended to like homework more than Caucasian American children did, and in fifth grade, Latino children liked school more than Caucasian American children did.

FIGURE 12.8

African American, Latino, and Caucasian American Mothers' Attitudes About Improving Children's Educational Performance

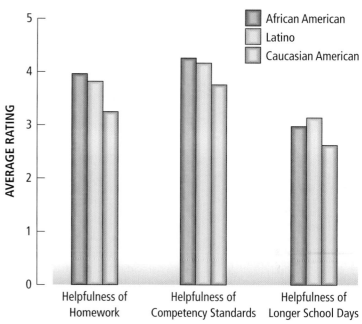

Notice how the data contradict the stereotyped belief that minority parents do not emphasize academic achievement and hold high standards. How do parents' attitudes influence children's school performance?

Source: Stevenson, Chen, and Uttal, 1990 (p. 517).

Latino and African American children and their mothers were very positive about education, and the mothers held high expectations about their children's future prospects for education (Stevenson et al., 1990). Compared to Caucasian American mothers and teachers, minority mothers and teachers were more positive about the value of homework, competency testing, and lengthening school days to improve educational opportunities for children (see Figure 12.8).

Given the positive attitudes that children and their mothers have about schooling in the elementary grades, it seems surprising that so many minority children experience school failure during junior high and high school. An important goal for future research is to discover what factors have a destructive effect on older minority children's school achievement.

How Do Language and Literacy Develop During the School Years?

By the time children enter school, they have mastered many of the basic building blocks of language. They have a large vocabulary, use many grammatical rules in their speech, adjust their speech to fit their listeners, and understand how to communicate many of their needs to others. During the school years, children's language skills continue to develop, but the

Is this how a 6-year-old would understand the sentence "Big Bird was followed by the children"? Why would a young child make this mistake while an older child would not?

changes are more subtle than those that occurred during the preschool years. Compared to the preschool child, the school-age child is able to communicate more effectively over a broader range of contexts, use and understand more complex grammatical forms, and think about better ways to communicate using language. Additionally, a dramatic advance occurs during these years—children learn to read.

Development of Syntax

During the school years, children's understanding and use of grammar expand to include more complex forms of sentences, such as sentences in the passive voice. If preschool children overhear, "Big Bird was followed by the children," they are likely to picture in their mind Big Bird following behind children, rather than the accurate scenario. Preschool children often are confused by a sentence in the passive voice, probably because they rely heavily on word order and interpret the sentence as being in the active voice. That is, they expect the object of the action to follow the verb in a sentence. By the age of 5, children understand passive constructions with action verbs ("was bitten"), but only during the school years do they come to understand such sentences employing non-action-oriented verbs ("was followed by"). Children's understanding of the passive voice continues to develop through the school years, but the full range of understanding is not usually acquired until adolescence (Bloom, 1998).

Some children learn to understand such sentences earlier, however. Children who speak Sesotho (an African dialect) understand passive constructions by age 3. Compared to English speakers, Sesotho speakers use passive constructions for sentences much more frequently. For instance, there is no way to ask a question except in a passive form. Instead of asking, "Who asked you?" a Sesotho child must say, "Whom were you asked by?" (de Villiers & de Villiers, 1992). This cultural difference suggests that children learn more quickly those forms of language to which they are exposed (Demuth, 1990).

Young children use a variety of strategies for understanding spoken language. One example is the **minimal distance principle (MDP),** in which children assume that the noun most closely preceding the verb is the subject of the sentence. For instance, using the MDP, children would correctly interpret the sentence "Aladdin told Jasmine to eat the bread" to mean that Jasmine will be the person eating the bread. However, the order of words in some sentences do not follow the rule, and when children use the MDP to help them understand such a sentence, they incorrectly interpret it. For example, if the MDP is applied to the sentence "Jasmine promised Aladdin to feed the dog," it will be misinterpreted to mean that Aladdin will feed the dog—when, in fact, the intended meaning is that Jasmine will feed the dog. It isn't until around 8 or 9 years of age that most children learn that *promise* sentences are exceptions to the MDP.

Development of Semantics

Children's understanding of word meanings continues to develop during the school years (Hoff-Ginsberg, 1997). They add new words to their vocabulary, and their understanding of these new words often is acquired by listening to the context in which the words are used. By third grade, children know about 20,000 words, and by fifth grade, they know about 40,000 words. Between first and third grade, children learn approximately 8 to 10 new words per day (Anglin, 1993).

Not all children learn that many words a day or have 40,000 words in their vocabulary by fifth grade, however. The variation among children is great, and the differences become larger with age. The variation is likely due in part to the relationship between reading and vocabulary size. Children who like to read when they are young develop larger vocabularies than other children do (Nagy, Anderson, & Herman, 1987), and then, because these children continue to read more than other children, they continue to learn more words (Robbins & Ehri, 1994).

School-age children become increasingly sophisticated in their ability to understand subtle aspects of meaning, such as the double meanings some words carry. Terms such as *cold,*

minimal distance principle (MDP)   *the assumption that the noun most closely preceding the verb is the subject of the sentence*

bright, and *sweet* have a physical meaning ("The pie is *sweet*") and also a psychological meaning ("She is a *sweet* person"). Not until children are 7 or 8 years old do they use these terms to refer to people, and complete mastery of these terms may not be achieved until a child reaches 12 years of age (Bloom, 1998).

Children also learn to understand the meanings expressed by idioms, which cannot be interpreted literally (see Figure 12.9). If 4-year-old Tara heard her mother say, "It's raining cats and dogs," she might run to the door and look to the sky to witness this amazing sight of dogs and cats falling from the sky. Or overhearing her father say, in a conversation about someone at work, "She hit the ceiling," Tara might imagine a woman pounding her fist on the ceiling. These and other English idioms are difficult for young children—and people learning English as a second language—to understand. Children misinterpret these sentences because they interpret them literally. For instance, when a third-grade child participating in a study of word meanings was asked the meaning of *moneybags,* the child said, "It means that money goes into bags, and they have like dollar signs on them, and usually people bring moneybags to rob banks and stuff" (Anglin, 1993, p. 110). To understand idioms, children must ignore the literal meaning of the words and instead rely solely on the context to infer the meaning of the phrase. They gradually develop an understanding of idioms, but full understanding does not occur until adolescence.

Development of Pragmatics

The basic knowledge that children acquired as preschoolers about the pragmatics of language is refined and expanded during the school years. Children become more skilled in these aspects of communication because they come to recognize more of the unwritten "rules" of conversations (Holzman, 1996).

During the school years, two changes in children's understanding of the pragmatics of language are particularly noteworthy. The first change is the school-age child's increased ability to maintain a conversation (Bloom, 1998). Older children will continue to converse on one topic longer than young children will. Also, unlike preschoolers, who maintain the flow of a topic by repeating information, older children introduce new and relevant information into a conversation to maintain the topic.

The second change is school-age children's growing ability to be sensitive and "repair" conversations when listeners do not understand what they are saying. Although preschool children have some ability to clarify messages to help listeners understand, they do not deal well with repeated requests to clarify messages. Older children, on the other hand, continue to add information to make their message clear to the listener. By 9 years of age, children also provide definitions or background information as cues to help listeners understand their statements (Ninio & Snow, 1996).

Children's Literacy

One of the most dramatic changes that occurs in many cultures during the school years is that children learn to read and write. Unlike speech, which is universal and is quickly and easily acquired by most children all over the world, reading and writing are not common to all cultures and usually require extensive training before they are learned (Liberman, 1996). Both reading and writing require that children develop many complex skills involving attention, perception, memory, and background knowledge.

Cracking the Code: Learning to Read

Reading depends on a complex set of skills that children learn gradually as they grow older (Adams, Treiman, & Pressley, 1998). These skills help children to crack the code of written words and their meanings.

FIGURE 12.9

Understanding Idioms

It's raining cats and dogs.

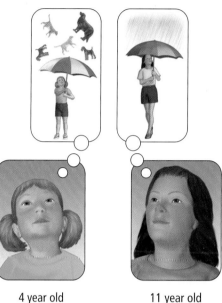

4 year old   11 year old

Younger children and children who are new speakers of English have difficulty with idioms. In this drawing, the 4-year-old girl does not understand the idiom, but the older girl does. Why do you think idioms are so difficult for younger children to understand?

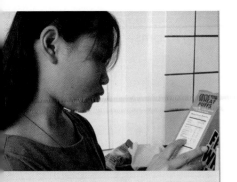

What skills has this child mastered to enable her to read?

Children move through phases in learning to read (Chall, Jacobs, & Baldwin, 1990). The first phase occurs during the preschool years. During this time, children master many of the skills required for reading, such as learning the letters of the alphabet, recognizing some words, and writing their names. The second phase starts when children are 7 to 8 years old, when they begin to read fluently. At this point, reading does not require as much effort as it did earlier. In the third phase, which arises between ages 9 and 13, children are able to use reading to obtain information. Reading becomes automatic enough so that they have the cognitive capacity to give more attention to the content of their reading. Instead of learning to read, children are now reading to learn (Hiebert & Raphael, 1996).

What skills do children need to learn to become successful readers? One important skill that children need to understand is that the written words they *see* are related to the language they *hear*. Just because a caregiver holds a book while conveying a story to a child does not mean the child understands that the book has in it the words to tell the story. Caregivers can help children understand this connection by showing children that they are reading words from the book and that the words provide the story to be told (Foorman et al., 1998).

Some of the skills involved in reading come easily to children. English-speaking children readily acquire the following specific prerequisite knowledge about reading:

- Words are read from left to right across the page.
- Words continue from the extreme right of one line to the extreme left of the next line down.
- Spaces between chunks of letters indicate words.

Other skills do not come so easily. Many children, for instance, have difficulty discriminating between letters. To do this, children must be able to recognize the unique form of each letter and its orientation on the page. Mastering the orientation of letters can be quite taxing for young children because few things in their world depend on orientation to define them. A child looks around and sees a cat; a cat is a cat, regardless of its position—lying down, sitting, or standing facing to the right or the left. The same cannot be said about letters. A *b* is not a *b* when it faces in the other direction; it becomes a *d*. Children's lack of attention to orientation can be seen in their earliest attempts at "writing"—the letters they draw are scattered on the page, slanted, and even placed on their sides. It is not surprising, then, that over 50 percent of 5- and 6-year-old children reverse letters and numbers. Only about 10 percent of 7-year-olds do so (Kaufman, 1980). Even after they learn letters, many children confuse those that differ only in orientation, such as *b* and *d* (Adams et al., 1998).

Another challenge for children is mastering phonemic awareness (see Chapter 6). To read a word, children must recognize the sounds associated with the letters and be able to blend these sounds together to form a word. The ability to recognize the correspondence between sounds and letters relates to reading achievement in the early grades (Bruck, 1992). Preschool children are not very aware of these correspondences, but school-age children become more skilled at recognizing them.

How can children's awareness of phonemes be improved? Exposure to nursery rhymes or other rhyming activities promotes phonemic awareness, as children hear the subtle variations in the sounds of similar words. Rhyming games also increase children's general awareness that words consist of various sounds (McBride-Chang, 1995). Phoneme deletion exercises, such as asking a child to say *cat* without the /c/ sound, can also improve children's understanding of phonemes. Training preschool and kindergarten children in phonemic awareness leads to improved reading skills up to four years later (Byrne & Fielding-Barnsely, 1995).

Children's Reading Readiness

Pushing children to read before they are ready may cause them to become discouraged. Instead, caregivers should be on the lookout for general cues that their children are ready to read. Following are some of the cues that indicate readiness to read (National Association for the Education of Young Children, 1998):

- Attempting to tell stories while scanning and turning pages in a book
- Understanding that stories start at the front of the book and move to the back in order, page by page
- Recognizing written labels or signs
- Pointing out individual letters
- Showing interest in seeing his or her name in print

Once children have shown that they are ready to read, caregivers can arrange many activities to encourage reading. The complex skills involved in reading are best practiced and learned in the social context of interactions with caregivers, peers, and siblings. Competence in reading is fostered by practice and experience in all language domains. Reading to children certainly encourages reading skills, but so do other language-related activities such as carrying on conversations with them.

Controversies About Teaching Children to Read

Reading has been taught in many different ways, but controversy today surrounds the relative merits of two methods (Freppon & Dahl, 1998). In the **phonics approach,** children are trained to translate letters and groups of letters into sounds. For instance, children practice sounding out words that they cannot initially pronounce. Only simple and basic materials are used to study individual words. In the **whole language approach,** learning to read is assumed to be a natural process that occurs most effectively in a print-rich environment. Children become readers by guessing the meanings of words based on each word's context within the passage and their prior knowledge (Smith, 1992). Associated with this approach is the idea of **emergent literacy,** which assumes that children naturally develop the skills involved in written and oral language over the years and gradually improve these skills as they grow older (Teale & Sulzby, 1985). Although many educators have adopted the whole language approach, research provides little support that this method facilitates children's reading (Vellutino, 1991).

Rather than focus on one approach to the exclusion of the other, some researchers argue that the best method is to incorporate aspects of both approaches (Pressley, 1998). For instance, the developmental approach to reading proposed by Spear-Swerling and Sternberg (1994) allows for changes in the method as children grow older and as their reading competencies change. In the earliest phase, children use visual cues to learn words. In the next phase, they make limited use of phonetic features of words. In the final phase, which begins at around 6 or 7 years of age and continues through adulthood, children achieve automatic word recognition. At this point, the most important skills to stress are those involving comprehension of the material (Adams et al., 1998).

The whole language and phonics approaches appear to help different kinds of children. The whole language approach particularly benefits children with low initial reading scores, whereas those with high initial reading scores benefit more from a phonics approach (Sacks & Mergendoller, 1997).

How Do School-Age Children Understand the Social World?

Children use their cognitive skills to solve a wide array of problems, ranging from conservation tasks to arithmetic problems, but they also use cognitive skills to help them understand people and their actions. As children progress through later childhood, their knowledge about people and social situations becomes increasingly sophisticated. This increased understanding of the social world contributes to more mature and responsible behavior and improved interactions with others.

Social Perspective Taking: Communicating with Others

Imagine 3-year-old Shannon trying to communicate to 3-year-old Michael that he should pick a particular stuffed toy rabbit out of a group of toys. Shannon might say, "Pick up the

phonics approach *technique used to teach reading, whereby children are trained to translate letters and groups of letters into sounds*

whole language approach *technique used to teach reading, based on the idea that learning to read is a natural process that occurs most effectively in a print-rich environment*

emergent literacy *educational approach based on the idea that children will naturally develop the skills involved in written and oral language and gradually improve these skills as they grow older*

FIGURE 12.10

Changes in How Children Think About Others

She's a girl who wears glasses and has a dog.

She's very friendly and seems fun.

3 year old   8 year old

As children grow older, their views of others change from being very focused on external features (what other people look like) to focus more on psychological and internal characteristics (what other people act like). What consequences do these changes have for the stability of children's expectations about other people?

one I like the most," not considering that Michael would not know which one was her favorite. To be able to effectively communicate with others, children (and adults) must be skilled in **social perspective taking**—the ability to move away from one's own perspective and recognize what others perceive.

In contrast to a child in the preoperational stage, children in the concrete operational stage are better able to view a wide variety of problems from another person's perspective. They are less egocentric and can both consider their own view and recognize that others see things from different vantage points. Children's understanding of others' perspectives extends into many domains; they now can communicate effectively with others because they can better imagine what others are thinking and seeing.

Similar to how they think about themselves, preschool children tend to think about others by focusing on external characteristics and temporary situations. School-age children show a more sophisticated understanding of people (Hala, 1997; Yuille, 1997). Preschoolers tend to refer to other people in very concrete terms (focusing on age, appearance, and possessions), seldom using abstract characteristics to describe others (Miller & Aloise, 1989). At around the age of 8, children's thinking about others becomes more refined, and they are more likely to think about others in abstract and internal psychological terms. For instance, an 8-year-old child will describe her friend as shy rather than simply saying that she is a girl.

Because of their focus on external characteristics and behavior, preschoolers tend to think that people change frequently; they do not observe the stability in personality that older children notice. A 10-year-old child is likely to believe that a girl in his class who shared her lunch with another child would probably help someone who was hurt, inferring from this one behavior that the girl is helpful in many situations (Rholes & Ruble, 1984).

Just as preschoolers cannot easily view a scene from another person's perspective, they generally cannot view social events from any perspective but their own. By late childhood, children come to recognize that two different people involved in a social interaction may have differing views and attitudes about the event. They still, however, may not use both points of view to understand the event the way an adolescent or adult might (Flavell & Miller, 1998).

Children's Understanding of Others' Beliefs and Feelings

As you learned in Chapter 9, a key feature of developing social skills is coming to understand that others have thoughts, feelings, and beliefs of their own. By school age, children have learned to "read minds"—that is, they are aware of others' thoughts, beliefs, knowledge, desires, and intentions (Hala & Carpendale, 1997).

Imagine a situation in which 9-year-old Iris watches her friend Lisa walk into the room and then turn around and walk out of the room. Iris, like most older children, can consider the existence of mental events, so she might guess that Lisa was looking for something she thought was in the room or that Lisa heard a noise in the room and was looking for the source. In either case, Iris is considering mentalistic explanations for the

On what basis are these girls likely to describe each other? How do their descriptions differ from those of preschool children?

actions that Lisa took. Mentalistic explanations are those that involve consideration of other people's mental states—their beliefs and thoughts. Not all children have the ability to consider mentalistic explanations. Some children, such as autistic children, are *mindblind*—they have no mentalistic explanations to help them understand others' actions. A mindblind person would have no explanation for Lisa's actions other than the suggestion that Lisa might carry out this action every day, and this explanation is likely to be proved wrong. Imagine how difficult it would be for a mindblind person to interpret other social events, especially a complex interaction involving several people. Most children, however, develop more sophisticated mentalistic concepts as they grow older and can readily understand that others experience feelings, emotions, and beliefs.

At what age do children use ethnicity to group people? Is ethnic awareness the same as prejudice?

Children's Understanding of Race and Prejudice

The images that come to mind when we think of prejudice tend to involve adults or adolescents. For instance, we might visualize neo-Nazi groups or members of the Ku Klux Klan. When people encounter prejudicial or racist attitudes in children, they are quick to attribute them to children's imitation of adults rather than to the children's own personal preferences. This attribution, however, has been questioned by research on race and prejudice, which indicates that the level of prejudice in children has not declined since the middle of the twentieth century, as it has in adults (Aboud, 1988).

Prejudice refers to having preconceived ideas about a person or group of people, often having to do with physical characteristics, ethnicity, or race. Some people respond to their prejudices with **discrimination**—acting in an unfavorable manner toward people because of their affiliation with a group. Awareness of ethnic and racial groups is considered a prerequisite for some types of prejudice and discrimination (Carter & Rice, 1997). When do children consciously recognize ethnicity in individuals?

Development of Understanding of Ethnicity

By 6 months of age, many infants can perceptually categorize people on the basis of physical appearance (Walsh, Katz, & Downey, 1991). Simply recognizing that some people look different does not indicate that a child understands ethnicity, however. But children show strong same-race peer preferences by 2 years of age, and these preferences become more clearly established in early grade school (Katz, 1992). By 4 years of age, children have considerable knowledge about racial stereotypes of African Americans and Caucasians (Levy & Katz, 1993). Although children distinguish between Caucasian and African American people by age 4, their recognition of other ethnic groups, such as Native Americans, Chinese Americans, or Latinos, is delayed for a few years, probably because the distinctive physical features of members of these groups can be less obvious (Aboud, 1988).

Perception of differences among other ethnic groups arises between the ages of 6 and 8 years. At this time, children begin to use ethnicity to group people together and to understand and make guesses about what people are like. For instance, they assume that people of the same race are similar in many ways despite the fact that they have different facial features or different shades of color, and they assume that people of different races are different in many ways even when they have many features in common (Ramsey, 1987). By age 11, children have incorporated more flexibility into their beliefs. No longer do children always perceive people to be different because they are of different races; children often find similarities based on individual features such as emotional expressions or abilities.

Awareness that different ethnic groups exist plays a role in the development of prejudice, but ethnic awareness does not determine prejudice (Carter & Rice, 1997). Children may hold stereotypes about and be prejudiced against groups that they cannot identify. Also, most people are aware of stereotypes, yet not all people apply this knowledge or act in prejudicial ways.

social perspective taking *the ability to move away from one's own perspective and recognize what others perceive*

prejudice *preconceived ideas about a person or group of people, often based on physical characteristics, ethnicity, or race*

discrimination *acting in an unfavorable manner toward people because of their affiliation with a group*

Theories of Prejudice Formation

The most widely held theory about the formation of prejudice is that children adopt their parents' prejudicial attitudes and behaviors. According to this theory, children learn prejudice from their parents either by direct instruction, as when a parent tells a child not to play with children of another race because they are not "good," or by observation of the parents' words or actions toward people of different races. The scientific evidence, however, suggests that children do not always adopt the prejudicial attitudes of their parents, and if they do, it is usually after 7 years of age (Branch & Newcombe, 1986). In addition, cases have been found in which children held prejudicial attitudes when their parents did not (Davey, 1983). For these reasons, it is unlikely that children's prejudice can be explained solely on the basis of learning from parents, other adults, or peers (Aboud & Doyle, 1996).

Theories of the development of prejudice also must account for the age-related changes observed in the development of children's prejudice (Black-Gutman & Hickson, 1996). An important shift in prejudice occurs at about 7 years of age. After 7 years of age, Caucasian American children often show a decline in prejudice (Augoustinos & Rosewarne, 2001) and minority children show a more widespread preference for their own group (Bigler & Liben, 1993).

A social–cognitive theory has been proposed to account for the development of prejudice. According to this theory, the ways in which children think about the social world around them are influenced by the level of cognitive development they have attained (Aboud, 1988). Early on, children's thinking is dominated by their emotions and preferences. Later, children begin to consider how similar or dissimilar other people are to themselves. Prejudice is related to the perceived degree of dissimilarity. People with different skin color, language, and/or clothing are noticeably different, and these perceptions dominate children's reactions. Finally, children begin to understand the difference between categories and individual qualities and learn to attend to more than one quality of a person at the same time (they realize that a person can have a different skin color but similar interests). Then they can use categories as the basis for determining ethnicity and individual qualities as the basis for forming preferences.

Thus, as children acquire more advanced modes of thinking, their views of others become less extreme and polarized. They become aware of individuals' internal qualities, understand that ethnicity is permanent and unchangeable, and realize that ethnic differences are reconcilable. In other words, because of changes in cognitive development, older

NURTURING CHILDREN
REDUCING PREJUDICE IN CHILDREN

What can be done to reduce prejudice in children? The answer to this question depends upon the age of the child. For children 4 to 7 years of age, the following suggestions may be helpful (Aboud, 1988; Katz, 1992):

■ Help children develop perspective-taking skills. Prejudice at this age is based on the egocentric belief that there is only one way of experiencing the world.

■ Help children develop a concern and compassion for others. Foster an ethic of caring rather than prejudice.

■ Increase children's exposure to people of other races. Children's preferences for people of their own race and their negative attitudes toward people of other races will decrease. These effects generally are stronger for Caucasian American children than for minority children, although interracial exposure has been found to decrease African American children's lack of trust in and suspicion of Caucasians.

For children 7 to 12 years of age, a different set of principles should be followed to reduce prejudice:

■ Encourage children to judge others on the basis of internal qualities rather than external attributes.

■ Help children attend to similarities in different groups. Pointing out the ways in which children are similar, even though they may look or act different, helps children identify qualities they can relate to and should reduce prejudice.

■ Help children recognize that their perspective may differ from those of others and that two different perspectives can both be valid. Children's acceptance of ethnic differences will be enhanced.

children's prejudice is reduced (Aboud, 1988; Black-Gutman & Hickson, 1996).

How Does Schooling Influence Children's Cognitive Development?

As children enter late childhood, schooling becomes a more and more important aspect of their intellectual (and social) life. Literally thousands of hours of a child's life are spent in the classroom. In addition to being influenced by what they do in the classroom, children are influenced by their schools' philosophies of education. Beliefs about the goals of education have varied; a strong emphasis on the basics in the early 1950s gave way to open classrooms in the 1960s, in which children explored and learned independently. Although the debate over teaching the basics versus encouraging thinking skills continues, some broad patterns can be identified. Trends in education today include an emphasis on making the child an active participant in the learning process and using child-relevant situations to teach thinking skills.

This teacher is demonstrating a science experiment. Describe some of the other ways in which teachers influence children's cognitive development.

Opportunities for Active Learning

Some teachers today, trained in the cognitive developmental theories of Piaget and Vygotsky, have adopted **constructivist theories of learning,** in which students are encouraged to actively participate in their own education. These teachers think of themselves as mentors for their students, encouraging them to discover and transform complex information for themselves (Paris, 2001; Steffe & Gale, 1995). Classroom environments that support children's autonomy improve academic performance as well as increasing children's sense of competence and self-esteem (Fry & Addington, 1984; Ryan & Grolnick, 1986). Research shows that constructivist approaches have been used effectively for teaching many different topics, including science (Neale, Smith, & Johnson, 1990) and reading (Rosenshine & Meister, 1997). The variety of techniques teachers use to encourage students to become actively involved with the material include the following (Slavin, 1997):

- In **cooperative learning,** students work together in groups to solve problems.
- In **discovery learning,** students are encouraged to discover principles for themselves.
- In **generative learning,** students are taught how to use specific methods of problem solving to integrate new information with preexisting information.

Multicultural and Multilingual Education

Schools are facing new challenges as they try to provide optimal educational experiences for the increasingly diverse students who are entering schools today. Educating children from various backgrounds will become an even more central issue in the future.

What is the best way to balance the educational issues of minority cultures with those of the larger culture? Some people believe that a focus on diversity may cause divisions among groups at a national level, whereas others assert that an emphasis on minority cultures will strengthen the national culture. The practices of educators mirror these different beliefs. Educational practices in the schools range from emphasizing minority cultures to focusing on human relationship skills.

The many definitions of **multicultural education** reflect the lack of agreement about how best to deal with a diverse population of students. Some definitions describe multicultural education as a curriculum that includes non-European perspectives—for instance, discussions of Latino authors and their works in an English class. Other, broader

constructivist theories of learning *educational approach in which students are encouraged to actively participate in their education*

cooperative learning *educational approach in which students work together in groups to solve problems*

discovery learning *educational approach that encourages students to discover principles for themselves*

generative learning *educational approach in which students are taught how to use specific methods of problem solving to integrate new information with preexisting information*

multicultural education *educational practices and curricula that present non-European perspectives or improve educational outcomes for students from a wide spectrum of backgrounds*

definitions suggest that multicultural education refers to policies and practices that improve educational outcomes for students from a wide spectrum of ethnic, religious, gender, and disability backgrounds (Banks, 1995; Banks & Banks, 1993). The types of programs using multicultural curricula vary considerably, and research efforts have been focused on assessing their effectiveness (Aboud & Levy, 2000; Bigler, 1999).

Some children have limited English proficiency (Hakuta & McLaughlin, 1996). By 2026, about 25 percent of children will come from families in which the primary language is not English (National Center for Education Statistics, 1998). What is the best way to help these children succeed in school? The issue of how to best educate students from diverse backgrounds with various language skills is especially a concern in the large US cities of Los Angeles, New York, Miami, and Atlanta. Consider, for instance, the question of whether immigrant children should take their classes in English or in their native language (see the Debating the Issue box).

Teachers' Bias in Achievement Expectations

Children differ from one another in many ways—sex, ethnicity, abilities, social class, and religion. Although in the ideal situation each child would receive equal attention and opportunities in school, this is not always the case.

When teachers are forming their ideas about each student in class, they use the students' own characteristics and sometimes rely on stereotypes to help them form impressions of girls' and boys' skills (Madon et al., 1998). Even in elementary school, teachers believe that boys possess greater scientific and math intellectual skills than girls do (Meece et al., 1982; Shepardson & Pizzini, 1992; Tiedemann, 2000). Teachers also have different ideas about what they consider undesirable classroom behavior for girls and boys (Borg, 1998).

Children's classroom performance is influenced by the general expectations teachers hold about their capabilities. Many studies have demonstrated that teachers have different expectations for and act differently toward students whom they believe to be high and low achievers, and one of the first was the classic study by Rosenthal and Jacobson (1968). For example, children who are expected to be high achievers are given more opportunities to participate in class and more time to respond. They also receive more praise for giving right answers and less criticism for giving wrong answers. Children who are not expected to perform well are given less opportunity to participate (Jussim, Madon, & Chatman, 1994; Kolb & Jussim, 1994). More recent research suggests that the influence of teachers' beliefs may be modest since the effects on student performance are relatively small; however, these effects tend to persist over a long time (Smith, Jussim, & Eccles, 1999). Also, these effects tend to be more pronounced for some children than for others: girls in mathematics appear to be more negatively influenced by low teacher expectations than girls in female-stereotypic classes (McKown & Weinsten, 2002).

Teachers behave differently toward boys than toward girls. In almost every way, boys receive more attention—both good and bad—from teachers. Teachers interact more frequently with boys than with girls (Ebbeck, 1984) and provide more feedback that serves to extend interactions with boys (Morse & Handley, 1985). Teachers interrupt girls more than boys (Hendrick & Stange, 1991). Boys receive more criticism from teachers than do girls. Boys are allowed to spend more time speaking in class than girls are, boys are permitted to call out answers more than girls are, and these effects are stronger in elementary school than in high school (Irvine, 1986; Meece, 1987; Sadker & Sadker, 1986; Wilkinson & Marrett, 1986). Are teachers more responsive to boys because boys volunteer more than girls? That does appear to be part of the answer: in elementary and middle school classes, girls and boys were equally likely to be called on when they volunteered (Altermatt, Jovanovic, & Perry, 1998).

Many teachers are not even aware of the preferential treatment they give to some children. This lack of awareness makes training in diversity and multicultural issues particularly important, to ensure that all children have equal opportunities for education.

DEBATING THE ISSUE

HOW SUCCESSFUL IS BILINGUAL EDUCATION?

 About 9 percent, or over 4 million children, enrolled in public schools have limited English language skills (Kindler, 2002). These children are at a disadvantage in academic achievement because they speak a language other than English in their homes, and the achievement gap for these students widens with age. By far, the largest group (about 77 percent) speaks Spanish, although children come from homes where many other languages are spoken, with Vietnamese and Hmong being the next largest groups. About one quarter of children end up in classes that teach only in English (Kindler, 2002).

Bilingual education consists of programs designed to teach English-language skills to children who have only limited proficiency in English. Educators agree about the need for bilingual education but do not agree on how to best accomplish it (Brisk, 1998; Greene, 1997; Greene, 1998; Krashen, 2000; McQuillan & Tse, 1996). One group of educators recommends that children be given training in English at an early age, usually by removing them from the classroom for special instruction (Lampert, 1984). These children then spend the remainder of their school day in regular classrooms, learning math and science in their non-native language (English). The advantage of this approach is that children receive early exposure to English, but the disadvantage is that children spend hours a day in classes in which they have difficulty understanding the language being used.

Another group of educators advocates conducting children's primary education in their native language— teaching them to read, write, and communicate effectively in that language before introducing them to English

(Willig, 1985). These educators believe that the skills children develop for thinking critically in their own language will easily translate into their new language (English). The advantage of this approach is that children do not fall behind in school because they receive instruction in all topics in their native language. The disadvantage is that these children are separated from other children for their schooling.

Research has demonstrated that high-quality bilingual education programs are effective (Brisk, 1998; Cummins, 2004; Greene, 1997) and enhance self-esteem in children (Wright & Taylor, 1995). Canadian studies suggest that bilingualism increases students' achievement in areas other than language (Bain & Yu, 1980). The type of program that is most beneficial to students remains unclear, however (Hakuta & McLaughlin, 1996). Some evidence suggests that children show good short-term gains from being trained early in English, but longer-term gains in academic ability seem to be promoted more by providing children with education in their native language (Willig, 1985). Furthermore, it is clear that it takes children four to seven years to become competent English speakers, but most programs involve only two to three years of training (Hakuta, Butler, & Witt, 2000; Hakuta & McLaughlin, 1996).

A complicating factor in bilingual education is the many different native languages that are represented in some school districts. For instance, 58 percent of California's school-age children are non-native English speakers. The large majority of these children are Spanish speaking, but more than 35 other languages also are represented, including (in order of their occurrence) Vietnamese, Filipino, Cantonese, Korean, Cambodian, Hmong, Mandarin, Lao, Armenian, Japan-

ese, and Farsi. There are not enough teachers available to teach this variety of languages in the California school system. Only in school districts with a large concentration of students from one or two language backgrounds is it possible to develop high-quality bilingual educational programs.

Bilingual education recently has come under attack. Critics contend that children are damaged by bilingual education because of their inability to learn English well enough (Rossell & Baker, 1996; Rothstein, 1998), although there is no foundation for this claim (Romaine, 1995). In response to these attacks, California passed a proposition that practically bans bilingual education in state schools, scrapping bilingual programs and replacing them with intensive one-year immersion courses (Cornwell, 1998). Experts argue that one year of English immersion is very unrealistic because it does not allow children enough time to learn English well enough to succeed in school (August & Hakuta, 1997; Hakuta et al., 2000).

THINKING IT THROUGH

1. What are the advantages and disadvantages of being educated in one's native language? What difficulties do schools face in trying to accomplish this?

2. Do you think that as the US population becomes more diverse, concerns about the effectiveness of bilingual education will increase? Why or why not?

3. Should all children in the United States learn to speak more than one language, as children in Europe do? Why or why not?

TABLE 12.2
The Numbers and Percentages of 0- to 21-Year-Olds with Disabilities, 2000

DISABILITY	INCIDENCE AMONG 0- TO 21-YEAR-OLDS	PERCENTAGE OF ALL DISABLED 0- TO 21-YEAR-OLDS	PERCENT INCREASE/ DECREASE IN INCIDENCE FROM 1990
Specific learning disabilities	2,789,000	46.1	3.1
Speech or language impairment	1,068,000	17.6	−14.2
Mental retardation	597,000	9.9	−11.6
Serious emotional disturbance	462,000	7.6	−7.3
Multiple disabilities	106,000	1.8	−1.1
Hearing impairments	70,000	1.2	0
Orthopedic impairments	69,000	1.1	10
Other health impairments	221,000	3.6	200
Visual impairments	26,000	.4	−20
Autism and brain injury*	67,000	1.1	1000
All disabilities	4,915,168	100	27.2

Source: Adapted from US Department of Education, 2000b.

What accommodations might be made to help this child receive a good educational experience in a regular classroom?

mainstreaming *inclusion of children with all sorts of disabilities in regular classrooms*

Unfortunately, few educators have become sensitized to the unequal treatment that children receive in the classroom (American Association of University Women, 1994).

Students with Special Needs

About 10 percent of the children in the educational system have special needs due to physical disabilities, emotional disturbances, or mental retardation (see Table 12.2). Most children with special needs are between the ages of 6 and 11 (46 percent) or 12 and 17 (41 percent) (US Department of Education, 2000). Another 5 percent have special needs because they are gifted or particularly talented. The educational needs of children vary, depending on their abilities.

Dramatic changes have occurred in the education of children with special needs over the past 25 years, largely due to the passage of Public Law 94–142, the Education for All Handicapped Children Act of 1975, and its extension, the Individuals with Disabilities Education Acts of 1990 and 1994. These bills state that every disabled child is entitled to a public education appropriate to the child's needs, at public expense.

One feature of this legislation that has had particular impact on educational practices is the mandate that children be educated in the least restrictive environment possible. Efforts to ensure that children spend as much time as possible in the "normal" academic environment have led to **mainstreaming**—including children with all sorts of disabilities in regular classrooms. For instance, a student with a disability might spend most of the day in a special class but attend one or two regular classes. Most schools do not integrate students with severe disabilities into regular classrooms, although there is a debate about the advantages and disadvantages of full inclusion of these students in regular classes. The advantages of full inclusion are the provision of a less restrictive learning environment for children with disabilities and the opportunity for all children to interact and become friends with children of varied abilities (Marks, 1997). The disadvantages are that the child with special needs may not receive adequate attention in the general education classroom, children with disabilities may become socially isolated, and teachers may not be prepared to work with these students (Kelly, 1992; Keogh & MacMillan, 1996).

Children with Physical Disabilities

Education for the child with physical disabilities must be tailored to meet the specific needs of the child. Some children require spaces accessible to wheelchairs but need no other assistance. Other children, such as those with cerebral palsy, may need someone to guide their fingers over a computer keyboard so that they can communicate because they have difficulties with speaking.

Children who are blind or deaf also have specific educational requirements. Until the 1970s, most blind and deaf children were educated in residential centers, but today most are educated in regular classrooms. Most commonly, blind children are provided with braille reading materials. However, many blind children can read print if it is enlarged sufficiently, in which case they can be educated more flexibly in regular classrooms than when only braille books can be used.

Children with Learning Disabilities

Learning disabilities are a group of neurological disorders that affect the brain's ability to receive, process, interpret, store, or respond to information. There are many different types of learning disabilities, and people vary tremendously in how much their schooling and daily living are affected by them. About 5 percent of US children—about 3 million—have a learning disability (US Department of Education, 2001).

Reading disabilities, such as **dyslexia,** are the most common type of learning disability. Dyslexia involves difficulties in processing language and is often noticed when children have serious difficulties in writing, reading, and spelling. A child who writes letters or words backward may have dyslexia. Although reading disabilities have been identified in children for many years, only in the past 10 to 15 years has solid evidence emerged about the nature of these disabilities and how to help children who have them.

Brain imaging studies show that brain functioning is different in children with dyslexia compared to normal-reading children. These differences are apparent in the parts of the brain that are activated during reading (Temple et al., 2001), and also in those that are activated during nonreading activities, suggesting that the processing limitations for children with dyslexia may be more widespread (Corina, Richards, Serafini, & Richards, 2001). At this point, it is difficult to interpret from the brain imaging studies the nature of the processing difficulties that underlie dyslexia (Pennington, 1999). Genetic studies suggest that no single gene is involved in dyslexia but rather a set of genes (Alarcon & DeFries, 1995; DeFries et al., 1997). Interventions to help children become better readers appear more effective for younger children and for those with less severe reading disabilities. For older children and those with more severe disabilities, interventions have resulted in mixed outcomes, although a combination of direct instruction and strategy training appears to be useful in improving reading abilities for these children (Lovett, Barron, & Benson, 2003).

If a child is suspected of having learning disabilities, do not try to wait it out; have the child evaluated as soon as possible, so interventions can be started early. A child who is being evaluated for learning disabilities will take an intelligence test to determine whether uneven patterns exist in the scores on the different components of IQ. Achievement tests may also be given to assess specific academic skills. Finally, a group of tests will be used to examine the child's processing abilities or disabilities. The results from these tests will be used to help design an intervention for the child. Depending on the level of difficulty the child has, different types of interventions may be tried and will likely include speech-language therapy to work on language disabilities. Parents and teachers can make additional modifications to help the child succeed. A teacher may change his or her teaching methods or use more variety in teaching to appeal to a broader range of abilities in the

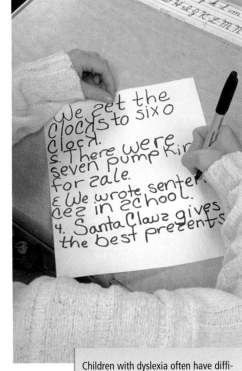

Children with dyslexia often have difficulty with reading and writing. In looking at this sample of writing, why might you suspect that the child could have dyslexia?

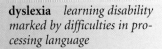

dyslexia *learning disability marked by difficulties in processing language*

child. Caregivers can help their children by providing quiet areas for reading, using audio-taped books, and buying large-print books.

Children with Attention-Deficit Hyperactivity Disorders

Eight-year-old Reese lives in a fast-moving world where sounds, images, and thoughts are constantly changing. He is easily bored and has difficulty keeping his mind on the tasks he needs to complete. He often is unable to sit still, plan ahead, or finish a task he has started, and sometimes he does not seem fully aware of what is going on around him. He tends to overreact, sometimes fighting with others who accidentally bump into him, and this has gotten him into trouble several times. Reese often loses things, and he seems to be careless and sloppy in his work and play.

The world that Reese lives in is shared by many other children. Reese has been diagnosed as having **attention-deficit hyperactivity disorder (ADHD)**, which is the most common mental disorder among children, affecting as many as 2 million American children. ADHD is marked by an inappropriately low level of attention and inappropriately high levels of impulsivity and activity. On the average, at least one child in every US classroom needs help for ADHD (Taylor, 1995). ADHD is diagnosed six times more often in boys than in girls (Arcia & Conners, 1998; Safer & Krager, 1994). Some children have attention deficit disorder without hyperactivity (ADD). These disorders can continue into adolescence and adulthood, causing a lifetime of frustration and pain.

In approximately half of the cases, onset of ADHD occurs before age 4. During the preschool years, caregivers notice that the child is very active and energetic (Taylor, 1995). Caregivers' complaints about a child's hyperactivity at age 3 are predictive of later childhood problems (Biederman et al., 1998).

In late childhood, the demands of school require prolonged attention every day. Some children cope with the transition well and meet the demands of school, even if they are still highly active and uncontrolled at home (Taylor, 1995). Other children, like Reese, who are inattentive and highly active, are at risk for failing to learn and for developing poor peer relationships (Greene et al., 2001). Because children with ADHD are likely to have problems in school, the disorder is frequently recognized when the child enters this environment.

As Reese's case shows, children with ADHD have difficulty staying on task and organizing and completing work. Their written work is often sloppy and characterized by impulsive, careless errors that result from not following directions or guessing without considering all the alternatives. Children with ADHD frequently do not seem to be listening to adults' instructions. Group situations and those that require sustained attention are the most difficult for these children (Jacobs, 1998).

Many children outgrow their hyperactivity after adolescence and escape later adjustment problems, but about one third continue to show attention problems into adulthood (Klein & Mannuzza, 1991). Those who continue to have problems with ADHD are also likely to have an explosive or immature personality (Barkley, Fischer, Edelbrock, & Smallish, 1990; Hechtman & Weiss, 1986).

ADHD can be difficult to accurately diagnose. Even pediatricians who treat children with ADHD find the diagnosis problematic (Kwasman, Tinsley, & Lepper, 1995). For ADHD to be diagnosed, a disturbance of at least six months' duration must occur prior to the age of 7, and at least eight symptoms must be present (see Table 12.3; American Psychiatric Association [APA], 2002). The challenge for pediatricians is to distinguish these characteristics from normal, age-appropriate attentional and active behaviors.

Scientists believe that biological factors influence ADHD. For example, brain imaging studies show that parts of the frontal lobe of the brain function at lower levels in children with ADHD, which in turn decreases their ability to inhibit their behavior and focus their attention (Castellanos, 1997). As a result, ADHD children are less able to regulate their activity in response to the demands of the situation (Barkley, 1997).

Evidence from several studies suggests a genetically inherited component to ADHD (Hewett et al., 1997; Quist & Kennedy, 2001). Consistent with the pattern expected in

attention-deficit hyperactivity disorder (ADHD) *a disorder marked by an inappropriately low level of attention and inappropriately high levels of impulsivity and activity*

TABLE 12.3
Characteristics of a Child with ADHD

Often fidgets with hands or feet or squirms in seat

Has difficulty remaining seated when required to do so

Is easily distracted by extraneous stimuli

Has difficulty awaiting a turn in game or group situations

Often blurts out answers to questions before they have been completed

Has difficulty following through on instructions from others

Has difficulty sustaining attention in tasks or play activities

Often shifts from one uncompleted activity to another

Has difficulty playing quietly

Often talks excessively

Often interrupts or intrudes on others

Often does not seem to listen to what is being said to him or her

Often loses things necessary for tasks or activities at school or home (toys, books, assignments, etc.)

Often engages in physically dangerous activities without considering the possible consequences

Source: American Psychiatric Association, 2002.

genetic disorders, if one monozygotic twin has ADHD, the other is likely to be hyperactive too; the same is not true of dizygotic twins (Nadder et al., 1998). Children who have ADHD usually have at least one close relative with the condition. At least one third of all fathers who had ADHD as a child have children with ADHD (Taylor, 1995).

Environmental factors involved in ADHD include poor maternal health during pregnancy, postmaturity (but *not* prematurity), long duration of labor, maternal use of alcohol and cigarettes, malnutrition during the first year of life, and chronic lead poisoning (Dulcan, 1989). These organic environmental factors affect the child's nervous system directly. Researchers also have identified various nonorganic environmental factors. For example, ADHD children are more common in families characterized by a considerable amount of hostility, either between parents or between parents and children (DuPaul, McGoey, Eckert, & VanBrakle, 2001; Lorys, Hynd, Lyytinen, & Hern, 1993). ADHD is associated with overstimulating, anxious, and intrusive styles of mothering, as well as with single-parent families (Carlson, Jacobvitz, & Sroufe, 1995; Jacobvitz & Sroufe, 1987). Furthermore, children with ADHD are more likely to come from families of low socioeconomic status (Pellegrini & Landers-Pott, 1996).

The most common way to treat many symptoms of ADHD is to use stimulant medications such as Ritalin. Parents naturally are concerned about having their young children take such strong medication. Many children begin treatment with Ritalin very early in life (Bowen, Fenton, & Rappaport, 1991), and parents often complain about the side effects (Pelham et al., 1999): insomnia, headaches, decreased appetite, nervousness, and sadness (Kwasman et al., 1995). Critics argue that many children who do not have true ADHD are medicated with Ritalin as a way to control their disruptive or simply active behavior (Taylor, 1995). Given these concerns, it becomes particularly important to consider what the research evidence shows about the effectiveness and the drawbacks of using medication to treat children with ADHD.

Do you think advertisers should try to convince parents that their children may need Ritalin to calm down? Decisions about whether a child should be given Ritalin require consultation with physicians, teachers, and parents, and the decision should not be made to simply calm down an active child.

High-quality medication treatment offers substantial benefits to those children who receive it (Jensen et al., 2001). When taking medication, children with ADHD become less negative and more responsive to parents; they also are less disruptive and impulsive in the classroom and when interacting with peers (Pelham et al., 1985; Whalen & Henker, 1991; Whalen et al., 1989). Medication also helps school performance; the children show improved attentional, writing, and learning skills (Dulcan, 1986; Pelham, Milich, & Walker, 1986).

These drugs, when properly supervised, are generally considered safe. Although they can be addictive to adolescents and adults if misused, these medications are not addictive to children and do not lead to later addiction. In fact, by reducing the negative experiences children with ADHD have with others in their environment, these drugs may actually help prevent later addictions (Taylor, 1995). These drugs do not make children "high," nor do they sedate them. Rather, they appear to help children control their hyperactivity, impulsiveness, and inattention.

There are drawbacks to these medications, however. It is difficult to predict how an individual child will respond to stimulants, so careful monitoring is required (Dulcan, 1989). Additionally, these medications appear to produce undesirable negative emotions such as sadness, depression, nervousness, and withdrawal in some children (Buhrmester et al., 1992). Because the medication alleviates the symptoms but does not cure ADHD, it is likely to be needed for a long time; about 80 percent of those who need medication as children also need it as adolescents, and about 50 percent continue to need it as adults (Taylor, 1995).

Like children on any medication, children on stimulants need to be monitored by a physician, and parents need to be informed about possible side effects. Generally speaking, the benefits of medication appear to outweigh the drawbacks (Greenhill, 2001).

Behavior management strategies, such as rewarding appropriate behavior and ignoring inappropriate behavior, also are effective strategies for dealing with ADHD, and they require the cooperation of parents and teachers (Dulcan, 1989). Diet therapies, such as restricting children's intake of food additives, have become popular, although the scientific evidence for their effectiveness is limited and complex (Breakey, 1997). Dietary treatments are most effective if there is direct evidence of an allergic disorder and changes in behavior associated with specific foods (Scahill & deGraft, 1997). For most children with ADHD, neither medication nor behavioral strategies alone are sufficient to normalize behavior and improve academic performance. Most professionals therefore use a combination of treatments for children with ADHD (Greene & Ablon, 2001).

Children with Mental Retardation

Even prior to the advent of IQ testing, many children were identified by their parents or teachers as having low levels of intellectual functioning, often because they did not adapt well to life's circumstances. IQ tests provide a means of classifying people according to degree of intellectual functioning. Used alone, however, IQ scores are not always highly predictive of adult functioning. For instance, some children with very low IQ scores have been quite successful in their daily living, usually because they have "street smarts" and a supportive environment (Kasari & Bauminger, 1998). Today **mental retardation** is defined broadly to include subaverage general intellectual functioning and impaired adaptive functioning, with onset during childhood (APA, 2002).

Four degrees of severity of intellectual impairment have been identified (see Table 12.4). A total of about 1 percent of the population falls into these categories, with more males than females being labeled as mentally retarded (APA, 2002). Mental retardation should not be considered a permanent feature of a person. Research has shown that many children labeled as mildly retarded "lose" their mental retardation as adults (Koegel & Edgerton, 1984). Some research suggests that even profoundly and severely retarded individuals can learn to live semi-independently, maintain employment, and develop social relationships (Mest, 1988).

mental retardation *condition characterized by subaverage general intellectual functioning and impaired adaptive functioning, with onset in childhood*

TABLE 12.4
Characteristics of Individuals with Various Degrees of Mental Retardation

DEGREE OF MENTAL RETARDATION	APPROXIMATE PERCENTAGE OF THE MENTALLY RETARDED	IQ SCORE	CHARACTERISTICS
Mild	85%	50–70	Acquire academic skills up to approximately sixth-grade level May become self-sufficient Can live successfully in the community
Moderate	10%	35–55	Acquire academic skills up to approximately second-grade level May be able to perform jobs, under supervision Adapt well to life in the community, but usually in supervised group homes
Severe	3–4%	20–40	Have limited academic skills May perform simple tasks, with close supervision Adapt well to life in the community, usually in group homes or with families
Profound	1–2%	Below 20 or 25	Require a highly structured environment with constant aid for optimal development Can perform simple tasks under close supervision May live in the community, in group homes, or with families

Source: American Psychiatric Association, 1994.

A leading known cause of mental retardation is very early prenatal events (30 percent), including exposure to teratogens (such as through maternal alcohol consumption). Environmental influences (such as lack of nurturance or cognitive stimulation) and other mental disorders (such as the onset of schizophrenia) account for many of the milder cases of mental retardation. About 10 percent of cases are due to genetic factors, such as Down syndrome, and health problems of childhood, such as lead poisoning and infections (Burack, Hodapp, & Zigler, 1998). The causes are unknown in about one third of the cases of mental retardation.

Today mentally retarded children are often integrated into general education classrooms, where they may receive specific step-by-step skill training, but these practices may not be the most effective. Research shows that it is more effective to teach these children cognitive skills, such as general problem-solving strategies and self-monitoring skills. Mentally retarded children have been taught, for instance, to use a specific strategy, apply it appropriately, and recognize the effort necessary to apply it. From these experiences, children learn how to behave in certain situations and grasp the importance of planning (Gordon, Saklofske, & Hildebrand, 1998). Other successful approaches are prevention directed, helping younger children who are at risk for being labeled mentally retarded. If these children learn adaptive strategies early, they may adapt more easily to school.

Gifted and Talented Children
Just as it is difficult to define *intelligence,* it is difficult to define *giftedness* (Gardner, 2000; Runco, 1997). The federal guidelines defining *giftedness* suggest that gifted children have outstanding abilities and need to have special programs and services beyond those that

TABLE 12.5

Students Enrolled in Regular Educational Programs and Gifted Programs

GROUP	PERCENTAGE OF GENERAL ENROLLMENT	PERCENTAGE OF ENROLLMENT IN GIFTED PROGRAMS
Caucasian Americans	71.2%	81.4 %
African Americans	16.2%	8.4 %
Latinos	9.1%	4.7 %
Asian Americans	2.5%	5.0 %

Source: Cohen, 1996.

This girl is considered a child prodigy. Why is it difficult for teachers to identify gifted children, and what kinds of programs should they receive in school to promote their skills?

acceleration programs *educational programs that encourage children to move rapidly through the usual coursework, compressing the time usually spent in each course*

enrichment programs *educational programs that encourage problem solving and creative activities through independent study or individualized instruction and mentoring*

most children receive. Gifted children may have a single ability or many, including general intellectual ability, specific academic aptitude, creative thinking, leadership ability, talents in the visual and performing arts, and motor skills (Keogh & MacMillan, 1996). For instance, Picasso possessed remarkable artistic talents even as a young child, but he was not a good student (Gardner, 1983).

Because teachers often identify children as gifted based on their school performance, they miss children who do not perform well in school or who are gifted in athletics, music, or performing arts. Some indication of these problems can be seen in Table 12.5, which compares the percentages of children from diverse backgrounds who are enrolled in gifted programs. Minority children are not included in gifted programs as often as Caucasian American children because of their tendency to come from disadvantaged backgrounds.

Gifted children are often bored and unchallenged by their school experiences. In some school districts, 60 percent of elementary school children scored above 80 percent on a test of the content of their math textbook *before* they had begun to use the book (Reis, 1989). If books present little or no challenge to the majority of students, it is clear that they will pose no challenge at all to gifted students.

Some gifted children attend special schools that focus on math and science or the arts. Other gifted children attend special classes in regular schools. The best kind of program for gifted children is still a matter of discussion and research. **Acceleration programs** encourage children to move rapidly through the usual coursework, compressing the time usually spent in each course. For instance, the Study of Mathematically Precocious Youth program speeds up the pace at which children learn mathematics so that they are taking advanced college-level math courses before they complete eighth grade (Stanley & Benbow, 1983). Acceleration programs have been very successful in increasing students' achievement and academic abilities.

In contrast, **enrichment programs** encourage problem solving and creative activities, often through independent study or programs with individualized instruction and mentoring (Renzulli, 1999). Children might be asked to conduct an extensive science project or to write a newspaper. The effects of these programs are less clear because the skills that children develop are difficult to assess (Keogh & MacMillan, 1996).

Children with Autism and Asperger Syndrome

Lawrence, the boy in the developmental mystery in the beginning of the chapter, is like many children with autism. He has difficulty communicating with others; he can repeat a well-practiced phrase, such as his name, but has great difficulty answering simple questions about topics such as what he likes to do. Autism is a developmental disorder of brain functioning. Children with autism have different symptoms that vary widely from child

TABLE 12.6
Symptoms of Autistic Disorders

COMMUNICATION SYMPTOMS	SOCIAL INTERACTION SYMPTOMS	BEHAVIOR SYMPTOMS
Delay in communication (e.g., not responding when spoken to)	Impairment in use of nonverbal behaviors (e.g., poor eye contact, not pointing out things of interest)	Preoccupation with one or more stereotypic patterns of interest (e.g., being obsessed with trains, collecting odd things, being hooked on certain TV shows)
Impaired ability to initiate or sustain a conversation with others (e.g., not knowing what to say to keep a conversation flowing)	Failure to develop peer relationships appropriate for age (e.g., unaware of presence of others or playing near but not interacting with other children)	Inflexible adherence to routines or rituals (e.g., insistence on sameness in ways toys are lined up or what is eaten for dinner)
Use of unusual vocabulary, echoing others' speech (e.g., repeating the same TV ad for hours)	Lack of spontaneous seeking to share enjoyment, interests, or achievements with others (e.g., not being excited when opening birthday presents)	Stereotyped or repetitive motor mannerisms (e.g., hand flapping, rocking, head rubbing)
Lack of make-believe play or appropriate social play (e.g., not being able to pretend to be cooking)	Lack of social give and take (e.g., not understanding that other people have feelings and can be hurt)	Persistent preoccupation with parts of objects (e.g., focus only on spinning wheels of toy car)

Source: American Psychiatric Association, 2000.

to child; they often include social difficulties, language delays, little or no evidence of imagination, and odd behaviors (see Table 12.6). Autism comprises a spectrum of disorders, ranging from very extreme symptoms to very mild ones. Children with autism vary in their intellectual level; about 75% of them are mentally retarded (Sigman & Capps, 1997). Other children with autism may be considered "high functioning," meaning that they suffer social and emotional problems but are not cognitively delayed and likely will develop fluent speech.

Asperger syndrome is a developmental disorder falling within the autistic spectrum. Like children with autism, children with Asperger syndrome have social difficulties but do not show significant delays in language or cognitive impairments; they often have impairments in fine and gross motor skills. There are similarities between high-functioning autistic children and children with Asperger syndrome, although the children with autism are more likely to have language delays and less likely to have motor development problems.

Most children with autism are diagnosed at age 3 or 4, although some are not diagnosed until age 12. Milder autistic disorders, such as Asperger syndrome, are often not noticed until a child starts school and his or her poor social skills become more obvious. The reported incidence of autism has been very difficult to determine since it varies widely, depending on a number of factors. Estimates range from about 1 in 500 to 1 in 1,000 cases diagnosed in the United States every year, and it occurs about three times more frequently in boys than in girls (NICHD, 2001). These figures are much higher than the earlier reports in the 1960s of 4 to 5 cases per 10,000 people, leading scientists to wonder whether an epidemic of autism is underway. There is no doubt that the number of cases has dramatically increased, but it is still unclear whether this is due to better diagnosis and reporting or to a real upsurge in the number of children who have this disorder (Fombonne, 2003).

Parents often report that they noticed unusual behavior in their child at around 18 months of age, but this reporting varies, often depending on the severity of the symptoms

(Baird, Cass, & Slonims, 2003). Research has demonstrated that children with autism can be identified from early videotapes of their behavior (e.g., lack of orienting to a person who says their name, lack of eye contact, engaging in repetitive behaviors; Osterling & Dawson, 1994). Certain indicators, such as no babbling or pointing by 12 months of age, no single words by 18 months, no two-word sentences by 24 months, and any loss of language signal that a child should be referred for further testing, but they are not absolute proof that autism is the problem. Early screening of behavior has yielded mixed results because there are many reasons that might explain these behaviors early in life (Baird et al., 2000). Some children with milder symptoms may not be identified until school age. Teachers should be aware of the symptoms that characterize children with autism at school age: abnormalities in language development, unusual vocabulary, inability to join in the play of other children, inappropriate behavior during play, difficulties in relating to adults, and lack of awareness of classroom norms (Le Couteur & Baird, 2003).

There are no specific biological tests, such as a blood test, for autism or Asperger syndrome; instead, diagnoses are made by observing the child's behavior, communication skills, and developmental progress. In a typical scenario, parents become concerned that their child does not seem normal; they go to the family physician, who may make an initial judgment that further evaluation is needed; and then a developmental pediatrician may be called upon to make the final evaluation. If autism is suspected, the specific needs of the child will be determined and appropriate support services will be determined. Many types of intervention have been used with children with autism, including behavioral training, using pictures for communication, exercise programs, social skills training, and speech and language therapy. The effectiveness of many of these treatments has not be determined. Nonetheless, many children with autism undergo a variety of therapeutic interventions, and some children show improvements over time (Baird et al., 2003).

Try It Out

1. Talk to a parent of a child who is learning to read. What are the caregivers doing to help the child? Do they express any concerns about how well their child is learning to read? What advice can you give to the caregivers to make reading easier and more enjoyable for their child?

2. Try some of the Piagetian tasks with an elementary school child. Does the child exhibit an understanding of conservation of liquid quantities but not more difficult types of conservation? Does the child show evidence of understanding seriation (see Figure 12.3)? Explain your answer.

3. Visit an elementary school during an art or music class. By simply watching or listening, can you identify children who appear to be particularly talented or creative? Ask the teacher for his or her definition of creativity in children, and find out what cues he or she uses to determine whether a child is particularly creative.

4. Talk to a child in elementary school about what she or he does in school, and try to determine the extent to which the child's teachers are using active thinking strategies. Does the child engage in projects that encompass several domains of learning (such as mathematics, language skills, and musical instruction)? What kind of reading instruction is stressed?

Key Terms and Concepts

acceleration programs (396)

attention-deficit hyperactivity disorder (ADHD) 392)

compensation (368)

constructivist theories of learning (387)

convergent thinking (376)

cooperative learning (387)
creativity (376)
discovery learning (387)
discrimination (385)
divergent thinking (376)
dyslexia (391)
emergent literacy (383)
enrichment programs (396)
generative learning (387)
mainstreaming (390)
mental retardation (394)

minimal distance principle (MDP) (380)
multicultural education (387)
phonics approach (383)
prejudice (385)
prodigies (376)
reversible thinking (365)
savants (376)
seriation (369)
social perspective taking (385)
whole language approach (383)

Sum It Up

How do school-age children think and solve problems?

- What must children be able to do in order to begin to solve conservation problems? (pp. 367–368)
- How do culture and community affect children's cognitive development? (p. 370)

What characteristics define children's intelligence and creativity?

- How is intelligence assessed? (p. 373)
- List and give an example of Gardner's eight frames of mind. (p. 375)

How do language and literacy develop during the school years?

- What two noteworthy changes in children's understanding of the pragmatics of language occur during the school years? (p. 381)

How do school-age children understand the social world?

- By what age do children begin to group people by ethnicity and race? (p. 385)

How does schooling influence children's cognitive development?

- List and describe the techniques teachers use to encourage students to become actively involved with schoolwork and learning. (p. 387)

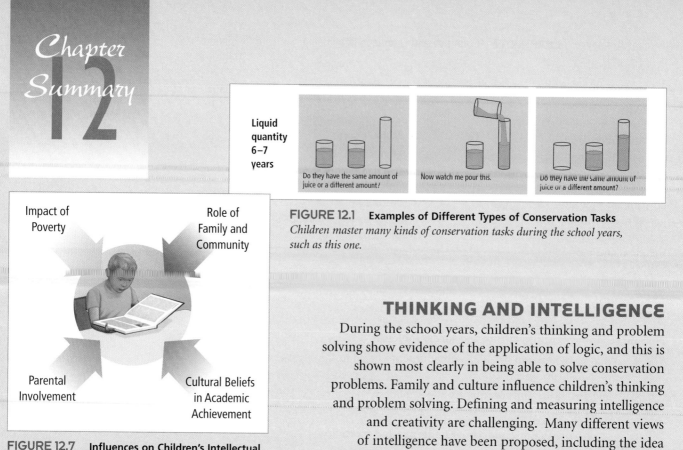

Liquid quantity 6–7 years

Do they have the same amount of juice or a different amount?

Now watch me pour this.

Do they have the same amount of juice or a different amount?

FIGURE 12.1 **Examples of Different Types of Conservation Tasks** *Children master many kinds of conservation tasks during the school years, such as this one.*

Impact of Poverty

Role of Family and Community

Parental Involvement

Cultural Beliefs in Academic Achievement

FIGURE 12.7 **Influences on Children's Intellectual Development** *Children vary in how quickly they learn to read.*

THINKING AND INTELLIGENCE

During the school years, children's thinking and problem solving show evidence of the application of logic, and this is shown most clearly in being able to solve conservation problems. Family and culture influence children's thinking and problem solving. Defining and measuring intelligence and creativity are challenging. Many different views of intelligence have been proposed, including the idea that there are multiple domains of intelligence. (Refer back to pages 367–379.)

LANGUAGE AND LITERACY

A major accomplishment for school-age children is learning to read. (Refer back to pages 379–383.)

What skills has this child mastered to enable her to read?

It's raining cats and dogs.

FIGURE 12.9 **Understanding Idioms** *Younger children and children who are new speakers of English have difficulty with idioms.*

4 year old   11 year old

English speaking children know the following about reading

- Words are read from left to right across the page
- Words continue from the extreme right on one line to the extreme left on the next line down
- Spaces between chunks of letters indicate words

3 year old   8 year old

FIGURE 12.10 **Changes in How Children Think About Others** *As children grow older, their views of others change from being very focused on external features (what other people look like) to focus more on psychological and internal characteristics (what other people act like).*

UNDERSTANDING THE SOCIAL WORLD

School-age children understand the internal and stable characteristics of personality and focus less on external appearances of others. (Refer back to pages 383–387.)

As children progress through the school years, they experience changes in their understanding of ethnic groups.

SCHOOLING AND COGNITIVE DEVELOPMENT

Children come to school with many different needs, and schools are required to provide an education that is suitable to those needs. (Refer back to pages 387–398.)

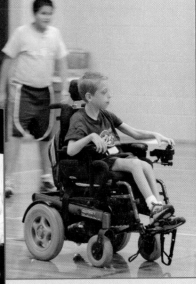

Children with special needs are guaranteed a free public education that is suitable to their needs.

TABLE 12.3
Characteristics of a Child with ADHD

Often fidgets with hands or feet or squirms in seat

Has difficulty remaining seated when required to do so

Is easily distracted by extraneous stimuli

Has difficulty awaiting a turn in game or group situations

Often blurts out answers to questions before they have been completed

Has difficulty following through on instructions from others

Has difficulty sustaining attention in tasks or play activities

Often shifts from one uncompleted activity to another

Has difficulty playing quietly

Often talks excessively

Often interrupts or intrudes on others

Often does not seem to listen to what is being said to him or her

Often loses things necessary for tasks or activities at school or home (toys, books, assignments, etc.)

Often engages in physically dangerous activities without considering the possible consequences

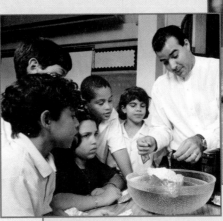

Many educators use student-centered activities to encourage children to think and solve problems rationally and creatively.

Social and Emotional Development in Late Childhood

13

Chapter Outline

How Do Children's Selves Develop During Late Childhood?
Erikson: Industry Versus Inferiority
Influences on Children's Perception of Self

How Do Emotions Develop During Late Childhood?
Fear and Anxiety in Late Childhood
Stress and Coping
Children's Responses to Community Violence

What Emotional and Psychological Disturbances Affect Children in Late Childhood?
Antisocial Behavior
Childhood Depression

What Changes Take Place in Moral Development During Late Childhood?
Piaget's Theory of Moral Development
Kohlberg's Theory of Moral Development
Culture and Morality
Gender and Morality

How Do Children's Family Relationships Change During Late Childhood?
Reduced Parent–Child Interaction
Reduced Parental Supervision
Increased Importance of Sibling Relationships
Only Children

What Factors Influence School-Age Children's Peer Relationships?
Peer Rejection
Bullying and Being Bullied
Development of Social Competence

How Does School Affect Social and Emotional Development in Late Childhood?
Influence of the School Environment
Influence of Teacher–Child Relationships

A DEVELOPMENTAL MYSTERY

Tom Burrell was just an ordinary 9-year-old boy—or so everyone thought. Then one day as he was walking to school with a group of classmates, everyone's view of Tom changed. In a canal that ran down the street toward the school, a young boy slipped and fell into the deep, rushing water. Unable to get out, he was being pulled down toward the drain. Many children were screaming or crying, and some were paralyzed with fear but not Tom. Sensing that something needed to be done, Tom jumped into the cold, rushing water and swam to the boy, grabbed him by the shirt, and pulled him to safety. Then someone noticed that the boy's dog also was trapped in the water. Tom again jumped in and rescued the dog.

The paramedics who arrived on scene were amazed that the young boy survived and gave all credit to Tom. When they heard that Tom also went back for the dog, they were even more amazed. When asked about becoming a hero, Tom said, "I knew something needed to be done. I didn't think about myself; I just wanted to help the boy and dog to be okay—so I jumped in there and tried to do something."

Several children witnessed the event—some older than Tom. Why was Tom the only one who acted and saved the day? What makes Tom different from the other children in this regard?

Tom's story is a mystery that is particularly applicable to late childhood, a distinctive period of development. Children assume new roles and acquire new capabilities that launch them into more complex and diverse environments, with increased expectations from adults. Many of these expectations revolve around children's behavior and adherence to social and moral standards. Tom's actions reflect the large individual differences in these competencies that are apparent during late childhood. Tom's reasoning about the situation reflects the more sophisticated social understanding that children develop at this time and the more advanced moral consciousness that becomes focused on the needs of others rather than strictly on one's own.

Late childhood also is the time when most children enter school, making new contacts with both older and younger children and a widening array of adults. The new environments and expanded interactions have major effects on children's social and emotional development. Most children meet these challenges with excitement and success, and some do so to an exceptional degree—like Tom. But some children become overwhelmed by these demands and changes—sometimes resulting in problem behaviors.

How Do Children's Selves Develop During Late Childhood?

Children's sense of self undergoes significant change during late childhood. For example, between 6 and 8 years of age, children begin to acknowledge that two traits or feelings can co-occur, but only sequentially; that is, one quality is initially experienced, followed by the other. By about age 8, children acknowledge that two opposing qualities of the self can exist simultaneously. However, at this age, children typically attach one quality to one situation and another quality to a different situation (such as "I'm smart in reading but dumb in math"). It is not until age 10 or later that children recognize simultaneous positive and negative qualities in the same situation—for instance, one can be both nice and mean to the same person or in the same situation (Harter, 1998). By late childhood, a child's self-concept reflects an understanding of enduring qualities and traits and is more accurate and realistic in its representations of the child and the child's characteristics (Schuster, Ruble, & Weinert, 1998).

FIGURE 13.1

Industry Versus Inferiority

Industry:
The pleasure she derives
from industry and success.

Inferiority:
The sense of failure that makes
her avoid opportunities for success.

Beginning around the time that children go to school, and
lasting until puberty, Erikson believed that children struggle with the psychosocial crisis of industry versus inferiority. Can you explain this crisis and the factors involved in
determining psychosocial development at this age?

Erikson: Industry Versus Inferiority

According to Erikson, beginning at around the time that children go to school, and lasting until puberty, children struggle
with the psychosocial crisis of industry versus inferiority.
Industry refers to the pleasure individuals derive in being
productive and successful. In contrast, **inferiority** refers to a
sense of failure that causes individuals to avoid opportunities
to succeed or makes them so nervous that their anxieties interfere with their ability to perform (Erikson, 1968; see Figure
13.1). Erikson argued that the primary task during this stage
was for a child to develop a capacity for industry while avoiding an excessive sense of inferiority. In the story at the beginning of this chapter, Tom's willingness to act heroically may
have resulted from his feelings of confidence and industry to
take control when the situation called for it.

This stage of Erikson's psychosocial development parallels Freud's latency stage—a time that Freud believed the
development of the children was quiet and dormant. But
Erickson did not think this was a rest period; children begin
school and must tame imagination and impulses and must
please others. During this stage, children begin to initiate projects, see them through to completion, and feel good about
what they have achieved. Children are learning to see the relation between perseverance and the pleasure of a job completed. Children have to learn to dedicate themselves to their
education and to learning the skills their social world requires
of them. During this time, teachers play an increased role in the child's development. If children are encouraged and reinforced for their initiative, they begin to feel industrious and
confident in their ability to achieve goals. If this initiative is not encouraged—if it is
restricted by parents or teachers—then the child begins to feel inferior, doubting his own
abilities.

Influences on Children's Perception of Self

How do children develop positive concepts and feelings about themselves? According to
research, children's self-concept and self-esteem are influenced by their family and peer
relationships, the environments in which they live, and some of their own characteristics
(Frome & Eccles, 1998).

Relationships with Caregivers and Peers

Children who have warm and secure relationships with their parents and other caregivers
generally have positive concepts and feelings about themselves. In contrast, children who
are rejected, overprotected, dominated, or neglected develop a negative self-concept and
low self-esteem (Kernis, Brown, & Brody, 2000; Mruk, 1999).

In addition, children with good peer relationships develop a positive self-concept and
positive self-esteem. Being accepted by peers affirms a sense of being liked. Having positive
peer relations also provides children with support and affection. In contrast, children who
are rejected by peers may develop doubts about being able to relate to others, which can
lead to low self-esteem, withdrawal, victimization, and aggression (Cordell, 1999; Egan &
Perry, 1998; Hartup, 1996).

Social and Cultural Conditions

How individuals view and feel about themselves is tied to the social and cultural conditions
in which they are raised (Miller, 2000; Watkins & Regmi, 1999). Children who are raised in

industry   *according to Kohlberg, pleasure derived from
being productive and successful*

inferiority   *according to
Kohlberg, a sense of failure that
causes performance anxiety*

stressful or threatening environments are at greater risk for developing a poor self-concept and low self-esteem. For example, as you learned in Chapter 1, children who live in poverty face a variety of stressors, such as violence, overcrowding, and inadequate nutrition, which do not affect more affluent children. These stressful conditions undermine individuals' sense of dignity, value, and self-worth. Conditions of abuse or neglect also damage children's self-esteem.

People in different cultures are strikingly different in how they see themselves (Raeff, 1997). For example, the North American representation of self is based on an appreciation of how one is different from others and the importance of asserting oneself. In contrast, the Japanese representation of self is based on fitting in with others and the importance of being connected with them (Markus & Kitayama, 1991). The factors that contribute to a positive self-concept and high self-esteem for North American children and Japanese children differ in accord with the cultural values and practices to which they are exposed. Japanese culture, for instance, values *suano*—a term used to describe the development of cooperation and the yielding of personal autonomy (White & LeVine, 1986). Unlike North Americans, the Japanese do not view *suano* as a sign of weakness; it is thought to reflect maturity, self-control, and healthy adaptation. For Japanese children, therefore, *suano* forms an important basis for self-concept and self-esteem. In Western cultures, however, independence and autonomy are highly valued. Consequently, the self-concepts and self-esteem of children in North America are determined in part by the degree to which the children reflect these characteristics (Markus & Kitayama, 1991).

Still, within North American cultures important differences exist among the values and practices of different subcultures (Frable, 1997). Various religious groups (such as the Quakers) and ethnic groups (such as Native Americans) explicitly value and promote interdependence to a greater extent than does the larger culture. In addition, children who live in small, rural communities are more likely to be exposed to values and practices that emphasize connectedness than are children growing up in larger metropolitan communities (Sampson, 1989).

Physical Appearance

Even at a young age, a person's physical appearance predicts self-esteem (Feingold, 1992). Individuals who are more physically attractive have higher levels of self-esteem than those who are less physically attractive, and this relationship is consistent throughout the life span (Harter, 1998). This correlation is just as high in special populations, such as the intellectually gifted and the learning disabled (Harter, 1993; Serketich & Dumas, 1997). Thus, from an early age, those who are judged to be attractive by societal standards receive more positive attention than do those judged to be less physically attractive. Young children are well aware of societal standards and incorporate them into their sense of self early in life.

The importance of physical appearance is first evident in infancy. Parents react to the physical appearance of their infants and toddlers, responding more positively to children who are more physically attractive (Langlois, 1981). During early childhood, girls and boys are equally satisfied with their appearance. Boys continue to evaluate their appearance positively as they move through the school years, but girls' evaluations begin to decline during elementary school (Harter, 1993). Girls' self-esteem also declines with age, and it becomes particularly low for those girls whose self-esteem hinges on their looks.

Society and the media place great importance on physical appearance at every age and for both sexes (Kilbourne, 1994; Wheeler & Kim, 1997). The standards are particularly narrow and rigid for women—emphasizing unrealistic ideals of thinness and desirable body characteristics (Henderson-King & Henderson-King, 1997). These standards are difficult for women and girls, even young girls, to live up to, and they create a situation in which females are likely to become dissatisfied with their physical appearance. In turn, their self-esteem may suffer.

FIGURE 13.2
Influences on Perception of Self

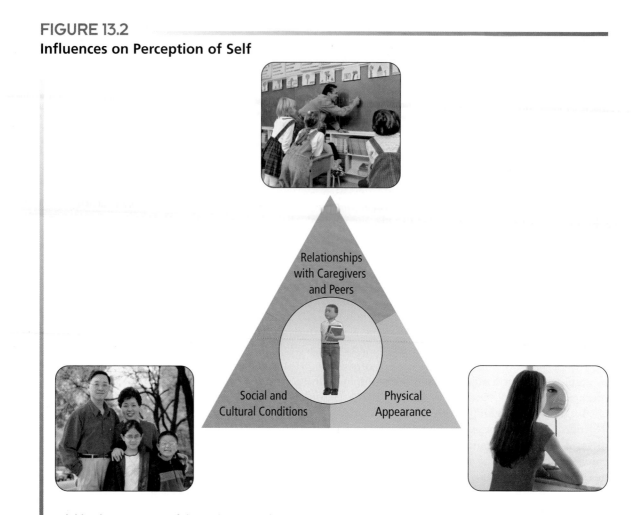

Children's perceptions of themselves are influenced by a variety of internal and external factors. Can you discuss the roles played by each factor identified in the figure in affecting how children come to see themselves?

How Do Emotions Develop During Late Childhood?

Eight-year-old Janet is a bright second-grader who is having problems. She cries every morning before going off to school, but if she is late for class, she also cries. She often is anxious, and she worries about what will happen to her at school. When she is called on in class, she gets nervous, stutters, and starts to cry. If the teacher marks something wrong on her math problems, she cries. She is afraid to talk to anyone or say anything during class. She feels as if she cannot cope with the stress of school and its demands. She is becoming more and more despondent and often is overwhelmed by sadness.

Janet's story reveals that children's emotional lives, as well as the environments that affect their emotional responses, become more complex and demanding during late childhood. Many school-age children have enhanced competencies and resources that they can call on to help them respond to these increased demands. Unfortunately, some children, like Janet, find themselves overwhelmed by their emotions and the demands made on them.

Fear and Anxiety in Late Childhood

As you can see in Janet's story, fear and anxiety become increasingly common in late childhood. This is not to say that these emotions are not apparent earlier in development, nor is it to say that fear and anxiety are typical of the emotional lives of most older children. But important developmental changes that take place in late childhood produce significant changes in the emotions of fear and anxiety.

Fear and anxiety evolved as warning signals and a way of mobilizing thought and action in response to psychological or physical dangers. Some causes of fear and anxiety are common to us all. Gray (1971) classified these as **innate fears**—fears that are inborn and reflexive. Innate fears are caused by intense stimuli (loud noises or severe pain), novelty (strange places and people), signals of danger (high places or darkness), and threatening or aggressive social interactions (Bowlby, 1973). Many day-to-day fears are extensions of these innate fears. Children's fear of ghosts or monsters, for example, may be an extension of the natural fear of darkness. Some fears are learned from others. For instance, children may come to fear snakes if their parents react fearfully toward snakes.

Fears that were common in infancy—such as fear of strangers or separation—decrease as children get older, whereas other fears increase. Classic studies of children's fears have shown that fear of animals, imaginary creatures, the dark, being left alone, death, and robbers all increase during the preschool years (Jersild & Holmes, 1935; Macfarlane, Allen, & Honzik, 1954). School-age children are less likely to fear imaginary things that look scary, but they are more likely to fear real-life events such as being attacked, being injured, or going on a roller coaster (Bauer, 1976). Between 7 and 8 years of age, as children master the concept of causality, they begin to fear things that might harm them. In addition, as children realize the importance of achievement and begin comparing themselves to others, they come to fear or worry about performing poorly or failing. Because school-age children tend to internalize negative experiences and information, their self-concept is more easily threatened than that of a younger child, leading to increased fear that their abilities are inadequate (Thompson, 1990). Throughout childhood, girls are more likely to express fear than boys are (Silverman, La Greca, & Wasserstein, 1995).

Using methods that tap brain functioning, researchers are now examining the brain processes involved in developing the regulation of fear and anxiety. These new techniques are opening new insights into the development of emotion regulation across late childhood. For example, Lewis and Steiben (2004) examined the brain waves of older children and found that certain amplitudes decreased with age and were related to the experience of anxiety. The researchers concluded that younger children spend more time and effort controlling their emotional responses in general, whereas older children focused their control of emotions more in anxiety-provoking situations. These findings are complex but confirm that across late childhood, children increasingly respond to fearful and anxious situations in more specific and controlled ways than do younger children. The findings also provide some evidence for a physiological basis (such as in the prefrontal cortex; Davidson, Putnam, & Larson, 2000) for the more apparent regulation of fear and anxiety during this period.

Older children are less fearful of things that look scary and increasingly become fearful about failing in their performance. Can you identify the developmental changes that contribute to this type of fear?

Stress and Coping

As Tom's story at the beginning of this chapter reveals, children respond differently to challenging situations. Fear and anxiety are just one type of emotional response to stress that children manifest. And how they respond to stressful situations has important consequences for their overall health, well-being, and development (Marriage & Cummins, 2004).

As children grow and change, their vulnerability to stress and the situations that produce it also changes. Events that cause stress in young children often appear innocuous to older children, and the situations that create stress in older children often leave young children unaffected. For example, young children may find being left alone overwhelmingly stressful, whereas older children generally do not. Older children, however, may become

innate fears   *fears that are inborn and reflexive*

Acculturative stress is associated with making a transition from one culture to another. What factors contribute to this type of stress?

stressed about an upcoming exam at school, whereas young children usually do not confront this kind of situation.

The ways in which older and younger children cope with stress also differ. Infants who are distressed by a loud noise may cope by crying out to elicit comfort and assistance from caregivers. Toddlers may cope with the fear of a stranger by clinging to their mother's skirt. Preschoolers may cope with a frightening scene on television by covering their eyes. And elementary school children may cope with the fear of performing in front of others during a recital by distracting themselves with thoughts of something pleasant.

Changes in Contexts That Cause Stress

Developmental changes in children's relations to their environments contribute to changes in the contexts that cause stress. Because infants rely on caregivers, it is not surprising that early forms of stress relate to issues of caregiver presence or absence (Gunnar & Brodersen, 1992). During the early preschool years, stress is more likely to be caused by caregivers' efforts to exercise discipline in order to get their children to obey and comply. During the late preschool years, children are more likely to come into contact with stressors that involve other children (Eisenberg, Fabes, & Guthrie, 1997; Naylor, Cowie, & del-Ray, 2001).

During late childhood, school increasingly becomes a source of stress (Skinner & Wellborn, 1997). Children in different countries perceive school as a source of trying and stressful experiences (Torsheim & Wold, 2001; Yamamoto, Soliman, Parsons, & Davies, 1987). The increased focus on intellectual skills, evaluation, and achievement elicits stressors—in the form of homework, tests, grades, and comparisons with classmates—that younger children do not face. School also is associated with increased stress related to peer relationships. Thus, the school context brings about changes in children's conceptions of themselves, in their relationships with peers and adults, and in the social situations in which they find themselves. Sometimes these changes disrupt the child's sense of well-being and consequently cause stress (Bryant, 1998).

Stress also may be produced when people move to a different culture (Myers & Rodriguez, 2003). The type of stress associated with making a transition from one culture to another is referred to as *acculturative stress* (Roysircar-Sodowsky & Maestas, 2000). When families immigrate to the United States, they often must learn a new language as well as adapt to new foods, traditions, and laws. Acculturation is a complex process of cultural adjustment that changes the conditions of one's life (Ager & Young, 2001). Because children have spent less time in their original culture, they acculturate faster than do their parents (Roysircar-Sodowsky & Maestas, 2002; Szapocznik & Kurtines, 1993). Although highly acculturated parents are likely to follow the parenting practices of their new culture (Dumka, Roosa, & Jackson, 1997), differences in rates of acculturation can lead to conflict within immigrant families, as parents and children develop conflicting cultural values and behaviors. Highly acculturated children may be critical of their less acculturated parents, seeing them as old-fashioned, traditional, and embarrassing (Gil, Vega, & Dimas, 1994). Thus, in addition to the demands placed on families and children when adapting to a new culture, familial differences in the degree of acculturation may represent a source of stress and conflict (Gil & Vega, 1996; Hovey, 2000).

Changes in Coping Skills

emotion-focused coping strategies *efforts to manage or reduce the emotional distress that is aroused in a stressful situation*

Older children's responses to stress are different from those of young children (see Figure 13.3). For example, older children are more likely to use **emotion-focused coping strategies**—efforts to manage or reduce the emotional distress (frustration, fear) that is aroused in stressful situations—than are younger children (Band & Weisz, 1988; Compas et al., 2001). Thinking of happy things and telling oneself that good things will come from the situation are examples of the emotion-focused coping strategies that increase over the

FIGURE 13.3
Developmental Changes in Stress and Coping

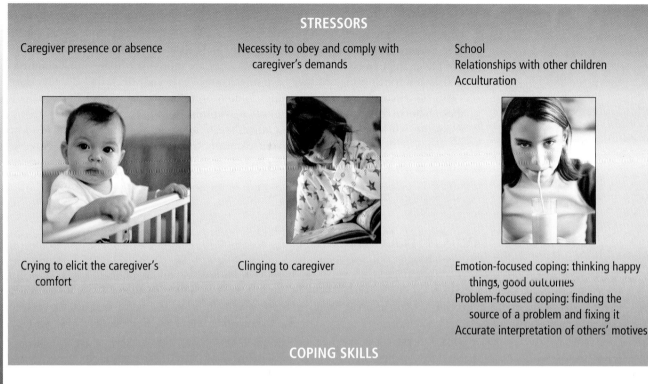

As children get older, the causes of stress change, as do the types of coping. Can you describe the factors that lead to such changes?

elementary school years. Because of their more advanced cognitive development, older children have a better understanding of stressful situations than young children do and can better use cognitive strategies (such as thinking of something pleasant) to cope with emotional distress (Eisenberg et al., 1997).

During late childhood, children also become more skilled in using **problem-focused coping strategies**—efforts to manage or modify the source of the stressful situation, such as finding a solution to the problem. As children develop better motor, communication, cognitive, and social skills, they are better able to effectively address and solve problems (Compas et al., 1999). Thus, when a child gets upset because his bicycle is broken, some children might try to fix the bike (problem-focused coping) whereas other children might try to distract themselves from the distress by watching television (emotion-focused coping). The degree to which these types of coping strategies are effective varies according to the individual child (can the child actually fix the broken bike?) and the context (is there something else that can be used to distract oneself?).

To cope effectively in situations involving other people, children need to understand the intentions of those involved. Understanding others' intentions is critical to developing a plan of action and interacting successfully with others (Kliewer, Fearnow, & Walton, 1998). Children who do not accurately interpret the intentions of others may cope ineffectively or inappropriately.

Research on aggressive children supports the importance of accurate interpretations of others' intentions. A child who interprets another's behavior as threatening and hostile is likely to respond aggressively, even when the other person's intentions are unclear (Crick, Grotpeter, & Bigbee, 2002; Dodge, 1991). For example, suppose two 9-year-olds, Ian and Mason, are playing on the school playground. Ian bumps into Mason, but Ian's intentions are unclear. Mason must decide whether or not Ian meant to hurt him. Mason concludes that Ian bumped into him on purpose, so he responds by pushing and hitting Ian. If Mason consistently makes this

problem-focused coping strategies *efforts to manage or modify the source of a stressful situation*

kind of interpretation, he will continue to respond to others in harmful ways. Some children are more likely than others to make inaccurate or inappropriate interpretations (MacBrayer, Milich, & Hundley, 2003). Children who have a tendency to interpret ambiguous behaviors as benign tend to be more prosocial than those who do not (Nelson & Crick, 1999). Generally, however, their advanced cognitive development and social experience permit school-age children to more accurately interpret the intentions and behaviors of other people.

Older children also cope better because they are more likely than young children to understand which situations they have some control over and which they do not (Harris, 1989). As discussed previously, young children overestimate their capabilities, including their ability to control situations. They often use problem-focused strategies in situations in which they will have little effect. These attempts can cause frustration; it is difficult to address the source of the problem when the source is uncontrollable. Older children are more likely to use coping strategies that accurately reflect the actual control they have in the situation.

NURTURING CHILDREN
HELPING CHILDREN COPE WITH DISASTER

On September 11, 2001, terrorists hijacked four US commercial aircraft and used three of them as missiles to attack the World Trade Center in New York and the Pentagon in Washington, DC. Thanks to the heroic efforts of passengers, the fourth aircraft was crashed in a rural area of Pennsylvania as terrorists prepared to target another site in Washington, DC. About 3,000 people lost their lives in the worst terrorist attack in history, and many more were affected by the aftermath of the ruin, destruction, and loss associated with these attacks. The media played the events of this day over and over, and many children were exposed to the intense emotions and reactions related to this attack.

Not surprisingly, children sense the anxiety and tension in adults around them. And, like adults, children experience the feelings of helplessness and lack of control that disaster-related stress can bring about. Unlike adults, however, children have little experience to help them place their current situation in perspective. How can parents and other concerned adults help children cope with such disasters? The following suggestions are adapted from the National Mental Health Association (2001).

Each child responds differently to a disaster, depending on his or her under-standing and maturity. It is easy to see how an event like that of September 11 can create a great deal of anxiety in children of all ages because they will interpret the disaster as a personal danger to themselves and those they care about. Whatever the child's age or relationship to the damage caused by the disaster, it's important that you be open about the consequences for your family and that you encourage the child to talk about it. Preschool children may show signs of anxiety in their behaviors. Behaviors such as bed-wetting, thumb sucking, baby talk, or a fear of sleeping alone may intensify or reappear in children who had previously outgrown them. Children may complain of stomachaches or headaches and be reluctant to go to school. It is important to remember that these children are not "being bad"—they are afraid. Children of this age need extra comfort and contact.

School-age children may ask many questions about the disaster. Be careful about providing false assurances—children of this age will know they are not true. Instead, remind children that they are safe now or that adults are working hard to make things safe. Remind children that disasters are very rare. Images of a disaster and the resulting damage are extremely frightening to children, so consider limiting the amount of media coverage they see. Do not be afraid to say "I don't know" to some of the questions children will have.

Adolescents can be encouraged to work out their concerns about a disaster. It is generally a good idea to talk about these issues, keeping the lines of communication open and remaining honest about the financial, physical, and emotional impact of the disaster on your family or on the community or nation. When adolescents are frightened, they may express their fear by acting out or regressing to habits they had when younger. Adolescents may turn to their friends for support. Encourage friends and families to get together and discuss the event to allay fears.

It is important for children to feel as safe and secure as possible in the face of upsetting events. Concrete supportive actions, such as collecting money or designing cards for victims, may be helpful. These activities focus children's attention and help teach them how to offer support in times of crisis. Caring and attentive adults can help children return to a normal routine that psychologically stabilizes the situation for them.

Resilience: Stress-Resistant Children

In any stressful situation, some children will come out relatively unscathed, whereas other children will be adversely affected. Several studies (Hetherington & Elmore, 2003; Nuechterlein, Phipps-Yonas, Driscoll, & Garmezy, 1990) have shown that children whose mothers had mental disorders (schizophrenia or depression) were at risk for problems with cognitive and social functioning. But equally important were the large numbers of children who showed little, if any, signs of problem behavior. These children were resistant to stress despite their mothers' mental disorders (Tebes, Kaufman, Adnopoz, & Racusin, 2001).

Findings such as these tell us that some children are more stress resistant than others. Stress-resistant children seem to have **resilience**—the capacity to bounce back or recover from stressful situations. Resilience reflects healthy functioning despite exposure to stressful events (Masten & Coatsworth, 1998; Reynolds, 1998).

Marian Radke-Yarrow and her colleagues (Radke-Yarrow & Sherman, 1990) studied children who cope well despite having been reared in chaotic and threatening conditions by a parent who was emotionally ill. Let's consider one of these resilient children.

Dominique is the second daughter in a family of four daughters. Her mother, who suffers from severe depression, supports her family through prostitution and welfare. Dominique's father appears intermittently in her life. He too suffers from depression and serious drug abuse. Dominique's mother, when not ill, is tough with her children. She yells at them much of the time and gets what she wants, even if she has to resort to physical violence. Dominique is healthy and sturdy and has been since birth. Her mother is proud of Dominique's health and appearance, spending hours keeping Dominique's hair stylishly braided.

Life in Dominique's family is very disorganized, with frequent moves, changes in caregivers, and limited opportunities to attend school. Despite these conditions, Dominique is curious, creative, outgoing, and charming. She also is doing well in school, and she reports being happy and unafraid. In essence, Dominique is surviving despite the chaotic environment in which she finds herself.

In Dominique's case, several factors protect her from the stressful and risky conditions in which she lives. Despite her mother's illness, Dominique has a warm relationship with her. Dominique's health and attractiveness are qualities that her mother values. Her mother prides herself on taking good care of her. Dominique also feels proud of her appearance and the fact that she can take care of herself when she needs to. Thus, Dominique has developed a positive self-concept and feelings of positive self-esteem. Dominique is popular with other children, and her teachers view her as independent and competent. This positive regard feeds back to her family life. It is a source of great joy to her mother, and Dominique receives praise for bringing home good school reports.

Resilient children like Dominique possess certain qualities that protect them and help them adapt to their stressful and demanding environments. These qualities also are valued by others. Other children possess qualities that lower their resilience. Recall from Chapter 7 that children who react more intensely and who are more temperamentally difficult, unpredictable, and moody also are less adaptable to stress than other children are (Carson & Bittner, 1994). In addition to being more vulnerable to stress, these children are viewed less positively by others than are children like Dominique.

Based on case studies like the one of Dominique, researchers have identified common characteristics of resilient children. Such children have above-average intelligence, possess attractive qualities that elicit positive responses in others, and have a positive place in the family (Henry, 2001; Masten & Coatsworth, 1998).

Children's Responses to Community Violence

Community violence is a major source of stress for many children (Garbarino, Hammond, Mercy, & Yung, 2004; Margolin & Gordis, 2004). In his book *There Are No Children Here*, Alex Kotlowitz (1991) tells the story of two boys growing up in an inner-city low-income housing project in Chicago. Lafeyette and Pharoah were 7 and 10 years of age when

resilience *the capacity to bounce back or recover from stressful situations*

TABLE 13.1
Common Characteristics of Resilient Children

RESILIENT CHILDREN GENERALLY . . .
Exhibit above-average intelligence
Possess attractive qualities that elicit positive responses in others
Have a positive place in their family

Kotlowitz began documenting their lives in a community filled with crime and violence. Kotlowitz (1991, p. 6) describes how Lafeyette and Pharoah often had to huddle on the floor of their tiny apartment as gunshots rang out nearby: "Pharoah shook with each gun pop, his eyes darting nervously from one end of the long hallway to the other. He clutched a garbage bag filled with aluminum cans he'd collected; his small body was curled up against the security of the cool concrete wall."

Children like Lafeyette and Pharoah face constant violence and danger in their neighborhoods. By some estimates (Berman, Silverman, & Kurtines, 2000), about 40 percent of the children in high-crime neighborhoods in US cities witness a homicide and more than two thirds witness a serious assault. Mothers in a housing project in Chicago identified shootings as their major safety concern for their children (Dubrow & Garbarino, 1989).

In war-torn countries such as Iraq, Israel, and Sudan, children regularly face traumatizing violence (Prinz & Feerick, 2003). For example, in Sarajevo during the war in the Balkans, where almost 25 percent of all children were wounded in the war, 97 percent of the children interviewed said they had experienced being shelled with bombs, 55 percent said they had been shot at by snipers, and 66 percent said they had been in situations where they thought they would die (UNICEF, 1993). In response to these conditions, 29 percent of the children in Sarajevo said they felt "unbearable sorrow" and 20 percent said they had constant terrifying dreams. In addition to the physical dangers, these children were confronted with other extremely adverse conditions—schools were destroyed, teachers were attacked and killed, food and water became scarce, and families were torn apart. Because of the violence, these children face both physical and psychological risks (Jones, Rrustemi, Shahini, & Uka, 2003).

How children respond to community violence depends on their developmental level (Straussner & Straussner, 1997). Because children's ability to control their environment is limited, safety is especially important to them (Garbarino, Dubrow, Kostelny, & Pardo, 1992; Myers-Walls, 2003). The younger the child, the more likely it is that safety issues are critical to her or his well-being (Garbarino, 1999). Children who experience traumatic violence prior to age 11 are three times more likely to have psychological problems (such as depression) than are children who experience such events after age 12 (Davidson & Smith, 1990). Children who experience traumatic violence and have been separated from their families (as is often the case for children in war-torn countries) are particularly susceptible to psychological impairment (Macksoud & Aber, 1996).

Older children also are vulnerable to community violence, but they respond to it differently than do younger children. Because of their increased ability to understand the dangerous situations they encounter, older children are more likely to recognize the significance of the events that take place around them. School-age children may become aggressive, as well as depressed, and may develop physical complaints, distortions in thought, and learning difficulties as a result of the violence they are exposed to (Garbarino et al., 1992; Henrich et al., 2004). They also may become increasingly distrustful of others. In Kotlowitz's (1991, p. 55) description of Lafeyette's response to the violent death of his friend, nicknamed Bird Leg, we see evidence of these kinds of responses:

> Bird Leg's funeral haunted him. He believed he had seen Bird Leg's spirit at a friend's apartment. "He was trying to tell us something," he told his mother. His face masked his troubles. It was a face without affect, without emotion. In Lafeyette it conveyed wariness. "I don't have friends," he told his mother. "Just associates. Friends you trust."

In the United States, exposure to community violence is greater for low-income children, who include a disproportionate number of minority children. According to one estimate (Gladstein, Slater-Rusonis, & Heald, 1992), 42 percent of inner-city African American children had seen someone shot, 25 percent had seen someone stabbed, and 23 percent had seen someone murdered. Latino and Native American children in the United States also are exposed to high rates of violence (Soriano, 1994; Yung & Hammond, 1994). For nonminority children, the percentages were half of those above.

One way to feel safe in a violent community is to identify with those who behave violently (Garbarino, 1999). Children growing up in violent communities often model themselves and their behavior on those individuals who cause the violence. In these communities, guns and knives are symbols of status, and their use often is positively reinforced (Bell, 1991). Exposure to violence puts children at risk of becoming violent themselves (Gorman-Smith & Tolan, 1998), feeding back into the cycle of community violence, victimization, and fear.

This picture depicts a funeral for a child. How does community violence undermine a child's sense of well-being? How might the responses of children exposed to urban violence relate to those of children in countries at war?

As discussed earlier, children can be quite resilient in the face of what appears to be overwhelming stress. But children's resilience is not unlimited. For many children, community violence may be "the last straw." Community violence can undermine children's development by providing constant reminders of their vulnerability and the inability of their families and communities to protect them (Milgram, 1998).

What Emotional and Psychological Disturbances Affect Children in Late Childhood?

Late childhood is a time when emotional and psychological problems often surface, especially in children who lack the skills necessary to cope with their increasingly demanding environments. For example, referrals for mental health services rise rapidly after the age of 5 (Zwaanswijk et al., 2003). School-age children's emotional and psychological problems become closely intertwined with their functioning in school, often interfering with their general educational development. Many of the emotional and psychological problems of adolescents and adults are direct outgrowths of disorders that appear during late childhood (Wallandar, Dekker, & Koot, 2003). Some of these problems may be self-correcting and need little intervention beyond that provided by parents or teachers. Others require professional help. Although a wide variety of emotional and psychological disturbances may occur, our discussion will focus on two of the most common problems: antisocial behavior and depression.

Antisocial Behavior

A pattern of behavior that is aggressive, defiant, uncooperative, irresponsible, or dishonest defines **antisocial behavior** (American Psychiatric Association, 2002). This pattern of behavior is disruptive to the individual, to his or her relationships, and to the community at large. Antisocial children often fail at school and are disliked by peers, teachers, and sometimes even their parents (Frick, 1998). Nearly half of all children referred to clinics for treatment are referred for antisocial behavior (Hinshaw & Lee, 2003). A history of antisocial behavior as a child is related to a wide array of adult mental health problems, including troubled marriages, failure at work, and crime (Dishion, French, & Patterson, 1995). Antisocial adults tend to rear antisocial children, thus perpetuating the cycle across generations (MacMillan, McMorris, & Krutschnitt, 2004; Steinhausen, Meier, & Angst, 1998).

Boys are much more likely than girls to be referred for treatment for antisocial behavior (Patterson, Reid, & Dishion, 1998), and this pattern has been found in a wide variety of cultures (Verhulst et al., 2003). This phenomenon may truly reflect higher rates of antisocial behavior in boys, or it may be due to biased perceptions—that is, these kinds of behaviors are expected more often among boys than among girls and therefore may be noticed more when boys display them. Gender differences in antisocial behavior become even more

antisocial behavior   *a pattern of behavior that is aggressive, defiant, uncooperative, irresponsible, and/or dishonest*

FIGURE 13.4
Progression of Antisocial Behaviors

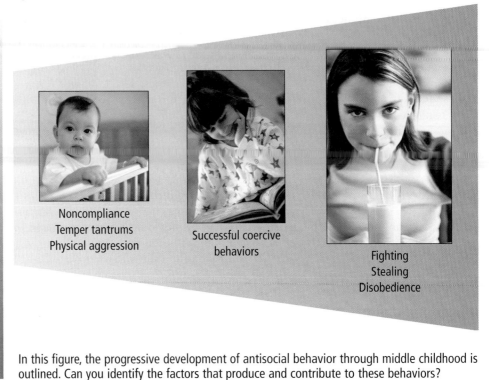

Noncompliance
Temper tantrums
Physical aggression

Successful coercive
behaviors

Fighting
Stealing
Disobedience

In this figure, the progressive development of antisocial behavior through middle childhood is outlined. Can you identify the factors that produce and contribute to these behaviors?

apparent during late childhood in settings that involve peer and school interactions (Sprague, Sugai, & Walker, 1998). For example, teachers generally find boys to be more antisocial than girls, although parents seldom report similar gender differences (Dishion & Andrews, 1996).

Antisocial children show a progression of coercive and aversive behaviors across childhood. As toddlers, antisocial children tend to be noncompliant, have frequent temper tantrums, and use physical aggression. As preschoolers, they continue to use these behaviors to coerce parents into letting them have their own way. When children use coercive behaviors to get their way and are successful, the antisocial behavior pattern is reinforced and maintained. School-age children extend their antisocial behavior into the school setting. Teachers report that these children often fight and steal and are disobedient (Patterson et al., 1998). Thus, over the course of a lifetime, antisocial behavior begins in the form of noncompliance with parental requests and frequent temper tantrums; progresses to fighting, stealing, and lying in late childhood; and culminates in noncompliance with authority and law in adolescence and adulthood (Bongers, Koot, van der Ende, & Verhulst, 2003).

Factors Affecting the Development of Antisocial Behavior

Diverse factors influence the development of antisocial behavior. The important influences can be grouped into four categories:

▧ *Biological factors:* Antisocial behavior is partially influenced by biological factors. Studies of identical twins reveal similar life-course patterns of antisocial behavior (Siminoff et al., 2004). However, the genetic component of antisocial behavior is demonstrated more clearly in adolescents and adults than in children (Plomin, Nitz, & Rowe, 1990). Studies also show that ADHD (see Chapter 12) and certain traits associated with a difficult temperament, such as impulsivity and irritability (see Chapter 7), are related to antisocial behavior patterns (Barkley, 1989; Schwartz, Snidman, & Kagan, 1996). Underlying these characteristics may be biochemical factors such as enzymes or neurotransmitters. Some researchers have proposed that antisocial children have an overactive reward system and an underactive inhibition system, resulting in impulsive and reward-seeking behavior (Fowles, 2003). Overactive reward systems and underactive inhibitory systems have been linked to the production of certain biochemicals, such as dopamine (Quay, 1988). However, in almost all of these studies, environmental factors such as the family have been identified as significant influences too (van der Valk, van den Oord, Verhulst, & Boomsma, 2003).

■ *Family factors:* Families contribute to children's antisocial behavior (Caspi et al., 2004; Patterson, 2002). Children who receive little parental supervision are more prone to antisocial behavior than are more closely supervised children, especially in high-risk urban neighborhoods (Shaw & Winslow, 1997). Antisocial behavior also is likely to be found in children who have few opportunities to engage in positive social interactions with parents (Snyder & Stoolmiller, 2002) and in children who observe physical spouse abuse (Jouriles et al., 1998). Having a parent who suffers from a mental illness is related to antisocial behavior too (Frick & Loney, 2002; Patterson et al., 1998); parents who are stressed, depressed, or antisocial generally use ineffective or inappropriate parenting practices, which contribute to antisocial behavior in their children (Brenner & Fox, 1998; Dadds & Salmon, 2003). Finally, children identified as insecurely attached are more prone to be antisocial if they come from high-risk backgrounds (Greenberg, Speltz, & DeKlyen, 1993).

■ *Peer relationships:* Experiences with peers promote antisocial behavior in three ways. First, children who have poor peer relationships are at risk for antisocial behavior because they lack positive experiences that help them learn how to control their antisocial impulses. Second, peers may act as models and reinforcers for antisocial behavior (Laird, Pettit, Dodge, & Bates, 1999). Third, antisocial children sometimes attract one another and form their own groups that then promote antisocial behavior (Granic & Dishion, 2003).

■ *Social milieu:* The degree to which children engage in antisocial behavior depends on their social environment. For example, antisocial behavior is more prevalent in urban than suburban areas and in low-income than middle-class neighborhoods (Crane, 1991). Moreover, the relationship between antisocial behavior and living in a stressful neighborhood increases over time because the stressful effects of such neighborhoods accumulate (Ingoldsby & Shaw, 2002). Elevated rates of antisocial behavior are found among minority children in the United States (Yung & Hammond, 1997), probably because they most often live in low-income urban areas (McLoyd, 1998b).

Treatments for Antisocial Behavior

Several forms of treatment have been developed for antisocial behavior. Some focus solely on the antisocial children, others on the family, and still others on the community. This diversity in emphasis reflects the fact that the treatment of antisocial children often requires the involvement of many people, including parents, peers, teachers, social workers, law enforcement officers, and judges. At present, no single treatment has been found to effectively address antisocial behavior problems (Lane, Beebe, Lambros, & Pierson, 2001). The difficulty of identifying a single effective treatment is due to the multiple causes of antisocial behaviors, representing a complex interplay of individual, family, peer, and societal factors (Reid & Eddy, 1997).

Treatment is more successful with children and families who are motivated to receive help. In many cases, however, the motivation is not there. The long-term treatment outcome for children with antisocial behavior problems also depends on the severity of the antisocial behavior. Children whose antisocial behavior is limited to minor or

FROM RESEARCH TO PRACTICE
HOW DO FAMILIES CONTRIBUTE TO CHILDREN'S ANTISOCIAL BEHAVIOR?

FROM RESEARCH . . .

Family interactions contribute to children's extreme aggression and antisocial behavior. Gerald Patterson (1982, 2002) proposed a model of family interaction to explain how children acquire these types of behaviors. Using social learning theory, Patterson came to the conclusion that the family interactions of antisocial children are different from those of typical children. He found that antisocial children are at least three times more likely than normal children to act aversively. Patterson determined that the problem can not be ascribed to the child alone but also to the way in which family members, particularly the parents, respond to the child. Based on his observations, Patterson described a model in which a cycle of coercive interactions takes place between parents and antisocial children.

In this cycle, aversive behavior is a characteristic of the whole family. Parents often respond to the aversive acts of the child with their own aversive acts, setting up an escalating cycle of retaliation and coercion. For example, a defiant boy may refuse to do his homework. In response to this defiance, the mother may scold and argue with the boy. In turn, the antisocial boy argues back and becomes increasingly brazen in his defiance. If the mother backs down at this point, the boy is negatively reinforced for such acts—his behavior is rewarded when the aversive situation ends because the mother backed down. This negative reinforcement—the mother stops her scolding—increases the chances the boy will use similar tactics in the future. Also, when the mother backs down from the argument, the aversive interaction ceases for her too. Thus, she also is negatively reinforced for giving in, which increases the chances that she will give in to her son's coercive attempts in the future, thereby setting the stage for the continuation of the cycle.

Having repeated this behavior thousands of times, children learn to use coercion to gain control over situations and eventually extend these behaviors to other people and other settings (Dishion et al., 1995). At the hub of this coercive cycle are the parents' inconsistent, harsh, and erratic attempts to set limits on their child. Often, families are not aware of this insidious cycle.

. . . TO PRACTICE

The coercive cycle in families can be changed. Patterson (1982) believes that intervention must include training to improve parents' skills at managing children's behavior. Parents are taught to recognize their role in the cycle and to respond more positively to children's good behavior. Training parents to use consistent, effective positive reinforcement, limit setting and supervision problem solving, and constructive communications has been found to be effective (Dishion & Kavanagh, 2003), although retraining is not easy and must involve the whole family.

THINKING IT THROUGH

1. According to Patterson's research, what pattern of behavior tends to develop between parents and their antisocial children? Describe this pattern using a concrete example.

2. What role does reinforcement play in Patterson's model?

3. Draw a diagram or flow chart based on Patterson's model that represents visually the coercive cycle by which children learn to use antisocial behaviors. At what points on your diagram could parents intervene to break the cycle?

isolated antisocial acts respond reasonably well to treatment. In contrast, children with severe and chronic antisocial problems do not respond positively to treatment (Graham, 1986). These findings highlight the importance of identifying ways to prevent antisocial behavior problems from developing (Capaldi, DeGarmo, Patterson, & Forgatch, 2002).

Childhood Depression

Childhood depression is a serious mental health problem; about 1 in 6 children experiences a depressive disorder at some time during childhood (National Institute of Mental Health [NIMH], 2000). Among young children, roughly equal numbers of boys and girls are classified as depressed. By the end of late childhood, however, girls outnumber boys 2 to 1 (NIMH, 2000). In the past 30 years, more children than ever before have been identified as depressed, and it is likely that there will be even more in the future as our ability to identify such children increases. To make matters worse, most depressed children do not receive treatment (Mufson & Moreau, 1997).

Childhood depressive disorders are conditions in which children display persistent negative moods and lack of pleasure in life. To be identified as clinically depressed, a child must exhibit four of the following eight symptoms on an almost daily basis (APA, 2002):

The child in this picture suffers from depression. Notice the sad and blank look on his face. What are some of the other signs of childhood depression? Can you identify some of the factors that contribute to the development of childhood depression?

- Significant weight loss or weight gain
- Insomnia (inability to sleep) or hypersomnia (oversleeping)
- Motor agitation or retardation
- Loss of interest or pleasure in usual activities
- Fatigue or loss of energy
- Feelings of worthlessness or excessive guilt
- Impairment in thinking or concentrating
- Reoccurring thoughts of suicide

Symptoms of depression vary with age. Because young children have difficulty with verbally expressing their feelings of depression, depression is more often inferred from their behavior, such as time spent crying or rocking, refusing food, or sleeping poorly. By the age of 6 or 7 years, children begin to describe their emotional state somewhat as adults do—they refer to themselves as being sad or miserable. By 7 or 8 years of age, depressed children experience a devalued view of themselves. Additionally, they may believe that their future holds little to be positive about—something young children have difficulty doing because of their focus on the here-and-now.

Although older children describe feelings of depression better than young children do, they may not admit to such feelings readily. Instead, they may display psychosomatic symptoms, especially headaches or stomachaches that result from emotional distress. They may complain of being bored or uninterested in activities. All children complain sometimes about being bored, but nondepressed children do so only when they have nothing to do. In contrast, depressed children are likely to say they are bored most of the time. Additionally, depressed children generally are not well engaged with school or with learning and thus have lower grades and academic achievement (Barrett & Waterfield, 1997). Depressed children may be irritable, withdrawn, and unable to cope with even minor frustrations. As a result, depression tends to be more prolonged and enduring in older children than in young children (Kashani, Rosenberg, & Reid, 1989).

Factors That Affect the Development of Childhood Depression

The causes of depression in children are not well understood, partly because childhood depression is not well defined and partly because we are just beginning to grasp its complexity. Despite these problems, the causes of depression can be grouped into three categories relating to biology, temperament, and social relationships.

 Genetic and biological factors: Several kinds of scientific evidence suggest that there is a genetic component to depression (Goodyear, 2001). Depressive symptoms are more common in children who have a history of depression in the family (Grabill, Griffith, & Kaslow, 2001; Puig-Antich et al., 1989). Additionally, the chance that a depressive disorder diagnosed in one twin is shared by the other was found to be about 50 percent for identical twins, compared to only about 25 percent for fraternal twins (Nurcombe, 1994). Other evidence points to the role of neurochemistry—the chemistry of the brain. Neurochemicals such as serotonin and norepinephrine have powerful effects on emotional states in adults and adolescents and are implicated in some types of childhood depression (Emslie, Weinberg, Kennard, & Kowatch, 1994).

FIGURE 13.5

Factors of Childhood Depression

Childhood depression is a serious problem and is produced by a variety of factors. This figure identifies some of these factors. Can you explain each and how it contributes to childhood depression?

■ *Temperament:* In the discussion of temperament in Chapter 7, you learned that some children are predisposed to react more intensely and with greater negative moods than others are. Thus, some children possess temperamental qualities that may predispose them to depression (Merikangas, Swendsen, Preisig, & Chazan, 1998). Children who are quiet and avoidant, slow to adapt to new situations, and prone to negative moods are likely to become depressed if they are stressed (Lengua, West, & Sandler, 1998; Thomas, Chess, & Birch, 1968). Children with difficult temperaments also are prone to feelings of hopelessness and low self-esteem (Bemporad, 1994).

■ *Family and social factors:* Children who are depressed often live in circumstances where they are undervalued or rejected. Parents who are emotionally unavailable to their children (perhaps because they themselves are depressed) or are critical and rejecting put their children at risk for depression (Nilzon & Palmerus, 1997). Children who are suffering abuse also are at risk for depression; however, children with a history of past abuse are no more likely to be depressed than are nonabused children (Kazdin, Moser, Colbus, & Bell, 1985). Children who have poor social skills and difficulty establishing meaningful relationships with others are prone to depression (Parker & Asher, 1987). Childhood depression also is associated with stressful life events, such as the loss of a parent (Goodyear, Kolvin, & Gatzanis, 1985). These findings suggest that depression in children often depends on the social situations in which they find themselves (Beardslee & Gladstone, 2001; Boyce et al., 1998).

Treatments for Childhood Depression

Most children with depression (about two thirds) improve substantially following treatment (Stark, Rouse, & Kurowski, 1994). Unfortunately, a significant number remain depressed for a considerable period of time. Treatment of childhood depression takes many forms, depending on the specific symptoms, the age of the child, and the cause of the depression. Reducing stressors that affect children can relieve their depression. Children who are depressed because of repeated failure at school may benefit from individualized instruction, tutoring, positive feedback, activities that promote peer acceptance and self-esteem, and counseling.

Antidepressant medications generally are used only for seriously depressed children and are only modestly effective (Wagner & Ambrosini, 2001). These medications were not developed for children, and there are few studies on their safe use with children. Many of these drugs have negative side effects such as nausea, dizziness, headache, and insomnia (Johnston & Fruehling, 1994). More recently, concern about increased suicides in children and teens has been noted (US Food and Drug Administration, 2004). These side effects were serious enough to lead the US Food and Drug Adminstration to advise manufacturers of antidepressants for children and teens to include a warning that alerts health care providers to the increased risk of suicidal thinking and behavior in children and adolescents being treated with these medications. Thus, children's use of antidepressants should be closely monitored by doctors and caregivers.

What Changes Take Place in Moral Development During Late Childhood?

A critical aspect of social and emotional development is the acquisition of moral values, intentions, and behaviors (Helwig & Turiel, 2002; Turiel, 1998). **Morality** is a set of principles or values that helps individuals distinguish right from wrong (Damon, 1988). Morality becomes a fundamental and important part of children's lives as soon as they start to develop relationships with others. Very early in life, children are aware of moral issues. As you learned in Chapter 10, young children and infants sometimes express concern about others' well-being and sometimes act prosocially. Young children also respond intensely

morality *a set of principles or values that helps individuals distinguish right from wrong*

when they feel their rights have been violated. Older children have an even more advanced understanding of fairness and justice, and they know that they are supposed to be responsible, honest, fair, kind, and cooperative to parents, siblings, teachers, friends, and strangers. Older children are also more capable of acting in moral ways as they are stronger, bigger, more independent, and more experienced than are younger children. Just consider Tom's story at the beginning of this chapter—had he been 3 years old instead of 9, it is unlikely he would have been motivated to accomplish his heroic feat!

Piaget's Theory of Moral Development

Although many theories address the issue of moral development (such as Freud's psychoanalytic concept of the superego; see Chapter 2), in recent years the cognitive developmental theories of Piaget and Kohlberg have been perhaps the most influential. Moral development provides an important example of the interconnectedness of developmental domains; advances in cognitive development and reasoning bring about important changes in how children interact with others and engage in moral behavior.

Piaget (1932/1965) based much of his theory of moral development on his observation and questioning of children as they played marbles. He believed that the essence of morality lies in respect for rules. While playing marbles, children must deal with issues of fairness, turn taking, reciprocity, and justice. By studying how children thought about and followed the rules of the marble game, Piaget believed he could discover the principles of moral development.

Piaget believed he could study the development of morality by observing children play games. How does children's game playing reflect their level of moral development?

Piaget's Stages of Moral Development

When preschoolers play a game, the point of the game is to have fun. They do not play systematically and do not have the intention to win. They make up their own rules and play the game according to whatever rules they like at the moment. Piaget labeled this stage of moral development the **premoral period**—the stage of moral development in which young children do not yet understand cooperative rules and goals associated with playing a game. Table 13.2 summarizes Piaget's stages of moral development and shows how children in these stages differ in terms of how they view rules, intentions, and punishment.

After age 5, children become concerned about playing by the rules and playing to win. During the period of concrete operations (between 6 and 10 years of age), children strictly adhere to rules—a stage of moral development that Piaget referred to as the **heteronomous morality stage.** Their moral decisions are based on the authority of others. Rules must be obeyed because they are sacred and unalterable. Any act that conforms to a rule is "good"; any act that does not conform is "bad." At this age, children have a sense of **moral realism**—judgments about morality are based on conforming to established rules set by powerful adults. Children between the ages of 6 and 10 react strongly to rule violations. Have you ever broken a rule in front of a child of this age, perhaps by jaywalking or parking in a no-parking zone? Even if you had a good reason for doing so, children in this stage often consider these actions to be wrong and react strongly.

In contrast to adolescents and adults, children between the ages of 6 and 10 years believe that right and wrong are determined by the consequences associated with an action. When an action results in positive consequences, it is "good"; when an action results in negative consequences, it is "bad," regardless of the intentions behind the action. Consider the following exchange between a kindergarten child and her teacher:

Katie: I told my dad the truth. I was fighting with my brother, and my dad came and said, "Who started this?" I said it happened by accident.
Teacher: Did your father believe you?
Katie: He really did.
Teacher: Was it an accident?
Katie: Kind of.
Teacher: Did you do it on purpose?
Katie: Yeah, but I didn't get yelled at. See, I told you it was an accident.

premoral period   *Piagetian stage of moral development in which young children do not yet understand cooperative rules and goals*

heteronomous morality stage   *Piagetian stage of moral development in which children adhere strictly to rules and base moral decisions on the authority of others*

moral realism   *the belief that morality is based on conforming to established rules set by powerful adults*

TABLE 13.2
Outline of Piaget's Stages of Moral Development

CONCEPT	PREMORAL PERIOD (BEFORE AGE 6)	HETERONOMOUS MORALITY STAGE (AGES 6 TO 10)	AUTONOMOUS MORALITY STAGE (AFTER AGE 10)
Adherence to rules	Have little concern for or awareness of rules Do not understand that rules are a cooperative agreement about how a game should be played	Obey rules because they are sacred and unchangeable Believe that being "right" means always following the rules Believe that rules are made by those who have absolute authority	Understand that rules are arbitrary social agreements that can be challenged or changed Understand that rules can be violated in the service of human needs
Intentionality	Are too egocentric to take others' intentions into account	Judge acts of goodness or badness in terms of the physical consequences and not the motivation behind them	Believe that morality is determined by one's intentions rather than the consequences of an act
Punishment	Act to avoid punishment and maximize rewards	Favor severe punishment regardless of the misdeed—punishment does not fit the crime Base judgments of good or bad on whether the act elicits punishment and how much punishment it elicits Think that misdeeds inevitably lead to punishment—immanent justice	Favor milder punishment if it helps the person see that her or his action was wrong Believe that punishment should fit the crime

Source: Adapted from Hoffman, 1970.

Because her father believed her and because she did not get yelled at, Katie defines her actions and intentions as truthful and moral. This is not the case for older children.

In his work with children, Piaget (1932/1965) relied on children's reasoning for information about the development of morality. For example, he asked children of different ages questions about the following two stories:

1. A little boy who is called John is in his room. He is called to dinner. He goes into the dining room. But behind the door there is a chair and on this chair there is a tray with 15 cups on it. John couldn't have known that all this was behind the door. He goes in, the door knocks against the tray, and the 15 cups fall to the floor and break!

2. Once there was a little boy named Henry. One day when his mother was out, he tried to get some jam out of the cupboard. He climbed up on a chair and stretched out his arm. But the jam was too high up and he couldn't reach it. While he was trying to get it, he knocked over a cup. The cup fell and broke on the floor!

In the first story, the child accidentally breaks 15 cups; in the second, the child breaks one cup in an attempt to sneak some jam while his mother is out. Who is naughtier?

Children in the heteronomous morality stage of moral development (between 6 and 10 years of age) answer that John is naughtier because he broke more cups. Their beliefs about morality are based on the consequences of the act. John broke more cups than Henry did. They do not take intentions into account. They believe that because John broke more cups than Henry did, he is likely to be punished more severely than Henry will be. Piaget referred to this belief of children in the stage of moral realism—that breaking a rule always leads to punishment—as **immanent justice.**

From the age of 11 years on, coinciding with the end of the concrete operational period (see Chapter 12), children's ideas about rules are no longer as rigid and constrained. Older

immanent justice   *the belief that breaking a rule always leads to punishment*

children's understanding of morality is based on the knowledge that rules can be changed if everybody agrees on the changes. Piaget refers to this stage of moral development, in which rules can be changed by the will of those involved in the game, as the **autonomous morality stage.**

Older children are likely to consider Henry to be the naughtier child because he was trying to sneak the jam. They take into account one's intentions and do not focus solely on the consequences of one's actions. Piaget argued that older children are more likely to believe that punishment should "fit the crime," whereas young children believe that punishment should always be severe, no matter what the misdeed might be. This more realistic view reflects children's increased flexibility and perspective taking as they move beyond concrete operational thinking and into formal operational thinking.

Evaluation of Piaget's Theory of Moral Development

The findings of several classic studies suggest that Piaget may have exaggerated young children's tendency to focus on *consequences* and overlook the *intentions* behind another's actions (Nelson-Le Gall, 1985; Schultz, Wright, & Schleifer, 1986). For example, even preschoolers evaluate a child who lied about a misdeed and got away with it more negatively than they do a child who told the truth and was punished for the misdeed (Bussey, 1992). Preschool children also judge a child who lied about a misdeed more negatively than they do a child who merely committed the misdeed. These findings are inconsistent with Piaget's belief that young children are moral realists. Because Piaget presented children with stories in which the information about the consequences of the actions was more obvious than the information about the children's intentions, young children tended to focus their attention on the information that was most obvious (Nelson, 1980). Young children have difficulty using subtle information about others' intentions, but when the intentions of another are made clear, they can and do use such information. By age 5, children understand that intentions and consequences are different kinds of information (Suber, 1982).

Although Piaget may have underestimated young children's ability to take into account the intentions of others, there is some support for his theory. For example, younger children's moral judgments depend on whether or not the misbehavior led to punishment. Children who were punished, regardless of whether they lied or told the truth, are more likely to be judged as bad than are children who behaved similarly but were not punished. In contrast, older children's judgments of goodness or badness are not influenced by whether the child was punished (Bussey, 1992).

Kohlberg's Theory of Moral Development

One theorist who was greatly influenced by Piaget and who contributed many new and important insights into the development of morality was Lawrence Kohlberg (1969, 1984). Kohlberg identified six stages of moral development, based on his interviews with children, adolescents, and adults. In these interviews, he presented moral dilemmas in which the respondent was required to choose between obeying a rule or law and taking some action that conflicted with the rule or law but served a need. Consider the following moral dilemma:

Judy was a 12-year-old girl. Her mother promised her that she could go to a special concert coming to their town if she saved up from baby-sitting and lunch money for a long time so she would have enough money to buy a ticket to the concert. She managed to save up the $5 the ticket cost plus another $3. But then her mother changed her mind and told Judy that she had to spend the money on new clothes for school. Judy was disappointed and decided to go to the concert anyway. She bought a ticket and told her mother that she had only been able to save $3. That Saturday she went to the performance and told her mother that she was spending the day with a friend. A week passed without her mother finding out. Judy then told her older sister, Louise, that she had gone to the performance and had lied to her mother about it. Louise wonders whether to tell their mother what Judy did. Should Louise, the older sister, tell

autonomous morality stage
Piagetian stage of moral development in which one believes that rules can be changed by the will of those involved

her mother that Judy had lied about the money or should she keep quiet? (Kohlberg, Colby, Gibbs, & Speicher-Dubin, 1978, p. 9)

Kohlberg was not interested in the specific answers respondents gave to the question—should Louise tell or not?—but instead focused on the reasons they gave to justify their answers to this moral dilemma. From his analysis of the reasons, Kohlberg identified three broad levels of moral development, with two stages at each level. These six stages are listed in Table 13.3, along with qualities that characterize each stage.

Kohlberg's Stages of Moral Development

At the first broad level of moral development, the **Preconventional Level,** morality is based on external forces. Children conform to rules to avoid punishment or to obtain personal rewards, and their reasoning reflects a belief that goodness or badness is determined by consequences. At the first stage within this level, *Punishment-and-Obedience Orientation,* obedience is valued for its own sake and the motivation for acting morally is to avoid punishment. Children have difficulty considering others' points of view. Actions are evaluated in terms of their physical consequences, such as the amount of damage done.

Here is an example of a stage 1 answer to the moral dilemma: "Louise should tell her mother about Judy's lie because if she doesn't, Louise is a liar." At this stage, Louise's telling her mother is justified based on the simple, or absolute, standard that not telling her mother would be a lie and Louise would be a liar if she did not tell. No reason is needed beyond the fact that it would be considered wrong not to do so. Children under age 10 typically are at this stage of moral development.

In stage 2 of this first level of moral development, *Instrumental-Purpose Orientation,* children believe that rules should be followed when it is in one's best interest to do so. Morality is based on serving one's own needs or interests. Children in stage 2 have some awareness of others' interests, but being right is considered only in relation to one's own needs.

Here is a typical stage 2 answer to the moral dilemma: "Louise should keep quiet because if she does, then Judy may keep quiet for Louise in the future." Louise's not telling is justified based on her self-interest and on an appreciation of the value of not telling their mom. Typically, stage 2 of moral development appears at age 13.

The next broad level of moral development is the **Conventional Level.** At this level, individuals strive to win praise and recognition for good conduct and for maintaining social order. Within this level, stage 3 morality—*Interpersonal Orientation*—reflects the belief that doing right is what pleases other people. Individuals are motivated to be seen by others as being nice and good. At this stage, individuals show more awareness of, and concern for, others' feelings and expectations than at earlier stages.

Here is an example of stage 3 reasoning: "Louise should not tell her mother about Judy's lie because telling would destroy Judy's trust and betray her confidence in Louise." According to this stage of moral development, Louise should not tell her mother because it is important that she maintain her relationship with her sister. The desire to be seen as being loyal and trustworthy is imperative. Stage 3 of moral development begins to appear in early adolescence (ages 13–14).

Stage 4 of moral development, *Social-Order-Maintenance Orientation,* reflects a belief that rules maintain the social order and that the social system will break down if people do not follow rules. At this stage, doing good involves following through on what you have agreed to do, for the good of the larger social system.

Here is an example of stage 4 reasoning: "Louise should not tell her mother because her mom promised Judy that she could use the money to go to the concert and her mom should keep her word. A promise should be sacred." This answer reflects concern about the promise that Judy's mother made to her. The mother is seen to have a duty, or obligation, to carry out her promise because society depends upon reliability and maintaining social contracts.

The third and highest broad level of moral development is the **Postconventional Level.** At this level, the individual is personally committed to a set of principles that are

Preconventional Level *first level of Kohlberg's theory of moral development, in which morality is based on external forces*

Conventional Level *second level of Kohlberg's theory of moral development, in which moral reasoning is based on winning praise and recognition for good conduct and maintaining the social order*

Postconventional Level *third level of Kohlberg's theory of moral development, in which judgments about morality are based on principles that the individual is personally committed to and that are shared by others*

TABLE 13.3
Kohlberg's Levels and Stages of Moral Development

	CONTENT OF STAGE		
STAGE	**WHAT IS RIGHT**	**REASONS FOR DOING RIGHT**	**SOCIAL PERSPECTIVE OF STAGE**
Preconventional Level			
Stage 1: Punishment-and-Obedience Orientation	Definitions of right and wrong are based on consequences. Rules should not be broken. Obedience is important for its own sake. Physical damage to persons and property should be avoided.	To avoid punishment Belief in the superiority of authority figures	Fails to consider others' points of view Cannot consider two points of view Considers actions in terms of their physical consequences
Stage 2: Instrumental-Purpose Orientation	Rules should be followed only when it is in one's immediate interest. Pragmatic reciprocity is the underlying principle: "You scratch my back; I'll scratch yours."	To serve one's own needs or interests	Is aware that others have interests they pursue and that these conflict Believes that being right is relative to one's needs
Conventional Level			
Stage 3: Interpersonal Orientation ("Good boy–Good girl" orientation)	Doing right is what pleases others. Being good means having good motives and showing concern about others. Being loyal, trustworthy, and respectful to others is important.	To be seen as a nice person by others To maintain rules and authority Belief in the Golden Rule	Is aware of shared feelings and expectations, which are more important than individual interests
Stage 4: Social-Order-Maintenance Orientation	One should conform to social rules in order to avoid disapproval by authorities. Doing good is fulfilling what one has agreed to do.	Belief that rules and law maintain the social order and are worth following To avoid breakdown in the system if rules are not followed	Takes the point of view of the larger social system Considers individual relations in terms of their place in the larger social system
Postconventional Level			
Stage 5: Social-Contract Orientation	Moral actions are usually those that reflect the will of the majority. Rules must be determined by democratic procedures and must be impartial. Some values must be upheld in any society, regardless of the majority opinion.	A sense of obligation to laws To uphold the social contract that protects all people's rights To do the greatest good for the greatest number of people	Is aware of values and rights prior to social contracts Recognizes that moral and legal points of view may conflict
Stage 6: Universal-Ethical-Principle Orientation*	Right and wrong are based on self-chosen ethical principles. Laws and social agreements are valid because they rest on such principles. When laws violate these principles, one should act in accordance with the principles rather than the laws. Principles are universal principles of justice: the equality of human rights and respect for others as individuals.	Belief in the validity of universal moral principles and a sense of personal commitment to them	Gives equal consideration to the rights of all human beings Has respect for the value and dignity of all people

*In later work, Kohlberg (1984) proposed that stage 6 is not distinguishable from stage 5 and suggested that the two be combined.

Source: Kohlberg, 1969; Rest, 1983.

shared with others but go beyond particular authority figures. Moral standards are internalized and become part of the individual. In stage 5, *Social-Contract Orientation,* moral actions are defined as those that reflect the will of the majority. Morality reflects a sense of obligation to uphold social laws and contracts that protect all people's rights. At this stage, individuals have an awareness of many points of view and have a desire to do the greatest good for the greatest number of people.

Here is an example of stage 5 reasoning: "Before you can say that Louise should tell her mother, you've got to consider the whole situation. Louise should respect her mother's point of view, but parents' expectations and rules should not violate what one believes to be right." Judgments about morality are no longer seen as black or white. Moral judgments focus on the obligation of each person and the recognition that everyone involved has rights.

The final stage of Kohlberg's theory of moral development is stage 6, *Universal-Ethical-Principle Orientation.* At this stage, right and wrong are based on self-chosen ethical principles. These are not concrete rules such as the Golden Rule, but rather are abstract moral principles of universal justice and respect for all individuals. When laws violate these moral principles, individuals should act in accordance with their principles rather than the law. At this stage, individuals consider the rights of all human beings.

Here is an example of the stage 6 level of reasoning: "One must always do what he or she thinks is right. If that means disobeying your parents, then so be it. Louise ought to do what she thinks a just person would do in this case, not do it just because of emotion or obligation." In this answer, the person recognizes that laws and social agreements are valid only because they rest on ethical principles. If a law violates these principles, one may disobey the law. Reasoning at this stage is based on universal principles and one's personal sense of commitment to them. Interestingly, none of Kohlberg's participants ever reached stage 6 (Kohlberg, 1981). Kohlberg described this stage as a "potential" stage and suggested that moral leaders such as Jesus, Gandhi, and Martin Luther King Jr. exemplify this level of moral reasoning. In later work, Kohlberg (1984) proposed that stage 6 is not distinguishable from stage 5 and suggested that the two be combined.

FIGURE 13.6

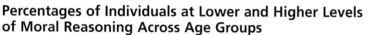

Percentages of Individuals at Lower and Higher Levels of Moral Reasoning Across Age Groups

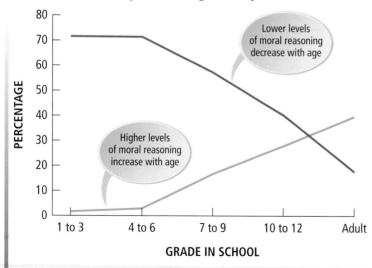

This figure shows that lower levels of moral reasoning decrease with age, whereas higher levels of moral reasoning increase with age. What factors might account for these changes? How do these data support Kohlberg's theory of moral development?

Source: Walker, 1989.

Evaluation of Kohlberg's Theory of Moral Development

Several longitudinal studies provide support for Kohlberg's stages (Colby, Kohlberg, Gibbs, & Lieberman, 1983; Walker, 1989). As children grow older, their level of moral development becomes more abstract and advanced. Figure 13.6 illustrates some of these findings. This figure depicts the percentages of children and adults who display lower levels of moral development (focus on consequences) and higher levels of moral development (emphasis on dignity and autonomy). As you can see, the percentage of individuals using lower-level reasoning decreases with age, whereas the percentage of individuals using higher-level reasoning increases with age (Walker, 1989).

Kohlberg argued that higher moral reasoning is based on a decline in egocentrism and an increase in perspective taking and abstract reasoning. As indicated in Table 13.3, children at the Preconventional Level show only a limited awareness of others' thoughts, needs, and intentions. Morality at the Conventional Level is characterized by an increased recognition of others' points of view, and moral reasoning at the Postconventional

Level is based on abstract principles and consideration of the rights of others. If Kohlberg was correct, there should be a correspondence between level of moral reasoning and cognitive development.

Formal tests of the relationship between level of moral reasoning and cognitive development generally support Kohlberg's theory—higher levels of cognitive development and role taking are related to higher levels of moral reasoning (Rest, 1983; Walker, 1988). But people with higher levels of cognitive development do not necessarily act more morally than those with lower levels of cognitive development (Blasi, 1983; Walker & Henning, 1997). Although a person in stage 5 will often act differently in moral situations than a person in stage 3 or 2, it is difficult to predict how that person will act based simply on knowledge of his or her level of moral reasoning, because other factors influence actual moral behavior. Moreover, at each stage there is considerable variability within an individual in the use of moral reasoning—individuals use moral concepts differently as they cycle through developmental and personal changes (Thoma & Rest, 1999).

Culture and Morality

According to Kohlberg, moral development was not learned by imitation or reinforcement. Nor did he believe that moral development was influenced by the specific content of the rules and laws of a culture. Rather, Kohlberg believed that morality was based on universal principles that developed in an invariant sequence, regardless of the culture in which a person was raised (Kohlberg, 1981).

Cross-cultural research provides evidence in support of Kohlberg's stages. Although stages 1 and 5 occur infrequently, stages 2, 3, and 4 can be found in many cultures (Eckensberger, 1994). Additionally, the sequence of stages is similar across different cultures (Snarey, 1985).

Moral themes, however, vary from culture to culture (Kahn, 1997). People in India, like people in many non-Western cultures, treat moral rules as part of the natural world. For example, Indian children consider violations of food customs more important than uncharitable behavior or stealing (Schweder, Mahapatra, & Miller, 1987). Violations of customs are serious moral offenses because they are considered to be as much a breach of natural moral principles as is an intentional act that harms someone. In contrast, American children view morality as a contract between people (Damon, 1988). Thus, Indian and American children have very different views of morality, and these cultural differences serve as a basis for differences in judgments about what is right and wrong.

Within American culture, there are differences in the moral values and orientations of different groups. For example, Mexican American children have a group orientation in which sharing, affiliation, and cooperation are highly valued moral qualities (Kagan, Knight, Martinez, & Santa, 1981). African American children generally focus on finding solutions to moral problems.

These differences in orientation influence how children respond to situations calling for moral judgments. In one study (Rotheram-Borus & Phinney, 1990), Mexican American and African American children were asked to identify what a person should do in certain moral situations, such as when someone asks for a loan, when someone is scolded by a teacher who is disappointed in that person, or when others are fighting. As you can see in Table 13.4, Mexican American children favored sharing money more often than African American children did. African American children were more inclined to stop a fight than were Mexican American children, who tended to feel bad or not want to get involved. After being scolded by a teacher, African American children favored apologizing more frequently than did Mexican American children, who were inclined to feel bad or angry. The differences generally are greater with age, perhaps reflecting the increased exposure older children have to the norms of their ethnic group (Rotheram-Borus & Phinney, 1990). Thus, moral development occurs as the result of the joint, reciprocal, and simultaneous influences of individual development and cultural socialization (Navaez, Getz, Rest, & Thoma, 1999).

TABLE 13.4
Children's Ideas of What Should Be Done in Different Moral Scenarios, by Ethnicity and Age

MORAL SCENARIO	THIRD-GRADERS		SIXTH-GRADERS	
	AFRICAN AMERICAN	MEXICAN AMERICAN	AFRICAN AMERICAN	MEXICAN AMERICAN
Asked to share money				
Share	24%	50%	76%	100%
Do not share	76%	50%	24%	0%
Scolded by teacher				
Apologize	28%	9%	62%	10%
Do something to change things	28%	18%	24%	14%
Feel bad	28%	36%	14%	67%
Get angry	16%	36%	0%	10%
Peers fighting				
Stop fight	48%	18%	62%	38%
Encourage fight	20%	23%	24%	10%
Feel bad	24%	45%	5%	24%
Do not get involved	8%	14%	10%	29%

Source: Rotheram-Borus and Phinney, 1990.

Gender and Morality

Carol Gilligan (1982, 1994) argued that just as people from different cultures vary in their ideas about morality, females and males differ in their moral judgments. Gilligan criticized Kohlberg's work based on two points. First, he studied only privileged, white men and boys. She felt that this caused a biased opinion against women. Secondly, in his stage theory of moral development, the male view of individual rights and rules was considered a higher stage than women's point of view of development in terms of its caring effect on human relationships. According to Gilligan, females rely on a morality of *caring* rather than of justice. The ethic of care is based on the assumption that people are not separate units with conflicting needs that require arbitration; rather, people are connected to one another. Based on an ethic of care, females place more emphasis on the maintenance of relationships, whereas males place more emphasis on law and order (Haste & Baddeley, 1991). These differences come from the sex-typed cultures in which males and females grow up (Skoe et al., 1999). In Gilligan's (1982) words, the sexes speak "in a different voice." Neither voice is louder or better; they are just different.

Generally, however, the scientific evidence does not support Gilligan's belief that males and females have different moral voices (Turiel, 1998). Although a few studies show gender differences in moral reasoning and show that girls are more likely to use an ethic of care than boys are (Skoe et al., 1993), the majority of studies do not find such differences (Walker, 1984, 1991). Even when differences are found, they are not consistent across boys and girls from different cultures or backgrounds (Skoe & Gooden, 1999). In addition, both boys and girls report more care reasoning when relationship issues are being discussed and more justice reasoning when nonrelationship issues (e.g., legal matters) are being discussed. Because women tend to report more relationship issues than do men, the greater care ethic used by women may be a result of the dilemmas they tend to face (Turiel, 1998). Thus, it appears that the ethics of justice and care are not in opposition to each other and that moral problems do not force a choice between them (Walker, 1995).

Although this gender debate is unsettled, Gilligan has raised interesting questions. She suggests, for example, that development may proceed along more than one line. One line of moral thought focuses on logic, justice, and social organization, the other on interpersonal relationships. If this is so, there is the possibility that these two lines at some point become integrated within each sex. Gilligan (1982) suggests that this integration is a major task of the adult years. Thus, despite the uncertain nature of the support for her model, Gilligan's work has contributed to an increased awareness that care is an integral component of moral reasoning.

How Do Children's Family Relationships Change During Late Childhood?

Although the family continues to play a significant role in school-age children's development, important changes take place that modify the nature of that role. The new abilities and competencies that develop during late childhood affect how children respond to their parents and how their parents respond to them. In a classic poll, when 7- and 10-year-old children were asked to identify the ten most important individuals in their lives, 80 percent included their mother and 79 percent included their father (Bryant, 1985). Siblings and other relatives also were important. Nonrelated peers appeared in the top 10 list 72 percent of the time, and 23 percent of the children identified at least one nonrelated adult in their top 10 list. This has changed little today—parents and other family members remain important figures in the lives of school-age children (Anderson & Cavallaro, 2002).

Reduced Parent–Child Interaction

As children enter late childhood, there is a decline in the amount of time they spend with their parents and in the amount of time their parents devote to them. Compared with parents of preschool-age children, parents of school-age children spend less than half as much time caring for, teaching, reading to, talking with, and playing with their children (Hill & Stafford, 1980).

Children's social interactions also change over the course of late childhood, becoming centered on activities that reach beyond the context of the family. Figure 13.7 displays the average number of hours per week that school-age children devote to different activities. As you can see, children spend a considerable amount of time involved in activities outside of the family—school, sports, and socializing. Children spend only about 30 minutes each week talking with family members (Hofferth & Sandberg, 2001). How the time is spent at home also changes. Older children spend more time studying, playing sports, and performing chores or housework, whereas young children spend more time playing and eating (Hofferth & Sandberg, 2001).

These changes reflect issues relevant to American and other Western cultures. In many non-Western societies, the period of late childhood is when children enter the workforce and begin contributing to the necessary functions of the family by assuming tasks such as caring for younger children or tending animals or crops. For example, in Kumasi, one of the leading market cities in central Ghana, it is common for 8- or 9-year-old children to participate in the local trade, selling goods on their own and contributing the proceeds to family needs (Clark, 1994). In societies like that of Kumasi, most of the issues that occupy Western parents and children are of little relevance.

Reduced Parental Supervision

Today's parents supervise their children less than parents did in the past. The decreased amount of supervision provided by parents comes at a cost. School-age children who are not well supervised by their parents are more likely to engage in antisocial and delinquent

FIGURE 13.7
How School-Aged Children (9–12 years) Spend Their Time

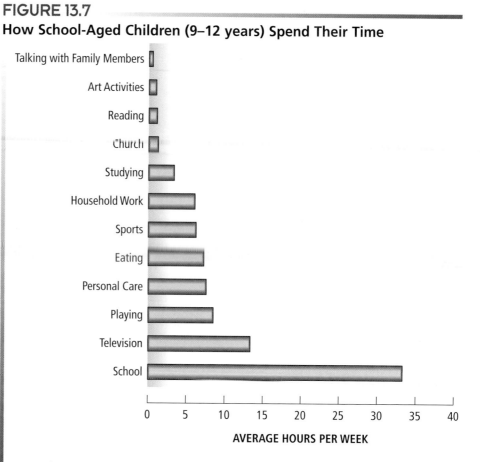

According to this figure, school and television account for a large part of school-age children's daily activities. How do the ways children spend their time change as they grow older? What factors account for those trends?

Source: Hofferth and Sandberg, 2001.

FIGURE 13.8
Labor Force Participation of Women: 1950–2001

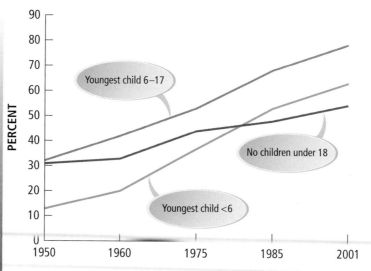

Notice the dramatic increase in labor force participation since 1950 for those women who have children. What changes have contributed to this increase?

Source: Hayghe, 1997; US Census Bureau, 2002.

behaviors than are children who are well supervised (Dishion et al., 1995). Adequate parental supervision deters such behaviors.

Economic conditions have contributed to the change in parental roles. Parental supervision has been reduced in part because of the increased participation of mothers in the paid workforce. Figure 13.8 illustrates how the number of women in the workforce grew between 1950 and 2001. As you can see in this figure, labor force participation by women is greatest among mothers of school-age children and has risen steadily since 1950. Although many families prefer to have a parent available to supervise children, few families can afford to forgo the additional income brought in when both parents work outside the home. Also, more women are now single mothers who must earn an income to provide for their children. And fewer families than in the past have access to extended family members who can provide after-school supervision. For these reasons, school-age children are increasingly likely to come home from school to a household where the mother and father are still at work.

The phrase **latchkey children** is used to describe children who are left unsupervised during the day or return home to an empty house after school. Each day, about 3.3 million school-age children in the United States are latchkey children (National Institute of Out-of-School Time, 2004). About 20 percent of 6- to 12-year-olds spend at least some time caring for themselves (Urban Institute, 2000).

Age is an important predictor of whether children are left to care for themselves. As you can see in Figure 13.9, as children get older, they are more likely to come home to an empty house. By the time a child reaches the teenage years, he or she is two to three times more likely to be a latchkey child than is a younger child, and this is particularly true for children whose mother works outside the home (US Census Bureau, 2002). Suburban children are about twice as likely to be latchkey children as are children living either in a city or a rural area. This may be because suburban parents feel safer in their neighborhoods or because they can rely on their neighbors to a greater extent than can people who live in cities or rural areas (Casper, Hawkins, & O' Connell, 1994).

Latchkey children are more likely than well-supervised children to be truant from school, feel stressed, receive poor grades, engage in risky behaviors, and use alcohol or tobacco (Dwyer et al., 1990). Such problems are particularly likely to arise when children are unsupervised and their parents do not know their whereabouts (Shulman et al., 1998). In contrast, enrollment in after-school care programs is associated with good grades and good peer relationships (Halpern, 1999). Thus, formal after-school care and supervision for children whose parents are not at home when they get out of school has the potential to protect children from possibly detrimental environments, particularly if the program is of high quality (Chung, de Kanter, & Stonehill, 2002; Noam, Miller, & Barry, 2002).

FIGURE 13.9
Percent of Children Who Are Latchkey Children, by Age

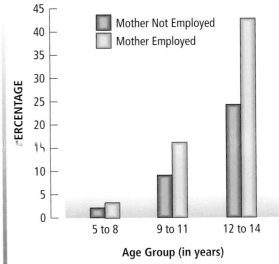

Notice the dramatic increase in the number of children older than 8 who are left alone after school, particularly for those children whose mothers are employed. What changes might contribute to parents' willingness to allow older children to take care of themselves after school? How does lack of supervision relate to children's behavior problems?

Increased Importance of Sibling Relationships

Not only do children's relationships with their parents begin to change during late childhood, but their relationships with their brothers and sisters also change during this time. By the time children enter school, those who have siblings spend considerably more time with them than they spend with their parents (Brody, 2004). According to one estimate, one third of siblings share a room, 25 percent share chores, and 50 percent report that playing with their siblings is a central activity (Bryant, 1982). During late childhood, siblings increasingly compare themselves to one another, and it is through these comparisons that

latchkey children *children who are left unsupervised during the day or return home to an empty house after school*

During late childhood, relationships between siblings change and become more important. Can you identify the reasons for this change?

siblings learn how they are different from one another. An age gap of 2 to 4 years heightens the differences between siblings (Dunn, 1983). Thus, sibling relationships provide children with opportunities to learn about themselves (Updegraff & Obeidallah, 1999).

Older siblings often take on some of the functions that parents serve, sometimes providing caretaking, comforting, and support (Brody, 2004). But does sibling caretaking substitute for parental caretaking? At least in the United States, the answer appears to be no. Sibling caretaking lacks the richness and complexity of the care provided by parents (Bryant, 1992). For instance, when children go to parents and to siblings to discuss emotionally stressful experiences, parents suggest more coping strategies than do siblings. Siblings may provide support or comfort, but it is not comparable to that provided by parents or other adult caregivers.

Only Children

Early in the twentieth century, the famous developmental psychologist G. Stanley Hall (see Chapter 1) was quoted as saying, "Being an only child is a disease in itself" (Fenton, 1928, p. 547). At that time, not having siblings was thought to be a type of social deprivation for children and was considered to have detrimental effects on their social development. The popular stereotype calls for an only child to be spoiled, insensitive, socially awkward, and egocentric. The research evidence, however, suggests that this belief is more popular myth than scientific fact (Richards & Goodman, 1996).

When findings from many studies were summarized, only children and children with siblings differed in just 2 out of 16 ways (Polit & Falbo, 1987). Only children scored higher than children with siblings on motivation to achieve and on self-esteem. Only children were just as likely as children with siblings to be resourceful, popular, self-reliant, and successful in their relationships as children and adults (Blake, 1989; Dawson, 1991). Despite G. Stanley Hall's concern about the detrimental effects of being an only child, there appear to be few differences between only children and those who have siblings (Falbo, 1992).

What Factors Influence School-Age Children's Peer Relationships?

With the increase in recent years in the number of working mothers and single-parent families, children today enter into peer groups earlier and for longer periods of time than their predecessors did. Peer relationships may therefore play a more important role today than in earlier times (Asher, 1990). The period of late childhood is a critical time for the development of these peer relationships. As you learned in Chapter 10, friendships become more stable and significant during late childhood, and children spend more time with their peers and friends. Most of this time is spent playing or socializing. As school-age children develop more advanced social, emotional, and cognitive skills, they become more adept at communicating with peers, understanding peers' behaviors and intentions, and coordinating their actions with those of others. Peer relationships also are important for children with disabilities, because they offer a context in which these children become valued members of a social circle (Salisbury & Palombaro, 1998). Thus, peer relationships represent important resources for children's successful adjustment (Ladd & Kochenderfer, 1998).

During late childhood, stable social groups emerge. By age 10 or 11, children report that most of their peer interactions take place in the context of these groups (Parker, Rubin, Price, & De Rosier, 1995). Although most children report being a member of a group, some do not, and those children who do not have good peer relationships are at risk for a variety of problem behaviors (Dodge et al., 2003; Rubin, Bukowski, & Parker, 1998).

Peer Rejection

Most children find interacting with peers rewarding and satisfying. Unfortunately, though, for some children, peer relationships are difficult, painful, and unsatisfying.

The number of children who have serious peer relationship problems during the school years varies, depending on the group that is assessed. In general, however, among average-achieving elementary school children, about 10 to 15 percent do not have any friends (Parker et al., 1995). But not all children who lack friends are the same. Two types of unpopular children have been identified. The first type is referred to as **rejected children**—those who are overtly disliked by their peers. The second type is referred to as **neglected children**—those who are reasonably well liked even though they lack friends. When children are asked to rate how much they like to play with other children, they like neglected children as much as they like most other children, but they do not like or want to play with rejected children (Asher, Rose, & Gabriel, 2001; Rubin et al., 1998). Rejected children are unpopular for long periods of time, and their status rarely changes. In contrast, neglected children's popularity and status may change from time to time or from situation to situation (Asher, 1990). Thus, rejected children have enduring difficulties in their peer relationships, whereas neglected children usually do not.

Additionally, rejected and neglected children have different emotional experiences with peers. Rejected children are more likely than neglected children to be lonely and feel victimized (McDougall, Hymel, Vaillancourt, & Mercer, 2001). When rejected and neglected children were asked if they would like to learn how to get along better with their peers, 48 percent of the rejected children said they would but only 16 percent of the neglected children said they would (Asher, Zelis, Parker, & Bruene, 1991). Rejected children are more isolated than neglected children are and therefore more emotionally distressed by poor peer relationships.

The research evidence suggests that certain behavioral, personality, and cognitive tendencies contribute to children's being rejected or neglected (Parker et al., 1995). For instance, rejected children are likely to be aggressive (Dodge et al., 2003), depressed (Little & Garber, 1995), and sometimes maltreated and abused at home (Bolger & Patterson, 2001). Neglected children have poor social skills and may be shy or withdrawn.

Based on such findings, it is clear that different strategies are needed to improve rejected and neglected children's peer relationships. For rejected children, an important aim of intervention is to reduce the aggressive and disruptive nature of their peer interactions (Waas & Graczyk, 1998). Roughly half of all rejected children are characterized as behaving in ways that interfere with the smooth functioning of the peer group (French, 1988). Altering the consequences for aggressive and disruptive behavior (such as removing any reinforcement received for such behaviors) and teaching self-control strategies (such as recognizing anger cues) can help rejected children generate more adaptive solutions to anger-arousing situations (Coie & Koeppl, 1990). For neglected children, helping them develop social skills that enhance the initiation and maintenance of peer interactions (such as teaching them effective skills for communicating) can improve their status among their peers (Mize & Ladd, 1990).

Bullying and Being Bullied

Paul was in the sixth grade, and it was his worst nightmare. He was teased about the way he looked and about his glasses. He was never invited to parties, ate lunch alone, and because no one spoke to him, he spoke to no one. In particular, a group of boys made fun of him, harassed him, used him as the target of their jokes, and threatened to "get" him almost every day after school. Paul remembers the sixth grade as the worst year of his life—afraid and anxious because of the bullies who tormented him.

Paul's story is sad but not unusual. Bullying is a problem at all levels of school, but it is an especially insidious problem during late childhood (Harris & Petrie, 2002). Late

rejected children *children who are overtly disliked by their peers*

neglected children *children who are reasonably well liked by their peers but lack friends*

Bullying at school is a significant problem for both boys and girls. Both bullies and their victims are at risk for poor adjustment. How does bullying affect the lives of bullies and their victims?

childhood is a time when children begin comparing themselves to others, learning what their strengths and weaknesses are, and growing increasingly concerned about what their peers think of them. When bullying occurs, as in Paul's case, it involves destructive and hurtful behaviors that can become insurmountable barriers to children in making positive connections with other students. Bullying and being victimized by bullies have been recognized as health problems for schoolchildren because of their association with a range of adjustment problems—such as poor mental health, violent behavior, and poor school performance (Juvonen, Graham, & Schuster, 2003).

Bullying is defined as aggressive behavior, repeated over time, that is intentionally harmful and occurs without provocation (Olweus, 1991). Bullying behaviors include not only physical aggression but also verbal harassment and public humiliation (such as name calling, spreading rumors, and ostracism; Olweus, 1978). Indeed, emotional and social bullying is a serious concern for children, and recent school shootings and violence suggest that it is not physical abuse by peers, but rather the inability to cope with social ridicule and rejection, that can fuel extreme outbursts of violence (CNN, 2002). For instance, the US Secret Service (2000) investigated characteristics of students involved in school shootings in the United States. Of the 37 different shootings investigated, 67 percent of the attackers said that they felt persecuted, bullied, threatened, attacked, or injured prior to the shooting.

Research on the degree to which boys and girls are bullied has been conducted in many different countries. In general, rates of bullying during elementary school vary from a low of 11 percent in Finland (Kumpulainen et al., 1998) to a high of almost 50 percent in Ireland (O'Moore & Kirkham, 2001). In a nationally representative study of older children in the United States, 13 percent were identified as bullies, 11 percent as victims, and 6 percent as bullies who also get bullied by others (Nansel et al., 2001). The highest rates of bullying occur in elementary school, with a steady decline as children get older. In general, more boys than girls bully others, and more boys than girls are victims of bullying (Olweus, 1996), although it depends on the type of bullying. For example, although boys are more likely to engage in physical bullying, gender differences in verbal or social bullying are less consistent (Espelage, Mebane, & Swearer, 2004).

Bullies and victims of bullying are both at risk for some adjustment problems (Dake, Price, & Telljohann, 2003). Bullies are likely to have behavior problems, perform poorly in school, and be more at risk for using cigarettes, alcohol, and drugs (Nansel et al., 2001). However, bullies often make friends easily and enjoy high social standing among their classmates, although classmates may not particularly want to spend time with them (Juvonen et al., 2003). It appears that the higher social prestige of bullies is due in part to the fear they induce in others. Regardless of the precise reason for their favorable social ranking, the high status poses a challenge for addressing bullying problems. When bullies are considered to be the "cool kids," it reinforces and encourages their behavior. Thus, those not involved in bullying may contribute to the problem.

Children who are victimized by bullies are more at risk for emotional and academic problems than are the bullies themselves. Bullied children have difficulty making friends, experience loneliness, and are anxious and depressed (Dake et al., 2003). Victims of bullying have been found to show increased rates of school absenteeism, physical health complaints, and feelings of hopelessness (Swearer, Grills, Haye, & Cary, 2004). Long-term studies of the effects of bullying indicate that even as adults, victims continue to feel angry and bitter about the bullying they suffered as children. Most said that they received no help at the time to stop the bullying. Compared to adults who did not experience bullying as children, adults who did experience it are more fearful of social relationships, are more likely to be loners, and have lower self-esteem (Kidscape, 1999). But the children who are most at risk from problems associated with bullying are those who both bully others and

bullying   *aggressive behavior, repeated over time, that is intentionally harmful and occurs without provocation*

DEBATING THE ISSUE

ARE SCHOOLS SAFE?

 Most Americans agree that schools should provide a safe environment for students. Feeling secure and safe enhances children's social and academic competence and increases their motivation to go to school. After the tragic events in 1999 at Columbine High School in Littleton, Colorado, it is clear that crime and victimization in the schools pose serious threats to students' and teachers' well-being. In the United States, an estimated 1.5 million violent crimes take place annually at schools (National Center for Education Statistics, 2004a). A large majority (71 percent) of students report having knowledge of someone's being bullied, physically attacked, or robbed at school, and more than half (56 percent) indicate that they witnessed such victimization (National Center for Education Statistics, 1995). In addition, most students (approximately 70 percent) report that drugs are easy to obtain at school (National Center for Education Statistics, 1998). In response to these kinds of statistics, most adults favor a zero-tolerance weapon and drug policy in schools (Gallup Organization, 1997), and such policies have reduced violence at schools. In fact, children are twice as likely to be victims of violent crime away from school than at school (National Center for Education Statistics, 2001b).

Attending school in an environment where disturbing and fearful events happen has an impact on students' sense of security. In one survey (National Center for Education Statistics, 2001b), worries about becoming a victim at school were found to be more common among middle and junior high school students (23 percent) than among senior high school students (16 percent). Threats of victimization and crime had motivated many students to develop strategies for avoiding harm. Students indicated that they took special routes to school, avoided certain parts of the school building or school grounds, stayed away from school-related events, stayed in groups while at school, or skipped school because they worried that someone might hurt or bother them. Minority children were more likely than nonminority children to indicate that they would stay away from school or school events to avoid being victimized. Although students develop coping strategies for dealing with victimization in school, this diverts energy that they could be using to play and learn.

THINKING IT THROUGH

1. How do children's concerns about their personal safety affect their motivation to attend school? What coping strategies do children develop to feel safe?

2. Did you feel safe in elementary school and junior high school? Recall events in which you were threatened or victimized by peers. How did these experiences affect you and your relationships with others? How did these experiences interfere with your schooling?

3. What do you think can be done to improve school safety?

---

are targets of bullying as well. These *bully-victims* seem to have the worst of both worlds—high levels of rejection, conduct problems, and school difficulties (Nansel et al., 2001). Victims who bully others also are at risk for future conduct problems and future violent and delinquent behavior (Juvonen et al., 2003).

These findings reveal the pervasive problems associated with bullying. And bullying does not affect just those directly involved. According to one national study of older children, 55 percent of children of ages 8 to 11 and 68 percent of those of ages 12 to 15 rated teasing and bullying as a big problem for people of their age (Kaiser Family Foundation, 2001). Effective intervention programs have been devised, but these must address change at the individual, group, and classroom level and must involve children, teachers, school officials, and parents (Olweus, Limber, & Mihalic, 1999). Based on existing research, the keys to a successful bullying prevention program include the following:

1. A commitment to changing the school norms with regard to bullying

2. Support from all adults for adopting comprehensive solutions

3. Recognizing that bullying prevention must be sustained and woven into the fabric of the school environment (Limber, 2004)

Development of Social Competence

The discussion of rejected, neglected, aggressive, and victimized children points out that some children are more skilled at being involved in social relationships with peers than others are. Popular children find it easy to make friends and influence playmates, manage conflicts, and make peers want to be with them. Other children lack these skills and as a result are isolated or excluded from peer relationships.

The term **social competence** refers to a child's ability to use age-appropriate social behaviors to enhance peer relationships without harming anyone (Schneider, 1993). Notice that this definition emphasizes that social competence is a developmental concept; what is socially competent at one stage of development may not be socially competent at another. Social competence is measured by the degree to which a child is accepted by his or her peers and the degree to which this acceptance is based on social behaviors that do not harm anyone. Teasing another child to gain the admiration of peers, for example, would not be considered a socially competent behavior because of the harm that is done to the child who is teased.

Social competence requires skills that foster smooth and satisfying interactions. Existing research demonstrates that socially competent children are skilled in at least four areas in which their less competent peers are not:

■ *Initiating social interactions:* Socially competent children initiate new relationships more gracefully than do less competent children. For example, socially competent children are adept at gaining entry into an existing peer group without being rejected (Rydell, Hagekull, & Bohlin, 1997). They integrate themselves into a group in ways that do not disrupt the ongoing activity (Dodge, Pettit, McClaskey, & Brown, 1986). Socially competent children also are more confident of their social skills and keep trying to make friends, even if they do not always succeed (Putallaz & Wasserman, 1990).

■ *Maintaining social interactions:* Once they form relationships, socially competent children are successful at maintaining them (Creasey, Jarvis, & Berk, 1998). They smile at, attend to, and comply with others more than do children who have less social competence. They also are more helpful and less aggressive than children with less social competence (Denham et al., 2001; Parker et al., 1995).

■ *Managing conflicts:* Socially competent children settle disputes effectively, without damaging their relationships. They are assertive but also recognize the importance of sharing and taking turns. In contrast, children low in social competence attempt to resolve conflicts with behaviors such as fighting, throwing a temper tantrum, or sulking and are less likely to suggest alternative ways of dealing with conflicts (Murphy & Eisenberg, 1996).

■ *Communicating for social purposes:* Socially competent children have well-developed communication skills (Farmer, 1997). They express themselves effectively and are good listeners. Because speech and language are important prerequisites of social competence, children with speech or language deficiencies or impairments often have low social competence (Rice, Hadley, & Alexander, 1993) and poor peer relations (Guralnick et al., 1996). Basic conversation and communication skills are necessary for initiating and maintaining positive social interactions with peers (Black & Hazen, 1990; Hadley & Schuele, 1995).

Children's social competence is influenced by a variety of factors. Children who are adaptable and positive and have well-regulated temperaments are more socially skilled than are children who are more temperamentally difficult (Eisenberg, Fabes, Guthrie, & Reiser, 2002). Children who have secure attachments with caregivers are more likely to form friendships and be popular with other children (Belsky & Fearon, 2002). In contrast, children whose parents are uninvolved and use harsh and inconsistent discipline tend to form insecure attachments and be low in social competence (Schmidt, Demulder, & Denham, 2002; Travillion & Snyder, 1993).

social competence *the ability to use age-appropriate social behaviors to enhance peer relationships without harming anyone*

FIGURE 13.10
Social Competence

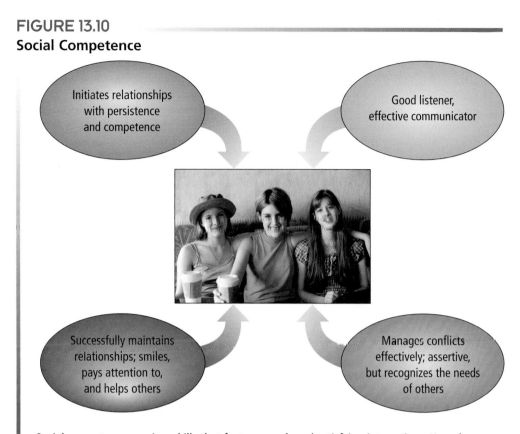

Social competence requires skills that foster smooth and satisfying interactions. How does social competence contribute to children's development and well-being?

Children who violate common expectations may be at risk for low popularity and low social competence. As you learned in Chapter 10, children generally play with same-sex peers, and violations of this pattern may have serious consequences for children. During late childhood, elaborate rules and rituals surround other-sex interaction. In general, contact with members of the other sex in public settings evokes negative reactions (Thorne, 2001; Thorne & Luria, 1986). Children often claim to be infected by the "germs" of the other sex (sometimes called *cooties*) and are teased for playing with someone of the other sex. Research shows that children who frequently cross gender boundaries in inappropriate ways have relatively low levels of social competence and are unpopular with peers (Sroufe, Bennett, Englund, & Urban, 1993).

The living conditions children experience influence their level of social competence. Children who are low in social competence are likely to experience adverse living conditions or to have experienced a negative life event recently (Hoglund & Leadbetter, 2004). Rejected children are likely to come from single-parent, low-income, unstimulating homes and are likely to have experienced stressful events in their families and schools. The more of these factors children experienced, the greater the chances that their social competence was adversely affected. For example, in one classic study (Patterson, Vaden, & Kupersmidt, 1991), the percentage of children who were rejected ranged from 18 percent of children who had no risk factors to almost 75 percent of those who experienced at least five risk factors. These findings point out that the stress of certain conditions and events can undermine children's social competence and their ability to form positive peer relationships.

How Does School Affect Social and Emotional Development in Late Childhood?

The most widely recognized function of school is to provide children with basic intellectual skills such as the ability to read, write, and do arithmetic. A less frequently discussed, but equally important, function is to further children's social and emotional development. Children must learn to cooperate with teachers and other children and to deal with a diverse population of peers (Ryan et al., 1995).

Influence of the School Environment

About 98 percent of children between the ages of 7 and 13 are enrolled in school, and this rate has held steady since the 1970s (National Center for Education Statistics, 2004b). Classes generally are organized with a single teacher, usually female, in charge of 20 to 30 same-age students. The total enrollment for many schools often exceeds several hundred children.

As indicated in Figure 13.11, the proportion of the school enrollment made up of ethnic minority students has increased. Thus, when children enter school today, they face an ethnically diverse environment, which provides both opportunities and challenges. Exposure to other children's personalities, values, behaviors, and customs requires new coping and interaction skills (Eisenberg et al., 1997). Because classmates tend to stay together from year to year, acceptance into the peer group becomes important, and not being accepted by one's schoolmates has negative consequences that can last for years (Parker et al., 1995).

The functioning and structure of the classroom affect children's emotional and social development. The classroom is generally task-oriented—daily classroom activities revolve around specific objectives. Preset performance standards are in place, and children's abilities to meet these standards vary. This structure focuses the attention of both the teacher and the students on differences in abilities and motivation, making competition and comparisons more likely than they were before children began school (Carlo et al., 1999). As you learned earlier in this chapter, the increased competition and focus on school performance sometimes cause fear and anxiety in children. But these pressures also produce feelings of pride and satisfaction when a school task is done well.

Children's responses to the increased demands of the school environment vary. Some children underestimate their school abilities, and they may undermine their own achievement by limiting their efforts in school, avoiding schoolwork, and spending extra time in other activities (such as music or sports). Focusing on nonacademic activities helps some children maintain a positive sense of self-worth (Paris & Cunningham, 1996). Other students, however, generalize their low perceptions of competence to other areas of achievement and may drop out or engage in antisocial behavior. Parents and teachers can unwittingly

FIGURE 13.11

School Enrollments of Children 5- to 17-Years-Old, by Ethnicity

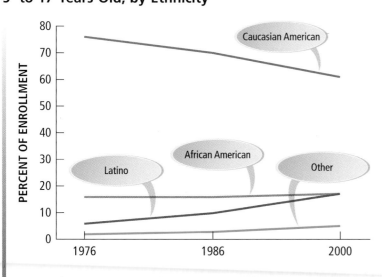

Notice the increase in the school enrollments of ethnic minorities. What changes account for these increases? What impact might these increases have on schools?

Source: Adapted from US Department of Education, 2002.

contribute to children's low perceptions of competence by over-emphasizing grades, achievement, and social comparisons as a basis for self-worth (Covington, 1992).

Other children form a different kind of school-related mis-perception about themselves: despite low or merely average school achievement, they have an extremely positive view of their school competence. This pattern appears in some inner-city minority students who have positive views of their competence and achievement even though they make low test grades (Stevenson et al., 1990). Such "illusions of competence" may result from unchallenging curricula or inflated praise by teachers and parents. Children with optimistic illusions may reduce their efforts and thereby lower their future achievement. Students who have an excessively pessimistic or optimistic view of their own competence, as a result of their experiences in school, may not invest appropriate effort in academic work and may have difficulty dealing with feedback that is not consistent with their perceptions of themselves (Paris & Cunningham, 1996).

In addition to helping students with their coursework, how can teachers promote children's learning? What factors influence how teachers respond to different children?

With age, children's understanding of school becomes more complex and complete (Buchanan-Barrow & Barrett, 1998). As they acquire a better understanding of school and its demands, they also learn a great deal about self-control. To become effective students, children must plan, evaluate, monitor, and revise their actions as they adapt to the demands of the school environment. Children who cannot or do not make these adjustments are at risk for poor school outcomes (Nicholls, 1992).

Influence of Teacher–Child Relationships

Teachers act as role models, caregivers, and mentors for children. Relationships between teachers and children have important effects on children's social and emotional development and their adaptation to the school environment. For example, children who have warm, secure, and positive relationships with teachers are more cognitively and socially competent (Howes, Matheson, & Hamilton, 1994; Tucker et al., 2002)—and the reverse is true as well; poor teacher–child relationships are predictive of behavior problems (Henricsson & Rydell, 2004). In addition, the quality of teacher–child relationships predicts children's social and academic outcomes years later (Hamre & Pianta, 2002; Howes, 2000). Sometimes, the quality of teacher–child relationships is more predictive of a child's behavior than is the quality of the child's relationships with his or her parents (Howes et al., 1994).

Teachers can have a significant influence on children's social development. This influence can be quite positive, encouraging feelings of competence and well-being. For example, teachers have been found to enhance positive outcomes for students if they (1) reduce the tendency of students to compare themselves with one another, (2) use cooperative interaction strategies in the classroom, (3) promote beliefs about students' competencies rather than their deficiencies, (4) increase chances for students to be successful, and (5) are warm, encouraging, and supportive (Shuell, 1996; Stipek, 1997). How teachers respond to and influence their students depends on many factors:

■ *Children's behaviors:* Teachers generally respond more positively to students who achieve, conform, and are agreeable and compliant. They give attention to students who make demands that are appropriate to classroom activities, but they are indifferent to students who are silent or withdrawn. Teachers also may reject children who make many demands that they consider illegitimate or who present behavior problems (Birch & Ladd, 1998; Zimmerman, 1998).

■ *Children's racial, ethnic, and socioeconomic backgrounds:* Teachers sometimes stereotype children on the basis of race, culture, and social class. For example, teachers may attribute failure in school to a child's class or ethnic background (Persell, 1993; Weinstein, 1998). Some teachers expect less from lower-class and minority children, even when these children have abilities similar to those of other children. Teachers act more positively toward students they hold in high esteem, and they spend more time interacting with students whom they expect to work hard and achieve more (Demaray & Elliot, 1998). Because teachers' expectations are influenced more by negative than by positive information about their students (Persell, 1993) and because stereotypes about children from lower-class and/or ethnic families are more likely to be negative than positive, children from these socially vulnerable backgrounds are more susceptible than other children to teachers' expectations and behaviors (Ferguson, 1998; McKown & Weinstein, 2002).

■ *Children's gender:* The available research supports the view that teachers treat boys and girls differently (Gray & Leith, 2004). Teachers generally give boys more attention than they give girls, and more freedom (Sadker & Sadker, 1994), and this pattern is seen in classrooms outside of the United States as well as within it (Einarsson & Granstroem, 2002). Teachers believe that boys possess greater school-related skills than girls do (Shepardson & Pizzini, 1992), so boys receive more approval, instruction, and time from their teachers (Duffy, Warren, & Walsh, 2001). Teachers believe that being nice and obedient is related to intellectual skills in girls but not in boys, although no research supports this argument (Gold, Crombie, & Noble, 1987). Thus, teacher–child relationships differ for boys and girls and are based on different qualities (Colwell & Lindsey, 2003).

As you can see, many aspects of school life affect older children, and they differ from children's experiences when they were younger. Many other changes occur during this time and set the stage for moving into the period of adolescence. It should also be clear that later childhood is not a period of "latency" (as Freud described it)—dynamic transitions, events, and developments occur that make it a significant period filled with important and significant changes.

Try It Out

1. Look through newspapers, magazines, or the Internet for a story in which heroism or extreme courage was displayed by a school-age child. How do such actions relate to moral development? What factors lead to heroism and courage? Draw some conclusions about the relationship between these types of behaviors and moral reasoning.
2. Describe how individual, familial, and social factors contribute to the problems of rejected children. What kinds of interventions and treatments might be effective in helping these children cope with their problems?
3. Interview school-age children about their experiences in school. Have them discuss their relationships with classmates and teachers. Ask them if they have ever experienced safety issues while at school (such as being threatened or seeing someone with a knife). Use the material in the chapter to draw some conclusions about the impact of these experiences and relationships on the children's development.

Key Terms and Concepts

antisocial behavior (413)
autonomous morality stage (421)
bullying (432)

Conventional Level (422)
emotion-focused coping strategies (408)
heteronomous morality stage (419)

immanent justice (420)
industry (404)
inferiority (404)
innate fears (407)
latchkey children (429)
morality (418)
moral realism (419)
neglected children (431)

Postconventional Level (422)
Preconventional Level (422)
premoral period (419)
problem-focused coping strategies (409)
rejected children (431)
resilience (411)
social competence (434)

Sum It Up

How do children's selves develop during late childhood?

- Describe the psychosocial crisis that Erikson proposed that occurs during late childhood. (p. 404)

How do emotions develop during late childhood?

- What types of fears do older children experience, and how do these differ from the fears of infants and young children? (p. 407)

What emotional and psychological disturbances affect children in late childhood?

- List and give an example of the factors affecting the development of antisocial behavior. (p. 414)

What changes take place in moral development during late childhood?

- List and give an example of each of the stages of moral development according to Piaget. (p. 419)

- List and give an example of each of the stages of moral development according to Kohlberg. (p. 423)

How do children's family relationships change during late childhood?

- How do sibling relationships provide children with opportunities to learn about themselves? (p. 430)

What factors influence school-age children's peer relationships?

- In what ways can bullying be prevented? (p. 433)

How does school affect social and emotional development in late childhood?

- What factors affect a teacher's influence on his or her students? (pp. 437–438)

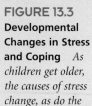

STRESSORS

Caregiver presence or absence

Necessity to obey and comply with caregiver's demands

School
Relationships with other children
Acculturation

Crying to elicit the caregiver's comfort

Clinging to caregiver

Emotion-focused coping: thinking happy things, good outcomes
Problem-focused coping: finding the source of a problem and fixing it
Accurate interpretation of others' motives

COPING SKILLS

FIGURE 13.3
Developmental Changes in Stress and Coping *As children get older, the causes of stress change, as do the types of coping.*

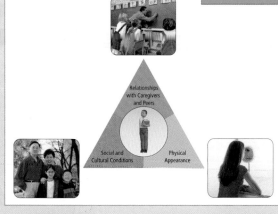

FIGURE 13.2 **Influences on Perception of Self**
Children's perceptions of themselves are influenced by a variety of internal and external factors.

DEVELOPMENT OF SELF AND EMOTIONS

Freud believed that development during late childhood was quiet and dormant. But Erikson did not think this was a rest period; children begin school and must tame imagination and impulses and also please others. Erikson argued that the primary task during this stage was for a child to develop a capacity for industry while avoiding an excessive sense of inferiority.

As children grow and change, their vulnerability to emotional stress and the situations that produce it also changes. Late childhood is a time when emotional and psychological problems often surface, especially in children who lack skills to cope with their increasingly demanding environments. (Refer back to pages 403–418.)

MORAL DEVELOPMENT

Children's moral development undergoes dramatic changes during late childhood. As they experience changes in cognitive and social development, older children begin to make moral judgments based less on rewards and punishments and more on internalized principles that underlie how good and just behaviors are defined. These judgments also underlie their actions. (Refer back to pages 418–427.)

TABLE 13.4
Children's Ideas of What Should Be Done in Different Moral Scenarios, by Ethnicity and Age

MORAL SCENARIO	THIRD-GRADERS		SIXTH-GRADERS	
	AFRICAN AMERICAN	MEXICAN AMERICAN	AFRICAN AMERICAN	MEXICAN AMERICAN
Asked to share money				
Share	24%	50%	76%	100%
Do not share	76%	50%	24%	0%
Scolded by teacher				
Apologize	38%	9%	62%	10%
Do something to change things	28%	18%	24%	14%
Feel bad	28%	36%	14%	67%
Get angry	10%	36%	0%	10%
Peers fighting				
Stop fight	48%	18%	62%	38%
Encourage fight	20%	23%	24%	10%
Feel bad	24%	45%	5%	24%
Do not get involved	8%	14%	10%	29%

Piaget believed he could study the development of morality by observing children play games.

Bullying at school is a significant problem for both boys and girls. Both bullies and their victims are at risk for poor adjustment.

SOCIAL RELATIONSHIPS

During late childhood, children spend less time with parents and more time with peers. Parental influence still remains strong, but friends and acquaintances take on increasing importance and influence, both positive and negative. (Refer back to pages 427–435.)

EFFECTS OF SCHOOL

During late childhood, school takes on greater importance. Although school involves the teaching of academic subjects, the school context brings children into contact with a larger number and variety of children and adults. Thus, school has important social as well as academic influences. (Refer back to pages 436–438.)

Teachers enhance outcomes for students when they minimize competition and promote cooperation and supportive relationships.

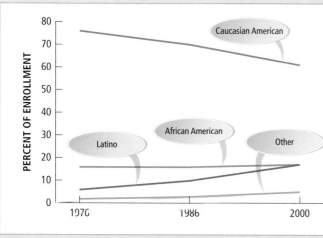

FIGURE 13.11 **School Enrollments of Children 5- to 17-Years-Old, by Ethnicity** *Notice the increase in the school enrollments of ethnic minorities.*

part

6

Adolescence

uring adolescence the complex interactions between biology and environment are particularly dramatic. Biological influences are apparent in physical changes, including growing taller, gaining weight, and developing to sexual maturity. Environmental influences come into play as family, friends, and significant others react to the changing adolescent. Virtually every aspect of development undergoes striking transformation—adolescents' bodies, relationships, thinking skills, and emotional understanding. As changes occur in one area, they in turn bring about changes in the others. Adolescents may not always understand or be prepared for these transitions, but with time and support, most learn to adapt.

No longer a child but still not an adult, adolescents struggle with issues of identity and independence. They also deal with many temptations and risky behaviors that can interfere with healthy development. Many teens experiment with alcohol, tobacco, drugs, sex, and crime; however, most do not abuse drugs or become promiscuous or delinquent. In fact, most teens lead happy and productive lives and eventually enter adulthood as well-adapted individuals.

Physical Development and Health in Adolescence

14

Chapter Outline

What Is Adolescence?
Historical Perspectives on Adolescence
Cultural Perspectives on Adolescence

How Do Adolescents Develop Physically and Sexually?
Brain Development
The Adolescent Growth Spurt
The Process of Puberty
Adolescents' Responses to Physical and Sexual Maturation
Psychological Reactions to Pubertal Events

What Are the Health and Safety Concerns of Adolescence?
Nutrition
Fitness and Sports Participation
Eating Disturbances and Disorders
Adolescents and Chronic Illnesses
Death in Adolescence
Sexual Health Concerns

A DEVELOPMENTAL MYSTERY

When Konner was a junior in high school, he felt he could do anything. He felt immune to bad things, as if they couldn't happen to him. He didn't worry about what he ate, how much he exercised, or the chances he took. He and his friends loved to drive fast, 20 or sometimes even 30 miles over the speed limit on side streets. Konner and his buddies would sometimes "car surf" after they drank—one of the guys would ride on the outside of the moving car. They would yell and laugh as their friends tried to hang on. But around Thanksgiving, the surfing almost turned tragic. One of Konner's friends lost his balance and fell off. The guys' laughter went silent when the friend did not get up—he was taken to the hospital, but it turned out that he had nothing more than some bruises and needed some stitches.

This accident caused Konner's parents to reflect on the risky behaviors the boys engaged in and the near-tragedy that resulted. Their activities seemed so common among kids their age. The parents wondered whether this high-risk horseplay was simply a part of the change that occurs during adolescence.

Adolescence is a time of great change. For many people, this period conjures up only negative images—a time when young people take drugs, become rebellious and disrespectful, are subject to "raging hormones," and engage in risky behaviors like those of Konner and his friends. The mystery his parents contemplated as to whether these behaviors are just the "facts" of adolescence reflect the commonly held idea that adolescence is a time of storm and stress. But this stereotype holds true for only a small minority of adolescents. Most make adjustments to cope with the changes in positive ways.

What Is Adolescence?

The period of adolescence covers a wide range of ages. A 13-year-old and a 17-year-old are both adolescents, but they experience very different worlds. Until recently, however, little distinction was made among adolescents of different ages because, compared to current norms, the period of adolescence was comparatively brief. In the early twentieth century, it was common for people to be married and have children by the age of 15 or 16. Consider the following personal account of 71-year-old David:

> My teen years were pretty typical. I went to school until I was 15 and then quit to help my dad in his store. Shortly after that, I met Elizabeth and we were married within a year. I had my first child when I was 17, and I remember having all our friends over for his first birthday. By that time, they were all married too, and many had children of their own. My adolescence didn't last too long. I was too busy working and taking care of my children. But I didn't mind; it was the thing to do in those days. (interview with author's grandparent)

Compared to David's experience, adolescence today, for many people in the United States, entails a much longer period of time. Most adolescents reach physical maturity earlier and delay adult responsibilities longer than they did in the past.

Adolescence often is defined as covering the period from about 11 years of age to about 19, although some psychologists maintain that adolescence extends into the adult years

FIGURE 14.1
The Wide Age Range of Adolescence

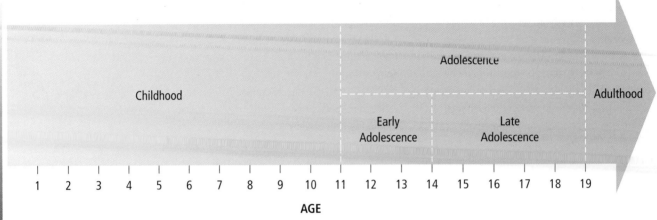

Adolescence encompasses a wide range of ages. Young teens differ in important ways from older teens. Can you identify some of these differences and the factors that contribute to them?

(Sheehy, 1995). Distinguishing between early adolescence (ages 11 to 14 years) and late adolescence (ages 15 to 19 years) is important because they represent different transitional periods (see Figure 14.1). During early adolescence, the individual is making the transition from childhood to adolescence. During late adolescence, the transition is from adolescence to adulthood (Sherrod, Haggerty, & Featherman, 1993). Thus, younger and older adolescents must deal with different developmental issues and tasks.

Physical changes occur very rapidly, and dramatic changes in appearance take place during early adolescence. Family members, friends, and teachers notice these changes and respond to adolescents based partly on how "grown up" they appear. In turn, adolescents' views of themselves are affected by these physical changes and how they are treated by others. Before we focus on adolescent physical development, it is important to understand how the concept of adolescence, and its study, came about.

Historical Perspectives on Adolescence

The term **adolescence** generally refers to the developmental period between childhood and adulthood. Although this transitional period was recognized by ancient Romans, Greeks, and Egyptians (Offer, Ostrov, Howard, & Atkinson, 1988), the concept of adolescence as we know it did not exist until the mid–nineteenth century. At that time, increased urbanization led to social and legal reforms that contributed to the social acceptance of adolescence as a stage of development. These reforms included the following:

- Child labor laws removed children and adolescents from factories and workplaces.
- Changes in criminal laws allowed courts to treat juveniles differently from adults. Children and adolescents are not subject to the same legal procedures and punishments as adults are.
- Mandatory public education placed large numbers of young people into schools and formally separated them from adults. Additionally, the age-graded school system separated children from adolescents.

In the twentieth century, as technology advanced, increasingly specialized skills were demanded from workers. More extensive and finely tuned education and training were needed to produce highly skilled workers, and these pressures continued to expand the time period of adolescence.

adolescence *the developmental period between childhood and adulthood*

Postponing adult responsibilities gives young people increased opportunities to explore different roles and values and to greatly extend their education. Not all youths take advantage of the time available for educational training and experimentation with different roles, though. Some adolescents, such as those who plan to work in jobs involving manual labor, resent being forced to continue studying "irrelevant" course materials in school and want to begin their adult roles. And extending adolescence has some negative consequences. For instance, it makes career choices more difficult for many adolescents, as the link between work and school becomes less obvious, and it increases the length of time young people are dependent on their parents, which may contribute to family conflict.

Today adolescents represent a smaller proportion of the US population than they did in the past. This trend reflects the declining birthrate and increased life expectancy of the US population. Although adolescents represent a relatively small and declining proportion of the US population, issues related to them—such as juvenile crime, substance abuse, and education—demand considerable time, attention, and resources.

In some cultures, such as the Penan culture in Borneo, from the time that children are 9 years old, they are expected to act like adults and participate in adult culture. Such cultural values tell us that adolescence is culturally defined and that age per se is not a good marker of adolescence or adulthood.

Cultural Perspectives on Adolescence

As a developmental period, adolescence varies from one culture to the next (Dusek, 1996). In less industrialized cultures, this period may be very brief, and adulthood may begin early. For instance, in some groups of African hunter-gatherers, adulthood is considered to begin once girls menstruate and boys participate successfully in a hunt (Abbott, 1997). Similarly, among the Punan Bah, a tiny ethnic group in the rain forest in Borneo, boys and girls are supposed to understand and participate in adult life from the age of 9 or 10. By age 13 or 14, Punan Bah members are expected to work on their own and take on the morals and responsibilities of the adult society (Nicolaisen, 1988). Like adolescence early in the twentieth century in the United States, the period of adolescence in Punan Bah society is considerably shorter (four to five years) than it is in present-day US society.

Many adolescents undergo initiations, or **rites of passage,** that mark their new status and roles within their community. The nature of these rites varies across cultures. In some African cultures, 13-year-old boys receive months of training in the basic skills needed for adulthood and then undergo circumcision to mark their new status (Dacey & Kenny, 1997). Young Australian Aboriginal adolescents do a walkabout, in which they leave their village and must survive on their own for six months. These rites of passage soften the blow of making an abrupt change to a new status. They inform the individuals of their new duties and roles, announce their status to the community, and provide a sense of belonging (Sebald, 1992).

Modern US society has nothing that corresponds in scope to the rites of passage experienced in other cultures; however, transition rituals mark changes in some domains. For instance, the *bar mitzvah* (or *bat mitzvah,* for girls) in Judaism marks the end of a boy's childhood within the religion, although it does not influence how the boy is treated by the rest of society.

In the United States, there are some markers of the transition into adult roles, but these occur later than, say, an Aboriginal walkabout, since adolescence in the United States extends for a longer time period. Also, these markers, such as the legal age for driving or voting, do not carry with them the same cultural significance as the rites of passage experienced by youth in other cultures.

Even in those cultures that have an expanded period of adolescence, the experience of adolescence is colored by variability in the societal expectations for youth. For example, as you will see, individual autonomy and independence are important goals of adolescent development in the United States. In contrast, because individual autonomy is valued less than group

rites of passage *initiations that mark an adolescent's new status and roles within the community*

In the Jewish religion, boys and girls go through a religious ceremony at the age of 13 that signifies the end of childhood. This rite of passage marks their new status and roles within the community.

cooperation in Chinese cultures, Chinese adolescents are not expected, and do not expect themselves, to act independently as early as Western adolescents do (Feldman & Rosenthal, 1994). Thus, Chinese and Western adolescents hold different concepts of themselves—concepts that reflect cultural variations in perceptions and beliefs about adolescence.

In some cultures, the notion of adolescence as a period of development separate from childhood and adulthood does not exist. The following comments are from a Samoan-born young woman:

> As a Samoan born, I had never heard of it [adolescence] until I came to New Zealand. I don't think it was part of my life because it is a Western concept, and from a non-Western society all those developmental stages didn't relate to me. All I know is that my aiga [family] and my community and my culture are important. They determine the way I behave, think, and feel. So adolescence as a developmental stage is foreign to our culture. (J. Kroger, 1996, p. 3)

Even subcultures within a country have different expectations for adolescents. For example, Amish and Hutterite children step from childhood expectations directly into adult roles and are less affected than other US youth by elements of the larger society that promote an extended period of adolescence (Sebald, 1992).

How Do Adolescents Develop Physically and Sexually?

Eleven-year-old Karen anxiously waits for her aunt to take off her shoes so that they can stand back to back to compare heights. Karen's feet have surpassed her aunt's in size over the past year, and now she wonders if she has grown taller. Karen is surprised that she and her aunt are the same height.

Karen is excited about the changes in her body. She is growing in height and weight, and her body is changing from its earlier childlike proportions to a more mature shape. Unlike the boys in her class, Karen is "growing like a weed"—she is undergoing the growth spurt of early adolescence. Later, the boys in her class will experience a similar growth spurt, and many will eventually become taller, heavier, and stronger than Karen.

The early adolescent years are marked by rapid physical growth and dramatic changes in appearance. In later adolescence, physical growth slows down. Recent research suggests that some of the most significant changes that take place during late adolescence are unseen changes occurring in the brain. Physical changes in brain development during adolescence may influence some of the behaviors associated with the teen years.

Brain Development

You may be surprised to learn that during adolescence, the brain continues to undergo physical changes, and these changes may be linked to adolescents' behavior. Dramatic transformations take place during adolescence in the prefrontal cortex and limbic brain regions. The amygdala, a part of the limbic system, grows quickly in response to testosterone during adolescence and is involved with feelings of fear and anger. Not surprisingly, boys change more than girls in this area of the brain (Giedd, 1997). This change may account for the increased aggressiveness and irritability often associated with adolescence. The prefrontal cortex is involved in the organization and planning of behavior and the anticipating of future events. People with damage to the prefrontal areas of the brain often have little concern for the past and future and are not good at sequencing events in time (Knight & Grabowecky, 2000). The limbic system plays a central role in the regulation of emotional behaviors and sexuality and is involved in the regulation of memory. These systems continue to develop during adolescence and early adulthood, which may contribute to changes in cognitive functioning (Benes, 2001; Casey, Giedd, & Thomas, 2000) and routine behaviors (such as sleep—see From Research to Practice). There is some speculation that the development of these areas and the systems associated with them may play a role in drug use, the lack of foresight some adolescents show, and the failure of some adolescents to recognize the consequences of their behavior (Spear, 2000).

Suppose you heard someone make insulting comments about a good friend. Your limbic system, which is involved in emotional responses, might respond by becoming angry, but other parts of the brain, particularly in the prefrontal cortex, would also become activated, to sort out why someone might think these things (even if they are wrong) and to provide brakes for the emotional system. The brain of the adolescent reacts differently. The limbic system responds, but the prefrontal cortex is less likely to do so. This pattern of response was demonstrated by researchers who showed photographs of faces expressing fear to both adults and adolescents. The adults could identify the expressions with much less difficulty than the adolescents. Also, the adults showed activation of the brain in both the limbic and the prefrontal areas, whereas the adolescents showed activation only in the limbic region (Baird et al., 1999). Interestingly, adolescents with conduct disorders have a particularly difficult time identifying expressions of sadness and fearfulness in others (Blair, James, & Coles, 2001).

Remember that one aspect of brain development is the increasing organization of the brain as neuronal connections are pruned, apparently strengthening the connections that remain. Research on developmental changes in brain structure and functions provides additional evidence of the importance of pruning. Studies of the prefrontal cortex illustrate that children and adolescents show more diffuse brain activity than adults do (Casey, Giedd, & Thomas, 2000; Giedd, 1997). As the areas of activation become more specialized, presumably they are able to direct attention and memory more effectively, and thus cognitive functioning improves (Luna et al., 2001).

FIGURE 14.2
Inside the Brain of a Teenager

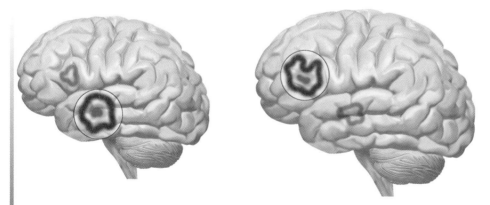

When interpreting emotions, teens (left image) rely more on the amygdala, whereas adults (right image) rely more on the frontal cortex. Teens seem not only to misread the feelings of others, but they react strongly from an area deep inside the brain that causes more of a "gut" emotional reaction than the adult brain does. This likely reflects the fact that a teen's frontal region is not fully connected with the emotional region. Such differences show that teens' brains are not yet fully developed, and some of their behaviors may result from this.

Source: PBS Frontline, 2004. Used with permission from Deborah Yurgelun-Todd.

FROM RESEARCH TO PRACTICE
ADOLESCENT SLEEP AND DEVELOPMENT

FROM RESEARCH . . .

Kimberly is a junior in high school. She sets her alarm clock to go off at 6:30 A.M., the latest possible time that allows her to shower and get to school, usually without eating breakfast. Her school day starts at 7:20 A.M., a common opening time for high schools in the United States. She often feels as if she is in a daze during her first few classes and has a hard time staying awake.

A growing body of research now suggests that Kimberly's fatigue is the result of a school schedule that is insensitive to her biological clock (Carskadon, 2002). During adolescence, teens have a physiological need for extra sleep that younger children do not need (Frieden & Smith, 2000). In other words, as teenagers move through adolescence, they need increasing amounts of sleep. Yet adolescents typically get less sleep as they mature (Wolfson & Carskadon, 1998).

Conventional wisdom suggests that the older you get, the less sleep you need. But new research contradicts this belief. Studies of teenagers who are allowed to get as much sleep as they need show no decline in sleep requirements with age. In fact, the reverse is true: older adolescents need more sleep than they did when they were younger. Late in adolescence, a hormonal shift pushes their preprogrammed period of wakefulness about an hour later than it was earlier in their teens. This shift is caused by a delay in the release of the hormone melatonin, which induces sleepiness and helps set the body's biological clock. As a result, teenagers need nine hours of sleep nightly, but few get this much (Richardson & Tate, 2002).

Risks for adolescents who do not get enough sleep include daytime sleepiness, susceptibility to accidents, mood and behavior problems, vulnerability to drug and alcohol use, and development of major sleep disorders (Carskadon, 1990; Wolfson et al., 1995). According to research, 20 percent of high school students fall asleep in school (Maas, 1995). Students with poor grades report that they get less sleep and go to sleep later on school nights than students with higher grades do (Wolfson & Carskadon, 2002). Sleep loss also results in grogginess, lack of attention in class, poor performance on exams, and disciplinary problems (Wahlstrom, 2002).

. . . TO PRACTICE

These findings led school officials in Edina, Minnesota, to change the start time for high school from 7:20 A.M. to 8:30 A.M. Teens now report sleeping more, and the extra rest has resulted in greater classroom participation and attentiveness, fewer absences due to illness, and fewer discipline problems (Center for Applied Research and Educational Improvement, 1997). Additionally, the Minneapolis Public Schools changed their start time to a later time for high school students and found similar results as the Edina study and provided the first test of the impact of school starting times on a large sample of teens (Wahlstrom, 2002).

These time changes also caused concerns, though. Many students were involved in extracurricular activities that began after school. Starting school later caused these students to work later into the night during the school week and lowered after-school participation in student activities, particularly among those who held after-school jobs. Additionally, certain meetings, practices, and events ended after dark, especially during the winter months, again lowering participation. Parents also faced difficulties adapting schedules when there were younger children in the family. Thus, despite the advantages, there are important disadvantages to consider (Wolfson, 2002).

Teens, parents, and educators also need to be more aware of good sleep hygiene practices. For example, parental control of children's sleep and wake time diminishes when children reach puberty (Mitru, Millrood, & Mateika, 2002). Although children have greater freedom to make their own decisions regarding bedtime, they may not be very good at doing what is best for them. Increased pressure by peers to engage in late-night activities, unsupervised television viewing, and increased access to telephones, computers, and the Internet may prevent teens from going to bed as early as they should (Carskadon, 1999). As a result, sleep hygiene education may increase the appreciation and understanding of the role of sleep in adolescent development.

THINKING IT THROUGH

1. What social and family factors might influence the amount of sleep an adolescent gets?

2. How can parents make certain that their teenagers get the sleep they need?

3. What other effects (both positive and negative) might result from changing the start time of high school to later in the day?

Imaging studies of the brains of adolescents and children have examined the degree of myelination of the neuronal connections. Remember from earlier chapters that myelination improves the speed of information transmission in the brain. Magnetic imaging studies done with children and adolescents of ages 4 to 17 found age-related increases in certain brain regions, suggesting a gradual development of the brain that continues through adolescence (Paus et al., 1999). Boys and girls undergo myelination in several regions at different rates, with girls showing more myelination in relay areas between the hippocampus (involved in emotions) and the frontal cortex (involved in higher functioning). These gender differences in brain development may be one of the reasons that adolescent girls show more reasoned and mature judgment, and more emotionality, than boys do (De-Bellis et al., 2001).

Does brain development during adolescence relate to changes in behavior? Some evidence now suggests that it does. Researchers argue that certain behaviors that are common among adolescents—such as risk-taking and independence seeking behaviors—may be promoted less by increases in pubertal hormones than by events occurring in brain development (Spear, 2000a). These neuronal changes, which often are transient, may predispose adolescents to behave in particular ways and make them particularly likely to use alcohol and other drugs than they are at other ages (Spear, 2002b). Particular sets of brain circuits involved in the development of addictions are the same as those that undergo rapid changes during adolescence. These changes motivate adolescents more than children or adults to have new experiences. But these conditions also reflect a less mature neurological system of inhibition, leading to impulsive actions and risky behaviors, including experimentation and abuse of addictive drugs.

For example, during adolescence, the human brain begins to release more chemicals associated with new experiences and the desire to repeat them. One of the chemicals is dopamine, a neurotransmitter involved in many forms of addiction. Activities that increase dopamine production are highly rewarding. Overall, this change in brain chemistry serves a positive purpose. During adolescence, teens need to increase their range of experiences and develop many new skills. Instead of playing with toy cars, for example, adolescents learn to drive a real car. They need experiences like these to become independent, self-regulating adults (Chambers, Taylor, & Potenza, 2003). The problem is that adolescent brains reinforce novel experiences in ways that are much stronger—and longer lasting—than those experienced by children or adults. Also, areas of the brain that adults use to weigh the risks of behaviors are still developing in adolescents. Thus, adolescent impulsivity and novelty seeking can be explained in part by maturational changes in frontal cortical and subcortical systems that produce chemical changes in adolescents' brains. These developmental processes may promote adaptation to adult roles but may also produce greater vulnerability to the addictive actions of drugs (Chambers & Potenza, 2003).

Although it is exciting to consider the effects of brain development on behavior, it is important to remember that the effects go both ways: the experiences that adolescents have also influence how the brain develops. Practice and experience help lay a solid foundation for brain development. Sports, computer games, reading, music, and learning a new language all set the stage for positive brain development; drinking and taking drugs may promote less positive brain development.

The Adolescent Growth Spurt

Girls and boys are approximately the same height until adolescence, when girls begin their growth spurt (see Figure 14.3). The average age at which girls begin this spurt is around 10½ years. Peak rates of growth are reached between ages 11 and 12, and growth tapers off by age 13 (Marshall & Tanner, 1986). During their spurt, girls grow about 3 inches per year, about twice as fast as they did before puberty. Growth slows down when girls reach **menarche,** the onset of their menstrual cycle. Most girls reach their adult height and weight by about age 15 or 16, but a few continue growing until they are 18 or 19 (Tanner, 1991).

On average, boys begin their growth spurt about two years later than do girls—at around 12½ years—and reach their peak rate of growth between ages 13 and 15. Boys

menarche *the onset of the menstrual cycle*

FIGURE 14.3

Pattern of Growth in Height for Boys and for Girls

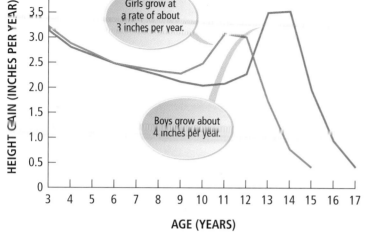

Notice how the graphs for boys and girls diverge at about 7 years of age. Girls' growth peaks at ages 11 and 12, whereas boys' growth peaks at 13 or 14. What factors account for these differences? How do these physical changes influence adolescents' interactions with others?

Source: Adapted from Tanner and Davies, 1985.

The young teens in this picture are the same age. Notice the dramatic differences in their heights and body shapes. The girls tend to be taller and more physically mature than the boys. What factors account for such differences?

puberty *developmental milestone reached when a person becomes sexually mature and capable of having children*

pubescence *the period of time during which sexual maturation takes place*

grow about 4 inches per year during their spurt, but during the peak growth time they may grow 6 to 8 inches in one year (Malina & Bouchard, 1991; Marshall & Tanner, 1986). Most boys reach their adult height at about 17 or 18 years of age, but some continue growing for several more years.

Weight changes also occur during the growth spurt. Early in adolescence, both sexes gain body fat; later, boys stop gaining fat while girls continue to gain it (Forbes, 1986). Although girls have somewhat more fat on their body even as children, during early adolescence the differences between the sexes become more pronounced. Boys and girls differ in the amounts of fat versus muscle they gain during the growth spurt, with boys gaining more muscle mass and girls gaining more body fat (Holliday, 1986; Malina, 1986). The fat that girls gain during adolescence is related to reproduction—their bodies gain enough stored energy to support pregnancy and nursing.

The growth spurt affects all parts of an adolescent's body, but different parts grow at different rates. An adolescent's hands, feet, head, and nose grow more quickly than the rest of the body. Only later do the arms, legs, and trunk reach adult size. Body proportions change from the narrow hips and shoulders of childhood to more sexually defined shapes, with girls developing broader hips and boys broader shoulders. Internal organs such as the lungs and heart also grow in size during adolescence. Large and noticeable individual differences characterize the timing and extent of growth during early adolescence. For instance, some girls begin their growth spurt as early as age 9, whereas others do not begin until 13 or 14. Boys may enter the growth spurt at age 10 or as late as 15. Many adolescents have some variation in their growth, with later or earlier than usual development of height or weight or sexual maturation.

Later in adolescence, the physical changes are much less pronounced. Both sexes continue to grow taller, but the rate of growth is slower than it was during the growth spurt of early adolescence. Both boys and girls may continue to gain muscle and fat on their bodies, but the changes associated with later adolescence are somewhat more evident in boys than in girls, who began their growth spurt earlier. Boys' voices deepen, and they continue to develop hair on their chins, cheeks, and bodies. Girls may show continued breast development. The exceptions to these patterns are the late-developing boys, who may be just beginning to show the physical changes associated with the adolescent growth spurt.

The Process of Puberty

The term most commonly associated with adolescent development is **puberty,** the developmental milestone reached when a person becomes sexually mature and capable of having children. Because sexual maturation actually takes place over several years, the term **pubescence** is used to refer to the time during which sexual maturation is taking place.

Puberty is not a single event but a progression of physical changes that usually begin in late childhood and culminate in early adolescence. These events include the development of the **primary sexual characteristics**—physical features directly related to reproduction, such as the ovaries, penis, and testes—and the development of **secondary sexual characteristics**—features that are outward manifestations of sexual development but are not directly involved in reproduction, such as breasts, facial and body hair, and an adult body shape.

Biological Influences on Pubertal Development

The physical changes that accompany puberty are influenced by biological factors; however, scientists have not identified one specific biological trigger for puberty. Instead, a complex interplay of the endocrine system, the nervous system, and the gonads leads to puberty, largely through the influence of hormones.

Hormones are released from the master gland of the endocrine system, called the pituitary gland. The hypothalamus, a part of the brain that sends signals to the pituitary gland and to the gonads, responds to levels of hormones in the body. The interplay among these components acts as a feedback loop, in which each part influences and reacts to each other part. For instance, the brain provides instructions to the endocrine system to maintain a certain level of hormones in the body. Depending on the levels of hormones in the bloodstream, the endocrine system will then increase or decrease the release of hormones.

The endocrine system, which circulates and regulates hormones within the body, develops before birth but stays relatively inactive until about the age of 7. At that time, the system gradually begins to secrete hormones into the bloodstream during sleep (Nottelmann et al., 1987). These hormones, called **gonadotropins,** travel to the brain, carrying messages about changes to the body. When they reach the brain, they stimulate the production of hormones by the sex glands, or gonads. Gradually, over about a 4- or 5-year span, the influence of these hormones becomes apparent in adolescents' bodies (Connolly, Paikoff, & Buchanan, 1996).

The hormonal changes during adolescence include increased levels of both sex hormones (testosterone and estrogen) and growth hormones. Boys and girls have approximately the same amounts of these sex hormones in their bodies throughout most of childhood, but during early adolescence this balance changes. In girls, the key hormone is estrogen, which is secreted in higher amounts through the stimulation of the ovaries. In boys, the key hormone is the androgen testosterone, which is secreted in higher amounts through stimulation of the testes. The relative amounts of these hormones in the body account for the physical changes associated with puberty. For instance, hair growth is related to androgens, and the onset of menstruation involves estrogen (Petersen, 1987).

Although the general sequence of events associated with puberty is predictable, the timing of these events varies considerably from one person to another (see Figure 14.4). Genetics plays a dominant role in the timing of puberty, as is evident in research showing that the events of puberty are more closely linked in time for monozygotic twins than for dizygotic twins or siblings (Tanner, 1989). It is unlikely, however, that genetic factors set a particular age for puberty to begin in an individual. Instead, each individual appears to have a genetically influenced predisposition to begin puberty within a certain age range and to move through the physical changes of puberty at a certain rate. Thus, genetic factors set upper and lower limits on the timing of puberty and on the rate of pubertal development.

FIGURE 14.4
Variations in Sexual Maturation

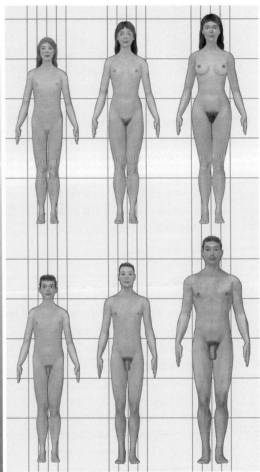

Notice how different the boys look and how different the girls look, even though they are of the same age (the females are about 13 years old, and the males are about 15 years old). Such comparisons reveal the large individual differences in the rates at which teens achieve sexual maturation.

Source: Tanner, 1975.

primary sexual characteristics *physical features directly related to reproduction, such as the ovaries, penis, and testes*

secondary sexual characteristics *features that are outward manifestations of sexual development but are not directly involved in reproduction, such as breasts, facial and body hair, and an adult body shape*

gonadotropins *chemical messengers that stimulate the production of hormones by the glands*

DEBATING THE ISSUE
DOES PUBERTY INTENSIFY ADOLESCENTS' GENDER ROLES?

 As their bodies mature and their interest in dating increases, young adolescents may consider it more important to act in ways that are consistent with gender-role expectations. Boys who do not act masculine enough or girls who do not act feminine enough may be less accepted by their peers (Egan & Perry, 2001). Because of the noticeable physical changes that occur during early adolescence, and others' reactions to these, boys and girls may feel compelled to fit into traditional gender roles (Huston & Alvarez, 1990). The idea that adolescents' sex-role behaviors and attitudes become more traditional in early adolescence is referred to as gender intensification (Hill & Lynch, 1983). Whether or not this actually occurs is not clear.

Some support for gender intensification has been found. For example, gender differences increase over the course of early adolescence (Galambos, Almeida, & Petersen, 1990), and girls have been found to spend more time in interpersonal activities and household chores, and less time playing sports, than they did before reaching puberty (Ruble et al.,

in press). Additionally, after puberty (but not before) girls are more likely to evidence depression than boys are (Wichstrom, 1999). Such differences are explained in part by developmental challenges for girls—pubertal development, dissatisfaction with weight and attainment of a mature female body, and increased importance of feminine sex-role identification. Moreover, the relation between school achievement and self-image increases during early adolescence for boys but decreases among girls (Roberts, Sarigiani, Newman, & Petersen, 1992). This sex difference is thought to occur because boys are pressured to excel in school, whereas girls are pressured to excel socially. Because boys and girls experience increasingly different socialization pressures and expectations during early adolescence, their behavior may come to reflect these differences.

Other studies do not support gender intensification (Watt, 2004), especially as related to changes in gender-role attitudes during early adolescence (Antill, Russell, Goodnow, & Cotton, 1993). In some cases, gender intensification occurs only for certain groups of children. For

instance, in a classic study of tomboys and non-tomboys, only the non-tomboys showed an increase in feminine preferences and activities during early adolescence (Plumb & Cowan, 1984).

Given all the changes occurring during adolescence, it is not surprising that there is considerable fluctuation in gender-role attitudes and behaviors throughout the adolescent years (Ruble et al., in press). Because puberty is a social as well as a physical event, the changes that it brings in gender roles are determined by the context in which they take place, puberty's timing and course, and the characteristics of individuals as they enter adolescence.

THINKING IT THROUGH

1. What pubertal changes may relate to gender intensification?

2. Is gender intensification desirable? How might it be avoided?

3. What factors might make some young adolescents more susceptible to gender intensification than others?

Environmental Influences on Pubertal Development

Environmental influences determine whether puberty occurs earlier or later within the genetically influenced age range for the onset of puberty—again illustrating the complex interplay of biological and environmental factors in human development (Connolly et al., 1996). Two powerful environmental influences are general health and nutrition. Adolescents who are healthy and who have received adequate nutrition throughout their early years are likely to enter puberty earlier. Adolescents who have been chronically ill may have delayed puberty (Brooks-Gunn, 1988). Children who are malnourished have delayed growth spurts and onset of puberty, possibly because of lower gonadotropin secretions (Hopwood et al., 1990). Girls who exercise strenuously (such as gymnasts, runners, and ballet dancers) and who have low levels of body fat often have delayed puberty (Bancroft & Reinisch, 1990). From an evolutionary perspective, girls appear to begin pubertal changes when their bodies have adequate fat to maintain pregnancy.

Although both biological and environmental factors are known to influence the timing of puberty, new evidence has given rise to speculation about how family experiences influence it. One controversial idea is that stressful family experiences trigger puberty. Based on evolutionary theories of development (Chapter 2), some researchers have speculated that early maturation may be an evolutionary mechanism that increases the chances of survival for girls who have a stressful family environment: by maturing early, they are able to leave their birth families and establish their own families earlier than other girls (Belsky, Steinberg, & Draper, 1991). Research supports the link between timing of maturation and family stress. Young girls raised in families that experience high levels of conflict reach puberty about six months earlier than girls from more harmonious homes (Belsky et al., 1991; Wierson, Long, & Forehand, 1993). However, the precise reasons for this effect and how it occurs are not yet fully understood (Graber, Brooks-Gunn, & Warren, 1995).

Girls raised in harmonious families tend to mature somewhat later than girls raised in stressful families. What evolutionary argument has been proposed to explain the early maturation of girls in stressful families?

Sex and Race Differences in Puberty

Just as girls and boys experience their growth spurts at different times, they also progress through puberty differently (see Figure 14.5). Girls begin and complete puberty about two years earlier than boys. Although it is commonly believed that menarche signals the beginning of puberty for girls, menarche actually occurs relatively late in pubertal development. The typical progression of pubertal changes in girls begins with breast growth and development. Between 8 and 10 years of age, enlarged breast buds develop, and the breasts continue to grow in size during adolescence. Growth of pubic hair is the second marker of puberty in girls, typically beginning at 10 to 12 years of age and continuing until the hair has formed the adultlike triangular pattern, usually by age 14. The third marker of puberty is the development of the female genitalia. The external sex organs—the labia, vulva, and clitoris—all increase in size and sensitivity. The internal sex organs—the ovaries and uterus—also grow rapidly. Menarche usually occurs about two years after the beginning of breast development. Typically, girls do not ovulate until about a year after menarche. The final pubertal changes for females include deepening of the voice and the tendency to have acne.

FIGURE 14.5
The Progression of Pubertal Events in Girls and Boys

GIRLS	•Breast buds appear.	•Pubic hair begins to grow. •Vagina, ovaries, uterus, and labia grow rapidly. •Breasts enlarge. •Growth spurt occurs.	•Menarche occurs. •Underarm hair grows.	•Breasts fill out. •Ova mature. •Girl becomes capable of conception (about 1 year after menarche). •Voice deepens.	
BOYS			•Testes and scrotum grow. •Pubic hair begins to grow.	•Penis enlarges. •Voice changes begin. •First ejaculation of semen occurs. •Underarm hair and hair on upper lip begin to grow. •Growth spurt occurs.	•Hair grows on cheeks, chin, body. •Marked changes occur in voice.
	8–10	10–12	12–13	13–16	16–18

YEARS OLD

Note the differences in the timing of pubertal events for boys and girls. Can you identify the factors that contribute to the start of puberty and the differences in the timing for boys and girls?

FIGURE 14.6

Cross-Cultural Comparisons of Changes in Age of Menarche

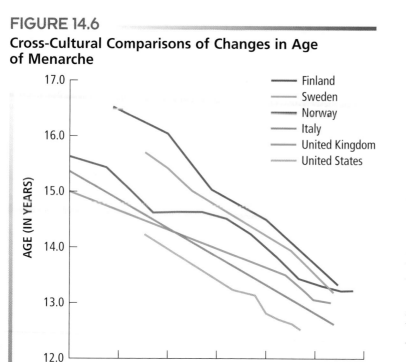

Notice that the age at which girls achieve menarche has been dropping consistently over the past century. How are these findings explained? What factors contribute to these patterns?

Source: W. A. Marshall and J. M. Tanner, *Human Growth,* 2/e, pp. 171–210, Figure 11.3. Kluwer Academic Publishers, Copyright 1986. Reprinted with kind permission of Springer Science and Business Media.

The age at which girls achieve puberty varies by race. According to the results of a large-scale study of over 18,000 children 3 to 12 years old, about 38 percent of African American girls and 11 percent of Caucasian American girls showed breast development by age 8 (Herman-Giddens et al., 1997). Thus, it appears that girls today are undergoing puberty about a year earlier than has been reported before, with African American girls beginning puberty from 1 to 2 years earlier than their Caucasian American peers. Why these recent trends are occurring is not yet understood.

The pattern of pubertal development for boys is more variable than that for girls, and events occur in a different order (Marshall & Tanner, 1986). In the most typical pattern for boys, the growth of the testes is the first marker, usually beginning at 11½ to 12 years of age. Growth of pubic hair may be next, although boys vary widely in the age at which this begins (10 to 15 years). About a year later, growth of the penis and scrotum usually occurs. Between ages 12 and 16, boys typically have their first ejaculation of seminal fluid, although mature sperm may not be produced until about age 15 (Caissy, 1994). About two years after the appearance of pubic hair, underarm and facial hair begin to appear. Facial hair first appears on the upper lip, then on the upper cheeks, and last on the chin and lower jaw. In males, body hair continues to develop well after puberty (Marshall & Tanner, 1986). A sometimes embarrassing aspect of adolescent male development is the change in voice that occurs as the larynx increases in size. Comparative studies show that, in contrast to girls, African American and Caucasian American boys exhibit no differences in pubertal development (Marshall & Tanner, 1986).

Generational Differences in Puberty

Children today achieve puberty, start the growth spurt, and reach adult height about three years earlier than children did 100 years ago. This generational trend is more apparent in girls than in boys (Papadimitriou, 2001). For instance, in the United States, the age at menarche has dropped about two to three years over the past century (Wyshak, 1983), with girls today reaching menarche at about 12.5 years (Herman-Giddens et al., 1997). This pattern is seen all over the world (see Figure 14.6).

One explanation for earlier maturation is improved nutrition and health care. These improvements may have reduced the time it takes for girls to reach a critical weight, which is regarded by some as the signal to the body to begin the adolescent growth spurt (Frisch, 1991). The trend toward earlier puberty and growth began with groups that had better nutrition, such as economically well-off adolescents. However, in many countries, such as the United States and Denmark, the differences among groups is now small, and the trend toward earlier puberty and growth spurts has ceased (Eveleth & Tanner, 1990; Helm & Grolund, 1998).

Adolescents' Responses to Physical and Sexual Maturation

Two elderly men watch as a young adolescent boy and girl hug and kiss each other in a movie theater. "Those kids' hormones are out of control," says one of the men.

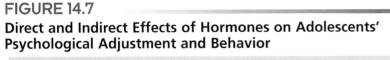

FIGURE 14.7

Direct and Indirect Effects of Hormones on Adolescents' Psychological Adjustment and Behavior

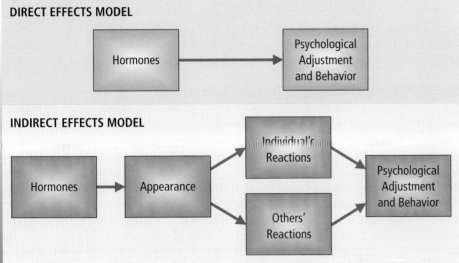

This figure depicts the influence of hormones on adolescents' adjustment and behavior. In the top model, hormones directly influence adjustment and behavior without any variables intervening. In the lower model, the effects of hormones on adjustment and behavior are mediated by the effects they have on the adolescent's appearance, which then influences how others behave, which then influences the adolescent's behavior and adjustment. Which model do you feel better depicts the ways in which hormones influence adolescents' adjustment and behavior?

Like the men at the movie theater, many people tend to blame hormones for adolescents' interest in the other sex, their moods swings, and their tendency to argue. This view, however, is inaccurate. Although the hormonal changes that trigger puberty are associated with changes in young adolescents' behavior, they are not direct causes of this behavior. Surprisingly little evidence suggests that hormones directly affect behavior. More support has been found for an indirect influence—hormonally triggered maturation brings about changes in an individual's self-concept and social interactions (Connolly et al., 1996). The indirect effects begin when hormones cause physical changes in the secondary sexual characteristics, which are visible signs of physical maturity. These signs then influence how others treat the adolescent. For instance, their parents' and peers' expectations for them change once adolescents undergo growth spurts because they seem older than other children. These changes influence the way they are treated. In turn, changes in how adolescents are treated influence how they feel about themselves (see Figure 14.7).

If a girl matures early and her father withdraws from her because he is uncomfortable with her emerging sexuality, she may feel rejected and begin to lose confidence in herself. On the other hand, a boy who matures early may be treated more like an adult by his teachers, thereby becoming more confident. In each case, it is not the biological changes at puberty that are causing the young adolescent's behavior. Instead, the meaning attributed to these changes by the young adolescent or by significant others influences the adolescent's behavior (Brooks Gunn & Warren, 1989).

Parents and their adolescent children can have different culture-based expectations about development. Hopi Indian girls know, for instance, that once they start to menstruate, they begin a new phase of life in which they may no longer roam at will but must instead stay at home. People in traditional Hopi society believe that running free is inappropriate

Although puberty is a physiological event that takes place in all individuals, one's culture defines its meaning and the customs surrounding it. Notice the elaborate décor and costume associated with this girl's transition to preadolescence.

after menarche because girls should guard their chastity and reputation and devote their time to preparing family meals. Girls also are expected to marry, which presents a dilemma: they must find a spouse while remaining secluded. Hopi girls are encouraged by their families to bring a new worker into the family in the form of a spouse, and yet they are not allowed the freedom to find that spouse. Although restrictions on freedom and pressure to marry make adolescence a trying time for Hopi girls, most learn to balance the expectations of their new status and adapt accordingly. Such responses to puberty, which vary across cultures, have important implications for interpersonal and personal adjustment.

Effects of Timing of Puberty in Boys and Girls

During adolescence, early-maturing boys are taller, heavier, and stronger than their peers, whereas late-maturing boys are shorter, thinner, and weaker. Because the traditional culture values strength and athleticism in men, early-maturing boys have an advantage. In light of their strength, these boys are likely to be better athletes than their peers and may feel more confident and competent, which can lead to increased self-esteem and elevated social status (Petersen, 1988; Simmons & Blyth, 1987). Late-maturing boys tend to be treated as though they were younger than their peers and may come to feel insecure about their own abilities (Caissy, 1994). They also are at risk for adjustment problems (Graber, Lewinsohn, Seeley, & Brooks-Gunn, 1997). Late-maturing boys also tend to be more dissatisfied with their body because they may weigh 25 to 30 pounds less and be 6 to 8 inches shorter than their peers (Alsaker, 1992).

Early-maturing boys are more likely than their peers to have problems at school and to use drugs and alcohol (Andersson & Magnusson, 1990; Duncan et al., 1985). One reason for these behaviors may be that early-maturing boys tend to make friends with older adolescents before they have had time to develop the strong coping skills they need to adjust to the physical changes of puberty (Alsaker, 1996). In contrast, late-maturing boys have the advantage of sufficient time in which to develop coping skills and values before they face the challenges of puberty (Susman, Koch, Maney, & Finkelstein, 1993).

Girls who mature early face a very different set of circumstances. Not only are they developing two or three years earlier than other girls; they also are four to six years ahead of the boys in their class. Being one of the first to enter puberty can be difficult, for there are no peers with whom to share the experience. Also, as early-maturing girls develop from slender preadolescents into fuller-breasted, wider-hipped adolescents, they may become concerned about the weight gain and increase in body fat that are normal to puberty. Some early-maturing girls perceive these changes as unattractive. The slim, long-legged body represents a standard of beauty that many young girls believe they must match in order to be accepted and considered attractive (Alsaker, 1996; Martin, 1996).

Because of dissatisfaction with the changes their body undergoes at puberty, early-maturing girls are at risk for eating disorders and disturbances (Koff & Rierdan, 1993). An exception to the poorer body image of early maturers is breast development: girls who develop breasts earlier tend to have a better body image, possibly because of the value placed on well-developed breasts in American society (Tobin-Richards, Boxer, & Petersen, 1983).

Early-maturing girls are more popular, have more older friends, gain more attention from older boys, and begin dating earlier than later-maturing girls. Like early-maturing boys, early-maturing girls tend to associate with older girls and boys, which may lead to use of alcohol and drugs (Tschann et al., 1994) and delinquency (Petersen, 1988). They also are more likely than their peers to be depressed, and they may do less well in school (Alsaker, 1992). Early onset of puberty seems to magnify preexisting behavior problems, so girls with earlier problems have the most difficulty adjusting (Ge, Conger, & Elder, 1996; Hayward, Killen, Wilson, & Hammer, 1997).

Late-maturing girls may have the best situation of all adolescents—they are not the first to enter a new stage and probably enter puberty at about the same time as many early-maturing boys. They are not the last to mature, since that position is held by late-maturing boys. Although these girls may have some initial doubts about their status, they have longer to learn to cope with the changes and more opportunities to share the experience with peers than do early-maturing girls.

Thus, early maturers of both sexes may be unprepared for the changes they experience; late maturers are less surprised by these changes and better informed. Late maturers have many mature role models, as well as family members who are prepared for the changes the adolescents undergo (Alsaker, 1996).

Individual characteristics—personality factors, attitudes, values, and prior experiences—play an important role in how adolescents respond to the physical changes that occur at puberty, the early or late timing of these changes, and the cultural expectations associated with them. For instance, one early-maturing girl may gravitate toward friends who are older and resemble her more, as they may make her feel more comfortable with her bodily changes. Through her older friends, she will be exposed to the norms and expectations for behavior among older adolescents (Alsaker, 1996). Another early-maturing girl, however, may continue to interact with same-age peers and thus respond quite differently to pubertal changes.

Outcomes for Early and Later Maturers

Several classic longitudinal studies have examined the characteristics of early and late maturers as they grow older and reach adulthood. These studies reveal that the early-maturing boys who enjoyed advantages over their peers take on more leadership roles later in life. They rate themselves as more responsible and warmer, but also as more rigid and conforming, than do other males (Jones & Mussen, 1958). Late-maturing boys, who are the last of their peers to mature, rate themselves as more rebellious, impulsive, and childish, but also as more creative. As adults, they hold fewer executive jobs, but they report being happier and having more successful marriages than do early-maturing males (Jones, 1965; Mussen & Jones, 1957).

Early-maturing girls, who face many challenges from adults and peers while dealing with puberty, continue to experience difficulties as they grow older. Although this certainly is not true of all early-maturing girls, as a group they complete fewer years of education and are more likely to develop negative attitudes about school (Alsaker, 1995). As young adults, they have more children than later-developing girls, especially if they developed relationships with older friends during adolescence (Magnusson, 1988). In middle age, they rate themselves as more self-directed and self-assured than later-developing girls do (Peskin, 1973).

TABLE 14.1
Issues and Outcomes for Early and Late Maturers

TIMING OF MATURATION	ISSUES	OUTCOMES
Early-maturing boys	Treated as older	Increased likelihood of behavior problems
	Make friends with older peers	Greater popularity because of sports abilities
	Greater athleticism	
Late-maturing boys	Treated as younger	Feelings of insecurity
		Adjustment problems
		Greater dissatisfaction with physical qualities
Early-maturing girls	Considerably ahead of peers in physical development	Increased risk for behavior problems
		Increased popularity with older boys
	More attractive to older boys	Date earlier
		Increased concern about physical appearance and weight
Late-maturing girls	Enter puberty about the same time that early-maturing boys do	Best adjustment of all adolescents
	Best prepared to handle changes	

Psychological Reactions to Pubertal Events

Puberty brings with it dramatic physical changes. Adolescents grow taller and gain weight, and their body proportions change. Girls begin to menstruate, and boys begin having wet dreams. How do adolescents react to the changes in the appearance and functioning of their bodies?

Reactions to Changes in Appearance

Adolescents expend considerable time and energy thinking about their appearance. One reason for this preoccupation is that adolescents are experiencing sudden changes in the way they look. Another source of adolescents' concern with their bodies is changes in their cognitive abilities, which cause them to focus more of their attention on themselves. This concern about appearance also is due in part to the positive characteristics attributed to attractive individuals. For example, research has demonstrated that people believe that attractive adolescents are successful, friendly, and intelligent (Lerner et al., 1990). Adolescents' body images also grow more important as they grow interested in the other sex; they want to be desirable to the other sex so that they will be able to get dates and be popular (Martin, 1996).

Adolescents' body images are shaped by societal expectations conveyed through magazines, television, and movies, as well as by people's responses to their appearance. For instance, hours of television viewing exposes adolescents to actors and actresses who tend to be young, attractive, and slim. The ideals concerning attractiveness for females are highly ingrained in our culture (Phelps et al., 1993). Girls know these standards by age 6 and believe that they relate to popularity. Being slim is a central feature of what it means to be attractive. At an early age, children develop negative stereotypes about overweight people (Counts, Jones, Frame, & Jarvie, 1986). Girls are more worried about being slim than boys are, and they are more critical of their own appearance. As you learned in reading about early- and late-maturing adolescents, early-maturing girls, in particular, have difficulty as they gain weight during puberty because they perceive this change as moving them away from the ideal of beauty in our culture (LaPorte, 1997). Despite all the societal pressures, though, many young girls develop a good body image, causing them to be less preoccupied than other girls with weight and with comparing themselves to others (Rosenbaum, 1993).

In this picture, R & B music artist Usher shows off his muscular physique. After puberty, boys become more concerned about muscularity and show increased preferences for larger and more muscular bodies. Can you identify the factors that contribute to this increased concern about boys' appearance and physique?

In the United States, the cultural expectation of long legs and a slim body, especially for girls and women, is a relatively recent notion. Even 25 years ago, the US ideal for women was more voluptuous and curvaceous. The pressure to be slim is related to socioeconomic class in the United States, with women of higher socioeconomic status being thinner than women of middle and lower socioeconomic status. Historically, however, being thin has been associated with a poor diet and with disease.

In recent years, greater attention has been paid to the impact of physical appearance of men and boys (Olivardia, Pope, Borowiecki, & Cohane, 2004). For example, after puberty boys become more concerned about muscularity and show increased preferences for larger, more muscular bodies (Cohane & Pope, 2001; Jones, 2004). For some, this increased concern becomes exaggerated and can develop into an obsessive focus on weight training and muscle enhancement (Choi, Pope, & Olivardia, 2002). After puberty, adolescent boys increasingly become preoccupied about their weight (Labre, 2002). Although not as great as is found for teen girls, this preoccupation is related to a variety of weight control behaviors—exercising, dieting, and steroid use. Dissatisfaction with one's body type increases after puberty due to the discrepancy in ideal versus real body types for boys (Jones, 2004). Thus, the pursuit of the ideal male body, which increases at puberty, has important consequences for adolescent boys as well girls (Ricciardelli & McCabe, 2004).

Within the United States, different ethnic groups hold varying standards for attractiveness. Some African American females report more flexible concepts of attractiveness, including "making what you've got work for you" (Parker et al., 1995). Caucasian American girls express a need to be "perfect" in their appearance, meaning they must have a flat stomach, little waist, and slim thighs to be attractive. In contrast, African American girls are less likely to focus on physical attributes, instead considering attitude, confidence, and grooming to be important to attractiveness. These more flexible and attainable standards for attractiveness may contribute to the better body images and lower risk of eating disorders among African American girls than among Caucasian American girls (Parker et al., 1995).

Reactions to Markers of Sexual Maturity

All I could think of was what I would feel if someone saw me buying sanitary napkins at the drugstore.

I was scared and embarrassed. I felt like everyone who looked at me could tell I was wearing one of those awful Kotex pads!

My mother and my school had prepared me for it, and although it was a surprise, it was kind of exciting to feel like I was a woman. (Dacey & Kenny, 1997, p. 83)

These girls have different ideas about what it means to be attractive. What standards of beauty do Caucasian American girls hold to? What standards characterize African American girls?

A milestone of puberty for girls is menarche. Most women vividly recall their first period (Gallant & Derry, 1995). But as the comments of the girls above indicate, responses to menarche are mixed. On the positive side, adolescent girls believe that menarche is a sign of maturity, signals their ability to have children, is a part of being a woman, and makes them more similar to other females. On the negative side, they find that it is a hassle because of the need to carry pads or tampons with them and the physical discomfort (McGrory, 1990; Ryan, Millstein, & Irwin, 1996).

Girls' adjustment to menarche is influenced by how prepared they are. Compared to girls who are prepared for menarche, unprepared girls report feeling more negative symptoms and have a more negative self-image (McGrory, 1990). Girls' prior expectations about menstruation also influence their feelings. Girls who expect pain and discomfort are more likely to report pain and discomfort once they begin menstruating (Brooks-Gunn & Ruble, 1982).

Two health problems related to menstruation may become issues for girls. **Dysmenorrhea** is the name for menstrual cramps and discomfort, and **premenstrual syndrome (PMS)** refers to a whole constellation of emotional and physical symptoms, such as backaches, headaches, moodiness, and water retention, that occurs before menstruation. Dysmenorrhea is caused by the uterus's release of a hormone called prostaglandin during menstruation. The resulting pain can be treated by taking antiprostaglandin medications. Many adolescent girls experience dysmenorrhea; over 90 percent report having cramps with their periods, and 64 percent say that cramps are moderate or severe (Wilson & Keye, 1989). Adolescent girls also report having the symptoms of PMS (Fisher, Trieller, & Napolitano, 1989). Although social expectancies influence girls' reporting of symptoms of PMS, this does not imply that the symptoms of PMS are not real. Instead, it may be that knowledge of impending menstruation sensitizes adolescent girls and women to certain physical and emotional symptoms associated with it.

Little research is available about boys' responses to puberty. An important marker of puberty for boys is their first ejaculation. Generally, boys are not well informed about ejaculation, and the little information they have is gained from peers or the media. Probably because ejaculation is associated with masturbation, boys are often secretive about their first ejaculation, seldom talking with others about it (Gaddis & Brooks-Gunn, 1985). In addition, boys' anxiety about puberty may be heightened by erections that occur frequently and without warning, sometimes causing guilt and embarrassment.

dysmenorrhea *menstrual cramps and discomfort*

premenstrual syndrome (PMS) *a whole constellation of emotional and physical symptoms, such as backaches, headaches, moodiness, and water retention, that occur before menstruation*

What Are the Health and Safety Concerns of Adolescence?

Adolescence is a period of enhanced awareness of and attention to well-being. For most adolescents, it is a time of optimal health, with low levels of chronic disease and low death rates. Adolescents describe themselves as being healthy overall. In a large-scale study of adolescents from Europe, Canada, and the United States, over 90 percent of adolescents described themselves as feeling healthy, although adolescents in the United States reported somewhat lower rates (Health Behavior in School-Aged Children, 2000).

Many of the major health issues for young adolescents center on their rapid growth and the changes associated with puberty and their increased independence and involvement in the social world. Because they may grow 4 to 8 inches per year, young adolescents need good nutrition, yet they often have inadequate diets. Societal norms make some adolescents, especially young girls, overly concerned about the normal changes associated with puberty (such as weight gain). This combination of societal expectations and normal developmental changes may lead to eating disturbances or, in rare cases, full-blown eating disorders. In reality, although adolescents are seldom sick, they are much more likely to die than are children. Accidents and injuries are the most likely cause of death during adolescence, especially for boys and for older rather than younger adolescents (CDC, 1998). Many of the fatalities among adolescents, such as those caused by accidents, homicides, and suicide, are preventable.

Nutrition

The rapid physical growth experienced by adolescents requires a high-quality diet. But the reality is that many adolescents' diets are far from adequate. Many adolescents skip meals, eat high-fat snacks, avoid eating fruits and vegetables, and have inadequate knowledge about nutrition (Hertzler & Frary, 1989). In a study of 120,000 young adolescents from 26 European countries, Canada, and the United States, adolescents living in the United States were found to be less likely to have a good diet than adolescents in other countries. US adolescents were less likely to eat fruits and vegetables each day and more likely to eat potato chips and french fries than students from other countries. The United States ranked among the top three countries for adolescent consumption of sweets and soft drinks each day (Health Behaviors of School-Aged Children, 2000).

Nutritional needs during adolescence vary widely, depending on rate of growth and amount of physical activity. For instance, a very active adolescent girl in the peak of her growth spurt may need 20 percent more calories than a younger girl (Ensminger, Ensminger, Konlande, & Robson, 1986). Not surprisingly, the most calories are needed during the peak of the growth spurt (Schebendach & Shenker, 1992). Adolescents who have inadequate food intake are at risk for a variety of psychological problems, school suspension, and peer relationship difficulties (Alaimo et al., 2000).

Because of the increased growth of muscles, young adolescent girls and boys need more protein than children do. Dramatic bone growth increases calcium requirements, but many adolescents consume less than the recommended amounts. Girls in particular fall far short in calcium consumption, consuming only about 60 to 78 percent of the required amount. Lack of adequate calcium may increase the likelihood of osteoporosis—a loss of density and weakening of the bones—in later life (Life Sciences Research Office, 1995; Schebendach & Shenker, 1992). Adolescents also require additional iron but often fail to eat foods that are rich in it. Lack of iron can lead to anemia and influence the ability to think, work, and adequately function (Beard, 1995).

The rapid physical growth experienced by adolescents requires a high-quality diet. But the reality is that many adolescents' diets are far from adequate. How does diet and nutrition affect adolescents' development?

Fitness and Sports Participation

Physical activity is an important part of a healthy lifestyle, and regular exercise is strongly associated with feeling healthy and confident, making friends, and spending time with friends. Despite Americans' preoccupation with fitness and health, many adolescents today weigh more than they should and do not exercise enough to be physically fit. US teens are less physically fit than adolescents in many other countries (Health Behaviors in School-Aged Children, 2000).

Physical Fitness in Adolescence

Physical fitness refers to a state of physical well-being that allows one to function effectively without undue fatigue. Four assessments are used to measure fitness, and boys' and girls' ratings in these categories change in different ways during adolescence:

- *Aerobic endurance:* During early adolescence, untrained boys and girls improve in aerobic endurance, which relates to the functioning of the heart and lungs. Girls then taper off, but boys continue to improve throughout adolescence (Gallahue & Ozmun, 1995). Training improves aerobic endurance and narrows the gap between girls and boys (Krahenbuhl, Skinner, & Korht, 1985).

- *Muscle strength and endurance:* Girls and boys are indistinguishable in muscle strength until adolescence, at which time boys' strength improves more rapidly than girls', probably because of boys' increased muscle growth. Girls and boys differ more on measures of upper-body strength (such as pull-ups) than they do on other measures of strength (such as sit-ups).

- *Muscle flexibility:* Beginning at age 10, girls are more flexible than boys, and they show more improvement than boys throughout adolescence (Gallahue & Ozmun, 1995). Flexibility peaks at age 17 but can be maintained through training.

- *Body fat:* Girls' percentage of body fat increases during adolescence, while boys' decreases (see Chapter 11). Despite the emphasis on fitness, a lack of activity and the popularity of fast foods have contributed to the fact that the average teen today carries more body fat than teens in 1960 did (Galluhue & Ozum, 1995).

This gymnast is demonstrating strength and flexibility. How do boys and girls differ in strength and flexibility during late adolescence?

Adolescents who are active have a lower percentage of body fat, greater muscle strength and endurance, and greater aerobic capacity (President's Council on Physical Fitness and Sports, 2001). With exercise, the heart becomes more efficient and pumps more blood with each beat, thus decreasing the rate at which it beats. Exercise also raises the level of "good" cholesterol and lowers blood pressure, thereby reducing the risk of heart disease. Obesity can be prevented through regular exercise. Exercise also steps up the effectiveness of the immune system, heightening people's resistance to disease (Malm, 2004).

Adolescents who exercise are more likely to be healthy adults. In a longitudinal study, female athletes had lower levels of breast cancer and reproductive system cancers than did nonathletes. Most of these athletes began their training before or during high school. Long-term exercise reduces the risk of serious diseases later in life (Kelder, Perry, Klepp, & Lytle, 1994). For instance, professional ballet dancers and weight lifters have stronger bones than do nonathletes, and strong bones lower the risk for osteoporosis later (Loucks, 1988).

Boys are more likely than girls to engage in vigorous physical activity. How does exercise enhance health and development? What can be done to increase fitness in adolescents?

In large-scale national studies of high school students' behavior, only 44 percent of senior boys and 27 percent of senior girls exercised either every day or almost every day, but nearly two thirds of all high school boys and about half of the girls exercised two or more times a week (CDC, 1998; Health Behaviors in School-Aged Children, 2000).

Adolescents and Organized Sports

During early adolescence, involvement in sports tends to peak. For example, compared to younger children and adults, 12- to 17-year-olds are more likely to participate in organized sports (such as football, softball, or soccer), bicycling, and swimming and are less likely to participate in aerobics, walking, and exercise with equipment. A dramatic increase has

physical fitness *a state of physical well-being that allows a person to function effectively without undue fatigue*

occurred over the past three decades in the number of girls participating in high school sports. In 1971, 4 percent of girls were active in high school athletics; recently the number has increased to 42 percent (CDC, 1998; President's Council, 1997).

In later adolescence, many teens, especially girls, drop out of sports. The factors that influence adolescents' involvement in sports include physical development, conflicts of interest, perceived skills, maturity, gender role expectations, and encouragement from family members and peers. Teens who continue to be involved in sports tend to be labeled "athletes" and often differ from their peers both in their physical development and in their confidence in their athletic abilities (President's Council, 1997). Females who continue to play sports tend to be popular, to be involved in more extracurricular activities, to have higher educational aspirations, and to be less likely to become delinquents (Melnick, Vanfossen, & Sabo, 1988).

The most popular sports among high school boys are basketball, track and field, baseball, and football; among girls, the most popular sports are basketball, track and field, volleyball, and softball (National Federation of State High School Associations, 2001). Male athletes who play football and basketball tend to be stronger and more physically developed than nonathletes. Adolescents of both sexes who are involved in gymnastics and track often are delayed in maturity; for instance, female gymnasts and figure skaters tend to enter puberty later than other girls (Malina & Bouchard, 1991).

Only a few studies have been done to assess the effects of sports participation on adolescents, but these studies suggest that involvement in sports can serve many functions. Some evidence suggests that sports are protective for females in that female athletes in a nationwide survey were less than half as likely as female nonathletes to get pregnant (5 percent and 11 percent, respectively). Female athletes also were more likely to be virgins, had their first intercourse later, and had sex less often than their nonathlete peers (Lehman & Koerner, 2004; Women's Sports Foundation, 1998). Sports also help adolescents develop social ties with others. Sports and other extracurricular activities integrate adolescents into the social world by connecting them with peers and adults in the community. Adolescents also are exposed to positive role models and have opportunities to engage in ethical behavior with other people. Young athletes derive support not only from connections with adults outside their family, such as coaches, but also from connections within their family. Athletic competitions provide a social setting in which family connections can be reaffirmed; parents often attend events to watch their sons and daughters compete and help their children cope with the pressures (Weiss & Hayashi, 1995). Parents and peers can provide support and encouragement for young athletes by having realistic expectations of them and avoiding negative evaluations of their performance (President's Council, 1997).

Sports participation, like other forms of exercise, may improve adolescents' mental health and psychological well-being (Pyle McQuivey, Brassington, & Steiner, 2003; Steiner et al., 2000). Teens who exercise regularly are less likely to be depressed and anxious than those who are sedentary (Landers & Petruzzello, 1994; Pastor, Balaguer, Pons, & Garcia-Merita, 2003). Exercise may be a protective factor, helping adolescents cope with stress. For instance, girls who exercise regularly are able to deal with high levels of stress better than girls who do not exercise regularly (Creswell & Hodge, 2004). Moderate levels of exercise are best for increasing mental health. Adolescents who exercise strenuously for long periods or who are in highly competitive sports contests may suffer negative moods, lose their ability to concentrate, and become depressed and anxious (Singer, 1992). Not surprisingly, teenage boys involved in contact sports (such as football, soccer, rugby, etc.) have more injuries than adolescents involved in other sports (Finch et al., 2002). Although team sport involvement has been linked to positive educational paths, it has also been linked to involvement in one type of risky behavior—drinking alcohol (Eccles & Barber, 1999; Lorente, Souville, Griffet, & Grelot, 2004). Furthermore, additional research is needed about the effects of intense training during adolescence and pressures from coaches and parents to succeed in sports (Marsh & Daigneault, 1999).

Additionally, sports serve as a vehicle for personal growth. Participation may improve adolescents' self-esteem and self-concept by helping them realize their particular strengths and improve their sense of mastery, concentration, and planning (Bowker, Gabdois, &

Cornock, 2003). Individual benefits depend on the type of sports involvement, attitudes about winning, and qualities of the coaches or adult leaders involved in the activity (Larson, 1994). For instance, athletes who use sports to measure their self-worth, especially boys, experience negative effects on their self-evaluation when they do poorly or when they lose. In contrast, athletes who use their sports performance to gain a sense of mastery are more likely to experience positive effects on their self-evaluation (Danish, Kleiber, & Hall, 1987; Duda, 1988).

Body image, which influences self-esteem, can be improved or denigrated through sports. Coaches sometimes discourage overweight adolescents from involvement in sports, which can negatively affect these adolescents' self-esteem. A young gymnast whose coach tells her she is too fat will feel worse rather than better about her body image. In contrast, when parents and coaches have a positive attitude toward adolescents' participation and appearance, adolescents feel better about their body as well as their accomplishments (President's Council, 1997).

Eating Disturbances and Disorders

The full spectrum of eating problems can be seen during adolescence. One of the most common problems, occurring in about 1 in 5 adolescents, is being overweight. Additionally, many adolescents have eating disturbances in which they eat too little or have unhealthy eating habits. A small group of adolescents—girls in particular—develop serious and life-threatening eating disorders such as anorexia and bulimia.

Obesity

About 14 percent of adolescents in the United States are seriously overweight, and this figure has doubled since the 1970s (CDC, 2001d), especially for adolescents who immigrated to the United States (Popkin & Udry, 1998). The reasons for the increase are unclear, although lack of exercise and poor eating habits contribute to the problem, as they do for younger children (see Chapter 11). Obesity in adolescence is related to a variety of serious health risks in later life (Vogt, 1999). For instance, overweight adolescents are more likely than their normal-weight peers to suffer heart disease, colon cancer, and arthritis and have generally poorer health as adults. About 75 percent of overweight adolescents become overweight adults (CDC, 2001d).

Many adolescents are concerned about their weight but attempt to control it in ineffective ways. Many adopt dieting as a strategy for weight control when increased physical activity is more likely to be beneficial. According to one health study, about one half of girls and one third of boys of ages 11 to 13 feel they should be dieting (Health Behavior in School-Aged Children, 2000).

Anorexia Nervosa

Sylvia is a 14-year-old adolescent who is 5 feet 6 inches tall but weighs only 85 pounds. She is not pleased with her appearance. Despite others' views that she is too skinny, Sylvia worries she is too fat. Because of this, she exercises frequently and eats little. Her diet is very restricted; she consumes only about 1,000 calories a day, mainly eating lettuce, carrots, and fruit. She has stopped having menstrual periods and often is sick. She has no idea that she is undernourished. Instead, Sylvia feels that she has a healthy fear of being fat and shows strong self-discipline because of her strict adherence to her low-calorie diet. Nonetheless, she is moody, depressed, and exhausted all the time. Sylvia suffers from anorexia and has had to be hospitalized to prevent starvation.

TABLE 14.2
Positive and Negative Effects of Teen Exercise and Sports Participation

Positive Effects

Improved physical and mental health

Enhanced self-esteem and sense of mastery

Improved social relationships

Enhanced perception of one's appearance and body image

Negative Effects

Increased risk of injury

Associated with increased consumption of alcohol

Increased stress and anxiety over competition and winning

Increased concern about body image

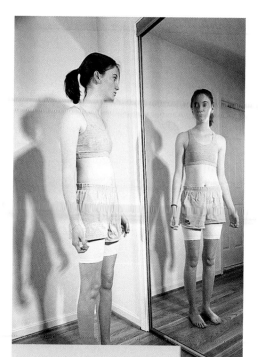

This young teenager is thin but still feels that she is overweight. Concern with being thin is a common characteristic in people with eating disorders and disturbances. What factors contribute to dramatically higher rates of eating disorders and disturbances among girls?

Anorexia nervosa is an eating disorder, occurring most often in young women, in which individuals eat very little but believe that they are fat. Food and weight become obsessions. Many people with anorexia eat less than 800 calories a day and only three or four different foods. A core symptom of this disorder is an unrelenting pursuit of thinness, usually beginning during adolescence (Bon-De-Matte, 1998). This illness is marked by psychological disturbances as well as physical symptoms. The essential symptoms include a dramatic loss of weight or failure to gain expected weight, an intense fear of gaining weight or becoming fat, a negative body image, and, for females, an absence of menstrual cycles (American Psychiatric Association, 2000).

Although it is commonly believed that individuals with anorexia have a distorted body image, research does not clearly support this belief. That is, individuals with anorexia perceive their body fairly accurately; nonetheless they have a negative body image since their ideal shape (what they *want* to look like) is much thinner than their actual shape. Furthermore, the particular focus of concern varies from girl to girl—some worry about the size of their abdomen or waist; others worry about having their inner thighs touch when they walk (Hsu & Sobkiewicz, 1991). People prone to anorexia are described as being overly perfectionistic, highly controlled, and "model children." Anorexia occurs nine times more often in females than in males and is more common in girls from middle-class and upwardly mobile families (Coupey, 1992; Silber, 1986).

Many factors relate to anorexia, but the extent to which they may cause the disorder is unclear. Also, wide individual differences exist in the causes of anorexia. Genetic predisposition plays a small role, but family relationships may play a larger role. Families of individuals with anorexia often have disturbed functioning (Morad, Kandel, & Merrick, 2004). For example, there is some evidence that parents of adolescents with anorexia tend toward intense and intrusive involvement in their children's lives, as a result of frustration and disappointment in their own lives. This parental overinvolvement leaves the children ill-equipped to cope with the challenges experienced during early adolescence (Fisher & Brone, 1991). Additionally, victims of anorexia tend to have certain psychological characteristics, including the following:

■ Personality traits such as shyness, social anxiety and fearfulness, overcontrol, passivity, and perfectionism

■ Loss of a family member early in life (Coupey, 1992)

■ Depression (Muratori, Viglione, Maestro, & Picchi, 2004)

Anorexia poses serious health hazards. Inadequate intake of calories may lead to poor growth, delayed sexual development, osteoporosis, and infertility. Anorexia can last for long periods of time, and death may result from starvation and its complications (Steinhausen, 2002).

Cultural beliefs concerning ideal weight and body shape appear to be important factors in the development of eating disorders. In industrialized cultures, where thinness is the societal ideal for women, anorexia and other eating disorders are more prevalent. In Argentina, for example, almost 1 in 10 girls suffers from a serious eating disorder—many more than in the United States. Health experts blame this "epidemic" on an obsession with thinness. In some parts of the world, the ideal body is heavier than it is in the United States (Booth, 1994). Being large and having body fat are emblems of wealth and fertility in many cultures. Among Africans, African Americans, Filipinos, Middle Easterners, and Native Americans, the ideal of attractiveness includes a higher level of body fat than it does among Caucasians. Being overweight in these cultures is a protective factor in overall health (Kittler & Sucher, 1998; Williamson, 1998).

In the United States, 1 percent of adolescents are diagnosed with anorexia (Katzman, 1996). This figure is higher for certain subcultures in the United States. For example, ath-

anorexia nervosa   *an eating disorder, occurring most often in young women, in which individuals eat very little but believe that they are overweight*

letic women and men such as dancers and gymnasts are at a higher risk for this disorder (Fombonne, 1995). An extreme example is the case of Heidi Guenther, a young dancer who was told by one of the directors of the Boston Ballet Company that she needed to lose weight. After a few months of intense dieting, Heidi collapsed and died, probably from complications of poor nutrition caused by anorexia. At the time of her death, she was 5 feet 5 inches tall but weighed only 100 pounds.

Treatment for anorexia must include consideration of both physical and psychological aspects of the disorder. Treatments that deal only with the weight loss, such as medication or surgery, are rarely effective (Agras et al., 2004). The most effective treatments involve structured programs with positive reinforcement for weight gain, as well as nutritional supplements, therapy to help the individual overcome the fear of getting fat, and family and group therapy, all of which are likely to be needed for several years (Agras et al., 2004).

Bulimia Nervosa

Like Sylvia's, Lisa's strange eating behavior began during adolescence. Lisa diets and exercises to lose weight, but unlike Sylvia, she regularly eats huge amounts of food; she maintains her normal weight by forcing herself to vomit. She feels lonely and isolated, and when things do not go well, she is overcome with an uncontrollable desire for sweets. She eats pounds of cake or cookies at a time and often does not stop until she is exhausted or in severe pain. Then, overwhelmed by guilt and disgust, she makes herself vomit. Lisa is bulimic.

Bulimia nervosa, an eating disorder characterized by secret eating binges and purges, often begins later in adolescence than anorexia does. During eating binges, people diagnosed with bulimia consume a large quantity of food over a short period of time and feel no control over their food consumption. People with bulimia have been known to eat over 7 pounds of food in a single binge (Lifshitz et al., 1991). Like Lisa, they often feel guilty and uncomfortable after a binge. To avoid gaining weight, and to reduce their anxiety and guilt, they purge themselves by vomiting, using laxatives, or exercising excessively. Table 14.3 compares the major symptoms of bulimia and anorexia.

TABLE 14.3
Comparison of Common Symptoms of Anorexia and Bulimia

SYMPTOMS	ANOREXIA	BULIMIA
Excessive weight loss	X	
Continuation of dieting although bone-thin	X	
Dissatisfaction with appearance	X	
Loss of monthly menstrual periods	X	X
Unusual interest in food	X	X
Development of strange eating rituals	X	X
Eating in secret	X	X
Obsession with exercise	X	X
Serious depression	X	X
Consumption of large amounts of food		X
Vomiting or use of drugs to stimulate defecation		X
Disappearance into bathroom for long periods of time		X
Abuse of drugs or alcohol		X

*Some individuals suffer from both anorexia and bulimia and have symptoms of both disorders.

Source: National Institute of Mental Health, 1994.

bulimia nervosa   *an eating disorder characterized by secret eating binges and purges*

Like people with anorexia, those with bulimia are persistently overconcerned with body shape and weight (Quadflieg & Fichter, 2003). Bulimia typically continues intermittently over many years, during which periods of normal eating are interspersed with binges and purges. Although prevalence estimates vary widely, about 2 to 5 percent of females and about 1 percent of males are diagnosed with bulimia (Boeck, 1992).

Personality, social, and cultural factors relate to bulimia. Individuals with bulimia often have family members who are obese and suffer from depression (Rastam & Gillberg, 1991). Individuals with bulimia tend to be depressed and have poor self-esteem (Brewerton, 2002). Like anorexia, bulimia is more likely to occur in adolescents from middle- and upper-class families and is more common where thinness is the ideal (Furnham & Alibhai, 1983) and where family relationships are conflicted and negative (Okon, Greene, & Smith, 2003).

Successful therapy for bulimia targets the physical and psychological aspects of the disorder. Bulimia is treated through behavior modification programs, nutrition education, medications for depression, and counseling (Phillips et al., 2003). Bulimia is most successfully treated when it is diagnosed early, but because people with bulimia maintain a normal body weight, they often are able to hide their illness from others for years.

Eating Disturbances

Although anorexia and bulimia are relatively rare, milder versions of these eating patterns, referred to as **eating disturbances,** are quite common in adolescents. For instance, some adolescents skip meals, avoid certain foods, or take in an inadequate number of calories (Lifshitz et al., 1991). Binge eating, but usually without purging, also is common. Eating disturbances are more common in adolescent girls than in any other group of people (Moore & Gullone, 1995; Page & Allen, 1995).

Why are eating disturbances so common? Even before puberty, US children have excessive concern with weight. In a study of 8- to 13-year-old children, over one third of the youngest children reported that they wanted to be thinner. By age 13, about 75 percent of the girls and 40 percent of the boys desired to be thinner (Maloney, McGuire, Daniels, & Specker, 1989). These weight-conscious children enter puberty already aware of the cultural belief that being thin is beautiful and healthy. Parental concerns and the media—especially television and fashion magazines—contribute to adolescents' weight concerns (Field et al., 2001). These concerns may be magnified by newly emerging cognitive abilities, which increase their attention and focus on themselves and their concerns about what others think of them, as will be discussed later in the chapter.

As you can see in Figure 14.8, by adolescence, eating and weight concerns are more pronounced among girls than among boys (CDC, 2001d), and this difference gets larger as young adolescents get older (Richards et al., 1990). Young girls, in particular, skip meals and avoid snacks or favorite foods to try to lose weight (CDC, 2001d; Stein & Reichert, 1990). Although taking laxatives, vomiting, and taking diet pills are uncommon and extreme dieting behaviors, girls are more likely to use these forms of dieting than boys are (CDC, 2001d).

Eating disturbances also may be common because adolescents in the United States weigh more now than in the past. This increase in body weight, coupled with the increased emphasis on thinness, may add to the dissatisfaction that many adolescents feel as they enter puberty and begin to gain weight. A longitudinal study of eating disturbances found that young adolescent girls with negative feelings about their body were more likely than their peers to develop eating problems when they gained weight (Attie & Brooks-Gunn, 1989). Thus, societal and developmental factors combine to increase the pressure for adolescents, particularly girls, to maintain a below-average body weight (Fombonne, 1995; Levine et al., 1994).

Changing relationships with others may influence the risk that an adolescent will develop eating disturbances. Dating increases concerns about one's popularity, appearance, and body image. For instance, young adolescent girls who have achieved menarche and

eating disturbances   *mild versions of eating disorders*

FIGURE 14.8

Sex Difference in Young Adolescents' Concerns About Weight and Eating, by Grade

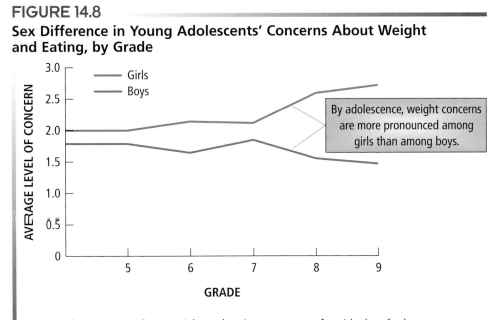

Notice that concerns about weight and eating are greater for girls than for boys at every age. Notice also how these concerns increase for girls and decrease for boys beginning in eighth grade. Can you explain the reasons for these differences and why these differences would be magnified around eighth grade?

Source: CDC, 2001d.

begun dating are more likely to develop eating disturbances than girls who are not dating (Cauffman & Steinberg, 1996). Interactions with mothers and fathers may buffer some girls from the stresses of puberty: girls who had better relationships with their parents, especially their fathers, had fewer weight and eating concerns and healthier eating habits than girls with strained relationships. Relationships with fathers are particularly important in conveying messages to daughters about whether their pubertal changes are acceptable (Field et al., 2001; Swarr & Richards, 1996).

As you learned in the discussion of adolescents' body images, ideals for attractiveness vary across ethnic groups. These differences may account for the research findings that Latino and Caucasian American students are more likely to think of themselves as being overweight than African American students are (CDC, 2001d).

Adolescents and Chronic Illnesses

Adolescents typically miss only about five days of school a year because of illness, and girls typically miss one more day of school than boys do. Only about 14 percent of all adolescents are chronically ill. Not surprisingly, adolescents who have chronic illnesses are more likely to miss school and are more limited in their activities than other adolescents (Coupey, 1992).

> *Patrick wears braces, is anxious to begin driving, and dreams of becoming a rock star. Like many other teens, Patrick struggles against his parents' protectiveness as he develops his own sense of self. He sometimes ignores his parents' advice. His parents say he is rebellious. The struggles that Patrick has with his parents could be deadly. Patrick has cystic fibrosis, a chronic disease that requires daily treatments and a strict regimen of pill taking—up to 30 pills a day. If Patrick ignores reminders about taking his pills or doing his treatments, he could die. "I hate bringing my pills to school 'cause I feel embarrassed," Patrick said. "No one else takes medicine. I'm the only one."*

Chronically ill adolescents like Patrick face many challenges. Patrick knows that he has to deal with these challenges every day for the rest of his life. He has to learn to cope with a life-threatening disease that requires constant attention. His health can deteriorate quickly if he forgets to take treatments or pills, and his mental health can be negatively affected by the continual struggle to manage his disease (Meuleners, Binns, Lee, & Lower, 2003).

The number of adolescents with chronic illnesses has increased, not because more children are identified as having these illnesses but because diseases that would have killed children 20 years ago now do not. Improved treatments have extended the life span of these children into adolescence and beyond. For instance, childhood cancer has been transformed from being almost uniformly fatal to being chronic and potentially curable.

Adolescents who test limits during their teens may engage in behaviors that are dangerous to their health. A diabetic teen may eat forbidden foods or take the wrong amount of insulin. Even adolescents who take responsibility for their own care and treatment may lack the knowledge to do so correctly. Errors in self-treatment are common among adolescents (Palardy et al., 1998).

Adolescents with chronic illnesses are at increased risk for psychological difficulties, especially depression. Nonetheless, the vast majority of these adolescents, even those with very serious diseases, are mentally healthy and well adjusted. The longer adolescents have a disease, the more likely it is that they will learn to cope with it (Olsson et al., 2003).

The entire family is affected by an adolescent's chronic disease. In addition to the time spent on medical treatments and the costs incurred, the family has to deal with dramatic changes in family functioning. The added stress may cause marital difficulties between parents and feelings of neglect and resentment among siblings (Wysocki & Green, 1997). However, families play a crucial role in helping adolescents adjust to a chronic disease. For instance, social support from family members has been found to help diabetic adolescents control their disease (Garrison & McQuiston, 1989).

Death in Adolescence

Most people assume that adolescence is a healthy and carefree time of life. In reality, although adolescents are seldom sick, they are much more likely to die than are children. Death rates for all age groups have decreased, but death rates for adolescents and young adults have declined the least. In fact, the death rates for African American males and Latino males and females have not decreased at all. Adolescents die at over twice the rate of infants and toddlers (from 1 to 4 years old) and almost five times the rate of children ages 5 to 14 (CDC, 2004a).

The newspapers are full of stories about adolescents who die violent deaths. Most deaths during adolescence, particularly later adolescence, stem from events that are preventable—accidents, homicides, and suicides. In 2001 in the United States, almost 13,000 teens ages 15–19 died; 75 percent of these deaths were due to accidents, homicides, and suicides (Annie E. Casey Foundation, 2004). Across adolescence, teens from ethnic and racial minorities are more likely to die than are Caucasian teens (see Figure 14.9)—revealing the fact that minority children live in more risky environments and engage in more risky behaviors.

FIGURE 14.9

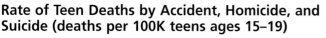

Rate of Teen Deaths by Accident, Homicide, and Suicide (deaths per 100K teens ages 15–19)

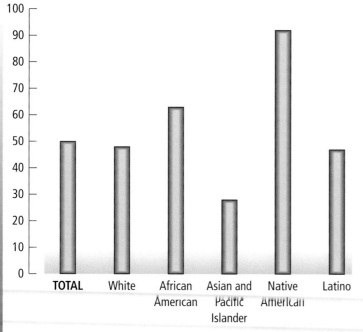

Notice the large differences in the rates of death across the different ethnic and racial groups. Can you identify what might contribute to these differences?

Source: Kids Count, 2004.

FIGURE 14.10

Deaths in Passenger Vehicles per 100,000 People

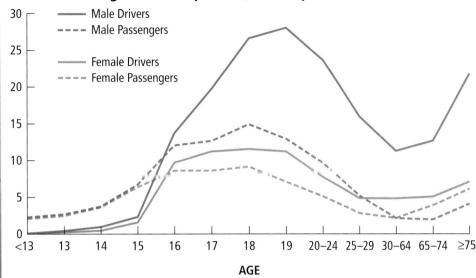

Notice the large sex difference in traffic fatalities that begins when teens start to drive. What factors account for such differences?

Source: US Department of Transportation, 2004.

Automobile Accidents

Driving or riding in an automobile is one of the riskiest activities for adolescents, killing almost 8,000 adolescents of 15–20 years of age per year (National Highway Traffic Safety Association, 2004). Auto-related deaths increase almost sixfold during adolescence, from about 5 per 100,000 for children under 15 to about 28 per 100,000 for older adolescents and young adults (National Center for Health Statistics, 2001c).

Across all ages of adolescence, more boys than girls die in car accidents—about 2 out of every 3 teenagers killed in motor vehicle crashes are males (US Department of Transportation, 2004). Across the life span, sex differences in traffic fatalities are largest during adolescence (see Figure 14.10). Research shows that teenagers are more likely than older drivers to speed, run red lights, make illegal turns, ride with an intoxicated driver, and drive after using alcohol and drugs, all of which contribute to their high accident rates (CDC, 2001c). In addition, adolescents engage in other activities that increase their risk of being hurt or killed. National surveys (CDC, 2001c) report high rates of risky behaviors among adolescents in high school (see Table 14.4).

Homicides

> It began as a typical dispute—two Texas teenagers talking trash over broken car windows. "And then I pulled out the gun," says Victor, 15, whose 1984 Cutlass had been damaged. "And he said, 'You ain't going to shoot me,' and I just started shooting, because he didn't think I would. It would have looked stupid if I pulled the gun and then didn't shoot him. I would have looked dumb." (Witkin, 1991, p. 29)

Victor's story is not that unusual. With children and adolescents having easy access to guns, even minor disputes can become lethal. US adolescents are particularly at risk for death by homicide. The United States has the highest homicide rate in the industrialized world: about 9 homicides per 100,000 people. Japan has the lowest rate: only about 1 homicide per 100,000 people.

TABLE 14.4
Risky Behaviors of Adolescents, Grades 9–12

BEHAVIOR	STATISTIC
Failure to use safety belts	16 percent of students rarely or never used a safety belt (seat belt) when riding with others.
Failure to wear motorcycle helmets	36 percent of students who had ridden motorcycles in the preceding 12 months rarely or never wore a helmet.
Failure to wear bicycle helmets	85 percent of students who had ridden bicycles during the preceding 12 months rarely or never wore a helmet.
Riding with a driver who has been drinking alcohol	33 percent of students had, during the preceding month, ridden with a driver who had been drinking alcohol.
Driving after drinking alcohol	13 percent of students had, during the preceding month, driven a vehicle after drinking alcohol.
Fighting at school	14 percent of students had, during the preceding 12 months, been involved in a fight at school.
Illegal steriod use	3 percent of teens said that they had, sometime in their lives, used illegal steriods to improve performance.
Taking laxatives or vomiting to lose weight	5 percent of teens said they had either taken laxatives or made themselves vomit to lose weight or control weight gain.

Source: Centers for Disease Control, 2001c.

As in Victor's story, most adolescent victims and murderers are males. Arrests of teenagers for murder rose dramatically during the 1980s and into the early 1990s. Although the number of arrests dropped in the late 1990s, homicides continue to occur at a high rate among young people. Males are much more likely to be murdered than females, and certain groups of males, such as young African American males, are much more likely than other groups to die from homicide. For instance, African American males between 14 and 24 years of age are about eight times more likely to die from homicide than are Caucasian American males (FBI, 2004). Typically, the murderer and the victim are of the same race (National Center for Health Statistics, 2001c).

The most common murder weapon is a gun—90 percent of homicides in the United States involve guns (FBI, 2004). Homicides are about twice as likely to occur in big cities as in rural or suburban areas, although most of the violence is concentrated only in small pockets of urban areas. The number of teen homicides over the past 15 years has contributed to the rising fear of crime, as adolescents are more likely than adults to kill or assault strangers.

In the past, children found a refuge from violent neighborhoods in their schools. Sadly, school is no longer a safe haven for children. Some schools have become violent places where murders occur (Kachur et al., 1996). In one survey, 7 percent of students said they had carried a weapon to school in the month before the survey, and 18 percent said they had carried a weapon somewhere (CDC, 2000b).

Because youth violence is so widespread, the US government has taken a key role in coordinating programs to deter violence (Dodge, 2001). Large-scale projects are under way in many cities to determine which interventions are effective in preventing and reducing aggressive and violent behavior (Cunningham & Henggeler, 2001). Most of the projects emphasize cooperative efforts among schools, health departments, and community partners.

Suicide

Suicide is the act of taking one's own life and is a major cause of death among adolescents. This is contrasted with **parasuicide,** which is a major risk factor for completed suicide, and is defined as any nonfatal self-injury, including suicide attempts and self-mutilation. It refers to a deliberate act of self-harm not resulting in death.

According to recent statistics, almost 11 out of every 100,000 adolescents between ages 15 and 24 die from suicide (CDC, 2004b). The suicide rate among adolescents has almost tripled since 1960, especially for Caucasian American males, but has been relatively unchanged since the 1990s (CDC, 2004c). Nationally, about 30 percent of high school students feel hopeless and about one fifth of these students think seriously about committing suicide during the year. Of even more

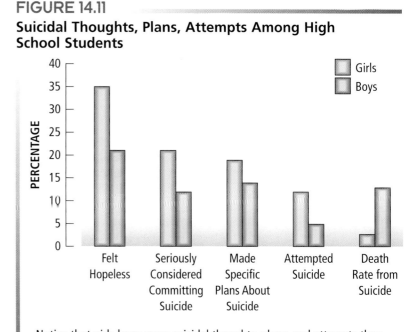

FIGURE 14.11

Suicidal Thoughts, Plans, Attempts Among High School Students

Notice that girls have more suicidal thoughts, plans, and attempts than boys. Why might this be so? Why do boys end up completing suicide more often that girls do?

Source: Centers for Disease Control, 2004c.

concern is the fact that about 15 percent of these adolescents make specific suicide plans, and about 3 percent are injured in a suicide attempt (CDC, 2004c). These rates are higher for girls than for boys (see Figure 14.11). Adolescent boys commit suicide about four times more often than girls, but girls attempt suicide about twice as often as boys do. A disturbing trend is that students in ninth grade were more likely to have made a suicide attempt than those in twelfth grade (CDC, 2004c). Fortunately, only a fraction of adolescents who attempt suicide are successful, with only 1 in 50 attempts resulting in death. Those who complete suicide are more likely to have had severe psychological problems (Jellinek & Snyder, 1998). For instance, when teens become so depressed that they lose interest in outside activities and friends, this downward spiral can culminate in suicide.

A number of studies reveal ethnic differences in the tendencies both to have suicidal thoughts and to make suicide attempts. Specifically, suicide risks tend to be higher for Native American and Latino teens and lower for Caucasian American and African American youths (CDC, 2004c). Numerous explanations have been suggested for the high suicide rates among American adolescents, including pressures to grow up fast, high rates of family instability, frequent residential mobility, and insecure economic futures (Cohen, Spirito, & Brown, 1996). The most prominent risk factors for attempting suicide during adolescence include the following (Cohen et al., 1996; Jellinek & Snyder, 1998):

- A psychiatric problem (such as depression), antisocial behavior, and substance abuse
- Belonging to a family that has a history of suicide
- Experiencing high levels of stress
- Experiencing family problems (such as parental rejection) or high levels of family conflict

suicide   *the act of taking one's own life*

parasuicide   *any nonfatal self-injury, including suicide attempts and self-mutilation*

Sexual Health Concerns

Before puberty, sexual activity consists primarily of self-exploration, masturbation, and interactions between boys and girls that entail holding hands, hugging, and playing games with sexual overtones (such as playing married partners). Once children reach puberty, however, sexual behavior becomes more explicit, ceases to be play, and increasingly becomes more adultlike (Graber & Archibald, 2001). This change has important implica tions for adolescents' health and well-being.

Sexually Transmitted Diseases

Adolescents' emerging sexuality puts them at particular risk for a wide variety of **sexually transmitted diseases (STDs),** which are diseases that may be transmitted from one person to another through sexual contact. Gonorrhea, syphilis, chlamydia, genital herpes, and HPV are all STDs. Sexual contact is not the only method for transmitting STDs. Some can be transmitted through such means as contaminated needles used in drug injections and contaminated blood used in transfusions. These diseases have serious long-term consequences, including decreased fertility later in life and death. One of the major concerns is that although the symptoms for STDs are often not obvious, the disease seriously damages the reproductive system nonetheless.

STDs are an epidemic in the United States and around the world. Young people are particularly at risk for contracting STDs. Approximately 19 million new cases of STDs occur each year in the United States, of which 9 million (48 percent) are among individuals between the ages of 15 and 24 years (Weinstock, Berman, & Cates, 2004). Of the sexually active population, 25 percent are 15 to 24 years old, yet this group accounts for the following:

- 48 percent of sexually transmitted diseases
- 60 percent of gonorrhea infections
- 74 percent of chlamydia infections
- 74 percent of HPV infections (Willard et al., 2004)

The total cost of the new cases of STDs that occur among 15- to 24-year-olds has been estimated to be $6.5 billion (Chesson et al., 2004). Thus, the large number of STDs acquired by persons of ages 15–24 creates not only a health burden but represents a substantial economic burden as well.

Rates for some STDs, such as gonorrhea, have decreased in the United States, but adolescents continue to be one of the age groups most likely to have the disease (CDC, 2000a). In a single act of unprotected sex with an infected partner, a teenage woman has a 1 percent risk of acquiring HIV, a 30 percent risk of getting genital herpes, and a 50 percent risk of contracting gonorrhea (Alan Guttmacher Institute, 1999). Teens' higher risk for these diseases may be due to the following:

- Multiple sexual partners rather than a single long-term relationship
- Unprotected intercourse
- High-risk partners

Some ethnic groups are more at risk than others for STDs. In the United States, African Americans are 10 to 30 times more likely than Caucasian Americans to contract STDs. There are no known biological reasons for the disparity; the risk factors likely to lead to these patterns are poverty, lack of access to health care, illicit drug use, negative attitudes toward condom use, and living in communities with high numbers of STD-infected people (PHS, 1996b).

AIDS

The same behaviors that put adolescents at risk for nondeadly STDs also increase their risk for acquired immunodeficiency syndrome (AIDS). In 1999, AIDS became the sixth leading

sexually transmitted diseases (STDs) *diseases that may be transmitted from one person to another through sexual contact*

FIGURE 14.12
Causes of AIDS in Adolescent Boys and Girls

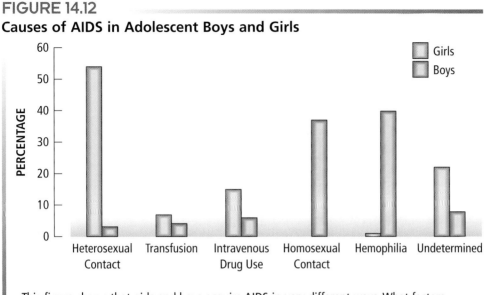

This figure shows that girls and boys acquire AIDS in very different ways. What factors account for girls' higher risk of contracting HIV infection through heterosexual transmission? Why are boys more likely to be exposed to HIV through hemophilia?

Source: Centers for Disease Control, 1996.

killer of US adolescents and young adults. Although the rates have leveled off for some age groups over the past few years, the number of HIV infection cases in adolescents has increased (CDC, 2003). Because of the long latency period (up to ten years) for HIV, the virus responsible for AIDS, many adolescents become infected but do not exhibit obvious symptoms of the disease until they are young adults. The higher rate of AIDS infections among young adults likely results from exposure to HIV during adolescence.

Certain groups of adolescents are more likely to test positive for HIV than other groups are. At highest risk are homosexuals, drug users, homeless or runaway adolescents, African American and Latino adolescents (CDC, 2001b), hemophiliacs, and inner-city youth. Additional risk factors for adolescents include having STDs, being sexually abused, selling sex for survival (to make money for food, drugs, or shelter), being sexually active without using condoms, and abusing alcohol (CDC, 2001b).

Figure 14.12 presents the major causes of AIDS in adolescents. As you can see, the causes vary for boys and girls. For boys, homosexual contact and having hemophilia are the two most likely sources of AIDS. In contrast, girls are much more likely to acquire AIDS through heterosexual contact (CDC, 2001b). Adolescent girls' immature reproductive systems may not produce progesterone consistently, and the lack of this hormone makes the mucus in the vagina a less effective barrier against all types of infections (Futterman & Hein, 1992).

Adolescent Contraceptive Use
A troubling finding is that American teenagers are less likely than their peers from other countries to regularly and effectively use contraception (Arnett & Balle-Jensen, 1993). Today, however, American teenagers use contraception more often than their counterparts in previous decades did. Between the late 1970s and the 1990s, for example, adolescents' condom use more than doubled (Herold & Marshall, 1996). Increased condom use also reflects concerns about "safe sex" and protection from AIDS. Recent evidence indicates that over 60 percent of sexually active adolescents used a condom during their last intercourse (CDC, 2004c). But the percentage of teens who use contraception varies according to age. The older girls are when they have sex for the first time, the greater the likelihood that they or their partners will use contraception. Additionally, the type of contraception used

during intercourse varies with age. Younger adolescents are more likely to use condoms, whereas older adolescents tend to prefer birth control pills (CDC, 2004c). Ethnic differences also exist in adolescent contraception use. For example, according to recent estimates, 73 percent of African American, 63 percent of Caucasian, and 57 percent of Latino adolescents reported that either they or their partner used condoms the last time they had sex (CDC, 2004c).

Although adolescents give various reasons for not using contraception (see Table 14.5), the most common reason is that they do not believe that they—or their partner—will get pregnant (Treboux & Bush-Rossnagel, 1991). This belief may reflect a personal fable that one is invulnerable to the consequences of sexual activity. Thus, adolescents' decision making about sexuality and contraception is influenced by their level of cognitive development.

The use of drugs and alcohol sometimes contributes to failure to use contraceptives. About one quarter of sexually active adolescents report that they used alcohol or drugs during their last sexual experience (CDC, 2004c). Boys were considerably more likely than girls to have used alcohol or drugs during their last sexual experience (30 versus 21 percent).

Contraceptive use involves complex decision making and planning. Available research indicates that successful use of contraception evolves out of a five-stage process (Byrne, 1983; Kelley, 1991):

- Acquiring, processing, and retaining contraceptive information
- Acknowledging the likelihood of sexual intercourse
- Obtaining the chosen contraception
- Communicating about contraceptive issues with one's partner
- Using the chosen method of contraception correctly

In recent years, increased emphasis on adolescent abstinence as a form of contraception has been advocated. However, once an adolescent becomes sexually active, it is unlikely that he or she will remain inactive for any length of time. For example, only about 27 percent of adolescents who are sexually active go without sex for three months (CDC, 2000a). Boys are more likely than girls to be abstinent (31 versus 24 percent), and younger adolescents are more likely than older adolescents to be abstinent (31 versus 22 percent). These sex and age differences in abstinence are likely due to the comparative lack of available sexual partners for boys and younger adolescents relative to girls and older adolescents.

Teen Pregnancy and Parenting

One of the potential outcomes of sexual activity is unintentional pregnancy. Pregnancy during adolescence brings dramatic emotions and dilemmas—how to tell parents, part-

TABLE 14.5
Reported Reasons Why Teenagers Do Not Use Contraception Regularly

Lack of availability of contraceptives
Inadequate knowledge about contraceptives, how to get them, and how to use them
Failure to identify pregnancy as a serious problem or one that should be prevented
False thinking that "pregnancy can't happen to me"
Reluctance to admit loss of virginity or sexual activity
Fear that parents will find out
Fear and embarrassment associated with buying contraceptives
Cost of contraception

Source: Coles and Stokes, 1985; Moore and Rosenthal, 1993.

ners, and friends; how to support a child; how to continue an education; and how to deal with being a parent. Adolescents must deal with these issues at a time when they are changing and may not be ready for such responsibilities (Martin, Hill, & Welsh, 1998).

In the United States, rates of teen pregnancy are exceptionally high. So much so, in fact, that one group has published an online clock that tabulates the number of teen pregnancies and births in the United States (http://www.cfoc.org/babyclock/clocksmaller.html). US teen pregnancy rates are the highest among developed nations, although the rate of US teen pregnancy has dropped since 1990 (CDC, 2004c). As you can see in Figure 14.13, the US teen birthrate is 5 times the rate in France, 14 times the rate in Japan, and 2 times the rate in England (Singh & Darroch, 2000).

Of the approximately 11 million teenage girls who are sexually active, about 1 million become pregnant each year (Henshaw, 2001). Eighty-five percent of these pregnancies are

FIGURE 4.13
Adolescent Birth Rates Worldwide

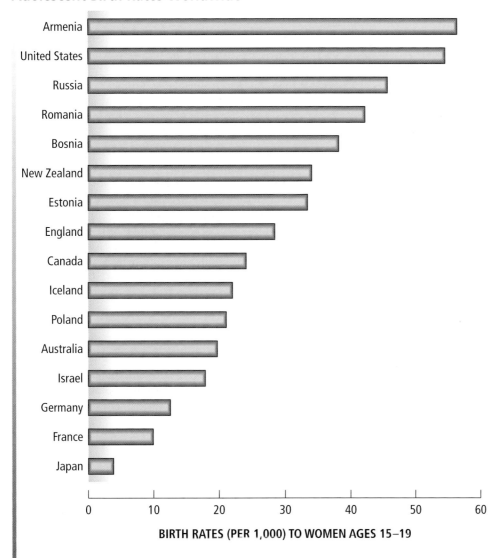

BIRTH RATES (PER 1,000) TO WOMEN AGES 15–19

As you can see in this graph, the percentage of births to adolescents varies dramatically among the different parts of the world. What cultural and social factors likely contribute to these differences? Why is the US rate so high compared to those of other countries?

Source: Singh and Darroch, 2000.

unintentional, and 76 percent occur outside of marriage (Kids Count, 2004). Ethnic–racial differences are apparent in teen pregnancy rates, with African American and Latino teens having over three times the rate of Caucasian teenagers. Additionally, African American and Latino teens are more likely than their Caucasian peers to say they want to become parents early in life (Trent & Crowder, 1997). Thus, ethnic differences in teen pregnancy may be due in part to differences in cultural norms, attitudes, and expectations about early pregnancy and parenthood (Miller, Benson, & Galbraith, 2001).

Teenagers who become pregnant rarely place their child for adoption. Instead, they either have an abortion or give birth and raise the child themselves. Only about 56 percent of all teen pregnancies result in the actual birth of a child. Of the total number of pregnancies, approximately 30 percent end in abortion and another 14 percent are miscarried or end in a stillbirth (Henshaw, 1999). Since the late 1980s, the proportion of teens giving birth has risen (Planned Parenthood, 2004). This may be due in part to a greater acceptance of out-of-wedlock births, as well as the federal government's policy of providing medical coverage for prenatal care and delivery services but not for abortion.

Repeat pregnancies are common during adolescence. Research (Gilmore et al., 1997) has shown that about half of the teenagers who become pregnant have a repeat pregnancy within 18 months of their first pregnancy, and 8 percent have more than one repeat pregnancy during that time. Younger adolescents and those with a history of behavior problems are more at risk for repeat pregnancies. Race, ethnicity, and social class are not associated with repeat pregnancies.

The life course for pregnant teens is not very optimistic. Can you identify the problems associated with teen pregnancy? What solutions can you think of to adequately address this issue?

Pregnancy during adolescence can have negative consequences for the mother, the father, and their children (Kids Count, 2004). Women who bear children during adolescence are likely to have fewer educational and job opportunities than their peers and to remain in poverty longer. Although it is illegal to exclude pregnant teenagers from public school, as many as 80 percent drop out and do not return (Manlove, 1998). An important social consequence of teen pregnancy is long-term dependency on public assistance (Kids Count, 2004).

Pregnant teens also are more vulnerable to health problems, such as toxemia, hemorrhaging, miscarriage, and even maternal death (Dell, 2001; Stevens-Simon & McAnarney, 1996). Infants born to adolescent mothers are more likely to be premature and to have low birthweight, birth defects, cognitive deficiencies, and impaired social–emotional development. A major contributor to these problems is lack of prenatal care—at least a third of pregnant teens receive inadequate prenatal care (Alan Guttmacher Institute, 2001). According to recent research, long-term consequences for children born to adolescent mothers include lower educational levels and less financial independence. In addition, children born to adolescent mothers are more likely to become teenage parents themselves (Hardy et al., 1997).

Adolescent pregnancy also puts teens at risk because of the demands associated with becoming an adolescent parent. Consider the following:

> *I haven't had a full night's sleep in a long time. I really miss that. I can't get her down when I need to do my homework. I'll sit there and play with her to make her happy. But I'll stay up till 2 or 3 o'clock in the morning doing homework. I have to support her and I'm proud of what I have done for her. I'm her mother, but I don't know what our future will be like. I do know that it's time for me to grow up. I want her to have a good life and not make the mistakes that me and her father have.* (Interview with 16-year-old Amber, mother of a 2-month-old daughter, adapted from Valdez, 1994)

As you can hear in Amber's words, she has conflicted feelings about being a young parent. Hope, fatigue, pride, determination, and uncertainty mark her life. Amber's determination to "grow up" reflects the fact that teen parents have to take on adult responsibilities, often before they have the physical, psychological, social, and economic abilities to do so. Compared to adults, adolescent parents are more likely to exhibit the following characteristics (Coley & Chase-Linsdale, 1998; Jorgensen, 1993):

- Lack of knowledge about child development
- Anxiousness and frustration about parenting
- Little interaction with their infants
- Negative exchanges with their children
- Negative attitudes toward parenting

Although teenage girls generally have difficulties taking on the responsibilities of being a parent, it also is true that they vary widely in their abilities to cope with child rearing. Given adequate support and access to resources, many teenage girls are capable of assuming these demanding responsibilities and of becoming effective mothers (Flanagan, 1998).

Less is known about teen dads, however. According to some estimates, about 28 percent of males become a father by the age of 19. The rate is substantially higher among minority teens (Thornberry et al., 2000). Boys who come from impoverished neighborhoods and are involved in problem behaviors are more apt to become teen fathers than other boys are. In addition, the parents of teen fathers are likely to have become parents at an early age and to have little formal education (Thornberry, Smith, & Howard, 1997).

Teenage fathers suffer many of the same adverse physical, psychological, educational, and occupational circumstances as teen mothers do. Teenage fathers are more likely than their peers to drop out of school, have an unstable work record, become depressed, engage in criminal behavior, and use drugs and alcohol. Many young fathers are cognitively and emotionally immature, have inaccurate expectations for their children, are ambivalent about being a father, and fail to become involved with their children (Marsiglio & Cohan, 1997).

A key element in how likely teen fathers are to remain involved with teen mothers and their children is whether the young males can secure stable employment and fulfill the breadwinner role. But this is no easy task.

The economic support and personal involvement of the father can have positive consequences for teen mothers and their children (Hawkins, Christiansen, Sargent, & Hill, 1995). However, many young fathers are psychologically unprepared for fatherhood (Fagan, Barnett, Bernd, & Whiteman, 2003), and their continued involvement with the mother often results in additional pregnancies (Marsiglio & Cohan, 1997). Both circumstances decrease the long-term stability and economic prospects of these families.

An alternative point of view is that the major disadvantages experienced by teenage mothers and fathers and their children—inadequate health care, poor nutrition, limited educational and career opportunities, troubled neighborhoods, and high family instability—result from poverty (Ross-Leadbeater & Way, 2001). Adolescents living in poverty are more likely to become parents during their teenage years and to develop long-term dependency on public assistance. Findings like these suggest that at least some of the problems associated with teenage parenting may be products of socioeconomic issues rather than a lack of maturity or competence on the part of adolescents.

Adolescent Sex Education

Most American teenagers know little about effective birth control. Certain myths about sexuality abound, such as the naive belief that a teenage girl cannot get pregnant during her first experience with sexual intercourse. To debunk these myths and provide basic information, many parents and professionals advocate school-based sex education. One roadblock to the effective implementation of sex education has been the stormy political debate over whether the primary focus of these programs should be the encouragement of abstinence or a comprehensive strategy that includes discussion of protection against pregnancy and sexually transmitted diseases. Abstinence-based programs seek to discourage teenage

NURTURING CHILDREN
CHARACTERISTICS OF EFFECTIVE SEX EDUCATION PROGRAMS

Sex education programs can be effective in helping teens make good decisions about sexuality. Based on the available research, sex education is most effective when it incorporates proven techniques. Ten elements of effective sex education programs have been identified (Kirby, 2001; SIECUS, 2001):

1. Focus on reducing one or more sexual behaviors that lead to unintended pregnancy or HIV/STD infection.

2. Base programs on theoretical approaches that have been demonstrated to influence other health-related behavior, and identify specific important sexual antecedents to be targeted.

3. Deliver and consistently reinforce a clear message about abstaining from sexual activity and/or using condoms or other forms of contraception. This appears to be one of the most important characteristics that distinguishes effective from ineffective programs.

4. Provide basic, accurate information about the risks of teen sexual activity and about ways to avoid intercourse or use methods of protection against pregnancy and STDs.

5. Include activities that address social pressures that influence sexual behavior.

6. Provide examples of and practice with communication, negotiation, and refusal skills.

7. Employ teaching methods designed to involve participants, and have them personalize the information.

8. Incorporate behavioral goals, teaching methods, and materials that are appropriate to the age, sexual experience, and culture of the students.

9. Maintain the program for a sufficient length of time (i.e., more than a few hours).

10. Select teachers or peer leaders who believe in the program, and then provide them with adequate training.

sexual activity and do not provide information about contraception. Assessments of these programs show that they do not have long-term effects on adolescent sexual behavior (SIECUS, 2001; Thomas, 2000).

The primary goals of comprehensive sex education programs are to assist young people in developing a positive view of sexuality, provide them with information about taking care of their sexual health, and help them acquire the skills needed to make satisfying and healthy sexual decisions. Sex education programs can be effective if they incorporate elements that have been proven to work (Kirby, 2001; SIECUS, 2001; see Nurturing Children box).

Sex education programs have the best outcomes when they are introduced before teens become sexually active and when information is included about both abstinence and contraception, as well as STD prevention. Research shows that sex education programs do not encourage sexual experimentation or increase sexual activity and that comprehensive approaches to sex education have been successful in helping young people postpone intercourse or use contraception (Kirby, 2001).

Try It Out

1. Review David's account of adolescence as a stage of development (page 445). In general, what considerations do you think led to efforts to differentiate stages of development? What historical trends contributed to defining adolescence in the United States? What considerations have led to differentiating early and late adolescence? How would you define adolescence as a stage of development?

2. Reflect on your own experiences with adolescent growth spurts, puberty, and the timing of onset of puberty. How did you, your parents, and your peers respond to your physical and sexual maturation? How did your maturation and others' responses to it affect your self-concept and self-esteem?

3. Collaborate with classmates to develop interview questions you could use as part of a clinical study on eating disturbances and eating disorders among adolescents. You want to discover how and when and in what social contexts these behaviors first began in your respondents. How could responses to your interview be used to develop an effective eating-disorders prevention program? What do you think should be the first three steps in any such program?

Key Terms and Concepts

adolescence (446)

anorexia nervosa (466)

bulimia nervosa (467)

dysmenorrhea (461)

eating disturbances (468)

gonadotropins (453)

menarche (451)

parasuicide (473)

physical fitness (463)

premenstrual syndrome (PMS) (461)

primary sexual characteristics (453)

puberty (452)

pubescence (452)

rites of passage (447)

secondary sexual characteristics (453)

sexually transmitted diseases (STDs) (474)

suicide (473)

Sum It Up

What is adolescence?

- What mid-nineteenth century social and legal reforms led to the acceptance of adolescence as a stage of development? (p. 446)

How do adolescents develop physically and sexually?

- How are teens' brains different than adults' in interpreting emotions? (p. 449)

- How do different ethnic groups approach standards of attractiveness? (pp. 460–461)

What are the health and safety concerns of adolescence?

- What four assessments are used to measure physical fitness during adolescence? (p. 463)

- What are the psychological characteristics associated with anorexia? (p. 466)

- What are the most prominent risk factors for attempting suicide during adolescence? (p. 473)

Chapter Summary 14

Childhood

Early
Adolescence

| 1 | 2 | 3 | 4 | 5 | 6 | 7 | 8 | 9 | 10 | 11 | 12 | 13 | 14 |

As a developmental period, adolescence varies from one culture to the next. In less industrialized cultures, the period of adolescence may be very brief and adulthood may begin early.

PERSPECTIVES ON ADOLESCENCE

Adolescence is a time of great change and covers a wide age range. A 13-year-old and a 17-year-old are both adolescents, but they experience very different worlds. The concept of adolescence as we know it did not exist until the mid–nineteenth century. Many adolescents undergo initiations, or rites of passage, that mark their new status and roles within their community. Although there are significant physical changes associated with the period of adolescence, these are defined by the culture in which the teen lives. (Refer back to pages 445–448.)

PHYSICAL AND SEXUAL DEVELOPMENT

The adolescent years are marked by rapid physical growth and dramatic changes in appearance. Brain development continues throughout adolescence and may contribute to some of the behavioral changes of adolescence. Puberty is the most visible marker of adolescence and represents a developmental milestone marking sexual maturity. The changes associated with puberty affect a teen's perception of himself or herself and how he or she is treated by others. Teens today tend to be larger, stronger, and heavier than teens in the past. (Refer back to pages 448–461.)

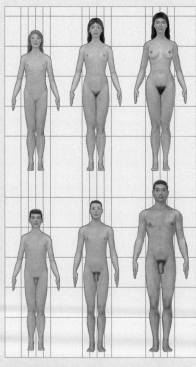

FIGURE 14.4 **Variations in Sexual Maturation**

TABLE 14.1
Issues and Outcomes for Early and Late Maturers

TIMING OF MATURATION	ISSUES	OUTCOMES
Early-maturing boys	Treated as older	Increased likelihood of behavior problems
	Make friends with older peers	Greater popularity because of sports abilities
	Greater athleticism	
Late-maturing boys	Treated as younger	Feelings of insecurity
		Adjustment problems
		Greater dissatisfaction with physical qualities
Early-maturing girls	Considerably ahead of peers in physical development	Increased risk for behavior problems
	More attractive to older boys	Increased popularity with older boys
		Date earlier
		Increased concern about physical appearance and weight
Late-maturing girls	Enter puberty about the same time that early-maturing boys do	Best adjustment of all adolescents
	Best prepared to handle changes	

Adolescence

Late Adolescence

Adulthood

15 16 17 18 19

FIGURE 14.1 The Wide Age Range of Adolescence *During early adolescence, the individual is making the transition from a child to an adolescent. During late adolescence, the transition is from an adolescent to an adult. Thus, younger and older adolescents must deal with different developmental issues and tasks.*

In the Jewish religion, boys and girls go through a religious ceremony at the age of 13 that signifies the end of childhood. This rite of passage marks their new status and roles within the community.

HEALTH AND SAFETY CONCERNS

For most adolescents, the teenage years are a period of optimal health. Deaths and injuries and other health problems are mostly due to accidents, suicide, violence, and inattention to health behaviors. Adolescents are sometimes at risk for poor health due to poor fitness, eating disturbances, accidents, and sexual behavior. (Refer back to pages 460–480.)

The rapid physical growth experienced by adolescents requires a high-quality diet. But the reality is that many adolescents' diets are far from adequate. How does diet and nutrition affect adolescents' development?

TABLE 14.5

Reported Reasons Why Teenagers Do Not Use Contraception Regularly

Lack of availability of contraceptives

Inadequate knowledge about contraceptives, how to get them, and how to use them

Failure to identify pregnancy as a serious problem or one that should be prevented

False thinking that "pregnancy can't happen to me"

Reluctance to admit loss of virginity or sexual activity

Fear that parents will find out

Fear and embarrassment associated with buying contraceptives

Cost of contraception

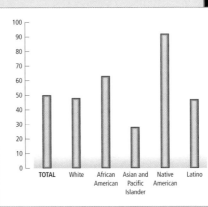

FIGURE 14.9 Rate of Teen Deaths by Accident, Homicide, and Suicide *Notice the large differences in the rates of death across the different ethnic and racial groups.*

483

Cognitive Development in Adolescence

15

Chapter Outline

How Do Adolescents Think and Reason?
Reaching Cognitive Maturity: Formal Operational Thinking
Adolescent Egocentrism
Social Cognition: Thinking About People and Relationships
Political and Religious Thinking

How Does School Influence Adolescent Development?
Adaptation to a Change in Schools
Transition to High School

What Factors Influence Adolescents' Perceptions of Academic Competence?
Gender Differences in Adolescents' Cognitive Abilities and Achievement
Explaining Gender Differences in Academic Abilities and Achievement
Cultural Influences on Academic Achievement

A DEVELOPMENTAL MYSTERY

Justin's mother marvels at the mysterious but wonderful changes she has seen in her 16-year-old son. In just the past few years, Justin has undergone a transformation. Whereas once he hardly showed any interest in current events in his country and around the world, Justin now has become active in local issues and concerned about politics in general. He belongs to the Sierra Club and worries about recycling, pollution, and the depletion of the ozone layer. He ponders deep questions about God and the meaning of life. Whereas once his mother had to beg him to occasionally read a book, Justin now devours science fiction. And though just a year ago he hardly cared about his looks, he now seems totally focused on them, and even a small blemish makes him upset, certain that everyone at school will notice it and stare at him. "My, how things have changed," mutters his mom. She wonders what produced these changes and how they could happen in such a short period of time.

As Justin's story reveals, during adolescence significant changes occur in how teens think about themselves as they experience the physical and social changes that characterize this period. This heightened consciousness is prompted in part by changes in their cognitive abilities. Adolescents also have a new perspective on the larger world. Justin's concerns about religion, politics, and the environment reflect transformations in how adolescents process information and reason about their worlds.

How Do Adolescents Think and Reason?

Justin's thinking reflects an interesting mix of abilities that accounts for some of his behavior. Like many adolescents, Justin has entered the last of Piaget's stages of cognitive development, the *formal operational stage*, and is now able to think logically about a wider range of situations than he could before. Broad environmental and social issues, such as what will happen if we run out of natural resources or whether assisted suicide should be made legal, become interesting to him because he can imagine many alternatives and perspectives. Religion and politics also typically become a significant focus. Justin also can use his new-found cognitive abilities to examine his own life. For most adolescents, the result is an intense inward focus and self-centeredness in their thinking.

Reaching Cognitive Maturity: Formal Operational Thinking

Justin's 9-year-old brother Gene recognizes that the amount of water stays the same when water is poured from a short, wide glass into a tall, narrow one, because he can apply basic logic to solve problems involving concrete objects. As a concrete operational thinker, Gene understands the principle of conservation of volume as it relates to liquids in containers. Justin, however, can apply logical operations more broadly to encompass hypothetical and abstract problems. As a formal operational thinker, Justin can imagine what it would be like to live on Mars, what would happen if the temperature on Earth got warmer, and how the universe began (Mueller, Overton, & Reene, 2001; Overton & Byrnes, 1991). Because formal operational thinkers can consider many alternatives and possibilities, they can be effective planners. Formal operational thinking appears from age 11 to 15, although it may not be completely developed until late adolescence (Niaz, 1997; Piaget, 1977).

FIGURE 15.1
Hypothetico-Deductive Reasoning

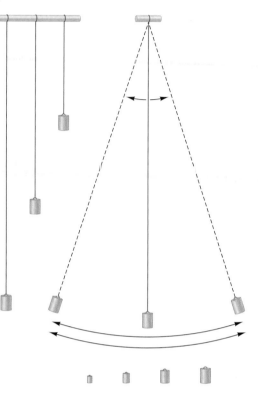

Inductive Phase
Formulate hypotheses:
"If I used shorter string,
the pendulum would swing faster."

Testing Phase
Carefully changing length of the
string but not changing anything
else, such as the weight or the height
from which the pendulum is dropped.

Deductive Phase
Assessing validity of hypotheses:
"After multiple tests, the speed of
the pendulum is inversely related
to the length of the string. My
hypothesis was correct."

Piaget presented children and adolescents with scientific problems to see how they reason and think. In the pendulum problem, differences in how adolescents and children tried to answer the scientific question were found. Can you identify these differences?

Source: "The Pendulum Problem" from *The Growth of Logical Thinking: From Childhood to Adolescence* by Jean Piaget and Barbel Inhelder. Copyright © 1958 by Basic Books, Inc. Reprinted by permission of Basic Books, a member of Perseus Books, L.L.C.

Hypothetico–Deductive reasoning

Justin is considered to have reached cognitive maturity, or the stage of formal operational thinking, because he can use **hypothetico–deductive reasoning,** which is the type of reasoning employed in science. This type of reasoning encompasses three phases of thinking (Small, 1990):

1. An inductive phase, which involves thinking about and generating possible hypotheses based on prior knowledge

2. A testing phase, which involves assessing the accuracy of the hypotheses

3. A deductive phase, which involves deriving conclusions from these hypotheses

Piaget used a pendulum problem to assess the thinking of children and adolescents (see Figure 15.1) (Inhelder & Piaget, 1958). Suppose Justin and Gene are given a pendulum; the length of the string by which it hangs can be varied, and the weights attached to the string can be changed. After being shown how the pendulum works, they are told that their goal is to discover the factor or factors that influence the rate at which the pendulum swings. Besides the weight and the length of the string, factors might include how high they hold a weight before releasing it and how much force they use to push the weight.

Recall from the description of scientific thinking in Chapter 2 how a scientist would solve this problem. A scientist would begin by generating a hypothesis—say, that a heavier

hypothetico–deductive reasoning   *the type of reasoning used in science*

weight will make the pendulum swing faster—and then systematically test the hypothesis. Although Gene and other children in the concrete operational stage can generate hypotheses (Ruffman, Perner, Olson, & Doherty, 1993), they have difficulty testing them, especially if the situation is complex (Kuhn, 1989). For instance, Gene is likely to change more than one factor at a time, making it hard to see which factor influences the swing of the pendulum. In contrast, Justin considers the whole structure of a problem and knows that he must systematically vary one factor while holding the others constant. Justin might try the heavier weight and then the lighter weight while maintaining the same string length, height from which the weight is released, and force of push. Gene and Justin will also differ in how they record their test data. Gene is less likely than Justin to keep track of the factors (Byrnes, 1988; Schauble, 1990) and more apt to forget the instances when testing disconfirms his hypotheses (Dunbar & Klahr, 1989; Foltz, Overton, & Ricco, 1995). Also, Gene may not change his hypothesis in light of new evidence, whereas Justin probably will (Kuhn et al., 1988; Strauss, 1998). For these reasons, Gene is less likely than Justin to determine the relevant factor or factors. Because Justin will try all variations of the factors, he will probably conclude that it is only the length of the string that matters (Small, 1990).

Reflective Abstraction

Formal operational thinkers also can think about their thinking. Piaget called this ability **reflective abstraction**—the ability to rearrange and rethink information already acquired (Piaget, 1971). According to Piaget, the ability to reflect upon the content of their thinking allows adolescents to draw new conclusions and insights through contemplation. Reflective abstraction provides more flexibility in thinking; formal operational thinkers can consider alternative solutions to problems based on their prior knowledge (Bjorklund, 1995). Using analogies is a good example of reflective abstraction. Adolescents' enhanced ability to construct relationships between objects is the result of reflective abstraction.

Using Formal Operational Reasoning

Applying hypothetico–deductive reasoning consistently to all sorts of problems is difficult. Careful analyses of adolescents' reasoning on different tasks often reveal that their reasoning varies from one problem to another and depends on the type of problem to be solved. Using many of the same tasks that Piaget and Inhelder had used, Martorano (1977) assessed formal operational thinking among sixth-, eighth-, tenth-, and twelfth-grade students. She found that although formal operational thinking emerges from 12 to 15 years of age, even the oldest students failed to use formal operational thinking consistently across all the tasks. Only 50 percent of tenth-graders succeeded in using formal operational thinking on the pendulum problem. Similarly, adolescents rely on different forms of reasoning, depending on their beliefs. When presented with information that is inconsistent with their beliefs, adolescents tend to use higher-order reasoning to reject the information; when presented with information that is consistent with their beliefs, they use quick processing and cognitive "shortcuts" to evaluate the information (Klaczynski, 2000).

Many studies confirm that adolescents and even adults do not always apply formal operational thinking. Even when tasks are made simple and the information is easy to obtain, not all adolescents ask for information to help them solve problems. Rather than apply formal operational thinking, adolescents often make decisions based on limited amounts of information (Linn, de Benedictis, & Delucchi, 1982). Adults also fail to use formal operational thinking consistently, especially in everyday problem solving. For instance, when adult grocery shoppers were asked to decide whether a 67-gram bottle of garlic powder at 77 cents was a better buy than a 35-gram bottle at 41 cents, only 20 percent of the shoppers used formal operational thinking to determine the price per gram for each, even when they had paper and pencil to calculate the difference. Most of the shoppers simply applied the informal rule that bigger amounts tend to be better values (Capon & Kuhn, 1979). They used a **heuristic**—that is, a shortcut for thinking.

reflective abstraction *the ability to rearrange and rethink information already acquired*

heuristic *a shortcut or rule of thumb used to help solve a problem*

Cross-Cultural Differences

Does the use of formal operational thinking vary across cultures? When Piagetian tests are given to individuals from non-Western cultures, evidence of formal operational thinking sometimes is not found. For example, when the pendulum problem was given to students in New Guinea, not a single student showed evidence of formal operational thinking (Kelly, 1977). These findings do not suggest that students in New Guinea are less intelligent. Instead, such differences may be due to cultural variations in formal schooling, how knowledge is represented, language processing, and beliefs about intellectual and cognitive processes. These differences suggest that formal operational thinking may not be universal (Altarriba, 1993; van de Vijver & Willemsen, 1993).

Another reason formal operational thinking may appear to be lacking in some cultures is researchers' failure to use problems indigenous to the culture. That is, the problems may be unfamiliar and not relevant to the culture. Thus, researchers who study formal operational thinking must take into account cultural differences as they decide how best to test for it.

Adolescent Egocentrism

In Chapter 9, you learned about the egocentric 3-year-old who hid her head under a blanket and thought no one could see her. She believed that everyone else saw the world exactly as she did. Adolescents show a different form of egocentrism—one that David Elkind (1967) called **adolescent egocentrism,** which reflects their belief that their thoughts and ideas are unique to them and are not understood by parents, teachers, or other adults. Adolescent egocentrism may account, in part, for some of the conflicts that arise between adolescents and their parents. As adolescents grow older, their self-centered beliefs about what they know evolve to become more realistic.

The Imaginary Audience

Because of their egocentric perspective, adolescents develop the mistaken idea that other people are as concerned with their feelings and behavior as they themselves are. Adolescents' self-consciousness translates into the feeling that they are on stage, with an **imaginary audience** watching their every move (Buis & Thompson, 1989; Vartanian, 1997). For example, when Michael feels uncomfortable at a party, he believes that all the other people know it; when he is proud of his athletic ability, he believes that everyone admires him. The influence of the imaginary audience peaks early in adolescence for girls and a bit later for boys (Vartanian & Powlishta, 1996). When formal operations become firmly established (at around 15 or 16 years of age), the egocentric use of an imaginary audience tends to diminish (Elkind, 1967). The imaginary audience is progressively modified by the reactions of the "real audience" of peers and significant adults. Research on the imaginary audience has failed to confirm some of Elkind's propositions. For example, some research has failed to find a relation between the imaginary audience and formal operational thinking (Jahnke & Blanchard-Fields, 1993), and other research suggests that young adolescents' concerns have their basis in a real rather than an imaginary audience (Bell & Bromnick, 2003).

The Personal Fable

Egocentrism is also expressed by creating a **personal fable**—a story adolescents tell themselves that is not quite true. This story usually emphasizes the uniqueness and invulnerability of the young adolescent (Elkind, 1967; Lapsley, 1993). Because of their central role in playing to an imaginary audience, young adolescents may come to believe that their feelings and experiences are unique in the history of humankind. As many adolescents' diaries can attest, only the teen writing the diary suffers with such agonizing intensity or experiences such exquisite pleasure. Adolescents also tend to see themselves as invincible, which may account for their tendency toward risk taking, such as drinking and driving or failing to use birth control. As adolescents gain more experience, especially once an intimate relationship has been formed, they see themselves in a more realistic light and the personal fable gradually fades. Nonetheless, the risk-taking behavior that emerges because of personal fables may have some long-term adaptive value in that it encourages adolescents to

adolescent egocentrism *an adolescent's belief that his or her thoughts and ideas are unique and are not understood by others*

imaginary audience *a characteristic of adolescents' self-consciousness, involving the feeling that they are on stage, with people watching their every move*

personal fable *a story adolescents tell themselves that emphasizes their uniqueness and invulnerability*

ideas. For example, whereas most young children in Judeo-Christian cultures tend to envision God in very concrete terms—an actual person who exists somewhere in physical space (such as heaven)—adolescents are capable of grasping a concept of God as a spiritual guide having no observable or physical form (Coles, 1990; Donelson, 1999).

Developmental changes in deference to authority figures are mirrored in religious thinking. When asked about their religious beliefs, young children often identify authority figures to justify their beliefs. For example, many young children raised as Christians say they believe in God because "the Bible tells me so." In contrast, a Christian adolescent considers religious issues in a more personal, abstract, and thoughtful way. He or she might provide the following rationale: "My religious beliefs help me to make choices in life. It seems like the Bible has more than one answer about many things, with some of the answers not being very clear. I make choices for myself." Because of changes in their thinking, teens begin to question the religious and political ideas they were taught during childhood, instead of simply relying on authority figures.

How Does School Influence Adolescent Development?

While adolescents are changing in appearance and thinking, they are also experiencing new schools and academic environments. At this time many adolescents enter new schools—going from elementary to middle or junior high school, and from these to senior high school. Although most adolescents adjust to the new environment without excessive problems, some do not make the transition smoothly and instead experience difficulty with school (Roeser, Eccles, & Freedman-Doan, 1999). A substantial portion of adolescents do not succeed in school, and from 15 to 30 percent drop out before completing high school.

Although most adolescents experience some stress as they change school environments, they do not all experience the same degree of stress. For example, adolescents who have close friends before and during the transition adapt more successfully to a new school environment than their friendless peers do (Fuligni et al., 2001). Students whose parents have a good understanding of adolescent development and parenting also tend to make a favorable transition to secondary school (Bronstein et al., 1996). Parents' perceptions influence how adolescents feel about their abilities in academic domains (Frome & Eccles, 1998). Once again, the importance of social support is apparent: adolescents who have social and personal support tend to cope successfully with changes in schools.

Adaptation to a Change in Schools

For some adolescents, the teen years are the beginning of a downward spiral that eventually leads to academic failure and dropping out of school. The spiral may begin with a marked decline in grades, common when students move out of elementary school. The greater the decline in grades, the greater the likelihood that the adolescent will fail and drop out of school (Simmons & Blyth, 1987). During this time, adolescents report feeling anxiety, frustration, helplessness, and a lack of confidence in school (Wigfield & Eccles, 2002). Teachers in post-elementary schools commonly complain that adolescent students are unmotivated, put little effort into their schoolwork, and seem generally disinterested in learning (Midgley, 1993). Although the changes associated with moving to middle or junior high school are not extreme for most adolescents, evidence suggests that students who experience declines in school performance and motivation are at risk for later school and social adjustment problems (Wigfield, Eccles, & Pintrich, 1996). One study found that adolescent girls who moved to a junior high school experienced losses in self-esteem, whereas those who stayed in the same school through eighth grade did not (Simmons & Blyth, 1987). These effects persisted: academically, the girls who moved to a junior high school during puberty were still behind the girls who did not, even after both groups made the transition to high school.

The large and impersonal nature of most junior high schools can have a detrimental effect on young teens. To address this problem, many educators advocate developmentally appropriate middle schools. What qualities need to be taken into account to help young teens when they leave elementary school?

Transition from Elementary School

One explanation for adolescents' school adjustment problems is that the transition from elementary school often occurs while they are adjusting to the physical changes of puberty (Simmons, Burgeson, Carlton-Ford, & Blyth, 1987). As you learned earlier in the previous chapter, hormonal adjustments associated with puberty bring on physical changes and powerful feelings that influence how adolescents see themselves and their relationships with others (Michael & Eccles, 2003). These changes and feelings influence motivation and performance in school. This is particularly true for girls because the school transition coincides with the onset of puberty—and possibly the initiation of dating. Although the effects for boys are not as severe, there is evidence that delaying the change of schools is beneficial for them, too (Simmons et al., 1987).

Declines in adolescents' school performance and interest also may be due to the failure of traditional junior high schools to provide developmentally appropriate educational environments for adolescents (Anderman et al., 2001; Roeser & Eccles, 2000). For instance, most junior high schools are larger, more impersonal, and more formal than elementary schools. Usually, each junior high school teacher specializes in one subject area and teaches many more students than does an elementary school teacher—making it difficult for the teacher to get to know and trust students (Wigfield, 1993). As a result, junior high school teachers emphasize control and discipline more, have less positive relationships with students, and provide adolescent students with fewer opportunities for independence (Midgley, Feldlaufer, & Eccles, 1988; Miller et al., 1990).

Because junior high school teachers must interact with a large number of students, they are not likely to notice individual declines in school interest and motivation. Thus, students can gradually slip onto less than optimal developmental pathways (Eccles et al., 1993). Also, teachers' expectations continue to influence students' achievement, particularly for low-achieving students (Madon, Jussim, & Eccles, 1997). A poor fit between the developmental needs of adolescents and the experiences provided to them by the school environment may partly explain the declines in school performance and motivation associated with the transition from elementary to junior high school (Eccles & Roesner, 2003).

To address the issues related to the transition to junior high, middle schools (serving children in grades six to eight) have been developed. Middle schools, designed to better meet the unique developmental needs of young adolescents (see boxed feature) are now the predominant form of school organization for adolescents. About 15,000 middle schools in the United States enroll more than 9 million students (Juvonen et al., 2004). These schools feature guidance and transition programs, team teaching, cooperative learning, career exploration, and athletics programs. Children who have more positive middle school experiences generally continue to have better attitudes and achievement for several years (Roeser, Eccles, & Sameroff, 1998). Although middle schools are more responsive to the needs of young adolescents, the problems associated with leaving elementary school persist—particularly for girls, who are likely to be undergoing the physical changes of puberty (Wigfield et al., 1996). Although the ideas behind the development of middle schools are logical and some children do benefit from such schools, evidence is accumulating that shows that separate elementary schools and middle schools cause transition problems for students that can negatively affect their developmental and academic progress. Part of the reason for these problems is that the implementation of the middle school concept has been less than adequate in most districts and schools. School systems that minimize transitions or provide more supportive environments for transitions are more likely to produce successful results for teens (Juvonen et al., 2004).

Transition to High School

During adolescence, most boys and girls transfer from a junior high or middle school to senior high. For many students, this transition is exciting and motivating and represents the next big step toward developing advanced academic skills and preparing for college. But as we just learned, school transitions can be difficult for many teens. High schools typically

NURTURING CHILDREN
DEVELOPMENTALLY APPROPRIATE MIDDLE SCHOOLS

Concern about the impact of junior high schools on young adolescents has focused attention on developing middle schools that better meet the needs of these students. Many teachers and school administrators believe that middle schools have great potential to positively influence students as they confront the wide range of choices and decisions (concerning issues such as gang membership, drug and alcohol use, and occupations) that arise during this period of development (McEwin, Dickinson, & Jacobson, 2004). What can parents and educators do to improve the ability of middle schools to meet the developmental needs of young adolescents? To address this question, researchers identified the following key components, or characteristics, of a developmentally appropriate middle school (Bottoms, Cooney, & Carpenter, 2003; National Middle School Association, 1995):

1. *Educators trained to understand the developmental qualities of young adolescents:* Educators must know how the developmental needs of young adolescents are distinct from those of children and older adolescents.
2. *An atmosphere of high expectations for all:* Teachers, parents, and students must have high expectations that empower students to learn, become intellectually engaged, and behave in keeping with responsible citizenship.
3. *Encouragement of family and community partnerships:* The need for open communication between schools and parent/community organizations and joint involvement in decisions about curriculum and instruction must be recognized.
4. *A positive school climate:* Teachers and administrators must recognize

that the school environment plays a role in young adolescents' ability to learn.
5. *Varied teaching approaches within the curriculum:* Teachers have to address the diverse needs of students with different learning styles, mental and physical maturation levels, and interests.
6. *Comprehensive guidance and support services:* Schools are responsible for providing young adolescents with more than instruction. Young adolescents, especially, need programs that provide for peer discussion, personal attention by professionals, and referral to specialists when needed.

are larger and more impersonal than junior high or middle schools. The large size and bureaucratic structure of high schools undermine the development of close relationships, particularly between teachers and students (Bryk, Lee, & Smith, 1990; Eccles & Roesner, 2003). These qualities weaken the motivation and involvement of many students, especially those not enrolled in the favored courses and those not expected to do well (Wigfield et al., 1996). Important differences among students begin to emerge during high school, which can lead to lower performance and school dropout. One new variable in this transition is that in most states, students are allowed to drop out and leave school at this time. The consequences of such a significant decision last long after high school.

Characteristics of High School Dropouts

At 16 years of age, Quanese moved from North Carolina to Connecticut. She felt out of place, had few friends, and was lonely and isolated. That summer she got pregnant and had to combine motherhood with school. During her junior year, her mother, with whom Quanese was very close, died. Quanese had to take on many of the household responsibilities that her mother had done. Six months before finishing her senior year, Quanese found the circumstances of her life too demanding to finish school and dropped out. The traumas she had experienced left her feeling as if she couldn't achieve anything. (Adapted from Royce, 1996)

Quanese is just one of the 1.5 million students who have dropped out of high school (US Census Bureau, 2003a). Annually, about 400,000 teens drop out of school (US Census Bureau, 2004a). This rate (about 10 percent of teens of 16 to 19 years of age) has declined

What factors contribute to whether students continue in school or drop out?

somewhat over the 1990s but has held generally constant and remains a concern. For many, like Quanese, the decision to drop out is related to life circumstances. For others, like Robert in the following story, dropping out is less a conscious decision than a consequence of personal behavior.

> *Robert was an OK student in junior high school. In his sophomore year, he began drinking and smoking pot. His drug use escalated, and he started hanging out with an older group. He'd rather be partying than in class, and his attendance became erratic. During his junior year, he found school to be less and less important. Ultimately, he gave up on it and dropped out.* (Adapted from Kramer, 1995)

As the examples of Robert and Quanese show, adolescents drop out of school for a variety of reasons. Table 15.2 lists some of the reasons given for leaving school before graduation; attitudes about school and academic performance are the most common reasons for both boys and girls. Studies show that low achievement, low ability, and low interest in school are characteristics of students who are likely to drop out (Jimerson et al., 2002; Rosenthal, 1998). These characteristics can be traced back to elementary school—elementary school children who do poorly, who are absent frequently, and who have attitude and behavior problems are more likely than their peers to drop out of high school (Barclay & Doll, 2001; Roeser et al., 1999). As children and young adolescents, they cannot leave school voluntarily, but they may disengage from school by not trying, acting out, or being truant (Alexander, Entwisle, & Kabbani, 2001). As older adolescents, they can decide for themselves, and many of these low-achieving students choose to leave school.

Table 15.2 also reveals that the reasons for dropping out differ for boys and girls. Like Quanese, girls are more likely to drop out because of social factors that influence or limit their choices, such as getting pregnant, getting married, or having to take care of the family. In contrast, as Robert's case suggests, boys are more likely to drop out because of behavior problems or getting expelled.

Race, ethnicity, and social class are all related to dropout rates. A worrisome number of minority students leave school before graduating. In some low-income, minority school districts in urban areas, as many as 50 percent or more of students leave school before obtain-

TABLE 15.2
Students' Reasons for Dropping Out of High School

REASON	PERCENTAGE OF BOYS CITING	PERCENTAGE OF GIRLS CITING
Did not like school	58	44
Did not get along with teachers	52	17
Was failing school	46	33
Could not keep up with schoolwork	38	25
Did not feel safe at school	19	12
Expelled	18	9
Friends dropped out	17	11
Had to get a job	15	16
Got married	5	23
Had to care for family	5	12
Was pregnant	—	31

Source: US Department of Education, 1997.

ing a high school diploma (Bryk et al., 1990). Examination of Figure 15.3 shows that the percentage of high school dropouts among African American, Latino, and Native American students, while not dramatically higher than that of Caucasian Americans, is nonetheless disproportionately high. Asian American students have the lowest percentage of dropouts.

Neighborhood and economic factors also contribute to teen dropout rates (Crowder & South, 2003). For example, adolescents living in poverty are five times more likely than those from affluent families to drop out of school. Students from families in the bottom 20 percent of the population's income levels represent over 30 percent of all dropouts (US Census Bureau, 2001e). Because racial and ethnic minority students are more likely to come from families with low incomes, their increased dropout rates are due in part to income level.

Cultural factors also are significant. For example, dropout rates of Latino youths are consistently high regardless of family income, but the dropout rate of Latino immigrants is two and a half times that of Latino youths born in the United States (US Department of Education, 1997). Proficiency in English is clearly a factor. The dropout rate of Latino students with limited English proficiency is over three times higher than that of Latino students who speak English well (US Census Bureau, 2001e). Bilingual education and English language learner programs improve the likelihood that these Latino students will stay in school. For students in these programs, the dropout rate is reduced (US Department of Education, 1997), but dropout rates are still considerably higher than those of other groups of high school students.

FIGURE 15.3
Percentage of High School Dropouts, by Race/Ethnicity

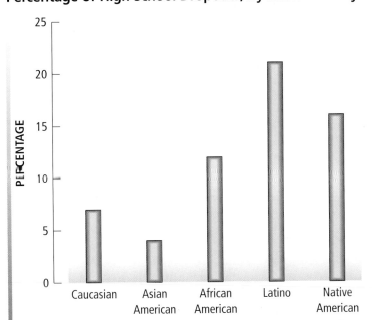

Notice that dropout rates differ by race/ethnicity. What are the consequences of dropping out of high school? How many dropouts eventually finish their high school education?

Source: US Census Bureau, 2003a.

Preventing High School Dropout

The consequences of dropping out can be profound. Leaving school before graduation seriously reduces an adolescent's chances of obtaining a well-paying job. In 2002, male dropouts earned about $22,000 per year and female dropouts earned about $13,000 per year—about one third less than high school graduates (US Census Bureau, 2004b). The economic and social costs of dropping out, both to the individual and to society, run into the billions of dollars (Cohen, 1998). Not only do individuals who drop out lose potential earnings, but society often must pay for extensive social services because dropouts are likely to need assistance or have behavior problems. High school dropouts make up nearly half of the heads of households on welfare and half of the prison population (Hao & Cherlin, 2004; Schwartz, 1995).

Many different programs have been developed to keep students in school. Effective dropout prevention programs have the following characteristics (Burt, Resnick, & Novick, 1998; Campbell, 2004; Gonzales et al., 2004):

- High expectations and standards for all students and programs to help at-risk youth meet these expectations

- Identification of potential dropouts as early as possible and early intervention to ensure school success

- Effective, flexible classroom instruction—a mix of academic instruction and experiential learning appears to be most effective

- Caring teachers with interest in and concern for at-risk youths
- Skills training and counseling necessary for success after graduation (such as occupational training and job counseling)
- Inclusion of families, peers, and the community in the program—peer tutors, parents, and local business and government agencies provide a broad support system for at-risk youths

Dropping out of school is not an irrevocable action. Nearly half of all dropouts eventually earn a high school diploma (US Department of Education, 1997). Some return to school, whereas others obtain some sort of equivalency credential. For example, both Quanese and Robert obtained their high school diplomas. After the birth of her second child, Quanese returned to school at age 22. She became a mentor in an adult education program to help inspire others to complete their education (Royce, 1996). Robert quit using drugs and passed the equivalency exam six years after he left school. Impressively, he applied to Yale University and was accepted (Kramer, 1995).

What Factors Influence Adolescents' Perceptions of Academic Competence?

As you have learned, how teens do in school critically affects their long-term success and adjustment. Students' performance in school is determined in part by the perceptions they have of their own academic abilities. During adolescence, these perceptions undergo important changes and are influenced by a wide variety of factors—such as gender, culture, and developmental level. For example, before entering adolescence, children are optimistic about their school-related abilities. In one classic study (Stipek, 1981), more than 80 percent of first-grade children thought they were the best student in the class! As students move beyond the elementary school years, their perceptions of their abilities become more realistic—and pessimistic (Paris & Cunningham, 1996). Furthermore, very young children are more confident about the extent to which they can improve their abilities than are older children. By fourth grade, children begin to doubt that they can become the best at their current worst activity (Freedman-Doan et al., 2000).

One reason is the increased emphasis on grades. Junior and senior high school teachers tend to apply higher standards in judging students' competence and in grading their performance than do elementary school teachers (Wigfield & Eccles, 2002). Additionally, students and teachers make more social comparisons concerning grades during junior high than they did during elementary school. Students therefore become more aware of how others do in school and more aware of their own level of performance. Interestingly, the drop in grades associated with the transition to middle-level schooling is not matched by a decline in young adolescents' performance on standardized achievement tests (Kavrell & Petersen, 1984). This finding suggests that grades are lower because of changes in grading practices and standards rather than a change in the rate of students' learning (Simmons & Blyth, 1987).

Gender Differences in Adolescents' Cognitive Abilities and Achievement

During childhood, boys and girls show few differences in specific cognitive abilities or achievement levels. But as they grow older, differences in these areas become apparent. Also, during adolescence, levels of girls' and boys' confidence in their academic skills change. For boys, confidence increases; for girls, confidence in their academic abilities drops (Halpern, 1992).

It is important to remember that compared to the very high variability from person to person within each sex, gender differences in cognitive abilities are very small. They account for only 1 to 5 percent of the variation. Furthermore, it is important to identify the origins of these gender differences—which may include family influences, cultural practices, and

DEBATING THE ISSUE

SHOULD TEENS WORK?

 Eighteen-year-old Dave wakes up at dawn, slurps some strawberry jam for a sugar rush, goes to high school until 2:30 P.M., hurries home to change and go off to his job at a clothing store where he works almost 30 hours a week. He gets home around 10:30, does maybe an hour of homework, and goes to bed around midnight. He's sacrificed some of his school life for his job, misses playing soccer and baseball, and he had to give up a challenging class because he had so little time for studying. (S. Waldman and K. Springen, 1992, p. 80)

For many adolescents like Dave, working is a major part of life. More than 5 million adolescents work—twice the rate of working adolescents in the 1950s. On average, boys work about 2 hours more than girls during the school year (17 versus 15 hours per week) and in the summer (24 versus 21 hours per week; US Department of Labor, 2000).

The jobs teens hold generally are low paying and involve retail sales, fast food, or unskilled labor. Most teens, like Dave, find their work intellectually dull, unchallenging, and monotonous. They rarely are allowed to act independently or make their own decisions while they work. The skills involved in most of these jobs are not very demanding (US Department of Labor, 2000). About 25 percent of their time is spent either cleaning or carrying things (Greenberger & Steinberg, 1986).

Many adults believe that work is a good way to keep adolescents out of trouble. It is assumed that getting a job helps teens accept responsibility, teaches them about the value of work and money, and prepares them for future adult roles. However, only 10 percent of high school seniors save most of their earnings for college, and only about 6 percent use most of their earnings to help pay for family living expenses (Waldman & Springen, 1992). Most teens use their earnings to buy clothing, music, or other items they desire.

Jobs can teach adolescents to be accepting and tolerant of others by forcing them to meet and interact with people of different social, racial, and cultural backgrounds (Waldman & Springen, 1992). Family economic conditions force some teens into the job market. Working can bring about positive outcomes if the adolescent contributes to the well-being of the family or is closely supervised by parents (Hansen & Jarvis, 2000; Shanahan, Mortimer, & Krueger, 2002). Also, students who are on the verge of dropping out or who are at risk for delinquency can be kept on track through a good job.

The critical number appears to be 20. Working fewer than 20 hours a week can give a teen higher self-esteem and a sense of responsibility, along with a paycheck. This teen can find the time needed to work by cutting the amount of time she or he spends watching television. Working more than 20 hours puts work too much at the center of a teen's life. Simple arithmetic explains why more than 20 hours of work is harmful. A teenager typically spends 35 hours a week in school and 10 hours a week doing homework; adding a 20-hour job results in a 65-hour work week (Resnick, 1997).

As in Dave's case, adolescents who work have less time available for homework and often struggle to keep up with their course work. Thus, students who work the most hours perform the most poorly in school (Paschall, Flewelling, & Russell, 2004). Additionally, students who work cut more classes, spend less time on homework, and have lower educational aspirations than those who do not work (Jimmerson, 1999).

Compared to adolescents in other industrialized countries such as Japan, more US adolescents work. They also work longer hours and have more spending money than do their counterparts in Japan. Given the impact that work has on teens' school performance, one reason for the lower achievement of US teens may be that they spend so much more of their time working than do their peers in comparable cultures.

School is not the only aspect of an adolescent's life that is affected by work. Adolescents who work also are more likely to have behavior problems and use alcohol or drugs (Bachman et al., 2003), get into arguments with their parents, get inadequate sleep and exercise, and fail to eat breakfast (Bachman & Schulenberg, 1993).

What is not clear is whether working more than 20 hours itself causes problematic outcomes or whether the adolescents who work these longer hours are, for example, less interested in school than their peers and more inclined to use drugs and alcohol before they enter the workforce. Longitudinal research that followed teens as they entered and dropped out of the workforce suggests that working directly contributes to these problems (Steinberg, Fegley, & Dornbusch, 1993). Even after controlling for differences among teenagers before they became employed, research suggests that taking on a job, particularly for more than 20 hours a week, diminishes teens' investment in school, increases rates of delinquency and drug use, and decreases feelings of self-reliance. When adolescents quit working, improvements in schooling and achievement were found. Thus, for too many teenagers, too much work may squander their future.

THINKING IT THROUGH

1. After reading this information, do you think teens should work? Why or why not?

2. What positive benefits for a teenager may come from working?

3. What social policy issues are related to teens in the workforce? How might policy be changed to ensure positive outcomes for teens who work?

How do the qualities of girls' interactions provide practice in using verbal skills?

differing hormone levels in girls and boys—and the means by which both sexes can be encouraged to develop a wide range of skills.

Gender Differences in Verbal Skills

Girls excel on a variety of verbal tasks, even in early childhood. Girls talk earlier, have larger vocabularies than boys do, and are less likely to have speech problems (Shucard, Shucard, & Thomas, 1987). Gender differences in reading comprehension appear during adolescence, with girls showing higher levels of comprehension (Hedges & Nowell, 1995). Overall, girls show somewhat higher scores in reading, writing, and spelling, and these differences persist into high school (Gleason & Ely, 2002). Although the gender differences in verbal skills are generally small, a few verbal skills show relatively large gender differences. In particular, females are much better than males at **associational fluency,** or producing synonyms for words (Hines, 1990). For example, given the word *vivacious,* girls and women can generate more words with similar meaning than boys and men can.

Gender Differences in Spatial–Visual Skills

Spatial–visual skills are the abilities involved in orienting oneself in the environment—for example, finding one's way or imagining how an object may be changed or rotated in space. For many years, researchers have reported that males outperform females in spatial–visual tasks (Maccoby & Jacklin, 1974), but in fact the sexes differ on only some of these tasks (Bosco, Longoni, & Vecchi, 2004). The types of tasks shown in Figure 15.4 are used to measure the three categories of spatial–visual skills (Halpern, 1992):

1. **Spatial perception** is the ability to locate the horizontal or vertical while ignoring distracting visual information.

2. **Mental rotation** is the ability to imagine how objects would appear if they were rotated or changed positionally.

3. **Spatial visualization** is the ability to find figures hidden within other figures.

Boys and girls differ least in spatial visualization. The greatest difference, favoring boys, is in mental rotation skills; it first appears at around the age of 10 or 11 (Linn & Petersen, 1986). Both girls and boys can mentally rotate objects; the gender difference lies in the speed with which the task is done (Newcombe, Mathason, & Terlecki, 2002). Boys' advantage in spatial perception is evident in their performance on the water-level task. In this task, a person is shown a drawing of a glass tilted at an angle and is asked to draw in the water line where it would be if the glass were half full. Based on the principle that the water level remains horizontal, we would expect that everyone would accurately draw a line parallel to the ground. But this is not so. In studies conducted in different countries, girls and women were more likely than boys and men to place the water line inaccurately (Halpern, 1992). The gender difference in the water-level task is moderately large, but training in this task can improve performance for both sexes and can eliminate the performance difference between girls and boys (Vasta, Nott, & Gaze, 1996).

Although large gender differences are found in some tests of spatial–visual skills, the few studies that have examined real-world applications of these skills find negligible differences. For instance, boys and men do not appear to be better at reading maps or finding their way in real environments than girls or women are (Pearson & Ferguson, 1989). It is interesting, however, that females and males use different strategies for way-finding and for giving directions. Females often rely on "route" strategies, attending to how to get from place to place and using landmarks as guides. Males tend to apply "orientation" strategies, using directional markers of north, south, and so forth (MacFadden, Elias, & Saucier, 2003).

Gender Differences in Math and Science Skills

Many girls lose confidence in their math and science abilities as they move through adolescence. This drop in confidence often precedes a drop in performance. Like visual–spatial

associational fluency *ability to produce synonyms for a given word*

spatial–visual skills *the cognitive abilities involved in orienting oneself in the environment*

spatial perception *the ability to locate the horizontal or vertical while ignoring distracting information*

mental rotation *the ability to imagine how objects would appear if their positions were rotated*

spatial visualization *the ability to find figures and shapes hidden within other figures*

skills, mathematical skills have many different components, and the extent to which boys and girls differ in math skills depends on the type of math ability considered (De Lisi & McGillicuddy-De Lisi, 2002; Hyde, Fennema, & Lamon, 1990). In the elementary school years, girls outperform boys in math. For example, in third grade, girls outperform boys in almost every type of math problem. The stronger performance of girls declines by sixth grade, however, and they start to lose pace compared with boys (Hyde et al., 1990; Marshall & Smith, 1987). Boys begin to outperform girls on standardized tests during early adolescence, and the differences increase during the adolescent years (Hyde et al., 1990; Ruble et al., in press). Differences are particularly pronounced in students with high math ability (Leder, 2004; Stanley & Benbow, 1982).

When girls' and boys' test-taking performance and grades in mathematics (as well as in other academic areas) are examined, an interesting difference emerges: for many boys the pattern is tests higher than grades, whereas for many girls the pattern is grades higher than tests (De Lisi & McGillicuddy-De Lisi, 2002; Dwyer & Johnson, 1997). These findings suggest that both sexes are competent in math but that they exhibit their skills differently.

As with math, girls and boys have similar scores on science proficiency tests at age 9, but boys outperform girls through adolescence (US Department of Education, 1996). This trend is not limited to the United States. As you can see in Figure 15.5, by eighth grade, boys outperformed girls in science in each country tested (International Association for the Evaluation of Educational Achievement, 1996), although girls in some countries outperformed boys in others.

Differences between boys' and girls' math and science performance have long been a source of concern. More boys than girls take advanced math and science, such as calculus and physics, and the number of girls studying math and science drops during high school (Status of Women Council, 1994). Additionally, many girls feel that they are not good at math and science and say that they do not like these subjects and experience anxiety about their abilities (Boaler, 2002). Girls' lack of confidence in their math and science abilities contributes to their lower performance (Schmader, Johns, & Barquissau, 2004). What is most troubling about these attitudes is that girls' grades in math and science are often equal to or better than those of their male peers (Jovanovic & Dreves, 1995). Girls can do math and science, but they are more likely than boys to opt out of advanced training in these areas and are thus less prepared for the many careers that involve math and science.

Female participation in math and science careers remains low—about 24 percent (National Science Foundation, 2002). By the time they enter high school, boys are more than twice as likely as girls to aspire to be scientists or engineers (Bae & Smith, 1996). Because

FIGURE 15.4
Tests of Spatial Ability

SPATIAL PERCEPTION
A Schematic Diagram of the Rod and Frame Test

Align a rod within these frames so that the rod is vertical.

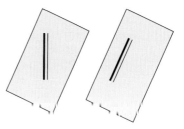

MENTAL ROTATION
Are these pairs of figures the same except for their orientation?

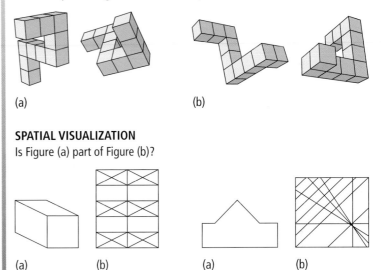

(a)   (b)

SPATIAL VISUALIZATION
Is Figure (a) part of Figure (b)?

(a)   (b)   (a)   (b)

This figure illustrates the three major forms of spatial abilities. In the spatial perception task, individuals are asked to put the rod in a vertical position within a tilted rectangular frame (as shown in the left frame). In the mental rotation task, individuals are asked to identify the pairs that are alike except for orientation. In the spatial visualization task, individuals are asked whether Figure (a) is part of Figure (b). How do these abilities differ from one another?

Source: Adapted from Halpern, 1992.

FIGURE 15.5

Average Science Proficiency of Eighth-Grade Boys and Girls, by Country

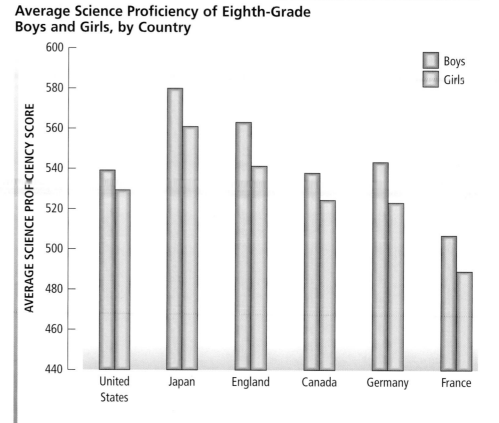

Notice that the gender differences in science proficiency exist in many countries. However, the absolute level of proficiency for girls in some countries, such as Japan, is higher than that of boys in other countries, such as Canada and the United States. What do these patterns indicate about the nature of this gender difference?

Source: International Association for the Evaluation of Educational Achievement, 2000.

How do boys and girls differ in mathematical abilities? What factors related to the learning environment of the classroom contribute to these differences? What other factors contribute to these differences? How can teachers help make mathematics more accessible to all adolescents?

overall cognitive differences between adolescent boys and girls are small or limited to very specific skills, other factors must account for the discrepancies between the numbers of men and women in math and science careers.

Explaining Gender Differences in Academic Abilities and Achievement

When Mattel Toy Company decided in 1992 to market the first talking Barbie doll, the doll's first words were "Math class is tough," "I love dressing up," and "Do you want to braid my hair?" The toy makers thought they were expressing the feelings of many school-age girls. They did not foresee the negative response of many parents and teachers to these first words. As a result, this talking Barbie never made it to store shelves (Jovanovic & Dreves, 1995).

The controversy surrounding talking Barbie and her comment about math highlights the issue of gender differences in academic performance and achievement. Why do boys and girls perform differently on some cognitive tasks (see Figure 15.6)?

Biological Influences on Boys' and Girls' Academic Achievement

Sex hormones may be involved in some gender differences because males and females differ in the relative concentrations of sex hormones. In prenatal development, differing levels of sex hormones affect the development of the brain—particularly how it is organized.

FIGURE 15.6
Explanations for Gender Differences in Academic Abilities and Achievement

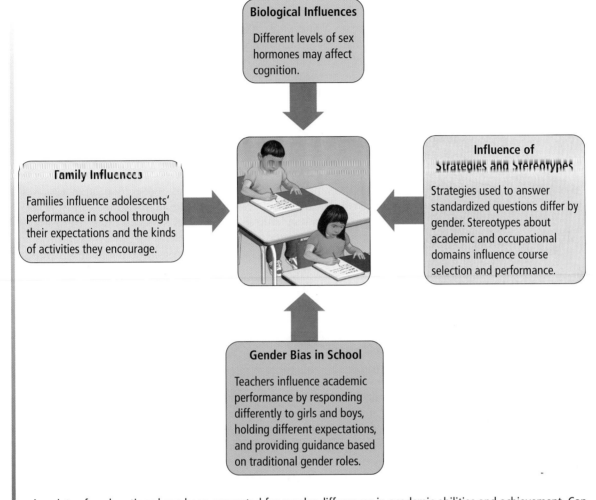

Biological Influences

Different levels of sex hormones may affect cognition.

Family Influences

Families influence adolescents' performance in school through their expectations and the kinds of activities they encourage.

Influence of Strategies and Stereotypes

Strategies used to answer standardized questions differ by gender. Stereotypes about academic and occupational domains influence course selection and performance.

Gender Bias in School

Teachers influence academic performance by responding differently to girls and boys, holding different expectations, and providing guidance based on traditional gender roles.

A variety of explanations have been suggested for gender differences in academic abilities and achievement. Can you identify these differences and how various approaches might explain them? Which explanation or set of explanations do you think best accounts for differences in boys' and girls' academic abilities and achievement?

Because brain organization can determine how information is received and processed and can sensitize the brain to circulating hormones later in development, early hormonal effects could influence intellectual abilities. Later in development, especially during adolescence, boys and girls have different levels of sex hormones circulating freely through the bloodstream, stimulating and regulating many biological functions. But do these hormones explain differences in boys' and girls' academic performance and interests?

Understanding the effects of hormones is complicated by the interrelationship of biological and environmental factors, which makes it difficult to separate out the effects due only to hormones (Halpern, 1997). For example, women with Turner's syndrome (see Chapter 3) have extremely low levels of androgens. These women possess normal intelligence but show specific problems in spatial–visual functioning. But these women also have certain behavioral and physical characteristics that might contribute to these findings. For example, they tend to have poor social skills (Halpern, 1992), which may decrease their social interactions so that they do not get as much attention or encouragement to develop their cognitive abilities. What appears to be a physiological response in Turner's women to low levels of hormones may be due in part to a social response to their behavior.

Although untangling the effects of hormones from environmental effects is difficult, some causal links between hormones and cognitive abilities have been suggested (Fitch & Bimonte, 2002). Individuals with disorders that influence the production of prenatal sex hormones often show patterns of cognitive abilities and behavior that differ from those of other members of their sex (Hines et al., 2003; Meyer-Bahlburg et al., 2004). For instance, girls with a disorder that causes increased prenatal production of male hormones show male-typical patterns of cognitive abilities (Hines, Brook, & Conway, 2004). Sex hormones also affect cognitive performance when they are given later in life. For instance, elderly men given male hormones to enhance their sexual functioning show improved scores on visual–spatial tests (Janowksy, Oviatt, & Orwoll, 1994).

Influence of Strategies and Stereotypes on Gender Differences in Academic Achievement

Two new lines of research provide some insights into gender differences in mathematics achievement. These findings may also relate to other areas of cognitive differences, which have yet to be investigated. The first line of research focuses on the strategies that girls and boys use to answer questions on standardized tests (De Lisi & McGillicuddy-De Lisi, 2002). It appears that girls perform better on conventional problems that involve applying computational approaches taught in school and assigning values to find the solutions. Boys, on the other hand, perform better on unconventional problems whose solutions require the use of insight, logic, or estimation. These findings may explain gender differences in grades and test performance. Classroom tests are more likely to involve solution methods that have been taught, and thus girls are likely to do well on them; standardized tests include these items but also include nonconventional items likely to favor boys' strategies (Gallagher & De Lisi, 1994; Gallagher et al., 2000).

To improve performance in mathematics for both sexes, it might be ideal for teachers to train students to adopt both types of strategies, depending on the kind of problem they face. Also, these findings illustrate how important it is to go beyond the basic information about a gender difference to explore the specific aspects of the difference.

The second line of research on gender differences in mathematics performance involves stereotypes. Although older adolescents hold more flexible beliefs than younger children do, adolescents have some stereotypic ideas about academic and occupational domains, and these may influence the courses they choose to take in school (Gleason & Ely, 2002). Students' ideas about their own competence in academic domains also are influenced by their beliefs about whether these domains are relevant and important for their future careers (Wigfield, Battle, Keller, & Eccles, 2002). Furthermore, stereotypes can exert a negative influence on performance indirectly. When stereotypes about their own groups are made salient, students may become anxious about or distracted by what others think about them, and this attitude can undermine their test-taking performance. Specifically, researchers have demonstrated—under controlled conditions—that when students are concerned about the stereotypes that other people have about their skills (when they are under a "stereotype threat"), they perform more poorly than when stereotypes are not salient (Steele, 1997). The negative influence of stereotype threat has been found for intelligence testing and race (Steele & Aronson, 1995) and for mathematics performance and gender (O'Brien & Crandall, 2003).

Family Influences on Boys' and Girls' Academic Achievement

Parents' beliefs have important influences on their children's academic achievement and performance (Drummond & Stipek, 2004; Fan & Chen, 2001). In fact, parents' beliefs about children's abilities in math and science have a greater impact on achievement and attitudes than do the children's earlier performance in those subjects (Eisenberg et al., 1996) and are predictive of children's academic performance years later (Bleeker & Jacobs, 2004).

Some parents convey stereotypic beliefs about cognitive abilities, varying their message depending on the sex of their child. Parents who believe that girls are less able than boys to do math or science are more likely to have daughters who believe that they will not do very

This boy is building a model. What other activities are boys encouraged to do, and how do these activities potentially contribute to interest in math and science?

This girl is cooking. What other activities are girls encouraged to do? Do you think girls' typical activities provide skills that will help them in math and science?

well in these subjects (Eccles et al., 2000; Yee & Eccles, 1988). When parents hold such beliefs, daughters are less likely to take math courses (Jacobs & Eccles, 1985). Conversely, sons are more likely to receive messages that they are supposed to do well in math and science because they have "natural talent" in these areas. Thus, parents' expectations influence their adolescents' expectations about their academic abilities, which then affect the adolescents' academic performance—those with higher expectations perform better (Jacobs, 1991).

Parents' influence on children's academic performance and attitudes can be traced to the activities parents provide and encourage. Opportunities to learn math and science principles are more likely to be provided to sons than to daughters. For example, parents provide more science-related equipment, such as microscopes and chemistry sets, to boys than to girls (Halpern, 1992). Parents also encourage their sons and daughters to participate in different activities and hobbies. Boys are encouraged more often than girls are to do math- or science-related activities at home (Eccles et al., 2000). Boys are encouraged to select leisure activities that involve science and math skills, such as making models, taking things apart, and helping with repairs around the house. In contrast, girls are likely to be encouraged to show interest in activities that involve domestic skills (Jacobs & Eccles, 2000).

Gender Bias in School

As you learned previously, when students are engaged in academic tasks, many teachers give more positive attention, praise, and feedback to boys than to girls (Einarsson & Granstroem, 2002). In a classic study, when teachers were asked if they treated boys and girls differently, most teachers say they did not (Sadker & Sadker, 1984). Thus, most teachers do not realize how their behavior may be affecting the behavior of male and female students.

The different expectations that teachers hold for boys and girls also influence students' academic performance and achievement. For example, teachers' standards for "good" students differ for girls and boys. Girls who conform to traditional gender stereotypes and are compliant and well-behaved are viewed by teachers as more capable than other girls (Gold, Crombie, & Noble, 1987). Yet teachers' evaluations of boys are not influenced by whether the boy is compliant. Thus, teachers' judgments of what constitutes a good student are based less on how well students do in school and more on gender-stereotyped attitudes and expectations (Worthington, 2002).

The guidance that students receive at school also is affected by gender stereotypes. School counselors tend to give conventional, gender-typed advice to students and do not encourage them to explore new fields (Owens, Smothers, & Love, 2003). The potential for peer ridicule adds to the pressure to avoid courses that do not fit gender stereotypes. Girls interested in math and science, for example, may be viewed as weird or unfeminine.

Although in recent decades great strides have been made in attempting to remedy sexism and stereotyping, schools and communities still have a long way to go to overcome gender bias.

Cultural Influences on Academic Achievement

When Huang Liu moved from China to the United States, he was surprised at how easy the math classes were. He also was surprised at how short the school year was. Huang Liu's reactions reveal important cultural differences in academic expectations and environments. Several decades of research have documented consistent differences in academic performance and motivation among students from various countries and different racial and ethnic groups. For example, students in the United States typically perform at lower levels than students from China, Hong Kong, Japan, and Korea (Stevenson, Chen, & Lee, 1993; Stevenson, Hofer, & Randel, 2000). Within the United States, Caucasian American students score higher than minority students, with the exception of Asian American students (Chen & Stevenson, 1995; Children's Defense Fund, 1992; Taylor, 1995). The reasons for these differences are complex, but such findings suggest that the beliefs, values, and experiences of different racial and ethnic groups influence the impact that schools have on students.

Cross-Cultural Studies

As you learned in Chapter 12, Stevenson and colleagues (Chen & Stevenson, 1995; Stevenson & Lee, 1990) compared the academic performance of US, Chinese, and Japanese students at age 7 and age 11. As you can see in Figure 15.7, Asian children outperformed US students in math, and these differences were magnified for young adolescents. Of the top 100 students at age 7, only 14 were American. By age 11, only 1 was American.

One reason for these differences is found in the cultural values of the groups of students. In many Asian countries, the connection between educational attainment and occupational success is stronger than it is in the United States. In Asian cultures, the centuries-old examination system is the means by which most governments select civil officials. To attend school beyond junior high, Chinese students must pass examinations; only a third of junior high students continue to high school (Chen & Stevenson, 1995). In Japan, acceptance to a prestigious university is considered a virtual guarantee of favorable employment. In contrast, in the United States, education is thought of as only one of many avenues to success. What ultimately is valued is occupational and financial success, regardless of how it is accomplished. When asked about their wishes for the future, 70 percent of students in China expressed wishes related to education, such as attending college or doing well in school, whereas only 10 percent of US students expressed a comparable wish (Stevenson & Stigler, 1992).

A second reason is found in differences in educational policies. The length of the school year

FIGURE 15.7

Cross-Cultural Comparison of Math Achievement

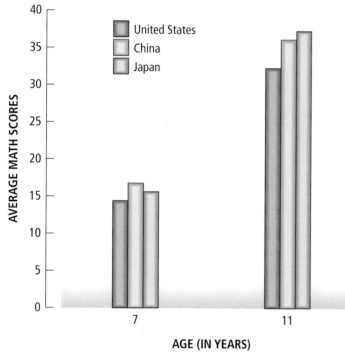

Notice that differences in math achievement among US, Chinese, and Japanese children are relatively small at age 7. But US children have noticeably lower average scores four years later. What factors contribute to these differences? What role does culture play in influencing these patterns?

Source: Reprinted from *Advances in Motivation and Achievement,* Vol. 9, C. Chen and H. W. Stevenson, "Culture and Academic Achievement," pp. 119–151, Copyright 1995, with permission from Elsevier Science.

is one reflection of a nation's values and commitment to education. In the United States, students attend school for 1,044 hours per year, compared to 1,655 hours for Chinese students and 1,466 hours for Japanese students (Stevenson & Lee, 1990). As each year passes, the accumulated difference in the amount of time students have spent in school translates into higher achievement. For instance, after ten years of schooling, Chinese children have received over 6,000 more hours of instruction than US children have, which amounts to an additional *six years* of schooling.

Cultural differences also exist in students' lives at home. Schoolchildren from the United States, China, and Japan allocate their time in different ways. The higher academic performance of Asian students may relate to the fact that they work longer and harder on their schoolwork. In Japan and China, students spend more time outside of school on academic activities and homework than do their counterparts in the United States. US children spend more of their out-of-school time engaged in social interactions with friends and family. US parents are tolerant of their children's spending large amounts of time on nonschool activities and believe that these activities help make them well-rounded individuals. Chinese and Japanese parents believe more strongly in education as the route to future happiness (Stevenson & Lee, 1990).

FIGURE 15.8

Comparison of Math Achievement of US Students from Different Ethnic Groups

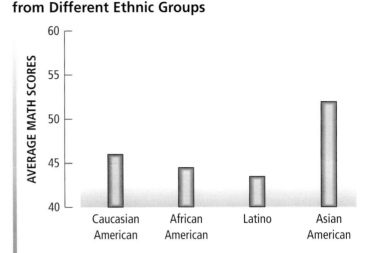

This figure depicts math achievement of US students from different ethnic groups. Asian American students clearly outperform their peers, and Caucasian American students outperform children of other US ethnic groups. What implications do these findings have for schools and social policy?

Source: Reprinted from *Advances in Motivation and Achievement*, Vol. 9, C. Chen and H. W. Stevenson, "Culture and Academic Achievement," pp. 119–151, Copyright 1995, with permission from Elsevier Science.

US Racial and Ethnic Differences

Within the United States, academic performance varies for different racial and ethnic groups. Figure 15.8 reveals that the math performance of 11-year-old Asian American students far outstripped that of any other ethnic group and that African American and Latino students had the lowest levels of performance (Chen & Stevenson, 1995). Whereas Caucasian American families value education less than Asian American families do, the same cannot be said of African American and Latino families. Like Asian American families, African American and Latino families place a high value on education. Despite this emphasis, the academic achievement of African American and Latino students is lower than that of either Asian American or Caucasian American students (Chen & Stevenson, 1995).

Many factors interfere with the translation of African Americans' and Latinos' high values for education into high levels of academic achievement (Graham & Taylor, 2002). The parents of these students do not put as much pressure on their children to achieve academically, relying more strongly on punishment as a disciplinary method than parents in the other groups do (Barber & Harmen, 2002). Parents who do not forcefully emphasize academic achievement and who routinely use punishment may undermine their children's motivation to learn independently (NICHD Child Care Research Network, 2004). Additionally, African American and Latino students enroll in fewer advanced courses, have more part-time jobs, watch more television, and have higher rates of absenteeism than other students do (Stevenson, Lee, & Mu, 2000). Racial discrimination and limited English proficiency also play roles in the lower school performance of US minorities.

School conditions contribute to racial and ethnic group differences. Thirty-seven percent of African American and 32 percent of Latino adolescents are enrolled in the largest city school districts in the United States, compared to 5 percent of Caucasian American and 22 percent of Asian American adolescents (Wigfield et al., 1996). More African American and Latino students live in impoverished neighborhoods, and the schools in these areas are

FROM RESEARCH TO PRACTICE
WHAT FACTORS PROMOTE THE ACADEMIC ACHIEVEMENT
OF ADOLESCENTS FROM IMMIGRANT FAMILIES?

FROM RESEARCH . . .

In the United States of America, every child is entitled—in fact, required—to receive an education, regardless of citizenship status. This mandate has created some stress and tension for the US school system because, as you have already learned (see Chapter 1), the United States has experienced a surge of immigration. Accompanying the increase in the size of the foreign-born population is a rise in the number of immigrant children and adolescents attending schools in the United States (Pong, 2003)—children of immigrants represent 20 percent of all children in this country, totaling about 10.5 million students in grades K–12 (Zigler & Finn-Stevenson, 2003). Because school success and achievement are so critical to children's future, they have been used to mark the degree of success immigrants have had in adapting to mainstream US culture.

Immigrant students face many challenges in attaining a sound education. Many come from homes in which English is not the main spoken language. For others, schooling has been interrupted by poverty or war in their home countries. Immigrant parents often know little about the workings of American schools and many themselves have received little formal education (Bhattacharya, 2000). Immigrant families also tend to settle in large urban areas that have troubled school systems (Zigler & Finn-Stevenson, 2003).

Despite these challenging conditions, many adolescents from immigrant families perform as well as or better than their native-born counterparts in school (Pong, 2003). The reasons for this phenomenon are unclear, but researchers have begun to examine it. One study of 1,100 senior and junior high school immigrant students of Latino, East Asian, Filipino, and European backgrounds who had a working knowledge of English provides some insight (Fuligni, 1997; Fuligni & Whitlow, 2004). The study examined academic achievement and values of adolescents of different generations: about 25 percent of the students were first-generation immigrants (neither the students nor their parents were born in the United States), about 40 percent were second-generation (students were born in the United States, but one or both parents were not), and the remainder were third-generation or greater (both the students and their parents were born in the United States).

The findings confirmed that students from immigrant families receive higher grades than those with native-born parents. One prominent factor in predicting academic performance in adolescents from immigrant families was students' interests, attitudes, and behaviors regarding education. Immigrant students consistently valued school and educational success more highly and spent more time on academic tasks (such as homework) than did native-born adolescents. These adolescents' strong motivation was supported by both the parents and peers, whether the families emigrated from Asia, Latin America, or Europe (Fuligni, 2001b). Generations more distant from the immigration experience showed ambivalence toward schooling and were more likely to become involved in problem behavior, however. Native-born teenagers also often doubted that academic endeavors would yield positive returns and questioned the opportunities available to them in American society (Suarez-Orozco & Suarez-Orozco, 1995). Across successive generations of immigrant families, adolescents' motivation and achievement declined.

. . . TO PRACTICE

Researchers (Midobuche, 2001; Zigler & Finn-Stevenson, 2003) are beginning to identify the factors that facilitate or limit immigrant children's success in school. In particular, schools and teachers play an important role. For example, schools that develop program services that are culturally sensitive and responsive enhance students' and parents' engagement in school. In addition, it is critical that language barriers be overcome. Immigrant students' communication barriers have received much attention, but less has been paid to communication barriers with immigrant parents who may speak little or no English. Providing information, materials, and feedback to parents in their native language can help them connect with schools—thereby enhancing the adjustment of their children and teens (Gonchas, 2001). Finally, recognition that immigrants are not a homogeneous group and instead represent incredible diversity in national background, education, and income status should motivate schools to tailor programs to the specific needs of various groups. A "one size fits all" approach is unlikely to work.

THINKING IT THROUGH

1. Why might first-generation immigrant adolescents and their families place higher value on education?

2. What experiences might cause later generations of immigrant students to lose interest in school?

3. What can communities do to enhance the likelihood that immigrant children will succeed in school?

less likely than schools serving advantaged populations to offer high-quality remedial services or advanced courses (Jordon & Cooper, 2003). Even children who are extremely motivated may find it difficult to perform well under these adverse conditions. Such findings suggest that economic conditions are important in explaining the differences in academic achievement and performance found between Caucasian American and Asian American students on the one hand and African American and Latino students on the other. Many African American and Latino students perform poorly in school not because they lack basic intellectual capacities or do not value education, but because of the economic and social conditions they grow up in (Jordon & Plank, 2000).

Try It Out

1. Formal operational thinking is a benchmark in cognitive development during adolescence. However, some cognitive researchers believe that this level of thinking is rare, even among adults. Describe or illustrate an experiment other than the pendulum problem that you think could help resolve questions about adolescents' and adults' use of formal operational thinking.
2. Arrange to interview adolescents about their perceptions of gender differences in academic abilities and their experiences with gender bias in school. Begin by designing specific questions. Then note what you think you will learn or what views you think you will hear most often, based on your own high school experiences. Compare respondents' perceptions and experiences with your predictions. How do you account for the similarities or differences you find in gender expectations?
3. Investigate dropout prevention and intervention programs and services in your state or in a school district near you. What makes these programs effective? What personal or professional role might you take in a dropout prevention program in your community?

Key Terms and Concepts

adolescent egocentrism (488)	mental rotation (500)	social cognition (489)
associational fluency (500)	moral domain (491)	social–conventional domain (492)
heuristic (487)	personal domain (492)	spatial perception (500)
hypothetico–deductive reasoning (486)	personal fable (488)	spatial visualization (500)
imaginary audience (488)	reflective abstraction (487)	spatial–visual skills (500)

Sum It Up

How do adolescents think and reason?

- Hypothetico–deductive reasoning encompasses what three phases of thinking? (p. 486)
- How do adolescents' views on other people change as they gain more experience in social situations? (pp. 489–490)

How does school influence adolescent development?

- What are the characteristics of effective high school dropout prevention programs? (p. 497)

What factors influence adolescents' perceptions of academic competence?

- What are the three categories of spatial-visual skills? (p. 500)
- What role does culture and ethnicity play in academic achievement? (pp. 506–509)

TABLE 15.1
Developmental Changes in Perspective Taking During Adolescence

STAGE	AGES (IN YEARS)	DESCRIPTION
Self-reflective and reciprocal perspective taking	7 to 12	Children can reflect on their own thoughts from another person's viewpoint but cannot hold both their own and the outside position simultaneously.
Third-person, or mutual, perspective taking	10 to 15	Adolescents can step outside their own viewpoint and those of others and assume the perspective of a neutral third person.
In-depth and symbolic perspective taking	12 to adult	Individuals are able to recognize multiple and more abstract levels of perspectives, including a societal perspective.

The egocentric perspective of adolescents leads them to feel as if they were the central focus of an imaginary audience. Egocentrism also results in the creation of personal fables that emphasize young adolescents' unique and vulnerable nature

THINKING AND REASONING

Compared to children, adolescents use more adultlike and sophisticated forms of thinking and reasoning. During adolescence formal operational thinking develops—the highest level of logical and abstract thought. Early in the stage, this transition is thought to lead to enhanced egocentrism and adolescents' focus on themselves. Later, adolescents use their higher levels of thought and reasoning to understand others and broader social, religious, and political issues. (Refer back to pages 485–492.)

SCHOOL AND DEVELOPMENT

While adolescents are changing in appearance and thinking, they are also experiencing changes in their schools and academic environments. This is a time when many adolescents enter new schools—going from elementary to middle or junior high school, and from these to senior high school. Although most adolescents adjust to their new environment without excessive problems, some do not make the transition smoothly and instead experience difficulty with school. Schools represent an important context for adolescent cognitive and academic development. (Refer back to pages 493–498.)

Adolescents who have social and personal support when changes in schools occur tend to cope successfully with the changes.

TABLE 15.2
Students' Reasons for Dropping Out of High School

REASON	PERCENTAGE OF BOYS CITING	PERCENTAGE OF GIRLS CITING
Did not like school	58	44
Did not get along with teachers	52	17
Was failing school	46	33
Could not keep up with schoolwork	38	25
Did not feel safe at school	19	12
Expelled	18	9
Friends dropped out	17	11
Had to get a job	15	16
Got married	5	23
Had to care for family	5	12
Was pregnant	—	31

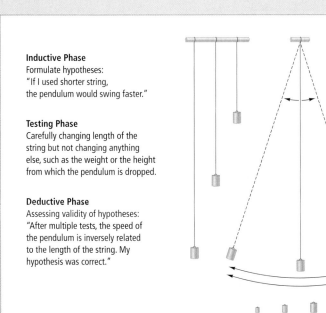

Inductive Phase
Formulate hypotheses:
"If I used shorter string, the pendulum would swing faster."

Testing Phase
Carefully changing length of the string but not changing anything else, such as the weight or the height from which the pendulum is dropped.

Deductive Phase
Assessing validity of hypotheses: "After multiple tests, the speed of the pendulum is inversely related to the length of the string. My hypothesis was correct."

As children grow older, they learn to apply their cognitive decision-making skills to social situations.

FIGURE 15.1 **Hypothetico-Deductive Reasoning** *Piaget presented children and adolescents with scientific problems to see how they reason and think. In the pendulum problem, differences in how adolescents and children tried to answer the scientific question were found.*

PERCEPTIONS OF ACADEMIC COMPETENCE

How teens do in school and the factors that affect that are critical determinants of their long-term success and adjustment. Students' performance in school is determined in part by the perceptions they have of their own academic abilities, by their gender and the stereotypes people hold about boys and girls, and by cultural factors. (Refer back to pages 498–509.)

FIGURE 15.7
Cross-Cultural Comparison of Math Achievement
The findings shown in these two figures highlight the important influence of cultural values and social conditions on school performance.

FIGURE 15.6
Explanations for Gender Differences in Academic Abilities and Achievement

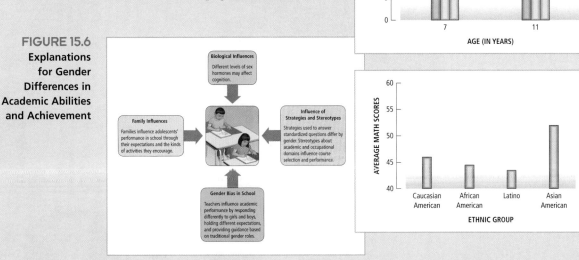

FIGURE 15.8
Comparison of Math Achievement of US Students from Different Ethnic Groups

511

Social and Emotional Development in Adolescence

Chapter Outline

16

How Do Older Adolescents Develop a Sense of Self and Identity?
Changes in Self-Concept During Adolescence
Self-Esteem During Adolescence
Gender Influences on Self-Development
Adolescent Identity Formation
Development of Adolescent Autonomy

How Do Family Relationships Change During Adolescence?
Parenting and Adolescent Development
The Bidirectionality of Parent–Adolescent Relationships
Parent–Adolescent Conflict

What Are the Characteristics of Adolescent Peer Relationships?
The Adolescent Peer Culture
Friendships During Adolescence
Peer Popularity and Rejection
Dating and Romantic Relationships
Sexual Relationships in Adolescence

How Do Mass Media Influence Adolescents' Development?
Popular Music
Computers

What Types of Behavior Problems Occur During Adolescence?
Antisocial Behavior
Depression
Substance Use and Abuse

What Factors Influence Adolescents' Vulnerability and Resilience?

A DEVELOPMENTAL MYSTERY

Tamara, who just turned 17, spends a lot of time playing softball and surfing the Internet to learn more about the people and events she studies in history, her favorite class. She sees herself as well-rounded, both athletic and bright, and she takes pride in her appearance. She has been seeing a boy her own age for almost three months but has not had sex yet. She wants to wait until she is older. After school, when she is not playing ball, Tamara works on the yearbook committee and volunteers at the DelMar Shelter. At the shelter, she works with younger teens from her neighborhood who have drug or alcohol problems. She gets to know peers who have had problems adjusting to stress and difficulties with their families and teachers. It helps put her own life in perspective. Tamara can hardly wait to graduate, go to college, and be on her own. But she wonders what will happen to the kids she works with at the shelter. She sees herself in some of them, and she feels mystified as to how her life turned out so well whereas the kids at the shelter are having so much trouble.

As children enter adolescence, they find themselves cast into many new roles and environments that are sometimes conflicting and confusing. Complicating the challenge of dealing with a changing social reality are the physical changes associated with puberty. As a result, adolescence is a period when relationships within and outside the family change dramatically. Like Tamara, adolescents begin to focus attention on establishing independence, building meaningful relationships with peers, and preparing for the future. In Western societies, the ability to function independently becomes increasingly important as children grow older (Fuligni, 1998). Because the United States is a society preoccupied with self-reliance, personal freedom, and individual success (Peterson, 1995), most adolescents receive a lot of encouragement to follow principles such as "look out for yourself," "make up your own mind," and "do your own thing." For most adolescents, like Tamara, the increased independence and responsibilities promote new strengths, identities, and competencies. But for some adolescents, such as those she works with at the shelter, this period is fraught with risk. The factors that contribute the mystery and confusion Tamara feels reflect a complex system of influences that affects adolescents' social and emotional development.

How Do Adolescents Develop a Sense of Self and Identity?

Compared to children, adolescents have a more complex sense of themselves, in part because of their advanced abilities to understand and imagine how others perceive and evaluate them (Harter, 1998). Their growing self-awareness results from interacting with, and receiving feedback from, a wider circle of significant others (peers, siblings, and teachers). They develop a more complete picture of themselves and a stronger sense of identity—who they are as people—and function more independently and autonomously than they did as children.

Changes in Self-Concept During Adolescence

The most fundamental change in adolescents' self-concepts is their development of a more differentiated view of themselves. As indicated in Table 16.1, adolescents tend to describe themselves in terms of eight domains—scholastic performance, athletic competence,

TABLE 16.1
Domains of Adolescents' and Children's Self-Concept

DOMAIN	USE BY ADOLESCENTS	USE BY CHILDREN
Scholastic	Yes	Yes
Athletic	Yes	Yes
Behavioral conduct	Yes	Yes
Social acceptance	Yes	Yes
Physical appearance	Yes	Yes
Job competence	Yes	No
Close friendships	Yes	No
Romantic appeal	Yes	No

Source: Adapted from Harter, 1998.

behavioral conduct, social acceptance, physical appearance, job competence, close friendships, and romantic appeal. In contrast, young children see themselves in terms of only the first five of these domains (Harter, 1998; see Table 16.1). The increased complexity of adolescents' view of self reflects their more advanced thinking skills and more diverse social environments, which encourage them to think about themselves in more complex ways as they take on new roles within their families, peer groups, schools, workplaces, and communities (Harter, 1999).

Fourteen-year-old Dylan's diary entry illustrates young adolescents' enhanced ability to understand that the way they view themselves changes to fit situations and individuals: "When I'm in math class, I feel smart and creative. Nothing bothers me. But when I have to write an English essay, I feel like an airhead. It's hard and I just don't think I've got what it takes." Like Dylan, adolescents view themselves in conflicting ways—as both "smart" and "an airhead"—depending on the situation. Because of their increased cognitive skills, young adolescents can now make distinctions in their self-concept by considering different circumstances (Harter, 2003).

Adolescents also distinguish between the **actual self**—how they see themselves now—and the **possible self**—how they wish to be in the future. For example, 15-year-old Jennifer aspires to be an artist, but she realizes that she does not yet have the necessary skills and must work hard to develop them if she is to succeed. Children, by contrast, have difficulty recognizing differences between where they are and where they want to be. Adolescents like Jennifer, who recognize a small or moderate difference between actual and possible selves, are likely to feel good about themselves and motivated to improve. In contrast, adolescents who face a large discrepancy between actual and possible selves are likely to feel frustrated, dissatisfied, and depressed. These individuals may experience a sense of hopelessness because they cannot imagine becoming what they want to be (Harter, 2003).

At the beginning of adolescence, the awareness of opposite traits within the self can cause distress and confusion (Harter, 2003). Adolescents at this very early stage frequently demonstrate all-or-none thinking and vacillate from one extreme view to another (Harter, 1998). Like Dylan, they may view themselves as brilliant at one point in time and a total airhead at another. But eventually, adolescents begin to understand that their core self, or personality, remains fairly consistent across time and situations. They can better integrate qualities of the self that seem inconsistent or that change from one setting to another. As you learned in Chapter 10, young children describe themselves in disconnected ways ("I'm quiet"; "I'm friendly"). In contrast, adolescents are much more likely to organize incongruent or even conflicting traits into a logically connected whole (Harter, 1999). Young adolescents are able to recognize that a consistency or coherence underlies their personality and

actual self *how adolescents see themselves*

possible self *how adolescents wish themselves to be in the future*

their actions. They are able to see how their seemingly contradictory qualities work together to reflect their true self.

Self-Esteem During Adolescence

Recall from Chapter 10 that self-esteem consists of the good or bad feelings one has about oneself. High self-esteem is thought to promote many positive outcomes, including academic achievement, popularity, and happiness. Most people believe that positive self-esteem is a protective factor that shelters adolescents from delinquency, academic failure, early sexual involvement, alcohol use, and depression (Salazar et al., 2004; Scheir, Botvin, Griffin, & Diaz, 2000). But research has not consistently supported these expectations (Deci & Ryan, 1995; Liu, Kaplan, & Risser, 1992). High self-esteem prevents some teens from developing realistic perceptions of the risks of their behaviors. In fact, some adolescents *enhance* their self-esteem by winning peer approval through involvement in high-risk behaviors (Damon, 1995). High self-esteem also leads some adolescents to feel entitled to status that they have not earned, as is seen sometimes among members of gangs, and can lead to violence when the sense of high self-esteem is threatened (Baumeister, Smart, & Boden, 1996; Costello & Dunaway, 2003).

Despite the inconsistencies in the research, self-esteem provides a way to assess young adolescents' feelings of personal well-being. Young adolescents' self-esteem is not entirely stable; it fluctuates considerably because they experience so many physical, cognitive, and social changes (Harter & Whitesell, 2003). But like their self-concept, adolescent self-esteem gradually becomes less subject to immediate experiences and events and more consistent (Zimmerman, Copeland, Shope, & Dielman, 1997).

Gender Influences on Self-Development

> *When Polly was a girl, she was energy in motion. She danced, did cartwheels and splits, played football, basketball, and baseball with the neighborhood boys. She yelled out orders and advice, shrieked for joy when she won a bet or heard a good joke, laughed with her mouth wide open. Then Polly had her first period and started junior high. She tried to keep up her old ways, but she was called a tomboy and chided for not acting more ladylike. She was excluded by her boy pals and by the girls, who were moving into makeup and romances. This left Polly confused and shaky. She had temper tantrums and withdrew from both boys' and girls' groups.* (Pipher, 1994, p. 17)

Because of their increased cognitive abilities, adolescents grow more capable of engaging in self-reflection and self-evaluation (Alfieri, Ruble, & Higgins, 1996). They spend a good deal of time imagining what others are thinking about them and feeling self-conscious. Girls might wear loose shirts and walk with a notebook hugged to their chest to hide their developing breasts. Boys worry about erections that develop at inconvenient times (Beal, 1994).

One way to cope with these feelings of self-consciousness is to blend in by doing what everyone else is doing. Although both boys and girls become more self-conscious during early adolescence, the increase is greater for girls (Richards, Crowe, Larson, & Swarr, 1998). Thus, for many girls like Polly, the beginning of adolescence is marked by a decrease in self-esteem and confusion about roles and self-concept (Quatman & Watson, 2001).

Young adolescent girls may suffer difficulties with their self-concept and self-esteem because of the important roles played by physical appearance and body image in peer acceptance (Polce, Myers, Kliewer, & Kilmartin, 2001). For example, the strongest predictor of a girl's popularity is being thin and pretty and wearing the "right" clothes (Adler, Kless, & Adler, 1992). A drop in self-esteem is particularly likely for girls who acknowledge that they base their self-esteem on their appearance (Harter, 2003). And few girls are so confident that they are unaffected by others' evaluations. Consider the case of Diane Sawyer, the television announcer. As a young teenager, Diane won a national beauty pageant. But

Teenage boys and girls differ in the importance they place on various qualities they use to define themselves. Can you identify some of these differences?

when she overheard a boy at a dance say, "Is that her? She's not so great," she ran back to her room and avoided dating for several years afterward (Bosworth, 1985).

In contrast, young adolescent boys place more value on what they do than what they look like. Adolescent boys generally have a stronger sense of self-confidence and competence about their appearance and physical abilities than do girls; girls place more value on their social selves than do boys (Eccles, Wigfield, Flanagan, & Miller, 1989). These deeply ingrained cultural beliefs put adolescent girls at a disadvantage in learning how to develop positive feelings about themselves and their bodies.

Adolescent girls' self-esteem also can be undermined by their experiences in school. Researchers have found that teachers may treat boys and girls differently. When boys and girls are engaged in academic tasks, teachers give more positive attention to the boys (Eisenberg et al., 1996). In addition, teachers praise boys more often, provide more feedback to them, and call on them more often to answer questions. Girls sit patiently with their hands raised, while boys grab teachers' attention—they are eight times more likely than girls to call out answers to questions. Girls who try these tactics may be ignored or admonished (Windass, 1989). Over time, girls come to feel less confident and begin to question how they feel about themselves.

Adolescent Identity Formation

One of the most important developmental tasks for adolescents is the formation of a sense of **identity,** defined as a sense of who one is, where one has been, and where one is going in life. Developing a sense of personal identity prepares people to deal with the challenges that arise later in development (Grotevant, 1998).

Identity formation does not begin or end during adolescence, but adolescents' increased ability to think abstractly about personal qualities and future possibilities makes identity issues a key focus of this period. Adolescents' expanding social world—a world of peers, school, work, leisure, and community involvements—provides motivation for developing a sense of identity (Erikson, 1968).

Erikson's Theory of Adolescent Identity Development

As you have learned throughout this text, Erikson believed that development involves psychosocial crises. During adolescence, the crisis revolves around identity issues. Adolescents

identity   *one's sense of who one is, where one has been, and where one is going in life*

begin making choices about who they are and who they want to be. If the challenges of this crisis are met successfully, adolescents form a secure sense of identity. To do so, adolescents must evaluate their personal assets and liabilities (Wallerstein & Goldberger, 1998).

Erikson believed that during adolescence, teens must resolve the crisis of identity versus **identity confusion.** During this period, adolescents explore possibilities and begin to form their own identity based on the outcome of their explorations. Identity—the sense of who one is—can be hindered, which results in a sense of confusion ("I don't know what I want to be when I grow up") about oneself and one's role in the world. If the challenges of the psychosocial identity crisis are not dealt with successfully, adolescents may develop an incomplete sense of self. These adolescents experience self-doubt, are preoccupied with their own concerns, and may be either too dependent on or excessively isolated from others (Erikson, 1980). Having a confused identity is like wandering aimlessly in search of oneself, without roots and lacking a vision for the future. Extreme forms of identity confusion leave individuals vulnerable to personality and behavioral disorders such as depression, delinquency, substance abuse, and suicide (Erikson, 1968).

These teenagers are exploring and experimenting with different roles, lifestyles, and interests. Erikson referred to this as the psychosocial moratorium. What role does this concept play in Erikson's theory, and how does this affect adolescent identity and development?

Forming an identity is a process and product of individual and social factors (Bosma & Kunnen, 2001). Adolescents use abstract thinking to assess their options and speculate about the future. In addition, they use their relationships with others as a kind of "mirror" that reflects back information about what they are like (Tarrant, 2003). Forming an identity provides adolescents with information about themselves, their direction in life, and their place in meaningful relationships (Meeus, Iedema, Helsen, & Vollebergh, 1999).

Erikson argued that adolescence should be a time of **psychosocial moratorium**—a period during which youths are reasonably free of adult responsibilities that might prevent them from adequately addressing identity issues. According to Erikson, adolescents in present-day Western societies should use this moratorium to consider who they are and their direction in life. An important part of this process is experimenting with a variety of roles, lifestyles, relationships, and value choices (Wallerstein & Goldberger, 1998).

Adolescents who experience a moratorium and are able to experiment with roles have an important advantage in identity formation (Erikson, 1968). When a period of experimentation does not occur, adolescents are at risk for identity confusion and may not realize their capabilities. As a result, they may be unprepared to enter adulthood. For example, identity-confused adolescents may not be ready for intimate adult relationships. According to Erikson, individuals must first develop a healthy sense of who they are before they are ready to engage in mature and intimate relationships with others.

Erikson (1959) believed that a sense of identity continuously develops throughout life. Identity issues may reemerge at any time and are subject to change. For adolescents, however, identity formation is particularly important because it gets them "on track" and moves them in a meaningful direction toward adulthood.

Marcia's Theory of Adolescent Identity Development

James Marcia (1987, 1993) expanded Erikson's theory, describing the basic processes involved in adolescent identity formation. Marcia proposed two essential aspects of an adolescent's search for identity:

- **Crisis/exploration** refers to the process of considering options, values, and goals. Making choices about life directions is an active process of searching among alternatives in religious beliefs, political views, sexuality, roles, and relationships. Because the term *crisis* implies that identity development is an unpleasant and disruptive experience, the term *exploration* often is used to provide a more neutral or even positive tone.

- **Commitment** refers to the making of voluntary choices about life directions from the many available options. By making these choices, adolescents become invested in their identity decisions.

identity confusion *an incomplete sense of self*

psychosocial moratorium *a period during which youths are reasonably free of adult responsibilities that might prevent them from adequately addressing identity issues*

crisis/exploration *the process of making choices about life directions by considering options, values, and goals*

commitment *the making of voluntary choices about life directions from among the many available options*

FIGURE 16.1
Marcia's Identity Status Categories

	Experienced Crisis/Exploration	Did Not Experience Crisis/Exploration
Made a Commitment	IDENTITY ACHIEVED	FORECLOSURE
Did Not Make a Commitment	MORATORIUM	IDENTITY CONFUSED

Marcia's theory of identity development involved different combinations of crisis/exploration and commitment. Can you describe the identity outcomes for the various combinations depicted in this figure?

Source: Marcia, 1993.

identity diffusion *identity status of those adolescents who have not explored or committed themselves to a specific identity choice*

foreclosure *identity status of those adolescents who have not explored alternatives but nonetheless have made a definite commitment to a specific identity*

moratorium *identity status of those adolescents who are actively exploring identity issues but have not yet made any firm commitment*

identity achieved *identity status of those adolescents who have experienced a period of exploration and crisis and have made a commitment*

The concepts of exploration and commitment are used to classify adolescents into four categories with respect to identity status (see Figure 16.1). These status categories provide a way to recognize adolescents who are in the different phases of identity development (Marcia, 1999):

- Adolescents who have not explored choices or committed themselves to a specific identity are considered **identity diffusion.** These adolescents may appear aimless and preoccupied, and they often lack confidence and positive views of themselves.

- Adolescents who have not explored alternatives but nonetheless have made a definite commitment to a specific identity are in **foreclosure.** In this case, the commitment has been made prematurely, without adequate searching or questioning. These teens may try to become what others want them to be rather than really deciding for themselves.

- Adolescents who are actively exploring identity issues but have not yet made any firm commitment are in **moratorium.** Adolescents must experience moratorium before developing a mature identity. This status may be uncomfortable, but it allows adolescents to consider a variety of ideas and behaviors.

- Adolescents who have experienced a period of exploration and crisis and have made a personal commitment to their choice are considered **identity achieved.** Identity-achieved adolescents experience greater self-acceptance and have a better sense of their own strengths and weaknesses.

Marcia believed that identity development is a process of moving or progressing from one status to another as issues related to who one is and what one wants to become are explored (Muuss, 1998). These categories do not take place in a definite order; regressions are common. For example, both foreclosed and identity-achieved adolescents may at some point return to the less advanced status of identity diffusion (Waterman, 1999). Identity issues reemerge at various times, and individuals may move back and forth among the various statuses as they experience different roles, environments, relationships, and challenges (Cote, 1996; Kroger, 2000).

Identity issues are not completely resolved during adolescence. Many continue into early adulthood and come up again at later periods of the life span (Tarrant, 2002)—such as deciding whether to get married or whether to become a parent. The important factor, however, is that adolescents start making constructive progress on identity formation. Identity-achieved adolescents are psychologically healthier than those classified in the other categories. Identity-achieved adolescents, for example, attain greater levels of achievement, morality, and intimacy than others do (Archer, 1993). Adolescents experiencing moratorium are likely to have problems with authority issues, whereas adolescents in foreclosure have a great need for social approval and a low level of autonomy. Those adolescents classified as identity-diffused are likely to be withdrawn, less intimate with peers, more neurotic, and less explorative in their interests and activities (Schmitt & Vondracek, 1999). Thus, adolescent identity status has important consequences for the quality of adolescents' adjustment and their relationships with others (Waterman, 1999).

Ethnic Identity

Because minority adolescents are raised in cultures with values and beliefs that differ from those of the mainstream culture, they often find the process of forming an identity to be particularly complicated. As a result, minority adolescents must work to integrate a sense of their own ethnicity into the identity they define. An important issue in ethnic identity development is how much the dominant culture appears to value or devalue the adolescent's ethnic heritage (Phinney & Rosenthal, 1992; Tomlinson-Clarke, 2001). The experiences minority youths have with prejudice, discrimination, and barriers to their educational, occupational, and economic progress contribute to this view of the dominant culture (Martinez & Dukes, 1997).

Together, these issues are reflected in one's **ethnic identity**—one's sense of belonging to an ethnic group. Ethnic identity involves thoughts, perceptions, feelings, and behavior that reflect ethnic group membership (Bernal & Knight, 1997; Phinney, 2000). It's components include the following (Phinney & Rosenthal, 1992; Spencer & Markstrom-Adams, 1990):

The sense of belonging to an ethnic group reflects one's ethnic identity. The young Latino teens congregating in this picture share common values, rituals, and interests. Can you identify the different components of ethnic identity?

- Identifying oneself as a member of an ethnic group
- Developing a sense of belonging to an ethnic group
- Forming attitudes (either positive or negative) toward one's ethnic group
- Having a sense of shared attitudes and values with an ethnic group
- Following the specific traditions and practices of an ethnic group (such as language, customs, and behavior)

Although members of different ethnic groups have different identity experiences, they share a common pathway (Phinney, Ong, & Madden, 2000; Umana-Taylor, Yazedjian, & Bamaca-Gomez, 2004). The first step along this pathway involves being either unidentified or prematurely identified with one's ethnic culture (ethnic identity diffusion). Next comes a period of exploring one's ethnicity (ethnic identity moratorium), followed by a period of commitment to a particular way of being an ethnic group member (ethnic identity achieved). As with the process of general identity development, ethnic identity issues may reappear at any time (Phinney, 2003).

Ethnic identity development is further complicated by the way in which ethnic identity issues are resolved. Four different ways of resolving identity issues have been identified (Phinney, 1996):

1. An individual who identifies with the majority culture and rejects his or her ethnic culture is defined as **assimilated.**

2. An individual who lives within the majority culture but feels alienated or like an outcast is considered **marginal.**

3. An individual who identifies only with his or her ethnic culture and rejects the majority culture is said to be **separated.**

4. An individual who identifies with both the majority and the minority culture is defined as **bicultural.**

Adolescents from different ethnic minorities report distinct outcomes with respect to ethnic identity. European American adolescents most frequently define themselves as assimilated, African American and Puerto Rican adolescents more frequently choose the separated category, and Mexican American adolescents and their Asian American peers more frequently define themselves as bicultural (Phinney et al., 1994). Once a secure ethnic identity is formed, adolescents in these different outcome groups are similar in mental health, self-esteem, grades, and social competence (Marsiglia et al., 2004).

ethnic identity *the sense of belonging to an ethnic group*

assimilated *identifying with the majority culture and rejecting one's ethnic culture*

marginal *living within the majority culture but feeling alienated or outcast*

separated *identifying only with one's ethnic culture and rejecting the majority culture*

bicultural *identifying with both the majority and the minority culture*

Parents represent one of the most important influences on the formation of ethnic identity. Secure ethnic identities are fostered in families in which parents do the following (Thornton, Chatters, Taylor, & Allen, 1990):

■ Teach adolescents to be proud of their heritage

■ Model participation in the ethnic community

■ Discuss ethnic issues with their adolescents

Like many of the general identity issues faced by adolescents, ethnic identity issues are likely to give rise to competing and ambivalent feelings. For example, a person can develop a preference for her or his own culture but also recognize the advantages of accepting the majority culture. Additionally, contextual factors influence ethnic identity development (Umana-Taylor, 2004; Umana-Taylor & Fine, 2004). For example, ethnic identity commitment was found to be greater for Native American teens enrolled in schools with a predominantly Native American student body than for those in schools with predominantly Caucasian American students (Lysne & Levy, 1997). In general, a central task for minority teenagers is to integrate their contrasting viewpoints into a unified sense of self.

Sexual Identity

I remember my first crush, this girl with dark hair. I was 15 and I felt terribly guilty about my feelings for her. I never felt like I fit in with the other girls. I don't know why for sure. I felt different. I knew at that time that I wasn't normal, and I wanted nothing more in the world than to be normal. So, I ignored my true feelings. I did everything I could to convince myself that I wasn't a lesbian and that my feelings were just a phase. (Holly, age 17)

Holly's story describes the feelings and thoughts of a teenager questioning her **sexual orientation,** determined by the sex of the sexual partners one is attracted to. A person with a sexual attraction to members of the other sex is **heterosexual** in orientation, whereas a person who is sexually attracted to members of the same sex is **homosexual** (gay or lesbian). Although figures vary, 5 to 10 percent of the population classify themselves as lesbian or gay (Savin-Williams, 2003). These figures may not be accurate because many homosexuals hide their sexual orientation out of fear of prejudice and discrimination (Rhode, 1997).

Few teens, whether heterosexual or homosexual, recall when they first became aware of their sexual orientation. Thus, development of sexual orientation appears to be more of a process than an event. Sexual orientation may be present before one has the ability to reflect upon and label sexual feelings and attractions. Studies of twins and gender-atypical children show that sexual orientation is determined early in life (Remafedi, 1991). Both hereditary and environmental factors have been implicated, but there is no consensus as to which is more influential.

During adolescence, sexual orientation and sexual behavior may be quite independent of each other. Adolescents engage in many forms of sexual activities, regardless of sexual orientation. For example, some lesbian and gay youths have extensive heterosexual experiences, whereas some heterosexual youths engage in prolonged homosexual behaviors (Savin-Williams & Diamond, 1999). Although "pre-gay" youths are more likely than others to engage in homosexual behaviors, they also frequently participate in heterosexual behaviors (Blumenfeld & Raymond, 1993).

As in Holly's case, awareness of same-sex attraction usually begins during adolescence. Because of their attraction to same-sex people, many gay and lesbian youths, like Holly, often feel different from most of their peers and come to believe that they are weird or abnormal. Homosexual experiences may occur prior to this awareness or may be delayed until years later. Labeling oneself as "homosexual" almost always occurs in late adolescence or early adulthood.

sexual orientation *characteristic determined by the sex of the sexual partners one is attracted to*

heterosexual *having a sexual attraction to members of the other sex*

homosexual *having a sexual attraction to members of the same sex*

Many gay and lesbian youths struggle because they are ostracized, rejected, teased, and abused by their peers (Savin-Williams & Cohen, 1996). For example, over half of the gay men in one study said they were victimized in junior and senior high school (Gross, Aurand, & Adessa, 1988). In another study (Hunter, 1990), over 40 percent of lesbian and gay youths said they had been physically attacked. In extreme cases, homosexual youths are the victims of terrible hate crimes. Recall the story of Matthew Shepard of Laramie, Wyoming, who was brutally attacked and killed in October 1998 because he chose not to hide his homosexuality. The verbal and physical abuses gays and lesbians endure cause great stress, are detrimental to their mental health, and often lead to school-related problems, substance abuse, prostitution, and even suicide (D'Augelli, 2003).

Five to 10 percent of teens identify themselves as gay or lesbian. How are gay or lesbian teens different from or similar to their heterosexual peers?

New findings show that gay and lesbian youths report an array of risk factors linked to suicidal thoughts and suicide attempts. In a study using nationally representative data, researchers found that youths with same-sex sexual orientations were twice as likely as their peers to attempt suicide and have suicidal thoughts (Russell & Joyner, 2001). The elevated risk of suicide among gay teens can be explained partly by risk factors that could affect any adolescent: depression, hopelessness, substance abuse, the recent suicide or attempted suicide of a family member or close friend, and experiences of victimization. However, the study showed that adolescent gays and lesbians reported experiencing significantly more of these factors. These findings provide strong evidence that sexual minority youths are more likely than their peers to think about and attempt suicide. The problems faced by gay and lesbian adolescents relate to the social and cultural contexts of sexuality and gender. Having supportive and accepting families and being comfortable with their sexual orientation help buffer gay and lesbian youths from the stress they face (D'Augelli, 2003).

In many important ways, lesbian and gay teens are similar to other adolescents. Levels of cognitive, physical, and self-concept development are not different for gay and straight youths (Boxer, Cohler, Herdt, & Irvin, 1993). In response to these facts, homosexuality was dropped as a mental disorder from the official diagnostic manual of the American Psychiatric Association in 1973. Furthermore, the belief that homosexual youths are promiscuous is not supported by scientific evidence—one quarter of gay and lesbian youths are virgins when they graduate from high school (Savin-Williams, 1995). Although lesbian and gay youths face difficulties (such as keeping their sexual orientation hidden from others for fear of retribution), most apparently adapt well and emerge from adolescence with positive views of themselves, their lives, and their future (Diamond & Savin-Williams, 2003).

Development of Adolescent Autonomy

As adolescents begin to separate themselves from their parents, they are encouraged to develop **autonomy**—the ability to govern oneself, make independent decisions, control one's feelings, and choose one's values. The desire for autonomy becomes especially prominent during late adolescence, as youths prepare to leave home and enter adulthood (Borman & Schneider, 1998; Silverberg & Gondoli, 1996).

Historically, this distancing process was thought to lead to conflict and turbulence in parent–adolescent relationships. According to contemporary interpretations, however, adolescent autonomy generally is not achieved through rebellion or rejection of parents. Adolescents assume their individuality while remaining connected to their parents (Silverberg & Gondoli, 1996). This interpretation provides a *constructive model* of the development of autonomy—one that emphasizes a balance between adolescents' needs to assert their individuality and to remain close and connected to others.

autonomy *the ability to govern oneself and make independent decisions*

FIGURE 16.2
Factors That Contribute to Adolescent Autonomy

Physical Changes
Greater autonomy comes from adolescents perceiving changes in how they are treated by others now that they are physically more mature.

Cognitive Changes
Greater autonomy comes from changes in the way adolescents think about problems and issues.

Social Changes
Greater autonomy results when parents are supportive and nurturing, and when teens are involved in diverse activities.

During adolescence, the desire for autonomy becomes prominent. Can you identify the different types of autonomy and how different factors may influence their development?

Forms of Autonomy

The development of autonomy is a complex process through which an individual becomes independent in three major areas:

- **Emotional autonomy** is the ability to understand oneself as a person who is emotionally distinct from one's parents. As adolescents become more autonomous, what they feel depends less on their parents and more on their own individual experiences and concerns (Garber & Little, 2001).

- **Behavioral autonomy** is the capacity to make and follow through with decisions regulating one's behavior (Sessa & Steinberg, 1991). This form of autonomy is the one that adolescents are most often aware of and is the source of many parent–adolescent conflicts (Collins, 1990).

- **Values autonomy** is the capacity to make judgments and choices with respect to personal beliefs and principles. This form of autonomy means that adolescents do not merely adopt the opinions and values of others but become committed to belief systems they choose voluntarily (Sessa & Steinberg, 1991).

As each form of autonomy develops, adolescents move toward a state of constructive autonomy, in which they question many of the ideas they were taught during childhood. During this time of exploration, adolescents identify their own choices apart from those imposed by authority figures (Chen & Dornbusch, 1998; Peterson, 1995).

emotional autonomy *the ability to understand oneself as a person who is emotionally distinct from one's parents*

behavioral autonomy *the capacity to make and follow through with decisions on regulating one's behavior*

values autonomy *the capacity to make judgments and choices about personal beliefs and principles*

Factors That Contribute to Adolescent Autonomy

Autonomy issues occur throughout life; they are not restricted to the period of adolescence (Baltes & Silverberg, 1994). During adulthood, for example, husbands and wives may struggle over how much time to spend together and how much time to invest in their individual careers. However, the period of adolescence is somewhat unique because the physiological changes of puberty bring autonomy issues to the forefront (see Figure 16.2). As adolescents acquire the physical characteristics of adults, parents and others are likely to view them as more mature, respond to them more as adults, and grant them more freedom (Connolly, Paikoff, & Buchanan, 1996). Perceiving these changes in how they are treated by others, adolescents feel they are mature enough for greater autonomy and responsibility.

Changes in the ways adolescents think about problems and issues also contribute to their greater autonomy. For example, the development of metacognitive and critical thinking skills promotes autonomy by enhancing adolescents' abilities to analyze their own thought processes, examine several aspects of a situation at the same time, consider more than one viewpoint, and question what they and others believe (Keating & Sasse, 1996; Smetana, 1988). These abilities permit greater flexibility in thought and independent decision making. Thus, changes in abstract thinking abilities pave the way for adolescents to define themselves as individuals.

Greater autonomy results when parents are supportive and nurturing (Smetana, 2002; Sroufe, 2002) and when they allow their teens to be involved in peer groups, work, and school activities (Silverberg & Gondoli, 1996). Becoming involved in diverse activities exposes adolescents to different viewpoints, values, and lifestyles. Adolescents may take this opportunity to evaluate their own beliefs and values and to assert or negotiate greater autonomy with authority figures. Thus, the social context in which adolescents develop affects the development of autonomy (Boykin-McElhaney & Allen, 2001).

How Do Family Relationships Change During Adolescence?

If you were like most teenagers, then, contrary to the stereotype, your family life was not marked by constant struggle and emotional distance. Instead, your family continued to be your primary source of influence and security. Although some adolescents do experience troubled family relationships, a large majority feel close to their parents, value their parents' opinions, believe that their parents love and care for them, and respect their parents as authority figures (Holmbeck, Paikoff, & Brooks-Gunn, 1995). Adolescents tend to agree with their parents on attitudes toward work, education, religion, and politics. In fact, differences of opinion are greater among adolescents than they are between adolescents and their parents (Gecas & Seff, 1990; Steinberg & Silk, 2002). If serious problems exist between parents and teens, these usually have their roots earlier in childhood (Dishion & Bullock, 2001).

Nonetheless, an important period of family change and adjustment occurs when children enter adolescence. Parents and young adolescents undergo challenging shifts in the established ways of dealing with one another (Steinberg, 2001). Families face the task of altering existing relationships to allow adolescents more involvement in social relationships beyond the family (such as with peers) and more independent decision making about lifestyle preferences. At the same time, parents must continue to supervise, protect, and provide guidance to reduce the chances that young teens will develop problem behaviors (Dishion & Bullock, 2001).

Families must therefore strike a balance between allowing changes that foster greater individual competence and maintaining stable connections that prevent adolescents from drifting into risky and problem behaviors (such as delinquency and drug use). As

This teenager and her mother are disagreeing about how the teen is dressed. Parent-adolescent conflict most often focuses on everyday lifestyle choices and rarely is destructive or abusive.

adolescence progresses, the relationship between parents and their teens must gradually evolve from one in which parents are clearly in charge to one in which greater equality and independence are granted to the teens (Avenevoli, Sessa, & Steinberg, 1999).

Parenting and Adolescent Development

As children become adolescents, parenting practices and patterns are likely to change. Adolescence can be disruptive for both adolescents and their families, as various tensions and dilemmas surface in new and sometimes unexpected ways. For example, teenagers have a greater need for privacy than they did when they were children. Thus, they are less likely to share their personal lives and more likely to become embarrassed or angry when their privacy is invaded. Another example is that adolescents begin to look for (and find) faults in their parents. Small children idealize their parents, but adolescents have a more realistic and critical view of them (Steinberg & Silk, 2003).

When adolescents and their parents handle these potentially disruptive situations successfully, teens become clearer about themselves, their goals, and their direction in life (Hauser et al., 1991). When teens do not cope successfully, serious problems can arise. Thus, how parents respond to the changes in the family that occur as their children enter adolescence plays an important role in helping their adolescents cope.

The physical changes, new cognitive abilities, and expanded social world of young adolescents stimulate parents to adjust the ways in which they relate to, discipline, and seek to guide them (Henricson & Roker, 2000; Steinberg, 1990). Children often enter adolescence quite dependent on their parents, but they exit this period in a more equal relationship with them. Parents and adolescents must renegotiate their relationships (Steinberg & Silk, 2003). For example, teens' and parents' influence within the family shifts. Mothers generally lose status in the family, whereas sons gain influence (Papini & Sebby, 1987). In the first few months after achieving puberty, daughters are treated more harshly than they were before they reached menarche and participate less in family activities (Steinberg, 1989). Most young teens and their families eventually make the necessary adjustments and adapt positively.

Support, Warmth, and Acceptance

Warm, supportive, and accepting parental behavior is associated with the development of social competence by adolescents and children of all ages (Carlo et al., 1999; Stafford & Bayer, 1993). Parents who hug, kiss, praise, and spend positive time with their adolescents foster close ties and communicate confidence in their adolescents' abilities (Fuligni & Eccles, 1993; Rohner, 1986). Adolescents who receive support and nurturance from their parents have high self-esteem and a well-developed identity and are less anxious, depressed, and aggressive than those who do not (Peterson & Haan, 1999; Scaramella, Conger, & Simons, 1999). Thus, supportive parent–adolescent relationships buffer teens from problem behaviors (Barnes et al., 2000). Warm, supportive parenting also prepares adolescents for intimate peer relationships (Laursen & Williams, 1997; Steinberg, 2001). Teens who have warm and close relationships with their parents select peers who reinforce rather than contradict parental values.

Induction

As you learned in Chapter 10, many parents influence their sons and daughters by using logical reasoning, or induction, to persuade them to accept the parental viewpoint (Stafford & Bayer, 1993). This moderate form of control legitimizes parental authority but does not produce hostile feelings. Parents may use induction to appeal to adolescents' concern for others, their desire to be mature, or their ability to understand and accept parents' points of view. Induction helps teens understand many things (Peterson & Haan, 1999):

- Why rules are necessary
- Why their misbehavior is unacceptable
- How their behavior affects others

- How their behavior might become more acceptable
- How they might make amends for any harm they caused

Parents who use induction do not impose their authority; they communicate confidence in adolescents' abilities to make good decisions and voluntarily comply. This parenting technique is more effective with young adolescents than with younger children because of adolescents' increased ability to think abstractly and consider several possibilities (Hill, 1987). Parents who rely on induction have teens with positive social values, high self-esteem, and good school performance (Aunola, Stattin, & Nurmi, 2000; Hoffman, 1994).

Monitoring and Supervision

"Where are you going?" "When will you be home?" "Whom will you be with?" These questions are commonly overheard in households with teenagers. Questions like these provide a way for parents to monitor and supervise their adolescents' schedules, peer associations, activities, and physical whereabouts. Effective monitoring requires that parents be involved in the lives of adolescents and maintain clear expectations about curfews, appropriate activities, acceptable peers, and places where they can and cannot go. Although some adolescents resist such monitoring and supervision, most affirm parents' legitimate authority to set rules and monitor their whereabouts (Smetana, 2000). Adolescents whose parents fail to monitor their activities are more likely to become involved in delinquency, antisocial behavior, early sexual activity, and drug use (Borawski et al., 2003; Miller, Benson, & Galbraith, 2001).

Punitiveness

Parental punitiveness refers to the use of force to influence children's behavior and qualities—either through spanking, slapping, or other forms of physical force or through nagging, name calling, or yelling (Straus & Donnelly, 1994; Turner & Finkelhor, 1996). Although parents are more likely to use physical punishment with younger children, over 40 percent of parents continue to use physical punishment frequently with their adolescents (Straus & Donnelly, 1994). When parents rely on physical or verbal punitiveness, their children may develop hostility toward them and may resist or reject their authority (Stafford & Bayer, 1993; Turner & Finkelhor, 1996). Adolescents may respond to parents' punitive behavior with their own punitive behaviors (such as yelling or insulting parents), thereby creating a cycle of punitive responses in the family (Patterson, Reid, & Dishion, 1998).

Adolescents whose parents use harsh punishment are likely to develop lower self-esteem and less advanced moral values than their peers. They also are more likely to have problems in school, use drugs, and develop behavior problems (Palmer & Hollin, 2001; Pettit et al., 2001).

The Bidirectionality of Parent–Adolescent Relationships

The emphasis on parental influence often leaves the impression that parent–adolescent relationships are a one-way street, with mothers and fathers dictating the flow of traffic that shapes who adolescents are. However, adolescents also influence their parents in many ways (Collins et al., 2000; Henry, Peterson, & Wilson, 1997). One example of the influence of teens is that parents adapt their parenting practices to adolescents' behaviors and personalities (Ambert, 1997; O'Connor & Dvorak, 2001). For instance, adolescents who defy, talk back to, communicate disrespect for, and even physically assault parents tend to stimulate parents to "crack down" on them with more forceful monitoring and punitiveness. If the result is better compliance and more peace, parents are likely to continue this coercive strategy, which appears on the surface to work (Ambert, 1997; Patterson, 1982).

Parents are increasingly using cell phones to keep tabs on their children's whereabouts and activities. Does monitoring decrease the risk of dangerous behaviors among adolescents?

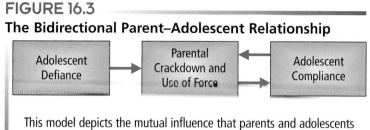

FIGURE 16.3
The Bidirectional Parent–Adolescent Relationship

This model depicts the mutual influence that parents and adolescents have on each other. When adolescents are defiant, they may stimulate parents to "crack down" on them. If the result is more compliance on the part of the adolescent, parents are likely to continue this coercive strategy.

This bidirectional relationship is illustrated in Figure 16.3.

In contrast, parents who view their adolescents as capable and trustworthy are more likely to use nonpunitive parenting practices. These parents tend to exercise more moderate monitoring and elicit more positive responses from their teens. Parents also may feel more positive about themselves when they view their adolescents as competent and responsive to rational and supportive approaches to parenting (Henry et al., 1997). These behaviors mutually reinforce the positive qualities of both parents and adolescents.

Parent–Adolescent Conflict

Despite the widespread notion that parents and adolescents spend much of their time battling each other in an endless power struggle, most research suggests that a more tranquil atmosphere is the norm in most homes. When differences do exist, they are more likely to revolve around personal lifestyle choices, such as styles of dress, hairstyles, tastes in music, and selection of leisure activities (Smetana, 2000; Steinberg, 1990). Although overt conflict between parents and adolescents is less frequent in Latino, Native American, and Asian American families than in Caucasian American families, those conflicts that do occur center on the same lifestyle issues and often are associated with the same outcomes (Bradford et al., 2004; Fuligni, 1998).

Adolescents and parents have their most intense conflicts during early adolescence, when adolescents try to become more independent before parents are ready to accept this change. These conflicts may be due in part to the changes brought on by puberty (Sagrestano, McCormick, Paikoff, & Holmbeck, 1999). Several studies indicate that conflicts intensify as adolescents reach the midpoint of puberty and try to distance themselves from parents (Laursen, Coy, & Collins, 1998; Paikoff & Brooks-Gunn, 1991). Conflicts also result from the different perceptions that parents and adolescents hold about day-to-day events (Larson & Richards, 1994). For example, a father may view his use of induction as a sensible way to persuade his 14-year-old daughter not to date an older boy. His daughter, however, may view his reasoning as an unfair intrusion into an area that she believes is none of his business. The daughter may define her father's stance as a violation of her privacy or an insult to her ability to make mature decisions. Most parent–adolescent conflicts are resolved by adolescents' giving in to parents. However, the number of unresolved conflicts and parents' use of punishment during such a conflict generally increase as adolescents get older because adolescents become less likely to give in (Smetana & Gaines, 1999).

Some developmental researchers view conflict as a process that fosters adaptive changes in parent–adolescent relationships (Collins, 1990). In early adolescence, teens often begin to "talk back" to their parents. They verbally question adult authority and may treat their parents with less respect. They may tell parents that "you can't tell me what to do" and may even use an occasional obscenity. These disrespectful behaviors are often disturbing and can be sources of conflict between parents and their young teens. But these parent–adolescent conflicts reflect the teen's attempt to assert his or her individuality (Lerner & Olson, 1994). Conflict encourages parents and adolescents to revise their expectations and renegotiate their relationship without fundamentally changing their feelings of being connected (Laursen & Collins, 1994). Parent–adolescent conflict may have greater consequences for parents than for teens, as parents' well-being may depend more on how they relate to their teens (Dekovic, 1999). Thus, conflict per se is not considered to be a critical factor in influencing outcomes for adolescents and their families. How conflict is managed and resolved appears to be more influential. For example, high rates of *intense* conflict characterize troubled parent–adolescent relationships and contribute to adolescents' greater involvement in deviant and antisocial behavior (Ambert, 1997; Patterson, Griesler, Vaden, & Kupersmidt, 1992).

FROM RESEARCH TO PRACTICE
WHAT ROLES DO MOTHERS AND FATHERS PLAY IN TEENS' PEER RELATIONSHIPS?

FROM RESEARCH . . .

Parents can play an important role in influencing the type and quality of their children's peer relationships. However, the nature of parental involvement in their children's social relationships differs across developmental periods. For example, during early childhood parents directly intervene in and supervise children's peer interactions; for older children and teens, parents may use a less direct approach, such as encouraging certain friendships and monitoring social activities. Although parents are thought to have considerable influence on children's peer relationships, little is known about the ways in which mothers and fathers involve themselves in their teenagers' peer relationships and the degree to which this involvement is related to the qualities of teens' friendships and peer experiences.

To address these issues, Kimberly Updegraff and colleagues (Updegraff, McHale, Crouter, & Kupanoff, 2001) collected information from 197 mothers, fathers, and firstborn teens (average age, 15 years). Family members participated in a home interview regarding parental involvement in adolescents' peer relationships (such as "time talking with my son/daughter about his/her friends" or "talking to the parents of his/her friends") and on the quality of the teens' peer relationships. In addition, each family participated in seven evening phone calls designed to provide information about daily home and personal activities. In these phone calls, information pertaining to the activities and events that took place in the home and with friends was obtained.

The results showed that mothers and fathers differed in their involvement in their teenagers' peer relationships. Specifically, mothers reported being more involved and were more knowledgeable about adolescents' peer interactions than were fathers. No differences were found, however, in the amount of time mothers and fathers spent with adolescents and their friends. Closer examination of the phone call information showed that parents' time spent with teens and their friends most commonly involved chauffeuring adolescents and their friends, attending sports events, and eating meals together. Although mothers may be more involved in traditional caregiving activities with their teens, which may contribute to their greater involvement and knowledge of peer interactions, fathers appear to share equally in leisure time with their teens and their friends.

Updegraff and colleagues made the important finding that direct parental involvement was related to positive peer relationships. This finding, however, was stronger for boys than girls. Thus, parents' direct peer involvement was more central to boys' than to girls' peer experiences. The authors concluded that because a boy's socialization experiences tend to encourage individuality and achievement, perhaps at the expense of intimate relationships with other teens, a mother's and father's efforts to facilitate a son's peer relationships may be particularly beneficial to his social development.

. . . TO PRACTICE

To promote positive peer relationships during adolescence, parents should consider a number of strategies. First, we know from previous research that parents who have close, strong emotional attachments with their children tend to have teens who are more socially competent. Spending time with teens and listening to them talk about their peer relationships are important qualities of positive parent–adolescent bonding. Although it is important to supervise and monitor teens' involvement with peers, it also is important to remember that part of growing up is choosing one's own friends. The more parents try to choose them for the teen, the more the teenager may rebel. If parents do not like their teenager's friends, invite them over and get to know them. Meeting them will give parents a sense of their personalities, what they are "into," and their family background. Be careful not to judge a teen's friends too quickly. Radical styles and unconventional appearances may be nothing more than a badge of identity. Being too judgmental may cause a teen to dismiss any snap judgments that parents offer. Adolescents may react negatively to any pressure or direct suggestions about whom they should hang out with. But there are many ways to learn more about their friends. Ask them what they like about a friend. Use examples from your own experiences. Having a good relationship with your teen, spending time together, and being involved in a teen's life allow communication about friends and other sensitive topics to become natural and expected.

THINKING IT THROUGH

1. How do societal expectations influence the ways that mothers and fathers interact and involve themselves in their teens' peer relationships?

2. What are the implications of these findings for the development of parenting programs for mothers and fathers of young teenagers?

The actresses in the movie *Mean Girls* are part of a clique. How do poor cliques differ from poor groups?

What Are the Characteristics of Adolescent Peer Relationships?

Adults and parents often worry that adolescents will be led astray by their peers or by peer pressure. Underlying this concern is the idea that adolescent peer groups are at odds with the desires and goals of parents and other adults. In almost a seductive fashion, peers are believed to lure adolescents away from social norms and parental wisdom toward behavior and activities that defy parental standards—bizarre dress, alcohol and drug use, promiscuous sex, and truancy. But in reality, although some adolescents are pressured by their peers to use drugs, skip school, and engage in delinquent activities, most are not. In fact, peers influence the development of important social, cognitive, and educational skills (Ambert, 1997; Brendgen, Bowen, Rondeau, & Vitaro, 1999). Thus, adolescent peer influences represent a combination of diverse and interrelated processes, most of which are constructive—though some are not.

DEBATING THE ISSUE

DO FRIENDS LEAD TEENS INTO TROUBLE?

As you have learned, teenagers are strongly influenced by their friends. One might draw the commonsense conclusion that adolescents who get involved with undesirable friends are more likely to get into trouble (Mruz, Hoza, & Bukowski, 2004). But do friends actually lead one another into trouble?

Two theoretical models have been debated—both trying to account for friends' apparent detrimental influences. The first model (the Peer Influence Model) suggests that associations with undesirable friends is the critical factor in influencing later behavior problems. In contrast, the second model (the Individual Characteristics Model) suggests that problem behavior during childhood leads to both later problem behavior and associations with undesirable friends. Thus, the first model proposes that undesirable peers cause later problem behavior whereas the second model proposes that undesirable friends or having no friend at all are by-products of earlier behavior problems.

To test these models, a longitudinal study of 868 Canadian boys was conducted (Vitaro et al., 1997). The friendships of the boys were assessed at ages 10 and 11 by asking the boys to identify their friends. Classmates then rated the aggressiveness and disruptiveness of these friends. Based on the ratings of friends, the

boys were allocated to one of four groups—aggressive–disturbing friends, average friends, nonaggressive–nondisturbing friends, and no friends. In addition, the boys rated their own involvement in problem behavior at ages 11, 12, and 13. The relationship between type of friend and the adolescents' problem behavior was then examined.

One of the key comparisons in this study focuses on the group of boys with no friends. According to the Peer Influence Model, boys who have no friends should not develop behavior problems. According to the Individual Characteristics Model, children with no friends should be at highest risk for behavior problems because their disruptive behavior contributes to a lack of friends.

The results provide partial support for both models. In support of the Peer Influence Model, boys who were moderately disruptive at ages 11–12 and had aggressive–disturbing friends had more behavior problems at age 13. However, data supporting the Individual Characteristics Model were found in the fact that boys who were highly disruptive at ages 11 and 12 had the most behavior problems at age 13, regardless of whether they had friends or the types of friends they had. Even highly disruptive boys who had nonaggressive–nondisturbing friends were as likely to develop behavior

problems as those who had aggressive–disturbing friends. Boys who were not disruptive were not influenced by their friends.

These findings suggest that multiple pathways may lead to problem behaviors. Boys who are highly disruptive before they enter adolescence do not need to be influenced by undesirable peers to develop later behavior problems. For boys who are moderately disruptive before adolescence, problem behavior is more likely if they associate with undesirable friends. Thus, friends' characteristics may influence some boys' developmental pathways to problem behavior, but this influence depends on those boys' individual characteristics.

THINKING IT THROUGH

1. Can you describe the basic difference between the Peer Influence Model and the Individual Characteristics Model? Draw a diagram that shows how these models relate to problem behavior.

2. Why was the "no friends" group so important in testing the two models?

3. How do you think the results would change if the study was done with girls rather than boys?

The Adolescent Peer Culture

Since World War II, adolescents have been spending more time with one another and less time with adults (Freeman, Csikszentmihalyi, & Larson, 1986). The emergence of an adolescent peer culture is the product of several social developments of the twentieth century (Brown & Larson, 2002; Modell & Goodman, 1990):

- Adolescence became a lengthy period of preparing for, but not participating in, the adult world. The absence of adult roles and responsibilities gave rise to the growth of youth cultures that give meaning and organization to the social world of adolescence.

- The development of low-wage jobs designed specifically for adolescents (such as those in the fast food industry) reinforced age segregation by creating work environments populated largely by teens.

- The growth of industries devoted to adolescents as consumers further contributed to adolescent culture by providing consumer items (clothing, pop music) designed specifically for this age group.

Adolescent peer culture is characterized by two kinds of peer groups. **Cliques** are small groups of peers, usually of the same sex and age, who interact on a regular basis. Common activities, shared interests, proximity, and familiarity form the foundation for the development of cliques. Cliques provide a stable social atmosphere in which members know each other well and engage in intimate friendships (Brown & Klute, 2003; Degirmencioglu, Urberg, Tolson, & Richard, 1998).

When a teen defines himself as a "nerd," he is telling everyone of his membership in a particular peer culture. He may be part of a clique, but he also is a member of a larger group characterized by stereotypes. **Crowds** are peer groups defined by members' activities and social standing. Crowds have larger and more diverse memberships than cliques do and are based on perceptions of social reputation (Ennett & Bauman, 1996). Members of crowds may or may not spend time in direct interaction. Crowds are distinguished from one another by lifestyle characteristics, such as members' clothing, activities, and traits (Brown, Mory, & Kinney, 1994).

Adolescents who become part of a particular crowd through clothing style, language, or choice of hangout engage in social experimentation that temporarily defines how they view themselves and how they are viewed by others. The typical American school is a major social arena for a great diversity of crowds (such as so-called jocks and nerds). In Table 16.2, you can see that adolescents use highly stereotyped images and descriptors to identify crowd members. Additionally, you can see that more adolescents think of themselves as normals or preps than as burnouts or jocks (Urberg, Degirmencioglu, Tolson, & Halliday-Scher, 2000).

Being a member of a particular crowd has consequences for adolescents' self-esteem and popularity. Members of more prestigious crowds, such as jocks, often have higher self-esteem than those in lower-status crowds, such as burnouts and brains (Brown & Lohr, 1987). Youths who are members of the high-status groups of preps and jocks spend more time with peers and friends than do those who are members of the low-status groups of burnouts and brains (Brown et al., 1994). These differences are not simply a function of crowd norms; they are the consequence of many factors—level of social skills, family experiences, personality, and so on (LaGreca, Prinstein, & Fetter, 2001). It is clear, however, that crowd affiliation is an important factor in influencing the patterns of identity and social relationships among members (Stone & Brown, 1999).

Adolescent peer cultures vary widely from one region, community, or school to another (Gecas & Seff, 1990). Whatever the lifestyle characteristics, though, all adolescent peer cultures do the following (Hartup, 1993; Rice, 1996):

- Provide ways of experimenting with different self-concepts
- Provide symbols of group membership
- Serve as symbols of independence from the adult world

cliques *small groups of peers, usually of the same sex and age, who interact with one another on a regular basis*

crowds *peer groups defined by members' activities and social standing*

TABLE 16.2
Descriptors of Various Adolescent Crowds

TYPE OF CROWD	PERCENTAGE IN CROWD	DESCRIPTORS
Preps	25	Have many friends
		Well known
		Invited to and attend social events
		Look good
		Are cool
		Have positive social principles
Jocks	9	Like sports
		Participate in physical activities
Brains or nerds	5	Have high academic skills and make good grades
		Are smart
Normals	47	Are average
		Go to social events and have fun
		Don't have problems
Whiggers	5	Wear baggy overalls
		Prefer rap music
		Use drugs/alcohol
Burnouts	5	Use drugs/alcohol
		Are aggressive
		Are not accepted by others
Alternatives	4	Wear black clothing
		Prefer heavy metal music
		Use drugs/alcohol

Source: Youniss, James, McLellan, Jeffrey A., and Strouse, Darcy. "We're Popular, but We're Not Snobs": Adolescents Describe Their Crowds. In *Personal Relationships During Adolescence,* ed. Montemayor et al., pp. 101–121. Copyright © 1994 by Sage Publications, Inc. Reprinted by permission of Sage Publications, Inc.

■ Serve as symbols of prestige or status within the peer world
■ Allow for the expression of personal beliefs, feelings, and values on topics that are important to adolescents (such as love, sexuality, dating relationships, substance use, and rebellion against adults)

Adolescent peer groups change as youths become more capable of intimacy. At the start of adolescence, peer activities revolve primarily around cliques or crowds composed of either males or females. One of the first changes begins during early adolescence when separate boy cliques and girl cliques come together for shared activities. Soon after, couples begin to form within the cliques. Clique leaders often initiate this transition to relationships with peers of the other sex, and they are followed by other members. Thus, same-sex cliques transform into mixed-sex cliques, but the activities of these mixed-sex cliques remain linked to the group as a whole.

Further change in peer relationships occurs during later adolescence when the cliques and crowds begin to dissolve and couples go their separate ways. Attention becomes focused on specific friendships or dating relationships rather than larger group interests. The safety and security of larger numbers is no longer a top priority, and the structure of adolescent peer groups becomes increasingly fragmented (Shrum, Cheek, & Hunter, 1988).

Friendships During Adolescence

Close friendships during adolescence provide a means for developing trust, security, and intimacy (Fischer, Munsch, & Greene, 1996). These issues are prominent throughout most of the life span, and adolescent friendships are important for making progress toward many of the psychological and social competencies that define mature intimacy and trust (Erikson, 1968).

During early adolescence, important changes take place in the qualities that define friendship (Updegraff et al., 2004). Friends become defined as those who share intimate thoughts, feelings, and expressions of support (Phillipsen, 1999). As you learned in Chapter 10, younger children define friends as those with whom they spend time and share activities. For example, a 9-year-old might describe a friend as someone who "plays games with me a lot." In contrast, a 14-year-old might describe a friend as someone who "listens to me and with whom I can talk about my private feelings" (Epstein, 1986).

During adolescence, friendships become more intense and intimate, based on sharing personal thoughts, feelings, and expressions of support. What factors account for this change in how friendships are defined?

Adolescents are more likely than younger children to share secrets, empathize, and cooperate with friends rather than compete with them (Buhrmeister, Goldfarb, & Cantrell, 1992). Knowledge of one's own and others' personal qualities increases, and this understanding fosters the ability to develop friendships based on mutual generosity, support, and helpfulness (Berndt & Perry, 1990).

Adolescents demand loyalty from friends and express anxiety over the possibility of being rejected. Because of this emphasis on having trustworthy, loyal, and supportive friends, adolescents often become angry and upset when friends talk behind their back and share their secrets with others (Berndt & Perry, 1990). Friendships can be "double-edged swords," providing joy, security, and support when they work, but also heartache, jealousy, and despair when they do not (Roth & Parker, 2001).

Although both boys and girls make progress toward more mature intimacy during adolescence, girls do so earlier and more thoroughly (Fischer et al., 1996). Compared to boys, adolescent girls express more interest in close friendships, have more intimate conversations with friends, are more concerned about receiving loyalty from friends, and express more anxiety about rejection (Bukowski, Gauze, Hoza, & Newcomb, 1993). Teen girls prefer more exclusive friendships, are more sensitive, and express greater empathy with friends than teen boys do (Brendgen, Markiewicz, Doyle, & Bukowski, 2001; Fischer et al., 1996). Adolescent girls also have higher expectations for intimacy in relationships with friends, but these expectations can be unrealistically high, leading to frustration and disappointment. In contrast, boys' friendships remain more focused on shared activities (Clark & Ayers, 1993).

Many of the gender differences in friendships are consistent with the ways girls and boys are socialized. Girls generally are socialized to be focused on interpersonal qualities and communication, whereas boys are encouraged to become autonomous and goal-oriented in their social lives (Ruble & Martin, 1998). For girls, intimacy is often expressed overtly through conversation and self-disclosure. Girls' activities with their friends focus primarily on sharing personal lifestyle qualities (clothing, makeup, and so forth) and aspects of heterosexual relationships (talking about boys; Seiffge-Krenke, 1993). For boys, the expression of support is often nonverbal (Black, 2000)—as one boy said, when he and his friends were down, they would get together and listen to heavy metal music (Arnett, 1991). This is due in part to the concern that boys have about being too intimate with other boys, fearing that close friendships might be mistaken for homosexual interest. Thus, differences in the expectations and interactions of adolescent girl friendships and boy friendships reflect their socialization contexts and experiences.

Peer Popularity and Rejection

Not all children are accepted by their peers. The same is true for adolescents. What makes some teens popular whereas others are outcasts? One answer focuses on adolescents' social skills. Popular adolescents have skills such as the following, which foster smooth and comfortable relationships (Wentzel & Erdley, 1993):

- The ability to act appropriately in a variety of social situations
- The ability to perceive and meet the needs of others
- Being agreeable and cheerful and having a sense of humor
- The ability to communicate effectively

Adolescents who are unpopular and rejected by their peers often lack these skills and have difficulty making others feel comfortable. But not all unpopular and rejected adolescents have the same problems. Aggressive adolescents may be unpopular because they are hostile and bully or badger others. Withdrawn adolescents may be unpopular because they are shy and timid (Hymel, Bowker, & Woody, 1993). Adolescents who are both aggressive and shy have problems controlling their hostility and aggression but also are hesitant or shy about making friends (Olweus, 2003; Pope & Bierman, 1999).

Unpopular and rejected adolescents are at risk for a variety of adverse consequences, such as depression, behavior problems, and academic difficulties (Olweus, 2003; Vitaro, Tremblay, & Bukowski, 2001), and these problems may have long-term effects (Giordano et al., 1998). But the problems vary for each type of rejected adolescent. Aggressive adolescents tend to make friends with one another, and their associations may foster even more aggressive behavior, placing them at risk for behavior problems and delinquency. Withdrawn adolescents tend to experience loneliness, low self-esteem, and diminished social competence. Adolescents who are classified as both aggressive and withdrawn are at greatest risk because they are vulnerable to the problems faced by both aggressive and withdrawn adolescents (Parkhurst & Asher, 1992; Rubin, LeMare, & Lollis, 1990).

Dating and Romantic Relationships

One of the biggest changes and challenges in adolescence is the development of dating and romantic relationships (Franiuk, 2004). Other-sex peers who previously seemed like aliens from another planet now become attractive. The boundaries between boys' and girls' worlds that were so vigorously defended early in development start to crumble in early adolescence. Today dating plays a different role in the lives of adolescents than it did in earlier historic periods (Furman & Shaffer, 2003). Several social changes have redefined dating relationships:

- Dating during adolescence is an end in itself, not a practice that frequently leads to marriage.
- Parents are less available to control and monitor adolescents' dating.
- Dating is less structured, more informal, and more focused on leisure-time activities.
- Dating is a means for sexual experimentation, especially when dating relationships last for a while and become exclusive.

On average, girls begin dating between 12 and 13 years of age, and boys begin a year or so later. Young adolescents usually date in small groups of couples, often meeting at the mall or at the movies. At this age, "going with" someone enhances an adolescent's status, but the relationship is often more form than content: the two may not talk to each other directly at school but pass along messages through intermediaries or over the phone (Beal, 1994). As adolescents mature and begin to drive cars and as their curfews become less confining, dating involves spending more time together as separate couples. During early adolescence, dating partners generally are chosen on the basis of membership in specific peer groups (Connolly, Furman, & Konarski, 2000). With age, partners are selected more on the basis of physical attraction, personal preferences, and personality qualities (Bouchey & Furman, 2003). Dating becomes more intimate as adolescents mature.

In early adolescence, dating and sexuality come to play a more prominent role in adolescents' daily lives. What changes occur during this period that increase the importance of intimate heterosexual relationships?

Despite the fact that only a few dating relationships last beyond adolescence, these relationships can be critically important to adolescents and their development (Davies & Windle, 2000; Shulman, Collins, & Knafo, 1997). Young adolescents learn about love, life, and emotions through dating, and they report that problems with boyfriends or girlfriends create more stress than family-related events do (Dornbusch et al., 1991). Adolescents who frequently date have been found to perform more poorly at school and to be at risk for depression (Quatman, Sampson, Robinson, & Watson, 2001). However, adolescents who never date are at risk for depression, excessive dependency on parents, and deficient social skills (Seiffge-Krenke, 1997). Thus, extremes in dating are related to problem behaviors in young teens.

There is evidence that adolescent boys and girls experience dating and romantic relationships differently (Leaper & Anderson, 1997). Boys emphasize the sexual aspects of dating and the physical attractiveness of the partner. Girls focus on the opportunities that dating relationships provide for closeness, self-disclosure, and communication (Furman & Wehner, 1997; Shulman & Seiffge-Krenke, 2001).

Sexual Relationships in Adolescence

Sexual maturation is one of the most distinctive transitions of adolescence, and the common perception is that this transition brings about unbridled passions that dominate adolescents' lives. How true is this? Sexuality is a key component of our lives and identities, and it seems to be everywhere. The variety of emotions evoked by sexuality—feelings of love, excitement, arousal, embarrassment, guilt, and anxiety—and the experiences associated with them often are among the most memorable of life.

Emerging Sexuality

During early adolescence, sexuality revolves around the adolescent's own body, particularly masturbation. Masturbation is the most common source of orgasm for young teens of both sexes, and it is the first source of ejaculation among 75 percent of adolescent boys. Most girls who masturbate do so around age 12, and most boys have their first experience at age 14 (Reinisch, 1990). Although masturbation persists into adulthood, it is more frequent among young adolescents.

Sexual interactions between boys and girls also begin during early adolescence. These early interactions often begin as curiosity and sex play. Over the course of adolescence, sexual behaviors become more and more a part of intimate relationships. This represents a significant advance in sexual behavior because it requires the ability to negotiate and share sexual experiences. Kissing, hugging, and fondling represent increasingly important and frequent behaviors between young adolescent boys and girls. By the time they get to high school, most adolescents change from sexual behavior focused on themselves to more interpersonal sexual behaviors, such as petting.

The most important sexual milestone that heterosexual adolescents achieve is the initiation of sexual intercourse. Teens who engage in sexual intercourse cross a line that irrevocably alters themselves and the nature of their relationships. Sexual intercourse for young adolescents generally is, however, a sporadic and rare experience. Fewer than 1 in 10 adolescents (7 percent) of both sexes engage in sexual intercourse before age 13, with a larger percentage of boys (10 percent) than girls (4 percent) doing so (CDC, 2004). Ethnic differences exist in early sexual activities—African American adolescents are more likely (19 percent) than Caucasian American (4 percent) or Latino (8 percent) adolescents to begin having sexual intercourse before age 13 (CDC, 2004).

The age at which adolescents begin to have sex is important for many reasons. Early sexual intercourse exposes one for a longer period to the risk of becoming pregnant. Another problem arises from the fact that development in the cognitive, emotional, and physical domains does not necessarily occur at the same rate. The earlier the onset of sexual intercourse, the greater the discrepancy between physical development and cognitive and emotional development. This discrepancy makes it more difficult for young adolescents to understand the consequences of their sexual behavior, and they are therefore less likely to use contraception to avoid an unintended pregnancy (Paikoff, McCormick, & Sagrestano, 2000). In addition, sexual activity that begins in early adolescence is likely to be part of a larger pattern of high-risk behavior, often including experimentation with drugs and alcohol (Miller, 1998; Miller et al., 1997). Initiation of intercourse at age 15 or earlier is associated with an increased incidence of both early pregnancy and sexually transmitted diseases. Many adolescent girls (70 percent) who had sex before they were 14 also report that the sexual experience was unwanted or involuntary (Moore, 1998); that is, most girls who engage in sex very early are victims of exploitation and not acting on their own wishes and desires (Elo, King, & Furstenberg, 1999).

Many factors influence adolescents' decisions to have sex. Although most teens will have sex before they leave high school, when asked when first intercourse should occur, most believe it is better to wait until they are at least 16 or older. This holds true for both boys and girls (National Center for Health Statistics, 1994).

Adolescents' reasons for waiting to have sex are listed in Table 16.3. As you can see, most of the reasons focus on either avoiding negative outcomes (such as pregnancy) or waiting until the right person comes along. Religious beliefs were identified by only a minority of adolescents. But remaining a virgin is difficult, and the likelihood of retaining virginity decreases as adolescents get older. For example, 91 percent of 12-year-olds are virgins and 70 percent of 15-year-olds are, but only 18 percent of 19-year-olds are (Singh & Darroch, 1999).

Sexual Attitudes and Behaviors of Adolescents

Compared to their counterparts in decades past, adolescents today generally are more accepting of sexual involvement before marriage (Irwin, 2004). The same is true for adults. Especially during the late 1960s and the 1970s, the sexual revolution led to more liberal attitudes toward sex (Gershman, 1997). This trend persists despite the rise of conservatism in the 1990s (Irwin, 2004).

Most adolescents begin having sex during their late teens, and the likelihood of being sexually active increases steadily with age. Moreover, this is consistent across a variety of industrialized countries (The Alan Guttmacher Institute, 2001; see Figure 16.4). By the age of 20, more than 80 percent of both males and females have had sex (Sonenstein et al., 1998). As noted in Chapter 15, ethnic differences exist in the percentages of sexually active teens (Upchurch, Levy-Storms, Sucoff, & Aneshensel, 1998). For example, African American high school students (67 percent) are substantially more likely to have had

TABLE 16.3
Adolescents' Reasons for Waiting to Have Sex

REASON	PERCENTAGE CITING REASON
1. Want to wait until I'm in a committed relationship	87
2. Worry about sexually transmitted diseases	85
3. Worry about pregnancy	84
4. Not old enough	84
5. Worry about AIDS	83
6. Haven't met the right person yet	80
7. Just not ready for sex	79
8. Want to wait until I'm married	71
9. Against my religion	40

Source: National Center for Health Statistics, 1994.

FIGURE 16.4

Comparison of Teenage Sexual Activity in Young Women from Industrialized Countries

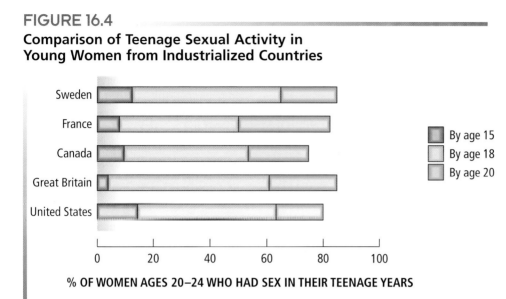

□ By age 15
□ By age 18
□ By age 20

% OF WOMEN AGES 20–24 WHO HAD SEX IN THEIR TEENAGE YEARS

Notice the relatively small differences across different countries. In general, most women begin sexual activity between 15 and 18. Can you identify the factors that influence the age at which teens begin to have sex?

Source: Alan Guttmacher Institute, 2004.

sexual intercourse than are either Caucasian American (42 percent) or Latino (51 percent) peers (CDC, 2004).

Traditionally, boys were much more likely than girls to experience sexual intercourse during adolescence. Today, however, that pattern is disappearing (Miller, Forehand, & Kotchick, 1999; Moreau, Ferron, Jeannin, & Dubois, 1996). Although boys begin having sexual intercourse earlier, girls close the gap and catch up with boys by late adolescence. Recent evidence indicates that among high school students, 48 percent of boys and 45 percent of girls are sexually active (CDC, 2004).

The pattern of sexuality for teenagers often begins with embraces and kisses, moves on to fondling, and culminates in sexual intercourse and other forms of reaching orgasm (Martin, 1996). African American teenagers tend to proceed more rapidly to intercourse. Ethnic differences reflect different cultural beliefs and expectations about sexuality and the role it plays in relationships (Upchurch et al., 1998).

A common misconception asserts that most adolescents are promiscuous, but this is not so. Only about 14 percent of high school students have had four or more sexual partners since becoming sexually active (CDC, 2004). Teenage boys (18 percent) are more likely than girls (11 percent) to have four or more partners. Ethnic differences again are apparent, with 29 percent of African American, 16 percent of Latino, and 11 percent of Caucasian American adolescents reporting four or more partners. Most youngsters, therefore, have few sexual partners during adolescence.

Correlates of Adolescent Sexual Attitudes and Behaviors

A large body of research has identified the factors associated with adolescent sexual activity (see Figure 16.5). Teens are more likely to have early and frequent sex if they live in disadvantaged communities, have low occupational and educational aspirations, and perform poorly in school (Irwin, 2004). Adolescents appear to have few incentives for delaying sexual intercourse when they have limited opportunities for upward mobility and reduced hopes for success.

What are the characteristics of the typical adolescent relationship? How likely is it that older adolescents will be sexually active in their intimate relationships?

FIGURE 16.5

Factors Associated with Adolescent Sexual Activity

- Socioeconomic factors
- Family relationships
- Peer influences
- Pressure from partner

This figure presents the factors associated with adolescent sexual activity. Can you describe how each one might influence teen sexual behavior?

Family relationships also play a role in teenage sexual activity (Crockett, Raffaelli, & Moilanen, 2003). Although parents and adolescents rarely talk about sex, discussions that do occur are most often between mothers and daughters (Miller, 1998). Fathers generally are less involved in these discussions and report feeling uncomfortable with talking about sex with their children. Thus, both boys and girls direct their questions about sex (usually about pregnancy and childbirth) to their mothers. When parents answer these questions, they usually do so on a one-time basis rather than as part of an ongoing dialogue (Raffaelli, Bogenschneider, & Flood, 1998).

The impact of discussions about sex depends on the messages conveyed. Parents who communicate permissive attitudes about sex may encourage early sexual activity. In contrast, parents who convey more strictly traditional or conservative attitudes often discourage this behavior in their teens, and parents who monitor and supervise their adolescents reduce the opportunities for early sexual activity (Paikoff, Luster, Villarruel, & Small, 1998). Teens whose parents are overly controlling and authoritarian, however, are more likely to rebel by engaging in early sexual activity. Thus, extreme levels of parental control (either high or low) often lead to earlier and higher rates of teenage sexual activity, particularly among teenage girls (Rodgers, 1999). Teenagers who enjoy close relationships with their parents and whose parents use moderate levels of control often postpone becoming sexually active (Davis & Friel, 2001; Doyle, Brendgen, Markiewicz, & Kamkar, 2003).

Peers may have more influence than the family on a teen's initial sexual experience and rate of sexual activity (Crockett et al., 2003). Teenagers' sexual attitudes are influenced by values and information conveyed by their peers. These values differ from adults', whose perceptions of adolescent sexuality are stereotypical. Adults tend to view teen sex as impulsive, irresponsible, shallow, impetuous, and transient (such as "puppy love"). Adolescents have a more positive view; they see their sexual and romantic involvements as spontaneous, honest, and meaningful.

When peers become sexually active, social norms are created that legitimize sex and make it more acceptable. Peer encouragement may occur when the best friends of teenagers either are believed to be—or actually are—sexually active (Rodgers, Rowe, & Buster, 1998). For instance, when teens who were sexually active were asked why they had not waited until they were older to have sex, the top reason given by both boys and girls was peer pressure (Keller, Duerst, & Zimmerman, 1996).

Pressure from one's partner also influences sexual behavior. Generally, adolescent females have sex with older males. According to one study, among girls who had their first voluntary intercourse before age 16, over half said that their first partner was older, with 34 percent saying that their first partner was at least 18 years old (CDC, 1997). Another study found that 65 percent of teen mothers had partners who were older than they were (Landry & Forrest, 1995), and the younger the mother, the greater the age difference between her and the father (Lindberg, Sonenstein, Ku, & Martinez, 1997). Additionally, teens who are younger than their partners are less likely to use contraception (Moore & Driscoll, 1997). Thus, teens who are involved with older boys or men may experience pressure to have sex so as to continue the relationship and may engage in risky sexual behaviors (Elo et al., 1999).

The Social–Psychological Context of Adolescent Sexuality

Sexuality during adolescence involves more than physiological responses and erotic sensations (Crockett et al., 2003). For most teenagers, sexuality is governed more by the social meanings and expectations that shape their behavior than by the biological urges associated with puberty (Christopher, 2001). Adolescent sexual activity is learned and maintained within everyday social relationships. Thus, an accurate view of teen sexuality recognizes complex social meanings, complicated feelings, difficult decision making, and elaborate behaviors shaped in part by the teenager's culture (Sharpe & Thomasina, 2003). A major challenge for adolescents is integrating this complex sexuality with the broader issue of establishing intimacy with another person (Erikson, 1968).

Some theorists suggest that sexual activity is socially scripted (Gagnon, 1990; Simon & Gagnon, 1986). Social scripting is evident in the different ways male and female adolescents are socialized for sexuality. Male sexual behavior tends to be more independent of intimate relationships and focused on physical gratification. Many boys first express themselves sexually through masturbation. Boys also tend to view early sexual experiences in terms of sexual conquest, peer status, and recreation rather than intimate relationships (Hendrick & Hendrick, 1995). The most common responses of teenage boys to their first sexual intercourse are feelings of excitement, satisfaction, happiness, and achieved status. Only later do they engage in sexual activity that involves close emotional ties (Martin, 1996).

For girls, however, the experiences and feelings associated with sexual behavior are quite different (Haka-Ikse, 1997). Teenage girls are less likely than boys to begin with masturbation (Martin, 1996), and social expectations and pressures are directed toward intimacy and relationship issues rather than sexual gratification. As a result, girls are more likely to experience their first sexual activity within the context of an emotional relationship. Teenage girls also are more likely than boys to report conflicted feelings about sex—often feeling guilty and anxious, as well as happy and excited (Brooks-Gunn & Paikoff, 1997).

Another example of social scripting is the **double standard**—social expectations for sexual attitudes and behavior that differ for males and females. Although the impact of the double standard has been declining (Orbuch & Sprecher, 2003), it continues to govern how teenagers express themselves sexually. Boys, for example, are supposed to value sex, pursue sex when opportunities arise, and be the sexual aggressors. In contrast, girls are expected to be more cautious, experience less enjoyment, and remain virgins as long as possible (Milhousen & Herold, 2001).

How Do Mass Media Influence Adolescents' Development?

Adolescents spend a significant portion of their time with mass media. According to some estimates, they spend about 8 hours a day with one or more of the mass media, sometimes as a primary activity, often as a secondary activity—for instance, listening to music while doing homework (Tarrant, North, & Hargreaves, 2000). Although television remains an important source of entertainment and information for adolescents, television viewing drops during adolescence by about 10 percent; the teen years are the only period of development in which television viewing declines (Liebert & Sprafkin, 1988). As they enter adolescence, youths spend more time with other media, such as music, computers, and video games.

Popular Music

Music is a pervasive phenomenon in the lives of many adolescents (Schwartz & Fouts, 2003). From the time they enter junior high school until they graduate from high school, teens spend over 10,000 hours listening to pop music (Thompson, 1993). Whereas television in many ways reflects adult society, music is more often associated with the values of youth. Thus, adolescents spend less time exposed to the mainstream adult messages presented on television and more time tuned to the teen-focused messages of popular music (Chapin, 2000). Many teens use music to shape their identity and to help define their social group. Some social groups are identified primarily by their choice of music.

Young teenagers listen to slightly over 3 hours of music daily, and girls tend to listen to music more than boys (Roberts & Christenson, 2001). African American youths listen to more music than Caucasian American youths, with African American teenage girls the most avid listeners, averaging about 7 hours a day (Hakanen, 1995).

double standard   *the imposition of different social expectations for males' and females' sexual attitudes and behavior*

During adolescence, music and other media play increasingly important roles. Can you identify the changes that bring about this interest in media other than television?

Music represents a significant topic of discussion among adolescents, and almost 80 percent consider music to be very important in their lives (Tarrant et al., 2000). In fact, teens cite musicians more frequently than athletes as their heroes, and they rate the influence of music higher than that of religion or books (Knight-Ridder/Tribune News Service, 1999). Liking and being able to talk about music are crucial to adolescents' peer relationships, and the heaviest music listeners spend more time with friends and less time with their families and schoolwork (Tarrant et al., 2000). Music affects emotions, and teens use music to enhance or intensify their mood or to change mood (Christenson & Roberts, 1998).

Much concern has been expressed over the time adolescents spend listening to music and its messages (Villani, 2001). As a result of the potentially negative influence of music containing violent, satanic, sexually explicit, and drug-related lyrics, warning labels are now found on many releases. But there is little evidence that popular music and its lyrics influence adolescents' behavior. Most adolescents do not attend to music lyrics—many do not even know the lyrics to their favorite songs (Roberts, Christenson, & Gentile, 2003). In addition, teenagers do not agree on the meanings of messages in popular songs (Pettegrew et al., 1995). Studies that examine the relation between adolescents' music and aggressive, sexual, or suicidal behavior fail to find significant relationships (Gardstrom, 1999; Scheel & Westfeld, 1999).

More recently, concern has been expressed about the influence of music videos. For example, the themes and images of "gangsta rap"—focusing on explicit sex and violence — have been the focus of much adult concern and attention. Is there cause for concern? A recent study suggests a link exists between preferences for rap music and adjustment problems for teens (Wingwood et al., 2003). In this study, researchers found that, compared with African American female teens who had less exposure to rap music videos, those who had greater exposure were 3 times more likely to have hit a teacher, more than 2.5 times more likely to have been arrested, and 2 times more likely to have had multiple sexual partners. They were also more than 1.5 times more likely to have acquired a new sexually transmitted disease, used drugs, and used alcohol over the 12-month follow-up period. These findings do not necessarily suggest that rap music *caused* teens to act in these ways—teens who are predisposed to act in these way may find rap music more appealing and gravitate to it. But it does point out the potential of violent rap videos to reinforce problem behaviors in teens. Such findings suggest that popular music is not only a central part of adolescent culture, but may also reflect or influence their values and behaviors.

Computers

Computers offer enormous opportunities to young people. They entertain, educate, and are now a vital part of daily living. With advances in computer networking, people have enhanced abilities to communicate and access information about an infinite variety of topics and ideas. Computer technology is now an integral part of education. In 1984, only 31 percent of all public schools provided access to computers. Now, almost all schools (98 percent) have some computers in classrooms. Unfortunately, because of lack of funding, public schools that serve low-income and minority students provide less access to computers—increasing the gap in education and technology training between these students and those from higher-

FIGURE 16.6

Percentage of Children Who Use Computers at Home or School, by Age

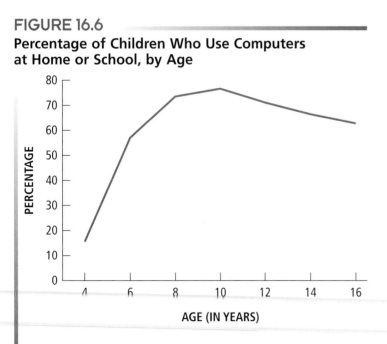

This figure shows how computer use increases through childhood and peaks during early adolescence. After that time, computer use drops off. Can you identify the factors that produce these changes?

Source: National Center for Education Statistics, 1996.

income school districts (Market Data Retrieval, 2001). Perceiving the benefits, many parents have bought computers for their children. Between 1984 and 2000, the number of American households with a computer increased over fourfold, from 8.2 percent to 51 percent (National Telecommunications and Information Administration, 1998; US Census Bureau, 2001a).

Use of Computers

Use of computers varies with age. As indicated in Figure 16.6, computer use increases dramatically between the ages of 4 and 10 years, when it peaks and begins to level off. For children, computers represent primarily a source of entertainment and basic learning. Although they continue to take advantage of these important functions, adolescents use the computer in more advanced ways—solving problems, doing homework, and communicating with others. Figure 16.7 presents the favorite computer activities of adolescents.

Adolescents' use of computers is determined in part by their availability. Over 82 percent of US households with incomes over $50,000 have access to a computer, whereas only about 23 percent of those with incomes under $15,000 do (US Census Bureau, 2001a). Access to computers also varies according to race and ethnicity, reflecting differences in socioeconomic status. Figure 16.8 illustrates this lack of equity: the rate of access of African American and Latino children is about half that of Caucasian American children. With computers playing an increasingly prominent role in everyday life, low-income minority children and adolescents are at a disadvantage because of this limited access.

Adolescents' Reactions to Computers

Adolescents generally believe that computers can be fun and form an important part of their lives. They also believe that computers can be used for harmful purposes and that they sometimes are intimidating.

Boys and girls react differently to computers (Wright et al., 2001). Put a computer in a classroom, and the boys will approach and use it. In contrast, the girls will often back away from it (Yelland & Lloyd, 2001). Boys tend to view computers as games and toys, whereas girls tend to view them as tools. Thus, boys will sit down at a computer and play, exploring its features with no particular purpose; girls will respond to its usefulness but are not particularly taken with the technology itself. When games were the main reason to use a computer, boys spent much more time with computers than girls did. Now that the array of nongame applications has widened, girls report using home computers as often, and with as much confidence, as boys do. Both boys and girls surf the Web for music and photos of movie stars, use e-mail and instant messaging to communicate with friends, and (especially in the case of teens) visit chat rooms (Shields & Behrman, 2000).

Computer software products manufactured for home use generally are designed with boys in mind (Levin & Barry, 1997). Many computer video games involve blasting alien invaders or fighting tough foes—contexts that demand aggression and dominance (Kirsh, 1998). In fact, a recent analysis of teen-rated video games found that over 90 percent of them contained violence (Haninger & Thompson, 2004). Even female characters tend to be violent, and almost half of the top-selling video games contain negative messages about or images of females (Children Now, 2000). The aggressive nature of computer games has been linked to

FIGURE 16.7

How Adolescents Spend Their Time on a Computer

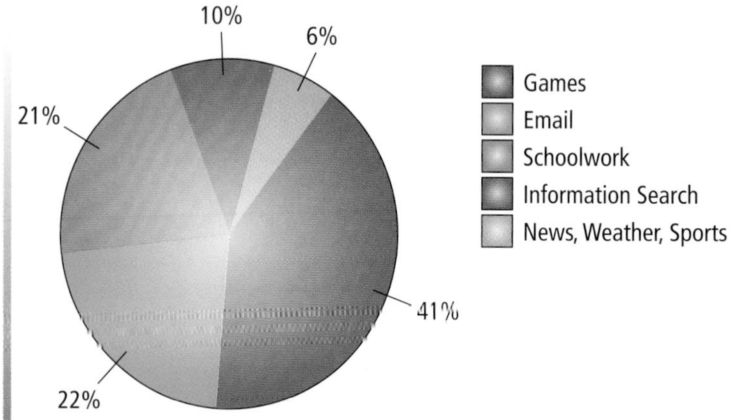

Notice that adolescents spend most of their computer time playing computer games. What reasons might explain this tendency? What does this say about the importance of computers in young adolescents' lives?

Source: Adapted from US Census Bureau, 2001a.

FIGURE 16.8

Percentage of US Households with Access to a Computer, by Ethnicity: 1984–2000

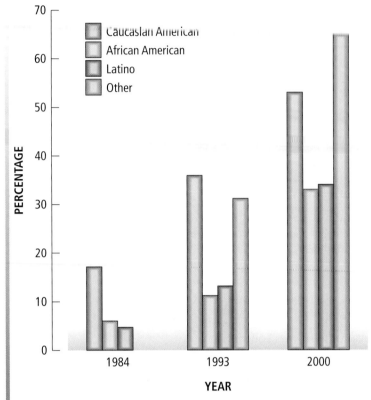

This figure illustrates how the percentage of US households with a computer has increased since 1984. Notice that this increase is greatest for Caucasian American and "other" households and lowest for African American and Latino households. What factors account for these differences among ethnic groups? How might lack of access affect African American and Latino children?

*Data were not available for the "Other" ethnic category in 1984.

Source: Adapted from National Telecommunications and Information Administration, 1998; US Census Bureau, 2001a.

increased aggressiveness in the children and adolescents who play them (Uhlmanna & Swanson, 2004), particularly for boys who are already more predisposed to act aggressively than girls are (Bartholow & Anderson, 2002). Although this matter raises concern, the effect of violent video games on aggression is less significant than the effect of viewed television violence (Sherry, 2001).

Computer games sometimes cause concern for parents because of the amount of time adolescents spend playing them, their seemingly addictive qualities, and the violent themes that characterize many of them. On average, American children who have home video games play with them about 1.5 hours a day. Next to television, video games are the second most popular form of entertainment among children (Mediascope, 1999). The most popular video games involve fantasy, sports, or violent competition (Dietz, 1998). Educational games make up only 2 percent of the sales of video games (Mediascope, 1999).

For some adolescents, computer games become all-consuming. There have been reports of adolescents who spend lunch money at video arcades or steal to get money to feed their computer game habit (Klein, 1984). Currently, research on the effects of computer games on children and adolescents is limited. However, the research that does exist suggests that most of the children and adolescents who play computer games frequently are no more maladjusted than those who play infrequently (Emes, 1997).

With the advent of the Internet, a global network of computers, people now have access to worldwide information 24 hours a day. According to some estimates, over 600 million people across the world (9 percent of the world's population) use the Internet (Nua Ltd., 2004). About 60 percent of the people in the United States use the Internet, and about 10 percent of these users are children and adolescents (Pew Internet and American Life Project, 2003). Currently, the number of households that are online is almost 70 million, and the percentage of children and adolescents using the Internet has increased to over 30 percent (US Census Bureau, 2001a). Internet use has increased, particularly among teenagers.

Teens are particularly attracted to the Internet for communication and recreation. For example, e-mail is how today's wired teens like to stay in touch with family and friends. Eighty-one percent of teens spend time sending e-mails (America Online, 2003). Instant messaging (IMing) also is a popular way to keep in touch; 70 percent of teens use it. In fact, today's teens prefer using the Internet to using the phone—56 percent of teens ages 18 and 19 indicate such preferences (America Online, 2003).

Teens also depend on the Internet as an educational resource. Fifty-eight percent of younger teens (12 to 17 years) consult online resources for guidance on homework assignments, whereas 61 percent of older teens (18 to 19 years) turn to the Internet for help completing their schoolwork. More than one quarter (26 percent) of younger teens go online to access news and current events. Sixty-one percent of older teens do the same (America Online, 2003). Such findings suggest that the Internet now is a central part of adolescents' daily lives.

Although the Internet has much to offer, the online world, like the rest of society, is made up of a broad array of people. Most are decent and respectful, but some are obnoxious and even exploitative, particularly of young people (Federal Bureau of Investigation [FBI], 1998). The Internet is not governed by any entity—almost no limits or checks control the kind of information that is available and who provides it. Because children and adolescents often are trusting and curious, they can be easy targets of online exploitation (Bremer & Rauch, 1998).

What Types of Behavior Problems Occur During Adolescence?

Although many adolescents experiment with some risky activities such as alcohol use and minor forms of deviant behavior (for example, curfew violations or vandalism), few of these problems are lasting or serious. Only a small percentage of adolescents are responsible for the more serious and dangerous activities (Loeber, Farrington, Stouthamer-Loeber, & Van-Kammen, 1998). Many youths become involved in deviant activities during adolescence; however, those with serious problem behaviors often show signs of difficulty earlier in their development (Simonoff et al., 2004).

Behavior problems may be thought of in terms of two general categories. **Externalizing problems** are psychological difficulties in which individuals "act out" against society through behavior such as truancy or substance abuse. **Internalizing problems** are psychological difficulties, such as anxiety or depressive disorders, in which individuals focus on or within themselves (Achenbach, 2002).

Adolescents often have multiple behavior problems. **Risk-taking behavior** is a syndrome associated with the co-occurrence of various acts, such as experimenting with drugs, having sex very early in adolescence, having sex without contraception, and engaging in delinquent and accident-inducing activities such as reckless driving (Jessor, 1992). Generally, adolescents tend to behave defiantly and unconventionally in their risk taking (Ketterlinus, Lamb, & Nitz, 1995). Defiant behavior may relate to underlying personality traits, such as sensation seeking; biologically inherited factors that predispose one to develop problem behaviors (Rodgers, Muster, & Rowe, 2001); social conditions, such as impoverished neighborhoods; or a combination of these (Ackerman et al., 2001). Needless to say, the precise factors that lead to behavior problems vary from adolescent to adolescent.

Antisocial Behavior

One large category of risk-taking behavior is antisocial behavior—behavior that conflicts with the norms of society. Antisocial behavior includes **delinquency,** a term widely used to refer to a variety of legally defined antisocial acts committed by juveniles. Although many delinquent acts, such as homicide or robbery, are illegal for both adults and juveniles, others, such as underage drinking, skipping school, and running away from home, are **status offenses**—acts that are illegal for juveniles but not for adults.

Adolescents and young adults violate the law more often than any other age group. Even if we ignore status offenses, violent crimes (such as assault, rape, and homicide) and property crimes (such as robbery, theft, and arson) increase during adolescence, peak during the high school years, and begin to decline in early adulthood. As Figure 16.9 shows, the rate of violent crime among juveniles increased until 1995 and then dropped (FBI, 2000).

Individuals under the age of 24 account for well over half of all violent crimes in the United States (FBI, 2000). A distressing trend is the growing tendency of adolescents to use weapons. One national survey of youth indicated that 17 percent of high school students had carried a weapon such as a gun, knife, or club at some time during the preceding 30 days (CDC, 2000b). Boys were almost five times more likely to do so than girls (29 percent versus 6 percent).

Depression

Over the past 35 years, the age of onset of depression has dropped. Depression is an internalizing disorder that now commonly begins during adolescence (Durant, 2004). Estimates of

externalizing problems   *psychological difficulties that involve acting out against society*

internalizing problems   *psychological difficulties, such as anxiety or depression, that involve a focus on or within the self*

risk-taking behavior   *a syndrome of multiple behavior problems*

delinquency   *the legal term for antisocial acts committed by juveniles*

status offenses   *acts that are illegal for juveniles but not for adults, such as running away from home*

FIGURE 16.9

Changes in Juvenile Violent Crime

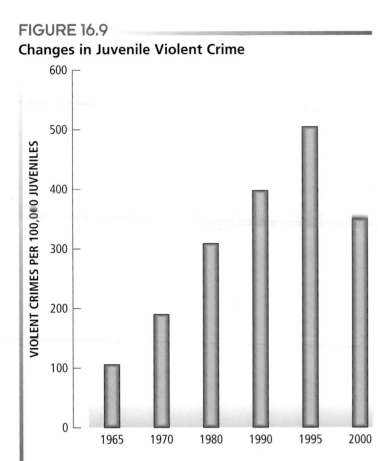

As you can see in this graph, juvenile violent crimes increased at a relatively steady rate between 1965 and 1995. What social, cultural, and family factors likely influenced the increased rates? Between 1995 and 2000, the rate dropped significantly. What changed over the past few years to decrease the rate?

Source: Federal Bureau of Investigation, 2000.

the prevalence of clinical depression range from 4 percent to 12 percent of adolescents (Kazdin & Marciano, 1998; Schwartz, Gladstone, & Kaslow, 1998), with older adolescents having higher rates (Garber, 2003). Depressed adolescents have symptoms such as dysphoria (sad mood), social withdrawal, fatigue, apathy, impaired school performance, feelings of hopelessness, sleep disturbances, eating disorders, concentration difficulties, and self-destructive impulses (American Psychiatric Association, 2000; Kazdin & Marciano, 1998). Before puberty, rates of depression are low and are equal for boys and girls. After puberty, girls report increased rates of depression (Cyranowski et al., 2000).

Although only a small percentage of teens are diagnosed with depression, a sizable percent report feeling extremely sad or hopeless. For example, in a nationwide study, about 28 percent of high school students said that they felt so sad or hopeless almost every day for over two weeks in a row that they stopped participating in some usual activities (CDC, 2000a). Overall, girls (36 percent) were significantly more likely than boys (21 percent) to feel this way, and this sex difference held for all racial/ethnic groups.

Evidence is growing that problems with hormonal activity in the brain and the nervous system often result in depression (Iosifescu & Renshaw, 2003). The onset of puberty and associated hormonal changes may influence adolescents' emotional states (Garber, 2003). Also, some teens seem prone to depression because they have cognitive mind-sets that cause them to define their circumstances in terms of hopelessness, pessimism, and self-blame (Garber, Weiss, & Shanley, 1993).

Depression is more common when adolescents are experiencing stressful transitions— changing schools, beginning to date, or facing disruptions in family relationships (such as parental divorce). Moreover, having a depressed parent increases the chances that an adolescent will suffer from depression (Harrington, 1996). In addition, parental behaviors and parenting styles affect adolescent depression (Davis, Sheeber, & Hops, 2002). For example, adolescent depression occurs more frequently in families that are low in warmth and high in conflict (Ge et al., 1994; Greenberger & Chen, 1996).

Although suicide is a serious health risk during adolescence (see Chapter 14), the relationship between suicide and depression is not straightforward (Metha, Chen, Mulvenon, & Dode, 1998). Some depressed youngsters are not suicidal, whereas other teenagers who are not depressed become suicidal (Aoki & Turk, 1997; Kazdin & Marciano, 1998). These findings indicate that depression and suicide are two related, but distinct, forms of internalizing disorders.

Substance Use and Abuse

Most teens try alcohol and other drugs. The majority will experiment and stop or will continue to use these substances casually without significant problems. Some will use them regularly, with varying degrees of physical, emotional, and social problems. Some will develop a dependency and will become destructive to themselves and others. Some will die, and some will cause others to die.

American adolescents grow up in a society that has contradictory attitudes about the use of drugs and alcohol. Governmental and law enforcement agencies seek to discourage adolescents from using illegal drugs, yet the media commonly associate dangerous and addictive substances, such as alcohol and tobacco, with images of prestige, style, and glamour. Although advertisements may not target adolescents, they present attractive and positive images of alcohol to all those who see them, including adolescents.

Describe the mixed messages adolescents are exposed to in their homes and in the media about drinking. How many adolescents try drinking and drugs?

Alcohol

Alcohol is the most commonly used and abused substance. The vast majority of high school students (about 80 percent) have had at least one alcoholic drink during their lifetime, and virtually all high school seniors have had some experience with alcohol (CDC, 2004). More than half of all high school students have had at least one drink of alcohol in the preceding month, with boys and girls showing similar patterns of use. New evidence suggests that the younger a teen is when he or she starts drinking, the greater the chance that he or she will develop problems with alcohol abuse and dependency at some point in life (Grant & Dawson, 1998). There are ethnic differences in alcohol consumption; generally higher levels of alcohol consumption exist among Latino and Caucasian American adolescents than among African American youngsters (see Figure 16.10). An especially troubling pattern is the high percentage (33 percent) of students in grades 8 through 12 who engage in heavy or binge drinking—consuming five or more drinks of alcohol on at least one occasion during the preceding month. Parents do little to dissuade adolescents from drinking. For example, fewer than one third of parents of tenth-graders give their children a clear "no use" message about alcohol (Johnson Institute, 1993).

At present, there is no known "safe dose" of alcohol for adolescents. Very little is known about the biological impact of alcohol on teens. However, pubertal changes, hormonal fluctuations, and incomplete muscle and body mass development may make adolescents more vulnerable to problems associated with alcohol than are adults. Because personal identity and social skills are still developing, "social drinking" may have more serious consequences for adolescents than it does for adults. Teens may learn to use alcohol to handle interpersonal relationships, deal with peer pressure, and control sexual impulses. Any use of intoxicants—even one beer—can have serious and unpredictable consequences for adolescents because of their low impulse control, emotional volatility, lack of a sense of limits, and feelings of invulnerability.

Often a dangerous tendency toward risky and unruly behavior characterizes teens who drink. Automobile accidents are the major cause of death among teenagers (see Chapter 14), with alcohol playing a significant role in about 40 percent of these fatalities. In 1998, over 8,278 adolescents from ages 15 through 20 died in alcohol-related crashes (National Highway Traffic Safety Administration, 2002). Adolescent drivers are still developing driving skills and are easily disoriented by alcohol or distracted by passengers who are drinking.

FIGURE 16.10
High School Students' Experiences with Alcohol

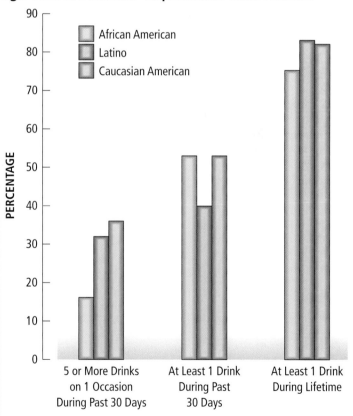

This graph shows that most adolescents have had some experience with alcohol, and about one third have engaged in heavy consumption in the past month. Notice that African American youth drink less than the other groups of adolescents do. What might account for these differences?

Source: Centers for Disease Control, 2000a.

Most people who smoke began during adolescence. What cognitive and social factors increase the likelihood that adolescents will engage in activities, such as smoking, that put their health at risk?

Tobacco

A large majority (58 percent) of high school students in the United States try tobacco during their teenage years (CDC, 2004). According to some estimates, as many as 3,000 teens start smoking each day, and ultimately 1,000 of these teens will die from conditions related to smoking (American Academy of Pediatrics, 1996). Most teens begin using tobacco before graduation from high school and soon after start to use it regularly (CDC, 2004). Thus, most people who are going to smoke are hooked by age 20. Additionally, early cigarette use is associated with heavier use; those who begin to use tobacco as young adolescents are among the heaviest users in late adolescence and adulthood (CDC, 2004).

Although smoking has been linked to lung cancer, heart disease, and various other diseases, many teenagers do not believe they are at risk for diseases associated with tobacco use. Studies reveal that less than half of high school students believe smoking is a great risk to health (Monitoring the Future, 2001). This is especially true for younger teens. Fewer than 40 percent of eighth-graders think "great risk" is entailed in smoking a pack or more per day. By twelfth grade, however, over 45 percent of students believe there is "great risk" in smoking.

The number of young adolescents using tobacco has risen, and rates among older adolescents remain high (Monitoring the Future, 2001). Overall, over one third of high school–age adolescents in the United States currently smoke or use smokeless tobacco. As shown in Figure 16.11, Caucasian American teenagers use tobacco more often than either African American or Latino youngsters (CDC, 2000a).

The development of tobacco use among adolescents progresses through five stages: forming positive attitudes and beliefs about tobacco, trying tobacco, experimenting with it, beginning to use it regularly, and becoming addicted to it. This process, which begins during early adolescence, generally takes place over a three-year period. Factors associated with tobacco use during adolescence include the following (CDC, 2000a):

- Low socioeconomic status
- Easy access to tobacco
- Peers' and siblings' use of tobacco
- Parental indifference
- Low academic achievement
- Low self-esteem
- Lack of knowledge of the health consequences of tobacco use

Young people face enormous pressures to use tobacco, and it is readily available to teens. By tenth grade, over 90 percent say they can get cigarettes easily if they want to. Despite efforts to limit access to cigarettes, the percentage of underage minors who buy their own cigarettes has actually increased since 1989 (from 58 to 68 percent). Each year in the United States, nearly 1 billion packs of cigarettes are sold to children under the age of 18 (CDC, 2004). Despite the widespread notion that parents can do little to prevent their teens from smoking, adolescents who perceive that both parents would respond negatively to, and be upset by, their smoking are less likely to smoke (Sargent & Dalton, 2001).

Illicit Drugs

Other than marijuana, illegal drugs are seldom used regularly by adolescents (National Institute on Drug Abuse [NIDA], 2000). Less than 4 percent of teenagers inject drugs (CDC, 2004). Daily use of stimulants, hallucinogens, LSD, PCP, inhalants, barbiturates, tranquilizers, cocaine, crack, steroids, and heroin also is relatively rare (less than 5 percent), although use of these drugs has increased since 1990 (NIDA, 2004c). Steroid use among adolescents also has increased since 1990. About 6 percent of adolescents have taken steroid pills or shots without a prescription one or more times during their lifetime (CDC, 2004). Use of illicit drugs is greatest among minority youths.

Marijuana use among adolescents has increased since 1990. Today about 40 percent of teens indicate they have tried marijuana (CDC, 2004). The number of adolescents who say they used marijuana in the preceding month has increased by more than 250 percent for eighth-graders since 1991 and by more than 150 percent for tenth-graders since 1992. In one year alone (1995 to 1996), marijuana use went from 9 percent to 11 percent among eighth-graders and from 17 percent to 20 percent among tenth-graders (NIDA, 2000). One reason for rising marijuana use may be a belief among teens that marijuana is not harmful to their health; only 43 percent of high school seniors say that marijuana is "very harmful" to their health. Adolescents can also obtain marijuana easily; almost three quarters say it is easy to get (Pride Surveys, 2003).

Across the country, teens enjoy all-night dance parties known as "raves" and increasingly encounter more than just music. Dangerous substances known collectively as *club drugs*—including ecstasy, GHB, and rohypnol—are gaining popularity. These drugs (see Table 16.4) are used by teens at a nightclub, rave, or trance scene. Raves and trance events are generally night-long dances, often held in warehouses. Many who attend do not use drugs, but those who use club drugs often are attracted to their generally low cost and to the intoxicating highs that are said to deepen the rave or trance experience (NIDA, 2004a).

FIGURE 16.11
High School Students' Tobacco Use

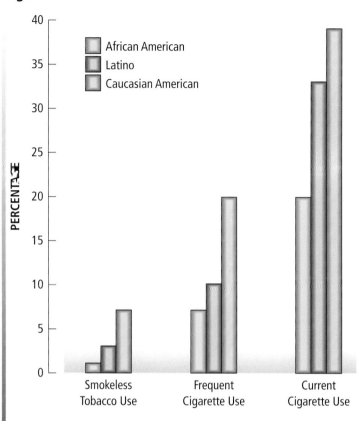

Caucasian American adolescents use tobacco more frequently than either Latino or African American adolescents. What factors may influence adolescents' use of tobacco products? What danger does early smoking pose for long-term health?

Source: Centers for Disease Control, 2000a.

TABLE 16.4
Popular Club Drugs for Teens

"X," "Adam," or "MDMA" (methylenedioxymethamphetamine) are slang names for *ecstasy,* which is a stimulant and a hallucinogen. Young people may use ecstasy to improve their moods or get energy to keep dancing; however, chronic abuse appears to damage the brain's ability to think and regulate emotion, memory, sleep, and pain.

"G," "liquid ecstasy," "Georgia home boy" or gamma-hydroxybutyrate (*GHB*) may be made in homes by using recipes with common ingredients. At lower doses, GHB can relax the user, but as the dose increases, the sedative effects may result in sleep and eventual coma or death.

"Roofie" or "roche" (*rohypnol*) is tasteless and odorless. It mixes easily in carbonated beverages. Rohypnol may cause individuals under the influence of the drug to forget what happened. Other effects include low blood pressure, drowsiness, dizziness, confusion, and stomach upset.

"Special K" or "K" (*ketamine*) is an anesthetic. Use of a small amount of ketamine results in loss of attention span, learning ability, and memory. At higher doses, ketamine can cause delirium, amnesia, high blood pressure, depression, and severe breathing problems.

"Speed," "ice," "chalk," or "meth" (*methamphetamine*) is often made in home laboratories. Methamphetamine use can cause serious health concerns, including memory loss, aggression, violence, psychotic behavior, and heart problems.

"Acid" or lysergic acid diethylamide (*LSD*) may cause unpredictable behavior, depending on the amount taken, where the drug is used, and the user's personality. A user might feel the following effects: numbness, weakness, nausea, increased heart rate, sweating, lack of appetite, "flashbacks," and sleeplessness.

Source: Adapted from Substance Abuse and Mental Health Services Administration, 2002.

Although national rates for visits to the hospital emergency rooms due to use of club drugs were low in 2002 (with none exceeding 2 mentions per 100,000 visits), significant increases in use of certain club drugs were apparent from 1995 to 2002. Visits due to ecstasy use, for example, increased from 421 in 1995 to 4,026 in 2002; GHB-related visits increased from 145 in 1995 to 3,330 in 2002 (Substance Abuse and Mental Health Services Administration, 2002). In particular, the use of ecstasy has risen sharply among teens and is growing in popularity even among seventh- and eighth-grade students (CDC, 2004). Research has shown that use of club drugs can cause serious health problems and, in some cases, even death. Used in combination with alcohol, these drugs can be even more dangerous (NIDA, 2004b).

Despite the increased attention to drug abuse, the percentage of students who say their parents talk to them about drugs has decreased. For example, the percentage of students who

FIGURE 6.12
Teens' Reasons for Using and Not Using Drugs

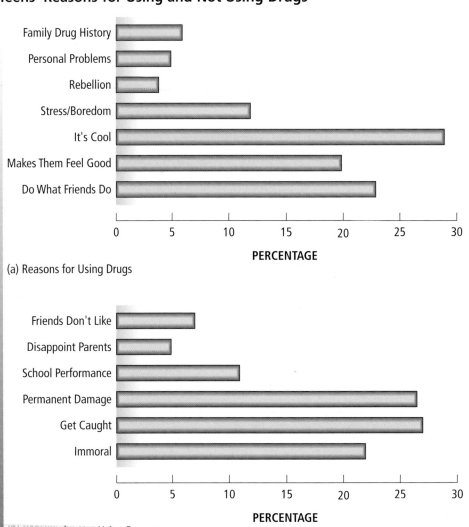

(a) Reasons for Using Drugs

(b) Reasons for Not Using Drugs

Many adults believe that adolescents use drugs because of personal problems and to rebel against their families. Adolescents report that they use drugs because it is cool and because their friends do. How might adolescents' reasons for using and not using drugs be helpful in planning prevention programs?

Source: National Center on Addiction and Substance Abuse, 1996.

NURTURING CHILDREN
PREVENTING TEENAGE DRUG USE

In 1937, the classic movie *Reefer Madness* told a horrifying story of the downfall of a youth who had a promising future—until he tried marijuana. But the film's message backfired, and today it is a cult favorite among young users of marijuana. Like many early efforts to scare teens away from drugs, *Reefer Madness* failed to have a positive impact.

Drug prevention has changed dramatically since then. Today thousands of schools, community organizations, houses of worship, and government agencies across the country are designing programs aimed at preventing alcohol, tobacco, and drug use among teens. Which programs are most effective? According to recent research (Dishion et al., 2002; NIDA, 2004c; Spoth, Redmond, Trudeau, & Shin, 2002), an effective teen drug prevention program should do the following:

- Target all forms of drug abuse, including the use of tobacco, alcohol, marijuana, and inhalants
- Include training in strategies to help teens resist drugs when offered and ways to strengthen personal commitment against drug use
- Utilize interactive methods in which peers have group discussions rather than listening to lectures
- Include a component for parents or caregivers that is designed to help them reinforce messages regarding drugs and their harmful effects
- Be long-term in nature, lasting over the school career, with repeated interventions to reinforce the original prevention goals
- Strengthen norms against drug use in all settings, including the family, school, and community
- Address the specific nature of the drug abuse problem in a local community
- Be age-specific, developmentally appropriate, and culturally sensitive
- Grow more intensive as the level of risk of the target population increases

said their parents talked to them often or a lot about the problems of drugs dropped from about 40 percent in 1991 to about 31 percent in 1997 (NPRIDE, 1997). Yet parents' warnings can be effective, leading to less drug use among adolescents. About 37 percent of teens who say their parents never talked to them about drugs used an illicit drug during the preceding year, compared to 26 percent of those whose parents spoke to them a lot about drugs.

Adolescents' reasons for using and not using drugs are complex and diverse. Figure 16.12 presents some of these reasons. As you can see, teens rarely say that they use drugs because they are stressed, rebellious, or have family or personal problems. Instead, they say they use drugs because it is "in" to do so and because it makes them feel good. Figure 16.12 also reveals that teens' main reasons for not using drugs are fear of getting caught, the damage drugs might do to them, and the idea that it is wrong to do so. Although teen drug use is influenced by peers, abstinence may have more to do with teens' relationships with parents and the degree to which parents monitor their activity and provide information about the physical and moral consequences of using drugs (National Center on Addiction and Substance Abuse, 1996).

Most drug use during adolescence is experimental and is not related to long-term problems. According to one longitudinal study, adolescents who engaged in some drug experimentation (primarily with marijuana) were the best-adjusted teens in the sample (Shedler & Block, 1990). Adolescents who used drugs frequently were maladjusted (had poor impulse control, were emotionally distressed), and adolescents who, by age 18, had never experimented with drugs were relatively anxious and lacking in social skills. These findings suggest that problem drug use may be a symptom, not a cause, of maladjustment.

What Factors Influence Adolescents' Vulnerability and Resilience?

Although teenagers today face increasing risks associated with drugs, unprotected sexual intercourse, violence, crime, and depression, no more than 20 percent of US adolescents have behavior or adjustment problems (Ebata, Petersen, & Conger, 1990). In addition, as

Late adolescence is a period of time in which many new responsibilities and challenges must be met. Most adolescents find these exciting and are resilient in the face of the increased demands of late adolescence. Can you identify the factors that contribute to resilience in adolescents?

you have already learned, many problems that arise during adolescence have their roots in earlier development. This fact is important because behavior problems that persist from childhood tend to be more severe and have different causes than those that develop during adolescence (Price & Lento, 2001).

Also, large individual differences exist in adolescents' abilities to cope with the stressors and temptations they face, and these abilities play a key role in whether outcomes are healthy or problematic. Individual qualities such as perseverance, intelligence, determination, and good health act as protective factors for adolescents who overcome adversity (Smokowski, Reynolds, & Bezruczko, 1999). From a transactional perspective, optimal coping results from a good balance between the characteristics of the individual and the demands of the situation. This balance changes across development. For example, according to a classic longitudinal study of coping, personal qualities (such as temperament) strongly influence outcomes early in development; school and cognitive factors are keys to adjustment during middle childhood; and during adolescence, the ability to develop interpersonal relationships is central to adjustment because the peer group and other aspects of the social context become more crucial (Werner & Smith, 1982).

The challenges and demands of adolescence create stresses that overwhelm some adolescents' abilities to cope and adapt. A 16-year-old who finds the demands of cliques and dating increasingly stressful may begin to drink alcohol as a way of coping. Drinking alcohol may enable this teen to continue to go to parties and interact socially, but it is unlikely to promote optimal social development. In addition, it is likely to make subsequent development more difficult (Bloom, 1998).

For most teens, the demands of adolescence bring opportunities that promote growth. Having a new peer group from which to select friends, experiencing more challenging learning environments in school, and taking on new responsibilities in the family and community are beneficial to most adolescents. Learning to drive and being able to accomplish more physically and intellectually demanding tasks also can be exciting. In fact, a certain amount of challenge and stress may be necessary for healthy development (Garbarino et al., 1992).

Adolescents' abilities to face these challenges and stressors are influenced greatly by their relationships. Warm and supportive relationships with parents serve as protective factors, even in the face of serious stress (Kiser, Ostoja, & Pruitt, 1998). Being liked and accepted by one's peers also serves a protective function. Having someone to talk to, confide in, and share with helps adolescents deal with the stressors of everyday life (Haveman & Wolfe, 1994). Positive relationships are particularly important for adolescents who are most at risk for developing behavior problems. Biological predispositions also contribute to adolescents' risk and resilience—some teens are inherently more vulnerable to environmental risks (Rutter, 2003). Table 16.5 lists some of the qualities that enhance adolescents' resilience and ability to cope.

Adolescence is a period in which teens prepare to enter adulthood. Physically, cognitively, socially, and emotionally, adolescents reach peak or near-peak levels. Because of these advances, they feel the need to function more independently, and parents and other adults give them more independence and responsibility.

Adolescence also is a period in which teens experiment and try out a wider variety of adultlike behaviors. Some promote and enhance development, and some impair it. Teens explore more educational and occupational opportunities, but they also experiment with drugs, alcohol, sexuality, and crime to a greater extent than they did when they were younger.

Teens' lives also become more complex as they experience more varied environments and people with different interests, skills, and backgrounds. In a classic study (Csikszentmihalyi & Larson, 1984), teens kept daily diaries about their lives. Seventeen-year-old Greg's diary entries for one week, shown in Figure 16.13, illustrate the complexity and variation in the individual and contextual issues that older teens face. As you can see, Greg's week was filled with thoughts and activities related to his education, job, friends, girlfriend, and family, as well as recreational drug use, entertainment, and sex. The issues Greg dealt with ranged from taking care of himself (getting himself fed) to social issues (equal rights) to

TABLE 16.5
Qualities That Enhance Adolescents' Resilience and Ability to Cope

QUALITY	DEFINITION
Support	Family support provides high levels of love and acceptance.
	Parental involvement provides help and advice when needed.
	Nonfamilial adult support provides advice and mentoring.
	School climate is positive.
Control	Parents have standards for appropriate conduct.
	Parents discipline teen when rules are violated.
	Teen is at home at least four nights a week.
	Best friends model responsible behavior.
Structured time use	Teen is involved in extracurricular school activities.
	Teen is involved in organizations or clubs outside of school.
	Teen is involved in religious programs or services.
Educational commitment	Teen is motivated to do well in school.
	Teen aspires to post–high school education.
	Teen's school performance is above average.
	Teen spends at least 6 hours per week doing homework.
Positive values	Teen places high personal value on helping other people.
	Teen is concerned about the conditions of others and their feelings.
	Teen values postponing sexual activity.
Social competence	Teen has the ability to stand up for what he or she believes in.
	Teen is good at making friends.
	Teen is good at making decisions and planning ahead.
	Teen has high self-esteem.
	Teen is optimistic about the future.

Source: Benson, 1993.

anxiety about dating and relationships (calling his girlfriend). His emotional states varied dramatically from day to day, ranging from relatively positive when he was with his friends at the mall to relatively negative when he was alone daydreaming or at work engaged in menial labor.

Today's adolescents have significant assets and strengths. Many of these strengths result from cumulative experiences acquired over the course of their lives. Because older adolescents are on the verge of becoming adults but are not quite there yet, it is easy to discount their skills and their potential contributions (Grotevant, 1998). The dynamic interplay of individual and contextual changes brings about greater adaptability and resourcefulness, as well as greater stress and demands for adjustment (Rutter, 2002). Fortunately, most adolescents are able to meet these challenges and become contributing, responsible, and competent adults.

Try It Out

1. Go to a local mall, and observe some teens. Notice their dress, conduct, and actions. What characteristics of and concerns about late adolescent social and emotional development can you identify? How do these fit with the stereotypes we hold about older teens?

FIGURE 16.13
17-Year-Old Greg's Weekly Diary Entries

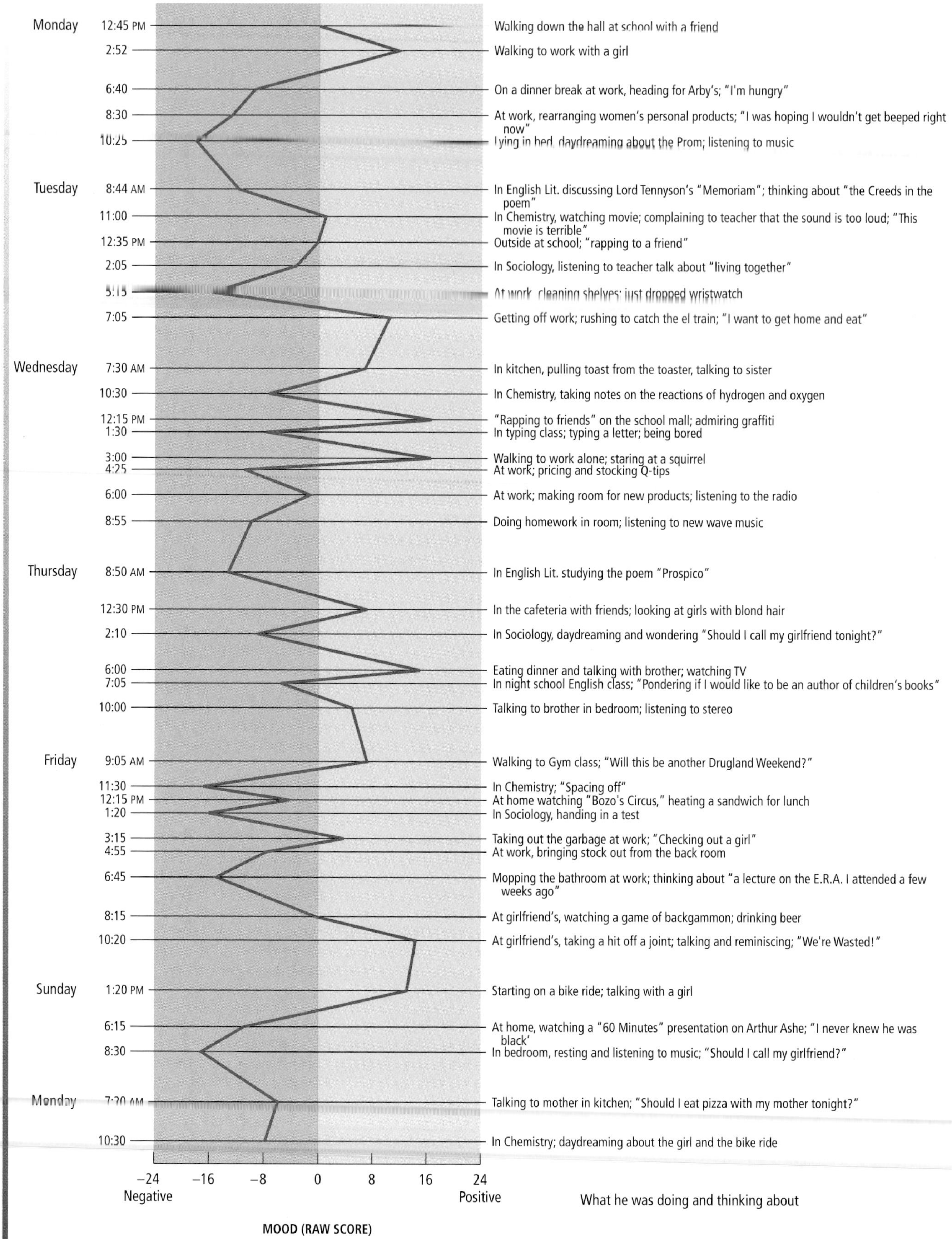

Day	Time	What he was doing and thinking about
Monday	12:45 PM	Walking down the hall at school with a friend
	2:52	Walking to work with a girl
	6:40	On a dinner break at work, heading for Arby's; "I'm hungry"
	8:30	At work, rearranging women's personal products; "I was hoping I wouldn't get beeped right now"
	10:25	Lying in bed, daydreaming about the Prom; listening to music
Tuesday	8:44 AM	In English Lit. discussing Lord Tennyson's "Memoriam"; thinking about "the Creeds in the poem"
	11:00	In Chemistry, watching movie; complaining to teacher that the sound is too loud; "This movie is terrible"
	12:35 PM	Outside at school; "rapping to a friend"
	2:05	In Sociology, listening to teacher talk about "living together"
	5:15	At work, cleaning shelves; just dropped wristwatch
	7:05	Getting off work; rushing to catch the el train; "I want to get home and eat"
Wednesday	7:30 AM	In kitchen, pulling toast from the toaster, talking to sister
	10:30	In Chemistry, taking notes on the reactions of hydrogen and oxygen
	12:15 PM	"Rapping to friends" on the school mall; admiring graffiti
	1:30	In typing class; typing a letter; being bored
	3:00	Walking to work alone; staring at a squirrel
	4:25	At work; pricing and stocking Q-tips
	6:00	At work; making room for new products; listening to the radio
	8:55	Doing homework in room; listening to new wave music
Thursday	8:50 AM	In English Lit. studying the poem "Prospico"
	12:30 PM	In the cafeteria with friends; looking at girls with blond hair
	2:10	In Sociology, daydreaming and wondering "Should I call my girlfriend tonight?"
	6:00	Eating dinner and talking with brother; watching TV
	7:05	In night school English class; "Pondering if I would like to be an author of children's books"
	10:00	Talking to brother in bedroom; listening to stereo
Friday	9:05 AM	Walking to Gym class; "Will this be another Drugland Weekend?"
	11:30	In Chemistry; "Spacing off"
	12:15 PM	At home watching "Bozo's Circus," heating a sandwich for lunch
	1:20	In Sociology, handing in a test
	3:15	Taking out the garbage at work; "Checking out a girl"
	4:55	At work, bringing stock out from the back room
	6:45	Mopping the bathroom at work; thinking about "a lecture on the E.R.A. I attended a few weeks ago"
	8:15	At girlfriend's, watching a game of backgammon; drinking beer
	10:20	At girlfriend's, taking a hit off a joint; talking and reminiscing; "We're Wasted!"
Sunday	1:20 PM	Starting on a bike ride; talking with a girl
	6:15	At home, watching a "60 Minutes" presentation on Arthur Ashe; "I never knew he was black"
	8:30	In bedroom, resting and listening to music; "Should I call my girlfriend?"
Monday	7:20 AM	Talking to mother in kitchen; "Should I eat pizza with my mother tonight?"
	10:30	In Chemistry; daydreaming about the girl and the bike ride

MOOD (RAW SCORE): −24 −16 −8 0 8 16 24

Negative — Positive

Source: From *Being Adolescent: Conflict and Growth in the Teenage Years* by Mihaly Csikszentmihalyi and Reed Larson. Copyright © 1984 by Basic Books, Inc. Reprinted by permission of Basic Books, a member of Perseus Books, L.L.C.

2. Describe your crowd or clique in middle school or junior high school. By what names or labels were crowds and cliques known in your school? What were the "rules" for membership or acceptance in a group?
3. Find some magazines, such as *Teen* or *Seventeen,* or some "webzines," such as *Teen People* (at http://www.teenpeople.com/) or *CyberTeens* (at http://www.cyberteens.com/), that are read primarily by teens. What insights do the features in these magazines provide about teens' development? Do teen boys and girls face different issues? What kinds of advertisements appear in these publications, and what do they tell you about issues related to adolescence?

Key Terms and Concepts

actual self (514)
assimilated (519)
autonomy (521)
behavioral autonomy (522)
bicultural (519)
cliques (529)
commitment (517)
crisis/exploration (517)
crowds (529)
delinquency (541)
double standard (537)
emotional autonomy (522)
ethnic identity (519)
externalizing problems (541)
foreclosure (518)
heterosexual (520)

homosexual (520)
identity (516)
identity achieved (518)
identity confusion (517)
identity diffusion (518)
internalizing problems (541)
marginal (519)
moratorium (518)
possible self (514)
psychosocial moratorium (517)
risk-taking behavior (541)
separated (519)
sexual orientation (520)
status offenses (541)
values autonomy (522)

Sum It Up

How do older adolescents develop a sense of self and identity?
- What eight domains do adolescents use to describe themselves? (p. 514)
- How are secure ethnic identities fostered in families? (p. 520)

How do family relationships change during adolescence?
- When parents use induction, what does it help teens to understand? (pp. 524–525)

What are the characteristics of adolescent peer relationships?
- What characteristics do all peer cultures share in common? (p. 529)

How do mass media influence adolescents' development?
- How do adolescents spend the majority of their time on the computer? (p. 539)

What types of behavior problems occur during adolescence?
- What factors are associated with tobacco use during adolescence? (p. 544)

What factors influence adolescents' vulnerability and resilience?
- What influences adolescents' abilities to face challenges and stressors? (p. 548)

FIGURE 16.2 **Factors That Contribute to Adolescent Autonomy** *During adolescence, the desire for autonomy becomes prominent.*

Physical Changes
Greater autonomy comes from adolescents perceiving changes in how they are treated by others now that they are physically more mature.

Cognitive Changes
Greater autonomy comes from changes in the way adolescents think about problems and issues.

Social Changes
Greater autonomy results when parents are supportive and nurturing, and when teens are involved in diverse activities.

Physical appearance and body image play important roles in the development of self-esteem and self-concept for young girls. Boys, on the other hand, place a higher premium on physical abilities.

SELF AND IDENTITY

Compared to children, adolescents have a more complex sense of themselves, in part because of their advanced abilities to understand and imagine how others perceive and evaluate them. Their growing self-awareness results from interacting with, and receiving feedback from, a wider circle of significant others (peers, siblings, and teachers). They develop a more complete picture of themselves because of the many changes that occur during early adolescence. Critically, adolescents begin to develop a stronger sense of identity—who they are as people—and function more independently and autonomously than they did as children. (Refer back to pages 513–523.)

FAMILY RELATIONSHIPS

Family relationships change during adolescence—teens and parents spend less time together, experience more tension, and have to renegotiate their relationships. Despite this, a large majority feel close to their parents, value their parents' opinions, believe that their parents love and care for them, and respect their parents as authority figures. Adolescents tend to agree with their parents on attitudes toward work, education, religion, and politics. Any serious problems between parents and teens usually have roots earlier in childhood. (Refer back to pages 523–527.)

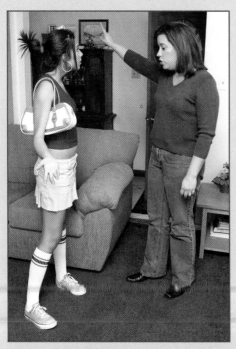

Parent-adolescent conflict most often focuses on everyday lifestyle choices and rarely is destructive or abusive.

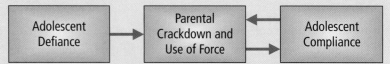

| Adolescent Defiance | → | Parental Crackdown and Use of Force | ← Adolescent Compliance → |

FIGURE 16.3 **The Bidirectional Parent–Adolescent Relationship** *This model depicts the mutual influence that parents and adolescents have on each other. When adolescents are defiant, they may stimulate parents to "crack down" on them. If the result is more compliance on the part of the adolescent, parents are likely to continue this coercive strategy.*

During adolescence, friendships become more intense and intimate, based on sharing personal thoughts, feelings, and expressions of support.

During adolescence, music and other media play increasingly important roles.

- Socioeconomic factors
- Family relationships
- Peer influences
- Pressure from partner

FIGURE 16.5 **Factors Associated with Adolescent Sexual Activity** *Sexual maturation is one of the most distinctive transitions of adolescence. During adolescence, most teens become sexually active.*

PEER RELATIONSHIPS AND MEDIA INFLUENCES

It is often believed that peers lure adolescents away from social norms and parental wisdom toward behavior and activities that defy parental standards. Adolescent peer relationships are important to teens, and their influences represent mostly constructive, diverse, and interrelated processes. Adolescents also spend a significant portion of their time with mass media. Although television remains an important source of entertainment and information, television viewing drops during adolescence, replaced with other media such as music, movies, and video games. (Refer back to pages 527–547.)

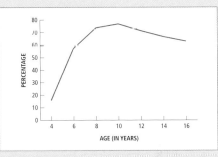

FIGURE 16.6 **Percentage of Children Who Use Computers at Home or School, by Age** *This figure shows how computer use increases through childhood and peaks during early adolescence. After that time, computer use drops off.*

VULNERABILITY AND RESILIENCE

Although many adolescents experiment with some risky activities, few of these are lasting or serious. Only a small percentage of adolescents are responsible for more serious and dangerous activities.

Despite the fact that teenagers face increasing risks associated with drugs, unprotected sex, violence, crime, and depression, relatively few US adolescents have behavior or adjustment problems. In addition, many problems that arise during adolescence have their roots in earlier development. Some teens seem more vulnerable to behavior problems, whereas others are quite resilient and seem to be protected from the negative effects of risky environmental circumstances. (Refer back to pages 547–549.)

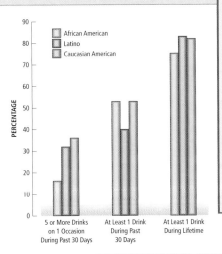

FIGURE 16.10 **High School Students' Experiences with Alcohol**

TABLE 16.5

Qualities That Enhance Adolescents' Resilience and Ability to Cope

QUALITY	DEFINITION
Support	Family support provides high levels of love and acceptance.
	Parental involvement provides help and advice when needed.
	Nonfamilial adult support provides advice and mentoring.
	School climate is positive.
Control	Parents have standards for appropriate conduct.
	Parents discipline teen when rules are violated.
	Teen is at home at least four nights a week.
	Best friends model responsible behavior.
Structured time use	Teen is involved in extracurricular school activities.
	Teen is involved in organizations or clubs outside of school.
	Teen is involved in religious programs or services.
Educational commitment	Teen is motivated to do well in school.
	Teen aspires to post–high school education.
	Teen's school performance is above average.
	Teen spends at least 6 hours per week doing homework.
Positive values	Teen places high personal value on helping other people.
	Teen is concerned about the conditions of others and their feelings.
	Teen values postponing sexual activity.
Social competence	Teen has the ability to stand up for what he or she believes in.
	Teen is good at making friends.
	Teen is good at making decisions and planning ahead.
	Teen has high self-esteem.
	Teen is optimistic about the future.

Glossary

acceleration programs educational programs that encourage children to move rapidly through the usual coursework, compressing the time usually spent in each course

accommodation changing a scheme to fit new information from the environment

active G-E correlation situation in which the child seeks out environments compatible with his or her genotype

actual self how adolescents see themselves

adolescence the developmental period between childhood and adulthood

adolescent egocentrism an adolescent's belief that his or her thoughts and ideas are unique and are not understood by others

age of viability the point at which postnatal survival is likely

alleles different forms of each gene

ambivalent attachment pattern characterized by inconsistent behavior toward a caregiver

amniocentesis a procedure used to determine whether genetic defects are present, in which amniotic fluid is collected and fetal cells are genetically tested

amnion a membrane that grows over the embryo and becomes filled with amniotic fluid, which protects the embryo

animism attributing lifelike qualities to objects that are not alive

anorexia nervosa an eating disorder, occurring most often in young women, in which individuals eat very little but believe that they are overweight

A-not-B error infants' tendency to search in the first hiding spot (A) while ignoring the second (B)

antisocial behavior a pattern of behavior that is aggressive, defiant, uncooperative, irresponsible, and/or dishonest

Apgar Scale a method of diagnosing potential problems in newborns, in which five vital signs are examined: respiration, reflex responsiveness, muscle tone, color, and heart rate

assimilated identifying with the majority culture and rejecting one's ethnic culture

assimilation directly processing information that fits a scheme

associational fluency ability to produce synonyms for a given word

associative play play in which various children engage, but with different goals

asthma a disease that causes difficulty with breathing

attachment theory explanation of development that focuses on the quality of the early emotional relationships developed between children and their caregivers

attachment an enduring emotional tie characterized by a tendency to seek and maintain closeness to a specific figure (the attachment figure), particularly under conditions of stress

attention-deficit hyperactivity disorder (ADHD) a disorder marked by an inappropriately low level of attention and inappropriately high levels of impulsivity and activity

auditory cortex the part of the brain that responds to complex musical tones

authoritarian parenting a style of parenting in which parents try to shape, control, and judge the behaviors and attitudes of their children according to rigid standards of conduct

authoritative parenting a style of parenting in which parents encourage verbal give-and-take and share with their children the reasons behind discipline and household rules

autonomous morality stage Piagetian stage of moral development in which one believes that rules can be changed by the will of those involved

autonomy the ability to govern oneself and make independent decisions

autosomes the first 22 pairs of chromosomes, which account for most of the body's cells

avoidant attachment pattern characterized by conspicuous avoidance of contact or interaction with the caregiver

axon long part of a neuron that is located at the cell base and sends messages to other neurons

babbling repeating consonant-vowel combinations, such as "mama" or "dada," two or more times

balanced polymorphism a kind of genetic diversity in which the genes that cause diseases provide certain genetic advantages as well as disadvantages

behavioral autonomy the capacity to make and follow through with decisions on regulating one's behavior

bicultural identifying with both the majority and the minority culture

blended family family structure formed when a widowed or divorced person remarries

Braxton-Hicks contractions mild, irregular contractions of the uterus experienced throughout pregnancy, especially during the last month or two

breech presentation fetal position in which the buttocks or feet lead the way

bulimia nervosa an eating disorder characterized by secret eating binges and purges

bullying aggressive behavior, repeated over time, that is intentionally harmful and occurs without provocation

canalized genetically limited phenotypic variation

carriers people who are heterozygous for a recessive disorder

case study method in which the researcher collects information about aspects of a person's life

centration the tendency to focus attention on the most obvious and striking characteristic of an object while ignoring others

cephalocaudal development the principle that growth occurs from the head downward

cesarean section procedure by which the fetus is delivered through an incision in the mother's abdomen

child development changes in physical, social, emotional, and intellectual functioning over time, from conception through adolescence

child-directed speech a special version of language that caregivers use with their children; also called motherese

chorion a membrane that grows to surround the embryo after about one month of development and helps form the placenta

chorionic villus sampling (CVS) a procedure used to assess genetic material in fetal cells, in which cells are removed from the projections on the chorionic membrane

chromosomes the structures on which genes reside

class inclusion part-whole relations of categories

classical conditioning Pavlov's theory of how responses to neutral stimuli become conditioned

clinical interview method in which the researcher asks detailed questions while interacting with the participant

cliques small groups of peers, usually of the same sex and age, who interact with one another on a regular basis

code switching the alternate use of two or more languages

cognitive development development of mental processes used to process information, grow in awareness, solve problems, and gain knowledge

cohort a group of individuals who are the same age or who experience similar events at the same time

cohort-sequential research design a cross-sectional study expanded so that data are collected from the same cohorts at different points in time

colostrum a pre-milk substance containing antibodies from the mother that protect the baby from infections

commitment the making of voluntary choices about life directions from among the many available options

compensation the understanding that one change can offset another

compliance obedience brought about by external pressures (such as the knowledge that one will be rewarded or punished for actions)

concrete operational stage Piaget's third stage of cognitive development (7 to 11 years), in which children begin to use logic to solve problems

conservation tasks tasks used to assess children's use of operations, in which children must decide whether a transformed object is the same as or different from what it was before

constructivist theories of learning educational approach in which students are encouraged to actively participate in their education

continuous development view of development as smooth and gradual

control group comparison group that is treated in the same way as the experimental group but does not receive the independent variable

control parameters the individual parts of a dynamic system

Conventional Level second level of Kohlberg's theory of moral development, in which moral reasoning is based on winning praise and recognition for good conduct and maintaining the social order

convergent thinking thinking that attempts to find a single correct answer to a problem

cooing making soft, repetitive vowel sounds such as "aah" and "ooh"

cooperative learning educational approach in which students work together in groups to solve problems

cooperative play play in which two or more children engage, with a common goal that requires social interaction

coordination of secondary circular reactions infants' ability to combine actions to solve simple problems

correlation coefficients calculated measures of the relations between variables

correlational study method in which researchers compare participants on two variables to determine whether the variables relate to each other

creativity novel and appropriate behavior that is different from what the person has done or seen before

crisis/exploration the process of making choices about life directions by considering options, values, and goals

critical periods periods of time during which a particular event or stimulus has to occur to have an impact on development

cross-sectional study method in which individuals of different ages are tested at the same point in time and the results from each age group are compared

crowds peer groups defined by members' activities and social standing

crowning the appearance of the top of the baby's head during birth

cruise in infant development, to move around while holding on to things for support

delinquency the legal term for antisocial acts committed by juveniles

demandingness the tendency of parents to exert firm control over children, requiring them to act in mature and appropriate ways

dendrites parts of a neuron that are located on the cell body and receive messages from other neurons

dependent variable the behavior thought to be affected by the independent variable

developmental domains the three main areas of development: physical, cognitive, and social-emotional development

discipline attempts by parents to alter children's behaviors or attitudes

discontinuous development view of development as abrupt and unstable, made up of qualitative stages and changes

discovery learning educational approach that encourages students to discover principles for themselves

discrimination acting in an unfavorable manner toward people because of their affiliation with a group

dishabituation renewed attention after habituation, caused by presentation of a new stimulus

disorganized/disoriented attachment pattern characterized by lack of a coherent strategy for handling separations from and reunions with the caregiver

display rules rules regarding how emotions should or should not be displayed

divergent thinking thinking that moves in many directions to produce many ideas or alternatives

dizygotic (DZ) twins twins who develop from two separate eggs fertilized by two separate sperm cells; fraternal twins

DNA a double helix consisting of two backbones, like a twisted ladder whose rungs are made up of chemical combinations; the basis of chromosomes

dominant gene a gene whose code is expressed when only one copy of the gene is present

double standard the imposition of different social expectations for males' and females' sexual attitudes and behavior

dual representation the ability to mentally represent something both as itself and standing for something else

dynamic systems theory a theory based on the idea that complex systems form from basic and simple conditions without adhering to a master plan for development

dyslexia learning disability marked by difficulties in processing language

dysmenorrhea menstrual cramps and discomfort

eating disturbances mild versions of eating disorders

ecological model Bronfenbrenner's model of the different spheres of influence

ectopic pregnancy a pregnancy that occurs outside the uterus

ego the part of the psyche that is the source of reason and operates within the conditions and demands of the real world

egocentric speech Piaget's term for speech directed toward the self

egocentrism the assumption, characteristic of most preschoolers, that their own perspective is shared by other people

embryonic stage the second stage of prenatal development, which begins at implantation and lasts until about eight weeks

emergent literacy educational approach based on the idea that children will naturally develop the skills involved in written and oral language and gradually improve these skills as they grow older

emotion regulation ability to alter emotional responses to a situation

emotional autonomy the ability to understand oneself as a person who is emotionally distinct from one's parents

emotion-focused coping strategies efforts to manage or reduce the emotional distress that is aroused in a stressful situation

empathy an emotional state that matches another person's emotional state—for instance, feeling bad because someone else is feeling bad

empirically based based on observation and experimentation

endogenous smile smile that is triggered by changes in nervous system activity and involves only the lower facial muscles

enrichment programs educational programs that encourage problem solving and creative activities through independent study or individualized instruction and mentoring

epidural block a common method for controlling the pain of labor, in which a local anesthetic is delivered to block pain in the region from the waist to the feet

episiotomy a small incision made in the skin below the vagina to prevent tearing of the vaginal tissues as the baby emerges

ethnic identity the sense of belonging to an ethnic group

ethnicity a group whose members share a common cultural heritage and a sense of belonging

ethological theory explanation of development that focuses on the causes and adaptive value of behavior, considering both the evolutionary history of the species and the social context

Event Related Potentials (ERP) a sharp increase in electrical activity in the brain that is created by exposure to a particular stimulus

evocative G-E correlation situation in which the child's genotype draws responses from others

evolutionary theories　explanations of development that focus on how behaviors promote the survival of the individual and the species

exogenous smile　smile that is triggered by external stimuli

exosystem　the part of the ecological model that represents the linkages among settings, one of which does not include the child, and how these influence development

expansion　taking young children's simplified language and adding complexity and completeness to it

experience-dependent plasticity　a shift in the wiring of the brain based on the type of environment the person is exposed to

experimental group　group that receives the independent variable

experimental study　method in which scientists bring people into a manipulated laboratory situation and then note the effects of the manipulation

expressive language style　language style focused on using words to regulate social interactions with adults

expressive language　children's ability to produce language

extended family　family structure consisting of one or more parents, one or more of the parents' children, and one or more other relatives living together in one household

externalizing problems　psychological difficulties that involve acting out against society

extinction　reducing unwanted behavior by withholding all positive consequences

fact　an objective, provable statement

failure to thrive (FTT)　a term used to describe infants and children who do not grow at the expected rates

false labor　moderately intense, rhythmic contractions late in the pregnancy

fast mapping　associating the sound of a word with the concept the word stands for, sometimes in a single exposure

fetal alcohol effects (FAE)　the effects, including mildly retarded physical development and learning disabilities, that may occur if a mother drinks moderately during pregnancy

fetal alcohol syndrome (FAS)　a constellation of problems, including physical deformities and intellectual deficits, that may occur if a mother drinks heavily during pregnancy

fetal stage　the third and final stage of prenatal development, which begins at about eight weeks and lasts until birth

foreclosure　identity status of those adolescents who have not explored alternatives but nonetheless have made a definite commitment to a specific identity

formal operational stage　Piaget's fourth stage of cognitive development (begins at around the age of 11), in which individuals are capable of applying logical principles to hypothetical and abstract situations

fragile X syndrome　a condition passed on by sex-linked transmission and characterized by protruding ears, prominent jaw, unusual speech, poor eye contact, and mild to moderate retardation

functional isolation　increased disengagement from social and physical environments that may result from a poor environment and inadequate nutrition

gametes　the sex cells (ova and sperm)

gender consistency　understanding that gender does not change despite changes in appearance or activities **gender stereotypes** beliefs people share about the typical characteristics of males and females

gender identity　understanding and acceptance that one is a boy or a girl

gender labeling　labeling oneself and others on the basis of gender group

gender schemas　mental representations about the cover

gender stability　understanding that gender is stable over time

gene-environment interactions　genetic sensitivity to particular environmental factors

generative learning　educational approach in which students are taught how to use specific methods of problem solving to integrate new information with preexisting information

genes　the portion of DNA that encodes specific genetic information

genetic imprinting　situation in which gene expression depends on the origins of the genes

genome　a person's complete set of DNA

genotype　a person's genetic code

germinal stage　the first stage of prenatal development, which begins at conception and lasts until the fertilized egg implants itself in the uterine wall

glial cells　cells that provide physical and functional support for neurons

goal-corrected partnership　an attachment relationship in which the child becomes a partner in planning how the relationship develops

gonadotrophins　chemical messengers that stimulate the production of hormones by the glands

goodness of fit　the match between a child's temperament and the demands of his or her environment

guilt　psychosocial crisis involving feelings of failure and becoming anxious when trying new things

habituation　decrease in attention to a repeatedly presented stimulus

heritability　an estimate of the degree to which variation of a characteristic in a population is influenced by genetic factors

heteronomous morality stage　Piagetian stage of moral development in which children adhere strictly to rules and base moral decisions on the authority of others

heterosexual　having a sexual attraction to members of the other sex

heterozygous　describing inheritance of a trait to which each parent has contributed a different copy of the gene

heuristic　a shortcut or rule of thumb used to help solve a problem

holophrases　individual words that convey as much meaning as whole sentences

homosexual　having a sexual attraction to members of the same sex

homozygous　describing inheritance of a trait to which both parents contributed identical copies of the gene

hostile aggression　aggression directed against another person, generally in retaliation for his or her actions

hypothetico-deductive reasoning　the type of reasoning used in science

id　the part of the psyche that is primitive and instinctual

identity　one's sense of who one is, where one has been, and where one is going in life

identity achieved　identity status of those adolescents who have experienced a period of exploration and crisis and have made a commitment

identity concept　the essential "sameness" of an object despite physical changes to it

identity confusion　an incomplete sense of self

identity diffusion　identity status of those adolescents who have not explored or committed themselves to a specific identity choice

image schemas　primitive notions, based on the visual appearance of objects, that lay a foundation for thinking about those objects

imaginary audience　a characteristic of adolescents' self-consciousness, involving the feeling that they are on stage, with people watching their every move

imminent justice　the belief that breaking a rule always leads to punishment

independent variable　condition that is assumed to be the cause of the behavior and is manipulated by the scientist

inductive reasoning　disciplinary techniques by which parents use reasoning and verbal communication for the purpose of changing children's behavior

industry　according to Kohlberg, pleasure derived from being productive and successful

infantile amnesia　inability to recall events that occurred very early in life

inferiority　according to Kohlberg, a sense of failure that causes performance anxiety

information processing theory　explanations for development that are based on the idea that people have limited capacities for learning but can flexibly apply strategies to find ways around those limitations

initiative　psychosocial crisis involving a willingness to take on responsibilities and learn new skills

innate fears　fears that are inborn and reflexive

instrumental aggression　aggression used for a specific purpose

internalization　obedience based on internal controls and standards that children have incorporated into their own expectations of themselves

internalizing problems　psychological difficulties, such as anxiety or depression, that involve a focus on or within the self

iron-deficiency anemia　a nutrient deficiency common among infants and toddlers

irreversibility   the inability to understand that an operation can be undone, returning something to its original form

karyotype   a photograph of chromosomes, used by geneticists to align each chromosome with the other member of its pair

kwashiorkor   a form of protein-energy malnutrition in which only protein is deficient

language acquisition device (LAD)   Chomsky's idea that there is a part of the brain that allows children to understand the properties of all human languages

latchkey children   children who are left unsupervised during the day or return home to an empty house after school

learning   changes that occur as the result of observation, experience, instruction, or practice

libido   the source of action and sexual desire

lightening   sensation that occurs when the fetus drops into the pelvic cavity, decreasing pressure on the mother's diaphragm

longitudinal study   method in which the same group of individuals is tested at different points in time

long-term memory   the part of the information processing system that has an unlimited capacity for storing information over long periods of time

love withdrawal   disciplinary techniques by which parents ignore, withhold affection from, or express lack of love for the child

low birthweight   term describing infants born after 37 weeks' gestation but weighing less than 5½ pounds

macrosystem   the outermost sphere of the ecological model, which represents societal values and attitudes

mainstreaming   inclusion of children with all sorts of disabilities in regular classrooms

marasmus   a form of protein-energy malnutrition involving severe body wasting

marginal   living within the majority culture but feeling alienated or outcast

maturation   changes brought about largely through the unfolding of a person's genetic code

meiosis   the process of cell replication undergone by ova and sperm; involves one duplication and one division of chromosomes, resulting in cells with a full set of genetic material, which undergo another division so that the final four cells each contain half the complement of chromosomes

menarche   the onset of the menstrual cycle

mental retardation   condition characterized by subaverage general intellectual functioning and impaired adaptive functioning, with onset in childhood

mental rotation   the ability to imagine how objects would appear if their positions were rotated

mesosystem   the middle sphere of the ecological model, which encompasses the connections among settings that include the child and how these connections influence the child

metabolic syndrome   a combination of obesity, high blood pressure, diabetes, and high cholesterol

microsystem   the inner sphere of the ecological model, which represents the immediate environment and includes influences such as physical objects, the structure of the environment, and the roles of and relationships among family members

minimal distance principle (MDP)   the assumption that the noun most closely preceding the verb is the subject of the sentence

mitosis   a type of cell division that gives rise to two daughter cells, each with identical chromosomes and genotypes; involves one duplication of chromosomes and one cell division.

molding   the pressing together, or even overlapping of the bones of the baby's skull, to accommodate passage through the birth canal

monozygotic (MZ) twins   twins who share the same genetic code because they developed from one fertilized egg, which divided into two separate individuals; identical twins

moral domain   issues that concern universal principles reflecting concepts of harm, welfare, and fairness

moral realism   the belief that morality is based on conforming to established rules set by powerful adults

morality   a set of principles or values that helps individuals distinguish right from wrong

moratorium   identity status of those adolescents who are actively exploring identity issues but have not yet made any firm commitment

multicultural education   educational practices and curricula that present non-European perspectives or improve educational outcomes for students from a wide spectrum of backgrounds

multiracial   a term used to describe people who are of two or more races

myelination   the process in which a neuron is sheathed in a smooth layer of fatty proteins (myelin)

natural selection   the process, in nature, whereby individuals who are best adapted to their surroundings survive and reproduce, and the adaptive characteristics of those individuals are passed on to the next generation

naturalistic study   method in which researchers observe the behavior of people in their natural environments

nature versus nurture debate   controversy over the extent to which biological/genetic and environmental factors influence development

negative reinforcement   removal of a negative or aversive stimulus, which increases the likelihood that a behavior will recur

neglect   failure to provide shelter, clothing, or protection for a child

neglected children   children who are reasonably well liked by their peers but lack friends

Neonatal Behavioral Assessment Scale   a measure commonly used to assess a newborn's responses to the environment

neonate   an infant who is in the first one to two months of life

neurodevelopmental approaches   explanations of development that focus on the relationship of brain development to behavior and thinking

neurons   the nerve cells that make up the communication system of the brain

night terrors   sleep disturbance characterized by repeated episodes of abrupt awakening, accompanied by intense anxiety, disorientation, unresponsiveness, and an inability to remember details about the event.

nuclear family   family structure in which the biological mother and father and their children live together

obesity   having a weight that is 20 percent more than ideal weight

object permanence   the concept that people and objects have an independent existence beyond one's own perception of them

onlooker play   play in which one child watches another child or children but does not directly participate

operant conditioning   learning based on the principle that the consequences of a behavior affect the likelihood that the behavior will be repeated

operations   actions internalized as symbols that can be reversed and coordinated

opinions   thoughts and feelings about a given topic

osteoporosis   a disease that involves a serious loss of bone density

overextension   the use of words to refer to objects or things that are outside the bounds of the category named by the word

overregularization   application of language rules when they do not apply

ovum   a human egg

parallel play   play in which two or more children engage in the same activity at the same time and place, but each child still plays separately

parasuicide   any nonfatal self-injury, including suicide attempts and self-mutilation.

parity   the number and spacing of children a woman bears

passive G-E correlation   situation in which parents provide a rearing environment that matches the child's own genotype

peak bone mass   the highest density of bone a person has in life

permissive parenting   a style of parenting in which parents make few demands on their children–they are accepting and tolerant of their children's impulses and desires

personal domain   issues that reflect personal preference and taste and are not socially regulated

personal fable   a story adolescents tell themselves that emphasizes their uniqueness and invulnerability

phenotype   the outward expression of the genotype

phonemes   the sounds of a language that are the basis for word construction

phonemic awareness   knowledge of permissible and nonpermissible strings of sounds in one's native language

phonics approach   technique used to teach reading, whereby children are trained to translate letters and groups of letters into sounds

physical abuse abuse that causes death, serious physical harm, or imminent risk of serious harm

physical development growth and change in a person's body and bodily functions

physical fitness a state of physical well-being that allows a person to function effectively without undue fatigue

pincer grasp using the forefinger and the thumb in opposition to pick up small objects

placenta the structure through which nutrients and waste products are exchanged between the mother and the developing embryo

placental barrier a line of protection for the unborn child, created by blood vessel walls that separate the maternal and fetal circulatory systems

polygenic transmission combined effect of multiple genes

positive reinforcement presentation of stimuli that increase the likelihood that a behavior will recur

possible self how adolescents wish themselves to be in the future

Postconventional Level third level of Kohlberg's theory of moral development, in which judgments about morality are based on principles that the individual is personally committed to and that are shared by others

postpartum depression intense feelings of sadness, anxiety, or despair experienced by a mother after the birth of a child

power assertion disciplinary techniques in which parents use physical force or threats of physical force to control children's behavior

pragmatics the practical rules guiding the use of verbal and nonverbal communication in differing situations

Preconventional Level first level of Kohlberg's theory of moral development, in which morality is based on external forces

prefrontal cortex the front part of the brain, which is involved in planning, social behavior, and working memory

prejudice preconceived ideas about a person or group of people, often based on physical characteristics, ethnicity, or race

premenstrual syndrome (PMS) a whole constellation of emotional and physical symptoms, such as backaches, headaches, moodiness, and water retention, that occur before menstruation

premoral period Piagetian stage of moral development in which young children do not yet understand cooperative rules and goals

preoperational stage Piaget's second stage of cognitive development (2 to 7 years), in which children begin to think in symbols but are egocentric and perceptually bound in their thinking

prereaching a child's effort to reach the arms toward an object without being able to contact it

pretend play play in which children let objects or persons symbolize things or people they are not

preterm or premature term describing infants born prior to 37 weeks' gestation

primary circular reactions repetitive actions that are centered on an infant's own body and motions

primary prevention efforts targeted at the population as a whole, to sensitize people to basic issues or to provide particular skills

primary sexual characteristics physical features directly related to reproduction, such as the ovaries, penis, and testes

private speech Vygotsky's term for speech directed toward the self, used when solving problems

problem-focused coping strategies efforts to manage or modify the source of a stressful situation

prodigies children who show exceptional abilities at a very young age in one domain of intelligence but not necessarily in others

prosocial behavior voluntary actions intended to benefit another person

proximodistal development the principle that body parts closer to the central axis of the body develop first, while those farther away from the center of the body develop later

psychoanalytic theories explanations of development that focus on the unconscious drives and forces that develop within the mind

psychological maltreatment emotional abuse caused by threatening harm or conveying to an individual that she or he is worthless, unloved, or unwanted

psychosexual development Freud's stage theory of development, based on how the libido is transformed into different structures and modes of expression

psychosocial crises in Erikson's lifespan theory, the struggles that occur at the various stages of development between two conflicting personality characteristics

psychosocial moratorium a period during which youths are reasonably free of adult responsibilities that might prevent them from adequately addressing identity issues

puberty developmental milestone reached when a person becomes sexually mature and capable of having children

pubescence the period of time during which sexual maturation takes place

punishment application of unpleasant consequences to decrease the likelihood that a behavior will be repeated

quickening fetal movements during pregnancy

race a group whose members share a genetic heritage

random assignment randomly assigning people to groups in a study so that the effects of uncontrolled variables will be the same for all groups

random sampling selecting participants for a study at random

range of reaction the range of possibilities of phenotypic variation displayed in response to different environments

rate-limiting component the slowest, or last-developing, part of a dynamic system

receptive language children's understanding of language

recessive gene a gene whose code is not expressed in the presence of a dominant gene

referential language style language style focused on developing a vocabulary that includes many object names

reflective abstraction the ability to rearrange and rethink information already acquired

reflexes simple, coordinated, unlearned responses

regulator genes genes that control the expression of other genes.

rejected children children who are overtly disliked by their peers

relational aggression aggression designed to damage someone's relationships with others, by withdrawing friendship, excluding someone from a group, and so on

relational play actions demonstrating an understanding of the relationship between two objects

resilience the capacity to bounce back or recover from stressful situations

responsiveness the tendency of parents to be warm, accepting, and willing to take into account the wishes and feelings of the child

reversible thinking the understanding that actions can be undone or reversed

risk-taking behavior a syndrome of multiple behavior problems

rites of passage initiations that mark an adolescent's new status and roles within the community

savants people who show exceptional abilities in one domain of intelligence but have retarded mental development in some other domains

scaffolding informal teaching methods that provide structure and support for children's thinking

schematic consistency the tendency of children's behavior and thinking to match their schemas

schemes cognitive guides, or blueprints, for processing information about the world

scripts concepts that people form about routines involved in everyday interactions and events

secondary circular reactions repetitive actions focused on the qualities of objects, such as the noises they make or their shapes and colors

secondary prevention efforts targeted at a specific segment of the population thought to be at high risk

secondary sexual characteristics features that are outward manifestations of sexual development but are not directly involved in reproduction, such as breasts, facial and body hair, and an adult body shape

secondhand smoke smoke that is released into the air by someone smoking

secure attachment pattern in which infants use their attachment figures as a secure base, obtaining comfort from their presence and becoming distressed by their absence

self-concept an individual's beliefs about the attributes and capacities she or he possess

self-conscious emotions   those emotions that involve injury to or enhancement of one's sense of self (such as pride and shame)

self-esteem   the value an individual attaches to the mental picture of himself or herself

semantic bootstrapping   children's use of word meaning to provide cues about syntax

semantics   the meanings associated with words

sensitive periods   periods of time that are optimal, but not necessary, for the development of certain behaviors or functions

sensorimotor stage   Piaget's first stage of cognitive development (0 to 2 years), in which the child relates to objects and people through his or her senses and motor skills

sensory register   the part of the information processing system that allows people to very briefly retain information taken in through the senses

separated   identifying only with one's ethnic culture and rejecting the majority culture

separation anxiety   a response in which negative protests accompany separation from attachment figures

seriation   the ordering of stimuli along a quantitative dimension (such as length).

sex chromosomes   the 23rd pair of chromosomes, which accounts for a person's sex

sexual abuse   abuse that involves engaging in sexual activity

sexual orientation   characteristic determined by the sex of the sexual partners one is attracted to

sexually transmitted diseases (STDs)   diseases that may be transmitted from one person to another through sexual contact

shaping   the process of rewarding behaviors that approximate the desired behavior

short-term memory   the part of the information processing system that holds information long enough for the person to evaluate and selectively act on the input

single-parent family   family structure in which children live with only their mother or their father

social cognition   thinking about people and interpersonal relationships

social communicative competence   the ability to effectively convey an intended message to others

social competence   the ability to use age-appropriate social behaviors to enhance peer relationships without harming anyone

social learning theory   Bandura's theory that individuals are greatly influenced by observing and imitating other people

social perspective taking   the ability to move away from one's own perspective and recognize what others perceive

social referencing   using caregivers as a source of information about how to respond in an uncertain emotional situation or condition.

social smile   smile that is triggered by social stimuli (such as the mother's face)

social-conventional domain   issues and actions that are defined as right or wrong because of a social agreement that they are so

social-emotional development   development of processes related to interactions with other people

socialization   the process by which children learn social roles and become members of groups

solitary play   play in which a child is alone, even if surrounded by other children

spatial perception   the ability to locate the horizontal or vertical while ignoring distracting information

spatial visualization   the ability to find figures and shapes hidden within other figures

spatial-visual skills   the cognitive abilities involved in orienting oneself in the environment

spermatogenesis   the process by which sperm develop

spermatozoa   mature spermatids that are fully functional and capable of fertilizing a human ovum

state of arousal   degree to which an infant is alert, attentive, or awake

static thinking   the tendency to attend more to the outcome than to the changes that produced the outcome

status offenses   acts that are illegal for juveniles but not for adults, such as running away from home

stepfamily   family structure formed when a person who has children from a former marriage remarries

Strange Situation   a procedure used to assess infants' attachment behavior under conditions of increasing stress due to separations from caregivers and strangers

stranger anxiety   a wary and fearful reaction to strangers

stuttering   having excessive disruptions in the rate, rhythm, and forward flow of speech

suicide   the act of taking one's own life.

superego   the part of the psyche that represents one's conscience, moral standards, and code of social conventions

survey study   method in which a number of people respond to a set of structured questions

symbolic representation   the use of mental symbols to represent objects

symbolic representations   mental representations of objects and people that can be manipulated in the mind

sympathy   feeling sorry or concerned for other people because of their emotional states or conditions

synapses   small gaps, or spaces, between the cells through which information is transmitted from one neuron to the next

synaptogenesis   the creation of new neural connections, or synapses

synchrony   degree to which caregiver's and baby's behaviors occur together and are coordinated to produce a state of mutual enjoyment and engagement

syntactic bootstrapping   children's use of the structure of sentences to provide cues about word meaning

syntax   the grammar, or rules, of a language

telegraphic speech   early language in which only highly informative words are used and less informative words are neglected

temperament   the predisposition to respond in certain enduring and characteristic ways to one's environment

teratogens   agents that cross the placental barrier and cause or increase the incidence of physical malformations and behavioral and cognitive deficits

tertiary circular reactions   subtle modifications infants make in their behavior with objects so as to explore the effects of those modifications

tertiary prevention   efforts directed at preventing or decreasing the reoccurrence of an event that has already occurred

theory of mind   the understanding of inner mental events–that people think, imagine, pretend, and wonder about the world around them

theory   a set of ideas structured to organize and explain facts

transactional perspective   the view that development occurs as the result of the interplay between the diverse qualities that individuals bring to their environments and the diverse environments that individuals experience

transductive reasoning   the inference that if two particular examples or events occur together, they must be causally related

transverse presentation   fetal position in which the shoulders and arms lead the way

type 2 diabetes   an insensitivity to insulin causing an imbalance in how the body handles sugar consumption

ultrasound   a procedure used to identify some developmental problems, in which video images of the fetus and the fetus's internal organs are produced from the echoes of sound waves

umbilical cord   the lifeline of the embryo, consisting of two arteries and one vein

underextension   the use of words to refer to fewer items than the word actually names

uninvolved parenting   a style of parenting in which parents make few demands of their children and are unresponsive or rejecting

values autonomy   the capacity to make judgments and choices about personal beliefs and principles

vernix caseosa   a white, waxy covering that provides the newborn child with protection from bacteria

vicarious reinforcement   learning by watching the consequences of other people's behaviors

visual cliff apparatus   a two-level "cliff" with a checkerboard pattern, covered with Plexiglas, used to create an illusion of depth

whole language approach   technique used to teach reading, based on the idea that learning to read is a natural process that occurs most effectively in a print-rich environment

zone of proximal development   Vygotsky's term for the distance between what a child can do unaided and what a child can do through interaction with skilled helpers

zygote   the fertilized ovum

References

A. C. Nielsen Media Research. (2003). *Television audience report.* New York: Author.

Abbott, S. (1997). Gender, status, and values among Kikuyu and Appalachian adolescents. In T. S. Weisner & C. Bradley (Eds.), *African families and the crisis of social change* (pp. 86–105). Westport, CT: Bergin & Garvey/Greenwood Publishing Group.

Abel, E. L. (1996). Introduction. In E. Abel (Ed.), *Fetal alcohol syndrome.* Boca Raton, FL: CRC Press.

Aber, J. L., Jones, S. M., & Cohen, J. (2000). The impact of poverty on the mental health and development of very young children. In C. H. Zeanah (Ed.), *Handbook of infant mental health* (pp. 113–128). New York: Guilford.

Aboud, F. E. (1988). *Children and prejudice.* New York: Blackwell.

Aboud, F. E., & Doyle, A. B. (1996). Parental and peer influences on children's racial attitudes. *International Journal of Intercultural Relations, 20,* 371–383.

Aboud, F. E., & Levy, S. R. (2000). Interventions to reduce prejudice and discrimination in children and adolescents. In S. Oskamp (Ed.), *Reducing prejudice and discrimination: The Claremont symposium on applied social psychology* (pp. 269–293). Mahwah, NJ: Erlbaum.

Abrams, S. M., Field, T., Scafidi, F., & Prodromidis, M. (1995). Newborns of depressed mothers. *Infants Mental Health Journal, 16,* 233–239.

Achenbach, T. M. (2002). Empirically based assessment and taxonomy across the life span. In J. J. Hudziak & J. E. Helzer (Eds.), *Defining psychopathology in the 21st century: DSM-V and beyond* (pp. 155–168). Washington, DC: American Psychiatric Publishing.

Ackerman, B. P., D'Eramo, K., Umylny, L., Schultz, D., & Izard, C. E. (2001). Family structure and the externalizing behavior of children from economically disadvantaged families. *Journal of Family Psychology, 15,* 288–300.

Acredolo, L., & Goodwyn, S. (1988). Symbolic gesturing in normal infants. *Child Development, 59,* 450–466.

Acredolo, L., & Goodwyn, S. (1996). *Baby signs.* New York: Contemporary Books.

Adair, R. H., & Bauchner, H. (1993). Sleep problems in childhood. *Current Problems in Pediatrics, 23,* 147–170.

Adams, M. J., Treiman, R., & Pressley, M. (1998). Reading, writing, and literacy. In W. Damon (Ed.), *Handbook of child psychology* (Vol. 4, pp. 275–356). New York: Wiley.

Adams, R. J. (1989). Newborn's discrimination among mid- and long-wave length stimuli. *Journal of Experimental Child Psychology, 47,* 130–141.

Adams, W. G., Gevai, J., Coffman, J., Palfrey, S., & Bauchner, H. (1998). Anemia and elevated lead levels in underimmunized inner-city children. *Pediatrics, 101,* 1–7.

Adler, P. A., Kless, S. J., & Adler, P. (1992). Socialization to gender roles: Popularity among elementary school boys and girls. *Sociology of Education, 65,* 169–187.

Administration for Children and Families. (2002). *Child maltreatment: 2002.* Washington, DC: Author.

Administration for Children and Families. (2002). *Head Start.* Washington, DC: Author.

Adolph, K. E. (1997). Learning in the development of infant locomotion. *Monographs of the Society for Research in Child Development 3,* Serial No. 251.

Ager, A., & Young, M. (2001). Cultivating the psychosocial health of refugees. In M. MacLachlan (Ed.), *Cultivating health: Cultural perspectives on promoting health* (pp. 177–197). New York: Wiley.

Agras, S., Brandt, H., Bulik, C., Dolan, S., Fairburn, C., Halmi, K., Herzog, D., Jimerson, D., Kaplan, A., Kaye, W., le-Grange, D., Lock, J., Mitchell, J., Rudorfer, M., Street, L., Striegel-Moore, R., Vitousek, K., Walsh, B., & Wilfley, D. (2004). Report of the National Institutes of Health workshop on overcoming barriers to treatment research in anorexia nervosa. *International Journal of Adolescent Medicine and Health, 35,* 509–521.

Aharoni, A., Keizer, L. C., Bouwmeester, H. J., Sun, Z., Alvarez-Huerta, M., Verhoeven, H. A., Blaas, J., van Houwelingen, A. M., De Vos, R. C., van der Voet, H., Jansen, R. C., Guis, M., Mol, J., Davis, R. W., Schena, M., van Tunen, A. J., & O'Connell, A. P. (2000). Identification of the SAAT gene involved in strawberry flavor biogenesis by use of DNA microarrays. *Plant Cell, 12,* 647–662.

Ainsworth, L. L. (1984). Contact comfort: A reconsideration of the original work. *Psychological Reports, 55,* 943–949.

Ainsworth, M. D. (1973). The development of infant–mother attachment. In B. M. Caldwell & H. N. Ricciuti (Eds.), *Review of child development research* (Vol. 3, pp. 1–94). Chicago: University of Chicago Press.

Ainsworth, M. D., Blehar, M. C., Waters, E., & Wall, S. (1978). *Patterns of attachment: A psychological study of the strange situation.* Hillsdale, NJ: Erlbaum.

Akbas, S. H., Ozben, T., Alper, O., Ugar, A., Yucel, G., & Luleci, G. (2001). Maternal serum screening for Down's syndrome. *Clinical Chemisty and Laboratory Medicine, 39,* 487–490.

Akhtar, N., Carpenter, M., & Tomasello, M. (1996). The role of discourse novelty in early word learning. *Child Development, 67,* 635–645.

Alaimo, K., Olson, C. M., & Frongillo, E. A. (2001). Food insufficiency and American school-aged children's cognitive, academic, and psychosocial development. *Pediatrics, 108,* 44–53.

Alan Guttmacher Institute. (1999). *Teen sex and pregnancy.* New York: Author.

Alan Guttmacher Institute. (2001). *Teenagers' sexual and reproductive health.* New York: Author.

Alan Guttmacher Institute. (2004). *The benefits of investing in sexual and reproductive health care.* New York: Author.

Alarcon, M., & DeFries, J. C. (1995). Quantitative trait locus for reading disability: An alternative test. *Behavior Genetics, 25,* 253.

Alessandri, S. M., Sullivan, M. W., Imaizumi, S., & Lewis, M. (1993). Learning and emotional responsivity in cocaine-exposed infants. *Developmental Psychology, 29,* 989–997.

Alexander, J. M., Bloom, S. L., McIntire, D. D., & Leveno, K. J. (1999). Severe preeclampsia and the very low birth weight infant: Is induction of labor harmful? *Obstetrics and Gynecology, 93,* 485–488.

Alexander, K. L., Entwisle, D. R., & Kabbani, N. S. (2001). The dropout process in life course perspective: Early risk factors at home and school. *Teachers College Record, 103,* 760–822.

Alfieri, T., Ruble, D. N., & Higgins, E. T. (1996). Gender stereotypes during adolescence: Developmental changes and the transition to junior high school. *Developmental Psychology, 32,* 1129–1137.

Alland, A. (1983). *Playing with form: Children draw in six cultures.* New York: Columbia University Press.

Allen, M. C. (1993). The high-risk infant. *Pediatric Clinics of North America, 40,* 479–490.

Allen, M. C. (1996). The neonatal neurodevelopmental examination. In A. J. Capute and P. J. Accardo (Eds.), *Developmental disabilities in infancy and childhood* (pp. 295–310). Baltimore, MD: Paul H. Brookes.

Allen, M. C., Donohue, P. K., & Dusman, A. E. (1993). The limit of viability—neonatal outcome of infants born at 22 to 25 weeks' gestation. *New England Journal of Medicine, 329,* 1597–1601.

Als, H., Duffy, F. H., McAnulty, G. B., Rivkin, M. J., Vajapeyam, S., Mulkern, R. V. Warfield, S. K., Huppi, P. S., Butler, S. C., Conneman, N., Fischer, C., & Eichenwals, E. C. (2004). Early experience alters brain function and structure. *Pediatrics, 113,* 846–857.

Alsaker, F. D. (1992). Pubertal timing, overweight, and psychological adjustment. *Journal of Early Adolescence, 12,* 396–412.

Alsaker, F. D. (1995). Timing of puberty and reactions to pubertal changes. In M. Rutter (Ed.), *Psychosocial disturbances in young people: Challenges for prevention* (pp. 37–82). New York: Cambridge University Press.

Alsaker, F. D. (1996). Annotation: The impact of puberty. *Journal of Child Psychology and Psychiatry, 37,* 249–258.

Altarriba, J. (1993). The influence of culture on cognitive processes. In J. Altarriba (Ed.), *Cognition and culture* (pp. 379–385). Amsterdam: North-Holland.

Altermatt, E. R., Jovanovic, J., & Perry, M. (1998). Bias or responsibility? Sex and achievement-level effects on teachers' classroom questioning practices. *Journal of Educational Psychology, 90,* 516–527.

Altmann, G. T. M. (2002). Statistical learning in infants. *Proceedings of the National Academy of Science, 99*(24), 15250–15251.

Amabile, T. M. (1993). What does a theory of creativity require? *Psychological Inquiry, 4,* 179–181.

Amabile, T. M. (2001). Beyond talent: John Irving and the passionate craft of creativity. *American Psychologist, 56,* 333–336.

Amato, M. (1997, April). Can this baby be soothed? *Child, 12,* 32–34.

Amato, P. R. (2000). The consequences of divorce for adults and children. *Journal of Marriage and the Family, 62,* 1269–1287.

Ambert, A. M. (1997). *Parents, children, and adolescents: Interactive relationships and development in context.* New York: Haworth Press.

America Online. (2003). *Youth wired survey.* Retrieved from http://media.aoltimewarner.com/media/newmedia/cb_press_view.cfm?release_num=55253423

American Academy of Pediatrics, Committee on Sports Medicine and Fitness and Committee on Injury and Poison Prevention. (2000). Swimming programs for infants and toddlers. *Pediatrics, 105,* 868–870.

American Academy of Pediatrics. (1991). *Recommendations for preventive pediatric health care.* Elk Grove, IL: American Academy of Pediatrics.

American Academy of Pediatrics. (1996). *Smoking: Straight talk for teens.* Elk Grove, IL: American Academy of Pediatrics.

American Academy of Pediatrics. (1998). In-line skating injuries in children and adolescents. *Pediatrics, 101,* 720–722.

American Academy of Pediatrics. (1999b). *2 to 4 years: Safety for your child.* Elk Grove, IL: American Academy of Pediatrics.

American Academy of Pediatrics. (2001). *Reduce the risk of SIDS.* Elk Grove, IL: American Academy of Pediatrics.

American Academy of Pediatrics. (2002). Skateboard and scooter injuries. *Pediatrics, 109,* 542–543.

American Academy of Pediatrics. (2003). AAP warns parents and pediatricians that fruit juice is not always the healthiest choice. Retrieved from http://www.aap.org/advocacy/archies/ mayjuice.htm

American Association of University Women. (1994). *Shortchanging girls, shortchanging America.* Washington, DC: Greenberg-Lake Analysis Group.

American College of Obstetricians and Gynecologists. (2000). *Planning your pregnancy and birth.* Chicago: American College of Obstetricians and Gynecologists.

American Dental Association. (2003). Oral health topic: Infants and children. Retrieved from http://www.ada.org/public/topics/infants.html

American Medical Association. (1996). *Physicians' guide to media violence.* Washington, DC: American Medical Association.

American Psychiatric Association. (1994). *Diagnostic and statistical manual of mental disorders* (4th ed.). Washington, DC: Author.

American Psychiatric Association. (2002). *Diagnostic and statistical manual of mental disorders* (4th ed., text revision). Washington, DC: Author.

American Psychological Association. (1993). *Violence and youth: Psychology's response. Volume I: Summary report of the American Psychological Association Commission on Violence and Youth.* Washington, DC: American Psychological Association.

American Red Cross. (2001). *Choosing quality child care.* Washington, DC: Author.

Anand, K. J. S., & Hickey, P. R. (1987). Pain and its effects in the human neonate and fetus. *New England Journal of Medicine, 137,* 1321–1329.

Anastasi, A. (1988). *Psychological testing.* New York: Macmillan.

Anderman, E. M., Eccles, J. S., Yoon, K. S., Roeser, R., Wigfield, A., & Blemnfeld, P. (2001). Learning to value mathematics and reading: Relations to mastery and performance-oriented instructional practices. *Contemporary Educational Psychology, 26,* 76–95.

Anders, T. F. (1979). Night-waking in infants during the first year of life. *Pediatrics, 63,* 860–864.

Anders, T. F., & Keener, M. (1985). Developmental course of nighttime sleep–wake patterns in full-term and premature infants during the first year of life: I. *Sleep, 8,* 173–192.

Anders, T. F., Goodlin-Jones, B. L., & Sadeh, A. (2000). Sleep disorders. In C. H. Zeanah (Ed.), *Handbook of infant mental health* (2nd ed., pp. 326–338). New York: Guilford.

Anders, T. F., Halpern, L. F., & Hua, J. (1992). Sleeping through the night: A developmental perspective. *Pediatrics, 90,* 554–560.

Anderson, D. R., Huston, A. C., Schmitt, K. L., Linebarger, D. L., & Wright, J. C. (2001). Early childhood television viewing and adolescent behavior: The recontact study. *Monographs of the Society for Research in Child Development, 66* (Whole No. 264).

Anderson, K. J., & Cavallaro, D. (2002). Parents or pop culture? Children's heroes and role models. *Childhood Education, 78,* 161–168.

Anderson, S. W., Bechara, A., Damasio, H., Tranel, D., & Damasio, A. R. (1999). Impairment of social and moral behavior related to early damage in human prefrontal cortex. *Nature Neuroscience, 2,* 1032–1037.

Andersson, B. (2003). Child care and its impact on children 0–2 years of age. In R. E. Tremblay & R. G. Barr (Eds.), *Encyclopedia on childhood development.* Montreal: Centre of Excellence for Early Childhood Development.

Andersson, T., & Magnusson, D. (1990). Biological maturation in adolescence and the development of drinking habits and alcohol abuse among young males: A prospective longitudinal study. *Journal of Youth and Adolescence, 19,* 33–41.

Ando, K. (1987, July). *The development of empathy in prosocial behavior.* Paper presented to the International Society for the Study of Behavioral Development, Tokyo.

Anglin, J. M. (1993). Vocabulary development. *Monographs of the Society for Research in Child Development, 58* (Whole No. 165).

Annett, M. (1993). Handedness and educational success: The hypothesis of a genetic balanced polymorphism with heterozygote advantage for laterality and ability. *British Journal of Developmental Psychology, 11,* 359–370.

Annie E. Casey Foundation. (2004). *Kids Count 2004.* Baltimore, MD: Author.

Antill, J. K., Russell, G., Goodnow, J. J., & Cotton, S. (1993). Measures of children's sex typing in middle childhood. *Australian Journal of Psychology, 45,* 25–33.

Antonucci, T. C., & Mikus, K. (1988). The power of parenthood: Personality and attitudinal changes during the transition to parenthood. In G. Y. Michaels & W. A. Goldberg (Eds.), *The transition to parenthood: Current theory and research* (pp. 62–84). New York: Cambridge University Press.

Aoki, W. T., & Turk, A. A. (1997). Adolescent suicide: A review of risk factors and implications for practice. *Journal of Psychology and Christianity, 16,* 273–279.

Apgar, V. A. (1953). Proposal for a new method of evaluation of the newborn infant. *Anesthesia and Analgesia, Current Research, 22,* 260.

Appel, A. E., & Holden, G. W. (1998). The co-occurrence of spouse and physical child abuse: A review and appraisal. *Journal of Family Psychology, 12,* 578–599.

Archer, S. L. (1993). Identity in relational contexts. In J. Kroger (Ed.), *Discussions on ego identity* (pp. 75–99). Hillsdale, NJ: Erlbaum.

Archibold, K. H., Giordani, B., Ruzicka, D. L., & Chervin, R. D. (2004). Cognitive executive dysfunction in children with mild sleep-ordered breathing. *Biological Research for Nursing, 5,* 168–176.

Arcia, E., & Conners, C. K. (1998). Gender differences in ADHD? *Journal of Developmental and Behavioral Pediatrics, 19,* 77–83.

Arditti, J. A., & Keith, T. Z. (1993). Visitation frequency, child support payment, and the father-child relationship postdivorce. *Journal of Marriage and the Family, 55,* 699–712.

Arend, R., Gove, F. L., & Sroufe, L. A. (1979). Continuity of individual adaptation from infancy to kindergarten: A predictive study of ego-resiliency and curiosity in preschoolers. *Child Development, 50,* 950–959.

Aries, E., & Moorehead, K. (1989). The importance of ethnicity in the development of identity in Black adolescents. *Psychological Reports, 65,* 75–82.

Aries, P. (1962). *Centuries of childhood.* New York: Vintage.

Arms, K. G., Davidson, J. K., & Moore, N. B. (1992). *Cultural diversity and families.* Dubuque, IA: Brown.

Arnett, J. (1991). Adolescents and heavy metal music: From the mouths of metalheads. *Youth and Society, 23,* 76–98.

Arnett, J., & Balle-Jensen, L. (1993). Cultural bases of risk behavior: Danish adolescents. *Child Development, 64,* 1842–1855.

Arnold, C. (1998). *Children and stepfamilies.* Washington, DC: Center for Law and Social Policy.

Arnold, T. K. (2004, October). The long shadow of Salk. *San Diego Magazine, 56*(12), 1–2.

Asher, S. R. (1990). Recent advances in the study of peer rejection. In S. R. Asher & J. D. Coie (Eds.), *Peer rejection in childhood* (pp. 3–16). Cambridge, England: Cambridge University Press.

Asher, S. R., Rose, A. J., & Gabriel, S. W. (2001). Peer rejection in everyday life. In M. R. Leary (Ed.), *Interpersonal rejection* (pp. 105–142). New York: Oxford University Press.

Asher, S. R., Zelis, K. M., Parker, J. G., & Bruene, C. M. (1991, April). *Self-referral for peer relationship problems among aggressive and withdrawn low-accepted children.* Paper presented at the biennial meeting of the Society for Research in Child Development, Seattle.

Ashley, J., & Tomasello, M. (1998). Cooperative problem-solving and teaching in preschoolers. *Social Development, 7,* 143–163.

Aslin, R. N. (1987). Visual and auditory development in infancy. In J. D. Osofsky (Ed.), *Handbook of infant development* (pp. 5–97). New York: Wiley.

Aslin, R. N., & Hunt, R. H. (2001). Development, plasticity, and learning in the auditory system. In C. A. Nelson & M. Luciana (Eds.), *Handbook of developmental cognitive neuroscience* (pp. 205–220). Cambridge, MA: MIT Press.

Aslin, R. N., Jusczyk, P. W., & Pisoni, D. B. (1998). Speech and auditory processing during infancy: Constraints on and precursors to language. In D. Kuhn & R. S. Siegler (Eds.), *Handbook of child psychology* (Vol. 2, pp. 147–198). New York: Wiley.

Association of SIDS and Infant Mortality Program. (1998). *Sudden infant death syndrome.* Minneapolis: Association of SIDS and Infant Mortality Program.

Astolfi, P., & Zonta, L. A. (1999). Risks of preterm delivery and association with maternal age, birth order, and fetal gender. *Human Reproduction, 14,* 2891–2894.

Atkin, C. (1983). Effects of realistic TV violence vs. fictional violence on aggression. *Journalism Quarterly, 60,* 615–621.

Atkin, L. C., Olvera, M. C., Givaudan, M., & Landeros, G. (1989). Neonatal and maternal perceptions of urban Mexican infants. In J. K. Nugent, B. M. Lester, & T. B. Brazelton (Eds.), *The cultural context of the infant* (Vol. 2, pp. 201–238). Norwood, NJ: Ablex.

Atkins, M. S., Osborne, M. L., Bennett, D. S., Hess, L., & Halperin, J. M. (2001). Children's competitive peer aggression during reward and punishment. *Aggressive Behavior, 27,* 1–13.

Atkinson, L., Niccols, A., Paglia, A., Coolbear, J., Parker, K. C. H., Poulton, L., Guger, S., & Sitarenios, G. (2000). A meta-analysis of time between maternal sensitivity and attachment assessments: Implications for internal working models in infancy/toddlerhood. *Journal of Social and Personal Relationships, 17,* 791–810.

Attie, I., & Brooks-Gunn, J. (1989). Development of eating problems in adolescent girls: A longitudinal study. *Developmental Psychology, 25,* 70–79.

Aube, J., Fleury, J., & Smetana, J. (2000). Changes in women's roles: Impact on and social policy implications for the mental health of women and children. *Development and Psychopathology, 12,* 633–657.

Augoustinos, M., & Rosewarne, D. L. (2001). Stereotype knowledge and prejudice in children. *British Journal of Developmental Psychology, 19,* 143–156.

August, D., & Hakuta, K. (1997). *Improving schooling for language-minority children: A research agenda.* Washington, DC: National Academy Press.

Aunola, K., Stattin, H., & Nurmi, J. E. (2000). Parenting styles and adolescents' achievement strategies. *Journal of Adolescence, 23,* 205–222.

Avenevoli, S., Sessa, F. M., & Steinberg, L. (1999). Family structure, parenting practices, and adolescent adjustment: An ecological examination. In E. M. Hetherington (Ed.), *Coping with divorce, single parenting, and remarriage: A risk and resiliency perspective* (pp. 65–90). Mahwah, NJ: Erlbaum.

Aviezer, O., Sagi, A., Resnick, G., & Gini, M. (2002). School competence in young adolescence: Links to early attachment relationships beyond concurrent self-perceived competence and representations of relationships. *International Journal of Behavioral Development, 26,* 397–409.

Avis, J., & Harris, P. L. (1991). Beliefs-desire reasoning among Baka children: Evidence for a universal conception of mind. *Child Development, 62,* 460–467.

Aylward, G. P. (1997). Conceptual issues in developmental screening and assessment. *Journal of Developmental and Behavioral Pediatrics, 18,* 340–349.

Azmitia, M., & Montgomery, R. (1993). Friendship, transactive dialogues, and the development of scientific reasoning. *Social Development, 2,* 202–221.

Azuma, H. (1986). Why study child development in Japan? In H. Sherman, H. Azuma, & K. Hakuta (Eds.), *Child development and education in Japan* (pp. 213–249). New York: Freeman.

Bachman, J. G., & Schulenberg, J. (1993). How part-time work intensity relates to drug use, problem behavior, time use, and satisfaction among high school seniors: Are these consequences or merely correlates? *Developmental Psychology, 29,* 220–235.

Bachman, J. G., Safron, D. J., Sy, S. R., & Schulenberg, J. E. (2003). Wishing to work: New perspectives on how adolescents' part-time work intensity is linked to educational disengagement, substance use, and other problem behaviors. *International Journal of Behavioral Development, 27,* 301–315.

Bae, Y., & Smith, T. M. (1996). *Women in mathematics and science.* Washington, DC: US Department of Education.

Baer, J. S., Sampson, P. D., Barr, H. M., Connor, P. D., & Streissguth, A. P. (2003). A 21-year longitudinal analysis of the effects of prenatal alcohol exposure on young adult drinking. *Archives of General Psychiatry, 60,* 377–385.

Baillargeon, R. (1987). Object permanence in 3½- and 4½-month-old infants. *Developmental Psychology, 23,* 655–664.

Baillargeon, R. (1994). How do infants learn about the physical world? *Current Directions in Psychological Science, 3,* 133–140.

Baillargeon, R., & Graber, M. (1988). Evidence of location memory in 8-month-old infants in a nonsearch AB task. *Developmental Psychology, 24,* 502–511.

Baillargeon, R., Spelke, E. S., & Wasserman, S. (1985). Object permanence in five-month-old infants. *Cognition, 20,* 191–208.

Bain, B., & Yu, A. (1980). Cognitive consequences of raising children bilingually. *Canadian Journal of Psychology, 34,* 304–313.

Baird, A. A., Gruber, S. A., Fein, D. A., Maas, L. C., Steingard, R. J., Renshaw, P. F., Cohen, B. M., & Yurgelun-Todd, D. A. (1999). Functional magnetic resonance imaging of facial affect recognition in children and adolescents. *Journal of the American Academy of Child and Adolescent Psychiatry, 38,* 195–199.

Baird, G., Cass, H., & Slonims, V. (2003). Diagnosis of autism. *British Medical Journal, 327,* 488–493.

Baird, G., Charman, T., Baron-Choen, S., Cox, A., Wheelwright, S., & Drew, A. (2000). A screening instrument for autism at 18 months of age: A six-year follow-up study. *Journal of the American Academy of Child and Adolescent Psychiatry, 39,* 694–702.

Baird, S. M., Campbell, D., Ingram, R., & Gomez, C. (2001). Young children with cri-du-chat: Genetic, developmental, and behavioral profiles. *Infant Toddler Intervention, 11,* 1–14.

Balcazar, H., Peterson, G. W., & Krull, J. L. (1997). Acculturation and family cohesiveness in Mexican American pregnant women: Social and health implications. *Family Community Health, 20,* 16–31.

Bales, D. W., & Sera, M. D. (1995). Preschoolers' understanding of stable and changeable characteristics. *Cognitive Development, 10,* 69–107.

Baltes, M. M., & Silverberg, S. B. (1994). The dynamics between dependency and autonomy: Illustrations across the life span. In D. L. Featherman & R. M. Lerner (Eds.), *Life-span development and behavior* (Vol. 12, pp. 41–90). Hillsdale, NJ: Erlbaum.

Baltimore, D. (2001). Our genome unveiled. *Nature, 409,* 814–816.

Bancroft, J., & Reinisch, J. (1990). *Adolescence and puberty.* New York: Oxford University Press.

Band, E. B., & Weisz, J. R. (1988). How to feel better when it feels bad: Children's perspectives on coping with everyday stress. *Developmental Psychology, 24,* 247–253.

Bandstra, E. S., Vogel, A. L., Morrow, C. E., Xue, L., & Anthony, J. C. (2004). Severity of prenatal cocaine exposure and child language functioning through age seven years: A longitudinal latent growth curve analysis. *Substance Use and Misuse, 39,* 25–59.

Bandura, A. (1977). *Social learning theory.* Englewood Cliffs, NJ: Prentice-Hall.

Banks, J. A. (1995). Multicultural education and the modification of students' racial attitudes. In W. D. Hawley & A. W. Jackson (Eds.), *Toward a common destiny: Improving race and ethnic relations in America* (pp. 315–339). San Francisco: Jossey-Bass.

Banks, J. A., & Banks, C. A. M. (1993). *Multicultural education.* Boston: Allyn & Bacon.

Banks, M. S. (1988). Visual recalibration and the development of contrast and optical flow. In A. Yonas (Ed.), *Perceptual development in infancy* (Vol. 20, pp. 145–196). Hillsdale, NJ: Erlbaum.

Barber, B. K., & Harmon, E. L. (2002). Parental psychological control of children and adolescents. In B. K. Barber (Ed.), *Intrusive parenting: How psychological control affects children and adolescents* (pp. 167–183). Washington, DC: American Psychological Association.

Bardin, C., Zelkowitz, P., & Papageorgious, A. (1997). Outcome for small-for-gestational-age and appropriate-for-gestational-age infants born before 27 weeks of gestation. *Pediatrics, 100,* 1–5.

Barkley, R. A. (1989). Attention deficit-hyperactivity disorder. In E. J. Mash & R. A. Barkley (Eds.), *Treatment of childhood disorders* (pp. 39–72). New York: Guilford.

Barkley, R. A. (1997). Attention-deficit/hyperactivity disorder, self-regulation, and time. *Journal of Developmental and Behavioral Pediatrics, 18,* 271–279.

Barkley, R. A., Fischer, M., Edelbrock, C. S., & Smallish, L. (1990). The adolescent outcome of hyperactive children diagnosed by research criteria: I. An 8-year prospective follow-up study. *Journal of the American Academy of Child and Adolescent Psychiatry, 29,* 546–557.

Barness, L. A., & Gilbert-Barness, E. (1992). Cause of death: SIDS or something else? *Contemporary Pediatrics, 9,* 13–31.

Barnett, S. W. (1998). Long-term cognitive and academic effects of early childhood education of children in poverty. *Preventive Medicine, 27,* 204–207.

Baron-Cohen, S. (2003). *The essential difference: The truth about the male and female brain.* Boulder, CO: Perseus.

Barr, H. M., Streissguth, A. P., Darby, B. L., & Sampson, P. D. (1990). Prenatal exposure to alcohol, caffeine, tobacco, and aspirin: Effects on fine and gross motor performance in 4-year-old children. *Developmental Psychology, 26,* 339–348.

Barr, R. G., Hopkins, B., & Green, J. A. (2000). *Crying as a sign, a symptom, and a signal: Clinical emotional and developmental aspects of infant and toddler crying.* New York: Cambridge University Press.

Barrett, M., & Eames, K. (1996). Sequential developments in children's human figure drawing. *British Journal of Developmental Psychology 14,* 219–236.

Barrett, M., & Waterfield, J. (1997). The hidden factor: An educational perspective on depression in learning. In K. N. Dwivedi & V. P. Varma (Eds.), *Depression in children and adolescents* (pp. 106–123). London: Whurr Publishers.

Bartholow, B. D., & Anderson, C. A. (2002). Effects of violent video games on aggressive behavior: Potential sex differences. *Journal of Experimental Social Psychology, 38,* 283–290.

Bartsch, K., & Wellman, H. M. (1995). *Children talk about the mind.* New York: Oxford University Press.

Bates, E., Carlson-Luden, V., & Bretherton, I. (1980). Perceptual aspects of tool using in infancy. *Infant Behavior and Development, 3,* 127–140.

Bates, E., Dale, P. S., & Thal, D. (1995). Individual differences and their implications for theories of language development (pp. 96–151), In P. Fletcher & B. MacWhinney (Eds.), *The handbook of child language.* Oxford, UK: Blackwell.

Bates, E., O'Connell, B., & Shore, C. (1987). Language and communication in infancy. In J. D. Osofsky (Ed.), *Handbook of infant development* (pp. 149–203). New York: Wiley.

Bates, E., Thal, D., & Janowsky, J. S. (1992). Early language development and its neural correlates. In I. Rapin & S. Segalowitz (Eds.), *Handbook of neuropsychology: Vol. 6, Child neurology.* (pp. 69–110). Amsterdam: Elsevier.

Bauer, D. H. (1976). An exploratory study of developmental changes in children's fears. *Journal of Child Psychology and Psychiatry, 17,* 69–74.

Baumeister, A. A., & Baumeister, R. F. (1989). Mental retardation. In C. G. Last & M. Hersen (Eds.), *Handbook of child psychiatric diagnosis* (pp. 61–94). New York: Wiley.

Baumeister, R. F., Smart, L., & Boden, J. M. (1996). Relation of threatened egotism to violence and aggression: The dark side of high self-esteem. *Psychological Review, 103,* 5–33.

Baumrind, D. (1967). Child care practices anteceding three patterns of preschool behavior. *Genetic Psychology Monographs, 75,* 43–88.

Baumrind, D. (1971). Current patterns of parental authority. *Developmental Psychology Monographs, 4* (1, Part 2).

Baumrind, D. (1989). Rearing competent children. In W. Damon (Ed.), *Child development today and tomorrow* (pp. 349–378). San Francisco: Jossey-Bass.

Baumrind, D. (1996). The discipline controversy revisited. *Family Relations, 45,* 405–414.

Baumrind, D., Larzelere, R. E., & Cowan, P. A. (2002). Ordinary physical punishment: Is it harmful? Comment on Gershoff (2002). *Psychological Bulletin, 128,* 580–589.

Baxter, M. P., & Dulberg, C. (1988). "Growing pains" in childhood—a proposal for treatment. *Journal of Pediatric Orthopaedics, 8,* 402–406.

Beal, C. R. (1994). *Boys and girls: The development of gender roles.* New York: McGraw-Hill.

Beard, J. (1995). One person's view of iron deficiency, development, and cognitive function. *American Journal of Clinical Nutrition, 62,* 709–710.

Beardslee, W. R., & Gladstone, T. R. G. (2001). Prevention of childhood depression: Recent findings and future prospects. *Biological Psychiatry, 49,* 1101–1110.

Beaudry, M., Simard, M., Drapeau, S., & Charbonneau, C. (2000). What happens to the sibling subsystem following parental divorce? In C. Violato & E. Oddone-Paolucci (Eds.), *The changing family and child development* (pp. 105–116). Aldershot, UK: Ashgate Publishing.

Beckman, D. A., & Brent, R. L. (1986). Mechanisms of known environmental teratogens: Drugs and chemicals. *Clinical Perinatology, 13,* 649–689.

Begley, S. (1996, February 19). Your child's brain. *Newsweek.*

Beitel, A. H., & Parke, R. D. (1998). Parental involvement in infancy: The role of maternal and paternal attitudes. *Journal of Family Psychology, 12,* 268–288.

Belamarich, P. F., Luder, E., Kattan, M., Mitchell, H. E., Islam, S., Lynn, H. S., & Crain, E. (2000). Do obese inner-city children with asthma have more symptoms than nonobese children with asthma? *Pediatrics, 106,* 1436–1441.

Bell, C. (1991). Traumatic stress and child in danger. *Journal of Health Care for the Poor and Underserved, 2,* 175–188.

Bell, J. H., & Bromnick, R. D. (2003). The social reality of the imaginary audience. *Adolescence, 38,* 205–219.

Bellinger, D.C., & Adams, H. F. (2001). Environmental pollutant exposures and children's cognitive abilities. In R. Sternberg & E. Grigorenko (Eds.), *Environmental effects on cognitive abilities* (pp. 157–188). Mahwah, NJ: Erlbaum.

Belsky, J. (1980). Child maltreatment: An ecological integration. *American Psychologist, 35,* 320–335.

Belsky, J. (1988). The "effects" of infant day care reconsidered. *Early Childhood Research Quarterly, 3,* 235–272.

Belsky, J. (1990). Parental and nonparental child care and children's socioemotional development: A decade in review. *Journal of Marriage and the Family, 52,* 885–903.

Belsky, J. (1993). Etiology of child maltreatment: A developmental–ecological analysis. *Psychological Bulletin, 114,* 413–434.

Belsky, J. (1996). Parent, infant, and social–contextual antecedents of father-son attachment security. *Developmental Psychology, 32,* 905–913.

Belsky, J. (1999). Infant–parent attachment. In L. Balter & C. S. Tamis-LeMonda (Eds.), *Child psychology: A handbook of contemporary issues* (pp. 45–63). Philadelphia: Psychology Press.

Belsky, J., & Cassidy, J. (1994). Attachment: Theory and evidence. In M. Rutter & D. Hay (Eds.), *Development through life* (pp. 373–402). Oxford, UK: Blackwell.

Belsky, J., & Fearon, R. M. P. (2002). Early attachment security, subsequent maternal sensitivity, and later child development: Does continuity in development depend upon continuity of caregiving? *Attachment and Human Development, 4,* 361–387.

Belsky, J., Spritz, B., & Crnic, K. (1996). Infant attachment security and affective–cognitive information processing at age 3. *Psychological Science, 7,* 111–114.

Belsky, J., Steinberg, L., & Draper, P. (1991). Childhood experience, interpersonal development, and reproductive strategy: An evolutionary theory of socialization. *Child Development, 62,* 647–670.

Belsky, J., Woodworth, S., & Crnic, K. (1996a). Trouble in the second year: Three questions about family interactions. *Child Development, 67,* 556–578.

Bem, S. L. (1981). Gender schema theory: A cognitive account of sex typing. *Psychological Review, 88,* 354–364.

Bem, S. L. (1983). Gender schema theory and its implications for child development: Raising gender-aschematic children in a gender-schematic society. *Signs, 8,* 598–616.

Bemporad, J. R. (1994). Dynamic and interpersonal theories of depression. In W. M. Reynolds & H. F. Johnston (Eds.), *Handbook of depression in children and adolescents* (pp. 81–95). New York: Plenum.

Benedek, E. P., & Brown, C. F. (1995). *How to help your child overcome your divorce.* Washington, DC: American Psychiatric Press.

Benes, F. (2001). The development of prefrontal cortex: The maturation of neurotransmitter systems and their interactions. In C. Nelson & M. Luciana (Eds.), *Handbook of developmental cognitive neuroscience* (pp. 79–92). Cambridge, MA: MIT Press.

Bennett, V. R., & Brown, L. K. (1993). The fetus. In V. R. Bennett & L. K. Brown (Eds.), *Myles textbook for midwives* (pp. 365–376). London: Churchill Livingstone.

Benson, P. (1993). *The troubled journal: A portrait of 6th–12th grade youth.* Minneapolis: The Search Institute.

Benson, P. L., Donahue, M. J., & Erickson, J. A. (1989). Adolescence and religion. In M. L. Lynn & D. O. Moberg (Eds.), *Research in the social scientific study of religion* (pp. 153–181). Greenwich, CT: JAI Press.

Berenbaum, S. A., & Snyder, E. (1995). Early hormonal influences on childhood sex-typed activity and playmate preferences: Implications for the development of sexual orientation. *Developmental Psychology, 31,* 31–42.

Berg, W. K., & Berg, K. M. (1987). Psychophysiological development in infancy: State, startle, and attention. In J. D. Osofsky (Ed.), *Handbook of infant development* (pp. 238–317). New York: Wiley.

Berk, L. E. (1994). Why children talk to themselves. *Scientific American, 272,* 78–83.

Berk, L. E., & Winsler, A. (1999). *Scaffolding children's learning: Vygotsky and early childhood education.* Washington, DC: National Association for the Education of Young Children.

Berko, J. (1958). The child's learning of English morphology. *Word, 14,* 150–177.

Berliner, L., & Elliot, D. M. (1996). Sexual abuse of children. In J. Briere, L. Berliner, J. A. Bulkley, C. Jenny, & T. Reid (Eds.), *The APSAC handbook on child maltreatment* (pp. 51–71). Thousand Oaks, CA: Sage.

Berman, C. M., Rasmussen, K. L. R., & Suomi, S. J. (1994). Responses of free-ranging rhesus monkeys to a natural form of social separation.

I. Parallels with mother–infant separation in captivity. *Child Development, 65,* 1028–1041.

Berman, S. L., Silverman, W. K., & Kurtines, W. M. (2000). Children's and adolescents' exposure to community violence, post-traumatic stress reactions, and treatment implications. *Journal of Disaster and Trauma Studies, 2000–1,* 1–11.

Bernal, J. (1973). Night waking in infants during the first fourteen months. *Developmental Medicine Child Neurology, 15,* 760–769.

Bernal, M. E., & Knight, G. P. (1997). Ethnic identity of Latino children. In J. G. Garcia & M. C. Zea (Eds.), *Psychological interventions and research with Latino populations* (pp. 15–38). Boston: Allyn & Bacon.

Berndt, T. J., & Perry, T. B. (1990). Distinctive features and effects of early adolescent friendships. In R. Montemayor, G. R. Adams, & T. Gullotta (Eds.), *From childhood to adolescence* (pp. 269–287). Newbury Park, CA: Sage.

Bertenthal, B. I. (1996). Origins and early development of perception, action, and representation. *Annual Review of Psychology, 47,* 431–459.

Bertenthal, B. I., & Campos, J. J. (1984). A reexamination of fear and its determinants on the visual cliff. *Psychophysiology, 21,* 413–417.

Bertenthal, B. I., & Clifton, R. K. (1998). Perception and action. In W. Damon (Ed.), *Handbook of child psychology* (Vol. 2, pp. 51–102). New York: Wiley.

Bertenthal, B. I., Proffitt, D. R., Kramer, S. J., & Spetner, N. B. (1987). Infants' encoding of kinetic displays varying in relative coherence. *Developmental Psychology, 23,* 171–178.

Bervall, A., Wessely, H., Forsman, A., & Hansen, S. (2001). A deficit in attentional set-shifting of violent offenders. *Psychological Medicine, 31,* 1095–1105.

Best, C. T. (1995). Learning to perceive the sound patterns of English. In C. Rovee-Collier & L. P. Lipsitt (Eds.), *Advances in infancy research* (pp. 122–156). Norwood, NJ: ABLEX.

Bettes, B. A. (1988). Maternal depression and motherese: Temporal and intonational features. *Child Development, 59,* 1089–1096.

Bhatia, T. K., & Ritchie, W. C. (1999). The bilingual child: Some issues and perspectives. In W. Ritchie & T. Bhatia, (Eds.), *Handbook of child language acquisition* (pp. 569–643). San Diego, CA: Academic Press.

Bhattacharya, G. (2000). The school adjustment of South Asian immigrant children in the United States. *Adolescence, 35,* 77–85.

Bialystock, E. (1999). Cognitive complexity and attentional control in the bilingual mind. *Child Development, 70,* 636–644.

Bialystock, E. (2001). *Bilingualism in development: Language, literacy, and cognition.* New York: Cambridge University Press.

Bialystock, E. (2002). Acquisition of literacy in bilingual children: A framework for research. *Language Learning, 52,* 159–199.

Biederman, J., Faraone, S. V., Taylor, A., Sienna, M., Williamson, S., & Fine, C. (1998). Diagnostic continuity between child and adolescent ADHD: Findings from a longitudinal clinical sample. *Journal of the American Academy of Child and Adolescent Psychiatry, 37,* 305–313.

Bier, J. A. B., Ferguson, A. E., Morales, Y., Liebling, J. A., Oh, W., & Vohr, B. R. (1997). Breastfeeding infants who were extremely low birth weight. *Pediatrics, 100,* 1–4.

Bigler, R. S. (1999). The use of multicultural curricula and materials to counter racism in children. *Journal of Social Issues, 55,* 687–705.

Bigler, R. S., & Liben, L. S. (1993). A cognitive-developmental approach to racial stereotyping and reconstructive memory in Euro-American children. *Child Development, 64,* 1507–1518.

Bijur, P. E., Trumble, A., Harel, Y., Overpeck, M. D., Jones, D., & Scheidt, P. C. (1995). Sports and recreation injuries in U.S. children and adolescents. *Archives of Pediatric and Adolescent Medicine, 149,* 1009–1016.

Biller, H. B. (1993). *Fathers and families.* Westport, CT: Greenwood.

Birch, S. H., & Ladd, G. W. (1998). Children's interpersonal behaviors and the teacher–child relationship. *Developmental Psychology, 34,* 934–946.

Bithoney, W. G., & Newberger, E. H. (1987). Child and family attributes of failure to thrive. *Journal of Developmental and Behavioral Pediatrics, 8,* 32.

Bjorklund, D. F. (1995). *Children's thinking.* Pacific Grove, CA: Brooks/Cole.

Bjorklund, D. F. (2000). *Children's thinking: Developmental function and individual differences.* Belmont, CA: Wadsworth/Thomson.

Bjorklund, D. F., Miller, P. H., Coyle, T. R., & Slawinski, J. L. (1997). Instructing children to use memory strategies: Evidence of utilization deficiencies in memory training studies. *Developmental Review, 17,* 411–442.

Bjorklund, D. F., & Pellegrini, A. D. (2000). Child development and evolutionary psychology. *Child Development, 71,* 1687–1708.

Black, B., & Hazen, N. L. (1990). Social status and patterns of communication in acquainted and unacquainted preschool children. *Developmental Psychology, 26,* 379–387.

Black, J. E. (1998). How a child builds its brain: Some lessons from animal studies of neural plasticity. *Preventative Medicine, 27,* 168–171.

Black, K. A. (2000). Gender differences in adolescents' behavior during conflict resolution tasks with best friends. *Adolescence, 35,* 499–512.

Black, M. M., Nair, P., Kight, C., Wachtel, R., Roby, P., & Schuler, M. (1994). Parenting and early development among children of drug-abusing women. *Pediatrics, 94,* 440–448.

Black-Gutman, D., & Hickson, F. (1996). The relationship between racial attitudes and social-cognitive development in children. *Developmental Psychology, 32,* 448–456.

Blair, R., James, R., & Coles, M. (2001). Expression recognition and behavioural problems in early adolescence. *Cognitive Development, 15,* 421–434.

Blake, J. (1989). *Family size and achievement.* Berkeley: University of California Press.

Bland, K. (1997, March 9). Infant abuse leaves lasting repercussions. *Arizona Republic,* pp. B1, B4.

Blasi, A. (1983). Moral cognition and moral action: A theoretical perspective. *Developmental Review, 3,* 178–210.

Blass, E. M., Ganchrow, J. R., & Steiner, J. E. (1984). Classical conditioning in newborn humans 2–48 hours of age. *Infant Behavior and Development, 7,* 223–235.

Blau, D. M. (2001). *The child care problem.* New York: Russell Sage Foundation.

Bleeker, M. M., & Jacobs, J. E. (2004). Achievement in math and science: Do mothers' beliefs matter 12 years later? *Journal of Educational Psychology, 96,* 97–109.

Bloch, H. (1990). Status and function of early sensory-motor coordination. In H. Bloch & B. I Bertenthal (Eds.), *Sensory-motor organization and development in infancy and early childhood* (pp. 163–178). Dordrecht, Netherlands: Kluwer.

Bloom, L. (1998). Language acquisition in its developmental context. In W. Damon (Ed.), *Handbook of child psychology* (Vol. 2, pp. 309–370). New York: Wiley.

Bloom, L., Margulis, C., Tinker, E., & Fujita, N. (1996). Early conversations and word learning: Contributions from child and adult. *Child Development, 67,* 3154–3175.

Bloom, L., Rocissano, L., & Hood, L. (1976). Adult–child discourse. *Cognitive Psychology, 8,* 521–552.

Blum, N.J., Taubman, B., & Osborne, M. L. (1997). Behavioral characteristics of children with stool toileting refusal. *Pediatrics, 99,* 50–53.

Blumenfeld, W. J., & Raymond, D. (1993). *Looking at gay and lesbian life.* Boston: Beacon Press.

Boaler, J. (2002). Paying the price for "sugar and spice": Shifting the analytical lens in equity research. *Mathematical Thinking and Learning, 4,* 127–144.

Boeck, M. A. (1992). Bulimia nervosa. In S. B. Friedman, M. Fisher, & S. K. Schonberg (Eds.), *Comprehensive adolescent health care* (pp. 232–237). St. Louis, MO: Quality Medical Publishing.

Boer, F. (1990). *Sibling relationships in middle childhood*. Leiden, Germany: DSWO University of Leiden Press.

Boer, F., Goedhart, T., & Treffers, P. D. A. (1992). Siblings and their parents. In F. Boer & J. Dunn (Eds.), *Children's sibling relationships* (pp. 41–54). Hillsdale, NJ: Erlbaum.

Bohannon, J. N., & Warren-Leubecker, A. (1989). Theoretical approaches to language acquisition. In J. Berko-Gleason (Ed.), *The development of language* (pp. 167–223). Columbus, OH: Merrill.

Bohlin, G., Hagekull, B., & Rydell, A. M. (2000). Attachment and social functioning: A longitudinal study from infancy to middle childhood. *Social Development, 9*, 24–39.

Bolger, K. E., & Patterson, C. J. (2001). Developmental pathways from child maltreatment to peer rejection. *Child Development, 72*, 549–568.

Bon-De-Matte, L. (1998). Anorexic syndrome in adolescence and anorexia. In P. Bria & A. Ciocca (Eds.), *Psychotherapeutic issues in eating disorders* (pp. 41–48). Rome, Italy: Abramowicz.

Bongers, I. L., Koot, H. M., van der Ende, J., & Verhulst, F. C. (2003). The normative development of child and adolescent problem behavior. *Journal of Abnormal Psychology, 112*, 179–192.

Booth, C. L., Rose-Krasnor, L., & Rubin, K. H. (1991). Relating preschoolers' social competence and their mothers' parenting behaviors to early attachment security and high-risk status. *Journal of Social and Personal Relationships, 8*, 363–382.

Booth, D. A. (1994). *Psychology of nutrition*. London: Taylor and Francis.

Booth, M. Z., & Matuga, J. (2003, July). Swazi children's families as reflected in their drawings: The impact of the home environment. *The African Symposium, 3*, 1–5.

Borawski, E. A., Ievers-Landis, C. E., Lovegreen, L. D., & Trapl, E. S. (2003). Parental monitoring, negotiated unsupervised time, and parental trust: The role of perceived parenting practices in adolescent health risk behaviors. *Journal of Adolescent Health, 33*, 60–70.

Borg, M. G. (1998). Secondary school teachers' perception of pupils' undesirable behaviours. *British Journal of Educational Psychology, 68*, 67–79.

Borke, H. (1975). Piaget's mountains revisited: Changes in the egocentric landscape. *Developmental Psychology, 11*, 240–243.

Borman, K., & Schneider, B. (1998). *The adolescent years*. Chicago: The National Society for the Study of Education.

Bornstein, M. H. (1989). Sensitive periods in development. *Psychological Bulletin, 105*, 179–197.

Bornstein, M. H., & Lamb, M. E. (1992). *Development in infancy* (3rd ed.), New York: McGraw-Hill.

Bornstein, M. H., & Ludemann, P. M. (1989). Habituation at home. *Infant Behavior and Development, 12*, 525–529.

Bornstein, M. H., Tal, J., & Tamis-LeMonda, C. S. (1991). Parenting in cross-cultural perspective: The United States, France, and Japan. In M. H. Bornstein (Ed.), *Cultural approaches to parenting* (pp. 69–90). Hillsdale, NJ: Erlbaum.

Bornstein, M. H., & Tamis-LeMonda, C. S. (1997). Maternal responsiveness and infant mental abilities. *Infant Behavior and Development, 20*, 283–296.

Borstelmann, L. J. (1983). Children before psychology: Ideas about children from antiquity to the late 1800s. In P. H. Mussen (Ed.), *Handbook of child psychology* (Vol. 1, pp. 1–40). New York: Wiley.

Borsting, E. (1994). Overview of vision and visual processing development. In M. Scheiman & M. Rouse (Eds.), *Optimetric measure of learning-related vision problems* (pp. 131–145). St. Louis, MO: Mosby.

Bosco, A., Longoni, A. M., & Vecchi, T. (2004). Gender effects in spatial orientation: Cognitive profiles and mental strategies. *Applied Cognitive Psychology, 18*, 519–532.

Boseley, S. (2004, June 30). Infertile woman expecting baby after ovarian tissue transplant. *The Guardian*, pp. 1–2.

Bosma, H. A., & Kunnen, E. S. (2001). Determinants and mechanisms in ego identity development: A review and synthesis. *Developmental Review, 21*, 39–66.

Boston Globe. (2003, May 27). Generation XL: An obesity epidemic.

Boston, M. B., & Levy, G. D. (1991). Changes and differences in preschoolers' understanding of gender scripts. *Cognitive Development, 6*, 412–417.

Bosworth, P. (1985, February). Diane Sawyer. *Ladies' Home Journal*, 28–34.

Bottoms, G., Cooney, S., & Carpenter, K. (2003). *Improving middle school*. Atlanta, GA: Southern Regional Education Board.

Bouchey, H. A., & Furman, W. (2003). Dating and romantic experiences in adolescence. In M. D. Berzonsky & G. R. Adams (Eds.), *Blackwell handbook of adolescence* (pp. 313–329). Malden, MA: Blackwell.

Bowen, R., Fenton, T., & Rappaport, L. (1991). Stimulant medication and attention deficit—hyperactivity disorder: The child's perspective. *AJDC, 145*, 291–295.

Bower, J. (1982). *Development in infancy*. San Francisco: Freeman.

Bower, M. (1995). *Thalidomide*. San Francisco: Project Inform.

Bowker, A., Gabdois, S., & Cornock, B. (2003). Sports participation and self-esteem: Variations as a function of gender and gender role orientation. *Sex Roles, 49*, 47–58.

Bowlby, J. (1969). *Attachment and loss, Vol. 1*. New York: Basic Books.

Bowlby, J. (1973). *Attachment and loss, Vol. 2*. New York: Basic Books.

Bowman, P. J., & Howard, C. (1985). Race-related socialization, motivation, and academic achievement: A study of Black youths in three-generation families. *Journal of the American Academy of Child Psychiatry, 24*, 134–141.

Boxer, A. M., Cohler, J. J., Herdt, G., & Irvin, F. (1993). Gay and lesbian youth. In P. H. Tolan & J. J. Cohler (Eds.), *Handbook of clinical research and practice with adolescents* (pp. 249–280). New York: Wiley.

Boyce, W. T., Frank, E., Jensen, P. S., Kessler, R. C., Nelson, C. A., Steinberg, L., & The MacArthur Foundation Research Network on Psychopathology and Development. (1998). Social context in developmental psychopathology. *Development and Psychopathology, 10*, 143–164.

Boykin-McElhaney, K., & Allen, J. P. (2001). Autonomy and adolescent social functioning: The moderating effect of risk. *Child Development, 72*, 220–235.

Brackbill, Y., McManus, K., & Woodward, L. (1985). *Medication in maternity: Infant exposure and maternal information*. Ann Arbor: University of Michigan Press.

Bradbard, M. R., Martin, C. L., Endsley, R. C., & Halverson, C. F. (1986). Influence of sex stereotypes on children's exploration and memory: A competence versus performance distinction. *Developmental Psychology, 22*, 481–486.

Bradford, K., Barber, B. K., Olsen, J. A., Maughan, S. L., Erickson, L. D., Ward, D., & Stolz, H. E. (2004). A multi-national study of interparental conflict, parenting, and adolescent functioning. *Marriage and Family Review, 35*, 107–137.

Bradley, R. H. (1999). The home environment. In S. L. Friedman & T. D. Wachs (Eds.), *Measuring environment across the life span: Emerging methods and concepts* (pp. 31–58). Washington, DC: American Psychological Association.

Bradley, R. H., Burchinal, M. R., & Casey, P. H. (2001). Early intervention: The moderating role of the home environment. *Applied Developmental Science, 5*, 2–8.

Bradley, R. H., & Caldwell, B. M. (1976). The relation of infants' home environments to mental test performance at fifty-four months: A follow-up study. *Child Development, 47*, 1172–1174.

Bradley, R. H., Caldwell, B. M., Rock, S. L., Ramey, C. T., Barnard, K. E., Gray, C., Hammond, M. A., Mitchell, S., Gottfried, A. W., Siegel, L. & Johnson, D. L. (1989). Home environment and cognitive development in the first three years of life: A collaborative study involving six sites and three ethnic groups in North America. *Developmental Psychology, 25,* 217–235.

Bradley, R. H., Whiteside, L., Mundfrom, D. J., Casey, P. H., Kelleher, K. J., & Pope, S. K. (1994). Early indications of resilience and their relation to experiences in the home environments of low birthweight, premature children living in poverty. *Child Development, 65,* 346–360.

Bradley, S. J., Gillian, D. O., Avinoam, B. C., & Zucker, K. J. (1998). Experiment of nuture: Abolatio penis at 2 months, sex reassignment at 7 months, and a psychosexual follow-up in young adulthood. *Pediatrics, 102,* 1–5.

Brage, S., Wedderkopp, N., Ekelund, U., Franks, P. W., Wareham, N J., Andersen, L. B., & Froberg, K. (2004). Features of the Metabolic Syndrome are associated with objectively measured physical activity and fitness in Danish children: The European Heart Study. *Diabetes Care, 27,* 2141–2148.

Braine, M. (1963). On learning the grammatical order of words. *Psychological Review, 70,* 323–348.

Brainerd, C. J., & Kaxzor, P. (1974). An analysis of two proposed sources of children's class inclusion errors. *Developmental Psychology, 10,* 633–643.

Branch, C. W., & Newcombe, N. (1986). Racial attitude development among young Black children as a function of parental attitudes: A longitudinal and cross-sectional study. *Child Development, 57,* 712–721.

Braungart-Rieker, J. M., Garwood, M. M., Powers, B. P., & Wang, X. (2001). Parental sensitivity, infant affect, and affect regulation: Predictors of later attachment. *Child Development, 72,* 252–270.

Braungart-Rieker, J. M., & Stifter, C. A. (1996). Infants' responses to frustrating situations: Continuity and change in reactivity and regulation. *Child Development, 67,* 1767–1779.

Braza, F., Braza, P., Carreras, M. R., & Munoz, J. M. (1997). Development of sex difference in preschool children: Social behavior during an academic year. *Psychological Reports, 80,* 179–188.

Brazelton, T. B. (1991). *Touchpoints: Your child's emotional and behavioral development.* Reading, MA: Addison-Wesley.

Brazelton, T. B., Nugent, K. J., & Lester, B. M. (1987). Neonatal behavioral assessment scale. In J. D. Osofsky (Ed.), *Handbook of infant development* (pp. 780–817). New York: Wiley.

Breakey, J. (1997). The role of diet and behavior in childhood. *Journal of Pediatric Child Health, 33,* 190–194.

Brederode, M. E. (1990). Research on Rua Sesamo, the Portuguese coproduction. In Children's Television Workshop (Ed.), *Sesame Street Research* (pp. 63–67). New York: Children's Television Workshop.

Bremer, J., & Rauch, P. K. (1998). Children and computers: Risks and benefits. *Journal of the American Academy of Child and Adolescent Psychiatry, 37,* 559–560.

Brendgen, M., Bowen, F., Rondeau, N., & Vitaro, F. (1999). Effect of friends' characteristics on children's social cognitions. *Social Development, 8,* 41–51.

Brendgen, M., Markiewicz, D., Doyle, A. B., & Bukowski, W. M. (2001). The relations between friendship quality, ranked-friendship preference, and adolescents' behavior with their friends. *Merrill-Palmer Quarterly, 47,* 395–415.

Brenner, R. A., Overpeck, M. D., Trumble, A. C., DerSimonian, R., & Berendes, H. (2001). Deaths attributable to injuries in infants, United States, 1983–1991. *Pediatrics, 103,* 968–974.

Brenner, V., & Fox, R. A. (1998). Parental discipline and behavior problems in young children. *Journal of Genetic Psychology, 159,* 251–256.

Brent, D., May, D.C., & Kundert, D. K. (1996). The incidence of delayed school entry. *Early Education & Development, 7,* 121–135.

Brewerton, T. D. (2002). Bulimia in children and adolescents. *Child and Adolescent Psychiatric Clinics of North America, 11,* 237–256.

Bridges, A. (1986). Actions and things: What adults talk about to 1-year-olds. In S. Kuczaj & M. Barrett (Eds.), *The development of word meaning* (pp. 225–255). New York: Springer.

Bridges, K. (1932). Emotional development in early infancy. *Child Development, 3,* 324–341.

Bridges, L. J., Connell, J. P., & Belsky, J. (1988). Similarities and differences in mother–infant and father–infant interaction in the strange situation. *Developmental Psychology, 24,* 92–100.

Bril, B., & Sabatier, C. (1986). The cultural context of motor development: Postural manipulations in the daily life of Bambara babies (Mali). *International Journal of Behavioral Development, 9,* 439–453.

Brisk, M. E. (1998). *Bilingual education.* Mahwah, NJ: Erlbaum.

Britner, P., & Reppucci, N. D. (1997). Prevention of child maltreatment: Evaluation of a parent education program for teen mothers. *Journal of Child and Family Studies, 6,* 165–175.

Brodsky, A. E., & DeVet, K. A. (2000). "You have to be real strong": Parenting goals and strategies of resilient, urban, African American, single mothers. *Journal of Prevention and Intervention in the Community, 20,* 159–178.

Brody, G. H. (2004). Siblings' direct and indirect contributions to child development. *Current Directions in Psychological Science, 13,* 124–126.

Brody, G. H., Stoneman, Z., MacKinnon, C. E., & MacKinnon, R. (1985). Role relationships and behavior between preschool-aged and school-aged sibling pairs. *Developmental Psychology, 21,* 124–129.

Brody, G. H., Stoneman, Z., & McCoy, J. K. (1992). Associations of maternal and paternal direct and differential behavior with sibling relationships: Contemporaneous and longitudinal analyses. *Child Development, 63,* 82–92.

Brodzinsky, D. M., Lang, R., & Smith, D. W. (1995). Parenting adopted children: Fathers and families. In M. H. Bornstein (Ed.), *Handbook of parenting* (Vol. 3, pp. 233–254). Mahwah, NJ: Erlbaum.

Bronfenbrenner, U. (1979). *The ecology of human development: Experiments by nature and design.* Cambridge, MA: Harvard University Press.

Bronfenbrenner, U. (1986). Ecology of the family as a context for human development: Research perspectives. *Developmental Psychology, 22,* 723–742.

Bronfenbrenner, U., & Ceci, S. J. (1994). Nature–nurture reconceptualized in developmental perspective: A bioecological model. *Psychological Review, 101,* 568–586.

Bronfenbrenner, U., & Evans, G. W. (2000). Developmental science in the 21st century: Emerging questions, theoretical models, research designs, and empirical findings. *Social Development, 9,* 115–125.

Bronfenbrenner, U., & Morris, P. A. (1998). The ecology of developmental processes. In W. Damon (Ed.), *Handbook of child psychology* (Vol. 1, pp. 993–1029). New York: Wiley.

Bronstein, P., Duncan, P., D'Air, A., Pieniadz, J., Fitzgerald, M., Abrams, C. L., Frankowski, B., Franco, O., Hunt, C., & Oh-Cha, S. Y. (1996). Family and parenting behaviors predicting middle school adjustment: A longitudinal study. *Family Relations, 45,* 415–426.

Brook, J. S., Brook, D. W., & Whiteman, M. (2000). The influence of maternal smoking during pregnancy on the toddler's negativity. *Archives of Pediatric and Adolescent Medicine, 154,* 381–385.

Brooks-Gunn, J. (1988). Antecedents and consequences of variations in girls' maturational timing. *Journal of Adolescent Health Care, 9,* 365–373.

Brooks-Gunn, J. (1995). Children in families in communities: Risk and intervention in the Bronfenbrenner tradition. In P. Moen, G. H. Elder, & K. Luscher (Eds.), *Examining lives in context: Perspectives on the ecology of human development* (pp. 467–519). Washington, DC: American Psychological Association.

Brooks-Gunn, J., & Paikoff, R. (1997). Sexuality and developmental transitions during adolescence. In J. Schulenberg & J. Maggs (Eds.),

Health risks and developmental transitions during adolescence (pp. 190–219). New York: Cambridge University Press.

Brooks-Gunn, J., & Ruble, D. (1982). The development of menstrual-related beliefs and behaviors during early adolescence. *Child Development, 53,* 1567–1577.

Brooks-Gunn, J., Klebanov, P. K., & Duncan, G. J. (1996). Ethnic differences in children's intelligence test scores. Role of economic deprivation, home environment, and maternal characteristics. *Child Development, 67,* 396–408.

Brooks-Gunn, J., & Warren, M. P. (1989). Biological and social contributions to negative affect in young adolescent girls. *Child Development, 60,* 40–55.

Brown, A. L., & Kane, M. J. (1988). Preschool children can learn to transfer: Learning to learn and learning by example. *Cognitive Psychology, 20,* 493–523.

Brown, A. L., Kane, M. J., & Long, C. (1989). Analogical transfer in young children: Analogies as tools for communication and exposition. *Applied Cognitive Psychology, 3,* 275–293.

Brown, B. B., & Klute, C. (2003). Friendships, cliques, and crowds. In M. D. Berzonsky & G. R. Adams (Eds.), *Blackwell handbook of adolescence* (pp. 330–348). Malden, MA: Blackwell.

Brown, B. B., & Larson, R. W. (2002). The kaleidoscope of adolescence: Experiences of the world's youth at the beginning of the 21st century. In R. W. Larson & B. B. Brown (Eds.), *The world's youth* (pp. 1–20). New York: Cambridge University Press.

Brown, B. B., & Lohr, M. J. (1987). Peer-group affiliation and adolescent self-esteem: An integration of ego-identity and symbolic-interaction theories. *Journal of Personality and Social Psychology, 52,* 47–55.

Brown, B. B., Mory, M. S., & Kinney, D. (1994). Casting adolescent crowds in a relational perspective. In R. Montemayor & G. R. Adams (Eds.), *Personal relationships during adolescence* (pp. 123–167). Thousand Oaks, CA: Sage.

Brown, J. R., & Dunn, J. (1992). Talk with your mother or your sibling? Developmental changes in early family conversations about feelings. *Child Development, 63,* 336–349.

Brown, J. V., Bakeman, R., Coles, C. D., Platzman, K. A., & Lynch, M. E. (2004). Prenatal cocaine exposure: A comparison of 2-year-old children in parental and nonparental care. *Child Development, 74,* 1282–1295.

Brown, J., & Pollitt, E., (1996). Malnutrition, poverty and intellectual development. *Scientific American, 274,* 38–43.

Brown, K. H., Robertson, A. D., & Akhtar, N. A. (1986). Lactational capacity of marginally nourished mothers: Infants' milk nutrient consumption and patterns of growth. *Pediatrics, 78,* 920–927.

Browne, J. V. (2000). Developmental care—considerations for touch and massage in the neonatal intensive care unit. *Neonatal Network, 19,* 1–10.

Bruck, M., (1992). Persistence of dyslexics' phonological deficits. *Developmental Psychology, 28,* 874–886.

Bruner, J. S. (1983). *Child's talk: Learning to use language.* New York: Norton.

Bryan, J. H., & Walbek, N. H. (1970). The impact of words and deeds concerning altruism upon children. *Child Development, 41,* 747–757.

Bryant, B. K. (1982). Sibling relationships in middle childhood. In M. E. Lamb & B. Sutton-Smith (Eds.), *Sibling relationships* (pp. 87–122). Hillsdale, NJ: Erlbaum.

Bryant, B. K. (1985). The neighborhood walk. *Monographs of the Society for Research in Child Development, 3* (Whole No. 210). Chicago: Society for Research in Child Development.

Bryant, B. K. (1998). Children's coping at school. In L. H. Meyer & H. Park (Eds.), *Making friends: The influence of culture and development* (Vol. 3, pp. 353–367). Baltimore, MD: Brookes Publishing.

Bryk, A. S., Lee, V. E., & Smith, J. B. (1990). High school organization and its effects on teachers and students: An interpretive summary of the

research. In J. Witte & W. Clure (Eds.), *Choice and control in American education* (pp. 135–226). London: Falmer Press.

Buchanan, A., & Hudson, B. (2000). *Promoting children's emotional well-being.* New York: Oxford University Press.

Buchanan, C. M., Maccoby, E. E., & Dornbusch, S. M. (1996). *Adolescents after divorce.* Cambridge, MA: Harvard University Press.

Buchanan-Barrow, B., & Barrett, M. (1998). Individual differences in children's understanding of the school. *Social Development, 7,* 250–268.

Bugental, D. B., & Goodnow, J. J. (1998). Socialization processes. In W. Damon (Ed.), *Handbook of child psychology* (Vol. 3, pp. 389–462). New York: Wiley.

Buhrmester, D. (1992). The developmental courses of sibling and peer relationships. In F. Boer & J. Dunn (Eds.), *Children's sibling relationships* (pp. 19–40). Hillsdale, NJ: Erlbaum.

Buhrmester, D., Goldfarb, J., & Cantrell, D. (1992). Self-presentation when sharing with friends and nonfriends. *Journal of Early Adolescence, 12,* 61–79.

Buhrmester, D., Whalen, C. K., Henker, B., MacDonald, V., & Hinshaw, S. P. (1992). Prosocial behavior in hyperactive boys: Effects of stimulant medication and comparison with normal boys. *Journal of Abnormal Child Psychology, 20,* 103–121.

Buis, J. M., & Thompson, D. N. (1989). Imaginary audience and personal fable: A brief review. *Adolescence, 24,* 773–781.

Bukowski, W. M., Gauze, C., Horz, B., & Newcomb, A. F. (1993). Differences and consistency between same-sex and other-sex peer relationships during early adolescence. *Developmental Psychology, 29,* 255–263.

Bullock, M. (1984). Preschool children's understanding of causal connections. *British Journal of Developmental Psychology, 2,* 139–142.

Bullock, M., & Gelman, R. (1979). Preschool children's assumptions about cause and effect: Temporal ordering. *Child Development, 50,* 89–96.

Bullock, M., Gelman, R., & Baillargeon, R. (1982). The development of causal reasoning. In W. F. Friedman (Ed.), *The developmental psychology of time* (pp. 209–253). New York: Academic Press.

Burack, J. A., Hodapp, R. M., & Zigler, E. (1998). *Handbook of mental retardation and development.* New York: Cambridge University Press.

Burchinal M., Lee, M., & Ramey, C. (1989). Type of day-care and preschool intellectual development in disadvantaged children. *Child Development, 60,* 128–137.

Burchinal, M. R., & Caskie, G. I. L. (2001). Maternal employment, child care, and cognitive outcomes. In E. L. Grigorenko & R. J. Sternberg (Eds.), *Family environment and intellectual functioning* (pp. 119–139). Mahwah, NJ: Erlbaum.

Burd, B. (1986). Infant swimming classes: Immersed in controversy. *The Physician and Sports Medicine, 14*(3), 239–244.

Burnett, J. W., Anderson, W. P., & Heppner, P. P. (1995). Gender roles and self-esteem: A consideration of environmental factors. *Journal of Counseling and Development, 73,* 323–326.

Burnham, M. M., Goodlin-Jones, B. L., Gaylor, E. E., & Anders, T. F. (2002). Use of sleep aids during the first year of life. *Pediatrics, 109,* 594–601.

Burt, M. R., Resnick, G., & Novick, E. R. (1998). *Building supportive communities for at-risk adolescents.* Washington, DC: American Psychological Association.

Buss, D. (1998). *Evolutionary psychology.* Boston: Allyn & Bacon.

Buss, K., & Goldsmith, H. H. (1998). Fear and anger regulation in infancy: Effects on the temporary dynamics of affective expression. *Child Development, 69,* 359–374.

Bussey, K. (1992). Lying and truthfulness: Children's definitions, standards, and evaluative reactions. *Child Development, 63,* 129–137.

Bussey, K., & Bandura, A. (1984). Influence of gender constancy and social power on sex-linked modeling. *Journal of Personality and Social Psychology, 47,* 1292–1302.

Bussey, K., & Bandura, A. (1992). Self-regulatory mechanisms governing gender development. *Child Development, 63,* 1236–1250.

Bussey, K., & Bandura, A. (1999). Social cognitive theory of gender development and differentiation. *Psychological Review, 106,* 676–713.

Bussey, K., & Perry, D. G. (1982). Same-sex imitation: The avoidance of cross-sex models or the acceptance of same-sex models? *Sex Roles, 8,* 773–785.

Butler, J., & Rovee-Collier, C. (1989). Contextual gating of memory retrieval. *Developmental Psychobiology, 22,* 533–552.

Byers, J. (1989). AIDS in children. Effects of neurological development and implications for the future. *Journal of Special Education, 23,* 5–16.

Byrne, B., & Fielding-Barnsley, R. (1995). Evaluation of a program to teach phonemic awareness to young children: A 2- and 3-year follow-up and a new preschool trial. *Journal of Educational Psychology, 87,* 488–503.

Byrne, D. (1983). Sex without contraception. In D. Byrne & W. A. Fisher (Eds.), *Adolescents, sex, and contraception* (pp. 3–31). Hillsdale, NJ: Erlbaum.

Byrnes, J. P. (1988). Formal operations: A systematic reformulation. *Developmental Review, 8,* 66–87.

Byrnes, J. P., & Fox, N. A. (1998). The educational relevance of research in cognitive neuroscience. *Educational Psychology Review, 10,* 297–342.

Cairns, R. B. (1998). The making of developmental psychology. In W. Damon (Ed.), *Handbook of child psychology* (Vol. 1, pp. 25–107). New York: Wiley.

Caissy, G. A. (1994). *Early adolescence.* New York: Insight Books.

Callanan, M. A. (1989). Development of object categories and inclusion relations: Preschoolers' hypotheses about word meanings. *Developmental Psychology, 25,* 207–216.

Camarota, S. (2001). *The impact of immigration on US population growth.* Washington, DC: US House of Representatives Subcommittee on Immigration, Border Security, and Claims.

Campbell, L. (2004). As strong as the weakest link: Urban high school dropout. *The High School Journal, 87,* 16–24.

Campos, F. (1996). *Latino, Hispanic, both, neither?* Austin: University of Texas Press.

Campos, J. J., Kermoian, R., & Zumbahlen, M. R. (1992). Socioemotional transformations in the family system following infant crawling onset. In N. Eisenberg & R. A. Fabes (Eds.), *Emotion and its regulation in early development* (pp. 25–40). San Francisco: Jossey-Bass.

Campos, M. M. (1992). Child care in Brazil. In M. E. Lamb, K. J. Sternberg, C. Hwang, & A. G. Broberg (Eds.), *Child care in context* (pp. 479–508). Hillsdale, NJ: Erlbaum.

Cangelosi, A., & Parisi, D. (2001). Computer simulation: A new scientific approach to the study of language evolution. In A. Cangelosi & D. Parisi (Eds.), *Simulating the evolution of language* (pp. 3–28). London: Sprinler.

Capaldi, D., DeGarmo, D., Patterson, G. R., & Forgatch, M. (2002). Contextual risk across the early life span and association with antisocial behavior. In G. R. Patterson & J. B. Reid (Eds.), *Antisocial behavior in children and adolescents: A developmental analysis and model for intervention* (pp. 123–145). Washington, DC: American Psychological Association.

Capon, N., & Kuhn, D. (1979). Logical reasoning in the supermarket: Adult females' use of proportional reasoning strategy in an everyday context. *Developmental Psychology, 15,* 450–452.

Caputo, R. K. (2003). Head Start, other preschool programs, and life success in a youth cohort. *Journal of Sociology and Social Welfare, 30,* 105–126.

Carey, W., & Jablow, M. M. (1999). *Understanding your child's temperament.* New York: Hungry Minds.

Carlo, G., Fabes, R. A., Laible, D., & Kupanoff, K. (1999). Early adolescence and prosocial/moral behavior II: The role of social and contextual influences. *Journal of Early Adolescence, 19,* 133–147.

Carlson, E. A., Jacobvitz, D., & Sroufe, L. A. (1995). A developmental investigation of inattentiveness and hyperactivity. *Child Development, 66,* 37–54.

Carlson, E. A., Sampson, M., & Sroufe, L. A. (2003). Implications of attachment theory and research for developmental–behavioral pediatrics. *Journal of Developmental and Behavioral Pediatrics, 24,* 364–379.

Carlton, M. P., & Winsler, A. (1999). School readiness: The need for a paradigm shift. *School Psychology Review, 28,* 338–352.

Carskadon, M. A. (1990). Patterns of sleep and sleepiness in adolescents. *Pediatrician, 17,* 5–12.

Carskadon, M. A. (1999). When worlds collide: Adolescent need for sleep versus societal demands. *Phi Delta Kappan, 80,* 348–353.

Carskadon, M. A. (Ed.). (2002). *Adolescent sleep patterns.* New York: Cambridge University Press.

Carson, D. K., & Bittner, M. T. (1994). Temperament and school-aged children's coping abilities and responses to stress. *Journal of Genetic Psychology, 155,* 289–302.

Carter, C., & Rice, C. L. (1997). Acquisition and manifestation of prejudice in children. *Journal of Multicultural Counseling and Development, 25,* 185–194.

Carter, D. B., & Middlemiss, W. A. (1992). The socialization of instrumental competence in families in the United States. In J. L. Roopnarine & D. B. Carter (Eds.), *Parent–child socialization in diverse cultures* (pp. 107–120). Norwood, NJ: Ablex.

Carter, M. C., Perzanowski, M. S., Raymond, A., & Platts-Mills, T. A. (2001). Home intervention in the treatment of asthma among inner-city children. *Journal of Allergy and Clinical Immunology, 108,* 732–737.

Cartwright, T., & Brent, M. R. (1997). Syntactic categorization in early language acquisition: Formalizing the role of distributional analysis. *Cognition, 63,* 121–170.

Case, R. (1992). Neo-Piagetian theories of child development. In R. Sternberg & C. Berg (Eds.), *Intellectual development* (pp. 161–196). New York: Cambridge University Press.

Case, R. (1998). The development of conceptual structures. In W. Damon (Ed.), *Handbook of child psychology* (Vol. 2, pp. 851–898). New York: Wiley.

Case, R., & Edelstein, W. (1993). *The new structuralism in cognitive development.* Basel, Switzerland: S. Karger, AG.

Case, R., & Okamoto, Y. (1996). Modeling the process of conceptual change in a continuously evolving hierarchical system. *Monographs of the Society for Research in Child Development, 61,* 283–295.

Casey, B. J., Giedd, J. N., & Thomas, K. M. (2000). Structural and functional brain development and its relation to cognitive development. *Biological Psychology, 54,* 241–257.

Casey, P. H. (1992). Failure to thrive. In M. D. Levine, W. B. Carey, & A. C. Crocker (Eds.), *Developmental-behavioral pediatrics* (pp. 375–383). Philadelphia: Saunders.

Casper, L. M., Hawkins, M., & O'Connell, M. (1994). *Who's minding the kids?* Washington, DC: US Census.

Caspi, A., Henry, B., McGee, R. O., Moffitt, T. E., & Silva, P. A. (1995). Temperamental origins of child and adolescent behavior problems: From age three to age fifteen. *Child Development, 66,* 55–68.

Caspi, A., Moffitt, T. E., Morgan, J., Rutter, M., Taylor, A., Arseneault, L., Tully, L., Jacobs, C., Kim-Cohen, J., & Polo-Tomas, M. (2004). Maternal expressed emotion predicts children's antisocial behavior problems. *Developmental Psychology, 40,* 149–161.

Caspi, A., & Silva, P. A. (1995). Temperamental qualities at age three predict personality traits in young adulthood: Longitudinal evidence from a birth cohort. *Child Development, 66,* 486–498.

Castellanos, F. X. (1997). Neuroimaging of attention-deficit hyperactivity disorder. *Child and Adolescent Psychiatric Clinics of North America, 6,* 383–411.

Cauffman, E., & Steinberg, L. (1996). Interactive effects of menarcheal status and dating on dieting and disordered eating among adolescent girls. *Developmental Psychology, 32,* 631–635.

Ceci, S. J., & Bruck, M. (1995). *Jeopardy in the courtroom.* Washington, DC: American Psychological Association.

Ceci, S. J., & Bruck, M. (1998). Children's testimony: Applied and basic issues. In W. Damon (Ed.), *Handbook of child psychology* (Vol. 4, pp. 713–774). New York: Wiley.

Center for Applied Research and Educational Improvement. (1997). *School start time study.* Minneapolis: University of Minnesota Press.

Center for Media Literacy. (1995). *Seven tips for TV viewing in the home.* Los Angeles: Author.

Center for the Evaluation of Risks to Human Reproduction (1999b, March 19). *Thalidomide.* Washington, DC: Author.

Center for the Evaluation of Risks to Human Reproduction. (1999a, March 19). *Folic acid.* Washington, DC: Author.

Centers for Disease Control. (1996). *HIV/AIDS Surveillance Report* (Vol. 8). Atlanta, GA: Author.

Centers for Disease Control. (1998). *Youth risk behavior surveillance—United States, 1997.* Washington, DC: Author.

Centers for Disease Control. (1999). *Immunization and infectious disease.* Washington, DC: Author.

Centers for Disease Control. (2000a). *Adolescent and school health.* Washington, DC: Author.

Centers for Disease Control. (2000b). *Gun deaths among children and teens drop sharply.* Author.

Centers for Disease Control. (2001a). *Births, marriages, divorces, and deaths for 1999–2001.* Washington, DC: Author.

Centers for Disease Control. (2001b). *HIV/AIDS Surveillance Report.* Washington, DC: Author.

Centers for Disease Control. (2001c). *Motor vehicle-related crashes among teenagers.* Washington, DC: Author.

Centers for Disease Control. (2001d). *Prevalence of overweight among children and adolescents: US, 1999.* Washington, DC: Author.

Centers for Disease Control. (2002a). *Injury fact book 2001–2002: Bicycle-related injuries.* Retrieved from http://www.cdc.gov/ncipc/fact_book/11_Bicycle_Related_Injuries.htm

Centers for Disease Control. (2003). *Assisted reproductive technology success rates: National summary and fertility clinic reports.* Washington, DC: US Department of Health and Human Services.

Centers for Disease Control. (2003). *Basic facts about asthma.* Washington, DC: Author.

Centers for Disease Control. (2003). *HIV/AIDS surveillance report.* Washington, DC: Author.

Centers for Disease Control. (2003a). *AIDS cases, deaths, and persons living with AIDS by years, 1985–2002—United States.* Retrieved from http://www.cdc.gov/hiv/stats/hasr1402/ cover.htm

Centers for Disease Control. (2003b). Physical activity levels among children aged 9–13 years—United States, 2002. *Morbidity and Mortality Weekly Report, 52*(33), 785–788.

Centers for Disease Control. (2004). *Vaccines: A safe choice.* Retrieved from http://www.cdc.gov/ nip/vacsafe/vacsafe-parents.htm

Centers for Disease Control. (2004). *Youth risk behavior surveillance.* Washington, DC: Author.

Centers for Disease Control. (2004a). *Asthma's impact on children and adolescents.* Retrieved from http://www.cdc.gov/asthma/children.htm

Centers for Disease Control. (2004a). *Children's blood levels in the United States.* Washington, DC: Author.

Centers for Disease Control. (2004a). *Deaths, 2002.* Washington, DC: Author.

Centers for Disease Control. (2004b). *Child passenger safety.* Retrieved from http://www.cdc.gov/ncipic/fact_book/13_Child_Passenger_Safety.htm

Centers for Disease Control. (2004b). *Health, 2003.* Washington, DC: Author.

Centers for Disease Control. (2004b). *Vaccines: A safe choice.* Washington, DC: Author.

Centers for Disease Control. (2004c). *Addressing asthma in schools.* Washington, DC: Author.

Centers for Disease Control. (2004c). *Measles outbreak in a boarding school—Pennsylvania, 2003.* Retrieved from http://www.cdc.gov/mmwr/preview/mmwrhtml/mm5314a3.htm

Centers for Disease Control. (2004c). *Youth risk behavior surveillance, 2003.* Washington, DC: Author.

Centers for Disease Control. (2004f). *Vision impairment.* Retrieved from http://www.cdc.gov/ ncbddd/dd/ddvi.htm.

Cernoch, J. M., & Porter, R. H. (1985). Recognition of maternal axillary odors by infants. *Child Development, 56,* 1593–1598.

Chabrol, H., Teissedre, F., Saint-Jean, M., Teisseyre, N., Roge, B., & Mullet, E. (2002). Prevention and treatment of post-partum depression: A controlled randomized study on women at risk. *Psychological Medicine, 32,* 1039–1047.

Chall, J. S., Jacobs, V. A., & Baldwin, L. E. (1990). *The reading crisis.* Cambridge, MA: Harvard University Press.

Chambers, R. A., & Potenza, M. N. (2003). Neurodevelopment, impulsivity, and adolescent gambling. *Journal of Gambling Studies, 19,* 53–84.

Chambers, R. A., Taylor, J. R., & Potenza, M. N. (2003). Developmental neurocircuitry of motivation in adolescence: A critical period of addiction vulnerability. *American Journal of Psychiatry, 160,* 1041–1052.

Chan, R. W., Raboy, B., & Patterson, C. J. (1998). Psychosocial adjustment among children conceived via insemination by lesbian and heterosexual mothers. *Child Development, 69,* 443–457.

Chandler, M., Fritz, A. S., & Hala, S. (1989). Small-scale deceit: Deception as a marker of two-, three-, and four-year-olds' early theories of mind. *Child Development, 60,* 1263–1277.

Chang, A. (2004, February 26). Schools across the US target vending machines in obesity controversy. Little Marais, MN: Organic Consumers Association.

Chapin, J. R. (2000). Adolescent sex and mass media: A developmental approach. *Adolescence, 35,* 799–811.

Charlesworth, R. (1989). "Behind" before they start? *Young Children, 44,* 5–13.

Chase, W. G., & Simon, H. A. (1973). Perception in chess. *Cognitive Psychology, 4,* 55–81.

Chase-Linsdale, P. L., Gordon, R. A., Coley, R. L., Wakschlag, L. S., & Brooks-Gunn, J. (1999). Young African American multigenerational families in poverty: The contexts, exchanges, and processes of their lives. In E. M. Hetherington (Ed.), *Coping with divorce, single parenting, and remarriage: A risk and resiliency perspective* (pp. 165–191). Mahwah, NJ: Erlbaum.

Chase-Linsdale, P. L., & Hetherington, E. M. (1990). The impact of divorce on life-span development: Short- and long-term effects. In D. L. Featherman & R. M. Lerner (Eds.), *Life span development and behavior* (Vol. 10, pp. 105–151). Hillsdale, NJ: Erlbaum.

Chatkupt, S., Lucek, P. R., Koenigsberger, M. R., & Johnson, W. G. (1992). Parental sex effect in spina bifida: A role for genomic imprinting? *American Journal of Medical Genetics, 144,* 508–512.

Chavkin, W. (2001). Cocaine and pregnancy. *Journal of the American Medical Association, 285,* 1626–1268.

Chen, C., & Stevenson, H. W. (1995). Culture and academic achievement. In M. L. Maher & P. R. Pintrich (Eds.), *Advances in motivation and achievement* (Vol. 9, pp. 119–151). Greenwich, CT: JAI Press.

Chen, J., & Kennedy, C. (2001). Television viewing and children's health. *Journal of the Society of Pediatric Nurses, 1,* 35–38.

Chen, Z. Y., & Dornbusch, S. M. (1998). Relating aspects of adolescent emotional autonomy to academic achievement and deviant behavior. *Journal of Adolescent Research, 13,* 293–319.

Chen, Z., & Siegler, R. S. (2000). Intellectual development in childhood. In R. J. Sternberg (Ed.), *Handbook of intelligence* (pp. 92–116). Cambridge, UK: Cambridge University Press.

Chess, S., & Thomas, A. (1999). *Goodness of fit: Clinical applications from infancy through adult life.* Philadelphia: Brunner/Mazel.

Chesson, H. W., Blandford, J. M., Gift, T. L., Tao, G., & Irwin, K. L. (2004). The estimated direct medical cost of sexually transmitted diseases among American youth. *Perspectives on Sexual and Reproductive Health, 36,* 11–19.

Chi, M. T. H. (1978). Knowledge structures and memory development. In R. S. Siegler (Ed.), *Children's thinking: What develops?* (pp. 73–96) Hillsdale, NJ: Erlbaum.

Chi, M. T. H., & Koeske, R. D. (1983). Network representation of a child's dinosaur knowledge. *Developmental Psychology, 19,* 29–39.

Child Trends. (2001). *School readiness: Helping communities get children ready for schools and schools ready for children.* Washington, DC: Author.

Children Now. (2000). *Girls and gaming.* Oakland, CA: Author.

Children's Defense Fund. (1992). *The state of America's children.* Washington, DC: Children's Defense Fund.

Children's Television Workshop. (1991). *What research indicates about the educational effects of Sesame Street.* New York: Author.

Chilman, C. S. (1993). Hispanic families in the United States. In H. P. McAdoo (Ed.), *Family ethnicity* (pp. 141–163). Newbury Park, CA: Sage.

Chisholm, J. S. (1983). *Navaho infancy: An ethological study of child development.* New York: Aldine.

Chisholm, J. S. (1989). Biology, culture, and the development of temperament: A Navajo example. In J. K. Nugent, B. M. Lester, & T. B. Brazelton (Eds.), *The cultural context of the infant* (Vol. 1, pp. 341–366). Norwood, NJ: Ablex.

Choi, P. Y., Pope, H. G., & Olivardia, R. (2002). Muscle dysmorphia: A new syndrome in weightlifters. *British Journal of Sports Medicine, 36,* 375–376.

Choi, S., & Gopnik, A. (1995). Early acquisition of verbs in Korean: A cross-linguistic study. *Journal of Child Language, 22,* 497–529.

Chomsky, N. (1965). *Aspects of the theory of syntax.* Cambridge, MA: MIT Press.

Chomsky, N. (1986). *Knowledge of language: Its nature, origin, and use.* New York: Praeger.

Christenson, P. G., & Roberts, D. F. (1998). *It's not only rock & roll: Popular music in the lives of adolescents.* Cresskill, NJ: Hampton Press.

Christofori, G., Naik, P., & Hanahan, D. (1995). Deregulation of both imprinted and expressed alleles of the insulin-like growth factor 2 during beta-cell tumorigenesis. *Nature Genetics, 10,* 196–201.

Christopher, F. S. (2001). *To dance the dance: A symbolic interactional exploration of premarital sexuality.* Mahwah, NJ: Erlbaum.

Chung, A. M., de Kanter, A. A., & Stonehill, R. M. (2002). Ensuring quality and sustainability in after-school programs. In B. M. Miller & G. G. Noam (Eds.), *Youth development and after-school time: A tale of many cities* (pp. 133–139). San Francisco: Jossey-Bass.

Cicchetti, D., Rogosch, F. A., & Toth, S. L. (1998). Maternal depressive disorder and contextual risk: Contributions to the development of attachment insecurity and behavior problems in toddlerhood. *Development and Psychopathology, 10,* 283–300.

Clark, E. V. (1981). Lexical innovations: How children learn to create new words. In W. Deutsch (Ed.), *The child's construction of language* (pp. 299–328). London: Academic Press.

Clark, E. V. (1993). *The lexicon in acquisition.* Cambridge, UK: Cambridge University Press.

Clark, E. V. (1997). Conceptual perspective and lexical choice in acquisition. *Cognition, 64,* 1–37.

Clark, G. (1994). *Onions are my husband: Survival and accumulation by West African market women.* Chicago: University of Chicago Press.

Clark, M. L., & Ayers, M. (1993). Friendship expectations and friendship evaluations. *Youth and Society, 24,* 299–313.

Clarke-Stewart, K. A. (1984). Day care: A new context for research and development. In M. Perlmutter (Ed.), *Parent–child interactions and parent–child relations in children's development* (Vol. 17, pp. 61–100). Hillsdale, NJ: Erlbaum.

Clarke-Stewart, K. A. (1989). Infant day care: Maligned or malignant? *American Psychologist, 44,* 266–273.

Clarke-Stewart, K. A. (1992). Consequences of child care for children's development. In A. Booth (Ed.), *Child care in the 1990s: Trends and consequences* (pp. 63–82). Hillsdale, NJ: Erlbaum.

Clarke-Stewart, K. A., Allhusen, V. D., & Clements, D.C. (1995). Nonparental caregiving. Fathers and families. In M. H. Bornstein (Ed.), *Handbook of parenting* (Vol. 3, pp. 151–176). Mahwah, NJ: Erlbaum.

Claxton, L. J., Keen, R., & McCarty, M. E. (2003). Evidence of motor planning in infant reaching behavior. *Psychological Science, 14,* 354–356.

Clinton, J. F. (1986). Expectant fathers at risk for couvade. *Nursing Research, 35,* 290–295.

Clubb, R. (1991). Chronic sorrow: Adaptation of parents with chronically ill children. *Pediatric Nursing, 17,* 461–466.

Cnattingius, S. (1994). The epidemiology of smoking during pregnancy: Smoking prevalence, maternal characteristics, and pregnancy outcomes. *Nicotine and Tobacco Research, 2,* 215–240.

Cnattingius, S., Bergstrom, R., Lipworth, L., & Kramer, M. S. (1998). Prepregnancy weight and the risk of adverse pregnancy outcomes. *New England Journal of Medicine, 388,* 147–152.

CNN. (2002). *What are kids saying about violence?* Retrieved July 30, 2002, from http://www.cnn.com/2002/HEALTH/parenting/07/30/young.bullies

Cohane, G. H., & Pope, H. G. (2001). Body image in boys: A review of the literature. *International Journal of Eating Disorders, 29,* 373–379.

Cohen, L. B. (2003). Commentary on part I: Unresolved issues in infant categorization. In D. H. Rakison & L. M. Oakes (Eds.), *Early category and concept development: Making sense of the blooming, buzzing confusion* (pp. 193–209). New York: Oxford University Press.

Cohen, L. M. (1996). Meeting the needs of gifted and talented minority language students. *ERIC Digest* (No. E480).

Cohen, M. A. (1998). The monetary value of saving a high-risk youth. *Journal of Quantitative Criminology, 14,* 5–53.

Cohen, Y., Spirito, A., & Brown, L. K. (1996). Suicide and suicidal behavior. In R. DiClemente & W. B. Hansen (Eds.), *Handbook of adolescent health risk behavior* (pp. 193–224). New York: Plenum.

Cohn, D. A., Lohrmann, B. C., & Patterson, C. (1985, April). *Loneliness and peer relations in young children.* Paper presented at the biennial meeting of the Society for Research in Child Development, Kansas City, MO.

Coie, J. D., & Dodge, K. A. (1998). Aggression and antisocial behavior. In W. Damon (Ed.), *Handbook of child psychology* (Vol. 3, 778–862). New York: Wiley.

Coie, J. D., & Koeppl, G. K. (1990). Adapting intervention to the problems of aggressive and disruptive rejected children. In S. R. Asher & J. D. Coie (Eds.), *Peer rejection in childhood* (pp. 309–337). Cambridge, UK: Cambridge University Press.

Colby, A., Kohlberg, L., Gibbs, J., & Lieberman, M. (1983). A longitudinal study of moral judgment. *Monographs of the Society for Research in Child Development, 48* (Whole No. 200).

Cole, E. B. (1992). *Learning and talking: A guide to promoting spoken language in hearing-impaired children.* Washington, DC: Alexander Graham Bell Association for the Deaf.

Cole, M. (1997). Cultural mechanisms of cognitive development. In E. Amsel & K. A. Renninger (Eds.), *Change and development* (pp. 245–263). Hillsdale, NJ: Erlbaum.

Coleman, M., Ganong, L., & Fine, M. (2000). Reinvestigating remarriage: Another decade of progress. *Journal of Marriage and the Family, 62,* 1288–1307.

Coles, C. (1994). Critical periods for prenatal alcohol exposure. *Alcohol Health and Research World, 18,* 22–29.

Coles, R. (1990). *The spiritual life of children.* Boston: Houghton Mifflin.

Coles, R., & Stokes, G. (1985). *Sex and the American teenager.* New York: Harper & Row.

Coley, R. L., & Chase-Linsdale, P. L. (1998). Adolescent pregnancy and parenthood. *American Psychologist, 53,* 152–166.

Colin, V. L. (1996). *Human attachment.* New York: McGraw-Hill.

Collaer, M. L., & Hines, M. (1995). Human behavioral sex differences: A role for gonadal hormone during early development? *Psychological Bulletin, 118*(1), 55–107.

Collier, J., Jr. (1988). Survival at Rough Rock: A historical overview of Rough Rock demonstration school. *Anthropology and Education Quarterly, 19,* 253–269.

Collins, W. A. (1990). Parent–child relationships in the transition to adolescence. In R. Montemayor, G. R. Adams, & T. Gullotta (Eds.), *From childhood to adolescence* (Vol. 2, pp. 85–106). Newbury Park, CA: Sage.

Collins, W. A., Maccoby, E. E., Steinberg, L., Hetherington, E. M., & Bornstein, M. H. (2000). Contemporary research on parenting: The case for nature and nurture. *American Psychologist, 55,* 218–232.

Coltrane, S. (1995). *Family man.* New York: Oxford University Press.

Colwell, M. J., & Lindsey, E. W. (2003). Teacher–child interactions and preschool children's perceptions of self and peers. *Early Child Development and Care, 173,* 249–258.

Committee on Pediatric AIDS. (1998). Surveillance of pediatric HIV infection. *Pediatrics, 101,* 315–319.

Compas, B. E., Connor-Smith, J. K., Saltzman, H., Thomsen, A. H., & Wadsworth, M. E. (1999). Getting specific about coping: Effortful and involuntary responses to stress in development. In M. Lewis & D. Ramsay (Eds.), *Soothing and stress* (pp. 229–256). Mahwah, NJ: Erlbaum.

Compas, B. E., Connor-Smith, J. K., Saltzman, H., Thomsen, A. H., & Wadsworth, M. E. (2001). Coping with stress during childhood and adolescence: Problems, progress, and potential in theory and research. *Psychological Bulletin, 127,* 87–127.

Comstock, G., & Paik, H. (1991). *Television and the American child.* New York: Academic Press.

Condry, J. (1989). *The psychology of television.* Hillsdale, NJ: Erlbaum.

Conger, R. D., Ge, X., Elder, G. H., Lorenz, F. O., & Simons, R. L. (1994). Economic stress, coercive family process, and developmental problems of adolescents. *Child Development, 65,* 541–561.

Connolly, J., Furman, W., & Konarski, R. (2000). The role of peers in the emergence of heterosexual romantic relationships in adolescence. *Child Development, 71,* 1395–1408.

Connolly, S. D., Paikoff, R. L., & Buchanan, C. M. (1996). Puberty: The interplay of biological and psychosocial processes in adolescence. In G. R. Adams & R. Montemayor (Eds.), *Psychosocial development during adolescence* (Vol. 8, pp. 259–299). Thousand Oaks, CA: Sage.

Connor, D. B., Knight, D. K., & Cross, D. R. (1997). Mothers' and fathers' scaffolding of their 2-year-olds during problem-solving and literacy interactions. *British Journal of Developmental Psychology, 15,* 323–338.

Consortium for Longitudinal Studies. (1983). *As the twig is bent . . . Lasting effects of preschool programs.* Hillsdale, NJ: Erlbaum.

Consumer Product Safety Alert. (2004). *Prevent child in-home drowning deaths.* Washington, DC: Author.

Consumer Product Safety Commission. (2001). *Nursery products report for 2000.* Washington, DC: Consumer Product Safety Commission.

Cook, T. D., Appleton, H., Conner, R. F., Shaffer, A., Tamkin, G., & Weber, S. (1975). *Sesame Street revisited.* New York: Russell Sage Foundation.

Cooksey, E. C., & Fondell, M. M. (1996). Spending time with his kids: Effects of family structure on fathers' and children's lives. *Journal of Marriage and the Family, 58,* 693–707.

Cooper, N.J., Sutton, A. J., Abrams, K. R., Wailoo, A., Turner, D., & Nicholson, K. G. (2003). Effectiveness of neuraminidase inhibitors in the treatment and prevention of influenza A and B: Systematic review and meta-analysis of randomized controlled trials. *British Medical Journal, 326,* 1235–1239.

Cooper, R. M., & Zubek, J. P. (1958). Effects of enriched and restricted early environments on the learning ability of bright and dull rats. *Canadian Journal of Psychology, 12,* 159–164.

Coopersmith, S. (1967). *The antecedents of self-esteem.* San Francisco: Freeman.

Coplan, R. J., & Rubin, K. H. (1998). Exploring and assessing nonsocial play in the preschool. *Social Development, 7,* 72–91.

Coplan, R. J., Rubin, K. H., Fox, N. A., Calkins, S. D., & Stewart, S. L. (1994). Being alone, playing alone, and acting alone: Distinguishing among reticence and passive and active solitude in young children. *Child Development, 65,* 129–137.

Copstick, S. M., Taylor, K. E., Hayes, R., & Morris, N. (1986). Partner support and the use of coping technique in labour. *Journal of Psychosomatic Research, 30,* 497–503.

Cordell, A. S. (1999). Self-esteem in children. In Carlock, C. J. (Ed), *Enhancing self-esteem* (pp. 287–376). Philadelphia: Accelerated Development, Inc.

Coren, S. (1993). *The left-hander syndrome.* New York: Vintage Books.

Coren, S., & Halpern, D. F. (1991). Left-handedness: A marker for decreased survival fitness. *Psychological Bulletin, 105,* 90–106.

Coren, S., & Porac, C. (1977). Fifty centuries of right-handedness. *Science, 198,* 631–632.

Corina, D. P., Richards, T. L., Serafini, S., Richards, A. L., Steury, K., Abbott, R. D., Echelard, D. R., Maravilla, K. R., & Berninger, V. W. (2001). FMRI auditory language differences between dyslexic and able reading children. *Neuroreport: For Rapid Communication of Neuroscience Research, 12,* 1195–1201.

Corkum, V., & Moore, C. (1998). The origins of joint visual attention in infants. *Developmental Psychology, 34,* 28–38.

Cornwell, T. (1998, June 12). California votes for English alone. *Times Educational Supplement,* 25.

Costello, B. J., & Dunaway, R. G. (2003). Egotism and delinquent behavior. *Journal of Interpersonal Violence, 18,* 572–590.

Cote, J. F. (1996). Sociological perspectives on identity formation. *Journal of Adolescence, 19,* 417–428.

Counts, C. R., Jones, C., Frame, C. L., & Jarvie, G. J. (1986). The perception of obesity by normal-weight versus obese school-age children. *Child Psychiatry and Human Development, 17,* 113–120.

Coupey, S. M. (1992). Anorexia nervosa. In S. B. Friedman & M. Fisher (Eds.), *Nutrition and eating disorders* (pp. 206–249). St. Louis, MO: Quality Medical Publishing.

Courchesne, E., Chisum, H., & Townsend, J. (1994). Neural activity-dependent brain changes in development: Implications for psychopathology. *Development and Psychopathology 6,* 697–722.

Covington, M. C. (1992). *Making the grade.* Cambridge, UK: Cambridge University Press.

Cowan, C. P., Cowan, P. A., Heming, G., Garrett, E., Coysh, W. S. & Curtis-Boles, H. (1985). Transitions to parenthood: His, hers, and theirs. *Journal of Family Issues, 6,* 451–481.

Cowden, J. E., Sayers, L. K., & Torrey, C. C. (1998). *Pediatric adapted motor development and exercise: An innovative, multisystem approach for professionals and families.* Springfield, IL: Thomas.

Cox, B. D., Ornstein, P. A., Naus, M. J., Maxfield, D., & Zimler, J. P. (1989). Children's concurrent use of rehearsal and organizational strategies. *Developmental Psychology, 25,* 619–627.

Cox, M. V. (1992). *Children's drawings.* New York: Penguin.

Cox, M., & Littleton, K. (1995). Children's use of converging obliques in their perspective drawings. *Educational Psychology, 15,* 127–139.

Cozby, P. C. (2004). *Methods in behavioral research* (8th ed.). New York: McGraw-Hill.

Crain, W. (1992). *Theories of development: Concepts and applications.* Englewood Cliffs, NJ: Prentice-Hall.

Crane, J. (1991). The epidemic theory of ghettos and neighborhood effects on dropping out and teenage childbearing. *American Journal of Sociology, 100,* 1226–1259.

Crane, J. P., LeFevre, M. L., Winborn, R. C., Evans, J. K., Ewigman, B. G., Bain, R. P., Frigoletto, F. D., & McNellis, D. (1994). A randomized trial of prenatal ultrasonographic screening: Impact on the detection, management, and outcome of anomalous fetuses. *American Journal of Obstetrics and Gynecology, 171,* 392–399.

Cratty, B. J. (1986). *Perceptual and motor development in infants and children.* Englewood Cliffs, NJ: Prentice-Hall.

Cratty, B. J. (1999). *Movement behavior and motor learning.* Ann Arbor, MI: Books on Demand.

Creasey, G. L., Jarvis, P. A., & Berk, L. E. (1998). Play and social competence. In O. N. Saracho & B. Spodek (Eds.), *Multiple perspectives on play in early childhood education* (pp. 116–143). Albany: State University of New York Press.

Cresswell, S., & Hodge, K. (2004). Coping skills: Role of trait sport confidence and trait anxiety. *Perceptual and Motor Skills, 98,* 433–438.

Crick, N. R., & Grotpeter, J. K. (1995). Relational aggression, gender, and social-psychological adjustment, *Child Development, 66,* 710–722.

Crick, N. R., Grotpeter, J. K., & Bigbee, M. A. (2002). Relationally and physically aggressive children's intent attributions and feelings of distress for relational and instrumental peer provocations. *Child Development, 73,* 1134–1142.

Crick, N. R., & Rose, A. J. (2000). Toward a gender-balanced approach to the study of social-emotional development: A look at relational aggression. In P. H. Miller & E. K. Scholnick (Eds.), *Toward a feminist developmental psychology* (pp. 153–168). Florence, KY: Taylor & Francis.

Crittenden, P. M. (1988). Distorted patterns of relationship in maltreating families. *Journal of Reproductive and Infant Psychology, 6,* 183–199.

Crittenden, P. M., & Ainsworth, M. D. (1989). Child maltreatment and attachment theory. In D. Cicchetti & V. Carlson (Eds.), *Child maltreatment* (pp. 432–463). Cambridge, UK: Cambridge University Press.

Crittenden, P. M., & Claussen, A. H. (2000). *The organization of attachment relationships: Maturation, culture, and context.* New York: Cambridge University Press.

Crockett, L. J., Raffaelli, M., & Moilanen, K. L. (2003). Adolescent sexuality: Behavior and meaning. In M. D. Berzonsky & G. R. Adams (Eds.), *Blackwell handbook of adolescence* (pp. 371–392). Malden, MA: Blackwell.

Crosser, S. (2004). When children draw. *Earlychildhood.com.* Retrieved from http:// www.Earlychildhood.com/articles/index

Crouter, A. C., McHale, S. M., & Tucker, C. J. (1999). Does stress exacerbate parental differential treatment of siblings? A pattern-analytic approach. *Journal of Family Psychology, 13,* 286–299.

Crowder, K., & South, S. J. (2003). Neighborhood distress and school dropout: The variable significance of community context. *Social Science Research, 32,* 659–698.

Crowell, J., & Treboux, D. (2001). Attachment security in adult partnerships. In C. Clulow (Ed.), *Adult attachment and couple psychotherapy* (pp. 28–42). Philadelphia: Brunner Routledge.

Csikszentmihalyi, M. (1991). An investment theory of creativity and its development. *Human Development, 34,* 32–34.

Csikszentmihalyi, M. (1996). *Creativity: Flow and the psychology of discovery and invention.* New York: HarperCollins.

Csikszentmihalyi, M., & Larson, R. (1984). *Being adolescent.* New York: Basic Books.

Cuffe, S. P., & Shugart, M. (2001). Child abuse and psychic trauma in children. In V. H. Booney & A. Pumariega (Eds.), *Clinical assessment of child and adolescent behavior* (pp. 328–357). New York: Wiley.

Culp, A. M., Osofsky, J. D., & O'Brien, M. (1996). Language patterns of adolescent and older mothers and their one-year-old children: A comparison study. *First Language, 16,* 61–75.

Cummings, E. M., & Davies, P. (1996). Emotional security as a regulatory process in normal development and the development of psychopathology. *Development and Psychopathology, 8,* 123–139.

Cummings, E. M., Goeke-Morey, M. C., & Papp, L. M. (2003). A family-wide model for the role of emotion in family functioning. In R. A. Fabes (Ed.), *Emotions and the family* (pp. 13–34). Binghamton, NY: Haworth.

Cummins, J. (2004). Language and literacy in bilingual children. *Journal of Child Language, 31,* 424–429.

Cunningham, F. G., Gant, N. F., Leveno, K. J., Gilstrap, L. C., Hauth, J. C., & Wenstrom, K. D. (2001). *Williams obstetrics.* New York: McGraw-Hill.

Cunningham, P. B., & Henggeler, S. W. (2001). Implementation of an empirically based drug and violence prevention and intervention program in public school settings. *Journal of Clinical Child Psychology, 30,* 221–232.

Curran, D. J., & Renzetti, C. M. (1996). *Social problems.* Boston: Allyn & Bacon.

Curran, J. M. (1999). Constraints of pretend play: Explicit and implicit rules. *Journal of Research in Childhood Education, 14,* 47–55.

Curtiss, S. (1977). *Genie: A psycholinguistic study of a modern-day "wild child."* New York: Academic Press.

Curtiss, S. (1989). The independence and task-specificity of language. In A Bornstein & J. Bruner (Eds.), *Interaction in human development* (pp. 105–137). Hillsdale, NJ: Erlbaum.

Cyranowski, J. M., Frank, E., Young, E., & Shear, K. (2000). Adolescent onset of the gender difference in lifetime rates of major depression. *Archives of General Psychiatry, 57,* 21–27.

D'Augelli, A. R. (2003). Lesbian and bisexual female youths aged 14 to 21: Developmental challenges and victimization experiences. *Journal of Lesbian Studies, 7,* 9–29.

Dacey, J., & Kenny, M. (1997). *Adolescent development.* Dubuque, IA: Brown and Benchmark.

Dadds, M. R., & Salmon, K. (2003). Punishment insensitivity and parenting: Temperament and learning as interacting risks for antisocial behavior. *Clinical Child and Family Psychology Review, 6,* 69–86.

Dahl, R. E. (1996). The impact of inadequate sleep on children's daytime cognitive functioning. *Seminars in Pediatric Neurology, 3,* 44–50.

Dainton, M. (1993). The myths and misperceptions of the stepmother identity: Descriptions and prescriptions for identity management. *Family Relations, 42,* 93–98.

Dake, J., Price, J., & Telljohann, S. (2003). The nature and extent of bullying at school. *The Journal of School Health, 73,* 173–180.

Daly, K. (1993). Reshaping fatherhood: Finding the models. *Journal of Family Issues, 14,* 510–530.

Damasio, A. R., & Damasio, H. (1992). Brain and language. *Scientific American, 14,* 597–611.

Damon, W. (1988). *The moral child.* New York: Free Press.

Damon, W. (1995). *Greater expectations: Overcoming the culture of indulgence in America's homes and schools.* New York: Free Press.

Daniels, D. H. (1998). Age differences in concepts of self-esteem. *Merrill-Palmer Quarterly, 44,* 234–258.

Danis, A., Bourdais, C., & Ruel, J. (2000). The co-construction of joint action between mothers and 2–4-month-old infants: The mother's role. *Infant and Child Development, 9,* 181–189.

Danish, S., Kleiber, D., & Hall, H. (1987). Enhancing motivation in the context of sport. In M. Maehr & D. Kleiber (Eds.), *Enhancing motivation* (pp. 211–238).Greenwich, CT: JAI Press.

Dannemiller, J. L. (2001). Brain-behavior relationships in early visual development. In C. A. Nelson & M. Luciana (Eds.), *Handbook of developmental cognitive neuroscience* (pp. 221–235). Cambridge, MA: MIT Press.

Dannemiller, J. L., & Stephens, B. R. (1988). A critical test of infant pattern preference models. *Child Development, 59,* 210–216.

Daro, D. (1996). Preventing child abuse and neglect. In J. Briere, L. Berliner, J. A. Bulkley, C. Jenny, & T. Reid (Eds.), *The APSAC handbook on child maltreatment* (pp. 343–358). Thousand Oaks, CA: Sage.

Daro, D. (2000). Child abuse prevention: New directions and challenges. In D. J. Hansen (Ed.), *Motivation and child maltreatment* (pp. 161–219). Lincoln: University of Nebraska Press.

Darwin, C. (1859). *On the origin of species.* London: J. Murray.

Darwin, C. (1877). Biographical sketch of an infant. *Mind, 2,* 285–294.

Dasen, P. R. (1973). Piagetian research in Central Australia. In G. E. Kearney, P. R. de Lacey, & G. R. Davidson (Eds.), *The psychology of Aboriginal Australians* (pp. 89–96). Sydney, Australia: Wiley.

Dasen, P. R. (1993). Culture and cognitive development from a Piagetian perspective. In W. J. Lonner & R. S. Malpass (Eds.), *Readings in psychology and culture* (pp. 141–150). Boston: Allyn & Bacon.

Datta, L. E. (1985). Benefits without gains: The paradox of the cognitive effects of early childhood programs and implications for policy. *Special Services in the Schools, 3,* 103–126.

Davey, A. G. (1983). *Learning to be prejudiced.* London: Edward Arnold.

Davidson, J., & Smith, R. (1990). Traumatic experiences in psychiatric outpatients. *Journal of Traumatic Stress Studies, 3,* 459–475.

Davidson, R. J., Putnam, K. M., & Larson, C. L. (2000). Dysfunction in the neural circuitry of emotion regulation: A possible prelude to violence. *Science, 289,* 591–594.

Davies, P. T., & Windle, M. (2000). Middle adolescents' dating pathways and psychosocial adjustment. *Merrill-Palmer Quarterly, 46,* 90–118.

Davis, B. E., Moon, R. Y., Sachs, H. C., & Ottolini, M. C. (1998). Effects of sleep position on infant motor development. *Pediatrics, 102,* 1135–1140.

Davis, B. T., Hops, H., Alpert, A., & Sheeber, L. (1998). Child responses to parental conflict and their effect on adjustment. *Journal of Family Psychology, 12,* 163–177.

Davis, B., Sheeber, L., & Hops, H. (2002). Coercive family processes and adolescent depression. In G. R. Patterson & J. B. Reid (Eds.), *Antisocial behavior in children and adolescents: A developmental analysis and model for intervention* (pp. 173–192). Washington, DC: American Psychological Association.

Davis, E. C., & Friel, L. V. (2001). Adolescent sexuality: Disentangling the effects of family structure and family context. *Journal of Marriage and the Family, 63,* 669–681.

Dawson, D. A. (1991). Family structure and children's mental health and well-being. *Journal of Marriage and the Family, 53,* 573–584.

Day, R. D., Peterson, G. W., & McCracken, C. (1998). Predicting spanking of younger and older children by mothers and fathers. *Journal of Marriage and the Family, 60,* 79–94.

De Houwer, A. (1995). Bilingual language acquisition. In P. Fletcher & B. MacWhinney (Eds.), *The handbook of child language* (pp. 219–250). Oxford, UK: Blackwell.

De Lisi, R., & McGillicuddy-De Lisi, A. V. (2002). Sex differences in mathematical abilities and achievement. In A. McGillicuddy-De Lisi & R. De Lisi (Eds.), *Biology, society, and behavior: The development of sex differences in cognition* (pp. 155–182). Westport, CT: Ablex.

de Quadros, C. A., (2004, February). Can measles be eradicated globally? *Bulletin of the World Health Organization, 82,* 134–138.

de Villiers, P., & de Villiers, J. (1992). Language development. In M. H. Bornstein & M. E. Lamb (Eds.), *Developmental psychology: An advanced textbook* (pp. 255–290). Hillsdale, NJ: Erlbaum.

De Wolff, M. S., & van IJzendoorn, M. H. (1997). Sensitivity and attachment: A meta-analysis of parental antecedents of infant attachment. *Child Development, 68,* 571–591.

Deak, G. O., & Maratsos, M. (1998). On having complex representations of things: Preschoolers use multiple words for objects and people. *Developmental Psychology, 34,* 224–240.

Deal, J. E., Halverson, C. F., & Wampler, K. S. (1989). Parental agreement on child-rearing orientations: Relations to parental, marital, and child characteristics. *Child Development, 60,* 1025–1034.

Deater-Deckard, K., Scarr, S., McCartney, K., & Eisenberg, M. (1994). Paternal separation anxiety: Relationships with parenting stress, child-rearing attitudes, and maternal anxieties. *Psychological Science, 6,* 341–346.

De-Bellis, M. D., Keshavan, M. S., Beers, S. R., Hall, J., Frustaci, K., Masalehdan, A., Noll, J., & Boring, A. M. (2001). Sex differences in brain maturation during childhood and adolescence. *Cerebral Cortex, 11,* 552–557.

DeCasper, A. J., & Spence, M. J. (1986). Prenatal maternal speech influences newborn's perception of speech sounds. *Infant Behavior and Development, 9,* 133–150.

Deci, E. L., & Ryan, R. M. (1995). Human autonomy: The basis for true self-esteem. In M. H. Kernis (Ed.), *Efficacy, agency, and self-esteem* (pp. 31–46). New York: Plenum.

Decker, M. D., Dewey, M. J., Hutcheson, R. H., & Schaffner, W. (1984). The use and efficacy of child restraint devices. *Journal of the American Medical Association, 252,* 2571–2575.

DeCorte, E., Greer, B., & Verschaffel, L. (1996). Mathematics teaching and learning. In D.C. Berliner & R. C. Calfee (Eds.), *Handbook of educational psychology* (pp. 491–549). New York: Macmillan.

Deford, F. (1986). *Alex: The life of a child.* New York: Signet/New American Library.

DeFries, J. C., Filipek, P. A., Fulker, D. W., Olson, R. K., Pennington, B. F., Smith, S. D., & Wise, B. W. (1997). Colorado learning disabilities research center. *Learning Disabilities Quarterly, 8,* 7–19.

Degirmencioflu, S. M., Urberg, K. A., Tolson, J. M., & Richard, P. (1998). Adolescent friendship networks: Continuity and change over the school year. *Merrill-Palmer Quarterly, 44,* 313–317.

Dekovic, M. (1999). Parent–adolescent conflict: Possible determinants and consequences. *International Journal of Behavioral Development, 23,* 977–1000.

Dekovic, M., & Janssens, J. M. (1992). Parents' child-rearing style and child's sociometric status. *Developmental Psychology, 28,* 925–932.

Dell, D. L. (2001). Adolescent pregnancy. In N. L. Stotland & D. E. Stewart (Eds.), *Psychological aspects of women's health care: The interface between psychiatry and obstetrics and gynecology* (pp. 95–116). Washington, DC: American Psychiatric Press.

Deloache, J. S. (1987). Rapid change in the symbolic functioning of very young children. *Science, 238,* 1556–1557.

DeLoache, J. S. (1991). Symbolic functioning in very young children: Understanding of pictures and models. *Child Development, 62,* 736–752.

DeLoache, J. S. (2000). Dual representation and young children's use of scale models. *Child Development, 71,* 329–338.

DeLoache, J. S., Cassidy, D. J., & Brown, A. L. (1985). Precursors of mnemonic strategies in very young children's memory. *Child Development, 56,* 125–137.

DeLoache, J. S., Kolstad, D. V., & Anderson, K. N. (1991). Physical similarity and young children's understanding of scale models. *Child Development, 62,* 111–126.

DeLoache, J. S., Pierroutsakos, S. L., & Troseth, G. (1997). The three R's of pictorial competence. In N. R. Vasta (Ed.), *Annals of child development* (pp. 1–48). Bristol, PA: Jessica Kingsley.

DeLoache, J. S., Pierroutsakos, S. L., & Uttal, D. H. (2003). The origins of pictorial competence. *Current Directions in Psychological Science, 12,* 114–118.

DeLongis, A., & Preece, A. (2002). Emotional and relational consequences of coping in stepfamilies. *Marriage & Family Review.*

Demaray, M. K., & Elliot, S. N. (1998). Teachers' judgments of students' academic functioning: A comparison of actual and predicted performance. *School Psychology Quarterly, 13,* 8–24.

DeMarie-Dreblow, D., & Miller, P. H. (1988). The development of children's strategies for selective attention: Evidence for a transitional period. *Child Development, 59,* 1504–1513.

DeMier, R. L., Hunan, M. T., Hatfield, R. F., Varner, M. W., Harris, H. B., & Maniello, R. L. (2000). A measurement model of perinatal stressors: Identifying risk for postnatal emotional distress in mothers of high-risk infants. *Journal of Clinical Psychology, 56,* 89–100.

Demuth, K. (1990). Maturation and the acquisition of the Sesotho passive. *Language, 65,* 56–81.

Denham, S. A. (1998). *Emotional development in young children.* New York: Guilford.

Denham, S. A., Mason, T., Caverly, S., Schmidt, M., Hackney, R., Caswell, C., & DeMulder, E. (2001). Preschoolers at play: Co-socializers of emotional and social competence. *International Journal of Behavioral Development, 25,* 290–301.

Denham, S. A., Renwick-DeBardi, S., & Hughes, S. (1994). Emotional communication between mothers and preschoolers: Relations with emotional competence. *Merrill-Palmer Quarterly, 40,* 488–508.

Denham, S. A., Zoller, D., & Couchoud, E. A. (1994). Socialization of preschoolers' emotion understanding. *Developmental Psychology, 30,* 928–936.

Department of Health and Human Services. (2003). *National survey on drug use and health.* Washington, DC: Author.

Deregowski, J. B. (1980). *Illusions, patterns, and pictures: A cross-cultural perspective.* London: Academic Press.

Devlin, B., Daniels, M., & Roeder, K. (1997). The heritability of IQ. *Nature, 338,* 468–471.

DeVries, M. (1984). Temperament and infant mortality among the Masai of East Africa. *American Journal of Psychiatry, 141,* 1189–1994.

DeVries, M., & Sameroff, A. J. (1984). Culture and temperament: Influences on temperament in three East African societies. *American Journal of Orthopsychiatry, 54,* 83–96.

Diamond, A. (1991). Frontal lobe involvement in cognitive changes during the first year of life. In K. R. Gibson & A. C. Petersen (Eds.), *Brain maturation and cognitive development: Comparative and cross-cultural perspectives* (pp. 127–180). New York: Aldine de Gruyter.

Diamond, A. (2000). Close interrelation of motor development and cognitive development and of the cerebellum and prefrontal cortex. *Child Development, 71,* 44–56.

Diamond, J. (1990, December). War babies. *Discovery,* 70–75.

Diamond, L. M., & Savin-Williams, R. C. (2003). The intimate relationships of sexual-minority youths. In M. D. Berzonsky & G. R. Adams (Eds.), *Handbook of adolescence* (pp. 393–412). Malden, MA: Blackwell.

Diamond, M., & Sigmundson, K. (1997). Sex reassignment at birth: Long-term review and clinical implications. *Archives of Pediatric Adolescent Medicine, 151,* 298–304.

Diehl, S. F., Moffitt, K. A., & Wade, S. M. (1991). Focus group interview with parents of children with medically complex needs: An intimate look at their perceptions and feelings. *Children's Health Care, 20,* 170–178.

Dietz, T. L. (1998). An examination of violence and gender role portrayals in video games. *Sex Roles, 38,* 423–444.

Dietz, W. H. (1998). Health consequences of obesity in youth: Childhood predictors of adult disease. *Supplement Pediatrics, 101,* 518–525.

Dietz, W. H. (2001). The obesity epidemic in young children: Reduce television viewing and promote playing. *British Medical Journal, 322,* 313–314.

Dietz, W. H., & Gortmaker, S. L. (1985). Do we fatten our children at the television set? Obesity and television viewing in children and adolescence. *Pediatrics, 75,* 807–812.

DiGirolamo, A. M., Geis, H. K., & Walker, C. E. (1998). Developmental issues. In R. T. Ammerman & J. V. Campo (Eds.), *Handbook of pediatric psychology and psychiatry* (pp. 1–22). Boston: Allyn & Bacon.

DiLalla, L. F., & Watson, M. W. (1988). Differentiation of fantasy and reality: Preschoolers' reactions to interruptions in their play. *Developmental Psychology, 24,* 286–291.

DiMaggio, P. (1997). Culture and cognition. *Annual Review of Sociology, 23,* 263–267.

DiPietro, J. (1981). Rough and tumble play: A function of gender. *Developmental Psychology, 17,* 50–58.

DiPietro, J. A., Hodgson, D. M., Costigan, K. A., & Johnson, T. R. B. (1996). Fetal antecedents of infant temperament. *Child Development, 67,* 2568–2583.

DiPietro, J. A., Larson, S. K., & Porges, S. W. (1987). Behavioral and heartrate pattern differences between breast-fed and bottle-fed neonates. *Developmental Psychology, 23,* 467–474.

Dishion, T. J. (1990). The peer context of troublesome child and adolescent behavior. In P. E. Leone (Ed.), *Understanding troubled and troubling youth* (pp. 128–153). Newbury Park, CA: Sage.

Dishion, T. J., & Andrews, D. W. (1996). A multicomponent intervention for families of young adolescents at risk: An analysis of short-term outcomes. *Journal of Consulting and Clinical Psychology, 63,* 538–548.

Dishion, T. J., & Bullock, B. M. (2002). Parenting and adolescent problem behavior: An ecological analysis of the nurturance hypothesis. In S. L. Ramey & J. G. Borkowski (Eds.), *Parenting and the child's world: Influences on academic, intellectual, and social-emotional development* (pp. 231–249). Mahwah, NJ: Erlbaum.

Dishion, T. J., French, D.C., & Patterson, G. R. (1995). The development and ecology of antisocial behavior. In D. Cicchetti & D. J. Cohen (Eds.), *Developmental psychopathology* (Vol. 2, pp. 421–471). New York: Wiley.

Dishion, T. J., & Kavanagh, K. (2003). *Intervening in adolescent problem behavior: A family-centered approach.* New York: Guilford.

Dishion, T., Kavanagh, K., Schneiger, A. K. J., Nelson, S., & Kaufman, N. (2002). Preventing early adolescent substance use: A family centered strategy for the public middle school. *Prevention Science, 3,* 191–202.

Dodge, K. A. (1991). Emotion and social information processing. In J. Garber & K. A. Dodge (Eds.), *The development of emotion: Regulation and dysregulation* (pp. 159–181). Cambridge, UK: Cambridge University Press.

Dodge, K. A. (2001). The science of youth violence prevention: Progressing from developmental epidemiology to efficacy to effectiveness to public policy. *American Journal of Preventive Medicine, 20,* 63–70.

Dodge, K. A., Lansford, J. E., Burks, V. S., Bates, J. E., Pettit, G. S., Fontaine, R., & Price, J. M. (2003). Peer rejection and social information-processing factors in the development of aggressive behavior problems in children. *Child Development, 74,* 374–393.

Dodge, K. A., Pettit, G. S., McClaskey, C. L., & Brown, M. M. (1986). Social competence in children. *Monographs of the Society for Research in Child Development* (Vol. 51, No. 2). Chicago: University of Chicago Press.

Doherty, W. J. (1997). The best of times and the worst of times: Fathering as a contested arena of academic discourse. In A. J. Hawkins & D. C. Dollahite (Eds.), *Generative fathering: Beyond deficit perspectives* (pp. 217–227). Newbury Park, CA: Sage.

Dollaghan, C. (1985). Child meet word: "Fast mapping" in preschool children. *Journal of Speech and Hearing Research, 28,* 449–454.

Dollberg, S., Fainaru, O., Mimouni, F. B., Shenhav, M., Lessing, J. B., & Kupferminc, M. (2000). Effect of passive smoking on neonatal nucleated red blood cells. *Pediatrics, 106,* 1–3.

Donahue, M. J. (1995). Religion and the well-being of adolescents. *Journal of Social Issues, 51,* 145–160.

Donaldson, M. (1978). *Children's minds.* New York: Norton.

Donelson, E. (1999). Psychology of religion and adolescents in the United States. *Journal of Adolescence, 22,* 187–204.

Donnez, J., Dolmans, M. M., Demylle, D., Jadoul, P., Pirard, C., Squifflet, J., Martinez-Madrid, B., & Van Langendonckt, A. (2004). Livebirth after orthotopic transplantation of cryopreserved ovarian tissue. *Lancet, 364,* 1405–1410.

Dornbusch, S. M., Mont-Reynaud, R., Ritter, P. L., Chen, Z. Y., & Steinberg, L. (1991). Stressful events and their correlates among adolescents of diverse backgrounds. In M. E. Colten & S. Gore (Eds.), *Adolescent stress: Causes and consequences* (pp. 111–130). New York: Aldine de Gruyter.

Doussard-Roosevelt, J. A., Porges, S. W., Scanlon, J. W., Alemmi, B., & Scanlon, K. B. (1997). Vagal regulation of heart rate in the prediction of development outcome for very low birth weight preterm infants. *Child Development, 68,* 173–186.

Dow, G. A., & Pick, H. L. (1992). Young children's use of models and photographs as spatial representations. *Cognitive Development, 7,* 351–363.

Doyle, A. B., Brendgen, M., Markiewicz, D., & Kamkar, K. (2003). Family relationships as moderators of the association between romantic relationships and adjustment in early adolescence. *Journal of Early Adolescence, 23,* 316–340.

Doyle, L. W., Rickards, A. L., Kelly, E. A., Ford, G. W., & Callanan, C. (1992). Breastfeeding and intelligence. *Lancet, 339,* 744–745.

Drewett, R. F. (1993). The infant's regulation of nutritional intake. In I. St. James-Roberts, G. Harris, & D. Messer (Eds.), *Infant crying, feeding, and sleeping: Development, problems, and treatments* (pp. 83–98). New York: Harvester Wheatsheaf.

Drummond, K. V., & Stipek, D. (2004). Low-income parents' beliefs about their role in children's academic learning. *Elementary School Journal, 104,* 197–213.

Dubrow, N. F., & Garbarino, J. (1989). Living in the war zone: Mothers and young children in a public housing development. *Child Welfare, 68,* 3–20.

Duda, J. (1988). The relationship between goal perspectives, persistence, and behavioral intensity among male and female recreational sport participants. *Leisure Sciences, 10,* 95–106.

Duffy, J., Warren, K., & Walsh, M. (2001). Classroom interactions: Gender of teacher, gender of student, and classroom subject. *Sex Roles, 45,* 479–593.

Dulcan, M. K. (1986). Comprehensive treatment of children and adolescents with attention deficit disorders: The state of the art. *Clinical Psychology Review, 6,* 539–569.

Dulcan, M. K. (1989). Attention deficit disorders. In C. G. Last & M. Hersen (Eds.), *Handbook of child psychiatric diagnosis* (pp. 95–128). New York: Wiley.

Dumka, L. E., Roosa, M. W., & Jackson, K. M. (1997). Risk, conflict, mothers' parenting, and children's adjustment in low-income, Mexican immigrant and Mexican American families. *Journal of Marriage and the Family, 59,* 309–323.

Dunbar, K., & Klahr, D. (1989). Developmental differences in scientific discovery processes. In D. Klahr & K. Kotovsky (Eds.), *Complex information processing: The impact of Herbert A. Simon* (pp. 109–143). Hillsdale, NJ: Erlbaum.

Duncan, P., Ritter, P., Dornbusch, S., Gross, R., & Carlsmith, J. (1985). The effects of pubertal timing on body image, school behavior, and deviance. *Journal of Youth and Adolescence, 14,* 227–236.

Duncan, R. M., & Pratt, M. W. (1997). Microgenetic change in the quantity and quality of preschoolers' private speech. *International Journal of Behavioral Development, 20,* 367–383.

Dunn, J. (1983). Sibling relationships in early childhood. *Child Development, 54,* 787–811.

Dunn, J. (1988). *The beginnings of social understanding.* Cambridge, MA: Harvard University Press.

Dunn, J. (1992). Sisters and brothers: Current issues in developmental research. In F. Boer & J. Dunn (Eds.), *Children's sibling relationships* (pp. 1–18). Hillsdale, NJ: Erlbaum.

Dunn, J. (2001). The development of children's conflict and prosocial behavior: Lessons from research on social understanding and gender. In J. Hill & B. Maughan (Eds.), *Conduct disorders in childhood and adolescence* (pp. 49–66). New York: Cambridge University Press.

Dunn, J., & Munn, P. (1987). The development of justification in disputes. *Developmental Psychology, 23,* 791–798.

Dunn, J., & Slomkowski, C. (1992). Conflict and the development of social understanding. In C. U. Shantz & W. W. Hartup (Eds.), *Conflict in child and adolescent development* (pp. 70–92). Cambridge, UK: Cambridge University Press.

DuPaul, G. J., McGoey, K. E., Eckert, T. L., & VanBrakle, J. (2001). Preschool children with attention-deficit/hyperactivity disorder: Impairments in behavioral, social, and school functioning. *Journal of the American Academy of Child and Adolescent Psychiatry, 40,* 508–515.

Durant, N. A. (2004). Adolescent depression: A guide for parents. *American Journal of Psychiatry, 161,* 1516.

Dusek, J. B. (1996). *Adolescent development and behavior.* Saddle River, NJ: Prentice-Hall.

Dweck, C. S., & Leggett, E. L. (1988). A social–cognitive approach to motivation and personality. *Psychological Review, 95,* 256–273.

Dwyer, C. A., & Johnson, L. M. (1997). Grades, accomplishments, and correlates. In W. Willingham & N. Cole (Eds.), *Gender and fair assessment* (pp. 127–156). Mahwah, NJ: Erlbaum.

Dwyer, K. M., Richardson, J. L., Danley, K. L., Hansen, W. B., Sussman, S. Y., Brannon, B., Dent, C. W., Johnson, C. A., & Flay, B. R. (1990). Characteristics of eighth-grade students who initiate self-care in elementary and junior high school. *Pediatrics, 86,* 448–454.

Eason, E., & Feldman, P. (2000). Much ado about a little cut: Is episiotomy worthwhile? *Obstetrics and Gynecology, 95,* 616–618.

Easterbrooks, M. A., & Goldberg, W. A. (1990). Security of toddler–parent attachment. In M. T. Greenberg, D. Cicchetti, & E. M. Cummings (Eds.), *Attachment in the preschool years* (pp. 221–244). Chicago: University of Chicago Press.

Eaton, W. O., & Enns, L. R. (1986). Sex differences in human motor activity level. *Psychological Bulletin, 100,* 19–28.

Ebata, A. T., Petersen, A. C., & Conger, J. (1990). The development of psychopathology in adolescence. In J. Rolf, A. S. Masten, D. Cicchetti, K. H. Nuechterlein, & S. Weintraub (Eds.), *Risk and protective factors in the development of psychopathology* (pp. 308–333). Cambridge, UK: Cambridge University Press.

Ebbeck, M. (1984). Equity for boys and girls: Some important issues. *Early Child Development and Care, 18,* 119–131.

Eccles, J. S., & Barber, B. L. (1999). Student council, volunteering, basketball, or marching band: What kinds of extracurricular involvement matter? *Journal of Adolescent Research, 14,* 10–43.

Eccles, J. S., Freedman-Doan, C., Frome, P., Jacobs, J., & Yoon, K. S. (2000). Gender-role socialization in the family: A longitudinal approach. In T. Eckes & H. Trautner (Eds.), *The developmental social psychology of gender* (pp. 333–360). Mahwah, NJ: Erlbaum.

Eccles, J. S., & Roeser, R. W. (2003). Schools as developmental contexts. In M. D. Berzonsky & G. R. Adams (Eds.), *Blackwell handbook of adolescence* (pp. 129–148). Malden, MA: Blackwell.

Eccles, J. S., Wigfield, A., Flanagan, C. A., & Miller, C. (1989). Self-concepts, domain values, and self-esteem: Relations and changes at early adolescence. *Journal of Personality, 57,* 282–310.

Eccles, J. S., Wigfield, A., Midgley, C. H., Reuman, D., MacIver, D., & Feldlaufer, H. (1993). Negative effects of traditional middle schools on students' motivation. *Elementary School Journal, 93,* 553–574.

Eckensberger, L. H. (1994). Moral development and its measurement across cultures. In W. J. Lonner & R. S. Malpass (Eds.), *Psychology and culture* (pp. 75–79). Boston: Allyn & Bacon.

Edens, J. F., & Cavell, T. A. (1999). A review and reformulation of adoptive relationships from an attachment perspective. *Adoption Quarterly, 3,* 43–70.

Edgeworth, J., & Carr, A. (2000). Child abuse. In A. Carr (Ed.), *What works with children and adolescents?: A critical review of psychological interventions with children, adolescents and their families* (pp. 17–48). Florence, KY: Taylor & Francis/Routledge.

Edwards, J. (2004). Bilingualism: Contexts, constraints, and identities. *Journal of Language and Social Psychology, 23,* 135–141.

Egan, S. K., & Perry, D. G. (1998). Does low self-regard invite victimization? *Developmental Psychology 34,* 299–309.

Egan, S. K., & Perry, D. G. (2001). Gender identity: A multidimensional analysis with implications for psychosocial adjustment. *Developmental Psychology, 37,* 451–463.

Egeland, B., & Sroufe, L. A. (1983). Developmental sequelae of maltreatment in infancy. In R. Rizley & D. Cicchetti (Eds.), *New directions for child development* (Vol. 11, pp. 77–72). San Francisco: Jossey-Bass.

Ehrle, J., Adams, G., & Tout, K. (2001). *Who's caring for our youngest children?* Washington, DC: The Urban Institute.

Eiberg, H., & Mohr, J. (1987). Major genes of eye color and hair color linked to LU and SE. *Clinical Genetics, 31,* 186–191.

Einarsson, C., & Granstroem, K. (2002). Gender-biased interaction in the classroom: The influence of gender and age in the relationship between teacher and pupil. *Scandinavian Journal of Educational Research, 46,* 117–127.

Eisenberg, A., Murkoff, H. E., & Hathaway, S. E. (1999). *What to expect when you're expecting.* New York: Workman.

Eisenberg, N. (1992). *The caring child.* Cambridge, MA: Harvard University Press.

Eisenberg, N., & Fabes, R. A. (1992). Emotion regulation and the development of social competence. In P. Clark (Ed.), *Emotion and social behavior* (Vol. 14, pp. 119–150). Newbury Park, CA: Sage.

Eisenberg, N., Fabes, R. A., & Spinrad, T. L. (2005). Prosocial development. In N. Eisenberg (Ed.), *Handbook of child psychology.* New York: Wiley.

Eisenberg, N., Fabes, R. A., Guthrie, I. K., & Reiser, M. (2002). The role of emotionality and regulation in children's social competence and adjustment. In A. Caspi & L. Pulkkinen (Eds.), *Paths to successful development: Personality in the life course* (pp. 46–70). New York: Cambridge University Press.

Eisenberg, N., Guthrie, I. K., Fabes, R. A., Shepard, S., Losoya, S., Murphy, B. C., Jones, S., Poulin, R., & Reiser, M. (2000). Prediction of elementary school children's externalizing problem behaviors from attentional and behavioral regulation and negative emotionality. *Child Development, 71,* 1367–1382.

Eisenberg, N., Martin, C. L., & Fabes, R. A. (1996). Gender development and gender effects. In D. Berliner & R. Calfee (Eds.), *Handbook of educational psychology* (pp. 358–398). New York: Macmillan.

Eisenberg, N., Zhou, Q., & Koller, S. (2001). Brazilian adolescents' prosocial moral judgment and behavior: Relations to sympathy, perspective taking, gender-role orientation, and demographic characteristics. *Child Development, 72,* 518–534.

Eisenberg, N., Fabes, R. A., & Guthrie, I. K. (1997). Coping with stress: The roles of regulation and development. In S. A. Wolchik & I. N. Sandler (Eds.), *Handbook of children's coping* (pp. 41–72). New York: Plenum.

Eisenberg, N., & Fabes, R. A. (1998). Prosocial development. In W. Damon (Ed.), *Handbook of child psychology* (Vol. 3, pp. 701–778). New York: Wiley.

Eisenberg, N., & Fabes, R. A. (1999). Emotion, emotion-related regulation, and quality of socioemotional functioning. In L. Balter & C. S. Tamis-LeMonda (Eds.), *Child psychology: A handbook of contemporary issues* (pp. 318–335). Philadelphia: Psychology Press.

Eisenberg, N., & Murphy, B. (1995). Parenting and children's moral development. In M. C. Bornstein (Ed.), *Handbook of parenting* (Vol. 4, pp. 227–257). Hillsdale, NJ: Erlbaum.

Eisenberg, N., & Strayer, J. (Eds.). (1987). *Empathy and its development.* Cambridge, UK: Cambridge University Press.

Elardo, R., & Bradley, R. H. (1981). The Home Observation for Measurement of the Environment (HOME) Scale: A review of research. *Developmental Review, 1,* 113–145.

Elardo, R., Bradley, R. H., & Caldwell, B. M. (1975). The relation of infants' home environments to mental test performance from six to thirty-six months: A longitudinal analysis. *Child Development, 46,* 71–76.

Elbert, T., Heim, S., & Rockstroh, B. (2001). Neural plasticity and development. In C. Nelson & M. Luciana (Eds.), *Handbook of developmental cognitive neuroscience* (pp. 191–202). Cambridge, MA: MIT Press.

Elder, G. H., Conger, R. D., Foster, E. M., & Ardelt, M. (1992). Families under economic pressure. *Journal of Family Issues, 13,* 5–37.

Elicker, J., Englund, M., & Sroufe, L. A. (1992). Predicting peer competence and peer relationships in childhood from early parent–child relationships. In R. D. Parke & G. W. Ladd (Eds.), *Family–peer relationships: Modes of linkage* (pp. 77–106). Hillsdale, NJ: Erlbaum.

Elkind, D. (1967). Egocentrism in adolescence. *Child Development, 38,* 1025–1033.

Elkind, D. (1987). *Miseducation: Preschoolers at risk.* New York: Knopf.

Elkind, D. (1988, January). Educating the very young: A call for clear thinking. *NEA Today,* 22–27.

Elo, I. T., King, R. B., & Furstenberg, F. F. (1999). Adolescent females: Their sexual partners and the fathers of their children. *Journal of Marriage and the Family, 61,* 74–84.

Emery, R. E. (1988). *Marriage, divorce, and children's adjustment.* Beverly Hills, CA: Sage.

Emery, R. E., & Laumann-Billings, L. (1998). An overview of the nature, causes, and consequences of abusive family relationships. *American Psychologist, 53,* 121–135.

Emes, C. E. (1997). Is Mr. Pac Man eating our children? *Canadian Journal of Psychiatry, 42,* 409–414.

Emslie, G. J., Weinberg, W. A., Kennard, B. D., & Kowatch, R. A. (1994). Neurobiological aspects of depression in children and adolescents. In W. M. Reynolds & H. F. Johnston (Eds.), *Handbook of depression in children and adolescents* (pp. 143–165). New York: Plenum.

Ennett, S. T., & Bauman, K. E. (1996). Adolescent social networks: School, demographic and longitudinal considerations. *Journal of Adolescent Research, 11,* 194–215.

Ensminger, A. H., Ensminger, M. E., Konlande, J. E., & Robson, J. R. K. (1986). *Food for health: A nutritional encyclopedia.* Clovis, CA: Peguis Press.

Epperson, C. N. (1999). Postpartum major depression: Detection and treatment. *American Family Physician, 59* 2247–2258.

Epstein, J. L. (1986). Friend selection: Developmental and environmental influences. In E. Mueller & C. Cooper (Eds.), *Process and outcome in peer relationships* (pp. 171–192). New York: Academic Press.

Epstein, L. G., Sharer, L. R., Oleske, J. M., Connor, E. M., Goudsmit, J., Bagdon, L., Robert-Guroff, M., & Koenigsberger, M. R. (1986). Neurologic manifestations of human immunodeficiency virus infection in children. *Pediatrics, 78,* 678–687.

Erel, O., Margolin, G., & John, R. S. (1998). Observed sibling interaction: Links with marital and the mother–child relationship. *Developmental Psychology, 34,* 288–298.

Erikson, E. H. (1959). *Identity and the life cycle in psychological issues* (Vol. 1). New York: International Universities Press.

Erikson, E. H. (1963). *Childhood and society.* New York: Norton.

Erikson, E. H. (1968). *Identity: Youth and crisis.* New York: Norton.

Erikson, E. H. (1969). *Gandhi's truth on the origins of militant nonviolence.* New York: Norton.

Erikson, E. H. (1980). *Identity and the life cycle.* New York: Norton.

Eron, L. D. (1982). Parent—child interaction, television violence, and aggression of children. *American Psychologist, 37,* 197–211.

Eron, L. D., Huesmann, L. R., Lefkowitz, M. M., & Walder, L. O. (1996). Does television violence cause aggression? In D. F. Greenberg (Ed.), *Criminal careers* (Vol. 2, pp. 311–321). Aldershot, UK: Dartmouth Publishing.

Escalette, M. E. W. (1989). A cross-cultural study of Nepalese neonatal behavior. In J. K. Nugent, B. M. Lester, & T. B. Brazelton (Eds.), *The cultural context of infancy* (Vol. 1, pp. 65–86). Norwood, NJ: Ablex Publishing.

Espelage, D. L., Mebane, S. E., & Swearer, S. M. (2004). Gender differences in bullying. In D. L. Espelage & S. M. Swearer (Eds.), *Bullying in American schools* (pp. 15–36). Mahwah, NJ: Erlbaum.

Espinoza, R. L., & Ehrlich, A. (1989). Personality, family relationships, and moral development in Chicano and black adolescent gang members. *Adolescent Psychiatry, 16,* 216–227.

Evans, G. W., & English, K. (2002). The environment of poverty: Multiple stressor exposure, psychophysiological stress, and socioemotional adjustment. *Child Development, 73,* 1238–1248.

Eveleth, P. B., & Tanner, J. M. (1990). *Worldwide variation in human growth.* Cambridge, UK: Cambridge University Press.

Eyler, F. D., & Behnke, M. (1999). Early development of infants exposed to drugs prenatally. *Clinical Perinatology, 26,* 107–150.

Ezzaki, A. (1990). Research on Iftah Ya Simsim, the Arabic coproduction. In Children's Television Workshop (Ed.), *Sesame Street research* (pp. 60–62). New York: Author.

Fabes, R. A., & Eisenberg, N. (1992). Young children's coping with interpersonal anger. *Child Development, 63,* 116–128.

Fabes, R. A., & Filsinger, E. E. (1988). Odor communication and parent–child interaction. In E. E. Filsinger (Ed.), *Biosocial perspectives on the family* (pp. 93–118). Newbury Park, CA: Sage.

Fabes, R. A., Carlo, G., Kupanoff, K., & Laible, D. (1999). Transition to adolescence and prosocial/moral development I: Individual processes. *Journal of Early Adolescence, 14,* 1–14.

Fabes, R. A., Eisenberg, N., Jones, S., Smith, M., Guthrie, I. K., Poulin, R., Shepard, S. A., & Friedman, J. (1999). Regulation, emotionality, and preschoolers' socially competent peer interactions. *Child Development, 70,* 432–442.

Fabes, R. A., Eisenberg, N., Smith, M. C., & Murphy, B. C. (1996). Getting angry at peers: Associations with liking of the provocateur. *Child Development, 67,* 942–956.

Fabes, R. A., & Eisenberg, N. (1996). *Meta-analysis of sex and differences in prosocial behavior.* Retrieved from http://www.asu.edu/clas/fhd/fabes/meta.pdf.

Fabes, R. A., Fultz, J., Eisenberg, N., Plumlee, T. M., & Christopher, F. S. (1989). The effects of rewards on children's prosocial motivation: A socialization study. *Developmental Psychology, 25,* 509–515.

Fabes, R. A., Gaertner, B. M., & Popp, T. K. (2005). Getting along with others: Social competence in early childhood. In K. McCartney & D. Phillips (Eds.), *Handbook of early childhood development* (pp. 000). New York: Blackwell.

Fabes, R. A., Martin, C. L., & Hanish, L. D. (2003). Qualities of young children's same-, other-, and mixed-sex play. *Child Development, 74,* 921–932.

Fabes, R. A., Martin, C. L., Hanish, L., & Updegraff, K. (2000). New criteria for evaluating child development research. *Child Development, 71,* 212–221.

Fabes, R. A., Martin, C. L., & Smith, M. (1994). Further perspectives on child development research: A reconsideration and a recall; Invited response to McKinney and Lerner's paper. *Family Sciences Research Journal, 23,* 43–56.

Fabris, C., Prandi, G., Perathoner, C., & Soldi, A. (1998). Neonatal drug addiction. *Panminerva Medicine, 40,* 239–243.

Fagan, J., Barnett, M., Bernd, E., & Whiteman, V. (2001). Prenatal involvement of adolescent unmarried fathers. *Fathering, 2003,* 283–302.

Falk, P. J. (1989). Lesbian mothers: Psychosocial assumptions in family law. *American Psychologist, 44,* 941–947.

Fallone, G., Owens, J. A., & Deane, J. (2002). Sleepiness in children and adolescents: Clinical implications. *Sleep Medicine Research, 6,* 207–306.

Fan, X., & Chen, M. (2001). Parental involvement and students' academic achievement: A meta-analysis. *Educational Psychology Review, 13,* 1–22.

Fanaroff, A. A., Martin, R. J., & Miller, M. J. (1994). Identification and management of high-risk problems in the neonate. In R. K. Creasy & R. Resnik (Eds.), *Maternal–fetal medicine: Principles and practice* (pp. 299–112). Philadelphia: W. B. Saunders.

Fang, J., Madhavan, S., & Alderman, M. H. (1999). Low birth weight: Race and maternal nativity-impact of community income. *Pediatrics, 103,* 1–6.

Fantuzzo, J., & Mohr, W. K. (2000). Pursuit of wellness in Head Start: Making beneficial connections for children and families. In D. Cicchetti & J. Rappaport (Eds.), *The promotion of wellness in children and adolescents* (pp. 341–369). Washington, DC: Child Welfare League of America.

Fantz, R. L., Ordy, J. M., & Udelf, M. S. (1962). Maturation of pattern vision in infants during the first six months. *Journal of Comparative and Physiological Psychology, 55,* 907–917.

Farber, N. (1994). Perceptions of pregnancy risk: A comparison by class and race. *American Journal of Orthopsychiatry, 64,* 479–484.

Farmer, M. (1997). Exploring the links between communication skills and social competence. *Educational and Child Psychology, 14,* 38–44.

Farrar, M. J. (1990). Discourse and the acquisition of grammatical morphemes. *Journal of Child Language, 17,* 607–624.

Farrar, M. J., & Goodman, G. S. (1992). Developmental changes in event memory. *Child Development, 63,* 173–187.

Federal Bureau of Investigation. (1998). *A parent's guide to Internet safety.* Washington, DC: Author.

Federal Bureau of Investigation. (2000). *Uniform crime reports: 2000.* Washington, DC: Author.

Federal Bureau of Investigation. (2004). *Supplementary homicide reports, 1976–2002.* Washington, DC: Author.

Federman, J. (1998). *National television violence study* (Vol. 3). Santa Barbara, CA: Center for Communication and Social Policy.

Feingold, A. (1992). Good-looking people are not what we think. *Psychological Bulletin, 111,* 304–341.

Feldman, D. H. (1999). The development of creativity. In R. J. Sternberg (Ed.), *Handbook of creativity* (pp. 169–186). Cambridge, UK: Cambridge University Press.

Feldman, R., Weller, A., Leckman, J. F., Kuint, J., & Eidelman, A. I. (1999). The nature of the mother's tie to her infant: Maternal bonding under conditions of proximity, separation, and potential loss. *Journal of Child Psychology and Psychiatry and Allied Disciplines, 40,* 929–939.

Feldman, S. S., & Rosenthal, D. A. (1994). Culture makes a difference . . . or does it? A comparison of adolescents in Hong Kong, Australia, and the United States. In R. K. Silbereisen & T. Eberhard (Eds.), *Adolescence in context* (pp. 99–124). New York: Springer-Verlag.

Fenson, C., Kagan, J., Kearsley, R. B., & Zelazo, P. R. (1976). The developmental progression of manipulative play in the first two years. *Child Development, 47,* 232–236.

Fenson, L., Dale, P. S., Reznick, J. S., Bates, E., Thal, D. J., & Pethick, S. J. (1994). Variability in early communicative development. *Monographs of the Society for Research in Child Development, 59* (Whole No. 242). Chicago: Chicago University Press.

Fenton, N. (1928). The only child. *Journal of Genetic Psychology, 35,* 546–556.

Ferber, R. (1985). *Solve your child's sleep problems.* New York: Simon & Schuster.

Ferber, R. (1986a). Sleepless child. In C. Guilleminault (Ed.), *Sleep and its disorders in children* (pp. 141–163). New York: Raven Press.

Ferber, R. (1986b). *Solve your child's sleep problems.* New York: Simon and Schuster.

Ferguson, R. E. (1998). Teachers' perceptions and expectations and the Black-White test score gap. In C. Jenks & M. Phillips (Eds.), *The Black-White test score gap* (pp. 273–317). Washington, DC: Brookings Institution.

Fergusson, D. M., Beautrais, A. L., & Silva, P. A. (1982). Breast-feeding and cognitive development in the first seven years of life. *Social Science Medicine, 16,* 1705–1708.

Fergusson, D. M., Horwood, L. J., & Lynskey, M. T. (1993). Maternal smoking before and after pregnancy: Effects on behavioral outcomes in middle childhood. *Pediatrics, 92,* 815–822.

Fernald, A. (1985). Four month old infants prefer to listen to motherese. *Infant Behavior and Development, 8,* 181–195.

Fernald, A. (1989). Intonation and communicative intent in mothers' speech to infants: Is the melody the message? *Child Development, 60,* 1497–1510.

Feynman, R. P. (1985). *"Surely you're joking, Mr. Feynman!"* Toronto: Bantam Books.

Field, A. E., Camargo, C. A., Taylor, C. B., Berkey, C. S., Roberts, S. B., & Colditz, G. A. (2001). Peer, parent, and media influences on the development of weight concerns and frequent dieting among preadolescent and adolescent girls and boys. *Pediatrics, 107,* 54–60.

Finch, C., Da-Costa, A., Stevenson, M., Hamer, P., & Elliott, B. (2002). Sports injury experiences from the Western Australian Sports Injury Cohort Study. *Australian and New Zealand Journal of Public Health, 26,* 462–467.

Fincham, F. D. (1998). Child development and marital relationships. *Child Development, 69,* 543–574.

Finkelman, B. (1995). *Physical and emotional abuse and neglect.* New York: Garland.

Fisch, S., Truglio, R. T., & Cole, C. F. (1999). The impact of *Sesame Street* on preschool children: A review and synthesis of 30 years' research. Media Psychology, 1, 165–190.

Fischer, J. L., Munsch, J., & Greene, S. M. (1996). Adolescence and intimacy. In G. R. Adams & R. Montemayor (Eds.), *Psychosocial development during adolescence* (Vol. 8, pp. 95–129). Thousand Oaks, CA: Sage.

Fischer, K. W., & Bidell, T. K. (1998). Dynamic relationship of psychological structures in action and thought. In W. Damon (Ed.), *Handbook of child psychology* (Vol. 1, pp. 467–562). New York: Wiley.

Fischer, K. W., & Rose, S. P. (1994). Dynamic development of coordination components in brain and behavior: A framework for theory and research. In G. Dawson & K. W. Fischer (Eds.), *Human behavior and the developing brain* (pp. 3–66). New York: Guilford.

Fisher, C. B., & Brone, R. J. (1991). Eating disorders in adolescence. In R. M. Lerner, A. C. Petersen, & J. Brooks-Gunn (Eds.), *Encyclopedia of adolescence* (Vol. 1, pp. 272–277). New York: Garland.

Fisher, M., Trieller, K., & Napolitano, B. (1989). Premenstrual symptoms in adolescents. *Journal of Adolescent Health Care, 10,* 369–375.

Fitch, R. H., & Bimonte, H. A. (2002). Hormone, brain, and behavior: Putative biological contributions to cognitive sex differences. In A. McGillicuddy-De Lisi & R. De Lisi (Eds.), *Biology, society, and behavior: The development of sex differences in cognition* (pp. 55–92). Westport, CT: Ablex.

Fitzgerald, B. (1999). Children of lesbian and gay parents: A review of the literature. *Marriage & Family Review, 29,* 57–75.

Fix, M., & Passell, J. S. (1994). *Immigration and immigrants: Setting the record straight.* Washington, DC: Urban Institute.

Flake, A. W., Roncarolo, M., Puck, J. M., Almeida-Porada, G., Evans, M. I., Johnson, M. P., Abella, E. M., Harrison, D. D., & Zanjani, E. D. (1996). Treatment of X-linked severe combined immunodeficiency by in utero transplantation of paternal bone marrow. *New England Journal of Medicine, 335,* 1806–1810.

Flanagan, P. (1998). Teen mothers: Countering the myths of dysfunction and developmental disruption. In C. G. Coll & J. L Surrey (Eds.), *Mothering against odds* (pp. 238–254). New York: Guilford Press.

Flavell, J. H. (1982). On cognitive development. *Child Development, 53,* 1–10.

Flavell, J. H. (1988). From cognitive connections to mental representations. In J. Astington, P. Harris, & D. Olson (Eds.), *Developing theories of mind* (pp. 244–267). New York: Cambridge University Press.

Flavell, J. H., Green, F. L., & Flavell, E. R. (1987). Development of knowledge about the appearance–reality distinction. *Monographs of the Society for Research in Child Development, 51* (Whole No. 212). Chicago: University of Chicago Press.

Flavell, J. H., Green, F. L., & Flavell, E. R. (1995). The development of children's knowledge about attentional focus. *Developmental Psychology, 31,* 706–712.

Flavell, J. H., & Miller, P. H. (1998). Social cognition. In W. Damon (Ed.), *Handbook of child psychology* (pp. 851–898). New York: Wiley.

Fleming, J., Challela, M., Eland, J., Hornick, R., Johnson, P., Martinson, I., Nativio, D., Nokes, K., Riddle, I., Steele, N., Sudela, K., Thomas, R., Turner, Q., Wheeler, B., & Young, A. (1994). Impact on the family of children who are technology dependent and cared for in the home. *Pediatric Nursing, 20,* 379–388

Fletcher, J. L., & Gordon, R. C. (1990). Perinatal transmission of bacterial sexually transmitted diseases: Part I. Syphilis and gonorrhea. *Journal of Family Practice, 30,* 448–456.

Focus on the Family. (1992). Oppressed minority or counterfeits? *Focus on the Family Citizen, 6,* 1–5.

Fodor, J. A. (1983). *The modularity of the mind.* Cambridge, MA: MIT Press.

Fogel, A. (1997). *Infancy.* Minneapolis, MN: West.

Fogel, A., Nwokah, E., Hsu, H. C., Dedo, J. Y., & Walker, H. (1993). Posture and communication in mother–infant interaction. In G. Savelsbergh (Ed.), *The development of coordination in infancy* (pp. 395–422). Amsterdam: Elsevier Science.

Fogel, A., & Thelen, E. (1987). Development of early expressive and communicative action: Reinterpreting the evidence from a dynamic systems perspective. *Developmental Psychology, 23,* 747–761.

Foltz, C., Overton, W. F., & Ricco, R. B. (1995). Proof construction: Adolescent development from inductive to deductive problem-solving strategies. *Journal of Experimental Child Psychology, 59,* 179–195.

Fombonne, E. (1995). Eating disorders: Time trends and possible explanatory mechanisms. In M. Rutter & D. J. Smith (Eds.), *Psychosocial disorders in young people: Time trends and their causes* (pp. 616–685). New York: Wiley.

Fombonne, E. (2003). The prevalence of autism. *Journal of the American Medical Association, 289,* 87–89.

Foorman, B. R., Francis, D. J., Fletcher, J. M., Schatschneider, C., & Mehta, P. (1998). The role of instruction in learning to read: Preventing reading failure in at-risk children. *Journal of Educational Psychology, 90,* 37–55.

Forbes, G. B. (1986). Body composition in adolescence. In F. Faulkner & J. M. Tanner (Eds.), *Human growth: A comprehensive treatise* (Vol. 2, pp. 119–145). New York: Plenum.

Fowler, W. (1986). Early experiences of great men and women mathematicians. *New Directions in Child Development, 32,* 87–109.

Fowles, D.C. (2003). Electrodermal hyporeactivity in psychopathy. In J. M. Hooley & M. F. Lenzenweger (Eds.), *Principles of experimental psychopathology* (pp. 255–268). Washington, DC: American Psychological Association.

Fox, G. L., Bruce, C., & Combs-Orne, T. (2000). Parenting expectations and concerns of fathers and mothers of newborn infants. *Family Relations, 49,* 123–131.

Fox, N. A., Kimmerly, N. L., & Schafer, W. D. (1991). Attachment to mother/attachment to father: A meta-analysis. *Child Development, 62,* 210–225.

Fox, R. A., & Solis-Camera, P. (1997). Parenting of young children by fathers in Mexico and the United States. *Journal of Social Psychology, 137,* 489–495.

Frable, D. S. (1997). Gender, racial, sexual, and class identities. *Annual Review of Psychology, 48,* 139–162.

Fracasso, M. P., Lamb, M. E., Schoelmerich, A., & Leyendecker, B. (1997). The ecology of mother-infant interaction in Euro-American and immigrant Central American families living in the United States. *International Journal of Behavioral Development, 20,* 207–217.

Franiuk, R. (2004). Adolescent romantic relations and sexual behavior: Theories, research, and practical implications. *Journal of Adolescence, 27,* 376–377.

Frank, D. A., Augustyn, M., Knight, W. G., Pell, T., & Zuckerman, B. (2001). Growth, development, and behavior in early childhood following prenatal cocaine exposure. *Journal of the American Medical Association, 285,* 1613–1625.

Frankel, K. A., & Bates, J. E. (1990). Mother–toddler problem solving: Antecedents in attachment, home behavior, and temperament. *Child Development, 61,* 810–819.

Fredrickson, B. L. (1998). Cultivated emotions: Parental socialization of positive emotions and self-conscious emotions. *Psychological Inquiry, 9,* 279–281.

Freedman, D. S., Dietz, W. H., & Srinivasan, S. R. (1999). The relation of overweight to cardiovascular risk factors among children and adolescents: The Bogalusa heart study. *Pediatrics, 103,* 1175–1182.

Freedman-Doan, C., Wigfield, A., Eccles, J. S., Blumenfeld, P., Arbreton, A., & Harold, R. D. (2001). What am I best at? Grade and gender differences in children's beliefs about ability improvement. *Journal of Applied Developmental Psychology, 21,* 379–402.

Freeman, M., Csikszentmihalyi, M., & Larson, R. (1986). Adolescence and its recollection. *Merrill-Palmer Quarterly, 32,* 167–185.

French, D.C. (1988). Heterogeneity of peer rejected boys: Aggressive and non-aggressive subtypes. *Child Development, 59,* 976–985.

Freppon, P. A., & Dahl, K. L. (1998). Balanced instruction: Insights and considerations. *Reading Research Quarterly, 33,* 240–251.

Freud, S. (1960). *The ego and the id* (J. Riviere, Trans.). New York: Norton. (Original work published 1923)

Freud, S. (1965). *A general introduction to psychoanalysis* (J. Riviere, Trans.). New York: Washington Square Books. (Original work published 1920)

Freund, L. S., Baker, L., & Sonnenschein, S. (1990). Developmental changes in strategic approaches to classification. *Journal of Experimental Child Psychology, 49,* 343–362.

Frick, P. J. (1998). *Conduct disorders and severe antisocial behavior.* New York: Plenum.

Frick, P. J., & Loney, B. R. (2002). Understanding the association between parent and child antisocial behavior. In R. D. Peters & R. J. McMahon (Eds.), *The effects of parental dysfunction on children* (pp. 105–126). New York: Kluwer.

Friedrich, L. K., & Stein, A. H. (1975). Prosocial television and young children: The effects of verbal labeling and role playing on learning and behavior. *Child Development, 46,* 27–38.

Friedrich-Cofer, L. K., Huston, A., Kipnis, D. M., Susman, E. J., & Clewett, A. S. (1979). Environmental enhancement of prosocial television content: Effects on interpersonal behavior, imaginative play, and self-regulation in a natural setting. *Developmental Psychology, 15,* 637–646.

Frisch, R. E. (1991). Puberty and body fat. In R. M. Lerner, A. C. Petersen, & J. Brooks-Gunn (Eds.), *Encyclopedia of adolescence* (Vol. 2). New York: Garland.

Frith, U. (1989). *Autism.* Oxford, UK: Oxford University Press.

Frolund, L. (1997). Early shame and mirroring. *Scandinavian Psychoanalytic Review, 20,* 35–57.

Frome, P. M., & Eccles, J. S. (1998). Parents' influence on children's achievement-related perceptions. *Journal of Personality and Social Psychology, 74,* 435–452.

Frost, J. L., Shin, D., & Jacobs, P. J. (1998). Physical environments and children's play. In O. N. Saracho & B. Spodek (Eds.), *Multiple perspectives on play in early childhood education* (pp. 255–294). Albany: State University of New York Press.

Fry, P. S., & Addington, J. (1984). Comparison of social problem solving of children from open and traditional classrooms: A two-year longitudinal study. *Journal of Educational Psychology, 76,* 318–329.

Fugger, E. F., Black, S. H., Keyvanfar, K., & Schulman, J. D. (1998). Births of normal daughters after MicroSort sperm separation and intrauterine insemination, in-vitro fertilization, or intracytoplasmic sperm injection. *Human Reproduction, 13,* 2367–2370.

Fujii, N., & Graybiel, A. M. (2003). Representation of action sequence boundaries by Macaque prefrontal cortical neurons. *Science, 301,* 1246–1249.

Fuligni, A. J. (1998). Authority, autonomy, and parent–adolescent conflict and cohesion: A study of adolescents from Mexican, Chinese, Filipino, and European backgrounds. *Developmental Psychology, 34,* 782–792.

Fuligni, A. J. (2001b). A comparative longitudinal approach to acculturation among children from immigrant families. *Harvard Educational Review, 71,* 566–578.

Fuligni, A. J., & Eccles, J. S. (1993). Perceived parent–child relationships and early adolescents' orientation toward peers. *Developmental Psychology, 29,* 622–632.

Fuligni, A. J., Eccles, J. S., Barber, B. L., & Clements, P. (2001). Early adolescent peer orientation and adjustment during high school. *Developmental Psychology, 37,* 28–36.

Fuligni, A. J., & Witkow, M. (2004). The postsecondary educational progress of youth from immigrant families. *Journal of Research on Adolescence, 14,* 159–183.

Furman, W. (1996). The measurement of friendship perceptions: Conceptual and methodological issues. In W. M. Bukowski, A. F. Newcomb, & W. W. Hartup (Eds.), *The company they keep: Friendships in childhood and adolescence* (pp. 41–65). Cambridge, UK: Cambridge University Press.

Furman, W., & Shaffer, L. (2003). The role of romantic relationships in adolescent development. In P. Florsheim (Ed.), *Adolescent romantic relations and sexual behavior.* Mahwah, NJ: Erlbaum.

Furman, W., & Wehner, E. A. (1997). Adolescent romantic relationships: A developmental perspective. In S. Shulman & W. A. Collins (Eds.), *Romantic relationships in adolescence* (pp. 21–36). San Francisco: Jossey-Bass.

Furnham, A., & Alibhai, M. (1983). Cross-cultural differences in the perception of female body shape. *Psychological Medicine, 13,* 829–837.

Furstenberg, F. F., & Cherlin, A. J. (1991). *Divided families.* Cambridge, MA: Harvard University Press.

Furstenberg, F. F., & Kiernan, K. E. (2001). Delayed parental divorce: How much do children benefit? *Journal of Marriage and the Family, 63,* 446–457.

Futterman, D., & Hein, K. (1992). AIDS and HIV infection. In S. B. Friedman, M. Fisher, & S. K. Schonberg (Eds.), *Comprehensive adolescent health care* (pp. 521–531). St. Louis, MO: Quality Medical Publishing.

Gaddis, A., & Brooks-Gunn, J. (1985). The male experience of pubertal change. *Journal of Youth and Adolescence, 14,* 61–70.

Gagnon, J. H. (1990). The explicit and implicit use of the scripting perspective in sex research. *Annual Review of Sex Research, 1,* 1–43.

Galambos, N. L., Almeida, D. M., & Petersen, A. C. (1991). Masculinity, femininity, and sex role attitudes in early adolescence. *Annual Progress in Child Psychiatry and Child Development, 5,* 77–91.

Gallagher, A. M., & De Lisi, R. (1994). Gender differences in scholastic aptitude test—mathematics problem solving among high ability students. *Journal of Educational Psychology, 86,* 204–211.

Gallagher, A. M., De Lisi, R., Host, P. C., McGillicuddy-De Lisi, A. V., Morely, M., & Cahalan, C. (2000). Gender differences in advanced mathematical problem solving. *Journal of Experimental Child Psychology, 75,* 165–190.

Gallahue, D. L., & Ozmun, J. C. (1995). *Understanding motor development.* Madison, WI: Brown & Benchmark.

Gallant, S. J., & Derry, P. S. (1995). Menarche, menstruation, and menopause: Psychosocial research and future directions. In A. L. Stanton & S. J. Gallant (Eds.), *The psychology of women's health* (pp. 199–259). Washington, DC: American Psychological Association.

Gallup Organization. (1997). *Public attitudes toward the public schools.* New York: Author.

Galotti, K. M., Pierce, B., Reimer, R. L., & Luckner, A. E. (2000). Midwife or doctor: A study of pregnant women making delivery decisions. *Journal of Midwifery and Women's Health, 45,* 320–329.

Gamble, T. J., & Zigler, E. (1989). The Head Start Synthesis Project. *Journal of Applied Developmental Psychology, 10,* 267–274.

Garbarino, J. (1999). The effects of community violence on children. In L. Balter & C. S. Tamis-LeMonda (Eds.), *Child psychology: A handbook of contemporary issues* (pp. 412–425). Philadelphia: Psychology Press.

Garbarino, J., & Stott, F. M. (1992). *What children can tell us.* San Francisco: Jossey-Bass.

Garbarino, J., Dubrow, N., Kostelny, K., & Pardo, C. (1992). *Children in danger.* San Francisco: Jossey-Bass.

Garbarino, J., Hammond, W. R., Mercy, J., & Yung, B. R. (2004). Community violence and children: Preventing exposure and reducing harm. In C. J. Schellenbach & K. I. Maton (Eds.), *Investing in children, youth, families, and communities* (pp. 303–320). Washington, DC: American Psychological Association.

Garber, J., & Little, S. A. (2001). Emotional autonomy and adolescent adjustment. *Journal of Adolescent Research, 16,* 355–371.

Garber, J., Weiss, B., & Shanley, N. (1993). Cognitions, depressive symptoms, and development in adolescence. *Journal of Abnormal Psychology, 102,* 47–57.

Garcia Coll, C. T. (1990). Developmental outcome of minority infants: A process-oriented look into our beginnings. *Child Development, 61,* 270–289.

Gardner, H. (1980). *Artful scribbles: The significance of children's drawing.* New York: Basic Books.

Gardner, H. (1983). *Frames of mind.* London: Heinemann.

Gardner, H. (1999). *Intelligence reframed: Multiple intelligences for the 21st century.* New York: Basic Books.

Gardner, H. (2000). The giftedness matrix: A developmental perspective. In R. Friedman & B. Shore (Eds.), *Talents unfolding: Cognition and development* (pp. 77–88). Washington, DC: American Psychological Association.

Gardner, H., & Hatch, T. (1989). Multiple intelligences go to school: Educational implications of the theory of multiple intelligences. *Educational Research, 18,* 4–9.

Gardstrom, S. C. (1999). Music exposure and criminal behavior: Perceptions of juvenile offenders. *Journal of Music Therapy, 36,* 207–221.

Garner, P. W., Jones, D.C., & Palmer, D. (1994). Social cognitive correlates of preschool children's sibling caregiving behavior. *Developmental Psychology, 30,* 905–911.

Garrison, W. T., & McQuiston, S. (1989). *Chronic illness during childhood and adolescence.* Newbury Park, CA: Sage.

Gauvain, M. (1998). Culture, development, and theory of mind: Comment on Lillard (1998). *Psychological Bulletin, 123,* 37–42.

Ge, X., Conger, R. D., & Elder, G. H. (1996). Coming of age too early: Pubertal influences on girls' vulnerability to psychological distress. *Child Development, 67,* 3386–3400.

Ge, X., Lorenz, F. O., Conger, R. D., Elder, G. H., & Simon, R. L. (1994). Trajectories of stressful life events and depressive symptoms during adolescence. *Developmental Psychology, 30,* 467–483.

Geary, D.C., & Bjorklund, D. F. (2000). Evolutionary developmental psychology. *Child Development, 71,* 57–65.

Gecas, V., & Seff, M. (1990). Social class and self-esteem: Psychological centrality, compensation, and the relative effects of work and home. *Social Psychology Quarterly, 53,* 165–173.

Gelman, R., & Baillargeon, R. (1983). A review of some Piagetian concepts. In P. Mussen (Ed.), *Handbook of child psychology* (Vol. 3, pp. 167–230). New York: Wiley.

Gelman, R., & Williams, E. M. (1998). Enabling constraints for cognitive development and learning: domain specificity and epigenesis. In W Damon (Ed.), *Handbook of child psychology* (pp. 575–630). New York: Wiley.

Gelman, S. A., & Taylor, M. (1984). How two-year-old children interpret proper and common names for unfamiliar objects. *Child Development, 55,* 1535–1540.

Georgieff, M. K., & Rao, R. (2001). The role of nutrition in cognitive development. In C. Nelson & M. Luciana (Eds.), *Handbook of developmental cognitive neuroscience* (pp. 491–504). Cambridge, MA: MIT Press.

Geraldson, B., & Hopkins, W. D. (1997). Children's lateralization on a finger-localization task. *Perceptual and Motor Skills, 84,* 1259–1264.

Gerris, J., de Neubourg, D., Magelschots, K., Van Royen, E., Vercruyssen, Barudy-Vasquez, J., Valkenburg, M., & Ryckaert, G. (2002). Elective single day 3 embryo transfer halves the twinning rate without decrease in the ongoing pregnancy rate of an IVF/ICSI programme. *Human Reproduction, 17,* 2626–2631.

Gershman, H. (1997). Sexual permissiveness and its consequences. In L. B. Schlesinger & E. Revitch (Eds.), *Sexual dynamics of anti-social behavior* (pp. 76–87). Springfield, IL: Thomas.

Gershoff, E. T. (2003). *Low income and the development of America's kindergartners.* New York: National Center for Children in Poverty.

Gershoff, E. T. (2002). Corporal punishment by parents and associated child behaviors and experiences: A meta-analytic and theoretical review. *Psychological Bulletin, 128,* 539–579.

Geschwind, N., & Galaburda, A. M. (1985). Cerebral lateralizations: Biological mechanisms, associations, and pathology: I. A hypothesis and a program for research. *Archives of Neurology, 42,* 428–459.

Geschwind, N., & Galaburda, A. M. (1987). *Cerebral lateralization: Biological mechanisms, associations, and pathology.* Cambridge, MA: MIT Press.

Gibbs, R. S., & Sweet, R. L. (1994). Clinical disorders. In R. K. Creasy & R. Resnik (Eds.), *Maternal–fetal medicine: Principles and practice* (pp. 355–411). Philadelphia: Saunders.

Giedd, J. N. (1997). Normal development. *Child and Adolescent Psychiatric Clinics of North America, 6,* 265–282.

Gil, A. G., & Vega, W. A. (1996). Two different worlds: Acculturation stress and adaptation among Cuban and Nicaraguan families. *Journal of Social and Personal Relationships, 13,* 435–456.

Gil, A. G., Vega, W. A., & Dimas, J. M. (1994). Acculturative stress and personal adjustment among Hispanic adolescent boys. *Journal of Community Psychology, 22,* 43–54.

Gilligan, C. (1982). *In a different voice: Psychological theory and women's development.* Cambridge, MA: Harvard University Press.

Gilligan, C. (1994). In a different voice: Women's conceptions of self and of morality. In B. Pulka (Ed.), *Caring voices and women's moral frames: Gilligan's view* (Vol. 6, pp. 1–37). New York: Garland.

Gillman, M. W., Rifas-Shiman, S. L., Camargo, C. A., Berkey, C. S., Frazier, A. L., Rockett, H. R., Field, A. E., & Colditz, G. A. (2001). Risk of overweight among adolescents who were breastfed as infants. *Journal of the American Medical Association, 285,* 2461–2467.

Gilmore, M. R., Lewis, S. M., Lohr, M. J., Spencer, M. S., & White, R. D. (1997). Repeat pregnancies among adolescent mothers. *Journal of Marriage and the Family, 59,* 536–550.

Ginsburg, H. J., & Miller, S. M. (1982). Sex differences in children's risk-taking behavior. *Child Development, 53,* 426–428.

Giordano, P. C., Cernkovich, S. A., Groat, H. T., Pugh, M. D., & Swinford, S. P. (1998). The quality of adolescent friendships: Long-term effects. *Journal of Health and Social Behavior, 39,* 55–71.

Gladstein, J., Slater-Rusonis, E., & Heald, F. (1992). A comparison of inner-city and upper-middle-class youths' exposure to violence. *Journal of Adolescent Health, 13,* 275–280.

Glass, R. H. (1994). Gamete transport, fertilization, and implantation. In R. K. Creasy & R. Resnik (Eds.), *Maternal–fetal medicine* (pp. 89–95). Philadelphia: Saunders.

Glastris, P. (1997, May 26). The alien payoff. *U.S. News & World Report,* 20–22.

Gleason, J. B. (1993). *The development of language.* New York: Macmillan.

Gleason, J. B., & Ely, R. (2002). Gender differences in language development. In A. McGillicuddy-De Lisi & R. De Lisi (Eds.), *Biology, society, and behavior: The development of sex differences in cognition* (pp. 127–154). Westport, CT: Ablex.

Gleason, J. B., Ely, R., Perlmann, R. Y., & Narasimhan, B. (1996). Patterns of prohibition in parent–child discourse. In D. I. Slobin & J. Gerhardt (Eds.), *Social interaction, social context, and language* (pp. 205–217). Mahwah, NJ: Erlbaum.

Gleitman, L. R., & Gillette, J. (1995). The role of syntax in verb learning. In P. Fletcher & B. MacWhinney (Eds.), *The handbook of child language* (pp. 413–427). Oxford, UK: Blackwell.

Gleitman, L. R., Newport, E. L., & Gleitman, H. (1984). The current status of the motherese hypothesis. *Journal of Child Language, 11,* 43–79.

Glover, V. (1997). Maternal stress or anxiety in pregnancy and emotional development of the child. *British Journal of Psychiatry, 171,* 105–106.

Goel, P., Radotra, A., Singh, I., Aggarwal, A., & Dua, D. (2004). Effects of passive smoking on outcome in pregnancy. *Journal of Postgraduate Medicine, 50,* 12–16.

Golan, M., Weizman, A., Apter, A., & Fainaru, M. (1998). Parents as exclusive agents of change in the treatment of childhood obesity. *American Journal of Clinical Nutrition, 67,* 1130–1135.

Gold, D., Crombie, G., & Noble, S. (1987). Relations between teachers' judgments of girls' and boys' compliance and intellectual competence. *Sex Roles, 16,* 351–358.

Goldberg, S. (1983). Parent-to-infant bonding: Another look. *Child Development, 54,* 1355–1382.

Goldberg, S., & DiVitto, B. (1995). Parenting children born preterm. In M. Bornstein (Ed.), *Handbook of parenting* (Vol. 1, pp. 209–231). Mahwah, NJ: Erlbaum.

Goldfield, B. (1987). The contributions of child and caregiver to referential and expressive language. *Applied Psycholinguistics, 8,* 267–280.

Goldfield, B., & Reznick, J. S. (1990). Early lexical acquisition: Rate, content, and the vocabulary spurt. *Journal of Child Language, 17,* 171–183.

Goldin-Meadow, C. (1997). When gestures and words speak differently. *Current Directions in Psychological Science, 6,* 138–143.

Goldin-Meadow, S., & Mylander, C. (1998). Spontaneous sign systems created by deaf children in two cultures. *Nature, 391,* 279–281.

Goldsmith, H. H., & Rieser-Danner, L. (1990). Assessing early temperament. In C. R. Reynolds & R. Kamphaus (Eds.), *Handbook of psychological and educational assessment of children* (Vol. 2, pp. 245–378). New York: Guilford.

Golinkoff, R. M., & Hirsh-Pasek, K. (1999). *How babies talk: The magic and mystery of language in the first three years of life.* New York: Plume.

Golinkoff, R. M., Hirsh-Pasek, K., Bloom, K., Smith, L. B., Woodward, A. L., Akhtar, N., Tomasello, M., & Hollich, G. (2000). *Becoming a word learner: A debate on lexical acquisition.* London: Oxford University Press.

Goncalves, M. (1990). *A representaca da escola feita pela crianca de baixa renda em sua primeira experància discente.* Paper presented at the 13th annual congress of ANPED, Belo Horizonte, Brazil.

Gonchas, G. Q. (2001). Structuring failure and success: Understanding the variability in latino school engagement. *Harvard Educational Review, 71,* 475–504.

Goncu, A. (1993). Development of intersubjectivity in social pretend play. *Human Development, 36,* 185–198.

Gonzales, N. A., Dumka, L. E., Deardorff, J., Carter, S., & McCray, A. (2004). Preventing poor mental health and school dropout of Mexican American adolescents following the transition to junior high school. *Journal of Adolescent Research, 19,* 1130–2131.

Goodman, G. S., Emery, R. E., & Haugaard, J. J. (1998). Developmental psychology and law: Divorce, child maltreatment, foster care, and adoption. In W. Damon (Ed.), *Handbook of child psychology* (Vol. 4, pp. 775–874). New York: Wiley.

Goodman, R. A., & Whitaker, H. A. (1985). Hemispherectomy: A review (1928–1981) with special reference to the linguistic abilities and disabilities of the residual right hemisphere. In C. T. Best (Ed.), *Hemispheric function and collaboration in the child* (pp. 121–156). Orlando, FL: Harcourt Brace Jovanovich.

Goodyear, I. M. (2001). *The depressed child and adolescent.* New York: Cambridge University Press.

Goodyear, I., Kolvin, I., & Gatzanis, S. (1985). Recent undesirable life events and psychiatric disorders in childhood and adolescence. *British Journal of Psychiatry, 147,* 517–533.

Gopnik, A. (1988). Three types of early words. *First Language, 8,* 49–70.

Gopnik, A., & Meltzoff, A. (1986). Relations between semantic and cognitive developments in the one-word stage: The specificity hypothesis. *Child Development, 57,* 1040–1053.

Gopnik, A., Meltzoff, A. N., & Kuhl, P. K. (1999). *The scientist in the crib: Minds, brains, and how children learn.* New York: Morrow.

Gopnik, A., & Wellman, H. M. (1994). The theory theory. In L. Hirschfeld & S. Gelman (Eds.), *Mapping the mind: Domain specificity in cognition and culture* (pp. 257–293). New York: Cambridge University Press.

Gordon, B., Saklofske, D. H., & Hildebrand, D. K. (1998). Assessing children with mental retardation. In V. H. Booney (Ed.), *Psychological assessment of children* (pp. 454–481). New York: Wiley.

Gorman-Smith, D., & Tolan, P. H. (1998). The role of exposure to community violence and developmental problems among inner-city youth. *Development and Psychopathology, 10,* 101–116.

Goswami, U. (1998). *Cognition in children.* Hove, UK: Psychology Press.

Gottesman, I. I. (1991). *Schizophrenia genesis: The origins of madness.* New York: Freeman.

Gottfried, A. W. (1985). Environment of newborns in special care units. In A. W. Gottfried & J. L. Gaiter (Eds.), *Infant stress under intensive care: Environmental neonatology* (pp. 251–257). Baltimore, MD: University Park Press.

Gottfried, A. W., Gottfried, A. E., Bathurst, K., & Guerin, D. W. (1994). *Gifted IQ: Early developmental perspectives.* New York: Plenum.

Gottlieb, G. (1997). *Synthesizing nature–nurture: Prenatal roots of instinctive behavior.* Mahwah, NJ: Erlbaum.

Gottman, J. M. (1983). How children become friends. *Monographs of the Society for Research in Child Development, 48* (Whole No. 201). Chicago: University of Chicago Press.

Gottwald, S. R., & Thurman, S. K. (1990). Parent–infant interaction in neonatal intensive care units: Implications for research and service delivery. *Infants and Young Children, 2,* 1–10.

Goubet, N., & Clifton, R. K. (1998). Object and event representation in 6½-month-old infants. *Developmental Psychology, 34,* 63–76.

Gould, E. (1999). Neurogenesis in adulthood: A possible role in learning. *Trends in Cognitive Sciences, 3,* 186–192.

Graber, J. A., & Archibald, A. B. (2001). Psychosocial change at puberty and beyond: Understanding adolescent sexuality and sexual orientation. In A. R. D'Augelli & C. J. Patterson (Eds.), *Lesbian, gay, and bisexual identities and youth: Psychological perspectives* (pp. 3–26). New York: Oxford University Press.

Graber, J. A., Brooks-Gunn, J., & Warren, M. P. (1995). The antecedents of menarcheal age: Heredity, family environment, and stressful life events. *Child Development, 66,* 346–359.

Graber, J. A., Lewinsohn, P. M., Seeley, J. R., & Brooks-Gunn, J. (1997). Is psychopathology associated with the timing of puberty? *Journal of the American Academy of Child and Adolescent Psychiatry, 36,* 1768–1776.

Graber, J. S. (2003). Puberty in context. In C. Hayward (Ed.), *Gender differences at puberty* (pp. 307–325). New York: Cambridge University Press.

Graber, J. J. S., Petersen, A. C., & Brooks-Gunn, J. (1996). Pubertal processes: Methods, measures, and models. In J. Graber, J. Brooks-Gunn, & A. Petersen (Eds.), *Transitions through adolescence: Interpersonal domains and context* (pp. 23–53). Mahwah, NJ: Erlbaum.

Grabill, C. M., Griffith, J. R., & Kaslow, N.J. (2001). Depression. In M. Hersen & V. B. Van Hasselt (Eds.), *Advanced abnormal psychology* (pp. 243–260). New York: Kluwer.

Graham, P. (1986). *Child psychiatry: A developmental approach.* Oxford, UK: Oxford University Press.

Graham, S. T., & Taylor, A. Z. (2002). Ethnicity, gender, and the development of achievement values. In J. Eccles & A. Wigfield (Eds.), *Development of achievement motivation* (pp. 121–146). San Diego, CA: Academic Press.

Granic, I., & Dishion, T. J. (2003). Deviant talk in adolescent friendships: A step toward measuring a pathogenic attractor process. *Social Development, 12,* 314–334.

Grant, B. (1993). Multiple pregnancy. In V. R. Bennett & L. K. Brown (Eds.), *Myles textbook for midwives* (pp. 365–376). London: Churchill Livingstone.

Grant, B. F., & Dawson, D. A. (1998). *Age of drinking onset predicts future alcohol abuse and dependence.* Washington, DC: National Institute on Alcohol Abuse and Alcoholism.

Grantham-McGregor, S., Ani, C., & Fernald, L. (2001). The role of nutrition in intellectual development. In R. Sternberg (Ed.), *Environmental effects on cognitive abilities* (pp. 119–155). Mahwah, NJ: Erlbaum.

Gray, C., & Leith, H. (2004). Perpetuating gender stereotypes in the classroom: A teacher perspective. *Educational Studies, 30,* 3–17

Gray, J. A. (1971). *The psychology of fear and stress.* New York: McGraw-Hill.

Gray, M. R., & Steinberg, L. (1999). Unpacking authoritative parenting: Reassessing a multidimensional construct. *Journal of Marriage and the Family, 61,* 574–587.

Gredler, G. R. (1997). Issues in early childhood screening and assessment. *Psychology in the Schools, 34,* 98–106.

Green, E. H. (1933). Friendships and quarrels among preschool children. *Child Development, 4,* 236–252.

Green, M. (1989). *Theories of human development.* New York: Prentice-Hall.

Greenberg, B. S., Edison, N., Korzenny, F., Fernandez-Collado, C., & Atkin, C. K. (1980). Antisocial and prosocial behaviors on television. In B. S. Greenberg (Ed.), *Life on television: Content analysis of U.S. television drama* (pp. 99–128). Norwood, NJ: Ablex Publishing.

Greenberg, M. T., Speltz, M. L., & DeKlyen, M. (1993). The role of attachment in early development of disruptive behavior problems. *Development and Psychopathology, 5,* 191–213.

Greenberger, E., & Chen, C. (1996). Perceived family relationships and depressed mood in early and late adolescence: A comparison of European and Asian Americans. *Developmental Psychology, 32,* 707–716.

Greenberger, E., & Steinberg, L. (1986). *When teenagers work: The psychological and social costs of adolescent employment.* New York: Basic Books.

Greene, B. (1984). *Good morning, merry sunshine.* New York: Penguin.

Greene, J. (1997). A meta-analysis of the Rossell and Baker review of bilingual education research. *Bilingual Research Journal, 21,* 103–122.

Greene, J. (1998). *A meta-analysis of the effectiveness of bilingual education.* Austin, TX: Tomas Rivera Policy Institute, University of Texas at Austin.

Greene, K., Rubin, D. L., Hale, J. L., & Walters, L. H. (1996). The utility of understanding adolescent egocentrism in designing health promotion messages. *Health Communication, 8,* 131–152.

Greene, R. W., & Ablon, J. S. (2001). What does the MTA study tell us about effective psychosocial treatment for ADHD? *Journal of Clinical Child Psychology, 30,* 114–212.

Greene, R. W., Biederman, J., Faraone, S. V., Monuteaux, M. C., Mick, E., DuPre, E. P., Fine, C. S., & Goring, J. G. (2001). Social impairment in girls with ADHD: Patterns, gender comparisons, and correlates. *Journal of the American Academy of Child and Adolescent Psychiatry, 40,* 704–710.

Greene, T. R. (1991). Text manipulations influence children's understandings of class inclusion hierarchies. *Journal of Experimental Child Psychology, 52,* 354–374.

Greenhill, L. L. (2001). Clinical effects of stimulant medication in ADHD. In M. V. Solanto & A. F. T. Arnsten (Eds.), *Stimulant drugs and ADHD: Basic and clinical neuroscience* (pp. 31–71). New York: Oxford University Press.

Greenough, W. T., & Alcantara, A. A. (1993). The roles of experience in different developmental information stage processes. In B. de Boysson-Bardies, S. de Schonen, P. Jusczyk, P. McNeilage, & J. Morton (Eds.). *Developmental neurocognition* (pp. 3–16). Dordrecht, Netherlands: Kluwer.

Greenough, W. T., & Black, J. E. (1992). Induction of brain structure by experience: Substrates for cognitive development. In M. R. Gunnar & C. A. Nelson (Eds.), *Developmental behavioral neuroscience* (pp. 155–200). Hillsdale, NJ: Erlbaum.

Greenough, W. T., & Black, J. (1992). Induction of brain structure by experience: Substrate for cognitive development. In M. R. Gunnar & C. A. Nelson (Eds.), *Minnesota symposia on child psychology 24: Developmental behavioral neuroscience* (pp. 155–200). Hillsdale, NJ: Erlbaum.

Greenough, W. T., Black, J. E., & Wallace, C. S. (1987). Experience and brain development. *Science, 58,* 539–560.

Greenspan, S. I., & Greenspan, N. T. (1985). *First feelings: Milestones in the emotional development of your baby and child.* New York: Viking.

Greenwald, R. L., Bank, L., Reid, J. B., & Knutson, J. F. (1997). A discipline-mediated model of excessively punitive parenting. *Aggressive Behavior, 23,* 259–280.

Griffin, D. W., & Bartholomew, K. (1994). Models of the self and other: Fundamental dimensions underlying measures of adult attachment. *Journal of Personality and Social Psychology, 67,* 430–445.

Griffin, R. S. (1998). *Sports in the lives of children and adolescents.* Westport, CT: Praeger.

Griffiths, M. (2004). Can videogames be good for your health? *Journal of Health Psychology, 9,* 339–344.

Grogan, S. (1999). *Body image.* London: Routledge.

Groome, L. J., Swiber, M. J., Atterbury, J. L., Bentz, L. S., & Holland, S. B. (1997). Similarities and differences in behavioral state organization during sleep periods in the infant before and after birth. *Child Development, 68,* 1–11.

Gross, L., Aurand, S., & Adessa, R. (1988). *Violence and discrimination against lesbian and gay people in Philadelphia and the Commonwealth of Pennsylvania.* Philadelphia: Philadelphia Lesbian and Gay Task Force.

Grossmann, K., Grossmann, K. E., Fremmer Bombik, E., Kindler, H., Scheuerer-Englisch, H., & Zimmermann, P. (2002). The uniqueness of the child–father attachment relationship: Fathers' sensitive and challenging play as a pivotal variable in a 16-year longitudinal study. *Social Development, 11,* 307–311.

Grotevant, H. D. (1998). Adolescent development in family contexts. In W. Damon (Ed.), *Handbook of child psychology* (Vol. 3, pp. 1097–1150). New York: Wiley.

Grusec, J. E. (1988). *Social development.* New York: Springer-Verlag.

Grusec, J. E., & Goodnow, J. J. (1994). Impact of parental discipline methods on the child's internalization of values: A reconceptualization of current points of view. *Developmental Psychology, 30,* 4–19.

Grusec, J. E., Dix, T., & Mills, R. (1982). The effects of type, severity, and victim of children's transgressions on maternal discipline. *Canadian Journal of Behavioural Sciences, 14,* 276–289.

Grusec, J. E., Goodnow, J. J., & Kuczynski, L. (2000). New directions in analyses of parenting contributions to children's acquisition of values. *Child Development, 71,* 205–211.

Grusec, J. E., & Lytton, H. (1988). *Social development: History, theory, and research.* New York: Springer-Verlag.

Guerin, D. W., Gottfried, A. W., & Thomas, C. W. (1997). Difficult temperament and behavior problems: A longitudinal study from 1.5 to 12 years. *International Journal of Behavioral Development, 21,* 71–90.

Guidubaldi, J. (1988). Differences in children's divorce adjustment across grade level and gender: A report from the NASP–Kent State Nationwide Project. In S. A. Wolchik & P. Karoly (Eds.), *Children of divorce* (pp. 185–232). New York: Gardner.

Gunnar, M. R. (1980). Contingent stimulation: A review of its role in early development. In S. Levine & H. Ursin (Eds.), *Coping and health* (pp. 316–345). New York: Plenum.

Gunnar, M. R. (1989). Studies of the human infant's adrenocortical response to potentially stressful events. *New Directions for Child Development, 45,* 3–18.

Gunnar, M. R., & Brodersen, L. (1992). Infant stress reactions to brief maternal separations in human and nonhuman primates. In T. M. Field, P. M. McCabe, & N. Schneiderman (Eds.), *Stress and coping in infancy and childhood* (pp. 1–18). Hillsdale, NJ: Erlbaum.

Gunnar, M. R., Bruce, J., & Grotevant, H. D. (2000). International adoption and institutionally reared children: Research and policy. *Development and Psychopathology, 12,* 677–694.

Gunnar, M. R., Fisch, R., Korsvik, S., & Donhowe, J. (1981). The effects of circumcision on serum cortisol and behavior. *Psychoneuroendocrinology, 6,* 269–275.

Gunnell, D. J., Frankel, S. J., Nanchahal, K., Peters, T. J., & Davey, S. G. (1998). Childhood obesity and adult cardiovascular mortality. *American Journal of Clinical Nutrition, 67,* 1111–1118.

Guo, S. S., Roches, A. F., Chumlea, W. C., Gardner, J. D., & Siervogel, R. M. (1994). The predictive value of childhood body mass index values for overweight at age 35. *American Journal of Clinical Nutrition, 59,* 810–819.

Guralnick, M. J., Connor, R. T., Hammond, M. A., Gottman, J. M., & Kinnish, K. (1996). The peer relations of preschool children with communication disorders. *Child Development, 67,* 471–489.

Gustafson, G. W., Wood, R. M., & Green, J. A. (2000). Can we hear the causes of infants' crying? In R. G. Barr, B. Hopkins, & J. A. Green (Eds.), *Crying as a sign, a symptom, and a signal: Clinical emotional and developmental aspects of infant and toddler crying* (pp. 8–22). New York: Cambridge University Press.

Hack, M., Klein, N. K., & Taylor, H. G. (1995). Long-term developmental outcomes of low birth weight infants. *The Future of Children, 5,* 176–196.

Hack, M., Taylor, H. G., Klein, N., & Eiben, R. (1994). Outcome of < 750 gm birthweight children at school age. *New England Journal of Medicine, 331,* 753–759.

Hadley, P. A., & Schuele, C. M. (1995). Verbal interactions with peers in a preschool language intervention classroom. In M. Rice & K. Wilcox (Eds.), *Building a language-focused curriculum for the preschool classroom* (pp. 105–125). Baltimore: Brookes.

Hagen, E. H. (1999). The functions of postpartum depression. *Evolution and Human Behavior, 20,* 325–359.

Haith, M. M. (1980). *Rules that babies look by: The organization of newborn visual activity.* Potomac, MD: Erlbaum.

Haith, M. M., & Benson, J. B. (1998). Infant cognition. In W. Damon (Ed.), *Handbook of child psychology* (Vol. 2, pp. 199–254). New York: Wiley.

Haka-Ikse, K. (1997). Female adolescent sexuality: The risks and management. In G. Creatsas & G. Mastorakos (Eds.), *Adolescent gynecology and endocrinology* (Vol. 816, pp. 446–470). New York: Academy of Sciences.

Hakanen, E. A. (1995). Emotional use of music by African American adolescents. *Howard Journal of Communication, 5,* 214–222.

Hakuta, K., & McLaughlin, B. (1996). Bilingualism and second language learning. In D.C. Berliner & R. C. Calfee (Eds.), *Handbook of educational psychology* (pp. 603–621). New York: Macmillan.

Hakuta, K., Butler, Y. G., & Witt, D. (2000). *How long does it take English learners to attain proficiency?* Berkeley, CA: University of California Linguistic Minority Research Institute. (ERIC Document Reproduction Service No. ED443275)

Hala, S. (1997). Theoretical and conceptual issues. In S. Hala (Ed.), *The development of social cognition* (pp. 3–34). East Sussex, UK: Psychology Press.

Hala, S., & Carpendale, J. (1997). All in the mind: Children's understanding of mental life. In S. Hala (Ed.), *The development of social cognition* (pp. 189–240). East Sussex, UK: Psychology Press.

Hall, D. G., & Graham, S. A. (1998). Beyond mutual exclusivity: Children use lexical form class information to constrain word-referent mapping. In E. V. Clark (Ed.), *Proceedings of the 29th Annual Child Language Research Forum* (pp. 181–190). Stanford, CA: Center for the Study of Language and Information.

Hall, J. A. (1984). *Nonverbal sex differences: Communication accuracy and expressive style.* Hillsdale, NJ: Erlbaum.

Hall, J. G. (1990). Genomic imprinting: Review and relevance to human diseases. *American Journal of Human Genetics, 46,* 857–873.

Halpern, D. F. (1992). *Sex differences in cognitive abilities.* Mahwah, NJ: Erlbaum.

Halpern, D. F. (1997). Sex differences in intelligence: Implications for education. *American Psychologist, 52,* 1091–1102.

Halpern, R. (1999). After-school programs for low-income children: Promise and challenges. *Future of Children, 9,* 81–95.

Hamers, J. F. (2004). A sociocognitive model of bilingual development. *Journal of Language and Social Psychology, 23*(1), 70–98.

Hamre, B. K., & Pianta, R. C. (2001). Early teacher–child relationships and the trajectory of children's school outcomes through eighth grade. *Child Development, 72,* 625–638.

Handley, H. M., & Morse, L. W. (1984). Two-year study relating adolescents' self-concept and gender role perceptions to achievement and attitudes toward science. *Journal of Research in Science Teaching, 21,* 599–607.

Haninger, K., & Thompson, K. M. (2004). Content and ratings of teen-rated video games. *Journal of the American Medical Association, 291,* 856–865.

Hansen, D. M., & Jarvis, P. A. (2000). Adolescent employment and psychosocial outcomes: A comparison of two employment contexts. *Youth and Society, 31,* 417–436.

Hao, L., & Cherlin, A. J. (2004). Welfare reform and teenage pregnancy, childbirth, and school dropout. *Journal of Marriage and Family, 66,* 179–194.

Hardy, J. B., Shapiro, S., Astone, N. M., Miller, T. L., Brooks-Gunn, J., & Hilton, S. C. (1997). Adolescent childbearing revisited: The age of inner-city mothers at delivery is a determinant of their children's self-sufficiency at age 27 to 33. *Pediatrics, 100,* 802–809.

Harkness, S., & Super, C. M. (1983). *The cultural structuring of children's play in a rural African community.* Paper presented at the annual meeting of the Association for the Anthropological Study of Play, Baton Rouge, LA.

Harlow, H. H. (1958). The nature of love. *American Psychologist, 12,* 673–685.

Harlow, H. H. (1959). Love in infant monkeys. *Scientific American, 200,* 68–74.

Harpin, V., Chellappah, G., & Rutter, N. (1983). Responses of the newborn infant to overheating. *Biology and the Neonate, 44,* 65–75.

Harrington, R. (1996). Family-genetic findings in child and adolescent depressive disorders. *International Review of Psychiatry, 8,* 355–368.

Harris, J. F., Durso, F. T., Mergler, N. L., & Jones, S. K. (1990). Knowledge base influences on judgments of frequency of occurrence. *Cognitive Development, 5,* 223–233.

Harris, J. R. (1995). Where is the child's environment? A group socialization theory of development. *Psychological Review, 102,* 458–489.

Harris, L. J. (1992). Left-handedness. In I. Rapid & S. J. Segalowitz (Eds.), *Handbook of neuropsychology* (Vol. 6, pp. 145–208). Amsterdam: Elsvier.

Harris, P. L. (1989). *Children and emotion.* Cambridge, MA: Blackwell.

Harris, P. L., & Kavanaugh, R. D. (1993). Young children's understanding of pretense. *Monographs of the Society for Research in Child Development, 58* (Whole No. 231). Chicago: University of Chicago Press.

Harris, P. L., Olthof, T., & Terwogt, M. M. (1981). Children's knowledge of emotion. *Journal of Child Psychology and Psychiatry and Allied Disciplines, 22,* 247–261.

Harris, S., & Petrie, G. (2002). A study of bullying in middle school. *NASSP Bulletin, 86,* 42–52.

Hart, B., & Risely, T. R. (1995). *Meaningful differences in the everyday experiences of young American children.* Baltimore, MD: Brookes.

Hart, C. H., DeWolf, D. M., Wozniak, P., & Burts, D.C. (1992). Maternal and paternal disciplinary styles: Relations with preschoolers' playgroup behavior orientations and peer status. *Child Development, 63,* 879–892.

Hart, S. N., Brassard, M. R., & Karlson, H. C. (1996). Psychological maltreatment. In J. Briere, L. Berliner, J. A. Bulkley, C. Jenny, & T. Reid (Eds.), *The APSAC handbook on child maltreatment* (pp. 72–89). Thousand Oaks, CA: Sage.

Harter, S. (1993). Causes and consequences of low self-esteem in children and adolescents. In R. F. Baumeister (Ed.), *Self-esteem: The puzzle of low self-regard* (pp. 87–116). New York: Plenum.

Harter, S. (1998). The development of self-representations. In W. Damon (Ed.), *Handbook of child psychology* (Vol. 3, pp. 553–618). New York: Wiley.

Harter, S. (1999). *The construction of the self: A developmental perspective.* New York: Guilford.

Harter, S. (2003). The development of self-representations during childhood and adolescence. In J. P. Tagney & M. R. Leary (Eds.), *Handbook of self and identity* (pp. 610–642). New York: Guilford.

Harter, S., & Whitesell, N. R. (2003). Beyond the debate: Why some adolescents report stable self-worth over time and situation, whereas others report changes in self-worth. *Journal of Personality, 71,* 1027–1058.

Hartl, D. L. (1994). Forensic DNA typing dispute. *Nature, 372,* 398–399.

Hartup, W. W. (1993). Adolescents and their friends. In B. Laursen (Ed.), *Close friendships in adolescence* (Vol. 60, pp. 3–22). San Francisco: Jossey-Bass.

Hartup, W. W. (1996). The company they keep: Friendships and their developmental significance. *Child Development, 67,* 1–13.

Hartup, W. W., & Stevens, N. (1999). Friendships and adaptation across the life span. *Current Directions in Psychological Science, 8,* 76–79.

Harwood, R. L., Miller, J. G., & Irizarry, N. L. (1995). *Culture and attachment.* New York: Guilford.

Harwood, R. L., Schoelmerich, A., Ventura-Cook, E., Schulze, P. A., & Wilson, S. A. (1996). Culture and class influences on Anglo and Puerto Rican mothers' beliefs regarding long-term socialization goals and child behavior. *Child Development, 67,* 2446–2461.

Hashima, P. Y., & Amato, P. R. (1994). Poverty, social support, and parental behavior. *Child Development, 65,* 394–403.

Hassold, T. J., & Patterson, D. (1998). *Down syndrome.* New York: Wiley.

Haste, H., & Baddeley, J. (1991). Moral theory and culture: The case of gender. In W. Kurtines & J. L. Gewirtz (Eds.), *Handbook of moral behavior and development* (Vol. 1, pp. 223–250). Hillsdale, NJ: Erlbaum.

Hatton, D. D., Bailey, D. B., Jr., Burchinal, M. R., & Ferrell, K. A. (1997). Development growth curves of preschool children with vision impairments. *Child Development, 68,* 788–806.

Hauser, M. D. (1999). Perseveration, inhibition, and the prefrontal cortex: A new look. *Current Opinion in Neurobiology, 9,* 214–222.

Hauser, S. T., Borman, E. H., Bowlds, M. K., Powers, S. L., Jacobson, A. M., Noam, G. I., & Knoebber, K. (1991). Understanding coping within adolescence. In E. M. Cummings & A. Greene (Eds.), *Lifespan developmental psychology: Perspectives on stress and coping* (pp. 177–194). Hillsdale, NJ: Erlbaum.

Hausfather, A., Toharia, A., LaRoche, C., & Engelsmann, F. (1997). Effects of age of entry, day-care quality, and family characteristics on preschool behavior. *Journal of Child Psychology and Psychiatry, 38,* 441–448.

Haveman, R., & Wolfe, B. (1994). *Succeeding generations.* New York: Russell Sage Foundation.

Hawkins, A. J., Christiansen, S. L., Sargent, K. P., & Hill, E. J. (1995). Rethinking fathers' involvement in child care: A developmental perspective. In W. Marsiglio (Ed.), *Fatherhood: Contemporary theory, research, and social policy* (pp. 41–56). Thousand Oaks, CA: Sage.

Hay, D. F., Castle, J., Davies, L., Demetriou, H., & Stimson, C. A. (1999). Prosocial action in very early childhood. *Journal of Child Psychology and Psychiatry and Allied Disciplines, 40,* 905–916.

Hayes, D. S., & Casey, D. M. (1992). Young children and television: The retention of emotional reactions. *Child Development, 63,* 1423–1436.

Hayghe, H. V. (1997, September). Developments in women's labor force participation. *Monthly Labor Review,* 41–47.

Hayne, H. (2003). Infant memory development: Implications for childhood amnesia. *Developmental Review, 24,* 33–73.

Hayne, H., & Rovee-Collier, C. (1995). The organization of reactivated memory in infancy. *Child Development, 66,* 893–906.

Hayne, H., Rovee-Collier, C., & Perris, E. E. (1987). Categorization and memory retrieval by three-month-olds. *Child Development, 58,* 750–767.

Haynes de Reght, H. L., Minkoff, H. L., Feldman, J., & Schwartz, R. H. (1986). Relation of private or clinic care to cesarean birth rate. *New England Journal of Medicine, 315,* 619–624.

Hayward, C., Killen, J. D., Wilson, D. M., & Hammer, L. D. (1997). Psychiatric risk associated with early puberty in adolescent girls. *Journal of the American Academy of Child and Adolescent Psychiatry, 36,* 255–262.

Health Behavior in School-Aged Children. (2000). In *Health policy for children and adolescents.* Geneva, Switzerland: World Health Organization.

Hearing, Speech, and Deafness Center. (2004). *Stuttering in children.* Retrieved from http:// www.hsdc.org/Child/Speech/stutter.htm

Hearold, S. (1986). A synthesis of 1043 effects of television on social behavior. In G. Comstock (Ed.), *Public communications and behavior* (Vol. 1, pp. 65–133). New York: Academic Press.

Hedges, L. V., & Nowell, A. (1995). Sex differences in mental test scores, variability, and numbers of high scoring individuals. *Science, 269,* 41–45.

Hediger, M. L., Overpeck, M. D., Kuczmarski, R. J., & Ruan, W. J. (2001). Association between infant breastfeeding and overweight in young children. *Journal of the American Medical Association, 285,* 2453–2460.

Heffer, R. W., & Kelley, M. L. (1987). Mothers' acceptance of behavioral interactions for children. *Behavior Therapy, 2,* 153–163.

Hegyi, T., Carbone, T., Anwar, M., Ostfeld, B., Hiatt, M., Koons, A., Pinto-Martin, J., & Paneth, N. (1998). The Apgar score and its components in the preterm infant. *Pediatrics, 101,* 77–81.

Helm, P., & Grolund, J. (1998). A halt in the secular trend toward earlier menarche in Denmark. *Acta Obstetrics and Gynecology Scandanavia, 77,* 198–200.

Helwig, C. C., & Turiel, E. (2002). Children's social and moral reasoning. In C. Hart & P. K. Smith (Eds.), *Handbook of childhood social development* (pp. 476–490). Maleden, MA: Blackwell.

Henderson-King, E., & Henderson-King, D. (1997). Media effects on women's body esteem: Social and individual difference factors. *Journal of Applied Social Psychology, 27,* 399–417.

Hendrick, J., & Stange, T. (1991). Do actions speak louder than words? An effect of the functional use of language on dominant sex role behavior in boys and girls. *Early Childhood Research Quarterly, 6,* 565–576.

Hendrick, S. S., & Hendrick, C. (1995). Gender differences and similarities in sex and love. *Personal Relationships, 2,* 55–65.

Hennessey, B. A., & Amabile, T. M. (1988). The conditions of creativity. In R. Sternberg (Ed.), *The nature of creativity: Contemporary psychological perspectives* (pp. 11–38). New York: Cambridge University Press.

Henrich, C. C., Schwab-Stone, M., Fanti, K., Jones, S. M., & Ruchkin, V. (2004). The association of community violence exposure with middle-school achievement: A prospective study. *Journal of Applied Developmental Psychology, 25,* 327–348.

Henricson, C., & Roker, D. (2000). Support for the parents of adolescents: A review. *Journal of Adolescence, 23,* 763–783.

Henricsson, L., & Rydell, A. M. (2004). Elementary school children with behavior problems: Teacher–child relations and self-perception. *Merrill-Palmer Quarterly, 50,* 111–138.

Henry, C. S., Peterson, G. W., & Wilson, S. M. (1997). Adolescent social competence and parental satisfaction. *Journal of Adolescent Research, 12,* 389–409.

Henry, D. L. (2001). Resilient children. *Social Work in Health Care, 34,* 283–298.

Henshaw, S. (1999). *Teenage pregnancy: Overall trends and state-by-state information.* New York: The Alan Guttmacher Institute.

Henshaw, S. (2001). *U.S. teenage pregnancy statistics with comparative statistics for women aged 20–24.* New York: The Alan Guttmacher Institute.

Hermand, D., Mullet, E., & Rompteaux, L. (1999). Societal risk perception among children, adolescents, adults, and elderly people. *Journal of Adult Development, 6,* 137–143.

Herman-Giddens, M. E., Slora, E. J., Wasserman, R. C., Bourdony, C. J., Bhapkar, M. V., Koch, G. G., & Hasemeier, C. M. (1997). Secondary sexual characteristics and menses in young girls seen in office practice: A study from the Pediatric Research in Office Settings Network. *Pediatrics, 99,* 505–512.

Herold, E. S., & Marshall, S. K. (1996). Adolescent sexual development. In G. R. Adams & R. Montemayor (Eds.), *Psychosocial development during adolescence* (Vol. 8, pp. 62–94). Thousand Oaks, CA: Sage.

Herrmann, D. J. (1998). The relationship between basic research and applied research in memory and cognition. In C. P. Thompson & D. J. Herrmann (Eds.), *Autobiographical memory* (pp. 13–27). Mahwah, NJ: Erlbaum.

Hertzler, A. A., & Frary, R. B. (1989). Food behavior of college students. *Adolescence, 24,* 349–356.

Hespos, S. J., & Baillargeon, R. (2001). Infants' knowledge about occlusion and containment events: A surprising discrepancy. *Psychological Science, 121,* 141–147.

Hetherington, E. M. (1999a). Should we stay together for the sake of the children? In E. M. Hetherington (Ed.), *Coping with divorce, single parenting, and remarriage: A risk and resiliency perspective* (pp. 93–116). Mahwah, NJ: Erlbaum.

Hetherington, E. M. (1999b). Social capital and the development of youth from nondivorced, divorced, and remarried families. In W. A. Collins & B. Laursen (Eds.), *Relationships as developmental contexts* (pp. 177–209). Mahwah, NJ: Erlbaum.

Hetherington, E. M., Bridges, M., & Insabella, G. M. (1998). What matters? What does not? Five perspectives on the association between marital transitions and children's adjustment. *American Psychologist, 53,* 167–184.

Hetherington, E. M., & Clingempeel, W. G. (1992). Coping with marital transitions. *Monographs of the Society for Research in Child Development, 57* (Whole No. 227). Chicago: University of Chicago Press.

Hetherington, E. M., & Elmore, A. M. (2003). Risk and resilience in children coping with their parents' divorce and remarriage. In S. S. Luthar (Ed.), *Resilience and vulnerability: Adaptation in the context of childhood adversities* (pp. 182–212). New York: Cambridge University Press.

Hetherington, E. M., Hagan, M. S., & Anderson, E. R. (1989). Marital transitions: A child's perspective. *American Psychologist, 44,* 303–312.

Hetherington, E. M., & Stanley-Hagan, M. (1999a). The adjustment of children with divorced parents: A risk and resiliency perspective. *Journal of Child Psychology and Psychiatry and Allied Disciplines, 40,* 129–140.

Hetherington, E. M., & Stanley-Hagan, M. (1999b). Stepfamilies. In M. E. Lamb (Ed.), *Parenting and child development in "nontraditional" families* (pp. 137–159). Mahwah, NJ: Erlbaum.

Hewett, J. K., Silberg, J. L., Rutter, M., Simonoff, E., Meyer, J. M., Maes, H., Pickles, A., Neale, M. C., Loeber, R., Erickson, M. T., Kendler, K. S., Heath, A. C., Turett, K. R., Reynolds, C. A., & Eaves, L. J. (1997). Genetics and developmental psychopathology. *Journal of Child Psychology and Psychiatry and Allied Disciplines, 38,* 943–963.

Hewlett, B. S. (1992). The parent–infant relationship and social–emotional development among Aka Pygmies. In J. L. Roopnarine & D. B. Carter (Eds.), *Parent–child socialization in diverse cultures* (pp. 223–244). Norwood, NJ: Ablex.

Heyman, R. E., & Slep, A. M. S. (2002). Do child abuse and interparental violence lead to adulthood family violence? *Journal of Marriage and Family, 64,* 864–870.

Hiebert, E. H., & Raphael, T. E. (1996). Psychological perspectives on literacy and extensions to educational practice. In D.C. Berliner & R. C. Calfee (Eds.), *Handbook of educational psychology* (pp. 550–562). New York: Macmillan.

Hill, A. J., & Pallin, V. (1998). Dieting awareness and low self-worth: Related issues in 8-year old girls. *International Journal of Eating Disorders, 24,* 405–413.

Hill, C. R., & Stafford, F. P. (1980). Parental care of children: Time diary estimates of quantity, predictability, and variety. *Journal of Human Resources, 15,* 219–239.

Hill, J. P. (1987). Research on adolescents and their families. In C. E. Irwin (Ed.), *Adolescent social behavior and health* (Vol. 13, pp. 13–31). San Francisco: Jossey-Bass.

Hill, J. P., & Lynch, M. E. (1983). The intensification of gender-related role expectations during early adolescence. In J. Brooks-Gunn & A. C. Petersen (Eds.), *Girls at puberty* (pp. 201–228). New York: Plenum.

Hines, M. (1990). Gonadal hormones and human cognitive development. In J. Balthazart (Ed.), *Hormones, brain, and behavior in vertebrates: 1. Sexual differentiation, neuroanatomical aspects, neurotransmitters and neuropeptides* (pp. 51–63). Basel, Switzerland: Barger.

Hines, M., Brook, C., & Conway, G. S. (2004). Androgen and psychosexual development: Core gender identity, sexual orientation, and recalled childhood gender role behavior in women and men with congenital adrenal hyperplasia (CAH) *Journal of Sex Research, 41,* 75–81.

Hines, M., Fane, B. A., Pasterski, V. L., Matthews, G. A., Conway, G. S., & Brook, C. (2003). Spatial abilities following prenatal androgen abnormality: Targeting and mental rotations performance in individuals with congenital adrenal hyperplasia. *Psychoneuroendocrinology, 28,* 1010–1026.

Hinshaw, S. P., & Lee, S. S. (2003). Conduct and oppositional defiant disorders. In R. A. Barkley & E. J. Mash (Eds.), *Child psychopathology* (2nd ed., pp. 144–198). New York: Guilford.

Hinshaw, S. P., Zupan, B. A., Simmel, C., Nigg, J. T., & Melnick, S. (1997). Peer status in boys with and without attention-deficit hyperactivity disorder. *Child Development, 68,* 880–896.

Hiscock, H., & Wake, M. (2001). Infant sleep problems and postnatal depression: A community-based study. *Pediatrics, 107,* 1317–1322.

Hitchins, M. P., & Moore, G. E. (2002, May 9). Genomic imprinting in fetal growth and development. *Expert Reviews in Molecular Medicine.* Retrieved from http:// www.expertreviews.org/0200457Xh.htm

Hobar, J. D., & Lucey, J. F. (1995). Evaluation of neonatal intensive care technologies. *The Future of Children, 5,* 139–161.

Hobel, C., & Culhane, J. (2003). Role of psychosocial and nutritional stress on poor pregnancy outcome. *American Society for Nutritional Sciences, 133,* 1709–1717.

Hochschild, A. R. (1997). *The time bind.* New York: Metropolitan Press.

Hodnett, E. D., & Osborn, R. W. (1989). Effects of continuous intrapartum professional support on childbirth outcomes. *Research in Nursing and Health, 12,* 289–297.

Hofferth, S. L., & Sandberg, J. F. (2001). How American children spend their time. *Journal of Marriage and Family, 63,* 295–308.

Hoff-Ginsberg, E. (1985). Some contributions of mothers' speech to their children's syntactic growth. *Journal of Child Language, 12,* 367–385.

Hoff-Ginsberg, E. (1986). Function and structure in maternal speech: Their relation to the child's development of syntax. *Developmental Psychology, 22,* 155–163.

Hoff-Ginsberg, E. (1997). *Language development.* Pacific Grove, CA: Brooks/Cole.

Hoffman, L. W., & Youngblade, L. M. (1999). *Mothers at work: Effects on children's well-being.* Cambridge, UK: Cambridge University Press.

Hoffman, M. L. (1970). Conscience, personality, and socialization techniques. *Human Development, 13,* 90–126.

Hoffman, M. L. (1994). Discipline and internalization. *Developmental Psychology, 30,* 26–28.

Hoffman, M. L. (2000). *Empathy and moral development: Implications for caring and justice.* New York: Cambridge University Press.

Hoglund, W. L., & Leadbeater, B. J. (2004). The effects of family, school, and classroom ecologies on changes in children's social competence and emotional and behavioral problems in first grade. *Developmental Psychology, 40,* 533–544.

Holbrook, M. C. (1996). *Children with visual impairments: A parents' guide.* Bethesda, MD: Woodbine House.

Holditch-Davis, B. P., Harris, B. G., Sandelowski, M., & Edwards, L. (1994). Beyond couvade: Pregnancy symptoms in couples with a history of infertility. *Health Care Women International, 15,* 537–548.

Hollich, G. J., Hirsh-Pasek, K., Golinkoff, R. M., Brand, R. J., Brown, E., Chung, H., Hennon, E., & Rocroi, C. (2000). Breaking the language barrier: An emergentist coalition model for the origins of word learning. *Monographs of the Society for Research in Child Development, 65*(3, Serial No. 262).

Holliday, M. A. (1986). Body composition and energy needs during growth. In F. Faulkner & J. M. Tanner (Eds.), *Human growth: A comprehensive treatise* (Vol. 2, pp. 101–117). New York: Plenum.

Holmbeck, G. N., Paikoff, R. L., & Brooks-Gunn, J. (1995). Parenting adolescents. In M. H. Bornstein (Ed.), *Handbook of parenting* (Vol. 1, pp. 91–118). Mahwah, NJ: Erlbaum.

Holzman, C., & Paneth, N. (1994). Maternal cocaine use during pregnancy and perinatal outcomes. *Epidemiology Review, 16,* 215–334.

Holzman, L. H. (1996). Pragmatism and dialectical materialism in language development. In H. Daniels (Ed.), *An introduction to Vygotsky* (pp. 75–98). London: Routledge.

Hondt, W., Cambier, A., & Vandewiele, M. (1989) The human being drawn by 7- to 13-year-old Senegalese pupils. *Journal of African Psychology, 1*(2), 49–62.

Hopkins, B. (1991). Facilitating early motor development: An intracultural study of West Indian mothers and their infants living in Britain. In J. Nugent, B. Lester, & T. Brazelton (Eds.), *The cultural context of infancy: Multicultural and interdisciplinary approaches to parent–infant relations* (pp. 93–143). Norwood, NJ: Ablex.

Hoppenbrouwers, T., Hodgman, J. E., Arawaka, K., Geidel, S. A., & Sterman, M. B. (1988). Sleep and waking states in infancy: Normative studies. *Sleep, 11,* 387–402.

Hopwood, N.J., Kelch, R. P., Hale, P. M., Mendes, T. M., Foster, C. M., & Beitins, I. Z. (1990). The onset of human puberty: Biological and environmental factors. In J. Bancroft & J. Reinisch (Eds.), *Adolescence and puberty* (pp. 29–49). New York: Oxford University Press.

Horn, J. L., & Trickett, P. K. (1998). Community violence and child development: A review of research. In P. K. Trickett & C. J. Schellenbach (Eds.), *Violence against children in the family and the community* (pp. 103–138). Washington, DC: American Psychological Association.

Horney, K. (1967). *Feminine psychology.* New York: Norton.

Horowitz, F. D. (2000). Child development and the PITS: Simple questions, complex answers, and developmental theory. *Child Development, 71,* 1–10.

Horsey, K. (2004, June). Success in ovarian tissue grafting. *BioNews,* pp. 1.

Horwood, L. J., & Fergusson, D. M. (1998, January). Breastfeeding and later cognitive and academic outcome. *Pediatrics, 101,* 1–7.

Hovey, J. D. (2000). Psychosocial predictors of acculturative stress in Mexican immigrants. *Journal of Personality, 134,* 490–502.

Howe, M. J. A. (1997). *IQ in question: The truth about intelligence.* London: Sage.

Howe, M. J. A. (1999). Prodigies and creativity. In R. J. Sternberg (Ed.), *Handbook of creativity* (pp. 431–446). Cambridge, UK: Cambridge University Press.

Howe, M. L., & Courage, M. L. (1997). The emergence and early development of autobiographical memory. *Psychological Review, 3,* 499–523.

Howes, C. (1988a). Peer interaction in young children. *Monographs of the Society for Research in Child Development, 53* (Whole No. 217). Chicago: University of Chicago Press.

Howes, C. (1988b). Relations between early child care and schooling. *Developmental Psychology, 24,* 53–57.

Howes, C. (1989). Friendships in very young children: Definition and functions. In B. H. Schneider, G. Attili, J. Nadel, & R. P. Weissberg (Eds.), *Social competence in developmental perspective* (pp. 127–130). Boston, MA: Kluwer.

Howes, C. (1990). Can the age of entry into child care and the quality of child care predict adjustment in kindergarten? *Developmental Psychology, 26*, 292–303.

Howes, C. (2000). Social–emotional classroom climate in child care, child–teacher relationships, and children's second-grade peer relations. *Social Development, 9*, 191–204.

Howes, C., Hamilton, C. E., & Matheson, C. C. (1994). Children's relationships with peers: Differential associations with aspects of the teacher/child relationship. *Child Development, 65*, 253–263.

Howes, C., & Matheson, C. C. (1992). Sequences in the development of competent play with peers: Social and pretend play. *Developmental Psychology, 28*, 961–974.

Howes, C., Matheson, C. C., & Hamilton, C. E. (1994). Maternal, teacher, and child care history correlates of children's relationships with peers. *Child Development, 65*, 264–273.

Hoyenga, K. B., & Hoyenga, K. T. (1993). *Gender related differences: Origins and outcomes.* Boston, MA: Allyn & Bacon.

Hoyt, C. (1996, April). Debunking the myth of the terrible toddler. *Child*, 50–52.

Hsu, L. K. G., & Sobkiewicz, T. A. (1991). Body image disturbance: Time to abandon the concept of eating disorders? *International Journal of Eating Disorders, 10*, 15–30.

Hubel, D., & Wiesel, T. (1979). Brain mechanisms of vision. *Scientific American, 241*, 150–162.

Hudson, J. A. (1990). The emergence of autobiographical memory in mother–child conversation. In R. Fivush & J. A. Hudson (Eds.), *Knowing and remembering in young children* (pp. 166–196). Cambridge, UK: Cambridge University Press.

Hudson, J. A., & Fivush, R. (1991). Planning in the preschool years: The emergence of plans from general event knowledge. *Cognitive Development, 6*, 393–415.

Hudson, J. A., Shapiro, L. R., & Sosa, B. B. (1995). Planning in the real world: Preschool children's scripts and plans for familiar events. *Child Development, 66*, 984–998.

Hudson, J. A., & Sheffield, E. G. (1998). Deja vu all over again: Effects of reenactment on toddlers' event memory. *Child Development, 69*, 51–67.

Huffman, L. C., Mehlinger, S. L., & Kerivan, A. S. (2000). *Risk factors for academic and behavior problems at the beginning of school.* Bethesda, MD: The Child Mental Health Foundations and Agencies Network.

Hughes, F. P. (1995). *Children, play, and development.* Boston: Allyn & Bacon.

Hulshoff-Pol, H. E., Hoek, H. W., Susser, E., Brown, A. S., Dingemans, A., Schnack, H. G., van-Haren, N., Ramos, L., Gispen-de-Wied, C. C., & Kahn, R. S. (2000). Prenatal exposure to famine and brain morphology in schizophrenia. *American Journal of Psychiatry, 157*, 1170–1172.

Hunter, F. T., McCarthy, M. E., MacTurk, R. H., & Vietze, P. M. (1987). Infants' social–constructive interactions with mothers and fathers. *Developmental Psychology, 23*, 249–254.

Hunter, J. (1990). Violence against lesbian and gay youths. *Journal of Interpersonal Violence, 5*, 295–300.

Hurt, H., Malmud, E., Betancourt, L. M., Brodsky, N. L., & Giannetta, J. M. (2001). A prospective comparison of developmental outcome of children with in utero cocaine exposure and controls using the Battelle Developmental Inventory. *Journal of Developmental and Behavioral Pediatrics, 22*, 27–34.

Hurtado, A. (1995). Variations, combinations, and evolutions. In R. E. Zambrana (Ed.), *Understanding Latino families* (pp. 40–61). Thousand Oaks, CA: Sage.

Hurtado, E. K., Claussen, A. H., & Scott, K. G. (1999). Early childhood anemia and mild/moderate mental retardation. *American Journal of Clinical Nutrition, 69*, 115–119.

Huston, A. C. (1983). Sex-typing. In E. M. Hetherington (Ed.), *Handbook of child psychology: Socialization, personality, and social development* (Vol. 4, pp. 388–467). New York: Wiley.

Huston, A. C. (1991). Children in poverty: Developmental and policy issues. In A. C. Huston (Ed.), *Children in poverty* (pp. 1–22). Cambridge, UK: Cambridge University Press.

Huston, A. C., & Alvarez, M. M. (1990). The socialization context of gender role development in early adolescence. In R. Montemayor & G. R. Adams (Eds.), *From childhood to adolescence* (pp. 156–179). Newbury Park, CA: Sage.

Huston, A. C., Donnerstein, E., Fairchild, H., Feshbach, N. D., Katz, P. A., Murray, J. P., Rubinstein, E. A., Wilcox, B., & Zuckerman, D. (1992). *Big world, small screen: The role of television in American society.* Lincoln: University of Nebraska Press.

Huston, A. C., & Wright, J. C. (1998). Mass media and children's development. In W. Damon (Ed.), *Handbook of child psychology* (Vol. 4, pp. 999–1058). New York: Wiley.

Huttenlocher, J. (1998). Language input and language growth. *Preventive Medicine, 27*, 195–199.

Huttenlocher, P. R. (1979). Synaptic density in human prefrontal cortex: Developmental changes and effects of aging. *Brain Research, 163*, 195–205.

Huttenlocher, P. R. (1990). Morphometric study of human cerebral cortex development. *Neuropsychologia, 28*, 517–527.

Huttenlocher, P. R. (1994). Synaptogenesis in human cerebral cortex. In G. Dawson & K. W. Fischer (Eds.), *Human behavior and the developing brain* (pp. 35–54). New York: Guilford.

Huttenlocher, P. R., & Dabholkar, A. S. (1997). Regional differences in synaptogenesis in human cerebral cortex. *Journal of Comparative Neurology, 387*, 167–178.

Hyde, J. S. (1984). How large are gender differences in aggression? A developmental meta-analysis. *Developmental Psychology, 20*, 722–736.

Hyde, J. S., Fennema, E., & Lamon, S. J. (1990). Gender differences in mathematics performance. *Psychological Bulletin, 107*, 139–155.

Hymel, S., Bowker, A., & Woody, E. (1993). Aggressive versus withdrawn unpopular children. *Child Development, 64*, 879–896.

Imperato-McGinley, J., Peterson, R. E., Gautier, T., & Sturla, E. (1979). Androgens and the evolution of male gender identity among male pseudohermaphrodites with 5-alpha-reductase deficiency. *New England Journal of Medicine, 300*, 123–127.

Ingoldsby, E. M., & Shaw, D. S. (2002). Neighborhood contextual factors and early-starting antisocial pathways. *Clinical Child and Family Psychology Review, 5*, 21–55.

Ingram, D. (1989). *First language acquisition.* New York: Cambridge University Press.

Inhelder, B., & Piaget, J. (1958). *The growth of logical thinking from childhood to adolescence.* New York: Basic Books.

Inhelder, B., & Piaget, J. (1964). *The growth of logical thinking in the child.* New York: Harper & Row.

Institute of Medicine. (1990). *Science and babies: Private decisions, public dilemmas.* Washington, DC: National Academy Press.

International Association for the Evaluation of Educational Achievement. (1996). *IEA's third international mathematics and science study.* Washington, DC: US Department of Education.

Intons-Peterson, M. J. (1988). *Children's concepts of gender.* Norwood, NJ: Ablex.

Iosifescu, D., & Renshaw, P. F. (2003). 31P-magnetic resonance spectroscopy and thyroid hormones in major depressive disorder. *Harvard Review of Psychiatry, 11*, 51–63.

Irvine, J. J. (1986). Teacher–student interactions: Effects of student race, sex, and grade level. *Journal of Educational Psychology, 78*, 14–21.

Irwin, C. E. (2004). Adolescent sexuality and reproductive health: Where are we in 2004? *Journal of Adolescent Health, 34,* 353–355.

Isabella, R. A. (1993). Origins of attachment: Maternal interactive behavior across the first year. *Child Development, 64,* 605–621.

Ishihara, K., & Miyahke, S. (1998). A longitudinal study of the development of daytime sleepiness in children. *Psychiatry and Clinical Neuroscience, 52,* 178–181.

Itard, J. (1972a). *Of the first developments of the young savage of Aveyron.* New York: Monthly Review Press. (Original work published 1801.)

Itard, J. (1972b). *Report of the progress of Victor of Aveyron.* New York: Monthly Review Press. (Original work published 1806.)

Izard, C. E., & Malatesta, C. Z. (1987). Perspective on emotional development I: Differential emotions theory of early emotional development. In J. D. Osofsky (Ed.), *Handbook of infant development* (pp. 419–494). New York: Wiley.

Jack, G. (2000). Ecological influences on parenting and child development. *British Journal of Social Work, 30,* 703–720.

Jacobs, E. H. (1998). *Fathering the ADHD child.* Northvale, NJ: Jason Aronson, Inc.

Jacobs, J. E. (1991). Influence of gender stereotypes on parent and child mathematics attitudes. *Journal of Educational Psychology, 83,* 518–527.

Jacobs, J. E., & Eccles, J. S. (1985). Gender differences in math ability: The impact of media reports on parents. *Educational Researcher, 14,* 20–25.

Jacobs, J. E., & Eccles, J. S. (2000). Parents, task values, and real-life achievement-related choices. In J. Harackiewicz & C. Sansone (Eds.), *Intrinsic and extrinsic motivation: The search for optimal motivation.*

Jacobs, R. A. (1997). Nature, nurture, and the development of functional specializations. *Psychonomic Bulletin and Review, 4,* 299–309.

Jacobson, S. W., Chiodo, L. M., & Jacobson, J. L. (1999). Breastfeeding effects on intelligence quotient in 4- and 11-year-old children. *Pediatrics, 103,* e71.

Jacobvitz, D., & Sroufe, L. A. (1987). The early caregiver–child relationship and attention-deficit disorder with hyperactivity in kindergarten: A prospective study. *Child Development, 58,* 1496–1504.

Jahoda, G. (1983). European "lag" in the development of an economic concept: A study in Zimbabwe. *British Journal of Developmental Psychology, 1,* 113–120.

Jain, A., Belsky, J., & Crnic, K. (1996). Beyond father behaviors: Types of dads. *Journal of Family Psychology, 10,* 432–442.

Jain, T., Missmer, S. A., & Hornstein, M. D. (2004). Trends in embryo-transfer practice and in outcomes of the use of assisted reproductive technology in the United States. *New England Journal of Medicine, 350,* 1639–1645.

Janowsky, J. S., Oviatt, S. K., & Orwoll, E. S. (1994). Testosterone influences spatial cognition in older men. *Behavioral Neuroscience, 108,* 325–332.

Jason, L. A., Kennedy, C. L., Hanaway, L., & Brackshaw, E. (1999). Television violence and children: Problems and solutions. In T. P. Gullotta & S. J. McElhaney (Eds.), *Violence in homes and communities: Prevention, intervention, and treatment. Issues in children's and families' lives* (Vol. 11, pp. 133–156). Thousand Oaks, CA: Sage.

Jellinek, M. B., & Snyder J. B. (1998). Depression and suicide in children and adolescents. *Pediatric Review, 19,* 255–264.

Jensen, P. S., Hinshaw, S. P., Swanson, J. M., Greenhill, L. L., Conners, C. K., Arnold, L. E., Abikoff, H. B., Elliott, G., Hechtman, L., Hoza, B., March, J. S., Newcorn, J. H., Severe, J. B., Vitiello, B., Wells, K., & Wigal, T. (2001). Findings from the NIMH Multimodal Treatment Study of ADHD (MTA): Implications and applications for primary care providers. *Journal of Developmental and Behavioral Pediatrics, 22,* 60–73.

Jersild, A., & Holmes, F. (1935). Children's fears. *Child Development Monographs* (Vol. 20). Chicago: University of Chicago Press.

Jessor, R. (1992). Risk behavior in adolescence: A psychosocial framework for understanding and action. In D. E. Rogers & E. Ginzberg (Eds.), *Adolescents at risk: Medical and social perspectives* (pp. 19–34). Boulder, CO: Westview Press.

Jimerson, S. R. (1999). On the failure of failure: Examining the association between early grade retention and education and employment outcomes during late adolescence. *Journal of School Psychology, 37,* 243–272.

Johnson Institute. (1993). *Drugs mean alcohol too.* Minneapolis, MN: Johnson Institute.

Johnson, D. E. (2001). The impact of orphanage rearing on growth and development. In C. A. Nelson (Ed.), *Minnesota Symposia on Child Psychology* (Vol. 27, pp. 23–57). New York: Erlbaum.

Johnson, D. J., Jaeger, E., Randolph, S. M., Cauce, A. M., & Ward, J. (2003). Studying the effects of early child care experiences on the development of children of color in the United States: Toward a more inclusive research agenda. *Child Development, 74,* 1227–1244.

Johnson, J. S., & Newport, E. L. (1989). Critical period effects in second language learning: The influence of maturational state on the acquisition of English as a second language. *Cognitive Psychology, 21,* 60–99.

Johnson, L. A., Welch, G. R., Keyvanfar, K., Dorfmann, A., Fugger, E. F., & Schulman, J. D. (1993). Gender preselection in humans? Flow cytometric separation of X and Y spermatozoa for the prevention of X-linked diseases. *Human Reproduction, 8,* 1733–1739.

Johnston, H. F., & Fruehling, J. J. (1994). Pharmacotherapy for depression in children and adolescents. In W. M. Reynolds & H. F. Johnston (Eds.), *Handbook of depression in children and adolescents* (pp. 365–397). New York: Plenum.

Johnston, J. R., Breunig, K., Garrity, C., & Baris, M. A. (1997). *Through the eyes of children.* New York: Free Press.

Jones, C. P., & Adamson, L. B. (1987). Language use in mother–child and mother–child–sibling interactions. *Child Development, 58,* 356–366.

Jones, D. C. (2004). Body image among adolescent girls and boys: A longitudinal study. *Developmental Psychology, 40,* 823–835.

Jones, L., Rrustemi, A., Shahini, M., & Uka, A. (2003). Mental health services for war-affected children: Report of a survey in Kosovo. *British Journal of Psychiatry, 183,* 540–546.

Jones, M. C. (1965). Psychological correlates of somatic development. *Child Development, 36,* 899–911.

Jones, M. C., & Mussen, P. H. (1958). Self-conceptions, motivations and interpersonal attitudes of early and late maturing girls. *Child Development, 29,* 491–501.

Jones, O. W., & Cahill, T. C. (1994). Basic genetics and patterns of inheritance. In R. K. Creasy & R. Resnik (Eds.), *Maternal–fetal medicine: Principles and practice* (pp. 103–189). Philadelphia: Saunders.

Jones, R. E. (1997). *Human reproductive biology.* New York: Academic Press.

Jones, S. S., Collins, K., & Hong, H. (1991). An audience effect on smile production in 10-month-old infants. *Psychological Science, 2,* 45–49.

Jonsson, B., & von Hofsten, C. (2003). Infants' ability to track and reach for temporarily occluded objects. *Developmental Science, 6,* 86–99.

Jordan, W. J., & Cooper, R. (2003). High school reform and Black male students: Limits and possibilities of policy and practice. *Urban Education, 38.*

Jordan, W. J., & Plank, S. B. (2000). Talent loss among high-achieving poor students. In M. G. Sanders (Ed.), *Schooling students placed at risk: Research, policy, and practice in the education of poor and minority adolescents* (pp. 83–108). Mahwah, NJ: Erlbaum.

Jorgensen, S. R. (1993). Adolescent pregnancy and parenting. In T. P. Gullotta & G. R. Adams (Eds.), *Adolescent sexuality* (Vol. 5, pp. 103–140). Newbury Park, CA: Sage.

Joseph, R. (2000). Fetal brain behavior and cognitive development. *Developmental Review, 20,* 81–98.

Josephson, W. L. (1995). *Television violence: A review of the effects on children of different ages.* Montreal: Department of Canadian Heritage.

Jouriles, E. N., McDonald, R., Norwood, W. D., Ware, H. S., Spiller, L. C., & Swank, P. R. (1998). Knives, guns, and interparent violence: Relations with child behavior problems. *Journal of Family Psychology, 12,* 178–194.

Jovanovic, J., & Dreves, C. (1995). *Math, science, and girls: Can we close the gender gap?* Urbana: University of Illinois Cooperative Extension Service.

Juffer, F., & Rosenboom, L. G. (1997). Infant–mother attachment of internationally adopted children in the Netherlands. *International Journal of Behavioral Development, 20,* 93–107.

Jusczyk, P. W. (1997). *The discovery of spoken language.* Cambridge, MA: Bradford.

Jussim, L., Madon, S., & Chatman, C. (1994). Teacher expectations and student achievement. In L. Heath & T. R. Scott (Eds.), *Applications of heuristics and biases to social issues* (Vol. 3, pp. 303–334). New York: Plenum.

Juvonen, J., Graham, S., & Schuster, M. A. (2003). Bullying among young adolescents: The strong, the weak, and the troubled. *Pediatrics, 112,* 1231–1237.

Juvonen, J., Le, V.-N., Kaganoff, T., Augustine, C., & Constant, L. (2004). *Challenges facing American middle schools.* Los Angeles: Rand Corporation.

Kachur, S. P., Stennies, G. M., Powell, K. E., Modzeleski, W., Stephens, R., Murphy, R., Kresnow, M., Sleet, D., & Lowry, R. (1996). School-associated violent deaths in the United States, 1992 to 1994. *Journal of the American Medical Association, 275*(22), 1729–1733.

Kagan, J. (1976). Emergent themes in human development. *American Scientist, 64,* 196.

Kagan, J. (1989). Temperamental contributions to social behavior. *American Psychologist, 44,* 668–674.

Kagan, J., Reznick, J. S., & Snidman, N. (1987). The physiology and psychology of behavioral inhibition in children. *Child Development, 58,* 1459–1473.

Kagan, J., Snidman, N., & Arcus, D. (1993). On the temperamental categories of inhibited and uninhibited children. In K. H. Rubin & J. B. Asendorpf (Eds.), *Social withdrawal, inhibition, and shyness in childhood* (pp. 19–30). Hillsdale, NJ: Erlbaum.

Kagan, S. L., & Neuman, M. J. (1998). Lessons from three decades of transition research. *Elementary School Journal, 87,* 365–379.

Kagan, S., Knight, G., Martinez, S., & Santa, P. (1981). Conflict resolution style among Mexican children. *Journal of Cross-Cultural Psychology, 12,* 222–232.

Kahn, A., Van De Merckt, D., & Rebuffat, E. (1989). Sleep problems in healthy preadolescents. *Pediatrics, 84,* 542–546.

Kahn, P. H. (1997). Bayous and jungle rivers: Cross-cultural perspectives on children's environmental moral reasoning. In H. D. Saltztein (Ed.), *Culture as a context for moral development* (pp. 23–37). San Francisco: Jossey-Bass.

Kaiser Family Foundation. (2001). *Talking with kids about tough issues.* Menlo Park, CA: Author.

Kalamas, A. D., & Gruber, M. L. (1998). Electrodermal responses to implied versus actual violence on television. *Journal of General Psychology, 125,* 31–37.

Kallen, K. (2000). Maternal smoking during pregnancy and infant head circumference at birth. *Early Human Development, 58,* 197–204.

Kalter, H. (2003). Teratology in the 20th century: Environmental causes of congenital malformations in humans and how their environmental causes were established. *Neurotoxicology and Teratology, 25,* 131–282.

Kapitanoff, S. H., Lutzker, J. R., & Bigelow, K. M. (2000). Cultural issues in the relation between child disabilities and child abuse. *Aggression and Violent Behavior, 5,* 227–244.

Karmiloff-Smith, A. (1992). *Beyond modularity: A developmental perspective on cognitive science.* Cambridge, MA: MIT Press.

Karpov, Y. V., & Haywood, H. C. (1998). Two ways to elaborate Vygotsky's concept of mediation. *American Psychologist, 53,* 27–36.

Kasari, C., & Bauminger, N. (1998). Social and emotional development in children with mental retardation. In J. A. Burack & R. M. Hodapp (Eds.), *Handbook of mental retardation and development* (pp. 411–433). New York: Cambridge University Press.

Kashani, J. H., Rosenberg, T. K., & Reid, J. C. (1989). Developmental perspectives in child and adolescent depressive symptoms in a community sample. *American Journal of Psychiatry, 146,* 871–876.

Kassianos, G. C. (1998). *Immunization: Childhood and travel health.* Malden, MA: Blackwell.

Katz, J. R. (2001). Playing at home: The talk of pretend play. In D. K Dickinson & P. O. Tabors (Eds.), *Beginning literacy with language: Young children learning at home and school* (pp. 53–73). Baltimore, MD: Brookes.

Katz, L., & Gottman, J. M. (1997). Buffering children from marital conflict and dissolution. *Journal of Child Clinical Psychology, 26,* 157–171.

Katz, P. (1992). *Progress report to NIMH.* Unpublished manuscript.

Katzman, D. K. (1996). Adolescent eating disorders. In R. H. A. Haslam & P. J. Valletutti (Eds.), *Medical problems in the classroom* (pp. 491–513). Austin, TX: Pro-Ed.

Kaufman, J., & Cicchetti, D. (1995). The effect of maltreatment on school age children's socioemotional development. *Developmental Psychology, 25,* 516–524.

Kaufman, L. (1980). Prime-time nutrition. *Journal of Community Health, 30,* 37–46.

Kaufman, N. L. (1980). Review of reversal errors. *Perceptual and Motor Skills, 51,* 55–79.

Kavrell, S. M., & Petersen, A. C. (1984). Patterns of achievement in early adolescence. In M. L. Maehr (Ed.), *Advances in motivation and achievement* (Vol. 4, pp. 1–35). Greenwich, CT: JAI Press.

Kazdin, A. E., & Marciano, P. L. (1998). Childhood and adolescent depression. In E. J. Mash & R. A. Barkley (Eds.), *Treatment of childhood disorders* (pp. 211–248). New York: Guilford.

Kazdin, A. E., Moser, J., Colbus, D., & Bell, R. (1985). Depressive symptoms among physically abused and psychiatrically disturbed children. *Journal of Abnormal Psychology, 94,* 298–307.

Kazura, K. (2000). Fathers' qualitative and quantitative involvement: An investigation of attachment, play, and social interactions. *Journal of Men's Studies, 9* 41–57.

Keating, D. P., & Sasse, D. K. (1996). Cognitive socialization in adolescence: Critical period for a critical habit of mind. In G. R. Adams & R. Montemayor (Eds.), *Psychosocial development during adolescence* (Vol. 8, pp. 232–258). Thousand Oaks, CA: Sage.

Keel, B. A., May, J. V., & DeJonge, C. J. (2000). *Handbook of assisted reproduction.* Boca Raton, FL: CRC Press.

Kehoe, E. J., & Macrae, M. (1998). Classical conditioning. In W. T. O'Donohue (Ed.), *Learning and behavior therapy* (pp. 36–58). Boston: Allyn & Bacon.

Keil, F. C. (1998). Cognitive science and the origins of thought and knowledge. In W. Damon (Ed.), *Handbook of child psychology* (Vol. 1, pp. 341–414). New York: Wiley.

Kelder, S. H., Perry, C. L., Klepp, K. I., & Lytle, L. L. (1994). Longitudinal tracking of adolescent smoking, physical activity, and food choice behaviors. *American Journal of Public Health, 84,* 1121–1126.

Keller, M. L., Duerst, B. L., & Zimmerman, J. (1996). Adolescents' views of sexual decision-making. *Journal of Nursing Scholarship, 28,* 125–130.

Kelley, K. (1991). Contraceptive behavior as a process. In R. M. Lerner, A. C. Petersen, & J. Brooks-Gunn (Eds.), *Encyclopedia of adolescence* (pp. 175–180). New York: Garland.

Kelley, M. L., Power, T. G., & Wimbush, D. D. (1992). Determinants of disciplinary practices in low-income Black mothers. *Child Development, 63*, 573–582.

Kelley, M. L., Sanchez-Hucles, J., & Walker, R. R. (1993). Correlates of disciplinary practices in working- to middle-class African-American mothers. *Merrill-Palmer Quarterly, 39*, 252–264.

Kellman, P. J., & Banks, M. S. (1998). Infant visual perception. In W. Damon (Ed.), *Handbook of child psychology* (Vol. 2, pp. 103–146). New York: Wiley.

Kellogg, R. (1970). Understanding children's art. In P. Cramer (Ed.), *Readings in development psychology today.* Delmar, CA: CRM.

Kelly, D. P. (1992). Hearing impairment. In M. D. Levine, W. B. Carey, & A. C. Crocker (Eds.), *Developmental–behavioral pediatrics* (pp. 510–518). Philadelphia: Saunders.

Kelly, J. B. (1994). The determination of child custody. *The Future of Children, 4*, 121–142.

Kelly, M. (1977). Papua New Guinea and Piaget: An eight-year study. In P. R. Dasen (Ed.), *Piagetian psychology: Cross-cultural contributions.* New York: Gardner.

Kempermann, G., Kuhn, H., & Gage, F. (1997). More hippocampal neurons in adult mice living in an enriched environment. *Nature, 386*, 493–495.

Kendall-Tackett, K. A., & Eckenrode, J. (1997). The effects of neglect on academic achievement and disciplinary problems. In G. K. Kantor & J. L. Jasinski (Eds.), *Out of darkness: Contemporary perspectives on family violence* (pp. 105–112). Thousand Oaks, CA: Sage.

Keogh, B. K., & MacMillan, D. L. (1996). Exceptionality. In D. C. Berliner & R. C. Calfee (Eds.), *Handbook of educational psychology* (pp. 311–330). New York: Macmillan.

Kernis, M. H., Brown, A., & Brody, G. H. (2000). Fragile self-esteem in children and its associations with perceived patterns of parent–child communication. *Journal of Personality, 68*, 225–252.

Kestenbaum, R., Farber, E. A., & Sroufe, L. A. (1989). Individual differences in empathy among preschoolers: Relation to attachment history. In N. Eisenberg (Ed.), *New directions for child development: Empathy and related emotional responses* (Vol. 44, pp. 51–64). San Francisco: Jossey-Bass.

Ketterlinus, R. D., Lamb, M. E., & Nitz, K. A. (1995). Adolescent nonsexual and sex-related problem behaviors: Their prevalence, consequences, and co-occurrence. In R. D. Ketterlinus & M. E. Lamb (Eds.), *Adolescent problem behaviors* (pp. 17–40). Hillsdale, NJ: Erlbaum.

Kidscape. (1999). *Long-term effects of bullying.* London: Author.

Kilbourne, J. (1994). Still killing us softly: Advertising and the obsession with thinness. In P. Fallon, M. Katzman, & S. Wooley (Eds.), *Feminist perspectives on eating disorders* (pp. 395–418). New York: Guilford.

Kilbride, P. L. (1980). Sensorimotor behavior of Baganda and Somia infants: A controlled comparison. *Journal of Cross-Cultural Psychology, 11*, 131–149.

Kimura, D. (1993). Sex differences in the brain. In *Mind and brain: Readings from Scientific American* (pp. 79–89). New York: Freeman.

Kindler, A. L. (2002). *Survey of the states' limited English proficiency students and available education programs and services: 1999–2000 summary report.* National Clearinghouse for English Language Acquisition and Language Instruction Education Programs. Washington, DC: US Department of Education.

King, M., & Yuille, J. (1987). Suggestibility and the child witness. In S. J. Ceci, D. Ross, & M. Toglia (Eds.), *Children's eyewitness memory* (pp. 24–35). New York: Springer-Verlag.

Kirby, D. (2001). *Emerging answers: Research findings on programs to reduce teen pregnancy.* Washington, DC: National Campaign to Prevent Teen Pregnancy.

Kirsh, S. J. (1998). Seeing the world through Mortal Kombat–colored glasses. *Childhood, 5*, 177–184.

Kirsh, S. J. (2003). The effects of violent video games on adolescents: The overlooked influence of development. *Aggression and Violent Behavior, 8*, 377–389.

Kiser, L. J., Ostoja, E., & Pruitt, D. B. (1998). Dealing with stress and trauma in families. *Child and Adolescent Psychiatric Clinics of North America, 7*, 87–103.

Kittler, P. G., & Sucher, K. P. (1998). *Food and culture in America: A nutrition handbook.* Belmont, CA: West/Wadsworth.

Klaczynski, P. A. (2000). Motivated scientific reasoning biases, epistemological beliefs, and theory polarization: A two-process approach to adolescent cognition. *Child Development, 71*, 1347–1366.

Klaus, M. H., & Kennell, J. H. (1982). *Parent-infant bonding.* St. Louis, MO: Mosby.

Klaus, M. H., Kennell, J. H., Plumb, N., & Zeuhlke, S. (1970). Human maternal behavior at the first contact with her young. *Pediatrics, 46*, 187–192.

Klebanoff, M. A., Levine, R. J., Der3imonian, R., Clemens, J. D., & Wilkins, D. G. (1999). Maternal serum paraxanthine, a caffeine metabolite, and the risk of spontaneous abortion. *New England Journal of Medicine, 341*, 1639–1644.

Klein, H. (1991). Couvade syndrome: Male counterpart to pregnancy. *International Journal of Psychiatry and Medicine, 21*, 57–69.

Klein, M. H. (1984). The bite of Pac-Man. *Journal of Psychohistory, 11*, 395–401.

Klein, P. D. (1997). Multiplying the problems of intelligence by eight: A critique of Gardner's theory. *Canadian Journal of Education, 22*, 377–394.

Klein, R. G., & Mannuzza, S. (1991). Long-term outcome of hyperactive children: A review. *Journal of the American Academy of Child and Adolescent Psychiatry, 30*, 383–387.

Kleinman, R. W., Murphy, J. M., Little, M., Pagano, M., Wehler, C. A., Regal, K., & Jellinek, M. S. (1998). Hunger in children in the United States: Potential behavioral and emotional correlates. *Pediatrics, 101*, e3.

Kliewer, W., Fearnow, M. D., & Walton, M. N. (1998). Dispositional, environmental, and context-specific predictors of children's threat perceptions in everyday stressful situations. *Journal of Youth and Adolescence, 27*, 83–100.

Klinefelter Syndrome and Associates. (2001). *Sex chromosomes variations.* Roseville, CA: Author.

Klinnert, M. D., Campos, J. J., Sorce, J. F., Emde, R. N., & Svejda, M. (1983). Emotions as behavior regulators: Social referencing in infancy. In R. Plutchik & H. Kelleman (Eds.), *Emotion: Theory, research, and experience: Emotions in early development* (Vol. 2, pp. 57–86). New York: Academic Press.

Knight, G., Fabes, R. A., & Higgins, D. (1996). Concerns about drawing causal inferences from meta-analyses of gender differences: An example in the study of aggression. *Psychological Bulletin, 119*, 410–421.

Knight, R. T., & Grabowecky, M. (2000). Prefrontal cortex, time, and consciousness. In M. S. Gazzaniga (Ed.), *The new cognitive neurosciences* (pp. 1319–1339). Cambridge, MA: MIT Press.

Knight-Ridder/Tribune News Service (1999, July 9). *Popular music's influence on teens is undeniable and sometimes negative.* New York: Author.

Kochanska, G. (1995). Children's temperament, mothers' discipline, and security of attachment: Multiple pathways to emerging internalization. *Child Development, 66*, 597–615.

Kochanska, G. (1997). Multiple pathways to conscience for children with different temperaments: From toddlerhood to age 5. *Developmental Psychology, 33*, 228–240.

Kochanska, G., & Askan, N. (1995). Mother–child mutually positive affect, the quality of child compliance to requests and prohibitions, and maternal control as correlates of early internalization. *Child Development, 66*, 236–254.

Kochanska, G., Coy, K. C., Tjebkes, T. I., & Husarek, S. J. (1998). Individual differences in emotionality in infancy. *Child Development, 69,* 375–390.

Kochanska, G., Murray, K. T., & Harlan, E. T. (2000). Effortful control in early childhood: Continuity and change, antecedents, and implications for social development. *Developmental Psychology, 36,* 220–232.

Koegel, P., & Edgerton, R. B. (1984). Black "six-hour retarded children" as young adults. In R. B. Edgerton (Ed.), *Lives in process: Mildly retarded adults in a large city* (pp. 145–171). Washington, DC: American Association on Mental Deficiency.

Koff, E., & Rierdan, J. (1993). Advanced pubertal development and eating disturbance in early adolescent girls. *Journal of Adolescent Health, 14,* 433–439.

Kohlberg, L. (1966). A cognitive-developmental analysis of children's sex role concepts and attitudes. In E. E. Maccoby (Ed.), *The development of sex differences* (pp. 82–173). Stanford, CA: Stanford University Press.

Kohlberg, L. (1969). Stage and sequence: The cognitive-developmental approach to socialization. In D. A. Goslin (Ed.), *Handbook of socialization theory and research* (pp. 347–480). Chicago: Rand McNally.

Kohlberg, L. (1981). *Essays on moral development: Vol. 1.* New York: Harper & Row.

Kohlberg, L. (1984). *Essays on moral development: Vol. 2.* New York: Harper & Row.

Kohlberg, L., & Kramer, R. (1969). Continuities and discontinuities in childhood and adult moral development. *Human Development, 12,* 3–120.

Kohlberg, L., Colby, A., Gibbs, J., & Speicher-Dubin, B. (1978). *Standard form scoring manual.* Cambridge, MA: Harvard University Center for Moral Education.

Kohn, A. (1993). *Punished by rewards.* Boston: Houghton Mifflin.

Kolb, K. J., & Jussim, L. (1994). Teacher expectations and underachieving gifted children. *Roeper Review, 17,* 26–30.

Kolko, D. J. (1996). Child physical abuse. In J. Briere, L. Berliner, J. A. Bulkley, C. Jenny, & T. Reid (Eds.), *The APSAC handbook on child maltreatment* (pp. 21–50). Thousand Oaks, CA: Sage.

Koller, H., Lawson, K., Rose, S. A., Wallace, I., & McCarton, C. (1997). Patterns of cognitive development in very low birth weight children during the first six years of life. *Pediatrics, 99,* 383–389.

Komsten, A. T., Skaalvik, E. M., & Espnes, G. A. (2004). Physical self-concept and sports: Do gender differences still exist? *Sex Roles, 50,* 119–127.

Kong, E. (1992). Early detection of cerebral motor disorders. *Medicine and Sports Science, 36,* 80–85.

Konner, M. (1991). Universals of behavioral development in relation to brain myelination. In K. R. Gibson & A. C. Petersen (Eds.), *Brain maturation and cognitive development: Comparative and cross-cultural perspectives* (pp. 181–224). New York: Aldine de Gruyter.

Kopp, C. B. (1992). Emotional distress and control in young children. In N. Eisenberg & R. A. Fabes (Eds.), *Emotion and its regulation in early development* (Vol. 55, pp. 41–57). San Francisco: Jossey-Bass.

Korbin, J. E., Coulton, C. J., Chard, S., Platt-Houston, C., & Su, M. (1998). Impoverishment and child maltreatment in African American and European American neighborhoods. *Development and Psychopathology, 10,* 215–233.

Korkman, M., Liikanen, A., & Fellman, V. (1996). Neurophysiological consequences of very low birth weight and asphyxia at term: Follow-up until school-age. *Journal of Clinical and Experimental Neuropsychology, 18,* 220–233.

Kornhaber, M. L. (2001). Howard Gardner. In J. Palmer (Ed.), *Fifty modern thinkers on education: From Piaget to present* (pp. 272–279). London: Routledge.

Korte, D., & Scaer, R. (1992). *A good birth, a safe birth.* Boston: Harvard Common Press.

Kotlowitz, A. (1991). *There are no children here.* New York: Doubleday.

Kowal, A., & Kramer, L. (1997). Children's understanding of parental differential treatment. *Child Development, 68,* 113–126.

Krahenbuhl, G. S., Skinner, J. S., & Korht, W. M. (1985). Developmental aspects of maximal aerobic power in children. *Exercise and Sport Science Review, 13,* 503.

Kramer, C. (1995, September 19). Former dropout makes new life at Yale. *Yale Daily News.*

Krashen, S. (2000). Bilingual education, the acquisition of English, and the retention and loss of Spanish. In A. Roca (Ed.), *Research on Spanish in the US: Linguistic issues and challenges* (pp. 432–444). Somerville, MA: Cascadilla Press.

Kraus, J. F., Peek-Asa, C., & Blander, B. (1997). Injury control: The public health approach. In R. Detels, W. W. Holland, J. McEwen, & J. Omenn (Eds.), *Textbook of public health* (3rd ed., pp. 1291–1306). New York: Oxford University Press.

Krauss, D. A., & Sales, B. D. (2001). The child custody standard: What do twenty years of research teach us? In S. O. White (Ed.), *Handbook of youth and justice* (pp. 411–435). New York: Kluwer.

Krechevsky, M., & Seidel, S. (1998). Minds at work: Applying multiple intelligences in the classroom. In R J. Sternberg & W. M. Williams (Eds.), *Intelligence, instruction, and assessment: Theory into practice* (pp. 17–42). Mahwah, NJ: Erlbaum.

Kroger, J. (2000). Ego identity status research in the new millennium. *International Journal of Behavioral Development, 24,* 145–148.

Kuchuk, A., Vibbert, M., & Bornstein, M. H. (1986). The perception of smiling and its experiential correlates in three-month-old infants. *Child Development, 57,* 1054–1061.

Kuczynski, L., Kochanska, G., Radke-Yarrow, M., & Girnius-Brown, O. (1987). A developmental interpretation of young children's noncompliance. *Developmental Psychology, 23,* 799–806.

Kuhn, D. (1989). Children and adults as intuitive scientists. *Psychological Review, 96,* 674–689.

Kuhn, D., Amsel, E., O'Loughlin, M., Schauble, L., Leadbeater, B., & Yotive, W. (1988). *The development of scientific reasoning skills.* San Diego, CA: Academic Press.

Kuhn, D., Nash, S. C., & Brucken, L. (1978). Sex role concepts of two- and three-year-old children. *Child Development, 49,* 445–451.

Kuhn, L., Kline, J., Ng, S., Levin, B., & Susser, M. (2000). Cocaine use during pregnancy and intrauterine growth retardation: New insights based on maternal hair tests. *American Journal of Epidemiology, 152,* 112–119.

Kumpulainen, K., Rasanen, E., Henttonnen, I., Almquest, F., Kresanov, K., Linna, S. I., Moilanen, I., Piha, J., Puura, K., & Tamminen, T. (1998). Bullying and psychiatric symptoms among elementary school–age children. *Child Abuse and Neglect, 22,* 705–707.

Kumra, S., Wiggins, E., Krasnewich, D., Meck, J., Smith, A. C. M., Bedwell, J., Fernandez, T., Jacobsen, L. K., Lenane, M., & Rapoport, J. L. (1998). Association of sex chromosome anomalies with childhood-onset psychotic disorders. *Journal of the American Academy of Child and Adolescent Psychiatry, 37,* 292–296.

Kurdek, L. A. (1988). Cognitive mediators of children's adjustment to divorce. In S. A. Wolchik & P. Karoly (Eds.), *Children of divorce* (pp. 233–266). New York: Gardner.

Kwasman, A., Tinsley, B. J., & Lepper, H. S. (1995). Pediatricians' knowledge and attitudes concerning diagnosis and treatment of attention deficit and hyperactivity disorders. *Archives of Pediatric and Adolescent Medicine, 149,* 1211–1216.

Labre, M. P. (2002). Adolescent boys and the muscular male body ideal. *Journal of Adolescent Health, 30,* 233–242.

Ladd, G. W., & Hart, C. H. (1992). Creating informal play opportunities: Are parents' and preschoolers' initiations related to children's competence with peers? *Developmental Psychology, 28,* 1179–1187.

Ladd, G. W., & Kochenderfer, B. J. (1998). Linkages between friendship and adjustment during early school transition. In W. M. Bukowski & A. F. Newcomb (Eds.), *The company they keep: Friendship in child-

hood and adolescence (pp. 322–345). New York: Cambridge University Press.

Lagercrantz, H., & Slotkin, T. A. (1986). The "stress" of being born. *Scientific American, 254,* 100–107.

LaGreca, A. M., Prinstein, M. J., & Fetter, M. D. (2001). Adolescent peer crowd affiliation: Linkages with health-risk behaviors and close friendships. *Journal of Pediatric Psychology, 26,* 131–143.

Laible, D., & Thompson, R. (2002). Mother–child conflict in the toddler years: Lessons in emotion, morality, and relationships. *Child Development,* 1187–1203.

Laird, R. D., Pettit, G. S., Dodge, K. A., & Bates, J. E. (1999). Best friendships, group relationships, and antisocial behavior in early adolescence. *Journal of Early Adolescence, 19,* 413–437.

Lamb, M. E. (1998). Nonparental child care: Context, quality, correlates, and consequences. In W. Damon (Ed.), *Handbook of child psychology* (Vol. 4, pp. 73–134). New York: Wiley.

Lamb, M. E. (1999). *Parenting and child development in "nontraditional" families.* Mahwah, NJ: Erlbaum.

Lamb, M. E., Sternberg, K. J., & Ketterlinus, R. D. (1992). Child care in the United States: The modern era. In M. E. Lamb, K. J. Sternberg, C. Hwang, & A. G. Broberg (Eds.), *Child care in context* (pp. 207–222). Hillsdale, NJ: Erlbaum.

Lampert, W. E. (1984). An overview of issues in immersion education. In Office of Bilingual and Bicultural Education (Ed.), *Studies in immersion education* (pp. 8–30). Sacramento: California Department of Education.

Landers, D. M., & Petruzzello, S. J. (1994). Physical activity, fitness and anxiety. In C. Bouchard, R. J. Shephard, & T. Stephens (Eds.), *Physical activity, fitness, and health* (pp. 868–882). Champaign, IL: Human Kinetics Publishers.

Landry, D. J., & Forrest, J. D. (1995). How much older are U.S. fathers? *Family Planning Perspectives, 27,* 159–165.

Lane, K. L., Beebe, M. E., Lambros, K. M., & Pierson, M. (2001). Designing effective interventions for children at-risk for antisocial behavior: An integrated model of components necessary for making valid inferences. *Psychology in the Schools, 38,* 365–379.

Lane, M. K., & Hodkin, B. (1985). Role of atypical exemplars of social and nonsocial superordinate categories within the class inclusion paradigm. *Developmental Psychology, 21,* 909–915.

Langendorfer, S. (1987). Separating fact from fiction in preschool aquatics. *National Aquatics Journal, 3,* 2–4.

Langer, J., & Killen, M. (1998). *Piaget, evolution, and development.* Mahwah, NJ: Erlbaum.

Langlois, J. H. (1981). Beauty and the beast: The role of physical attractiveness in the development of peer relations and social behavior. In S. S. Brehm, S. S. Kassin, & F. X. Gibbons (Eds.), *Developmental social psychology* (pp. 47–63). New York: Oxford University Press.

Langlois, J. H., & Downs, A. C. (1980). Mothers, fathers and peers as socialization agents of sex-typed play behaviors in young children. *Child Development, 51,* 1237–1247.

Langlois, J. H., Ritter, J. M., Roggman, L. A., & Vaughn, L. S. (1991). Facial diversity and infant preferences for attractive faces. *Developmental Psychology, 27,* 79–84.

Langlois, J. H., Roggman, L. A., Casey, R. J., Ritter, J. M., Rieser-Danner, L. A., & Jenkins, V. Y. (1987). Infant preferences for attractive faces: Rudiments of a stereotype? *Developmental Psychology, 23,* 363–369.

LaPorte, D. J. (1997). Gender differences in perceptions and consequences of an eating binge. *Sex Roles, 36,* 479–489.

Lapsley, D. K. (1993). Toward an integrated theory of adolescent ego development. *American Journal of Orthopsychiatry, 63,* 562–571.

Larson, R. (1994). Youth organizations, hobbies, and sports as developmental contexts. In R. Silbereisen & E. Todt (Eds.), *Adolescence in context: The interplay of family, school, peers, and work in adjustment* (pp. 46–65). New York: Springer-Verlag.

Larson, R., & Richards, M. H. (1994). *Divergent realities: The emotional lives of mothers, fathers, and adolescents.* New York: Basic Books.

Lassen, K., & Oei, T. P. (1998). Effects of maternal cigarette smoking during pregnancy on long-term physical and cognitive parameters of child development. *Addictive Behavior, 23,* 635–653.

Laursen, B., & Collins, W. A. (1994). Interpersonal conflict during adolescence. *Psychological Bulletin, 115,* 197–209.

Laursen, B., & Williams, V. A. (1997). Perceptions of interdependence and closeness in family and peer relationships among adolescents with and without romantic partners. In S. Shulman & W. A. Collins (Eds.), *Romantic relationships in adolescence* (pp. 3–20). San Francisco: Jossey-Bass.

Laursen, B., Coy, K. C., & Collins, W. A. (1998). Reconsidering changes in parent–child conflict across adolescence. *Child Development, 69,* 817–832.

Lautenbacher, S. (2004). Sex differences in pain inhibition and pain summation in humans. *International Journal of Sex Differences in Health, Disease, and Aging, 2,* 21–25.

Lavigne, J. V., Arend, R., Rosenbaum, D., Smith, A., Weissbluth, M., Binns, H. J., & Christoffel, K. K. (1999). Sleep and behavior problems among preschoolers. *Journal of Developmental and Behavioral Pediatrics, 20,* 164–169.

Le Couteur, A., & Baird, G. (2003). National initiative for autism: Screening and assessment (NIASA). *National autism plan for children.* London: National Autistic Society. Available at www.nas.org.uk/profess/niasa.html

Le Couteur, A., & Baird, G. (2003). National initiative for autism: Screening and assessment (NIASA). In *National autism plan for children.* London: National Autistic Society. Retrieved from www.nas.org.uk/profess/niasa.html

Leach, P. (1997). *Your baby and child.* New York: Knopf.

Leaper, C., & Anderson, K. J. (1997). Gender development and heterosexual romantic relationships during adolescence. In S. Shulman & W. A. Collins (Eds.), *Romantic relationships in adolescence* (pp. 85–104). San Francisco: Jossey-Bass.

Leaper, C., Anderson, K. J., & Sanders, P. (1998). Moderators of gender effects on parents' talk to their children: A meta-analysis. *Developmental Psychology, 34,* 3–27.

Lederman, S. A., Akabas, S. R., & Moore, B. J. (2004). Editor's overview of the conference on preventing childhood obesity. *Pediatrics, 114,* 1139–1145.

Lee, C. M., & Gotlib, I. H. (1995). Mental illness and the family. In L. L'Abate (Ed.), *Handbook of developmental family psychology and psychopathology* (pp. 243–264). New York: Wiley.

Lee, L. C. (1992). Day care in the People's Republic of China. In M. E. Lamb, K. J. Sternberg, C. Hwang, & A. G. Broberg (Eds.), *Child care in context* (pp. 355–392). Hillsdale, NJ: Erlbaum.

Leger, D. W., Thompson, R. A., Merritt, J. A., & Benz, J. J. (1996). Adult perception of emotion intensity in human infant cries: Effects of infant age and cry acoustics. *Child Development, 67,* 3238–3249.

Legerstee, M., Anderson, D., & Schaffer, A. (1998). Five- and eight-month-old infants recognize their faces and voices as familiar and social stimuli. *Child Development, 69,* 37–50.

Lehman, S. J., & Koerner, S. S. (2004). Adolescent women's sports involvement and sexual behavior/health: A process-level investigation. *Journal of Youth and Adolescence, 33,* 443–455.

Leinbach, M. D., & Fagot, B. I. (1993). Categorical habituation to male and female faces: Gender schematic processing in infancy. *Infant Behavior and Development, 16,* 317–332.

Leinbach, M. D., Hort, B. E., & Fagot, B. I. (1997). Bears are for boys: Metaphorical associations in young children's gender stereotypes. *Cognitive Development, 12,* 107–130.

Leiter, J., & Johnsen, M. C. (1997). Child maltreatment and school performance declines: An event-history analysis. *American Educational Research Journal, 34,* 563–589.

Lemons, J. A., Bauer, C. R., Oh, W., Korones, S. B., Papile, L., Stoll, B. J., Verter, J., Temprosa, M., Wright, L. L., Ehrenkranz, R. A., Fanaroff, A. A., Stark, A., Carlo, W., Tyson, J. E., Donovan, E. F., Shankaran, S., & Stevenson, D. K. (2001). Very low birth outcomes of the National Institute of Child Health and Development Neonatal Research Network, January 1995 through December 1996. *Pediatrics, 107,* 1–14.

Longua, L. J., West, S. G., & Sandler, I. (1998). Temperament as a predictor of symptomatology in children. *Child Development, 69,* 164–181.

Lenneberg, E. (1967). *Biological foundations of language.* New York: Wiley.

Lepper, M. R., & Henderlong, J. (2000). Turning "play" into "work" and "work" into "play": 25 years of research on intrinsic versus extrinsic motivation. In C. Sansone & J. M. Harackiewicz (Eds.), *Intrinsic and extrinsic motivation: The search for optimal motivation and performance* (pp. 257–307). San Diego: Academic Press.

Lerner, R. M., Delaney, M., Hess, L. I., Jovanovic, J., & von Eye, A. (1990). Early adolescent physical attractiveness and academic competence. *Journal of Early Adolescence, 10,* 4–20.

Leslie, A. M. (1987). Pretense and representation: The origins of "theory of mind." *Psychological Review, 94,* 412–426.

Lester, B. M. (1985). There's more to crying than meets the ear. In B. M. Lester & C. F. Z. Boukydis (Eds.), *Infant crying* (pp. 1–28). New York: Plenum.

Leve, L. D., & Fagot, B. I. (1997). Gender-role socialization and discipline processes in one- and two-parent families. *Sex Roles, 36,* 1–21.

Leventhal, E. A., Leventhal, H., Shacham, S., & Easterling, D. V. (1989). Active coping reduces reports of pain from childbirth. *Journal of Consulting and Clinical Psychology, 57,* 365–371.

Leventhal, J. M., Forsyth, B. W. C., Qi, K., Johnson, L., Schroeder, D., & Votto, N. (1997). Maltreatment of children born to women who used cocaine during pregnancy. *Pediatrics, 100,* 1–6.

Levin, B. B., & Barry, S. M. (1997). Children's views of technology: The role of age, gender, and school setting. *Journal of Computing in Childhood Education, 8,* 267–290.

Levine, M. P., Smolak, L., Moodey, A. F., Shuman, M. D., & Hessen, L. D. (1994). Normative developmental challenges and dieting and eating disturbances in middle school girls. *International Journal of Eating Disorders, 15,* 11–20.

LeVine, R. A., Dixon, S., LeVine, S., Richman, A., Leiderman, P. H., Keefer, C. H., & Brazelton, T. B. (1994). *Child care and culture: Lessons from Africa.* Cambridge, UK: Cambridge University Press.

Levinger, B. (1986). *Schoolfeeding programs in developing countries: An analysis of actual and potential impact.* Washington, DC: USAID.

Levy, G. D. (1999). Gender-typed and non-gender-typed category awareness in toddlers. *Sex Roles, 41,* 851–873.

Levy, G. D., & Katz, P. A. (1993, March). *Differences in preschoolers' race schemas.* Paper presented at the biennial meeting of the Society for Research in Child Development, New Orleans, LA.

Levy, J., & Heller, W. (1992). Gender differences in human neuropsychological function. In A. A. Gerall & H. Moltz (Ed.), *Sexual differentiation* (Vol. 11, pp. 245–274). New York: Plenum.

Lewis, C., & Lamb, M. E. (2003). Fathers' influences on children's development: The evidence from two-parent families. *European Journal of Psychology of Education, 18,* 211–228.

Lewis, H. B. (1987). The role of shame in depression in women. In R. Formanek & A. Gurian (Eds.), *Women and depression* (pp. 182–199). New York: Springer.

Lewis, M. (1993). Self conscious emotions: Embarrassment, pride, shame, and guilt. In M. Lewis & J. M. Haviland (Eds.), *Handbook of emotions* (pp. 563–573). New York: Guilford.

Lewis, M., Alessandri, S. M., & Sullivan, M. W. (1992). Differences in shame and pride as a function of children's gender and task difficulty. *Child Development, 63,* 630–638.

Lewis, M., & Brooks-Gunn, J. (1979). *Social cognition and the acquisition of self.* New York: Plenum.

Lewis, M., & Steiben, J. (2004). Emotion regulation in the brain: Conceptual issues and directions for developmental research. *Child Development, 75,* 371–376.

Lewis, M., Sullivan, M. W., Stanger, C., & Weiss, M. (1989). Self-development and self-conscious emotions. *Child Development, 60,* 146–156.

Lewit, E. M., & Baker, L. S. (1995). School readiness. *Future of Children, 5,* 128–139.

Li, R., Ogden, C., Ballew, C., Gillespie, C., & Grummer-Strawn, L. (2002). Prevalence of exclusive breastfeeding among US infants. *American Journal of Public Health, 92,* 1107–1110.

Li, X., Adam, G., Cui, H., Sandtedt, B., Ohlsson, R., & Ekstron, T. (1995). Expression, promotor usage, and imprinting status of insulin-like growth factor II (IGF2) in human hepatoblastoma: Uncoupling of IGF2 and H10 imprinting. *Oncogene, 11,* 221–229.

Liberman, A. M. (1996). *Speech: A special code.* Cambridge, MA: MIT Press.

Lieberman, P. (1984). *The biology and evolution of language.* Cambridge, MA: Harvard University Press.

Liebert, R. M., & Sprafkin, J. (1988). *The early window: Effects of television on children and youth.* New York: Pergamon.

Life Sciences Research Office. (1995). *Third report on nutrition monitoring in the United States.* Washington, DC: US Government Printing Office.

Lifshitz, F., Finch, N. M., & Lifshitz, J. Z. (1991). *Children's nutrition.* Boston: Jones and Bartlett.

Lillard, A. S. (1993). Pretend play skills and the child's theory of mind. *Child Development, 64,* 1–15.

Lillard, A. S. (1998). Ethnopsychologies: Cultural variations in theories of mind. *Psychological Bulletin, 123,* 3–32.

Lillo-Martin, D. (1999). Modality effects and modularity in language acquisition: The acquisition of American Sign Language. In W. Ritche & T. Bhatia (Eds.), *Handbook of child language acquisition* (pp. 531–567). San Diego: Academic Press.

Limber, S. P. (2004). Implementation of the Olweus bullying prevention program in American schools. In D. L. Espelage & S. M. Swearer (Eds.), *Bullying in American schools* (pp. 351–364). Mahwah, NJ: Erlbaum.

Lindberg, L. D., Sonenstein, F. L., Ku, L., & Martinez, G. (1997). Age differences between minors who give birth and their adult partners. *Family Planning Perspectives, 29,* 61–66.

Lindley, A. A., Becker, S., Gray, R. H., & Herman, A. A. (2000). Effect of continuing or stopping smoking during pregnancy on infant birth weight, crown–heel length, head circumference, ponderal index, and brain: body weight ratio. *American Journal of Epidemiology, 152,* 219–225.

Linn, M. C., de Benedictis, T., & Delucchi, K. (1982). Adolescent reasoning about advertisements: Preliminary investigations. *Child Development, 53,* 1599–1613.

Linn, M. C., & Petersen, A. C. (1986). A meta-analysis of gender differences in spatial ability: Implications for mathematics and science achievement. In J. S. Hyde & M. C. Linn, (Eds.), *The psychology of gender: Advances through meta-analysis* (pp. 67–101). Baltimore, MD: The Johns Hopkins University Press.

Lipsey, M. W. (1995). What do we learn from 400 research studies on the effectiveness of treatment with juvenile delinquents? In J. McGuire (Ed.), *What works? Reducing reoffending* (pp. 63–78). New York: Wiley.

Lipsitt, L. P., Engen, T., & Kaye, H. (1963). Developmental changes in the olfactory threshold of the neonate. *Child Development, 34,* 371–376.

Little, S., & Garber, J. (1995). Aggression, depression, and stressful life events predicting peer rejection in children. *Development and Psychopathology, 7,* 845–856.

Liu, X., Kaplan, H. B., & Risser, W. (1992). Decomposing the reciprocal relationships between academic achievement and general self-esteem. *Youth and Society, 24,* 123–148.

Liu, X., Liu, L., & Wang, R. (2003). Bed sharing, sleep habits, and sleep problems among Chinese school-aged children. *Sleep, 26,* 839–844.

Liu, X., Zhenxiao, S., Uchiyama, M., Shibui, K., Kim, K., & Okawa, M. (2000). Prevalence and correlates of sleep problems in Chinese schoolchildren. *Sleep, 23,* 1–10.

Livesley, W. J., & Bromley, D. B. (1973). *Person perception in childhood and adolescence.* London: Wiley.

Lo Turco, J. L. (2000). Neural circuits in the 21st century: Synaptic networks of neurons and glia. *Proceedings of the National Academy of Science, 97,* 8196–8197.

Locke, J. (1964). *Some thoughts concerning education.* Woodbury, NH: Barron's Educational Series. (Original work published 1690)

Lockwood, P., & Kunda, Z. (1997). Superstars and me: Predicting the impact of role models on the self. *Journal of Personality and Social Psychology, 73,* 91–103.

Loeber, R., & Hay, D. (1997). Key issues in the development of aggression and violence from childhood to early adulthood. *Annual Review of Psychology, 48,* 371–410.

Loeber, R., Farrington, D. P., Stouthamer-Loeber, M., & Van-Kammen, W. B. (1998). *Antisocial behavior and mental health problems.* Mahwah, NJ: Erlbaum.

Logsdon, M. C., McBride, A. B., & Birkimer, J. C. (1994). Social support and postpartum depression. *Research in Nursing & Health, 17,* 449–457.

Lohaus, A. K., Keller, H., Ball, J., Elben, C., & Volker, S. (2001). Maternal sensitivity: Components and relations to warmth and contingency. *Parenting Science and Practice, 1,* 267–284.

Lord, W. D., Boudreaux, M. C., & Lanning, K. V. (2001). Investigating potential child abduction cases. *FBI Law Enforcement Bulletin, 70,* 1–12.

Lorys, V. A. R., Hynd, G. W., Lyytinen, H., & Hern, K. (1993). Etiology of attention deficit hyperactivity disorder. In J. L. Matson (Ed.), *Handbook of hyperactivity in children* (pp. 47–65). Boston: Allyn & Bacon.

Loucks, A. B. (1988). Osteoporosis prevention begins in childhood. In E. W. Brown & C. F. Branta (Eds.), *Competitive sports for children and youth* (pp. 213–223). Champaign, IL: Human Kinetics Books.

Lovelace, V. O., & Huston, A. C. (1983). Can television teach prosocial behavior? *Prevention in Human Services, 2,* 93–106.

Lovett, M. W., Barron, R. W., & Benson, N. J. (2003). Effective remediation of word identification and decoding difficulties in school-age children with reading disabilities. In H. L. Swanson, K. Harris, & S. Graham. (Eds.), *Handbook of learning disabilities* (pp. 273–292). New York: Guilford.

Lozoff, B., Jimenez, E., Hagen, J., Mollen, E., & Wolf, A. W. (2000). Poorer behavioral and developmental outcomes more than 10 years after treatment for iron deficiency in infancy. *Pediatrics, 105,* 51.

Lozoff, B., Klein, N. K., Nelson, E. C., McClish, D. K., Manuel, M., & Chacon, M. E. (1998). Behavior of infants with iron-deficiency anemia. *Child Development, 69,* 24–36.

Lubeck, S., DeVries, M., Nicholson, J., & Post, J. (1997). Head Start in transition. *Early Education and Development, 8,* 219–244.

Lucas, A., Morely, R., Cole, T. J., Lister, G., & Leeson-Payne, C. (1992). Breast milk and subsequent intelligence quotient in children born before preterm. *Lancet, 339,* 261–264.

Luna, B., Thulborn, K. R., Munoz, D. P., Merriam, E. P., Garver, K. E., Minshew, N.J., Keshavan, M. S., Genovese, C. R., Eddy, W. F., & Sweeney, J. A. (2001). Maturation of widely distributed brain function subserves cognitive development. *Neuroimage, 13,* 786–793.

Lutzker, J. R. (1998). *Handbook of child abuse research and treatment.* New York: Plenum.

Lutzker, J. R. (2000). Child abuse. In V. B. Van Hasselt & M. Hersen (Eds.), *Aggression and violence* (pp. 54–66). Boston: Allyn & Bacon.

Lye, D. N. (1999). *Scholarly research on post-divorce parenting and child well-being.* Seattle, WA: Washington State Domestic Relations Commission.

Lynch, M. D. (1981). Self-concept development in childhood. In M. D. Lynch, A. A. Norem-Hebeisen, & K. Gergen (Eds.), *Self-concept: Advances in theory and research* (pp. 110–143). Cambridge, MA: Ballinger.

Lysne, M., & Levy, G. D. (1997). Differences in ethnic identity in Native American adolescents as a function of school context. *Journal of Adolescent Research, 12,* 372–388.

Lytton, H., & Romney, D. M. (1991). Parents' differential socialization of boys and girls: A meta-analysis. *Psychological Bulletin, 109,* 267–296.

Lyytinen, P., Poikkeus, A. M., & Laakso, M. L. (1997). Language and symbolic play in toddlers. *International Journal of Behavioral Development, 21,* 289–302.

Maas, J. (1995, November). *Asleep in the fast lane.* Paper presented at the Master's Forum, Minneapolis, MN.

MacBrayer, E. K., Milich, R., & Hundley, M. (2003). Attributional biases in aggressive children and their mothers. *Journal of Abnormal Psychology, 112,* 698–708.

Maccoby, E. E. (1980). *Social development.* San Diego, CA: Harcourt Brace Jovanovich.

Maccoby, E. E. (1990). Gender and relationships. *American Psychologist, 45,* 513–520.

Maccoby, E. E. (1998). *The two sexes: Growing up apart, coming together.* Cambridge, MA: Belknap Press.

Maccoby, E. E., Depner, C. E., & Mnookin, R. H. (1990). Coparenting in the second year after divorce. *Journal of Marriage and the Family, 52,* 141–155.

Maccoby, E. E., & Jacklin, C. N. (1974). *The psychology of sex differences.* Stanford, CA: Stanford University Press.

Maccoby, E. E., & Jacklin, C. N. (1980). Sex differences in aggression: A rejoinder and reprise. *Child Development, 51,* 964–980.

Maccoby, E. E., & Martin, J. A. (1983). Socialization in the context of the family. In E. M. Hetherington (Ed.), *Handbook of child psychology: Vol. 4. Socialization, personality, and social development* (pp. 1–101). New York: Wiley.

Maccoby, E. E., & Mnookin, R. H. (1992). *Dividing the child: Social and legal dilemmas of custody.* Cambridge, MA: Harvard University Press.

Macdonald, S. C., Pertowski, C. A., & Jackson, R. J. (1996). Environmental public health surveillance. *Journal of Public Health Management Practices, 2,* 45–49.

MacFadden, A., Elias, L., & Saucier, D. (2003). Males and females scan maps similarly, but give directions differently. *Brain and Cognition, 53,* 297–300.

MacFarlane, A. (1975). Olfaction in the development of social preferences in the human neonate. *Ciba Foundation Symposium, 33,* 103–117.

Macfarlane, J. W., Allen, L., & Honzik, M. P. (1954). *A developmental study of the behavior problems of normal children between twenty-one months and fourteen years.* Berkeley: University of California Press.

Mackey, M. C. (1990). Women's preparation for the childbirth experience. *Maternal and Child Nursing Journal, 19,* 143–173.

MacKinnon, C. E. (1989). Sibling interactions in married and divorced families: Influence of ordinal position, socioeconomic status, and play context. In C. A. Everett (Ed.), *Children of divorce* (pp. 221–234). New York: Haworth.

Macksoud, M. S., & Aber, J. L. (1996). The war experiences and psychosocial development of children in Lebanon. *Child Development, 67,* 70–88.

MacLean, P. D. (1985). Brain evolution relating to family, play, and the separation call. *Archives of General Psychiatry, 42,* 405–417.

Macmillan, R., McMorris, B. J., & Kruttschnitt, C. (2004). Linked lives: Stability and change in maternal circumstances and trajectories of antisocial behavior in children. *Child Development, 75,* 205–220.

MacWhinney, B. (1989). Competition and lexical categorization. In R. Corrigan, F. Eckman, & M. Noonam (Eds.), *Linguistic categorization* (pp. 195–241). Amsterdam: John Benjamin.

Madole, K. L., Oakes, L. M., & Cohen, L. B. (1993). Developmental changes in infants' attention to function and form–function correlations. *Cognitive Development, 8,* 189–209.

Madon, S., Jussim, L., & Eccles, J. (1997). In search of the powerful self-fulfilling prophecy. *Journal of Personality and Social Psychology, 72,* 791–809.

Madon, S., Jussim, L., Keiper, S., Eccles, J. S., Smith, A., & Palumbo, P. (1998). The accuracy and power of sex, social class, and ethnic stereotypes: A naturalistic study in person perception. *Personality and Social Psychology Bulletin, 24,* 1304–1318.

Magai, C., Hunziker, J., Mesias, W., & Culver, L. C. (2000). Adult attachment styles and emotional biases. *International Journal of Behavioral Development, 24,* 301–309.

Magnusson, D. (1988). *Individual development from an interactional perspective: A longitudinal study.* Hillsdale, NJ: Erlbaum.

Magnusson, D. (1995). Individual development: A holistic, integrated model. In P. Moen, G. H. Elder, & K. Luscher (Eds.), *Examining lives in context* (pp. 19–60). Washington, DC: American Psychological Association.

Maier, S. E., & West, J. R. (2001). Drinking patterns and alcohol-related birth defects. *Alcohol Research and Health, 25,* 168–174.

Main, M., & Solomon, J. (1990). Procedures for identifying infants as disorganized/disoriented during the Ainsworth Strange Situation. In M. Greenberg, D. Cicchetti, & M. Cummings (Eds.), *Attachment in the preschool years* (pp. 121–160). Chicago: University of Chicago Press.

Malatesta, C. Z. (1990). The role of emotions in the development and organization of personality. In R. A. Thompson (Ed.), *Socioemotional development* (Vol. 36, pp. 1–56). Lincoln: University of Nebraska Press.

Malina, R. M. (1986). Growth of muscle tissue and muscle mass. In F. Faulkner & J. M. Tanner (Eds.), *Human growth: A comprehensive treatise* (Vol. 2, pp. 77–99). New York: Plenum.

Malina, R. M., & Bouchard, C. (1991). *Growth, maturation, and physical activity.* Champaign, IL: Human Kinetics.

Malm, C. (2004). Exercise immunology: The current state of man and mouse. *Sports Medicine, 34,* 555–566.

Maloney, M. J., McGuire, J., Daniels, S. R., & Specker, B. (1989). Dieting behavior and eating attitudes in children. *Pediatrics, 84,* 482–489.

Malson, L. (1972). *Wolf children and the problem of human nature.* New York: Monthly Review Press.

Mander, R. (2000). The meanings of labour pain or the layers of an onion? A woman-oriented view. *Journal of Reproductive and Infant Psychology, 18,* 133–141.

Mandler, J. M. (1990). A new perspective on cognitive development in infancy. *American Scientist, 78,* 236–243.

Mandler, J. M. (1992). The foundations of conceptual thought in infancy. *Cognitive Development, 7,* 273–285.

Mandler, J. M. (1993). On concepts. *Cognitive Development, 8,* 141–148.

Mandler, J. M. (2003). Conceptual categorization. In D. H. Rakison & L. M. Oakes (Eds.), *Early category and concept development: Making sense of the blooming, buzzing confusion* (pp. 103–131). New York: Oxford University Press.

Mandler, J. M., & Bauer, P. (1988). The cradle of categorization: Is the basic level basic? *Cognitive Development, 3,* 247–264.

Mandler, J. M., Bauer, P. J., & McDonough, L. (1991). Separating the sheep from the goats: Differentiating global categories. *Cognitive Psychology, 23,* 263–298.

Mange, E. J., & Mange, A. P. (1994). *Basic human genetics.* Sunderland, MA: Sinauer.

Mangelsdorf, S. C., Plunkett, J. W., Dedrick, C. F., Berlin, M., Meisels, S. J., McHale, J. L., & Dichtellmiller, M. (1996). Attachment security in very low birth weight infants. *Developmental Psychology, 32,* 914–920.

Manlove, J. (1998). The influence of high school dropout and school disengagement on the risk of school-age pregnancy. *Journal of Research on Adolescence, 8,* 187–220.

Manners, P. (1999). Are growing pains a myth? *Australian Family Physician, 28,* 427–428.

Maratsos, M. (1998). The acquisition of grammar. In W. Damon (Ed.), *Handbook of child psychology* (Vol. 2, pp. 421–467). New York: Wiley.

March of Dimes. (2000). *Birth defects.* White Plains, NY: Author.

March of Dimes. (2001). *Prenatal care.* White Plains, NY: Author.

March of Dimes. (2004). *Birth defects.* White Plains, NY: Author.

March of Dimes. (2004). *Nutrition today matters tomorrow.* White Plains, NY: Author.

Marcia, J. (1987). The identity status approach to the study of ego identity development. In K. Yardley & T. Honess (Eds.), *Self and identity: Perspectives across the lifespan* (pp. 161–171). New York: Routledge & Kegan Paul.

Marcia, J. E. (1993). The relational roots of identity. In J. Kroger (Ed.), *Discussions on ego identity* (pp. 101–120). Hillsdale, NJ: Erlbaum.

Marcia, J. E. (1999). Representational thought in ego identity, psychotherapy, and psychosocial developmental theory. In I. Sigel (Ed.), *Development of mental representation: Theories and applications* (pp. 391–414). Mahwah, NJ: Erlbaum.

Marcus, G. F., Pinker, S., Ullman, M., Hollander, M., Rosen, T. J., & Xu, F. (1992). Overregularization in language acquisition. *Monographs of the Society for Research in Child Development, 57* (Whole No. 228). Chicago: University of Chicago Press.

Marcus, G. F., Vijayan, S., Rao, S. B., & Vishton, P. M. (1999). Rule learning by seven-month-old infants. *Science, 283,* 77–80.

Margolin, G., & Gordis, E. B. (2004). Children's exposure to violence in the family and community. *Current Directions in Psychological Science, 13,* 152–155.

Margolin, G., Gordis, E. B., Medina, A. M., & Oliver, P. H. (2003). The co-occurrence of husband-to-wife aggression, family-of-origin aggression, and child abuse potential in a community sample: Implications for parenting. *Journal of Interpersonal Violence, 18,* 413–440.

Marín, G. (1994). The experience of being a Hispanic in the United States. In W. J. Lonner & R. S. Malpas (Eds.), *Psychology and culture* (pp. 23–28). Boston: Allyn & Bacon.

Market Data Retrieval. (2001). *Technology in education 2001.* Shelton, CT: Market Data Retrieval.

Markman, E. M. (1989). *Categorization and naming in children: Problems of induction.* Cambridge, MA: MIT Press.

Marks, S. B. (1997). Reducing prejudice against children with disabilities in inclusive settings. *International Journal of Disability, Development, and Education, 44,* 117–131.

Markson, L., & Bloom, P. (1997). Evidence against a dedicated system for word learning in children. *Nature, 385,* 813–815.

Markus, H. R., & Kitayama, S. (1991). Culture and the self: Implications for cognition, emotion, and motivation. *Psychological Review, 98,* 224–253.

Marques-Bruna, P., & Grimshaw, P. N. (1997). 3-dimensional kinematics of overarm throwing action of children age 15 to 30 months. *Perceptual and Motor Skills, 84,* 1267–1283.

Marriage, K., & Cummins, R. A. (2004). Subjective quality of life and self-esteem in children. *Social Indicators Research, 66,* 107–122.

Marsh, H. W., & Redmayne, R. S. (1994). A multidimensional physical self-concept and its relation to multiple components of physical fitness. *Journal of Educational Psychology, 16,* 45–55.

Marsh, J. S., & Daigneault, J. P. (1999). The young athlete. *Current Opinions in Pediatrics, 11,* 84–88.

Marshall, S. P., & Smith, J. D. (1987). Sex differences in learning mathematics: A longitudinal study with item and error analyses. *Journal of Educational Psychology, 79,* 372–383.

Marshall, W. A., & Tanner, J. M. (1986). Puberty. In F. Faulkner & J. M. Tanner (Eds.), *Human growth: A comprehensive treatise* (pp. 171–210). New York: Plenum.

Marsiglia, F. F., Kulis, S., & Hecht, M. L. (2004). Ethnicity and ethnic identity as predictors of drug norms and drug use among adolescents in the US Southwest. *Substance Use and Misuse, 39,* 1061–1094.

Marsiglio, W., & Cohan, M. (1997). Young fathers and child development. In M. E. Lamb (Ed.), *The role of the father in child development* (pp. 227–244). New York: Wiley.

Marsiglio, W., Hutchinson, S., & Cohan, M. (2000). Envisioning fatherhood: A social psychological perspective on young men without kids. *Family Relations, 49,* 133–142.

Martin, C. A., Hill, K. K., & Welsh, R. (1998). Adolescent pregnancy, a stressful life event. In T. W. Miller (Ed.), *Children of trauma* (pp. 141–160). Madison, CT: International Universities Press.

Martin, C. L. (1989). Children's use of gender-related information in making social judgments. *Developmental Psychology, 25,* 80–88.

Martin, C. L. (1991). The role of cognition in understanding gender effects. In H. Reese (Ed.), *Advances in child development and behavior* (Vol. 23, pp. 113–149). San Diego, CA: Academic Press.

Martin, C. L. (1994). Cognitive influences on the development and maintenance of gender segregation. In C. Leaper (Ed.), *Childhood gender segregation* (pp. 35–52). San Francisco: Jossey-Bass.

Martin, C. L., Eisenbud, L., & Rose, H. (1995). Children's gender-based reasoning about toys. *Child Development, 66,* 1453–1471.

Martin, C. L., & Fabes, R. A. (2001). The stability and consequences of young children's same-sex peer interactions. *Developmental Psychology, 37,* 431–446.

Martin, C. L., & Halverson, C. F. (1981). A schematic processing model of sex typing and stereotyping in children. *Child Development, 52,* 1119–1134.

Martin, C. L., & Halverson, C. F. (1983). Gender constancy: A methodological and theoretical analysis. *Sex Roles, 9,* 775–790.

Martin, C. L., Woods, C. H., & Little, J. K. (1990). The development of gender stereotype components. *Child Development, 61,* 1891–1904.

Martin, K. (1996). *Puberty, sexuality, and the self: Boys and girls at adolescence.* New York: Routledge.

Martin, L. M. (2000). The compatibility of Vygotsky's theoretical framework with the developmental-interaction approach. In N. Nager & E. Shapiro (Eds.), *Revisiting a progressive pedagogy: The developmental-interaction approach. Early childhood education* (pp. 73–93). Albany: State University of New York Press.

Martindale, C. (2001). Oscillations and analogies: Thomas Young, MD, FRS, genius. *American Psychologist, 56,* 342–345.

Martinez, R. O., & Dukes, R. L. (1997). The effects of ethnic identity, ethnicity, and gender on adolescent well-being. *Journal of Youth and Adolescence, 26,* 503–516.

Martinez-Frias, M. L., Bermejo, E., Rodriguez-Pinilla, E., & Frias, J. L. (2004). Risk for congenital anomalies associated with different sporadic and daily doses of alcohol consumption during pregnancy. *Birth Defects Research, 70,* 194–200.

Martini, M. (1994). Peer interaction in Polynesia: A view from the Marquesas. In J. L. Roopnarine, J. E. Johnson, & F. H. Hooper (Eds.), *Children's play in diverse cultures* (pp. 73–103). New York: State University of New York Press.

Martins, C., & Gaffan, E. A. (2000). Effects of early maternal depression on patterns of infant-mother attachment: A meta-analytic investigation. *Journal of Child Psychology and Psychiatry and Allied Disciplines, 41,* 737–746.

Martlew, M., & Connolly, K. J. (1996). Human figure drawings by schooled and unschooled children in Papua New Guinea. *Child Development, 67,* 2743–2762.

Martorano, S. C. (1977). A developmental analysis of performance on Piaget's formal operations task. *Developmental Psychology, 13,* 666–672.

Marzolf, D. P., & DeLoache, J. S. (1994). Transfer in young children's understanding of spatial representations. *Child Development, 64,* 1–15.

Masataka, N. (1996). Perception of motherese in a signed language by 6-month-old deaf infants. *Developmental Psychology, 32,* 874–879.

Mason, M. A. (1998). The modern American stepfamily: Problems and possibilities. In M. A. Mason (Ed.), *All our families: New policies for a new century* (pp. 95–116). New York: Oxford University Press.

Massey, C. M., & Gelman, R. (1988). Preschoolers' ability to decide whether a photographed unfamiliar object can move itself. *Developmental Psychology, 24,* 307–317.

Masten, A. S., & Coatsworth, J. D. (1998). The development of competence in favorable and unfavorable environments. *American Psychologist, 53,* 205–220.

Masten, A. S., & Curtis, W. J. (2000). Integrating competence and psychopathology: Pathways toward a comprehensive science of adaptation in development. *Development and Psychopathology, 12,* 529–550.

Maurer, D., & Barrerra, M. E. (1981). Infants' perception of natural and distorted arrangements of a schematic face. *Child Development, 52,* 196–202.

Maurer, D., & Lewis, T. L. (2001). Visual acuity and spatial contrast sensitivity: Normal development and underlying mechanisms. In C. A. Nelson & M. Luciana (Eds.), *Handbook of developmental cognitive neuroscience* (pp. 237–252). Cambridge, MA: MIT Press.

May, D.C., & Kundert, D. K. (1997). School readiness practices and children at-risk. *Psychology in the Schools, 34,* 73–84.

Mayo Clinic. (2003). Raising an active child: Ideas for parents. Retrieved from http:// mayoclinc.com/invoke.cfm?id=FL00030

Mazur, E. (1993). Developmental differences in children's understanding of marriage, divorce, and remarriage. *Journal of Applied Developmental Psychology, 14,* 191–212.

McAdoo, H. P. (1993). *Family ethnicity.* Newbury Park, CA: Sage.

McBride-Chang, C. (1995). What is phonological awareness? *Journal of Educational Psychology, 87,* 179–192.

McCauley, E., Kay, T., Ito, J., & Treder, R. (1987). The Turner syndrome: Cognitive deficits, affective discrimination, and behavior problems. *Child Development, 58,* 464–473.

McClelland, D.C. (1993). Intelligence is not the best predictor of job performance. *Current Directions in Psychological Science, 2,* 5–6.

McCloskey, L. A., Figueredo, A. J., & Koss, M. P. (1995). The effects of systemic family violence on children's mental health. *Child Development, 66,* 1239–1261.

McCormick, M. C., Gortmaker, S. L., & Sobol, A. M. (1990). Very low birth weight children: Behavior problems and school difficulty in a national sample. *Journal of Pediatrics, 117,* 687–693.

McDermott, D. (2001). Parenting and ethnicity. In M. J. Fine & S. W. Lee (Eds.), *Handbook of diversity in parent education: The changing faces of parenting and parent education* (pp. 73–96). San Diego, CA: Academic Press.

McDonnell, L. M., & Hill, P. T. (1993). *Newcomers in American schools: Meeting the educational needs of immigrant youth.* Santa Monica, CA: Rand.

McDougall, P., Hymel, S., Vallancourt, T., & Mercer, L. (2001). The consequences of childhood peer rejection. In M. R. Leary (Ed.), *Interpersonal rejection* (pp. 213–247). New York: Oxford University Press.

McEwin, C. K., Dickinson, T. S., & Jacobson, M. G. (2004). *Programs and practices in K–8 schools: Do they meet the educational needs of young adolescents?* Westerville, OH: National Middle School Association.

McFarlane, M., Doueck, H. J., & Levine, M. (2002). Preventing child abuse and neglect. In B. L. Bottoms & M. B. Kovera (Eds.), *Children, social science, and the law* (pp. 322–341). New York: Cambridge University Press.

McGlaughlin, A., & Grayson, A. (2001). Crying in the first year of infancy: Patterns and prevalence. *Journal of Reproductive and Infant Psychology, 19,* 47–59.

McGrath, M. P., Wilson, S. R., & Franssetto, S. (1995). Why some forms of induction are better than others at encouraging prosocial behavior. *Merrill-Palmer Quarterly, 41,* 347–360.

McGrory, A. (1990). Menarche: Responses of early adolescent females. *Adolescence, 25,* 265–270.

McGuigan, W. M., Vuchinich, S., & Pratt, C. C. (2000). Domestic violence, parents' view of their infant, and risk for child abuse. *Journal of Family Psychology, 14,* 613–624.

McHale, S. M., Crouter, A. C., McGuire, S., & Updegraff, K. A. (1995). Congruence between mothers' and fathers' differential treatment of siblings: Links with family relations and children's well-being. *Child Development, 66,* 116–128.

McHale, S. M., Updegraff, K. A., Jackson-Newsom, J., Tucker, C. J., & Crouter, A. C. (2000). When does parents' differential treatment have negative implications for siblings? *Social Development, 9,* 149–172.

McKenna, J., Mosko, S., Richard, C., Drummond, S., Hunt, L., Cetel, M. B., & Arpaia, J. (1994). Experimental studies of infant–parent co-sleeping: Mutual physiological and behavior influences and their relevance to SIDS. *Early Human Development, 38,* 187–201.

McKown, C., & Weinstein, R. S. (2002). Modeling the role of child ethnicity and gender in children's differential response to teacher expectations. *Journal of Applied Social Psychology, 32,* 159–184.

McKusick, V. A. (1998). *Mendelian inheritance in man: A catalog of human genes and genetic disorders (12th ed.). Baltimore, MD: Johns Hopkins University Press.*

McLoyd, V. C. (1998a). Children in poverty. In W. Damon (Ed.), *Handbook of child psychology* (Vol. 4, pp. 135–208). New York: Wiley.

McLoyd, V. C. (1998b). Socioeconomic disadvantage and child development. *American Psychologist, 53,* 185–204.

McLoyd, V. C., Cauce, A. M., Takeuchi, D., & Wilson, L. (2000). Marital processes and parental socialization in families of color: A decade review of research. *Journal of Marriage and the Family, 62,* 1070–1093.

McManus, I. C., & Bryden, M. P. (1992). The genetics of handedness, cerebral dominance, and lateralization. In I. Rapin & S. J. Segalowitz (Eds.), *Handbook of neuropsychology* (Vol. 6, pp. 115–144). Amsterdam: Elsevier.

McPherson, S. L., & Thomas, J. R. (1989). Relation of knowledge and performance in boys' tennis: Age and expertise. *Journal of Experimental Child Psychology, 48,* 190–211.

McQuillan, J. & Tse, L. (1996). Does research really matter? An analysis of media opinion on bilingual education, 1984–1994. *Bilingual Research Journal, 20,* 1–27.

Meadow-Orlans, K. P., & Spencer, P. E. (1999). Maternal sensitivity and the visual attentiveness of children who are deaf. *Early Development and Parenting, 5,* 213–223.

Meaney, M. J. (1988). The sexual differentiation of social play. *Trends in Neuroscience, 7,* 54–58.

Measelle, J. R., Ablow, J. C., Cowan, P. A., & Cowan, C. P. (1998). Assessing young children's views of their academic, social, and emotional lives. *Child Development, 69,* 1556–1576.

Medeiros, D. M. (2003). Get used to it! Children of gay and lesbian parents. *Archives of Sexual Behavior, 32,* 490–491.

Mediascope. (1999). *Video game violence.* Studio City, CA: Author.

Meece, J. L. (1987). The influence of school experiences on the development of gender schemata. *New Directions for Child Development, 38,* 57–73.

Meece, J. L., Parsons, J. E., Kaczala, C. M., Goff, S. B., & Futterman, R. (1982). Sex differences in math achievement: Toward a model of academic choice. *Psychological Bulletin, 91,* 324–348.

Meeus, W., Iedema, J., Helsen, M., & Vollebergh, W. (1999). Patterns of adolescent identity development: Review of literature and longitudinal analysis. *Developmental Review, 19,* 419–461.

Mellou, E. (1996). Can creativity be nurtured in young children? *Early Child Development and Care, 119,* 119–130.

Melnick, M. J., Vanfossen, B. E., & Sabo, D. F. (1988). Developmental effects of athletic participation among high school girls. *Sociology of Sport Journal, 5,* 22–36.

Meltzer, D. (1981). *Birth: An anthology of ancient texts, songs, prayers, and stories.* San Francisco: North Point Press.

Meltzoff, A. N. (1995). What infant memory tells us about infantile amnesia: Long-term recall and deferred imitation. *Journal of Experimental Child Psychology, 59,* 497–515.

Meltzoff, A. N., & Moore, M. K. (1994). Imitation, memory, and the representation of persons. *Infant Behavior and Development, 17,* 83–99.

Melzak, S. (1992). The secret life of children who have experienced physical aggression and violence. In V. P. Varma (Ed.), *The secret life of vulnerable children* (pp. 101–129). New York: Routledge.

Mendelsohn, A. L., Dreyer, B. P., Fierman, A. H., Rosen, C. M., Legano, L. A., Kruger, H. A., Lim, S. W., & Courtlandt, C. D. (1998). Low-level lead exposure and behavior in early childhood. *Pediatrics, 101,* 1–6.

Mennella, J. A., Jagnow, C. P., & Beauchamp, G. K. (2001). Prenatal and postnatal flavor learning by human infants. *Pediatrics, 107,* 1–12.

Menyuk, P. (1988). *Language development: Knowledge and use.* New York: HarperCollins.

Menyuk, P., Liebergott, J. W., & Schultz, M. C. (1995). *Early language development in full-term and premature infants.* Hillsdale, NJ: Erlbaum.

Mercer, R. T., Ferketich, S., May, K., DeJoseph, J., & Sollid, D. (1988). Further exploration of maternal and paternal fetal attachment. *Research in Nursing and Health, 11,* 83–95.

Merikangas, K. R., Swendsen, J. D., Preisig, M. A., & Chazan, R. Z. (1998). Psychopathology and temperament in parents and offspring: Results of a family study. *Journal of Affective Disorders, 51,* 63–74.

Merriman, W. E., & Bowman, L. L. (1989). The mutual exclusivity bias in children's word learning. *Monographs of the Society for Research in Child Development, 54* (Whole No. 130). Chicago: University of Chicago Press.

Mervis, C. A., Yeargin-Allsopp, M., Winter, S., & Boyle, C. (2000). Aetiology of childhood vision impairment in metropolitan Atlanta, 1991–1993. *Pediatric and Perinatal Epidemiology, 14,* 70–77.

Mest, G. M. (1988). With a little help from their friends: Use of social support by persons with retardation. *Journal of Social Issues, 44,* 117–125.

Metha, A., Chen, E., Mulvenon, S., & Dode, I. (1998). A theoretical model of adolescent suicide risk. *Archives of Suicide Research, 4,* 115–133.

Meuleners, L., Binns, C. W., Lee, A., & Lower, A. (2002). Perceptions of the quality of life for adolescents with a chronic illness by teachers, parents, and health professionals: A Delphi study. *Child-Care, Health, & Development, 51,* 341–350.

Meyer-Bahlburg, H., Dolezal, C., Baker, S., Carlson, A. D., Obeid, J. S., & New, M. I. (2004). Prenatal androgenization affects gender-related behavior but not gender identity in 5 to 12-year-old girls with congenital adrenal hyperplasia. *Archives of Sexual Behavior, 33,* 97–104.

Miami Herald. (1998, January 22). Divorce rates across the world,

Michael, A., & Eccles, J. S. (2003). When coming of age means coming undone: Links between puberty and psychosocial adjustment among European American and African American girls. In C. Hayward (Ed.), *Gender differences at puberty* (pp. 277–303). New York: Cambridge University Press.

Midgley, C. M. (1993). Motivation and middle level schools. In M. L. Maehr & P. R. Pintrich (Eds.), *Advances in motivation and achievement* (Vol. 8, pp. 217–274). Greenwich, CT: JAI Press.

Midgley, C. M., Feldlaufer, H., & Eccles, J. S. (1988). The transition to junior high school. *Journal of Youth and Adolescence, 17,* 543–562.

Midobuche, E. (2001). More than empty footprints in the sand: Educating immigrant children. *Harvard Educational Review, 71,* 529–535.

Mikulincer, M., Shaver, P. R., & Pereg, D. (2003). Attachment theory and affect regulation. *Motivation and Emotion, 27,* 77–102.

Milgram, N. A. (1998). Children under stress. In T. H. Ollendick & M. Hersen (Eds.), *Handbook of child psychopathology* (pp. 505–553). New York: Plenum.

Milhausen, R., & Herold, E. S. (2001). Reconceptualizing the sexual double standard. *Journal of Psychology and Human Sexuality, 13,* 63–83.

Miller, A. L., Volling, B. L., & McElwain, N. L. (2000). Sibling jealousy in a triadic context with mothers and fathers. *Social Development, 9,* 433–457.

Miller, B. C. (1998). *Family matters: A research synthesis of family influences on adolescent pregnancy.* Washington, DC: The National Campaign to Prevent Teen Pregnancy.

Miller, B. C., Benson, B., & Galbraith, K. A. (2001). Family relationships and adolescent pregnancy risk: A research synthesis. *Developmental Review, 21,* 1–38.

Miller, B. C., Norton, M. C., Curtis, T., Hill, E. J., Schvaneveldt, P., & Young, M. H. (1997). The timing of sexual intercourse among adolescents: Family, peer, and other antecedents. *Youth and Society, 29,* 54–83.

Miller, C. L., Eccles, J. S., Flanagan, C., Midgley, C. M., Feldlaufer, H., & Goldsmith, R. (1990). Parents' and teachers' beliefs about adolescence: Effects of sex and experience. *Journal of Youth and Adolescence, 19,* 363–394.

Miller, E. K., & Cohen, J. D. (2001). An integrative theory of prefrontal cortex function. *Annual Review of Neuroscience, 24,* 167–202.

Miller, H. M. (2000). Cross-cultural validity of a model of self-worth: Application to Finnish children. *Social Behavior and Personality, 28,* 105–118.

Miller, J. G. (1986). Early cross-cultural commonalities in social explanation. *Developmental Psychology, 22,* 514–520.

Miller, K. S., Forehand, R., & Kotchick, B. A. (1999). Adolescent sexual behavior in two ethnic minority samples. *Journal of Marriage and the Family, 61,* 85–98.

Miller, N. B., Cowan, P. A., Cowan, C. P., Hetherington, E. M., & Clingempeel, W. G. (1993). Externalizing in preschoolers and early adolescents: A cross-study replication of a family model. *Developmental Psychology, 29,* 4–18.

Miller, P. A., Kozu, J., & Davis, A. C. (2001). Social influence, empathy, and prosocial behavior in cross, cultural perspective. In R. B. Cialdini & W. Wosinska (Eds.), *The practice of social influence in multiple cultures* (pp. 63–77). Mahwah, NJ: Erlbaum.

Miller, P. H. (1993). *Theories of developmental psychology.* New York: Freeman.

Miller, P. H., & Aloise, P. A. (1989). Young children's understanding of the psychological causes of behavior: A review. *Child Development, 60,* 257–285.

Millikan, R. G. (1998). A common structure for concepts of individuals, stuffs, and real kinds: More mama, more milk, and more mouse. *Behavioral and Brain Sciences, 21,* 55–100.

Minton, C., Kagan, J., & Levine, J. A. (1971). Maternal control and obedience in the two-year-old. *Child Development, 42,* 1873–1894.

Mintz, J. (1995). Self in relation to other: Preschoolers' verbal social comparisons within narrative discourse. In L. L. Sperry & P. A. Smiley (Eds.), *Exploring young children's concepts of self and other through conversation* (pp. 61–74). San Francisco: Jossey-Bass.

Mischel, W. (1966). A social-learning view of sex differences in behavior. In E. E. Maccoby (Ed.), *The development of sex differences* (pp. 57–81). Stanford, CA: Stanford University Press.

Mitru, G., Millrood, D. L., & Mateika, J. H. (2002). The impact of sleep on learning and behavior in adolescents. *Teachers College Record, 104,* 704–726.

Miyake, K., Chen, S., & Campos, J. J. (1985). Infant temperament, mother's mode of interaction, and attachment in Japan: An interim report. In I. Bretherton & E. Waters (Eds.), *Growing points of attachment theory and research* (pp. 276–297). Chicago: Society for Research in Child Development.

Mize, J., & Ladd, G. W. (1990). Toward the development of successful social skills training for preschool children. In S. R. Asher & J. D. Coie (Eds.), *Peer rejection in childhood* (pp. 338–364). Cambridge, UK: Cambridge University Press.

Mize, J., & Pettit, G. S. (1997). Mothers' social coaching, mother–child relationship style, and children's peer competence: Is the medium the message? *Child Development, 68,* 312–332.

Moerk, E. L. (1989). The LAD was a lady and the tasks were ill-defined. *Developmental Review, 9,* 21–57.

Molfese, V. J., & Molfese, D. L. (2000). *Temperament and personality development across the lifespan.* Mahwah, NJ: Erlbaum.

Monahan, S. C., Buchanan, C. N., Maccoby, E. E., & Dornbusch, S. M. (1993). Sibling differences in divorced families. *Child Development, 63,* 152–168.

Money, J., & Ehrhardt, A. A. (1972). *Man and woman; Boy and girl.* Baltimore: Johns Hopkins University Press.

Monitoring the Future. (2001). *Monitoring the Future national survey results on drug use, 1975–2000.* Bethesda, MD: National Institute on Drug Abuse.

Monk, C., Fifer, W. P., Myers, M. M., Sloan, R. P., Trien, L., & Hurtado, A. (2000). Maternal stress responses and anxiety during pregnancy: Effects on fetal heart rate. *Developmental Psychobiology, 36,* 67–77.

Montour, K. (1977). William James Sidis, the broken twig. *American Psychologist, 32,* 265–279.

Moon, C., Cooper, R. P., & Fifer, W. P. (1993). Two-day-olds prefer their native language. *Infant Behavior and Development, 16,* 495–500.

Moore, K. A., & Driscoll, A. (1997). *Partners, predators, peers, protectors: Males and teen pregnancy.* Washington, DC: Child Trends Inc.

Moore, K. L. (1998). *The developing human: Clinically oriented embryology,* (6th ed.). Philadelphia: Saunders.

Moore, S., & Rosenthal, D. (1993). *Sexuality in adolescence.* London: Routledge.

Moore, S. M., & Gullone, E. (1995). Fear of weight gain: Its correlates among school-aged adolescents. *Psychological Reports, 76,* 1305–1306.

Morad, M., Kandel, I., & Merrick, J. (2004). Anorexia and bulimia in the family. *International Journal of Adolescent Medicine and Health, 16,* 89–90.

Moreau, G. F., Ferron, C., Jeannin, A., & Dubois, A. F. (1996). Adolescent sexuality: The gender gap. *AIDS Care, 8,* 641–653.

Morelli, G. A., Rogoff, B., Oppenheim, D., & Goldsmith, D. (1992). Cultural variation in infants' sleeping arrangements. *Developmental Psychology, 28,* 604–613.

Morelli, G. A., & Verhoef, H. (1999). Who should help me raise my child? A cultural approach to understanding nonmaternal child care decisions. In L. Balter & C. S. Tamis-LeMonda (Eds.), *Child psychology: A handbook of contemporary issues* (pp. 491–509). Philadelphia: Psychology Press.

Morris, K. (1998). Short course of AZT halves HIV-1 perinatal transmission. *Lancet, 351,* 651.

Morris, R. J., & Kratochwill, T. R. (1998). Childhood fears and phobias. In R. J. Morris & T. R. Kratochwill (Eds.), *The practice of child therapy* (pp. 91–131). Boston: Allyn & Bacon.

Morris, T. W., & Levinson, E. M. (1995). Relationship between intelligence and occupational adjustment and functioning. *Journal of Counseling and Development, 73,* 503–514.

Morrison, F. J., Alberts, D. M., & Griffith, E. M. (1997). Nature-nurture in the classroom: Entrance age, school readiness, and learning in children. *Developmental Psychology, 33,* 254–262.

Morrongiello, B. A., & Rocca, P. T. (1989). Visual feedback and anticipatory hand orientation during infants' reaching. *Perception and Motor Skills, 69,* 787–802.

Moss, E., St. Laurent, D., & Parent, S. (1999). Disorganized attachment and developmental risk at school age. In J. Solomon & C. George (Eds.), *Attachment disorganization* (pp. 160–186). New York: Guilford.

Mrug, S., Hoza, B., & Bukowski, W. M. (2004). Choosing or being chosen by aggressive–disruptive peers: Do they contribute to children's externalizing and internalizing problems? *Journal of Abnormal Child Psychology, 32,* 53–65.

Mruk, C. (1999). *Self-esteem research, theory, and practice.* New York: Springer.

Mueller, U., Overton, W. F., & Reene, K. (2001). Development of conditional reasoning: A longitudinal study. *Journal of Cognition and Development, 2,* 27–49.

Mufson, L., & Moreau, D. (1997). Depressive disorders. In R. T. Ammerman & M. Hersen (Eds.), *Handbook of prevention and treatment with children and adolescents* (pp. 403–430). New York: Wiley.

Muller, T., & Espenshade, T. J. (1985). *The fourth wave: California's newest immigrants.* Washington, DC: Urban Institute Press.

Munakata, Y. (1998). Infant perseveration and implications for object permanence theories: A PDP model of the AB task. *Developmental Science, 1,* 161–184.

Munakata, Y., McClelland, J. L., Johnson, M. H., & Siegler, R. S. (1997). Rethinking infant knowledge: Toward an adaptive process account of successes and failures in object permanence tasks. *Psychological Review, 104,* 686–713.

Munn, P., & Dunn, J. (1988). Temperament and the developing relationship between siblings. *International Journal of Behavioral Development, 12,* 433–451.

Muratori, F., Viglione, V., Maestro, S., & Picchi, L. (2004). Internalizing and externalizing conditions in adolescent anorexia. *Psychopathology, 37,* 92–97.

Muret-Wagstaff, S., & Moore, S. G. (1989). The Hmong in America: Infant behavior and rearing practices. In J. K. Nugent, B. M. Lester, & T. B. Brazelton (Eds.), *The cultural context of infancy* (Vol. 1, pp. 319–340). Norwood, NJ: Ablex.

Murphy, B. C., & Eisenberg, N. (1996). Provoked by a peer: Children's anger-related responses and their relations to social functioning. *Merrill-Palmer Quarterly, 42,* 103–124.

Murphy, W. D., & Smith, T. A. (1996). Sex offenders against children. In J. Briere, L. Berliner, J. A. Bulkley, C. Jenny, & T. Reid (Eds.), *The APSAC handbook on child maltreatment* (pp. 175–191). Thousand Oaks, CA: Sage.

Murray, J. P. (1995). Children and television violence. *Kansas Journal of Law & Public Policy, 4,* 7–14.

Murray, L., & Trevarthen, C. (1986). The infant's role in mother–infant communication. *Journal of Child Language, 13,* 15–29.

Mussen, P. H., & Jones, M. C. (1957). Self-concepts, motivations, and interpersonal attitudes of late and early maturing boys. *Child Development, 28,* 243–256.

Must, A. & Strauss, R. S. (1999). Risk and consequences of childhood and adolescent obesity. *International Journal of Obesity, 23* (Suppl 2): S2–S11.

Muuss, R. E. (1998). Marcia's expansion of Erikson's theory of identity formation. In R. E. Muuss & H. D. Porton (Eds.), *Adolescent behavior and society* (pp. 260–270). New York: McGraw-Hill.

Myers, A., Sampson, A., Weitzman, M., Rogers, B., & Kayne, H. (1989). School breakfast program and school performance. *American Journal of Diseases of Childhood, 143,* 1234–1239.

Myers, B. J. (1984). Mother–infant bonding: The status of this critical-period hypothesis. *Developmental Review, 4,* 240–274.

Myers, H. F., & Rodriguez, N. (2003). Acculturation and physical health in racial and ethnic minorities. In P. B. Organista & K. M. Chun (Eds.), *Acculturation: Advances in theory, measurement, and applied research* (pp. 163–185). Washington, DC: American Psychological Association.

Myers-Walls, J. A. (2003). Children as victims of war and terrorism. *Journal of Aggression, Maltreatment, and Trauma, 8,* 41–62.

Nadder, T. S., Silberg, J. L., Eaves, L. J., Maes, L. J., & Meyer, J. M. (1998). Genetic effects on ADHD symptomatology in 7- to 13-year-old twins. *Behavioral Genetics, 28,* 83–99.

Nagy, W. E., Anderson, R. C., & Herman, P. A. (1987). Learning word meanings from context during normal reading. *American Educational Research Journal, 24,* 237–270.

Naigles, L. R. (1990). Children use syntax to learn verb meanings. *Journal of Child Language, 17,* 357–374.

Nansel, T., Overpeck, M., Pilla, R., Ruan, W., Simmons-Morton, B., & Scheidt, P. (2001). Bullying behaviors among US youth: Prevalence and association with psychosocial adjustment. *Journal of the American Medical Association, 285,* 2094–2100.

Nash, J. M. (1997, February 3). Fertile minds. *Time,* 49–62.

Nathanielsz, P. W. (1995). The role of basic science in preventing low birth weight. *The Future of Children, 5,* 57–70.

National Association for the Education of Young Children. (1998). Learning to read and write. *Young Children, 53,* 30–46.

National Cancer Institute. (2001, October). *Risks associated with smoking cigarettes with low machine-measures yields of tar and nicotine.* Smoking and Tobacco Control Monograph No. 13 (NIH Publication No. 02–5074). Bethesda, MD: US Department of Health and Human Services, National Institutes of Health, National Cancer Institute.

National Center for Children in Poverty. (1999). *Poverty and brain development in early childhood.* New York: Author.

National Center for Education Statistics. (1995). *Student victimization at school.* Washington, DC: US Department of Education.

National Center for Education Statistics. (1996). *Youth indicators, 1996.* Washington, DC: US Department of Education.

National Center for Education Statistics. (1998). *Condition of education.* Washington, DC: US Department of Education.

National Center for Education Statistics. (1999). *Parent and family involvement in education.* Washington, DC: US Department of Education.

National Center for Education Statistics. (2001a). *Digest of education statistics, 2000.* Washington, DC: US Department of Education.

National Center for Education Statistics. (2001b). *Indicators of school crime and safety.* Washington, DC: US Department of Education.

National Center for Education Statistics. (2003). *National household education surveys of 2001.* Washington, DC: Author.

National Center for Education Statistics. (2004). *Crime and safety in America's public schools.* Washington, DC: US Department of Education.

National Center for Educational Statistics. (2002). *The condition of education.* Washington, DC: Author.

National Center for Health Statistics, in collaboration with the National Center for Chronic Disease Prevention and Health Promotion. (2000). *CDC growth charts: United States.* Washington, DC: Author.

National Center for Health Statistics. (1990). *International divorce rates.* Washington, DC: Author.

National Center for Health Statistics. (1994). *Health, United States, 1993.* Washington, DC: Author.

National Center for Health Statistics. (1995). Advance report of final divorce statistics. *Monthly Vital Statistics Report, 43,* 1–32.

National Center for Health Statistics. (1996). *Health, United States, 1995.* Hyattsville, MD: Public Health Service.

National Center for Health Statistics. (2001a). *Births, 2000.* Washington, DC: Author.

National Center for Health Statistics. (2001b). *Entering kindergarten.* Washington, DC: Author.

National Center for Health Statistics. (2001c). *Healthy people, 2000.* Washington, DC: Author.

National Center for Health Statistics. (2003a). *Births: Final data for 2002.* Washington, DC: Author.

National Center for Health Statistics. (2003b). *Health, United States 2003.* Washington, DC: Author.

National Center for Health Statistics. (2003c). *National vital statistics reports* (Vol. 52). Washington, DC: Author.

National Center for Injury Prevention and Control. (2004). *Child passenger safety.* Washington, DC: Author.

National Child Abuse and Neglect Data System. (2001). *Child maltreatment 1999: Reports from the states to the National Child Abuse and Neglect Data System.* Washington, DC: US Government Printing Office.

National Clearinghouse on Child Abuse and Neglect. (1999). *Child abuse and neglect fact sheet.* Washington, DC: Author.

National Down Syndrome Society. (2000). *About Down syndrome.* New York: Author.

National Federation of State High School Associations. (2001). *Athletics participation summary: 1999–2000.* Indianapolis, IN: National Federation of State High School Associations.

National Highway Traffic Safety Administration (2002) *Young drivers: 2002.* Washington, DC: Author.

National Highway Traffic Safety Association. (2004). *Young drivers.* Washington, DC: Author.

National Institute of Arthritis and Musculoskeletal and Skin Diseases. (2002, August) *Kids and their bones: A guide for parents.* Bethesda, MD: National Institute of Arthritis and Musculoskeletal and Skin Diseases.

National Institute of Mental Health. (1994). *Eating disorders.* Washington, DC: Author.

National Institute of Mental Health. (2000). *Depression in children and adolescents.* Bethesda, MD: Author.

National Institute of Out-of-School Time. (2004). *Facts on children and youth in out-of-school time.* Boston, MA: National Institute on Out-of-School Time.

National Institute on Drug Abuse. (2000). *Monitoring the future.* Washington, DC: Author.

National Institute on Drug Abuse. (2004a). *Club drugs.* Washington, DC: Author.

National Institute on Drug Abuse. (2004b). *Ecstasy abuse.* Washington, DC: Author.

National Institute on Drug Abuse. (2004c). *Lessons from prevention research.* Washington, DC: Author.

National Issues Forum. (1989). *The day care dilemma.* Dubuque, IA: Kendall/Hunt Publishing.

National Mental Health Association. (2001). *Helping children handle disaster-related anxiety.* Alexandria, VA: Author.

National Middle School Association. (1995). *Developmentally responsive middle level schools.* Columbus, OH: Author.

National Research Council and Institute of Medicine. (2000). *From neurons to neighborhoods: The science of early childhood development.* Washington, DC: National Academy Press.

National Research Council. (1998). *The new Americans: Economic, demographic, and fiscal effects of immigration.* Washington, DC: Author.

National Research Council. (2001). *Getting to positive outcomes for children in child care.* Washington, DC: National Academy Press.

National Science Foundation. (2002). *Science and engineering indicators.* Washington, DC: Author.

National Telecommunications and Information Administration. (1998). *Falling through the Net II.* Washington, DC: Author.

National Vital Statistics Reports. (2003). Deaths: Final data for 2001. Centers of Disease Control. Retrieved from http://www.cdc.gov/nchs/data/nvsr52/nvsr52_03.pdf

National Vital Statistics Reports. (2003). *Deaths. Final data for 2001.* Washington, DC: Centers for Disease Control.

Natsopoulos, D., Kiosseoglou, G., Xeromeritou, A., & Alevriadou, A. (1998). Do the hands talk on mind's behalf? Differences in language ability between left- and right-handed children. *Brain Language, 64,* 182–214.

Navaez, D., Getz, I., Rest, J. R., & Thoma, S. J. (1999). Individual moral judgment and cultural ideologies. *Developmental Psychology, 35,* 478–488.

Naylor, P., Cowie, H., & del-Rey, R. (2001). Coping strategies of school children in response to being bullied. *Child Psychology and Psychiatry Review, 6,* 114–120.

Neale, D.C., Smith, D., & Johnson, V. G. (1990). Implementing conceptual change teaching in primary science. *Elementary School Journal, 91,* 109–131.

Neiger, B. L. (2002). The re-emergence of thalidomide. *Teratology, 62,* 432–435.

Nelson, C. A., & Bloom, F. E. (1997). Child development and neuroscience. *Child Development, 68,* 970–987.

Nelson, D. A., & Crick, N. R. (1999). Rose-colored glasses: Examining the social information processes of prosocial young adolescents. *Journal of Early Adolescence, 19,* 17–38

Nelson, K. (1973). Structure and strategy in learning to talk. *Monographs of the Society for Research in Child Development, 38* (Whole No. 149). Chicago: University of Chicago Press.

Nelson, K. (1986). *Event knowledge: Structure and function in development.* Hillsdale, NJ: Erlbaum.

Nelson, K. (1993). The psychological and social origins of autobiographical memory. *Psychological Science, 4,* 1–8.

Nelson, K., & Fivush, R. (2004). The emergence of autobiographical memory: A social cultural developmental theory. *Psychological Review, 111,* 486–511.

Nelson, K. E. (1981). Individual differences in language development. *Developmental Psychology, 17,* 170–187.

Nelson, S. A. (1980). Factors influencing young children's use of motives and outcomes as moral criteria. *Child Development, 51,* 823–829.

Nelson-Le Gall, S. A. (1985). Motive-outcome matching and outcome foreseeability: Effects on attribution of intentionality and moral judgments. *Developmental Psychology, 21,* 332–337.

Nemours Foundation. (2002). *KidsHealth: Preventing abductions.* Retrieved from http://kidshealth.org/

Neveus, T., Hetta, J., Cnattingius, S., Tuvemo, T., Kackgren, G., Olsson, U., & Stenberg, A. (1999). Depth of sleep and sleep habits among enuretic and incontinent children. *Acta Paediatric, 88,* 748–752.

Newcomb, A. F., & Bagwell, C. L. (1995). Children's friendship relations: A meta-analytic review. *Psychological Bulletin, 117,* 306–347.

Newcombe, N., Mathason, L., & Terlecki, M. (2002). Maximization of spatial competence: More important than finding the cause of sex differences. In A. McGillicuddy-De Lisi & R. De Lisi (Eds.), *Biology, society, and behavior: The development of sex differences in cognition* (pp. 155–182). Westport, CT: Ablex.

Newman, L. F., & Buka, S. L. (1991). Every child a learner. *American Educator, 42,* 27–33.

Newport, E. L. (1991). Contrasting concepts of the critical period for language. In S. Carey & R. Gelman (Eds.), *The epigenesis of mind: Essays on biology and cognition* (pp. 111–130). Hillsdale, NJ: Erlbaum.

Newport, E. L., & Meier, R. P. (1985). The acquisition of American Sign Language. In D. I. Slobin (Ed.), *The cross-linguistic study of language acquisition.* (Vol. 1, pp. 881–938). Hillsdale, NJ: Erlbaum.

Niaz, M. (1997). How early can children understand some form of "scientific reasoning"? *Perceptual and Motor Skills, 85,* 1272–1274.

NICHD. (2001). *Autism facts.* Washington, DC: Author.

NICHD Early Child Care Research Network. (2002). Early child care and children's development prior to school entry. *American Educational Research Associations, 39,* 133–164.

NICHD Early Child Care Research Network. (2003a). Does amount of time spent in child care predict socioemotional adjustment during the transition to kindergarten? *Child Development, 74,* 976–1005.

NICHD Early Child Care Research Network. (2003b). Modeling the impacts of child care quality on children's preschool cognitive development. *Child Development, 74,* 1454–1475.

NICHD Early Child Care Research Network. (2004). Multiple pathways to academic achievement. *Harvard Educational Review, 74,* 1–28.

Nicholls, J. G. (1992). Students as educational theorists. In D. Schunk & J. Meece (Eds.), *Student perceptions in the classroom* (pp. 267–286). Hillsdale, NJ: Erlbaum.

Nicholson, J. M., Fergusson, D. M., & Horwood. L. J. (1999). Effects on later adjustment of living in a stepfamily during childhood and adolescence. *Journal of Child Psychology and Psychiatry and Allied Disciplines, 40,* 405–416.

Nicolaisen, I. (1988). Concepts and learning among the Punan Bah of Sarawak. In G. Johoda (Ed.), *Acquiring culture: Cross cultural studies of child development* (pp. 193–222). London: Croom Helm.

Nieman, R. H., & Gaithright, J. F. (1981). *The long-term effects of ESEA Title I preschool and all-day kindergarten.* Cincinnati, OH: Cincinnati Public Schools.

Nilzon, K. R., & Palmerus, K. (1997). The influence of familial factors on anxiety and depression in childhood and early adolescence. *Adolescence, 32,* 935–943.

Ninio, A., & Snow, C. E. (1996). *Pragmatic development.* Boulder, CO: Westview.

Noam, G. G., Miller, B. M., & Barry, S. (2002). Youth development and afterschool time: Policy and programming in large cities. In B. M. Miller & G. G. Noam (Eds.), *Youth development and after-school time: A tale of many cities* (pp. 9–18). San Francisco: Jossey-Bass.

Norgaard, J. P., Djurhuus, J. C., Watanabe, H., Stenberg, A., & Lettgen, B. (1997). Experience and current status of research into the pathophysiology of nocturnal enuresis. *British Journal of Urology, 79,* 825–835.

Nosphitz, J. D., & King, R. A. (1991). *Pathways of growth: Essentials of child psychiatry.* New York: Wiley.

Nottelmann, E. D., Susman, E. J., Blue, J. H., Inoff-Germain, G. D., Dorn, L. D., Loriaux, D. B., Cutler, G. P., & Chrousos, G. P. (1987). Gonadal and adrenal hormone correlates of adjustment in early adolescence. In R. Lerner & T. Foch (Eds.), *Biological–psychological interactions in early adolescence* (pp. 303–321). Hillsdale, NJ: Erlbaum.

Nozza, R. J. (1995). Estimating the contribution of nonsensory factors to infant–adult differences in behavioral thresholds. *Hearing Research, 91,* 72–77.

Nsamenang, A. B. (1987). A West African perspective. In M. E. Lamb (Ed.), *The father's role: Cross-cultural perspectives* (pp. 273–293). Hillsdale, NJ: Erlbaum.

Nsamenang, A. B. (1992). *Human development in cultural context: A third world perspective.* Newbury Park, CA: Sage.

Nsamenang, A. B., & Laosebikan, S. (1981, April). *Father–child relationship and the development of psychopathology.* Paper presented to the Nigerian Psychological Society Conference, Jos, Nigeria.

Nua Ltd. (2004). *How many online?* Retrieved from http://www.nua.ie/surveys/how_many_online/

Nuechterlein, K. H., Phipps-Yonas, S., Driscoll, R., & Garmezy, N. (1990). Vulnerability factors in children at risk: Anomalies in attentional functioning and social behavior. In J. E. Role & A. S. Masten (Eds.), *Risk and protective factors in the development of psychopathology* (pp. 445–479). New York: Cambridge University Press.

Nurcombe, B. (1994). The validity of the diagnosis of major depression in childhood and adolescence. In W. M. Reynolds & H. F. Johnston (Eds.), *Handbook of depression in children and adolescents* (pp. 61–77). New York: Plenum.

Nyiti, R. M. (1982). The validity of "cultural differences" explanations for cross-cultural variation in the rate of Piagetian cognitive development. In D. Wagner & H. Stevenson (Eds.), *Cultural perspectives on child development* (pp. 167–202). New York: Freeman.

O'Brien, L. T., & Crandall, C. S. (2003). Stereotype threat and arousal: Effects on women's math performance. *Personality and Social Psychology Bulletin, 29,* 782–789.

O'Brien, M., Roy, C., Jacobs, A., Macaluso, M., & Peyton, V. (1999). Conflict in the dyadic play of 3-year-old children. *Early Education and Development, 10,* 289–313.

O'Connor, B. P., & Dvorak, T. (2001). Conditional associations between parental behavior and adolescent problems: A search for personality–environment interactions. *Journal of Research in Personality, 35,* 1–26.

O'Malley, K. D., & Nanson, J. (2002). Clinical implications of a link between fetal alcohol spectrum disorder and attention-deficit hyperactivity disorder. *Canadian Journal of Psychiatry, 47,* 349–354.

O'Moore, M., & Kirkham, C. (2001). Self-esteem and its relationship to bullying behavior. *Aggressive Behavior, 27,* 269–283.

O'Neill, D. B., & Micheli, L. J. (1988). Overuse injuries in the young athlete. *Clinical Sports Medicine, 7,* 591–610.

Oakes, L. M., & Madole, K. L. (2003). Principles of developmental change in infants' category formation. In D. H. Rakison & L. M. Oakes (Eds.), *Early category and concept development: Making sense of the blooming, buzzing confusion* (pp. 131–158). New York: Oxford University Press.

Oakes, L. M., Plumert, J. M., Lansink, J. M., & Merryman, J. D. (1996). Evidence for task-dependent categorization in infancy. *Infant Behavior and Development, 19,* 425–440.

Oates, R. K., Peacock, A., & Forrest, D. (1985). Long-term effects of nonorganic failure to thrive. *Pediatrics, 75,* 36–40.

Oberklaid, F., Amos, D., Liu, C., Jarman, F., Sanson, A., & Prior, M. (1997). "Growing pains": Clinical and behavior correlates in a community sample. *Developmental and Behavioral Pediatrics, 18,* 102–106.

Oddone-Paolucci, E., Genuis, M. L., & Violato, C. (2001). A meta-analysis of the published research on the effects of child sexual abuse. *Journal of Psychology, 135,* 17–36.

Offer, D., Ostrov, E., Howard, K. I., & Atkinson, R. (1988). *The teenage world: Adolescents' self image in ten countries.* New York: Plenum.

Office of Immigration Statistics. (2002). *Yearbook of Immigration Statistics.* Washington, DC: Author.

Office of Management and Budget. (1995). Standards for the classification of federal data on race and ethnicity. *Federal Register, 60,* 44673–44693.

Office of Minority Health. (1998). *Ethnic disparities in health.* Washington, DC: Author.

Office of the Surgeon General. (2000). *Children's oral health.* Washington, DC: US Department of Health and Human Services.

Ogbu, J. U. (1991). Immigrant and involuntary minorities in comparative perspective. In M. G. Gibson & J. U. Ogbu (Eds.), *Minority status and schooling* (pp. 131–156). New York: Garland.

Ogbu, J. U. (1994). From cultural differences to differences in cultural frame of reference. In P. Greenfield & R. Cocking (Eds.), *Cross-cultural roots of minority child development* (pp. 365–391). Hillsdale, NJ: Erlbaum.

Ogden, C. L., Flegal, K. M., Carroll, M. D., & Johnson, C. L. (2002). Prevalence and trends in overweight among US children and adolescents, 1999–2000. *Journal of the American Medical Association 288,* 1728–1732.

Okon, D. M., Greene, A. L., & Smith, J. E. (2003). Family interactions predict intraindividual symptom variation for adolescents with bulimia. *International Journal of Eating Disorders, 34,* 450–457.

Oktay, K., Buyuk, E., Veeck, L., Zaninovic, N., Xu, K., Takeuchi, T., Opsahl, M., & Rosenwaks, Z. (2004). Embryo development after heterotopic transplantation of cryopreserved ovarian tissue. *Nature, 363,* 837–840.

Olivardia, R., Pope, H. G., Borowiecki, J. J., & Cohane, G. H. (2004). Biceps and body image: The relationship between muscularity and self-esteem, depression, and eating disorder symptoms. *Psychology of Men and Masculinity, 5,* 112–120.

Olsson, C. A., Bond, L., Johnson, M. W., Forer, D. L., Boyce, M. F., Sawyer, S. M. (2003). Adolescent chronic illness: A qualitative study of psychosocial adjustment. *Academy of Medicine Singapore, 32,* 43–50.

Olweus, D. (1978). *Aggression in the schools: Bullies and whipping boys.* Washington, DC: Hemisphere.

Olweus, D. (1991). Bully/victim problems among schoolchildren: Basic facts and effects of a school based intervention. In D. Pepler & K. I. Rubin (Eds.), *The development and treatment of childhood aggression* (pp. 411–448). Hillsdale, NJ: Erlbaum.

Olweus, D. (1996). Bully/victim problems at school: Facts and effective intervention. *Reclaiming Children and Youth, 5* 15–22.

Olweus, D. (2003). Social problems in school. In G. Bremner & A. Slater (Eds.), *An introduction to developmental psychology* (pp. 434–454). Malden, MA: Blackwell.

Olweus, D., Limber, S. P., & Mihalic, S. (1999). *The bullying-prevention program.* Boulder, CO: Center for the Study and Prevention of Violence.

Opler, E. M. (1995). *Myths and tales of Jicarilla Apache.* Mineola, NY: Dover Publications.

Orbuch, T. L., & Sprecher, S. (2003). Attraction and interpersonal relationships. In J. Delamater (Ed.), *Handbook of social psychology* (pp. 339–362). New York: Kluwer.

Ornstein, P. A., Naus, M. J., & Liberty, C. (1975). Rehearsal and organizational processes in children's memory. *Child Development, 46,* 818 830.

Ortiz, V. (1995). The diversity of Latino families. In R. E. Zambrana (Ed.), *Understanding Latino families* (pp. 18–29). Thousand Oaks, CA: Sage.

Osterling, J., & Dawson, G. (1994). Early recognition of children with autism: A study of first birthday home video tapes. *Journal of Autism and Developmental Disorders, 24,* 247–259.

Otake, M., & Schull, W. J. (1984). In utero exposure to A-bomb radiation and mental retardation. *British Journal of Radiology, 57,* 409–414.

Overton, W. F. (1998). Developmental psychology: Philosophy, concepts, and methodology. In W. Damon (Ed.), *Handbook of child psychology* (Vol. 1, pp. 107–188). New York: Wiley.

Overton, W. F., & Byrnes, J. P. (1991). Cognitive development. In R. M. Lerner, A. C. Petersen, & J. Brooks-Gunn (Eds.), *Encyclopedia of adolescence* (Vol. 1, pp. 151–156). New York: Garland.

Owens, E. B., & Shaw, D. S. (2003). Poverty and early childhood adjustment. In S. S. Luthar (Ed.), *Resilience and vulnerability: Adaptation in the context of childhood adversities* (pp. 267–292). New York: Cambridge University Press.

Owens, R. E. (1996). *Language development: An introduction.* Boston: Allyn & Bacon.

Owens, S. L., Smothers, B. C., & Love, F. E. (2003). Are girls victims of gender bias in our nation's schools? *Journal of Instructional Psychology, 30,* 131–136.

Padilla, M. T. (1997, May 14). Tiger Woods helps bring multiracial issue to fore. *Arizona Republic,* pp. 1, 2.

Page, R. M., & Allen, O. (1995). Adolescent perceptions of body weight and weight satisfaction. *Perceptual and Motor Skills, 81,* 81–82.

Paik, H., & Comstock, G. (1994). The effects of television violence on antisocial behavior: A meta-analysis. *Communication Research, 21,* 516–546.

Paikoff, R. L., Brooks-Gunn, J., & Warren, M. P. (1991). Effects of girls' hormonal status on depressive and aggressive symptoms over the course of one year. *Journal of Youth and Adolescence, 20,* 191–215.

Paikoff, R. L., McCormick, A., & Sagrestano, L. M. (2000). Adolescent sexuality. In L. T. Szuchman & F. Muscarella (Eds.), *Psychological perspectives on human sexuality.* New York: Wiley.

Paisley, T. S., Joy, E. A., & Price, R. J. (2003). Exercise during pregnancy. *Current Sports Medicine Reports, 2,* 325–330.

Palardy, N., Greening, L., Ott, J., Holderby, A., & Atchinson, J. (1998). Adolescents' health attitudes and adherence to treatment for insulin-dependent diabetes mellitus. *Journal of Developmental and Behavioral Pediatrics, 19,* 31–37.

Palmer, E. J., & Hollin, C. R. (2001). Sociomoral reasoning, perceptions of parenting, and self-reported delinquency in adolescents. *Applied Cognitive Psychology, 15,* 85–100.

Papadimitrious, A. (2001). Sex differences in the secular changes in pubertal maturation. *Pediatrics, 108,* 65.

Papini, D. R., & Sebby, R. A. (1987). Adolescent pubertal status and affective family relationships: A multivariate assessment. *Journal of Youth and Adolescence, 16,* 1–15.

Parens, E., & Knowles, L. P. (2003, July/August). Reprogenetics and public policy: Reflections and recommendations. *Hastings Center Report, 33, 3.*

Paret, I. (1983). Night waking and its relationship to mother–infant interaction in nine-month-old infants. In J. Call, E. Galenson, & R. Tyson (Eds.), *Frontiers of infant psychiatry* (pp 171–177) New York: Basic Books.

Paris, S. G. (2001). Classroom applications of research on self-regulated learning. *Educational Psychologist, 36,* 89–101.

Paris, S. G., & Cunningham, A. E. (1996). Children becoming students. In D.C. Berliner & R. C. Calfee (Eds.), *Handbook of educational psychology* (pp. 117–147). New York: Macmillan.

Parke, R. D. (1995). Fathers and families. In M. H. Bornstein (Ed.), *Handbook of parenting* (Vol. 3, pp. 27–64). Mahwah, NJ: Erlbaum.

Parke, R. D., & Buriel, R. (1998). Socialization in the family. In W. Damon (Ed.), *Handbook of child psychology* (Vol. 3, pp. 463–552). New York: Wiley.

Parker, B., McFarlane, J., & Socken, K. (1994). Abuse during pregnancy: Effects on maternal complications and birth weight in adult and teenage women. *Obstetrics and Gynecology, 84,* 323–328.

Parker, J. G., & Asher, S. R. (1987). Peer relations and later personal adjustment: Are low-accepted children at risk? *Psychological Bulletin, 102,* 357–389.

Parker, J. G., Rubin, K. H., Price, J., & De Rosier, M. E. (1995). Peer relationships, child development, and adjustment: A developmental psychopathology perspective. In D. Cicchetti & D. J. Cohen (Eds.), *Developmental psychopathology* (Vol. 2, pp. 96–161). New York: Wiley.

Parkhurst, J. T., & Asher, S. R. (1992). Peer rejection in middle school. *Developmental Psychology, 28,* 231–241.

Parten, M. (1933). Social play among preschool children. *Journal of Abnormal and Social Psychology, 28,* 136–147.

Paschall, M. J., Flewelling, R. L., & Russell, T. (2004). Why is work intensity associated with heavy alcohol use among adolescents? Journal of Adolescent Health, 34, 79–87.

Pastor, Y., Balaguer, I., Pons, D., & Garcia-Merita, M. (2003). Testing direct and indirect effects of sports participation on perceived health in Spanish adolescents between 15 and 18 years of age. *Journal of Adolescence, 26,* 717–730.

Pasupathi, M., Staudinger, U. M., & Baltes, P. B. (2001). Seeds of wisdom: Adolescents' knowledge and judgment about difficult life problems. *Developmental Psychology, 37,* 351–361.

Pathways Awareness Foundation. (2004). Assure the best for your baby's physical development. Retrieved from http://www.pathways awareness.org/publications/brochure/PAFBabyOKPDForder.pdf

Patterson, C. J. (1992). Children of lesbian and gay parents. *Child Development, 63,* 1025–1042.

Patterson, C. J. (2002). Lesbian and gay parenthood. In M. H. Bornstein (Ed.), *Handbook of parenting: Being and becoming a parent* (Vol. 3, pp. 317–338). Mahway, NJ: Erlbaum.

Patterson, C. J. (2003). Children of lesbian and gay parents. In L. D. Garnets & D. C. Kimmel (Eds.), *Psychological perspectives on lesbian, gay, and bisexual experiences* (pp. 497–548). New York: Columbia University Press.

Patterson, C. J., & Chan, R. W. (1999). Families headed by lesbian and gay parents. In M. E. Lamb (Ed.), *Parenting and child development in "nontraditional" families* (pp. 191–219). Mahwah, NJ: Erlbaum.

Patterson, C. J., Fulcher, M., & Wainright, J. (2002). Children of lesbian and gay parents: Research, law, and policy. In B. L. Bottoms & M. Bull Kovera (Eds.), *Children, social science, and the law* (pp. 176–199). New York: Cambridge University Press.

Patterson, C. J., Griesler, P. C., Vaden, N. A., & Kupersmidt, J. D. (1992). Family economic circumstances, life transitions, and children's peer relations. In R. D. Parke & G. W. Ladd (Eds.), *Family–peer relationships: Modes of linkage* (pp. 385–424). Hillsdale, NJ: Erlbaum.

Patterson, C. J., Vaden, N. A., & Kupersmidt, J. B. (1991). Family background, recent life events, and peer rejection during childhood. *Journal of Social and Personal Relationships, 8,* 347–361.

Patterson, G. R. (1982). *Coercive family process.* Eugene, OR: Castalia.

Patterson, G. R. (2002). The early development of coercive family process. In G. R. Patterson & J. B. Reid (Eds.), *Antisocial behavior in children and adolescents: A developmental analysis and model for intervention* (pp. 25–44). Washington, DC: American Psychological Association.

Patterson, G. R., Reid, J. B., & Dishion, T. J. (1998). *Antisocial boys.* Eugene, OR: Castalia.

Patterson, G. R., & Yoerger, K. (1993). Developmental models for delinquent behavior. In S. Hodgins (Ed.), *Crime and mental disorder* (pp. 140–172). Newbury Park, CA: Sage.

Paul, R. (1991). Profiles of toddlers with slow expressive language development. *Topics in Language Disorders, 11,* 1–13.

Paul, R., Spangle-Looney, S., & Dahm, P. S. (1991). Communication and socialization skills in ages 2 and 3 in late-talking young children. *Journal of Speech and Hearing Research, 4,* 858–865.

Paus, T., Zijdenbos, A., Worsley, K., Collins, D. L., Blumenthal, J., Giedd, J. N., Rapoport, J. L., & Evans, A. C. (1999). Structural maturation of neural pathways in children and adolescents: In vivo study. *Science, 283,* 1908–1911.

PBS Frontline. (2004). *Inside the teen brain: Interview with Deborah Yurgelun-Todd.* Retrieved from http://www.pbs.org/wgbh/pages/frontline/shows/teenbrain/interviews/todd.html

Pearson, J. L., & Ferguson, L. R. (1989). Gender differences in patterns of spatial ability, environmental cognition, and math and English achievement in late adolescence. *Adolescence, 24,* 421–431.

Pelham, W. E., Aronoff, H. R., Midlam, J. K., Shapiro, C. J., Gnagy, E. M., Chronis, A. M., Onyango, A. N., Forehand, G., Nguyen, A., & Waxmonsky, J. (1999). A comparison of Ritalin and Aderall: Efficacy and time-course in children with ADHD. *Pediatrics, 103,* 1–14.

Pelham, W. E., Bender, M. E., Caddell, J., Booth, S., & Moorer, S. H. (1985). Methylphenidate and children with attention deficit disorder: Dose effects on classroom academic and social behavior. *Archives of General Psychiatry, 42,* 948–952.

Pelham, W. E., Milich, R., & Walker, J. L. (1986). Effects of continuous and partial reinforcement and methylphenidate on learning in children with attention deficit disorder. *Journal of Abnormal Psychology, 95,* 319–325.

Pellegrini, A. D., & Landers-Pott, M. (1996). Children, classroom context and activity and attention to tasks. *Emotional and Behavioral Difficulties, 1,* 29–35.

Pellegrini, A. D., & Smith, P. K. (1998). Physical activity play: The nature and function of a neglected aspect of play. *Child Development, 69,* 577–598.

Pennington, B. F. (1999). Toward an integrated understanding of dyslexia: Genetic, neurological, and cognitive mechanisms. *Development and Psychopathology, 11,* 629–654.

Peracchio, L. A. (1993). Young children's processing of a televised narrative: Is a picture really worth a thousand words? *Journal of Consumer Research, 20,* 281–293.

Perez Granados, D. R., & Callanan, M. A. (1997). Parents and siblings as early resources for young children's learning in Mexican-descent families. *Hispanic Journal of Behavioral Sciences, 19,* 3–33.

Perris, E. E., Myers, N. A., & Clifton, R. K. (1990). Long-term memory for a single infancy experience. *Child Development, 61,* 1796–1807.

Perry, D. G., Perry, L. C., & Rasmussen, P. (1986). Cognitive social learning mediators of aggression. *Child Development, 57,* 700–711.

Persell, C. H. (1993). Social class and educational equality. In J. A. Banks & C. A. M. Banks (Eds.), *Multiculture education: Issues and perspectives* (pp. 71–89). Boston: Allyn & Bacon.

Perusse, D., Neale, M. C., Heath, A. C., & Eaves, L. J. (1994). Human parental behavior: Evidence for genetic influence and potential implication for gene-culture transmission. *Behavioral Genetics, 24,* 327–335.

Peskin, H. (1973). Influence of the developmental schedule of puberty on learning and ego development. *Journal of Youth and Adolescence, 2,* 273–290.

Peters, H. E., Argys, L. M., Maccoby, E. E., & Mnookin, R. H. (1993). Enforcing divorce settlements: Evidence from child support compliance and award modifications. *Demography, 30,* 719–735.

Petersen, A. C. (1987). The nature of biological-psychosocial interactions: The sample case of early adolescence. In R. M. Lerner & T. T. Foch (Eds.), *Biological-psychological interactions in early adolescence* (pp. 35–61). Hillsdale, NJ: Erlbaum.

Petersen, A. C. (1988). Adolescent development. *Annual Review of Psychology, 39,* 583–607.

Peterson, G. W. (1995). The need for common principles in prevention programs for children, adolescents, and families. *Journal of Adolescent Research, 10,* 470–485.

Peterson, G. W., & Haan, D. (1999). Socializing children and parents in families. In M. Sussman, S. Steinmetz, & G. W. Peterson (Eds.), *Handbook of marriage and the family* (pp. 455–501). New York: Plenum.

Peterson, J. L., & Zill, N. (1986). Parent-child relationships and behavior problems in children. *Journal of Marriage and the Family, 48,* 295–307.

Pettegrew, J., Lewis, L. A., Brown, J. D., Schulze, L., Zook, K. B., Perry, I., Rose, T., & Ledbetter, J. (1995). Music videos and rap music: Cultural conflict and control in the age of the image. In G. Dines & J. M. Humez (Eds.), *Gender, race, and class in media* (pp. 479–544). Thousand Oaks, CA: Sage.

Pettit, G. S., Bates, J. E., & Dodge, K. A. (1997). Supportive parenting, ecological context, and children's adjustment. *Child Development, 68,* 908–923.

Pettit, G. S., Laird, R. D., Dodge, K. A., Bates, J. E., & Criss, M. M. (2001). Antecedents and behavior-problem outcomes of parental monitoring and psychological control in early adolescence. *Child Development, 72,* 583–598.

Pew Internet and American Life Project. (2003). *Internet use in the United States.* Washington, DC: Author.

Phelan, K. J., Khoury, J., Kalkwarf, H. J., & Lanphear, B. P. (2001). Trends and patterns of playground injuries in United States children and adolescents. *Ambulatory Pediatrics, 1,* 227–233.

Phelps, L. A., Johnston, L. S., Jimenesez, D. P., Wilczenski, F. L., Andrea, R. K., & Healy, R. W. (1993). Figure preference, body dissatisfaction, and body distortion in adolescence. *Journal of Adolescent Research, 8,* 297–310.

Phillips, D., Lande, J., & Goldberg, M. (1990). The state of childcare regulation: A comparative analysis. *Early Childhood Research Quarterly, 5,* 151–179.

Phillips, E. L., Greydanus, D. E., Pratt, H. D., & Patel, D. R. (2003). Treatment of bulimia nervosa: Psychological and psychopharmacologic considerations. *Journal of Adolescent Research, 18,* 261–279.

Phillipsen, L. C. (1999). Associations between age, gender, and group acceptance and three components of friendship quality. *Journal of Early Adolescence, 19,* 438–464.

Phinney, J. S. (1996). Understanding ethnic diversity: The role of ethnic identity. *American Behavioral Scientist, 40,* 143–152.

Phinney, J. S. (2000). Identity formation across cultures: The interaction of personal, societal, and historical change. *Human Development, 43,* 37–31.

Phinney, J. S. (2003). Ethic identity and acculturation. In P. B. Organista & K. M. Chun (Eds.), *Acculturation: Advances in theory, measurement, and applied research* (pp. 63–81). Washington, DC: American Psychological Association.

Phinney, J. S., DuPont, S., Espinosa, C., Revill, J., & Sanders, K. (1994). Ethnic identity and American identification among ethnic minority youths. In A. M. Bouvy & F. J. R. van de Vijver (Eds.), *Journeys into cross-cultural psychology* (pp. 167–183). Amsterdam: Swets & Zeitlinger.

Phinney, J. S., Ong, A., & Madden, T. (2000). Cultural values and intergenerational value discrepancies in immigrant and non-immigrant families. *Child Development, 71,* 528–539.

Phinney, J. S., & Rosenthal, D. A. (1992). Ethnic identity in adolescence. In G. R. Adams & T. P. Gullotta (Eds.), *Adolescent identity formation* (Vol. 4, pp. 145–172). Newbury Park, CA: Sage.

Piaget, J. (1952). *The origins of intelligence in children.* New York: Norton.

Piaget, J. (1963). *The origins of intelligence in children* (M. Cook, Trans.). New York: Norton. (Original work published 1936.)

Piaget, J. (1965). *The moral judgment of the child.* New York: Free Press. (Original work published 1932.)

Piaget, J. (1969). *The child's conception of time* (A. J. Pomerans, Trans.). London: Routledge. (Original work published 1946.)

Piaget, J. (1971). *Biology and knowledge.* Chicago: University of Chicago Press.

Piaget, J. (1977). *The development of thought.* New York: Viking.

Piaget, J., & Inhelder, B. (1958). *The growth of logical thinking from childhood to adolescence.* New York: Basic Books.

Pinker, S. (1984). *Language learnability and language development.* Cambridge, MA: Harvard University Press.

Pinker, S. (1994). *The language instinct.* New York: HarperCollins.

Pipher, M. (1994). *Reviving Ophelia.* New York: Grosset/Putnam.

Planned Parenthood. (2004). *Pregnancy and childbearing among U.S. teens.* New York: Author.

Plimpton, C. E., & Regimbal, C. (1992). Differences in motor proficiency according to gender and race. *Perceptual and Motor Skills, 74,* 399–402.

Plomin, R. (1994). *Genetics and experience: The interplay between nature and nurture.* Thousand Oaks, CA: Sage.

Plomin, R., DeFries, J. C., & McClearn, G. E. (1990). *Behavioral genetics: A primer.* New York: Freeman.

Plomin, R., DeFries, J. C., McClearn, G. E., & Rutter, M. (1997). *Behavioral genetics.* New York: Freeman.

Plomin, R., Fulker, D. W., Corley, R., & DeFries, J. C. (1997). Nature, nurture, and cognitive development from 1 to 16 years: A parent–offspring adoption study. *Psychological Science, 8,* 442–447.

Plomin, R., Nitz, K., & Rowe, D.C. (1990). Behavior genetics and aggressive behavior in childhood. In M. Lewis & S. Miller (Eds.), *Handbook of development psychology* (pp. 119–133). New York: Plenum.

Plumb, P., & Cowan, G. (1984). A developmental study of stereotyping and androgynous activity preference of tomboys, nontomboys, and males. *Sex Roles, 10,* 703–712.

Plunkett, J. W., Meisels, S. J., Stiefel, G. S., Pasick, P. L., & Roloff, D. W. (1986). Patterns of attachment among preterm infants of varying biological risk. *Journal of the American Academy of Child Psychiatry, 25,* 794–800.

Polce, L. M., Myers, B. J., Kliewer, W., & Kilmartin, C. (2001). Adolescent self-esteem and gender: Exploring relations to sexual harassment, body image, media influence, and emotional expression. *Journal of Youth and Adolescence 30,* 225–244.

Polit, D. F., & Falbo, T. (1987). Only children and personality development: A quantitative review. *Journal of Marriage and the Family, 49,* 309–325.

Pollak, S. D., & Sinha, P. (2002). Effects of early experience on children's recognition of facial displays of emotion. *Developmental Psychology, 38,* 784–791.

Pollitt, E., Golub, M., Gorman, K., Grantham-McGregor, S., Levitsky, D., Schurch, B., Strupp, B., & Wachs, T. (1996). A recommendation of the effects of undernutrition on children's biological, psychosocial, and behavioral development. *Society for Research in Child Development Social Policy Report, 10,* 1–23.

Pomerantz, E. M., Ruble, D. N., Frey, K. S., & Greulich, F. (1995). Meeting goals and confronting conflict: Children's changing perceptions of social comparison. *Child Development, 66,* 723–738.

Pong, S. (2003). *Immigrant children's school performance.* Retrieved from http://www.pop.psu.edu/general/pubs/working_papers/psu-pri/wp 0307.pdf

Pooler, W. S. (1991). Sex of child preferences among college students. *Sex Roles, 25,* 569–576.

Pope, A. W., & Bierman, K. L. (1999). Predicting adolescent peer problems and antisocial activities: The relative roles of aggression and dysregulation. *Developmental Psychology, 35,* 335–346.

Popkin, B. M., & Udry, J. R. (1998). Adolescent obesity increases significantly in second and third generation U.S. immigrants. *Journal of Nutrition, 128,* 701–706.

Porac, C., Coren, S., & Searleman, A. (1986). Environmental factors in hand preference formation. *Behavior Genetics, 16,* 251–261.

Porter, R. H., Cernoch, J. M., & McLaughlin, F. J. (1983). Maternal recognition of neonates through olfactory cues. *Physiology and Behavior, 30,* 151–154.

Porter, R. H., Makin, J. W., Davis, L. B., & Christensen, K. M. (1992). Breast-fed infants respond to olfactory cues from their own mother and unfamiliar lactating females. *Infant Behavior and Development, 15,* 85–93.

Posada, G., Gao, Y., Wu, F., Posada, R., Tascon, M., Schoelmerich, A., Sagi, A., Kondo-Ikemura, K., Haaland, W., & Synnevaag, B. (1995). The secure-base phenomenon across cultures: Children's behavior, mothers' preferences, and experts' concepts. In E. Waters, B. Vaughan, G. Posada, & K. Kondo-Ikemura (Eds.), *Caregiving, cultural, and cognitive perspectives on secure-base behavior and working models* (pp. 27–48). Chicago: Society for Research in Child Development.

Posner, M. J., & Rothbart, M. K. (2000). Developing mechanisms of self-regulation. *Development and Psychopathology, 12,* 427–441.

Potts, R., Doppler, M., & Hernandez, M. (1994). Effects of television content on physical risk-taking in children. *Journal of Experimental Child Psychology, 58,* 321–331.

Poulin, F., Cillessen, A. H. N., Hubbard, J. A., Coie, J. D., Dodge, K. A., & Schwartz, D. (1997). Children's friends and behavioral similarity in two social contexts. *Social Development, 6,* 224–236.

Powell, G. F., Low, J. F., & Speers, M. A. (1987). Behavior as a diagnostic aid in failure to thrive. *Journal of Developmental Behavioral Pediatrics, 8,* 18–24.

Power, F. C., Higgins, A., & Kohlberg, L. (1989). *Lawrence Kohlberg's approach to moral education.* New York: Columbia University Press.

Power, T. G., McGrath, M. P., Hughes, S. O., & Manire, S. H. (1994). Compliance and self-assertion: Young children's responses to mothers versus fathers. *Developmental Psychology, 30,* 980–989.

Prechtl, H. F. R., Einspieler, C., Cloni, G., Bos, A. F., Ferrari, F., & Sontheimer, D. (1997). An early marker for neurological deficits after perinatal brain lesions. *Lancet 349,* 1361–1364.

Prectl, H. F. R., & Beintema, D. (1965). *The neurological examination of the full-term newborn infant.* London: William Heinemann Medical Books.

Present, P. (1987). *Child drowning study: A report on the epidemiology of drowning in residential pools to children under age five.* Washington, DC: Consumer Product Safety Commission.

President's Council on Physical Fitness and Sports. (2001, March). Healthy people 2010: Physical activity and fitness. *Research Digest, Series 3, No. 13.*

Pressley, M. (1998). *Reading instruction that works: The case for balanced teaching.* New York: Guilford.

Price, D. W. W., & Goodman, G. S. (1990). Visiting the wizard: Children's memory for a recurring event. *Child Development, 61,* 664–680.

Price, J. M., & Lento, J. (2001). The nature of child and adolescent vulnerability: History and definitions. In R. E. Ingram & J. M. Price (Eds.), *Vulnerability to psychopathology: Risk across the lifespan* (pp. 20–38). New York: Guilford.

PRIDE Surveys. (2003). Bowling Green, KY: Author.

Prinz, R. J., & Feerick, M. M. (2003). Children exposed to community violence or war/terrorism. *Clinical Child and Family Psychology Review, 6,* 221–222.

Prugh, D. G., Staub, E. M., Sands, H. H., Kirschbaum, R. M., & Lenihan, E. A. (1953). A study of the emotional reactions of children in families to hospitalization and illness. *American Journal of Orthopsychiatry, 23,* 70–106.

Prysak, M., & Castronova, F. C. (1998). Elective induction versus spontaneous labor. *Obstetrics and Gynecology, 92,* 47–52.

Public Broadcasting Service. (1999). *The PBS audience.* Alexandria, VA: Publication Broadcasting Service.

Public Broadcasting Service. (2003). *Using television in the home.* Washington, DC: Author.

Puig-Antich, J., Geotz, D., Davies, M., Kaplan, T., Davies, S., Ostrow, L., Asnis, L., Toomey, J., Iyengar, S., & Ryan, N. (1989). A controlled family history study of prepubertal major depressive disorder. *Archives of General Psychiatry, 46,* 406–418.

Putallaz, M., & Wasserman, A. (1990). Children's entry behavior. In S. R. Asher & J. D. Coie (Eds.), *Peer rejection in childhood* (pp. 60–89). Cambridge, UK: Cambridge University Press.

Pyle, R. P., McQuivey, R. W., Brassington, G. S., & Steiner, H. (2003). High school student athletes: Associations between intensity of participation and health factors. *Clinical Pediatrics, 42,* 697–701.

Quadflieg, N., & Fichter, M. M. (2003). The course and outcome of bulimia nervosa. *European Journal of Child and Adolescent Psychiatry, 12,* 99–109.

Quatman, T., & Watson, C. M. (2001). Gender differences in adolescent self-esteem: An exploration of domains. *Journal of Genetic Psychology, 16,* 93–117.

Quatman, T., Sampson, K., Robinson, C., & Watson, C. M. (2001). Academic, motivational, and emotional correlates of adolescent dating. *Genetic, Social, and General Psychology Monographs, 127,* 211–234.

Quay, H. C. (1988). Attention-deficit disorder and the behavioral inhibition system. In L. M. Bloomingdale & J. Sergeant (Eds.), *Attention deficit disorder. Criteria, cognition, intervention* (pp. 117–126). New York: Pergamon.

Quinn, P. C. (2002). Early categorization: A new synthesis. In U. Goswami (Ed.), *Blackwell handbook of childhood cognitive development* (pp. 84–101). Oxford, UK: Blackwell.

Quinn, P. C. (2003). Concepts are not just for objects: Categorization of spatial relation information by infants. In D. H. Rakison & L. M. Oakes (Eds.), *Early category and concept development: Making sense of the blooming, buzzing confusion* (pp. 50–70). New York: Oxford University Press.

Quinn, P. C., & Eimas, P. D. (1996). Perceptual organization and categorization in young infants. *Journal of Experimental Child Psychology, 69,* 151–174.

Quist, J. F., & Kennedy, J. L. (2001). Genetics of childhood disorders: ADHD. Part 7: The serotonin system. *Journal of the American Academy of Child and Adolescent Psychiatry, 40,* 253–256.

Radke-Yarrow, M., & Sherman, T. (1990). Hard growing: Children who survive. In J. Rolf, A. S. Masten, D. Cicchetti, K. H. Nuechterlein, & S. Weintraub (Eds.), *Risk and protective factors in the development of psychopathology* (pp. 97–119). Cambridge, UK: Cambridge University Press.

Raeff, C. (1997). Cultural values, children's social interactions, and the development of an American individualistic self. *Developmental Review, 17,* 205–230.

Raffaelli, M., Bogenschneider, K., & Flood, M. F. (1998). Parent–teen communication about sexual topics. *Journal of Family Issues, 19,* 315–333.

Rakison, D. H. (2003). Parts, motion, and the development of the animate–inanimate distinction in infancy. In D. H. Rakison & L. M. Oakes (Eds.), *Early category and concept development: Making sense of the blooming, buzzing confusion* (pp. 159–192). New York: Oxford University Press.

Rakison, D. H., & Poulin-Dubois, D. (2001). Developmental origin of the animate–inanimate distinction. *Psychological Bulletin, 127,* 209–228.

Ramsey, P. G. (1987). Young children's thinking about ethnic differences. In J. S. Phinney & M. J. Rotheram (Eds.), *Children's ethnic socialization* (pp. 56–72). Beverly Hills, CA: Sage.

Rastam, M., & Gillberg, C. (1991). The family background in anorexia nervosa: A population-based study. *Journal of the American Academy of Child and Adolescent Psychiatry, 30,* 283–289.

Rathus, S. A., Nevid, J. S., & Fichner-Rathus, L. (1993). *Human sexuality in a world of diversity.* Boston: Allyn & Bacon.

Rauschecker, J. P. (1999). Auditory cortical plasticity: A comparison with other sensory systems. *Trends in Neurosciences, 22,* 74–80.

Raver, C. C., & Zigler, E. F. (1997). New perspectives on Head Start. *Early Childhood Research Quarterly, 12,* 363–385.

Rechtschaffen, A., Bergmann, B. M., Kushida, C. A., & Gilliland, M. A. (2602). Sleep deprivation in the rat. *Sleep, 25,* 68–87.

Reder, P., & Duncan, S. (2000). Child abuse and parental mental health. In P. Reder & M. McClure (Eds.), *Family matters: Interfaces between child and adult mental health* (pp. 166–179). London: Routledge.

Reichman, N. E., & Pagnini, D. L. (1997). Maternal age and birth outcomes. *Family Planning Perspectives, 29,* 268–272.

Reid, J. B., & Eddy, J. M. (1997). The prevention of antisocial behavior: Some considerations in the search for effective interventions. In D. M. Stoff & J. Breiling (Eds.), *Handbook of antisocial behavior* (pp. 343–356). New York: Wiley.

Reik, W., Collick, A., Norris, M. L., Barton, S. C., & Surani, M. A. H. (1987). Genomic imprinting determines methylation of parental alleles in transgenic mice. *Nature, 328,* 248–251.

Reinisch, J. M. (1990). *The Kinsey Institute new report on sex: What you must know to be sexually literate.* New York: St. Martin's Press.

Reis, S. M. (1989). Reflections on policy affecting the education of gifted and talented students. *American Psychologist, 44,* 399–408.

Reisman, J. E. (1987). Touch, motion, and proprioception. In P. Salapatek & L. Cohen (Eds.), *Handbook of infant perception* (Vol. 1, pp. 265–303). New York: Academic Press.

Remafedi, G. (1991). Adolescent homosexuality. In R. M. Lerner, A. C. Petersen, & J. Brooks-Gunn (Eds.), *Encyclopedia of adolescence* (pp. 504–507). New York: Garland.

Renzulli, J. S. (1999). What is this thing called giftedness, and how do we develop it? A twenty-five year perspective. *Journal for the Education of the Gifted, 23,* 3–54.

Repacholi, B. M., & Gopnik, A. (1997). Early reasoning about desires: Evidence from 14- and 18-month-olds. *Developmental Psychology, 33,* 12–21.

Rescorla, L., & Schwartz, E. (1990). Outcome of toddlers with specific expressive language impairment. *Applied Psycholinguistics, 11,* 393–408.

Resnick, M. D. (1997). *Adolescents and work*. Unpublished data, University of Minnesota.

Rest, J. R. (1983). Morality. In J. H. Flavell & E. M. Markman (Eds.), *Handbook of child psychology* (Vol. 3, pp. 556–629). New York: Wiley.

Reuter, M. A., Conger, R. D., & Ramisetty-Mikler, S. (1999). Assessing the benefits of a parenting skills training program: A theoretical approach to predicting direct and moderating effects. *Family Relations, 48*, 67–77.

Reynolds, A. J. (1998). Resilience among black urban youth: Prevalence, intervention effects, and mechanisms of influence. *American Journal of Orthopsychiatry, 68*, 84–100.

Reynolds, M. A., Schieve, L. A., Martin, J. A., Jeng, G., & Macaluso, M. (2003). Trends in multiple births conceived using assisted reproductive technology, United States, 1997–2000. *Pediatrics, 111*, 1159–1162.

Rheingold, H. L. (1982). Little children's participation in the work of adults: A nascent prosocial behavior. *Child Development, 53*, 114–125.

Rhode, M. (1997). *Sexual orientation*. Seattle, WA: Friends Project.

Rholes, W. S., & Ruble, D. N. (1984). Children's understanding of dispositional characteristics of others. *Child Development, 33*, 550–560.

Ricciardelli, L. A., & McCabe, M. P. (2001). Children's body image concerns and eating disturbance: A review of the literature. *Clinical Psychology Review, 21*, 325–344.

Ricciardelli, L. A., & McCabe, M. P. (2004). A biopsychosocial model of disordered eating and the pursuit of muscularity in adolescent boys. *Psychological Bulletin, 130*, 179–205.

Rice, E. P. (1996). *The adolescent: Development, relationships, and culture*. Boston: Allyn & Bacon.

Rice, M. L. (1990). Preschoolers QUIL: Quick incidental learning of words. In G. ContiRamsden & C. Snow (Eds.), *Children's language* (Vol. 7, pp. 171–195). Hillsdale, NJ: Erlbaum.

Rice, M. L., Hadley, P. A., & Alexander, A. (1993). Social biases toward children with specific language impairment: A correlative causal model of language limitations. *Applied Psycholinguistics, 14*, 445–471.

Rice, M. L., Huston, A. C., Truglio, R. T., & Wright, J. C. (1990). Words from *Sesame Street*: Learning vocabulary while viewing. *Developmental Psychology, 26*, 421–428.

Richards, H., & Goodman, R. (1996). Are only children different? A study of psychiatric referrals. *Journal of Child Psychology and Psychiatry, 37*, 753–757.

Richards, M. H., Casper, R. C., & Larson, R. (1990). Weight and eating concerns among pre- and young adolescent boys and girls. *Journal of Adolescent Health, 11*, 203–209.

Richards, M. H., Crowe, P. A., Larson, R., & Swarr, A. (1998). Developmental patterns and gender differences in the experience of peer companionship during adolescence. *Child Development, 69*, 154–163.

Richardson, G. A., Hamel, S. C., Goldschmidt, L., & Day, N. L. (1999). Growth of infants prenatally exposed to cocaine/crack: Comparison of a prenatal care and a no prenatal care sample. *Pediatrics, 104*, 18–22.

Richardson, G. S., & Tate, B. A. (2002). Factors influencing sleep patterns of adolescents. In M. A. Carskadon (Ed.), *Adolescent sleep patterns* (pp. 33–45). New York: Cambridge University Press.

Richman, N., Stevenson, J. E., & Graham, P. (1982). *Preschool to school: A behavioral study*. London: Academic Press.

Ridley, M. (1999). *Genome: The autobiography of a species in 23 chapters*. New York: HarperCollins.

Rieber, R. W., & Hall, M. J. (1998). *The collected works of L. S. Vygotsky*. New York: Plenum.

Rimm-Kaufman, S. E., Pianta, R. C., & Cox, M. J. (2000). Teachers' judgments of problems in the transition to kindergarten. *Early Childhood Research Quarterly, 15*, 147–166.

Robbins, C., & Ehri, L. C. (1994). Reading storybooks to kindergartners helps them learn new vocabulary words. *Journal of Educational Psychology, 86*, 54–64.

Roberts, D. F., & Christenson, P. G. (2001). Popular music in childhood and adolescence. In D. G. Singer & J. L. Singer (Eds.), *Handbook of children and the media* (pp. 395–414). Thousand Oaks, CA: Sage.

Roberts, D. F., Christenson, P. G., & Gentile, D. A. (2003). The effects of violent music on children and adolescents. In Gentile (Ed.), *Media violence and children* (pp. 153–170). Westport, CT: Praeger.

Roberts, L. R., Sarigiani, P. A., Petersen, A. C., & Newman, J. L. (1993). Gender differences in the relationship between achievement and self-image during early adolescence. In R. A. Pierce & M. A. Black (Eds.), *Life span development* (pp. 126–139). Dubuque, IA: Kendall/Hunt.

Roberts, W., & Strayer, J. (1996). Empathy, emotional expressiveness, and prosocial behavior. *Child Development, 67*, 449–470.

Robertson, J. A. (1996). Legal uncertainties in human egg donation. In C. B. Cohen (Ed.), *New ways of making babies* (pp. 175–187). Bloomington: Indiana University Press.

Robinson, A., Goodman, S., & O'Brien, D. (1984). Genetic and chromosomal disorders, including inborn errors of metabolism. In C. H. Kempe, H. K. Silver, & D. O'Brien (Eds.), *Current pediatric diagnosis and treatment* (pp. 322–367). Los Altos, CA: Lange Medical.

Robinson, J. A., McKenzie, B. E., & Day, R. H. (1996). Anticipatory reaching by infants and adults: The effect of object features and apertures in opaque and transparent screens. *Child Development, 67*, 2641–2657.

Robinson, T. N. (1998). Does television cause childhood obesity? *Journal of the American Medical Association, 279*, 959–960.

Robinson, T. N. (1999). Reducing children's television viewing to prevent obesity: A randomized controlled trial. *Journal of the American Medical Association, 27*, 1561–1567.

Robinson, T. N., & Killen, J. D. (1995). Ethnic and gender differences in the relationships between television viewing and obesity, physical activity, and dietary fat intake. *Journal of Health Education, 26*, S91–S98.

Robinson, T. N., & Killen, J. D. (2001). Obesity prevention for children and adolescents. In J. K. Thompson & L. Smolak (Eds.), *Body image, eating disorders, and obesity in youth* (pp. 261–292). Washington, DC: American Psychological Association.

Rochat, P. (1989). Object manipulation and exploration in 2- to 5-month-old infants. *Developmental Psychology, 25*, 871–884.

Roche, A. F. (1979). Secular trends in human growth, malnutrition, and development. *Monographs of the Society for Research in Child Development, 44* (Whole No. 179). Chicago: University of Chicago Press.

Rodgers, B. R. (1999). Parenting processes related to sexual risk-taking behaviors of adolescent males and females. *Journal of Marriage and the Family, 61*, 99–109.

Rodgers, J. L., Muster, M., & Rowe, D.C. (2001). Genetic and environmental influences on delinquency: DF analysis of NLSY kinship data. *Journal of Quantitative Criminology, 17*, 145–168.

Rodgers, J. L., Rowe, D.C., & Buster, M. (1998). Social contagion, adolescent sexual behavior, and pregnancy. *Developmental Psychology, 34*, 1096–1113.

Roeser, R. W., & Eccles, J. S. (2000). Schooling and mental health. In A. Sameroff & M. Lewis (Eds.), *Handbook of developmental psychopathology* (pp. 135–156). New York: Kluwer/ Plenum.

Roeser, R. W., Eccles, J. S., & Freedman-Doan, C. (1999). Academic functioning and mental health in adolescence: Patterns, progressions, and routes from childhood. *Journal of Adolescent Research, 14*, 135–174.

Roeser, R. W., Eccles, J. S., & Sameroff, A. J. (1998). Academic and emotional functioning in early adolescence: Longitudinal relations, patterns, and prediction by experience in middle school. *Development and Psychopathology, 10*, 321–352.

Roffey, S., Majors, K., & Tarrant, T. (1997). Friends—who needs them? *Educational and Child Psychology, 14*, 51–56.

Rogoff, B. (1990). *Apprenticeship in thinking: Cognitive development in social context*. New York: Oxford University Press.

Rogoff, B. (1998). Cognition as a collaborative process. In D. Kuhn & R. S. Siegler (Eds.), *Handbook of child psychology* (Vol. 2, pp. 679–744). New York: Wiley.

Rogoff, B., Mistry, J., Goncu, A., & Mosier, C. (1993). Guided participation in cultural activity by toddlers and caregivers. *Monographs of the Society for Research in Child Development, 58* (Whole No. 179). Chicago: University of Chicago Press.

Rohner, R. P. (1986). *The warmth dimension: Foundations of parental acceptance–rejection theory*. Beverly Hills, CA: Sage.

Romaine, S. (1995). *Bilingualism* (2nd ed.). Oxford, UK: Blackwell.

Ronnqvist, L., & von Hofsten, C. (1994). Neonatal finger and arm movements as determined by a social and an object context. *Early Development and Parenting, 3,* 81–94.

Roopnarine, J. L., Lasker, J., Sacks, M., & Stores, M. (1998). The cultural contexts of children's play. In O. N. Saracho & B. Spodek (Eds.), *Multiple perspectives on play in early childhood education* (pp. 194–219). Albany: State University of New York Press.

Root, A. W. (2000). Precocious puberty. *Pediatric Review, 21,* 10–19.

Roper Organization. (1993). Survey of March 13–27, 1993. *Roper Reports, 93.*

Rosander, K., & von Hofsten, C. (2004). Infants' emerging ability to represent occluded object motion. *Cognition, 9,* 1–22.

Rose, A. J., & Asher, S. R. (2000). Children's friendships. In C. Hendrick & S. Hendrick (Eds.), *Close relationships: A sourcebook* (pp. 47–57). Thousand Oaks, CA: Sage.

Rose, S. A., & Blank, M. (1974). The potency of context in children's cognition. *Child Development, 45,* 499–502.

Roseboom, T. J., van der Meulen, J. H. P., Ravelli, A. C. J., Osmond, C., Barker, D. J. P., & Bleker, O. P. (2003). Perceived health status of adults after prenatal exposure to the Dutch famine. *Paediatric and Perinatal Epidemiology, 17,* 391–397.

Rosenbaum, M. B. (1993). The changing image of the adolescent girl. In M. Sugar (Ed.), *Female adolescent development* (pp. 62–80). New York: Brunner/Mazel.

Rosenblith, J. F. (1992). *In the beginning: Development from conception to age two*. Newbury Park, CA: Sage.

Rosenshine, B., & Meister, C. (1997). Cognitive strategy instruction in reading. In S. A. Stahl & D. A. Hayes (Eds.), *Instructional models in reading* (pp. 85–107). Mahwah, NJ: Erlbaum.

Rosenstein, D., & Oster, H. (1988). Differential facial responses to four basic tastes in newborns. *Child Development, 59,* 1555–1568.

Rosenthal, B. S. (1998). Non-school correlates of dropout: An integrative review of the literature. *Child and Youth Services Review, 20,* 413–433.

Rosenthal, M. K. (1999). Out-of-home child care research: A cultural perspective. *International Journal of Behavioral Development, 23,* 477–518.

Rosenthal, R., & Jacobson, L. (1968). *Pygmalion in the classroom*. New York: Holt, Rinehart and Winston.

Ross, H. S., & Conant, C. L. (1992). The social structure of early conflict: Interaction, relationships, and alliances. In C. U. Shantz & W. W. Hartup (Eds.), *Conflict in child and adolescent development* (pp. 153–186). Cambridge, UK: Cambridge University Press.

Rossell, C. H., & Baker, K. (1996). The educational effectiveness of bilingual education. *Research in the Teaching of English, 30*(1), 7–74.

Rosser, P. L., & Randolph, S. M. (1989). Black American infants: The Howard University normative study. In J. K. Nugent, B. M. Loctor, & T. B. Brazelton (Eds.), *The cultural context of infancy* (Vol. 1, pp. 133–165). Norwood, NJ: Ablex.

Ross-Leadbeater, B. J., & Way, N. (2001). *Growing up fast: Transitions to early adulthood of inner-city adolescent mothers*. Mahwah, NJ: Erlbaum.

Rossner, S. (1998). Childhood obesity and adulthood consequences. *Acta Pediatrics, 87,* 1–5.

Roth, M. A., & Parker, J. G. (2001). Affective and behavioral responses to friends who neglect their friends for dating partners: Influences of gender, jealousy, and perspective. *Journal of Adolescence, 24,* 281–296.

Rothbart, M. K. (1989). Temperament and development. In G. Kohnstamm, J. Bates, & M. K. Rothbart (Eds.), *Temperament in childhood* (pp. 187–247). Chichester, UK: Wiley.

Rothbart, M. K., & Bates, J. E. (1998). Temperament. In W. Damon (Ed.), *Handbook of child development* (Vol. 3, pp. 105–176). New York: Wiley.

Rothbart, M. K., & Mauro, J. A. (1990). Questionnaire approaches to the study of infant temperament. In J. W. Fagen & J. Colombo (Eds.), *Individual differences in infancy: Reliability, stability, and prediction* (pp. 411–429). Hillsdale, NJ: Erlbaum.

Rothbaum, F., Weisz, J., Pott, M., Miyake, K., & Kazuo, G. (2000). Attachment and culture: Security in the United States and Japan. *American Psychologist, 55,* 1093–1104.

Rothenberg, S. J., Manalo, M., Kiang, J., Khan, F., Cuellar, R., Reyes, S., Sanchez, M., Reynoso, B., Aguilar, A., Diaz, M., Acosta, S., Jauregui, M., & Johnson, C. (1999). Maternal blood lead level during pregnancy in South Central Los Angeles. *Archives of Environmental Health, 54,* 151–157.

Rotheram-Borus, M. J., & Phinney, J. S. (1990). Patterns of social expectations among Black and Mexican-American children. *Child Development, 61,* 542–556.

Rothstein, R. (1998). Bilingual education: The controversy. *Phi Delta Kappan, 79,* 672.

Rousseau, J. J. (1911). *Emile* (B. Foxley, Trans.). London: Dent. (Original work published 1762.)

Rovee-Collier, C. K., Enright, M., Lucas, D., Fagan, J., & Gekoski, M. J. (1981). The forgetting of newly acquired and reactivated memories of 3-month-old infants. *Infant Behavior and Development, 4,* 317–331.

Rovee-Collier, C. K., & Fagen, J. W. (1981). The retrieval of memory in early infancy. *Advances in Infancy Research, 1,* 225–254.

Rovee-Collier, C. K., & Shyi, C. W. G. (1992). A functional and cognitive analysis of infant long-term retention. In M. L. Howe, C. J. Brainerd, & V. F. Reyna (Eds.), *Development of long-term retention* (pp. 456–494). New York: Springer-Verlag.

Rovet, J., Netley, C., Keenan, M., Bailey, J., & Stewart, D. (1996). The psychoeducational profile of boys with Klinefelter syndrome. *Journal of Learning Disabilities, 29,* 180–196.

Rowland, T. W. (1991). Effects of obesity on aerobic fitness in adolescent females. *American Journal of Diseases of Children, 145,* 764–768.

Royce, L. (1996, June 19). Grad's degree late, but sweet. *Danbury News-Times.*

Roysircar, G., & Maestas, M. L. (2002). Assessing acculturation and cultural variables. In S. Okazaki & K. S. Kurasaki (Eds.), *Asian American mental health: Assessment theories and methods* (pp. 77–94). New York: Kluwer.

Rubin, K. H., & Asendorpf, J. B. (1993). Social withdrawal, inhibition, and shyness in childhood: Conceptual and definitional issues. In K. H. Rubin & J. B. Asendorpf (Eds.), *Social withdrawal, inhibition, and shyness in childhood* (pp. 3–18). Hillsdale, NJ: Erlbaum.

Rubin, K. H., Bukowski, W., & Parker, J. G. (1998). Peer interactions, relationships, and groups. In W. Damon (Ed.), *Handbook of child psychology* (Vol. 3, pp. 619–700). New York: Wiley.

Rubin, K. H., LeMare, L. J., & Lollis, S. (1990). Social withdrawal in childhood: Developmental pathways to peer rejection. In S. R. Asher & J. D. Coie (Eds.), *Peer rejection in childhood* (pp. 217–249). New York: Cambridge University Press.

Ruble, D. N., & Dweck, C. S. (1995). Self-perceptions, person conceptions, and their development. In N. Eisenberg (Ed.), *Social development* (Vol. 15, pp. 109–139). Thousand Oaks, CA: Sage.

Ruble, D. N., & Martin, C. L. (1998). Gender development. In W. Damon (Ed.), *Handbook of child psychology* (Vol. 3, pp. 933–1016). New York: Wiley.

Ruble, D., Martin, C. L., & Berenbaum, S. (in press). Gender development. In W. Damon (Ed.), *Handbook of child psychology.* New York: Wiley.

Rudy, D., & Grusec, J. E. (2001). Correlates of authoritarian parenting in individualist and collectivist cultures and implications for understanding the transmission of values. *Journal of Cross-Cultural Psychology, 32,* 202–212.

Ruff, H. A. (1986). Components of attention during infants' manipulative exploration. *Child Development, 57,* 105–114.

Ruffman, T., Perner, J., Olson, D. R., & Doherty, M. (1993). Reflecting on scientific thinking: Children's understanding of the hypothesis–evidence relation. *Child Development, 64,* 1617–1636.

Runco, M. A. (1997). Is every child gifted? *The Roeper School, 19,* 220–224.

Runco, M. A. (1999). A longitudinal study of exceptional giftedness and creativity. *Creativity Research Journal, 12,* 161–164.

Runco, M. A., & Pritzker, S. R. (1999). *The encyclopedia of creativity.* San Diego, CA: Academic Press.

Russ, S. W. (1996). Development of creative process in children. In M. Runco (Ed.), *Creativity from childhood through adulthood: The developmental issues. New directions for child development* (pp. 31–42). San Francisco: Jossey-Bass.

Russell, S. T., & Joyner, K. (2001). Adolescent sexual orientation and suicide risk: Evidence from a national study. *American Journal of Public Health, 91,* 1276–1281.

Rutter, M. (2002). The interplay of nature, nurture, and developmental influences: The challenge ahead for mental health. *Archives of General Psychiatry, 59,* 996–1000.

Rutter, M. (2003). Genetic influences on risk and protection: Implications for understanding resilience. In S. S. Luthar (Ed.), *Resilience and vulnerability: Adaptation in the context of childhood adversities* (pp. 489–509). New York: Cambridge University Press.

Rutter, M., Dunn, J., Plomin, R., Simonoff, E., Pickles, A., Maughan, B., Ormel, J., Meyer, J., & Eaves, L. (1997). Integrating nature and nurture: Implications of person–environment correlations and interactions for developmental psychopathology. *Development and Psychopathology, 9,* 335–364.

Ryan, A. S. (1997). The resurgence of breastfeeding in the United States. *Pediatrics, 99,* 1–6.

Ryan, B. A., Adams, G. R., Gullotta, T. P., Weissberg, R. P., & Hampton, R. L. (1995). *The family-school connection.* Thousand Oaks, CA: Sage.

Ryan, R. M., & Grolnick, W. S. (1986). Origins and pawns in the classroom: Self-report and projective assessments of individual differences in children's perceptions. *Journal of Personality and Social Psychology, 50,* 550–558.

Ryan, S. A., Millstein, S. G., & Irwin, C. E. (1996). Puberty questions asked by early adolescents. *Journal of Adolescent Health, 19,* 145–152.

Rydell, A. M., Hagekull, B., & Bohlin, G. (1997). Measurement of two social competence aspects in middle childhood. *Developmental Psychology, 33,* 824–833.

Rymer, R. (1993). *Genie: A scientific tragedy.* New York: HarperPerennial.

Rys, G. S., & Bear, G. G. (1997). Relational aggression and peer relations: Gender and developmental issues. *Merrill-Palmer Quarterly, 43,* 87–106.

Saarni, C. (1984). An observational study of children's attempts to monitor their expressive behavior. *Child Development, 55,* 1504–1513.

Saarni, C., Mumme, D. L., & Campos, J. J. (1998). Emotional development: Action, communication, and understanding. In W. Damon (Ed.), *Handbook of child psychology* (Vol. 3, 237–310). New York: Wiley.

Sabogal, F., Marín, G., & Otero-Sabogal, R. (1987). Hispanic familism and acculturation: What changes and what doesn't? *Hispanic Journal of Behavioral Sciences, 9,* 397–412.

Sacks, C. H., & Mergendoller, J. R. (1997). The relationship between teachers' theoretical orientation toward reading and student outcomes in kindergarten children with different initial reading abilities. *American Educational Research Journal, 34,* 721–739.

Sacks, J. J., Smith, J. D., Kaplan, K. M., Lambert, D. A., Sattin, W., & Sikes, K. (1989). The epidemiology of injuries in Atlanta day-care centers. *Journal of the American Medical Association, 262,* 1641–1645.

Sacks, O. (1970). *The man who mistook his wife for a hat.* New York: Harper & Row.

Sadeh, A., Gruber, R., & Raviv, A. (2002). Sleep, neurobehavioral functioning, and behavior problems in school-age children. *Child Development, 73,* 405–417.

Sadeh, A., Raviv, A., & Gruber, R. (2000). Sleep patterns and sleep disruptions in school-age children. *Developmental Psychology, 36,* 291–300.

Sadker, M., & Sadker, D. (1986, March). Sexism in the classroom: From grade school to graduate school. *Phi Delta Kappan,* 512–515.

Sadker, M., & Sadker, D. (1994). *Failing at fairness: How America's schools cheat girls.* New York: Scribner.

Sadler, T. W. (2000). *Langman's medical embryology.* Philadelphia: Lippincott Williams & Wilkins.

Safer, D. J., & Krager, J. M. (1994). The increased rate of stimulant treatment for hyperactive/inattentive students in secondary schools. *Pediatrics, 94,* 462–464.

Saffran, J. R., Aslin, R. N., & Newport, E. L. (1996). Statistical learning by 8-month-old infants. *Science, 274,* 1926–1928.

Saffron, L. (1996). *What about the children?* New York: Wellington House.

Sagberg, R. (1999). Road accidents caused by drivers falling asleep. *Accident Analysis and Prevention, 31,* 639–649.

Sagi, A., & Hoffman, H. L. (1976). Empathic distress in the newborn. *Developmental Psychology, 12,* 15–176.

Sagrestano, L. M., McCormick, S. H., Paikoff, R. L., & Holmbeck, G. N. (1999). Pubertal development and parent–child conflict in low-income, urban, African American adolescents. *Journal of Research on Adolescence, 9,* 85–107.

Sahin, N. (1990). Research on Susam Sokagi, the Turkish coproduction. In Children's Television Workshop (Ed.), *Sesame Street research* (pp. 68–72). New York: Children's Television Workshop.

Sahlman, S. (2002). *Immigration to the US: 2002 Update.* Washington, DC: Population Resource Center.

Salazar, L. F., DiClemente, R. J., Wingood, G. M., Crosby, R. A., Harrington, K., Davies, S., Hook, E. W., & Oh, M. K. (2004). Self-concept and adolescents' refusal of unprotected sex: A test of mediating mechanisms among African American girls. *Prevention Science, 5,* 137–149.

Salihu, H. M., Boos, R., & Schmidt, W. (1997). A report on 158 cases of transcervical chorionic villus sampling. *Archives of Gynecology and Obstetrics, 259,* 91–95.

Salisbury, C. L., & Palombaro, M. M. (1998). Friends and acquaintances: Evolving relationships in an inclusive elementary school. In L. H. Meyer & H. Park (Eds.), *Making friends: The influence of culture and development* (Vol. 3, pp. 81–104). Baltimore, MD: Brookes.

Salovey, P., & Sluyter, D. J. (1997). *Emotional development and emotional intelligence.* New York: Basic Books.

Sameroff, A. J. (1987). The social context of development. In N. Eisenberg (Ed.), *Contemporary topics in developmental psychology* (pp. 273–291). New York: Wiley.

Sameroff, A. J. (1989). Principles of development and psychopathology. In A. J. Sameroff & R. N. Emde (Eds.), *Relationship disturbances in early childhood* (pp. 17–32). New York: Basic Books.

Sampaio, R. C., & Truwit, C. L. (2001). Myelination in the developing human brain. In C. A. Nelson & M. Luciana (Eds.), *Handbook of developmental cognitive neuroscience* (pp. 35–44). Cambridge, MA: MIT Press.

Sampson, E. E. (1989). The challenge of social change for psychology: Globalization and psychology's theory of the person. *American Psychologist, 44*, 914–921.

Samuels, C. A., & Ewy, R. (1985). Aesthetic perception of faces during infancy. *British Journal of Developmental Psychology, 3*, 221–228.

Samuels, H. R. (1980). The effect of an older sibling on infant locomotor exploration of a new environment. *Child Development, 51*, 607–609.

Samuelson, L. K., & Smith, L. B. (1998). Memory and attention make smart word learning. *Child Development, 69*, 94–104.

Sander, L. W., Julia, H. L., Stechler, G., & Burns, P. (1972). Continuous 24-hour interactional monitoring in infants reared in two caretaking environments. *Psychosomatic Medicine, 34*, 270–282.

Sanders, M. R., Cann, W., & Markie-Dadds, C. (2003). The triple P-positive parenting program: A universal population-level approach to the prevention of child abuse. *Child Abuse Review, 12*, 155–171.

Sands, R., Tricker, J., Sherman, C., Armatas, C., & Maschette, W. (1997). Disordered eating patterns, body image, self-esteem, and physical activity in preadolescent school children. *International Journal of Eating Disorders, 21*, 59–166.

Sandy, S. V., & Cochran, K. M. (2000). The development of conflict resolution skills in children: Preschool to adolescence. In M. Deutsch & P. T. Coleman (Eds.), *The handbook of conflict resolution: Theory and practice* (pp. 316–342). San Francisco: Jossey-Bass.

Sapienza, C., & Hall, J. G. (1995). Genome imprinting in human disease. In C. Scriver, A. Beaudet, W. Sly, and D. Valle (Eds.), *The metabolic and molecular basis of inherited disease* (7th ed., pp. 437–458). New York: McGraw Hill.

Sargent, J. D., & Dalton, M. (2001). Does parental disapproval of smoking prevent adolescents from becoming established smokers? *Pediatrics, 108*, 1256–1262.

Sattler, J. M. (2001). *Assessment of children: Cognitive applications.* San Diego, CA: Sattler.

Savin-Williams, R. C. (1995). An exploratory study of pubertal maturation timing and self-esteem among gay and bisexual male youths. *Developmental Psychology, 31*, 56–64.

Savin-Williams, R. C. (2003). Are adolescent same-sex romantic relationships on our radar screen? In P. Florsheim (Ed.), *Adolescent romantic relations and sexual behavior: Theory, research, and practical implications* (pp. 325–336). Mahway, NJ: Erlbaum.

Savin-Williams, R. C., & Cohen, K. M. (1996). Psychosocial outcomes of verbal and physical abuse among lesbian, gay, and bisexual youths. In R. C. Savin-Williams & K. M. Cohen (Eds.), *The lives of lesbians, gays, and bisexuals: Children to adults* (pp. 181–200). Fort Worth, TX: Harcourt Brace.

Savin-Williams, R. C., & Diamond, L. M. (1999). Sexual orientation. In W. K. Silverman & T. H. Ollendick (Eds.), *Developmental issues in the clinical treatment of children* (pp. 241–258). Boston: Allyn & Bacon.

Savin-Williams, R. C., & Esterberg, K. G. (2000). Lesbian, gay, and bisexual families. In D. H. Demo & K. R. Allen (Eds.), *Handbook of family diversity* (pp. 197–215). New York: Oxford University Press.

Scahill, L., & deGraft, J. A. (1997). Food allergies, asthma, and attention deficit hyperactivity disorder. *Journal of Child and Adolescent Psychiatric Nursing, 10*, 36–42.

Scaramella, L. V., Conger, R. D., & Simons, R. L. (1999). Parental protection influences and gender specific increases in adolescent internalizing and externalizing problems. *Journal of Research on Adolescence, 9*, 111–141.

Scarr, S. (1998). American child care today. *American Psychologist, 53*, 95–109.

Scarr, S., & McCartney, K. (1984). How people make their own environment: A theory of genotype–environment effects. *Child Development, 54*, 424–435.

Schaefer, C. E., & DiGeronimo, T. F. (1995, September). Understanding anger. *Child*, 48–55.

Schauble, L. (1990). Belief revision in children: The role of prior knowledge and strategies for generating evidence. *Journal of Experimental Child Psychology, 49*, 31–57.

Schebendach, J., & Shenker, I. R. (1992). Nutrition. In S. B. Friedman, M. Fisher, & S. K. Schonberg (Eds.), *Comprehensive adolescent health care* (pp. 206–212). St. Louis, MO: Quality Medical Publishing.

Scheel, K. R., & Westefeld, J. S. (1999). Heavy metal music and adolescent suicidality: An empirical investigation. *Adolescence, 34*, 253–273.

Scheier, L. M., Botvin, G. J., Griffin, K. W., & Diaz, T. (2000). Dynamic growth models of self-esteem and adolescent alcohol use. *Journal of Early Adolescence, 20*, 178–209.

Schepher-Hughes, N. (1987). Basic strangeness: Maternal estrangement and infant death. In C. Super (Ed.), *The role of culture in developmental disorders* (pp. 131–153). San Diego, CA: Academic Press.

Scher, M. S., Richardson, G. A., & Day, N. L. (2000). Effects of prenatal cocaine/crack and other drug exposure on electroencephalographic sleep studies at birth and one year. *Pediatrics, 105*, 39–48.

Schiff-Myers, N. (1988). Hearing children of deaf parents. In D. Bishop & K. Mogford (Eds.), *Language development in exceptional circumstances* (pp. 47–61). New York: Churchill Livingstone.

Schlosser, E. (2002). *Fast food nation: The dark side of the all-American meal.* New York: HarperCollins.

Schlottmann, A. (1999). Seeing it happen and knowing how it works: How children understand the relation between perceptual causality and underlying mechanisms. *Developmental Psychology, 35*, 303–317.

Schmader, T., Johns, M., & Barquissau, M. (2004). The costs of accepting gender differences: The role of stereotype endorsement in women's experience in the math domain. *Sex Roles, 50*, 835–850.

Schmidt, M. E., Demulder, E. K., & Denham, S. (2002). Kindergarten social–emotional competence: Developmental predictors and psychosocial implications. *Early Child Development and Care, 172*, 451–462.

Schmitt, R. E., & Vondracek, F. W. (1999). Breadth of interests, exploration, and identity development in adolescence. *Journal of Vocational Behavior, 55*, 298–317.

Schneider, B. (1993). *Children's social competence in context.* New York: Pergamon.

Schneider, K. (1997). Development of emotions and their expression in task-oriented situations in infants and preschool children. In U. C. Segerstrale & P. Molnar (Eds.), *Nonverbal communication: Where nature meets culture* (pp. 109–130). Hillsdale, NJ: Erlbaum.

Schneider, W., & Bjorklund, D. F. (1998). Memory. In W. Damon (Ed.), *Handbook of child psychology* (Vol. 2, pp. 467–521). New York: Wiley.

Schothorst, P. F., & van Engeland, H. (1996). Long-term behavioral sequelae of prematurity. *Journal of the American Academy of Child and Adolescent Psychiatry, 35*, 175–183.

Schuell, T. J. (1996). Teaching and learning in a classroom context. In R. C. Calfee & D. Berliner (Eds.), *Handbook of educational psychology* (pp. 726–764). New York: Macmillan.

Schultz, R. T., Wright, K., & Schleifer, M. (1986). Assignment of moral responsibility and punishment. *Child Development, 57*, 177–184.

Schur, E. A., Sanders, M., & Steiner, H. (2000). Body dissatisfaction and dieting in young children. *International Journal of Eating Disorders, 27*, 74–82.

Schuster, B., Ruble, D. N., & Weinert, F. E. (1998). Causal inferences and the positivity bias in children: The role of the covariation principle. *Child Development, 69*, 1577–1596.

Schutte, N. S., Malouff, J. M., Post-Gordon, J. C., & Rodasta, A. L. (1988). Effects of playing video games on children's aggressive and other behaviors. *Journal of Applied Social Psychology, 18*, 103–109.

Schwartz, C. E., Snidman, N., & Kagan, J. (1996). Early childhood temperament as a determinant of externalizing behavior in adolescence. *Development and Psychology, 8*, 527–537.

Schwartz, J. A., Gladstone, T. R. G., & Kaslow, N. J. (1998). Depressive disorders. In T. H. Ollendick & M. Hersen (Eds.), *Handbook of child psychopathology* (pp. 269–289). New York: Plenum.

Schwartz, K. D., & Fouts, G. T. (2003). Music preferences, personality style, and developmental issues of adolescents. *Journal of Youth and Adolescence, 32,* 205–213.

Schwartz, W. (1995). School dropouts: New information about an old problem. *ERIC Digest* (No. ED 386 515).

Schwebel, D. C., Plumert, J. M., & Pick, H. L. (2000). Integrating basic and applied developmental research: A new model for the twenty-first century. *Child Development, 71,* 222–230.

Schweder, R. A., Mahapatra, M., & Miller, J. G. (1987). Culture and moral development. In J. Kagan & S. Lamb (Eds.), *The emergence of morality in young children* (pp. 1–83). Chicago: University of Chicago Press.

Scopesi, A., Zanobini, M., & Carossino, P. (1997). Childbirth in different cultures: Psychophysical reactions of women delivering in US, German, French, and Italian hospitals. *Journal of Reproductive and Infant Psychology, 15,* 9–30.

Sebald, H. (1992). *Adolescence: A social psychological analysis.* Englewood Cliffs, NJ: Prentice-Hall.

Sedlak, A. J., & Broadhurst, D. D. (1996). *Executive summary of the Third National Incidence Study of Child Abuse and Neglect.* Washington, DC: US Department of Health and Human Services.

Sedlak, A. J., Finkelbor, D., Hammer, H., & Schultz, D. J. (2002). NISMART: National incidence studies of missing, abducted, runaway, and throwaway children. Washington, DC: US Department of Justice.

Segall, M. H., Dasen, P. R., Berry, J. W., & Poortinga, Y. H. (1990). *Human behavior in global perspective: An introduction to cross-cultural psychology.* New York: Pergamon.

Seidenberg, M. S. (1997). Language acquisition and use: Learning and applying probabilistic constraints. *Science, 275,* 1599–1603.

Seifer, R., & Schiller, M. (1995). The role of parenting sensitivity, infant temperament, and dyadic interaction in attachment theory and assessment. *Monographs of the Society for Research in Child Development, 60,* 146–174.

Seifer, R., Schiller, M., Sameroff, A. J., Resnick, S., & Riordan, K. (1996). Attachment, maternal sensitivity, and infant temperament during the first year of life. *Developmental Psychology, 32,* 12–25.

Seiffge-Krenke, I. (1993). Close friendship and imaginary companions in adolescence. *New Directions in Child Development, 60,* 73–87.

Seiffge-Krenke, I. (1997). The capacity to balance intimacy and conflict: Differences in romantic relationships between healthy and diabetic adolescents. In S. Shulman & W. A. Collins (Eds.), *Romantic relationships in adolescence* (pp. 53–68). San Francisco: Jossey-Bass.

Sell, M. A., Ray, G. E., & Lovelace, L. (1995). Preschool children's comprehension of a *Sesame Street* video tape: The effects of repeated viewing and previewing instructions. Educational Technology Research and Development, 43, 49–60.

Selman, R. L. (1980). *The growth of interpersonal understanding.* New York: Academic Press.

Selman, R. L., Beardslee, W., Schultz, L. H., Krupa, M., & Podorefsky, D. (1986). Assessing adolescent interpersonal negotiation strategies: Toward the integration of structural and functional models. *Developmental Psychology, 22,* 450–459.

Selman, R. L., Lavin, D. R., & Brion-Meisels, S. (1982). Troubled children's use of self-reflection. In F. C. Serafica (Ed.), *Social-cognitive development in context* (pp. 375–421). London: Methuen.

Serketich, W. J., & Dumas, J. E. (1997). Adults' perceptions of the behavior of competent and dysfunctional children based on the children's physical appearance. *Behavior Modification, 21,* 457–469.

Sessa, F. M., & Steinberg, L. (1991). Family structure and the development of autonomy during adolescence. *Journal of Early Adolescence, 11,* 38–55.

Shanahan, M. J., Mortimer, J. T., & Krueger, H. (2002). Adolescence and adult work in the twenty-first century. *Journal of Research on Adolescence, 12,* 99–120.

Sharpe, T. H., & Thomasina, H. (2003). Adolescent sexuality. *Family Journal Counseling and Therapy for Couples and Families, 11,* 210–215.

Shavinina, L. (1997). Extremely early high abilities, sensitive periods, and development of giftedness. *High Ability Studies, 8,* 247–258.

Shaw, D., & Winslow, E. B. (1997). Precursors and correlates of antisocial behavior from infancy to preschool. In D. M. Stoff & J. Breiling (Eds.), *Handbook of antisocial behavior* (pp. 148–158). New York: Wiley.

Shedler, J., & Block, J. (1990). Adolescent drug use and psychological health: A longitudinal inquiry. *American Psychologist, 45,* 612–630.

Sheehy, G. (1995). *New passages: Mapping your life across time.* New York: Random House.

Shelley-Sireci, L. M., & Ciano-Boyce, C. (2002). Becoming lesbian adoptive parents: An explanatory study of lesbian adoptive, lesbian birth, and heterosexual adoptive parents. *Adoption Quarterly, 6,* 33–43.

Shepard, L. A. (1997). Children are not ready to learn? The invalidity of school readiness testing. *Psychology in the Schools, 34,* 85–97.

Shepardson, D. P., & Pizzini, E. L. (1992). Gender bias in female elementary teachers' perceptions of the scientific ability of students. *Science Education, 76,* 147–153.

Sherrod, L. R., Haggerty, R. J., & Featherman, D. L. (1993). Introduction: Late adolescence and the transition to adulthood. *Journal of Research on Adolescence, 3,* 216–226.

Sherry, J. L. (2001). The effects of violent video games on aggression: A meta-analysis. *Human Communication Research, 27,* 409–431.

Shettles, L., & Rorvik, D. M. (1984). *How to choose the sex of your baby.* New York: Doubleday.

Shields, M. K., & Behrman, R. E. (2000). Children and computer technology: Analysis and recommendations. *Future of Children, 10,* 191–196.

Shifflett, K., & Cummings, E. M. (1999). A program for educating parents about the effects of divorce and conflict on children. *Family Relations, 48,* 79–89.

Shrum, W., Cheek, N. H., & Hunter, S. M. (1988). Friendship in school: Gender and racial homophily. *Sociology of Education, 61,* 227–239.

Shucard, D. W., Shucard, L. L., & Thomas, D. G. (1987). Sex differences in electrophysiological activity in infancy: Possible implications for language development. In S. U. Philips, S. Steele, & C. Tanz (Eds.), *Language, gender, and sex in a comparative perspective* (pp. 278–295). Cambridge, UK: Cambridge University Press.

Shulman, S., Kedem, P., Kaplan, K. J., Sever, I., & Braja, M. (1998). Latchkey children: Potential sources of support. *Journal of Community Psychology, 26,* 185–197.

Shulman, S., & Seiffge-Krenke, I. (2001). Adolescent romance: Between experience and relationships. *Journal of Adolescence, 24,* 417–428.

Shurkin, J. N. (1992). *Terman's kids.* Boston: Little, Brown.

Shute, N. (1997, November 10). No more hard labor. *U.S. News & World Report,* 92–95.

Shutt, E., Miller, M., Schreck, C., & Brown, N. (2004). Reconsidering the leading myths of stranger child abduction. *The Justice Professional, 17,* 127–134.

Shwe, H., & Markman, E. M. (1997). Young children's appreciation of the mental impact of their communicative signals. *Developmental Psychology, 33,* 630–636.

Sidebotham, P. (2000). Patterns of child abuse in early childhood: A cohort study of the "children of the nineties." *Child Abuse Review, 9,* 311–320.

SIECUS. (2001). *Issues and answers: Facts on sexuality education.* Washington, DC: Author.

Siegler, R. S. (1996). *Emerging minds: The process of change in children's thinking.* New York: Oxford University Press.

Siegler, R. S. (1998). *Children's thinking.* New York: Prentice-Hall.

Siegler, R. S., & Shipley, C. (1995). Variation, selection, and cognitive change. In T. Simon & G. Halford (Eds.), *Developing cognitive competence: New approaches to process modeling* (pp. 31–76). Hillsdale, NJ: Erlbaum.

Sigman, M., & Capps, L. (1997). *Children with autism: A developmental perspective.* Cambridge, MA: Harvard University Press.

Sigman, M., Beckwith, L., Cohen, S. E., & Parmelee, A. H. (1989). Stability in the biosocial development of the child born preterm. In M. H. Bornstein & N. A. Krasnegor (Eds.), *Stability and continuity in mental development* (pp. 29–42). Hillsdale, NJ: Erlbaum.

Signorella, M. L., Bigler, R. S., & Liben, L. S. (1998). A meta-analysis of children's memories for own-sex and other-sex information. *Journal of Applied Developmental Psychology, 18,* 429–445.

Signorella, M. L., & Liben, L. S. (1984). Recall and reconstruction of gender-related pictures: Effects of attitudes, task difficulty, and age. *Child Development, 55,* 393–405.

Silber, T. J. (1986). Anorexia nervosa in blacks and Hispanics. *International Journal of Eating Disorders, 5,* 121–128.

Silverberg, S. B., & Gondoli, D. M. (1996). Autonomy in adolescence: A contextual perspective. In G. R. Adams & R. Montemayor (Eds.), *Psychosocial development during adolescence* (Vol. 8, pp. 12–61). Thousand Oaks, CA: Sage.

Silverman, W. K., La Greca, A. M., & Wasserstein, S. (1995). What do children worry about? Worries and their relation to anxiety. *Child Development, 66,* 671–686.

Simeon, D. T., & Grantham-McGregor, S. (1990). Nutritional deficiencies and children's behavior and mental development. *Nutrition Research Reviews, 3,* 1–24.

Simmons, R. G., & Blyth D. A. (1987). *Moving into adolescence: The impact of pubertal change and school context.* New York: Aldine de Gruyter.

Simmons, R. G., Burgeson, R., Carlton-Ford, S., & Blyth, D. (1987). The impact of cumulative change in early adolescence. *Child Development, 58,* 1220–1234.

Simon, W., & Gagnon, J. H. (1986). Sexual scripts: Permanence and change. *Archives of Sexual Behavior, 15,* 97–120.

Simonoff, E., Elander, J., Holmshaw, J., Pickles, A., Murray, R., & Rutter, M. (2004). Predictors of antisocial personality: Continuities from childhood to adult life. *British Journal of Psychiatry, 184,* 118–127.

Simons, R. L., Johnson, C., & Conger, R. D. (1994). Harsh corporal punishment versus quality of parental involvement as an explanation of adolescent maladjustment. *Journal of Marriage and the Family, 56,* 591–607.

Simons-Morton, B. G., Taylor, W. C., Snider, S. A., & Huant, I. W. (1993). The physical activity of fifth-grade students during physical education classes. *American Journal of Public Health, 83,* 262–264.

Simonton, D. K. (1994). *Greatness: Who makes history and why.* New York: Guilford.

Simpson, J. L., & Elias, S. (1994). Fetal cells in maternal blood: Overview and historical perspective. *Annals of the New York Academy of Sciences, 731,* 1–8.

Singer, D. G., & Singer, J. L. (2001). *Handbook of children and the media.* Thousand Oaks, CA: Sage.

Singer, L. T., Arendt, R., Minnes, S., Farkas, K., Salvator, A., Kirchner, H. L., & Kliegman, R. (2002). Cognitive and motor outcomes of cocaine-exposed infants. *Journal of the American Medical Association, 287,* 1952–1960.

Singer, L. T., Minnes, S., Short, E., Arendt, R., Farkas, K., Lewis, B., Klein, N., Russ, S., Min, M. O., & Kirchner, H. L. (2004). Cognitive outcomes of preschool children with prenatal cocaine exposure. *Journal of the American Medical Association, 291,* 2448–2456.

Singer, L. T., Salvator, A., Guo, S., Colling, M., Lilen, L., & Baley, J. (1999). Maternal psychological distress and parenting stress after the birth of a very low-birth-weight infant. *Journal of the American Medical Association, 28,* 799–805.

Singer, R. S. (1992). Physical activity and psychological benefits: A position statement of the International Society of Sport Psychology (ISSP). *The Sports Psychologist, 6,* 199–203.

Singer, W. (1995). Development and plasticity of cortical processing architectures. *Science, 270,* 758–764.

Singh, S., & Darroch, J. E. (1999). Trends in sexual activity among adolescent American women: 1982–1995. *Family Planning Perspectives, 31,* 211–219.

Sinha, R., Fisch, G., Teague, B., Tamborlane, W. V., Banyas, B., Allen, K., Savoye, M., Rieger, V., Taksali, S., Barbetta, G., Sherwin, R. S., & Caprio, S. (2002). Prevalence of impaired glucose tolerance among children and adolescents with marked obesity. *New England Journal of Medicine, 346,* 802–810.

Sizer, F., & Whitney, E. (1997). *Nutrition: Concepts and controversies.* Belmont, CA: West.

Skinner, B. F. (1957). *Verbal behavior.* New York: Appleton-Century-Crofts.

Skinner, E. A., & Wellborn, J. G. (1997). Children's coping in the academic domain. In S. A. Wolchik & I. N. Sandler (Eds.), *Handbook of children's coping* (pp. 387–422). New York: Plenum.

Skoe, E. E., & Gooden, A. (1993). Ethic of care and real-life moral dilemma content in male and female early adolescents. *Journal of Early Adolescence, 13,* 154–167.

Skoe, E. E., Hansen, K. L., Morch, W. T., Bakke, I., Hoffmann, T., Larsen, B., & Aasheim, M. (1999). Care-based moral reasoning in Norwegian and Canadian early adolescents: A cross-national comparison. *Journal of Early Adolescence, 19,* 280–291.

Skogstad, W. (2003). The importance of fathers. *Psychoanalytic Psychotherapy, 17,* 178–181.

Skuse, D., Wolke, D., & Reilly, S. (1992). Failure to thrive: Clinical and developmental aspects. In H. Remschmidt & M. H. Schmidt (Eds.), *Developmental psychopathology* (pp. 46–71). Goettingen, Germany: Hogrefe & Huber.

Slade, A., & Wolf, D. P. (1994). *Children at play: Clinical and developmental approaches to meaning and representation.* New York: Oxford University Press.

Slater, A., Mattock, A., Brown, E., & Bremner, G. J. (1991). Form perception at birth: Cohen and Younger revisited. *Journal of Experimental Child Psychology, 51,* 395–406.

Slavin, R. E. (1997). When does cooperative learning increase student achievement? In E. Dubinsky & D. Mathews (Eds.), *Readings in cooperative learning for undergraduate mathematics* (pp. 71–84). Washington, DC: The Mathematical Association of America.

Sleep, J. (1993). Physiology and management of the second stage of labor. In V. R. Bennett & L. K. Brown (Eds.), *Myles textbook for midwives* (pp. 199–215). London: Churchill Livingstone.

Slep, A. M. S., & O'Leary, S. G. (2001). Examining partner and child abuse: Are we ready for a more integrated approach to family violence? *Clinical Child and Family Psychology Review, 4,* 87–107.

Slotkin, T. A., Kudlacz, E. M., Hou, Q. C., & Seidler, F. J. (1990). Maturation of the sympathetic nervous system: Role in neonatal physiological adaptations and in cellular development of peripheral tissues. In J. M. Cuezva, A. M. Pascual-Leone, & M. S. Patel (Eds.), *Endocrine and biochemical development of the fetus and neonate* (pp. 67–75). New York: Plenum.

Slotkin, T. A., & Seidler, F. J. (1989). Catecholamines and stress in the newborn. In O. Zinder & S. Berznitz (Eds.), *Molecular biology of stress* (pp. 133–142). New York: A. R. Liss.

Small, M. Y. (1990). *Cognitive development.* San Diego, CA: Harcourt Brace Jovanovich.

Smetana, J. G. (1988). Adolescents' and parents' conceptions of parental authority. *Child Development, 59,* 321–335.

Smetana, J. G. (2000). Middle-class African American adolescents' and parents' conceptions of parental authority and parenting practices: A longitudinal investigation. *Child Development, 71,* 1672–1686.

Smetana, J. G. (2002). Culture, autonomy, and personal jurisdiction in adolescent–parent relationships. *Advances in Child Development and Behavior, 29,* 51–87.

Smetana, J. G., & Gaines, C. (1999). Adolescent–parent conflict in middle-class African American families. *Child Development, 70,* 1447–1463.

Smith, A. E., Jussim, L., & Eccles, J. S. (1999). Do self-fulfilling prophecies accumulate, dissipate, or remain stable over time? *Journal of Personality and Social Psychology, 77,* 548–565.

Smith, B. A., & Blass, E. M. (1996). Taste-mediated calming in premature, preterm, and full-term human infants. *Developmental Psychology, 32,* 1084–1089.

Smith, F. (1992). Learning to read: The never-ending debate. *Phi Delta Kappan, 74,* 432–441.

Smith, G. A., Bowman, M. J., Luria, J. W., & Shields, B. J. (1997). Baby-walker-related injuries continue despite warning labels and public education. *Pediatrics, 100,* 1–7.

Smith, G. A., & Shields, B. J. (1998). Trampoline-related injuries to children. *Archives of Pediatric and Adolescent Medicine, 152,* 694–699.

Smith, P. K., & Green, M. (1974). Aggressive behavior in English nurseries and playgroups: Sex differences and response of adults. *Child Development, 45,* 211–214.

Smitsman, A. W. (2001). Action in infancy—perspective, concepts, and challenges: The development of reaching and grasping. In G. Bremner & A. Fogel (Eds.), *Blackwell handbook of infant development* (pp. 71–98). Malden, MA: Blackwell.

Smokowski, P. R., Reynolds, A. J., & Bezruczko, N. (1999). Resilience and protective factors in adolescence: An autobiographical perspective from disadvantaged youth. *Journal of School Psychology, 37,* 425–448.

Smolin, L. A., & Grosvenor, M. B. (2000). *Nutrition: Science and applications.* Fort Worth, TX: Saunders.

Smulders, B. (1999). *The Dutch midwivery system.* Camperdown, Australia: Birth International.

Snarey, J. R. (1985). Cross-cultural universality of social–moral development: A critical review of Kohlbergian research. *Psychological Bulletin, 92,* 202–232.

Snow, C. E. (1990). Building memories: The ontogeny of autobiography. In D. Cicchetti & M. Beeghly (Eds.), *The self in transition* (pp. 213–242). Chicago: University of Chicago Press.

Snow, C. W. (1989). *Infant development.* Englewood Cliffs, NJ: Prentice-Hall.

Snyder, H. N. (1996). The juvenile court and delinquency cases. *The Future of Children, 6,* 53–63.

Snyder, J., & Stoolmiller, M. (2002). Reinforcement and coercion mechanisms in the development of antisocial behavior: The family. In G. R. Patterson & J. B. Reid (Eds.), *Antisocial behavior in children and adolescents: A developmental analysis and model for intervention* (pp. 65–100). Washington, DC: American Psychological Association.

Soberon, H. (1996). *Latino, Hispanic, both, neither?* Gainesville: University of Florida.

Socolar, R. R. S., & Stein, R. E. K. (1996). Maternal discipline of young children: Context, belief, and practice. *Journal of Developmental and Behavioral Pediatrics, 17,* 1–8.

Solis, J. (1995). The status of Latino children and youth: Challenges and prospects. In R. E. Zambrama (Ed.), *Understanding Latino families* (pp. 62–84). Thousand Oaks, CA: Sage.

Sonenstein, F. L., Ku, L., Lindberg, L. D., Turner, C. F., & Pleck, J. H. (1998). Changes in sexual behavior and condom use among teenaged males. *American Journal of Public Health, 88,* 956–959.

Soriano, F. I. (1994). U.S. Latinos. In L. D. Eron, J. H. Gentry, & P. Schlegel (Eds.), *Reason to hope: A psychosocial perspective on violence and youth* (pp. 119–132). Washington, DC: American Psychological Association.

Sotos, J. F. (1997). Genetic-disorder with overgrowth. *Clinical Pediatrics, 36,* 37–49.

Spear, L. P. (2000). Modeling adolescent development and alcohol use in animals. *Alcohol Research and Health, 24,* 115–123.

Spear, L. P. (2002a). The adolescent brain and age-related behavioral manifestations. *Neuroscience and Biobehavioral Reviews, 24,* 417–463.

Spear, L. P. (2002b). The adolescent brain and the college drinker: Biological basis of propensity to use and misuse alcohol. *Journal of Studies on Alcohol, 14,* 71–81.

Spear-Swerling, L., & Sternberg, R. J. (1994). The road not taken: An integrative theoretical model of reading disability. *Journal of Learning Disabilities, 27,* 91–103.

Spelke, E. S. (1992). Origins of knowledge. *Psychological Review, 99,* 605–632.

Spelke, E. S., Breinlinger, K., Macomber, J., & Jacobson, K. (1992). Origins of knowledge. *Psychological Review, 99,* 605–632.

Spelke, E. S., & Hespos, S. J. (2002). Conceptual development in infancy: The case of containment. In N. L. Stein et al. (Eds.), *Representation, memory, and development: Essays in honor of Jean Mandler* (pp. 223–246). Mahwah, NJ: Erlbaum.

Spelke, E. S., & von Hofsten, C. (2001). Predictive reaching for occluded objects by 6-month-old infants. *Journal of Cognition and Development, 2,* 261–281.

Spencer, M. B. (1990). Development of minority children: An introduction. *Child Development, 61,* 267–269.

Spencer, M. B., & Markstrom-Adams, C. (1990). Identity processes among racial and ethnic minority children in America. *Child Development, 61,* 290–310.

Spoth, R. L., Redmond, D., Trudeau, L., & Shin, C. (2002). Longitudinal substance initiation outcomes for a universal preventive intervention combining family and school programs. *Psychology of Addictive Behaviors, 16,* 129–134.

Sprafkin, J., Gadow, K. D., & Abelman, R. (1992). *Television and the exceptional child: A forgotten audience.* Hillsdale, NJ: Erlbaum.

Sprague, J., Sugai, G., & Walker, H. (1998). Antisocial behavior in schools. In T. S. Watson & F. M. Gresham (Eds.), *Handbook of child behavior therapy* (pp. 451–474). New York: Plenum.

Sroufe, L. A. (1977). *Knowing and enjoying your baby.* Englewood Cliffs, NJ: Prentice-Hall.

Sroufe, L. A. (2002). From infant attachment to promotion of adolescent autonomy. In S. L. Ramey & J. G. Borkowski (Eds.), *Parenting and the child's world: Influences on academic, intellectual, and social-emotional development* (pp. 187–202). Mahwah, NJ: Erlbaum.

Sroufe, L. A., Bennett, C., Englund, M., & Urban, J. (1993). The significance of gender boundaries in preadolescence: Contemporary correlates and antecedents of boundary violation and maintenance. *Child Development, 64,* 455–466.

Sroufe, L. A., Carlson, E. A., Levy, A. K., & Egeland, B. (2003). Implications of attachment theory for developmental psychopathology. In M. E. Hertzig & E. A. Farber (Eds.), *Annual progress in child psychiatry and child development* (pp. 43–61). New York: Brunner-Routledge.

Sroufe, L. A., & Waters, E. (1976). The ontogenesis of smiling and laughing: A perspective on the organization of development in infancy. *Psychological Review, 83,* 173–189.

Sroufe, L. A., & Waters, E. (1977). Attachment as an organizational construct. *Child Development, 48,* 1184–1199.

St. James-Roberts, I. (1993). Infant crying: Normal development and persistent crying. In I. St. James-Roberts, G. Harris, & D. Messer (Eds.), *Infant crying, feeding, and sleeping* (pp. 7–25). London: Harvester Wheatsheaf.

St. James-Roberts, I., & Halil, T. (1991). Infant crying patterns in the first year: Normative and clinical findings. *Journal of Child Psychology and Psychiatry, 32,* 951–968.

St. James-Roberts, I., & Plewis, I. (1996). Individual differences, daily fluctuations, and developmental changes in amounts of infant waking, fussing, crying, feeding, and sleeping. *Child Development, 67,* 2527–2540.

Stack, D. M., & LePage, D. E. (1996). Infants' sensitivity to manipulations of maternal touch during face-to-face interactions. *Social Development, 5,* 41–55.

Stafford, L., & Bayer, C. L. (1993). *Interaction between parents and children.* Newbury Park, CA: Sage.

Stang, H. J., Snellman, L. W., Condon, L. M., Conroy, M. M., Liebo, R., Brodersen, L., & Gunnar, M. R. (1997). Beyond dorsal penile nerve block: A more humane circumcision. *Pediatrics, 100,* 1–6.

Stangor, C., & McMillan, D. (1992). Memory for expectancy-congruent and expectancy-incongruent information. *Psychological Bulletin, 111,* 42–61.

Stangor, C., & Ruble, D. N. (1989). Differential influences on gender schemata and gender constancy on children's information processing and behavior. *Social Cognition, 7,* 353–372.

Stanley, B. K., Weikel, W. J., & Wilson, J. (1986). The effects of father absence on interpersonal problem-solving skills of nursery school children. *Journal of Counseling and Development, 64,* 383–385.

Stanley, J. C., & Benbow, C. P. (1982). Huge sex ratios at upper end. *American Psychologist, 37,* 972.

Stanley, J. C., & Benbow, C. P. (1983). SMPY's first decade: Ten years of posing problems and solving them. *Journal of Special Education, 17,* 11–25.

Stark, K. D., Rouse, L. W., & Kurowski, C. (1994). Psychological treatment approaches for depression in children. In W. M. Reynolds & H. F. Johnston (Eds.), *Handbook of depression in children and adolescents* (pp. 275–307). New York: Plenum.

State vs. *Michaels,* Superior Court, Essex County (New Jersey, 1988).

Status of Women Council. (1994). *Girls and science.* Yellowknife, NWF: Author.

Steele, C. M. (1997). A threat in the air: How stereotypes shape intellectual identity and performance. *American Psychologist, 52,* 613–629.

Steele, C. M., & Aronson, J. A. (1995). Stereotype threat and the intellectual test performance of African Americans. *Journal of Personality and Social Psychology, 69,* 797–811.

Steffe, L. P., & Gale, J. E. (1995). *Constructivism in education.* Hillsdale, NJ: Erlbaum.

Stein, D. M., & Reichert, P. (1990). Extreme dieting behaviors in early adolescence. *Journal of Early Adolescence, 10,* 108–121.

Stein, M. T., Bennett, F. C., & Abbott, M. B. (2004). Early delay in motor development. *Journal of Developmental and Behavioral Pediatrics, 22,* 93–98.

Stein, N. L., & Trabasso, T. (1989). Children's understanding of changing emotional states. In C. Saarni & P. L. Harris (Eds.), *Children's understanding of emotion* (pp. 50–77). New York: Cambridge University Press.

Steinberg, L. (1989). Pubertal maturation and parent–adolescent distance. In G. R. Adams & R. Montemayor (Eds.), *Biology of adolescent behavior and development* (pp. 71–97). Newbury Park, CA: Sage.

Steinberg, L. (1990). Autonomy, conflict, and harmony in the family relationship. In S. S. Feldman & G. R. Elliot (Eds.), *At the threshold* (pp. 255–276). Cambridge, MA: Harvard University Press.

Steinberg, L. (2001). We know some things: Parent-adolescent relationships in retrospect and prospect. *Journal of Research on Adolescence, 11,* 1–19.

Steinberg, L., Fegley, S., & Dornbusch, S. M. (1993). Negative impact of part-time work on adolescent adjustment: Evidence from a longitudinal study. *Developmental Psychology, 29,* 171–180.

Steinberg, L., Mounts, N. S., Lamborn, S. D., & Dornbusch, S. M. (1991). Authoritative parenting and adolescent adjustment across varied ecological niches. *Journal of Research on Adolescence, 1,* 19–36.

Steiner, H., McQuivey, R. W., Pavelski, R., Pitts, T., & Kraemer, H. (2000). Adolescents and sports: Risk or benefit? *Clinical Pediatrics, 39,* 161–166.

Steinhausen, H. C., Meier, M., & Angst, J. (1998). The Zurich long-term outcome study of child and adolescent psychiatric disorders in males. *Psychological Medicine, 28,* 275–383.

Stephens, M. B., Montefalcon, R., & Lane, D. A. (2000). The maternal perspective on prenatal ultrasound. *Journal of Family Practice, 49,* 601–604.

Stern, D. (1992). *Diary of a baby.* New York: Basic Books.

Sternberg, R. J. (1985). *Beyond IQ.* New York: Cambridge University Press.

Sternberg, R. J., & Wagner, R. K. (1993). The g-ocentric view of intelligence and job performance is wrong. *Current Directions in Psychological Science, 2,* 1–5.

Stevenson, H. W. (1998a). Cultural interpretations of giftedness: The case of East Asia. In R. C. Friedman & K. B. Rogers (Eds.), *Talent in context* (pp. 61–77). Washington, DC: American Psychological Association.

Stevenson, H. W. (1998b). A study of three cultures: Germany, Japan, and the United States. *Phi Delta Kappan, 79,* 524–529.

Stevenson, H. W., Chen, C., & Lee, S. (1992). Chinese families. In J. L. Roopnarine & D. B. Carter (Eds.), *Parent–child socialization in diverse cultures* (pp. 17–34). Norwood, NJ: Ablex.

Stevenson, H. W., Chen, C., & Lee, S. (1993). Mathematics achievement in Chinese, Japanese, and American children. *Science, 259,* 53–58.

Stevenson, H. W., Chen, C., & Uttal, D. (1990). Beliefs and achievement: A study of black, white, and Hispanic children. *Child Development, 61,* 508–523.

Stevenson, H. W., Hofer, B. K., & Randel, B. (2000). Mathematics achievement and attitudes about mathematics in China and the West. *Journal of Psychology in Chinese Societies, 1,* 1–16.

Stevenson, H. W., & Lee, S. (1990). Contexts of achievement. *Monographs of the Society for Research in Child Development, 55* (Whole No. 221). Chicago: University of Chicago Press.

Stevenson, H. W., Lee, S., & Mu, X. (2000). Successful achievement in mathematics: China and the United States. In P. G. Heymans & C. F. M. Lieshout (Eds.), *Developing talent across the life span* (pp. 167–183). Philadelphia: Psychology Press.

Stevenson, H. W., & Stigler, J. W. (1992). *The learning gap.* New York: Summit Books.

Stevenson, H. W., Lee, S., & Mu, X. (2000). Successful achievement in mathematics: China and the United States. In C. F. M. van Lieshout & P. G. Heymans (Eds.), *Developing talent across the life span* (pp. 167–183). Philadelphia: Psychology Press.

Stevens-Simon, C., & McAnarney, E. R. (1996). Adolescent pregnancy. In R. J. DiClemente & W. B. Hansen (Eds.), *Handbook of adolescent health risk behavior* (pp. 313–332). New York: Plenum.

Stipek, D. J. (1981). Children's perceptions of their own and their classmates' ability. *Journal of Educational Psychology, 73,* 404–410.

Stipek, D. J. (1997). Success in school—for a head start in life. In J. Burack & S. S. Luthar (Eds.), *Developmental psychopathology: Perspectives on adjustment; risk, and disorder* (pp. 75–92). New York: Cambridge University Press.

Stipek, D. J., Recchia, S., & McClintic, S. (1992). Self-evaluation in young children. *Monographs of the Society for Research in Child Development, 57* (Whole No. 226). Chicago: University of Chicago Press.

Stockhammer, T. F., Salzinger, S., Feldman, R. S., & Mojica, E. (2001). Assessment of the effect of physical child abuse within an ecological framework: Measurement issues. *Journal of Community Psychology, 29,* 319–344.

Stone, M. R., & Brown, B. B. (1999). Identity claims and projections: Descriptions of self and crowds in secondary school. In J. A. McLellan & M. J. V. Pugh (Eds.), *The role of peer groups in adolescent social identity: Exploring the importance of stability and change* (pp. 7–20). San Francisco: Jossey-Bass.

Stores, G. (1999). Children's sleep disorders: *Modern approaches. Developmental Medicine and Child Neurology, 41,* 568–573.

Straus, M. A., & Donnelly, D. A. (1994). *Beating the devil out of them: Corporal punishment in American families.* New York: Lexington Books.

Strauss, R., & Goldberg, W. A. (1999). Self and possible selves during the transition to fatherhood. *Family Psychology, 13,* 244–259.

Strauss, R. S. (2000). Childhood obesity and self-esteem. *Pediatrics, 105,* 1–5.

Strauss, R. S., & Pollack, H. A. (2001). Epidemic increase in Childhood overweight. *Journal of the American Medical Association, 286,* 2845–2848.

Strauss, S. (1998). Cognitive development and science education: Toward a middle level model. In W. Damon (Ed.), *Handbook of child psychology* (Vol. 4, pp. 357–399). New York: Wiley.

Straussner, J. H., & Straussner, S. L. A. (1997). Impact of community and school violence on children. In N. K. Phillips & S. L. A. Straussner (Eds.), *Children in the urban environment* (pp. 61–77). Springfield, IL: Thomas.

Streissguth, A. P. (1997). *Fetal alcohol syndrome.* Baltimore: Brookes.

Streissguth, A. P., Bookstein, F. L., Barr, H. M., Sampson, P. D., O'Malley, K., & Young, J. K. (2004). Risk factors for adverse life outcomes in fetal alcohol syndrome and fetal alcohol effects. *Journal of Developmental and Behavioral Pediatrics, 25,* 228–238.

Strelau, J. (1994). The concepts of arousal and arousability as used in temperament studies. In J. E. Bates & T. D. Wachs (Eds.), *Temperament: Individual differences at the interface of biology and behavior* (pp. 117–143). Washington, DC: American Psychological Association.

Striefel, S., Robinson, M. A., & Truhn, P. (1998). Dealing with child abuse and neglect within a comprehensive family-support program. In J. R. Lutzker (Ed.), *Handbook of child abuse and treatment* (pp. 267–289). New York: Plenum.

Stringer, P. (1998). One night Vygotsky had a dream: Implications for educational psychologists. *Educational and Child Psychology, 15,* 14–20.

Strom, R., Strom, S., Strom, P., & Collinsworth, P. (1994). Parent competence in families with gifted children. *Journal for the Education of the Gifted, 18,* 39–54.

Stromswold, K. (2000). The cognitive neuroscience of language acquisition. In M. Gazzaniga (Ed.), *The new cognitive neurosciences* (2nd ed., pp. 897–932). Cambridge, MA: MIT Press.

Suarez-Orozco, C., & Suarez-Orozco, M. M. (1995). *Transformations: Immigration, family life, and achievement motivation among Latino adolescents.* Palo Alto, CA: Stanford University Press.

Suber, C. F. (1982). Separable effects of motives, consequences, and presentation order on children's moral judgments. *Developmental Psychology, 18,* 257–266.

Substance Abuse and Mental Health Services Administration. (2002). *Club drugs.* Washington, DC: Authors.

Suecoff, S. A., Avner, J. R., Chou, K. J., & Crain, E. F. (1999). A comparison of New York city playground hazards in high- and low-income areas. *Archives of Pediatrics & Adolescent Medicine, 153,* 363–366.

Summerfield, L. M. (2000). Promoting physical activity and exercise among children. Retrieved from http://www.kidsource.com/kidsource/content4/pormote.phyed.html

Super, C. M., & Harkness, S. (1991). The development of affect in infancy and childhood. In M. Woodhead & R. Carr (Eds.), *Becoming a person: Child development in social context* (Vol. 1, pp. 56–73). London: Routledge.

Surgeon General. (1996). *Physical activity and health.* Washington, DC: US Department of Health.

Susman, E. J., Koch, P. B., Maney, D. W., & Finkelstein, J. W. (1993). Health promotion in adolescence: Developmental and theoretical considerations. In R. M. Lerner (Ed.), *Early adolescence: Perspectives on research, policy, and intervention* (pp. 247–260). Hillsdale, NJ: Erlbaum.

Susman-Stillman, A., Kalkose, M., Egeland, B., & Waldman, I. (1996). Infant temperament and maternal sensitivity as predictors of attachment security. *Infant Behavior and Development, 19,* 33–47.

Sutton, A. J., Abrams, K. R., & Jones, D. R. (2001). An illustrated guide to the methods of meta-analysis. *Journal of Evaluation in Clinical Practice, 7,* 135–148.

Sutton, A. J., Lambert, P. C., Hellmich, M., Abrams, K. R., & Jones, D. R. (2000). Meta-analysis in practice. In D. A. Berry & D. K. Stangl (Eds.), *Meta-analysis in medicine and health policy* (pp. 359–390). New York: Marcel Dekker.

Sutton, H. E. (1988). *An introduction to human genetics.* San Diego, CA: Harcourt Brace Jovanovich.

Sutton-Smith, B. (1994). Does play prepare the future? In J. H. Goldstein (Ed.), *Toys, play, and child development* (pp. 130–146). Cambridge, UK: Cambridge University Press.

Sutton-Smith, B. (1998). *The ambiguity of play.* Cambridge, MA: Harvard University Press.

Swain, J. L., Stewart, T. A., & Leder, P. (1987). Parental legacy determines methylation and expression of autosomal transgene: A molecular mechanism for parental imprinting. *Cell, 50,* 719–727.

Swarr, A. E., & Richards, M. H. (1996). Longitudinal effects of adolescent girls' pubertal development, perceptions of pubertal timing, and parental relations on eating patterns. *Developmental Psychology, 32,* 636–646.

Swearer, S. M., Grills, A. E., Haye, K. M., & Cary, P. T. (2004). Internalizing problems in students involved in bullying and victimization. In D. L. Espelage & S. M. Swearer (Eds.), *Bullying in American schools* (pp. 63–84). Mahwah, NJ: Erlbaum.

Synnott, A. (1988). Little angels, little devils: A sociology of children. In G. Handel (Ed.), *Childhood socialization* (pp. 25–43). Hawthorne, NY: Aldine de Gruyter.

Szagun, G. (1992). Children's understanding of the feeling experience and causes of sympathy. *Journal of Child Psychology and Psychiatry, 33,* 1183–1191.

Szapocznik, J., & Kurtines, W. (1993). Family psychology and cultural diversity: Opportunities for theory, research, and application. *American Psychologist, 48,* 400–407.

Taffel, S. M., Placek, P. J., & Moien, M. (1989). Cesarean section rate levels off in 1987. *Family Planning Perspective, 21,* 227–228.

Tager-Flusberg, H. (1994). *Constraints on language acquisition: Studies of atypical children.* Mahwah, NJ: Erlbaum.

Takahashi, K. (1990). Are the key assumptions of the "Strange Situation" procedure universal? A view from Japanese research. *Human Development, 30,* 23–30.

Tamis-LeMonda, C. S., Bornstein, M. H., Cyphers, L., Toda, S., & Ogino, M. (1992). Language and play at one year: A comparison of toddlers and mothers in the United States and Japan. *International Journal of Behavioral Development, 15,* 33–45.

Tangney, J. P. (1990). Sharing shame and guilt. *Contemporary Social Psychology, 14,* 83–88.

Tangney, J. P. (1999). The self-conscious emotions: Shame, guilt, embarrassment, and pride. In T. Dalgleish & M. J. Power (Eds.), *Handbook of cognition and emotion* (pp. 541–568). New York: Wiley.

Tanner, J. M. (1975). Growth and endocrinology of the adolescent. In L. Gardner (Ed.), *Endocrine and genetic diseases of childhood* (pp. 77–121). Philadelphia: Saunders.

Tanner, J. M. (1978). *Physical growth from conception to maturity.* London: Open Books.

Tanner, J. M. (1989). *Fetus into man.* Cambridge, MA: Harvard University Press.

Tanner, J. M. (1991). Growth spurt, adolescent I. In R. M. Lerner, A. C. Petersen, & J. Brooks-Gunn (Eds.) *Encyclopedia of adolescence* (Vol. 1, pp. 277–303). New York: Garland.

Tanner, J. M., & Davies, P. S. (1985). Clinical longitudinal standards for height and height velocity for North American children. *Journal of Pediatrics, 107,* 317–329.

Tappan, M. B. (1998). Sociocultural psychology and caring pedagogy: Exploring Vygotsky's "hidden curriculum." *Educational Psychologist, 33,* 23–33.

Taras, H. L., Sallis, J. F., Patterson, T. L., Nader, P. R., (1989). Televisions' influence on children's diet and physical activity. *Journal of Developmental and Behavioral Pediatrics, 10,* 176–180.

Tarrant, M. (2002). Adolescent peer groups and social identity. *Social Development, 11,* 110–123.

Tarrant, M., North, A. C., & Hargreaves, D. J. (2000). English and American adolescents' reasons for listening to music. *Psychology of Music, 28,* 166–173.

Tarullo, L. B., Zill, N., Resnick, G., Kim, K., O'Donnell, K., Sorongon, A., McKey, R. H., Samant, S. P., O'Brien, R., D'Elio, M. A., & Vaden-Kiernan, M. (2003). *Head Start FACES 2000: A whole-child perspective on program performance.* Washington, DC: Administration for Children and Families, US Department of Health and Human Services.

Tasker, F. (2002). Lesbian and gay parenting. In A. Coyle & C. Kitzinger (Eds.), *Lesbian and gay psychology: New perspectives* (pp. 81–97). Malden, MA: Blackwell.

Tatzer, E., Schubert, M. T., Timischl, W., & Simbruner, G. (1985). Discrimination of taste and preference for sweet in premature babies. *Early Human Development, 12,* 23–30.

Taubman, B. (1997). Toilet training and toileting refusal for stool only: A prospective study. *Pediatrics, 99,* 54–58.

Taylor, E. (1995). Dysfunctions of attention. In D. Cicchetti & D. J. Cohen (Eds.), *Developmental psychopathology* (Vol. 2, pp. 243–273). New York: Wiley.

Taylor, H. G., Klein, N., & Hack, M. (1994). Academic functioning in < 750 gm birthweight children who have normal cognitive abilities: Evidence for specific learning disabilities. *Pediatric Research, 35,* 289.

Taylor, J. A., & Bell, D. A. (1998). *Gene–gene–environment: New insight into smoking-induced bladder cancer.* Washington, DC: NIEHS.

Taylor, M., & Carlson, S. M. (1997). The relation between individual differences in fantasy and theory of mind. *Child Development, 68,* 436–455.

Taylor, M., & Hort, B. C. (1990). Can children be trained to make the appearance–reality distinction? *Cognitive Development, 5,* 89–99.

Taylor, R. D. (1995). Social contextual influence on family relations: Adolescent adjustment and competence in African-American families. In M. L. Maher & P. R. Pintrich (Eds.), *Advances in motivation and achievement* (Vol. 9, 229–253). Greenwich, CT: JAI Press.

Teale, W. H., & Sulzby, E. (1985). *Emergent literacy: Writing and reading.* Exeter, NH: Heinemann.

Tebes, J. K., Kaufman, J. S., Adnopoz, J., & Racusin, G. (2001). Resilience and family psychosocial processes among children of parents with serious mental disorders. *Journal of Child and Family Studies, 10,* 115–136.

Telama, R., Yang, X., Laakso, L., & Viikari, J. (1997). Physical activity in childhood and adolescence as predictors of physical activity in young adulthood. *American Journal of Preventive Medicine, 13,* 317–323.

Tellegen, A. (1988). The analysis of consistency in personality assessment. *Journal of Personality, 56,* 621–663.

Temple, E., Poldrack, R. A., Salidis, J., Deutsch, G. K., Tallal, P., Merzenich, M. M., & Gabrieli, J. (2001). Disrupted neural responses to phonological and orthographic processing in dyslexic children: An fMRI study. *Neuroreport: For Rapid Communication of Neuroscience Research, 12,* 299–307.

Terman, L. M. (1925). *Genetic studies of genius.* Stanford, CA: Stanford University Press.

Terman, L. M., & Oden, M. H. (1959). *The gifted group in midlife: Thirty-year follow-up of the superior child.* Stanford, CA: Stanford University Press.

Teti, D. M. (1992). Sibling interaction. In V. B. Van Hesselt & M. Hersen (Eds.), *Handbook of social development* (pp. 201–228). New York: Plenum.

Teti, D. M., Sakin, J. W., Kucera, K., Corns, K. M., & Eiden, R. D. (1996). And baby makes four: Predictors of attachment security among preschool-age firstborns during the transition to siblinghood. *Child Development, 67,* 579–596.

The Urban Institute. (2004). *Crossing borders: The impact of immigration.* Washington, DC: Author.

Thelen, E. (1989). Self-organization in developmental processes: Can systems approaches work? In M. Gunnar & E. Thelen (Eds.), *Systems in development* (Vol. 22, pp. 77–117). Hillsdale, NJ: Erlbaum.

Thelen, E., Corbetta, D., Kamm, K., Spencer, J. P., Schneider, K., & Zernicke, R. F. (1993). The transition to reaching: Mapping intention and intrinsic dynamics. *Child Development, 64,* 1058–1098.

Thelen, E., & Smith, L. B. (1994). *A dynamic systems approach to the development of cognition and action.* Cambridge, MA: MIT Press.

Thelen, E., & Smith, L. B. (1998). Dynamic systems theories. In W. Damon (Ed.), *Handbook of child psychology* (Vol. 1, pp. 563–633). New York: Wiley.

Thiedke, C. C. (2001). Sleep disorders and sleep problems in childhood. *American Family Physician, 63,* 277–284.

Thiedke, C. C. (2003). Nocturnal enuresis. *American Family Physician, 67,* 1499–1506.

Thoma, S. J., & Rest, J. R. (1999). The relationship between moral decision making and patterns of consolidation and transition in moral judgment development. *Developmental Psychology, 35,* 323–334.

Thoman, E. B. (1990). Sleeping and waking state in infants: A functional perspective. *Neuroscience and Biobehavioral Review, 14,* 93–107.

Thoman, E. B., & Whitney, M. P. (1989). Sleep states of infants monitored in the home: Individual differences, developmental trends, and origins of diurnal cyclicity. *Infant Behavior and Development, 12,* 59–75.

Thoman, E. B., & Whitney, M. P. (1990). Behavior states in infants: Individual differences and individual analyses. In J. Colombo & J. Fagen (Eds.), *Individual differences in infancy: Reliability, stability, prediction* (pp. 113–136). Hillsdale, NJ: Erlbaum.

Thomas, A., & Chess, S. (1970). The origins of personality. *Scientific American, 223,* 102–109.

Thomas, A., & Chess, S. (1977). *Temperament and development.* New York: Brunner/Mazel.

Thomas, A., & Chess, S. (1985). The behavioral study of temperament. In J. Strelau, F. Farley, & A. Gale (Eds.), *The biological bases of personality and behavior* (Vol. 1, pp. 213–225). Washington, DC: Hemisphere.

Thomas, A., Chess, S., & Birch, H. G. (1968). *Temperament and behavior disorders in childhood.* New York: New York University Press.

Thomas, J. R., & French, K. E. (1985). Gender differences across age in motor performance: A meta-analysis. *Psychological Bulletin, 98,* 260–282.

Thomas, K., Ricciardelli, L. A., & Williams, R. J. (2000). Gender traits and self-concept as indicators of problem eating and body dissatisfaction among children. *Sex Roles, 43*(7/8), 441–458.

Thomas, M. H. (2000). Abstinence-based programs for prevention of adolescent pregnancies. *Journal of Adolescent Health, 26,* 5–17.

Thomas, R. M. (1996). *Comparing theories of child development.* Belmont, CA: Wadsworth.

Thomas, R. M. (2000). *Comparing theories of child development.* Belmont, CA: Wadsworth.

Thompson, J. K., Heinberg, L. J., Altabe, M., & Tantleff-Dunn, S. (1999). *Exacting beauty: Theory, assessment, and treatment of body image disturbances.* Washington, DC: American Psychological Association.

Thompson, K. P. (1993). Media, music, and adolescents. In R. M. Lerner (Ed.), *Early adolescence: Perspectives on research, policy, and intervention* (pp. 407–418). Hillsdale, NJ: Erlbaum.

Thompson, R. A. (1990). Emotion and self-regulation. In R. A. Thompson (Ed.), *Socioemotional development: Nebraska symposium on motivation* (Vol. 36, pp. 383–483). Lincoln: University of Nebraska Press.

Thompson, R. A. (1991). Infant day care: Concerns, controversies, choices. In J. V. Lerner & N. L. Galambos (Eds.), *Employed mothers and their children* (pp. 9–36). New York: Garland.

Thompson, R. A. (1998). Early sociopersonality development. In W. Damon (Ed.), *Handbook of child psychology* (Vol. 3, pp. 25–104). New York: Wiley.

Thompson, R. A. (1999). Early attachment and later development. In J. Cassidy & P. R. Shaver (Eds.), *Handbook of attachment* (pp. 265–286). New York: Guilford.

Thompson, R. A., & Nelson, C. A. (2001). Developmental science and the media: Early brain development. *American Psychologist, 56,* 5–15.

Thornberry, T. P., Smith, C. A., & Howard, G. J. (1997). Risk factors for teenage fatherhood. *Journal of Marriage and the Family, 59,* 505–520.

Thornberry, T. P., Wei, E. H., Stouthamer-Loeber, M., & Dyke, J. V. (2000). *Teenage fatherhood and delinquent behavior.* Washinton, DC: Office of Juvenile Justice and Delinquency Prevention.

Thorne, B. (2001). Girls and boys together . . . but mostly apart: Gender arrangements in elementary schools. In R. Satow (Ed.), *Gender and social life* (pp. 153–166). Boston, Ma: Allyn & Bacon.

Thorne, B., & Luria, Z. (1986). Sexuality and gender in children's daily worlds. *Social Problems, 33,* 176–190.

Thornton, M. C., Chatters, L. M., Taylor, R. J., & Allen, W. R. (1990). Sociodemographic and environmental correlates of racial socialization by Black parents. *Child Development, 61,* 401–409.

Thorogood, P. (1997). *Embryos, genes, and birth defects.* New York: John Wiley.

Thorp, J. A., & Breedlove, G. (1996). Epidural analgesia in labor: An evaluation of risks and benefits. *Birth, 23,* 63–83.

Thorpe, K. J., Dragonas, T., & Golding, J. (1992). The effects of psychosocial factors on the mother's emotional well-being during early parenthood: A cross-cultural study of Britain and Greece. *Journal of Reproductive and Infant Psychology, 10,* 205–217.

Tiedemann, J. (2000). Parents' gender stereotypes and teachers' beliefs as predictors of children's concept of the mathematical ability in elementary school. *Journal of Educational Psychology, 92,* 144–151.

Tiggemann, M., & Wilson-Barrett, E. (1998). Children's figure ratings: Relationship to self-esteem and negative stereotyping. *International Journal of Eating Disorders, 23,* 83–88.

Tilford, C. A., Kuroda-Kawaguchi, T., Skaletsky, H., Rozen, S., Brown, L. G., Rosenberg, M., McPherson, J. D., Wylie, K., Sekhon, M., Kucaba, T. A., Waterston, R. H., & Page, D.C. (2001). A physical map of the human Y chromosome. *Nature, 409,* 943–945.

Tinsworth, D. K., McDonald, J. E. (2001). *Injuries and deaths associated with children's playground equipment.* Washington, DC: US Consumer Product Safety Commission.

Tobin-Richards, M. H., Boxer, A. M., & Petersen, A. C. (1983). The psychological significance of pubertal change: Sex differences in perceptions of self during early adolescence. In J. Brooks-Gunn & A. C. Petersen (Eds.), *Girls at puberty* (pp. 113–134). New York: Plenum.

Tomada, G., & Schneider, B. H. (1997). Relational aggression, gender, and peer acceptance: Invariance across culture, stability over time, and concordance among informants. *Developmental Psychology, 33,* 601–609.

Tomasello, M. (1992). The social bases of language acquisition. *Social Development, 1,* 67–87.

Tomasello, M. (1999). The cultural ecology of young children's interactions with objects and artifacts. In E. Winograd, R. Fivush, & W. Hirst (Eds.), *Ecological approaches to cognition: Essays in honor of Ulric Neisser, Emory symposia in cognition* (pp. 153–170). Mahwah, NJ: Erlbaum.

Tomasello, M., & Akhtar, N. (1995). Two-year-olds use pragmatic cues to differentiate reference to objects and actions. *Cognitive Psychology, 10,* 201–224.

Tomasello, M., & Mannie, S. (1985). Pragmatics of sibling speech to one-year-olds. *Child Development, 56,* 911–917.

Tomasello, M., Strosberg, R., & Akhtar, N. (1996). Eighteen-month-old children learn words in non-ostensive context. *Journal of Child Language, 23,* 157–176.

Tomlinson-Clarke, S. (2001). Education and identity within a psychological and sociocultural context. In N. K. Shimahara & I. Z. Holowinsky (Eds.), *Ethnicity, race, and nationality in education: A global perspective* (pp. 193–210). Mahwah, NJ: Erlbaum.

Torgan, C. (2002, June). Childhood obesity on the rise. *The NIH Word on Health,* 1–2.

Torney-Purta, J. (1992). Cognitive representations of the political system in adolescents: The continuum from pre-novice to expert. In H. Haste & J. Torney-Purta (Eds.), *The development of political understanding* (pp. 11–25). San Francisco: Jossey-Bass.

Torney-Purta, J. (1994). Dimensions of adolescents' reasoning about political and historical issues: Ontological switches, development processes, and situated learning. In M. Carretero & J. F. Voss (Eds.), *Cognitive and instructional processes in history and the social sciences* (pp. 103–122). Hillsdale, NJ: Erlbaum.

Torrance, E. P. (1966). *Torrance Tests of Creativity.* Princeton: Personnel Press.

Torrance, E. P. (1988). The nature of creativity as manifest in its testing. In R. Sternberg (Ed.), *The nature of creativity: Contemporary psychological perspectives* (pp. 43–75). New York: Cambridge University Press.

Torsheim, T., & Wold, B. (2001). School-related stress, school support, and somatic complaints: A general population study. *Journal of Adolescent Research, 16,* 293–303.

Toselli, M., Farneti, P., & Salzarulo, P. (1998). Maternal representation and care of infant sleep. *Early Development and Parenting, 7,* 73–78.

Travillion, K., & Snyder, J. (1993). The role of maternal discipline and involvement in peer rejection and neglect. *Journal of Applied Developmental Psychology, 14,* 37–57.

Treboux, D. A., & Bush-Rossnagel, N. A. (1991). Age differences in adolescent sexual behavior, sexual attitudes, and contraceptive use. In R. M. Lerner, A. C. Petersen, & J. Brooks-Gunn (Eds.), *Encyclopedia of adolescence* (pp. 1018–1021). New York: Garland.

Tremblay, R. E. (2001). The development of physical aggression during childhood and the prediction of later dangerousness. In G. Pinard & L. Pagani (Eds.), *Clinical assessment of dangerousness: Empirical contributions* (pp. 47–65). New York: Cambridge University Press.

Trent, K., & Crowder, K. (1997). Adolescent birth intentions, social disadvantage, and behavioral outcomes. *Journal of Marriage and the Family, 59,* 523–535.

Trice, A. D., & Rush, K. (1995). Sex-stereotyping in four-year-olds' occupational aspirations. *Perceptual and Motor Skills, 81,* 701–702.

Trickett, P. K., & Kuczynski, L. (1986). Children's misbehavior and parental discipline in abusive and non-abusive families. *Developmental Psychology, 57,* 115–123.

Trickett, P. K., & McBride-Chang, C. (1995). The developmental impact of different forms of child abuse and neglect. *Developmental Review, 15,* 331–337.

Trommsdorff, G. (1995). Person–context relations as developmental conditions for empathy and prosocial action: A cross-cultural analysis. In T. A. Kindermann & J. Valsiner (Eds.), *Development of person–context relations* (pp. 113–146). Hillsdale, NJ: Erlbaum.

Tronick, E. Z. (1989). Emotions and emotional communication in infants. *American Psychologist, 44,* 112–119.

Tschann, J. M., Adler, N. E., Irwin, C. E., Millstein, S. G., Turner, R. A., & Kegeles, S. M. (1994). Initiation of substance use in early adolescence: The roles of pubertal timing and emotional distress. *Health Psychology, 13,* 326–333.

Tucker, C. M., Zayco, R. A., Herman, K. C., Reinke, W. M., Trujillo, M., Carraway, K., Wallack, C., & Ivery, P. D. (2002). Teacher and child variables as predictors of academic engagement among low-income African American children. *Psychology in the Schools, 39,* 477–488.

Turiel, E. (1983). *The development of social knowledge: Morality and convention.* Cambridge, UK: Cambridge University Press.

Turiel, E. (1998). The development of morality. In W. Damon (Ed.), *Handbook of child psychology* (Vol. 3, pp. 863–932). New York: Wiley.

Turner Syndrome Society of the United States. (2001). *Resources and research.* Houston, TX: Author.

Turner, H. A., & Finkelhor, D. (1996). Corporal punishment as a stressor among youth. *Journal of Marriage and the Family, 58,* 155–166.

Uauy, R., & Peirano, P. (1999). Breast is best: Human milk is optimal food for brain development. *American Journal of Clinical Nutrition, 70,* 433–434.

Ullian, E. M., Sapperstein, S. K., Christopherson, K. S., & Barres, B. A. (2001). Control of synapse number by glia. *Science, 291,* 657–661.

Umana-Taylor, A. J. (2004). Ethnic identity and self-esteem: Examining the role of social context. *Journal of Adolescence, 27,* 139–146.

Umana-Taylor, A. J., & Fine, M. A. (2004). Examining ethnic identity among Mexican-origin adolescents living in the United States. *Hispanic Journal of Behavioral Sciences, 26,* 36–59.

Umana-Taylor, A. J., Yazedjian, A., & Bamaca-Gomez, M. (2004). Developing the ethnic identity scale using Eriksonian and social identity perspectives. *Identity, 4,* 9–38.

UNAIDS. (2002). Children on the brink, 2002: A joint report on orphan estimates and program strategies. New York: UNICEF.

Ungerer, J. A., Brody, L. R., & Zelazo, P. R. (1978). Long-term memory for speech in 2- to 4-week-old infants. *Infant Behavior and Development, 1,* 177–186.

UNICEF. (1993). *Psychosocial programme: Emergency in former Yugoslavia.* New York: Author.

UNICEF. (2001). *The state of the world's children.* New York: Author.

UNICEF. (2003). *Comparative analysis of child maltreatment in rich nations.* New York: Author.

Upchurch, D. M., Levy-Storms, L., Sucoff, C. A., & Aneshensel, C. S. (1998). Gender and ethnic differences in the timing of first sexual intercourse. *Family Planning Perspectives, 30,* 121–127.

Updegraff, K. A., & Obeidallah, D. A. (1999). Young adolescents' patterns of involvement with siblings and friends. *Social Development, 8,* 52–69.

Updegraff, K. A., Helms, H. M., McHale, S. M., Crouter, A. C., Thayer, S. M., & Sales, L. H. (2004). Who's the boss? Patterns of perceived control in adolescents' friendships. *Journal of Youth and Adolescence, 33,* 403–420.

Updegraff, K. A., McHale, S. M., Crouter, A. C., & Kupanoff, K. (2001). Parents' involvement in adolescents' peer relationships: A comparison of mothers' and fathers' role. *Journal of Marriage and the Family, 63,* 655–668.

Uranova, N. A., Vostrikov, V. M., Orlovskaya, D. D., & Rahmanova, V. I. (2004). Oligodendroglial density in the prefrontal cortex in schizophrenia and mental disorders: A study from the Stanley Neuropathology Consortium. *Schizophrenia Research, 67,* 269–275.

Urban Institute. (2000). *Child care patterns of school-age children with employed mothers.* Washington, DC: Author.

Urberg, K. A., Degirmencioglu, S. M., Tolson, J. M., & Halliday-Scher, K. (2000). Adolescent social crowds. *Journal of Adolescent Research, 15,* 427–455.

US Census Bureau. (2001a). *Home computers and Internet use in the US.* Washington, DC: US Census Bureau.

US Census Bureau. (2001b). *Living arrangements of children.* Washington, DC: Author.

US Census Bureau. (2001c). *Overview of race and Hispanic origin.* Washington, DC: Author.

US Census Bureau. (2001d). *Population projections of the United States.* Washington, DC: Author.

US Census Bureau. (2001e). *School enrollment, 1999.* Washington, DC: Author.

US Census Bureau. (2002). *Health insurance coverage: 2000.* Washington, DC: Author.

US Census Bureau. (2002). *Labor force, employment, and earnings.* Washington, DC: Author.

US Census Bureau. (2002). *Who's minding the kids?* Washington, DC: Author.

US Census Bureau. (2003). *America's families and living arrangements.* Washington, DC: Author.

US Census Bureau. (2003a). *School enrollment.* Washington, DC: Author.

US Census Bureau. (2004a). *Current population survey.* Washington, DC: Author.

US Census Bureau. (2004b). *Educational attainment in the US.* Washington, DC: Author.

US Consumer Product Safety Commission. (2001). *Scooter data.* Retrieved from http://www.cpsc.gov/pr/prscoot.html

US Department of Agriculture. *Dietary Guidelines for Americans.* (2000). Washington, DC: Author.

US Department of Agriculture. (2004). *The food guide pyramid for young children.* Washington, DC: Author.

US Department of Education. (1993). *Public school kindergarten teachers' views on children's readiness for school.* Washington, DC: Author.

US Department of Education. (1996). *Achievement of U.S. students in science, 1969 to 1994; mathematics, 1973 to 1994; reading, 1971 to 1994; writing, 1984 to 1994.* Washington, DC: Author.

US Department of Education. (1997). *Dropout rates in the United States: 1995.* Washington, DC: Author.

US Department of Education. (1998). *Kindergarten class of 1998–1999: Early Childhood Longitudinal Study.* Washington, DC: National Center for Education Statistics.

US Department of Education. (2000). *Implementation of the Individuals with Disabilities Education Act.* Washington, DC: Author.

US Department of Education. (2001). Elementary and secondary education: An international perspective. Washington, DC: Author.

US Department of Energy Human Genome Program. (2004). *DNA: The molecule of life.* Retrieved from http://www.ornl.gov/sci/techresources/Human_Genome/graphics/slides/01-0085jpg.shtml

US Department of Health and Human Services. (1999). *Child maltreatment 1998: Reports from the states to the National Child Abuse and Neglect Data System.* Washington, DC: Author.

US Department of Health and Human Services. (2001). *Trend in children's oral health.* Retrieved from http://www.mchoralhealth.org/PDFs/OHTrendsfactsheet.pdf

US Department of Health and Human Services. (2004). *Child maltreatment.* Washington, DC: Author.

US Department of Labor. (2000). *Report on the youth labor force.* Washington, DC: Author.

US Department of Labor. (2001). *Employment characteristics of families.* Washington, DC: Author.

US Department of Labor. (2004). *Women in the labor force.* Washington, DC: Author.

US Department of Transportation. (2004). *Traffic fatalities.* Washington, DC: Author.

US Environmental Protection Agency. (1992). *Respiratory health effects of passive smoking: Lung cancer and other disorders.* Washington, DC: Author.

US Environmental Protection Agency. (2004). *Asthma and indoor environments*. Washington, DC: Author.

US Food and Drug Administration. (2004, October 15). *Suicidality in children and adolescents being treated with antidepressant medications*. Washington, DC: Authors.

US Office of Special Education Programs: IDEA Part B child count. (2002). *Number served (ages 6 to 21), by disability and state*. Retrieved from http://www.ideadata.org/tables26th/ar_aa3/ htm

US Secret Service. (2000). *Report on the prevention of targeted violence in school*. Washington, DC: US Department of Treasury.

US State Department. (2000). *International adoptions*. Washington, DC: US Government Printing Office.

USDA. (1998). *Healthy eating index and nutrition information*. (1998). Washington, DC: Author.

Valdez, E. O. (1996). Chicano families and urban poverty: Familial strategies of cultural retention. In R. M. De Anda (Ed.), *Chicanas and Chicanos in contemporary society* (pp. 63–74). Boston: Allyn & Bacon.

Valdez, J. (1994, September 18). Teen pregnancy: Interviews and statistics. *Arizona Republic*.

Valent, F., Brusaferro, S., & Barbone, F. (2001). A case-crossover study of sleep and childhood injury. *Pediatrics, 107*, 1–7.

Van Beveren, T. T., Little, B. B., & Spence, M. J. (2000). Effects of prenatal cocaine exposure and postnatal environment on child development. *American Journal of Human Biology, 12*, 417–428.

van de Vijver, F. J. R., & Willemsen, M. E. (1993). Abstract thinking. In J. Altarriba (Ed.), *Cognition and culture* (pp. 317–342). Amsterdam: North-Holland.

van der Valk, J. C., van den Oord, E. J. C. G., Verhulst, F. C., & Boomsma, D. I. (2003). Genetic and environmental contributions to stability and change in children's internalizing and externalizing problems. *Journal of the American Academy of Child and Adolescent Psychiatry, 42*, 1212–1220.

Van Griffin, K., & Haith, M. M. (1984). Infant visual response to gestalt geometric forms. *Infant Behavior and Development, 7*, 335–346.

van IJzendoorn, M. H., Schuengel, C., & Bakermans, J. J. (1999). Disorganized attachment in early childhood: Meta-analysis of precursors, concomitants, and sequelae. *Development and Psychopathology, 11*, 225–249.

Van Naarden, K., Decoufle, P., & Caldwell, K. (2000). Prevalence and characteristics of children with serious hearing impairment in metropolitan Atlanta, 1991–1993. *Pediatrics, 106*, 616–617.

Vandell, D. L., & Wolfe, B. (2000). *Child care quality: Does it matter and does it need to be improved?* Washington, DC: US Government Printing Office.

Vandewater, E. A. (2004, October). *Media use and children's health*. Invited talk given at Arizona State University, Tempe, AZ.

Vandewater, E. A., Shim, M., & Caplovitz, A. G. (2004). Linking obesity and activity level with children's television and video game use. *Journal of Adolescence, 27*, 71–85.

Van-Evra, J. P. (1998). *Television and child development*. Mahwah, NJ: Erlbaum.

van-Laar, C. The paradox of low academic achievement but high self-esteem in African American students: An attributional account. *Educational Psychology Review, 12*, 33–61.

Vartanian, L. R. (1997). Separation—individuation, social support, and adolescent egocentrism. *Journal of Early Adolescence, 17*, 245–270.

Vartanian, L. R. (2000). Revising the imaginary audience and personal fable constructs of adolescent egocentrism. *Adolescence, 35*, 639–661.

Vartanian, L. R., & Powlishta, K. K. (1996). A longitudinal examination of the social–cognitive foundations of adolescent egocentrism. *Journal of Early Adolescence, 16*, 157–178.

Vasta, R., Knott, J., & Gaze, C. (1996). Can spatial training erase the gender differences on the water-level task? *Psychology of Women Quarterly, 20*, 549–567.

Vellutino, F. R. (1991). Introduction to three studies on reading acquisition: Convergent findings on theoretical foundations of code-oriented versus whole-language approaches to reading instruction. *Journal of Educational Psychology, 83*, 437–443.

Verbeek, P., Hartup, W. W., & Collins, W. A. (2000). Conflict management in children and adolescents. In F. Aureli & F. B. M. de Waal (Eds.), *Natural conflict resolution* (pp. 34–53). Berkeley: University of California Press.

Verhulst, F. C., Achenbach, T. M., Erol, N., Lambert, M. C., Leung, P. W. L., Silva, M., van der Ende, J., Zilber, N., & Zubrick, S. R. (2003). Comparisons of problems reported by youths from seven countries. *American Journal of Psychiatry, 160*, 1479–1485.

Verschueren, K., Buyck, P., & Marcoen, A. (2001). Self-representations and socioemotional competence in young children: A 3-year longitudinal study. *Developmental Psychology, 37*, 126–134.

Vik, T., Bakketeig, L. S., Trygg, K. U., Lund-Larsen, K., & Jacobsen, G. (2003). High caffeine consumption in the third trimester of pregnancy. *Paediatric and Perinatal Epidemiology, 17*, 324–331.

Villani, S. (2001). Impact of media on children and adolescents: A 10-year review of the research. *Journal of the American Academy of Child and Adolescent Psychiatry, 40*, 392–401.

Vitaro, F., Tremblay, R. E., & Bukowski, W. M. (2001). Friends, friendships and conduct disorders. In J. Hill & B. Maughan (Eds.), *Conduct disorders in childhood and adolescence. Cambridge child and adolescent psychiatry* (pp. 346–378). New York: Cambridge University Press.

Vitaro, F., Tremblay, R. E., Kerr, M., Pagant, L., & Bukowski, W. M. (1997). Disruptives, friends' characteristics, and delinquency in early adolescence: A test of two competing models of development. *Child Development, 68*, 676–689.

Vogt, C. J. (1999). A model of risk factors involved in childhood and adolescent obesity. In A. J. Goreczny & M. Hersen (Eds.), *Handbook of pediatric and adolescent health psychology* (pp. 221–234). Boston: Allyn & Bacon.

Volling, B. L., & Elins, J. L. (1998). Family relationships and children's emotional adjustment as correlates of maternal and paternal differential treatment. *Child Development, 69*, 1640–1656.

Volling, B. L., McElwain, N. L., Notaro, P., & Herrera, C. (2002). Parents' emotional availability and infant emotional competence: Predictors of parent–infant attachment and emerging self-regulation. *Journal of Family Psychology, 16*, 447–465.

Volling, B. L., Youngblade, L. M., & Belsky, J. (1997). Young children's social relationships with siblings and friends. *American Journal of Orthopsychiatry, 67*, 102–111.

von Hofsten, C. (1983). Catching skills in infancy. *Journal of Experimental Psychology: Human Perception and Performance, 9*, 75–85.

von Hofsten, C. (1984). Developmental changes in the organization of prereaching movements. *Developmental Psychology, 20*, 378–388.

von Hofsten, C., & Lindhagen, K. (1979). Observations of the development of reaching for moving objects. *Journal of Experimental Child Psychology, 28*, 158–173.

von Hofsten, C., & Spelke, E. S. (1985). Object permanence and object-directed reaching in infancy. *Journal of Experimental Psychology: General, 114*, 198–212.

von Hofsten, C., Vishton, P., Spelke, E. S., Feng, Q., & Rosander, K. (1998). Predictive action in infancy: Tracking and reaching for moving objects. *Cognition, 67*, 255–285.

von Kries, R., Koletzko, B., Sauerwald, T., von Mutius, E., Barnert, D., Grunert, V., & von Voss, H. (1999). Breast feeding and obesity: Cross sectional study. *British Medical Journal, 319*, 147–150.

Vygotsky, L. S. (1978). *Mind in society* (A. Blunden & N. Schmolze, Trans). Cambridge, MA: Harvard University Press. (Original work published 1930.)

Vygotsky, L. S. (1986). *Thought and language* (A. Kozulin, Trans.). Cambridge, MA: MIT Press. (Original work published 1934.)

Waas, G. A., & Graczyk, P. A. (1998). Group intervention for the peer-rejected child. In K. C. Stoiber & T. R. Kratochwill (Eds.), *Handbook of group intervention for children and families* (pp. 141–158). Boston: Allyn & Bacon.

Wachs, T. D. (1992). *The nature of nurture.* Newbury Park, CA: Sage.

Wachs, T. D. (1995). Relation of mild-to-moderate malnutrition to human development: Correlational studies. *Journal of Nutrition Supplement, 125,* 2245S–2254S.

Wachs, T. D., & King, B. (1994). Behavioral research in the brave new world of neuroscience and temperament: A guide to the biologically perplexed. In J. E. Bates & T. D. Wachs (Eds.), *Temperament: Individual differences at the interface of biology and behavior* (pp. 307–336). Washington, DC: American Psychological Association.

Wachs, T. D., & Kohnstamm, G. A. (2001). *Temperament in context.* Mahwah, NJ: Erlbaum.

Wagner, K. D., & Ambrosini, P. J. (2001). Childhood depression: Pharmacological therapy/treatment. *Journal of Clinical Child Psychology, 30,* 88–97.

Wahlstrom, K. L. (2002). Accommodating the sleep patterns of adolescents within current educational structures: An uncharted path. In M. A. Carskadon (Ed.), *Adolescent sleep patterns* (pp. 172–197). New York: Cambridge University Press.

Wakeley, A., Rivera, S., & Langer, J. (2000a). Can young infants add and subtract? *Child Development, 71,* 1525–1534.

Wakeley, A., Rivera, S., & Langer, J. (2000b). Not proved: Reply to Wynn. *Child Development, 71,* 1537–1539.

Walco, G. (1997). Growing pains (commentary). *Developmental and Behavioral Pediatrics, 18,* 107–108.

Waldman, S., & Springen, K. (1992). Too old, too fast? *Newsweek,* 80–88.

Walk, R. D., & Gibson, E. J. (1961). A comparative and analytical study of visual depth perception. *Psychological Monographs, 15* (Whole No. 519).

Walker, K., Taylor, E., McElroy, A., & Phillip, D. (1995). Familial and ecological correlates of self-esteem in African American children. In M. N. Wilson (Ed.), *African American family life: Its structural and ecological aspects* (pp. 23–34). San Francisco: Jossey-Bass.

Walker, L. J. (1988). The development of moral reasoning. *Annals of Child Development, 5,* 33–78.

Walker, L. J. (1989). A longitudinal study of moral reasoning. *Child Development, 60,* 157–166.

Walker, L. J. (1995). Sexism in Kohlberg's moral psychology? In W. M. Kurtines & J. L. Gewirtz (Eds.), *Moral development* (pp. 83–107). Boston: Allyn & Bacon.

Walker, L. J., & Henning, K. H. (1997). Moral development in the broader context of personality. In S. Hala (Ed.), *The development of social cognition* (pp. 297–327). Hove, UK: Psychology Press.

Walker, N. C., & O'Brien, B. (1999). The relationship between method of pain management during labor and birth outcomes. *Clinical Nursing Research, 8,* 119–134.

Wallander, J. L., Dekker, M., & Koot, H. M. (2003). Psychopathology in children and adolescents with intellectual disability: Measurement, prevalence, course, and risk. In L. M. Glidden (Ed.), *International review of research in mental retardation* (Vol. 26, pp. 93–134). San Diego, CA: Academic Press.

Wallerstein, J. S., & Corbin, S. B. (1999). The child and the vicissitudes of divorce. In R. M. Galatzer-Levy & L Krasu (Eds.), *The scientific basis of child custody decisions* (pp. 73–95). New York: Wiley.

Wallerstein, J. S., & Kelly, J. B. (1975). The effects of parental divorce: Experiences of the preschool child. *Journal of the American Academy of Child Psychiatry, 14,* 600–616.

Wallerstein, J. S., & Kelly, J. B. (1976). The effects of parental experiences of the child in later latency. *American Journal of Orthopsychiatry, 46,* 256–269.

Wallerstein, J. S., & Kelly, J. B. (1980). *Surviving the breakup: How children and parents cope with divorce.* New York: Basic Books.

Wallerstein, J. S., & Lewis, J. (1998). The long-term impact of divorce on children: A first report from a 25-year study. *Family and Conciliation Courts Review, 36,* 368–383.

Wallerstein, R. S., & Goldberger, L. (1998). *Ideas and identities: The life and work of Erik Erikson.* Madison, CT: International Universities Press.

Walsh, P. E., & Stolberg, A. L. (1989). Parental and environmental determinants of children's behavioral, affective and cognitive adjustment to divorce. *Journal of Divorce, 12,* 265–282.

Walsh, P. V., Katz, P. A., & Downey, E. P. (1991, April). *A longitudinal perspective on race and gender socialization in infants and toddlers.* Paper presented at the biennial meeting of the Society for Research in Child Development, Seattle, WA.

Wapner, R. J. (1997). Chorionic villus sampling. *Obstetrics and Gynecology Clinics of North America, 24,* 83–110.

Warfield, C. (2002, October 25–November 7). Where can I turn? I need more answers: Following the path to no limitations. Chicago Network, *City Talk.*

Wasz-Hockert, O., Michelsson, K., & Lind, J. (1985). Twenty-five years of Scandinavian cry research. In B. M. Lester & C. F. Z. Boukydis (Eds.), *Infant crying* (pp. 349–354). New York: Plenum.

Watamura, S. E., Donzella, B., Alwin, J., & Gunnar, M. R. (2003). Morning-to-afternoon increases in cortisol concentrations for infants and toddlers at child care: Age differences and behavioral correlates. *Child Development, 74*(4), 1006–1020.

Waterman, A. S. (1988). Identity status theory and Erikson's theory. *Developmental Review, 8,* 185–208.

Waterman, A. S. (1999). Issues of identity formation. *Developmental Review, 19,* 462–479.

Watkins, D., & Regmi, M. (1999). Self-concepts of mountain children of Nepal. *Journal of Genetic Psychology, 160,* 429–435.

Watkins, J., & Peabody, P. (1996). Sports injuries in children and adolescents treated at a sports injury clinic. *Journal of Sports Medicine and Physical Fitness, 36,* 43–48.

Watson, J. B., & Raynor, R. (1920). Conditioned emotional reactions. *Journal of Experimental Psychology, 3,* 1–14.

Watt, H. M. (2004). Development of adolescents' self-perceptions, values, and task perceptions according to gender and domain in 7th- through 11th-grade Australian students. *Child Development, 75,* 1556–1574.

Weber-Fox, C., & Neville, H. (1996). Maturational constraints on functional specializations for language processing: ERP and behavior evidence in bilingual speakers. *Journal of Cognitive Neuroscience, 9,* 231–256.

Wedemeyer, N. V., Bickhard, N. H., & Cooper, R. G. (1989). The development of structural complexity in the child's concept of family: The effect of cognitive stage, sex, and intactness of family. *The Journal of Genetic Psychology, 150,* 342–357.

Wegener, D. H., & Aday, L. A. (1989). Home care for ventilator-assisted children: Predicting family stress. *Pediatric Nursing, 15,* 271–376.

Weinberg, R. A. (1989). Intelligence and IQ: Landmark issues and great debates. *American Psychologist, 44,* 98–104.

Weinstein, R. A. (1998). Promoting positive expectations in schooling. In N. M. Lambert & B. L. McCombs (Eds.), *How students learn* (pp. 81–111). Washington, DC: American Psychological Association.

Weinstock, H., Berman, S., & Cates, W. (2004). Sexually transmitted diseases among American youth: Incidence and prevalence estimates. *Perspectives on Sexual and Reproductive Health, 36,* 6–10.

Weiss, B., & Dodge, K. A. (1992). Some consequences of early harsh discipline: Child aggression and a maladaptive social information processing style. *Child Development, 63,* 1321–1335.

Weiss, M. R., & Hayashi, C. T. (1995). All in the family: Parent–child influences in competititve youth gymnastics. *Pediatric Exercise Science, 7,* 36–48.

Wellman, H. M. (1990). *The child's theory of mind.* Cambridge, MA: MIT Press.

Wellman, H. M., & Gelman, S. A. (1998). Knowledge acquisition in foundational domain. In W. Damon (Ed.), *Handbook of child psychology* (Vol. 2, pp. 523–574). New York: Wiley.

Wellman, H. M., & Woolley, J. D. (1990). From simple desires to ordinary beliefs: The early development of everyday psychology. *Cognition, 35,* 245–275.

Wentworth, N., Benson, J. B., & Haith, M. (2000). The development of infants' reaches for stationary and moving targets. *Child Development, 71,* 576–601.

Wentzel, K. R., & Erdley, C. A. (1993). Strategies for making friends: Relations to social behavior and peer acceptance in early adolescence. *Developmental Psychology, 29,* 819–826.

Werker, J. F., & Tees, R. C. (1984). Cross-language speech perception: Evidence for perceptual reorganization during the first year of life. *Infant Behavior and Development, 7,* 49–63.

Werker, J. F., & Vouloumanos, A. (2001). Speech and language processing in infancy: A neurocognitive approach. In C. A. Nelson & M. Luciana (Eds.), *Handbook of developmental cognitive neuroscience* (pp. 269–280). Cambridge, MA: MIT Press.

Werker, J. F., Marcus, G., Mehler, J., Neville, H., & Sebastian-Galles, N. (2004, March 18–20). Human infant speech perception and language acquisition: Rules vs. statistics (workshop summary). Banff International Research Station conference. Retrieved from http://www.pims.math.ca/ibrs/workshops/2004/04w2552

Werner, E. E., & Smith, R. S. (1982). *Vulnerable but invincible: A longitudinal study of resilient children and youth.* New York: McGraw-Hill.

Whalen, C. K., & Henker, B. (1991). Therapies for hyperactive children: Comparisons, combinations, and compromises. *Journal of Consulting and Clinical Psychology, 59,* 126–137.

Whalen, C. K., Henker, B., Buhrmester, D., Hinshaw, S. P., Huber, A., & Laski, K. (1989). Does stimulant medication improve the peer status of hyperactive children? *Journal of Consulting and Clinical Psychology, 57,* 545–549.

Wheeler, L., & Kim, Y. (1997). What is beautiful is culturally good: The physical attractiveness stereotype has different content in collectivistic cultures. *Personality and Social Psychology Bulletin, 23,* 795–800.

Whitaker, R. C., Wright, J. A., Pepe, M. S., Seidel, K. D., & Dietz, W. H. (1997). Predicting obesity in young adulthood from childhood and parental obesity. *New England Journal of Medicine, 337,* 869–873.

White, M. J., & Glick, J. E. (2000). Generation status, social capital, and the routes out of high school. *Sociological Forum, 15,* 671–691.

White, M., & LeVine, R. A. (1986). What is an *Ii ko* (good child)? In H. Stevenson, H. Azuma, & K. Hakuta (Eds.), Child development and education in Japan (pp. 55–62). New York: Freeman.

Whitehead, B. D., & Popenoe, D. (2003). *Marriage and children.* Piscataway, NJ: Rutgers University Press.

Whiting, B. B., & Edwards, C. P. (1988). *Children of different worlds: The formation of social behavior.* Cambridge, MA: Harvard University Press.

Whiting, B. B., & Whiting, J. W. M. (1975). *Children of six cultures: A psychocultural analysis.* Cambridge, MA: Harvard University Press.

Wiblkinson, L. C., & Marrett, C. B. (Eds.). (1986). *Gender influences in classroom interaction.* New York: Academic Press.

Wichstrom, L. (1999). The emergence of gender difference in depressed mood during adolescence: The role of intensified gender socialization. *Developmental Psychology, 35,* 232–245.

Widerstrom, A. H., Mowder, B. A., & Sandall, S. R. (1991). *At-risk and handicapped newborns and infants: Development, assessment, and intervention.* Englewood Cliffs, NJ: Prentice-Hall.

Widom, C. S. (2001). Child abuse and neglect. In S. O. White (Ed.), *Handbook of youth and justice* (pp. 31–47). New York: Kluwer.

Wierson, M., Long, P. J., & Forehand, R. L. (1993). Toward a new understanding of early menarche: The role of environmental stress in pubertal timing. *Adolescence, 28,* 913–924.

Wiese, D., & Daro, D. (1996). *Current trends in child abuse reporting and fatalities.* Chicago: National Committee to Prevent Child Abuse.

Wigfield, A. (1993). Why should I learn this? In M. L. Maehr & P. R. Pintrich (Eds.), *Advances in motivation and achievement* (Vol. 8, pp. 99–138). Greenwich, CT: JAI Press.

Wigfield, A., Battle, A., Keller, L. B., & Eccles, J. S. (2002). Sex differences in motivation, self-concept, career aspiration, and career choice: Implications for cognitive development. In A. McGillicuddy-De Lisi & R. De Lisi (Eds.), *Biology, society, and behavior: The development of sex differences in cognition* (pp. 93–124). Westport, CT: Ablex.

Wigfield, A., & Eccles, J. S. (2002). The development of competence beliefs, expectancies for success, and achievement values from childhood through adolescence. In J. S. Eccles & A. Wigfield (Eds.), *Development of achievement motivation* (pp. 91–120). San Diego, CA: Academic Press.

Wigfield, A., Eccles, J. S., & Pintrich, P. R. (1996). Development between the ages of 11 and 25. In D. C. Berliner & R. C. Calfee (Eds.), *Handbook of educational psychology* (pp. 148–185). New York: Macmillan.

Wikander, B., & Helleday, A. (1996). The excessively crying infant: The mother–infant relationship. *Early Child Development and Care, 124,* 11–23.

Wilcox, M. J., Hadley, P. A., & Ashland, J. E. (1996). Communication and language development in infants and toddlers. In M. J. Hanson (Ed.), *Atypical infant development* (pp. 365–402). Austin, TX: Pro-Ed.

Wilcox, M. J., & Terrell, B. Y. (1985). Child language behavior: The acquisition of social communicative competence. In C. S. McLoughlin & D. F. Gullo (Eds.), *Young children in context* (pp. 40–65). Springfield, IL: Thomas.

Wilkinson, A. (1976). Counting strategies and semantic analysis as applied to class inclusion. *Cognitive Psychology, 8,* 64–85.

Willett, J. B., Singer, J. D., & Martin, N. C. (1998). The design and analysis of longitudinal studies of development and psychopathology in context. *Development and Psychopathology, 10,* 395–426.

Williamson, L. (1998). Eating disorders and the cultural forces behind the drive for thinness. *Social Work in Health Care, 28,* 61–73.

Willig, A. (1985). A meta-analysis of selected studies on the effectiveness of bilingual education. *Review of Educational Research, 55,* 269–317.

Wilson, B. J., & Smith, S. L. (1998). Children's responses to emotional portrayals on television. In P. A. Andersen & L. K. Guerrero (Eds.), *Handbook of communication and emotion* (pp. 533–569). San Diego, CA: Academic Press.

Wilson, C., & Keye, W. (1989). A survey of adolescent dysmenorrhea and premenstrual symptom frequency. *Journal of Adolescent Health Care, 10,* 317–322.

Wilson, G. S. (1989). Clinical studies of infants and children exposed prenatally to heroin. *Annals of the New York Academy of Sciences, 562,* 183–194.

Wilson, R. D. (2000). Amniocentesis and chorionic villus sampling. *Current Opinion in Obstetrics and Gynecology, 12,* 81–86.

Wimmer, H., & Perner, J. (1983). Beliefs about beliefs: Representation and constraining function of wrong beliefs in young children's understanding of deception. *Cognition, 13,* 103–128.

Windass, A. (1989). Classroom practices and organization. In C. Skelton (Ed.), *Whatever happens to little women?* (pp. 38–49). Milton Keynes, UK: Open University Press.

Winer, G. A. (1980). Class inclusion reasoning in children: A review of the empirical literature. *Child Development, 51,* 309–328.

Wingwood, G. M., Tolson, J. M., & Halliday-Scher, K. (2003). A prospective study of exposure to rap music videos and African American female adolescents' health. *American Journal of Public Health, 93,* 437–439.

Winner, E. (1986). Where pelicans kiss seals. *Psychology Today, 20,* 25–35.

Winsler, A., Diaz, R. M., & Montero, I. (1997). The role of private speech in the transition from collaborative to independent task performance in young children. *Early Childhood Research Quarterly, 12,* 59–79.

Wisniewski, L., & Marcus, M. D. (1998). Childhood obesity. In V. B. Van Hasselt & M. Hersen (Eds.), *Handbook of psychological treatment protocols for children and adolescents* (pp. 179–201). Mahwah, NJ: Erlbaum.

Witkin, G. (1991, April 8). Kids who kill. *U.S. News and World Report.*

Wolf, A. E. (1996, October). Tantrums. *Child,* 42–46.

Wolf, D. P. (1990). Being of several minds: Voices and versions of the self in early childhood. In D. Cicchetti & M. Beeghly (Eds.), *The self in transition* (pp. 183–212). Chicago: University of Chicago Press.

Wolff, P. H. (1963). Observations on the early development of smiling. In B. Foss (Ed.), *Determinants of infant behavior* (Vol. 2, pp. 113–138). London: Methuen.

Wolff, P. H. (1969). The natural history of crying and other vocalizations in early infancy. In B. M. Foss (Ed.), *Determinants of infant behavior* (Vol. 4, pp. 97–112). London: Methuen.

Wolfner, G. D., & Gelles, R. J. (1993). A profile of violence toward children: A national study. *Child Abuse & Neglect, 17,* 197–212.

Wolfson, A. R. (2002). Bridging the gap between research and practice: What will adolescents' sleep/wake patterns look like in the 21st century? In M. A. Carskadon (Ed.), *Adolescent sleep patterns* (pp. 198–219). New York: Cambridge University Press.

Wolfson, A. R., & Carskadon, M. A. (2002). Understanding adolescents' sleep patterns and school performance: A critical appraisal. *Sleep Medicine Reviews, 7,* 491–506.

Wolfson, A. R., Tzischinsky, O., Brown, C., Darley, C., Acebo, C., & Carskadon, M. A. (1995). Sleep, behavior, and stress at the transition to senior high school. *Sleep Research, 24,* 5–20.

Women's Sports Foundation. (1998). *Sport and teen pregnancy.* New York: Author.

Wong, D. L., & Perry, S. E. (1998). *Maternal child nursing care.* St. Louis, MO: Mosby.

Wood, J. N., & Grafman, J. (1999). Human prefrontal cortex: Processing and representational perspectives. *Nature Reviews Neuroscience, 4,* 139–147.

Woodward, A. L., & Markman, E. M. (1998). Early word learning. In W. Damon (Ed.), *Handbook of child psychology* (Vol. 2, pp. 371–420). New York: Wiley.

Woodward, E. H., & Gridina, N. (2001). *Media in the home.* Philadelphia: Annenberg Public Policy Center.

Woodworth, S., Belsky, J., & Crnic, K. (1996). The determinants of fathering during the child's second and third years of life: A developmental analysis. *Journal of Marriage and the Family, 58,* 679–692.

Woolley, J. D., & Wellman, H. M. (1990). Young children's understanding of realities, nonrealities, and appearances. *Child Development, 61,* 946–961.

World Health Organization. (1997). *WHO global database on child growth and malnutrition.* Geneva, Switzerland: Author.

World Health Organization. (1999). *Care of the umbilical cord: A review of the evidence.* Geneva, Switzerland: Author.

World Health Organization. (2004, October). One million polio vaccinators, 80 million children, 23 countries: Africa launches largest ever immunization campaign. Retrieved from http://www.who.int/mediacentre/news/releases/2004/pr69/en/

Worthington, A. C. (2002). The impact of student perceptions and characteristics on teaching evaluations. *Assessment and Evaluation in Education, 27,* 49–64.

Wright, J. C., Huston, A. C., Vandewater, E. A., Bickham, D. S., Scantlin, R. M., Kotler, J. A., Yelland, N., & Lloyd, M. (2001). Virtual kids of the 21st century: Understanding the children in schools today. *Information Technology in Childhood Education Annual, 12,* 175–192.

Wright, S. C., & Taylor, D. M. (1995). Identity and the language of the classroom. *Journal of Educational Psychology, 87,* 241–252.

Wright, V. C., Schieve, L. A., Reynolds, M. A., Jeng, G., & Kissin, D. (2004). Assisted reproductive technology surveillance—United States, 2001. *Morbidity and Mortality Report, 53,* 1220.

Wynn, K. (2000). Findings of addition and subtraction in infants are robust and consistent: Reply to Wakely, Rivera, and Langer. *Child Development, 71,* 1535–1536.

Wyshak, G. (1983). Secular changes in age at menarche in a sample of US women. *Annals of Human Biology, 10,* 75–78.

Wysocki, T., & Green, P. (1997). Self-management of childhood diabetes in family context. In D. S. Gochman (Ed.), *Handbook of health behavior research II: Provider determinants* (pp. 169–187). New York: Plenum.

Xu, F. (2003). Numerosity discrimination in infants: Evidence for two systems of representations. *Cognition, 89,* B15–B25.

Yagel, S., Anteby, E., Hochner-Celnikier, D., Ariel, I., Chaap, T., & Ben-Neriah, Z. (1998). The role of midtrimester target fetal organ screening combined with the "triple test" and maternal age in the diagnosis of trisomy 21. *American Journal of Obstetrics and Gynecology, 178,* 40–44.

Yamamoto, K., Soliman, A., Parsons, J., & Davies, O. L., Jr. (1987). Voices in unison: Stressful events in the lives of children in six countries. *Journal of Child Psychology and Psychiatry, 28,* 855–864.

Yanai, J., Steingart, R. A., Snapir, N., Gvaryahu, G., Rozenboim, I., & Katz, A. (2000). The relationship between neural alterations and behavioral deficits after prenatal exposure to heroin. In S. F. Ali (Ed.), *Neurobiological mechanisms of drugs of abuse* (Vol. 914, pp. 402–411). New York: New York Academy of Sciences.

Yang, C. K., & Hahn, H. M. (2002). Cosleeping in young Korean children. *Journal of Developmental Behavioral Pediatrics, 23,* 151–457.

Yankelovich, S., & White, C. (1989). *The role of Sesame Street among children in poverty.* New York: Children's Television Workshop.

Yee, D. K., & Eccles, J. S. (1988). Parents' perceptions and attributions for children's math achievement. *Sex Roles, 19,* 317–333.

Yelland, N., & Lloyd, M. (2001). Virtual kids of the 21st century: Understanding the children in schools today. In D. Shade (Ed.), *Information technology in childhood education* (pp. 175–192). Norfolk, VA: AACE.

Yenen, S. (1997). *Turkish odyssey.* Ankara, Turkey: Serif Yenen.

Yetman, N. R. (1991). *Majority and minority.* Boston: Allyn & Bacon.

Yin, R. K. (1994). Discovering the future of the case study method in evaluation research. *Evaluation Practice, 15,* 283–290.

Young, J. (1996). *Developmental care of the premature baby.* Philadelphia: Balliere Tindall.

Young, L. R., & Nestle, M. (1995). Portion sizes in dietary assessment: Issues and implications, *Nutrition Reviews, 53,* 149–158.

Young, L. R., & Nestle, M. (2002). *The contribution of expanding portion sizes to the US obesity epidemic. American Journal of Public Health, 92,* 246–249.

Younger, B. A., & Fearing, D. D. (1999). Parsing items into separate categories: Developmental change in infant categorization. *Child Development, 70,* 291–303.

Youniss, J. (1980). *Parents and peers in social development.* Chicago: University of Chicago Press.

Youniss, J., McLellan, J. A., & Strouse, D. (1994). "We're popular, but we're not snobs": Adolescents describe their crowds. In R. Montemayor, G. R. Adams, & T. P. Gullotta (Eds.), *Personal relationships during adolescence* (pp. 101–122). Thousand Oaks, CA: Sage.

Yuan, L. L., & Ganetsky, B. (1999). A glial–neuronal signaling pathway revealed by mutations in a neurexin-related protein. *Science, 283,* 1343–1344.

Yuille, N. (1997). Children's understanding of traits. In S. Hala (Ed.), *The development of social cognition* (pp. 273–296). East Sussex, UK: Psychology Press.

Yung, B. R., & Hammond, W. R. (1994). Native Americans. In L. D. Eron, J. H. Gentry, & P. Schlegel (Eds.), *Reason to hope: A psychosocial perspective on violence and youth* (pp. 133–144). Washington, DC: American Psychological Association.

Yung, B. R., & Hammond, W. R. (1997). Antisocial behavior in minority groups. In D. M. Stoff & J. Breiling (Eds.), *Handbook of antisocial behavior* (pp. 474–495). New York: Wiley.

Zahn-Waxler, C., Radke-Yarrow, M., Wagner, E., & Chapman, M. (1992). The development of concern for others. *Developmental Psychology, 28,* 1038–1047.

Zaiwalla, Z., & Stein, A. (1993). The physiology of sleep in infants and young children. In I. St. James-Roberts, G. Harris, & D. Messer (Eds.), *Infant crying, feeding and sleeping: Development, problems, and treatment* (pp. 135–149). New York: Harvester Wheatsheaf.

Zeanah, C. H., Nelson, C. A., Fox, N. A., Smyke, A. T., Marshall, P., Parker, S. W., & Koga, S. (2003). Designing research to study the effects of institutionalization on brain and behavioral development: The Bucharest Early Intervention Project. *Development and Psychopathology, 15,* 885–907.

Zebrowitz, L., & Montepare, J. M. (1992). Impressions of babyfaced individuals across the lifespan. *Developmental Psychology, 28,* 1143–1152.

Zebrowitz, L., Kendall-Tackett, K., & Fafel, J. (1991). The impact of children's facial maturity on parental expectations and punishments. *Journal of Experimental Child Psychology, 52,* 221–238.

Zeifman, D., Delany, S., & Blass, E. M. (1996). Sweet taste, looking, and calm in 2- and 4-week-old infants: The eyes have it. *Developmental Psychology, 32,* 1090–1099.

Zero to Three. (1997). *Parents speak: Nationwide Survey Among Parents of zero-to-three-year-olds.* Washington, DC: Author.

Zero to Three. (2004). *Choosing quality child care.* Washington, DC: Author.

Zeskind, P. S. (1985). A developmental perspective on infant crying. In B. M. Lester & C. F. Z. Boukydis (Eds.), *Infant crying* (pp. 158–186). New York: Plenum.

Zigler, E. (1999). Head Start is not child care. *American Psychologist, 54,* 142.

Zigler, E., & Finn-Stevenson, M. (2003). *Portrait of 4 schools: Meeting the needs of immigrant students and their families.* New Haven, CT: Yale Center in Child Development and Social Policy.

Zigler, E. F., Finn-Stevenson, M., & Hall, N. W. (2002). *The first three years and beyond: Brain development and social policy.* New Haven, CT: Yale University Press.

Zigler, E., & Gilman, E. (1998). *The legacy of Jean Piaget.* Mahwah, NJ: Erlbaum.

Zigler, E., & Styfco, S. J. (1998). Applying the findings of developmental psychology to improve early childhood intervention. In S. G. Paris & H. M. Wellman (Eds.), *Global prospects for education* (pp. 345–365). Washington, DC: American Psychological Association.

Zill, N. (1999). Promoting educational equity and excellence in kindergarten. In R. C. Pianta & M. J. Cox (Eds.), *The transition to kindergarten* (pp. 67–108). Baltimore, MD: Brookes.

Zillmann, D. (1982). Television viewing and arousal. In D. Pearl, L. Bouthilet, & J. Lazar (Eds.), *Television and behavior* (Vol. 2, pp. 53–67). Washington, DC: US Government Printing Office.

Zimmerman, B. F. (1998). Classroom disruption: Educational theory as applied to perception and action in regular and special education. In A. Rotatori & J. Schwenn (Eds.), *Advances in special education* (Vol. 11, pp. 77–98). Greenwich, CT: JAI Press.

Zimmerman, M. A., Copeland, L. A., Shope, J. T., & Dielman, T. E. (1997). A longitudinal study of self-esteem: Implications for adolescent development. *Journal of Youth and Adolescence, 26,* 117–141.

Zogby International. (2001). *Assessment of views on immigration.* Oakland, CA: Diversity Alliance for a Sustainable America.

Zurbriggen, E. L., & Freyd, J. J. (2004). The link between child sexual abuse and risky sexual behavior: The role of dissociative tendencies, information-processing effects, and consensual sex decision mechanisms. In L. J. Koenig & L. S. Doll (Eds.), *From child sexual abuse to adult sexual risk: Trauma, revictimization, and intervention* (pp. 135–157). Washington, DC: American Psychological Association.

Zwaanswijk, M., Verhaak, P. F. M., Bensing, J. M., van der Ende, J., & Verhulst, F. C. (2003). Help seeking for emotional and behavioural problems in children and adolescents. *European Child and Adolescent Psychiatry, 12,* 153–161.

Name Index

Abbott, M. B., 155
Abbott, S., 447
Abel, E. L., 100
Abelman, R., 334
Aber, J. L., 412
Aber, J. R., 377
Ablon, J. S., 394
Ablow, J. C., 300
Aboud, F. E., 385, 387
Abrams, K. R., 48
Abrams, S. M., 114
A. C. Nielsen Media
  Research, 332
Achenbach, T. M., 541
Acredolo, L., 188
Adair, R. H., 259
Adams, G., 229
Adams, H. F., 157
Adams, M. J., 381, 382,
  383
Adams, R. J., 143
Adams, W. G., 264
Adamson, L. B., 197
Aday, L. A., 124
Addington, J., 387
Adessa, R., 521
Adler, P., 515
Adler, P. A., 515
Administration for Chil-
  dren and Families,
  238, 292
Adnopoz, J., 411
Adolph, K. E., 152
Ager, A., 408
Agras, S., 467
Aharoni, A., 73
Ainsworth, M., 208, 217,
  219, 222
Ainsworth, M. D., 222,
  225, 315
Akabas, S. R., 355
Akbas, S. H., 79
Akhtar, N., 187, 285
Akhtar, N. A., 159
Alaimo, K., 351, 462
Alan Guttmacher Insti-
  tute, 474, 478, 534
Alarcon, M., 391
Alberts, D. M., 291
Alcantara, A. A., 139
Alderman, M. H., 121
Alessandri, S. M., 102,
  213
Alevriadou, A., 253
Alexander, A., 282, 434
Alexander, J. M., 113
Alexander, K. L., 496
Alfieri, T., 515
Alibhai, M., 468
Allen, J. P., 523
Allen, L., 149, 407
Allen, M. C., 120
Allen, M. S., 100

Allen, O., 468
Allen, W. R., 520
Allhusen, V. D., 231
Almeida, D. M., 454
Alpert, A., 322
Als, H., 141
Altabe, M., 352
Altarriba, J., 488
Altermatt, E. R., 388
Altmann, G. T. M., 193
Alvarrez, M. M., 454
Alwin, J., 217
Amabile, T. M., 377
Amato, M., 209
Amato, P. R., 318, 322
Ambert, A. M., 525, 526,
  528
Ambrosini, P. J., 418
American Academy of
  Pediatrics, 147,
  157, 158, 159,
  263–264, 344, 350,
  360, 544
American Association of
  University
  Women, 390
American College of
  Obstetricians and
  Gynecologists, 105
American Dental Associ-
  ation, 344
American Medical Asso-
  ciation, 39
American Psychiatric
  Association, 332,
  392, 414, 466, 542
American Psychological
  Association, 394,
  417
American Red Cross, 232
America Online, 540
Anastasi, A., 374
Anderman, E. M., 494
Anders, T. F., 134, 135
Andersen, E. R., 324
Anderson, C. A., 521
Anderson, D., 144
Anderson, D. R., 332
Anderson, K. J., 427, 533
Anderson, K. N., 270
Anderson, R. C., 380
Anderson, S. W., 247
Anderson, W. P., 307
Andersson, B., 232
Ando, K., 313
Andrews, D. W., 414
Aneshensel, C. S., 534
Anglin, J. M., 189, 282,
  380, 381
Angst, J., 414
Ani, C., 257
Annett, M., 253

Annie E. Casey Founda-
  tion, 470
Antill, J. K., 454
Antonucci, T. C., 115
Aoki, W. T., 542
Apgar, V., 119
Appel, A. E., 236
Archbold, K. H., 261
Archer, S. L., 518
Archibald, A. B., 474
Arcia, E., 392
Arcus, D., 218
Ardelt, M., 318
Arditti, J. A., 323, 325
Arend, R., 228
Argys, L. M., 323
Aries, E., 303
Aries, P., 12
Arms, K. G., 18
Arnett, J., 475, 531
Arnold, J., 324
Arnold, T. K., 358
Aronson, J. A., 504
Asendorp, J. B., 218
Asher, S. R, 326, 327
Asher, S. R., 326, 418,
  430, 431, 532
Ashland, J. E., 285
Ashley, J., 311
Askan, N., 318
Aslin, R. N., 142, 144,
  145, 185, 186
Association of SIDS and
  Infant Mortality
  Programs, 159
Astolfi, P., 104
Ater, A., 355
Atkin, C., 333
Atkin, L. C., 210
Atkins, M. S., 312
Atkinson, L., 225
Atkinson, R., 446
Attie, I., 468
Aube, J., 231
Augoustinos, M., 386
August, D., 389
Aunola, K., 525
Aurand, S., 521
Avenevoli, S, 524
Aviezer, O., 228
Avinoam, B. C., 302
Avis, J., 280
Avner, J. R., 361
Ayers, M., 531
Aylward, G. P., 10
Azmitia, M., 326
Azuma, H., 317

Bachman, J. G., 499
Baddeley, J., 426
Bae, Y., 501
Baer, J. S., 100
Bagwell, C. F., 326, 327

Bailey, D. B., Jr., 250
Baillargeon, R., 173, 174,
  177, 274
Bain, B., 389
Baird, A. A., 449
Baird, G., 398
Baird, S. M., 209
Baker, K., 389
Baker, L., 272
Baker, L. S., 291
Bakermans, J. J., 225
Balaguer, I., 464
Balcazar, H., 158
Baldwin, LE., 382
Bales, D. W., 300
Balle-Jenson, L., 475
Baltes, M. M., 523
Baltes, P. B., 3
Baltimore, D., 63
Bamaca-Gomez, M., 519
Bancroft, J., 454
Band, E. B., 408
Bandstra, E. S., 102
Bandura, A., 38, 306, 307
Bank, L., 317
Banks, C. A. M., 388
Banks, J. A., 388
Banks, M. S., 142, 145
Barber, B. K., 507
Barber, B. L., 464
Barbone, F., 261
Bardin, C., 120
Baris, M. A., 320
Barkley, R. A., 392, 415
Barness, L. A., 159
Barnett, M., 479
Barnett, S. W., 292
Baron-Cohen, S., 249
Barquissau, M., 501
Barr, H. M., 101
Barr, R. G., 209
Barrera, M. E., 144
Barrett, M., 252, 417
Barron, R. W., 391
Barry, S., 429
Barry, S. M.
Bartholomew, K., 219
Bartholow, B. D., 540
Bartsch, K., 280
Bates, E., 178, 191, 192,
  195, 216
Bates, J. E., 214, 228, 315,
  415
Bathurst, K., 378
Battle, A., 304
Bauchner, H., 264
Bauer, D. H., 407
Bauer, P., 178
Bauman, K. E., 529
Baumeister, A. A., 21, 377
Baumeister, R. F., 21, 377,
  515
Bauminger, N., 394

Baumrind, D., 316, 318,
  319
Baxter, M. P., 346
Bayer, CL. 524,525
Beal, C. R., 515, 532
Bear, G. G., 313
Beard, J., 462
Beardslee, W. R., 418
Beauchamp, G. K., 146
Beaudry, M., 331
Beautrais, A. L., 160
Becker, S., 101
Beckman, D. A., 99
Beckwith, L., 134
Beebe, M. E., 415
Begley, S., 136
Behrman, R. E., 539
Beitel, A. H., 228
Belamarich, P. F., 352
Bell, C., 414
Bell, D. A., 75
Bell, J. H., 488
Bell, R., 418
Bellinger, D.C., 157
Belsky, J., 115, 221, 226,
  228, 231, 232, 234,
  237, 238, 319, 330,
  434, 455
Bem, S. L., 304, 307
Bemporad, J. R., 418
Benbow, C. P., 396, 501
Benedek, E. P., 322
Benes, F., 449
Bennett, C., 435
Bennett, F. C., 155
Benson, B., 478, 525
Benson, J. B., 155, 173
Benson, N.J., 391
Benson, P. L., 492
Benz, P. J., 209
Berenbaum, S., 454, 501
Berenbaum, S. A., 306
Berg, K. M., 134
Berg, W. K., 134
Bergstrom, R., 105
Berk, L. E., 275, 434
Berko, J., 284
Berliner, L., 234
Berman, C. M., 13
Berman, S., 474
Berman, S. L., 412
Bermejo, E., 99
Bernal, J., 135
Bernal, M. E., 519
Bermejo, E.,
Berndt, L., 475
Berndt, T. J., 531
Berry, J. W., 370
Bertenthal, B. I., 143, 144,
  145, 250
Best, C. T., 185
Bettes, B. A., 197
Bezruczko, N., 548
Bhatia, T. K., 286, 287

Bhattacharya, G., 508
Bialystock, E., 286
Bickhard, N. H., 321
Biderman, J., 392
Bier, J. A. B., 122
Bierman, K. L., 532
Bigbee, M. A., 409
Bigelow, K. M., 235
Bigler, R. S., 304, 307,
  386, 388
Bijur, P. E., 350
Biller, H. B., 115
Bimonte, H. A., 504
Binet, A., 373
Binns, C. W., 470
Birch, H. G., 418
Birch, S. H., 437
Birkimer, J. C., 114
Bithoney, W. G., 162
Bittner, M. T., 411
Bjorklund, D. F., 31–32,
  42, 173, 181, 182,
  184, 272, 273, 371,
  373
Black, B., 434
Black, J. E., 139, 140, 141,
  341
Black, K. A., 531
Black, M. M., 30
Black, S. H., 68
Black-Gutman, D., 386,
  387
Blair, R., 449
Blake, J., 430
Bland, K., 234
Blander, B., 261
Blank, M., 274
Blasi, A., 425
Blass, E. M., 145, 181
Blau, D. M., 232
Bleeker, M. M., 504
Blehar, M. C., 222
Bloch, H., 155
Block, J., 547
Bloom, F. E., 140
Bloom, L., 186, 187, 191,
  196, 284, 285, 286,
  380, 381, 548
Bloom, P., 187
Bloom, S. L., 113
Blum, N.J., 157
Blumenfeld, W. J., 520
Blyth, D., 494
Blyth, D. A., 150, 190, 190
Boaler, J., 501
Boden, J. M., 515
Boeck, M. A., 468
Boer, F., 331
Bogenschneider, R., 536
Bohannon, J. N., 196
Bohlin, G., 228, 434
Bon-De-Matte, L., 466

Bongers, I. L., 414
Boomsma, D. I., 415
Boos, R., 78
Booth, C. L., 228
Booth, D. A., 466
Borawski, E. A., 525
Borg, M. G., 388
Borke, H., 274
Borman, K., 521
Bornstein, M. H., 141, 144, 179, 181, 208, 228
Borowiecki, J. J., 460
Borstelmann, L. J., 11
Borsting, E., 246
Bosco, A., 500
Boseley, S., 82
Bosma, H. A., 517
Boston, M. B., 305
Bosworth, P., 516
Bottoms, G., 495
Botvin, G. J., 515
Bouchard, C., 452, 464
Bouchey, H. A., 532
Boudreaux, M. C., 362
Bourdais, C., 156
Bowen, F., 528
Bowen, J., 393
Bower, J., 208
Bower, M., 99
Bowker, A., 532
Bowlby, J., 32, 217, 219, 407
Bowman, L. L., 190
Bowman, M. J., 157
Bowman, P. J., 303
Boxer, A. M., 458, 521
Boyce, W. T., 418
Boykin-McElhaney, K., 523
Boyle, C., 346
Brackbill, Y., 109
Brackshaw, E., 333
Bradbard, M. R., 305
Bradford, K., 526
Bradley, R. H., 21, 44, 120, 121, 288
Bradley, S. J., 302
Brage, S., 353
Braine, M., 191
Brainerd, C. J., 272
Branch, C. W., 386
Brassard, M. R., 234
Brassington, G. S., 464
Braungart-Rieker, J. M., 215, 225
Braza, F., 305
Braza, P., 305
Brazelton, T. B., 109, 119, 120, 208
Breakey, J., 394
Brederode, M. E., 294
Breedlove, G., 109
Bremer, J., 541
Bremner, G. J., 181
Brendgen, M., 528, 531, 536
Brenner, B., 415
Brenner, R. A., 157
Brent, D., 291
Brent, M. R., 191
Brent, R. L., 99
Bretherton, I., 178
Breunig, K., 320
Brewerton, T. D., 468
Bridges, K., 205
Bridges, L. J., 226, 283
Bridges, M., 322
Bril, B., 148
Brion-Meisels, S., 491
Brisk, M. E., 389

Britner, P., 239
Broadhurst, D. D., 234, 235
Brodersen, L., 408
Brodsky, A. E., 303
Brody, G. H., 331, 404, 429, 430
Brody, L. R., 182
Brodzinsky, D. M., 219
Bromley, D. B., 489
Bromnick, R. D., 488
Brone, R. J., 466
Bronfenbrenner, U., 23, 43, 44
Bronstein, P., 493
Brook, C., 504
Brook, D. W., 101
Brook, J. S., 101
Brooks-Gunn, J., 21, 44, 212, 352, 377, 454, 455, 457, 458, 461, 468, 523, 526, 537
Brown, A., 404
Brown, A. L., 277, 371
Brown, B. B., 529
Brown, C. F., 322
Brown, E., 181
Brown, J., 257
Brown, J. R., 286, 330
Brown, J. V., 102, 122
Brown, K. H., 159
Brown, L. K., 473
Brown, M., 361
Brown, M. M., 434
Bruce, C., 115
Bruce, J., 23
Bruck, M., 279, 382
Brucken, L., 304
Bruene, C. M., 431
Bruner, J. S., 179, 196
Brusaferro, S., 261
Bryan, J. H., 315
Bryant, B. K., 408, 427, 429, 430
Bryden, M. P., 253
Bryk, A. S., 495, 497
Buchanan, A., 314
Buchanan, C. M., 325, 453, 523
Buchanan, C. N., 323
Bugental, D. B., 315
Buhrmester, D., 331, 394, 531
Buis, J. M., 488
Buka, S. L., 101
Bukowski, W., 430
Bukowski, W. M., 528, 531, 532
Bullock, B. M., 523
Bullock, M., 274
Burack, J. A., 395
Burchinal, M., 289
Burchinal, M. R., 232, 250, 288
Burd, B., 158
Burgeson, R., 494
Buriel, R., 315, 322
Burnett, J. W., 307
Burnham, M. M., 135
Burt, M. R., 497
Burts, D.C., 317
Bush, George H., 291
Bush-Rossnagel, N. A., 476
Buss, A., 214
Buss, D., 31
Buss, K., 210
Bussey, K., 306, 307, 421
Buster, M., 536
Butler, J., 183
Butler, Y. G., 389

Buyck, P., 299
Byers, J., 98
Byrne, B., 382
Byrne, R., 476
Byrnes, J. P., 341, 485

Cahill, T. C., 77, 78
Cairns, R. B., 14
Caissy, G. A., 456, 458
Caldwell, B. M., 44
Caldwell, K., 345
Callanan, M. A., 190, 331
Camarota, A., 19
Cambier, A., 252
Campbell, D., 209
Campbell, L., 497
Campos, F., 19
Campos, J. A., 144, 205
Campos, J. J., 23, 145, 152, 153, 226, 233
Cangelosi, A., 32
Cann, W., 239
Cantrell, D., 531
Capaldi, D., 416
Capon, N., 487
Capps, L., 367, 397
Caputo, R. K., 231
Carey, W., 215
Carlo, G., 314, 436, 524
Carlson, E. A., 228, 393
Carlson, S. M., 280
Carlson-Luden, V., 178
Carlton, M. P., 291
Carlton-Ford, S., 494
Carossino, P., 116
Carpendale, J., 384
Carpenter, A., 495
Carpenter, M., 187
Carr, A., 239
Carreras, M. R., 305
Carroll, M. D., 352
Carskadon, M. A., 450
Carson, D. K., 411
Carter, C., 385
Carter, D. B., 317
Carter, M. C., 263–264
Cartwright, T., 191
Cary, P. T., 97, 98
Case, R., 40, 41, 274, 341
Casey, B. J., 449
Casey, D. M., 333
Casey, P. H., 162, 288
Caskie, G. I. L., 232
Casper, L. M., 429
Caspi, A., 214, 215, 415
Cass, H., 398
Cassidy, D. J., 277
Cassidy, J., 228
Castellanos, F. X., 392
Castronova, F. C., 113
Cates, W., 474
Cauce, A. M., 316
Cauffman, E., 469
Cavallaro, D., 427
Cavell, T. A., 2109
Ceci, S. J., 23, 279
Center for Applied Research and Educational Improvement, 450
Center for Media Literacy, 333
Center for the Evaluation of Risks to Human Reproduction, 99
Centers for Disease Control, 84, 98, 157, 262, 264, 320, 344, 346, 348, 350, 352, 354, 355, 358, 359, 360, 462, 463, 465,

468, 469, 470, 472, 473, 474, 475, 476, 477, 478, 506, 533, 535, 536, 541, 542, 543, 544, 545, 546
Cernoch, J. M., 147
Chabrol, H., 114
Chall, J. S., 382
Chambers, R. A., 451
Chan, R. W., 17
Chandler, M., 280
Chang, A., 353
Chapin, J. R., 537
Chapman, M., 313
Charbonneau, C., 331
Charlesworth, R., 290
Chase, W. G., 278
Chase-Lindsale, P. L., 318, 321, 322, 479
Chatkup, S., 71
Chatman, C., 300
Chatters, L. M., 520
Chavkin, W., 102
Chazan, R. Z., 418
Cheek, N. H., 530
Chellappa, G. H., 147
Chen, C., 317, 379, 506, 507, 542
Chen, E., 542
Chen, J., 354
Chen, M., 379, 504
Chen, S., 226
Chen, Z., 370
Chen, Z. Y., 522
Cherlin, A. J., 321, 322, 323, 325, 497
Chervin, R. D., 261
Chess, S., 214, 215, 216
Chesson, H. W., 474
Chi, M. T. H., 278
Children Now, 539
Children's TV Workshop, 294, 295
Child Trends, 291
Chilman, C. S., 303
Chiodo, L. M., 160
Chisholm, J. S., 148, 210
Chisum, H., 139
Choi, P. Y., 460
Choi, S., 197
Chomsky, N., 193–194, 195
Chou, K. J., 361
Christensen, K. M., 147
Christenson, P. G., 537, 538
Christiansen, S. L., 479
Christofori, G., 71
Christopher, F. S., 537
Christopherson, K. S., 246
Chung, A. M., 429
Cicchetti, D., 225, 234
Clark, A. T., 187, 193
Clark, E. V., 190, 283
Clark, G., 427
Clark, M. L., 531
Clarke-Stewart, K. A., 231, 289
Claussen, A. H., 32, 226, 257
Claxton, L. J., 155
Clements, D.C., 231
Clifton, R. K., 174, 183, 250
Clingempeel, W. G., 319, 320
Clubb, R., 124
Cnattingius, S., 101, 105
CNN, 432
Coatsworth, J. D., 411

Cochran, K. M., 311
Coffman, J., 264
Cohan, M., 115, 479
Cohane, G. H., 460
Cohen, J., 377
Cohen, J. D., 247
Cohen, K. M., 521
Cohen, L. B., 175, 178
Cohen, M. A., 497
Cohen, S. E., 134
Cohen, Y., 473
Cohler, J. J., 521
Cohn, D. A., 326
Coie, J. D., 312, 431
Colbus, D., 418
Colby, A., 422, 424
Cole, C. F., 294
Cole, E. B., 196
Cole, M., 281
Coleman, M., 324
Coles, C., 100
Coles, M., 449
Coles, R., 493
Coley, R. L., 479
Colin, V. L., 219, 220, 221, 224, 228, 229
Collaer, M. L., 306
Collins, A., 208
Collins, W. A., 311, 522, 525, 526
Collinsworth, P., 378
Coltrane, S., 228
Colwell, M. J., 438
Combs-Orne, T., 115
Committee on Pediatric AIDS, 98
Compas, B. E., 408, 409
Comstock, G., 294, 333
Conant, C. L., 311
Concu, A., 276
Condry, J., 332
Conger, J., 547
Conger, R. D., 239, 315, 318, 458, 524
Connell, J. P., 226
Connenschein, S., 272
Conners, C. K., 392
Connolly, J., 532
Connolly, K. J., 253
Connolly, S. D., 453, 454, 457, 523
Connor, D. B., 179
Consortium for Longitudinal Studies, 293
Consumer Product Safety Alert, 264
Consumer Product Safety Commission, 350, 360
Conway, G. S., 504
Cook, T. D., 294
Cooksey, E. C., 228
Cooney, R., 495
Cooper, R., 509
Cooper, R. G., 321
Cooper, R. M., 73
Cooper, R. P., 146
Coopersmith, S, 300, 301
Copeland, L. A., 515
Coplan, R. J., 329
Copstick, S. M., 112
Corbetta, D., 155
Corbin, S. B., 323
Cordell, A. S., 404
Coren, S., 253, 254
Corina, D. P., 391
Corkum, V., 180
Corley, R., 8
Cornwell, T., 389
Costello, B. J., 515
Costigan, K. A., 214

Cote, J. F., 518
Cotton, S., 454
Couchoud, E. A., 314
Counts, C. R., 460
Coupey, S. M., 466, 469
Courage, M. L., 184
Courchesne, E., 139
Covington, M. C., 437
Cowan, C. P., 115, 300
Cowan, G., 454
Cowan, P. A., 300, 316
Cowden, J. E., 347
Cowi, H., 408
Cox, B. D., 252
Cox, M. J., 291
Coy, K. C., 205, 526
Coyle, T. R., 371
Cozby, P. C., 50, 51
Crain, F., 361
Crain, W., 36, 37, 39
Crandall, C. S., 504
Crane, J., 415
Crane, J. P., 78
Cratty, B. J., 131, 138, 141, 152, 245, 250, 251, 252, 254, 347, 348
Creasey, G. L., 434
Creswell, S., 464
Crick, N. R., 313, 409, 410
Crittenden, P. M., 32, 225, .226
Crnic, K., 115, 228, 319
Crockett, L. J., 536
Crombie, G., 438, 505
Cross, D. R., 179
Crosser, S., 253
Crouter, A. C., 331, 527
Crowder, K., 478, 497
Crowe, P. A., 515
Crowell, J., 32
Csikszentmihalyi, M., 328, 376, 529, 548
Cuffe, S. P., 238
Culhane, J., 6
Culp, A. M., 197
Culver, L. C., 316
Cummings, E. M., 239, 310, 322, 327
Cummins, J., 389
Cunningham, A. E., 436, 437, 498
Cunningham, P. B., 98, 103, 104, 107, 109, 113, 473
Curran, D. J., 18
Curran, J. M., 328
Curtis, W. J., 3
Curtiss, S., 49, 197, 199
Cyranowski, J. M., 542

Dabholkar, A. S., 139
Dacey, J., 447, 461
Dadds, M. R., 415
Dahl, K. L., 383
Dahl, R. E., 259
Daigneault, R. S., 464
Dainton, M., 15
Dake, J., 432
Dale, P. S., 191
Dalton, M., 544
Daly, K., 115
Damasio, A. R., 194
Damasio, H., 194
Damon, W., 314, 418, 425, 515
Daniels, D. H., 301
Daniels, M., 9
Daniels, S. R., 468

Danis, A., 156
Danish, S., 465
Dannemiller, J. L., 142, 143, 144
Dansen, P. R, 370
Darby, B. L., 101
Daro, D., 235, 238
Darroch, J. E., 534
Darwin, C., 13, 14, 31, 32, 33, 49
Dasen, P., 372
Datta, L. E., 292
D'Augelli 03, 521
Davidson, J., 412
Davidson, J. K., 18
Davidson, R. J., 407
Davies, O. L., Jr., 408
Davies, P., 322
Davies, P. T., 533
Davis, A. C., 313
Davis, B., 542
Davis, B. E., 151
Davis, B. T., 322
Davis, E. C., 536
Davis, L. B., 147
Dawson, D. A., 430, 543
Dawson, G., 398
Day, N. L., 102
Day, R. D., 315, 319
Day, R. H., 156
Deak, G. O., 190
Deal, J. E., 315
Deane, J., 261
Deater-Deckard, K., 221
De-Bellis, M. D., 451
de Benedictis, T., 487
DeCasper, A. J., 145
Decker, M. D., 264
DeCorte, E., 378
Decoufle, P., 345
Deford, F., 69
DeFries, J. C., 8, 71, 76, 391
DeGarmo, D., 416
Degirmencioflu, S. M., 529
Degirmencioglu, S. M., 529
deGraf, J. A., 394
de Houwer, A., 287
DeJong, C. J., 84
de Kanter, A. A., 429
Dekker, M., 414
DeKlyen, M., 415
Dekovic, M., 319, 526
Delany, S., 145
DeLisi, D., 504
De Lisi, R., 501, 504
Dell, D. L., 478
DeLoache, J. S., 270, 271, 277
DeLongis, A., 15
del Ray, R., 408
Delucchi, K., 487
Demaray, M. K., 438
DeMarie-Dreblow, D., 277
DeMier, R. L., 124
Demulder, E. K., 434
Demuth, K., 380
Denham, S., 434
Denham, S. A., 309, 314, 434
Department of Health and Human Services, 238
Depner, C. E., 325
Deregowski, J. B., 374
De Rosier, M. E., 430
Derry, P. S., 461
Descartes, R., 287
DeVet, K. A., 303
deVilliers, J., 193, 380
deVilliers, P., 193, 380

Devlin, B., 9
DeVries, M., 23, 217, 292
Dewey, M. J., 264
DeWolf, D. M., 317
De Wolff, M. W., 225
Diamond, A., 171, 174, 341
Diamond, J., 6
Diamond, L. M., 520, 521
Diamond, M., 302
Diaz, R. M., 275
Diaz, T., 515
Dickinson, T. S., 495
Diehl, S. F., 124
Dielman, T. E., 515
Dietary Guidelines for Americans, 351
Dietz, W. H., 352, 354, 355, 540
DiGeronimo, T. F., 211
DiGirolamo, A. M., 342
DiLalla, L. F., 281
DiMaggio, P., 281
Dimas, J. M., 408
DiPietro, J., 348
DiPietro, J. A., 160, 214
Dishion, T., 416
Dishion, T. J., 331, 414, 415, 429, 523, 525, 527
DiVitto, B., 124
Dix, T., 317
Dode, I., 542
Dodge, K. A., 312, 315, 409, 415, 430, 431, 434, 472
Doherty, M., 487
Doherty, W. J., 115, 228
Dollaghan, C., 189
Donahue, M. J., 492
Donaldson, M., 274
Donelson, E., 493
Donhow, J. E., 147
Donnelly, D. A., 525
Donnez, J., 82
Donohue, P. K., 100
Donzella, B., 217
Doosard-Rousevelt, J. A., 121
Doppler, M., 333
Dornbusch, S. M., 319, 323, 325, 499, 522, 533
Doueck, H. J., 239
Dow, G. A., 270
Downey, E. P., 385
Downs, A. C., 305
Doyle, A. B., 385, 386, 387, 531, 536
Doyle, L. W., 160
Dragonas, T., 107
Drapeau, S., 331
Draper, P., 455
Dreves, C., 501, 502
Drewett, R. F., 158
Driscoll, A., 536
Driscoll, R., 411
Drummond, K. W., 504
Dubois, A. F., 535
Dubrow, N., 412
Dubrow, N. F., 412
Duda, J., 165
Duerst, B. L., 536
Duffy, J., 438
Dukes, R. L., 519
Dulberg, C., 346
Dulcan, M. K., 393, 394
Dumas, J. E., 405
Dumka, L. E., 408
Dummins, R. A., 407
Dunaway, R. G., 515
Dunbar, K., 487
Dunbar, K., 487
Duncan, G. J., 21, 377
Duncan, P., 458

Duncan, R. M., 275, 280, 331
Duncan, S., 235, 237
Dunn, J., 280, 286, 311, 330, 331, 430
DuPaul, G. K., 393
Durant, N. A., 541
Durso, F. T., 278
Dvorak, T., 525
Dweck, C. S., 300, 301
Dwyer, C. A., 501
Dwyer, K. M., 429

Eames, K., 252
Eason, E., 110
Easterbrooks, M. A., 228
Easterling, D. W., 112
Eaton, W. O., 305
Eaves, L. J., 117
Ebata, A. T., 547
Ebbeck, M., 388
Eccles, J. S., 281, 388, 404, 464, 493, 494, 498, 504, 505, 524
Eckenrode, J., 238
Eckensberger, L. H., 425
Eckert, T. L., 393
Eddy, J. M., 415
Edelbrock, C. S., 392
Edelstein, W., 40
Edens, J. F., 219
Edgerton, R. B., 394
Edgeworth, J., 239
Edwards, C. P., 135, 305
Edwards, J., 287
Edwards, L., 106
Egan, S. K., 404, 454
Egeland, B., 225, 228, 320
Ehrhardt, A. A., 302
Ehri, L. C., 380
Ehrle, J., 229
Ehrlich, A., 303
Eiben, R., 121, 122
Eiberg, H., 67
Eimas, P. D., 176
Einarsson, C., 438, 505
Eisebud, L., 305
Eisenberg, A., 94
Eisenberg, M., 221
Eisenberg, N., 48, 105, 114, 311, 312, 313, 314–315, 408, 409, 434, 436, 504, 516
Elardo, R., 44
Elbert, T., 33
Elder, G. H., 318
Elias, L., 500
Elias, S., 79
Elicker, J., 228
Elins, J. L., 331
Elkind, D., 12, 290, 488
Elliot, D. M., 234
Elliot, S. N., 438
Elmore, A. M., 411
Elo, I. T., 534, 536
Ely, R., 500, 504
Emery, R. E., 235, 239, 322
Emes, C. E., 540
Emslie, G. J., 417
Endsley, R. C., 305
Engelsmann, F., 231
Engen, T., 116
English, K., 21
Enns, L. R., 305
Ennett, S. T., 529
Ensminger, A. H., 462
Ensminger, M. E., 462
Entwisle, D. R., 496
Epperson, C. N., 114
Epstein, J. L., 98, 531

Erdley, C. A., 532
Erel, O., 331
Erickson, J. A., 492
Erikson, E. H., 35, 49, 205, 206, 211, 299, 404, 516–517, 531, 537
Eron, L. D., 334
Espelage, D. L., 432
Espenshade, T. J., 15
Espinoza, R. L., 303
Esterberg, K. G., 17
Evans, G. W., 21, 44
Eveleth, P. B., 456
Ewy, R., 144
Ezzaki, A., 294

Fabes, R. A., 4, 46, 47, 50, 213, 305, 308, 310, 312, 313, 314, 316, 326, 327, 402, 408
Fabris, C., 102
Fafel, J., 32
Fagan, J., 479
Fagen, J. W., 182
Fagot, B. I., 182, 304, 317
Fainaru, M., 355
Falbo, T., 430
Falk, P. J., 17
Fallone, G., 261, 262
Fan, X., 379, 504
Fanaroff, A. A., 120
Fang, J., 121
Fantuzzo, J., 293
Fantz, R. L., 142
Farber, E. A., 314
Farber, N., 489
Farmer, M., 434
Farneti, P., 134
Farrar, M. J., 278, 287
Farrington, D. P., 541
Fearing, D. D., 178
Fearnow, M. D., 409
Fearon, R. M. P., 434
Featherman, D. L., 446
Federal Bureau of Investigation, 472, 541
Federman, J., 332, 333
Feerick, M. M., 412
Fegley, S., 499
Feingold, A., 405
Feldlaufer, H., 494
Feldman, J., 113
Feldman, P., 110
Feldman, R., 124, 377, 378
Feldman, R. S., 238
Feldman, S. S., 448
Fellman, V., 121
Fennema, E., 501
Fenson, C., 178, 284
Fenton, N., 430
Fenton, T., 393
Ferber, R., 135, 136
Ferguson, L. R., 500
Ferguson, R. E., 438
Fergusson, D. M., 101, 160, 324
Fernald, A., 145, 186
Fernald, L., 257
Ferrell, K. A., 250
Ferron, C., 535
Feter, M. D., 529
Feynman, R. P., 373
Fichner-Rathus, L., 81
Fichter, M. M., 468
Field, A. E., 468, 469
Field, T., 114
Fielding-Barnsely, R., 382
Fifer, W. P., 146
Filsinger, E. E., 146
Finch, C., 464
Finch, N. M., 159, 350
Fincham, F. D., 323

Fine, M., 324
Fine, M. A., 520
Finkelhor, D., 525
Finkelman, B., 234
Finkelstein, J. W., 458
Finn-Stevenson, M., 508
Fisch, R., 147
Fischer, J. L., 531
Fischer, K. W., 40, 246
Fischer, M., 392
Fisch, S., 294
Fisher, C. B., 466
Fisher, M., 461
Fitch, R. H., 504
Fitzgerald, B., 17
Fivush, R., 184, 278
Fix, M., 19
Flake, A. W., 80
Flanagan, C. A., 516
Flanagan, P., 479
Flavell, E. R., 280, 281
Flavell, J. H., 10, 280, 281, 384, 489
Flegal, K. M., 352
Fleming, J., 123
Fletcher, J. L., 98
Fleury, J., 231
Flewelling, R. I., 499
Focus on the Family, 17
Fodor, J. A., 194
Fogel, A., 106, 116, 152, 156
Foltz, C., 487
Fombonne, E., 397, 467, 468
Fondell, M. M., 228
Foorman, B. R., 382
Forbes, G. B., 452
Forehand, R., 535
Forehand, R. L., 455
Forgatch, M., 416
Forrest, D., 162
Forrest, J. D., 536
Foster, E. M., 318
Fouts, G. T., 537
Fowler, W., 76, 287
Fowles, D. C., 415
Fox, G. L., 115
Fox, N. A., 229, 341
Fox, R. A., 318, 415
Frable, D. S., 302, 405
Fracasso, M. P., 228
Frame, C. L., 460
Franiuk, R., 532
Frank, D. A., 102
Frankel, K. A., 228
Franssetto, S., 316
Fredrickson, B. L., 213
Freedman, D. S., 352
Freedman-Doan, C., 493, 498
Freeman, M., 529
French, D. C., 414, 431
French, K. E., 305, 347
Freppon, P. A., 383
Freud, S., 33, 35–36, 419, 438
Freund, L. S., 272, 368
Frey, K. S., 301
Freyd, J. J., 238
Frias, J. L., 99
Frick, P. J., 414, 415
Friedrich, L. K., 334
Friedrich-Cofer, L. K., 334
Friel, L. V., 536
Frisch, R. E., 456
Frith, U., 8
Fritz, A. S., 280
Frolund, L., 212
Frome, P. M., 404, 493
From Research to Practice, 261
Frongillo, E. A., 351

Frost, J. L., 329
Fruehling, J. J., 418
Fry, P. S., 387
Fugger, E. F., 68
Fujii, N., 247
Fujita, N., 285
Fulcher, M., 17
Fuligni, A. J., 493, 508, 513, 524, 526
Fulker, D. W., 9
Furman, W., 326, 523, 532, 533
Furnham, A., 468
Furstenberg, F. F., 321, 322, 323, 325, 534
Futterman, D., 475

Gabriel, S. W., 431
Gaddis, A., 461
Gadow, K. D., 334
Gaertner, B. M., 327
Gaffan, E. A., 225
Gage, F., 141
Gagnon, J. H., 537
Gaines, C., 526
Gaithright, J. F., 292
Galaburda, A. M., 253
Galambos, N. L., 454
Galbraith, K. A., 478, 525
Gale, J. E., 387
Gallagher, A. M., 504
Gallahue, D. L., 151, 158, 342, 463
Gallant, S. J., 461
Gallup Organization, 433
Galotti, K. M., 112
Gamble, T. J., 293
Ganchrow, J. R., 181
Gandhi, M., 49
Ganetsky, B., 246
Ganong, L., 324
Garbarino, J., 50, 279, 411, 412, 414, 548
Garber, J., 431, 522, 542
Garcia Coll, C. T., 15, 20
Garcia-Merita, M., 464
Gardner, H., 252, 375, 376, 395, 396
Gardstrom, S. C., 538
Garmezy, N., 411
Garner, P. W., 314
Garrison, W. T., 470
Garrity, C., 320
Garwood, M. M., 225
Gatzanis, S., 418
Gauss, K., 288
Gautier, T., 302
Gauvain, M., 280
Gauze, C., 531
Gaylor, E. E., 135
Gaze, C., 500
Ge, X., 458, 542
Geary, D.C., 31
Gecas, V., 523, 529
Geis, H. K., 342
Gelles, R. J., 235
Gelman, R., 177, 274
Gelman, S. A., 190, 280
Gentile, D. A., 538
Genuis, M. L., 238
Georgieff, M. K., 254, 257
Geraldson, B., 251
Gerris, J., 85
Gershman, H., 534
Gershoff, E. T., 20, 48, 316
Geschwind, N., 253
Getz, I., 425
Geva, J., 264
Gibbs, J., 422, 424
Gibbs, R. S., 97, 98
Gibson, E. J., 154
Giedd, J. N., 448, 449
Gil, A. G., 408

Gilbert-Barness, E., 159
Gillberg, C., 468
Gillette, J., 283
Gillian, D. O., 302
Gilligan, C., 426–427
Gillman, M. W., 160
Gilman, E., 40
Gilmore, M. R., 478
Gini, M., 228
Ginsburg, H. J., 305
Giordani, B., 261
Giordano, P. C., 532
Girnius-Brown, O., 317
Givaudan, M., 210
Gladstein, J., 412
Gladstone, T. R. G., 418, 542
Glass, R. H., 83
Glastris, P., 19
Gleason, J. B., 184, 285, 300, 504
Gleitman, H., 196
Gleitman, L. R., 196, 283
Glover, V., 104
Goedhart, T., 331
Goeke-Morey, M. C., 310
Goel, P., 101
Golan, M., 355
Gold, D., 438, 505
Goldberg, M., 230
Goldberg, S., 117, 124
Goldberg, W. A., 115, 228
Goldberger, L., 35, 517
Goldfarb, J., 531
Goldfield, B., 283
Golding, J., 107
Goldin-Meadow, S., 199
Goldschmidt, L., 102
Goldsmith, D., 135
Goldsmith, H. H., 210, 217
Golinkoff, R. M., 187
Gomez, C., 209
Goncalves, M., 233
Gonchas, G. Q., 508
Goncu, A., 213
Gondoli, D. M., 521, 523
Gonzales, N. A., 497
Gooden, A., 426
Goodlin-Jones, B. L., 135
Goodman, G. S., 235, 278
Goodman, R., 430
Goodman, R. A., 140
Goodman, S., 76
Goodnow, J. J., 315, 316, 454
Goodwyn, S., 188
Goodyear, I., 418
Goodyear, I. M., 417
Gopnick, A., 144, 178, 187, 197
Gopnik, A., 173, 177, 178
Gordis, E. B., 411
Gordon, B., 395
Gordon, R. C., 98
Gorman-Smith, D., 44, 414
Gortmaker, S. L., 122, 354, 355
Goswami, U., 368
Gotlib, I. H., 320
Gottesman, I. I., 9
Gottfried, A. E., 378
Gottfried, A. W., 122, 216, 378
Gottlieb, G., 8
Gottman, J. M., 322, 326, 327
Gottwald, S. R., 122
Goubet, N., 174
Gould, E., 141
Gove, F. L., 228
Graber, J., 352

Graber, J. A., 455, 458, 474
Graber, M., 173
Grabill, C. M., 417
Grabowecky, M., 448–449
Graczyk, P. A., 431
Graham, P., 330, 416
Graham, S., 432
Graham, S. A., 190
Graham, S. T., 507
Granic, I., 415
Granstroem, K., 438, 505
Grant, B., 91
Grant, B. F., 543
Grantham-McGregor, S., 257, 351
Gray, C., 438
Gray, J. A., 407
Gray, M. R., 319
Graybiel, A. M., 247
Grayson, A., 209
Gredler, G. R., 291
Green, E. H., 312
Green, F. L., 280, 281
Green, J. A., 209
Green, M., 33, 35, 38, 312
Green, P., 470
Greenberg, B. S., 334
Greenberg, M. T., 415
Greenberger, E., 499, 542
Greene, A. L., 468
Greene, B., 119, 134, 207
Greene, J., 389
Greene, K., 489
Greene, R. W., 392, 394
Greene, S. M., 531
Greene, T. R., 272
Greenhill, L. L., 394
Greenough, W. T., 139, 141
Greenspan, N. T., 207
Greenspan, S. I., 207
Greenwald, R. L., 317
Greer, B., 378
Greulich, F., 301
Gridina, N., 332
Griesler, P. C., 526
Griffin, D. W., 219
Griffin, K. W., 515
Griffin, R. S., 350
Griffith, E. M., 291
Griffith, J. R., 417
Grills, A. E., 432
Grinshaw, P. N., 251
Grogan, S., 352
Grolnick, W. S., 387
Grolund, J., 456
Groome, L. J., 133
Gross, L., 521
Grossman, K., 229
Grosvenor, M. B., 160, 161, 162, 255
Grotevant, H. D., 23, 516, 549
Grotpeter, J. K., 313
Gruber, M. L., 333
Gruber, R., 259, 261
Grusec, J., 315
Grusec, J. E., 317, 319
Grusec, J. W., 312, 316, 317, 325
Guerin, D. W., 216, 378
Guidubaldi, J., 321
Gullone, E., 468
Gunnar, M. R., 23, 116, 147, 217, 221, 408
Gunnell, D. J., 352
Guo, S. S., 352
Guralnick, M. J., 434
Gustafson, G. W., 209
Guthrie, I. K., 213, 314, 408

Haan, D., 5224
Hack, M., 100, 121, 122
Hadley, P. A., 282, 285, 434
Hagan, A. M., 324
Hagekull, B., 228, 434
Hagen, E. H., 114
Haggerty, R. J., 446
Hahn, H. M., 260
Haith, M., 155
Haith, M. M., 142, 143, 173
Haka-Ikse, K., 537
Hakanen, E. A., 537
Hakuta, K., 388, 389
Hala, S., 280, 384, 489
Hale, J. L., 489
Halil, T., 209
Hall, D. G., 190
Hall, G. S., 14, 430
Hall, H., 465
Hall, J. A., 305
Hall, J. G., 71
Hall, M. J., 41
Hall, N. W., 238
Halliday-Scher, K., 529
Halpern, D. F., 253, 498, 500, 503, 505
Halpern, L. F., 134
Halpern, R., 429
Halverson, C. F., 281, 304, 305, 307, 315
Hamel, S. C., 102
Hamers, J. F., 287
Hamilton, C. E., 232, 437
Hammer, L. D., 458
Hammond, W. R., 411, 414, 415
Hamre, B. K., 437
Hanaway, L., 333
Haninger, K., 539
Hanish, L., 47
Hansen, D. M., 499
Hao, L., 497
Hardy, J. B., 478
Hargreaves, D. J., 537
Harkness, S., 207, 328
Harlan, E. T., 216
Harlow, H. H., 221
Harmon, E. L., 507
Harpin, V., 147
Harrington, R., 542
Harris, B. G., 106
Harris, J. F., 278
Harris, J. R., 5
Harris, L. J., 253
Harris, P. L., 280, 281, 309, 410
Harris, S., 431
Hart, B., 196
Hart, C. H., 317, 327
Hart, S. N., 234
Harter, S., 300, 403, 405, 513, 514, 515
Hartup, W. W., 311, 325, 326, 404, 529
Harwood, R. L., 23, 227
Hashima, P. Y., 318
Hassold, T. J., 76
Haste, H., 426
Hatch, T., 376
Hathaway, S. E., 94
Hatton, D. D., 250
Haugaard, J. J., 235
Hauser, M. D., 247
Hauser, S. T., 524
Hausfather, A., 231
Haveman, R., 548
Hawkins, A. J., 479
Hawkins, M., 429
Hay, D., 312
Hay, D. F., 314
Hayashi, C. T., 464
Haye, K. M., 432

Hayes, D. S., 333
Hayes, R., 112
Hayne, H., 183, 184
Haynes de Reght, H. L., 113
Hayward, C., 458
Haywood, H. C., 275
Hazen, N. L., 434
Heald, F., 412
Health Behaviors in School-Aged Children, 462, 465
Hearing, Speech, and Deafness Center, 345
Hearold, S., 333
Heath, A. C., 117
Hedges, L. W., 500
Hediger, M. L., 160
Heffer, R. W., 316
Hegyi, T., 119
Heim, S., 33
Hein, K., 475
Heinberg, L. J., 352
Helleday, A., 211
Helledorn, B., 254
Helm, P., 456
Helsen, M., 517
Helwig, C. C., 418
Henderlong, J., 328
Henderson-King, D., 405
Henderson-King, E., 405
Hendrick, C., 537
Hendrick, J., 388
Hendrick, S. S., 537
Henggeler, S. W., 473
Henker, B., 394
Hennessey, B. A., 377
Henning, K. H., 425
Henrich, C. C., 412
Henricson, C., 524
Henricsson, L., 437
Henry, C. S., 525, 526
Henry, D. L., 411
Henshaw, S., 477, 478
Heppner, P. P., 307
Herdt, G., 521
Herman, A. A., 101
Herman, P. A., 380
Hermand, D., 489
Herman-Giddens, M. E., 456
Hern, K., 393
Hernandez, M., 333
Herold, E. S., 475, 537
Herrera, C., 233
Herrmann, D. J., 47
Hespos, S. J., 177, 177R
Hetherington, E. M., 319, 320, 321, 322, 324, 325, 411
Hewett, J. K., 392
Hewlett, B. S., 318
Heyman, R. E., 236
Hickey, P. R., 147
Hickson, F., 386, 387
Hiebert, E. H., 382
Higgins, A., 492
Higgins, D., 312
Higgins, E. T., 515
Hildebrand, D. K., 395
Hill, A. J., 352
Hill, C. R., 427
Hill, E. J., 479
Hill, J. P., 454, 525
Hill, K. K., 477
Hill, P. T., 19
Hines, M., 306, 500, 504
Hinshaw, S. P., 319, 414
Hiscock, H., 114
Hitchens, M. P., 71
Hobar, J. D., 122
Hobel, C., 6
Hochschild, A. R., 16

Hodapp, R. M., 395
Hodge, K., 464
Hodgson, D. M., 2
Hodkin, B., 229
Hodnett, E. D., 112
Hofer, B. K., 506
Hofferth, S. L., 427
Hoff-Ginsberg, E., 196, 287, 380
Hoffman, H. L., 313
Hoffman, L. W., 231
Hoffman, M. L., 313, 314, 525
Hoglund, W. L., 435
Holbrook, M. C., 346
Holden, G. W., 236
Holditch-Davis, B. P., 106
Hollich, G. J., 187
Holliday, M. A., 452
Hollin, C. R., 525
Holmbeck, G. N., 523, 526
Holmes, F., 407
Holzman, C., 30
Holzman, L. H., 381
Hondt, W., 252
Hong, H., 208
Honzik, M. P., 407
Hood, L., 285
Hopkins, B., 209, 254
Hopkins, W. D., 251
Hoppenbrouwers, T., 134
Hops, H., 322, 542
Hopwood, N.J., 454
Horn, J. L., 44
Horney, K., 35
Hornstein, M. D., 85
Horowitz, F. D., 45, 47
Horsey, K., 82
Hort, B. C., 281
Hort, B. E., 304
Horwood, L. J., 101, 160, 324
Horz, B., 531
Hou, Q. C., 116
Hovey, J. D., 408
Howard, C., 303
Howard, G. J., 479
Howard, K. I., 446
Howe, M. J. A., 378
Howe, M. L., 184, 374
Howes, C., 232, 289, 326, 327, 329, 437
Hoyenga, K. B., 306
Hoyenga, K. T., 306
Hoyt, C., 211
Hoza, B., 528
Hsu, L. K. G., 466
Hua, J., 134
Huant, I. W., 349
Hubel, D., 141
Hudson, B., 314
Hudson, J. A., 182, 278
Huesmann, L. R., 334
Huffman, L. C., 291
Hughes, F. P., 328
Hughes, S., 314
Hughes, S. O., 314
Hulshoff-Pol, H. E., 6
Hundley, M., 410
Huniziker, J., 316
Hunt, R. J., 142, 144, 145
Hunter, F. T., 180
Hunter, J., 521
Hurtado, A., 23
Hurtado, E. K., 257
Hurt, H., 102
Hurtado, A., 23
Husarek, S. J., 205
Huston, A. C., 294, 305, 318, 332, 333, 334, 377, 454
Hutcheson, R. H., 264
Hutchinson, S., 115

Huttenlocher, J., 285
Huttenlocher, P. R., 139, 195, 246
Hyde, J. S., 312, 501
Hymel, S., 532
Hynd, G. W., 393
Hynel, S., 431

Iedema, J., 517
Imaizumi, S., 102
Imperato-McGinley, J., 302
Individuals with Disabilities Education Acts of 1990, 390
Ingoldsby, E. M., 415
Ingram, D., 197, 282
Ingram, R., 209
Inhelder, B., 273, 368, 486
Insabella, G. M., 322
Institute of Medicine, 81, 84
International Association for the Evaluation of Educational Achievement, 501
Intons-Peterson, M. J., 304
Iosifescu, D., 542
Irizarry, N. L., 227
Irvin, F., 521
Irvine, J. J., 388
Irwin, C. E., 461, 534, 535
Isabella, R. A., 225
Ishihara, K., 259
Itard, J., 7, 8, 29–30
Ito, J., 77
Izard, C. E., 208

Jablow, M. M., 215
Jack, G., 318
Jacklin, C. N., 305, 312, 500
Jackson, K. M., 408
Jackson, R. J., 263
Jacobs, E. H., 392
Jacobs, J. E., 281, 504, 505
Jacobs, P. J., 329
Jacobs, R. A., 8, 33
Jacobs, V. A., 382
Jacobson, J. L., 160
Jacobson, L., 388
Jacobson, M. G., 495
Jacobson, S. W., 160
Jacobvitz, D., 393
Jagnow, C. P., 146
Jahoda, G., 370
Jain, A., 228
Jain, T., 85
James, R., 449
Janowsky, J. S., 195, 504
Janssens, J. M., 319
Jarvie, G. J., 460
Jarvis, P. A., 434, 499
Jason, L. A., 333
Jeannin, A., 535
Jellinek, M. B., 473
Jersild, A., 407
Jessor, R., 541
Jimerson, S. R., 496, 499
John, R. S., 331
Johns, M., 501
Johnsen, M. C., 238
Johnson, C., 315
Johnson, D. E., 23, 246
Johnson, D., 233
Johnson, J. S., 195
Johnson, L., 68
Johnson, L. A., 68
Johnson, L. M., 501
Johnson, M. H., 173
Johnson, T. R. B., 214
Johnson, V. G., 387
Johnson Institute, 543

Johnston, C. L., 352
Johnston, H. F., 418
Johnston, J. R., 320
Jones, C., 460
Jones, C. P., 197
Jones, D.C., 314
Jones, D. R., 48
Jones, L., 412
Jones, M. C., 459
Jones, OW, 77, 78
Jones, R. E., 81, 83, 91, 94, 107, 108, 110
Jones, S. K., 278
Jones, S. M., 377
Jones, S. S., 208
Jonsson, B., 155
Jordon, W. J., 509
Jorgensen, S. R., 479
Joseph, R., 94
Josephson, W. L., 334
Jouriles, E. N., 415
Jovanovic, J., 388, 501, 502
Joy, E. A., 105
Joyner, K., 521
Juffer, F., 219
Jusczyk, P. W., 142, 144
Jussim, L., 388, 494
Juvonen, J., 432, 433, 494

Kabbani, N. S., 496
Kachur, S. P., 472
Kagan, J., 17, 178, 218, 221, 315, 415
Kagan, S., 425
Kagan, S. L., 293
Kahn, A., 260
Kaiser Family Foundation, 433
Kalamas, A. D., 333
Kalkose, M., 225
Kalkwarf, H. J., 361
Kallen, K., 101
Kalter, H., 99
Kamkar, K., 536
Kandel, I., 466
Kane, M. J., 371
Kapitanoff, S. H., 235
Kaplan, H. B., 515
Karlson, H. C., 234
Karmiloff-Smith, A., 173
Karpov, Y. V., 275
Kasari, C., 394
Kashani, J. H., 417
Kaslow, N.J., 417, 542
Kassianos, G. C., 262
Katz, J. R., 328
Katz, L., 322
Katz, P., 385, 386
Katz, P. A., 385
Katzman, D. K., 466
Kaufman, J., 234
Kaufman, J. S., 411
Kavanagh, K., 416
Kavanaugh, R. D., 281
Kavrell, S. M., 498
Kaxzor, P., 272
Kay, T., 77
Kaye, H., 146
Kazdin, A. E., 418, 542
Kazura, K., 228
Kearsley, R. B., 178
Keating, D. P., 523
Keel, P. A., 84, 85
Keen, R., 155
Keener, M., 134
Kehoe, E. J., 36
Keil, F. C., 42
Keith, T. Z., 323
Kelder, S. H., 463
Keller, L. B., 504
Keller, M. L., 536
Kelley, K., 476
Kelley, M. L., 316, 318

Kellman, P. J., 142, 145
Kellogg, R., 252
Kelly, D. P., 391
Kelly, J. B., 321
Kelly, M., 488
Kelly, M. L., 316
Kempermann, G., 141
Kendall-Tackett, K., 32
Kendall-Tackett, K. A., 238
Kennard, B. D., 417
Kennedy, C., 354
Kennedy, C. L., 333
Kennedy, J. L., 392
Kennell, J. H., 219
Kenny, M., 447, 461
Keogh, B. K., 391, 396
Kerivan, A. S., 291
Kermoian, R., 23, 152
Kernis, M. H., 404
Kestenbaum, R., 314
Ketterlinus, R. D., 230, 541
Keye, W., 461
Keyvanfa, K. R., 68
Khoury, J., 361
Kidscape, 432
Kids Count, 478
Kiernan, K. E., 321
Kilbourne, J., 405
Kilbride, P. L., 254
Killen, J. D., 349, 354, 355, 458
Killen, M., 39
Kilmartin, C., 515
Kim, Y., 405
Kimberly, N. L., 229
Kimura, D., 305
Kindler, A. L., 389
King, B., 214, 215
King, M., 279
King, R. A., 246
King, R. B., 534
Kinney, D., 529
Kiosseoglou, G., 253
Kirby, D., 480
Kirkham, C., 432
Kirsh, S. J., 539
Kiser, L. J., 548
Kitayama, S., 405
Kittler, P. G., 466
Klaczynski, P. A., 487
Klahr, D., 487
Klaus, M. H., 117, 219
Klebanoff, M. A., 101
Klebanov, P. K., 21, 377
Kleiber, D., 465
Klein, H., 106
Klein, M. H., 540
Klein, N., 121, 122
Klein, N. K., 121
Klein, P. D., 376
Klein, R. G., 392
Kleinfelter Syndrome & Associates, 77
Kleinman, R. W., 351
Klepp, K. I., 463
Kless, S. J., 515
Kliewer, W., 409, 515
Klinnert, M. D., 208
Klute, C., 529
Knight, D. K., 179
Knight, G., 312, 422, 425
Knight, G. P., 519
Knight, R. T., 448–449
Knight-Ridder/Tribune News Service, 538
Knott, J., 500
Knowles, L. P., 68
Knutson, J. R., 317
Koch, P. B., 458
Kochanska, G, 216
Kochanska, G., 205, 317, 318

Kochenderfer, B. J., 430
Koegel, P., 394
Koeppie, G. K., 431
Koerner, S. S., 464
Koeske, R. D.
Koff, E., 458
Kohlberg, L., 227, 302, 419, 421–425, 492
Kohn, A., 316
Konnstamm, G. A., 217
Kolb, K. J., 388
Kolko, D. J., 234, 235
Koller, H., 121
Koller, S., 313
Kolstad, D. V., 270
Kolvin, E., 418
Konarski, R., 532
Kong, E., 155
Konlande, J. E., 462
Konner, M., 139, 247
Koot, H. M., 414
Kopp, C. B., 211
Korbin, J. E., 238
Korht, W. M., 463
Korkman, M., 121
Kornhaber, M. L., 376
Korsvik, S., 147
Korte, D., 112, 113
Kostelny, K., 412
Kotchick, B. A., 535
Kotlowitz, A., 411, 412
Kowal, A., 331
Kowatch, R. A., 417
Kozu, J., 313
Krager, J. M., 392
Krahenbuhl, G. S., 463
Kramer, C., 496, 498
Kramer, L., 331
Kramer, M. S., 105
Kramer, S. J., 144
Krashen 00, S., 389
Kraus, J. F., 261
Krauss, D. A., 323
Krechevsky, M., 376
Kroger, J., 518
Krueger, H., 499
Krull, J. L., 158
Krutschnitt, C., 414
Ku, L., 536
Kuchuk, A., 144
Kuczmarski, R. J., 160
Kuczynski, L., 317
Kudlacz, E. M., 116
Kuhl, P. K., 177
Kuhn, D., 304, 487
Kuhn, H., 141
Kuhn, L., 102
Kuipanoff, K., 490
Kumpulainen, K., 432
Kumra, S., 78
Kunda, Z., 307
Kundert, D. K., 291
Kunnen, E. S., 517
Kupanoff, K., 314, 527
Kupersmidt, B., 435
Kupersmidt, J. B., 526
Kurdek, L. A., 321
Kurowski, C., 418
Kurtines, M., 408
Kurtines, W. M., 412
Kwasman, A., 392, 393

Laakso, L., 350
Laasko, M. L., 328
Labre, M. P., 460
Ladd, G. W., 327, 430, 431, 437
Lagercrantz, H., 116
LaGreca, A. M., 407, 529
Laible, D., 314, 327, 490
Laird,R. D., 415
Lamaze, F., 111–112
Lamb, M. E., 228, 230, 232, 318, 541

Lamborn, S. D., 319
Lambros, K. M., 415
Lamon, S. J., 501
Lampert, W. E., 389
Lande, J., 230
Landeros, G., 210
Landers, D. M., 464
Landers-Pott, M., 393
Landry, D. J., 356
Lane, D. A., 78
Lane, K. L., 415
Lane, M. K., 272
Lang, R., 219
Langendorfer, S., 158
Langer, J., 39, 175
Langlois, J. H., 144, 305, 405
Lanning, K. V., 362
Lanphear, B. P., 361
Lansink, J. M., 178
Laosebikan, S., 106
LaPorte, D. J., 460
Lapsley, D. K., 488
LaRoche, C., 231
Larson, C. L., 407
Larson, R., 465, 515, 526, 529, 548
Larson, R. W., 529
Larson, S. K., 160
Larzelere, R. E., 316
Lasker, J., 329
Lassen, K., 101
Laumann-Billings, L., 239
Laursen, B., 524, 526
Lautenbacher, S., 48
Lavigne, J. V., 135
Lavin, D. R., 491
Leach, P., 156
Leadbetter, B. J., 435
Leaper, C., 48, 533
Leboyer, F., 112
Le Couteur, A., 398
Leder, P., 71
Lederman, S. A., 355
Lee, A., 470
Lee, C. M., 320
Lee, L. C., 233
Lee, M., 289
Lee, S., 317, 378, 379, 506
Lee, S. S., 414
Lee, V. E., 495
Lefkowitz, M. M., 334
Leger, D. W., 209
Legerstee, M., 144
Lehman, S. J., 464
Leinbach, M. D., 182, 304
Leiter, J., 238
Leith, H., 438
LeMare, L. J., 532
Lemons, J. A., 120
Lengua, L. J., 418
Lenneberg, E., 194
Lento, J., 548
LePage, D. E., 208
Lepper, H. S., 392
Lepper, M. R., 328
Lerner, R. M., 460
Leslie, A. M., 281
Lester, B. M., 109, 120, 289
Leve, L. D., 317
Leveno, K. J., 113
Leventhal, E. A., 112
Leventhal, H., 112
Leventhal, J. M., 30, 102
Levin, B. B., 539
Levine, J. A., 315
Levine, M., 239
Levine, M. P., 468
LeVine, R. A., 233, 405
Levinger, B., 351
Levinson, E. M., 374

Levy, G. D., 178, 305, 385, 520
Levy, J., 305–306
Levy, S. R., 388
Levy-Storms, L., 534
Lewinsohn, P. M., 458
Lewis, C., 228
Lewis, J., 321
Lewis, M., 102, 212, 213
Lewis, M. D., 107
Lewis, T. L., 142
Lewit, E. M., 291
Leyendecker, B., 228
Li, R., 161
Li, X., 71
Liben, L. S., 304, 307, 386
Liberman, A. M., 381
Liberty, C., 371
Liebergott, J. W., 197
Lieberman, M., 424
Lieberman, P., 184
Liebert, R. M., 332, 537
Life Sciences Research Office, 161, 462
Lifshitz, F., 159, 161, 162, 350, 355, 467, 468
Lifshitz, J. Z., 159, 350
Liikanen, A., 121
Lillard, A., 280
Lillard, A. S., 270
Lillo-Martin, D., 199
Limber, S. P., 433
Lind, J., 209
Lindberg, L. D., 536
Lindhagen, K., 155
Lindley, A. A., 101
Lindsey, E. W., 438
Linn, M. C., 487, 500
Linsdale, P. L., 479
Lipsey, M. W., 48
Lipsitt, L. P., 146
Lipworth, L., 105
Little, B. B., 102
Little, J. K., 304
Little, S., 431
Little, S. A., 522
Littleton, K., 252
Liu, L., 260
Liu, X., 260, 515
Livesley, W. J., 489
Lloyd, M., 539
Lockwood, P., 307
Loeber, R., 312, 541
Logsdon, M. C., 114
Lohaus, A. K., 226
Lohrmann, B. C., 326
Lollis, S., 532
Loney, B. R., 415
Long, C., 371
Long, P. J., 455
Longoni, A. M., 500
Lord, W. D., 362
Lorys, V. A. R., 393
Lo Turco, J. L., 246
Loucks, A. B., 463
Love, F. E., 505
Lovelace, L., 294
Lovelace, V. O., 334
Lovett, M. W., 391
Low, J. F., 162
Lonen Ms, 170
Lozoff, B., 257
Lubeck, S., 292
Lucas, A., 160
Lucey, J. F., 122
Luckner, A. E., 112
Ludemann, P. M., 181
Luna, B., 449
Luria, J. W., 157
Luria, Z., 435
Lutzker, J. R., 234, 235, 238
Lye, D. N., 325

Lynch, M. D., 300
Lynch, M. E., 454
Lynskey, M. T., 101
Lysne, M., 520
Lytle, L. L., 463
Lytle, L.l., 463
Lytton, H., 215, 307, 312
Lyytinen, H., 393
Lyytinen, P., 328

Maas, J., 450
McAdoo, H. P., 18
McAnarney, E. R., 478
MacBrayer, E. K., 410
McBride, A. B., 114
McBride-Chang, C., 238, 382
McCabe, M. P., 352, 460
McCarthy, M. E., 180
McCartney, K., 74, 75, 221
McCarty, M.E., 155
McCauley, E., 77
McClaskey, C. L., 434
McClearn, G. E., 77, 78
McClelland, D.C., 374
McClelland, J. L., 173
McClintic, S., 213, 300
McCloskey, L. A., 238
Maccoby, E. E., 46, 221, 312, 318, 319, 321, 323, 325, 327, 500
McCormick, A., 534
McCormick, M. C., 122
McCormick, S. H., 526
McCoy, J. K., 331
McCracken, C., 315, 319
McDermott, D., 303
McDonald, J. E., 361
Macdonald, S. C., 263
McDonnell, L. M., 19
McDonough, L., 272
McDougall, P., 431
McElroy, A., 303
McElwain, N. L., 233, 331
McEwin, C. K., 495
MacFadden, A., 500
MacFarlane, A., 147
McFarlane, J., 107
Macfarlane, JW, 407
McFarlane, M., 239
McGillicuddy-De Lisi, A. V., 501, 504
McGlaughlin, A., 209
McGoey, K. E., 393
McGrath, M. P., 316
McGrath, M. P., 314
McGrory, A., 461
McGuigan, W. M., 236
McGuire, J., 468
McGuire, S., 331
McHale, H. M., 527
McHale, S. M., 331
McIntire, D. D., 113
McKenna, J., 136
McKenzie, B. E., 156
Mackey, M. C., 112
MacKinnon, C. E., 331
MacKinnon, R., 331
McKown, C., 388, 438
Macksoud, M. S., 412
McLaughlin, B., 388, 389
McLaughlin, F. J., 147
MacLean, P. D., 33
McLoyd, V. C., 216, 319, 377, 415
McManus, I. C., 253
McMillan, D., 304
MacMillan, D. L., 391, 396
MacMillan, R., 414
McMorris, B. J., 414
McPherson, S. L., 371
McQuillan, J., 389

McQuiston, S., 470
McQuivey, R. W., 464
Macrae, M., 36
MacTurk, R. H., 180
MacWhinney, B., 190
Madden, T., 519
Madhavan, S., 121
Madole, K. L., 175, 178
Madon, S., 388, 494
Maestas, M. L., 408
Maestro, S., 466
Magai, C., 316
Magnusson, D., 4, 44, 458, 459
Mahapatra, M., 425
Maier, S. E., 100
Main, M., 225
Majors, K., 326
Makin, J. W., 147
Malatesta, C. Z., 205, 208
Malina, R. M., 452, 464
Malm, C., 463
Maloney, M. J., 468
Malson, L., 7
Mander, R., 116
Mandler, J. M., 177, 178, 272, 278
Maney, D. W., 458
Mange, A. P., 9, 66, 70, 71, 76, 79
Mange, E. J., 9, 66, 70, 71, 76, 79
Mangelsdorf, S. C., 226
Manire, S. H., 314
Manlove, J., 478
Manners, P., 346
Mannie, S., 285
Mannuzza, S., 392
Manus, K., 109
Maratsos, M., 190, 194
March of Dimes, 6, 75, 76, 79, 98, 99, 101, 105
Marcia, J., 517–518
Marciano, P. L., 542
Marcoen, A., 299
Marcus, G. F., 190, 193, 284
Marcus, M. D., 352
Margolin, G., 236, 331, 411
Margulis, C., 285
Marin, G., 303
Market Data Retrieval, 539
Markie-Dadds, C., 239
Markiewicz, D., 531, 536
Markman, E. M., 177, 187, 189, 190, 280
Marks, S. B., 390
Markson, L., 187
Markstrom-Adams, C., 519
Markus, H. R., 405
Marques-Bruna, P., 251
Marriage, K., 407
Marsh, H. W., 349, 464
Marshall, S. K., 475
Marshall, S. P., 501
Marshall, W. A., 451, 452, 456
Marsiglia, F. F., 519
Marsiglio, W., 115, 479
Martin, C. A., 177
Martin, C. L., 24, 46, 47, 281, 304, 305, 306, 307, 454, 531
Martin, J. A., 318, 319
Martin, J., 458, 460, 535, 537
Martin, L. M., 275
Martin, N. C., 53
Martin, R. J., 120
Martindale, C., 377

Martinez, G., 536
Martinez, R. O., 519
Martinez, S., 425
Martinez-Frias, M. L., 99
Martini, M., 330
Martins, C., 225
Martorano 77, 487
Marzolf, D. P., 270
MasatakN., 196
Mason, M. A., 324
Massey, C. M., 274
Masten, A. S., 3, 411
Mateika, J. H., 450
Mathason, L., 500
Matheson, C. C., 329, 2323
Mattock, A., 181
Maurer, D., 142, 144
Mauro, I. A., 214
May, D.C., 291
May, J. V., 84
Mayo Clinic, 355
Mazur, E., 321
Meadow-Orlans, K. P., 226
Meaney, M. J., 305
Measelle, J. R., 300
Mebane, S. E., 432
Medeiros, D. M., 17
Mediascope, 540
Medina, A. M., 236
Meece, J. L., 388
Meeus, W., 517
Mehlinger, S. L., 291
Meier, M., 414
Meier, R. P., 199
Meister, C., 387
Mellou, E., 377
Melnick, M. J., 464
Meltzer, D., 107
Meltzoff, A., 178, 187
Meltzoff, A. N., 183
Melzak, S., 237
Mendelsohn, A. L., 264
Mennella, J. A., 146
Menyuk, P., 185, 186, 197
Mercer, L., 431
Mercer, R. T., 106
Mercy, J., 411
Mergendoller, J. R., 383
Mergler, N. L., 278
Merikangas, K. R., 418
Merrick, J., 466
Merriman, W. E., 190
Merritt, J. A., 209
Merryman, J. D., 178
Mervis, C. A., 346
Mesias, W., 316
Mest, G. M., 394
Metha, A., 542
Meuleners, L., 470
Meyer-Bahlburg, H., 504
Michael, A., 494
Micheli, L. J., 350
Michelsson, K., 209
Middlemiss, W. A., 317
Midgley, C. M., 493, 494
Midobuche, E., 508
Mihalic, S., 433
Mikulincer, M., 228
Mikus, K., 115
Milgram, N. A., 414
Milhouwen, R., 537
Milich, R., 394, 410
Miller, A. L., 331
Miller, B. C., 478, 525, 534, 536
Miller, B. M., 429
Miller, C., 516
Miller, C. L., 494
Miller, E. K., 247
Miller, H. M., 404
Miller, J. G., 227, 425, 490

Miller, K. S., 535
Miller, M., 361
Miller, M. J., 120
Miller, N. B., 320
Miller, P. A., 313
Miller, P. H., 30, 39, 277, 371, 384, 489
Miller, S. M., 305
Millikan, R. G., 177
Millrood, D. L., 450
Mills, R., 317
Millstein, S. G., 461
Minkoff, H. L., 113
Minton, C., 315
Mintz, J., 301
Mischel, W., 306
Missmer, S. A., 85
Mistry, J., 276
Mitru, G., 450
Miyake, K., 226
Miyake, S., 259
Mize, J., 327, 431
Mnookin, R. H., 321, 323, 325
Moerk, E. L., 195
Moffitt, K. A., 124
Mohr, J., 67
Mohr, W. K., 293
Moilanen, K. L., 536
Mojica, E., 238
Molfese, D. L., 215
Molfese, V. J., 215
Monahan, S. C., 323
Money, J., 302
Monitoring the Future, 544
Monk, C., 104
Montefalson, R., 78
Montepare, J. M., 32
Montero, I., 275
Montgomery, R., 326
Montour, K., 5
Moon, C., 146
Moon, R. Y., 151
Moore, B. J., 355
Moore, C., 180
Moore, G. E., 71
Moore, K. A., 536
Moore, K. L., 83, 94, 534
Moore, M. K., 183
Moore, N. B., 18
Moore, S. G., 110
Moore, S. M., 468
Moorehead, K., 303
Morah, M., 466
Moreau, D., 417
Moreau, G. F., 535
Morelli, G. A., 136
Morelli, G. A., 135, 233
Morris, N., 112
Morris, P. A., 44
Morris, RJ, 98
Morris, T. W., 374
Morrison, F. J., 291
Morrongiello, B. A., 155
Mortimer, J. T., 495
Mory, M. W., 529
Moser, J., 418
Mosier, C., 276
Moss, E., 225
Mounts, N. S., 319
Mowder, B. A., 122
Mrug, S., 528
Mruk, C., 301, 404
Mu, X., 379, 507
Mueller, U., 485
Mufson, L., 417
Muller, T., 15
Mullet, E., 489
Mulvenon, S., 542
Mumme, D., 144, 205
Munakata, Y, 173
Munakata, Y., 42
Munn, P., 311, 331

Munoz, J. M., 305
Munsch, J., 531
Muratori, F., 466
Muret-Wagstaff, S., 110
Murkoff, H. E., 94
Murphy, B. C., 311, 313, 434
MurphyB, 317
Murphy, W. D., 235
Murray, J. P., 332
Murray, K. T., 216
Murray, L., 179
Mussen, P. H., 459
Must, A., 352
Muster, M., 541
Muus, R. E., 518
Myers, A., 351
Myers, D. B., 117, 515
Myers, H. R., 408
Myers, N. A., 183
Myers-Walls, J. A., 412
Mylander, C., 199

Nadder, T. S., 393
Nagy, W. E., 380
Naigles, L. R., 283
Nansel, T., 432, 433
Nanson, J., 100
Napolitano, B., 461
Narasimhan, B., 285
Nash, J. M., 8, 136, 140, 141
Nash, S. C., 304
Nathanieisz, P. W., 107
National Association for the Education of Young Children, 382
National Cancer Institute, 264
National Center for Children in Poverty, 21
National Center for Education Statistics, 229, 291, 388, 433, 436
National Center for Health Statistics, 91, 98, 101, 102, 103, 110, 112, 113, 119, 120, 157, 158, 324, 471, 472, 534
National Center for Injury Prevention and Control, 263–264
National Center on Addiction and Substance Abuse, 547
National Clearinghouse on Child Abuse and Neglect, 234
National Down Syndrome Society, 76
National Federation of State High School Associations, 464
National Highway Traffic Safety Administration, 471, 543
National Institue of Mental Health, 416
National Institute of Arthritis and Musculoskeletal and Skin Diseases, 344
National Institute of Child Health and Development, 230, 231, 232
National Institute of Out-of-School Time, 429

Munoz continued...
National Institute on Drug Abuse, 544, 545, 546
National Issues Forum, 229
National Mental Health Association, 410
National Middle School Association, 495
National Research Council, 16, 19
National Research Council and Institute of Medicine, 199
National Science Foundation, 501
National Telecommunications and Information Administration 539
Natsopoulos, D., 253
Naus, M. J., 371
Navaez, D., 425
Naylor, P., 408
Neale, D.C., 387
Neale, M. C., 117
Neiger, B. L., 99
Nelson, C. A., 140, 141
Nelson, D. A., 410
Nelson, K., 184, 277, 278, 283
Nelson, K. E., 187
Nelson, S. A., 421
Nelson-Le Gall, S. A., 421
Nemours Foundation, 362
Nestle, M., 353
Neuman, M. J., 293
Neveus, T., 347
Nevid, J. S., 81
Neville, H., 199
Newberger, E. H., 162
Newcomb, A. F., 326, 327, 531
Newcombe, N., 386, 500
Newman, L. F., 101, 490
Newport, E., 195
Newport, E. L., 11, 173, 186, 196, 199
Newton, I., 33
NHANES, 161
Niaz, M., 485
NICHD, 397
NICHD Child Care Research Network, 507
Nicholls, J. G., 437
Nicholson, J., 292
Nicholson, J. M., 324
Nicolaisen, J., 447
Nieman, R. H., 292
Nilzon, K. R., 418
Ninio, A., 285, 381
Nitz, K., 414
Nitz, K. A., 541
Noam, G. G., 429
Noble, S., 438, 505
Norgaard, J. P., 347
North, A. C., 537
Nosphitz, J. D., 246
Notaro, P., 233
Nottelmann, E. D., 453
Novick, J. R., 497
Nowell, A., 500
Nozza, R. J., 145
NPRIDE, 547
Nsamenang, A. B., 106
Nua Ltd., 540
Nuechterlein, K. H., 411
Nugent, K. J.
Nurcombe, B., 417
Nurmi, J. E., 525
Nyiti, R. M., 370

National Institute on... continued
Oakes, L. M., 175, 178
Oates, R. K., 162
Obeidallah, D. A., 430
Oberklaid, R., 346
O'Brien, B., 109
O'Brien, D., 76
O'Brien, L. T., 504
O'Brien, M., 197, 311
O'Connell, B., 187
O'Connell, M., 429
O'Connor, B. P., 525
Oddone-Paolucci, E., 238
Oden, M. H., 55
Oei, T. P., 101
Offer, D., 446
Office of Immigration Statistics, 19
Office of Management and Budget, 20
Office of Management and the Budget, 19
Office of Minority Health, 98
Office of the Surgeon General, 344
Ogbu, J. U., 303, 374
Ogden, C. L., 352
Okamoto, Y., 41
Okon, D. M., 468
Oktay, K., 82
O'Leary, S. G., 236
Olivardia, R., 460
Oliver, P. H., 236
Olson, C. M., 351
Olson, D. R., 487
Olsson, C. A., 470
Olthof, T., 309
Olvera, J. D., 210
Olweus, D., 432, 433, 532
O'Malley, K. D., 100
O'Moore, M., 432
O'Neill, D. B., 350
Ong, A., 519
Oper, O. 95, 117
Oppenheim, D., 135
Orbuch, T. L., 537
Ordy, J. M., 142
Ornstein, P. A., 371
Ortiz, V., 18
Orwoll, E. S., 504
Osborn, R. W., 112
Osborne, M. L., 157
Osofsky, J. D., 197
Oster, H., 145
Osterling, J., 398
Ostoja, E., 548
Ostrov, E., 446
Otake, M., 103
Otero-Sabogal, R., 303
Ottolini, M. C., 151
Overbeck, M. D., 160
Overton, S. F., 487
Overton, W. F., 46, 485
Oviatt, S. K., 504
Owens, E. B., 21
Owens, J. A., 261
Owens, R. E., 184, 185, 186, 192, 196, 284, 285, 287
Owens, S. L., 505
Ozmun, J. C., 151, 158, 342, 463

Padilla, M. T., 20
Paertowski, C. A., 264
Page, R. M., 468
Pagnini, D. L., 103
Paik, H., 294, 333
Paikoff, R., 537
Paikoff, R. L., 453, 523, 526, 534
Paisley, T. S., 105
Palardy, N., 470
Palfry, S., 264

Pallin, V., 352
Palmer, D., 314
Palmer, E. J., 525
Palmerus, K., 418
Palombaro, M. M., 430
Paneth, N., 30
Papadimitriou, A., 456
Papageorgious, A., 120
Papini, D. R., 524
Papp, L. M., 310
Pardo, C., 412
Parens, E., 68
Parent, S., 225
Paret, I., 135
Paris, S. G., 387, 436, 437, 498
Parisi, D., 32
Parke, R. D., 228, 315, 322
Parker, B., 107
Parker, J. G., 326, 418, 430, 431, 434, 436, 461, 531
Parkhurst, J. T., 532
Parmelee, A. H., 134
Parsons, J., 408
Parten, M., 328
Pascal, B., 288
Paschall, M. J., 499
Passell, J. S., 19
Paster, Y., 464
Pasupathi, M., 3
Patterson, C., 326
Patterson, C. J., 17, 415, 435, 526
Patterson, D., 76
Patterson, G. 82, 416
Patterson, G. R., 414, 415, 416, 525
Paul, R., 192
Paus, T., 451
Pavlov, I., 36
Peabody, P., 350
Peacock, A., 162
Pearson, J. L., 500
Peek-Asa, C., 261
Peirano, P., 159
Pelham, W. E., 393, 394
Pellegrini, A. D., 31–32, 305, 328, 393
Pennington, B. F., 391
Peracchio, L. A., 333
Perathoner, C., 102
Pereg, D., 228
Perez-Granados, D. R., 331
Perlmann, R. Y., 285
Perner, J., 280, 487
Perris, E. E., 183
Perry, C. L., 463
Perry, D. G., 307, 333
Perry, L. C., 333
Perry, M., 388
Perry, P. G., 531
Perry, S. E., 81, 83, 91, 94, 108, 111
Persell, C. H., 438
Perusse, D., 117
Perzanowski, M. A., 263–264
Peskin, H., 459
Peters, H. E., 323
Petersen, A. C., 352, 453, 454, 458, 498, 500, 547
Peterson, G. W., 158, 315, 319, 522, 524, 525
Peterson, J. L., 322
Peterson, R. E., 302
Petit, G. S., 315
Petrie, G., 431
Petruzzello, S. J., 464
Pettegrew, J., 538

Pettit, G. S., 327, 415, 434, 525
Pew Internet and American Life Project, 540
Phelan, K. J., 361
Phelps, L. A., 460
Phillip, D., 303
Phillips, D., 230
Phillips, E. L., 468
Phillipsen, L. C., 531
Phinney, J. S., 425, 519
Phipps-Yonas, S., 411
Physical Self Description Questionnaire (PSDQ), 349
Piaget, J., 10, 13, 39–42, 49, 50, 167, 168, 169, 170, 171, 172, 174, 177, 269–273, 275, 312, 367, 368, 387, 419–421, 485
Pianta, R. C., 291, 437
Picchi, L., 466
Pick, H. L., 47, 270
Pierce, R., 112
Pierroutsakos, S. L., 270, 271
Pierson, M., 415
Pinker, S., 194, 195, 284
Pintrich, P. R., 493
Pipher, M., 515
Pisoni, D. B., 142, 144, 145, 185
Pizzini, E. L., 388, 438
Plank, S. B., 509
Planned Parenthood, 478
Plato, 11, 12
Platts-Mill, T. A., 263–264
Plewis, I., 209
Plimpton, C. E., 348
Plomin, R., 8, 9, 70, 71, 76, 77, 78, 214, 414
Plumb, N., 117
Plumb, P., 454
Plumert, J. M., 47, 178
Plunkett, J. W., 124
Poikkeus, A. M., 328
Polce, L. M., 515
Polit, D. F., 430
Pollack, H. A., 352
Pollak, S. D., 248
Pollitt, E., 256, 257
Pomerantz, E. M., 300, 301
Pong, S., 508
Pons, D., 4646
Pooler, W. S., 68
Poortinga, Y. H., 370
Pope, H. G., 460
Pope, W. S., 532
Popenoe, D., 320
Popkin, B. M., 465
Popp, T. K., 327
Porac, C., 253, 254
Porges, S. W., 160
Porter, R. H., 147
Posada, C., 219
Posner, M. J., 216
Post, J., 292
Potenza, M. N., 451
Potts, R., 333
Poulin, F., 327
Poulin-Dubois, D., 274
Powell, G. F., 162
Power, F. C., 492
Power, T. G., 314, 316
Powers, B. P., 225
Powlishta, K. K., 488
Prandi, G., 102
Pratt, C. C., 236
Pratt, M. W., 275
Prechtl, H. F. R., 155

Preece, A., 15
Preisig, MA., 418
Present, P., 264
President's Council, 464, 465
President's Council on Physical Fitness and Sports, 463
Pressley, M., 381, 383
Price, D. W. W., 278
Price, J., 430, 432
Price, J. M., 548
Price, R. J., 105
Pride Surveys, 545
Prinstein, M. J., 529
Prinz, R. J., 412
Pritzker, S. R., 376
Prodromidis, M., 114
Proffitt, D. R., 144
Prugh, D. G., 44
Pruitt, D. B., 548
Prysak, M., 113
Public Broadcasting Service, 294, 333
Public Law 94–142 (Education for All Handicapped Children Act of 1975), 390
Puig-Antich, J., 417
Putallaz, M., 434
Putnam, K. M., 407
Pyle, R. P., 464

Quadflieg, N., 468
Quatman, T., 515, 533
Quay, H. C., 415
Quinn, P. C., 176, 177
Quist, J. F., 392

Raboy, B., 17
Racusin, G., 411
Radke-Yarrow, M., 313, 317, 411
Raeff, C., 405
Raffaelli, M., 536
Rakison, D. H., 176, 274
Ramey, C., 289
Ramisetty-Mikler, S., 239
Ramsey, P. G., 385
Randel, B., 506
Randolph, S. M., 254
Rao, R., 254, 257
Rao, S. B., 193
Raphael, T. E., 382
Rappaport, I., 393
Rasmussen, K. L. R., 13
Rasmussen, P, 333
Rastam, M., 468
Rathus, S. A., 81
Rauch, P. K., 541
Rauschecker, J. P., 248
Raver, C. C., 292, 293
Raviv, A., 259, 261
Ray, G. E., 294
Raymond, A., 263–264
Raymond, D., 520
Raynor, R., 36
Recchia, S., 213, 300
Rechtschaffen, A., 258
Reder, P., 235, 237
Redmayne, R. S., 349
Redmond, D., 547
Reene, K., 485
Regimbal, C., 348
Regmi, M., 404
Reichert, 468
Reichman, N. E., 103
Reid, J. B., 317, 414, 415, 525
Reid, J. C., 417
Reik, W., 71
Reilly, S., 209
Reimer, R. L., 112

Reinisch, J., 454
Reinisch, J. M., 533
Reis, S. M., 396
Reisman, J. E., 147
Remafedi, G., 520
Renshaw, P. F., 542
Renwick-DeBardi, S., 314
Renzetti, C. M., 18
Renzulli, J. S., 396
Repacholi, B. M., 144, 178
Reppucci, N. D., 239
Rescorla, L., 192
Resnick, G., 228, 497
Resnick, M. D., 499
Rest, J. R., 425
Reuter, M. A., 239
Reynolds, A. J., 411, 548
Reynolds, M. A., 84
Reznick, J. S., 217, 283
Reznick, J. S., 314
Rhode, M., 520
Rholes, W. S., 384
Ricciardelli, L. A., 352, 460
Ricco, R. B., 487
Rice, E. P., 529
Rice, M. L., 187, 281, 282, 294, 434
Richard, P., 529
Richards, A. L., 391
Richards, H., 430
Richards, M. H., 468, 469, 515, 526
Richards, T. L., 391
Richardson, G. A., 102
Richman, N., 330
Ridley, M., 64
Rieber, R. W., 41
Rierdan, J., 458
Rieser-Danner, L., 217
Rimm-Kaufman, S. E., 291
Risley, T. R., 196
Risser, W., 515
Ritchie, W. C., 286, 287
Ritter, J. M., 144
Rivera, S., 175
Robbins, C., 380
Roberts, D. F., 537, 538
Roberts, L. R., 454
Roberts, W., 313
Robertson, A. D., 159
Robertson, J. A., 85
Robinson, A., 76
Robinson, C., 533
Robinson, J. A., 136, 156
Robinson, M. A., 239
Robinson, T. N., 349, 354, 355
Robson, J. R. K., 462
Rocca, P. T., 155
Rochat, P., 156
Roche, A. F., 133
Rocissano, L., 285
Rockstroh, B., 33
Rodgers, B. R., 536
Rodgers, J. L., 536, 541
Rodriguez, JN., 408
Rodriquez-Pinilla, E., 99
Roeder, K., 9
Roeser, R. W., 493, 494, 495, 496
Roffey, S., 326
Roggman, L. A., 144
Rogoff, B., 135, 179, 180, 276, 281
Rogosch, F. A., 225
Rohner, R. P., 524
Roker, D., 524
Romaine, S., 389
Romney, D. M., 307
Rompteaux, L., 489
Rondeau, N., 528

Ronnqvist, L., 155
Roopnarine, J. L., 329
Roosa, M. W., 408
Roper Organization, 18
Rorvik, D. M., 68
Rose, A. J., 313, 326, 327, 431
Rose, H., 305
Rose, S. A., 274
Rose, S. P., 246
Rose-Krasnor, L., 228
Rosenbaum, M. B., 460
Rosenberg, T. K., 417
Rosenblith, J. F., 89, 97, 208
Rosenboom, L. G., 219
Rosenboom, T. J., 6
Rosenshine, B., 387
Rosenstein, D., 145
Rosenthal, B. S., 496
Rosenthal, D. A., 448, 519
Rosenthal, M. K., 233
Rosenthal, R., 388
Rosewarne, D. L., 386
Rossner, S., 352
Roth, M. A., 531
Rothbart, M. K., 214, 216
Rothbaum, F., 226
Rothenberg, S. J., 103
Rotheram-Borus, M. J., 425
Rothstein, R., 389
Rouse, L. W., 418
Rovee-Collier, C., 182, 183, 184
Rovet, J., 77
Rowe, D.C., 414, 541
Rowland, T. W., 354
Royce, L., 495, 498
Roysircar, G., 408
Ruan, W. J., 160
Rubin, D. L., 489
Rubin, K. H., 218, 228, 329, 430, 431, 532
Ruble, D. N., 300, 301, 304, 305, 307, 384, 403, 454, 501, 515, 531
Rudy, D., 319
Ruel, J., 156
Ruff, H. A., 177
Ruffman, T., 487
Runco, M. A., 376, 377, 395
Rush, K., 306
Russ, S. W., 377
Russell, G., 454
Russell, S. T., 521
Russell, T., 499
Rutter, M., 8, 10, 70, 548, 549
Rutter, N., 147
Ruzicka, D. L., 261
Ryan, A. S., 161
Ryan, B. A., 436
Ryan, R. M., 387
Ryan, S. A., 461
Rydell, A. M., 228, 434, 437
Rymer, R., 192, 198
Rys, G. S., 313

Saarni, C., 144, 205, 309
Sabatier, C., 148
Sabo, D. F., 464
Sabogal, F., 303

Sachs, H. C., 151
Sacks, C. H., 383
Sacks, J. J., 361
Sacks, M., 329
Sacks, O., 371
Sadeh, A., 135, 259, 261
Sadker, D., 388, 438, 505
Sadker, M., 388, 438, 505
Sadler, T. W., 96
Safer, D. J., 392
Saffran, J. R., 186, 193
Saffron, L., 17
Safkin, J., 334
Sagberg, R., 261
Sagi, A., 228, 313
Sagrestano, L. M., 526, 534
Sahin, N., 294
Sahlman, S., 19
St. James-Roberts, I., 209
St. Laurent, D., 225
Saklofske, D. H., 395
Salazar, L. F., 515
Sales, B. D., 323
Salihu, H. M., 78
Salisbury, C. L., 430
Salmon, K., 415
Salovey, P., 374
Salzarulo, P., 134
Salzinger, S., 238
Sameroff, A. J., 22, 23, 494, 495
Sampaio, R. C., 138
Sampson, E. E., 405
Sampson, K., 533
Sampson, M., 228
Sampson, P. D., 101
Samuels, C. A., 144
Samuels, H. R., 250
Samuelson, L. K., 187
Sanchez-Hucles, J., 318
Sandall, S. R., 122
Sandberg, J. F., 427
Sandelowski, M., 106
Sander, L. W., 134
Sanders, M., 352
Sanders, M. R., 239
Sanders, P., 48
Sandler, I., 418
Sands, R., 352
Sandy, S. V., 311
Santa, P., 425
Sapienza, C., 71
Sapperstein, S. K., 246
Sargent, JD., 544
Sargent, K. P., 479
Sarigiani, P. A., 454
Sasse, D. K., 523
Sattler, J. M., 373
Saucier, D., 500
Savin-Williams, R. C., 17, 520, 521
Sawyer, D., 515–516
Sayers, L. K., 347
Scaer, R., 112, 113
Scafidi, R., 114
Scahill, L., 394
Scaramella, L. V., 524
Scarr, S., 74, 75, 221, 230
Schaefer, C. E., 211
Schafer, W. D., 229
Schatter, A., 144
Schaffner, K., 264
Schebendach, J., 462
Scheel, K. R., 538
Scheier, L. M., 515
Schepher, N., 217
Scher, M. S., 102
Schiff-Myers, N., 199
Schiller, M., 226
Schleifer, M., 421
SchlosserE., 353
Schlottmann, A., 277
Schmader, T., 501

Schmidt, R. E., 434
Schmidt, W., 78
Schmitt, R. E., 518
Schneider, B., 434, 521
Schneider, B. H., 313
Schneider, K., 208
Schneider, W., 181, 182, 184
Schoelmerich, A., 228
Schothorst, P. F., 121
Schreck, C., 361
Schubert, M. T., 145
Schuele, C. M., 434
Schuengel, C., 225
Schulenberg, J., 499
Schull, W. J., 103
Schulman, J. D., 68
Schultz, M. C., 197
Schultz, R. T., 421
Schur, F. A., 352
Schuster, B., 403
Schuster, M. A., 432
Schwartz, C. E., 415
Schwartz, E., 192
Schwartz, J. A., 542
Schwartz, K. D., 537
Schwartz, R. H., 113
Schwartz, W., 497
Schwebel, D.C., 47
Schweder, R. A., 425
Scopesi, A., 116
Scott, K. G., 257
Searleman, A., 254
Sebald, R. L., 447, 448
Sebby, R. A., 524
Sedlak, A. J., 234, 235
Seeley, J. R., 458
Seff, M. A., 523, 529
Segall, M. H., 370
Seidel, S., 376
Seidenberg, M. S., 194
Seidler, F. J., 116
Seifer, R., 226
Seiffge-Krenke, I., 531, 533
Sell, M. A., 294
Selman, R. L., 490, 491
Sera, M. D., 300
Serafini, S., 391
Serketich, W. J., 405
Sessa, F. M., 522, 524
Shacham, S., 114
Shaffer, L., 532
Shahini, M., 412
Shanahan, M. J., 499
Shanley, N., 542
Shapiro, L. R., 278
Sharpe, T. H., 537
Shaver, P. R., 228
Shavinina, L., 11
Shaw, D. S., 21, 415
ShawWinslow, 415
Shedler, J., 547
Sheeber, L., 322, 542
Sheehy, G., 446
Sheffield, E. G., 182
Shenker, I. R., 462
Shepard, L. A., 291
Shepardson, D. P., 388, 438
Sherman, T., 411
Sherrod, L. R., 446
Sherry, J. L., 540
Shettles, L., 60
Shields, B. J., 157, 330
Shields, M. K., 539
Shifflett, K., 239
Shin, C., 547
Shin, D., 329
Shipley, C., 371
Shope, J. T., 515
Shore, C., 187
Shrum, W., 530
Shucard, D. W., 500

Shucard, L. L., 500
Shugart, M, 238
Shulman, S., 429, 533
Shurkin, J. N., 55
Shute, N., 109, 112
Shutt, E., 361
Shwe, H., 280
Shyi, C. W. G., 182
Sidebotham, P., 235
SIECUS, 480
Siegler, R. S., 42, 173, 274, 277, 278, 367, 370, 371, 375
Sigman, M., 134, 367, 397
Sigmundson, K., 302
Signorella, M. L., 304, 307
Silber, T. J., 466
Silva, P. A., 160, 214, 215
Silverberg, S. B., 521, 523
Silverman, W. K., 407, 412
Simbruner, G., 145
Simeon, D. T., 257
Simmons, R. G., 458, 493, 494, 498
Simon, H. A., 278
Simon, T., 373
Simon, W., 537
Simonoff, E., 414, 541
Simons, R. L., 315, 524
Simons-Morton, B. G., 349
Simonton, D. K., 375, 376
Simpson, J. L., 79
Singer, D. G., 334
Singer, J. D., 53
Singer, J. L., 334
Singer, L. T., 102, 124
Singer, R. S., 464
Singer, W., 139
Singh, S., 534
Sinha, P., 248
Sinha, R., 352
Sizer, F., 161, 256, 350, 351
Skinner, B. F., 38, 192, 193
Skinner, E. A., 408
Skinner, J. S., 463
Skoe, E. E. A., 426
Skogstad, W., 228
Skuse, D., 209
Slade, A., 328
Slater, A., 181
Slater-Rusonis, E., 412
Slavin, R. E., 387
Slawinski, J. L., 371
Sleep, J., 109
Slep, A. M. S., 236
Slonims, V., 398
Slotkin, T. A., 116
Sluyter, D. J., 374
Small, M. Y., 174, 486, 487
Smallish, L., 392
Smart, L., 515
Smetana, J., 231
Smetana, J. G., 317, 523, 525, 526
Smith, A. E., 388
Smith, B. A., 145
Smith, C. A., 179
Smith, D., 307
Smith, D. W., 219
Smith, F., 383
Smith, G. A., 157, 350
Smith, J. B., 495
Smith, J. D., 501
Smith, J. E., 468
Smith, L. B., 10, 44, 152, 187
Smith, M., 24, 313

Smith, P. K., 305, 312, 328
Smith, R., 412
Smith, R. S., 548
Smith, S. L., 333
Smith, T. A., 235
Smith, T. M., 501
Smitsman, A. W., 155
Smokowski, P. R., 548
Smolin, L. A., 160, 161, 162, 255
Smothers, B. C., 505
Smulders, B., 116
Snarey, J. R., 425
Snider, S. A., 349
Snidman, N., 217, 415
Snow, C. E., 285, 300, 381
Snow, C. W., 208, 209
Snyder, E., 306
Snyder, H. N., 316
Snyder, J., 415, 434
Snyder, JB., 473
Soberon, H., 19
Sobkiewicz, T. A, 466
Sobol, A. M., 122
Socolar, R. R. S., 317
Socken, K., 107
Soldi, A., 102
Soliman, A., 408
Solis-Camera, P., 318
Solomon, J., 225
Sonenstein, F. L., 534, 536
Soriano, F. I., 414
Sosa, B. B., 278
Sotos, J. F., 77
South, S. J., 497
Spangle-Looney, S., 192
Spear, L., 449, 451
Spear-Swerling, L., 383
Specker, B., 468
Speers, M. A., 162
Speicher-Dubin, B., 422
Spelke, E. S., 155, 174, 177
Speltz, M. L., 415
Spence, M. J., 145, 393
Spencer, J. P., 155
Spencer, M. B., 20, 519
Spencer, P. E., 226
Spetner, N. B., 144
Spinrad, T. L., 4
Spirito, A., 473
Spoth, R. L., 547
Sprafkin, J., 32, 537
Sprague, J., 414
Sprecher, S., 537
Springel, K., 499
Spritz, B., 228
Sroufe, L. A., 207, 208, 224, 228, 314, 320, 393, 435, 523
Stack, D. M., 208
Stafford, F. P., 427
Stafford, L., 524, 525
Stang, H. J., 147
Stange, T., 388
Stangor, C., 212, 304, 307
Stanley, B. K., 323
Stanley, J. C., 396, 501
Stanley-Hagan, M., 321, 325
Stark, K. D., 418
Stattin, H., 525
Status of Women Council, 501
Staudinger, U. M., 3
Steele, C. M., 504
Steffe, L. P., 387
Steiben, J., 407
Stein, A., 134
Stein, A. H., 334
Stein, D. M., 468
Stein, M. T., 155
Stein, N. L., 212

Stein, R. E. K., 317
Steinberg, L., 319, 455, 499, 522, 524, 526
Steiner, H., 352, 464
Steiner, J. E., 181
Steinerg, L., 469
Steinhausen, H. C., 414, 466
Stephens, B. R., 144
Stephens, M. B., 78
Stern, D., 142
Sternberg, K. J., 230
Sternberg, R., 374
Sternberg, R. J., 374, 383
Stevens, N., 326
Stevenson, H. W., 317, 378, 379, 437, 506, 507
Stevenson, J. E., 330
Stevens-Simon, C., 478
Stewart, T. A., 71
Stifter, C. A., 215
Stigler, J. W.
Stipek, D., 437, 504
Stipek, D. J., 213, 300, 498
Stockhammer, T. F., 238
Stolberg, A. L., 322
Stone, B. B., 529
Stone, M. R., 529
Stonehill, R. M., 429
Stoneman, Z., 331
Stores, G., 260
Stores, M., 329
Stott, F. M., 50, 279
Stouthamer-Loeber, M., 541
Straus, M. A., 525
Strauss, R., 115
Strauss, R. A., 352
Strauss, R. S., 352
Strauss, S., 487
Straussner, J. H., 412
Straussner, S. L. A., 412
Strayer, J., 313
Streissguth, A. P., 99, 101
Strelau, J., 214
Striefel, S., 239
Stringer, P., 42
Strom, P., 378
Strom, R., 378
Strom, S., 378
Stromswold, K., 199
Strosberg, R., 187
Sturla, E., 302
Styfco, S. J., 292
Suarez-Orozco, C., 508
Suarez-Orozco, M. M., 508
Suber, C. F., 421
Substance Abuse and Mental Health Services Administration, 546
Sucher, K. P., 466
Sucoff, C. A., 534
Suecoff, S. A., 361
Sugai, G., 414
Sullivan, M. W., 102, 212, 213
Sulzby, E., 383
Summerfield, L. M., 355
Suomi, S. J., 13
Super, C. M., 207, 328
Surgeon General, 348
Susman, E. J., 458
Susman-Stilman, A., 225
Sutton, A. J., 48
Sutton, H. E., 78
Sutton-Smith, B., 213
Swain, J. L., 71
Swarr, A., 515
Swarr, A. E., 469

Swearer, S. M., 432
Sweet, R. L., 97, 98
Swendsen, J. D., 418
Synnott, A., 13
Szagun, G., 314
Szapocznik, J., 408

Tager-Flusberg, H., 76
Takahashi, K., 226
Takeuchi, D., 316
Tal, J., 208
Tamis-LeMonda, C. S., 179, 208, 228, 329
Tangney, J. P., 212, 213
Tanner, J. M., 245, 247, 451, 452, 453, 456
Tantleff-Dunn, S., 352
Tappan, M. B., 275
Taras, H. L., 354
Tarrant, M., 517, 518, 537, 538
Tarrant, T., 326
Tarullo, L. B, 292, 293
Tasker, F., 17
Tatzer, E., 145
Taubman, B., 156, 157
Taylor, A. Z., 507
Taylor, D. M., 389
Taylor, E., 303
Taylor, H. G., 121
Taylor, J. A., 75
Taylor, J. R., 451
Taylor, K. E., 112
Taylor, M., 190, 280, 281
Taylor, R. D., 393, 394, 506
Taylor, R. J., 520
Taylor, W. C., 349
Teale, W. H., 383
Tebes, J. K., 411
Tees, R. C., 185
Telama, R., 350
Tellegen, A., 9
Telljohann, S., 432
Temple, E., 391
Terlecki, M., 500
Terman, L., 55
Terman, L. M., 55
Terrell, B. Y., 282
Terwogt, M. M., 309
Teti, D. M., 330
Thal, D., 191, 195
Thelen, E., 10, 44, 45, 152, 155
Thiedke, C. C., 259, 260, 346, 347
Thoma, S. J., 425
Thoman, E. B., 133, 134
Thomas, A., 214, 215, 216, 418
Thomas, C. W., 216
Thomas, D. G., 500
Thomas, J. R., 305, 347, 371
Thomas, K., 352
Thomas, K. M., 449
Thomas, M. H., 480
Thomas, R. M., 31, 276
Thomasina, M., 537
Thompson, D. N., 488
Thompson, J. K., 352
Thompson, K. M., 539
Thompson, K. P., 537
Thompson, R., 327
Thompson, R. A., 32, 141, 209, 219, 220, 221, 228, 231, 407

Tiedemann, J., 388
Tiggemann, M., 352
Tilford, C. A., 66
Timischl, W., 145
Tinker, E., 285
Tinsley, B. J., 392
Tinsworth, D. K., 361
Tjebkes, T. L., 205
Tobin-Richards, M. H., 458
Toharia, A., 231
Tolan, P. H., 44, 414
Tolson, J. M., 529
Tomada, G., 313
Tomasello, M., 187, 270, 285, 311
Tomlinson-Clarke, S., 519
Torgan, C., 352, 355
Torney-Purta, J., 492
Torrance, E. P., 376
Torrey, C. C., 347
Torsheim, T., 408
Toselli, M., 134
Toth, S. L., 225
Tout, K., 229
Townsend, J., 139
Trabaso, T., 212
Travillion, K., 434
Treboux, D., 32
Treboux, D. A., 476
Treder, R., 77
Treffers, P. D. A., 331
Treiman, R., 381
Tremblay, R. E., 312, 532
Trent, K., 478
Trevarthen, C., 179
Trice, A. D., 306
Trickett, P. K., 44, 238, 317
Trieller, K., 461
Trommsdorff, G., 313
Tronick, E. Z., 309
Troseth, G., 270, 271
Trudeau, L., 547
Truglio, R. T., 294
Truhn, P., 239
Truwit, C. L., 138
Tschann, J. M., 458
Tse, L., 389
Tucker, C. J., 331
Tucker, C. M., 437
Turiel, E., 418, 426, 491–492
Turk, A. A., 542
Turner, H. A., 525
Turner Syndrome Society of the US, 77

Uauy, R., 159
Udelf, M. S., 142
Udry, J. R., 465
Uka, A., 412
Ullian, E. M., 246
Umana-Taylor, A. J., 519, 520
UNAIDS, 359, 360
Ungerer, A., 182
UNICEF, 158, 239, 256, 257, 412
United States Secret Service, 432
Upchurch, D. M., 534, 535
Updegraff, K., 47
Updegraff, K. A., 331, 430, 527
Updegraff, N. A., 531
Urban, J., 435
Urban Institute, 19, 429
Urberg, K. A., 529
U.S. Census Bureau, 14, 15, 16, 18, 20, 157,

229, 230, 429, 495, 497, 539
U.S. Department of Agriculture, 255, 351
U.S. Department of Education, 291, 390, 391, 497, 501
U.S. Department of Health and Human Services, 102, 344
U.S. Department of Justice, 325
U.S. Department of Labor, 16, 229, 231, 499
U.S. Department of Transportation, 471
U.S. Environmental Protection Agency, 264
U.S. Food and Drug Administration, 418
U.S. Office of Special Education Programs, 345
U.S. Public Health Service, 474
U.S. State Department, 23
Uttal, D., 379

Vaden, N. A., 435, 526
Vaillancourt, T., 431
Valdez, E. O., 303
Valent, F., 261
Van Beveren, T. T., 102
VanBrakle, J., 393
Vandell, D. L., 230, 232
van den Oord, E. J. C. G., 415
van der Ende, J., 414
van der Valk, J. C., 415
van de Vijver, F. J. R., 488
Vandewater, E. A., 348, 354
Vandewiele, M., 252
van Engeland, H., 121
Van-Evra, J. P., 332
Vanfossen, B. E., 464
Van Griffin, K., 143
van IJzendoorn, M. H., 225

Van-Kammen, W. B., 541
van-Laar, C., 303
Van Naarden, K., 345
Vartanian, L. R., 488, 489
Vasta, R., 500
Vaughn, L. S., 144
Vecchi, T., 500
Vega, W. A., 408
Vellutino, F. R., 383
Verbeek, P., 311
Verhoef, H., 233
Verhulst, F. C., 414, 415
Verschaffel, L., 378
Verschueren, K., 299
Vibbert, M., 144
Vietze, P. M., 180
Viglione, V., 466
Viikari, J., 350
Vijayan, S., 193
Vik, T., 101
Villani, S., 538
Violato, C., 238
Vishton, P. M., 193
Vitaro, F., 528, 532
Vogt, C. J., 465
Vollebergh, W., 517
Volling, B. L., 233, 330, 331
Vondracek, F. W., 518
von Hofsten, C., 144, 155
von Kries, R., 160
Vouloumanos, A., 145
Vuchinich, S., 236
Vygotsky, L., 41, 179, 196, 274–275, 276, 387

Waas, G. A., 431
Wachs, T. D., 9, 11, 214, 215, 217, 257
Wade, S. M., 124
Wagner, E., 313
Wagner, K. D., 418
Wagner, R. K., 374
Wahlstrom, K. L., 450
Wake, M., 114
Wakeley, A., 175
Walbek, N. H., 315
Walco, G., 346
Walder, L. O., 334
Waldman, S., 499
Walerstein, J. S., 321
Walk, R. D., 144
Walker, C. E., 342
Walker, H., 414
Walker, J. L., 394

Walker, K., 303
Walker, L. J., 424, 425
Walker, N. C., 109
Walker, R. R., 318
Wall, S., 222
Wallace, C. S., 139, 141
Wallandar, J. K., 414
Wallerstein, J. S., 321, 323
Wallerstein, R. S., 35, 517
Walsh, M., 438
Walsh, P. E., 322
Walsh, P. V., 385
Walters, L. H., 489
Walton, M. N., 409
Wampler, K. S., 315
Wang, R., 260
Wang, X., 225
Wapner, R. J., 78
Warheld, C., 154
Warren, K., 438
Warren, M. P., 455, 457
Warren-Leubecker, A., 196
Wasserman, A., 434
Wasserman, S., 174
Wasserstein, S., 407
Wasz-Hockert, O., 209
Watamura, S. E., 217
Waterfield, J.
Waterman, A. S., 518
Waters, E., 208, 222, 224
Watkins, D., 404
Watkins, J., 350
Watson, C. M., 515, 533
Watson, J. B., 36
Watson, M. W., 281
Watt, J. L., 454
Way, N., 479
Weber-Fox, C., 199
Wedemeyer, N. V., 321
Wegener, D. H., 124
Wehner, E. A., 533
Weikel, W. K., 323
Weinberg, R. A., 374
Weinberg, W. A., 4
Weinert, F. E., 403
Weinright, J., 17
Weinstein, R. S., 438
Weinsten, R. S., 438
Weinstock, H., 474
Weiss, B., 315, 542
Weiss, M., 212
Weiss, M. R., 464
Weisz, J. R., 408
Weizman, A., 355

Wellborn, J. G., 408
Wellman, H. M., 173, 212, 280, 281
Welsh, C., 477
Wentworth, N., 155
Wentzel, K. R., 532
Werker, J., 193
Werker, J. F., 145, 185
Werner, E. E., 548
West, J. R., 100
West, S. G., 418
Westfeld, J. S., 538
Whalen, C. K., 394
Wheeler, L., 405
Whitaker, H. A., 140
Whitaker, R. C., 352
White, C., 294
White, M., 405
Whitehead, B. D., 320
Whiteman, M., 101
Whiteman, V., 479
Whitesell, N. R., 515
Whiting, B. B., 135, 305, 312
Whiting, J. W. M., 312
Whitkow, M., 508
Whitney, E., 161, 256, 350, 351
Whitney, M. P., 133, 134
Wichstrom, L., 454
Widerstrom, A. H., 122
Widom, C. S., 234, 235
Wierson, M., 455
Wiese, D., 235
Wiesel, T., 141
Wigfield, A., 493, 494, 495, 498, 504, 507, 516
Wikander, B., 211
Wilcox, M. J., 282, 285
Wilkinson, A., 272
Willemsen, M. E., 488
Willett, J. B., 53
Williams, E. M., 177
Williams, R. J., 352
Williams, V. A., 524
Williamson, L., 466
Willig, A., 389
Wilson, B. J., 333
Wilson, C., 102, 461
Wilson, D. M., 458
Wilson, J., 323
Wilson, L., 316
Wilson, R. D., 79
Wilson, S., 525

Wilson, S. R., 316
Wilson-Barrett, E., 352
Wimbush, D. D., 316
Wimmer, H., 280
Windass, A., 516
Windle, M., 533
Winer, G. A., 272
Wingwood, G. M., 538
Winner, E., 252
Winsler, A., 275, 291
Winter, S., 346
Wisniewski, L., 352
Witkin, G., 471
Witt, D., 389
Wold, B., 408
Wolf, A. E., 210
Wolf, D. P., 300, 328
Wolfe, B., 230, 232, 548
Wolff, P. H., 207, 209
Wolfner, G. D., 235
Wolfson, A. R., 450
Wolke, D., 209
Women's Sports Foundation, 464
Wong, D. L., 81, 83, 91, 94, 108, 111
Wood, R. M., 209
Woods, C. H., 304
Woods, T., 20
Woodward, A. L., 187, 189, 190
Woodward, E. H., 332
Woodward, L., 109
Woodworth, S., 115, 319
Woody, E., 532
Woolley, J. D., 212, 281
World Health Organization, 117, 257, 359
Worthington 02, 505
Wozniak, P., 317
Wright, J. C., 294, 333, 539
Wright, K.421
Wright, S. C., 389
Wright, V. C., 84
Wyshak, G., 456
Wysocki, T., 470

Xeromeritou, A., 253

Yagel, S., 104
Yamamoto, K., 408
Yanai, J., 102
Yang, C. K., 260
Yang, X., 350

Yankelovich, S., 294
Yazedjian, A., 519
Yeargin-Allsopp, M., 346
Yee, D. K., 505
Yelland, N., 539
Yenen, S., 117
Yetman, N. R., 18
Yin, R. K., 49
Young, J., 122
Young, L. R., 353
Young, M., 408
Youngblade, L. M., 231, 330
Younger, B. A., 178
Youniss, J., 327
Yu, A., 389
Yuan, L. L., 246
Yuille, J., 279
Yuille, N., 384
Yung, B. R., 411, 414, 415

Zahn-Waxler, C., 313
Zaiwalla, Z., 134
Zanobini, M., 116
Zeanah, C. H., 141
Zebrowitz, L., 32
Zeifman, D., 145
Zelazo, P. R., 178, 182
Zelis, K. M., 431
Zelkowitz, P., 120
Zero to Three, 4, 232
Zeskind, P. S., 209
Zeuhlke, S., 117
Zhou, Q., 313
Zigler, E., 40, 238, 292, 293, 395, 508
Zigler, E. F., 292, 293
Zill, N., 4, 322
Zillmann, D., 333
Zimmerman, B. F., 437
Zimmerman, J., 536
Zimmerman, M. A., 515
Zogby International, 19
Zoller, D., 314
Zonta, L. A., 104
Zubek, J. P., 73
Zucker, K. J., 302
Zumbahlen, M. R., 23, 152
Zurbriggen, E. L., 238
Zwaanswijk, M., 414

Subject Index

Abduction, of children, 361–362
Abortion, 478
  spontaneous, 101
Abstinence, 476, 479, 480, 547
Abstract thinking, 517
Academic achievement
  in adolescence, 494, 498–509
  biological influences on, 502–504
  changing schools and, 493–494
  cultural influences on, 378–379, 506–509
  family influences on, 504–505
  gender differences in, 498–501, 502–506
  of immigrant children, 19
  increased competition and, 436, 437
  parental roles in, 378–379
  teachers' expectations and, 388–390
Acceleration programs, 396
Acceptance, in adolescence, 524
Accidents
  avoiding, 157
  bicycle and scooter, 360
  in early childhood, 261, 263–264
  in late childhood, 350, 360–361
  motor vehicle, 360, 471, 543
Accommodation, 39, 40
Acculturation, 408
Acquired immune deficiency syndrome (AIDS),
    359–360, 474–475
Acrual self, 514
Active G-E correlation, 74–75
Adaptation, 32
Addictions, development of, 451
Adolescence
  academic achievement in, 494, 498–509
  behavior problems in, 541–547
  challenges and demands of, 548
  chronic illness in, 469–470
  cognitive abilities in, 485–493, 498, 504–505
  cultural differences in, 447–448
  death in, 462, 470–473, 475, 543
  definition of, 445–448
  depression in, 470
  drugs and alcohol in, 476
  early, definition of, 446
  eating disorders in, 458, 465–468
  family relationships in, 523–537
  gender identity in, 520–521
  growth spurt in, 451–452
  health in, 458, 462–480
  historical perspective on, 14, 446–447
  identity in, 35, 513–523
  mass media influence on, 537
  nutrition in, 454, 462
  parenting in, 476–479
  peer relationships in, 524, 527, 528–537
  physical development in, 446, 448–461
  pregnancy in, 476–479
  safety in, 462–480
  school influences in, 493–498
  sexual behavior in, 533–537
  sexual health concerns in, 474–480
  sexual maturation in, 456–459
  social cognition in, 489–492
  social development in, 513

sports in, 462–465
suicide in, 473
working in, 499
  see also Puberty
Adolescent autonomy, 521–523
Adolescent egocentrism, 488–489
Adolescent peer culture, 529–530
Adoption(s), 478
  international, 24
Adoption studies, 8
African Americans, 18
  academic achievement of, 379, 507
  adolescence and, 460–461
  death rates of, 470, 472
  exposure to violence, 412–413
  family relationships of, 15, 303
  identity and, 519
  moral values of, 425, 426
  racial stereotypes of, 385
  self-esteem in, 303
  sexual activity of, 533, 534–535
  sexual health of, 475, 478
Afterbirth, 108
After-school care programs, 429
Age
  and memory, 184
  and moral scenarios, 426
  and pregnancy, 103
  and size, 49
Age of viability, 94
Age-related stages, 4
Aggression, 312–313
  in adolescence, 532
  bullying, 431–433
  gender differences in, 312–313
  hostile, 312
  instrumental, 312
  relational, 313
  in response to aggression, 409–410
  on television, 332–333, 334
AIDs. See Acquired immune deficiency syndrome
    (AIDS)
Ainsworth's Strange Situation, 222
Alcohol, 99–100, 123, 476, 543
  and prenatal development, 96, 99–100, 123
Alleles, 67
All-night dance parties, 545
Alpha fetoprotein (AFP), 78
Ambivalent attachment, 224
American culture, 425
American Psychological Association, 52
American Sign Language, 199
Amino acids, 71
Amnesia, infantile, 182, 184
Amniocentesis, 78, 79
Amnion, 91
Amniotic fluid, 79, 91, 96
Amygdala, 448
Anal stage, 34
Analytical intelligence, 374
Anatolia, 117
Androgens, 306
Angelman syndrome, 71
Anger, 308

in infants, 210–211
Animal studies, 73
Animism, 273
Anorexia nervosa, 465–467
Antidepressant medications, 418
Antisocial behavior, 413–416
  ADHD and, 414
  in adolescence, 541
  development of, 414–415
  family factors in, 415, 416
  gender differences in, 413–414
  in late childhood, 413–418, 436–437
  peer relationships and, 415
  progressive development of, 414
  temperament and, 414
  treatments for, 415–416
Anxiety
  assessment of, 54
  in late childhood, 406–407
  in preschool children, 410
Apgar Scale, 119
Appearance
  in adolescence, 460–461
  in early childhood, 245–246
  in late childhood, 342, 405
  of newborns, 118–119
Applied developmental research, 47
Arousal
  measuring, 54
  states of, 133–134
Asian Americans, 20
  academic achievement of, 378–379, 506
  drop outs, 497
  family relationships of, 15
  population of, 18
Asperger syndrome, 396–398
Assimilation, 39, 40, 519
Association, learning through, 180–181
Associational fluency, 500
Associative play, 329
Asthma, 262–263
Attachment, 217–229
  ambivalent, 224
  assessing patterns of, 221–225
  avoidant, 224
  caregiver sensitivity and, 225–226
  consequences of, 227–228
  development of, 219–221
  disorganized/disoriented, 225
  to fathers, 228–229
  infant characteristics and, 226
  in infants, 32
  insecure, 228, 231
  phases of, 219–221
  role of culture in, 226–227
  secure, 222–224, 225, 228, 434
  survival value of, 32
Attachment theory, 32, 217, 219
Attention, 38
Attention deficit disorder (ADD), 392
Attention-deficit hyperactivity disorder (ADHD),
    392–394
  characteristics of children with, 393
  treatment for, 393–394

Attractiveness, infant preference for, 144
Auditory cortex, 248
Australian Aborigines, 447
Authoritarian parenting, 318
Authoritative parenting, 319
Autism, 249, 385, 396–398
Autonomous morality, 420, 421
Autonomy, 521–523
    adolescent, 521–523
    forms of, 522
Autonomy versus shame and doubt, 212
Autosomal recessive disease, 69
Autosomes, 65, 66, 70
Aversive behavior, 416
Avoidant attachment, 224
Axon, 137, 246
AZT, 98

Babbling, 186, 187
Babinski reflex, 151
Baby signs, 188
Balance, in motor development, 250
Balanced polymorphism, 70
Baldness, 70
Bandura's social learning theory, 38–39
Bar mitzvah, 447
Baumrind's parenting styles, 318–320
Bed-wetting, 346–347
Behavior, origins of, 29
Behavioral autonomy, 522
Behavioral measures, 54
Behavior management, for ADHD, 394
Beliefs, understanding others', 384–385
Beta thalassemia, 70
Bias
    cultural, 35
    gender, 505–506
    in interviews, 50
    teacher, 388, 437–438, 505–506
    test, 374
Bicultural, 519
Bicycle accidents, 360
Bilingual children, language development in, 286–287
Bilingual education, 389, 497
Biological-based theories, 31–33
    of gender development, 306
    of language development, 193–195
Birth control. See Contraceptive use
Birth defects, 71, 79, 96, 98, 105
Birthing centers, 111
Birthing practices, 117
Birth rates
    adolescence, worldwide, 477
    by age and race, 104
Birth rituals, 117–118
Birth(s)
    multiple, 91
    twin, 91, 92
    see also Childbirth
Blacks, 18, 19, 20. See also African Americans
Bladder control, in infants and toddlers, 156
Bladder disorders, 75, 346–347
Blind children, 226, 391
Blind infants, 226
Blinking, 150
Blood type, 73
Body fat, 245, 255
Body image
    in adolescence, 458, 460–461, 465, 469
    eating disorders and, 458, 460, 465–468
    in late childhood, 405
    see also Obesity
Body movements, sensorimotor stage, 168
Body proportions, 452
Body size
    in early childhood, 245–246, 255
    in late childhood, 342
Bonding, 117, 219
Bone health, 342–344
Bowel control, in infants, 156
Bowlby's theory of attachment, 32, 217, 219
Brain
    hemispheres of, 139, 246, 253
    language-related areas of, 194, 199

Brain damage, 75, 194, 247, 376
Brain development, 33
    in adolescence, 448–451
    cigarettes and, 101
    disruptions in growth, 140–141
    in early childhood, 246–248
    environmental effects on, 140–141
    features of, 139
    gender differences in, 451
    growth spurt in, 246
    in infants, 134, 136–141, 174, 195
    key structures in, 139
    in late childhood, 341–342
    myelination, 246–247
    in newborns, 137
    prefrontal, 247
    prenatal, 141
    research on, 141
    in toddlers, 195
Brain plasticity, 8, 139–140, 141, 248
Braxton-Hicks contractions, 109
Brazelton's Neonatal Behavioral Assessment, 119
Breaking water, 109
Breast-fed children, 159–160
Breast-feeding, 122
    benefits of, 159–161
    prevalence of, 161
Breech presentation, 113
Bronfenbrenner's ecological theory, 43–44
Bulimia nervosa, 467–468
Bullying, 431–433
Bully-victims, 432–433

Caffeine, 100–101
Calcium deficiency, 342, 462
Canalized, 73
Cancer, 71, 72, 73, 75, 82, 470
Capillaries, 93
Carcinogens, 101
Caregivers. See Parents, Family relationships, Parent-
        child relationships
Caring, 314
Carriers, 69
Case studies, 49
Catching, 251
Catecholamines, 116
Categories, 272–273, 274, 368
Cell division, 65–66
Cells, 64, 65
Central nervous system, 93
Centration, 271, 272
Cephalocaudal development, 94
Cerebral cortex, 139
Cervix, 109
Cesarean section, 112–113
Chemical hazards, 103
Chemotherapy, 81
Chicanos, 20. See also Latinos
Chicken pox, 357
Child abductions, 361–362
Child abuse, 233–239
    characteristics of abusers, 102, 235–238
    definitions of, 234
    ecological model of, 237
    effects of, 198, 235, 238, 248
    incidence of, 234
    preventing, 238
Childbirth, 107–113
    birthing methods, 110–112
    birth process, 107–110
    by cesarean section, 112–113
    complications of, 22, 112–113
    cultural differences in, 116–118
    father's perspective of, 115
    induced labor and, 113
    mother's perspective of, 114
    newborn's perspective of, 116
    stages of, 108
Child custody arrangements, 323–324, 325
Child development
    critical issues in, 5–11
    definition of, 4–5
Child-directed speech, 196–197
Childhood. See Early childhood; Late childhood

Childhood obesity, 352–356
Child labor, 12, 446
Child mortality, 70, 263
Child neglect, 102, 234, 431
Child prodigy, 376, 3964
Chinese culture, 448, 506
Chorion, 93
Chorionic villus sampling (CVS), 78, 79
Chromosomal disorders, 78, 96
Chromosomes, 64, 65–66, 82
Chronic illness, 469–470
Cigarettes, 96–97, 101, 264, 544
Cilia, 82
Civil disobedience, 492
Classical conditioning, 36–37
Classification, 272–273
Class inclusion, 272
Clinical interviews, 49–50
Cliques, 529, 530
Club drugs, 545
Cocaine, 30, 102
Codeine, 102
Code switching, 286
Coercive cycle, 416
Cognition-based theories, 36–39, 307
Cognitive development, 4, 39–41
    cultural influences on, 281–282
    culture as a context for, 180, 370
    in early childhood, 269–282
    early intervention and, 290–295
    gender differences in, 307
    in infancy and toddlerhood, 167–180
    in late childhood, 367, 387–398
    Piaget's theory of cognitive development, 39–41,
            167–172, 269–274, 367–371
        concrete operational stage in, 40–41, 367–371,
                384
            formal operational stage, 40–41, 485–488
            preoperational stage, 40–41, 269–274, 369
            sensorimotor stage, 40–41, 167–172, 269
            stages in, 40–41, 177
    reaching maturity in, 485–488
    schooling and, 387–398
    social context of, 179–180, 274–275, 276
Cognitive developmental theories, 39–41
    Kohlberg's, 307
    Piaget's, 167–172, 269–274, 367–371
    Vygotsky's, 41–42
Cohort, 52
Cohort-sequential research designs, 54
Colon cancer, 72
Color-blindness, 70, 71
Colostrum, 159
Columbine High School, 433
Commitment, 517
Communication, intentional, 186
Compensation, 368
Competence, 301–302
    illusions of, 437
Compliance, 315
Computer games, 540
Computers, 538–541
Conception, 65, 80–84
Concepts
    children's understanding of, 368
Concepts, understanding, 272–273, 274
Concrete operational stage, 40, 41, 367–371, 384
Concrete operations, 367
Conditioned response, 36
Conditioned stimulus, 36
Condoms, 475–476
Conflict, 311
    in parent-adolescent relationship, 526
Congenital adrenal hyperplasia (CEH), 306
Congenital rubella syndrome, 98
Conscience, 216
Consequences, 421
Conservation, 368, 369, 485
    conservation tasks, 271
Constructivist theories of learning, 387
Contextual theories, 43–45
Contingency, learning through, 180–181
Continuity versus discontinuity, 10
Continuous development, 10

Contraceptive use, 475–476, 480, 533–534
Contractions, 109
Control group, 51
Control parameters, 44
Conventional Level, of moral development, 422
Convergent thinking, 376
Conversation, 381
Conversational rules, 285
Cooing, 186, 187
Cooperative learning, 387
Cooperative play, 329
Coordination, in early childhood, 251
Coping, 548, 549
    with disaster, 410
Coping skills, 408, 409
    changes in, 408–410
    emotion-focused, 409
Corporal punishment, 316
Correlational studies, 50–51
Correlation coefficients, 50
Correlations, positive and negative, 51
Cosleeping, 135–136, 260
Couvade, 106–107
Crack, 102
"Crack" babies, 29
Crawling, 151
Creative intelligence, 375
Creativity, 376–377
    assessment of, 376
    components of, 377
Creches, 233
Creeping, 151
Crime, 412, 541
Crisis/exploration, 517
Critical period, 10–11
    for language development, 194–195, 198
Cross-sectional studies, 52–54
Crowds, 529, 530
    descriptors of, 530
Crowning, 110
Cruise, 152
Crying, infant, 209–211, 214
Cultural bias, 35
Cultural contexts, of cognitive development, 180, 370
Cultural differences
    in academic achievement, 506–509
    in adolescence, 447–448, 457–458
    in attachment, 226
    in birthing methods, 110
    in body image, 466
    in care giving environments, 23
    in childbirth, 116–118
    in children's reasoning, 372
    in cognitive development, 281–282
    in discipline, 315–316, 317–318
    in laughing and smiling, 208
    in motor development, 148–149, 254
    in parental beliefs, 23
    in parenting, 319–320
    in perception of temperament, 217
    in physical development, 245–246
    in play, 329–330
    in pregnancy and birth, 106, 107
    in scaffolding, 179, 180
    in self-esteem, 303
    in sense of self, 405
    in sleep patterns, 135–136
    in use of day care, 233
    in use of formal operational thinking, 488
Cultural diversity. See Diversity
Cultural influences, 18
Culture, and morality, 425
Cystic fibrosis, 69–70

"Dance of perception," in newborns, 147
Darwin's theory of evolution, 31–32
Dating, 532–533
Day care
    effects of, 230–232
    guidelines for quality, 232–233
    influence on development, 229–233
    patterns of use, 229–230
Deaf children, 198, 199, 391

Death
    in adolescence, 462, 470–473, 475, 543
    in early childhood, 70, 263
    in late childhood, 357, 360
    see also Infant mortality
Defense mechanisms, 34
Deferred imitation, 183, 270
Delinquency, 48, 541
Demandingness, 318
Dendrites, 136–137
Dental health, 344
Dependent variables, 51
Depression, 416–418
    in adolescence, 470, 541–542
    family and social factors in, 418
    genetic and biological factors in, 417
    in late childhood, 416–418
    symptoms of, 417
    temperament and, 418
    treatments for, 418
Depressive disorders, 417
Depth, perception of, 144–145
Developmental changes, 48
    influences on, 5–8
    permanent, 7
Developmental domains, 4
Developmental milestones, 151
Developmental problems, 153–155
Developmental science, 54–56
    topics in, 46–47
Diabetes, 72, 352
Dietary Guidelines for Americans, 351
Dilation of cervix, 108, 109
Disabilities. See Special needs children
Disaster, coping with, 410
Discipline
    choice of, 318
    consistent, 315
    cultural differences in, 317–318
    factors influencing the use of, 317
    power assertion and, 315–316
    of young children, 315–318
    see also Punishment
Discontinuous development, 10
Discovery learning, 387
Discrimination, 385
    against gays and lesbians, 521
Diseases
    chronic, 469–470
    contagious, 262
    in early childhood, 262–263
    in late childhood, 356–360
    obesity and, 352
    prenatal development and, 97–98
Dishabituation, 181–182
Disorganized/disoriented attachment, 222, 223, 225
Display rules, 309–310
Divergent thinking, 376
Diversity
    of child development, 21–24
    cultural, 227
    focus on, 387–388
    racial and ethnic, 18–20
    recognizing in research, 20
Divorce, 29
    adjustment to, 322–323
    child custody arrangements in, 323–324, 325
    effects of, 320–325, 331
Divorce rates
    by country, 320
    in the U.S., 320
Dizygotic (DZ) twins, 9, 393
DNA (deoxyribonucleic acid), 63, 64–65
Domains of social knowledge, 491–492
Domestic violence, 236
Dominant genes, 67
Dominant traits, 67–69
Dominant transmission, 67–69
Dopamine, 451
Double standard, 537
Down Syndrome, 75, 76, 77, 79, 395
    maternal age and, 104
Drawing
    cultural influences on, 252–253

    developmental changes in, 252
Drop outs
    characteristics of, 495–497
    prevention of, 497–498
    race, ethnicity, and rates of, 496
Drowning, 264
Drugs
    club, 545
    fertility, 91
    illicit, 544–547
    ten reasons for using /not using, 546
Drug use and abuse, 496, 542–547
    in adolescence, 476
    parental warnings against, 547
    in pregnancy, 98–103
    prenatal development and, 98–103
    prevention programs for, 547
Dual representation, 270–271
Dynamic systems theory, 44–45, 152
Dyslexia, 391
Dysmenorrhea, 461
Dysphoria, 542

Early adolescence. See Adolescence
Early childhood, 245–334
    body size and appearance in, 245–246, 255, 342
    brain development in, 246–248
    cognitive development in, 269–282
    concept of gender in, 302–307
    early intervention programs in, 287–295
    eating habits in, 254–256
    effects of divorce in, 320–325
    emotional development in, 308–315
    friendship in, 326–327
    health and safety in, 261, 262–265
    language development in, 282–287
    memory in, 276–277
    motor development in, 249–254
    nutritional needs in, 254–256
    parental influences in, 315–325
    play in, 328–330
    preschool in, 287–295
    self-awareness in, 299–302
    sibling relationships in, 325–333, 330–331
    sleep patterns in, 258–262
    social development in, 314–315
Early childhood education. See Preschool
Early Head Start, 293
Eating disorders, 458, 462, 465
Eating disturbances, 468
Eating habits, in early childhood, 254–256
Ecological theory, 43–44
Ectoderm, 93
Ectopic pregnancy, 91
Education. See School(s)
Ego, 33
Egocentric speech, 275
Egocentrism, 40, 273, 274, 488–489
Ejaculation, 81, 83, 461
Elaboration, 371
El Mal. See Huntington's disease
Embarrassment, 212
Embryonic stage, 89, 91–94
Embryo transfer, 84
Emergent literacy, 383
Emotional autonomy, 522
Emotional development
    in early childhood, 308–315
    in infancy and toddlerhood, 205–213
    in late childhood, 406–413
Emotion-focused coping strategies, 408–409
Emotion regulation, 308–311, 407
Emotions
    display rules and, 309–310
    negative, 308–309
    play and, 213
    prosocial, 313–314
    television viewing and, 332–334
    temperament and, 310
Empathy, 313
Empirically based, 30–31
Endocrine system, 104–105, 453
Endoderm, 93
Endogenous smile, 207

Enrichment programs, 396
Environment, 3
Environmental factors
    in ADHD, 393
    in brain development, 140–141
    in development, 5
    diversity of, 23
    in puberty, 454–455
Environmental hazards, 264–265
    prenatal development and, 103
Environment-based theories, 193
Epidural block, 109
Epigenetic principle, 35
Epileptic seizures, 8
Episiotomy, 110
Erection, 461, 515
Erikson's psychosocial theory, 35–36, 211–212,
    299–300
Erikson's theory of adolescent identity development,
    516–517
Estrogen, 453
Ethic of care, 426
Ethics, in research, 51, 52
Ethnic diversity, 18–20
Ethnic identity, 518–520, 520
Ethnicity, 18
    and academic achievement, 507–509
    and child-care arrangements, 230
    children's understanding of, 385
    and dropping out, 497
    moral scenarios and, 426
    poverty and, 21
    school enrollments by, 436
    and sexual activity, 535
Ethological theory, 32
Event-related brain potentials (ERPs), 200
Event related potential (ERP), 248
Evocative G-E correlation, 74
Evolution, Darwin's theory of, 31–32
Evolutionary theories, 31–32
Exercise
    in adolescence, 463, 464
    during pregnancy, 105
    recommended level of, 355
Exogenous smile, 207
Exosystem, 43, 44
Expansion, 197
Experience
    and cognitive abilities, 370
    and later development, 6
Experience-dependent events, 140
Experience-dependent plasticity, 248
Experience-expectant events, 140
Experimental group, 51
Experimental study, 51
Experiments, laboratory, 49
Experts, memory, 278
Expressive language, 186, 283
Externalizing problems, 541
Extinction, 38
Eyewitness testimony, of children, 278, 279

Faces
    infant preference for, 144
    perception of, 143–144
Facial expressions, of infants, 32
Facts, 30
Failure to thrive (FTT), 162
Fallopian tube, 82
Family and Medical Leave Act, 231
Family relationships
    in adolescence, 523–537
    in late childhood, 427–430
Family(s)
    academic achievement and, 504–505
    antisocial behavior and, 415, 416
    blended, 15
    children's conception of, 321
    depression and, 418
    extended, 15
    giftedness and, 377–378
    nuclear, 14
    single-parent, 14–15

step-, 15, 324
Family structure
    changes in, 14–16
    race and, 14–16
Fast mapping, 187
Fathers
    attachment to, 228–229
    expectant, 107
Fear(s), 308
    in adolescence, 410
    bullies and, 432
    of failure, 407
    in infancy, 222, 223, 231, 407
    innate, 407
    in late childhood, 406–407
Federal Bureau of Investigation (FBI), 362
Feelings, understanding others', 384–385
Fertility drugs, 91
Fertility treatment, for cancer, 83
Fertilization, 82–83
Fetal alcohol effects (FAE), 99–100
Fetal alcohol syndrome (FAS), 99, 123
Fetal stage, 90, 94–96
Fetology, 80
Fetus, 116
    expulsion of, 109–110
    growth and change of, 95
    treatment of diseased, 80
Fine motor skills
    in early childhood, 251–253
    in late childhood, 347
    milestones in, 250–251
Fitness. See Physical fitness
Folate, 105
Follicular phase, 81
Food choices, 354. See also Nutrition; Obesity
Food pyramid, 351
Foreclosure, 518
Formal operational stage, 40, 41, 485–488
Frames of mind, 375–376
Fraternal twins, 9
Freud's psychosexual theory, 33–35, 404
Friendship
    in adolescence, 531
    in early childhood, 326–327
    in late childhood, 430
    race and, 327
    same sex, 327
    in toddlerhood, 326
Functional isolation, 257

Galvanic skin response, 54
Gamete intrafallopian transfer (GIFT), 84
Gametes, 65
Gardner's theory of multiple intelligences, 375
Gay parents, 17
Gays, 520–521
Gender, concept of, 302–307
Gender bias, in school, 505–506
Gender consistency, 302
Gender development, 306–307
Gender differences, 305
    in academic achievement, 498–501, 502–506
    in adolescence, 520–521
    in brain development, 451
    in math and science skills, 500–502
    in morality, 426–427
    in puberty, 454, 455–456, 458–459
    in self-esteem, 515–516
    sex hormones and, 502–504
    in spatial-visual skills, 500, 501
    in verbal skills, 500
Gender identity, 302, 305
    in early childhood, 302
    reinforcement of, 305
Gender labeling, 302
Gender roles, 306–307
    puberty and, 454
Gender schemas, 307–308
Gender stability, 302
Gender stereotypes, 304, 505–506
Gender-typed play, 304–306
Gene-environment interactions, 75

Gene expression, 72–74
    range of reaction and, 73
General Social Survey, 50
Generation XL, 352
Generative learning, 387
Genes, 64, 65–66
    dominant, 67
    recessive, 67, 69
    regulator, 72–73
Genetic counseling, 79–80
Genetic diseases, 68
    detection of, 78–80
Genetic disorders, 71, 306
Genetic factors, 9
    in development, 63–72
    in growth patterns, 131–133
    in puberty, 453–454
Genetic imprinting, 71
Genetic map, 64
Genetic predisposition, 73, 74
Genetic technology, 78–79
Genetic transmission, 66–72
Genital stage, 34
Genome, 63–64
Genomes to Life Project, 72
Genotypes, 67
Germinal stage, 89, 90–91
Gestures, 186
Giardia, 158
Gifted and talented children, 4, 395–396
    gifted, defined, 395–396
    longitudinal study of, 55
    role of the family and, 377–378
Gifted programs, 396
Glial cells, 246
Global Polio Eradication Initiative, 358
Goal-corrected partnership, 315
Gonadotropins, 453
Goodness of fit, 215
Grammar, 193, 198, 283–285, 380
Grasping, 155–156
Gratification, immediate, 33
Gross motor skills, 149–155
    in early childhood, 249–254
    in late childhood, 347
    milestones in, 250–251
    see also Motor development
Growing pains, 346
Growth patterns, in infants and toddlers, 131–133
Growth spurt, in adolescence, 451–452, 456
Guilt, 299–300
Guns, 472

Habituation, 181–182
Handedness, 253–254
Hate crimes, 521
Head, lifting the, 149
Head Start, 290–293
Health
    in adolescence, 458, 462–280
    in early childhood, 261, 262–265
    in infancy, 157–162
    in late childhood, 342–347, 352–362, 356–362
    sexual, 474–480
Hearing problems, 344–345
Height
    in adolescence, 451–452
    growth charts for, 132, 343
Helping, 314
Hemispheres, of the brain, 139, 246, 253
Hemophilia, 70
Heritability, 9
Heroin, 102–103
Heteronomous morality stage, 419, 420
Heterosexual, 520
Heterozygous, 67
Heuristic, 487
High school, 494–498
Hispanics, 19, 20
    population of, 18
    see also Latinos
HIV. See Human immunodeficiency virus (HIV)
Holophrases, 187

Home environment, 288–289
Home Observation for Measurement of the Environment (HOME), 288
Homicides, 471–473
Homosexual, 520
Homozygous, 67
Hopi Indian girls, 457
Hormones, 81, 306, 453
Hostile aggression, 312
Human Genome Project (HGP), 63–64
Human immunodeficiency virus (HIV), 98, 359–360, 475
Hunger, 34, 351
    in infants, 147
Huntington's disease, 63, 68, 71
Hyponatremia, 158
Hypothalamus, 453
Hypotheses
    testing, 55
Hypotheses, formulating, 46
Hypothetico-deductive reasoning, 486–487
Hypotonia, 153

Identical twins, 8–9
Identity
    in adolescence, 35, 513–523, 516–521
        Erikson's theory of, 516–517
        ethnic, 518–520, 520
        gender, 302, 520–521
        sexual, 520–521
Identity achieved, 518
Identity concept, 271
Identity confusion, 517
Identity development
    Erikson's theory of, 516–517
    Marcia's theory of, 517–518
Identity diffusion, 518
Idioms, 381
Image schemas, 178
Imaginary audience, 488
Immigrants, 18
    academic achievement of, 508
    acculturation of, 408
    illegal, 19
    population of, 19
    undocumented, 19
Imminent justice, 420
Immune system, 80
Immunizations, 157
Impression formation, 489–490
Imprinting, 11
Independent variables, 51
Individual Characteristics Model, 528
Individual differences
    in development, 11
    in twins, 11
Individuals with Disabilities Education Acts of 1990, 390
Induction, 524–525, 526
Inductive reasoning, 316–317
Industry versus inferiority, 404
Infantile amnesia, 182
Infant mortality, 157, 158
    historical trends in, 111
Infants
    arousal states in, 133–134
    brain development in, 136–141
    breast-fed, 147
    cognitive development in, 167–180
    continuity of development in, 10
    emotions in, 205–213
    failure to thrive, 162
    fine motor skills in, 155–156
    health and safety and, 157–162
    language development in, 184–192
    learning and remembering in, 180–184
    low-birthweight, 102, 120, 122
    memory in, 182–184
    motor development in, 148–157
    nutritional needs of, 158–162
    perception of, 144–145
    perceptual development in, 142–147
    physical development in, 131–136

sense of taste, smell, and touch, 145–147
    sleep patterns in, 133–136
    temperament in, 213–217
    weaning and feeding, 161–162
    see also Mother-infant relationship; Newborns
Infectious diseases, 97–98
Inferiority, industry versus, 404
Infertility, 83–84
Information processing
    in infants and toddlers, 180–184
    in late childhood, 370–371
Information processing theory, 42–43, 276–278
Initiative versus guilt, 299–300
Injuries, 350, 360–361
    playground, 361
    sports, 350
    see also Accidents
Innate morality, 13
Innate theories, 193–195
Instrumental aggression, 312
Intellectual development, 289
    family and cultural influences on, 377–379
    poverty and, 377
    see also Intelligence(s)
Intelligence quotient (IQ), 373. See also IQ scores
Intelligence(s)
    analytical, 374
    components of, 374–376
    creative, 375
    defining, 395
    development of, 9
    environmental factors in, 9
    and IQ scores, 373
    measuring, 373
    multiple, 375–376
    Piaget's view of, 39–40
    practical, 375
    racial and ethnic differences in, 21
    triarchic theory of, 374
    see also Intellectual development
Intelligence tests, 373
    cultural bias in, 374
Intentional communication, 186
Intentionality, 420
Intentions, 421
    understanding others', 409–410, 421
Internalization, 315, 541
Internet, 540–541
    for communication and recreation, 540
    resources of, 540–541
Interviews, clinical, 49–50
Intonation, 186
Intracytoplasmic sperm injection (ICSI), 84
Intrauterine insemination, 84
Intrinsic motivation, 377
In vitro fertilization (IVF), 68, 84
IQ scores
    distribution of, 373
    early intervention and, 292
    of gifted children, 55
    intelligence and, 373
    mental retardation and, 76, 394, 395
    understanding the limits of, 373–374
Iron-deficiency anemia, 257
Irreversibility, 271

Jahara of South America, 116
Japanese culture, 405, 506
Joint attention, 179–180
Joint custody, 324, 325
Jumping, 250–251
Junior high school, 494, 495
Junk food, 353, 354
Juvenile delinquency, 48, 541

Karyotype, 65–66, 79
Kindergarten, 287, 290
Klinefelter's syndrome, 76
Kohlberg's theory of cognitive development, 307
Kohlberg's theory of moral development, 421–425, 492
    evaluation of, 424–425
    levels of, 422–425
    stages of, 421, 423

Kumasi, 427
Kwashiorkor, 256–257

Labor. See Childbirth
Laboratory experiments, 49
Lamaze childbirth, 111–112
Language
    expressive, 186
    first words, 186–187
    receptive, 186
    see also Language development
Language acquisition, 31–32
    computer simulation of, 31–32
Language acquisition device (LAD), 193
Language development
    in bilingual children, 286–287
    conversation rules and, 285
    critical periods for, 11, 194–195, 198
    delayed, 23
    early and late talkers, 191–192
    in early childhood, 282–287
    first sentences, 191
    helping strategies for, 287
    language styles and, 283
    in late childhood, 379–383
    milestones in, 185
    resilient and fragile aspects of, 198–200
    social context of, 285–286
    theories of, 192–193
Language disorders, 194
Latchkey children, 429
Late childhood, 341–438
    accidents and injuries in, 350, 360–361
    brain development in, 341–342
    emotional development in, 406–412, 413–418, 436–438
    family relationships in, 427–430
    health in, 342–347, 352–355, 356–362
    language and literacy development in, 379–383
    moral development in, 418–427
    motor development in, 347–350
    nutritional needs in, 350–356
    obesity in, 352–356
    peer relationships in, 430–435
    psychological problems in, 413–418
    safety in, 356–362
    sense of self in, 403–406
    sibling relationships in, 429–430
    social development in, 383–387, 434–435, 436–438
Latency period, 438
Latency stage, 34, 404
Latinos, 19
    academic achievement of, 379, 507
    death rates of, 470
    drop-out rates, 497
    exposure to violence, 413
    family in, 303
    identity and, 519
    self-esteem in, 303
    sexual health of, 475, 478
    suicide among, 473
    use of day care, 230
Laughter, 207, 208
Lead poisoning, 264, 395
Learning
    constructivist theories of, 387
    cooperative, 387
    cultural contexts of, 180
    discovery, 387
    environment factors in, 6
    generative, 387
    how to learn, 371
    in infants and toddlers, 180–184
    to read, 381–382
Learning-based theories, 36–39, 48
    constructivist, 387
    of language development, 192–193
    objections to, 193
    see also Cognitive-based theories
Learning disabilities, 391–392. See also Special needs children
Least restrictive environment, 390

Leboyer childbirth, 112
Leprosy, 99
Lesbian parents, 17
Lesbians, 521
Libido, 33
Lightening, 108
Limbic system, 448, 449
Limited English proficiency, 388, 389
    and academic achievement, 507
    and dropping out, 497
Literacy development
    in late childhood, 379–383, 381–383
    reading and, 380
Locke's *tabula rasa*, 12–13
Longitudinal studies, 53
Long-term memory, 42, 276
Love withdrawal, 316
Low-birthweight, 6, 21, 102, 122
    by race/ethnicity, 120
Low-income households, 21, 231
Luteal phase, 81

Macrosystem, 43, 44
Mainstreaming, 390
Malnourishment, 198, 454
Malnutrition, 162, 256–258
Mapping, fast, 187
Marasmus, 256–257
Marcia's theory of adolescent identity development, 517–518
Marginal, 519
Marijuana, 544–545, 547
Marriage
    interracial, 20
    same-sex, 17
Mass media. *See* Television
    influence on adolescent development, 537–541
Masturbation, 533
Maternal age, 103
Maternal employment, 16, 229–233, 427–429
Maternal mortality, historical trends in, 111
Maternal stress, 104
Math skills
    cross-cultural comparison of, 506
    gender differences in, 500–502
Mattel Toy Company, 502
Maturation, 5, 455
    timing of, 459
Measles, 262, 357–358
Meiosis, 65, 66
Melatonin, 450
Memory
    aids for, 183–184
    components of, 276–277
    in infants and toddlers, 180–184
    in late childhood, 371
    long-term, 42, 182–184, 276
    metacognition and, 277, 280
    short-term, 42, 276
    strategies for, 277, 371
Menarche, 451, 455, 461
    age of, 456
Menstrual phase, 82
Menstruation, 451, 453
Mentalistic explanations, 384–385
Mental retardation, 71, 75, 76
    causes of, 99–100, 105, 395
    degrees of severity of, 394–395
    IQ scores and, 394, 395
    poverty and, 21
Mental rotation, 500, 501
Mesoderm, 93
Mesosystem, 43, 44
Meta-analysis, 48
Metabolic syndrome, 352–353
Metacognition, 277, 280, 371
Mexican Americans, 15, 20
    moral values of, 425, 426
    see also Latinos
Microsystem, 43, 44
Middle Ages, 12
Middle school, 495
Midwives, 110, 116
Mindblind, 385

Minimal distance principle (MDP), 380
Miscarriage, 100, 104
Mitosis, 65, 66
Modeling, 38
Molding, 110
Monozygotic (MZ) twins, 8–9, 393
Moral development
    Kohlberg's theory of, 421–425, 492
    in late childhood, 418–427
    Piaget's theory of, 419–421
Moral dilemmas, 421–422, 492
Moral domain, 491–492
Morality, 216, 418
    culture and, 425
    gender and, 426–427
    research on, 425
Moral realism, 419
Moratorium, 518
Moro reflex, 149, 151
Morphine, 102
Mother-child relationship, 411
Mother-infant relationship, 22
Mothers, working, 16
Motivation
    intrinsic, 377
    reinforcement and, 39
Motor development
    in early childhood 24254
    fine motor skills, 155–156
    gross motor skills, 149–155
    individual differences in, 148
    in infants and toddlers, 148–157
    in late childhood, 347–350
    milestones in, 250–251
    typical and atypical, 154, 162
Motor reproduction, 39
Motor skills, 347–348
Motor vehicle accidents, 360, 471, 543
Mr. Rogers' Neighborhood, 334
Multicultural education, 387–388
Multilingual education, 387–388
Multiple intelligences, 375–376
Multiple pregnancies, 91
Multiracial, 20
Mumps, 358
Muscle growth, 452, 460, 462
Music training, 248
Music videos, 538
Myelination, 138, 246–247, 341, 451

National Association for the Education of Young
    Children (NAEYC), 232
National Center for Missing and Exploited Children, 362
National Child Abuse and Neglect Data System, 235
National Health Interview Survey, 50
National Institutes of Health, 64
Native Americans
    ethnic identity of, 520
    exposure to violence, 413
    interdependence of, 405
    suicide and, 473
Naturalistic studies, 50
Nature versus nurture debate, 7–8, 11, 13, 72, 177. *See
    also* Environmental factors
Negative reinforcement, 38
Neglect, child, 102, 198, 234. *See also* Child abuse
Neglected children, 431
Neonatal Behavioral Assessment Scale, 119
Neonatal intensive care, 100, 122
Neonate, 118. *See also* Newborns
Neo-Piagetians, 40
Nervous system, 94
Neural tube, 93
Neural tube defects, 105
Neurochemistry, 417
Neurodevelopmental approaches, 33
Neuronal connections, 136–140, 449–451
Neurons, 136–137
    connections among, 137–139
Newborns
    addicted, 102
    behavioral assessment of, 119–120
    caregiving and, 123–124

    characteristics of, 118–120
    high-risk, 123–124
    low birthweight and preterm, 120, 121–122
    perception in, 142–143, 145
    physical appearance of, 118–119
    reflexes in, 149, 150
    at risk, 120–121
    senses of, 145–147
    see also Infants
Niche building, 74
Night terrors, 260–261
Nocturnal enuresis, 346–347
Norepinephrine, 417
NREM (non-rapid eye movement) sleep, 258
Nuclear family, 14
Number concepts, infants' understanding of, 175
Nurture, fostering in children, 4. *See also* Nature
    versus nurture debate
Nutrition
    in adolescence, 454, 462
    deficiencies and problems, 6, 256–257, 258
    in early childhood, 254–256
    in infancy, 133, 158–162
    in late childhood, 350–351
    during pregnancy, 105
    prenatal care and, 100
    in toddlerhood, 133
    USDA recommended foods, 350–351
Obedience, 315
Obesity, 352–356
    in adolescence, 465
    causes of, 353–355
    in children, 159–160
    health consequences of, 352
    in late childhood, 352–356
Object permanence, 40, 170, 171, 173–175
Onlooker play, 328
Only children, 430
Operant conditioning, 38, 181
Operations, 270
Opinions, 30
Oral health, 344
Oral stage, 34
Organization, in memory, 371
Origin of Species (Darwin), 13
Osteoporosis, 342
Ovarian tissue transplant, 82
Overactive reward systems, 415
Overextension, 189–190
Overregularization, 284
Overweight, 460
Ovulation, 80, 82
Ovum, 81
Oxytocin, 107

Pader-Willi syndrome, 71
Pain, in newborns, 147
Palmar grasping reflex, 149, 150
Parallel play, 329
Parasuicide, 473
Parent-adolescent relationship, 476–479, 524–525, 548
    bidirectionality of, 525
    conflict in, 526
Parental supervision, in late childhood, 427–429
Parent-child relationship, 117
    academic achievement and, 378–379
    in adolescence (*see* Parent-adolescent
        relationship)
    and cognitive development, 287–288
    in late childhood, 427
Parenting styles, 318–320
Parents
    adoptive, 219
    discipline by, 315–318
    of gifted children, 378
    same-sex, 17
    as teachers, 287–288
    see also Parent-child relationship
Parity, 104–105
Passive G-E correlation, 74
Passive voice, 380
Patterns
    infant preference for, 142

perception of, 143
Peak bone mass, 342
Peer Influence Model, 528
Peer relationships
    in adolescence, 524, 527, 528–537
    and antisocial behavior, 415
    in early childhood, 325–333
    in late childhood, 404, 408, 430–435
    parental role in, 327, 527
    same-sex, 435
Perception
    of depth, 144–145
    in early cognitive development, 175–178
    of emotional expression, 144
    of faces, 143–144
    of moving objects, 144
    of objects, 176–178
    of self
Perceptual development, in infants, 142–147
Performance, versus competence, 173
Permissive parenting, 13, 319
Personal domain, 492, 493
Personal fable, 488–489
Personality, 35, 214, 514–515
Phallic stage, 34
Phenotypes, 67, 72, 73
Phenylalanine, 75
Phenylketonuria (PKU), 7, 75
Philosophical roots, 12–13
Phonemes, 184
Phonemic awareness, 186, 382
Phonics approach, 383
Physical abuse, 234
Physical appearance. See Appearance
Physical development, 4
    in adolescence, 448–461, 456–459
    in early childhood, 245–248
    in infants and toddlers, 131–136, 405
    in late childhood, 340–362
    see also Motor development
Physical disabilities, 391. See also Special needs children
Physical education classes, 354
Physical fitness
    in adolescence, 462–465
    in late childhood, 347–350
    reasons for lack of, 348–349
Physiological measures, 54
Piaget's theory of cognitive development, 39–41,
        167–172, 269–274, 367–371
    concrete operational stage in, 40–41, 367–371,
        384
    formal operational stage, 40–41, 485–488
    preoperational stage, 40–41, 269–274, 369
    sensorimotor stage, 40–41, 167–172, 269
    stages in, 40–41, 177
Piaget's theory of moral development, 419–421
    evaluation of, 421
    stages in, 419, 420
Pincer grasp, 156
Pitocin, 113
Pituitary gland, 453
Placenta, 93
    expulsion of, 108, 110
Placental barrier, 96
Play
    associative, 329
    cooperative, 329
    cultural differences in, 329–330
    in early childhood, 280–281, 328–330
    gender-typed, 304–306
    infant, 213
    onlooker, 328
    parallel, 329
    pretend, 326, 328–329, 330
    pretend and real, 280–281
    relational, 178
    rough-and-tumble, 348
    same-sex, 46
    social, 328–329
    solitary, 328, 329
Playground injuries, 361
Polio, 262, 358–359
Political thinking, 492–493

Polygenic transmission, 72
Popularity, 531–532
Popular music, 537–538
Population, of the U.S., 18
Positive reinforcement, 38
Possible/impossible events, 173–175
Possible self, 514
Postconventional Level, of moral development,
        422–424, 492
Postpartum depression, 114
Poverty, 20–21
    cycle of, 21
    ethnicity and, 21
    health and safety and, 157
    and intellectual development, 377
    mental retardation and, 21
    teen parenting and, 479
Power assertion, in discipline, 315–316, 317–318
Practical intelligence, 375
Pragmatics, 185, 381
Precausal reasoning, 272
Preconventional Level, of moral development, 422
Predisposition. See Heritability
Prefrontal cortex, 246, 247, 341, 448, 449
Pregnancy
    in adolescence, 476–479
    age and, 103
    alcohol and, 99–100, 123
    cultural influences on, 106–107
    drugs in, 102–103
    ectopic, 91
    environmental problems during, 96–107
    malnutrition during, 6
    men's responses to, 106–107
    multiple, 91
    risk of, 534
    smoking in, 101
    women's responses to, 106
Preimplantation genetic diagnosis (PGD), 68
Prejudice, 385
    children's understanding of, 385
    development of, 386
    reducing, 386
    social-cognitive theory of, 386
Premature birth, 21, 120, 122, 478
Prematurity, 120
Premenstrual syndrome (PMS), 461
Premoral period, 419, 420
Prenatal care, 98, 100, 105
    inadequate or lack of, 478
Prenatal development, 89–90
    alcohol and, 99–100, 123
    diseases and, 97
    early timetable of, 90
    environmental hazards and, 103
    environmental problems and, 96–107
    growth and change of fetus and mother, 95
    maternal conditions and, 103–105
    milestones and characteristics of, 92–93
    protective factors in, 105–106
    stages of, 89–96
Prenatal hormones, 249
Prenatal malnutrition, 6
Prenatal senses, 147
Preoperational stage, 40, 41, 269–274, 369
Prereaching, 155
Preschool, 16–17, 282–295
Preschoolers. See Early childhood
Pretend play, 280–281, 326, 328–329, 330
Preterm births, 122
    by race/ethnicity, 120
    see also Premature birth
Pride, 211–213
Primary circular reaction, 168–169
Primary prevention, 238
Primary sexual characteristics, 453
Privacy, right to, 52
Private speech, 41, 275
Problem solving
    in early childhood, 269–282, 275
    in infants and toddlers, 170–172
    strategies, 371
    use of logical principles in, 367–368
Prodigies, 4, 376, 396

Progesterone, 475
Project Head Start. See Head Start
Projective measures, 55
Prosocial behavior, 313–325
    in early childhood, 334
    effect of television viewing on, 334
Prostaglandins, 1007
Protection from harm, 52
Proteins, 64
Proximodistal development, 94
Pruning, 139, 140
Psychoanalysis, 34, 35
Psychoanalytic theories, 33–35
Psychological maltreatment, 234
Psychosexual development, Freud's theory
    of, 33–35
Psychosocial crises, 35
Psychosocial development, 211–212
Psychosocial moratorium, 517
Psychosocial theory, 35, 36, 200, 300, 404
Puberty, 5, 452–461
    biological influences in, 453
    environmental factors in, 454–455
    gender roles and, 454
    genetic factors in, 453–454
    psychological reactions to, 460–461
    race differences in, 455–456
    sex differences in, 454, 455–456, 458–459
Public Law 94–142, Education for All Handicapped
        Children Act of 1975, 390
Public television, 294–295
Puerto Rican Americans, 18. See also Latinos
Punan Bah, 447
Punishment, 38
    in adolescence, 525
    corporal, 316
    in moral development, 420, 421
    see also Discipline
Punitiveness, 525

Quickening, 94

Race, 18
    children's understanding of, 385
    family structure and, 14–16
Racial differences
    in academic achievement, 507–509
    in motor development, 254
    in puberty, 455–456
Racial diversity, 18–20
Racial stereotypes, 385
Radiation, 103
Radiation treatments, 81
Random assignment, 51
Random sampling, 51
Range of reaction, 73
Rap music, 538
Rate-limiting component, 45
Raven Progressive Matrices Test, 374
Raves, 545
Reaching, 155
Read, learning to, 381–382
Reading
    and literacy development, 380
    methods of teaching, 383
    prerequisite knowledge for, 382
    by race-ethnicity, 289
Reading disabilities, 391–392
Reading readiness, 382–383
    defined, 291
Reasoning
    cultural differences in, 372
    formal operational, 487
    hypothetico-deductive, 486–487
    inductive and deductive, 272
    precausal, 272
    transductive, 272
Receptive language, 186
Recessive genes, 67, 69
Recessive traits, 67
Recessive transmission, 69–70
Reefer Madness (movie), 547
Referential language, 283
Reflective abstraction, 487

Reflexes
    in infants, 148
    in newborns, 149, 150
    salivation, 36
Reflexive schemes, 168
Regulator genes, 72–73
Rehabilitation, 48
Rehearsal, 371
Reinforcement
    motivation and, 39
    negative, 416
Reinforcement-based theories, of language develop-
        ment, 192
Rejection
    in adolescence, 531–532
    in childhood, 431, 435
Relational aggression, 313
Relational play, 178
Religious thinking, 492–493
Remarriage, children's adjustment to, 324–325
REM (rapid eye movement) sleep, 258
Reproductive technologies, 83–84
Research
    controlled variables in, 51, 54–56
    ethics in, 51, 52
    strategies, 47–54
    topics in, 46–47
Research designs, 47–54
Research methods, 8–10, 46, 52–54
    measurement of behavior, 54–56
Resilience, 411, 412
    in adolescence, 547–549
Responsiveness, 318
Retention, 39
Reversible thinking, 368
Risk-taking behavior, 88, 451, 464, 470–471, 515,
        536, 541
Ritalin, 393–394
Rites of passage, 447
Rooting reflex, 149, 150
Rousseau's innate morality, 13
Rubella, 97–98
Rules, 420
Running, 250–251

Sadness, 308
Safety
    in adolescence, 462–480
    bullying and, 433
    day care and, 232
    in early childhood, 261
    infant, 157–162
    in late childhood, 350, 356–362
    personal, 361–362, 433
    in sports, 350
Salivation, 36
Same-sex marriage, 17
Same-sex parents, 17
Same-sex play, 46
Samoans, 448
Sampling, random, 51
Savants, 376
Scaffolding, 179, 197, 275
Schemas, 178
Schematic consistency, 307–308
Schemes, 39, 168, 269–274, 367–371
Schizophrenia, 9
School(s), 493–498
    and adolescence, 493–498
    changing, 493–494
    influence of, 436, 493–498
    preschool, 16–17, 202–206
    readiness for, 291
    as a source of stress, 408
    transitions, 494
Science skills, gender differences in, 500–502
Scientific method, 46
Scientific reasoning, 46
Scientific theories, 30
Scooter accidents, 360
Scripts, 277–278

Secondary circular reactions, 169
Secondary prevention, 238
Secondary sexual characteristics, 453, 455–456
Secondhand smoke, 264
Second-language learning, 195, 200
Secure attachment, 222–224, 434
Sedentary lifestyles, 354
Self
    perception of, 404–406
    sense of, 403–406, 469, 513–523
Self-awareness, 212
    in early childhood, 299–302
Self-concept
    in adolescence, 513–515
    development of, 300
    domains of, 514
    environmental factors in, 405
    in late childhood, 403–406
    negative, 404
    physical, 349
    sex differences in, 349
Self-conscious emotions, 211–213
Self-control, 437
Self-esteem
    in adolescence, 515
    cultural differences in, 303
    in early childhood, 301–302
    gender differences in, 515–516
    high, 515
    low, 404, 405, 515
    sex differences in, 405
Self-perception, influences on, 406
Self-reports, 54–55
Semantic bootstrapping, 284
Semantics, 184, 380–381
Sense of self, 403–406, 469
    in adolescence, 513–523
Sensitive periods, 11
Sensorimotor stage, 40, 41, 269
    substages of, 167–172
Sensory register, 42
Sensory storage, 276
Sentences, 283–285
    first, 191
Separated, 519
Separation anxiety, 221
Seriation, 369–370
Serotonin, 417
Sesame Street (PBS), 294–295, 334
Severe combined immunodeficiency, 80
Sex cells, 65
Sex chromosomal abnormalities, 76–78
Sex chromosomes, 66, 70
Sex determination, 66, 67, 82
    by preselection, 68
Sex differences. See Gender differences
Sex education, 479–480
Sex hormones, 453, 502, 503
    and cognitive abilities, 504
Sex-linked transmission, 70–71
Sex selection, 68
Sexual abuse, 234, 279
Sexual attitudes and behaviors, in adolescence,
        534–535
    correlates of, 535–536
Sexual characteristics, 453, 455, 456
Sexual development, 448–461
Sexual identity, 302, 520–521
Sexual intercourse, 533–534, 535
Sexuality
    emerging, 533–534
    social psychological context of, 536–537
Sexually transmitted diseases (STDs), 98, 474, 480,
        534
Sexual maturation, 152, 156–159
Sexual orientation, 520
Sexual relationships, 533–537
Shame, 211–213
Shaping, 38
Sharing, 314
Short-term memory, 42, 276

Shyness, 218
Sibling relationships
    differences in quality of, 331
    dynamics of, 330–331
    in early childhood, 325–333, 330–331
    in late childhood, 429–430
    parental favoritism and, 331
Sickle cell anemia, 70, 80
Simpatia, 303
Single-parent families, 14–15, 230, 322
Sitting, 149–151
Skeletal system, 7
Sleep
    problems with, 259–262
    requirements for, 258–259
Sleepiness, 261–262
Sleep patterns
    in adolescence, 449, 450
    cosleeping, 260
    in early childhood, 258–262
    in infancy, 134–136, 259–260
    in newborns, 134
    for toddlers, 135
Smell, sense of, 142, 146–147
Smiling, 206–208
Smoking, 96–97, 101, 264, 544
Social cognition, 489–492
Social communicative competence, 282
Social competence, 434–435
Social contexts, of cognitive development, 179–180
Social-conventional domain, 492, 493
Social development
    and adjustment, 5
    in early childhood, 314–325
    in late childhood, 434–435
    television viewing and, 332–334
Social-emotional development, 4
Social interaction
    deficits in, 249
    influence of, 41–42
Social interactions
    in early childhood, 273
    infant, 184
    in infants, 179–180
    initiating, 434
    maintaining, 434
Social interaction theories, 196
Socialization, 7, 314–315
Social learning theories, 38–39, 306–307
Social perspective taking, 383–384
    in adolescence, 490–491
Social play, 328–329
Social policy, in child development, 23–24
Social referencing, 208
Social rules, 311
Social scripting, 537
Social smile, 208
Social support, during pregnancy, 106
Society for Research in Child Development, 52
Solitary play, 328, 329
Sound(s)
    distinguishing, 184–186
    frequency of, 345
    infant perception of, 145, 184
    newborns' localization ability, 145
    prenatal exposure to, 145
    of speech, 185–186
Spanking, 315–316
Spatial perception, 500, 501
Spatial skills, 305, 376
Spatial visualization, 500, 501
Spatial-visual skills, 500, 501
Special needs children, 390–398
    with autism and asperger syndrome, 396–398
    gifted and talented, 395–396
    mainstreaming, 390
    see also specific disabilities
Speech
    distinguishing sounds of, 185–186
    producing sounds of, 186, 187
Speech problems, 345

Sperm, 82, 83
Spermatogenesis, 82
Spermatozoa, 82
Spina bifida, 71, 105
Sports
   in adolescence, 462–465
   influence of participation in, 350
   in late childhood, 348–350
   safety in, 350
Stage theories, 10, 34
Standing, 151
State of arousal, 133
State v. Michaels, 279
Static thinking, 271
Status offenses, 541
Step-families, 15, 324–325
Stepping, 150
Stereotypes
   gender, 304
   racial, 385
Sternberg's triarchic theory of intelligence, 374–376
Steroids, 544–545
Stressful transitions, 542
Stranger anxiety, 221
Strange Situation, 222, 223, 225, 226, 231
Stress
   acculturative, 408
   causes of, 407, 408
   coping with, 408, 409
   disaster-related, 410
   in late childhood, 407–411
   obesity and, 355
   vulnerability to, 407
Stress hormones, 116
Stress-resistent children, 411
Study of Mathematically Precocious Youth program, 396
Stuttering, 345
Substance use and abuse, 542–547. See also Drug use and abuse
Sucking reflex, 149, 150
Sudden infant death syndrome (SIDS), 151, 157, 159
Suicide, 418, 521
   in adolescence, 473, 542
Superego, 33–34, 35
Support, in adolescence, 524
Surrogate mothers, 84
Survey studies, 50
Swimming, 264
   in infancy, 158
   infant, 151
Symbolic representation, 172, 269–271
Symbols, understanding, 270–271
Sympathy, 313
Synaptic connections, 137, 341
Synaptogenesis, 137
Synchrony, 225
Syntactic Bootstrapping, 283
Syntax, 184–185, 380
Syphilis, 98
Systematic desensitization, 37

Tabula Rasa, 12–13
Talented children. See Gifted and talented children
Taste, sense of, 142, 145–146
Tay Sachs disease, 70
Teacher bias, 388, 437–438, 505–506
Teacher-child relationships, 437–438
Teachers
   influence on social development, 437
   parents as, 287–288
Telegraphic speech, 191
Television
   public, 294–295
   violence on, 51
Television viewing
   of disasters, 410
   and family life, 332
   impact on children's behavior, 39
   influence on emotional development, 332–334
   limiting, 355

and obesity, 354
and physical fitness, 348–349
and prosocial behavior, 334
and social development, 332–334
supervision of, 333
of violence and aggression, 50, 332–333, 334
Temperament
   antisocial behavior and, 414
   consistency of, 215
   depression and, 418
   emotion regulation and, 310–311
   in infancy and toddlerhood, 213–217
   infant development and, 215–217
   of siblings, 331
   structure of, 214–215
Teratogens, 96–97, 103
Tertiary circular reactions, 171
Tertiary prevention, 238–239
Test bias, 374
Testosterone, 94, 306, 448, 453
Test scores, by income group, 21
Thalidomide, 98–99
Theories
   evaluating, 30–31
   usefulness of, 29–3146
   use of, 29–31
Theory of mind, 278–280
There Are No Children Here (Kotlowitz), 411–412
Thinking
   cultural influences on, 281–282
Thinness, 105, 160, 165–166, 168
Three-mountain task, 273
Throwing, 251
Tobacco, 544. See also Smoking
Toddlerhood
   cognitive development in, 167–180
   emotions in, 205–213
   feeding, 161–162
   language development in, 184–192
   learning and remembering in, 180–184
   memory in, 182–184
   motor development in, 148–157
   physical development in, 131–136
   sleep patterns in, 135
   temperament in, 213–217
   see also Infants
Toilet training, 156
Touch, sense of, 147
Traits
   conflicting, 514–515
   dominant and recessive, 67
   stability over time, 300
   temperamental, 216
Trance events, 545
Transactional perspective, 21–22
Transductive reasoning, 272
Transition, 109
Transverse presentation, 113
Treatment programs, assessment of, 48
Triarchic theory of intelligence, 374–376
Trisomy-X syndrome, 77
Truancy, 429
Trust, developing a sense of, 206
Trust versus mistrust, 35, 206
Turner's syndrome, 76–77, 503
Twins, 8–9
   increase in rates of, 84
Twin studies, 8–9
Type 2 diabetes, 352

Ulnar grasp, 156
Ultrasound imaging, 78
Umbilical cord, 93, 110
Unconditioned response, 36
Unconditioned stimulus, 36
Unconscious, 34
Underactive inhibitory systems, 415
Underextension, 190
Undernourishment, 256–258
Undernutrition, 162, 351–352
Uninvolved parenting, 319–320

U.S. Census Bureau, 50
U.S. Department of Agriculture, 68, 350–351
U.S. Department of Energy, 64
U.S. Department of Health and Human Services, 120
U.S. Food and Drug Administration (FDA), 99
U.S. Public Health Service, 105
Uterus, 91, 94, 109

Vaccinations, 157, 262, 357, 359
Vagina, 94
Values, importance of, 24
Values autonomy, 522
Variables
   controlled, 51
   dependent, 51
   independent, 51
Vending machines, school, 353
VERB, 355–356
Verbal skills, 305
   gender differences in, 500
Vernix caseosa, 118
Vicarious reinforcement, 38
Victimization, 235, 238, 431–432, 433
Victor, Wild Boy of Aveyron, 7–8, 29, 35, 49
Video games, 540
Violence
   community, 411–413
   domestic, 236
   explanation for, 5
   television, 332–333, 334
   traumatic, 412
   in video games, 540
   youth, 472–473
   see also Child abuse and neglect
Violent crime, 541
Viral diseases, 97
Vision, in newborns and infants, 142–143
Vision problems, 346
Visual acuity, 142–143
Visual cliff apparatus, 144–145
Visual development, 250
Vocabulary development
   in early childhood, 282–283
   in infants and toddlers, 187–188
Voice, change in, 456
Vulnerability, in adolescence, 547–549
Vygotsky's theory of cognitive development, 41–42, 276
   social interaction and, 274–275

Walking, 152
   implications of, 152–153
   infant, 44–45
Weaning, 161–162
Weight
   in adolescence, 452, 468–469
   growth charts for, 132, 343
   helping children lose, 355–356
   see also Eating disorders; Nutrition; Obesity
Whole language approach, 383
Wild Boy of Aveyron, 7–8, 29, 35, 49
Word meanings, 184–185, 187–191
   learning levels of, 190–191
Working, in adolescence, 499
Working women, 16, 229–233, 427–429
Worthiness, 301–302
Writing, 382

X chromosomes, 66, 70, 76
X-linked diseases, 68
X-linked transmission, 70
XYY syndrome, 77

Y chromosome, 70, 76

Zone of proximal development, 42, 179
Zygote, 90, 91

$\mathcal{P}$hoto $\mathcal{C}$redits